TABLE B MEASURES OF U.S. INCOME, PRICES, AND FEDERAL GOVERNMENT FINANCE

Year	National Income	Personal Income	Disposable Income	Chain-Type Price Index		Consumer Price Index			
	Billions of Dollars			*Index Number*	*Percent Change*	*Index Number*	*Percent Change*		
1959	410.4	393.5	349.0	23.0	–	29.1	0.7	-12.8	287.5
1960	426.2	411.7	362.9	23.3	1.3	29.6	1.7	0.3	290.5
1961	441.2	429.1	378.8	23.6	1.3	29.9	1.0	-3.3	292.6
1962	475.3	456.1	401.3	23.9	1.3	30.2	1.0	-7.1	302.9
1963	502.6	479.1	421.1	24.2	1.3	30.6	1.3	-4.8	310.3
1964	540.2	513.5	457.6	24.6	1.7	31.0	1.3	-5.9	316.1
1965	587.8	555.8	493.9	25.0	1.6	31.5	1.6	-1.4	322.3
1966	644.4	604.7	533.7	25.7	2.8	32.4	2.9	-3.7	328.5
1967	680.7	649.7	571.9	26.6	3.5	33.4	3.1	-8.6	340.4
1968	742.4	713.5	621.4	27.7	4.1	34.8	4.2	-25.2	368.7
1969	800.9	778.2	668.4	29.0	4.7	36.7	5.5	3.2	365.8
1970	836.6	836.1	727.1	30.6	5.5	38.8	5.7	-2.8	380.9
1971	904.0	898.9	790.2	32.1	4.9	40.5	4.4	-23.0	408.2
1972	999.2	987.3	855.3	33.5	4.4	41.8	3.2	-23.4	435.9
1973	1125.3	1105.6	965.0	35.4	5.7	44.4	6.2	-14.9	466.3
1974	1206.7	1213.3	1054.2	38.5	8.8	49.3	11.0	-6.1	483.9
1975	1295.5	1315.6	1159.2	42.2	9.6	53.8	9.1	-53.2	541.9
1976	1447.5	1455.4	1273.0	44.6	5.7	56.9	5.8	-73.7	629.0
1977	1616.3	1611.4	1401.4	47.5	6.5	60.6	6.5	-53.7	706.4
1978	1839.2	1820.2	1580.1	50.9	7.2	65.2	7.6	-59.2	776.6
1979	2053.3	2049.7	1769.5	55.3	8.6	72.6	11.3	-40.7	829.5
1980	2216.1	2285.7	1973.3	60.4	9.2	82.4	13.5	-73.8	909.1
1981	2470.2	2560.4	2200.2	66.1	9.4	90.9	10.3	-79.0	994.8
1982	2569.2	2718.7	2347.3	70.2	6.2	96.5	6.2	-128.0	1137.3
1983	2761.4	2891.7	2522.4	73.2	4.3	99.6	3.2	-207.8	1371.7
1984	3132.7	3205.5	2810.0	75.9	3.7	103.9	4.3	-185.4	1564.7
1985	3351.5	3439.6	3002.0	78.6	3.6	107.6	3.6	-212.3	1817.5
1986	3516.5	3647.5	3187.6	80.6	2.5	109.6	1.9	-221.2	2120.6
1987	3778.1	3877.3	3363.1	83.1	3.1	113.6	3.6	-149.8	2346.1
1988	4108.6	4172.8	3640.8	86.1	6.8	118.3	4.1	-155.2	2601.3
1989	4362.1	4489.3	3894.5	89.7	4.2	124.0	4.8	-152.5	2868.0
1990	4611.9	4791.6	4166.8	93.6	4.3	130.7	5.4	-221.2	3206.6
1991	4719.7	4968.5	4343.7	97.3	4.0	136.2	4.2	-269.4	3598.5
1992	4950.8	5264.2	4613.7	100.0	2.8	140.3	3.0	-290.4	4002.1
1993	5194.4	5479.2	4789.3	102.6	2.6	144.5	3.0	-255.1	4351.4
1994	5495.1	5750.2	5018.8	105.0	2.3	148.2	2.6	-203.1	4643.7
1995	5799.2	6101.7	5307.4	107.5	2.4	152.4	2.8	-163.9	4921.0

SOURCE: *Economic Report of the President,* February, 1996 and *Economic Indicators,* March, 1996.

Fourth Edition

Economics

A Contemporary Introduction

William A. McEachern

Professor of Economics

University of Connecticut

SOUTH-WESTERN College Publishing

An International Thomson Publishing Company

ABOUT THE COVER DESIGN

The cover illustrates "Networking Around Earth," a painting by Alan Cober. The image demonstrates many concepts at once—global economic growth, the rise of information technology, the interconnectedness of local cultures and economies. Similarly, the new edition of *Economics: A Contemporary Introduction* integrates in every chapter international economic issues, real-world examples, and today's most promising new information technology, the Internet. Copyright © Alan Cober/SIS.

Publishing Team Director: Jack C. Calhoun
Acquisitions Editors: Jack C. Calhoun/John Alessi
Developmental Editors: Dennis Hanseman/Kurt Gerdenich
Marketing Manager: Scott D. Person
Project Manager: Justified Left—A Publishing Alliance
Production House: WordCrafters Editorial Services, Inc.
Composition: General Graphic Services, Inc.
Cover and Internal Designer: Joseph M. Devine
Internal Photo Researcher: Feldman & Associates
Chapter Opener Photo Researchers: Jennifer Mayhall/Alix Roughen
Team Assistants: Cory Broadfoot, Kristen Meere

HB83DA
Copyright © 1997
by South-Western College Publishing
Cincinnati, Ohio

Library of Congress Cataloging-in-Publication Data

McEachern, William A.
    Economics : a contemporary introduction / William A. McEachern. —
4th ed.
        p.   cm.
    Includes bibliographical references and index.
    ISBN 0-538-85514-2
    1. Economics.   I. Title.
HB171.5.M475   1997
330—dc20   96-21299
                                                                                    CIP

1 2 3 4 5 6 7 8 9 0 VH 5 4 3 2 1 0 9 8 7 6
Printed in the United States of America

I(T)P International Thomson Publishing
South-Western College Publishing is an ITP Company.
The ITP trademark is used under license.

To Pat

Preface

Economics has a short history but a long past. As a distinct discipline, economics has been studied for only a few hundred years, yet civilizations have confronted the economic problem of scarce resources but unlimited wants for millenia. Economics, the discipline, may be centuries old, but it is new every day. Each day offers fresh evidence to support or reshape evolving economic theory. In *Economics: A Contemporary Introduction,* I draw upon my 25 years of teaching principles to convey the vitality, timeliness, and evolving nature of economics.

Remember the last time you were in an unfamiliar neighborhood and had to ask for directions? Along with the directions came the standard comment "You can't miss it!" So how come you missed it? Because the "landmark" that was obvious to the neighborhood resident who gave the directions might as well have been invisible to you, a stranger. Writing a principles text is much like giving directions. The author must be familiar with the material, but familiarity can also dull one's perceptions, making it difficult to see things through the fresh eyes of a principles student. Some authors try to compensate by telling all they know, in the process overwhelming the student with so much detail that the central point gets lost. Other authors take a minimalist approach by offering little of what students may already know intuitively, and instead talking abstractly about good x and good y, units of labor and units of capital, or the proverbial widget. This turns economics into a foreign language.

Students typically arrive the first day of class with 18 or more years of experience with economic institutions, economic events, and economic choices. Each student grew up in a household—the central economic institution. As consumers, students are familiar with fast-food restaurants, movie theaters, car dealers, and dozens of stores at the mall. Most students have been resource suppliers—more than half held jobs while in high school. Students also have experienced government: For example, they know about sales taxes, drivers licenses, speed limits, and public education. And, from imported cars to emerging markets around the globe, students are growing more aware of the rest of the world.

Thus, students have abundant experience with economic institutions, economic events, and economic choices. They may not recognize the economic content of this experience, but they possess this knowledge nonetheless. Yet some principles authors neglect this rich lode of student experience, and instead try to create for the student a new world of economics. Such an approach fails to make the connection between economics and what Alfred Marshall called "the ordinary business of life."

Good directions rely on landmarks familiar to us all—a stoplight, a fork in the road, a white picket fence. Likewise, a good textbook builds bridges from the familiar to the new. I try to build such bridges. How? *In essence, I try to "lead by example"—I provide examples that draw on the students' common experience.* I try to create graphic pictures that need little explanation, thereby eliciting from the reader that light of recognition, that *"Aha!"*. Examples should be self-explanatory; they should convey the point quickly and directly. Having to explain an example is like having to explain a joke—the point gets lost. Throughout, I provide just enough intuitive information and institutional detail to get the point across without overwhelming the student. My emphasis is on economic ideas, not economic jargon.

Since instructors can cover only a fraction of the textbook material in class, principles texts should, to the extent possible, be self-explanatory, thereby providing instructors with greater flexibility to emphasize topics of special interest. My approach is to start where students are, not where we would like them to be. For example, to explain the division of labor, rather than refer to Adam Smith's pin factory, I call attention to the division of labor at McDonald's. To explain resource substitution, rather than referring to abstract units of labor and capital, I discuss a specific example, such as labor-capital combinations for washing a car—ranging from a drive-through car wash (much capital and little labor) to a Saturday-morning-send-the-band-to-Disney-World–charity car wash (little capital and much labor).

THE FOURTH EDITION

Introductory Chapters. Topics common to both macroeconomics and microeconomics are covered in the first four chapters. Limiting the introductory material to four chapters saves precious class time, particularly at institutions where students can take macro and micro courses in either order (and hence are likely to end up repeating the introductory chapters). New case studies in the introductory chapters aim to draw students into the material and include discussions of marginal analysis in the computer industry, the market for professional basketball, specialization on the Internet, and the global market for automobiles.

Macroeconomic Chapters. Since there is no consensus about which macroeconomic model explains the economy best, some textbooks present a smorgasbord of alternative macroeconomic approaches, leaving it to the student to choose among them. Students, however, lack sufficient background to evaluate the alternatives, so competing theories often seem unrelated and confusing. Rather than dwell on the differences among competing schools of thought, I use the aggregate demand and aggregate supply model to focus on the fundamental distinction between the *active approach,* which views the economy as essentially stable and self-correcting, and the *passive approach,* which views the economy as unstable and in need of government intervention.

Wherever possible, I rely on the students' experience and intuition to explain the theory behind macroeconomic abstractions such as aggregate demand and aggregate supply. For example, to explain how employment can temporarily exceed its natural rate, I note how students, as the term draws to a close, can temporarily shift into high gear to study for final exams and finish term papers. I have made the graphs more readable and more intuitively obvious by using numbers rather than letters. And to convey a feel for the size of the U.S. economy, I usually list trillions of dollars rather than billions of dollars. For example, students have an easier time grasping a change in real GDP expressed as an increase from $7.0 trillion to $7.2 trillion rather than as an increase from Y to Y'. This edition measures real output in chained (1992) dollars, reflecting the most recent revisions by the Bureau of Economic Analysis.

In light of the renewed interest in economic growth, I have moved up the chapter on economic growth to follow the introductory macroeconomic chapter. Emerging issues of macroeconomics that receive coverage in this edition include "green" accounting, coordination failures, real business cycle theory, asymmetric information in banking, and the convergence of national economies. Some other timely issues discussed in case studies include counterfeiting, computer banking, growth rates around the world, hysteresis and high unemployment in Europe, industrial policy, balancing the federal budget, computers and GDP growth, and the link between central bank independence and inflation around the world.

Microeconomic Chapters. My approach to microeconomics underscores the role of time and information in production and consumption. For example, both time and information are scarce resources and, as such, are valued by consumers and producers. The microeconomic presentation also reflects the growing interest in the economic institutions that underpin impersonal market activity. More generally, I try to convey the intuition that most microeconomic principles operate like gravity: Market forces work whether or not individual economic actors understand them.

Emerging microeconomic issues covered in this revision reflect the growing recognition of market imperfections. Topics include optimal search theory, the lemons problem, the winner's curse, adverse selection, signaling, screening, moral hazard, and the principal-agent problem. Other timely microeconomic topics discussed include game theory, rent seeking, the market for pollution rights, efficiency wages, economies of scope, and the bounds of the firm. Timely case studies include discussions of auction markets, experimental economics, demand curves in the animal world, economies of scale at McDonald's, the De Beers diamond monopoly,

Postal Service productivity, architects and derived demand, outsourcing, the costly strike at Caterpillar, air pollution in Mexico City, the destruction of the tropical rainforest, campaign financing, and "ending welfare as we know it."

Where possible, I have tried to clarify terminology. For example, the Third Edition used the terms *total fixed cost, total variable cost,* and *total cost.* In the Fourth Edition, these terms are more simply *fixed cost, variable cost,* and *total cost.* As another example, the expression *marginal resource cost* was abbreviated in the Third Edition to MRC and *marginal revenue product* to MRP. But since the "R" in each abbreviation represents a different word, some students could be confused by the abbreviations. In the Fourth Edition, I do not abbreviate these expressions. You may be thinking, "Why is he telling us about such minor details?" I am telling you because a lack of attention to such details can result in unnecessary confusion.

International Chapters. This revision reflects the growing impact of the world economy on U.S. economic welfare. International issues are introduced early and are discussed often. For example, the rest of the world is introduced as an economic actor in Chapter 1 and comparative advantage and the production possibilities frontier are each discussed from a global perspective in Chapter 2. The international coverage is not simply an afterthought but is woven into the text to enhance the entire presentation. For example, students gain greater perspective about such topics as economic growth, unemployment, inflation, government deficits and debt, central banks, unionization trends, antitrust laws, pollution, environmental laws, tax rates, and the distribution of income if the U.S. experience is compared with that of other countries around the world.

And recent trends in the competitive structure of the U.S. economy cannot be fully understood without examining the role of imports, trade barriers, and trade agreements. Likewise, students can better understand how free markets allocate resources when problems confronting the transitional economies around the world are examined. In addition to integrating coverage of international topics throughout, there are three chapters devoted exclusively to the international issues. One of these three focuses on developing and transitional economies. International case studies include discussion of Mexico's peso problem, privatizing foreign aid, the World Trade Organization, and purchasing power parity and the price of a Big Mac.

ORGANIZATION

In many principles textbooks, chapters are interrupted by boxed material, parenthetical explanations, and other distractions that disrupt the flow of the chapter. Segregating material from the mainstream of a chapter leaves students uncertain about when or if this material should be read. In contrast, this book has a natural flow. Each chapter opens with a motivating paragraph and a list of key ideas, then tells a compelling story, using logical sections and subsections. Qualifying footnotes are used sparingly, and parenthetical explanations are used hardly at all. Moreover, case studies appear in the natural sequence of the chapter. Students can thus read each chapter smoothly from beginning to end. In this edition I have adopted a "just-in-time" philosophy; the idea is to introduce material as it is needed to develop an argument, not before. Overall, the Fourth Edition is a bit leaner, economic jargon has been reduced, and many tables have been converted to charts and graphs.

The Fourth Edition includes as an option material referencing the Internet, a valuable resource with more potential today than perhaps any other available on campus. Over 22 million distinct World Wide Web sites exist around the world, most with many levels, multiple materials, and colorful graphics. Computer users can "point and click" to navigate between pages within a site and among different sites. The Internet can be a powerful learning tool, a resource that has its place in the economics curriculum. Although Internet addresses and related material supplement each chapter, this is all optional. *Instructors who choose not to rely on the Internet-related material can still utilize in full all other features of the textbook.* The book is designed to be used either way.

Each chapter includes the following features.

Case Studies. Each chapter contains two case studies, or extended examples, that connect economic theory to the real world. Case studies are carefully integrated into the presentation of the text, so the discussion flows uninterrupted. Exercises related to the case studies are included with the end-of-chapter questions and problems. Accompanying every case study is an interactive Internet example offering one or more World Wide Web site addresses for students to visit, explore, or browse materials related to the case study. These "links" are optional tools for discovering the latest information, or for visiting online the major actors of the case study. These links also appear within the McEachern Economics Web site (**http://www.thomson.com/mceachern/**).

Net Bookmarks. In addition to the interactive Internet examples tied to the case studies, every chapter includes a Net Bookmark. Similar to the interactive Internet examples, Net Bookmarks offer students the option to explore World Wide Web resources tied to key concepts in the chapter. Rather than relying only on sites that offer data—as useful as these sites are to economists—I have chosen sites based on their economic relevance and interest to principles students. These links are also contained conveniently within the McEachern Economics Web site (**http://www.thomson.com/mceachern/**).

End-of-Chapter Material. Each chapter contains both a *Conclusion* and a *Summary*. The Conclusion draws the discussion to a close; the Summary reviews the key points. Each chapter ends with, on average, 20 questions and problems. Many questions are analytical, requiring the student to perform calculations or to draw graphs. Suggested answers to questions and problems are provided in the *Instructor's Manual*. New to this edition are *Using the Internet Problems,* which offer students the opportunity to use Internet resources to solve economic problems. These problems are contained within the McEachern Economics Web site.

Appendixes. Several end-of-chapter appendixes provide more detailed treatment of various topics. The appendix to Chapter 1, for example, is recommended for all students unfamiliar with variables, graphs, slopes, and the like. Other appendixes are optional in the sense that subsequent material does not rely on them. Including additional material in this way offers the instructor greater flexibility of coverage with no loss of continuity.

Marginal Definitions and Glossary. Important economic terms appear in boldface type and are defined in the body of the text. These terms are also defined in the margins and listed alphabetically in the *Glossary,* which appears at the end of the book, just before the index.

CLARITY BY DESIGN

In many textbooks, the design of the pages—the layout of the page and the use of color—is usually an afterthought, without regard to how students read and understand a textbook. By contrast, this book has a natural flow and a systematic use of color. No element of the design is wasted, and all elements work efficiently together for the maximum pedagogical value.

Page Design. By design, each element of the chapter builds upon the next. From the opening, motivating paragraph to the conclusion and summary, each chapter has a consistent flow. Case studies, as do photographs and Net Bookmarks, appear in the natural sequence of the chapter. Although each chapter contains numerous examples and features, none is set off in a box. Students can thus read each chapter smoothly from beginning to end without a hitch. In addition, every effort has been made to present students with an open, readable page design. The size of the print, the length of the text line, and the amount of "white space" are all optimal for students encountering college textbooks for the first time. Nearly all graphs are accompanied by captions that explain the key features.

Use of Color. Color is used systematically within graphs, charts, and tables to ensure that students quickly and easily comprehend these exhibits. Throughout the book, demand curves are blue and supply curves are red. In comparative statics, the curves determining the final equilibrium point are darker than the initial curves. Color shading highlights the underlying data for easy recognition, such as measures of economic profit or loss, tax incidence, consumer and producer surplus, and the welfare effects of tariffs and quotas. In short, color is more than mere face entertainment—it is employed consistently and with forethought as a pedagogical aid.

THE SUPPORT PACKAGE

The teaching and learning support package accompanying *Economics: A Contemporary Introduction* provides instructors and students with focused, accurate, and innovative supplements to the textbook.

Student Supplements

Study Guide. The *Study Guide* is available for the hardbound text, as well as in Macro and Micro versions. Each *Study Guide* chapter includes the following: (1) an introduction; (2) a chapter outline, with definitions of all terms; (3) a discussion of the chapter's main points; (4) a "lagniappe," or bonus, which supplements the material in the chapter and includes a "Question to Think About"; (5) a list of key terms; (6) a variety of true or false, multiple choice, and discussion questions; and (7) answers to all of these questions. Visit the McEachern Economics Web site for more details (**http://www.thomson. com/mceachern**), or visit your local bookstore.

Virtual Economics: Principles and Applications. *Virtual Economics,* created by Willie Belton, Richard Cebula, and John McLeod, Jr., all of the Georgia Institute of Technology, is a self-contained CD-Rom economics adventure. Using a flexible, modular approach and an engaging, multimedia format, students experience the world of economics firsthand. *Virtual Economics* combines cutting-edge presentations with powerful graphing manipulation software and realistic simulations to provide students with the latest tools for learning economics—all with just a click of the mouse.

***EconoGuide* Student Software.** Students have an opportunity to apply what they have learned and test their knowledge of economic concepts with *EconoGuide,* a Windows-based tutorial and assessment software program. The software is fully copyable and networkable.

McEachern Economics Web Site. As mentioned already, the Internet can be a powerful learning tool. To get the most from this promising tool, students and educators need what is provided with the Fourth Edition—well-defined applications in the text and in supplementary materials, as well as clear directions for their use. The Fourth Edition offers a structured tour of economic resources on the Internet. Over 140 interactive examples and exercises in the text— Case Study Interactive Examples, Net Bookmarks, and Using the Internet Problems—provide a clear map to relevant and interesting sites. Many addresses will take students around the world. These applications are interesting but simple to use. And, to keep references to Internet sites current and accurate, technical support for these applications is provided by South-Western College Publishing within the McEachern Economics Web site (**http://www. thomson.com/mceachern**). Also at the McEachern Economics Web site, students can print a chapter from the *Study Guide,* download the software for free, join the Internet Student Discussion Group (as can instructors join the Internet Instructor Discussion Group), and take advantage of other benefits associated with using the Fourth Edition. *Importantly, nothing about these applications requires a detailed knowledge of the Internet.* All this material represents optional paths for further study and exploration. Nothing more is needed than curiosity and access to e-mail and the World Wide Web.

Graphing Primer. The *Graphing Primer* shows students how to construct and interpret graphs that appear in the text.

Instructor Supplements

Test Bank A. Thoroughly revised for relevancy and consistency, *Test Bank A* contains over 7,000 questions in multiple choice, true or false, and short-answer formats. New to this edition are over 150 short-answer questions.

Test Bank B. Coordinated by the author of *Test Bank A, Test Bank B* offers 2,000 original questions.

MicroExam A* and *MicroExam B. *MicroExam A* and *MicroExam B* offer the printed *Test Banks A* and *B* in electronic form for instant test generation. The easy-to-use software allows you to edit questions and print graphs.

Hypermedia Electronic Presentation Software for Windows. For each chapter of McEachern, *Hypermedia Electronic Presentation Software* provides instructors with a self-contained lecture resource. The software allows instructors to shift curves and display lecture notes and materials from the text.

PowerPoint Slides. Key materials from the text, as well as additional instructional materials, are available on *PowerPoint* slides to help enhance lectures and integrate technology into the classroom,

Transparency Acetates. Over 150 tables and graphs from the book are reproduced as full-color transparency acetates. Many of the acetates are "hinged" so that instructors may build complex graphs step by step.

CNBC Video Library. Hard-hitting, real-world business and economic events come to life in the classroom through exclusive CNBC videos. Short and long video clips are included for each chapter to highlight issues discussed in the text.

Teaching Assistance Manual. The *Teaching Assistance Manual* provides additional support beyond the *Instructor's Manual* and may be especially useful to new instructors, graduate assistants, and teachers interested in generating more class discussion. This manual offers (1) overviews and outlines of each chapter; (2) chapter objectives and quiz material; (3) material for class discussion; (4) topics warranting special attention; (5) supplementary examples; and (6) "What if?" discussion questions. Four appendixes provide guidance on (a) presenting material; (b) generating and sustaining class discussions; (c) preparing, administering, and grading quizzes; and (d) coping with the special problems confronting foreign graduate assistants.

The Teaching Economist. Since 1990 I have edited *The Teaching Economist,* a newsletter aimed at making teaching more interesting and more fun. The newsletter discusses new and imaginative ways to present topics—for example, how to "sensationalize" economic concepts, useful resources on the Internet, economic applications from science fiction, and more generally, ways to teach just for the fun of it. A regular feature of *The Teaching Economist,* "The Grapevine," offers teaching ideas suggested by colleagues from across the country. (Past issues of *The Teaching Economist* are reprinted at the end of the *Teaching Assistance Manual.*)

ACKNOWLEDGMENTS

Many people contributed to this book's development. I gratefully acknowledge the insightful comments of those who reviewed material for the Fourth Edition:

Richard K. Anderson
Texas A&M University

James Q. Aylesworth
Lakeland Community College

Klaus G. Becker
Texas Tech University

Scott Bloom
North Dakota State University

Rebecca R. Cline
Middle Georgia College

John A. Edgren
Eastern Michigan University

Paul G. Farnham
Georgia State University

Edward N. Gamber
Lafayette College

G. Robert Gillette
University of Kentucky

Philip E. Graves
University of Colorado at Boulder

Simon Hakim
Temple University

Brigid Harmon
University of Cincinnati

Dennis L. Hoffman
Arizona State University

Joyce P. Jacobsen
Wesleyan University

Nake M. Kamrany
University of Southern California

Faik Koray
Louisana State University

Denis Patrick Leyden
University of North Carolina, Greensboro

C. Richard Long
Georgia State University

Robert J. Rossana
Wayne State University

Ted Scheinman
Mt. Hood Community College

Calvin D. Siebert
University of Iowa

David E. Spencer
Brigham Young University

William J. Swift
Pace University

Thomas TenHoeve
Iowa State University

Percy O. Vera
Sinclair Community College

Donald A. Wells
University of Arizona

Robert Whaples
Wake Forest University

Michael D. White
St. Cloud State University

Kenneth Woodward
Saddleback College

Edward G. Young
University of Wisconsin, Eau Claire

I also thank those who have offered comments on previous editions:

Polly Reynolds Allen
University of Connecticut

Ted Amato
University of North Carolina at Charlotte

Thomas Andrews
Temple University

Dale G. Bails
Iowa Weslyan College

Maurice Ballabon
CUNY Baruch

Andy Barnett
Auburn University

Richard Barnett
SUNY at Buffalo

David W. Brasfield
Murray State University

Jurgen Brauer
Augusta College

Gardner Brown Jr.
University of Washington

Robert K. Brown
Texas Tech University

Judy C. Butler
Baylor University

Giorgio Canarella
California State University at Los Angeles

Charles Callahan III
SUNY College at Brockport

Richard Cebula
Georgia Institute of Technology

Larry A. Chenault
Miami University

Larry R. Clarke
Brookhaven College

Steven A. Cobb
Xavier University

James Peery Cover
University of Alabama

James M. Cox
DeKalb College

Jerry L. Crawford
Arkansas State University

Joseph Daniels
Marquette University

Elynor G. Davis
Georgia Southern University

Susan M. Davis
SUNY College at Buffalo

A. Edward Day
University of Central Florida

David H. Dean
University of Richmond

Janet S. Deans
Chestnut Hill College

David A. Denslow
University of Florida

Donald S. Elliot Jr.
Southern Illinois University

G. Rod Erfani
Transylvania University

Gisela Meyer Escoe
University of Cincinnati

Mark Evans
California State University at Bakersfield

Eleanor R. Fapohunda
SUNY College at Farmingdale

Mohsen Fardmanesh
Temple University

Rudy Fichtenbaum
Wright State University

T. Windsor Fields
James Madison University

Rodney Fort
Washington State University

Michael P. Gallaway
University of Texas at Austin

Gary M. Galles
Pepperdine University

Grant W. Gardner
Southern Methodist University

Adam Gifford
California State University at Northridge

J. Robert Gillette
Texas A&M University

Art Goldsmith
Washington and Lee University

Daniel M. Gropper
Auburn University

Robert Halvorsen
University of Washington

Nathan Hampton
St. Cloud State University

William T. Harris
University of Delaware

William R. Hart
Miami University

Baban Hasnat
SUNY College at Brockport

James R. Hill
Central Michigan University

Jane Smith Himarios
University of Texas at Arlington

Bruce C. Horning
Vanderbilt University

Janice Holtkamp
Iowa State University

Calvin Hoy
County College of Morris

Shane Hunt
Boston University

Beth Ingram
University of Iowa

David D. Jaques
California State University at Pomona

Nancy Jianakoplos
Colorado State University

John Kane
SUNY College at Oswego

Walter H. Kemmsies
Memphis State University

D. Mark Kennet
Tulane University

Faik Koray
Louisiana State University

Joseph D. Kotaska
Monroe Community College

Joseph M. Lammert
Raymond Walters College

Laraine Lomax
Northeastern University

Ana Maria Lomperis
North Carolina State University

Richard Long
Georgia State University

Thomas M. Maloy
Muskegon Community College

Gabriel Manrique
Winona State University

Robert A. Margo
Vanderbilt University

Wolfgang Mayer
University of Cinncinati

J. Harold McClure Jr.
Villanova University

John M. McDowell
Arizona State University

Floyd B. McFarland
Oregon State University

James McLain
University of New Orleans

Martin I. Milkman
Murray State University

Milton G. Mitchell
*University of Wisconsin at
Oshkosh*

Kathryn A. Nantz
Fairfield University

Andrew J. Policano
*University of Wisconsin-
Madison*

Kellie Poyas
Colorado State University

Reza Ramazani
St. Michaels University

Carol H. Rankin
Xavier University

Mitch Redlo
*Monroe Community
College*

John J. Reid
Memphis State University

Diane Lim Rogers
*Pennsylvania State
University*

Mark Rush
University of Florida

Richard Saba
Auburn University

Rexford Santerre
Bentley College

Peter M. Schwarz
*University of North
Carolina at Charlotte*

Lee J. Van Scyoc
*University of Wisconsin at
Oshkosh*

Donna E. Shea
Bentley College

Steven M. Sheffrin
*University of California,
Davis*

Roger Sherman
University of Virginia

William F. Shughart II
University of Mississippi

Philip A. Smith
DeKalb College

V. Kerry Smith
*North Carolina State
University*

Janet Speyrer
University of New Orleans

George Spiva
University of Tennessee

Houston H. Stokes
*University of Illinois at
Chicago*

Robert J. Stonebreaker
*Indiana University of
Pennsylvania*

Thomas TenHoeve
Iowa State University

Stuart E. Theil
*Washington State
University*

Jin Wang
*University of Wisconsin at
Stevens Point*

Gregory H. Wassall
Northeastern University

William Weber
Eastern Illinois University

David R. Weinberg
Xavier University

Michael D. White
St. Cloud State University

Richard D. Winkelman
Arizona State University

Peter Wyman
*Spokane Falls Community
College*

Mesghena Yasin
Morehead State University

Leland B. Yeager
Auburn University

William Zeis
Bucks Community College

I relied on the division of labor based on comparative advantage to prepare the most complete teaching package on the market today. John Pisciotta of Baylor University authored the *Hypermedia Electronic Presentation Software for Windows*. John Lunn of Hope College authored the *Study Guide*. Robert Toutkoushian of the University System of New Hampshire authored the *Instructor's Manual*. And Robert Catlett of Emporia State University coordinated *Test Bank A* and *Test Bank B*. I thank all of my colleagues for their contributions to the project.

The talented staff at South-Western College Publishing provided invaluable editorial, administrative, and sales support. I would especially like to acknowledge the help of Dennis Hanseman and Kurt Gerdenich, Developmental Editors, and Joe Devine, the book's designer. Brigid Harmon, an economist who was closely involved with a previous edition as Developmental Editor, wrote the marginal notes for the *Annotated Instructor's Edition*. Sue Ellen Brown of Justified Left was the Project Manager, and Ann Mohan of WordCrafters was Project Editor. I thank Jack Calhoun, the Publishing Team Director, Scott Person, the Marketing Manager, and John Alessi, the Acquisitions Editor. I also appreciate the support of South-Western's dedicated service and sales force, for they contributed in a significant way to the gratifying success of the Third Edition, which made the Fourth Edition possible. Finally, I owe a special debt to my wife, Pat, who offered abundant encouragement and support along the way.

William A. McEachern

Brief Contents

PART 1		Chapter Number in	
INTRODUCTION TO ECONOMICS		Macroeconomics A Contemporary Introduction	Microeconomics A Contemporary Introduction
1 The Art and Science of Economic Analysis	1	1	1
2 Some Tools of Economic Analysis	25	2	2
3 The Market System	43	3	3
4 The Economic Actors: Households, Firms, Governments, and the Rest of the World	67	4	4

PART 2			
FUNDAMENTALS OF MACROECONOMICS			
5 Introduction to Macroeconomics	89	5	
6 Productivity and Growth	110	6	
7 Unemployment and Inflation	130	7	
8 Measuring Economic Aggregates	152	8	
9 Consumption and Aggregate Expenditure	177	9	
10 Aggregate Expenditure and Demand-Side Equilibrium	205	10	
11 Aggregate Supply	230	11	

PART 3			
FISCAL AND MONETARY POLICY			
12 Fiscal Policy	255	12	
13 Money and the Financial System	276	13	
14 Banking and the Money Supply	299	14	
15 Monetary Theory and Policy	320	15	
16 The Policy Debate: Active or Passive?	343	16	
17 Budgets, Deficits, and Public Policy	369	17	

PART 4

INTRODUCTION TO THE MARKET SYSTEM

18	Elasticity of Demand and Supply	393	5
19	Consumer Choice and Demand	420	6
20	Production and Cost in the Firm	447	7

PART 5

MARKET STRUCTURE AND PRICING

21	Perfect Competition	474	8
22	Monopoly	503	9
23	Monopolistic Competition and Oligopoly	526	10

PART 6

RESOURCE MARKETS

24	Resource Markets	550	11
25	Human Resources: Labor and Entrepreneurial Ability	576	12
26	Unions and Collective Bargaining	593	13
27	Capital, Interest, and Corporate Finance	616	14
28	Imperfect Information, Transaction Costs, and Market Behavior	637	15

PART 7

MARKET FAILURE AND PUBLIC POLICY

29	Economic Regulation and Antitrust Activity	656	16
30	Public Choice	678	17
31	Externalities and the Environment	698	18
32	Income Distribution and Poverty	721	19

PART 8

THE INTERNATIONAL SETTING

33	International Trade	745	18	20
34	International Finance	774	19	21
35	Developing and Transitional Economies	798	20	22

Contents

PART 1
INTRODUCTION TO ECONOMICS

1 The Art and Science of Economic Analysis 1

The Economic Problem: Scarce Resources But Unlimited Wants 2
Resources 2   Goods and Services 3   Economic Actors 4   Microeconomics and Macroeconomics 4

The Art of Economic Analysis 5
Rational Self-Interest 5   Economic Analysis Is Marginal Analysis 5   Case Study: Marginal Analysis in the Computer Industry 6   Choice Requires Time and Information 7

The Science of Economic Analysis 7
The Role of Theory 8   The Scientific Method 8   Economists Tell Stories 9   Case Study: A Yen for Vending Machines 9   Predicting Average Behavior 10   Normative Versus Positive Analysis 10   Some Pitfalls of Faulty Economic Analysis 11   If Economists Are So Smart, Why Aren't They Rich? 12

Appendix: Understanding Graphs 16
Drawing Graphs 17   The Slopes of Straight Lines 19   The Slope Depends on How Units Are Measured 19   The Slopes of Curved Lines 19   Curve Shifts 21   The 45-Degree Ray from the Origin 22

2 Some Tools of Economic Analysis 25

Choice and Opportunity Cost 26
Opportunity Cost 26   Case Study: The Opportunity Cost of College 26   Opportunity Cost Is Subjective 27   Sunk Cost and Choice 28

Specialization, Comparative Advantage, and Exchange 28
The Law of Comparative Advantage 29   Absolute and Comparative Advantage 29   Specialization and Exchange 30   Division of Labor and Gains from Specialization 30   Case Study: Evidence of Specialization 31

The Economy's Production Possibilities 32
Efficiency and the Production Possibilities Frontier 32   Inefficient and Unattainable Production 34   Shape of the Production Possibilities Frontier 34   What Shifts the Production Possibilities Frontier? 35   What We Can Learn from the PPF 37   Three Questions Each Economic System Must Answer 37

Economic Systems 38
Pure Capitalism 38   Command Economy 39   Mixed and Transitional Economies 39   Economies Based on Custom or Religion 40

3 The Market System 43

Demand 44
The Law of Demand 44   The Demand Schedule and Demand Curve 45

Changes in Demand 47
Changes in Consumer Income 47   Changes in the Prices of Related Goods 48   Changes in Consumer Expectations 49   Changes in the Number or Composition of Consumers 49   Changes in Consumer Tastes 49

Supply 50
The Supply Schedule and Supply Curve 50

Changes in Supply 51
Changes in Technology 52   Changes in the Prices of Relevant Resources 53   Changes in the Prices of Alternative Goods 53   Changes in Producer Expectations 53   Changes in the Number of Producers 53

Demand and Supply Create a Market 54
Markets 54   Specialized Markets 54   Market Equilibrium 55   Markets Allocate Resources 55

Changes in Equilibrium Price and Quantity 57
Impact of Changes in Demand 57   Impact of Changes in Supply 58   Simultaneous Changes in Demand and Supply 59   Case Study: The Market for Professional Basketball 60

xv

Disequilibrium Prices   61
Price Floors 62   Price Ceilings 62   Case Study: Toys Are Serious Business 63

4 The Economic Actors: Households, Firms, Governments, and the Rest of the World   67

The Household   68
The Evolution of the Household 68 Households Maximize Utility 68 Households as Resource Suppliers 68 Households as Demanders of Goods and Services 70

The Firm   70
Transaction Costs and Evolution of the Firm 70   Why Do Firms Specialize? 71   Why Does Household Production Still Exist? 72 Case Study: The Electronic Cottage 73   Kinds of Firms 73   Nonprofit Institutions 75

The Government   76
The Role of Government 76   Government's Structure and Objectives 77   Size and Growth of U.S. Government 78   Sources of Government Revenue 80   Tax Principles and Tax Incidence 81

The Rest of the World   82
International Trade 82   Exchange Rates 83   Trade Restrictions 83 Case Study: The World of Automobiles 84

PART 2
FUNDAMENTALS OF MACROECONOMICS

5 Introduction to Macroeconomics   89

The National Economy   90
What's Special about the National Economy? 90   Similarities Between the Human Body and the Economy 90   Testing New Theories 91   Knowledge and Performance 92

Economic Fluctuations and Growth   93
Economic Fluctuation Analysis 93 Case Study: The Global Economy 96   Leading Economic Indicators 98

Aggregate Demand and Aggregate Supply   98
Aggregate Output and the Price Level 98   Aggregate Supply Curve 100   Equilibrium 100

A Short History of the U.S. Economy   101
The Great Depression and Before 101   The Age of Keynes: Between the Great Depression and the Early 1970s 103   The Great Stagflation 104   Experience Since 1980 104   The Twin Deficits 106   Case Study: Half Century of Price Levels and Real GDP 106

6 Productivity and Growth   110

U.S. Productivity   111
What Is Productivity? 111   Labor Productivity 111   The Per-Worker Production Function 112   Long-Term Productivity Growth 113   The Recent Slowdown in Productivity Growth 114

Why the Slowdown in Labor Productivity Growth?   115
Rate of Capital Formation 115   Changes in the Labor Force 115 Changing Composition of Output 116   Increased Role of Government 116   Huge Budget Deficits 117

Research and Development   118
Basic and Applied Research 118   Expenditures for Research and Development 118   Patents and Productivity 120   Case Study: Computers and Productivity 120

Other Issues of Technology and Growth   122
Industrial Policy 122   Case Study: Picking Technological Winners 122   Does Technological Change Lead to Unemployment? 123 Output Per Capita 124   Do Economies Converge? 125

7 Unemployment and Inflation   130

Unemployment   131
Measuring Unemployment 131   Changes over Time in Unemployment Statistics 133   Unemployment in Various Groups 134 Duration of Unemployment 135   Unemployment Differences across the Country 135   Case Study: Poor King Coal 136 Types of Unemployment 136   The Meaning of Full Employment 138   Unemployment Insurance 138   International Comparisons of Unemployment 139   Problems with Official Unemployment Figures 139

Inflation   140
Case Study: Hyperinflation in Brazil 140   Two Sources of Inflation 142   A Historical Look at Inflation and the Price Level 143   Anticipated versus Unanticipated Inflation 143   The Transaction Costs of Variable Inflation 144   Adapting to Relative Price Changes 144   International Comparisons of Inflation 145   Inflation and Interest Rates 147   Why Is Inflation So Unpopular? 148

8 Measuring Economic Aggregates   152

The Product of a Nation   153
National Income Accounts 153   GDP Based on the Expenditure Approach 154   Composition of Aggregate Expenditure 155 GDP Based on the Income Approach 155

Limitations of National Income Accounting 157
Some Production Is Not Included in GDP 157 Leisure, Quality, and Variety 158 Case Study: Tracking a $ Trillion Economy 159 Gross Domestic Product Ignores Depreciation 160 GDP Does Not Reflect All Costs 160 GDP Values All Output Equally 161

Accounting for Price Changes 161
Price Indexes 162 Consumer Price Index 162 Problems with the CPI 163 GDP Price Index 164 Moving from Fixed Weights to Chain Weights 165 Case Study: Computer Prices and GDP Estimation 165 Real GDP Estimates 166

Appendix A: A Closer Look at National Income Accounts 171
National Income 171 Personal Income 171 Disposable Income 172 Summary of National Income Accounts 172 Summary Income Statement of the Economy 172

Appendix B: The Chain-Weighted Index 174
Real GDP Index 174 GDP Price Index 175

9 Consumption and Aggregate Expenditure 177

Early Views of the Macroeconomy 178
The Classical View 178 Keynes and the Great Depression 178

The Circular Flow of Income and Expenditure 179
The Income Half of the Circular Flow 179 The Expenditure Half of the Circular Flow 181 Leakages Equal Injections 182 Planned Investment versus Actual Investment 182

Consumption 183
An Initial Look at Income and Consumption 183 The Consumption Function 184 Marginal Propensities to Consume and to Save 185 MPC, MPS, and the Slope of the Consumption and Savings Functions 186 Nonincome Determinants of Consumption 188 Case Study: The Life-Cycle Hypothesis 190

Investment 191
The Demand for Investment 192 From Micro to Macro 193 Planned Investment and the Economy's Level of Income 193 Nonincome Determinants of Investment 194 Case Study: Variability of Consumption and Investment 195

Government 196
Government Purchase Function 196 Net Taxes 196

Net Exports 197
Net Exports and Income 198 Nonincome Determinants of Net Exports 198

Appendix: Variable Net Exports 202
Net Exports and Income 202 Shifts in Net Exports 203

10 Aggregate Expenditure and Demand-Side Equilibrium 205

Aggregate Expenditure and Income 206
The Components of Aggregate Expenditure 206 Quantity of Real GDP Demanded 207 When Output and Planned Spending Differ 209 Leakages Equal Planned Injections 209

The Simple Spending Multiplier 210
Effects of an Increase in Aggregate Expenditure 210 The Spending Multiplier and the Circular Flow 212 Numerical Value of the Spending Multiplier 213 Case Study: Hard Times in Connecticut 214

Changes in the Price Level 215
A Higher Price Level 215 A Lower Price Level 217 The Multiplier and Shifts in Aggregate Demand 217 Case Study: Not Enough Saving 219

Appendix A: Variable Net Exports 224
Net Exports and the Spending Multiplier 225 A Change in Autonomous Spending 226

Appendix B: Algebra of Income and Expenditure 227
The Aggregate Expenditure Function 227 A More General Form of Income and Expenditure 227 Introducing Variable Net Exports 228

11 Aggregate Supply 230

Aggregate Supply in the Short Run 231
Labor Supply and Aggregate Supply 231 Potential Output and the Natural Rate of Unemployment 232 Actual Price Level Higher than Expected 233 Why Costs Rise When Output Exceeds Potential 233 The Price Level, Real Wages, and Labor Supply 234 Actual Price Level Lower than Expected 234 The Short-Run Aggregate Supply Curve 235

Equilibrium in the Short Run and Long Run 236
Actual Price Level Higher than Expected 237 Actual Price Level Lower than Expected 239 Tracing Potential Output 241 Evidence on Aggregate Supply 241 Case Study: Output Gaps and Wage Flexibility 242

Changes in Aggregate Supply 244
Increases in Aggregate Supply 244 Decreases in Aggregate Supply 246 Case Study: Why Is Unemployment So High in Europe? 247

Appendix: The Market for Resources 251
The Market for Labor 251 Changes in the Expected Price Level 252 Potential GDP 253

PART 3
FISCAL AND MONETARY POLICY

12 Fiscal Policy   255

Theory of Fiscal Policy   256
Changes in Government Purchases 256   Changes in Net Taxes 257
Changes in Net Taxes and Government Purchases Combined 259

Including Aggregate Supply   260
Fiscal Policy with a Contractionary Gap 260   Fiscal Policy with
an Expansionary Gap 261   Automatic Stabilizers 264   From the
Golden Age to Stagflation 265   Fiscal Policy and the Natural
Rate of Unemployment 265   Lags in Fiscal Policy 266   Discre-
tionary Policy and Permanent Income 266   Feedback Effects of
Fiscal Policy on Aggregate Supply 267   Giant U.S. Budget
Deficits of the 1980s and 1990s 267   Case Study: The Supply-
Side Experiment 267   Case Study: Discretionary Policy and Pres-
idential Elections 269

**Appendix: The Algebra of
Demand-Side Fiscal Policy   273**
Net-Tax Multiplier 273   The Multiplier When Both G and NT
Change 273   The Multiplier with a Proportional Income Tax 274
Including Variable Net Exports 274

13 Money and the
Financial System   276

The Evolution of Money   277
Barter and the Double Coincidence of Wants 277   Earliest Money
and Its Functions 277   Problems with Commodity Money 279
Coins 279   Money and Banking 280   Paper Money 281   The
Value of Money 282   When Money Performs Poorly 282   Case
Study: When the Monetary System Breaks Down 283

Financial Institutions in the United States   284
Commercial Banks and Thrifts 284   Development of the Dual
Banking System 284   Birth of the Federal Reserve System 285
Powers of the Federal Reserve System 285   Banking During the
Great Depression 286   Roosevelt's Reforms 287   Branch Banking
Restrictions 289   The Quiet Life of Depository Institutions 290

Recent Problems with Depository Institutions   290
Depository Institutions Were Losing Deposits 291   Bank Deregu-
lation 291   Bailing Out the Thrifts 292   Case Study: Easy Money,
Empty Buildings 292   Commercial Banks Were Also Failing 293

14 Banking and the
Money Supply   299

Banks, Their Deposits, and the Money Supply   300
Banks Are Financial Intermediaries 300   Money and Liquidity 301
Other Deposits 301

How the Banking System Works   303
Starting a Bank 303   Reserve Accounts 304   Liquidity versus Profitability 305   The Fed's Balance Sheet 306   Case Study: Tracking
the Supernote 307

How Banks Create Money   309
Creating Money Through Excess Reserves 309   Summary of
Rounds 312   Case Study: Banking on the Net 313   Another Pos-
sibility 314   Excess Reserves, Reserve Requirements, and Money
Expansion 314   Limitations on Money Expansion 316   Multiple
Contraction of Money 316   Change in the Discount Rate 316

15 Monetary Theory and Policy   320

Money and the Economy: The Indirect Channel   321
The Demand for Money 321   Money Demand and Interest Rates
322   Supply of Money and the Equilibrium Interest Rate 323

Money and Aggregate Demand   324
Interest Rates and Planned Investment 324   Money and the Slope
of the Aggregate Demand Curve 326   Adding Aggregate Supply
328   Fiscal Policy with Money 329

Money and the Economy: The Direct Channel   330
The Equation of Exchange 330   The Quantity Theory of Money
331   Case Study: The Money Supply and Inflation 332   What
Determines the Velocity of Money? 333   How Stable Is Velocity? 334

Money Supply versus Interest Rate Targets   335
Contrasting Policies 336   Targets Until 1982 337   Targets after
1982 337   Case Study: International Finance 338

16 The Policy Debate:
Active or Passive?   343

Active Policy versus Passive Policy   344
Closing a Contractionary Gap 344   Closing an Expansionary Gap
345   Problems with Active Policy 346   The Problem of Lags 347
Review of Policy Perspectives 348   Case Study: Presidential Economics 349

Role of Expectations   350
Monetary Policy and Expectations 350   Anticipating Monetary
Policy 352   Policy Credibility 354   Case Study: Central Bank In-
dependence and Price Stability 355

The Phillips Curve   356
Short-Run Phillips Curve 358   Long-Run Phillips Curve 359   The
Natural Rate Hypothesis 360   Evidence of the Phillips Curve 361

Policy Rules versus Discretion 362
Rationale for Rules 362 Rules and Rational Expectations 363
Theory of Real Business Cycles 363

17 Budgets, Deficits, and Public Policy 369

The Federal Budget Process 370
The Presidential Role in the Budget Process 370 The Congressional Role in the Budget Process 370 Problems with the Budget Process 371 Suggested Budget Reforms 373

Federal Budget Deficits 373
Rationale for Deficits 373 Budget Philosophies and Deficits 374

Deficits in the 1980s 374 Deficit Reduction Measures 375 Case Study: The 1996 Federal Budget Deadlock 376 Why Deficits? Why Now? 377 The Relationship between Deficits and Other Aggregate Variables 378 Crowding Out and Crowding In 380 The Twin Deficits 380 Deficits in Other Countries 382

The Ballooning National Debt 382
The National Debt since World War II 382 Debt Relative to GDP 384 An International Perspective on National Debt 384 Interest Payments on the Debt 384 Interest Payments and Seigniorage 385 Who Bears the Burden of the Debt? 385 Case Study: An Intergenerational View of Deficits and Debt 387

Reducing the Deficit 388
Line-Item Veto 388 Balanced Budget Amendment 389

PART 4
INTRODUCTION TO THE MARKET SYSTEM

18 Elasticity of Demand and Supply 393

Price Elasticity of Demand 394
Calculating Price Elasticity of Demand 394 Categories of Price Elasticity of Demand 396 Elasticity and Total Revenue 396 Price Elasticity and the Linear Demand Curve 397 Constant-Elasticity Demand 398

Determinants of the Price Elasticity of Demand 400
Availability of Substitutes 400 Proportion of the Consumer's Budget Spent on the Good 401 A Matter of Time 401 Elasticity Estimates 402 Case Study: Pharmaceutical Prices across Countries 403

Price Elasticity of Supply 405
Categories of Supply Elasticity 405 Determinants of Supply Elasticity 407

Elasticity and Tax Incidence: An Application 408
Demand Elasticity and Tax Incidence 408 Supply Elasticity and Tax Incidence 410

Other Elasticity Measures 411
Income Elasticity of Demand 411 Case Study: The Demand for Food and "The Farm Problem" 412 Cross-Price Elasticity of Demand 415

19 Consumer Choice and Demand 420

Utility Analysis 421
Tastes and Preferences 421 The Law of Diminishing Marginal Utility 421

Measuring Utility 422
Units of Utility 422 Utility Maximization in a World without Scarcity 424 Utility Maximization in a World of Scarcity 425 The Utility-Maximizing Conditions 426 Deriving the Law of Demand from Marginal Utility 426 Case Study: Demand in the Animal World 428 Consumer Surplus 429 Market Demand and Consumer Surplus 431 Case Study: The Marginal Value of Free Medical Care 432

The Role of Time in Demand 433

Appendix: Indifference Curves and Utility Maximization 438
Consumer Preferences 438 The Budget Line 441 Consumer Equilibrium at the Tangency 442 Effects of a Change in Income 443 Effects of a Change in Price 443 Income and Substitution Effects 443

20 Production and Cost in the Firm 447

Cost and Profit 448
Explicit and Implicit Costs 448 Alternative Measures of Profit 448

Production in the Short Run 450
Fixed and Variable Resources 450 The Law of Diminishing Marginal Returns 450 The Total and Marginal Product Curves 453

Costs in the Short Run 453
Total Cost and Marginal Cost in the Short Run 453 Average Cost in the Short Run 456 The Relationship between Marginal Cost and Average Cost 456 Summary of Short-Run Cost Curves 459

Costs in the Long Run 459
The Long-Run Average Cost Curve 459   Economies of Scale 461
Diseconomies of Scale 461   Case Study: At the Movies 462
Economies and Diseconomies of Scale at the Firm Level 463   Case
Study: Billions and Billions of Burgers 464

Appendix: A Closer Look at Production and Costs 468
The Production Function and Efficiency 468   Isoquants 469   Isocost Lines 470   The Choice of Input Combinations 471   The Expansion Path 472

PART 5
MARKET STRUCTURE AND PRICING

21 Perfect Competition   474

An Introduction to Perfect Competition   475
Perfectly Competitive Market Structure 475   Demand under Perfect Competition 475

Short-Run Profit Maximization   476
Total Revenue Minus Total Cost 477   Marginal Cost Equals Mar-
ginal Revenue in Equilibrium 479   Measuring Profit in the Short
Run 479

Minimizing Short-Run Losses   480
Fixed Cost and Minimizing Losses 480   Marginal Cost Equals Mar-
ginal Revenue 481   Shutting Down in the Short Run 483   The
Firm and Industry Short-Run Supply Curves 483   Case Study:
Auction Markets 486

Perfect Competition in the Long Run   487
Zero Economic Profit in the Long Run 487   The Long-Run Adjustment to a Change in Demand 488

The Long-Run Supply Curve   491
Constant-Cost Industries 492   Increasing-Cost Industries 492   Decreasing-Cost Industries 494

Perfect Competition and Efficiency   495
Productive Efficiency 495   Allocative Efficiency 495   Gains from
Voluntary Exchange through Competitive Markets 496   Case
Study: Experimental Economics 498

22 Monopoly   503

Barriers to Entry   504
Legal Restrictions 504   Economies of Scale 504   Control of Essential Resources 505   Case Study: Are Diamonds Forever? 505

Revenue for the Monopolist   506
Demand and Marginal Revenue 506   The Gain and Loss from Selling One More Unit 507   Revenue Curves 508

Firm Costs and Profit Maximization   510
Profit Maximization 510   Short-Run Losses and the Shutdown
Decision 513   Long-Run Profit Maximization 514   Contestable
Markets 514

Monopoly and the Allocation of Resources   515
Price and Output under Perfect Competition 515   Price and
Output under Monopoly 515   Allocative and Distributive Ef-
fects 516

Problems Estimating the Welfare Cost of Monopoly   517
Why the Welfare Loss of Monopoly Might Be Lower 517   Why
the Welfare Loss of Monopoly Might Be Higher 517   Case Study:
The Mail Monopoly 518

Models of Price Discrimination   519
Conditions for Price Discrimination 519   Examples of Price Dis-
crimination 519   A Model of Price Discrimination 521   Perfect
Price Discrimination: The Monopolist's Dream 521

23 Monopolistic Competition
and Oligopoly   526

Monopolistic Competition   527
Characteristics of Monopolistic Competition 527   Product Differ-
entiation 527   Short-Run Profit Maximization or Loss Minimiza-
tion 528   Zero Economic Profit in the Long Run 530   Case
Study: Fast Forward 531   Monopolistic Competition and Perfect
Competition Compared 532

An Introduction to Oligopoly   534
Varieties of Oligopoly 534   Case Study: The Unfriendly Skies 535
Economies of Scale 535   High Cost of Entry 536

Models of Oligopoly   537
Collusion and Cartels 537   Price Leadership 539   Cost-Plus Pric-
ing 540   Game Theory 541   The Kinked Demand Curve 542
Summary of Models 545   Comparison of Oligopoly and Perfect
Competition 545   Mergers and Oligopoly 546

PART 6
RESOURCE MARKETS

24 Resource Markets 550

The Once-Over 551
Resource Demand 551 Resource Supply 551

The Demand and Supply of Resources 552
The Market Demand Curve 552 The Market Supply Curve 553 Temporary and Permanent Resource Price Differences 553 Opportunity Cost and Economic Rent 556

A Closer Look at Resource Demand 558
The Firm's Demand for One Resource 558 Marginal Revenue Product 559 Marginal Resource Cost 561 Shifts in the Demand for Resources 563 Case Study: The Derived Demand for Architects 564 Price Elasticity of Resource Demand 565 Hiring Resources as a Price Searcher 566 Summarizing Resource Markets 568 Optimal Use: More than One Resource 568 Case Study: The McMinimum Wage 570

Distribution of Resource Earnings 572

25 Human Resources: Labor and Entrepreneurial Ability 576

Labor Supply 577
Labor Supply and Utility Maximization 577 Wages and Individual Labor Supply 579 Nonwage Determinants of Labor Supply 581 Market Supply of Labor 583 Why Wages Differ 583 Case Study: Comparable Worth 584

Entrepreneurial Ability 586
The Entrepreneur Can Supply Other Resources 586 Why Entrepreneurs Often Invest in the Firm 587 Entrepreneurship and Theories of Profit 587 Profit and the Supply of Entrepreneurs 588 Case Study: IBM's Lotus Position 589

26 Unions and Collective Bargaining 593

A Brief History of the U.S. Labor Movement 594
Early Labor Organizations 594 A New Deal for Labor 595 The Labor Movement after World War II 595

Collective Bargaining and Other Tools of Unionism 596
Collective Bargaining 596 The Strike 596 Case Study: Hard Ball at Caterpillar 597

Union Wages and Employment 598
Inclusive, or Industrial, Unions 598 Exclusive, or Craft, Unions 600 Increasing Demand for Union Labor 600 Case Study: Featherbedding on Broadway 602 Bilateral Monopoly 603

Other Union Objectives 605
Maximizing the Total Wage Bill 605 Maximizing Economic Rent 606 Summary of Union Objectives 608

Recent Trends in Union Membership 608
Public Employee Unions 609 Competition from Nonunion Suppliers 610 Industry Deregulation 611 Unions and Technological Change 611 A Fight for Survival 611

27 Capital, Interest, and Corporate Finance 616

The Role of Time in Consumption and Production 617
Production, Saving, and Time 617 Consumption, Saving, and Time 618 Optimal Investment 619 Investing in Human Capital 622 The Demand for Loanable Funds 622 Why Interest Rates Differ 623

Present Value and Discounting 625
Present Value of Payment One Year Hence 625 Present Value for Payments in Later Years 626 Present Value of an Income Stream 626 Present Value of an Annuity 627 Case Study: The Million-Dollar Lottery 627

Corporate Finance 628
Corporate Stock and Retained Earnings 629 Corporate Bonds 629 Securities Exchanges 629

Corporate Ownership and Control 630
Managerial Behavior in Large Corporations 630 Constraints on Managerial Discretion 631 The Market for Corporate Control 632 Case Study: Campeau Bets the Store 633

28 Imperfect Information, Transaction Costs, and Market Behavior 637

The Rationale for the Firm and the Scope of Its Operation 638
The Firm Reduces Transaction Costs 638 The Boundaries of the Firm 639 Case Study: The Trend toward Outsourcing 643 Economies of Scope 644

Market Behavior with Imperfect Information 644
Optimal Search with Imperfect Information 644 The Winner's Curse 646

Market Behavior with Asymmetric Information 647
Hidden Characteristics: The "Lemon" Problem 648 Hidden Actions: The Principal-Agent Problem 648 Adverse Selection 649 Moral Hazard 649 Coping with Asymmetric Information 650 Asymmetric Information in Labor Markets 650 Adverse Selection Problems in Labor Markets 651 Signaling and Screening 651 Case Study: The Reputation of a Big Mac 652

PART 7
MARKET FAILURE AND PUBLIC POLICY

29 Economic Regulation and Antitrust Activity   656

Business Behavior and Public Policy   657
Government Regulation of Business 657

Regulating Natural Monopolies   657
Unregulated Profit Maximization 658   Setting Price Equal to Marginal Cost 659   Subsidizing the Natural Monopolist 659   Setting Price Equal to Average Cost 660   The Regulatory Dilemma 660

Alternative Theories of Economic Regulation   660
Producers Have a Special Interest in Economic Regulation 661   Case Study: Rail and Truck Regulation and Deregulation 662   Case Study: Airline Regulation and Deregulation 665

Antitrust Laws   667
Origins of Antitrust Policy 667   Antitrust Law Enforcement 668   Per Se Illegality and the Rule of Reason 669   Mergers and Public Policy 669

Competitive Trends in the U.S. Economy   671
Market Competition over Time 671   Recent Competitive Trends 673   Problems with Antitrust Legislation 673

30 Public Choice   678

The Economy as a Game   679
Fairness of the Game 679   Kinds of Games 679   Rules and Behavior 680

Public Choice in Direct Democracy   680
Median Voter Model 680   Logrolling 682   Cyclical Majority 682

Representative Democracy   683
Goals of the Participants 684   Rational Ignorance 684   Distribution of Costs and Benefits 685   Case Study: Farm Subsidies: Negative-Sum Game 685   Rent Seeking 688   Case Study: Campaign Finance Reform 690

The Underground Economy   691

Bureaucracy and Representative Democracy   692
Ownership and Funding of Bureaus 692   Ownership and Organizational Behavior 693   Bureaucratic Objectives 693   Private versus Public Production 694

31 Externalities and the Environment   698

Externalities and the Common Pool Problem   699
Renewable Resources 699   External Costs with Fixed Technology 700   External Costs with Variable Technology 702   Resolving the Common Pool Problem 703   Case Study: Destruction of the Tropical Rain Forests 705   The Coase Analysis of Externalities 707   A Market for Pollution Rights 708   Positive Externalities 710

Environmental Protection in the United States   712
Air Pollution 712   Case Study: City in the Clouds 713   Water Pollution 714   Hazardous Waste and the Superfund 714   Solid Waste: "Paper or Plastic?" 715

32 Income Distribution and Poverty   721

The Distribution of Household Income   722
The Lorenz Curve 723   Why Do Incomes Differ? 725

Poverty and the Poor   725
Official Poverty Level 726   Programs to Help the Poor 727   Welfare Expenditures and the Rate of Poverty 729

Who Are the Poor?   730
Poverty and Age 731   Poverty and Public Choice 731   Poverty and Gender 732   Poverty and Discrimination 734   Affirmative Action 735

Undesirable Consequences of Income Assistance   736
Work Disincentives 736   Does Welfare Cause Dependency? 737

Welfare Reform   738
Recent Reforms 738   Case Study: "Ending Welfare As We Know It" 740   Case Study: The Homeless 741

PART 8
THE INTERNATIONAL SETTING

33 International Trade   745

The Gains from Trade   746
A Profile of Imports and Exports 746   Production Possibilities

without Trade 746   Consumption Possibilities Based on Comparative Advantage 748   Reasons for International Specialization 750

Trading on the World Market   751
What If World Price Is Above Domestic Equilibrium Price? 752

What If World Price Is Below the Domestic Equilibrium Price? 753
The Rest of the World 754   Determining the World Price 754
Consumer and Producer Surplus 755   The Net Effect of Trade on
Social Welfare 757

Trade Restrictions   758
Tariffs 758   Import Quotas 759   Other Trade Restrictions 762
Freer Trade by Multilateral Agreement 763   Case Study: The
World Trade Organization 763   Common Markets 764

Arguments for Trade Restrictions   765
National Defense Argument 765   Infant Industry Argument 765
Antidumping Argument 766   Jobs and Income Argument 767
Declining Industries Argument 768   Problems with Protection 768
Case Study: Enforcing Trade Restrictions 769

34 International Finance   774

Balance of Payments   775
International Economic Transactions 775   Merchandise Trade Balance 775   Balance on Goods and Services 776   Unilateral Transfers 777   Capital Account 777   Statistical Discrepancy 778
Deficits and Surpluses 778

Foreign Exchange Rates and Markets   780
Foreign Exchange 780   Demand for Foreign Exchange 781   Sup-
ply of Foreign Exchange 782   Determining the Exchange Rate 782
Arbitrageurs and Speculators 784   Purchasing Power Parity 784
Case Study: The Big Mac Index 785   Flexible Exchange Rates 787
Fixed Exchange Rates 787   Enforcing a Rate Ceiling 788   En-
forcing a Rate Floor 789   Case Study: Mexico's Peso Problems 790

**History and Development of the International
Monetary System   792**
The Bretton Woods Agreement 792   Demise of the Bretton
Woods System 793   The Current System: Managed Float 793

35 Developing and Transitional Economies   798

Worlds Apart   799
Developing Countries 799   Classifications of Economies 799
Health and Nutrition 801   High Birth Rates 803   Women in De-
veloping Countries 805

Productivity: Key to Development   805
Low Labor Productivity 805   Technology and Education 806   Inefficient Use of Labor 806   Natural Resources 808   Financial Institutions 808   Capital Infrastructure 808   Entrepreneurial Ability
809   Government Monopolies 809

International Trade and Development   809
Import Substitution versus Export Promotion 810   Migration and
the Brain Drain 811   Trade Liberalization and Special Interests 811

Foreign Aid and Economic Development   811
Foreign Aid 812   Does Foreign Aid Promote Economic Development? 812   Case Study: Privatizing Foreign Aid 813

Transitional Economies   814
Types of Economic Systems 814   Enterprises and Soft Budget
Constraints 814   Case Study: Ownership and Resources Use 815

Markets and Institutions 816
Institutions and Economic Development 817   The "Big Bang"
Versus Gradualism 817   Privatization 818

Glossary   825

Index   837

Photo Credits   855

About the Author

William A. McEachern is Professor of Economics at the University of Connecticut. Since 1973 he has taught principles of economics and in 1980 developed a series of annual workshops for teaching assistants. He has given teaching workshops around the country. He earned an undergraduate degree *cum laude* in the honors program from Holy Cross College and an M.A. and a Ph.D. from the University of Virginia. He has authored several books and monographs in public finance, public policy, and industrial organizations. His research has appeared in edited volumes as well as journals such as *Economic Inquiry, National Tax Journal, Southern Economic Journal, Journal of Industrial Economics, Kyklos, Quarterly Review of Economics and Business, Challenge,* and *Public Choice.* He is Editor-in-Chief of *The Connecticut Economy: A University of Connecticut Quarterly Review* and has advised federal, state, and local governments on policy matters and directed a bipartisan commission examining Connecticut's finances. Professor McEachern has been quoted in publications such as *The Wall Street Journal, New York Times, Christian Science Monitor,* and *USA Today.* He has received the University of Connecticut's Faculty Award for Distinguished Public Service.

Photo by Peter Morenus/UConn

The Art and Science of Economic Analysis

Y ou have been reading and hearing about economic issues for years—unemployment, inflation, oil prices, the federal deficit, college tuition, housing prices. When the explanations of these issues go into any depth, some people tune out the same way they do when the weather forecaster tries to provide an in-depth analysis of high-pressure fronts colliding with moisture carried in from the coast. What many people fail to realize is that economics is much more lively than the dry accounts offered by the news media. Economics is about making choices, and you make economic choices every day—choices about whether to get a part-time job or focus more on your studies, live in a dorm or off-campus, take a course in accounting or one in history, pack a lunch or buy a Big Mac. You, the economic decision maker, are the subject of this book, and you already know much more economics than you realize. You bring to the subject a rich personal experience, experience that will be tapped throughout the book to reinforce your understanding of the basic ideas. This chapter will introduce you to the art and science of economic analysis. Topics discussed in this chapter include:

- The economic problem
- Marginal analysis
- Rational self-interest

- Scientific method
- Normative versus positive analysis
- Pitfalls of economic thinking

THE ECONOMIC PROBLEM: SCARCE RESOURCES BUT UNLIMITED WANTS

Would you like a new car, a nicer home, better meals, more free time, a more interesting social life, more spending money, more sleep? Who wouldn't? Even if you can satisfy some of these desires, others will keep popping up. *The problem is that, although your wants, or desires, are virtually unlimited, the instruments at your disposal to satisfy these wants—your resources—are scarce.* A resource is *scarce* when there is not enough of it to satisfy people's wants. Because of scarce resources, you must choose from among your many wants and, whenever you choose, you must forgo satisfying some other wants.

The problem of scarce resources but unlimited wants is faced to a greater or lesser extent by each of the more than five billion people around the world. It is faced by taxicab drivers, farmers, brain surgeons, shepherds, students, politicians—by everybody. The taxicab driver uses the cab and other scarce resources, such as knowledge of the city, driving skills, and time, to earn income. This, in turn, can be exchanged for housing, groceries, clothing, trips to Disney World, and other goods and services that help satisfy some of the driver's unlimited wants.

Economics is the study of how people choose to allocate their scarce resources in order to produce, exchange, and consume goods and services in an attempt to satisfy their unlimited wants. We shall first consider what we mean by resources, next examine goods and services, and finally focus on the heart of the matter: economic choice, which arises from scarcity.

Economics The study of how people choose to use their scarce resources in an attempt to satisfy their unlimited wants

Resources

Resources are the inputs used to produce the goods and services that humans want. Goods and services are scarce because resources are scarce. We can divide resources divide into four broad categories: land, labor, capital, and entrepreneurial ability. **Land** represents not only land in the conventional sense of plots of ground, but all other natural resources—all so-called gifts of nature, including bodies of water, trees, oil reserves, minerals, and even animals. **Labor** comprises the broad category of human effort, both physical and mental. Labor includes the effort of both the cab driver and the brain surgeon. Note that labor itself comes from a more fundamental resource: *time.* Time is really the ultimate raw material of life. Without it we can accomplish nothing. We allocate our time to alternative uses: we can *sell* our time as labor, or we can *spend* our time doing other things such as sleeping, reading, or watching TV.

Land Plots of ground and other natural resources used to produce goods and services

Labor The physical and mental effort of humans used to produce goods and services

Capital represents human creations used to produce goods and services. We often distinguish between physical capital and human capital. *Physical capital* consists of roads, airports, buildings, machinery, tools, and other manufactured items employed to produce goods and services. Physical capital includes the driver's cab, the surgeon's scalpel, the farmer's tractor, the interstate highway system, and the building where your economics class meets. *Human capital* consists of the knowledge and skill people acquire to enhance their labor productivity, such as the taxi driver's knowledge of the city's streets or the surgeon's knowledge of human biology.

Capital All buildings, equipment, and human skill used to produce goods and services

A special kind of human skill is called **entrepreneurial ability**—that rare talent required to dream up a new product or find a better way to produce an

Entrepreneurial ability Managerial and organization skills combined with the willingness to take risks

existing one. The entrepreneur tries to discover and act on profitable opportunities by hiring resources and assuming the risk of business success or failure. The largest firms in the world today, such as Ford, IBM, and Microsoft, each began as an idea in the mind of an individual entrepreneur.

Resource owners are usually paid for the *time* their resources are employed by entrepreneurs, so resource payments have a time dimension, as in a wage of $10 per hour or rent of $600 per month. Resource owners are paid **rent** for their land, **wages** for their labor, and **interest** for their capital. The entrepreneur's effort is rewarded by **profit,** which is the difference between total revenue from sales and the total cost of the resources employed. The entrepreneur *claims* the *residual*—what's left over—after resource suppliers get paid. Sometimes the entrepreneur suffers a loss.

Goods and Services

Resources are combined in a variety of ways to produce goods and services. A farmer, a tractor, fifty acres of land, seeds, and fertilizer produce a good: corn. One hundred musicians, musical instruments, some chairs, a conductor, a musical score, and a music hall combine to produce a service: Beethoven's Fifth Symphony. Corn is a **good** because it is something we can see, feel, and touch; it requires scarce resources to produce; and it is used to satisfy human wants. The book you now hold, the chair you are sitting in, the clothes you are wearing, and your next meal are all goods. The performance of the Fifth Symphony is a **service** because it is not something tangible, yet it uses scarce resources to satisfy human wants. Lectures, movies, concerts, phone calls, on-line computer services, dry cleaning, and haircuts are all services.

Because goods and services require scarce resources, they are themselves scarce. A good or service is **scarce** if the amount people desire exceeds the amount that is available at a zero price. Since we cannot have all the goods and services we would like, we must continually choose among them. We must choose among more pleasant living quarters, better meals, nicer clothes, more reliable transportation, faster computers, and so on. Making choices in a world of scarcity means we must pass up some goods and services.

A few goods and services are considered *free* because the amount freely available (that is, available at a zero price) exceeds the amount people desire. For example, air and seawater are often considered free because we can breathe all the air we want and have all the seawater we can haul away. Yet, despite the old saying that "The best things in life are free," most goods and services are scarce, not free, and even those that appear to be free come with strings attached. For example, *clean* air and *clean* seawater have become increasingly scarce because the atmosphere has been used as a gas dump and the ocean as a sewer. *Goods and services that are truly free are not the subject matter of economics. Without scarcity, there would be no economic problem.*

Sometimes we mistakenly think of certain goods as free because they involve no apparent cost to us. Those subscription cards that keep falling out of magazines appear to be free. At least it seems we would have little difficulty rounding up about three thousand if necessary! Producing them, however, uses up scarce resources, resources drawn away from competing uses, such as producing higher-quality magazines. You may have heard the expression "There is no such thing as a free lunch." There is no free lunch because all

Rent *The payment resource owners receive for the use of their land*

Wages *The payment resource owners receive for their labor*

Interest *The payment resource owners receive for the use of their capital*

Profit *The return resource owners receive for their entrepreneurial ability; the total revenue from sales minus the total cost of resources employed by the entrepreneur*

Good *A tangible item that is used to satisfy wants*

Service *An intangible activity that is used to satisfy wants*

Scarce *When the amount people desire exceeds the amount available at a zero price*

Net Bookmark

Yahoo!, a directory of computerized links to the World Wide Web, was the creation of Jerry Yang and David Filo, Ph.D. candidates in electrical engineering at Stanford University. In their words, Yahoo! "began as an idea, grew into a hobby and lately has turned into a full-time passion." Visit Yahoo! at **http://www.yahoo.com/**.

goods and services involve a cost; producing a lunch draws scarce resources away from the production of other goods and services. A Russian proverb makes a similar point, but with more bite: "The only place you find free cheese is in a mousetrap."

Economic Actors

There are four types of actors, or participants, in the economy: households, firms, governments, and the rest of the world. *Households* play the leading role. As consumers, households demand the goods and services produced; as resource owners, households supply land, labor, capital, and entrepreneurial ability to firms, to governments, and to the rest of the world. *Firms, governments,* and *the rest of the world* are supporting actors because they demand the resources that households supply and supply the goods and services that households demand. The rest of the world includes foreign households, firms, and governments, which supply resources and products to U.S. markets and demand resources and products from U.S. markets.

Market A set of arrangements through which buyers and sellers carry out exchange at mutually agreeable terms

Markets are the means by which buyers and sellers carry out exchange. Markets are often physical places, such as a supermarket, department store, or shopping mall. Markets also include the mechanisms by which buyers and sellers communicate, such as classified ads, radio and television ads, cyberspace, and face-to-face bargaining. These market mechanisms provide information about the quantity, quality, and price of products offered for sale. Goods and services are bought and sold in **product markets;** resources are bought and sold in **resource markets.** The most important resource market is the labor market, or job market. Think of your experience looking for a job, and you get some idea of this market.

Product market A market in which goods and services are exchanged

Resource market A market in which resources are exchanged

Microeconomics and Macroeconomics

Although you have made thousands of economic choices, if you are like most people, you have seldom thought about your own economic behavior. For example, why did you choose to spend your scarce resource—*time*—reading this book right now rather than doing something else? **Microeconomics** is the study of your economic behavior and the economic behavior of others making choices about such matters as what to buy and what to sell, how much to work and how much to play, how much to borrow and how much to save. Microeconomics examines what factors influence individual economic choices and how the choices of various decision makers are coordinated by markets. For example, microeconomics explains how price and output are determined in individual markets, such as the market for breakfast cereal or the market for sports equipment.

Microeconomics The study of the economic behavior in particular markets, such as the market for computers or for unskilled labor

You have also likely given little thought to the factors that influence your own economic choices or how these choices link up with those made by hundreds of millions of others in the U.S. economy to determine economy-wide aggregates such as gross production, employment, and growth. **Macroeconomics** studies the performance of the economy as a whole. Whereas microeconomics studies the individual pieces of the economic puzzle, as reflected, for example, by particular markets, macroeconomics puts all the pieces together to focus on the big picture.

Macroeconomics The study of the economic behavior of entire economies

THE ART OF ECONOMIC ANALYSIS

An economy results from the choices of millions of individuals attempting to satisfy their unlimited wants. Because these choices lie at the very heart of the economic problem—the problem of coping with scarce resources but unlimited wants—they deserve a closer look. Developing an understanding of the factors that shape economic choices is the first step toward mastering the art of economic analysis.

Rational Self-Interest

A key economic assumption is that individuals, in making choices, rationally select alternatives they perceive to be in their best interests. By *rational* we mean simply that people try to make the best choices they can under the circumstances. People may not know with certainty which alternative will turn out to be the best. They simply select the alternatives they *expect* will yield them the most satisfaction and happiness.

This reliance on *rational self-interest* should not be viewed as blind materialism, pure selfishness, or greed. We all know people who are attuned to station WIIFM (What's In It For Me?). But, for most of us, self-interest often includes the welfare of our family, our friends, and perhaps the poor of the world. Even so, our concern for others is influenced by economic considerations. We may volunteer to drive a friend to the airport on Saturday afternoon, but we are less likely to offer a ride if the plane leaves at 6:00 A.M. We are more likely to donate our old clothes than our new ones to organizations such as Goodwill Industries. We tend to give more to our favorite charities if our contributions are tax deductible. *The point is that the notion of self-interest does not rule out concern for others; it simply means that concern for others is to some extent influenced by the same economic factors that affect other economic choices.* The lower the personal cost of helping others, the more help we offer.

Economic Analysis Is Marginal Analysis

Economic choice usually involves some adjustment to the existing situation, the status quo. The software producer must decide whether to revise or discontinue one of its word processing programs. The town manager must decide whether to hire another worker for street maintenance. Your favorite jeans are on sale, and you must decide whether to buy another pair. You are wondering whether you should carry an extra course next term. You have just finished dinner and must decide whether to have dessert.

Economic choice is based on a comparison of the expected marginal cost and the expected marginal benefit of the change under consideration. **Marginal** means "incremental" or "decremental"; it refers to a change in an economic variable, a change in the status quo. *You, as a rational decision maker, will change the status quo as long as your expected marginal benefit from the change exceeds your expected marginal cost.* For example, you compare the marginal benefit you expect from eating dessert with its marginal cost—the extra money, extra time, and extra calories.

Typically the change under consideration is small, but a marginal choice can involve a major economic adjustment, as in the decision to quit school and get a job. For a firm, a marginal choice might mean producing a new product, building a plant in Mexico, or even filing for bankruptcy. By focusing on the

Marginal A term meaning "incremental" or "decremental"; used to describe the result of a small change in an economic variable

effect of a marginal adjustment to the status quo, the economist is able to cut the analysis of economic choice down to manageable size. Rather than confront a bewildering economic reality head-on, the economist can begin with a marginal choice, then see how this choice affects a particular market and helps shape the economic system as a whole. Consider the marginal choices in the following case study.

CASE STUDY

Marginal Analysis in the Computer Industry

Location:

To learn more about the computer industry, visit Microsoft Corporation (http://www.microsoft.com/), Apple Computer, Incorporated (http://www.apple.com/), and Power Computing Corporation (http://www.powercc.com/).

One of most dynamic markets in the economy today is that for computer hardware and software. In this case study we examine three marginal decisions faced by three producers in this market.

Microsoft Network. August 24, 1995 was a significant day in the computer world. It was the day that Microsoft Corporation launched its new operating system, Windows 95. The earlier version of Windows was the dominant operating system for computers throughout the world, and the new and improved version was expected to extend Microsoft's market lead. As the release day approached, one decision remained: Should the new system include software that would allow users to subscribe to Microsoft Network, the firm's new on-line computer service? The problem was that the U.S. Justice Department was threatening legal action against Microsoft if the company used its dominance in operating systems to become dominant in on-line services. So the marginal *cost* of including the connecting software as part of Windows 95 was the risk of federal intervention. The marginal *benefit* of including the connecting software was that Microsoft would thereby gain entry into the growing on-line market. Microsoft decided that the marginal benefit outweighed the marginal cost; the on-line capability became part of Windows 95. Windows 95 turned out to be a smash hit, with seven million copies sold in the first five weeks.

Send in the Clones. Apple's Macintosh computer is highly regarded by experts for its ease of use and its sophisticated capabilities. Yet Macs account for fewer than one in ten personal computers in use. How come? More than a decade ago, when both Apple and IBM were creating the personal computer market, IBM allowed other firms to produce lower-cost clones of the IBM-PC, whereas Apple allowed no cloning of its Mac. Thanks to the clones, IBM-type machines began to dominate the market, so software developers found these machines a more attractive target. With more software available for them, IBM-type machines became even more popular. The decision whether or not to allow clones was a marginal decision for both Apple and IBM. As a result of those decisions, IBM-type machines gained the dominant share of the market. Apple recently rethought its position and decided to allow the Mac to be cloned, as we'll see next.

Pricing the Mac Clone. Why would Apple allow other firms to produce cheaper versions of its own successful model? First, as we've seen, Macs had a dwindling share of the market and, with the introduction of Windows 95, which was used on IBM-type machines, Macs were in danger of getting even less attention from software developers. Second, Apple earned license fees by selling the right to produce Mac clones. In the spring of 1995, Power Computing introduced the first Mac clone, the Power 100. That company's marginal decision was what price to charge. The clone was initially priced about $1,000 below a comparable Mac. About three months later, Power Computing aggressively cut its price by 30 percent. The lower price made the clone a hit. The lower price also put pressure on Apple to keep its prices down.

Sources: Don Clark, "U.S. Plans No Action Against Microsoft Before Launch of Windows 95 System," *The Wall Street Journal,* 9 August 1995; Jim Carlton, "Microsoft Profits Soar 58% on Strength of Windows 95," *The Wall Street Journal,* 18 October 1995; Steven Levy, "How Apple Became Avis," *Newsweek,* 21 August 1995; Sebastian Rupley, "Apple's Day in the Sun," *PC Magazine,* August 1995.

Marginal Analysis in the Computer Industry
continued

Choice Requires Time and Information

Rational choice takes time and requires information, but both time and information are scarce and valuable. If you have any doubts about the time and information required to make choices, talk to someone who recently purchased a home, a car, or a personal computer. Talk to a corporate official deciding whether to introduce a new product or build a new factory. Consider your own experience in selecting a college. You probably talked to friends, relatives, teachers, and guidance counselors. You likely looked at school catalogs and college guides. You may have visited campuses to meet with the admissions staff and with anyone else willing to talk. The decision took time and money, and it probably involved aggravation and anxiety.

Because information is costly to acquire, we are often willing to pay others to gather and digest it for us. The markets for college guidebooks, stock analysts, travel agents, real estate brokers, career counselors, restaurant guidebooks, and *Consumer Reports* magazine indicate our willingness to pay for information that will improve our economic choices.

To review: The art of economic analysis focuses on how individuals use their scarce resources in an attempt to satisfy their unlimited wants. Rational self-interest guides individual choice. Choice involves a comparison of the marginal cost and marginal benefit of alternative actions, a comparison that requires time and information.

THE SCIENCE OF ECONOMIC ANALYSIS

Economists use the science of economic analysis to develop theories, or models, that help to explain how economic choices are made and how the economy works. An **economic theory,** or **economic model,** is a simplification of economic reality that *is used to make predictions about the real world.* A theory, or model, captures the important elements of the problem under study; it need not spell out every detail and interrelation. In fact, the more details a theory con-

Economic theory, economic model A simplification of reality used to make predictions about the real world tains, the more unwieldy it becomes and the less useful it may be. The world we live in is so complex that we must simplify if we want to make any sense of things. A theory can be presented verbally, graphically, or mathematically.

The Role of Theory

People often don't understand the role of theory. Perhaps you have heard someone say "Oh, that's fine in theory, but in practice it's another matter." The implication is that the theory provides little aid in practical matters. People who say this fail to realize that they are merely substituting their own theory for a theory they either do not believe or do not understand. They are really saying "I have my own theory, which works better.'

All of us employ theories, however poorly defined or understood. Someone who pounds on the Pepsi machine that just ate his quarter has a crude theory about how that machine works and what just went wrong. One version of that theory might be "The quarter drops through a series of whatchamacallits, but sometimes the quarter gets stuck. *If* I pound on the machine, *then* I can free up the quarter and send it on its way." Evidently this theory works well enough that many individuals continue to pound on machines that fail to perform (a real problem for the vending machine industry). Yet if you asked this mad pounder to explain his "theory" about how the machine operates, he would look at you as if you were crazy.

The Scientific Method

To study economic problems, economists employ a process of theoretical investigation called the *scientific method,* which consists of four steps.

Step One. The first step is to identify and define the key variables that are relevant to the economic problem under consideration. A **variable** is a measure, such as the *price* of Pepsi or the *quantity* of Pepsi, that can take on different possible values. The variables of concern become the basic elements of the theory, so they must be selected with care.

Variable A measure, such as price or quantity, that can take on different possible values

Step Two. The second step is to specify the assumptions under which the theory is to apply. Assumptions lay out the framework for the theory. One major category of assumptions is the **other-things-constant assumption**—in Latin, the *ceteris paribus* assumption. The idea is to identify the variables of interest, then to focus exclusively on the relation among them, assuming that nothing else of importance will change—in other words, that other things will remain constant. For example, suppose that we are interested in how the price of Pepsi influences the amount purchased. To isolate the relation between the price of Pepsi and the quantity purchased, we assume that there are no changes in other important variables such as consumer income, the price of Coke, and the average temperature.

Other-things-constant assumption The assumption, when focusing on key economic variables, that other variables remain unchanged

We also make assumptions about individual behavior; these are called **behavioral assumptions.** Perhaps the most fundamental behavioral assumption is that of rational self-interest. As noted earlier, we assume that individual decision-makers rationally pursue their self-interest and make choices accordingly. Rationality implies that each consumer buys the products expected to maximize his or her level of satisfaction. Rationality also implies that each firm sup-

Behavioral assumption An assumption that describes the expected behavior of economic actors plies the products expected to maximize that firm's profit. These kinds of assumptions are called behavioral assumptions because they specify how we expect economic actors to behave.

Step Three. The third step is to formulate a **hypothesis,** which is a theory about how key variables relate to each other. For example, one hypothesis holds that *if* the price of Pepsi goes up, other things constant, *then* the quantity purchased will decline. Thus, the hypothesis becomes a prediction of what will happen to the quantity purchased if the price goes up. The purpose of this theory, like that of any theory, is to make predictions about the real world.

Hypothesis A statement about relationships among key variables

Step Four. The validity of a theory is tested by confronting its predictions with evidence. To test a hypothesis, the fourth step, we must focus attention on the variables in question, while at the same time carefully controlling for other effects. The test will lead us either to reject the theory as inconsistent with the evidence or to continue using the theory until another one comes along that predicts even better. Even though theory may not predict well at all times, it may still predict better than competing theories.

Economists Tell Stories

Despite economists" reliance on the scientific method for developing and evaluating theories, economic analysis is perhaps as much art as science. Observing some phenomenon in the real world, isolating the key variables, formulating a theory to explain how these variables relate, and devising an unambiguous way to test the predictions all involve more than simply an understanding of economics and the scientific method. Carrying out these steps requires a good intuition for identifying, relating, measuring, and testing theories.

Economic analysis also calls for the imagination of a storyteller. Economists explain theories by telling stories about how they think the world works. To tell a compelling story, the economist relies on case studies, anecdotes, parables, and the personal experience of the listener. Throughout this book you will hear stories that bring you closer to the ideas under consideration, such as the story about the Pepsi machine mentioned earlier. These stories help breathe life into economic theory and allow you to personalize abstract ideas. For example, here is a case study about the popularity of vending machines in Japan.

CASE STUDY

A Yen for Vending Machines

The rate of unemployment is usually much lower in Japan than in the United States. For example, in 1995 Japan's unemployment rate was 3.2 percent, compared to 5.6 percent in the United States. A low Japanese birth rate and tight controls on immigration have limited the availability of even unskilled workers in Japan. Because labor there is relatively scarce and therefore costly, Japanese retailers rely on vending machines to sell goods. Vending machines obviously eliminate the need for a sales clerk. Japan has more vending machines per capita than any other country in the world—more than twice as many as in the United States and nearly ten times as many as in Europe.

A low unemployment rate is not the only reason vending machines are more popular in Japan than in the United States. As noted earlier, in the United

A Yen for Vending Machines
continued

Location:

To learn more about the economics of the vending industry, visit American Coin-Op Services (http://acs.buffnet.net/). For information about Japan's economy, visit the Japan Economic Foundation (JEF) (http://www.jef.or.jp/). For an online tour of Japan, visit "Japanese Information," a service of Nippon Telegraph and Telephone Corporation (http://www.ntt.jp/japan/index.html).

States it is common practice to shake down vending machines that perform poorly. Such abuse results in a greater probability that the machines will malfunction in the future, leading to yet more abuse. In Japan, however, vending machines get more respect—in part because Japanese vending machines are more sophisticated and more reliable and in part because of the lower crime rate there and greater respect for property. For example, the automobile theft rate in Japan is only one twentieth the U.S. rate.

So Japanese consumers use vending machines with greater frequency. Sales per machine in Japan are double the U.S. level. In Japan vending machines sell a wide range of products including video cassettes, whisky, hot pizza, and even dating services. Despite the relative abundance of vending machines in Japan currently, their use is expected to continue to grow.

Sources: Nicholas Kristof, "In Japan, Chicken Little Lays the Golden Egg," *New York Times,* 30 July 1995; "Push-Button Lover," *The Economist,* 16 November 1991; "Economic Indicators," *The Economist,* 5 August 1995; and VENNET, an Internet site about vending machines (http://wave.sheridan.wy.us/~jtrucano/index.html).

The case study conveys two points. First, producers combine resources in a way that conserves the resource that is relatively more costly, in this case labor. Second, the customs and conventions of the marketplace may differ across countries, and this may result in different types of economic arrangements, such as the more extensive use of vending machines in Japan than in the United States.

Predicting Average Behavior

The task of an economic theory is to predict the effect of an economic change on economic choices and, in turn, the effect of these choices on particular markets or on the economy as a whole. Does this mean that economists try to predict the behavior of particular consumers or producers? No, because any particular individual may behave in an unpredictable way. But the unpredictable actions of numerous individuals tend to cancel one another out, so the *average behavior* of groups can be predicted more accurately. For example, a college instructor cannot predict very well which particular students will be absent on a given day but can predict fairly precisely what percentage of the class will be absent. Likewise, if Burger King cuts the price of Whoppers in half, the manager can better predict how much Whopper sales will increase than how a particular customer will respond. *The random actions of individuals tend to offset one another, so the average behavior of a large group can be predicted more accurately than the behavior of a particular individual.* Consequently, economists focus on the average behavior of people in groups—for example, as Whopper consumers—rather than on the specific behavior of a particular economic actor.

Normative Versus Positive Analysis

Economists, through their simplifying models, try to explain how the world works. Sometimes economists concern themselves not with how the world does work but with how it *should* work. Compare these two statements: "The

U.S. unemployment rate is 5.6 percent" and "The U.S. unemployment rate should be lower." The first is called a **positive economic statement** because it is an assertion about economic reality that can be supported or rejected by reference to the facts. The second statement is called a **normative economic statement** because it reflects an opinion, and an opinion is merely that—it cannot be shown to be true or false by reference to the facts. Positive statements concern what *is;* normative statements concern what, in someone's opinion, *should be.* Positive statements do not have to be true, but they must be subject to verification or refutation by reference to the facts.

Positive economic statement A statement that can be proved or disproved by reference to facts

Normative economic statement A statement that represents an opinion, which cannot be proved or disproved

Theories are expressed as positive statements, such as "If the price increases, the quantity demanded will decrease." Most of the disagreement among economists involves normative questions about the appropriate role of government rather than statements of positive analysis. To be sure, many theoretical issues still remain unresolved, but most economists agree about most fundamental theoretical principles—that is, about positive economic analysis. For example, in a survey of 464 U.S. economists, only 6.5 percent disagreed with the statement "A ceiling on rents reduces the quantity and quality of housing available." This is a positive statement because it can be shown to be consistent or inconsistent with the evidence. In contrast, there was much less agreement on normative statements such as "The distribution of income in the United States should be more equal." Half the economists surveyed "generally agreed," a quarter "generally disagreed," and a quarter "agreed with provisos."[1]

Some Pitfalls of Faulty Economic Analysis

Economic analysis, like other forms of scientific inquiry, is subject to common mistakes in reasoning that can cause the unwary to draw faulty conclusions. We will discuss three possible sources of confusion.

The Fallacy That Association Is Causation. Does something like this sound familiar: "The stock market was up today as traders reacted favorably to higher profits reported by General Motors"? Although stock market analysts typically claim that millions of stock market transactions spring from a single event, such simplifications are often misleading and even wrong. To assume that event A caused event B simply because B followed A in time is to commit the **fallacy that association is causation,** a common error. The fact that one event precedes another or that the two occur simultaneously does not necessarily imply that one causes the other. Do not confuse subsequence with consequence. Remember: *Association is not necessarily causation.*

Association-is-causation fallacy The incorrect idea that if two variables are associated in time, one must necessarily cause the other

The Fallacy of Composition. Standing up at a football game to get a better view does not work if others stand as well. Arriving early to get in line for concert tickets does not work if many others arrive early as well. Running to the exit to flee a burning theater will have tragic results if many others run as well. These are examples of the **fallacy of composition,** which is an erroneous belief that what is true for the individual, or for the part, is also true for the group, or the whole.

Fallacy of composition The incorrect belief that what is true for the individual, or part, must necessarily be true for the group, or whole

1   Richard M. Alston, et al., "Is There a Consensus Among Economists in the 1990s?," *American Economic Review* 82 (May 1992): pp. 203–209, Table 1.

The Mistake of Ignoring the Secondary Effects. In many cities, public officials, because of concern about rising rents, have imposed rent controls on apartments. The *primary effect* of this policy, the effect on which policymakers focus, is to keep rents from rising. Over time, however, fewer new apartments get built because the rental business becomes less profitable. Moreover, existing rental units deteriorate because owners cannot afford to pay for maintenance. Thus, the quantity and quality of housing may well decline as a result of what appears to be a reasonable measure to keep rents from increasing. The policymakers" mistake was to ignore the **secondary effects** of their policy. Economic actions have secondary effects that often turn out to be more important than the primary effects. Secondary effects may develop more slowly and may not be obvious, but good economic analysis takes them into account.

Secondary effects Unintended consequences of economic actions that develop slowly over time as people react to events

If Economists Are So Smart, Why Aren't They Rich?

Why aren't economists rich? Well, some of them are. Until his recent death, Taikichiro Mori, of Japan, a former economics professor, was reportedly the wealthiest person in the world. Some economists earn as much as $25,000 per appearance on the lecture circuit. Others earn thousands a day as consultants. Economists have been appointed to cabinet positions, including Secretaries of Commerce, Defense, Labor, State, and Treasury. Former Presidents Reagan and Bush majored in economics. Economics is the only social science and the only business discipline for which the prestigious Nobel Prize is awarded, and pronouncements by economists are reported in the media daily.

An economic columnist for the *New York Times* wrote that "Businessmen employ economists in large numbers or consult them at high fees, believing that their cracked crystal balls are better than none at all. The press pursues the best-known seers. While many laymen may be annoyed by economists, other social scientists *hate* them—for their fame, Nobel Prizes, and ready access to political power."[2] Despite its critics, the economics profession thrives because its models usually do a better job of making economic sense out of a confusing world than do alternative approaches.

But not all economists are wealthy, nor is personal wealth the objective of the discipline. In a similar vein, not all doctors are healthy (some of them even smoke cigarettes); not all carpenters live in perfectly built homes; not all marriage counselors are happily married; and not all child psychologists have well-adjusted children.

Robert E. Lucas, Jr., Professor of Economics at the Universtiy of Chicago, was awarded the 1995 Nobel Prize in Economic Sciences for his contributions to macroeconomic theory.

CONCLUSION

This textbook describes how economic factors affect individual choices and how all these choices come together to shape the economic system. Economics is not the whole story, and economic factors are not always the most important. But economic factors have important and predictable effects on individual choices, and these choices affect the way we live. Economics is a

---

2   Leonard Silk, *Economics in Plain English* (New York: Simon and Schuster, 1978), p. 17 (emphasis in original).

challenging discipline, but it is also an exciting and rewarding one. The good news is that you already know a great deal about economics. To use this knowledge, however, you must cultivate the art and science of economic analysis. You must be able to simplify the real world to isolate the key variables and then tell a persuasive story about how these variables relate.

An economic relation can be expressed in words, represented as a table of quantities, described by a mathematical equation, or illustrated as a graph. The appendix to this chapter provides an introduction to the use of graphs. You may find the appendix unnecessary. If you are already familiar with relations among variables, slopes, tangents, and the like, you can probably just browse. If you have little recent experience with graphs, you may benefit from a more careful reading, with pencil and paper in hand.

In the next chapter we will introduce some key ideas of economic analysis. Subsequent chapters will use these ideas to explore economic problems and to explain economic behavior that may otherwise appear puzzling. You must walk before you can run, however, and in the next chapter you will take those first wobbly steps.

SUMMARY

1. Economics is the study of how people choose to use their scarce and limited resources to produce, exchange, and consume goods and services in an attempt to satisfy their unlimited wants. The economic problem arises from the conflict between scarce resources and unlimited wants. If wants were limited or if resources were not scarce, there would be less need to study economics.

2. Economic resources are combined in a variety of ways to produce goods and services. Major categories of resources include (1) land, representing all natural resources, (2) labor, (3) capital, and (4) entrepreneurial ability. Because economic resources are scarce, only a limited number of goods and services can be produced with them; therefore, choices must be made.

3. Microeconomics focuses on choices in households, firms, and governments and how these choices affect particular markets, such as the market for used cars. Each choice is assumed to be guided by rational self-interest. Choice typically requires time and information, both of which are scarce and valuable. Whereas microeconomics examines the individual pieces of the puzzle, macroeconomics steps back to consider the big picture—the performance of the economy as a whole in terms of aggregate measures such as total production, employment, the price level, and growth.

4. Economists use theories, or models, to help predict the effects that changes in economic factors will have on choices and, in turn, the effects these choices will have on particular markets and on the economy as a whole. Economists employ the scientific method to study economic problems by (1) isolating the key variables, (2) specifying the assumptions under which the theory operates, (3) hypothesizing how, according to the theory, the variables relate, and (4) testing the theory by comparing its predictions with the evidence. A theory may not work perfectly, but it will be used as long as it predicts better than competing theories.

5. Positive economic analysis is aimed at discovering how the world works. Normative economic analysis is concerned more with how, in someone's opinion, the world should work. Economic analysis, if not pursued carefully, can result in inaccurate conclusions arising from the fallacy that association is causation, the fallacy of composition, and ignorance of the secondary effects.

QUESTIONS AND PROBLEMS

1. **(Definition of Economics)** What determines whether a resource is considered scarce? What is the importance of this scarcity to the definition of economics?

2. **(Resources)** Determine which category of resources each of the following belongs in:
   a. A taxicab
   b. Computer software

c. One hour of legal counsel
d. A parking lot
e. A forest
f. The Mississippi River
g. An individual bringing a new way of manufacturing steel to the market

3. **(Goods and Services)** Explain why each of the following should *not* be considered "free" for the economy as a whole:
   a. Food Stamps
   b. U.S. aid to developing countries
   c. Corporate charitable contributions
   d. Noncable television programs
   e. Public high school education

4. **(Economic Actors)** Which economic actors play the leading role in the economic system? Which actors play supporting roles? In what sense are they considered supporting actors?

5. **(Micro Versus Macro)** Indicate whether each of the following analyses would be considered microeconomics or macroeconomics:
   a. Determining the price of an automobile
   b. The impact of tax policies on the total level of consumption in the economy
   c. A household's decisions regarding allocating its disposable income among various goods and services
   d. A worker's decision regarding how many hours to work each week
   e. Determining the rate of inflation in the economy
   f. Appropriate government policies to affect the level of employment

6. **(Micro Versus Macro)** Some economists believe that in order to really understand macroeconomics, one must fully understand microeconomics. How does microeconomics relate to macroeconomics?

7. **(Rational Self-Interest)** Discuss the impact of rational self-interest on each of the following decisions:
   a. Whether to attend college full time or enter the full-time workforce
   b. Whether to buy a new or used textbook
   c. Whether to attend a local college or an out-of-town college

8. **(Marginal Analysis)** A small pizza store must decide whether to increase the radius of its delivery area by a mile. What considerations must be taken into account if such a decision is to contribute to profitability?

9. **(The Value of Time)** Economists often attempt to measure the value of time by using wage rates or average salary levels. According to these measures, the value of time in growing economies is always rising. How does the growing value of time affect the types of products and services being introduced into the economy? How might this increase in the value of time be related to the widespread use of microwave ovens, video cassette recorders, McDonald's, and automatic tellers at banks?

10. **(Pitfalls of Economic Thinking)** Using the discussion of pitfalls in economic thinking, identify the fallacy or mistake in thinking in each of the following statements:
    a. Raising taxes will always increase government revenues.
    b. Whenever there is a recession, imports tend to decrease. Thus, to stop a recession, we should increase imports.
    c. Raising steel tariffs helps the U.S. steel industry, and therefore the entire economy is helped.
    d. Air bags in automobiles can reduce accidental death from collision. Therefore, air bags in cars make good economic sense.
    e. Gold sells for about $400 per ounce. Therefore, the U.S. government could sell all of the gold in Fort Knox at $400 per ounce and eliminate the national debt.

11. **(Role of Theory)** What good is economic theory if it cannot predict an individual's behavior?

12. **(Rational Self-Interest)** If behavior is governed by rational self-interest, why do people give to charitable institutions?

13. **(Rational Decision Making)** Information necessary to make good decisions is often costly to obtain. Yet your own interests can best be served by rationally weighing all options available to you, which requires completely informed decision making. Does this mean that making uninformed decisions is irrational? How do you determine what amount of information is the right amount of information?

14. **(Normative Versus Positive Analysis)** Indicate whether each of the following statements is normative or positive:
    a. The U.S. unemployment rate dropped below 6 percent in 1995.
    b. Inflation is too high in the United States.
    c. The U.S. government should increase the minimum wage.
    d. U.S. trade restrictions cost consumers $19 billion annually in higher prices.

15. **(Association Versus Causation)** Suppose I observe that communities with lots of doctors tend to have relatively high rates of illness. I conclude, therefore, that doctors cause illness. What's wrong with this reasoning?

16. **(Marginal Analysis in the Computer Industry)** What factors would Apple have considered in determining whether or not to allow Macintosh clones?

17. **(A Yen for Vending Machines)** Do vending machines conserve any other resources besides labor? Does your answer offer any additional insight into the widespread use of vending machines in Japan?

18. **(A Yen for Vending Machines)** Suppose you had the choice of purchasing identically priced lunches at an automat (vending machines only) or a cafeteria. Which would you typically prefer? Why?

Using the Internet

19. Visit the White House home page—**http://www. whitehouse.gov/**. Look under the "Publications" subheading for the briefings on economic policy. In a paragraph or two, summarize the most recent briefing. Who gave the briefing? Is the subject matter macroeconomics or microeconomics? Is the analysis primarily normative or positive?

Appendix
UNDERSTANDING GRAPHS

Take out a pencil and a blank piece of paper. Go ahead, do it. Put a point in the middle of the paper. This will be the point of departure, called the **origin.** With your pencil at the origin, draw a straight line off to the right; this line is called the **horizontal axis.** The value of the variable *x* measured along the horizontal axis increases as you move to the right of the origin. Now mark off this line into increments of, say, 5 units each from 0 to 20. Returning to the origin, draw another line straight up; this line is called the **vertical axis.** Similarly, the value of the variable *y* measured along the vertical axis increases as you move upward. Again, mark off this line into increments of 5 units each from 0 to 20.

Within the space framed by the axes, you can plot possible combinations of the variables measured along each axis. Each point identifies a value measured along the horizontal, or *x,* axis and a value measured along the vertical, or *y* axis. For example, place point *a* in your graph to reflect the combination where *x* equals 5 units and *y* equals 15 units. Likewise, place point *b* in your graph to reflect 10 units of *x* and 5 units of *y*. Now compare your results with those shown in Exhibit 1.

A **graph** is a picture showing how variables relate, and a picture can be worth a thousand words. Consider Exhibit 2, which shows the U.S. annual unemployment rate between 1900 and 1995. The year is measured along the horizontal axis, and the unemployment rate along the vertical axis. Exhibit 2 is a **time-series graph** because it shows the value of a variable, in this case the unemployment rate, over time. If you had to describe the information presented in Exhibit 2 in words, the explanation would take pages and would be mind-numbing. The picture shows not only how one year compares to the next, but also how one decade compares to another and how the rate has trended over time. The eye can wander over the hills and valleys to observe patterns that would be hard to convey in words. The sharply

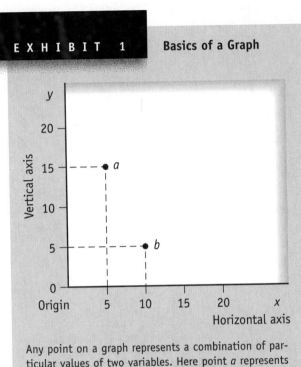

EXHIBIT 1   **Basics of a Graph**

Any point on a graph represents a combination of particular values of two variables. Here point *a* represents the combination of 5 units of variable *x* (measured on the horizontal axis) and 15 units of variable *y* (measured on the vertical axis). Point *b* represents 10 units of *x* and 5 units of *y*.

higher unemployment rate during the Great Depression of the 1930s is unmistakable. The graph also shows that the average unemployment rate has drifted upward since the 1940s. *Graphs convey information in a compact and efficient way.*

This appendix shows how graphs express a variety of relations among variables. Most of the graphs of interest in this book reflect the relation between two economic variables, such as the year and the unemployment rate, the price of a product and the quantity demanded, or the cost of production and the quantity supplied. Because we focus on just two

U.S. Unemployment Rate Since 1900

EXHIBIT 2

A time-series graph depicts the behavior of some economic variable (here, the unemployment rate) over time.

Sources: *Historical Statistics of the United States,* 1970, and *Economic Report of the President,* February 1996

variables at a time, we usually assume that other relevant variables remain constant.

We often observe that one thing appears to depend on another. The time it takes you to drive home depends on your average speed. Your weight depends on how much you eat. The amount of Pepsi purchased depends on its price. A **functional relation** exists between two variables when the value of one variable *depends* on the value of another variable. The value of the **independent variable** determines the value of the **dependent variable.** The price of Pepsi, the independent variable, determines how much consumers buy, the dependent variable. This is not to say that other factors, such as consumer incomes, the price of Coke, and the weather do not affect how much Pepsi consumers buy, but we typically focus on the relation between the two key variables, assuming that other factors remain unchanged. The task of the economist is to isolate economic relations and determine the direction of causality, if any. Recall that one of the pitfalls of economic thinking is the erroneous belief that association is causation. We can-

not conclude that, simply because two events are related in time, the first event causes the second. There may be no relation between the two events.

Drawing Graphs

Consider a very simple relation. Suppose you are planning to drive across country and want to determine how far you will travel each day. You estimate that your average speed will be 50 miles per hour. Possible combinations of driving time and distance traveled appear in Exhibit 3. One column lists the hours driven per day, and the next column gives the number of miles traveled per day, assuming an average speed of 50 miles per hour. The distance traveled, the dependent variable, depends on the number of hours driven, the independent variable. We identify combinations of hours driven and distance traveled as *a, b, c,* and so on. We can plot these combinations as a graph in Exhibit 4, with hours driven per day measured along the horizontal axis and total distance traveled along the vertical axis. Each combination of hours driven and distance traveled is repre-

EXHIBIT 3	Schedule Relating Distance Traveled to Hours Driven

	Hours Driven per Day	Distance Traveled per Day (miles)
a	1	50
b	2	100
c	3	150
d	4	200
e	5	250

sented by a point in Exhibit 4. For example, point *a* shows that when you drive for only 1 hour, you travel only 50 miles. Point *b* indicates that when you drive for 2 hours, you travel 100 miles. By connecting the points, or combinations, we create a line running upward and to the right. Held constant along this line is the average speed of 50 miles per hour.

EXHIBIT 4	Graph Relating Distance Traveled to Hours Driven

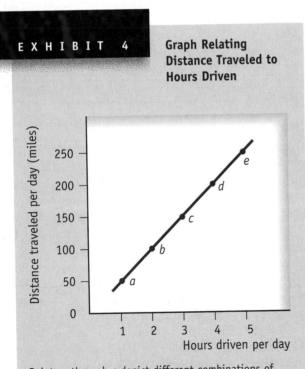

Points *a* through *e* depict different combinations of hours driven per day and the corresponding distances traveled. Connecting these points creates a graph.

EXHIBIT 5	Hypothetical Demand Curve for Pepsi

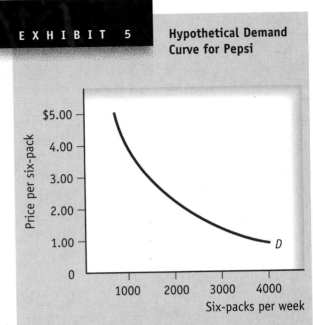

The demand curve shows an inverse, or negative, relation between price and quantity demanded. The curve slopes downward from left to right, indicating that the quantity demanded increases as the price falls.

Types of relations between variables include the following: (1) As one variable increases, the other increases too, as in Exhibit 4, in which case there is a **positive,** or **direct, relation** between the variables; (2) as one variable increases, the other decreases, in which case there is a **negative,** or **inverse, relation;** and (3) as one variable increases, the other remains unchanged, in which case the two variables are said to be *independent,* or *unrelated.*

In later chapters we will consider demand, a key economic idea. The *demand curve* shows the relation between the quantity of a product demanded and the price of that product, other things constant. Exhibit 5 depicts the relation between the price of Pepsi and the quantity of Pepsi demanded per week. This demand curve is identified simply as *D.* As you can see, more Pepsi is demanded at lower prices than at higher prices: there is an inverse, or negative, relation between price and quantity demanded. Inverse relations are expressed by downward-sloping curves. One of the advantages of graphs is that they easily convey the relation between variables. We need not examine the particular combinations of numbers; we need only focus on the shape of the curve.

Incidentally, economists usually measure price, the independent variable, along the vertical axis and quantity demanded, the dependent variable, along the horizontal axis. This arrangement appears odd to mathematicians, who usually put the independent variable on the horizontal axis and the dependent variable on the vertical axis. In another context, however, the cost of production is the dependent variable and quantity produced the independent variable, so for consistency economists measure dollar amounts on the vertical axis and quantity on the horizontal axis.

The Slopes of Straight Lines

A more precise way to describe the shape of a curve is to measure its slope. The **slope** of a line indicates how much the vertical variable changes for a given increase in the horizontal variable. Specifically, the slope between any two points along any straight line is the vertical change between these two points divided by the horizontal increase, or

$$\text{Slope} = \frac{\text{Change in the vertical distance}}{\text{Increase in the horizontal distance}}$$

For brevity, we refer to the slope as the *rise over the run,* where the *rise* is the vertical change and the *run* is the horizontal increase.

Each of the four panels in Exhibit 6 indicates the vertical change, given a 10-unit increase in the horizontal variable. In panel (a), the vertical distance increases by 5 units when the horizontal distance increases by 10 units. The slope of the line in panel (a) is therefore 5/10, or 0.5. Notice that the slope in this case is a positive number because the relation between the two variables is positive, or direct. This slope indicates that for every 1-unit increase in the horizontal variable, the vertical variable increases by 0.5 units. The slope, incidentally, does not imply causality; the increase in the horizontal variable does not necessarily cause the increase in the vertical variable. The slope simply indicates in a uniform way the relation between an increase in the horizontal variable and the associated change in the vertical variable.

In panel (b), the vertical distance declines by 7 units when the horizontal distance increases by 10 units, so the slope equals −7/10, or −0.7. The slope in this case is a negative number, because the two variables have a negative, or inverse, relation. In

panel (c), the vertical variable remains unchanged as the horizontal variable increases by 10, so the slope equals 0/10, or 0. These two variables are unrelated. Finally, in panel (d), the vertical variable can take on any value, although the horizontal variable remains unchanged. In this case any change in the vertical measure, for example a 10-unit change, is divided by 0, since the horizontal value does not change. Any change divided by 0 is infinitely large, so we say that the slope of a vertical line is infinite. Again, the two variables are unrelated.

The Slope Depends on How Units Are Measured

The mathematical value of the slope depends on the units of measurement on the graph. For example, suppose copper tubing costs $1 per foot to produce. Graphs depicting the relation between output and total cost are shown in Exhibit 7. In panel (a), total cost of production increases by $1 for each 1-foot increase in the amount of tubing produced. Thus, the slope in panel (a) equals 1/1, or 1. If the cost remains the same but the unit of measurement is not *feet* but *yards,* the relation between output and total cost is as depicted in panel (b). Now total cost increases by $3 for each 1-yard increase in output, so the slope equals 3/1, or 3. Because of differences in the units used to measure copper tubing, the two panels reflect different slopes, even though the cost of tubing is $1 per foot in each panel. So keep in mind that *the slope will depend in part on the unit of measurement.*

As noted earlier, economic analysis usually involves *marginal analysis,* such as the marginal cost of producing one more unit of output. The slope is a convenient device for measuring marginal effects because it reflects the change in total cost along the vertical axis for each 1-unit change along the horizontal axis. For example, in panel (a) of Exhibit 7, the marginal cost of another *foot* of copper tubing is $1, which also equals the slope of the line. In panel (b), the marginal cost of another *yard* of tubing is $3, which, again, is the slope of that line. Because of its applicability to marginal analysis, the slope has special significance in economics.

The Slopes of Curved Lines

The slope of a straight line is the same everywhere along the line, but the slope of a curved line varies at different points along the curve. Consider the curve in Exhibit 8. To find the slope of that curved line at

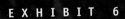

EXHIBIT 6   **Alternative Slopes for Straight Lines**

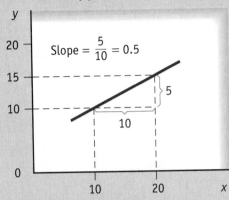

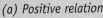

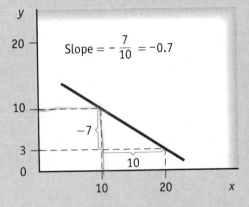

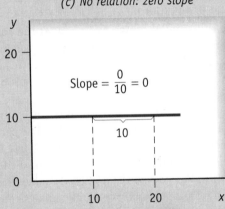

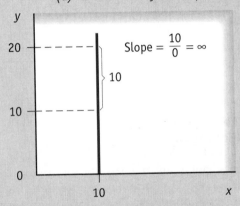

The slope of a line indicates how much the vertically measured variable changes for a given increase in the variable measured on the horizontal axis. Panel (a) shows a positive relation between two variables; the slope is 0.5, a positive number. Panel (b) depicts a negative, or inverse, relation. When the x variable increases, the y variable decreases; the slope is −0.7, a negative number. Panels (c) and (d), represent situations in which two variables are unrelated. In panel (c), the y variable always takes on the same value; the slope is 0. In panel (d), the x variable always takes on the same value; the slope is infinite.

a particular point, draw a straight line that just touches the curve at that point but does not cut or cross the curve. Such a line is called a **tangent** to the curve at that point. The slope of the tangent is the slope of the curve at that point. Consider the line *AA*, which is tangent to the curve at point *a*. As the horizontal value increases from 0 to 10 along *AA*, the vertical value drops from 40 to 0. Thus, the vertical change divided by the horizontal change equals −40/10, or −4, which is the slope of the curve at point *a*. This

slope is negative because the curve slopes downward at that point. Alternatively, consider *BB*, a line drawn tangent to the curve at point *b*. The slope of *BB* is the change in the vertical divided by the change in the horizontal, or −10/30, which equals −0.33. As you can see, the curve depicted in Exhibit 8 gets flatter as the horizontal variable increases, so the value of its slope approaches zero.

Other curves, of course, will reflect different slopes as well as different changes in the slope along

Slope Depends on the Unit of Measure   E X H I B I T   7

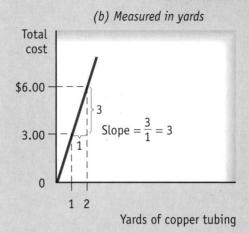

(a) Measured in feet

Total cost

$6.00

5.00

$\text{Slope} = \dfrac{1}{1} = 1$

0

5 6

Feet of copper tubing

(b) Measured in yards

Total cost

$6.00

3.00

$\text{Slope} = \dfrac{3}{1} = 3$

0

1 2

Yards of copper tubing

The value of the slope depends on the units of measure. In panel (*a*), output is measured in feet of copper tubing; in panel (*b*), output is measured in yards. Although the cost of production is $1 per foot in each panel, the slope is different in the two panels because copper tubing is measured using different units.

E X H I B I T   8   **Slopes at Different Points on a Curved Line**

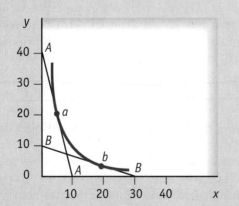

The slope of a curved line varies from point to point. At a given point, such as *a* or *b*, the slope of the curve is equal to the slope of the straight line that is tangent to the curve at that point.

the curve. Downward-sloping curves have a negative slope, and upward-sloping curves, a positive slope. Sometimes curves are more complex, having both positive and negative ranges. For example, consider the hill-shaped curve in Exhibit 9. For relatively small values of *x*, there is a positive relation between *x* and *y*. As the value of *x* increases, however, its positive relation with *y* diminishes, eventually becoming negative. We can divide the curve into two segments: (1) the segment between the origin and point *a*, where the slope is positive, and (2) the segment of the curve to the right of point *a*, where the slope is negative. The slope of the curve at point *a* is 0. The U-shaped curve in Exhibit 9 represents the opposite relation: *x* and *y* are negatively related until point *b* is reached; thereafter they are positively related. The slope equals 0 at point *b*.

Curve Shifts

Economic analysis often involves shifts in the curves, or the relations, under consideration. Exhibit 10 depicts a hypothetical demand curve, *D*, for Pepsi. The curve reflects the inverse relation between the price of Pepsi and the quantity demanded per week, other things constant. Suppose an increase in consumer income makes consumers demand more Pepsi at each

Curves with Both Positive and Negative Ranges

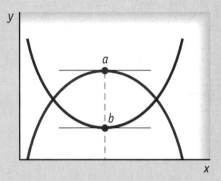

Some curves have both positive and negative slopes. The hill-shaped curve has a positive slope to the left of point *a*, a slope of 0 at point *a*, and a negative slope to the right of that point. The U-shaped curve starts off with a negative slope, has a slope of 0 at point *b*, and has a positive slope to the right of that point.

The 45-degree Line from the Origin

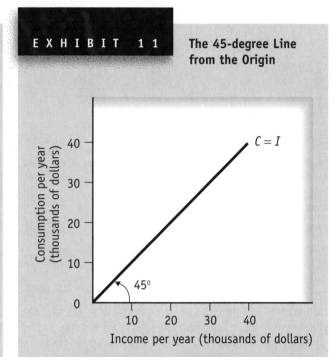

The 45-degree line extending from the origin has a slope equal to 1. At each point along the line, the value of what is measured on the horizontal axis (here, annual income) is equal to the value of what is measured on the vertical axis (annual consumption).

Shift in the Demand Curve for Pepsi

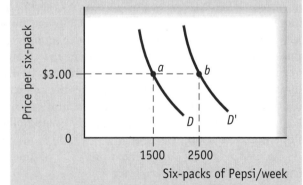

The demand curve *D* shifts to the right to *D'* because higher consumer income increases the demand for Pepsi. After the shift in the demand curve, more Pepsi is demanded at each price. For example, at a price of $3 per six-pack, the quantity demanded per week increases from 1500 to 2500.

price level. As a result, the demand curve for Pepsi shifts to the right, from *D* to *D'*, indicating that more Pepsi is demanded at each price. For example, the original demand curve indicates at point *a* that 1500 six-packs of Pepsi were demanded per week when the price was $3 per six-pack. After the increase in income, the amount demanded at that price increases to 2500 six-packs per week, as reflected by point *b*. Conversely, we could trace the effects of a decrease in consumer income on the demand for Pepsi. A decrease in income would shift the demand for Pepsi to the left, so less Pepsi would be demanded at each price.

The 45-Degree Ray from the Origin

Speaking of income, suppose we want to trace the relationship between income and consumption. Exhibit 11 measures annual household income on the horizontal axis and annual consumption spending on the vertical axis. Suppose this household spends all its income on consumption, regardless of the level of

The 45-degree Line as a Reference Line

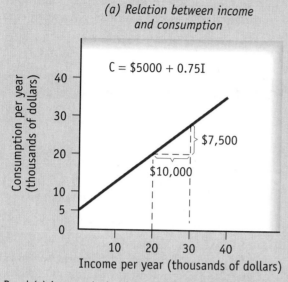

(a) Relation between income
and consumption

C = $5000 + 0.75I

$7,500

$10,000

Consumption per year (thousands of dollars)

Income per year (thousands of dollars)

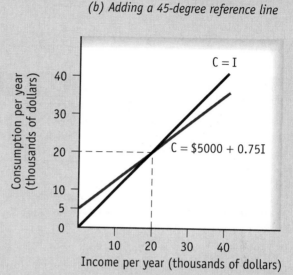

(b) Adding a 45-degree reference line

C = I

C = $5000 + 0.75I

Consumption per year (thousands of dollars)

Income per year (thousands of dollars)

Panel (a) is a graph showing the relation between household income and household consumption. When income is 0, consumption is $5,000, as households borrow or dip into savings. For each $10,000 increase in income, consumption increases by $7,500. The slope of the line is 0.75. Panel (b) introduces a 45-degree reference line showing all points where income and consumption are equal. The two lines intersect at $20,000. At income levels less than $20,000 consumption exceeds income. At income levels exceeding $20,000, consumption is less than income.

income. In this case the relation between income and consumption could be expressed by a 45 degree line drawn from the origin, which has a slope equal to 1. A straight line from the origin is called a **ray.** As you can see, along such a line, consumption always equals income. This relationship between consumption and income can be expressed by the equation $C = I$, where C is consumption and I is income.

In reality, household consumption does not usually equal income. At relatively low levels of income, households borrow or dip into savings, so consumption usually exceeds income. And at relatively high levels of income, households save some income, so consumption is usually less than income. Panel (a) of Exhibit 12 shows a line reflecting a more realistic relation between consumption and income. Consider first the point where this line cuts the vertical axis; this point is called the vertical **intercept,** which in this case reflects consumption of $5,000. Hence, when income is zero, the household, by borrowing or relying on savings, still spends $5,000 per year.

Consumption increases as income increases. In fact, for the consumption line in Exhibit 12, each $10,000 increase in income increases consumption by $7,500. Thus the slope of the consumption line is the rise over the run, or $7,500/$10,000, which reduces to 0.75. This consumption line can be expressed algebraically as $C = $5,000 + 0.75I$, where, again, C is consumption and I is income. So at any level of income, consumption equals $5,000 plus 0.75 times the level of income. For example, if income is $40,000, consumption equals $5,000 plus 0.75 times $40,000, or $5,000 plus $30,000, or $35,000. So when income equals $40,000, consumption is $35,000, which is less than income.

In Exhibit 12(b) we again present the consumption line $C = $5,000 + 0.75I$, but, to add perspective, we include the 45 degree ray introduced earlier. By comparing the consumption line with the 45 degree reference line, we can quickly determine the relation between consumption and income. For example, at points along the consumption line where income is below $20,000, consumption exceeds income, which means the household borrows or relies on savings. At points along the consumption line where income exceeds $20,000, consumption is less than income, which means the household saves some income. Where income equals $20,000, the two lines intersect, meaning that consumption equals income. So the 45 degree ray from the origin provides a handy reference tool to compare relative magnitudes on each axis. The one requirement for use of this tool is that the same units be measured on each axis, such as dollars in this case.

With this we close our once-over of graphs. Return to this appendix when you feel you need to review.

APPENDIX QUESTIONS

1. **(Use of Graphs)** Graph the relationship $TC = 10 + 12Q$, where TC = total cost (in dollars) and Q = dozens of eggs.
   a. What is the intercept?
   b. What is the slope?
   c. How would the slope change if you graphed total cost against single eggs rather than dozens of eggs?
   d. What is the marginal cost of an egg?

2. **(Use of Graphs)** Suppose you have collected the following data on automobiles:

Observation	Mileage	Weight	Transmission
1	40 mpg	1,500 lb	manual
2	30 mpg	2,500 lb	manual
3	20 mpg	1,500 lb	automatic
4	10 mpg	2,500 lb	automatic

   a. An engineer looking at the second and third observations might conclude that mileage improves when auto weight increases. What is wrong with this analysis?
   b. Draw a graph relating auto weight (on the horizontal axis) to mileage (on the vertical axis) for cars with manual transmissions.
   c. How would changing the transmission influence your graphs?

3. **(Use of Graphs)** A demand curve shows a relation between the price of an item and the quantity demanded.
   a. Construct a demand curve based on the following data:

Quantity Demanded	Price	Income of Demander
0	$50	$100
10	$40	$150
15	$20	$100
20	$10	$100

   b. What is the vertical intercept?
   c. What is the slope?

Some Tools of Economic Analysis

2

In the first chapter we learned that because of scarcity, we must make choices. And whenever we choose, we must pass up at least one alternative. We also learned that choices are guided by rational self-interest and require both time and information. The first chapter said little, however, about how to analyze economic choices. In this chapter we develop a framework for evaluating economic alternatives. First, we consider the cost involved in selecting one alternative over others. Next, we develop tools to explore the production choices available to individuals and to the economy as a whole. Finally, we consider how different economies address the economic choices they confront—choices about what goods and services to produce, how to produce them, and for whom to produce them. Topics discussed in this chapter include:

- Opportunity cost
- Division of labor
- Comparative advantage
- Specialization

- Production possibilities frontier
- Three economic questions
- Economic systems

CHOICE AND OPPORTUNITY COST

Consider a decision you just made: the decision to read this chapter now rather than use the time to study for another course, sleep, watch TV, or do something else. Suppose your best alternative to reading now is getting some sleep, so the cost of reading is passing up the opportunity to sleep. Because of scarcity, whenever you make a choice, you must pass up other opportunities; you must incur an *opportunity cost.*

Opportunity Cost

Opportunity cost The value of the best alternative forgone when an item or activity is chosen

The **opportunity cost** of the chosen item or activity is the benefit expected from the *best alternative* that is forgone. You might think of opportunity cost as the *opportunity lost.* Sometimes opportunity cost can be measured in terms of money, although, as we shall see, money is usually only part of the cost.

How many times have you heard people say they did something because they "had nothing better to do"? They actually mean they had no attractive alternatives, so they were sacrificing very little to undertake the chosen activity. Yet, according to the idea of opportunity cost, people *always* do what they do because they have nothing better to do. The choice selected seems, at the time, preferable to all other possible choices. You are reading this chapter right now because you have nothing better to do. In fact, you are attending college for the same reason: College appears more attractive than your best alternative. Consider the opportunity cost of attending college in the following case study.

CASE STUDY

The Opportunity Cost of College

Location:

To learn more about the costs and benefits of attending college, visit the U.S. Department of Education (http://www.ed.gov/) or browse the *Academe This Week,* a weekly online journal provided by the Chronicle of Higher Education (http://chronicle.merit.edu/).

What is your opportunity cost of attending college this year? What was the best alternative you gave up to attend college? If you already had a job, you have a good idea of the income you gave up to attend college. Suppose you expected to earn $16,000 a year from a full-time job. As a college student, you could still work part time during the school year and full time during the summer. Suppose as a college student you earn a total of $7,000 during the year. Thus, by attending college this year you are giving up net earnings of $9,000 ($16,000 − $7,000).

There is also the direct cost of college itself. Suppose you are paying $8,000 this year for tuition, fees, and books at a public university. This money is therefore unavailable to you (or your family) to spend elsewhere. So the opportunity cost of paying for tuition, fees, and books is the forgone benefit expected from the alternative goods and services that money could have purchased. Opportunity cost would be much higher at private institutions.

Expenses for room and board are not opportunity costs, because even if you had not attended college, you would still have to live somewhere and eat something. Likewise, whether or not you attended college, you would still face outlays for items such as entertainment, clothes, and laundry. Such expenses do not represent an opportunity cost of attending college. They are personal upkeep costs that arise regardless of what you are doing. For simplicity, let's assume that room, board, and personal expenses are the same whether or not you attend college, so they are not an opportunity cost of college. Thus, the forgone earnings of $9,000 plus the $8,000 for tuition, fees, and books yield an opportunity cost of attending college this year of $17,000.

This analysis assumes that other things are constant. If, in your view, attending college is more of a pain than you expected the best alternative to be, the opportunity cost of attending college is even higher. That is, if you are one of those people who find college difficult, often boring, and in most ways more unpleasant than a full-time job, then the cost in money terms understates your true opportunity cost. Not only are you incurring the added expense of college, you are also forgoing a more pleasant quality of life. If, on the contrary, you think the wild and crazy life of a college student is more enjoyable on balance than a full-time job, then $17,000 overstates your true opportunity cost, because the best alternative involves a less satisfying quality of life.

Evidently, you view college as a wise investment in your future even though it is costly and perhaps even painful. For you, the net benefit expected from college—that is, the total benefit minus the total cost—exceeds that expected from the best alternative, and that is why you, as a rational decision maker, are attending college. In fact, a growing share of college students are going into debt to finance their education.

Sources: Ellen Graham, "Study Now, Pay Later: Students Pile on Debt," *The Wall Street Journal,* 11 August 1995; and CollegeNET, the "Internet Guide to Colleges and Universities" (**http://www.collegenet.com/**).

The Opportunity Cost of College
continued

Opportunity Cost Is Subjective

Opportunity cost is subjective. Only the individual chooser can estimate the expected value of the best alternative. The chooser seldom knows the actual value of the forgone alternative, since, by definition, that alternative is "the road not taken." Thus, if you give up an evening of pizza and conversation with friends to work on a term paper, you will never know exactly the value of what you gave up. You know only what you *expected*. Evidently, you expected the net benefit of working on that paper to be greater than the net benefit you expected from your best alternative. Incidentally, focusing on only the *best* alternative forgone makes all other alternatives irrelevant.

Calculating Opportunity Cost Requires Time and Information. People rationally choose the alternative that promises the highest expected net benefit. This does not mean that people exhaustively calculate costs and benefits for all possible alternatives. Since acquiring information about alternatives is often costly and time consuming, people usually make choices based on limited or even incorrect information. Indeed, some choices may turn out to be poor ones (for example, you went on a picnic and it rained; the movie you rented was boring; the shoes you bought gave you sore feet). At the time you made the choice, however, you thought you were making the best use of all your scarce resources, including the time required to gather and evaluate information about your alternatives.

Time is the Ultimate Constraint. The Sultan of Brunei is among the world's richest people, based on the huge oil revenues that flow into his tiny country. His palace has 2,000 rooms, with walls of fine Italian marble. His throne room is the size of a football field. And he owns 150 Rolls-Royces.[1] Supported by such wealth, he would appear to have overcome the economic problem caused by scarce resources but unlimited wants. However, even though the Sultan can buy whatever he wants, he has limited *time* in which to enjoy his acquisitions. If he pursues one activity, he cannot at the same time do something else, so each activity he undertakes has an opportunity cost. Consequently, the Sultan must choose from among the competing uses of his scarcest resource, time. Though your alternatives may not be as exotic as the Sultan's, you, too, face a time constraint (especially during final exams).

Opportunity Cost May Vary with Circumstance. Opportunity cost depends on the alternatives. This is why you are less likely to study on a Saturday night than on a Tuesday night. On a Saturday night the opportunity cost of studying is greater, because you have more attractive alternatives and usually the expected net benefit of at least one of these alternatives exceeds the expected net benefit from studying. Suppose you choose a movie for Saturday night. The opportunity cost of the movie is the value of your best alternative, which might be attending a sporting event. For some of you, studying on Saturday night may be well down the list of alternatives—perhaps ahead of reorganizing your closet, but behind watching trucks being unloaded at the supermarket.

Although opportunity cost is subjective, in some circumstances money paid for goods and services becomes a good approximation of their opportunity cost. The monetary cost definition, however, may leave out some important elements, particularly the time involved. Watching a video costs you not only the rental fee but also the time and travel expense to get it, watch it, and return it.

Sunk Cost and Choice

Sunk Cost A cost that must be incurred no matter what; hence, a cost that is irrelevant when an economic choice is being made

Suppose you have just finished shopping for groceries and are wheeling your grocery cart up to a row of checkout counters. How do you decide which line to join? You pick the line you think will involve the least time. Suppose that after waiting for 10 minutes in a line that barely moves, you notice that another line has disappeared. Do you switch to the open cashier, or do you think, "Since I have already spent 10 minutes in this line, I'm going to stay in this line"? The 10 minutes you already waited represents a **sunk cost,** which is a cost that you cannot recover regardless of what you do. You should ignore sunk costs in making economic choices, because your choice has no impact on sunk cost. Therefore, you should switch to the open cashier. *Economic decision makers should consider only those costs that are affected by the choice. Sunk costs are by definition not affected by the choice and are therefore irrelevant.* The irrelevance of sunk costs is underscored by Shakespeare's Lady Macbeth, who advised, "Things without all remedy should be without regard: What's done is done." A modern variant is the proverb " There is no sense crying over spilt milk."

SPECIALIZATION, COMPARATIVE ADVANTAGE, AND EXCHANGE

Suppose you live in the dormitory, where your meals and chores are taken care of. You and your roommate have such busy schedules that you each can spare

---

1   These figures are reported by Kieran Cooke in "Sultan's Swing to Reform," London *Financial Times,* 4 August 1995.

only about an hour per week for such mundane tasks as typing and ironing. Each of you must turn in a three-page typewritten paper every week, and you each prefer to have your shirts ironed if you have the time. Suppose you take 10 minutes to type one page, or half an hour to type the three-page paper. Your roommate is from the hunt-and-peck school and takes about 20 minutes per page, or an hour for the three pages. But your roommate is talented at ironing and can iron a shirt in 5 minutes flat (or should that be, iron that flat in five minutes). You take about twice as long, or 10 minutes, to iron a shirt.

During the hour available each week for typing and ironing, the typing takes priority. If you each do your own typing and ironing, your roommate takes the entire hour to type the paper and so has no time left for ironing. You type your paper in a half hour and iron three shirts in the remaining half hour. Thus, with each of you performing your own tasks, the combined output is two typed papers and three ironed shirts.

The Law of Comparative Advantage

Before long, you each realize that total output would increase if you did all the typing and your roommate did all the ironing. In the hour available for these tasks, you type both papers and your roommate irons twelve shirts. As a result of specialization, total output has increased by nine shirts. You strike a deal to exchange your typing for your roommate's ironing, so you each end up with a typed paper and six ironed shirts. Thus, *each of you is better off as a result of specialization and exchange.* By specializing in the tasks that each does best, you and your roommate employ the **law of comparative advantage,** which states that the individual with the lower opportunity cost for producing a particular output should specialize in producing that output.

Law of comparative advantage *The individual or country with the lowest opportunity cost of producing a particular good should specialize in producing that good.*

Absolute and Comparative Advantage

The gains from specialization and exchange in the previous example seem obvious. A more interesting case arises if you are not only a faster typist but also a faster ironer. Suppose we change the example so that your roommate now takes 12 minutes to iron a shirt, compared to your 10 minutes. You now have an absolute advantage in both tasks, since each takes you less time than it does your roommate. More generally, having an **absolute advantage** means being able to produce a product using fewer resources than other producers use.

Absolute advantage *The ability to produce something with fewer resources than other producers use*

Does your absolute advantage in both activities mean specialization is no longer a good idea? Recall that the law of comparative advantage states that the individual with *the lower opportunity cost* of producing a particular good should specialize in producing that good. You still take 10 minutes to type a page and 10 minutes to iron a shirt, so your opportunity cost of typing one page is ironing one shirt. Your roommate takes 20 minutes to type a page and 12 minutes to iron a shirt, so your roommate could iron 20/12, or 1 2/3, shirts in the time taken to type one page. So your opportunity cost of typing one page is ironing one shirt, and your roommate's opportunity cost is ironing 1 2/3 shirts. *Because your opportunity cost of typing is lower than your roommate's, you have a comparative advantage in typing.*

Although you have an absolute advantage in both tasks, your **comparative advantage** calls for specializing in the task for which you have the lower opportunity cost—in this case, typing. If neither of you specialized, you could

Comparative advantage *The ability to produce something at a lower opportunity cost than other producers face*

type one paper and iron three shirts; your roommate could still type just the one paper. Your combined output would be two papers and three shirts.

If you each specialized according to the law of comparative advantage, in an hour you could type both papers and your roommate could iron five shirts. Thus, specialization increases total output by two ironed shirts. Even though you are better at both tasks than your roommate, you are comparatively better at typing. Put another way, your roommate, although worse at both tasks, is not quite as poor at ironing as at typing. Don't think this is simply common sense. Common sense would lead you to do your own ironing and typing, since you are more skilled at both. *Absolute advantage focuses on who uses the fewest resources, but comparative advantage focuses on what else those resources could have been used to produce—that is, on the opportunity cost of those resources.*

The law of comparative advantage applies not only to individuals but also to firms, regions of a country, and countries. Those individuals, firms, regions, or countries with the lowest opportunity cost of producing a particular good should specialize in producing that good. Because of such factors as climate, the skills of the workforce, and capital and natural resources available, certain parts of the country and certain parts of the world have a comparative advantage in producing particular goods. From Apple computers in California's Silicon Valley to oranges in sunny Florida, from VCRs in Korea to bananas in Honduras—*resources are allocated most efficiently across the country and around the world when production and trade conform to the law of comparative advantage.*

Specialization and Exchange

In the previous example you and your roommate each specialized, then exchanged your output. No money was involved. In other words, you engaged in barter. **Barter** is a system of exchange in which products are traded directly for other products. Barter works satisfactorily in very simple economies where there is little specialization and few different goods to trade. But for economies with greater specialization, *money* plays an important role in facilitating exchange. Money serves as a *medium of exchange* because it is the one thing that everyone is willing to accept in return for all goods and services.

Because of specialization and comparative advantage, most people consume little of what they produce and produce little of what they consume. People specialize in particular activities, such as plumbing or carpentry, and exchange their products for money, which in turn they exchanged for output produced by others. Did you make a single article of the clothing you are now wearing? Probably not. Consider the degree of specialization that goes into a cotton shirt. Some farmer in a warm climate grew the cotton and sold it to someone who spun it into thread, who sold it to someone who wove it into fabric, who sold it to someone who made the shirt, who sold it to a wholesaler, who sold it to a retailer, who sold it to you. Your shirt or blouse was produced by many specialists.

Division of Labor and Gains from Specialization

Picture a visit to McDonald's: "Let's see, I'll have a Big Mac, an order of fries, and a chocolate shake." About a minute later your order is ready. Consider how long it would take you to prepare the same meal yourself. It would take at least 15 minutes to make a homemade version of the Big Mac with all its special ingredients. Peeling, slicing, and frying the potatoes would take another 15 minutes. With the ice cream on hand, you should be able to make the shake in

Barter *The direct exchange of one good for another without the use of money*

Because we produce little of what we consume—books, for example—and consume little of what we produce, we need to use money as a medium of exchange.

5 minutes. In all, it would take you at least an hour to buy the ingredients, prepare the meal, and clean up afterward.

Why is the McDonald's meal faster, cheaper, and, for some people, better than one you could make yourself? Why is fast food so fast? The manager of McDonald's is taking advantage of the gains resulting from the **division of labor.** Rather than have each worker prepare an entire individual meal, McDonald's separates meal preparation into various tasks and has individuals specialize in these separate tasks. This division of labor allows the group to produce much more than it could if each person tried to prepare an entire meal. Instead of each worker doing it all and making a total of, say, 20 complete meals in an hour, 10 workers specialize and produce more like 500 meals per hour.

Division of labor The organization of production of a single good into separate tasks in which people specialize

How is this increase in productivity possible? First, the manager can assign tasks according to individual preferences and abilities—according to comparative advantage. The employee with the toothy smile and pleasant personality can handle the customers up front; the employee with the strong back but few social graces can handle the 50-pound sacks of potatoes out back. Second, a worker who performs the same task again and again gets better at it. Experience is a good teacher. The employee operating the cash register, for example, becomes better at handling the special problems that arise in dealing with customers. Third, there is no time lost in moving from one task to another. Finally, and perhaps most important, the **specialization of labor** allows for the introduction of more sophisticated production techniques, techniques that would not make economic sense on a smaller scale. For example, McDonald's does not prepare each milkshake separately, but mixes ingredients in a machine that shakes gallons at a time. Such machines would be impractical in the home. The specialization of labor allows for the introduction of specialized machines, and these machines make each worker more productive.

Specialization of labor Focusing an individual's efforts on a particular product or a single task

To review: The specialization of labor takes advantage of individual preferences and natural abilities, allows workers to develop more experience at a particular task, reduces the time required to shift between different tasks, and permits the introduction of labor-saving machinery. Specialization and the division of labor occur not only among individuals, but also among firms, regions, and indeed entire countries. The clothing production mentioned earlier might often involve growing cotton in one country, turning the cotton into cloth in another, sewing the clothing in a third country, and marketing that clothing in a fourth country.

We should also note that specialization can create problems, since doing the same thing for 8 hours a day often becomes tedious. Consider, for example, the assembly line worker whose task is to tighten a particular bolt. Such a job could drive that worker nuts. Repetitive motion can also lead to injury. Thus, the gains from breaking production down into individual tasks must be weighed against the problems caused by assigning workers to repetitive and tedious jobs. Specialization is discussed in the following case study.

CASE STUDY

Evidence of Specialization

Evidence of specialization is all around us. A trip to the shopping mall will quickly reveal the degree to which sellers specialize. Retailers specialize in everything from luggage to stationery; restaurants specialize in cuisine ranging from Chinese food to pizza. If you let your fingers do the walking through the

Evidence of Specialization
continued

Location:

To discover specialized stores on the Internet—like this herb shop—use the Lycos search engine (http://www.lycos.com/) or visit "The Internet Mall" (http://www.internet-mall.com/).

Yellow Pages, you will find thousands of separate specializations; for example, under "Physicians" alone you will find dozens of medical specialties. Or, without moving a muscle, you can appreciate the division of labor within a single industry by watching the credits roll at the end of the next film you see. Listed by specialization are the dozens and sometimes hundreds of people who worked on the movie—everyone from the gaffer to the assistant location scout.

Perhaps the newest way to explore specialization and the division of labor is on the Internet's World Wide Web, where there are millions of individual sites, most of which reflect some specialized product or activity. By using a search engine such as Lycos (originally developed at Carnegie Mellon University), you can type in any specialty to identify the number of sites that refers to that specialty. For example, according to Lycos, 862 sites refer to "butchers," 4,443 refer to "bakers," and 1,617 refer to "candles," or candlestick makers. In comparison, "entrepreneurs" are found at 3,923 sites, including information about collegiate entrepreneurs, the best businesses to start, plus a free electronic magazine called *The Virtual Entrepreneur* (see "Sources" below for the Internet addresses).

From "abattoirs" (slaughterhouses) to "zookeepers," the Internet identifies more specialties than any other single reference in the world. Where else could you find 601 references to "comedians," including three sites devoted exclusively to Jim Carrey? The Internet represents an easy way to track specialization.

Sources: Lycos technology is developed and marketed by Lycos, Inc., an independent operating company of CMG Information Services. "The Internet Mall" is a trademark of Intuitive Systems. Visit *The Virtual Entrepreneur* at http://emporium.turnpike.net/B/bizopp/index.html. For information on collegiate entrepreneurs, visit the Association of Collegiate Entrepreneurs (ACE) (http://www.is.csupomona.edu/ace/). For tips on the best businesses to start, visit the Entrepreneurial Edge Online Journal (http://www.edgeonline.com).

THE ECONOMY'S PRODUCTION POSSIBILITIES

The focus to this point has been on how individuals choose to use their scarce resources to satisfy their unlimited wants—more specifically, how they specialize based on comparative advantage. This emphasis on the individual has been appropriate because the world of economics is driven by the choices of individual decision makers, whether they are consumers, producers, or public officials. Just as resources are scarce for the individual, they are scarce for the economy as a whole (no fallacy of composition here). An economy has millions of different resources, which can be combined in all kinds of ways to produce millions of possible goods and services. In this section we step back from the immense complexity of the real economy to develop a simple model that presents the economy's production options.

Efficiency and the Production Possibilities Frontier
Here are the model's simplifying assumptions:

1. To reduce the analysis to manageable proportions, we limit the output to just two broad classes of products; in our example they are consumer goods,

such as pizzas and haircuts, and capital goods—physical capital such as factories, and human capital, such as college degrees.

2. The focus is on production during a given time period—in this case, a year.
3. The available supplies of resources in the economy are fixed in both quantity and quality during the time period.
4. Society's knowledge about how these resources can be combined to produce output—that is, the available *technology*—does not change during the year.

The point of these assumptions is to freeze the economy in time to focus on the economy's production alternatives based on the resources and technology available during that time.

Given the resources and the technology available in the economy, **the production possibilities frontier,** or **PPF,** identifies the various possible combinations of the two classes of goods that can be produced when all available resources are employed efficiently. The economy's PPF for consumer goods and capital goods is shown by the curve *AF* in Exhibit 1, where *A* identifies the amount of consumer goods produced per year if all the economy's resources are used efficiently to produce consumer goods, and *F* identifies the amount of cap-

Production possibilities frontier A curve showing all alternative combinations of goods that can be produced when available resources are used efficiently

The Economy's Production Possibilities Frontier

EXHIBIT 1

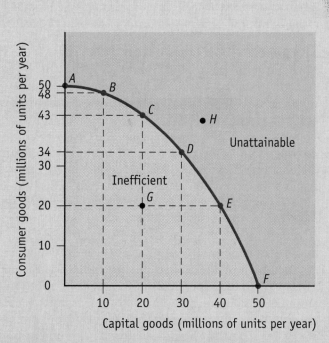

If the economy uses its available resources and technology fully and efficiently in producing consumer goods and capital goods, it will be on its production possibilities frontier curve *AF*. The PPF is bowed out to illustrate the law of increasing opportunity cost: additional units of capital goods require the economy to sacrifice more and more units of consumer goods. Note that more consumer goods must be given up in moving from *D* to *E* than in moving from *A* to *B*, although in each case the gain in capital goods is 10 million units. Points inside the PPF, such as *G*, represent inefficient use of resources. Points outside the PPF, such as *H*, represent unattainable combinations.

ital goods produced per year if all the economy's resources are used efficiently to produce capital goods. Points along the curve between *A* and *F* identify the possible combinations of the two types of goods that can be produced when all the economy's resources are used efficiently to produce both types of goods. *Resources are said to be employed efficiently when no change in the way the resources are combined could increase the production of one type of good without decreasing the production of the other type of good.* **Efficiency** involves getting the maximum possible output from available resources.

Inefficient and Unattainable Production

Efficiency The condition that exists when there is no way resources can be reallocated to increase the production of one good without decreasing the production of another

Points along the production possibilities frontier indicate the various possible combinations of outputs that can be produced when all available resources are employed efficiently. Points inside the PPF, such as *G* in Exhibit 1, represent combinations that either do not employ resources fully or employ them inefficiently. Note that point *C* yields more consumer goods and no fewer capital goods than *G*. And point *E* yields more capital goods and no fewer consumer goods than *G*. Indeed, any point along the PPF between *C* and *E*, such as point *D*, yields both more consumer goods and more capital goods than *G*. Hence, point *G* is inefficient; by using resources more efficiently or by using previously idle resources, the economy can produce more of one good without reducing the production of the other good.

Points outside the PPF, such as *H* in Exhibit 1, represent *unattainable* combinations, given the resources and the technology available. Thus *the PPF not only reflects efficient combinations of production but also identifies the border between inefficient combinations inside the frontier and unattainable combinations outside the frontier.*

Shape of the Production Possibilities Frontier

Focus again on point *A* in Exhibit 1. Although all resources are employed efficiently at point *A*, certain resources contribute little to the production of consumer goods. Any movement along the PPF involves giving up some of one good to get more of the other. Movements down the curve indicate that the opportunity cost of more capital goods is fewer consumer goods. For example, moving from point *A* to point *B* increases the amount of capital goods produced from none to 10 million units and reduces production of consumer goods from 50 million to 48 million units, a decline of only 2 million units. Increasing production of capital goods to 10 million units causes the production of consumer goods to fall little, because capital production initially draws upon resources, such as heavy machinery used to build factories, that add little to production of consumer goods but are quite productive in capital goods.

As shown by the dashed lines in Exhibit 1, each additional 10 million units of capital goods reduces consumer goods by more and more. Larger and larger amounts of consumer goods must be sacrificed because, as more capital goods are produced, the resources drawn away from consumer goods are those that are better suited to the production of consumer goods. *The opportunity cost increases as the economy produces more capital goods, because the resources in the economy are not all perfectly adaptable to the production of both types of goods.*

Law of increasing opportunity cost As more of a particular good is produced, larger and larger quantities of an alternative good must be sacrificed if the economy's resources are already being used efficiently

The shape of the production possibilities frontier reflects the law of increasing opportunity cost. If the economy uses all resources efficiently, the **law of increasing opportunity cost** states that as more of one good is produced, larger and larger quantities of the alternative good must be sacrificed. The PPF derives its bowed-out shape from the law of increasing opportunity cost. For example, whereas the first 10 million units of capital goods have an opportunity cost of only 2 million units of consumer goods, the final 10 million—that is, the increase from point E and point F—have an opportunity cost of 20 million units of consumer goods. Notice that the *slope* of the PPF indicates the opportunity cost of an additional unit of capital. As we move down the curve, the slope gets steeper, reflecting the higher opportunity cost of capital in terms of consumer goods.

The law of increasing opportunity cost also applies when moving from the production of capital goods to the production of consumer goods. When the economy concentrates on capital goods, as at point F, certain resources, such as cows and agricultural land, contribute little directly to the production of capital goods. (What's worse, cows foul the work area if allowed to hang around the factories.) Thus, the move from point F to point E involves little opportunity cost of forgone capital goods. As more consumer goods are produced, however, resources that are better suited to the production of capital goods must switch to the production of consumer goods, reflecting the law of increasing opportunity cost. Incidentally, if resources were perfectly adaptable to alternative uses, the PPF would be a straight line, reflecting a constant opportunity cost along the PPF.

What Shifts the Production Possibilities Frontier?

When we construct the production possibilities frontier, we assume that the amount of resources available in the economy and the level of technology are constant. Over time, however, the PPF may shift as a result of changes in resource availability or in technology. A shift outward in the PPF reflects economic growth.

Changes in Resource Availability. If people decide to work longer hours, the PPF will shift outward, as depicted in panel (a) of Exhibit 2. An increase in the size or the health of the labor force, an increase in the skills of the labor force, or an increase in the availability of other resources, such as new oil discoveries, will also shift the PPF outward. In contrast, a decrease in the availability or the quality of resources will shift the PPF inward, as depicted in panel (b). For example, in 1990 Iraq invaded Kuwait, setting oil fields ablaze and destroying much of Kuwait's physical capital, thereby shifting Kuwait's PPF inward . In West Africa the encroaching sands of the Sahara each year cover and destroy thousands of square miles of productive farmland, shifting the PPF of that economy inward.

The new PPFs in both panels (a) and (b) appear to be parallel to the original PPF, indicating that the resource that changed is equally adaptable to production of either good. For example, electrical power can be used in the production of both consumer goods and capital goods. If, however, a resource is better suited to the production of consumer goods, then an increase in the supply of that resource will shift the PPF more along the consumer goods axis than along the capital goods axis, as shown in panel (c). Panel (d) shows the effect of an increase in a resource better suited to capital goods.

Increases in the Capital Stock. An economy's production possibilities frontier depends in part on the stock of human and physical capital. The more capital an

EXHIBIT 2   **Shifts in the Economy's Production Possibilities Frontier**

(a) Increase in available resources

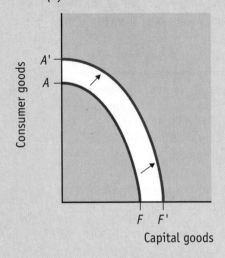

(b) Decrease in available resources

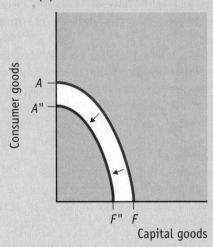

(c) Increase in resource or technological advance that benefits consumer goods

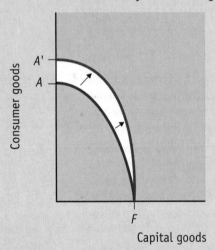

(d) Increase in resource or technological advance that benefits capital goods

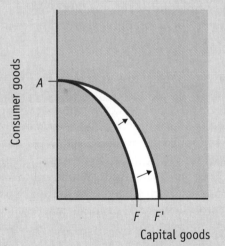

When the resources available to an economy change, the PPF shifts. If more resources become available, the PPF shifts outward, as in panel (a), indicating that more output can be produced. A decrease in available resources causes the PPF to shift inward, as in panel (b). Panel (c) shows a change affecting consumer goods production. More consumer goods can now be produced at any given level of capital goods. Panel (d) shows a change affecting capital goods production.

economy accumulates one period, the more output can be produced in the next period. Thus, increased production of capital goods this period (for example, by more education in the case of human capital or more machines in the case of physical capital) will increase the economy's PPF next period.

Effects of Technological Change. Another type of change that could shift the economy's PPF outward is a technological discovery that employs available resources more efficiently. Some discoveries enhance the production of both products, such as an innovation that manages resources more efficiently, as shown in panel (a) of Exhibit 2. The effect of a technological advance in the production of consumer goods, such as genetically altered seeds that double crop production, is reflected by an outward shift in the PPF along the consumer goods axis, as shown in panel (c) of Exhibit 2. Panel (d) shows the result of a technological advance in the production of capital goods, such as the development of a CD-ROM for self-instruction that enhances the production of human capital.

What We Can Learn from the PPF

The production possibilities frontier demonstrates several ideas introduced so far. The first is *efficiency:* The PPF describes the efficient combinations of output that are possible, given the economy's resources and technology. The second is *scarcity:* Given the resource and the technology, the economy can produce only so much. The PPF slopes downward, indicating that as the economy produces more of one good, it produces less of the other good. This tradeoff demonstrates *opportunity cost.* The bowed-out shape of the PPF reflects the *law of increasing opportunity cost,* which arises because not all resources are perfectly adaptable to the production of all goods. Because society must somehow choose a specific combination of output—a single point—along the PPF, the PPF also underscores the need for *choice.* That choice will determine not only current consumption but also the capital stock available next period. How society goes about choosing a particular combination will depend upon the nature of the economic system, as we will see in the next section. Finally, a shift outward in the PPF reflects *economic growth.*

Three Questions Each Economic System Must Answer

Every point along the economy's production possibilities frontier is an efficient combination of output. Whether the economy produces efficiently and how the economy selects the most preferred combination will depend on the decision-making rules employed. Regardless of how decisions are made, each economy must answer three fundamental questions: What goods and services will be produced? How will they be produced? And for whom will they be produced? An **economic system** is the set of mechanisms and institutions that resolve the what, how, and for whom questions. The criteria used to distinguish among economic systems are (1) who owns the resources, (2) what decision-making process is used to allocate resources and products, and (3) what types of incentives guide economic actors.

Economic system The set of mechanisms and institutions that resolve the what, how, and for whom questions

What Goods and Services Will Be Produced? Many of us take for granted the incredible number of choices that go into deciding what gets produced—everything from which new kitchen appliances are introduced and which aspiring novelists get published to which roads get built. Although different economies resolve these and millions of other questions using different decision-making rules and mechanisms, all economies must somehow make such choices.

How Will Goods and Services Be Produced? The economic system—or, more specifically, individual decision makers in the economic system—must determine how output is to be produced. Which resources should be used, and how should they be combined to produce each product? How much labor should be used and at what skill levels? What kinds of machines should be used? What type of fertilizer should be used to grow the best strawberries? Should the factory be built in the city or closer to the interstate highway? Again, billions of individual decisions determine which resources are employed and how these resources are combined.

For Whom Will Goods and Services Be Produced? Finally, who will actually consume the goods and services produced? The economic system must determine how to allocate the fruits of production among the population. Should equal amounts be provided to everyone? Should the weak and the sick receive more? Should those willing to wait in line the longest receive more? Should goods be allocated according to height? Weight? Religion? Age? Gender? Race? Strength? Political connections? The value of resources supplied? The question "For whom will goods and services be produced?" is often referred to as the *distribution question.*

Although we discussed the three economic questions separately, they are closely interwoven. The answer to one depends very much on the answers to the others. For example, an economy that distributes goods and services in uniform amounts to all will, no doubt, answer the what-is-to-be-produced question differently from an economy that somehow allows each person to choose a unique combination. Laws about resource ownership and the extent to which the government attempts to coordinate economic activity determine the "rules of the game"—the set of conditions that shape individual incentives and constraints. Along a spectrum ranging from the most free to the most regimented type of economic system, *pure capitalism* would be at one end and the *command economy* would be at the opposite end.

ECONOMIC SYSTEMS

Pure Capitalism

Under **pure capitalism,** the rules of the game include the private ownership of all resources and the coordination of economic activity based on the price signals generated in free, unrestricted markets. Any income derived from the use of land, labor, capital, or entrepreneurial ability goes exclusively to the individual owners of those resources. Owners have *property rights* to the use of their resources and are therefore free to sell those resources to the highest bidder. Producers are free to make and sell whatever output they think will be profitable. Consumers are free to buy whatever goods they can afford. All this voluntary buying and selling is coordinated by unrestricted markets, where buyers and sellers make their wishes known. Market prices guide resources to their highest-valued use and direct goods and services to consumers who value them the most.

Under pure capitalism, markets answer the what, how, and for whom questions. Markets transmit information about relative scarcity, provide individual incentives, and distribute income among resource suppliers. No single individual or small group coordinates these activities. Rather, it is the voluntary

Net Bookmark What products do Internet users need? Mark Andreessen, co-founder and Vice President of Technology for Netscape Communications, developed NCSA Mosaic, a popular software Internet browser, while an undergraduate at the University of Illinois. To discover more about Andreessen and Netscape Communications, visit "Welcome to Netscape" (http://www.netscape.com/).

Pure capitalism An economic system characterized by private ownership of resources and the use of prices to coordinate economic activity in unregulated markets

choices of many buyers and sellers responding only to their individual incentives and constraints that direct resources and products to those who value them the most. According to Adam Smith (1723–1790), one of the first to explain the allocative role of markets, market forces coordinate as if by an "invisible hand"—an unseen force that harnesses the pursuit of self-interest to direct resources where they earn the greatest payoff. According to Smith, *although each individual pursues his or her self-interest, the invisible hand promotes the general welfare.* Pure capitalism is sometimes called *laissez-faire* capitalism; translated from the French, this phrase means "to let do," or to let people do as they choose without out government intervention. Thus, *under pure capitalism, voluntary choices based on rational self-interest are made in unrestricted markets to answer the questions what, how, and for whom.*

As we shall see in later chapters, pure capitalism has its flaws. Most notable are the following:

1. There is no central authority that can protect property rights, enforce contracts, and otherwise ensure that the rules of the game are followed
2. People with no resources to sell may starve
3. Producers may try to monopolize markets by eliminating the competition
4. So-called public goods, such as national defense, will not be produced by private firms because private firms cannot prevent those who fail to pay from enjoying the benefits of public goods.

Command Economy

In a **command economy,** resources are directed and production is coordinated based on the "command," or central plan, of government rather than by markets. At least in theory, there is public, or communal, ownership of property. Government planners, as representatives of all the people, determine, for example, how much steel, how many cars, how many homes, and how many loaves of bread to produce. They also determine how to produce these goods and how to allocate them.

Command economy An economic system characterized by public ownership of resources and centralized economic planning

In theory, the command economy incorporates individual choices into collective choices, which, in turn, are reflected in central planning decisions. In practice, command economies also have flaws. Most notably:

1. Running an economy is so complicated that some resources are used inefficiently
2. Since nobody in particular owns resources, people have less incentive to employ them in their highest valued use
3. Central plans may reflect more the preferences of central planners than those of society
4. Each individual has less personal freedom in making economic choices.

Mixed and Transitional Economies

No country on earth exemplifies either type of economic system in its pure form. Economic systems have been growing more alike over time, with the role of government increasing in capitalist economies and the role of markets increasing in command economies The United States represents a **mixed capitalist economy,** with government directly accounting for about one-third of all economic activity. What's more, government regulates the private sector in

Mixed capitalist economy An economic system characterized by private ownership of some resources and public ownership of other resources. Some markets are unregulated and others are regulated.

a variety of ways. Most other advanced industrial nations, such as Germany, Japan, Great Britain, and Canada, also have mixed capitalist economies.

Countries with command economies are currently introducing more market incentives. For example, about 20 percent of the world's population lives in the People's Republic of China, which grows more decentralized, or market oriented, each year. The former Soviet Union has dissolved into 15 independent republics, and most of these are trying to privatize what had been state-owned enterprises to turn production decisions over to market forces. From Hungary to Mongolia, the transitions to market economies now underway in former command economies will shape the 21st century.

Economies Based on Custom or Religion

Finally, some economic systems are shaped largely by custom or religion. For example, laws of the Muslim religion limit the rate of interest that can be earned on certain investments. Caste systems in India and elsewhere restrict occupation choice. More generally, religion, custom, and family relations play important roles in organizing and coordinating economic activity. Your own pattern of consumption and choice of occupation may be influenced by some of these factors.

CONCLUSION

Although economies can answer the three economic questions in a variety of ways, this text will focus primarily on the mixed form of capitalism found in the United States. This type of economy blends private choice, guided by the price system in competitive markets, with public choice, guided by democracy in political markets. The study of mixed capitalism grows more relevant as former command economies try to develop market economies.

If you were to quit right now, you would already know more economics than most people. But to understand market economies, you must learn how markets work, as you will in the next chapter, which introduces the market interaction of demand and supply.

SUMMARY

1. Resources are scarce, but human wants are unlimited. Since we cannot satisfy all wants, we must choose, and choice always involves an opportunity cost. The opportunity cost of the selected option is the forgone benefit from the best alternative.

2. The law of comparative advantage states that the individual, firm, region, or country with the lowest opportunity cost of producing a particular good should specialize in the production of that good. Specialization according to the law of comparative advantage promotes the most efficient use of resources.

3. The specialization of labor increases efficiency by (1) taking advantage of individual preferences and natural abil-

ities, (2) allowing each worker to develop more experience at a particular task, (3) reducing the time required to move between different tasks, and (4) allowing for the introduction of more specialized capital and production techniques.

4. The production possibilities frontier shows the productive capabilities of the economy when all resources are used efficiently. The frontier's bowed-out shape reflects the law of increasing opportunity cost, which arises because some resources are not perfectly adaptable to the production of different goods. Over time, the frontier can shift in or out as a result of changes in the availability of resources or in technology. The frontier demonstrates several economic concepts, including efficiency,

scarcity, the law of increasing opportunity cost, the need for choice, and economic growth.

5. All economic systems, regardless of their decision-making process, must answer three fundamental questions: What is to be produced? How is it to be produced? and For whom is it to be produced? Nations answer the questions differently, depending on who owns their resources and how economic activity is coordinated.

QUESTIONS AND PROBLEMS

1. **(Opportunity Costs)** Discuss the ways in which the following conditions might affect the opportunity cost of going to a movie tonight:
   a. You have a final exam tomorrow.
   b. School will be out for one month starting today.
   c. The same movie will be shown on TV tomorrow night.
   d. The school dance or concert is the same night as the movie.

2. **(Opportunity Costs)** "You should never buy pre-cooked frozen foods because you are paying for the labor costs of preparing food." Is this statement always true, or can it be invalidated by the principle of comparative advantage?

3. **(Opportunity Costs)** Indicate whether each of the following statements is true or false, explaining your answer:
   a. The opportunity cost of an activity includes the sum of the benefits of all alternatives passed up.
   b. Opportunity cost is an objective measure.
   c. When making choices, people exhaustively gather all available information about the costs and benefits of alternative choices.
   d. A decision maker seldom knows the actual value of a forgone alternative and must base decisions on expected values.

4. **(Production Possibilities)** In response to an increase of illegal aliens, Congress made it a federal offense to hire illegal aliens. How will the measure affect the U.S. production possibilities frontier? Will all industries be affected equally?

5. **(Production Possibilities)** "If society decides, by way of the marketplace, to use its resources fully (that is, to keep the economy on the production possibilities frontier), then future generations will be worse off because they will not be able to use these resources." If this assertion is true, full employment of resources may not be a good thing. Comment on the validity of this assertion.

6. **(Production Possibilities)** Under what conditions is it possible to increase production of one good without decreasing production of another good?

7. **(Production Possibilities)** Suppose that there are two resources in the economy (labor and capital) and two goods (wheat and cloth). Capital is relatively more useful in producing wheat, and labor is relatively more useful in producing cloth. If the supply of capital falls by 10 percent and the supply of labor increases by 10 percent, how will the PPF for wheat and cloth change?

8. **(Comparative and Absolute Advantage)** Indicate whether each of the following would cause the economy's PPF to shift inward or outward:
   a. An increase in average vacation time.
   b. An increase in immigration.
   c. A decrease in the average retirement age.
   d. The migration of skilled workers to other countries.

9. **(Specialization)** Explain how the specialization of labor can lead to increased productivity.

10. **(Comparative and Absolute Advantage)** Consider the following information concerning the production of wheat and cloth in the United States and England:

Labor Hours Required to Produce One Unit

	England	United States
Wheat	2	1
Cloth	6	5

   a. What is the opportunity cost of wheat in England? In the United States?
   b. Which country has a comparative advantage in wheat? In cloth?
   c. Which country has an absolute advantage in wheat? In cloth?
   d. Which country should specialize in the production of wheat? Of cloth?

11. **(Production Possibilities)** Suppose a production possibilities frontier includes the following data points:

Cars	Washing Machines
0	1,000
100	600
200	0

a. Graph the production possibilities frontier, assuming that it has no curved segments.
b. What is the cost of a car when 50 cars are produced?
c. What is the cost of a car when 150 cars are produced?
d. What is the cost of a washing machine when 50 cars are produced? 150 cars?
e. What do your answers tell you about opportunity costs?

12. **(Sunk Cost)** You go to a restaurant and buy an expensive meal. Halfway through, in spite of feeling full, you decide to clean your plate. After all, you think, you paid for the meal, so you are going to eat all of it. What's wrong with this thinking?

13. **(Production Possibilities)** Under what conditions would an economy be operating inside its PPF? Outside its PPF?

14. **(Opportunity Cost)** Suppose that in an hour George can either write one poem or mow two lawns, and Martha can either write two poems or mow three lawns. Construct a daily production possibility frontier for George *and* Martha, assuming each works an 8-hour day.

15. **(Economic Questions)** What basic economic questions must be answered in a barter economy? In a primitive economy? In pure capitalism? In a command economy?

16. **(Comparative Advantage)** Suppose that you are a doctor and also a good car mechanic. Why should you pay someone to repair your car?

17. **(Production Possibilities Frontier)** Suppose that government deficits drive up the cost of borrowing money so that businesses no longer can afford to fund research and development. How might this affect the production possibilities frontier?

18. **(Evidence of Specialization)** Provide some examples of specialized markets or retail outlets. What makes a medium like the World Wide Web conducive to specialization?

19. **(The Opportunity Cost of College)** During the Vietnam War period, colleges and universities were literally overflowing with students. Was this bumper crop of undergraduates caused by a greater expected return on a college education or by a change in the opportunity cost of attending college? Explain.

20. **(The Opportunity Cost of College)** Suppose that the minimum wage was increased to $10 per hour. What impact, if any, do you think this would have on the opportunity cost of attending college?

Using the Internet

21. Use the Lycos search engine (**http://www.lycos.com/**) to determine the number of web sites in which the word "economics" appears. Do the same for "economist" and "entrepreneur." What is the most unusual web site you find in your search for "entrepreneur"?

The Market System

3

Why do vine-ripened tomatoes cost more in January than in August? Demand and supply. Why do roses cost more on Valentine's Day than during the rest of the year? Demand and supply. Why do surgeons earn more than butchers? You guessed it: Demand and supply. Many economic questions boil down to the workings of demand and supply. Indeed, some believe that if you programmed a computer to respond "demand and supply" to economic questions, you could put many economists out of work.

Demand and supply are the most fundamental and the most powerful of all economic tools. An understanding of the two will take you far in mastering the art and science of economic analysis. This chapter will introduce you to the underpinnings of demand and supply and show you how the two interact in competitive markets. As you will see, the correct analysis of demand and supply takes skill and care. The chapter uses graphs extensively, so you may want to refer to the appendix of Chapter 1 for a refresher. Topics discussed in this chapter include:

- Demand and quantity demanded
- Supply and quantity supplied
- Markets

- Equilibrium price and quantity
- Changes in demand and in supply
- Disequilibrium

DEMAND

How much Pepsi will consumers buy per week if the price is $3 per six-pack? If the price is $2? If it's $4? The answers reveal the relationship between the price of Pepsi and the quantity purchased. Such a relationship is called the *demand* for Pepsi. **Demand** indicates the quantity of a product that consumers are both *willing* and *able* to buy at each possible price during a given period of time, other things constant. Because demand reflects a specific period of time, such as a day, a week, or a month, think of demand as the desired *rate* of purchase during that time period at each possible price. Also, note the emphasis on *willing* and *able*. You may be *able* to buy a motorcycle at a price of $2,000 because you can afford one, but you may not be *willing* to buy one if motorcycles do not interest you.

Demand A relation showing the quantities of a good consumers are willing and able to buy at various prices during a given period of time, other things constant

The Law of Demand

In a remote region of western Pennsylvania is a poorly lit, run-down yellow building known as Pechin's Mart. The aisles are unmarked and strewn with half-empty boxes arranged in no apparent design. The sagging roof leaks when it rains. Why do shoppers come from as far away as Maryland and put up with the chaos and the grubbiness to buy as many groceries as they can haul away? The store has violated nearly all the rules of retailing, yet it thrives, with annual sales more than four times the national average. The store thrives because it follows a rule merchants have known for thousands of years: Its prices are the lowest around.

You as a consumer have little trouble understanding that people will buy more at a lower price than at a higher price. Sell the product for less, and the world will beat a path to your door. This relation between the price of a product and the quantity demanded is an economic law. The **law of demand** states that the quantity of a product demanded in a given time period varies inversely with its price, other things constant. Thus, the higher the price, the smaller the quantity demanded; the lower the price, the greater the quantity demanded.

Law of demand The quantity of a good demanded is inversely related to its price, other things constant

Demand, Wants, and Needs. Consumer *demand* and consumer *wants* are not the same thing. As we have seen, wants are unlimited. You may *want* a Mercedes-Benz 300, but the price of $70,000 is likely beyond your budget (that is, the quantity you demand at that price is zero). Nor is *demand* the same as *need*. You may *need* a new muffler for your car, but if the price is $200, you may decide "I am not going to pay a lot for this muffler." Apparently, you have better ways to spend your money. If, however, the price of mufflers drops enough—say, to $90—then you are both willing and able to buy one.

The Substitution Effect of a Price Change. What explains the law of demand? Why, for example, is more demanded when the price is lower? The explanation begins with scarce resources meeting unlimited wants. Many goods and services are capable of satisfying particular wants. For example, you can satisfy your hunger with pizza, tacos, burgers, chicken, or dozens of other dishes. Similarly, you can satisfy your desire for warmth in the winter with warm clothing, a home-heating system, a trip to Hawaii, or in many other ways. Clearly, some ways of satisfying your wants will be more appealing to you than others (a trip to Hawaii is more fun than warmer clothing). In a world without scarcity, there would be no prices, so you would always choose the most attractive alternative. Scarcity, however, is a reality, and the degree of scarcity of one good relative to another helps determine each good's *relative* price.

Notice that the definition of demand includes the "other-things-constant" assumption. Among "other things" assumed to remain constant are the prices of other goods. When the price of one good declines and other prices remain constant, this good becomes relatively cheaper. Consumers are more *willing* to purchase the good when its relative price falls; they tend to substitute this now-cheaper good for other goods. For example, if the price of pizza drops, you tend to eat more pizza and less of other foods. This is called the **substitution effect** of a price change. On the other hand, an increase in the price of one good, other things constant, causes consumers to substitute other goods for the higher-priced good. Remember, *it is the change in the relative price—the price of one good relative to the prices of other goods—that causes the substitution effect.* If all prices increased by the same percentage, there would be no change in relative prices and no substitution effect.

Substitution effect *When the price of a good falls, consumers will substitute it for other goods, which are now relatively more expensive*

The Income Effect of a Price Change. A fall in the price of a product increases the quantity demanded for a second reason. Suppose you earn $30 a week from a part-time job and spend all your income on pizza, buying three a week at $10 per pizza. What if the price drops to $5? At that price you can now afford six pizzas a week with your income. The decrease in the price of pizza has increased your **real income**—that is, your income measured in terms of the goods and services it can buy. The price reduction, other things constant, increases the *purchasing power* of your income, thereby increasing your *ability* to purchase pizza. The quantity of pizza you demand will likely increase because of this **income effect** of a price decrease. You may not increase your quantity demanded to six pizzas, but you would be able to.

Real income *Income measured in terms of the goods and services it can buy*

More generally, because of the income effect of a price decrease, other things constant, consumers typically increase their quantity demanded. Conversely, an increase in the price of a good, other things constant, reduces real income, thereby reducing the *ability* to purchase all goods. Because of the income effect of a price increase, consumers typically reduce their quantity demanded.

Income effect *A fall in the price of a good increases consumers' real income, making them more able to purchase all goods, so the quantity demanded increases*

The Demand Schedule and Demand Curve

Demand can be expressed as a *demand schedule* or as a *demand curve*. Panel (a) of Exhibit 1 shows a hypothetical demand schedule for milk. When we describe demand, we must specify the units being measured and the time period being considered. In our example, the price is for a quart of milk, and the period is a month. The milk is of uniform quality, in this case grade A homogenized whole milk. The schedule lists possible prices, along with the quantity demanded at each price. At a price of $1.25 per quart, for example, consumers demand 8 million quarts per month. As you can see, the lower the price, other things constant, the greater the quantity demanded. If the price drops as low as $0.25 per quart, consumers demand 32 million quarts per month. As the price of milk falls, consumers substitute milk for other goods. And as the price of milk falls, the real income of consumers increases, causing them to increase the quantity of milk demanded.

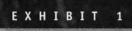

EXHIBIT   1   The Demand Schedule and Demand Curve for Milk

(a) Demand schedule

	Price per Quart	Quantity Demanded per Month (millions of quarts)
a	$1.25	8
b	1.00	14
c	0.75	20
d	0.50	26
e	0.25	32

(b) Demand curve

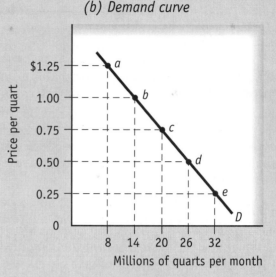

The market demand curve, *D*, shows the quantity of milk demanded, at various prices, by all consumers.

Demand curve *A curve showing the quantities of a commodity demanded at various possible prices, other things constant*

The demand schedule in panel (a) appears as a **demand curve** in panel (b), with price on the vertical axis and the quantity demanded per month on the horizontal axis. Each combination of price and quantity demanded listed in the demand schedule in panel (a) is a point in panel (b). Point *a,* for example, indicates that if the price is $1.25 consumers demand 8 million quarts per month. These points connect to form the demand curve for milk, labeled *D.* Note that the demand curve slopes downward, reflecting the *law of demand:* Price and quantity demanded are inversely related, other things constant. Assumed to be constant along the demand curve are the prices of other goods. Thus along the demand curve for milk, the price of milk changes *relative to the prices of other goods.* The demand curve shows the effect of a change in the *relative price* of milk—that is, relative to other prices, which do not change.

Take care to distinguish between the *demand* for milk and the *quantity demanded.* The *demand* for milk is not a specific quantity but the entire relation between price and quantity demanded—that is, the demand schedule or demand curve. An individual point on the demand curve shows the *quantity demanded* at a particular price. For example, at a price of $0.75 per quart, the quantity demanded is 20 million quarts. When the price of milk changes, say, from $0.75 to $1.00, this change is shown in Exhibit 1 by a movement along the demand curve—in this case from point *c* to point *b.* Any movement along a demand curve reflects a *change in quantity demanded,* not a change in demand.

The law of demand applies to the millions of products sold in grocery stores, department stores, clothing stores, drug stores, music stores, book stores, travel agencies, and restaurants, and through Yellow Pages, classified ads, cyberspace, stock markets, real estate markets, job markets, and all other markets. The law of demand applies even to choices that seem more personal than economic, such as whether or not to own a pet. For example, after New York City passed a dog-litter law, owners had to follow their dogs around the city's sidewalks with scoopers, plastic bags, or whatever else would do the job. Because the law raised the cost of owning a dog, the quantity demanded decreased. The number of dogs left at animal shelters doubled. Many dogs were simply abandoned by their owners, raising the number of strays in the city. The law of demand predicts such behavior.

It is useful to distinguish between *individual demand,* which is the demand of an individual consumer, and *market demand,* which is the sum of the individual demands of *all* consumers in the market. In most markets there are many consumers, sometimes millions. Unless otherwise noted, when we talk about demand, we will be referring to market demand, as in Exhibit 1.

CHANGES IN DEMAND

A given demand curve isolates the relation between the price of a good and the quantity demanded when other factors that could affect demand remain unchanged. What are these other factors and how do changes in them affect demand? Variables that can affect market demand are (1) consumer income, (2) the prices of related goods, (3) consumer expectations, (4) the number and composition of consumers in the market, and (5) consumer tastes. Let's consider how a change in each affects demand.

Changes in Consumer Income

Exhibit 2 shows *D,* the market demand curve for milk. This demand curve assumes a given level of consumer income. Suppose consumer incomes increase. Consumers will then be willing and able to purchase more milk at each price, so the demand for milk will increase; the demand curve shifts to the right from D to D'. For example, at a price of $1.00, the quantity demanded increases from 14 million to 20 million quarts per month, as indicated by the movement from point *b* on D to point *g* on D'.

An increase in the demand for milk also means that consumers are willing and able to pay a higher price for each *quantity* of milk. For example, consumers were initially willing and able to pay $1.00 per quart for 14 million quarts, as reflected by point *b*. After the increase in income, consumers are willing and able to pay $1.25 per quart for 14 million quarts, as reflected by point *f* on the new demand curve, which is directly above point *b* on the original demand curve. In short, *an increase in demand—that is, a shift to the right or a shift upward in the demand curve—means that consumers are willing and able to buy more units at each price and to pay more per unit at each quantity.*

We classify goods into two broad groupings, depending on how demand for the good responds to changes in income. The demand for **normal goods** increases as income increases. Because the demand for milk increases when consumer income increases, milk is a normal good. Most goods are normal goods. In contrast, the demand for **inferior goods** actually declines as income increases. Examples of inferior goods include ground chuck, trips to the Laundromat, and bus rides. As income increases, consumers tend to switch from consuming these inferior goods to consuming normal goods (steak, their own

If the incomes of milk consumers increase, these consumers will be willing and able to purchase more milk at any given price. As a result, the demand for milk will increase.

Normal good A good for which demand increases as consumer income rises

Inferior good A good for which demand decreases as consumer income rises

EXHIBIT 2

An Increase in the Market Demand for Milk

An increase in the demand for milk is reflected by an outward shift in the demand curve. After the increase in demand, the quantity of milk demanded at a price of $1 per quart increases from 14 million quarts (point *b*) to 20 million quarts (point *g*). Another way to interpret the shift is to say that the maximum price consumers are willing to pay for 14 million quarts has increased from $1 per unit (at point *b*) to $1.25 per unit (at point *f*).

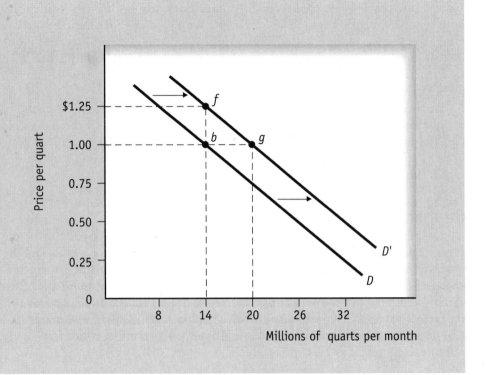

washers and dryers, automobile or plane rides), so the demand curve for inferior goods shifts to the left.

Changes in the Prices of Related Goods

As noted already, the prices of other goods are assumed to be constant along a given demand curve. Let's now bring these other goods into the picture. There are various ways of trying to satisfy any particular want. Consumers choose among substitutes partly on the basis of their relative prices. Consider two substitutes, milk and juice. Obviously, they are not perfect substitutes (you wouldn't pour juice on cereal or use it to make hot chocolate). Yet an increase in the price of juice, other things constant, will prompt some consumers to buy less juice and more milk. Two goods are **substitutes** if an increase in the price of one leads to an increase in the demand for the other, and conversely, if a decrease in the price of one leads to a decrease in the demand for the other.

Two goods are complements if they are used in combination to satisfy some particular want. Milk and chocolate chip cookies, computer hardware and software, popcorn and movies, and airline tickets and rental cars are complements. Two goods are **complements** if a decrease in the price of one leads to an increase in the demand for the other. For example, a decrease in the price of computers leads to an increase in the demand for software. Most pairs of goods selected at random are *unrelated*—for example, milk and housing, pizza and socks, and dental floss and golf equipment.

Substitutes Goods that are related in such a way that an increase in the price of one leads to an increase in the demand for the other

Complements Goods that are related in such a way that an increase in the price of one leads to a decrease in the demand for the other

Changes in Consumer Expectations

Another factor assumed to be constant along a given demand curve is consumer expectations about factors that influence demand, such as future income and the future price of the good. A change in consumer expectations can change demand. For example, a consumer who learns about a future pay increase may increase current demand in anticipation of that pay increase. In anticipation of a steady paycheck, a college senior who lands a job may buy a new car even before graduation. Changes in price expectations can also affect demand. For example, if consumers come to believe that home prices will jump next year, some will increase their demand for housing this year, before prices go up. On the other hand, expectations of a lower price in the future will encourage some consumers to postpone purchases, thereby reducing current demand.

Changes in the Number or Composition of Consumers

As mentioned earlier, market demand is the sum of the individual demands of all consumers in the market. If the number of consumers in the market changes, demand will change. For example, if the population grows, the demand for food will increase. Even if the total population remains the same, demand could change as a result of a change in the composition of the population. For example, if the number of retired couples increases, the demand for recreational vehicles will probably increase. If the baby population booms, the demand for baby food, baby clothes, and playpens will jump.

Changes in Consumer Tastes

Do you like anchovies on your pizza? How about sauerkraut on your hot dog? Is music to your ears more likely to be new wave, country, heavy metal, rap, reggae, jazz, or classical? Choices in food, clothing, movies, music, reading—indeed, all consumer choices—are influenced by consumer tastes. **Tastes** are nothing more than your likes and dislikes as a consumer. Tastes are assumed to be constant along a given demand curve. What determines tastes? Who knows? Economists certainly don't, nor do they spend much time worrying about it. They recognize, however, that tastes are important in shaping demand.

Tastes Consumer preferences

Economists assume that tastes are relatively stable. Because a change in tastes is so difficult to isolate from other economic changes, we should be reluctant to attribute a change in demand to a change in tastes. In our analysis of consumer demand, we will assume that tastes are given and are relatively stable over time. We know, for example, that younger people usually prefer rock music, whereas older people tend to prefer other kinds of music. The music piped into shopping malls tends to be so-called easy-listening music, a choice designed to discourage younger people from hanging around the mall any longer than required to do their shopping.

If we could not assume that tastes are relatively stable, we would be tempted to attribute any change in demand to a change in tastes. For example, the question "Why did the demand for milk change?" could be answered by saying "Obviously, the taste for milk changed." But since it is usually difficult to verify such an assertion, we use the change-in-tastes explanation sparingly and only after ruling out other possible changes. At times, we *can* trace a change in tastes to a specific event. For example, after the American Heart Association linked cholesterol to heart disease, the sales of eggs, which are high in cholesterol, fell by 25 percent. As another example, the demand for fur coats has dropped sharply because animal-rights activists have campaigned against wearing fur.

Remember, a movement along a given demand curve is called a **change in quantity demanded.** A change in quantity demanded results from a change in *price,* other things constant. A shift in the demand curve is called a **change in demand.** A change in demand results from a change in one of the *nonprice* determinants of demand, such as a change in income, a change in the price of related goods, a change in consumer expectations, a change in the number or composition of consumers, or a change in consumer tastes.

Change in quantity demanded A movement along the demand curve in response to a change in the price, other things constant

Change in demand A shift in a given demand curve caused by a change in one of the nonprice determinants of demand for the good

SUPPLY

Just as demand is the relation between price and quantity demanded, supply is the relation between price and quantity supplied. Specifically, **supply** indicates how much of the good producers are both *willing* and *able* to offer for sale per period at each possible price, other things constant. The **law of supply** states that the quantity supplied is usually directly related to its price, other things constant. Thus, the lower the price, the smaller the quantity supplied; the higher the price, the greater the quantity supplied.

Supply A relation showing the quantities of a good producers are willing and able to sell at various prices during a given time period, other things constant

Law of supply The quantity of product supplied in a given time period is usually directly related to its price, other things constant

Supply curve A curve showing the quantities of a good supplied at various prices, other things constant

The Supply Schedule and Supply Curve

Exhibit 3 presents the market *supply schedule* and market **supply curve,** S, for milk, showing the quantities of milk supplied at various possible prices by thousands of dairy farmers. As you can see, price and quantity supplied are directly, or positively, related. Producers offer more for sale at a higher price than at a lower price, so the supply curve slopes upward.

There are two reasons producers tend to offer more goods for sale when the price is higher. First, as the price of a good increases, other things constant, a producer is more *willing* to supply the good. Prices act as signals to existing and potential suppliers about the relative rewards for producing various goods. An increase in the price of milk provides farmers with a profit incentive to shift some resources out of the production of other goods, such as corn, for which the price is now relatively lower, and into milk, for which the price is now relatively higher. *A higher milk price attracts resources from lower-valued uses to the higher-valued use.*

A second reason the supply curve tends to slope upward is that higher prices increase the producer's *ability* to supply the good. The law of increasing opportunity cost states that the opportunity cost of additional output rises as output increases—that is, the *marginal* cost of production increases as output increases. Since producers face a higher marginal cost for additional output, they must receive a higher price for that output to be *able* to increase the quantity supplied. For example, when milk production is low, farmers are able to employ resources that are well suited to the task. As output increases, however, producing the additional increments of milk draws on resources that may be better suited to producing other goods. To feed additional cows, for example, a farmer may have to convert a corn field into a pasture. Therefore, additional output has a higher opportunity cost. *Higher milk prices make farmers more able to draw resources away from alternative uses.* Similarly, a higher price for gasoline in-

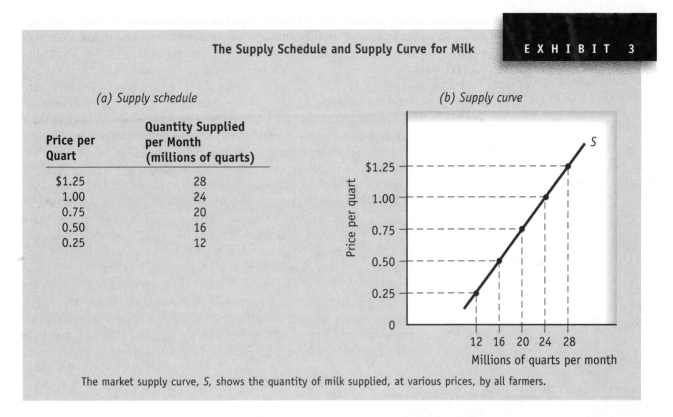

The Supply Schedule and Supply Curve for Milk

EXHIBIT 3

(a) Supply schedule

Price per Quart	Quantity Supplied per Month (millions of quarts)
$1.25	28
1.00	24
0.75	20
0.50	16
0.25	12

(b) Supply curve

The market supply curve, S, shows the quantity of milk supplied, at various prices, by all farmers.

creased oil companies' ability to explore in less accessible locations, such as the remote jungles of the Amazon, the stormy waters of the North Sea, and the frozen tundra of Alaska and Siberia.

Thus, a higher price makes producers more *willing* and more *able* to increase the quantity of goods offered for sale. Producers are more *willing* because production of the higher-priced good is now relatively more attractive than the alternative uses of the resources involved. Producers are more *able* because the higher price allows them to cover the higher marginal costs typically involved with higher rates of production.

As with demand, we distinguish between *individual* supply and *market* supply. Market supply is the sum of the amount supplied at each price by all the individual suppliers. Unless otherwise noted, when we talk about supply, we will be referring to market supply. We also distinguish between *supply* and *quantity supplied*. Supply is the relation between the price and quantity supplied, as reflected by the entire supply schedule or supply curve. Quantity supplied refers to a particular amount offered for sale at a particular price, as reflected by a point on a given supply curve.

CHANGES IN SUPPLY

The supply curve expresses the relation between the price of a good and the quantity supplied, other things constant. Assumed constant along a supply curve are the nonprice determinants of supply, including (1) the state of technology,

(2) the prices of relevant resources, (3) the prices of alternative goods, (4) producer expectations, and (5) the number of producers in the market. We will consider how a change in each of these determinants of supply will affect the supply curve.

Changes in Technology

Recall from Chapter 2 that the state of technology represents the economy's stock of knowledge about how to combine resources most efficiently. Along a given supply curve, technology is assumed to remain unchanged. If a more efficient technology is discovered, production costs will fall, so suppliers will be more willing and more able to supply the good at each price. Consequently, supply will increase, as reflected by a shift to the right of the supply curve. For example, suppose a new milking machine called The Invisible Hand has a soothing effect on cows; cows find the new machine so "udderly" delightful that they produce more milk. Such a technological advance increases the market supply of milk, as shown by the shift from S to S′ in Exhibit 4.

Notice that just as a change in demand can be interpreted in two different ways, so can a change in supply. First, an increase in supply means that dairy farmers supply more milk at each possible price. For example, when the price is $1.00 per quart, the amount of milk supplied increases from 24 million to 28 million quarts per month, as shown in Exhibit 4 by the movement from point

EXHIBIT 4

An Increase in the Supply of Milk

An increase in the supply of milk is reflected by a shift to the right in the supply curve, from S to S′. After the increase in supply, the quantity of milk supplied at a price of $1 per quart increases from 24 million quarts (point h) to 28 million quarts (point i). Another way to interpret the shift is to say that it shows a reduction in the minimum price suppliers require in order to produce 24 million quarts. Previously, a price of $1 per quart was required (point h); after the increase in supply, suppliers require a price of only $0.75 per quart (point j).

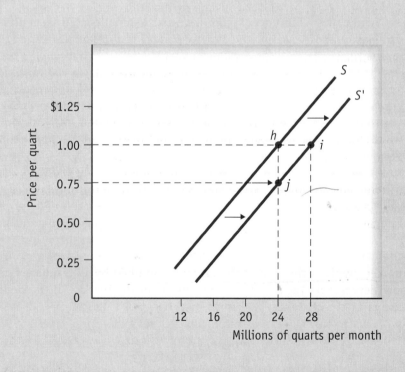

h to point *i*. Second, an increase in supply means that farmers are willing and able to supply the same quantity at a lower price. For example, farmers originally supplied 24 million quarts when the price was $1.00 per quart; on the new supply curve, that same quantity is supplied for only $0.75 per quart, as shown by the movement from point *h* to point *j*.

Changes in the Prices of Relevant Resources

Relevant resources are those employed in the production of the good in question. For example, suppose the price of cow fodder falls. This lower resource price reduces the cost of milk production. Dairy farmers are therefore more willing and able to supply milk. The supply curve for milk shifts to the right, or shifts down, as shown in Exhibit 4. On the other hand, an increase in the price of a relevant resource reduces supply. For example, higher electricity rates increase the cost of lighting the barn and operating the milking machines. These higher production costs decrease supply.

Relevant resources Resources used to produce the good in question

Changes in the Prices of Alternative Goods

Nearly all resources have alternative uses. The farmer's field, tractor, barn, and labor could produce a variety of crops. **Alternative goods** are goods that use some of the same resources as are used to produce the good under consideration. For example, as crop prices increase so does the opportunity cost of dairy farming. Some farmers will shift out of dairy farming and into crop farming, so the supply of milk will decrease, or shift to the left. On the other hand, a fall in the price of an alternative good, such as crops, will make milk production relatively more attractive. As resources shift into milk production, the supply of milk will increase, or shift to the right.

Alternative goods Other goods that use some of the same types of resources used to produce the good in question

Changes in Producer Expectations

Changes in producer expectations about market factors can change current supply. For example, a farmer expecting higher prices for milk in the future may begin to expand the dairy today, thereby increasing the current supply of milk, shifting the supply of milk to the right. When a good can be stored easily (crude oil, for example, can be left in the ground), expecting higher prices in the future prompts producers to reduce their current supply and await the higher price. Their decrease in supply is reflected by a shift to the left in the supply curve. Thus, an expectation of higher prices in the future could either increase or decrease the current supply, depending on the nature of the good under consideration. More generally, any change expected to affect future profitability, such as a change in business taxes, could change current supply.

Changes in the Number of Producers

Since market supply is the sum of the amounts supplied by all producers, market supply depends on the number of producers in the market. If the number of producers increases, supply will shift to the right; if the number decreases, supply will shift to the left. For example, during the 1980s the number of stores renting movie videos mushroomed, so the supply of videos available for rent increased sharply, shifting the supply curve to the right.

Finally, note the distinction between (1) a **change in quantity supplied,** which is the producer response to a change in the *price* of the good, other things constant, and is represented as a movement along a given supply curve, and (2)

Change in quantity supplied A movement along the supply curve in response to a change in the price, other things constant

Change in supply *A shift in a given supply curve caused by a change in one of the nonprice determinants of the supply of the good*

a **change in supply,** which is the response to a change in one of the *nonprice* determinants of supply, and is represented as a shift in the entire supply curve.

We are now ready to bring demand and supply together.

DEMAND AND SUPPLY CREATE A MARKET

Suppliers and demanders have different views of price, because demanders *pay* the price and suppliers *receive* it. Thus, a higher price tends to be bad news for consumers but good news for producers. As the price rises, consumers reduce their quantity demanded and producers increase their quantity supplied. How is this conflict between producers and consumers resolved?

Markets

A product's market sorts out the conflicting price perspectives of suppliers and demanders. A *market,* a term first introduced in Chapter 1, is a mechanism that coordinates the independent intentions of buyers and sellers. A market represents all the arrangements used to buy and sell a particular good or service. A market reduces the **transaction costs** of exchange—the costs of time and information required for exchange. For example, suppose you are looking for a summer job. One approach would be to go from employer to employer looking for openings. This would be time consuming and could involve extensive travel. Better yet, you could pick up a copy of the local newspaper and read the help-wanted ads. These ads, which are one element of the job market, reduce the transaction costs required to bring workers and employers together.

Transaction costs *The costs of time and information required to carry out market exchange*

The coordination that occurs through markets takes place not because of some central plan but because of Adam Smith's "invisible hand." For example, most of the auto dealers in your community tend to locate together, usually on the outskirts of town, where land is cheaper. The dealers congregate not because someone told them to or because they like one another's company but because each wants to be where customers shop for cars—that is, near other dealers. Similarly, stores group together downtown and in shopping malls to be where shoppers shop. Disney World, Sea World, Universal Studios, and the planned Universal City locate together in Orlando to be where tourists tour. Similar theme parks have located in the Los Angeles area for the same reason.

Specialized Markets

Markets can encompass the entire world, such as the market for crude oil or the market for wheat, or they can be as narrow as the competing gas stations at an intersection. Some markets are specialized; others are more general. In Quincy Market, a shopping center in Boston, one store sells nothing but kites. In a rural community outside Boston, a general store sells everything from hammers to pork chops. Why do some stores specialize and others sell many different products?

Adam Smith gave us the answer more than 200 years ago, when he noted that *the degree of specialization is limited by the extent of the market.* The larger the market—that is, the greater the potential number of customers—the greater the specialization. Quincy Market attracts millions of shoppers each year. Even if just a tiny fraction of them buys kites, the kite store can thrive. The general store, however, relies on a much smaller customer base (the several dozen homes scattered across the surrounding countryside) so it must offer a wider range of goods to earn a profit. Thus, specialty stores are more likely to locate in major population areas than in rural communities. In cyberspace, the Internet's World Wide Web has the potential for reaching millions of customers, which is why some sellers on the Web are quite specialized. For example, one sells nothing but juggling equipment.

Market Equilibrium

To see how a market works, let's bring together market supply and market demand. Exhibit 5 shows the demand for and supply of milk, using schedules in panel (a) and curves in panel (b). To get things started, suppose the price initially is $1.00 per quart. At that price producers supply 24 million quarts per month, but consumers demand only 14 million quarts per month. The quantity supplied exceeds the quantity demanded, resulting in an *excess quantity supplied,* or a **surplus,** of 10 million quarts per month. This unsold milk tells producers that the price is too high. Unless the price falls, the surplus will continue and milk will sour on store shelves. The suppliers' desire to eliminate the surplus puts downward pressure on the price, as reflected by the arrow pointing downward in panel (b). As the price falls, producers reduce their quantity supplied and consumers increase their quantity demanded. As long as quantity supplied exceeds quantity demanded, the surplus will force the price lower.

Alternatively, suppose the price is initially $0.50 per quart. You can see from Exhibit 5 that at that price consumers demand 26 million quarts per month but producers supply only 16 million quarts per month, resulting in an *excess quantity demanded,* or a **shortage,** of 10 million quarts per month. Producers notice that the quantity supplied has quickly sold out and customers are grumbling because milk is no longer available. Empty store shelves, frustrated consumers, and profit-seeking producers create market pressure for a higher price, as reflected by the arrow pointing upward in panel (b). As the price rises, producers increase their quantity supplied and consumers reduce their quantity demanded. The price will continue to rise as long as quantity demanded exceeds quantity supplied.

Thus, a surplus creates downward pressure on the price, and a shortage creates upward pressure on the price. As long as quantity demanded and quantity supplied differ, this difference will force a price change, which in turn will change quantity demanded and quantity supplied. Note that a shortage or a surplus must always be defined at a particular price. There is no such thing as a general shortage or a general surplus.

When the quantity consumers are willing and able to buy equals the quantity producers are willing and able to sell, the market is in equilibrium. In **equilibrium,** the independent plans of both buyers and sellers exactly match, so market forces will exert no pressure to change price and quantity. In panel (b) of Exhibit 5, the demand and supply curves intersect at the *equilibrium point,* identified as point *c.* The *equilibrium price* is $0.75 per quart, and the *equilibrium quantity* is 20 million quarts per month. At that price and quantity, the market *clears.* There is no shortage and no surplus, so there is no pressure for change.

Markets Allocate Resources

Note that the market finds equilibrium through the independent actions of thousands, or even millions, of buyers and sellers. Prices are signals of relative

The World Wide Web, with its connection to millions of customers around the globe, allows very specialized clients—like jugglers—to cheaply and effectively market their services. For example, visit the Raspyni Brothers Juggling Team (http://www.raspyni.com/).

Surplus An excess of quantity supplied over quantity demanded at a given price

Shortage An excess of quantity demanded over quantity supplied at a given price

Equilibrium The condition that exists in a market when the plans of the buyers match the plans of the sellers

EXHIBIT 5

Equilibrium in the Milk Market

Market equilibrium occurs at a price at which the quantity demanded by consumers is equal to the quantity supplied by producers. This is shown at point *c*. At prices above the equilibrium price, the quantity supplied exceeds the quantity demanded; at these prices there is a surplus, and there is a downward pressure on the price. At prices below equilibrium, quantity demanded exceeds quantity supplied; the resulting shortage puts upward pressure on the price.

(a) Market schedules

Millions of Quarts per Month

Price per Quart	Quantity Demanded	Quantity Supplied	Surplus or Shortage	Price Will
$1.25	8	28	Surplus of 20	Fall
1.00	14	24	Surplus of 10	Fall
0.75	20	20	Equilibrium	Remain the same
0.50	26	16	Shortage of 10	Rise
0.25	32	12	Shortage of 20	Rise

(b) Market curves

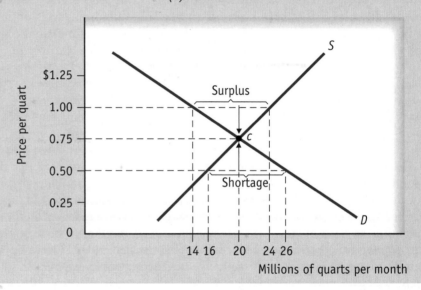

scarcity. The equilibrium price rations the product to those consumers who are willing and able to pay that price. In one sense the market is personal, because each consumer and each producer makes a personal decision regarding how much to buy or sell at a given price. In another sense the market is impersonal, because it requires no conscious coordination among consumers or producers. *Impersonal market forces synchronize the personal and independent decisions of many individual buyers and sellers to determine equilibrium price and quantity.*

Markets allocate scarce resources to their highest-valued use. The measure of value is consumers' willingness and ability to pay. In a market economy, those unable to pay go without. Many view this feature of the market system as a flaw. Some observers are troubled, for example, because U.S. consumers spend billions each year on pet food when some people do not have enough to eat. On your next trip to the supermarket, notice how much shelf space is devoted to pet products—often an entire aisle. Petsmart, a chain store for pet products, sells 12,000 different items.

CHANGES IN EQUILIBRIUM PRICE AND QUANTITY

Equilibrium is the combination of price and quantity at which the intentions of demanders and suppliers exactly match. Once a market reaches equilibrium, that price and quantity will continue to prevail unless one of the determinants of demand or supply changes. A change in any one of these determinants will usually change equilibrium price and quantity in a predictable way, as we shall see.

Impact of Changes in Demand

In Exhibit 6, demand curve D and supply curve S intersect to yield the initial equilibrium price of $0.75 per quart and the initial equilibrium quantity of 20 million quarts of milk per month. Suppose that one of the determinants of demand changes in a way that increases demand, shifting the demand curve to the right from D to D'. Any of the following changes could increase the demand for milk: (1) an increase in consumer income (because milk is a normal good); (2) an increase in the price of a substitute, such as juice, or a decrease in the price of a complement, such as cereal; (3) a change in consumers' expectations that encourages them to buy more milk now; (4) an increase in the number of consumers; (5) a change in consumer tastes—based, for example, on a growing awareness that the calcium in milk builds stronger bones.

After the increase in demand to D', as reflected in Exhibit 6, the quantity demanded at the initial price of $0.75 is 30 million quarts, which exceeds the quantity supplied of 20 million quarts by 10 million quarts. This shortage puts

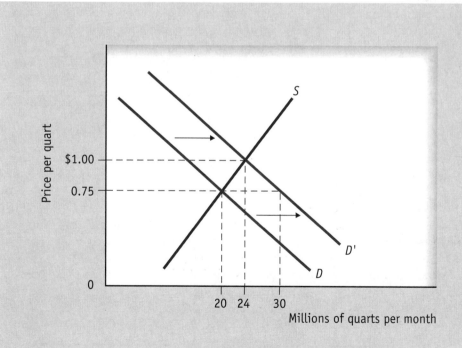

EXHIBIT 6

Effects of an Increase in Demand

After an increase in demand shifts the demand curve from D to D', quantity demanded exceeds quantity supplied at the old price of $0.75 per quart. As the price rises, quantity supplied increases along supply curve S, and quantity demanded falls along demand curve D'. When the new equilibrium price of $1.00 per quart is reached, the quantity demanded will once again equal the quantity supplied. Both price and quantity are higher following the increase in demand.

upward pressure on the price. As the price increases, the quantity demanded decreases along the new demand curve, D', and the quantity supplied increases along the supply curve S until the two quantities are in equilibrium once again. The new equilibrium price is $1.00 per quart, and the new equilibrium quantity is 24 million quarts per month. Thus, given an upward-sloping supply curve, an increase in demand increases both equilibrium price and quantity. A decrease in demand lowers both equilibrium price and quantity. We can summarize these results as follows: *Any change in demand, with the upward-sloping supply curve held constant, will change equilibrium price and quantity in the same direction as the change in demand.*

Impact of Changes in Supply

Consider now the impact of a change in supply. In Exhibit 7, as before, we begin with demand curve D and supply curve S to yield the initial equilibrium price of $0.75 per quart and the initial equilibrium quantity of 20 million quarts. Suppose one of the determinants of supply changes, resulting in a supply increase from S to S'. Changes that could increase the supply of milk include: (1) a technological advance in milk production; (2) a reduction in the price of a relevant resource; (3) a decline in the price of an alternative good; (4) a change in expectations that encourages farmers to supply more milk now; or (5) an increase in the number of dairy farmers.

After the increase in supply in Exhibit 7, the amount supplied at the initial equilibrium price of $0.75 increases from 20 million to 30 million quarts, resulting in a 10-million-quart surplus. This surplus forces the price down. As the price falls, the quantity supplied declines along the new supply curve and the quantity demanded increases until a new equilibrium point is established. The new equilibrium price is $0.50 per quart, and the new equilibrium quantity is 26 million quarts. The increase in supply reduces the equilibrium price but increases the equilibrium quantity.

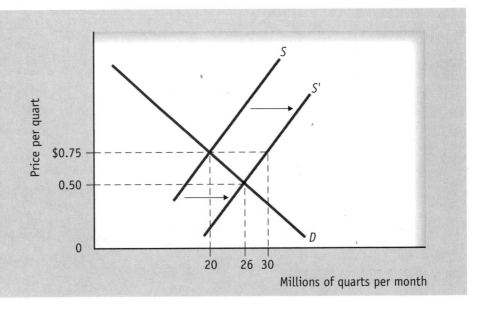

EXHIBIT 7

Effects of an Increase in Supply

An increase in supply is depicted as a shift to the right in the supply curve, from S to S'. As the new equilibrium, quantity is greater and price is lower than before the increase in supply.

Alternatively, a reduction in supply—that is, a shift to the left in the supply curve—increases equilibrium price but reduces equilibrium quantity. Thus, *a shift in the supply curve, with the demand curve unchanged, changes equilibrium quantity in the same direction as the change in supply but changes equilibrium price in the opposite direction.* An easy way to remember this is to picture the supply curve moving along a given downward-sloping demand curve. As the supply curve shifts up to the left, or decreases, price increases but quantity decreases; as the supply curve shifts down to the right, or increases, price decreases but quantity increases.

Simultaneous Changes in Demand and Supply

As long as only one curve shifts, we can say for sure what will happen to equilibrium price and quantity. If both curves shift, however, the outcome is less obvious. For example, suppose both demand and supply increase, as in Exhibit 8. Note that in panel (a) demand increases more than supply, and in panel (b) supply increases more than demand. In both panels, equilibrium quantity increases. The change in equilibrium price, however, depends on the size of the increase in demand *relative* to the increase in supply. If the increase in demand is greater, as in panel (a), equilibrium price increases from P to P'. If the increase in supply is greater, as in panel (b), equilibrium price decreases from P to P''.

Conversely, if both demand and supply decrease, the equilibrium quantity decreases, but again we cannot say what will happen to the equilibrium price unless we examine the relative shifts. (You can use Exhibit 8 to consider de-

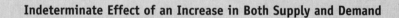

Indeterminate Effect of an Increase in Both Supply and Demand   E X H I B I T 8

(a) Shift in demand dominates   *(b) Shift in supply dominates*

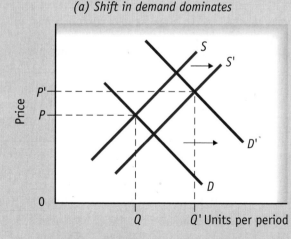
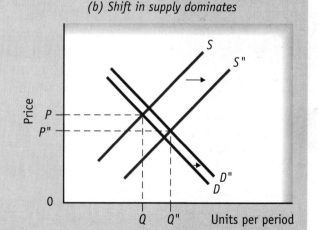

When both supply and demand increase, the quantity exchanged—the equilibrium quantity—also increases. The effect on price depends on which curve shifts farther. In panel (a), the shift in demand is greater than the shift in supply; as a result, the price rises. In panel (b), the shift in supply is greater, so the price falls.

creases in demand and supply by viewing D' and S' as the initial curves.) If the decrease in demand exceeds the decrease in supply, the price will fall. If the decrease in supply exceeds the decrease in demand, the price will rise.

If demand and supply move in opposite directions, then, without reference to particular shifts, we cannot say what will happen to the equilibrium quantity. We can say what will happen to the equilibrium price. *The equilibrium price will increase if demand increases and supply decreases, and the equilibrium price will decrease if demand decreases and supply increases.* These results are no doubt confusing, but Exhibit 9 summarizes the four possible combinations of changes. Using Exhibit 9 as a reference, work through some hypothetical shifts in demand and supply to develop an understanding of the results. Then consider the effect of an increase in demand for professional basketball in the following case study.

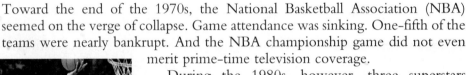

Toward the end of the 1970s, the National Basketball Association (NBA) seemed on the verge of collapse. Game attendance was sinking. One-fifth of the teams were nearly bankrupt. And the NBA championship game did not even merit prime-time television coverage.

During the 1980s, however, three superstars turned the league around. Michael Jordan, Larry Bird, and "Magic" Johnson brought new life to the sagging game and attracted millions of new fans. Since 1980, total attendance has doubled, the number of NBA teams has increased from 22 to 29 (with new franchises selling for record amounts), the value of television broadcast rights has jumped sharply, and so has the merchandise value of team logos.

The NBA is more popular than ever. Celebrities such as Jack Nicholson and Spike Lee have become fixtures in court-side seats (seats that sell for as much as $500 per game). Basketball's popularity also increased around the world. The NBA formed global marketing alliances with Coca-Cola, McDonald's, and IBM, and the 1995 NBA finals were televised in 164 countries.

NBA players are the key resource in the production of NBA games. The growth in demand for pro basketball, coupled with a collective bargaining agreement that gave players more than half of total revenue, jacked up average player salaries tenfold, from $170 thousand in 1980 to $1.7 million in 1995. Basketball players are now the highest paid team professionals in the United States; their average pay is more than double that in pro football and pro hockey.

The primary source of talent for the NBA is college basketball. College games, especially the NCAA tournament (nicknamed "March Madness"), serve to heighten interest in the NBA, because fans can follow top collegiate players to the professional ranks. Top college prospects sign multiyear contracts that can exceed $2 million per year. Such numbers attract talented players earlier and earlier in their college years, since top players who remain in college risk a costly injury. For example, in 1995 most of the top draft choices were underclassmen, and one top pick was even drafted after high school. Because of basketball's worldwide popularity, talented players who fail to make the NBA often can sign high-paying contracts overseas.

The attractive pay earned by the top players stems from the limited supply of those with such talent combined with a large and growing demand for that talent. Rare talent alone is not enough. For example, top rodeo riders and top bowlers also possess rare talent, but the demand for their talent is not great enough to support pay anywhere near NBA levels. Both supply and demand determine the average pay level.

Sources: John Helyar, "Pro Basketball Loses Its 'Feel Good' Image in Nasty Labor Dispute," *The Wall Street Journal,* 7 August 1995; *The American Almanac: Statistical Abstract of the United States: 1994-1995,* Bureau of the Census, (Austin, Texas: The Reference Press, 1994).

**The Market for
Professional Basketball**
continued

DISEQUILIBRIUM PRICES

A surplus exerts downward pressure on the price; a shortage exerts upward pressure on the price. However, markets do not always attain equilibrium quickly. During the time required for adjustment, the market is said to be in disequilibrium. **Disequilibrium** is usually a temporary phase while the market gropes for equilibrium. For example, popular toys, best-selling books, and chart-busting compact discs often sell out and are unavailable, at least temporarily. On the other hand, some new products bomb, so they pile up unsold on store shelves. Sometimes, however, often as a result of government intervention in markets, disequilibrium can last a long time, as we will see next.

Disequilibrium Usually a temporary mismatch between quanitity supplied and quantity demanded as the market seeks equilibrium

		Change in Demand	
		Demand increases	Demand decreases
Change in supply	Supply increases	Equilibrium price change is indeterminate. Equilibrium quantity increases.	Equilibrium price falls. Equilibrium quantity change is indeterminate.
	Supply decreases	Equilibrium price rises. Equilibrium quantity change is indeterminate.	Equilibrium price change is indeterminate. Equilibrium quantity decreases.

EXHIBIT 9

Effects of Changes in Both Supply and Demand

When the supply and demand curves shift in the same direction, equilibrium quantity also shifts in that direction; the effect on equilibrium price depends on which curve shifts more. If the curves shift in opposite directions, equilibrium price will move in the same direction as demand; the effect on equilibrium quantity depends on which curve shifts more.

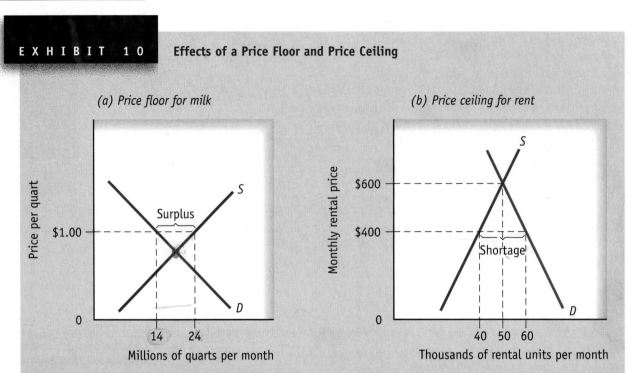

EXHIBIT 10   Effects of a Price Floor and Price Ceiling

(a) Price floor for milk

(b) Price ceiling for rent

If a price floor is established above the equilibrium price, a permanent surplus will result. A price floor established at or below the equilibrium price will have no effect. If a price ceiling is established below the equilibrium price, a permanent shortage will result. A price ceiling established at or above the equilibrium price will have no effect.

Price Floors

Prices are sometimes established at a level above the equilibrium value. For example, the federal government often regulates the prices of agricultural commodities in an attempt to ensure farmers a higher and more stable income than they would otherwise earn. To achieve higher prices, the federal government sets a **price floor,** or a *minimum* selling price above the equilibrium price. Panel (a) of Exhibit 10 shows the effect of a $1.00 per quart price floor. At that price farmers supply 24 million quarts of milk per month, but consumers demand only 14 million quarts. Thus the price floor results in a surplus of 10 million quarts. This surplus, unless somehow eliminated, will force the price downward. So, as part of the price support program, the government usually agrees to buy the surplus milk to take it off the market. The federal government, in fact, spends billions of dollars each year buying and storing surplus agricultural products.

Price floor A minimum legal price below which a good or service cannot be sold

Price Ceilings

Sometimes public officials try to keep prices below their equilibrium values by establishing a **price ceiling,** or a *maximum* selling price. For example, concern about the rising cost of rental housing in some cities prompted legislation to impose rent ceilings. Panel (b) depicts the demand and supply for rental housing in a hypothetical city; the vertical axis shows the monthly rent and the hori-

Price ceiling A maximum legal price above which a good or service cannot be sold zontal axis shows the number of rental units. The equilibrium, or market-clearing, rent is $600 per month, and the equilibrium quantity is 50,000 housing units.

Suppose the government sets a maximum rent of $400 per month. At that ceiling price, 60,000 rental units are demanded, but only 40,000 are supplied, resulting in a housing shortage of 20,000 units. Because of such excess demand, the rental price no longer provides sufficient rationing of housing to those who most value housing. Consequently, other rationing devices emerge to deal with the housing shortage, such as waiting lists, political connections, and the willingness to pay under-the-table charges, such as "key fees," "finder's fees," excessive security deposits, and the like.

Effective price floors and ceilings distort market forces. Price floors above the equilibrium price create surpluses, and price ceilings below the equilibrium price create shortages. Various nonprice allocation devices emerge to cope with the disequilibrium resulting from the market interference. Government is not the only source of disequilibrium, however, as shown in the following case study.

CASE STUDY

Toys Are Serious Business

Location:

NPD Toy Services, a marketing information source for the U.S. toy and video games industry, helps manufacturers and sellers better understand the market for new toys. To learn more about NPD Toy Services, visit the NPD Group, Inc. (http://www.npd.com/toys.htm).

Toys are a $20 billion business in the United States, but the business is not that much fun for toy makers. Each year thousands of new toys are introduced and thousands are dropped. Most toys don't make it from one season to the next, turning out to be costly failures. A few have staying power, such as G.I. Joe, who could collect military retirement pay based on more than 30 years of service, Barbie, who is pushing 35, and the Wiffle Ball, still a hit after 40 years.

Store buyers must order in February for Christmas delivery. Can you imagine the uncertainty of this market? Who, for example, could have anticipated the phenomenal success of Nintendo and Barney? Or how about the Cabbage Patch Kids frenzy of a decade ago? Over 20 million of the Kids sold for about $30 each, but there was still a shortage at that price. To prevent the near riots that broke out each time a new shipment arrived, stores established waiting lists to allocate their monthly allotments. But the wait could be up to eight months. Classified ads offered dolls for as much as $250. Some car dealers and furniture stores promised a free doll with a major purchase. The shortage attracted boatloads of counterfeit dolls from overseas. Some of these illegal aliens were detained at the border, but many more made it through.

A more recent hot entry into the toy market has been the Mighty Morphin Power Rangers. Between 1993 and 1994, the manufacturer expanded production tenfold, with 11 new factories churning out nearly $1 billion worth of Rangers. Still, at a selling price of $13, the quantity demanded exceeded quantity supplied.

Apparently, suppliers of the Cabbage Patch Kids and the Power Rangers have supply curves that are relatively flat, or horizontal, for they responded to a greater than expected demand for their products, not by increasing the price

Toys are Serious Business
continued

but by increasing the quantity supplied at that price. Eventually, market equilibrium was achieved, but in the meantime disequilibrium prevailed.

Despite these phenomenal successes, most of the thousands of new toys introduced each year are expensive flops. Lately, toy makers have tried to reduce their market risk by linking new toys to movie characters, such as those in Batman, The Lion King, and Pocahontas. But since toy production must begin long before a movie is released, there is no guarantee that the movie upon which the toy is based will be successful. Without a successful movie, the toy linked to that movie has little chance. For example, because the movie *Stargate* went nowhere, so did toys based on that movie.

The point is that there is much uncertainty about the market for new products such as toys. Suppliers can only guess what the demand will be, so they must feel their way in deciding how much to produce and what price to charge.

Sources: "Ranger Shortage, Year 2," *New York Times,* 11 December 1994; "Cabbage Patch Comeback Kids," *Business Week,* 14 August 1995; and "Toy Makers' Addiction to Hollywood Figures Reshapes Kids Play," *The Wall Street Journal,* 13 July 1995. Visit the Virtual Toy Store Directory at http://www.halcyon.com/uncomyn/home.html; or visit FAO Schwarz at http://www.faoschwarz.com/.

CONCLUSION

Although a market usually involves the interaction of many buyers and sellers, few markets are consciously designed. Just as the law of gravity works whether or not we understand Newton's principles, market forces operate whether or not market participants understand demand and supply. These forces arise naturally, much the way car dealers congregate on the outskirts of town.

Demand and supply are the foundation of a market economy. To build on that foundation, we must take a closer look at key economic decision-makers in the economy. In the next chapter we focus on the four economic actors: households, firms, governments, and the rest of the world.

SUMMARY

1. Demand is a relationship between the price of a good and the quantity consumers are willing and able to buy per period, other things constant. According to the law of demand, the price of a good varies inversely with the quantity demanded, so the demand curve slopes downward.

2. A demand curve slopes downward for two reasons. A decrease in the price of a good (1) makes consumers more *willing* to substitute this good for other goods and (2) increases the real income of consumers, making them more *able* to buy the good.

3. Assumed to be constant along a demand curve are (1) consumer income, (2) the prices of related goods, (3) consumer expectations, (4) the number and composition of consumers in the market, and (5) consumer tastes. A change in any one of these could change demand.

4. Supply is a relationship between the price of a good and the quantity producers are willing and able to sell per period, other things constant. According to the law of supply, price and quantity supplied are usually directly related, so the supply curve typically slopes upward. The supply curve slopes upward because higher prices (1) make producers more *willing* to supply this good than alternative goods and (2) make producers more *able* to cover the higher marginal cost associated with greater output rates.

5. Assumed to be constant along a supply curve are (1) the state of technology, (2) the prices of relevant resources, (3) the prices of alternative goods, (4) producer expectations, and (5) the number of producers. A change in any one of these will change supply.

6. Demand and supply come together in the market for a given product. Markets provide information about the price, quantity, and quality of the product for sale. They also reduce the transaction costs of exchange—the costs of time and information required to undertake exchange. The interaction of demand and supply guides resources and products to their highest-valued use.

7. The market equilibrium reconciles the independent intentions of buyers and sellers. Equilibrium will continue unless there is a change in one of the determinants of demand or supply. Disequilibrium is usually a temporary phase while markets seek equilibrium, but sometimes it lasts longer.

QUESTIONS AND PROBLEMS

1. **(Demand and Quantity Demanded)** According to the text, what variables increase the demand for normal goods? Explain why a reduction in the price of a normal good does *not* increase the demand for the good.

2. **(Substitution and Income Effects of a Price Change)** Distinguish between the substitution and income effects of a price change. If a good's price increases, does each effect have a positive or negative impact on the quantity demanded?

3. **(Shifting Demand)** Using supply and demand curves, show the effect of each of the following events on the market for cigarettes:
   a. A cure for lung cancer is found.
   b. There is an increase in the price of cigars and pipes.
   c. There is a substantial increase in wages in states that grow tobacco.
   d. A fertilizer that increases the yield per acre of tobacco is discovered.
   e. There is a substantial rise in the price of matches and cigarette lighters.
   f. An embargo is placed on foreign tobacco products.

4. **(Substitutes and Complements)** For each of the following pairs, indicate whether the goods are substitutes, complements, or unrelated:
   a. Peanut butter and jelly.
   b. Private and public transportation.
   c. Coke and Pepsi.
   d. Alarm clocks and automobiles.
   e. Golf clubs and golf tees.

5. **(Equilibrium)** Determine whether each of the following statements is true or false. Then provide a short explanation for your answer.
   a. At equilibrium, all sellers can find buyers.
   b. At equilibrium, no buyer is willing and able to buy more than that buyer is being sold.
   c. At equilibrium, there is no pressure on the market to produce or consume more than is being sold.

   d. At prices *above* equilibrium, the quantity exchanged is larger than the quantity demanded.
   e. At prices *below* equilibrium, the quantity exchanged is equal to the quantity supplied.

6. **(Equilibrium)** What are the effects on the equilibrium price and quantity of steel if the wages of steelworkers rise and the price of aluminum rises?

7. **(Supply and Demand)** How did each of the following affect the world price of oil? (Use basic supply and demand analysis.)
   a. Tax credits for home insulation.
   b. Completion of the Alaskan oil pipeline.
   c. Decontrol of oil price ceilings.
   d. Discovery of oil in Mexico and the North Sea.
   e. Mass production of smaller rather than larger automobiles.
   f. Increased use of nuclear power.

8. **(Price Floor)** There is considerable interest in whether the minimum wage rate contributes to teenage unemployment. Draw a supply and demand diagram for the unskilled labor market, and discuss the effects of a minimum wage. Who is helped, and who is hurt?

9. **(Price Ceiling)** Discuss the effect on the market for gasoline if the government establishes an effective price ceiling. Assume that the gasoline market was initially in equilibrium.

10. **(Demand)** Explain the effect of an increase in consumer incomes on demand for a good.

11. **(Equilibrium)** If a price is not an equilibrium price, there will be a tendency for it to move to its equilibrium value. Regardless of whether the price was too high or too low to begin with, the adjustment process will increase the quantity of the good purchased. Explain, using a supply-demand diagram.

12. **(Income Effects)** When you move along the demand curve, you must hold income constant. Yet one factor that can cause a change in the quantity demanded is an "income effect." Explain.

13. **(Equilibrium)** Consider the following supply and demand graph. Assume that demand and supply are initially at D^1 and S^1. What are the equilibrium price and quantity? If demand increases to D^2, what are the new equilibrium price and quantity? What results if the government does not allow the price to change when demand increases?

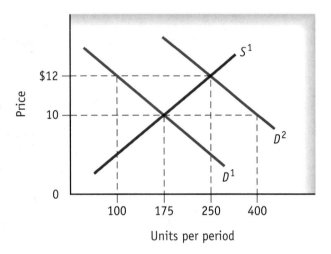

14. **(Price Ceilings)** Suppose the supply and demand curves for rental housing units have the typical shapes, and that rent control establishes a rent level below the equilibrium level.
    a. What happens to the quantity of housing consumed?
    b. Who gains from rent control?
    c. Who loses from rent control?

15. **(Demand and Supply)** What happens to the equilibrium price and quantity of ice cream in response to each of the following? Explain your answers.

a. An increase in the price of grain.
b. A decrease in the price of beef.
c. New concerns about the fat content of ice cream and an increase in the price of sugar used to produce ice cream.

16. **(Equilibrium)** In 1994, Procter & Gamble introduced a new over-the-counter pain reliever called Aleve. What effect would this have had on the market equilibrium for Tylenol?

17. **(Markets)** Discuss the role of markets in coordinating the independent decisions of buyers and sellers.

18. **(The Market for Professional Basketball)** Discuss the changes in supply and demand included in the case study on professional basketball.

19. **(Toys Are Serious Business)** Use a supply and demand graph to analyze the situation in the market for Mighty Morphin Power Rangers toys. Keep in mind the shortage at the $13 selling price, the development of new factories, and the continued shortage.

Using the Internet

20. Considering a career? How many job listings are there for your field of study in the most recent Sunday edition of the *Chicago Tribune* (**http://www. careerpath.com**)? Thinking about a vacation? How much does a week's stay on the Gold Coast, Queensland, Australia, cost? Visit the Pelican Cove Waterfront Apartments (**http://AusWeb.com.au/tourism/ pel-cove/**) to find out. The prices are in Australian dollars with approximate U.S. dollar conversions. For an exact conversion, use The Universal Currency Convertor (**http://www.xe.net/currency/**).

The Economic Actors: Households, Firms, Governments, and the Rest of the World

To develop a better understanding of how the economy works, you must become more acquainted with key players in the economy. In this chapter we examine the four main groups of economic actors: households, firms, governments, and the rest of the world. You already know more than you realize about these actors. You grew up in a *household*. You have been around *firms* all your life, such as stores, restaurants, and service outlets. You know a lot about *governments,* from taxes to public education. And you have a growing awareness of *the rest of the world,* from foreign cars to the Internet's World Wide Web. This chapter will begin with your abundant personal experience with the economic actors to consider their structure, organization, and objectives. At the end of the chapter, a section entitled "A Closer Look" examines the interconnections among the four actors. Topics discussed in this chapter include:

- Evolution of the household
- Evolution of the firm
- Household production versus firm production
- Role of government

- Government spending and taxation
- International trade and finance
- Trade restrictions

THE HOUSEHOLD

Households play the starring role in the economy. First, they demand goods and services from product markets and thereby determine what gets produced. Second, households supply land, labor, capital, and entrepreneurial ability to resource markets. As demanders of goods and services and suppliers of resources, households make all kinds of choices, such as what to buy, how much to save, where to live, and where to work. Although a household usually consists of several individuals, each household is considered as acting as a single decision maker; we will refer to that decision maker as the *householder.*

The Evolution of the Household

In earlier times, when the economy was primarily agricultural, a farm household was largely self-sufficient. Individual family members specialized in specific farm tasks. With the introduction of new seed varieties, fertilizers, and labor-saving machinery, farm productivity increased sharply. Fewer farmers were needed to grow enough food to feed a nation. Simultaneously, the growth of urban factories increased the demand for factory labor. As a result, people moved from farms to cities, where they were far less self-sufficient.

Households have evolved in other ways. For example, in 1950 only about 15 percent of married women with children under 18 years of age were in the U.S. labor force. Now, because of higher levels of education among married women and an increased demand for labor, more than half of married women with young children are in the labor force. Rising wages increased the opportunity cost of working in the home.

The rise of the two-earner household has affected the family as an economic unit. Less production occurs in the home, and more goods and services are demanded from the market. For example, child-care services and fast-food restaurants have displaced some household production. The rise of the two-worker family therefore reduced the advantages of specialization within the household—a central feature of the farm family. Nonetheless, some production still occurs in the home, as we will explore in a later section.

Households Maximize Utility

There are about 100 million households in the United States. All those who live under one roof are considered part of the same household. What exactly do householders attempt to accomplish in making decisions? Economists assume that people attempt to maximize their level of satisfaction, sense of well-being, or overall welfare. For the sake of brevity, we say that householders attempt to maximize the household's **utility.** Householders, like other economic actors, are viewed as rational decision makers, meaning that they try to act in the household's best interests and would not deliberately select an option expected to make them worse off. Utility maximization depends on each household's subjective goals, not on some objective standard. The subjectivity of utility allows for a wide range of behavior, all consistent with utility maximization. For example, some households maintain a neat home with a well-groomed lawn; others pay no attention to their home and use the lawn as a junkyard.

Utility The satisfaction received from consuming a good or service or a collection of goods and services; satisfaction, sense of well-being

Households as Resource Suppliers

Householders use their limited resources in an attempt to satisfy their unlimited wants. They can use these resources to produce goods and services in their homes. For example, they can prepare their own meals or fix that leaky roof.

EXHIBIT 1

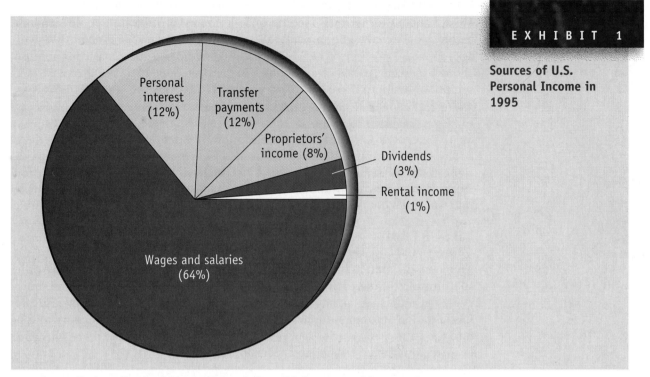

Source: "Business Situation," *Survey of Current Business,* U.S. Department of Commerce, January 1996.

Or they can sell these resources in the resource market and use the income to buy goods and services in the product market. The most valuable resource sold by most households is labor.

Exhibit 1 shows the sources of personal income received by U.S. households in 1995, when personal income totaled $6 trillion. As you can see, 64 percent, or about two-thirds, of personal income is from wages and salaries. Tied for second place at 12 percent are interest earnings and transfer payments (to be discussed shortly), followed by proprietors' income at 8 percent. *Proprietors* are people who work for themselves rather than for employers; farmers, plumbers, and doctors are often self-employed. Only a tiny fraction of personal income comes from rents and dividends. *The majority of personal income in the United States is from labor earnings rather than from the ownership of other resources such as capital or land.*

Because of poor education, disability, discrimination, or bad luck, some households have few valuable resources to sell. Also, female householders make up a growing share of all householders, and many single mothers find their education and job opportunities limited because of child-care responsibilities. Society has made the political decision that individuals in such circumstances are entitled to some form of public assistance. Consequently, government gives some households **transfer payments,** which are outright grants from the government to entitled households. *Cash transfers* are monetary payments, such as Aid to Families with Dependent Children or Social Security benefits. *In-kind transfers,* such as food stamps, Medicare, and Medicaid, fund specific goods and services.

Transfer payments Cash or in-kind benefits given to individuals as outright grants from the government

Households as Demanders of Goods and Services

What happens to personal income once it comes into the household? Personal income is allocated among personal consumption, saving, and taxes. On average, about 80 percent of U.S. personal income goes to personal consumption, about 5 percent is saved, and about 15 percent goes to taxes. Personal consumption sorts into three broad categories: (1) *durable goods,* such as automobiles and refrigerators; (2) *nondurable goods,* such as food, clothing, and gasoline; and (3) *services,* such as housing, electricity, and medical care. Durable goods make up 13 percent of U.S. personal consumption, nondurables make up 30 percent, and services make up 57 percent. The service sector is the fastest growing, because many activities—such as meal preparation and child care—which formerly were produced in the household are now often purchased in the market.

THE FIRM

Members of households once built their own homes, made their own clothes and furniture, grew their own food, and amused themselves. Over time, however, the efficiency arising from comparative advantage resulted in a greater specialization among resource suppliers. But why was the firm necessary to capture the gains arising from specialization? In this section we explore why *firms* evolved to produce this greater specialization.

Transaction Costs and Evolution of the Firm

Suppose a consumer wanted to buy a sweater. Why couldn't that consumer take advantage of specialization by relying on one household to grow the wool, another to spin the wool into yarn, and a third to knit the yarn into a sweater? The consumer would have to reach separate agreements with each specializing household about quantity, quality, and price. How much wool would be needed? How much time would be required to spin the wool into yarn and to knit the yarn into a sweater? Transacting each contract would require substantial amounts of time and information. These *transaction costs* could easily erase the efficiency gains arising from the greater specialization.

Instead of negotiating with each specialist, the consumer could simply purchase the sweater from someone who would do all that bargaining. The consumer could buy the sweater from an *entrepreneur* who contracted for all the resources necessary to knit a sweater. The entrepreneur, by arranging for the production of many sweaters rather than just one, was thereby able to reduce the transaction costs per sweater.

The Cottage Industry ERA. For hundreds of years, profit-seeking entrepreneurs relied on "putting out" raw material such as wool and cotton to rural households that turned this raw material into finished goods. The system developed in the British Isles, where workers' simple thatched cottages served as tiny factories specializing in one stage of production. This approach to production, which came to be known as the *cottage industry* system, still exists in some parts of the world.

The Industrial Revolution. As the British economy expanded in the 18th century, entrepreneurs began to organize the various stages of production under one roof. Technological developments increased the productivity of each worker and contributed to the shift of employment from rural areas to urban factories. *Work therefore became organized in large, centrally powered factories, which promoted a more efficient division of labor, the direct supervision of production, reduced transportation costs, and the use of machines far bigger than anything that had been used in the home.* The development of large-scale factory production, known as the *Industrial Revolution,* began in Great Britain around 1750 and spread to the rest of Europe, North America, and Australia.

The Firm. So production has evolved from self-sufficient, rural households through the cottage industry system, where specialized production occurred in the household, to the current system of handling much production under one roof. Today, entrepreneurs combine resources in firms such as factories, mills, offices, stores, and restaurants. **Firms** are economic units formed by profit-seeking entrepreneurs who combine land, labor, and capital to produce goods and services. *Firms that operate on a large scale often achieve lower production costs per unit and lower transaction costs in hiring and directing a variety of resources.* Just as we assume that householders attempt to maximize utility, we assume that firms attempt to *maximize profit.* Profit, the entrepreneur's reward, is total revenue minus the total cost of production.

Why Do Firms Specialize?

If the firm is such an efficient device for combining resources under one roof, why aren't all phases of production combined in a single firm? For example, why do sweater producers purchase wool from other firms rather than raise their own sheep? Or why do most sweater producers sell their finished products to wholesalers and retailers rather than directly to households? To answer these questions, we must consider the costs and benefits of coordinating activity within the firm versus coordinating activity through markets.

Although firms are convenient devices for assembling and coordinating specialized resources under one roof, the gains from this coordination are limited. Like other people, entrepreneurs have *bounded rationality,* which means that they face limits on their ability to monitor all the specialized resources, exercise quality control at each stage, and keep track of the entire process. As the entrepreneur brings together more and more specialized resources, the cost of all this internal coordination grows. At some point the cost of adding one more activity exceeds the benefit, so things start to go wrong. The entrepreneur tries to become a jack-of-all-trades, but ends up a master of none. Thus, entrepreneurs and the firms they create become more efficient by purchasing certain specialized inputs from other firms. *The market, relying only on the profit-maximizing motives of each entrepreneur, guides resources through the intermediate steps "as if by an invisible hand," coordinating the task of linking one firm's output with another firm's input to produce the final good.*

Consequently, a firm is often more efficient if it specializes in a single product or in a limited range of products. For instance, many seasoned travelers are wary of eating at a hotel's restaurant, despite its convenience, because of the difficulty of operating both a nice hotel and a fine restaurant. Different entrepreneurs have different opinions about their abilities to coordinate production in

Net Bookmark

In 1903, Ford Motor Company began with 10 employees in a converted Detroit wagon factory. Today, Ford employs over 338,000 workers around the world. Ford's 1916 Highland Park assembly plant is shown here. For more about the history of Ford, visit Ford Worldwide Connection (http://www.ford.com/) and the Henry Ford Museum Online (http://hfm.umd.umich.edu/).

Firms *Economic units, formed by profit-seeking entrepreneurs, that use hired resources to produce goods and services for sale*

the firm, so some hotels have restaurants and some do not. Often the hotel restaurant is owned and operated by an entirely different firm.

Why Does Household Production Still Exist?

If firms are such convenient units for reducing the production and transaction costs of bringing together specialized resources, why doesn't all production occur within firms? Why are activities such as house cleaning and meal preparation still undertaken primarily by households, not by firms? Indeed, some people repair their own cars, paint their own homes, and perform many other tasks that are also performed by firms. Why hasn't all production shifted to firms?

If a householder's opportunity cost of performing a task is below the market price, the householder usually performs that task. Thus, householders with the lowest opportunity cost of time will tend to do more for themselves. For example, janitors typically mow their own lawns; physicians do not. Consider some reasons for household production.

No Skills or Specialized Resources Are Required. Some activities require so few skills or specialized resources that households find it cheaper to do these jobs themselves. Sweeping the floor requires only a broom and some time and so is usually performed by household members. Sanding the floor, however, involves costly machinery and special skills, so this service is usually purchased in the market. Similarly, although you wouldn't hire someone to brush your teeth, repairing a tooth is another matter. Households usually perform tasks that demand neither particular skills nor specialized machinery.

Household Production Avoids Taxes. Governments tax income, sales, and other market transactions. Suppose you are trying to decide whether to paint your home or hire a painter. If the income tax rate is one-third, a painter who requires $2,000 net of taxes to do the job must charge you $3,000 to net $2,000 after paying $1,000 in taxes. You must earn $4,500 before taxes in order to have $3,000 after taxes to pay the painter. Thus, you must earn $4,500 so that the painter can net $2,000 after taxes. If you paint the house yourself, no taxes are imposed. The tax-free nature of do-it-yourself activity favors household production over market purchases.

Household Production Reduces Transaction Costs. Lining up bids from painting contractors, hiring a contractor, negotiating terms, and monitoring job performance all take time and require information. Doing the job yourself reduces these transaction costs. Household production also allows for more personal control over the final product than is available through a market transaction. For example, some people prefer home-cooked meals to restaurant food, in part because home-cooked meals can be prepared according to individual tastes.

Technological Advances Increase Household Productivity. Technological breakthroughs are not confined to market production. Vacuum cleaners, dishwashers, microwave ovens, and other modern appliances reduce the time and often the skill required to perform household tasks. Also, modern technologies such as VCRs, cable TV, and computer games produce home entertainment. In fact, microchip-based technologies have shifted some production from the firm back to the household, as discussed in the following case study.

The Industrial Revolution shifted production from rural cottages to large, centrally powered, urban factories. But the Information Revolution spawned by the invention of the microchip is decentralizing the acquisition, analysis, and transmission of information. These days people who say they work at the home office are often referring not to corporate headquarters but to the room just off their kitchen.

People with a personal computer, a modem, a fax machine, an Internet connection, and an e-mail address are ready for business. They can send a memo via fax or e-mail to colleagues around town, around the country, or around the world. With the right software, they can work on a document with a team of colleagues from around the world. They can also buy or sell thousands of products from securities to hot sauce. And they can do all this without leaving home.

In fact, an office does not even have to be in a specific place. With the use of laptop computers, cellular telephones, voice mail, e-mail, and portable fax machines, some people now work in a *virtual* office, which has no permanent location—"deals on wheels," so to speak.. For example, accountants at Ernst & Young spend most of their time in the field. When workers need to return to the headquarters, they call a few hours ahead to reserve an office in what is called a "hoteling system." The office *concierge* puts a nameplate on an available office and programs the telephone and voice mail. The hoteling system has sharply reduced the demand for headquarters space and has saved firms millions of dollars.

Sources: John Eckhouse, "Tired of the Rat Race? Make Money with Your Mouse," *HomePC,* 1 August 1995; Andrea Savari, "Mapping the Future of the Virtual Office," *Electrical Engineering Times,* 31 July 1995; and Michael Fillon, "Bringing the Office Home," *Information Week,* 22 May 1995. As an example of sales over the Internet, visit Hot Hot Hot, "the Net's coolest hot sauce shop" (http://www.hot.presence.com/g/p/H3/).

CASE STUDY

The Electronic Cottage

Location:

To tour a virtual office, visit KPMG's Virtual Office (http://www.rad.kpmg.com/). To explore a virtual law firm, visit Thierman Virtual Law Firm (http://www.dnai.com/tvlf/).

Kinds of Firms

There are about 25 million businesses in the United States. Two-thirds of these are small retail businesses, small service operations, part-time home-based businesses, and small farms. Each year nearly a million new firms are started, many of which fail. Entrepreneurs organize firms in one of three ways: as a sole proprietorship, as a partnership, or as a corporation. Let's examine the advantages and disadvantages of each.

Sole Proprietorships. The simplest form of business organization is the **sole proprietorship,** a single-owner firm. A self-employed plumber, electrician, farmer, or family physician is an example. A sole proprietorship is easy to organize; the sole proprietor simply opens for business by, for example, taking out a classified ad announcing availability for carpentry, snow plowing, or lawn mowing.

Sole proprietorship A firm with a single owner who has the right to all profits and who bears unlimited liability for the firm's debts

The owner is in complete control. The owner, however, faces *unlimited liability* for any business debts and could lose everything, including a home and other assets. Also, since the sole proprietor has no partners or other financial backers, raising enough money to get the business up and running can be difficult. One final disadvantage is that sole proprietorships usually go out of business upon the death of the proprietor. Sole proprietorships are the most common form of business organization, accounting most recently for 74 percent of all U.S. businesses. Because this type of firm is typically small, however, proprietorships generate a small portion of all U.S. business sales—only 6 percent.

Partnerships. A more complicated form of business organization is the **partnership,** which involves two or more individuals who agree to contribute resources to the business in return for a share of the profit or loss. Law, accounting, and medical partnerships typify this business form. Partners have strength in numbers and often find it easier than the sole proprietor to raise sufficient funds to get the business going. But the partners may not always agree. Also, each partner usually faces unlimited liability for all the debts and claims against the partnership, so one partner could lose everything because of another's mistake. Finally, the death or departure of one partner may disrupt the firm's continuity and could require a complete reorganization. The partnership is the least common form of U.S. business organization, making up only 8 percent of all firms and accounting for just 4 percent of all business sales.

Partnership A firm with multiple owners who share the firm's profits and each of whom bears unlimited liability for the firm's debts

Corporations. By far the most important form of business organization is the corporation. The **corporation** is a legal entity established through articles of incorporation. The owners of the corporation are issued shares of stock entitling them to corporate profits in proportion to their stock ownership. A major advantage of the corporate form is that many individuals—hundreds or even thousands—can pool their money, so incorporating represents the easiest way to amass large sums of money to finance the firm. Also, stockholders have *limited liability,* meaning their liability for any losses is limited to the value of their stock. A final advantage of this form of organization is that the corporation has a life separate and apart from those of the owners. The corporation continues to exist even if ownership changes hands, and it can be taxed and sued as if it were a person.

Corporation A legal entity owned by stockholders whose liability is limited to the value of their stock

The corporate form has some disadvantages as well. A stockholder's ability to influence corporate policy is limited to voting for a board of directors, which oversees the operation of the firm. Each share of stock usually carries with it one vote; the typical stockholder of a large corporation owns only a tiny fraction of the shares and thus has little say. Whereas the income from sole proprietorships and partnerships is taxed only once, corporate income is taxed twice: first as corporate profits and second as stockholder income, either as corporate dividends or as realized capital gains. A *realized capital gain* is any increase in the market value of a share that occurs between the time the share is purchased and the time it is sold.

A hybrid type of corporation has evolved to take advantage of the limited liability feature of the corporate structure, while reducing the impact of double taxation. The *S corporation* provides owners with limited liability, but corporate

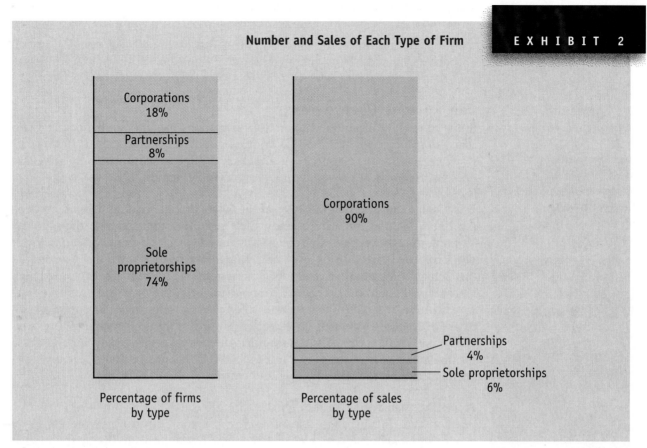

Number and Sales of Each Type of Firm

EXHIBIT 2

Corporations
18%

Partnerships
8%

Sole
proprietorships
74%

Percentage of firms
by type

Corporations
90%

Partnerships
4%

Sole proprietorships
6%

Percentage of sales
by type

Source: *The American Almanac: Statistical Abstract of the United States, 1995–1996,* U.S. Bureau of the Census, 1995.

profits are taxed only once—as income on each shareholder's personal income tax return. To qualify as an S corporation, a firm must have no more than 35 stockholders and must have no foreign or corporate stockholders.

Corporations make up only 18 percent of all U.S. businesses, but because they tend to be much larger than the other two forms of business, corporate sales represent 90 percent of all business sales. Exhibit 2 shows, by type of U.S. firm, the percentage of firms and the percentage of total sales. *The sole proprietorship is the most important in terms of total numbers, but the corporation is the most important in terms of total sales.*

Nonprofit Institutions

To this point we have considered firms that maximize profit. Some institutions, such as nonprofit hospitals, the Red Cross, the Salvation Army, churches, synagogues, mosques, and perhaps the college you are attending, are private organizations that do not have profit as an explicit objective. Yet even nonprofit institutions must somehow pay for the resources they employ. Revenue sources typically include some combination of voluntary contributions and service charges, such as college tuition and hospital bills. Although there are millions of nonprofit institutions, when we talk about firms in this book, we will be referring to for-profit firms.

THE GOVERNMENT

You might think that production by firms and by households could satisfy all consumer demands. Why must yet another economic institution get into the act?

The Role of Government

Sometimes the unrestrained operation of markets has undesirable results. Too many of some goods and too few of other goods may be produced. In this section we consider the sources of **market failure** and how society's welfare could at times be improved by government intervention.

Market failure *A condition that arises when unrestrained operation of markets yields socially undesirable results*

Establishing and Enforcing the Rules of the Game. Private markets depend on people like you to voluntarily employ their resources to maximize their utility. What if you were repeatedly robbed of your paycheck on your way home from work, or what if your employer told you after a week's work that you would not be paid? Why bother working? The system of private markets would break down if you could not safeguard your private property or if you could not enforce contracts. Governments play a role in *safeguarding private property* through police protection and in *enforcing contracts* through a judicial system. More generally, governments try to make sure that market participants play fair and abide by the "rules of the game." These rules of the game are established by government and by the customs and conventions of the market.

Promoting Competition. Although the "invisible hand" of competition usually promotes an efficient allocation of resources, some firms try to avoid competition through *collusion*, which is an agreement among firms to divide the market or to fix the market price. Or an individual firm may try to eliminate the competition by using unfair business practices. For example, to drive out local competitors, a large firm may temporarily sell at a price below its cost. *Government antitrust laws try to promote competition by prohibiting collusion and other anticompetitive practices.*

For the sake of efficiency, the electric utility in your community is a natural monopoly. Because the utility is a monopoly, however, it faces government regulation.

Regulating Natural Monopolies. Competition usually keeps the product price lower than it is when the product is sold by a **monopoly,** a sole supplier to the market. In a few cases, however, a monopoly can produce and sell the product for less than several competing firms could sell it. For example, electricity is supplied more efficiently by a single firm that wires the community than by competing firms running their own wires. When it is cheaper for one firm to serve the market than for two or more firms to do so, that firm is called a **natural monopoly.** But since a natural monopoly faces no competition, it tends to charge a higher price than is optimal from society's point of view. Therefore, the government usually regulates the monopoly, forcing it to lower the price.

Monopoly *A sole producer of a product for which there are no good substitutes*

Natural monopoly *One firm that can serve the entire market at a lower per-unit cost than can two or more firms*

Providing Public Goods. So far in this book we have been talking about private goods, which have two important features. First, private goods are *rival* in consumption, meaning that the amount consumed by one person is unavailable for others to consume. For example, when you and some friends share a pizza, each slice you eat is one less slice available to the others. Second, the supplier of a private good can easily *exclude* those who fail to pay. Only paying customers get a pizza. Thus, private goods also have a feature called *excludability*. In contrast, **public goods,** such as national defense and a system of justice, are *nonrival* in consumption. One person's consumption does not diminish the amount available to others. What's more, once produced, public goods are available to all; suppliers cannot easily prevent those who fail to pay from consuming them. For example, national defense is *nonexcludable*—it is available to all regardless of who pays for it and who does not. Because public goods are *nonrival* and *nonexcludable,* private firms usually cannot supply them profitably. The government, however, has the authority to collect taxes for public goods.

Dealing with Externalities. Market prices reflect the *private* costs and benefits of producers and consumers. But sometimes production or consumption imposes costs or benefits on third parties—on those who are neither supplier nor demander in the market transaction. For example, a paper mill fouls the air breathed by nearby residents, but the price of paper as determined in the private market fails to reflect the cost of such pollution to society. Since these pollution costs are outside, or *external* to, the market activity, they are called *externalities*. An **externality** is a cost or a benefit that falls on third parties and is consequently ignored by the two parties to the market transaction. A *negative externality* imposes on third parties an external cost, such as factory pollution or jet noise. A *positive externality* confers on third parties an external benefit, such as results from safer driving or better education. *Because market prices do not reflect externalities, governments often employ taxes, subsidies, and regulations to discourage negative externalities and to encourage positive externalities.*

A More Equal Distribution of Income. As noted earlier, some people, because of a lack of education, mental or physical disabilities, or perhaps the need to care for small children at home, may be unable to earn enough to support themselves. Since resource markets do not necessarily guarantee each household even a minimum level of income, transfer payments reflect society's attempt to provide a basic standard of living to all citizens. Nearly all citizens agree that, through government transfer payments, society should alter some of the results of the market by redistributing income to the poor. (Notice the normative nature of this statement.) Where differences of opinion arise is in deciding just how much redistribution should occur and what form it should take.

Full Employment, Price Stability, and Economic Growth. The government, through its ability to tax and spend and its control of the money supply, attempts to promote full employment, price stability, and an adequate rate of growth in the economy. The government's pursuit of these objectives through taxing and spending is called **fiscal policy** and through regulating the money supply is called **monetary policy.** These policies are examined in the study of macroeconomics.

Government's Structure and Objectives

The United States has a *federal system* of government, meaning that responsibilities are shared across levels of government. The state government grants some powers to local government and surrenders some powers to the national, or

Public good A good that is available for all to consume, regardless of who pays and who does not

Externality A cost or a benefit that falls on third parties and is therefore ignored by the two parties to the market transaction

Fiscal policy The use of government purchases, transfer payments, taxes, and borrowing to influence aggregate economic activity

Monetary policy Regulation of the money supply in order to influence aggregate economic activity

federal, government. As the system has evolved, the federal government has primary responsibility for the security of the nation and the stability of the economy. State governments fund higher education, prisons, and, with aid from the federal government, highways, and aid to the needy. Local governments' responsibilities include primary and secondary education, plus police and fire protection.

Difficulty in Defining Government Objectives. We assume that households maximize utility and firms maximize profit, but what do governments—or, more specifically, government decision makers—attempt to maximize? One problem with focusing on the U.S. government's objectives is that the federal system consists of not one but many governments—more than 80,000 separate jurisdictions in all. What's more, because the federal government relies on offsetting, or countervailing, powers among the *executive, legislative,* and *judicial* branches, it does not act as a single, consistent, decision maker. Even within the federal executive branch, there are so many agencies and bureaus that at times they seem to work at cross purposes. For example, at the same time the U.S. Surgeon General requires health warnings on cigarettes, the U.S. Department of Agriculture subsidizes tobacco farmers. Given this thicket of jurisdictions, branches, and bureaus of government, one useful theory of government behavior is that elected officials try to maximize the number of votes they will get in the next election. Thus, we can assume that elected officials are *vote maximizers.* In this theory, vote maximization guides the decisions of elected officials who, in turn, control government employees.

Voluntary Exchange Versus Coercion. Market exchange relies on the voluntary behavior of buyers and sellers. If you don't like tofu, no problem—just don't buy any. But in political markets the situation is different. Under any voting rule except unanimous consent, there will be some government coercion. Public choices are enforced by the police power of the state. Those who fail to pay their taxes could go to jail, even if they object to the programs funded by the taxes.

Absence of Market Prices. Another distinguishing feature of governments is that the selling price of public output is usually either zero or some amount below its cost. If you are now attending a state college or university, your tuition probably covers less than half of the total cost of providing your education. (Why are taxpayers willing to subsidize your education?) Since the revenue side of the government budget is usually separate from the expenditure side, there is no necessary link between the cost and benefit of a public program. For a private exchange to occur, however, the expected benefit must at least equal the cost.

Size and Growth of U.S. Government

One way to track the role of government over time is by measuring government's share of the U.S. *gross domestic product,* or *GDP,* which is the total value of all final goods and services produced in the United States. In 1929, the year the Great Depression began, government spending, mostly by state and local governments, accounted for just 10 percent of GDP. The federal government at that time played a minor role. In fact, during the country's first 150 years, federal spending, except during times of war, never exceeded 3 percent of GDP.

EXHIBIT 3

Government Spending in U.S. Since 1929 as Percentage of Gross Domestic Product

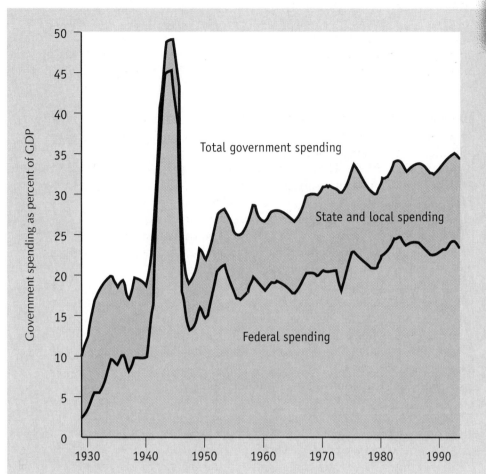

Source: *Economic Report of the President,* February 1996 and January 1964.

The Great Depression, World War II, and a change in mainstream macroeconomic thinking increased the role of the federal government in the economy. Exhibit 3 shows government spending as a percentage of gross domestic product, with a breakout between federal spending and state and local spending. Note the spike in federal spending during World War II and the steady rise since then in government spending as a percentage of the gross domestic product. Government spending in 1995 was 34 percent of GDP, with 23 percent by the federal government and 11 percent by state and local governments. In comparison, government spending as a percent of GDP in 1995 was 36 percent in Japan, 42 percent in the United Kingdom, 47 percent in Canada, 49 percent in Germany, 54 percent in France, and 55 percent in Italy.[1]

Thus, spending by the U.S. federal government accounts for about two-thirds of all government spending. Exhibit 4 provides a detailed look at the composition of U.S. federal spending since 1940. As you can see, the percent-

---

1   Figures for foreign countries are from the Organization for Economic Cooperation and Development (OECD).

EXHIBIT 4

Percentage Composition of Federal Outlays Since 1940 (share of total)

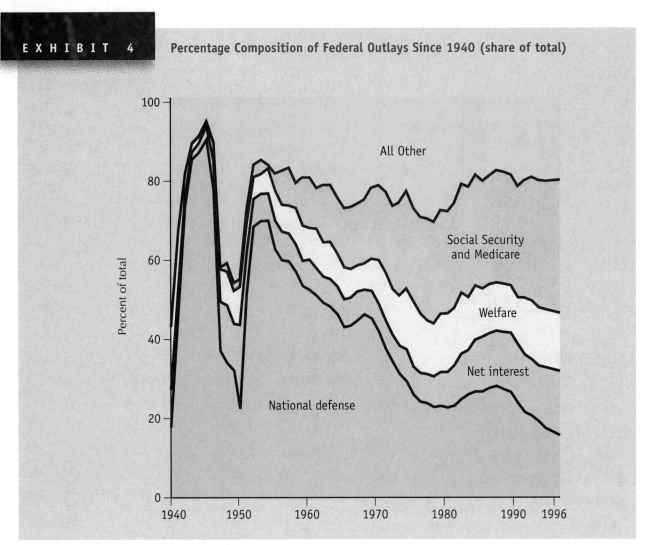

Source: *Economic Report of the President,* February 1996.

age of federal spending allocated to defense was high during World War II and during the Korean War of the early 1950s. Since the mid-1950s, defense spending has declined as a percentage of all federal spending, and spending on Social Security and Medicare, programs aimed primarily at the elderly, has increased, now accounting for one-third of the federal budget. For the last two decades, welfare spending, which consists of cash and in-kind transfer payments, has remained relatively constant as a percentage of all federal spending; welfare spending accounts for one-seventh of the federal budget.

Sources of Government Revenue

Taxes provide the bulk of revenue at all levels of government. The federal government relies primarily on the individual income tax, state governments rely on income and sales taxes, and local governments rely on the property tax. In addition to taxes, other revenue sources include user charges—such as highway tolls—and borrowing, particularly at the federal level, where recent deficits

EXHIBIT 5

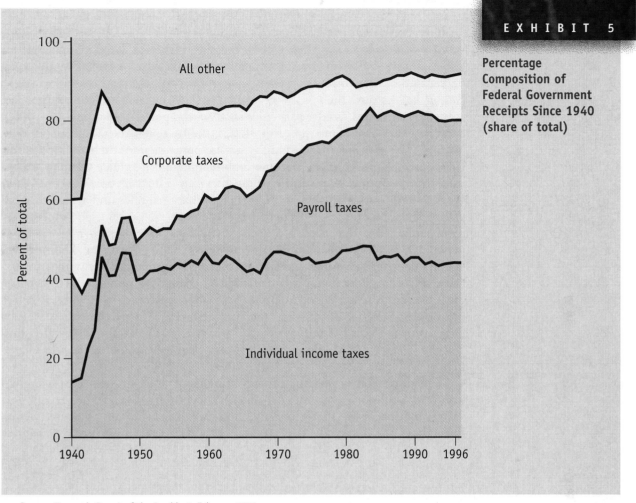

Percentage Composition of Federal Government Receipts Since 1940 (share of total)

Source: *Economic Report of the President,* February 1996.

have been substantial. Some states also sell lottery tickets and liquor to raise money.

Exhibit 5 focuses on sources of federal receipts since 1940. The individual income tax has accounted for about 45 percent of federal revenues since after World War II. In the early 1950s, payroll taxes accounted for only about 10 percent of federal receipts, compared to 36 percent in 1995. *Payroll taxes* are deducted from paychecks to support Social Security, unemployment benefits, and medical care for the elderly. Corporate income taxes and revenue from other sources, such as *excise,* or sales, taxes, have declined as a share of the total since the 1950s.

Tax Principles and Tax Incidence

The structure of a tax is often justified on the basis of one of two general principles. First, a tax could relate to the individual's *ability to pay,* so those with a greater ability pay more taxes. Income or property taxes often rely on this principle. Or, second, a tax could relate to the *benefits received* from the government activity funded by the tax. For example, the tax on gasoline funds highway construction and maintenance, thereby linking tax payment to road use.

Tax incidence The distribution of tax burden among tax payers.

Tax incidence indicates who actually bears the burden of the tax. One way of evaluating tax incidence is by measuring the tax as a percentage of income. Under *proportional taxation,* taxpayers at all income levels pay the same percentage of their income in taxes. A proportional income tax is also called a *flat-rate tax,* because the tax as a percentage of income remains constant, or flat, as income increases. Under *progressive taxation,* the percentage of income paid in taxes increases as income increases; that is, the marginal tax rate increases with income. The *marginal tax rate* indicates what percentage of each additional dollar of income goes to taxes. Because high marginal rates reduce the after-tax return from working or investing, high rates can reduce people's incentives to work and to invest. In 1995, there were five marginal rates under the U.S. federal personal income tax—15 percent, 28 percent, 31 percent, 36 percent, and 39.6 percent—so that tax is progressive. Finally, under *regressive taxation,* the percentage of income paid in taxes decreases as income increases: The marginal tax rate declines as income increases. Most U.S. payroll taxes are regressive, because they are a flat rate up to a certain level of income, above which the marginal rate drops to zero. For example, Social Security taxes in 1996 were levied on the first $62,700 of workers' income. Half the 12.4 percent tax is paid by employers and half by employees (the self-employed pay the entire amount). But the 2.9 percent Medicare tax is proportional, because it applies to all earnings.

This discussion of revenue sources brings to a close, for now, our examination of the role of government in the U.S. economy. Government has a pervasive influence on the economy, and discussions of its role are woven throughout the book.

THE REST OF THE WORLD

Thus far we have focused on institutions within the United States—that is, on *domestic* households, firms, and governments. This initial focus was appropriate because our primary objective has been to understand the workings of the U.S. economy, which is by far the largest national economy in the world. But the rest of the world affects what U.S. households consume and what U.S. firms produced. For example, Asian economies such as those of Japan and South Korea supply U.S. markets with autos, electronic equipment, and other manufactured goods, thereby affecting U.S. prices, wages, and profits. Likewise, political unrest in the Persian Gulf can drive up the price of oil. Foreign actors, therefore, have a profound effect on the U.S. economy—on what we consume and what we produce. The *rest of the world* consists of the households, firms, and governments in more than 170 sovereign countries throughout the world, ranging from countries with fewer people than any of the United States, to the People's Republic of China, with nearly five times the U.S. population.

International Trade
In Chapter 2 you learned about comparative advantage and the gains from specialization. These gains explain why households stopped trying to do every-

thing for themselves and began to specialize. International trade arises for the same reasons. *International trade occurs because the opportunity cost of producing specific goods differs among countries.* Americans import raw materials such as crude oil, diamonds, and coffee beans and finished goods such as cameras, VCRs, and automobiles. U.S. producers export sophisticated products such as computers, aircraft, and movies, as well as agricultural products such as wheat and corn.

International trade between the United States and the rest of the world has increased in recent decades. In 1970 U.S. exports of goods and services amounted to only 7 percent of the gross domestic product. That figure has since increased to 11 percent. The chief U.S. trading partners in 1995 order of importance were Canada, Japan, Mexico, Great Britain, Germany, France, South Korea, and Taiwan.

The **merchandise trade balance** equals the value of exported goods minus the value of imported goods. Goods in this case are distinguished from services, which show up in another trade account. For the last two decades the United States has experienced a merchandise trade *deficit,* meaning that the value of U.S. imported goods has exceeded the value of U.S. exported goods. Just as a household must cover its spending, so too must a nation. The deficit in our merchandise trade balance must be offset by a surplus in one or more of the other *balance-of-payments* accounts. A nation's **balance of payments** is the record of all economic transactions between its residents and residents of the rest of the world. The balance of payments consists of several accounts, such as the merchandise trade balance. Since 1982 Americans have been consuming more than they have been producing and have been borrowing from abroad to finance the difference.

Merchandise trade balance The value of a country's exported goods minus the value of its imported goods during a given time period

Balance of payments A record of all economic transactions between residents of one country and residents of the rest of the world during a given time period

Exchange Rates

The lack of a common currency complicates trade between countries. How many U.S. dollars buy a Mercedes selling for 100,000 marks? An American buyer cares only about the dollar cost; the German manufacturer cares only about the marks received. To facilitate trade between nations, a market for foreign exchange has developed. **Foreign exchange** is the currency of another country needed to carry out international transactions. The supply and demand for foreign exchange come together in *foreign exchange markets* to determine an equilibrium exchange rate. The *exchange rate* measures the price of one currency in terms of another. For example, the exchange rate between U.S. dollars and German marks might indicate that one mark exchanges for 72 cents. The greater the demand for a particular foreign currency or the smaller the supply, the higher its exchange rate—that is, the more dollars it will cost. The exchange rate affects the prices of imports and exports and thus helps shape the flow of foreign trade.

Foreign exchange The currency of another country needed to carry out international transactions

Trade Restrictions

Although there are clear gains from international specialization and exchange, nearly all countries restrict trade. These restrictions can take the form of (1) **tariffs,** which are taxes on imports or exports; (2) **quotas,** which are legal limits on the quantity of a particular good that can be imported or exported; and (3) other restrictions, such as the agreement by Japanese car manufacturers to limit their exports to the United States.

Tariff A tax on imports or exports

Quota A legal limit on the quantity of a particular product that can be imported or exported

If specialization according to comparative advantage is so beneficial, why do most countries restrict trade? Restrictions benefit certain domestic producers that lobby their governments for these benefits. For example, U.S. textile manufacturers have sought and received from Congress protective legislation restricting textile imports, thereby raising U.S. textile prices. These higher prices harm domestic consumers, but consumers are usually unaware of this harm. Trade restrictions interfere with the free flow of products across borders and tend to harm the overall economy. Trade restrictions in the auto industry are discussed in the following case study.

CASE STUDY

The World of Automobiles

Location:

About one-quarter of car sales in the United States are imports, with Japanese manufacturers accounting for most of this amount. To learn more about the Japanese automobile industry, browse "CarMag: Internet CarMagazine Japan" (http://www.carmag.co.jp/) or visit the "Data Center," part of Toyota Motor Corporation's "Toyota Internet Drive" (http://www.toyota.co.jp/Data_center/index.html).

The U.S. auto industry is huge, with annual sales of more than $250 billion, an amount exceeding the gross domestic product of 90 percent of the world's economies. The industry employs directly about 800,000 people, plus another 900,000 people in 30,000 auto dealerships. The supplier-manufacturing-assembly network involves more than 4,000 plants in 48 states.

The import share of U.S. auto sales was only 0.4 percent in the decade following World War II. In 1973, however, the suddenly powerful Organization of Petroleum Exporting Countries (OPEC) more than tripled oil prices. In response to the higher price of gasoline, Americans scrambled for more fuel-efficient automobiles, which were sold primarily by foreign manufacturers, especially the Japanese. As a result, imports jumped to 21 percent of U.S. auto sales by 1980.

In the early 1980s, at the urging of the Big Three auto makers (General Motors, Ford, and Chrysler), the Reagan administration persuaded Japanese producers to accept "voluntary" import quotas limiting the number of Japanese automobiles they exported to the United States. The quotas, or supply restrictions, drove up the price of Japanese imports, and U.S. auto producers used this as an opportunity to raise their own prices. Experts estimate that the so-called "protection" from foreign competition cost U.S. consumers over $15 billion.

The quotas had two effects on Japanese producers. First, faced with a strict limit on the number of cars they could export to the United States, they began shipping more upscale models instead of subcompacts. Second, the quotas encouraged Japanese producers to establish manufacturing plants in the United States. By making autos in the United States, Japanese auto makers also reduced the problem of a rising value of the yen relative to the dollar, which made cars produced in Japan more expensive in the United States. Japanese-owned auto plants in the United States now account for one-quarter of U.S. car production. Toyota even sells some U.S.-built cars in Japan, such as the Avalon, a new luxury car. Two German auto makers, Mercedes and BMW, have also built plants here.

Imports still make up about one-quarter of U.S. car sales, with Japanese manufacturers accounting for most of this. Imports include cars produced abroad by foreign firms but sold under the names of U.S. firms, such as the

Dodge Colt (produced in Japan by Mitsubishi), Chevrolet's Geo Storm (produced in Japan by Isuzu) and Geo Metro (produced in Japan by Suzuki), and the Pontiac LeMans (produced in South Korea by Daewoo).

The Big Three also produce around the world. In fact, Ford is the largest auto maker in Australia, Great Britain, Mexico, and Argentina; General Motors ranks second in western Europe, Canada, Australia, and Germany. The most hotly contested markets now are in China, India, and Latin America, where the potential is enormous.

Sources: Walter Adams and James Brock, "Automobiles," in *The Structure of American Industry,* 9th ed. (Englewood Cliffs, N.J.: Prentice Hall, 1995): pp. 65–92; Robert L. Simison, "GM Sees End to Market-Share Drop," *The Wall Street Journal,* 10 August 1995; Valerie Reitman, "Toyota Names a Chief Likely to Shake Up Global Auto Business," *The Wall Street Journal,* 11 August 1995.

The World of Automobiles
continued

CONCLUSION

In this chapter we examined four economic actors: households, firms, governments, and the rest of the world. Domestic households are by far the most important, for they, along with foreign households, supply all the resources and demand all the goods and services produced. But government spending accounts for a growing share of economic activity. In recent years the U.S. economy has come to depend more on the rest of the world both as a market for U.S. goods and as a source of products. The links among the four actors are examined in "A Closer Look," which appears at the end of the chapter.

SUMMARY

1. Most household income arises from the sale of labor, and most household income is spent on personal consumption, which consists of spending on durable goods, nondurable goods, and services—the fastest-growing portion of personal consumption. Income not spent on personal consumption is either saved or paid as taxes.

2. Firms are convenient devices for bringing together specialized resources. But as a firm grows larger, the net benefits of organizing production within the firm often diminish. At some point market exchange becomes a more efficient way to coordinate production. Markets, relying only on the profit motives of each firm, guide resources through the intermediate stages required to produce the final good.

3. Firms can be organized in three different ways: as sole proprietorships, partnerships, or corporations. Because corporations are typically large, they account for the bulk of all sales by U.S. firms.

4. When private markets yield socially undesirable results, government may intervene to address these market failures. Government programs are designed to (1) protect private property and enforce contracts; (2) promote competition; (3) regulate natural monopolies; (4) provide public goods; (5) discourage negative externalities and encourage positive externalities; (6) provide for greater equality in the distribution of income; and (7) promote full employment, price stability, and growth.

5. In the United States, the federal government relies primarily on the personal income tax, states rely on income and sales taxes, and localities rely on the property tax. A tax is often justified by basing it (1) on the individual's ability to pay or (2) on the benefits the taxpayer receives from the activities financed by the tax.

6. The rest of the world is also populated by households, firms, and governments. Trade requires foreign exchange markets to establish exchange rates between currencies. The balance of payments summarizes the transactions between the residents of one country and the residents of the rest of the world. Despite the benefits from comparative advantage, nearly all countries impose trade restrictions to protect specific domestic industries.

7. The circular flow model (which appears after the end-of-chapter questions) shows the flow of resources, products, income, and expenditures through the economy. As you will see, this model shows that the prices of goods and services are determined in the product markets and the prices of resources are determined in the resource markets.

QUESTIONS AND PROBLEMS

1. **(Evolution of the Household)** Indicate whether each of the following would increase or decrease the opportunity costs for mothers who elect to forgo paid employment outside the home. Explain your answers.
   a. Higher levels of education.
   b. Higher unemployment rates for women.
   c. Higher average pay levels for women.
   d. Lower demand for labor in areas that traditionally employ mainly women.

2. **(Households as Demanders of Goods and Services)** Classify each of the following as a durable good, nondurable good, or service:
   a. A gallon of milk.
   b. A lawn mower.
   c. A VCR.
   d. A manicure.
   e. A pair of shoes.
   f. An eye exam.
   g. A personal computer.
   h. A neighborhood teenager mowing a lawn.

3. **(Household Production)** Technological breakthroughs have made household production possible in some cases. What are some technological advances that have made household production of entertainment possible?

4. **(Household Production)** Many households supplement their food budget by cultivating small vegetable gardens. Explain how each of the following might affect this kind of household production:
   a. Both husband and wife are professionals earning high salaries.
   b. The household is located in the city rather than in the country.
   c. The household is located in the South rather than in the North.
   d. The household is located in a region where there is a high sales tax on food.
   e. The household is located in a region that has a high property tax rate.

5. **(Evolution of the Firm)** Explain how production after the Industrial Revolution differed from production under the cottage industry system.

6. **(Corporations)** Why did the institution of the firm appear after the advent of the Industrial Revolution in the 19th century? What type of business organization existed before this?

7. **(Sole Proprietorship)** What are the disadvantages of the sole proprietorship form of business?

8. **(Kinds of Firms)** Rank the three types of businesses according to their total number in the United States. Then rank them according to their percentage of total sales in the United States.

9. **(Government)** Often it is said that government is necessary when private markets fail to work effectively and fairly. Based on your reading of the text, discuss how private markets might break down.

10. **(Government)** Complete each of the following sentences:
    a. When the private operation of markets leads to overproduction or underproduction of some goods, this is known as a(n) _____.
    b. Goods that are nonrival and nonexcludable are known as _____.
    c. _____ are cash or in-kind benefits given to individuals as outright grants from the government.
    d. A(n) _____ confers an external benefit to third parties to a market transaction.
    e. _____ refers to the government's pursuit of full employment and price stability through variations in taxing and government spending.

11. **(Tax Rates)** Suppose taxes are related to income level as follows:

Income	Taxes
$1,000	$200
$2,000	$350
$3,000	$450

    a. What percentage of income is paid in taxes at each level?
    b. Is the tax progressive, proportional, or regressive?
    c. What is the marginal tax rate on the first $1,000 of income? The second $1,000? The third $1,000?

12. **(Externality)** Suppose a good has an external cost associated with its production. What's wrong with letting the market decide how much should be produced?

13. **(International Trade)** Distinguish between tariffs and quotas. Who benefits from and who is harmed by such trade restrictions on imports?

14. **(Household Productivity)** Although technology has enhanced the ability of households to increase home production of many forms of activities, the more traditional forms of household production (e.g., meal preparation, laundry) have increasingly been handled outside the household unit. Can you explain this phenomenon?

15. **(Government Revenue)** What are the different sources used to provide government revenue in the United States? Which types of taxes are of greatest importance at each level of government? What two types of taxes provide the most revenue to the U.S. federal government?

16. **(International Trade)** Why does international trade occur? What measures the level of economic transactions between the residents of one country and the residents of the rest of the world? What does it mean to run a deficit in the merchandise trade balance?

17. **(Objectives of the Economic Actors)** In economic analysis, what are the assumed objectives of households, firms, and the government?

18. **(Household Production)** What factors does a householder consider when deciding whether to produce a good or service at home rather than buying it in the marketplace?

19. **(The Electronic Cottage)** How has the development of personal computer hardware and software reversed some of the trends brought on by the Industrial Revolution?

20. **(The World of Automobiles)** What factors contributed to the building of automobile factories in the United States by Japanese producers?

Using the Internet

21. Visit the Financial Times Group (**http://www.usa. ft.com/**) and examine "Highlights from the FT," or the *Financial Times*. Briefly summarize (1) a news story about the American economy; (2) a news story about the European economy; and (3) a news story about the Asia/Pacific economy.

Introduction to Macroeconomics

In macroeconomics we think big—not about the demand and supply for chewing gum but the demand and supply for everything produced in the economy; not about the price of floppy disks but the average price of all products sold in the economy; not about consumption by the Jackson household but consumption by all households; not about the investment by General Motors but the investment by all firms in the economy.

We are concerned not only with what determines such big-picture measures as the level of the economy's prices, employment, and production but also with understanding their movement over time. We are especially interested in what makes an economy grow over time, for a growing economy usually means more job opportunities and more goods and services available—in short, an improving standard of living. What determines the economy's ability to use resources productively, to adapt, to grow? Macroeconomists develop and test theories about how the economy as a whole works—theories they can use to predict the consequences of economic policies and events. Topics discussed in this chapter include:

- The national economy
- Economic fluctuations
- Aggregate demand and aggregate supply

- Short history of U.S. economy
- Demand-side economics
- Supply-side economics

THE NATIONAL ECONOMY

Economy The structure of economic life or economic activity in a community, a region, a country, a group of countries, or the world

Macroeconomics concerns the overall performance of the economy. The term **economy** describes the structure of economic life or economic activity in a community, a region, a country, a group of countries, or the world. We could talk about the St. Louis economy, the Missouri economy, the Midwest economy, the U.S. economy, the North American economy, or the world economy. We measure the economy's performance in different ways, such as the number of workers employed, their average earnings, or the size and number of firms. The most often used measure of an economy's performance is the *gross product,* which measures the market value of final goods and services produced in a particular geographical region during a given time period, usually one year. If the focus is the Missouri economy, we consider the gross *state* product. If the focus is the U.S. economy, we consider the gross *domestic* product. We can use the gross product to track the same economy over time or to compare different economies at the same time.

What's Special about the National Economy

The national economy deserves special attention. Here's why. If you were to drive west on Interstate 10 in Texas, you would hardly notice crossing the state line into New Mexico. If, however, you took the Juarez exit off I-10 south into Mexico, you would be stopped at the border, asked for identification, and could be searched. You would become quite aware that you were crossing an international border. Like most countries, the United States and Mexico usually allow freer movement of people and goods *within* their borders than *across* their borders.

The differences between the United States and Mexico are far greater than the differences between Texas and New Mexico. For example, each country has its own culture and language, its own communication and transportation systems, its own system of government, its own currency, and, most importantly, its own "rules of the game"—that is, its own regulations, customs, and conventions for conducting economic activity both within and across its borders.

The focus of macroeconomics is the performance of the national economy, including how the national economy interacts with other economies around the world. To get some idea of the complex nature of the U.S. economy, consider a profile of households, firms, governments, and the rest of the world. In the United States, there are about 100 million households, about 25 million businesses, and about 80,000 separate governments. These numbers offer snapshots of economic actors, but the economy is a moving picture—too complex to describe in snapshots. This is why we use theoretical models to simplify the key relationships. Let's begin with an analogy.

Similarities Between the Human Body and the Economy

Consider the similarities and differences between the human body and the economy. The body consists of millions of cells, each performing particular functions yet each linked to the operation of the entire body. Similarly, the economy is composed of millions of economic units, each acting with some independence yet each interconnected with the economy as a whole. The economy, like the body, is continually renewing itself, with new households, new businesses, and new foreign competitors.

Blood circulates throughout the body, facilitating the exchange of vital nutrients among cells. Similarly, **money** circulates throughout the economy, facilitating the exchange of resources and products among individual economic units. In fact, money is called a *medium of exchange*. In Chapter 9, we will see that the pattern traced by the movement of money, products, and resources throughout the economy is a *circular flow,* as is the pattern traced by the movement of blood and nutrients throughout the body.

Money Something accepted as a medium of exchange

Flows and Stocks. Just as the same blood recirculates again and again in the body, the same money recirculates to finance many transactions. The same dollars you spend on muffins are spent by the baker on butter, then spent by the dairy farmer on work boots. The dollars *flow* through the economy. To measure a flow, we use a **flow** variable. A flow variable is measured per period of time, such as heartbeats per minute or your average spending per week. We often distinguish between a flow variable and a *stock* variable. A **stock** variable represents an amount of something at a particular time, such as the amount of blood in your body or the number of dollars in your wallet right now.

Flow A variable that measures the amount of something over an interval of time, such as the amount of money you spend on food per week

Stock A variable that measures the amount of something at a particular point in time, such as the amount of money you have right now

Role of Expectations. In both medicine and macroeconomics, *expectations* play an important role. For example, if the patient expects a medicine to work, it often does work, even if it is only a sugar pill, or placebo. A similar mechanism operates in the economy. Suppose, for example, that all firms expect greater demand for their products. To expand output, firms buy more capital and hire more labor. As a result, households, as resource suppliers, earn more and so increase their demand for goods and services. Thus, producers may help bring about the very prosperity they expect. Negative expectations can also be self-fulfilling. If firms expect demand to fall, they invest less and hire fewer workers. As a result, household incomes decline, reducing the demand for goods and services.

Differences of Opinion. Both in medicine and in macroeconomics, matters are subject to different interpretations. First, experts within each field may differ on what ails the patient or the economy. An old medical saying holds that a correct diagnosis is half the cure. In macroeconomics, for example, experts may disagree about what's the problem. Second, even when experts within a field agree about what's wrong, they may disagree on what to do about it. Medical researchers, however, have two big advantages over macroeconomists: (1) they have collected vastly more information about their subject, and (2) they can test their theories in a laboratory setting.

Testing New Theories

Physicians and other natural scientists can test theories using controlled experiments. Macroeconomists, however, have no laboratory and little ability to run experiments of any kind. Granted, they can study different economies throughout the world, but each economy is unique, so comparisons across countries are tricky. Controlled experiments also provide scientists something seldom available to macroeconomists—the chance, or serendipitous, discovery (such as penicillin). But with only one patient—the U.S. economy—the macroeconomist cannot introduce particular policies in a variety of ways. Cries of "Eureka!" are seldom heard from macroeconomists.

Knowledge and Performance

Throughout history, little was known about human biology, yet many people nonetheless enjoyed good health. For example, the fact that blood circulates in our bodies was not discovered until 1638; it took another 150 years to figure out why. Similarly, over the millennia various complex economies have developed and flourished, though at the time there was little understanding or even concern about how these economies worked.

The economy is much like the body; as long as it functions smoothly, we need not understand its operation. But if a problem develops—high inflation, severe unemployment, or sluggish growth, for example—we must know how a healthy economy works before we can consider if and how the problem can be corrected. We need not know every detail of the economy, just as we need not know every detail of the body. But we must understand the essential relationships among key economic variables. For example, we would like to know the extent to which the economy is self-organizing and self-adjusting. Does the economy work well enough on its own, or does it often perform poorly? If the economy does perform poorly, what are the policy options and can we be sure that the proposed remedy won't do more harm than good?

When doctors did not understand how the body works, the cure was often worse than the disease. Much of the history of medicine describes misguided attempts to deal with maladies. As recently as the 19th century, for example, medical "remedies" included "bleeding, cupping, violent purging, the raising of blisters by vesicant ointments, the immersion of the body in either ice water or intolerably hot water, endless lists of botanical extracts evoked up and mixed together under nothing more than pure whim."[1] Even today, medical care is based on less scientific evidence than we think. According to one researcher, only one in seven medical interventions is supported by reliable scientific evidence.[2]

Likewise, national policymakers sometimes implemented the wrong economic prescription because of a flawed theory about how the economy works. At one time, for example, a nation's economic vitality was thought to spring from the stock of precious metals the nation accumulated in the public treasury. This theory spawned a policy called *mercantilism,* which held that, as a way of accumulating gold and silver, a nation should sell more output to foreigners than it bought from them. To achieve this, nations restricted imports by such devices as tariffs and import quotas. But these restrictions reduced international trade, thereby reducing the gains from specialization that arise from trade. Another flawed economic theory prompted President Herbert Hoover to introduce a major tax *increase* when the nation was suffering through the Great Depression. Policymakers have since learned that such a policy does more harm than good.

---

1   As described by Lewis Thomas in *The Youngest Science: Notes of a Medicine Watcher* (New York: Viking Press, 1983), p. 19.

2   See Sherwin Nuland, "Medical Fads: Bran, Midwives and Leeches," *New York Times,* 25 January 1995.

We all have some acquaintance with cycles in nature—the changing seasons, the ebb and flow of the tides, the regular movements of celestial bodies, the biorhythms of the body. As we shall see, the economy also has a rhythm of its own.

ECONOMIC FLUCTUATIONS AND GROWTH

Economic activity, like cycles in nature, fluctuates in a fairly regular way. The U.S. economy and other industrial market economies historically have experienced alternating periods of expansion and contraction in the level of economic activity. **Economic fluctuations** are the rise and fall of economic activity relative to the long-term growth trend of the economy. These economic fluctuations, which are also referred to as *business cycles,* vary in length and intensity, yet some features appear common to all. These ups and downs usually involve the entire nation and often the world, and they affect nearly all dimensions of economic activity, not simply employment and production levels.

Economic Fluctuation Analysis

Perhaps the easiest way to understand economic fluctuations is to examine their components. During the 1920s and 1930s, Wesley C. Mitchell, director of the National Bureau of Economic Research (NBER), analyzed economic fluctuations. In simplest terms, the economy, according to Mitchell, has two phases: periods of expansion and periods of contraction. Before World War II, some contractions were so severe that they were called depressions. Although there is no official definition, a **depression** is a sharp reduction in the nation's total production accompanied by high unemployment lasting more than a year. A milder contraction is called a **recession,** which the NBER identifies as a period of decline in total output and employment usually lasting six months to a year. Prior to World War II, the economy experienced both recessions and depressions. Since World War II, there have been recessions but no depressions.

Despite these ups and downs, the U.S. economy has grown sharply over the long run. Measured by the amount of goods and services produced, the economy today is more than six times larger than it was in 1940, with an average annual growth rate of 3.4 percent per year. Production tends to increase over the long run because of (1) increases in the amount and quality of resources, (2) better technology, and (3) improvements in the "rules of the game" that facilitate production and exchange. Exhibit 1 shows such a long-term growth trend as an upward-sloping straight line. Economic fluctuations reflect movements around this growth trend. A recession begins after the previous expansion has reached its *peak* and continues until the economy reaches a *trough.* The period between the peak and the trough is a *recession* and the period between the trough and the subsequent peak is an **expansion.**

The U.S. economic record appears in Exhibit 2, which shows the annual percentage change in economic activity relative to the long-term trend during the last hundred years. As you can see, the fluctuations vary widely in duration

Net Bookmark

Wesley C. Mitchell, former director of the National Bureau of Economic Research (NBER). Founded in 1920, the (NBER) is a private, nonprofit, nonpartisan research organization dedicated to promoting a better understanding of how the economy works. Visit the NBER at http://nber.harvard.edu/.

Economic fluctuations The rise and fall of economic activity relative to the long-term growth trend of the economy; also called business cycles

Depression A severe reduction in an economy's total production accompanied by high unemployment lasting more than a year

Recession A period of decline in total output usually lasting at least six months and marked by contractions in many sectors of the economy

Expansion A phase of economic activity during which there is an increase in the economy's total production

EXHIBIT 1

Hypothetical Business Fluctuations

Business fluctuations reflect movements of economic activity around a trend line that shows long-term growth. A recession (shown in red) begins after a previous expansion (shown in gold) has reached its peak and continues until the economy reaches a trough. An expansion begins when economic activity starts to increase and continues until the economy reaches a peak.

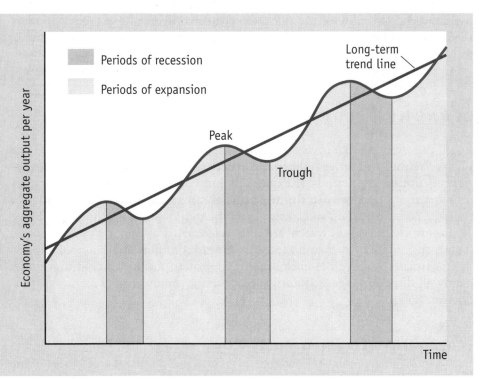

EXHIBIT 2   Historical Business Fluctuations in the United States

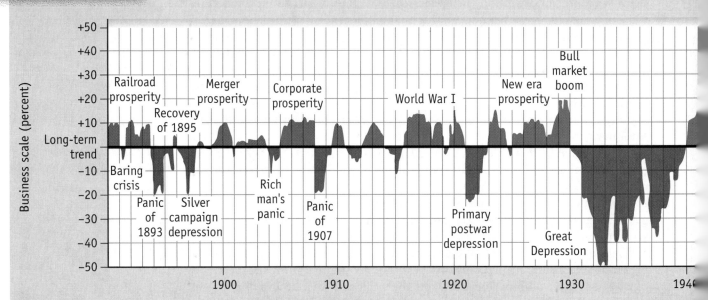

This historical chart shows the phases of business fluctuations since 1890. The vertical scale indicates the percentage by which the level of business activity exceeded or fell short of the long-term trend.

Source: "American Business Activity from 1790 to Today," Ameritrust Corporation, January 1988. Updated by author.

and in rate of change. The big declines during the Great Depression of the 1930s and the sharp gains during World War II stand in stark contrast. Analysts at NBER have been able to track the U.S. economy back to 1854. Since then, the country has experienced 31 full peak-to-trough fluctuations. No two have been exactly alike. The longest expansion on record lasted 106 months, from 1961 to 1969, a stretch that included the Vietnam War. The longest *peacetime* expansion began in November 1982 and continued for nearly eight years until a recession began in August 1990. The longest contraction lasted 65 months, from 1873 to 1879.

Since 1933, the U.S. economy has completed 11 cycles of peaks and troughs. During this period, peacetime expansions averaged about $3\frac{1}{2}$ years and peacetime recessions about 1 year; wartime expansions were longer. The entire cycle lasts about $4\frac{1}{2}$ years on average. Recent research suggests that the average length of an entire cycle was about the same during the 50 years before World War II as during the 50 years after it, though periods of contractions tended to be longer prior to World War II.[3] Again, despite the ups and downs, the economy has grown significantly over the long term, so the growth during expansions more than offsets the decline during recessions. As we will see in the next chapter, this growth rate has not been uniform, but it has been

3   See the research of Christina D. Romer, "Is the Stabilization of the Postwar Economy a Figment of the Data?" *American Economic Review* 76 (June 1986): 314–34, and Mark W. Watson, "Business-Cycle Durations and Postwar Stabilization of the U.S. Economy," *American Economic Review* 84 (March 1994): 24–46.

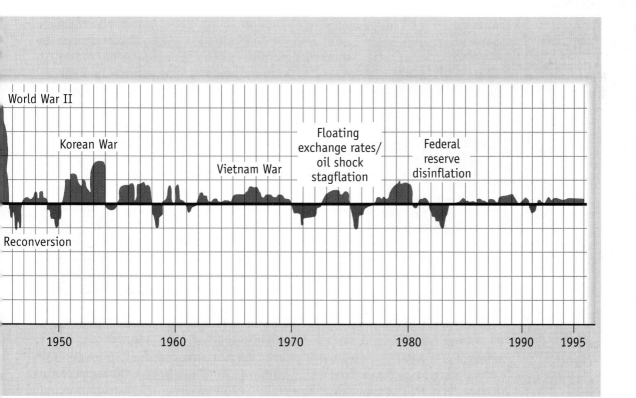

nonetheless impressive—since 1940 the economy has doubled in size every 21 years on average.

The intensity of the economic fluctuations varies from region to region across the United States. For example, a recession hits hardest those regions that produce durable goods, such as automobiles, major appliances, and computers; with the onset of a recession, the demand for these items falls more than the demand for nondurable goods.

Because of seasonal fluctuations and random disturbances, the economy does not move smoothly through phases of economic fluctuations. We cannot always distinguish between temporary blips in economic activity and actual turning points in the cycle. The drop in production in a particular month may be the result of a snowstorm or a poor harvest rather than the onset of a recession. Turning points—peaks and troughs—are thus identified by the NBER only after the fact. Since a recession usually involves declining output for two consecutive quarters, a recession is not so designated until at least six months after it begins.

As noted earlier, the U.S. economy's ups and downs usually involve the entire nation; indeed, business fluctuations seem to be linked across economies around the world. The following case study compares the year-to-year change in aggregate output in the United States with two other leading economies, the United Kingdom and Japan.

CASE STUDY

The Global Economy

Location:

The Organization for Economic Development (OECD) is a forum for monitoring economic trends in its 25 member countries, which include the United States, United Kingdom, and Japan. The OECD is the world's largest source of comparative data on the industrial economies. Visit the OECD at http://www.oecd.org/.

Though economic fluctuations are not perfectly synchronized across countries, a link is often apparent. Consider the recent experience in three leading economies—the United States, Japan, and the United Kingdom (or U.K.). Exhibit 3 shows the year-to-year percentage change in their total output, which is called their *real GDP*. At first the exhibit may look like just so much static electricity, but if you spend a little time following the growth changes in each country, you will begin to see similarities.

For example, U.S. real GDP declined in 1980, 1982, and 1991, reflecting recessions during those years. The deepest U.S. recession was in 1982, when output declined by 2.2 percent. The United Kingdom experienced recessions in roughly the same years, though in the early 1980s it had one long recession rather than the two shorter ones experienced in the United States. Although Japan did not suffer a recession in the early 1980s, the growth of its real GDP fell from 5.5 percent in 1979 to 2.7 percent in 1983. Japan's growth rate peaked at 6.2 percent in 1988 and then declined to −0.2 percent in 1993.

One problem with this linkage of business fluctuations across economies is that these swings tend to reinforce one another. For example, if other economies around the world slump about the same time as the U.S. economy, then foreigners purchase fewer U.S. products, thus reducing U.S. exports and deepening the U.S. recession. Likewise, U.S. consumers purchase fewer foreign

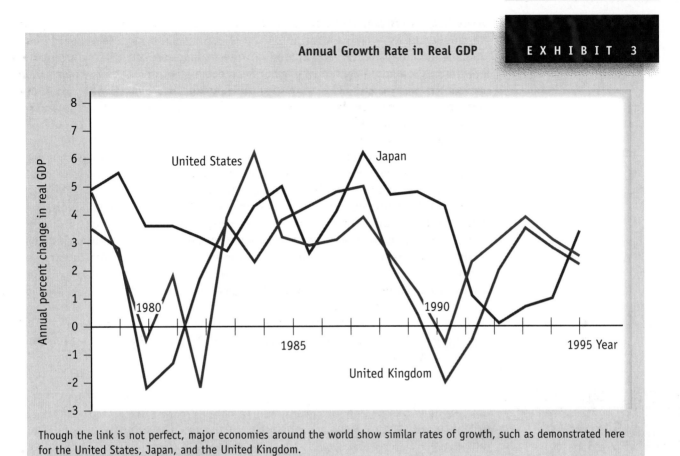

Annual Growth Rate in Real GDP

EXHIBIT 3

Though the link is not perfect, major economies around the world show similar rates of growth, such as demonstrated here for the United States, Japan, and the United Kingdom.

Source: Organization for Economic Cooperation and Development.

products, thus reinforcing the recessions in foreign economies. Expansions are also mutually reinforcing across countries. As we'll see, however, an economy can have too much of a good thing, for an overheated economy can experience problems with inflation.

Although year-to-year fluctuations in output are important, even more important is an economy's average growth rate in output over the long run. Between 1978 and 1995, the U.S. economy grew on average by 2.4 percent per year, compared to 3.4 percent in Japan and 2.2 percent in the United Kingdom. These growth rates may seem similar, but tiny differences compound over the years. For example, between 1978 and 1995, the United States grew by a total of 50 percent, Japan grew by 77 percent, and Great Britain grew by 45 percent. So Japan's economy grew half again as fast as the U.S. economy; this difference translates into millions of jobs and hundreds of billions of dollars worth of output. We will focus more on economic growth in the next chapter.

Sources: Annual growth data from *Economic Report of the President,* February 1996; Robert Steiner, "Japan's GDP Rose Even as Yen Surged," *The Wall Street Journal,* 19 September 1995; and the Organization for Economic Cooperation and Development.

The Global Economy
continued

Leading Economic Indicators

Certain events foreshadow a turning point in economic activity. Months before a recession is fully under way, changes in the *leading economic indicators* point to the coming storm. In the early stages of a recession, business slows down, orders for machinery and equipment slip, and the stock market, in anticipation of lower profits, turns down. The confidence consumers have in the economy also begins to sag, and households reduce their spending on big-ticket items such as automobiles and housing. All these activities are called *leading economic indicators* because they are the first variables to predict, or *lead to,* a downturn. Upturns in leading indicators point to an economic recovery. But leading indicators cannot predict precisely *when* turning points will occur.

Our introduction to economic fluctuations has been largely mechanical, focusing on the history and measurement of these fluctuations. We have not discussed the reasons behind the fluctuations, in part because such a discussion requires a firmer footing in macroeconomic theory and in part because the causes remain in dispute. In the next section we begin to lay the foundation for a macroeconomic framework by introducing a key model of analysis.

AGGREGATE DEMAND AND AGGREGATE SUPPLY

The economy is so complex that we need to simplify, or to abstract from the millions of relationships, in order to isolate the important elements under consideration. We must step back from all the individual economic transactions to survey the resulting mosaic. We begin with the familiar tools of demand and supply.

Aggregate Output and the Price Level

The demand for food shows the relationship between the relative price of food and the quantity of food demanded. When we consider the demand for food, we must take into account a diverse array of products—milk, bread, fruit, vegetables, meat, and so on. Moving from the demand for a specific product, milk, to the demand for a general product, food, is not conceptually difficult. Likewise, we can make the transition from the demand for food, housing, clothing, entertainment, or medical care to the demand for all output produced in the economy—the demand for aggregate output. **Aggregate output** is the total quantity of goods and services produced in the economy during a given time period. A unit of aggregate output is a composite measure of all output in the same sense that a unit of food is a composite measure of all food.

Aggregate demand is the relationship between the average price level of *all* goods and services in the economy and the quantity of *all* goods and services demanded. The **price level** in the economy is a composite measure reflecting the prices of food, housing, clothing, entertainment, medical care, and all other output. In earlier chapters, we talked about the price of a particular product, such as milk, *relative to the prices of other products.* Here we talk about the *average price* of all goods and services produced in the economy.

You are more familiar than you think with these aggregate measures. Media reports of economic growth or an economic slowdown refer to changes in the *gross domestic product,* or *GDP,* the most common measure of aggregate out-

Aggregate output The total quantity of final goods and services produced in an economy during a given time period

Aggregate demand The relationship between the price level in the economy and the quantity of aggregate output demanded, other things held constant

Price level A composite measure reflecting the prices of all goods and services in the economy relative to prices in a base year put. The gross domestic product measures the market value of all final goods and services produced in the United States during a given time period, usually a year. The economy's price level relates to the "cost of living" so often mentioned in news reports. Two common measures of the price level are (1) the *consumer price index,* which tracks changes in the prices of the "basket" of goods and services consumed by the typical family, and (2) the *GDP price index,* which tracks the average price of all items in the gross domestic product. The GDP *price index* is used to "deflate" the gross domestic product—that is, to eliminate any year-to-year growth in GDP due solely to changes in the average price level. After deflation, remaining changes are thus changes in real output. After deflating GDP for price changes, we end up with what is called the *real* gross domestic product.

In Chapter 8, you will learn how the economy's price level is computed. All you need to know now is that the economy's price level reflects average prices in a particular year relative to the average prices in a base year, or a reference year. The price level in the *base year* is set at a benchmark value of 100 and the price levels in other years are expressed relative to the base-year price level. For example, in 1995 the U.S. GDP price index was 108, indicating that the price level that year was 8 percent higher than its value of 100 in the base year of 1992.

Aggregate Demand Curve

The **aggregate demand curve** shows the relationship between the price level in the economy and the aggregate output demanded, other things constant. Exhibit 4 pictures a hypothetical aggregate demand curve, *AD*. The horizontal axis measures aggregate output as real GDP, or real gross domestic product. The vertical axis measures an index of the economy's price level (relative to a 1992 base year price level of 100).

The aggregate demand curve in Exhibit 4 reflects an inverse relationship between the price level in the economy and the quantity of aggregate output demanded. As the price level falls, other things constant, households demand more washers and Wheaties, firms demand more trucks and typewriters, governments demand more computer software and military hardware, and the rest of the world demands more U.S. grain and U.S. aircraft.

The reasons behind this inverse relationship will be examined more closely in later chapters. Here we provide some quick intuition. The quantity of aggregate output demanded depends in part on household *wealth.* Some wealth is usually held in a savings account. A reduction in the price level, other things constant, increases the purchasing power of a given amount of savings. Therefore, households feel richer as the price level decreases, so they increase the quantity of aggregate output demanded. Conversely, an increase in the price level decreases the purchasing power of a given amount of savings. Because households feel poorer when the price level increases, they decrease the quantity of aggregate output demanded.

Among the factors held constant along a given aggregate demand curve are the price levels in other countries as well as the exchange rates between the dollar and foreign currencies. When the U.S. price level falls, U.S. products become cheaper relative to foreign products. Consequently, households, firms, and governments both here and abroad increase their quantity of U.S. output

Aggregate demand curve A curve representing the relationship between the economy's price level and the amount of aggregate output demanded per period of time, other things held constant

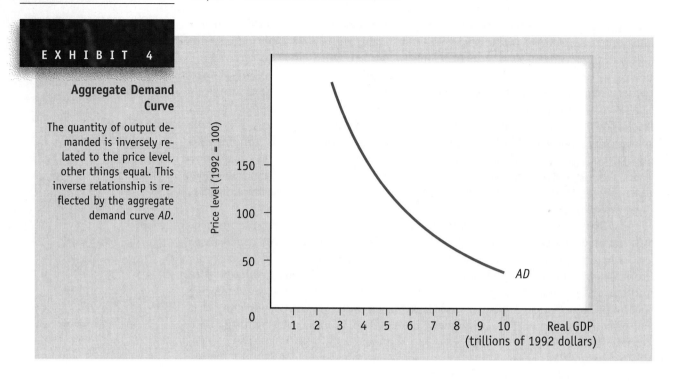

EXHIBIT 4

Aggregate Demand Curve

The quantity of output demanded is inversely related to the price level, other things equal. This inverse relationship is reflected by the aggregate demand curve *AD*.

demanded. On the other hand, a higher U.S. price level makes U.S. goods relatively more costly compared to foreign goods, so the quantity of U.S. output demanded decreases.

Aggregate Supply Curve

Aggregate supply curve   A curve representing the relationship between the economy's price level and the amount of aggregate output supplied per period of time, other things held constant

The **aggregate supply curve** shows the quantity of aggregate output that producers are willing and able to supply at each price level, other things constant. How does the quantity supplied respond to changes in the price level? The upward-sloping supply curve, *AS,* in Exhibit 5 depicts a positive relationship between the price level and the quantity of aggregate output that producers supply, other factors that affect supply held constant. Held constant along an aggregate supply curve are (1) resource owners' willingness and ability to supply resources, (2) the state of technology, and (3) the "rules of the game" in the economy, which provide production incentives. For example, wage rates are assumed to be constant along the supply curve. With wages constant, firms find a higher price level more profitable so they increase the quantity of output supplied. *Whenever the prices firms receive rise more than the cost of production, firms find it profitable to expand output as the price level increases, so the aggregate output supplied varies directly with the economy's price level.*

Equilibrium

The intersection of the aggregate demand and aggregate supply curves determines the equilibrium levels of price and aggregate output in the economy. Exhibit 5 is a rough depiction of aggregate demand and supply in 1995; the equilibrium price level in 1995 was 108 (compared to a price level of 100 in the base year of 1992). The equilibrium real GDP in 1995 was $6.7 trillion (measured in 1992 dollars).

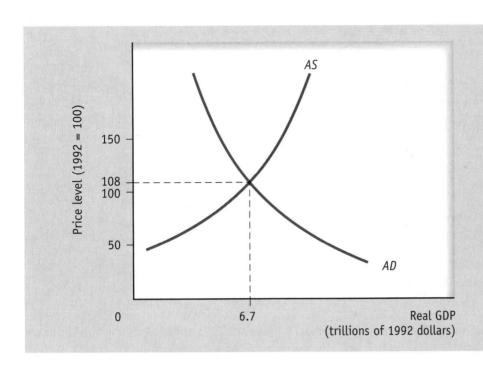

EXHIBIT 5

Aggregate Demand and Supply

The total output of the economy and its price level are determined at the intersection of the aggregate demand and aggregate supply curves. The equilibrium reflects real GDP and the price level for 1995, using 1992 as the base year.

Though employment is not measured directly along the horizontal axis, firms must usually hire more workers to produce more output. So higher levels of real GDP are beneficial because (1) more people in the economy are employed and fewer are unemployed, and (2) more goods and services become available in the economy.

Perhaps the best way to understand aggregate demand and aggregate supply is to apply these tools to the U.S. economy. In the following section we simplify U.S. economic history to review changes in the price and output levels over time.

A SHORT HISTORY OF THE U.S. ECONOMY

The history of the U.S. economy can be crudely divided into three economic eras: (1) prior to and including the Great Depression, (2) after the Great Depression to the early 1970s, and (3) since the early 1970s. The first era was marked by a series of economic recessions and depressions, culminating in the Great Depression of the 1930s. These depressions were often accompanied by a falling price level. The second era was one of generally strong economic growth, with only moderate increases in the price level. The third era was characterized by problems with both unemployment and a higher price level.

The Great Depression and Before

Prior to World War II, the U.S. economy alternated between periods of prosperity and sharp economic decline. As noted earlier, the longest contraction on record occurred between 1873 and 1879, when 80 railroads went bankrupt and most of the steel industry was shut down. During the depression of the 1890s,

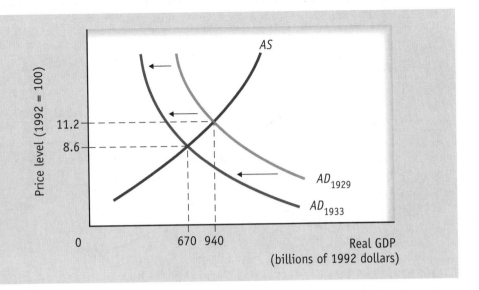

EXHIBIT 6

The Decrease in Aggregate Demand between 1929 and 1933

The Great Depression of the 1930s can be represented by a shift to the left of the aggregate demand curve, from AD_{1929} to AD_{1933}. In the resulting depression, real GDP fell from $940 billion to $670 billion, and the price level dropped from 11.2 to 8.6.

In 1933, the Great Depression left one-quarter of eligible workers without jobs, the highest recorded unemployment rate in the history of the United States.

the unemployment rate topped 18 percent. In October 1929 the stock market crashed, beginning what was to become the deepest economic contraction in our nation's history—the Great Depression of the 1930s.

In terms of aggregate demand and aggregate supply, the Great Depression can be viewed as a shift to the left in the aggregate demand curve, as shown in Exhibit 6. AD_{1929} is the aggregate demand curve in 1929, before the onset of the depression. Real GDP in 1929 was $940 billion (measured in dollars of 1992 purchasing power) and the price level was 11.2, relative to a base-year (1992) price level of 100. (Thus the average price level in 1929 was only 11.2 percent of the level in 1992.) By 1933 the aggregate demand curve had decreased to AD_{1933}.[4] Why did aggregate demand fall so sharply? Though the causes are still debated, grim business expectations, a drop in consumer spending, and a sharp decline in the nation's money supply each contributed to the drop in aggregate demand.

Because of this decline in aggregate demand, both the price level and real GDP declined. Between 1929 and 1933, the price level decreased by 24 percent, from 11.2 to 8.6, and real GDP fell by 29 percent, from $940 billion to $670 billion. As aggregate output declined, the unemployment rate jumped, climbing from about 3 percent in 1929 to 25 percent in 1933, the highest U.S. rate ever recorded.

Prior to the Great Depression, government policy was based primarily on the *laissez-faire* philosophy of Adam Smith. Smith, you may recall, argued in his book *The Wealth of Nations* that if people were allowed to pursue their self-interest in free markets, resources would be guided as if by an "invisible hand" to produce the greatest, most efficient level of aggregate output. Though the U.S. economy had suffered several sharp contractions since the beginning of the

---

4   The aggregate supply curve probably also shifted somewhat during the period, but for simplicity we assume it was unchanged. Most economists agree that the shift in the aggregate demand curve was the dominant factor.

19th century, most economists of the day viewed these as a natural phase of the economy—unfortunate but therapeutic and essentially *self-correcting*.

The Age of Keynes: Between the Great Depression and the Early 1970s

The Great Depression was so severe, however, that it stimulated new thinking about how the economy worked (or didn't work). In 1936, John Maynard Keynes (1883–1946) published *The General Theory of Employment, Interest, and Money,* perhaps the most famous economics book of this century. In it, he argued that aggregate demand was inherently unstable, in part because investment decisions were often guided by the unpredictable "animal spirits" of business expectations. He saw no natural forces operating to ensure that the economy, even if allowed a reasonable time to adjust, would return to a higher level of aggregate output and employment.

Keynes proposed that the government shock the economy out of its depression by increasing aggregate demand. He recommended an *expansionary fiscal policy* to deal with contractions. This could be achieved directly by increasing government spending, or indirectly by cutting taxes to stimulate the primary components of private-sector demand, consumption and investment. Either action would likely result in a government budget deficit. A **government budget deficit** is a flow variable that measures, for a particular period, the amount by which total government expenditures exceed total government revenues.

Government budget deficit A flow variable that measures the amount by which total government expenditures exceed total government revenues in a particular period

To see what Keynes had in mind, imagine federal budget policies that increase aggregate demand in Exhibit 6, shifting the aggregate demand curve to the right, back to its original position. Such a shift would raise the equilibrium level of aggregate output and employment. According to the Keynesian prescription, the miracle drug of government fiscal policy—changes in government spending and taxes—was needed to compensate for what he viewed as the inherent instability of private spending, especially investment. If demand in the private sector declined, Keynes said the government should pick up the slack. We can think of the Keynesian approach as **demand-side economics** because it focused on how changes in aggregate demand could promote full employment. Keynes argued that government spending could be just the tonic to jolt the economy out of its depression and back to health.

Demand-side economics Macroeconomic policy that focuses on changing aggregate demand as a way of promoting full employment and price stability

The U.S. economy languished during the 1930s, but when World War II broke out, huge federal budget deficits financed the war. The war-related demand stimulated output and employment, seeming to confirm the powerful impact that government spending could have on the economy. Immediately after the war, memories of the Great Depression were still vivid. Trying to avoid another depression, Congress approved the *Employment Act of 1946,* which imposed a clear responsibility on the federal government to foster, in the language of the act, "maximum employment, production, and purchasing power." The act also requires the president to report annually on the state of the economy and to appoint a *Council of Economic Advisers,* a three-member group with a professional staff, to provide the president economic advice.

The economy seemed to prosper during the 1950s largely without the help of expansionary fiscal policies. The decade of the 1960s, however, proved to be the *Golden Age of Keynesian economics,* a period when fiscal policymakers thought

Inflation A sustained increase in the economy's average price level

they could "fine-tune" the economy to avoid recessions. During the 1960s, nearly all developed economies of the world enjoyed low unemployment and healthy growth in output with only modest **inflation,** a sustained increase in the price level. In short, the U.S. economy was booming and was on top of the world.

The economy was on such a roll that toward the end of the 1960s, some economists began to think economic fluctuations were a thing of the past. As a sign of the times, the federal government changed the name of a publication called *Business Cycle Developments* to *Business Conditions Digest*. In the early 1970s, however, fluctuations returned with a fury. Worse yet, the problem of recession was compounded by inflation, which increased during the recessions of 1974–75 and 1979–80. Until then, inflation was limited primarily to periods of expansion. Confidence in demand-side policies was shaken, and the expression "fine-tuning" passed from economists' vocabularies. What ended the Golden Age of Keynesian economics?

The Great Stagflation

During the late 1960s, the federal government escalated the war in Vietnam and increased spending on social programs at home. These simultaneous efforts stimulated aggregate demand enough that in 1968 the *inflation rate,* the annual percentage increase in the price level, jumped to 4.1 percent, after averaging only 2.1 percent during the previous decade. Inflation climbed to 4.7 percent in 1969 and to 5.5 percent in 1970. These rates, though not unusual by today's standards, were so alarming at the time that in 1971 President Richard Nixon introduced measures to freeze prices and wages.

Stagflation A contraction, or stagnation, of a nation's output accompanied by inflation

The freeze was eliminated in 1973, about the time that crop failures around the world caused grain prices to soar. To compound these problems, the Organization of Petroleum Exporting Countries (OPEC) pushed up the world price of oil. The resulting reduction in aggregate supply, shown in Exhibit 7 by the shift to the left in the aggregate supply curve, from AS_{1973} to AS_{1975}, created the so-called **stagflation** of the 1970s, meaning a *stag*nation, or contraction, in the economy's aggregate output combined with in*flation,* or a rise, in the economy's price level. Between 1973 and 1975, real GDP declined by about $40 billion, while the price level jumped nearly 20 percent from 35.4 to 42.2. The unemployment rate climbed from 4.9 percent in 1973 to 8.5 percent in 1975.

Stagflation appeared again at the end of the 1970s, partly as a result of another boost in oil prices. Between 1979 and 1980, real GDP declined; at the same time, the price level increased by 9.2 percent. Macroeconomics has not been the same since. Because the problem of stagflation was primarily on the supply side, not on the demand side, the demand-management prescriptions of Keynes seemed ineffective. If government stimulated aggregate demand, this would worsen inflation.

Experience Since 1980

Increasing aggregate supply seemed an appropriate way to combat stagflation, for such a move would both lower inflation and increase output and employment. Attention therefore turned from aggregate demand to aggregate supply.

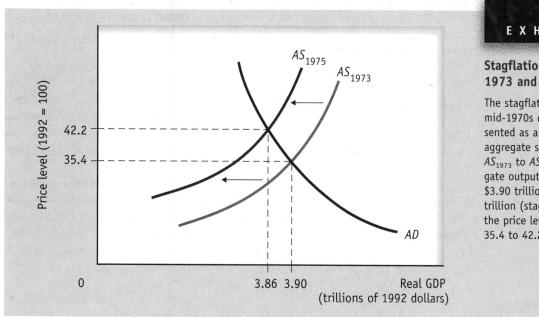

EXHIBIT 7

Stagflation between 1973 and 1975

The stagflation of the mid-1970s can be represented as a reduction in aggregate supply from AS_{1973} to AS_{1975}. Aggregate output fell from $3.90 trillion to $3.86 trillion (stagnation), and the price level rose from 35.4 to 42.2 (inflation).

A key idea behind so-called **supply-side economics** was that the federal government, by lowering tax rates, would increase after-tax earnings and thereby provide resource owners with incentives to increase their supply of labor and other resources. This greater resource supply would increase aggregate supply. According to advocates of the supply-side approach, the increase in aggregate supply would achieve the happy result of increasing real GDP and reducing the price level. But this was easier said than done.

Supply-side economics Macroeconomic policy that focuses on increasing aggregate supply through tax cuts or other changes to increase incentives to produce

To provide economic incentives and thereby increase aggregate supply, in 1981 President Ronald Reagan and Congress cut personal income tax rates by 23 percent. Their hope was that aggregate output would increase enough that the lower tax rate would actually result in more tax revenue. Put another way, the tax cuts would stimulate enough of an expansion of the economic pie that the government's smaller share of the bigger pie would exceed what had been its larger share of the smaller pie.

But before the tax cut went into effect, recession hit and the unemployment rate climbed to nearly 10 percent of the workforce. After the recession, the economy began the longest peacetime expansion on record. During the rest of the 1980s, output grew, unemployment declined, and inflation remained relatively low. During this period, however, the growth in federal spending exceeded the growth in federal tax revenues, so the federal budget deficit swelled.

The annual federal deficit worsened with the onset of the recession in 1990. Even though that recession officially ended in March of 1991, the deficit continued to grow. By 1992 the deficit topped $290 billion. In early 1993, President Bill Clinton pushed through tax increases and budget cuts aimed at reducing budget deficits. By 1994 these measures combined with an improving economy to reverse the growth in deficits, at least temporarily. Still, these annual deficits accumulated as a huge federal debt. **Government debt** is a stock variable that mea-

Government debt A stock variable that measures the net accumulation of prior budget deficits sures the net accumulation of prior deficits. Measured relative to GDP, the federal debt climbed from 34 percent in 1980 to about 80 percent in 1995.

The Twin Deficits

On the international scene, the higher price of imported oil meant Americans were spending more on imports than they received for their exports. The U.S. trade balance deteriorated during the 1980s, with the trade deficit exceeding $140 billion in 1987. These annual trade deficits meant that foreigners were accumulating dollars from their net sales to the United States. Foreigners used this money to invest in U.S. firms, to buy U.S. stocks and bonds, and to buy other U.S. assets such as real estate.

Thus, there were twin deficits during the 1980s and 1990s—the federal budget deficit and the balance-of-trade deficit. The rest of the world took the dollars accumulated because of our trade deficits and lent them back to us, thereby helping us finance the federal budget deficits.

We close with a case study that summarizes the price and output movements in the U.S. economy during the last half century.

CASE STUDY

A Half Century of Price Levels and Real GDP

Location:

To explore *Economic Reports of the President* from previous years, visit the UMSL Library Gopher at the University of Missouri–St. Louis (gopher://gopher.umsl.edu:70/11/library/govdocs/erps). For the *Economic Report* from the most current year, visit the "Office of Management and Budget," as maintained by the Government Printing Office (http://www.access.gpo.gov/omb/index.html).

In Exhibit 8, we trace the combination of the price level and real GDP since 1947. Aggregate demand and aggregate supply curves are shown only for 1947 and 1995, but all the points in the series reflect such intersections. Years of growing real GDP are indicated as blue points and years of declining real GDP as red points. Despite 8 recessions since 1947, the upward long-term trend in the economy is unmistakable: real GDP, measured in 1992 dollars, has climbed from $1.4 trillion in 1947 to $6.7 trillion in 1995—a fivefold increase in production. The price level has risen faster, climbing from only 16.8 in 1947 to 107.7 in 1995—a twelvefold increase.

Because the population is growing all the time, the economy must generate new jobs each year just to employ the additional people entering the labor force. For example, the U.S. population has doubled from 144 million in 1947 to about 265 million in 1995. During that same period the number of people employed in the economy more than doubled, from 57 million in 1947 to 126 million in 1995. Thus, during the last half century, the U.S. economy has been an impressive job machine.

Not only has the number of people working more than doubled, but the average level of education has also increased. Employment of other resources in the economy, especially capital, has also increased sharply. What's more, the level of technology has improved steadily, thanks to developments such as the computer chip, so that machines have become much more sophisticated. The availability of more and higher-quality human capital and physical capital has increased the productivity of each worker, leading to the fivefold increase in real GDP since 1947.

Since real GDP has grown more quickly than the population, real GDP *per capita* has climbed as well, nearly tripling between 1947 and 1995. The United

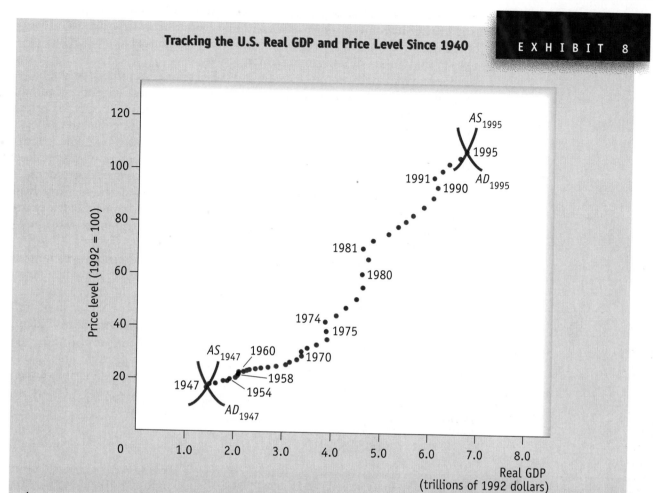

Tracking the U.S. Real GDP and Price Level Since 1940

EXHIBIT 8

As you can see, both the price level and real GDP have increased sharply since 1940. The blue points indicate years of growing real GDP and the red points are years of declining real GDP. Real GDP was about six times higher in 1995 than in 1940, and the price level was twelve times higher.

States is the largest economy in the world and is also among the world leaders in real GDP per capita. U.S. productivity and growth are examined more closely in the next chapter.

Source: *Survey of Current Business* 76 (Jan./Feb. 1996); figures for 1947–1958 are author's estimates based on chain-weighted approach.

A Half Century of Price Levels and Real GDP

continued

CONCLUSION

During the 1960s, Keynesian demand-side policies dominated. When stagflation limited the relevance of demand-side economics, interest shifted to other approaches, including supply-side economics. As we shall see, however, there are more than two sides to this story.

Different economists may have different interpretations of the events discussed in this chapter. At this point there is no dominant macroeconomic theory about how the economy works. Some books lay out the competing theories, leaving it to the reader to choose sides. Rather than describe each theory of the economy in detail, we will attempt to integrate theories whenever possible to find the common ground among them.

Because macroeconomists have no test subjects and cannot rely on serendipitous discoveries, they hone their craft by developing models of the economy and then observing the economy's performance for evidence to support or refute these models. In this sense macroeconomics is largely retrospective, always looking at recent history for hints about which model works best. The macroeconomist is like a traveler with a view only of the road behind, who must find the way using a collection of poorly drawn maps. The traveler must continually check each map (or model) against the landmarks passed, to see if one map appears more consistent with the terrain than the others. Each new batch of information about the economy's performance causes macroeconomists to shuffle through their "maps" to reevaluate their models.

In macroeconomics there is often an emphasis on what can go wrong with the economy. Problems associated with faltering economic growth, unemployment, and inflation capture much of the attention in macroeconomic theory and policy. In the next chapter we begin to "get the lay of the land" by considering in greater detail the record of economic growth in the United States. In the following chapter we discuss two problems confronting the economy: unemployment and inflation. Our approach to growth, unemployment, and inflation at this stage of the textbook will be more descriptive than prescriptive. We must understand how a healthy economy operates before we can consider remedial policies when the economy fails in some important way.

SUMMARY

1. The focus of macroeconomics is the national economy. A standard way of gauging an economy's performance is by measuring the gross domestic product, or GDP—the value of final goods and services produced during a year.

2. Economic fluctuations are the rise and fall of economic activity relative to the economy's long-term growth trend. The economy has two phases: periods of expansion and periods of contraction. Though no two economic fluctuations are the same, contractions average about a year, and expansions average about $3\frac{1}{2}$ years.

3. The aggregate demand curve slopes downward, reflecting a negative, or inverse, relationship between the price level and the quantity of aggregate output demanded. The aggregate supply curve slopes upward, reflecting a positive, or direct, relationship between the quantity of aggregate output supplied and the price level. The intersection of the two curves determines the economy's equilibrium price and output levels.

4. The Great Depression prompted Keynes to argue that the economy was inherently unstable, largely because the components of private spending, particularly business investment, were erratic. Keynes did not believe that depressions were self-correcting. He argued that whenever aggregate demand declined, the federal government should spend more or tax less. His demand-side policies dominated macroeconomics between World War II and the late 1960s.

5. During the 1970s, higher energy prices and global crop failures reduced aggregate supply. The result was stagflation, the troublesome combination of declining production and higher inflation. Demand-side policies appeared less effective in an economy suffering from a reduction in aggregate supply.

6. Supply-side tax cuts in the early 1980s were supposed to increase aggregate supply, thereby increasing output while dampening inflation. But federal spending increased faster than federal revenues, resulting in huge budget deficits, which continued through the 1980s and into the 1990s.

QUESTIONS AND PROBLEMS

1. **(Stocks and Flows)** Wages and profits are considered flows. The money supply and the federal debt are considered stocks. Explain why this is the case. What is the relationship between the federal budget deficit and the federal debt? What is the difference between annual investment and the value of the capital stock?

2. **(Economic Fluctuations)** Describe the various components of the economy's regular fluctuations over time. Since the economy fluctuates, is there no long-term growth?

3. **(Leading Economic Indicators)** Define *leading economic indicators* and give some examples.

4. **(Economic Fluctuations)** Explain why the National Bureau of Economic Research (NBER) identifies the turning points in the economy only after they occur.

5. **(Aggregate Demand and Supply)** Explain why a decrease in the aggregate demand curve results in a lower level of employment, given a fixed aggregate supply.

6. **(Stagflation)** Discuss some causes of the stagflations of 1973 and 1979. What differences are there between these episodes of stagflation and the Great Depression of the 1930s?

7. **(Aggregate Demand and Supply)** Is it possible for prices to fall while production and employment rise? If so, how might this happen?

8. **(Aggregate Demand and Aggregate Supply)** How do aggregate demand and aggregate supply curves differ from the demand and supply curves discussed in Chapter 3?

9. **(Aggregate Demand and Supply)** Use an aggregate demand-supply diagram to predict the change in aggregate output and price under each of the following conditions, *ceteris paribus:*
   a. A decrease in wealth
   b. An increase in the price of OPEC oil
   c. An increase in the level of technology

10. **(Aggregate Demand Curve)** Describe the relationship illustrated by the aggregate demand curve. Why does this relationship hold?

11. **(Supply-Side Economics)** One supply-side measure pushed by the Reagan administration was a cut in income tax rates. Use an aggregate demand-supply diagram to show what the effect was intended to be. Indicate what might happen if such tax cuts also generated a change in aggregate demand.

12. **(Twin Deficits)** What is meant by the "twin deficits"? Why are they related?

13. **(Aggregate Demand)** In Chapter 3, we learned that demand curves have a negative slope because of, among other reasons, a "substitution effect." Does the same kind of "substitution effect" influence the slope of the aggregate demand curve? Explain your answer.

14. **(Aggregate Demand and Aggregate Supply)** Indicate whether each of the following would generate a leftward or rightward shift in the aggregate demand or aggregate supply curve:
   a. A change in the average price level
   b. A decrease in the level of household wealth
   c. An increase in the supply of resources
   d. An increase in wage rates

15. **(Demand-Side Economics)** What is the relationship between demand-side economics and federal budget deficits?

16. **(The Global Economy)** How are economic fluctuations linked across national economies?

17. **(A Half Century of Price Levels and Real GDP)** Real GDP increased sixfold between 1940 and 1995. The price level, however, increased twelvefold during the same period. Does this mean that the rising price level masked an actual decline in output? Why or why not?

18. **(A Half Century of Price Levels and Real GDP)** Why is it important for real GDP to rise over time?

Using the Internet

19. Review the *Summary of Commentary on Current Economic Conditions by Federal Reserve District* (Beige Book), available through the Federal Reserve Bank in Minneapolis (**http://woodrow.mpls.frb.fed.us/economy/beige/beigeb.html**).

   a. Summarize the national economic conditions for the last month. Overall, is the economy healthy? Why or why not?
   b. Go to the district report applicable to your home town. Summarize the economic conditions for the last month. Is the economy in your district healthy? Why or why not?

6

Productivity and Growth

CHAPTER

Two centuries ago, most Americans were employed in agriculture, in jobs where the hours were long and rewards unpredictable. Nonagricultural workers had it no better; they worked from sunrise to sunset for a wage that bought only the bare necessities. There was little intellectual stimulus and little contact with the outside world. A typical worker's home in the year 1790 is described as follows: "Sand sprinkled on the floor did duty as a carpet.... What a stove was he did not know. Coal he had never seen. Matches he had never heard of.... He rarely tasted fresh meat.... If the food of an artisan would now be thought coarse, his clothes would be thought abominable."[1]

The single most important factor determining a nation's standard of living in the long run is the productivity of its resources. A nation prospers by getting more from its resources. Even relatively small increases in the growth of productivity can, if maintained for years, have large effects on living standards. Growing productivity is therefore key to a higher standard of living. In the last two centuries, there has been a tremendous increase in U.S. productivity and in the variety of products available. This growth in productivity has kept the U.S. standard of living ahead of that of nearly every other nation on earth.

For the last two decades, however, U.S. productivity *growth* has slowed down. This slowdown could threaten continued prosperity and will affect the standard of living you experience during your lifetime. In this chapter we consider the sources of economic growth and examine the recent slowdown in productivity growth. We also consider the government's role in fostering economic growth and productivity.

We should note at the outset that, though the *growth* in U.S. productivity has recently lagged behind the historical trend and behind the growth in most other industrial countries, the *level* of productivity still ranks U.S. workers first in the world. So this chapter is more about the growth in productivity than about the level of productivity. The chapter is more about the future economic leadership of the United States than about our current top ranking. Topics discussed in this chapter include:

- Labor productivity
- Slowdown in productivity growth
- Technological change
- Research and development
- Growth policies

---

1   E. L. Bogart, *The Economic History of the United States* (New York: Longmans, Green, and Co., 1912), pp. 157–58.

U.S. PRODUCTIVITY

Economic growth is a complicated process that we do not yet fully understand. Since before Adam Smith inquired into the *Wealth of Nations,* economists have been trying to discover what makes some economies prosper while others founder. Because the capitalist economy is not the product of conscious design, it does not divulge its secrets readily, nor can it easily be manipulated in pursuit of growth objectives. We cannot simply push here and pull there to achieve the desired result. Changing the economy is not like remodeling a home by moving a wall out to expand the kitchen. Since we have no clear copy of the economy's blueprint, we cannot make changes to specifications.

What Is Productivity?

Productivity measures how efficiently resources are employed. In simplest terms, the greater the productivity, the more goods and services can be produced from a given amount of resources. **Productivity** is defined as the ratio of a specific measure of output to a specific measure of input. It usually reflects an average, expressing total output divided by the total input of a specific kind of resource. For example, *labor productivity* is the output per unit of labor and is measured as total output divided by the number of units of labor employed to produce that output.

Productivity The ratio of a specific measure of output to a specific measure of input

We can talk about the productivity of any resource, such as land, labor, or capital. When agricultural products made up the bulk of total output, land productivity, or bushels of grain per acre, was the key measure of economic welfare. Where soil was rocky and barren, people were less prosperous than where soil was fertile and fruitful. Even today, in many developing countries throughout the world, the productivity of the soil determines the standard of living. Industrialization and trade, however, have liberated many economies from dependence on soil quality. Today some of the world's richest economies have little land or have land of poor fertility.

Labor Productivity

Labor is the resource most commonly used in measuring productivity. Why labor? First, it accounts for a relatively large share of the cost of production. Second, the quantity of labor is more easily measured than other inputs, whether we speak of hours per week or full-time workers per year. Statistics about employment and hours worked are more readily available and more reliable than those about other resources used.

The resource most responsible for increasing labor productivity is capital. For example, consider the difference between digging a ditch with your bare hands and digging it with a shovel. Now compare that shovel to a backhoe. The addition of capital makes the digger more productive. As mentioned in Chapter 1, there are two broad categories of capital: human capital and physical capital. *Human capital* is the accumulated knowledge, skill, and experience of the labor force. As individual workers acquire more human capital, their productivity, and hence their income, grows, which is why surgeons earn more than butchers and accountants earn more than file clerks. You are reading this book right now to enhance your human capital. *Physical capital* includes the machines, buildings, roads, airports, communication networks, and other manu-

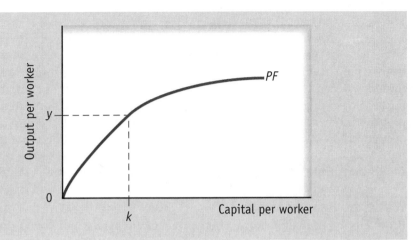

EXHIBIT 1

Per-Worker Production Function

The per-worker production function, *PF,* shows the direct relationship between the amount of capital per worker, *k,* and the output per worker, *y.* The bowed shape of *PF* reflects the law of diminishing marginal returns.

Per-worker production function
The relationship between the amount of capital per worker in the economy and the output per worker

factured creations used to produce goods and services. As a nation accumulates more capital per worker, labor productivity tends to increase and the nation grows richer.

The Per-Worker Production Function

We can express the relation between the amount of capital per worker and the output per worker as an economy's **per-worker production function.** Exhibit 1 shows the relation between the amount of capital per worker, measured along the horizontal axis, and output per worker, or labor productivity, measured along the vertical axis, other things held constant including the level of technology. The production function, *PF,* slopes upward from left to right because an increase in the amount of capital per worker helps each produce more output. For example, a bigger truck makes the truck driver more productive. Any point on the curve shows the relation in the economy between the amount of capital per worker and the output per worker. For example, when there are *k* units of capital per worker, the output per worker in the economy is *y.*

As the quantity of capital per worker increases, the output per worker increases as well but at a diminishing rate, as reflected by movement along the per-worker production function. The diminishing slope of this curve reflects the *law of diminishing marginal returns,* which when applied to capital says that the larger the capital stock per worker already is, the less additional output can be gained by increasing the capital stock per worker still more. For example, adding more trucks to a shipping company initially increases the productivity of drivers. Once all drivers have trucks, however, additional trucks add little or nothing. Thus, given the level of technology and the supply of other resources, the additional gains from more capital accumulation eventually diminish.

Held constant along a per-worker production function is the level of technology prevailing in the economy. Technological change usually improves the *quality* of capital and represents a major source of increasing productivity. For example, an automobile is more efficient than a horse and buggy, a word processor is more efficient than a typewriter, a Lotus spreadsheet is more efficient than a pencil and paper, and a fiber-optics telephone line is more efficient

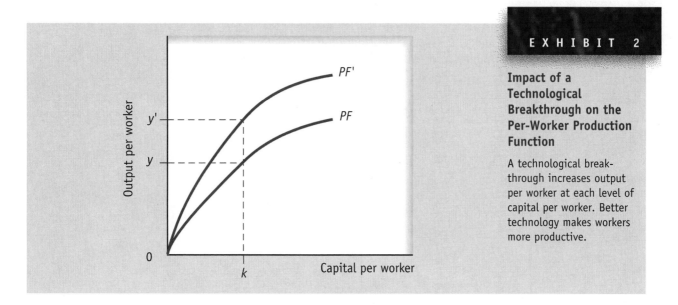

Impact of a Technological Breakthrough on the Per-Worker Production Function

A technological break-through increases output per worker at each level of capital per worker. Better technology makes workers more productive.

than copper wire. Improving technology is reflected in Exhibit 2 by an upward rotation in the per-worker production function from *PF* to *PF'*. As a result of a technological breakthrough, more output is produced at each level of capital per worker. For example, when there are *k* units of capital per worker, the improvement in technology increases the output per worker in the economy from *y* to *y'*.

Thus, two kinds of changes in capital improve worker productivity: (1) an increase in the *quantity* of capital, as reflected by a movement along the curve, and (2) an improvement in the *quality* of capital, as reflected by technological change that rotates the curve upward. Over time, improvements in per-capita output, otherwise known as the standard of living, result from both more capital per worker and better capital per worker.

Long-Term Productivity Growth

Exhibit 3 offers a long-run perspective on growth in the United States, showing annual productivity growth over the last 125 years as measured by real output per work hour. Productivity growth is averaged by decade, beginning with the 1870s and ending with 1990 through 1995. The huge dip in productivity growth during the 1930s due to the Great Depression and the rebound during the 1940s due to World War II are unmistakable. During the entire 125-year period, labor productivity grew by an average of 2.1 percent per year. This may not seem like much, but because of the power of compounding, output per work hour grew about 1,240 percent during the 125-year span. To put this in perspective, suppose that in 1870 a roofing worker could shingle a roof in a day. If roofers experienced a 1,240 percent increase in their labor productivity, the 1995 version of that worker could shingle 12.4 *more* roofs in a day.

Over long periods, small differences in productivity growth rates have significant impacts on the economy's ability to produce and, therefore, on the standard of living. For example, if productivity growth had averaged 1.1 percent instead of 2.1 percent, output per work hour since 1870 would have increased by only 290 percent, not 1,240 percent. On the other hand, if productivity had increased an

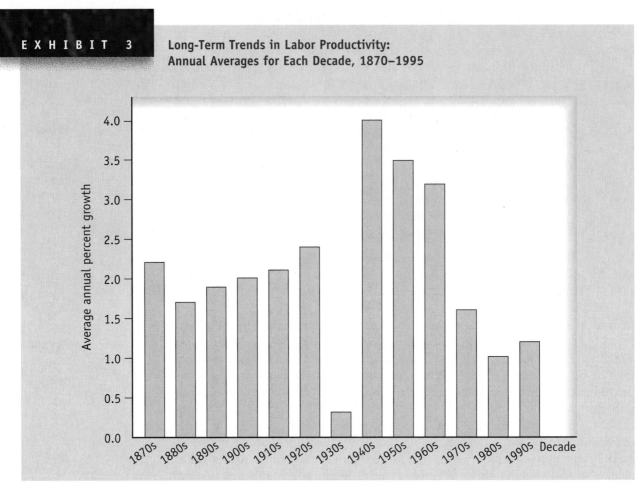

EXHIBIT 3

Long-Term Trends in Labor Productivity: Annual Averages for Each Decade, 1870–1995

Sources: Prior to 1950, Angus Maddison, *Phases of Capitalist Development* (New York: Oxford University Press, 1982); 1950 to 1989, *Economic Report of the President,* February, 1996; since 1960, figures based on chain-weighted derivation of labor productivity. Figures for 1990s are through 1995.

average of 3.1 percent per year, output per work hour since 1870 would have increased by 4,440 percent! The wheels of progress seem to grind slowly but they grind very fine, and the cumulative effect can be awesome.

Higher productivity can easily make up for output losses during recessions. For example, an economy with an average annual growth in productivity of 2.0 percent instead of 1.5 percent can in a decade increase output by more than $400 billion, which can more than make up for the output lost during three typical recessions. This cumulative power of productivity growth is why economists now focus less on short-term fluctuations in output and more on long-term growth.

The Recent Slowdown in Productivity Growth

You can see in Exhibit 3 the decade-by-decade slowdown in the growth of productivity since the 1940s. By breaking the data down into time periods other than decades, we can better examine productivity since World War II. The growth rate of output per labor hour declined from an average of 3.0 percent per year between 1948 and 1972 to 1.2 percent per year between 1972 and 1995. *Thus, the rate of growth in labor productivity since 1972 has been less than half what it was during the quarter century following World War II and, except for the Great Depression, less than it was in any decade during the previous century.*

Such a slowdown in labor productivity growth usually means the standard of living also grows more slowly. For example, between 1948 and 1972, median family income adjusted for inflation more than doubled. But between 1972 and 1995, real median family income grew only about 5 percent. Make no mistake, workers in the United States are still the most productive in the world, but the slowdown in recent productivity growth has narrowed our world lead. The long-run implications of the recent slowdown are serious. If, during the next century, productivity were to grow by only 1.2 percent (the average between 1972 and 1995) instead of 2.1 percent (the average for the last 125 years), output per worker would increase only 230 percent instead of 700 percent.

WHY THE SLOWDOWN IN LABOR PRODUCTIVITY GROWTH?

A thorough explanation of the recent slowdown in productivity growth should not only account for the overall trend from period to period but also explain differences in productivity growth across economic sectors. No one has yet developed such an explanation. All we have are possible reasons for the slowdown. Nonetheless, possible contributors to the slowdown are worth discussing because they give us a better understanding of what factors influence productivity.

Factors that economists believe may have contributed to the slowdown in productivity growth include (1) reduced growth in capital formation, (2) changes in the labor force, (3) the changing composition of output, (4) an expanding role of government, (5) higher federal budget deficits, and (6) reduced spending on research and development. This last possibility is potentially so important that it warrants extensive discussion. But let's begin by examining the first five factors.

Rate of Capital Formation

As already noted, the productivity of labor depends in part on the amount of capital supporting each worker. Increases in the ratio of capital to labor—what's called capital *deepening*—added about 0.8 percentage points per year to the growth in productivity since 1972. Prior to 1972, capital deepening contributed a tiny bit more to productivity growth. So a reduction in the contribution of capital deepening explains only a tiny part of the post-1972 slowdown in productivity growth. Investment spending as a percentage of GDP increased beginning in 1993, and this trend should pay off with more capital deepening for the rest of the decade.

Changes in the Labor Force

An important component in the production function is the quality of labor—the skill level and education level of workers. Some economists argue that changes in the composition of the labor force have contributed to the decline in productivity growth. Individuals just entering the labor force are typically less productive because they have fewer skills and less work experience than those already in the labor force. As long as the proportion of new workers remains constant over time, their presence should not affect productivity measures. But if the share of employment accounted for by new workers increases, as it has since 1966, then productivity growth may suffer. Moreover, the skill level of immigrants coming to this country since 1970 has on average been lower than it was prior to 1970. The average job experience of workers has declined slightly in the last three decades, slightly reducing the average productivity growth.

But the increase in the number of less experienced workers has been offset by the increase in the years of education of the work force as a whole. In the last three decades, the average educational attainment of the work force has increased by about two years. New entrants to the labor force are much better educated than workers retiring from the labor force. The percentage of high school graduates enrolling in college after graduation climbed from 49 percent in 1980 to 62 percent in 1992.

So work force quality has declined because of an increase in the proportion of workers with less experience. But work force quality has increased because of the increased quantity of workers' education. On net, changes in work force quality appear to bear little or no responsibility for the post-1972 slowdown in productivity growth.

Changing Composition of Output

Average productivity will decline if workers shift from sectors where substantial capital formation and technological change take place to sectors where capital formation and technological change are less important. Labor productivity can be increased more easily in the goods-producing sector (manufacturing, construction, and farming), where machines can be readily introduced, than in the service sector (government, education, transportation, finance, health care, and retailing), where machinery is less important. For example, there are more opportunities for technological change when producing automobiles than when producing haircuts.

Since 1948, productivity has grown by an average of 2.8 percent in the goods-producing sector but by only 1.4 percent in the service sector. The goods-producing sector's share of total employment, however, has declined from about 40 percent in 1948 to about 20 percent today. *The service sector's growing share of the labor force has lowered the growth rate of productivity in the economy as a whole.*

Most economists who have explored the issue agree that the shift from high-productivity to low-productivity sectors accounts for some of the slowdown. Some claim the shift is responsible for more than half the decline. Still other economists argue that labor productivity in the service sector is frequently underestimated because output in that sector is often poorly defined and poorly measured. For example, computer technology has increased productivity sharply in the banking industry, but the federal government does not compute labor productivity in this sector.

Increased Role of Government

Another factor cited as a source of slower productivity growth is the more pervasive role of government in the economy, both in its regulatory function and more generally in its impact on the direction of economic activity. Government regulation grew sharply between the mid-1960s and the late 1970s. In one 3-year period, five major regulatory bodies were established by the federal government, including the Environmental Protection Agency and the Occupational Safety and Health Administration. Some regulation may have a positive effect on worker productivity. For example, better worker health and a safer work environment can increase productivity and reduce worker turnover. But other regulations may divert resources from direct production and thereby reduce productivity. For example, requirements for greater safety in coal mines have been cited as a source of lackluster productivity in that industry. The control of toxic emissions, the improvement of safety in the workplace, and the like may ultimately increase the quality of life in the nation, but they add little to output as measured by GDP per worker.

Since the late 1970s, however, many industries—including trucking, airlines, and telecommunications, which had been heavily regulated by the government—have been deregulated. So while some sectors of the economy have become more regulated since 1972, other sectors have become less regulated.

One way to view government's role in the economy in a wider context is to look at the relationship between economic growth and the share of GDP that goes to the federal government. During the half century prior to 1929, the federal government's role was relatively modest compared to the half century since 1948. But during both periods real GDP grew by about the same amount. Output per worker grew slightly more during the more recent half century. The point is that *it is too simplistic to conclude that a growing role of government is a major obstacle to economic growth and productivity.*

Huge Budget Deficits

In his first State of the Union address, President Clinton argued that large federal deficits were responsible for the declining growth in labor productivity. He said that to finance the deficits, the federal government must borrow huge amounts, thereby "crowding out" other borrowers who could invest in physical capital, human capital, and research and development. By raising tax rates and reducing the growth rate in government spending, Clinton proposed reducing the federal deficit as a way of increasing productivity and growth.

Despite President Clinton's assertion, the link between federal deficits and labor productivity growth remains unclear. For example, between 1973 and 1981, federal deficits averaged less than $50 billion per year; between 1982 and 1995, federal deficits averaged $200 billion per year. But during both periods, labor productivity averaged about the same. Nobody would argue that huge deficits boost labor productivity, especially over the long term, but we cannot simply attribute the recent slowdown in productivity growth to higher federal deficits.

Ironically, despite the growing federal deficits, government investments in roads, bridges, and airports—so-called *public capital*—has declined. In 1970, the value of the nation's public capital stock was about 50 percent compared to GDP; this figure has declined to about 40 percent today. Some argue that declining investment in the public infrastructure serves as a drag on productivity growth. For example, the failure to invest sufficiently in airports and in the air traffic control system has resulted in congested airports and flight delays.

Perhaps the single most important contributor to productivity growth is technological change. In the next section we examine research and development, the fuel for technological change.

RESEARCH AND DEVELOPMENT

Simon Kuznets, who won the Nobel Prize in part for his analysis of the sources of economic growth, claimed that technological change and the ability to apply this change to all aspects of production were the driving forces behind modern economic growth in developed market economies. Kuznets argued that changes in the *quantities* of labor and capital accounted for only one-tenth of the increase in economic growth. Nine-tenths of the increase was a result of improvements in the *quality* of inputs.

Basic and Applied Research

A major contributor to productivity growth has been an improvement in the quality of human and physical capital. In terms of human capital, this quality improvement results from more education and more job training. In terms of physical capital, quality improvement results from better technology embodied in this capital. For example, because of extensive investments in cellular transmission, new satellites, and fiber optics technology, labor productivity in the telecommunications industry increased by an average of 5.5 percent per year in the 1970s and 1980s.

Improvements in technology arise from scientific discovery, which is the result of research. We distinguish between basic research and applied research. **Basic research,** the search for knowledge without regard to how that knowledge will be used, is a first step toward technological advancement. In terms of economic growth, however, scientific discoveries are meaningless until they are implemented—which requires applied research. **Applied research** seeks to answer particular questions or to apply scientific discoveries to the development of specific products. Since technological breakthroughs may or may not have commercial possibilities, basic research has less of an immediate payoff than applied research. But basic research likely yields a higher rate of return to society as a whole than does applied research.

If a technological breakthrough is thought to have economic value in the marketplace, it becomes *embodied* in new capital. Such technological innovation increases the productivity of other resources by permitting them to be combined in more efficient ways, so total output is increased. *From the wheel to assembly-line robots, capital embodies the fruits of scientific inquiry and serves as the primary engine for economic growth.*

Expenditures for Research and Development

Since technological advances spring from the process of research and development (R&D), expenditures on R&D represent one measure of the economy's efforts to improve productivity through technological discovery. One way to track R&D activity is to measure these expenditures relative to GDP. Exhibit 4 shows R&D expenditures in the United States as a percent of GDP since 1960. Federally supported R&D is distinguished from private R&D, which consists primarily of industry outlays plus a small amount by the private non-

---

Net Bookmark

Has a failure to invest sufficiently in air-traffic control systems harmed the U.S. economy through congested airports and flight delays? For different perspectives, visit the National Air Traffic Controllers Association (http://www.natca.org/) and the Center for Advanced Aviation System Development (CAASD), sponsored by the Federal Aviation Administration (http://www.caasd.org/). Also visit the Office of Airline Information (http://www.bts.gov/), part of the Department of Transportation's Bureau of Transportation Statistics (BTS), for airline "on-time statistics" among airports.

Basic research The search for knowledge without regard to how that knowledge will be used

Applied research Research that seeks to answer particular questions or to apply scientific discoveries to the development of specific products

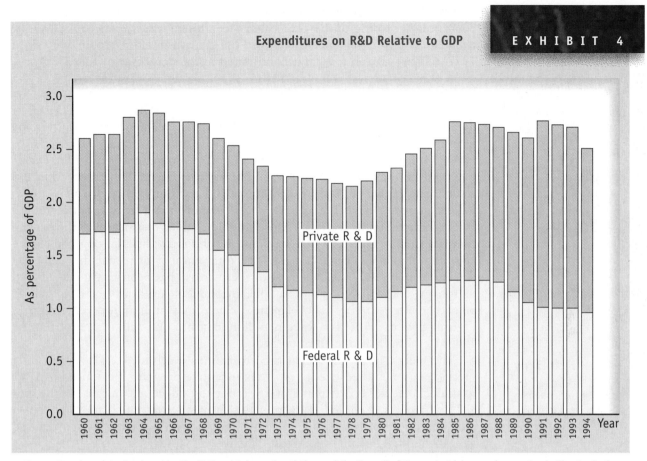

Expenditures on R&D Relative to GDP   E X H I B I T   4

Source: Based on data developed by the National Science Foundation and the Council of Economic Advisers and appearing in Chapter 3 of the *Economic Report of the President,* February 1995.

profit sector. Federally supported R&D (on the bottom of each bar) fell from a high of nearly 2 percent of GDP in 1964 to about 1 percent most recently. Private R&D (on the top of each bar) has grown slightly from about 1 percent of GDP between 1960 and 1972 to about 1.5 percent most recently.

As you can see from Exhibit 4, total R&D expenditures relative to GDP dipped in the 1970s, bottoming out about 1978. Some economists believe that the slowdown during the 1970s proved costly to the economy in terms of forgone growth opportunities. This dip was due largely to the drop in federal outlays. Research suggests, however, that a dollar of federally supported R&D contributes less to economic growth than does a dollar of company-supported R&D,[2] perhaps because most federally supported R&D has military objectives. Thus, although the decline in federal R&D may have contributed to the slowdown in productivity growth during the 1970s, the impact would have been greater had the decline in R&D occurred primarily in the private sector.

In dollar terms, U.S. investment in R&D was most recently greater than that in Japan, Germany, and France combined. Even relative to GDP, the

---

2   See, for example, Zvi Griliches, "Productivity, R&D, and Basic Research at the Firm Level in the 1970s," *American Economic Review* 76 (March 1986): pp. 141–54.

United States and Japan were tied for first place among major industrialized countries. According to the U.S. Labor Department, investment in R&D contributed about 0.2 percentage points to the growth in labor productivity since 1972, which was about what it contributed in the decade prior to 1972.

Patents and Productivity

The fruit of R&D is inventions and technological breakthroughs. Did the slowdown in R&D expenditures during the 1970s influence inventive activity? One measure of inventive activity is the number of patents granted by the U.S. Patent Office, the agency established by Congress to grant inventors the exclusive rights to their discoveries. In fact, there is a strong relation both within and across firms between R&D expenditures and the number of patents granted. Patents granted per year fell during the 1970s, dropping from about 75,000 in 1971 to about 50,000 by 1979. More troubling still is that nearly all the decline came in patents granted to U.S. corporations and individuals (as opposed to foreign corporations and individuals). The total number of patents has since increased to over 100,000, but most of the increase has been in patents granted to foreign corporations. For example, there has been sharp growth in U.S. patents granted to the major Japanese electronics and motor vehicle firms. Overall, patents granted to foreigners climbed from one-fifth of the total in the 1960s to more than one-third today.

The federal government has tried to stimulate private R&D by providing special investment tax incentives. A tax incentive program introduced in 1981 to stimulate new R&D expenditures was not cost effective.[3] Because of the special tax benefits accorded R&D outlays, firms became much more liberal in their definitions of R&D. The incentive program was substantially restructured in 1989 and has become more cost effective.

The most dramatic technological development in recent years has been the information revolution powered by the computer chip. The following case study considers the impact of computers on economic growth.

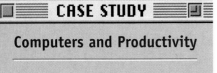

CASE STUDY
Computers and Productivity

The first commercially sold computer was introduced over 40 years ago. Since then, the price of computing power has dropped to less than 0.0005 of what it was when first introduced. So the computing capability that cost $10,000 in the mid-1950s costs less than $5 today.

U.S. companies are way ahead of nearly all other countries in high-technology industries ranging from software to biotechnology. And personal computers are moving beyond word processing and spreadsheet analysis to help people work together. For example, design engineers in California can use the Internet to try out new ideas with marketers in New York, cutting development time in half. Sales representatives on the road can use laptop computers to log orders and provide customer service. U.S. insurance companies can coordinate data entry done as far away as Europe to handle claims more efficiently. Computers not only improve the quality and safety in the automobile and airline industries but also increase the versatility of machines, which can be reprogrammed for differ-

---

3   Edwin Mansfield, "The R&D Tax Credit and Other Technology Policy Issues," *American Economic Review* 76 (May 1986): pp. 190–94.

ent tasks. Research suggests that workers who use computers on the job earn 10 to 15 percent higher wages than similar workers who don't.

It's been said that we can see computers everywhere except in the productivity statistics. Why hasn't U.S. productivity shot up in response to the growing use of computers? If all the direct and related contributions of computers are included, the average annual growth contribution of computers from 1987 to 1993 comes to one-half a percentage point. To be sure, this represents a substantial addition to growth, but it's disappointingly small for a technology that seems to hold so much promise.

Computers and Productivity
continued

Location:

Half of the Americans using computers are under 17 years of age. Hence, designing learning tools to take advantage of this competency with computers is itself a growing industry. Visit Cooperative Media Group, a developer of educational and entertainment new media (http://www.cmg.com/).

One problem is that despite all we hear about the computer revolution, computers are *not yet* everywhere. For example, though spending on computers represents a growing fraction of all investment, only about 2 percent of the U.S. capital stock consists of computers and peripheral equipment. In contrast, previous technological revolutions captured a much larger share of investment. In 1890, for example, railroads accounted for about one-fifth of the U.S. capital stock. Another problem is that many of the benefits of computers affect unmeasured attributes of output. For example, computers improve communications among workers with links such as e-mail, and enhance consumer convenience with devices such as automatic teller machines.

An optimistic view is that the big productivity gains from information technology are still to come as people learn to use computers more effectively and as fresh applications are developed. Whenever new technologies are introduced, productivity often falls initially as workers try to master new and unfamiliar skills. But over time, experience starts paying off. What's more, the technology itself improves and become more user friendly.

Of the 100 million Americans who used computers at home, school, or work in 1995, half were 17 years of age or younger. As these computer-literate people enter the workforce, the rates of return to computer applications should improve. (As a sign of the times, Taco Bell models its cash registers after Nintendo.) According to this view, change takes time. For example, Thomas Edison designed the first electrical power plant in 1882, but it took another four decades before U.S. companies converted from steam to electricity.

But critics of this sunnier view note that there is no evidence that the rates of return to computers have increased and that there has been little recent increase in the growth trend of computers as a fraction of the capital stock. Even in the most optimistic scenario, computers are expected to add about one percentage point to the annual growth rate of U.S. real GDP.

Sources: Michael Meyer, "Considering the PC Paradox," *Newsweek*, 27 February 1995, pp. 48–49; S. D. Oliner and D.E. Sichel, "Computers and Output Growth Revisited: How Big Is the Puzzle?" *Brookings Papers on Economic Activity*, No. 2 (1994): pp. 273–317; and Alan B. Krueger, "How Computers Have Changed the Wage Structure: Evidence from Microdata, 1984–1989," *Quarterly Journal of Economics*, February 1994, pp. 33–60.

One final thought before turning to other matters. Productivity growth since 1972 appears slow compared to the high growth rates immediately following World War II. But many economists believe that the rapid growth between 1948 and 1972 occurred because the economy was catching up after the crushing depression. Such growth, they say, should not be used as the benchmark against which to judge current growth rates. Between 1972 and 1995, U.S. productivity, though still below the historical average, was close to growth rates experienced in other industrial economies. What's more, productivity growth rates during the 1990s were slightly above rates for the 1980s. The U.S. economy is considered the world's most competitive, and Americans continue to enjoy the highest standard of living in the world.

OTHER ISSUES OF TECHNOLOGY AND GROWTH

In this section we consider some other issues of technology and growth, beginning with the government's ability to identify and nurture technologies of the future.

Industrial Policy

In recent years, policymakers have debated whether or not the federal government should become more involved in shaping the nation's technological future. One concern is that technologies of the future often require huge sums to develop and implement, sums that individual firms cannot always raise. Another concern is that some technological breakthroughs benefit other industries, but the firm that develops the breakthrough may not be in a position to reap benefits from these spillover effects, so individual firms may underinvest in such research. The proposed solution is more government involvement.

Industrial policy The policy that government, using taxes, subsidies, and regulations, should nurture the industries and technologies of the future to give domestic industries an advantage over foreign competition

Industrial policy is the idea that government, using taxes, subsidies, and regulations, should nurture the industries and technologies of the future to give domestic industries an advantage over foreign competition. The objective is to secure a leading role for domestic industry in the future. One example of European industrial policy is Airbus Industrie, a four-nation aircraft consortium. With an estimated $20 billion in aid from European governments, the aircraft producer has taken business away from McDonnell-Douglas and has become Boeing's main challenger. When Airbus seeks business orders around the world, it can draw on its government backing to promise special terms, such as landing rights at key European airports and an easing of regulatory constraints. U.S. producers have no such ties to government and therefore no such goodies to offer. Industrial policy is discussed in the following case study.

CASE STUDY

Picking Technological Winners

U.S. industrial policy over the years has been aimed at creating the world's most advanced military industry. For example, the Defense Advanced Research Projects Agency tried to help develop new technologies, such as computer graphics, semiconductors, and computer-controlled machine tools. With the demise of the Soviet Union, however, defense technologies have become less important. Some argue that U.S. industrial policy should shift from a military to a civilian focus. President Bill Clinton promised during his campaign that he would establish a powerful agency to help finance and coordinate R&D for what he called "cutting-edge products and technologies." He also proposed bringing together businesses, universities, and laboratories to carry out R&D in civilian technologies.

Skeptics wonder whether the same government that has brought us huge deficits should be trusted to identify emerging technologies and to pick the firms that will lead the way. Critics of industrial policy believe the market is a better allocator of scarce resources than the government. For example, the costly attempt of European governments to develop the supersonic transport did not work out. As another example, in the early 1980s the U.S. government spent $1 billion to help military contractors try to develop a high-speed computer circuit. But Intel, a company receiving no federal support, was the first to develop the circuit.

There is also concern that an industrial policy would evolve into another government giveaway program. Rather than going to the most promising technologies, the money and the competitive advantages would be awarded based on political influence. Critics also wonder how wise it is to sponsor corporate research when beneficiaries may share their expertise with foreign companies and may even build factories abroad. Sematech, for example, is a U.S. government–backed alliance of companies in the semiconductor industry. One of its members, Advanced Micro Devices, teamed up with a Japanese company to make semiconductors in Japan.

Professor Gene Grossman of Princeton University, after surveying the available evidence on industrial policy, concluded that the government's track record at backing winners has been poor. He says there are better alternatives to industrial policy, such as tax incentives for all R&D, that do not require the targeting of specific industries. Many economists would prefer to let IBM, Hewlett-Packard, or some upstart gamble on the important technologies of the future.

Sources: Steven Greenhouse, "The Calls for Industrial Policy Grow Louder," *New York Times,* 19 July 1992, p. 5; Gene Grossman, "Promoting Industrial Activities: A Survey of Recent Arguments and Evidence," *OECD Economic Studies* (Spring 1990): pp. 87–125; and Richard Rapaport, "The Playground of Big Science," *Wired,* October 1995, pp. 152–59, 215.

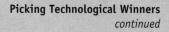

Picking Technological Winners
continued

Location:

For information about the Advanced Research Projects Agency (ARPA), the central research and development organization for the Department of Defense, visit "ARPA" (http://www.arpa.mil/). For information about Intel Corporation, visit "Welcome to Intel!" (http://www.intel.com/). For information about Sematech, a consortium of American semiconductor manufacturers, visit "Sematech" (http://www.sematech.org/public/home.html).

Does Technological Change Lead to Unemployment?

Technological change can sometimes free resources for new uses. For example, now that fiber-optics technology has become the most efficient means of communicating, the copper from existing telephone lines becomes available for other uses. In fact, AT&T controls most of the world's known stock of copper in the form of existing wires and cables that will gradually be replaced by fiber-optics cables.

Technological change often reduces the number of workers needed to produce a given amount of output. Consequently, some observers fear that new technology will throw people out of work and lead to higher unemployment. True, technological change can lead to unemployment in some industries, and can thus create dislocations as workers must find new jobs. But technology can also increase production and employment by making products more affordable. For example, the introduction of the assembly line made automobiles more af-

New fiber-optic cables, designed to handle a high amount of traffic and capable of delivering high-quality messages, are replacing traditional copper cables.

fordable to the average household, stimulating production and employment in that industry. Even in industries where some workers are displaced by machines, those who keep their jobs are more productive. As long as wants are unlimited, displaced workers will usually find jobs producing other goods and services demanded in a growing economy. More generally, as labor productivity rises, so do wages and, ultimately, consumption.

Although data from the 19th century are sketchy, there is no evidence that the unemployment rate is any higher today than it was 125 years ago. Since then, worker productivity has increased more than twelvefold and the length of the average work week has dropped more than one-third. Though technological change may displace some workers in the short run, the long-run benefits include higher real incomes on average and more leisure—in short, a higher standard of living.

If technological change causes more unemployment, then the slowdown in productivity growth that has occurred over the last two decades should have resulted in lower unemployment. But, in fact, the unemployment rate has drifted up during the last two decades when compared to the high-productivity growth decades of the 1950s and 1960s. And if technological change causes more unemployment, then unemployment rates should be lower where modern technology has not yet been introduced, such as in developing countries. But, in fact, unemployment rates are typically much higher in such countries, and those who are employed there earn relatively little because they are not very productive.

Again, there is no question that technological change often creates job dislocations in the short run, as workers scramble to adjust to a new environment. Some workers with specialized skills made obsolete by technology may not be able to find a job that pays as well as the one they lost. These temporary dislocations are one price of progress. Over time, however, most displaced workers find other jobs, often in new industries created by technological change.

Output Per Capita

So far we have focused on growth resulting from increased labor productivity—that is, growth achieved by getting more output from each hour worked. The growth in the economy depends on both the growth in labor productivity and in the quantity of labor. The economy may grow by employing more workers, by getting more hours from the existing work force, or both. *Output per capita* captures the combined effects of growing productivity and a growing workforce. If the workforce grows faster than the population as a whole, output per capita can increase faster than productivity per worker.

Exhibit 5 presents the average growth in *real GDP per capita* between 1948 and 1995 for the United States and the six other leading industrial countries. (These seven are known as the *G-7 countries*.) In keeping with what we have learned about the growth rate in productivity, the period is divided into two intervals: 1948 to 1972 and 1972 to 1995. As you can see, during the first interval, the U.S. growth rate trailed all the others. The 2.4 percent U.S. annual growth rate between 1948 and 1972 was only about half the 4.7 percent average for the six other countries listed. Why was the U.S. rate so relatively low? With the exception of Canada, the six other developed countries were starting from low levels of output and productivity after being ravaged by World War II, so it was easier for these countries to show an improvement.

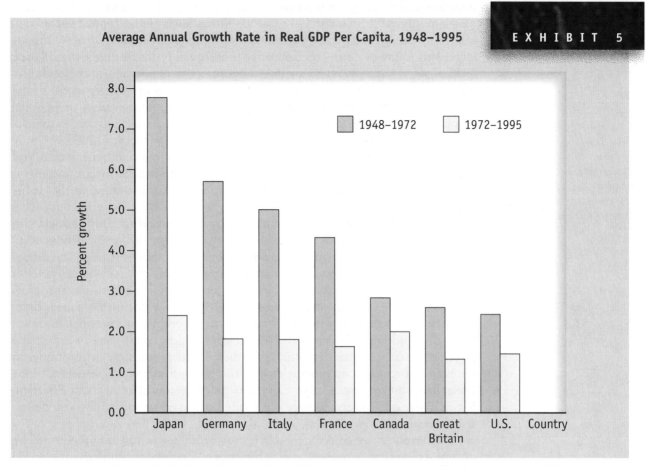

Average Annual Growth Rate in Real GDP Per Capita, 1948–1995

EXHIBIT 5

Sources: Organization for Economic Cooperation and Development; *Economic Report of the President,* February 1996.

During the more recent period, the U.S. growth rate was still lower than that in most other countries listed, but the average difference was smaller. The U.S. annual growth rate of 1.4 percent between 1972 and 1995 was only 0.4 percentage points below the 1.8 percent average growth rate for the six other countries. In fact, between the periods 1948–1972 and 1972–1995, the U.S. annual growth rate declined from 2.4 percent to 1.4 percent, but growth rates for the six other countries declined on average from 4.7 percent to 1.8 percent. Japan's growth rate fell by two-thirds, from 7.8 percent to 2.4 percent, between those two periods.

Note that between 1972 and 1995 the U.S. growth rate of GDP per capita averaged about 1.4 percent per year, while the growth rate in output per labor hour averaged only 1.2 percent per year. What explains the difference? *During that period, the growth in employment exceeded the growth in population, so output per capita grew faster than output per labor hour.*

Do Economies Converge?

How could it be that the United States, with one of the highest levels of productivity in the world, is also among the countries where productivity is growing least rapidly? Some observers suggest that this is to be expected. The slow-growing leader, fast-growing follower pattern may simply reflect the dynamics of technological "catch-up." Leader countries such as the United States will find their productivity growth limited by the rate of creation of new knowledge. But follower countries can grow more quickly by closing some of their technological gap—by, for example, buying computers when they previously had none. Until 1995, the United States, which makes up just 5 percent of the world's population, accounted for the majority of home purchases of personal computers. But home computer sales in Europe and Asia-Pacific are now taking off and are expected to nearly double U.S. sales by the year 2000.[4]

Convergence A theory that economies around the world will grow more alike over time, with poorer countries catching up with richer countries

The **convergence** theory argues that economies around the world will grow more alike, with poorer countries catching up with richer countries. It is easier to copy new technology once it is developed than to develop that technology in the first place. Countries that start out far behind have the advantage of being able to increase their productivity by copying existing technology. But economies that are already using the latest technology can boost productivity only with a steady stream of technological breakthroughs.

The convergence theory says that less developed countries will grow faster than more developed countries. The empirical evidence for this theory is mixed. On one hand, among the most developed countries of the world, there has been convergence since 1950. Productivity levels in countries such as Japan, Germany, and France have grown closer to the U.S. level.[5] Newly industrialized East Asian countries have invested heavily in technology acquisition and human resources and are quickly closing the gap with the world leaders. On the other hand, since 1950 some of the very poorest countries of Latin America, Africa, Asia, and Eastern Europe have failed to close the gap with more developed countries.

One reason why convergence may not occur is the vast differences in the quality of human capital across countries. Whereas technology is indeed portable, the knowledge, skill, and training often required to take advantage of that technology are not. Countries with a high level of human capital can make up for other shortcomings. For example, the physical capital stock in Japan and Germany was mostly destroyed during World War II. But the two countries retained enough of their well-educated and highly skilled labor force to become industrial leaders again in little more than a generation.[6] Some countries simply do not have the human capital needed to identify and absorb new technology. And some countries lack the stable macroeconomic environment and the established institutions needed to help nurture economic growth.

CONCLUSION

The disappointing growth rate over the last 20 years, and the resulting anxieties that so many Americans have about their own and their children's economic

---

4   See Jim Carlton, "Foreign Markets Give PC Markets a Hearty Hello," *The Wall Street Journal,* 15 September 1995.
5   See the discussion by Howard Pack, "Endogenous Growth Theory: Intellectual Appeal and Empirical Shortcomings," *Journal of Economic Perspectives* 8 (Winter 1994): pp. 55–72.
6   Further issues of economic development are discussed in the final chapter, entitled "Developing and Transitional Economies."

prospects, place the spotlight on efforts to increase the economy's growth and productivity. The productivity of an economy depends on the availability and quality of various resources, the level of technology, methods for organizing production, the energy and enterprise of entrepreneurs and workers, and a variety of institutional and social factors that affect the incentives and behavior of various resource suppliers. These factors interact to determine the level and growth of productivity.

The factors that contribute to productivity are strongly correlated with one another. A country with low productivity will probably be deficient in the quality of its work force, in the quantity or quality of its physical capital, and in the level of its technology. Similarly, a country with high productivity is likely to excel in all measures.

If U.S. productivity grows at a rate of 2.1 percent per year, which has been the long-term trend, output per worker will double every 33 years, so 100 years from now each hour of labor will produce about eight times more real goods and services than it produces today. But if our productivity growth averages 1.2 percent per year, the average between 1972 and 1995, output per worker will double only every 58 years; 100 years from now each hour of labor will yield only 3.3 times what it produces today. In the long run, small differences in productivity growth will determine whether the United States remains an economic leader or becomes a second-rate economy.

The growth in the economy depends on both the growth in labor productivity and in the quantity of labor. The growth in the quantity of labor in the United States is expected to be somewhat slower in the future than it has been in the past two decades, primarily because of a decline in the growth of the working-age population. On balance, the economy over the next decade should grow about as fast as it has over the past two decades, with a modest increase in the growth of labor productivity offsetting some of the decline in growth of the working-age population.

One final point bears repeating: Though the *growth* in U.S. productivity has in recent decades lagged behind the growth in other industrial countries, our *level* of productivity is still the highest in the world. U.S. workers are still the most productive on earth, and the U.S. standard of living remains among the highest in the world. Real per-capita income in the United States is one-third higher than it is in Japan and in other developed economies. In fact, real per-capita income in the United States is about 20 times greater than it is for over half the human race. So don't confuse our *level* of productivity, which remains tops, with our *growth* in productivity, which has slowed in the last two decades.

SUMMARY

1. Because the population is continually increasing, an economy must produce more goods and services simply to maintain its standard of living, as measured by the output per capita. If output grows faster than the population, the standard of living will rise.

2. Over the last 125 years, labor productivity has grown an average of 2.1 percent per year. Output per hour of work was 1,240 percent greater in 1995 than in 1870. Research suggests that the *quality* of labor and capital is much more important than the *quantity* of these resources. Productivity growth has slowed somewhat in the last two decades, especially in comparison to the robust growth during and immediately following World War II.

3. A variety of factors could explain the recent decline in productivity growth, including (1) a slower rate of growth in physical capital formation, (2) an increase in the share of less experienced workers, (3) the changing composition of output, (4) growth in government regulations, (5) higher federal deficits, and (6) a decline in research and development expenditures.

QUESTIONS AND PROBLEMS

1. **(Labor Productivity)** Complete each of the following:
   a. Total output of a nation _____ by the number of units of labor employed to produce that output is known as labor productivity.
   b. The resource most responsible for increasing labor productivity is _____, which includes both _____ _____ and ____ _____ _____.
   c. According to the _____ _____ _____ _____, when additional units of capital are added to a fixed amount of labor, a decreasing amount of additional output is created.
   d. The relation between the amount of capital per worker and the output per worker is illustrated by the economy's _____ _____ _____.

2. **(Labor Productivity)** What are the two kinds of changes in capital that would improve labor productivity? How would each type be illustrated with a per-worker production function? What determines the slope of the per-worker production function?

3. **(Productivity)** As discussed in the text, per capita GDP levels in many developing countries depend on land productivity. However, many richer economies have either little land or land of poor quality. What are some of the countries that you would consider dependent on land productivity? What countries are rich despite poor land resources, and why is land productivity no longer of primary importance in those countries? How would you categorize the United States?

4. **(Slowdown in Labor Productivity Growth)** What is the relationship between labor productivity and (a) the rate of capital formation, (b) skill and education levels, and (c) the composition of output? How have each of these contributed to the slowdown in U.S. labor productivity growth since 1972?

5. **(Government Regulation and Productivity)** Government regulation of U.S. industry has increased significantly since the mid-1960s. How does the concept of opportunity cost explain how this may have contributed to the slowdown in productivity growth?

6. **(Basic and Applied Research)** Distinguish between basic and applied research. Relate this to the human genome project—research to develop a complete map of the human chromosomes showing the location of every gene.

7. **(Patents)** U.S. patents provide the developer of a new process or product with exclusive rights to their development for 17 years. Why is patent protection necessary to encourage research and development?

8. **(Industrial Policy)** Define industrial policy. What reasons are given in support of industrial policy?

9. **(Technological Change and Employment)** Explain how technological change can lead to unemployment in certain industries. How can it lead to increased employment?

10. **(Technology and Productivity)** What measures can government take to promote the development of practical technologies?

11. **(Output per Capita)** The U.S. central bank, the Federal Reserve, has defined sustainable growth (growth that does not lead to accelerating inflation) as 2.5 percent to 2.8 percent. The range is determined by adding the annual growth rate of the labor force to the average yearly increase in labor productivity. Based on the information in the chapter, explain this method of determining sustainable growth.

12. **(Output per Capita)** Explain how output per capita can grow faster than the growth in labor productivity.

13. **(Converging Economies)** Explain the convergence theory. Under what circumstances may convergence fail to occur?

14. **(Productivity)** What factors might contribute to a low level of productivity in an economy? What is the impact of low productivity on the economy's standard of living?

15. **(Productivity and the Standard of Living)** Productivity changes are certainly important in determining long-term changes in living standards, yet other factors also play a role. Do you think the increasing importance

of international trade in the U.S. national accounts can be changing the way productivity growth is linked to improved living standards?

16. **(Computers and Productivity)** How has the increased use of computers affected U.S. productivity in the last few years? Is the contribution of computers expected to increase or decrease in the near future? Explain.

17. **(Picking Technological Winners)** What has been the central focus of U.S. industrial policy in the past? Is that the appropriate focus in the present?

18. **(Picking Technological Winners)** What are the arguments against having a U.S. industrial policy?

Using the Internet

19. Visit "A Word from Wall Street," a monthly survey of 16 Wall Street economists performed by BankAmerica Corporation (**http://www.bankamerica.com/ econ_indicator/wallov.html**). Review "Survey on the State of the Economy One Year Out." Which is more likely: The economy one year from today will be experiencing a boom, healthy growth, slowdown, or stagflation? Review other materials derived from this survey. Do you see a justification for this prediction?

7

Unemployment and Inflation

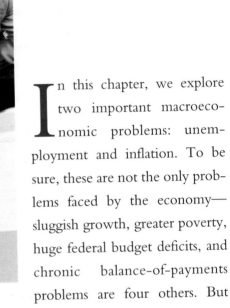

In this chapter, we explore two important macroeconomic problems: unemployment and inflation. To be sure, these are not the only problems faced by the economy—sluggish growth, greater poverty, huge federal budget deficits, and chronic balance-of-payments problems are four others. But lower unemployment and lower inflation would go a long way to help diminish the effects of other economic problems. Although unemployment and inflation are often related, we will initially describe each separately. Our focus will be more on the extent and consequences of these problems than on their causes. The causes of each and the relationship between the two will become clearer in later chapters as you learn more about how the economy works.

As this chapter will show, not all unemployment nor all inflation harms the economy. Even in a healthy economy, a certain amount of unemployment reflects the voluntary choices of workers and employers seeking their best opportunities. And inflation that is fully anticipated creates fewer distortions than does unanticipated inflation. Topics discussed in this chapter include:

- Measuring unemployment
- Frictional, structural, seasonal, and cyclical unemployment
- Meaning of full employment
- Sources and consequences of inflation
- Relative price changes
- Nominal and real interest rates

UNEMPLOYMENT

"They scampered about looking for work. . . . They swarmed on the highways. The movement changed them; the highways, the camps along the road, the fear of hunger and the hunger itself, changed them. The children without dinner changed them, the endless moving changed them."[1] No question, a long stretch of unemployment can have a profound effect on an individual or a family. The most obvious loss is a steady paycheck, but the unemployed often suffer a loss of self-esteem. Moreover, researchers have found that unemployment appears to be linked to a greater incidence of crime and to a variety of afflictions including heart disease, suicide, and mental illness. However much people complain about their jobs, they rely on these jobs not only for income but also for part of their personal identity. The loss of a job usually involves some loss of that identity.

In addition to these personal costs, unemployment imposes a cost on the economy as a whole, since fewer goods and services are produced. When the economy does not generate enough jobs to employ all those who are willing and able to work, that unemployed labor service is lost forever. *This lost potential output coupled with the economic and psychological damage to unemployed workers and their families represents the real cost of unemployment.* As we begin our analysis of unemployment, keep in mind that unemployment statistics reflect millions of individuals with their own stories. For some, unemployment is a brief break between jobs. For others, a long stretch of unemployment can have a profound effect on their families' stability and economic welfare.

Measuring Unemployment

The unemployment rate is perhaps the most widely reported measure of the nation's economic health. What does the unemployment rate measure, what are the sources of unemployment, and how does unemployment change over time? These are some of the questions explored in this section. To start, we will consider how unemployment is measured.

We begin with the U.S. noninstitutional adult population, which consists of all persons 16 years of age and older, except those who are institutionalized, such as in prisons or mental hospitals. In this chapter, when we refer to the *adult population,* we will mean the noninstitutional adult population. The **labor force** consists of those in the adult population who are either working or looking for work. Those looking for work are considered unemployed. More specifically, the Bureau of Labor Statistics counts people as unemployed if they have no job but have looked for work at least once in the preceding four weeks. The unemployment rate measures the percentage of those in the labor force who are unemployed. Thus, the **unemployment rate** equals the number unemployed—that is, those without jobs who are looking for work—divided by the number in the labor force.

Only a fraction of adults not working are considered unemployed. The others may have retired, may have chosen to remain at home to care for small children or perform household tasks, or may be full-time students. The "idle rich" may pursue a life of leisure. Others may be unable to work because of long-term illness or disability. Finally, some people may have become so discouraged

Net Bookmark

The Bureau of Labor Statistics, an agency within the Department of Labor, is the principal fact-finding agency for the federal government in the field of labor economics and statistics. Visit the BLS (**http://stats.bls.gov/**).

Labor force All noninstitutionalized individuals 16 years of age and older who are either working or actively looking for work

Unemployment rate The number of unemployed individuals expressed as a percentage of the labor force

---

1 John Steinbeck, *The Grapes of Wrath* (New York: Viking Press, 1939), p. 392.

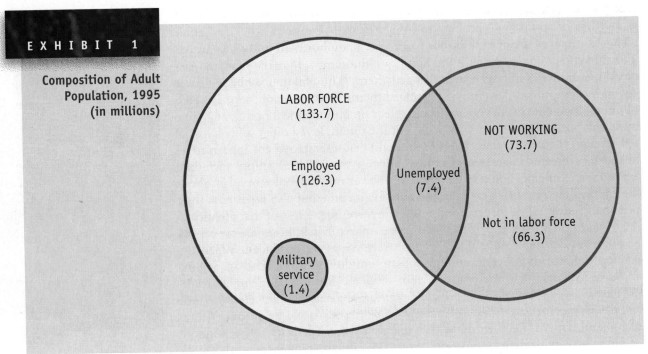

EXHIBIT 1

Composition of Adult Population, 1995 (in millions)

LABOR FORCE (133.7)

NOT WORKING (73.7)

Employed (126.3)

Unemployed (7.4)

Not in labor force (66.3)

Military service (1.4)

Source: *Economic Report of the President,* February 1996; not drawn to scale.

Discouraged worker A person who has dropped out of the labor force because of lack of success in finding a job

by an unfruitful job search that they have given up their search in frustration. Since these so-called **discouraged workers** have, in effect, dropped out of the labor force, they are not counted as unemployed. Also, some individuals who are working part time would prefer to work full time, yet all part-time workers are counted as employed. *Because the official unemployment rate does not include discouraged workers and counts all part-time workers as employed, the true extent of unemployment in the economy tends to be understated.*

These definitions are illustrated in Exhibit 1, where circles represent the various groups and subgroups, and the number of individuals in each category and subcategory is listed in parentheses (in millions). The circle on the left depicts the entire U.S. labor force, including both those who are employed and those who are unemployed. The circle on the right represents those in the adult population who, for whatever reason, are not working. These two circles reflect the entire adult population.[2] Their overlap identifies the number of *unemployed* workers—that is, the number in the labor force who aren't working.

Unemployment Rate. You can see from the circles in Exhibit 1 that all those who are unemployed are counted as not working, but not all those who are not working are counted as unemployed. The number of individuals in each category and subcategory is listed in parentheses (in millions). Of the 133.7 million in the labor force in 1995, 7.4 million were unemployed. The unemployment rate is found by dividing the number unemployed by the number in the labor force; in 1995, the unemployment rate averaged 5.5 percent.

---

2   Prior to the 1940 census, "workers" could include anyone 10 years of age or older. In 1940, age 14 became the lower limit, and in 1966 the lower limit was raised to 16, where it remains.

Labor Force Participation Rate. The labor force participation rate indicates the proportion of adults who are in the labor force. In Exhibit 1, the U.S. adult population equals those in the labor force (133.7 million) plus those not in the labor force (66.3 million)—a total of 200.0 million. The **labor force participation rate** therefore equals the number in the labor force divided by the adult population, or 66.8 percent (133.7/200.0). So, on average, about two of three adults are in the labor force.

Civilian Unemployment Rate. Individuals in military service are depicted by the small circle identifying that subset of the labor force. Since all those in the military are considered employed (even those who "only stand and wait"), this small circle does not intersect the "not working" circle. Official unemployment statistics often distinguish between the overall unemployment rate, which was just discussed, and the civilian unemployment rate, which is found by dividing the number unemployed by the civilian labor force. Until the reporting method was changed during the Reagan administration, military personnel were not included in the labor force. Including them lowers the official unemployment rate below the civilian unemployment rate. The reporting method was changed again under the Clinton administration to exclude military personnel from the labor force. Thus, the unemployment rate now reported is the civilian unemployment rate.

Over the last 30 years, the number of working-age women in the work force has increased from less than 40 percent to about 60 percent.

Labor force participation rate
The ratio of the number in the labor force to the population of working age

Changes over Time in Unemployment Statistics

The adult population changes slowly over time. The only way to join that group is to become 16 years of age, be deinstitutionalized, or immigrate to the United States. The only way to leave the adult population is to die, become institutionalized, or emigrate from the United States to another country. Since 1950, the adult population in the United States has grown by an average of 1.6 percent per year.

Moving in and out of the labor force is easier than moving in and out of the adult population. Thus, the labor force participation rate can change more quickly than the adult population. One striking development since World War II has been the convergence in the labor force participation rates of men and women. Three decades ago, fewer than 40 percent of working-age women were in the work force; today that rate is about 60 percent. The largest increase in labor activity occurred among younger women, but sizable gains also took place for women in their forties and fifties. The labor force participation rate among men has declined from 83 percent in 1960 to about 75 percent today, primarily because of earlier retirement.

What changes even more quickly over time than labor force participation or the adult population is the unemployment rate. Exhibit 2 depicts the U.S. civilian unemployment rate since 1900, with shading to indicate years of recession or depression. As you can see, the rate rises during recessions and falls during expansions. Perhaps the most striking feature of the graph is the dramatic jump that occurred during the Great Depression, when the unemployment rate peaked at 25 percent.

Note that since the end of World War II there has been an upward trend in the unemployment rate (a trend line has been superimposed on the data). Between 1947 and 1970, for example, the rate averaged 4.7 percent, never reaching 6.9 percent any year during that stretch. Since 1970, however, the unemployment rate has averaged 6.9 percent, never falling as low as 4.7 percent.

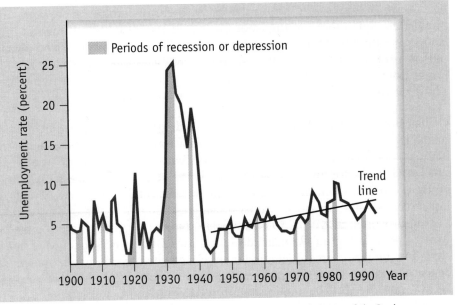

Sources: *Historical Statistics of the United States,* 1970; and *Economic Report of the President,* February 1996.

EXHIBIT 2

The U.S. Civilian Unemployment Rate since 1900

Since 1900 the unemployment rate has fluctuated widely, rising during recessions and falling during expansions. During the Great Depression of the 1930s, the rate rose as high as 25.2 percent. Since 1950 there has been an upward trend in the unemployment rate.

(Later in this section, we examine some possible reasons why the unemployment rate has increased.) These numbers imply that on average since 1970, about 2.5 million more people have been unemployed at any given time than was the case between 1947 and 1970. We should also note, however, that the labor force grew sharply between these two periods because of a growing population and a rising female labor force participation rate. Thus, although the number of unemployed increased, the number employed increased as well, growing by over 45 million since 1970. In fact, the United States since 1970 has been considered an "astounding job machine," and has been the envy of the world. At the same time that the U.S. economy was creating over 45 million jobs, the industrialized countries of Western Europe experienced little employment growth.

Unemployment in Various Groups

The overall unemployment rate says nothing about who is unemployed or for how long. Even a low rate of unemployment often hides wide differences in unemployment rates across age, race, gender, and geographical area. Unemployment rates since 1972 for different groups appear in Exhibit 3. Each panel presents the unemployment rate by race and by gender; panel (a) considers those 20 years of age and older, and panel (b) those 16 to 19 years old. Years of recession are shaded. As you can see, rates are higher among blacks than among whites, and rates are higher among teenagers than among those age 20 and older. During recessions, the rates of all groups climbed. For all groups, rates peaked during the recession of 1982. Unemployment also varies by occupational group. Historically, professional and technical workers have experienced lower unemployment rates than blue-collar workers, especially construction workers.

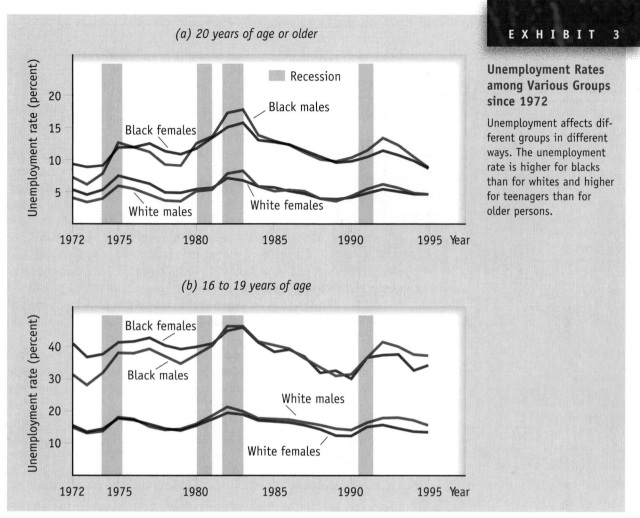

EXHIBIT 3

Unemployment Rates among Various Groups since 1972

Unemployment affects different groups in different ways. The unemployment rate is higher for blacks than for whites and higher for teenagers than for older persons.

Source: *Economic Report of the President,* February 1996.

Duration of Unemployment

Any given unemployment rate says little about how long people have been unemployed—that is, the *average duration of unemployment.* The average duration of unemployment in 1995 was 16.6 weeks. Some were unemployed longer than others: 36 percent were unemployed fewer than 5 weeks; 32 percent from 5 to 14 weeks; 15 percent from 15 to 26 weeks; and 17 percent 27 weeks or longer. Typically, a rise in the unemployment rate is due to both a larger number of unemployed and a longer average duration of unemployment.

Unemployment Differences across the Country

The national unemployment rate masks much variance in rates across the country. For example, during 1988, when the U.S. unemployment rate averaged only 5.5 percent, more than 100 counties had unemployment rates exceeding 15 percent, and 30 counties had rates exceeding 25 percent. To look behind the numbers, we examine one county's experience with high unemployment in the following case study.

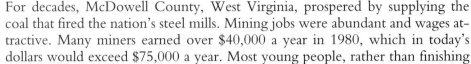

For decades, McDowell County, West Virginia, prospered by supplying the coal that fired the nation's steel mills. Mining jobs were abundant and wages attractive. Many miners earned over $40,000 a year in 1980, which in today's dollars would exceed $75,000 a year. Most young people, rather than finishing their educations, became miners (more than half of those over age 25 are high school dropouts). The mining companies dominated the county, owning most of the property and discouraging other types of economic development.

But between 1980 and 1985, the value of the dollar rose relative to foreign currencies, so American steel became more expensive overseas and foreign steel became cheaper in the United States. Steel imports increased by 56 percent between 1980 and 1985. As the world's demand for U.S. steel fell, so did the demand for the coal needed to produce that steel. Coal mines in McDowell County shut down, and by 1988 the official unemployment rate for the county had reached a whopping 32 percent. Local officials claimed the actual rate was even higher. According to the 1990 census, half those under 18 lived in poverty, as did 36 percent of those 18 to 64 years of age.

The county tried to attract new industry—even a nuclear-waste dump—but met with little success. The county's poor roads and bridges and a labor force trained only for mining scared off potential employers. In short, the county had all its eggs in one basket, but the basket fell.

Sources: Alan Murray, "Unemployment Tops 25% in Some Regions Mired in Deep Poverty," *The Wall Street Journal,* 21 April 1988; and Walter Adams, "Steel," *The Structure of American Industry,* Walter Adams and James Brock, eds. (Englewood Cliffs, N.J.: Prentice Hall, 1995), pp. 93–118. Recent employment figures for McDowell County can be found at Internet site http://musom.mu.wvnet.edu/0u:/wvvhs/54047.html.

Types of Unemployment

Consider all the ways people can become unemployed. They may quit or get fired from their jobs. They may be looking for a first job because they just turned sixteen or graduated. Or they may be reentering the labor force after an absence. An examination of the reasons behind unemployment during 1995 indicates that 47 percent of those unemployed lost their previous jobs, 11 percent quit their previous jobs, 8 percent were entering the labor market for the first time, and 34 percent were reentering the market. *Thus, 53 percent were unemployed either because they quit their jobs or because they were just joining or rejoining the labor force.*

Pick up any metropolitan newspaper and thumb through the classified pages. The "Help Wanted" section may run more than 40 pages and include more than 10,000 jobs, listed alphabetically from accountants to x-ray technicians. Why, when millions are unemployed, are so many jobs unfilled? To understand this paradox, we must take a closer look at the reasons behind unemployment. We distinguish four types of unemployment, based on the source: frictional, structural, seasonal, and cyclical.

Frictional Unemployment. Just as employers do not often hire the first applicant who comes through the door, workers do not always accept their first job offer. Both employers and job applicants need time to explore the job market. Employers need time to find out about the talent available, and job seekers need time to find out about opportunities. The time required to bring together labor suppliers and labor demanders results in **frictional unemployment.** Although unemployment often creates economic and psychological hardships, not all unemployment is necessarily bad. Frictional unemployment does not usually last long and results in a better match-up between workers and jobs, so the entire economy becomes more efficient.

Structural Unemployment. A second reason job vacancies and unemployment can occur simultaneously is that unemployed workers often do not have the skills demanded by employers or do not live in the area where their skills are in demand. In 1995, for example, the Lincoln Electric Company in Euclid, Ohio, could not fill 200 job openings because few of the thousands who applied could operate computer-controlled machines. Unemployment arising from a mismatch of skills or geographic location is called **structural unemployment.** Structural unemployment occurs because changes in tastes, technology, taxes, or competition reduce the demand for certain skills and increase the demand for other skills. In our dynamic economy, some people are stuck with skills that are no longer demanded, such as the coal miners in West Virginia. For example, automatic teller machines have put many bank tellers out of work. And computers have reduced the demand for middle managers (in 1994, one in four out-of-work managers had been unemployed for more than 6 months[3]).

Whereas most frictional unemployment is short-term and voluntary, structural unemployment poses more of a problem because workers must seek jobs elsewhere or must develop the skills that are in demand. For example, unemployed bank tellers and middle managers must seek work in other industries or in other regions. Moving to where the jobs are is easier said than done. People prefer to remain near friends and relatives. Those laid off from high-wage jobs may be reluctant to leave the area because they hope to be rehired. Families in which one spouse is still employed may not want to give up one job to seek two jobs elsewhere. Finally, the available jobs may be in areas where the cost of living is much higher. So the unemployed often stay put.

Seasonal Unemployment. Unemployment caused by seasonal changes in labor supply and demand during the year is called **seasonal unemployment.** During cold winter months, demand falls off for farmhands, lifeguards, golf instructors, lawn-care specialists, and dozens of other seasonal occupations. Likewise, the tourist trade in places such as Miami and Phoenix wilts in the summer heat. The Christmas season increases the demand for sales clerks, postal carriers, and Santa Clauses. Those with seasonal jobs know they will probably be unemployed in the off-season. Some may even have purposely chosen a seasonal occupation. To eliminate seasonal unemployment, we might have to outlaw

Frictional unemployment Unemployment that arises because of the time needed to match qualified job seekers with available job openings

Structural unemployment Unemployment that arises because (1) the skills demanded by employers do not match the skills of the unemployed, or (2) the unemployed do not live where the jobs are located

Seasonal unemployment Unemployment caused by seasonal shifts in labor supply and demand

---

3 Even when displaced managers find new jobs, they often take a pay cut. See Fred Bleakley, "Job Searches Still Last Months, or Years, for Many Middle-Aged Middle Managers," *The Wall Street Journal,* 18 September 1995.

winter and abolish Christmas. Monthly employment statistics are "seasonally adjusted" to smooth out the bulges that result from seasonal factors.

Cyclical Unemployment. As production declines during recessions, many firms reduce their demand for inputs, including labor. **Cyclical unemployment** is the increase in unemployment that occurs during recessions. Between 1932 and 1934, when unemployment averaged about 24 percent, there was clearly much cyclical unemployment. Between 1942 and 1945, when the unemployment rate averaged only 1.6 percent, there was no cyclical unemployment. Government policies that stimulate aggregate demand during recessions are aimed at reducing cyclical unemployment.

Cyclical unemployment Unemployment that occurs because of declines in the economy's aggregate production during recessions

The Meaning of Full Employment

When economists talk about "full employment," they do not mean zero unemployment. In an ever-changing economy such as ours, shifts in demand and changes in technology alter the supply and demand for existing products. Consequently, even when the economy is at **full employment,** there will be some frictional, structural, and seasonal unemployment. After all, nearly half of those unemployed have quit their last job or are new entrants or reentrants into the labor force. A large proportion of this group could be counted among the frictionally unemployed.

Full employment The level of employment when there is no cyclical unemployment

Most economists believe that unemployment of the frictional-structural-seasonal variety has risen since the late 1950s, perhaps from 4 percent to 5 or 6 percent; that high an unemployment rate would now constitute full employment. Why did this increase occur? The full employment level may have changed over time because of changes in the composition of the labor force and more general changes in the structure of the economy. Since the 1950s, the composition of the labor force has shifted. Today, groups that have historically experienced lower unemployment rates comprise a smaller proportion of the labor force. For example, the group that experiences the lowest average unemployment in the labor force—white males 20 years of age and older—made up about two-thirds of all workers in 1955. Now they make up only about half of the labor force.

Unemployment Insurance

As noted earlier, unemployment often imposes an economic and psychological hardship on those unemployed. For a variety of reasons, however, the burden of unemployment may not be as severe today as during the Great Depression. Today, a large proportion of households have two workers in the labor force, so even if one household member becomes unemployed, another is likely to have a job, a job that often provides health insurance and other benefits. When a household has more than one person in the labor force, the economic shock of unemployment is cushioned to some extent.

Moreover, workers who lose their jobs now often receive unemployment benefits. In response to the massive unemployment of the Great Depression, Congress passed the Social Security Act of 1935, which provided unemployment insurance financed by a tax on employers. Unemployed workers who meet certain qualifications can receive **unemployment insurance** for up to 6 months, provided they actively seek employment. During recessions, benefits are often extended beyond six months in states with especially high unemployment rates. The insurance is aimed primarily at those who have lost jobs. Not

Unemployment insurance Temporary income provided to unemployed workers who actively seek employment and who meet other qualifications

covered are those just entering or reentering the labor force, those who quit their last job, or those fired for just cause such as excessive absenteeism or theft. Because of these restrictions, only about half of all unemployed workers receive unemployment benefits.

Unemployment insurance usually replaces more than half of a person's take-home pay. In 1995, for example, an average of $187 per week was paid to the unemployed who received benefits. Because unemployment benefits reduce the opportunity cost of remaining unemployed, they may reduce incentives to find work. For example, if you faced the choice of washing dishes for a take-home pay of $200 per week or collecting $150 per week in unemployment benefits, which would you choose? Evidence suggests that unemployed workers who receive insurance benefits tend to search less actively than those without such benefits. Therefore, although unemployment insurance provides a safety net for the unemployed, it may also reduce the urgency of finding work, thereby increasing unemployment. On the plus side, unemployment insurance may allow for a higher-quality search, since the insured job seeker has "walking-around" money and need not take the first job that comes along.

International Comparisons of Unemployment

Consider unemployment rates around the world. In 1995, when the U.S. civilian unemployment rate was 5.6 percent, it was 9.5 percent in Canada, 9.3 percent in Germany, 12.1 percent in France, 8.8 percent in the United Kingdom, 12 percent in Italy, and 3.2 percent in Japan. We should view international comparisons with caution, however, because the definitions of unemployment may differ across countries with respect to age limits, the criteria used to determine whether a person is looking for work, the way layoffs are treated, how those in the military are counted, and in other subtle ways. These differences can affect estimates of unemployment. For example, most countries in North and South America and some European countries base their unemployment estimates on periodic surveys of the labor force. The U.S. Bureau of Labor Statistics surveys 60,000 individuals around the nation each month. Experts believe that such extensive surveys yield the most reliable results.

But most other countries, including Germany, Great Britain, and a majority of less-developed countries, base official estimates on registrations with government employment offices. Reliance on such self-reporting tends to underestimate the actual level of unemployment, particularly in less-developed countries where there are few jobs, no unemployment benefits, and hence no real reason to bother registering as unemployed with the government. Centrally planned economies, such as North Korea and Cuba, usually do not publish unemployment rates.

In Japan, many firms offer an implicit promise to provide employment security for life. As a result, some employees there may do little or no work yet are still carried on the company's payroll. Other employment practices differ across countries. For example, Germany imposes penalties on firms for "socially unjustified" layoffs, and Swedish law makes it harder to lay off Swedish citizens than foreign workers.

Problems with Official Unemployment Figures

Official unemployment statistics are not without their problems. As we saw earlier, not counting discouraged workers in the official labor force understates un-

Underemployment *A situation in which workers are overqualified for their jobs or work fewer hours than they would prefer*

employment. Official employment data also ignore the problem of **underemployment,** which arises because people are counted as employed even if they can find only part-time jobs or they are vastly overqualified for the job, as when someone with a Ph.D. in English can find employment only as a bookstore clerk. Counting overqualified and part-time workers as employed tends to understate the actual amount of unemployment.

On the other hand, because unemployment insurance and some welfare programs require recipients to seek employment, some people may act as if they are looking for work just to qualify for such programs. If these people do not in fact want to find a job, their inclusion among the unemployed tends to overstate the official unemployment figures. *On net, however, most experts believe that official U.S. unemployment figures tend to underestimate unemployment because of the exclusion of discouraged workers and because underemployed workers are counted as employed.* Despite several qualifications and limitations, the unemployment rate is a useful measure of unemployment trends over time.

We turn next to the second major concern in today's economy: inflation.

INFLATION

We begin our discussion of inflation with a case study that highlights the cost of high inflation by focusing on the recent experience of Brazil.

CASE STUDY

Hyperinflation in Brazil

Location:

What is the latest news on the economy in Brazil? Visit the Brazilian Embassy in London (http://www.demon.co.uk/Itamaraty/body.html) or review "News From Brazil", a monthly magazine about Brazil. (http://www.earthlink.net/~brazzil/).

During the six years between 1988 and 1994, year-to-year inflation rates in Brazil were 1,300 percent, 2,900 percent, 440 percent, 1,000 percent, 1,260 percent, and 1,740 percent. Six years of such inflation meant that prices in 1994 were about *4 million* times higher than in 1988! To put this in perspective, if that inflation rate had prevailed in the United States, the price of a gallon of gasoline would have climbed from $1.25 in 1988 to $5 million in 1994. A pair of jeans that sold for $35 in 1988 would have cost $140 million in 1994!

With the value of the Brazilian cruzeiro cheapening by the hour, people understandably did not want to hold cruzeiros. As soon as workers were paid, they tried either to buy goods and services before prices increased or to exchange cruzeiros for a more stable currency, such as the U.S. dollar. With such wild inflation, everyone, including merchants, had difficulty keeping track of prices. Price differences among sellers of the same product became greater, prompting shoppers to incur the "shoe-leather cost" of walking around in search of the lowest price.

The huge increase in the average price level meant that wads of money were needed to carry out even the simplest transactions. Think again in terms of dollars. To carry the equivalent of $20 in preinflated spending power for pizza and a movie, you would have to load yourself down with $80 million. Even in $100 bills, this amount of currency would weigh nearly a ton. That's one fat wallet! Because carrying even small amounts of spending money became physically impossible, Brazilian officials issued currencies in larger and larger denominations. Between the mid-1980s and 1994, new currency denominations were issued on five separate occasions. Each new currency was worth a large multiple of the previous one. For example, the 1994 issue of the new *cruzeiro real* exchanged for 2,750 of the cruzeiro it replaced. New currency issues made transactions easier.

Lugging money around, shopping for the lowest price, and constant preoccupation with money matters all take time and energy away from production. Thus, high and unpredictable inflation leads to wasteful activity, such as immediately converting each day's pay into another currency or into goods and services, that is rational for each individual but unproductive for the economy as a whole.

Sources: "Brazil: Another Try," *The Economist* 9 July–15 July 1994, p. 44; and "Brazil," *Britannica Book of the Year* (Encyclopaedia Britannica: Chicago, 1994), pp. 570–71.

Hyperinflation in Brazil
continued

We have already discussed inflation in different contexts. *Inflation* is a sustained increase in the average level of prices. If the price level bounces around—moving up one month, falling back another—any particular increase in the price level would not necessarily be called inflation. Very high inflation, as in Brazil, is called **hyperinflation.** A sustained *decrease* in the average level of prices is called **deflation.** And a reduction in the rate of inflation is called *disinflation.*

We typically measure inflation on an *annual* basis. The annual *inflation rate* equals the percentage increase in the average price level from one year to the next. For example, between 1994 and 1995, the U.S. consumer price index increased by 2.8 percent. In this section, we first consider two sources of inflation. We then examine the extent and consequences of inflation in the United States and around the world.

Hyperinflation **A very high rate of inflation**

Deflation **A sustained decrease in the price level**

Two Sources of Inflation

Inflation can be depicted as a continuing increase in the economy's price level resulting from an increase in aggregate demand or a decrease in aggregate supply. Panel (a) of Exhibit 4 shows that an increase in aggregate demand raises the price level from P to P'. Inflation resulting from an increase in aggregate demand is often called **demand-pull inflation.** In such cases, a rising aggregate demand curve *pulls up* the price level. To generate continuous demand-pull inflation, the aggregate demand curve would have to keep shifting out along a given aggregate supply curve.

Alternatively, inflation can arise from a reduction in aggregate supply, as shown in panel (b) of Exhibit 4, where a shift to the left in the aggregate supply curve raises the price level. For example, crop failures and reductions in the supply of oil during the 1970s reduced aggregate supply, thereby raising the price level. Inflation stemming from a decrease in aggregate supply is often called **cost-push inflation,** suggesting that an increase in the cost of production has *pushed up* the price level. A decrease in aggregate supply usually leads not only to a higher price level but also to a falling level of output, a combination that was identified in Chapter 5 as *stagflation.* Again, to generate sustained and continuous cost-push inflation, the aggregate supply curve would have to keep shifting to the left along a given aggregate demand curve, which is most unlikely.

Demand-pull inflation **A sustained rise in the price level caused by increases in aggregate demand**

Cost-push inflation **A sustained rise in the price level caused by reductions in aggregate supply**

EXHIBIT 4

Inflation Caused by Shifts in the Aggregate Demand and Aggregate Supply Curves

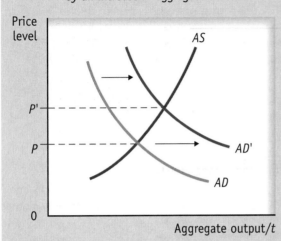

(a) Demand-pull inflation: inflation induced by an increase in aggregate demand

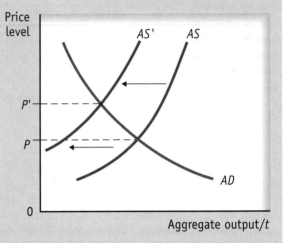

(b) Cost-push inflation: inflation induced by a decrease in aggregate supply

Panel (a) illustrates demand-pull inflation. An outward shift of the aggregate demand to AD' "pulls" the price level up from P to P'. Panel (b) shows cost-push inflation, in which a decrease in aggregate supply to AS' "pushes" the price level up from P to P'.Figure caption

A Historical Look at Inflation and the Price Level

The consumer price index is the measure of the price level you most often encounter, so we accord it some attention here. As you will learn in the next chapter, the **consumer price index,** or **CPI,** measures the cost of a fixed "market basket" of consumer goods and services over time. Exhibit 5 indicates the movement of the price level in the United States since 1900, as measured by the consumer price index. Panel (a) shows the *level* of prices in each year, which is measured by an index relative to the base period. As you can see, the price level was not much higher in 1940 than in 1900. Since 1940, however, it has risen steadily, especially during the 1970s.

Of most concern is not the level of prices but year-to-year changes in that level. Panel (b) shows the annual *rate of change* in the CPI, or the annual rate of *inflation* or *deflation,* since 1900. The decade of the 1970s was not the only period of high inflation during this century. Inflation also exceeded 10 percent from 1917 to 1920, in 1942, and in 1947—periods associated with world wars. Prior to World War II, inflation was primarily a wartime phenomenon and was usually followed by deflation. Such an inflation–deflation cycle has characterized war and peace stretching back over the last two centuries. In fact, between the Revolutionary War and World War II, the price level declined in about as many years as it increased. At the end of World War II, the price level was about where it had been at the end of the Civil War.

So inflation is nothing new; the price level has varied for as far back as we have records. But prior to World War II, periods of inflation and deflation

Consumer price index (CPI) A measure of the cost of a fixed "market basket" of consumer goods and services

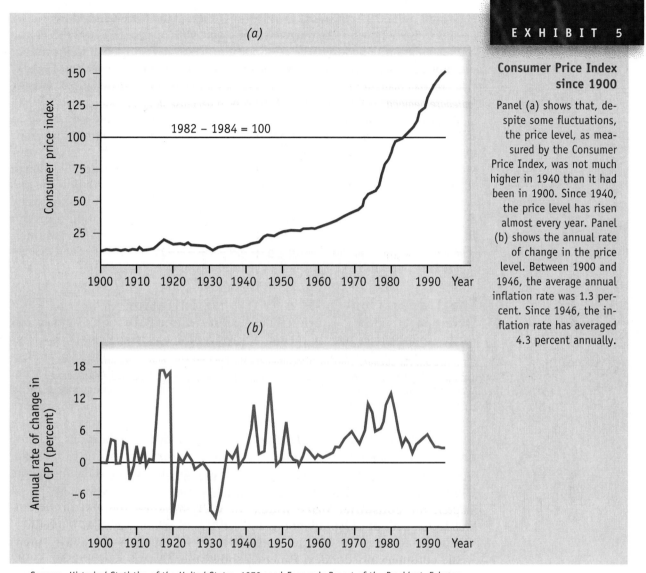

(a)

1982 – 1984 = 100

(b)

Sources: *Historical Statistics of the United States,* 1970; and *Economic Report of the President,* February 1996.

EXHIBIT 5

Consumer Price Index since 1900

Panel (a) shows that, despite some fluctuations, the price level, as measured by the Consumer Price Index, was not much higher in 1940 than it had been in 1900. Since 1940, the price level has risen almost every year. Panel (b) shows the annual rate of change in the price level. Between 1900 and 1946, the average annual inflation rate was 1.3 percent. Since 1946, the inflation rate has averaged 4.3 percent annually.

evened out over the long run. Therefore, people had good reason to believe the dollar would retain its purchasing power when averaged over the long term. Since World War II, however, the price level has increased by an average of 4.3 percent per year. That may not sound like much, but it translates into a *sevenfold* increase in the consumer price index since 1946. Put another way, today's dollar can purchase one-seventh the real goods and services that a dollar of 1946 could purchase. Inflation has reduced confidence in the value of the dollar over the long term.

Anticipated Versus Unanticipated Inflation

What is the effect of inflation on the economy's performance? *Unanticipated inflation* creates more problems for the economy than does *anticipated inflation*. To the extent that inflation is higher or lower than anticipated, it arbitrarily creates economic winners and losers. If inflation is higher than expected, the winners are all those who had contracted to buy for a price that did not reflect the higher inflation. The losers are all those who contracted to sell at that price. If inflation is lower than expected, the situation is reversed: the winners are all those who contracted to sell at a price that anticipated higher inflation, and the losers are all those who contracted to buy at that price.

Suppose inflation next year is expected to be 3 percent, and you agree to sell your labor for a *nominal,* or money, wage that is 3 percent higher than your nominal wage this year. In this case you expect your *real* wage—that is, your wage measured in dollars of constant purchasing power—to remain unchanged. If inflation turns out to be 3 percent, you and your employer will both be satisfied with your nominal wage increase of 3 percent. If inflation turns out to be 5 percent, your real wage will fall and you will be a loser. If inflation turns out to be only 1 percent, your real wage will increase and you will be a winner. *The arbitrary gains and losses arising from unanticipated inflation is one reason that inflation is so unpopular.*

The Transaction Costs of Variable Inflation

During long periods of price stability, people correctly believe that they can predict future prices and can therefore plan accordingly. Money is an important link between the present and the future. Uncertainty about inflation undermines the ability of money to serve as such a link. When inflation accelerates unexpectedly, the purchasing power of the dollar declines unexpectedly and the future value of the dollar becomes more uncertain. Since the future is more cloudy, planning becomes more difficult.

Firms that deal with the rest of the world face added complications, for they must not only attempt to plan for U.S. inflation, but also anticipate how the value of the dollar might change relative to foreign currencies. Inflation uncertainty and the resulting exchange-rate uncertainty increase the difficulty of making international business decisions. In this more uncertain environment, managers must shift their attention from worrying about productivity to anticipating the effects of inflation and exchange-rate variations on the firm's finances. Some economists suspect that the high and variable inflation rate in the United States during the 1970s and early 1980s contributed to the slower growth rate of the economy during that period.

Inflation forces individuals and firms to try to guard against unexpected changes in the dollar's value. For example, they adopt cost-of-living adjustments in wage settlements. During the 1970s, the variable-rate home mortgage began replacing the fixed-rate mortgage typically offered by banks. The interest rate on a variable-rate mortgage varies from year to year, depending on the market rate of interest, which depends in part on the rate of inflation. Lenders became more apprehensive about inflation over the long term, so they wanted to get their money back sooner. Thus, the average duration of loans decreased. The transaction costs of drawing up contracts, particularly long-term contracts, increased.

Adapting to Relative Price Changes

Inflation has been defined as a sustained rise in the price level. This definition, however, misses an important problem with inflation: not all prices change at the same rate. Even with no inflation, some prices would go up and some would go down, reflecting the workings of supply and demand for different products. During the last two decades, for example, the price level in the United States roughly tripled, yet the prices of color televisions, VCRs, pocket calculators, computers, and many other items declined steadily. Because the prices of various goods change by different amounts, *relative prices* change. Whereas the price level describes the terms by which some representative bundle of goods is exchanged for *money,* relative prices describe the terms by which individual goods are exchanged for *one another.*

Inflation does not necessarily cause the changes in relative prices, but inflation can obscure these changes. During periods of volatile inflation, there is greater uncertainty about the price of one good relative to another—that is, about relative prices. In his Nobel Prize address, Milton Friedman noted, "The more volatile the rate of general inflation, the harder it becomes to extract the signal about relative prices from the absolute prices; the broadcast about relative prices is, as it were, being jammed by the noise coming from the inflation broadcast."[4] But relative price changes are important for allocating the economy's resources efficiently.

If all prices moved together, producers could simply link the selling prices of their goods to the overall inflation rate. Since not all prices move in unison, however, tying a particular product's price to the overall inflation rate may result in a price that is too high or too low based on market conditions. The same is true of agreements by employers to raise wages in accord with inflation. If the price of an employer's product lags behind the inflation rate, the employer will be hard-pressed to increase wages by the rate of inflation. Consider the problem confronting oil producers who had signed labor contracts agreeing to pay their workers cost-of-living wage increases. In some years those employers had to provide pay increases at a time when the price of oil was falling like a rock.

International Comparisons of Inflation

In 1995, the U.S. inflation rate as measured by consumer prices was 2.8 percent, compared to −0.1 percent in Japan, 2.0 percent in Germany, 1.7 percent in France, 3.5 percent in the United Kingdom, 5.4 percent in Italy, and 2.2 percent in Canada. Exhibit 6 presents the trends since 1967 in consumer prices in these seven industrialized countries, the *G-7 countries.* Periods of U.S. recessions are shaded. Note that all countries except Germany experienced a "spike" in inflation during the oil crisis of 1974. Since 1985, inflation has been relatively low except in the United Kingdom, where the rate climbed above 10 percent during the first half of 1990. Inflation has been much higher in Argentina, Bolivia, Brazil, and in the emerging transitional economies of Eastern Europe and the former Soviet Union.

As with unemployment statistics, the quantity and quality of data collected to track movements in the price level vary across countries. Governments in less-developed countries sample fewer products and measure prices only in the capital city. Whereas some 400 items are sampled in the United States, as few as 30 might be sampled in some less developed countries.

---

4   Milton Friedman, "Nobel Lecture: Inflation and Unemployment," *Journal of Political Economy* 85 (June 1977): p. 467.

EXHIBIT 6   **International Consumer Prices**

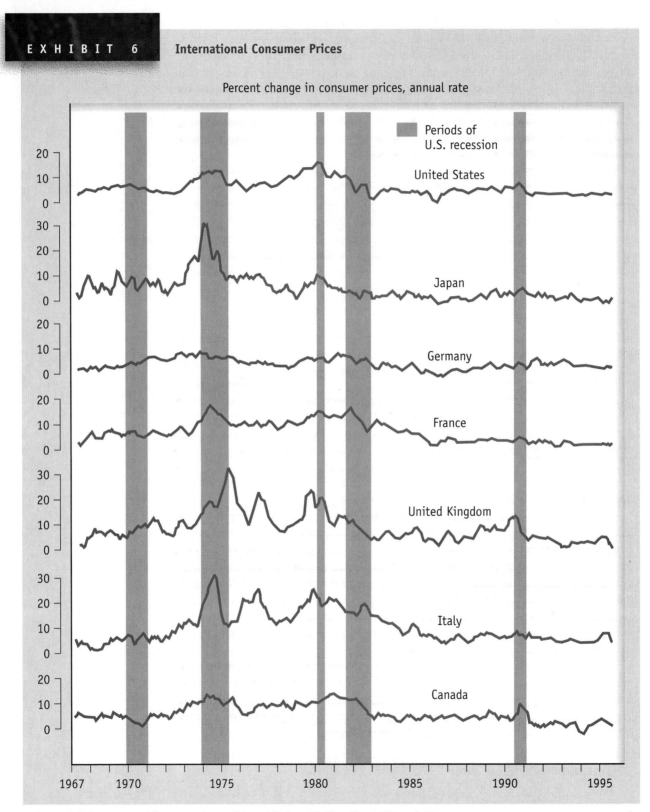

Percent change in consumer prices, annual rate

Periods of U.S. recession

United States

Japan

Germany

France

United Kingdom

Italy

Canada

1967   1970   1975   1980   1985   1990   1995

Source: U.S. Department of Commerce, *Survey of Current Business* 75 (Nov./Dec. 1995): p. C-25.

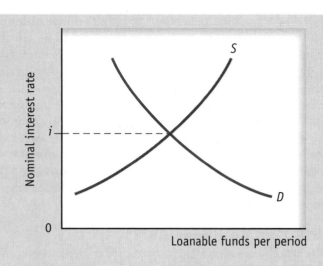

EXHIBIT 7

The Market for Loanable Funds

The upward-sloping supply curve, *S,* shows that more funds are supplied to financial markets at higher interest rates. The downward-sloping demand curve, *D,* shows that the quantity of loanable funds demanded is greater at lower interest rates. The two curves intersect to determine the equilibrium interest rate, *i.*

Inflation and Interest Rates

No discussion of inflation would be complete without a consideration of the role of interest. **Interest** is the dollar amount paid to lenders to forgo present consumption and imposed on borrowers. The **interest rate** is the interest per year as a percentage of the amount loaned. For example, if the interest rate is 5 percent, the interest is $5 per year for a $100 loan. The greater the interest rate, other things constant, the greater the reward for lending money. Thus the quantity of money people are willing to lend increases as the interest rate rises, other things constant. The supply of *loanable funds* therefore slopes upward, as indicated by line *S* in Exhibit 7.

These funds are demanded by households, firms, and governments to finance purchases, such as homes, buildings, and machinery, and in the case of governments, to finance deficits. The lower the interest rate, other things constant, the lower the opportunity cost of borrowing funds. Hence, the quantity of loanable funds demanded increases as the interest rate falls, other things constant. The demand for loans therefore slopes downward, as indicated by curve *D* in Exhibit 7. The downward-sloping demand curve for loanable funds and the upward-sloping supply curve intersect at the equilibrium point to yield the equilibrium nominal rate of interest, *i.*

The **nominal rate of interest** measures interest in terms of the dollars paid even if inflation erodes the value of those dollars. The nominal rate of interest is the rate that appears on the borrowing agreement; it is the rate discussed in the news media and is often of political significance. The **real rate of interest** is the nominal rate of interest minus the inflation rate:

$$\text{Real rate} = \text{nominal rate} - \text{inflation rate}$$

For example, if the nominal rate of interest is 5 percent and the annual rate of inflation is 3 percent, the real rate of interest is only 2 percent. Under these conditions, if you lend $100 for a year, you would earn a nominal interest in-

Interest The dollar amount paid to lenders to forgo present consumption and imposed on borrowers

Interest rate Interest per year as a percentage of the amount loaned

Nominal rate of interest The interest rate expressed in current dollars as a percentage of the amount loaned

Real rate of interest The interest rate expressed in dollars of constant purchasing power as a percentage of the amount loaned; the nominal rate of interest minus the inflation rate come of $5 per year but a real interest income of only $2 per year. If there were no inflation, the nominal rate of interest and the real rate of interest would be identical. But with inflation, the real rate of interest will be less than the nominal rate of interest. The real rate of interest, however, is known only after the fact—that is, only after inflation actually occurs. The nominal rate of interest is always positive; the real rate could turn out to be negative.

Because the future is uncertain, lenders and borrowers must form expectations about inflation, and base their willingness to lend and to borrow on these expectations. Other things held constant, the higher the *expected* rate of inflation, the higher the nominal rate of interest that lenders would require and that borrowers would be willing to pay. Lenders and borrowers base their decisions on the *expected* real interest rate, which equals the nominal rate of interest minus expected inflation.[5]

Why Is Inflation So Unpopular?

Whenever the price level increases, more must be spent to buy the same goods and services. If you think of inflation only in terms of spending, you consider only the problem of paying those higher prices. But if you think of inflation in terms of the higher money incomes that result, you see that higher prices mean higher receipts for resource suppliers. When viewed from the income side, inflation is not so bad.

If every higher price is received by some resource supplier, why are people so troubled by inflation? Presidents Ford and Carter could not control inflation and were turned out of office. Inflation fell significantly during the Reagan administration, and President Reagan was reelected in a landslide, even though the level of unemployment was higher during his first term than during President Carter's tenure. During the 1988 presidential election, George Bush won in part by reminding voters what the rate of inflation was the last time a Democrat had been president. Since then, inflation has been so low that it has not been a campaign issue.

One difference between inflation and unemployment is that, at any particular time, unemployment affects only a fraction of the labor force, fewer than one in 10 workers. In contrast, inflation affects everyone, whether in or out of the labor force, employed or unemployed, buying or selling goods, borrowing or lending money. *People are often more concerned with inflation than with unemployment because more people are affected by inflation.* Also, whereas people view their higher incomes as just reward for their labor, they see inflation as a penalty that unjustly robs them of purchasing power. Most people do not stop to realize that, unless real output per worker increases, higher wages *must* result in higher prices. Prices and wages are simply two sides of the same coin. To the extent that nominal wages on average keep up with inflation, most workers do not suffer a loss of real income as a result of inflation.

Although inflation affects everyone, it hits hardest those whose incomes are fixed in nominal terms. For example, pensions are often fixed and are eroded by inflation; retirees who rely on fixed nominal interest income also see their incomes eroded by unanticipated inflation.

---

5   Although the discussion has implied that there is only one rate of interest, there are actually many rates. Rates differ depending on such factors as the risk and the maturity of different loans.

In summary, to the extent that the level and composition of inflation are fully anticipated by all market participants, inflation is of less concern in macroeconomic analysis than when inflation is unanticipated. Unanticipated inflation arbitrarily redistributes income and wealth from one group to another and reduces the ability to make long-term plans. The more variable and unpredictable inflation is, the greater the difficulty of negotiating long-term contracts. The overall productivity of the economy falls, because people must spend more time coping with the uncertainty created by inflation and less time producing goods and services.

CONCLUSION

This chapter has focused on two macroeconomic problems: unemployment and inflation. Though we have discussed them separately, they are related in a variety of ways, as we will see in later chapters. Politicians sometimes add the unemployment rate to the rate of inflation to come up with what they refer to as the "misery index." In 1980, for example, an unemployment rate of 7.1 percent combined with a CPI increase of 13.6 percent to yield a misery index of 20.6—a number that explains why President Carter was not reelected that year. By 1984 the misery index had dropped to 11.8 and by 1988 to 9.6; Republicans retained the White House in both elections. In 1992, the index climbed slightly to 10.4 percent, an increase that spelled trouble for President Bush.

In Chapter 8, we learn how to measure economic activity and how to adjust data for inflation. In subsequent chapters, we build a model of the economy by developing aggregate demand and aggregate supply curves. Once we have some idea how a healthy economy works, we can consider the policy options in the face of high unemployment or high inflation.

SUMMARY

1. The unemployment rate equals the number of people looking for work divided by the number in the labor force. The overall unemployment rate masks differences in rates among particular groups. The lowest rate is among adult white males; the highest rate is among black teenagers.

2. There are four types of unemployment. Frictional unemployment arises because employers and qualified job seekers need time to find one another. Structural unemployment arises because changes in taste, technology, taxes, and competition reduce the demand for certain skills. Seasonal unemployment stems from the effects of the weather and the calendar on certain industries, such as construction and agriculture. Cyclical unemployment comes from the decline in production during recessions. Full employment occurs when cyclical unemployment is zero.

3. Unemployment imposes both an economic and a psychological burden on the unemployed. For some people,

this burden is reduced by unemployment insurance, which typically replaces more than half of their take-home pay. Unemployment insurance provides a safety net for some people who are unemployed, but it also may reduce their incentive to find work.

4. Inflation is a sustained rise in the average level of prices. Demand-pull inflation results from an increase in aggregate demand. Cost-push inflation results from a decrease in aggregate supply. Until World War II, both increases and decreases in the price level were common, but since then the price level has steadily increased.

5. Anticipated inflation causes fewer distortions in the economy than does unanticipated inflation. Unanticipated inflation arbitrarily creates winners and losers, and forces people to spend more time and energy coping with the effects of inflation. The negative effects of high and variable inflation on an economy's productivity can be observed in countries, such as Brazil, that have experienced hyperinflation.

6. Because not all prices change by the same amount during inflationary periods, people have difficulty keeping track of relative prices. Uncertainty about relative prices makes economic activity more costly and more risky.

7. The intersection of the supply and demand curves for loanable funds indicates the equilibrium interest rate. The nominal rate of interest equals the real rate of interest plus the rate of inflation. The higher the expected inflation rate, the higher the nominal rate of interest.

QUESTIONS AND PROBLEMS

1. **(Labor Force)** Refer to Exhibit 1 in this chapter to determine whether the following are true or false.
   a. Some people who are officially unemployed are not in the labor force.
   b. Some people in the labor force are not working.
   c. All people who are not unemployed are in the labor force.
   d. Some people who are not working are not unemployed.

2. **(Types of Unemployment)** Indicate whether each of the following would be considered frictional, structural, seasonal, or cyclical unemployment:
   a. A UPS employee who is hired for the Christmas season and laid off after Christmas.
   b. A worker who is laid off due to reduced demand for aggregate output.
   c. A worker in the typewriter manufacturing industry who becomes unemployed as the increased popularity of personal computers reduces demand for typewriters.
   d. A new college graduate who is looking for employment during the summer after graduation.

3. **(Measuring Unemployment)** Indicate the impact on each of the following if 2 million formerly unemployed workers decide to return to school full time and stop looking for work:
   a. The labor force participation rate.
   b. The size of the labor force.
   c. The unemployment rate.

4. **(Unemployment in Various Groups)** Does the overall unemployment rate provide an accurate picture of the impact of unemployment for all U.S. population groups?

5. **(The Meaning of Full Employment)** When the economy is considered to be at full employment, is the unemployment rate at 0 percent? Why or why not? How would you expect an increase in unemployment insurance to affect the full employment figure?

6. **(Inflation)** Using the concepts of aggregate supply and demand, explain why inflation usually rises during wartime.

7. **(Inflation)** If actual inflation is higher than anticipated inflation, who will lose purchasing power and who will gain?

8. **(Source of Inflation)** Distinguish between the two sources of inflation.

9. **(Real Interest Rates)** During much of the 1970s, real interest rates in the United States were negative. How can bankers and other lenders conduct business when they are lending at negative interest rates? What caused lenders to lend consistently at rates that were too low?

10. **(Inflation and Interest Rates)** Calculate the real interest rate for each of the following situations. If borrowers and lenders are anticipating an inflation rate of 3 percent, who gains or loses in each situation?
    a. The nominal interest rate is 10 percent and inflation is zero.
    b. The nominal interest rate is 10 percent and inflation is 5 percent.
    c. The nominal interest rate is 10 percent and prices are falling at a rate of 5 percent.

11. **(Unemployment Rate)** Suppose that the U.S. noninstitutional adult population is 180 million and the labor force participation rate is 65 percent.
    a. What is the size of the U.S. labor force?
    b. If 70 million of the adult population are not working, what is the unemployment rate?
    c. If the number of adults in the military is 2 million, what is the civilian unemployment rate?

12. **(Problems with Official Unemployment Figures)** Explain why most experts believe that official U.S. unemployment figures tend to underestimate unemployment.

13. **(Inflation)** Explain why steady inflation is likely to be less harmful to an economy than a situation in which inflation rates fluctuate a lot.

14. **(Inflation and Relative Price Changes)** What does the consumer price index measure? Does the index indicate changes in relative prices? Why or why not?

15. **(Nominal Versus Real Interest Rates)** Using a supply-demand diagram for loanable funds (like Exhibit 8), show what happens to nominal interest rates and the equilibrium quantity of loans when both borrowers and lenders increase their estimates of the expected inflation rate from 5 percent to 10 percent.

16. **(The Transaction Costs of Variable Inflation)** What changes occurred in U.S. labor and financial markets in response to the variable inflation of the 1970s?

17. **(Inflation and Interest Rates)** For much of 1992, the spread between short- and long-term interest rates on U.S. government debt was at record levels. Could this be explained, at least in part, by anticipated inflation?

18. **(Nominal Versus Real Interest Rates)** Explain as carefully as you can why borrowers would be willing to pay a higher rate of interest if they expected the inflation rate to increase in the future.

19. **(Inflation Costs)** Suppose that the rate of inflation is constant and known with certainty so that all time-related contracts can be indexed perfectly for inflation, and therefore no risk from inflation exists. What kinds of problems might still exist if the inflation rate was exceedingly high?

20. **(Poor King Coal)** Is the unemployment in McDowell County frictional, structural, or cyclical? Why?

21. **(Wild Inflation in Brazil)** In countries like Brazil that are having massive inflation problems, the increased use of another country's currency (like the U.S. dollar) becomes common. Why do you suppose this happens?

22. **(Wild Inflation in Brazil)** Suppose that the exchange rate between cruzeiros and the U.S. dollar is fixed (e.g., 1 dollar = 10,000 cruzeiros). What would this policy do to international trade between the two countries?

Using the Internet

23. Through the Bureau of Labor Statistics (**http://stats.bls.gov/**), find the monthly unemployment rates for the last 12 months (look within "Economy at a Glance"). Do you notice any economic trends? Now examine the last two quarterly unemployment rates for the region of the country you are currently in (look within "Regional Information" and then "Regional Economy"). How does your region compare to the nation as a whole?

8

Measuring Economic Aggregates

Although Americans account for only 5 percent of the world's population, they produce one-quarter of the world's output. In this chapter you will learn how economists keep track of the billions of economic transactions that constitute the U.S. economy—the largest and most complex economy in the history of the world. The scorecard is the *national income accounting system,* which reflects the performance of the economy as a whole by reducing a huge network of economic activity to a few aggregate measures. This chapter focuses on the most important measure of economic activity: the gross domestic product, or GDP—a term already introduced.

As we shall see, the value of total output can be measured either from the total spending on aggregate output or from the total income generated by producing that output. We examine both approaches, show how they are equivalent, and learn how to adjust for changes in the price level over time.

The major components and important equalities built into the national income accounts are offered here as another way of understanding how the economy works—not as a foreign language to be mastered before the next exam. The emphasis here is more on economic intuition than on accounting precision. The main part of this chapter provides the background sufficient for later chapters. More details about the national income accounts are offered in the appendix. Topics discussed in this chapter include:

- Gross domestic product
- National income accounts
- Expenditure and income approaches

- Limitations of national income accounting
- Consumer price index
- GDP price index

THE PRODUCT OF A NATION

How do we measure the economy's performance? During much of the 17th and 18th centuries, when the dominant economic policy was mercantilism, many thought that economic prosperity was best measured by the stock of precious metals a nation accumulated. Francois Quesnay was the first to measure economic activity as a *flow*. In 1758 he published his *Tableau Économique,* which described the circular flow of goods and income among different sectors of the economy. His insight was probably inspired by his knowledge of the circular flow of blood in the body—Quesnay was the court physician to King Louis XV of France.

Rough measures of national income were developed in England more than 200 years ago, but detailed calculations built up from microeconomic data were refined in the United States during the Great Depression. The resulting *national income accounting system* organizes huge quantities of data collected from a variety of sources around the country. These data are summarized, assembled into a coherent framework, and reported periodically by the federal government. The U.S. national income accounts are the most widely reported and among the most highly regarded in the world and have earned their developer, Simon Kuznets, a Nobel Prize.

National Income Accounts

How do the national income accounts keep track of the economy's incredible variety of goods and services, from work boots to guitar lessons? The **gross domestic product,** or **GDP,** measures the market value of all final goods and services produced during a year by resources located in the United States, regardless of who owns those resources. Thus, for example, GDP includes U.S. production by foreign firms, but excludes foreign production by U.S. firms.[1]

The national income accounts are based on a double-entry bookkeeping system in which sales of aggregate output are recorded on one side and resource payments are recorded on the other side. GDP can be measured either by total spending on U.S. production or by total income received from that production. The **expenditure approach** involves adding up the aggregate expenditure on all final goods and services produced during the year. The **income approach** involves adding up the aggregate income earned during the year by those who produce that output.

The gross domestic product includes only **final goods and services,** which are goods and services sold to the final, or ultimate, user. A toothbrush, a pair of contact lenses, and a bus ride are examples of final goods and services. Whether a sale is to the final user often depends on who buys the product. Your purchase of chicken from the grocer is reflected in GDP. When a Kentucky Fried Chicken franchise purchases chicken, however, this transaction is not directly recorded in GDP because the franchise is not the final consumer. Only when the chicken is deep fried and sold to consumers is a sale recorded as part of GDP.

Gross domestic product, or GDP The market value of all final goods and services produced by resources located in the United States, regardless of who owns those resources

Expenditure approach A method of calculating GDP by adding up expenditures on all final goods and services produced during the year

Income approach A method of calculating GDP by adding up all payments to owners of resources used to produce output during the year

Final goods and services Goods and services sold to final, or ultimate, users

---

1   Prior to 1992, the federal government's measure of output was *gross national product,* or *GNP,* which measures the market value of all goods and services produced by resources supplied by U.S. residents and firms, regardless of the location of the resources.

Intermediate goods are those items purchased for additional processing and resale, such as goods bought by grocers as stock for the store.

Intermediate goods and services Goods and services purchased for further reprocessing and resale

Consumption All household purchases of final goods and services

Investment The purchase of new plants, equipment, buildings, and net additions to inventories

Physical Capital Manufactured items used to produce goods and services

Inventories Producers' stocks of finished or in-process goods

Intermediate goods and services are those purchased for additional processing and resale, such as the chicken purchased by a franchise. This additional processing may be imperceptible, as when the corner grocer buys canned goods to stock the shelves. Or the intermediate goods can be dramatically altered, as when paint and canvas are transformed into a work of art.

Sales of intermediate goods and services are excluded from GDP to avoid the problem of *double counting,* which is counting an item's value more than once. For example, suppose the grocer buys a can of tuna for $0.60 and sells it for $1.00. If GDP included both the intermediate transaction of $0.60 and the final transaction of $1.00, that can of tuna would be counted twice in GDP, and the recorded value of $1.60 would be $0.60 more than the final value of the good. Hence, the gross domestic product counts only the final value of the product. The GDP also ignores the value of secondhand goods, such as used cars, existing homes, and used textbooks. These goods were counted as part of GDP in the year they were produced. (But the brokerage services provided by used-car dealers, realtors, and bookstores are included in GDP.)

GDP Based on the Expenditure Approach

As noted already, one way to measure the value of GDP is to add up all spending on final goods and services produced in the economy during the year. The easiest way to understand the spending approach to GDP is to divide aggregate expenditure into its four components: consumption, investment, government purchases, and net exports. We will discuss each in turn.

Consumption, or more specifically, *personal consumption expenditures,* consists of purchases of final goods and services by households during the year. Consumption is the largest spending category and the easiest to understand. Along with services such as dry cleaning and haircuts, consumption includes purchases of nondurable goods, such as soap and soup, and durable goods, such as TVs, CD players, and furniture. Durable goods are those expected to last at least three years. Consumption accounts for about two-thirds of the total spending on final goods and services.

Investment, or more specifically, *gross private domestic investment,* consists of spending during the year on current output that is not used for present consumption. The most important category of investment is new **physical capital,** such as new buildings and new machinery purchased by firms and used to produce goods and services. Investment in the United States accounts for about one-sixth of gross domestic product, although, as we'll see, investment fluctuates from year to year. Investment includes new residential construction but excludes household purchases of durable goods, such as furniture. Investment also excludes purchases of existing buildings and financial assets, such as stocks and bonds.

Changes in firms' inventories are another category of investment. **Inventories** are stocks of goods in process, such as computer parts, and stocks of finished goods, such as new computers. Inventories help manufacturers deal with unexpected changes in the supply of their resources or in the demand for their products. A *net* increase in inventories during the year counts as investment, since inventories are not used for current consumption. Conversely, a net decrease in inventories during the year counts as negative investment, or *disinvestment,* since net inventory reductions represent the sale of output already credited to a prior year's GDP.

Government purchases, or more specifically, *government consumption and gross investment,* include spending by all levels of government for goods and services—from clearing snowy roads to clearing court dockets, from library books to the librarian's pay. Government purchases account for about one-fifth of the total spending in the United States. Government purchases, and therefore GDP, do not include transfer payments, such as Social Security and welfare benefits. Such payments reflect an outright grant from the government to recipients and are not true purchases by the government or true earnings by the recipients.

The final component of aggregate expenditure results from the interaction of the U.S. economy with the rest of the world. **Net exports** equal the value of U.S. exports minus the value of U.S. imports. Net exports include the value of not only merchandise trade—that is, goods, or stuff you can drop on your feet—but also services, or so-called *invisibles,* such as tourism, insurance, accounting, and consulting. In only 4 of the last 35 years has the value of U.S. exports exceeded the value of its imports, meaning net exports were positive in only those 4 years. In all other years, the value of imports exceeded the value of exports, meaning net exports have been negative.

With the expenditure approach, the nation's **aggregate expenditure** equals the sum of consumption, C, investment, I, government purchases, G, and net exports, which is the value of exports, X, minus the value of imports, M, or $(X - M)$. Summing these spending components yields aggregate expenditure, or GDP:

$$C + I + G + (X - M) = \text{Aggregate expenditure} = \text{GDP}$$

Composition of Aggregate Expenditure

Exhibit 1 presents the percentage breakdown of each spending component in the United States since 1959. As you can see, consumption's share of GDP changed little from year to year, but there has been a modest trend upward from an average of 61 percent during the 1960s to 68 percent during the 1990s. Investment bounced around the most from year to year, with no particular trend in terms of its share of GDP. Government purchases trended down from an average of 27 percent in the 1960s to 20 percent in the 1990s. Incidentally, in Chapter 4 you learned that all government spending has been increasing relative to GDP. The sharp growth in transfer payments, especially Social Security, accounts for all that growth (recall that transfer payments are not included in government purchases).

As noted already, net exports have been negative in all but four years since 1959. Negative net exports means that the sum of consumption, investment, and government purchases exceeds GDP, the amount produced in the U.S. economy. So U.S. spending exceeds U.S. GDP by the amount reflected as negative net exports. Since the spending components must sum to GDP, *negative net exports are expressed by that portion of spending that exceeds 100 percent of GDP.*

GDP Based on the Income Approach

The expenditure approach sums, or aggregates, spending on production. The income approach sums, or aggregates, income arising from that production.

Net Bookmark

Should the government, the largest single purchaser in the United States, use its buying power to influence how the private marketplace behaves? For example, should the government invest in "green" technologies, such as solar energy? For one perspective on this issue, visit the Government Purchasing Project, a nonprofit organization (http://www.essential.org/orgs/GPP/GPP.html).

Government purchases Spending for goods and services by all levels of government

Net exports The value of a country's exports minus the value of its imports

Aggregate expenditure Total spending on final goods and services during a given time period

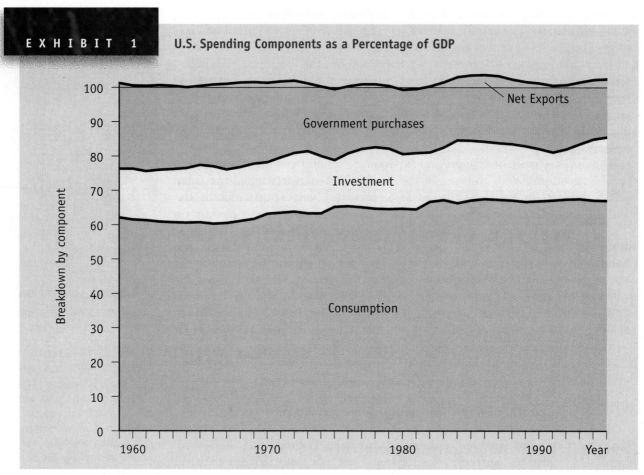

EXHIBIT 1   U.S. Spending Components as a Percentage of GDP

Source: *Economic Report of the President,* February 1996; and U.S. Department of Commerce, *Survey of Current Business,* March 1996.

Double-entry bookkeeping ensures that the value of aggregate output equals the total income paid for resources used to produce that output: the wages, rent, interest, and profit arising from production. The price of a Hershey Bar® reflects income to all the resource suppliers who bring the candy bar to the grocer's shelf. **Aggregate income** equals the sum of all the income earned by resource suppliers in the economy. Thus, we can say that

$$\text{Aggregate expenditure} = \text{GDP} = \text{aggregate income.}$$

The finished product is usually processed by several firms on its way to the consumer. Wooden furniture, for example, starts as raw timber, which is cut by one firm, milled by another, made into furniture by a third, and retailed by a fourth. Double counting can be avoided either by including only the market value of furniture when sold by a retailer or by *calculating the value added at each stage of production.* The **value added** by each firm equals that firm's selling price minus the amount paid for inputs from other firms. The value added at each stage represents income to resource suppliers at that stage. *The sum of the value added at all stages equals the market value of the final good, and the sum of the value*

Aggregate income *The sum of all income earned by resource suppliers in an economy during a given time period*

Value added *The difference at each stage of production between the value of a product and cost of intermediate goods bought from other firms*

EXHIBIT 2

Stage of Production	Sale Value (1)	Cost of Intermediate Goods (2)	Value Added (3)
Logger	$ 20	—	$ 20
Miller	50	$ 20	30
Manufacturer	120	50	70
Retailer	200	120	80
			$200

Computation of Value Added for a New Desk

added for all final goods and services equals the GDP based on the income approach. For example, suppose you buy a wooden desk for $200. Because you are the ultimate user of this desk, $200 is the final market value added directly into GDP. Consider the history of that desk. Suppose the tree that gave its life for your studies was cut into a log that was sold to a miller for $20. That log was milled into lumber and sold to a manufacturer for $50, who made your desk and sold it to a retailer for $120, who sold it to you for $200.

Column (1) of Exhibit 2 lists the selling price at each stage of production. If all of these transactions were added together, the desk would add a total of $390 to GDP. To avoid double counting, we include only the value added at each stage of production, listed in column (3) as the difference between the purchase price and the selling price. Again, the value added at each stage equals the income to all who supplied resources at that stage. For example, the $80 in value added by the retailer represents income to all who contributed resources at that final stage, from the newspaper that carried the retailer's advertising to the truck driver who provided "free delivery" of your desk. The value added at all stages totals $200—which is both the final market value of the desk and the total income earned by all resource suppliers along the way.

LIMITATIONS OF NATIONAL INCOME ACCOUNTING

Imagine the difficulty of developing an accounting system that must capture the subtleties of a complex and dynamic economy, such as the United States'. In the interest of clarity and simplicity, some features of the economy are neglected; others receive perhaps too much weight. In this section, we examine some limitations of the national income accounting system, beginning with productive activity that is not captured by GDP.

Some Production Is Not Included in GDP

With some minor exceptions, GDP includes only those products that are sold in markets. It thus misses all do-it-yourself household production. Household services not purchased in the market are excluded from GDP—child care, meal preparation, house cleaning, even "do-it-yourself" home repair and maintenance. Thus an economy in which householders are largely self-sufficient will have a lower GDP than will an otherwise similar economy in which households specialize and sell goods and services to one another.

This irregularity of the national income accounts has influenced the growth of GDP in recent decades. During the 1950s, more than 80 percent of mothers with small children stayed at home caring for the family, but all this care added not one whit to GDP. Today more than half of mothers with small children are in the work force, where their market labor is reflected in GDP. GDP has increased both because more mothers have market jobs and because household services, such as meals and child care, are now more frequently purchased in markets rather than provided by householders. In less developed economies, more economic activity is "do-it-yourself." Because official GDP figures ignore most home production, these figures understate the household goods and services produced in less developed countries.

Underground economy An expression used to describe all market exchange that goes unreported either because it is illegal or because those involved want to evade taxes

GDP also ignores production where no official records are kept. The **underground economy** is an expression used to describe all market exchange that goes unreported either because the activity itself is illegal, or because those involved want to evade taxes on otherwise legal activity. Although there are no official estimates on the extent of the underground economy, most economists agree that it is substantial. Recent estimates of the underground economy range from 5 percent to 15 percent of GDP.[2] A Census Bureau study suggests that the nation's underground economy amounts to about 7.5 percent of GDP, which in 1996 would have been about $500 billion.

Even though some production is not reflected in GDP, the *imputed income* from certain activities that do not pass across recorded markets is included. Income must be imputed, or estimated, because market exchange does not occur. For example, included in GDP is an *imputed rental income* that homeowners receive from home ownership, even though no rent is actually paid or received. (This imputed income is discussed in the appendix to this chapter.) Also included in GDP is an imputed dollar amount for (1) wages paid *in kind,* such as employers' payments for employees' medical insurance and (2) food produced on the farm for that farm family's own consumption. The national income accounts therefore reflect some economic production that does not involve market exchange.

Leisure, Quality, and Variety

The average work week is much shorter now than it was at the turn of the century, so people work less to produce today's output. The increase over the years in the amount of leisure available has resulted in a higher quality of life. But leisure time is not reflected in GDP because leisure is not explicitly bought and sold in a market. The quality and variety of products available have also improved over the years, as a result of technological advances and competition, yet most of these improvements are not reflected in GDP. For example, improvements have occurred in televisions, recording systems, computers, running shoes, tires, and so on. Also, new products are introduced each year. *The gross domestic product fails to reflect (1) changes in the availability of leisure time, (2) changes in the quality of existing products, and (3) changes in the availability of new*

---

2   See Joel F. Houston, "The Underground Economy: A Troubling Issue for Policymakers," Federal Reserve Bank of Philadelphia *Business Review* (September/October 1987): 3–12.

products. The special problem of measuring production in an economy shaped by changing technology is discussed in the following case study.

CASE STUDY

Tracking a $7 Trillion Economy

Location:

To learn more about tracking the U.S. economy, visit the Bureau of the Census (http://www.census.gov/), the Bureau of Economic Analysis (http://www.bea.doc.gov/), and the Bureau of Labor Statistics (http://stats.bls.gov/).

Ever since Article I of the U.S. Constitution required a decennial population census, the federal government has been gathering statistics. The three main statistics-gathering agencies are the Bureau of the Census, the Bureau of Economic Analysis, and the Bureau of Labor Statistics. Since 1980, real GDP has increased by about 50 percent, employment has increased by more than 25 million, and real foreign trade has more than doubled. Yet the federal budget for statistics-gathering agencies has declined in real terms. Only 0.2 percent of the federal budget goes toward keeping track of the economy.

Federal budget cuts have eliminated some data-collection efforts and have slowed down others. For example, computations of monthly international trade statistics have become so overwhelming that as many as half of the imports counted for a particular month reflect a "carryover" from previous months. Some agencies must do more with the same staff. For example, in 1980 the Bureau of Labor Statistics had 18 analysts to monitor productivity in 95 different industries. The number of industries they track now exceeds 175, but the number of analysts remains unchanged.

The traditional ways of monitoring economic activity were originally developed in the 1930s and 1940s, when manufacturing dominated. Manufacturing output is relatively easy to measure because the output is tangible, such as automobiles or toasters. But service output, such as financial advice or on-line computer services, is intangible, and is therefore more difficult to measure.

Because services are intangible, measures for the service sector tend to be less reliable than those for the manufacturing sector. Measures of service output often fail to reflect improvements in the speed or quality of services. For example, computerized checkout systems not only record sales information more efficiently but allow retailers to track inventory and order new supplies. Or consider the Wisconsin trucking firm that uses on-board computers in its trucks to map the most efficient routes and to remap the routes should priorities change. The firm has become so efficient that the number of ton-miles (tonnage times miles) carried per month has declined. Yet, according to government statisticians, these truck drivers are less productive because ton-miles is how output is measured.

Government statisticians have no way of measuring output in a wide range of industries including banking, medicine, software, legal services, wholesale trade, and communications. For example, the output growth in banking is assumed equal to the increase in hours worked in the industry, so labor productivity is assumed to be zero, even though research suggests that labor productivity has grown by an average of 2 percent per year in the industry. In medicine, productivity measures have no way to reflect the benefits of new surgical procedures that are safer and require less recuperation time than earlier procedures.

There are indications that output and productivity in the service sector may be rising faster than official records show. For example, capital investment in the service sector has risen substantially in recent years—far more than in the manufacturing sector. And the United States has experienced growing trade surpluses in services, suggesting that the U.S. service sector is competitive and relatively productive, at least when compared to services produced abroad. In contrast, the trade balance on goods has been in deficit, and this deficit has been growing.

Sources: Alfred Malabre and Lindley Clark, "Productivity Statistics for the Service Sector May Understate Gains," *The Wall Street Journal,* 12 August 1992; "The Real Truth about the Economy," *BusinessWeek,* 7 November 1994, pp. 110–118; and Lee Burton, "Big Six's Shift to Consulting Accelerates," *The Wall Street Journal,* 21 September 1995.

Gross Domestic Product Ignores Depreciation

Depreciation The value of capital stock used up during a year in producing GDP

Net domestic product Gross domestic product minus depreciation

In the course of producing GDP, some capital wears out, such as the delivery truck that finally dies, and some capital becomes obsolete, such as an outmoded computer. A new truck that logs a hundred thousand miles its first year has been subject to wear and tear and therefore has a diminished value as a resource. A truer picture of the *net* production that actually occurs during the year is found by subtracting this *depreciation* from GDP. **Depreciation** measures the value of the capital stock that is used up or becomes obsolete in the production process. The gross domestic product is called "gross" because it fails to take into account this depreciation. **Net domestic product** equals gross domestic product minus depreciation—the value of the capital stock used up in the production process.

We can now distinguish between two definitions of investment. *Gross investment* measures the value of all investment during the period. Gross investment is used in computing GDP. *Net investment* equals gross investment minus depreciation. The economy's production possibilities depend on what happens to net investment. If net investment is negative—that is, if depreciation exceeds gross investment—the capital stock declines, so its contribution to output will decline as well. If net investment is zero, the capital stock remains constant, as does its contribution to output. And if net investment is positive, the capital stock grows, as does its contribution to output.

As the names imply, the *gross* domestic product (GDP) reflects *gross* investment and the *net* domestic product (NDP) reflects *net* investment. Developing a figure for depreciation involves much guesswork. For example, what is the appropriate measure of depreciation for the parking lots at Disney World, the metal display shelves at Wal-Mart, the 5,000-gallon casks used to age wine in the Napa Valley, or the Library of Congress building?

GDP Does Not Reflect All Costs

Some production and consumption degrades the quality of our environment. Trucks and automobiles pump carbon monoxide into the atmosphere. Housing developments displace forests. Paper mills foul the lungs and burn the eyes. These negative externalities—costs that fall on those not directly involved in the transactions—are largely ignored in GDP accounting, even though they diminish the quality of life and may limit future production. To the extent that growth in GDP also involves growth in such negative externalities, a rising GDP may not be as attractive as it would first appear.

Although the national income accounts reflect the depreciation of the buildings, machinery, vehicles, and other manufactured capital, this accounting ignores the depletion of natural resources, such as standing timber, fish stocks, soil fertility, and the like. So manufactured capital stock is depreciated but the natural capital stock is not. For example, suppose intensive farming raises farm productivity temporarily but depletes the fertility of the soil. The additional farm production adds to GDP, but the soil's lost fertility is ignored. The U.S. Commerce Department is now in the process of developing so-called "green" accounting to reflect the impact of production on air pollution, water pollution, lost trees, soil depletion, and the loss of other natural resources.

GDP Values All Output Equally

In GDP, the market price of output is the measure of its value. Therefore, each dollar spent purchasing handguns or attack dogs is counted in GDP the same as each dollar spent purchasing baby formula or fresh fruit. Positive economic analysis tries to avoid making value judgments about how people choose to spend their money. Because the level of GDP provides no information about its composition, some economists question whether GDP is a good measure of the nation's economic welfare. For example, at a time when many people in the nation are hungry and homeless, Americans spend billions of dollars on tobacco products, even though these products are linked to illness and death.

Despite the limitations and potential inaccuracies associated with official GDP estimates, the trend of GDP over time provides a fairly accurate picture of the overall movement of the U.S. economy. Inflation, however, distorts the direct comparability of dollar amounts from one year to the next. In the next section we examine how to adjust GDP for changes in the economy's price level.

ACCOUNTING FOR PRICE CHANGES

As we noted earlier, the national income accounts are based on the market values of the goods and services produced in a particular year. The gross domestic product measures the value of output in *current dollars*—that is, in the dollar values at the time the output is produced. When GDP is based on current dollars, the national income accounts measure the *nominal value* of national output. Hence, the current-dollar GDP, or **nominal GDP,** is based on the prices prevailing when the output is produced.

Nominal GDP GDP based on prices prevailing at the time of the transaction; current-dollar GDP

Real GDP A measure of GDP that removes the impact of price changes from changes in nominal GDP

The system of national income accounting based on current, or nominal, dollars allows us to make comparisons among income or expenditure components in a particular year. Since the economy's price level changes over time, however, current-dollar comparisons across years make less sense. For example, between 1979 and 1980, nominal GDP increased by about 9 percent. That sounds impressive, but the economy's price level rose more. Hence, the growth in nominal GDP between 1979 and 1980 resulted entirely from inflation. **Real GDP**—that is, GDP measured in terms of actual production—in fact declined.

If nominal GDP increases in a given year, part of this increase may simply be the result of inflation—pure hot air. To make meaningful comparisons of GDP across years, we take out the hot air, or *deflate* nominal GDP. To focus on *real* changes in production, we eliminate changes due solely to changes in the price level. To do this, we must devise a way to compare the price level in one year with the price level in another year.

Price Indexes

To compare the price level over time, let's first establish a point of reference, a base year to which prices in other years can be compared. An *index number* compares the value of some variable in a particular year to its value in a base, or reference, year. To see how index numbers work, consider the simplest case imaginable. Suppose bread is the only good produced in the economy. As a reference point against which to measure price changes, we choose the price of bread in some specified year. The year selected is called the **base year;** prices in other years are expressed in terms of the base-year price.

Base year The year with which other years are compared when constructing an index; the index equals 100 in the base year, or base period

Suppose the base year is 1994, when a loaf of bread in our simple economy sold for $1.25. Let's say the price of bread increased to $1.30 in 1995, and to $1.40 in 1996. We construct a *price index* by dividing each year's price by the price in the base year and then multiplying by 100, as shown in Exhibit 3. For 1994, the base year, we divide the base price of bread by itself, $1.25/$1.25, which equals 1, so the price index in the base year equals $1 \times 100 = 100$. *The price index in the base year is always 100.* The price index in 1995 is $1.30/$1.25, which equals 1.04, which when multiplied by 100 equals 104. In 1996, the index is $1.40/$1.25, or 1.12, which when multiplied by 100 equals 112. Thus, the index in 1995 is 4 percent higher than in the base year; in 1996 it is 12 percent higher than in the base year.

The price index not only permits comparisons between the base year and any other year but also allows for comparisons between any two years. For example, what if you were presented with the indexes for 1995 and 1996 and asked what happened to the price level between the two years? By dividing the 1996 price index by the 1995 price index, 112/104, you would find that the price level rose by 7.7 percent.

This section has shown how to develop a price index assuming we already know the price level each year. Determining the price level is a bit more involved, as we now see.

Consumer Price Index

Consumer price index (CPI) A measure over time of the cost of a fixed "market basket" of consumer goods and services

The price index most familiar to you is the **consumer price index,** or **CPI,** which measures changes over time in the cost of buying the "market basket" of goods and services purchased by a typical family. Changes in the cost of this bas-

EXHIBIT 3	Year	Price of Bread in Current Year (1)	Price of Bread in Base Year (2)	Price Index (3) = (1)/(2) × 100
Hypothetical Example of a Price Index (base year = 1994)	1994	$1.25	$1.25	100
	1995	1.30	1.25	104
	1996	1.40	1.25	112

Hypothetical Market Basket Used to Develop the Consumer Price Index

EXHIBIT 4

Good or Service	Quantity in Market Basket (1)	Prices in Base Year (2)	Cost of Basket in Base Year (3) = (1) × (2)	Prices in Current Year (4)	Cost of Basket in Current Year (5) = (1) × (4)
Twinkies	365 packages	$ 0.49/package	$178.85	$ 0.45	$ 164.25
Fuel Oil	500 gallons	1.00/gallon	500.00	1.50	750.00
Cable TV	12 months	20.00/month	240.00	20.00	240.00
			$918.85		$1,154.25

ket are often referred to as changes in the "cost of living." For simplicity, suppose a typical family's market basket for the year includes 365 packages of Twinkies, 500 gallons of fuel oil, and 12 months of cable TV service. Prices in the base year are listed in column (2) of Exhibit 4. The total cost of each product in the base year is found by multiplying price times quantity, as shown in column (3). The cost of the market basket in the base year is shown at the bottom of column (3) to be $918.85.

Current-year prices are listed in column (4). Notice that not all prices changed by the same amount since the base year. The price of fuel oil increased by 50 percent, but the price of Twinkies declined. The cost of purchasing that same basket in the current year is $1,154.25, shown as the total of column (5). To compute the consumer price index for the current year, we simply divide the total cost in the current year by the total cost of that same basket in the base year, $1,154.25/$918.85, then multiply by 100. This yields a price index of 125.6. We could say that between the base year and the current year, the "cost of living" increased by 25.6 percent, although not all prices increased by the same percentage.

The federal government uses the years 1982 to 1984 as the base period for calculating the CPI for a market basket of about four hundred items. The CPI is reported monthly based on price data collected from about 18,000 sellers in 56 localities across the country. In reality, of course, each household consumes a unique market basket, so we could theoretically develop 100 million CPIs—one for each U.S. household.

Problems with the CPI

There is no perfect way to measure changes in the price level. As we have already noted, the quality and variety of products are, on average, improving all the time, so some price increases may be as much a reflection of quality improvements as of inflation. For example, the computing power per dollar spent on personal computers has increased sharply in the last decade. There is a *quality bias* in the CPI, since it assumes that quality remains relatively constant over time even though quality has generally improved. *As a result of underestimating quality improvements, the CPI overstates the true extent of inflation.*

The CPI tends to overstate inflation for another reason. Recall that the CPI holds constant over time the kind and amount of goods and services in the typical market basket. Since not all items in the market basket experience the same rates of price change, relative prices change over time. A family would respond to changes in relative prices by consuming less of the relatively more expensive goods and more of the relatively cheaper goods. But, because the CPI holds the composition of the market basket constant, it ignores consumer adjustments to changes in relative prices. *The CPI calculations thus imply uneconomical consumer behavior, thereby overstating the true extent of inflation experienced by the typical family.*

CPI has also failed to keep up with the consumer shift toward discount outlets. Government statisticians consider goods sold at discount retailers as distinct from similar or identical goods sold by traditional retailers. The discounter is assumed to be offering a different good, one with lower services and consumer amenities. Hence the discounter's lower price does not translate into a reduction in the cost of living.

A panel of five prominent economists recently evaluated the CPI for Congress. The panel concluded that the index overstates increases in the cost of living by about 1 percent per year. This 1 percent breaks down as follows: (1) failure to reflect improving quality adds 0.2 percent; (2) failure to reflect consumer adjustments to relative price changes adds 0.3 percent; (3) failure to reflect new products in a timely way adds 0.3 percent; and (4) failure to include the shift toward discount outlets adds 0.2 percent.

The CPI is of more than academic concern because changes in an array of payments ranging from labor union agreements to Social Security benefits are linked to the index. This 1 percent annual overestimation of the annual CPI increase means the Social Security program pays out billions more than is required to keep up with the cost of living. Overstating the CPI also distorts measures that use the CPI to adjust for inflation, such as real median family income. For example, based on the official CPI, the real median family income has increased only about 5 percent in the last two decades. If we correct for a 1 percent upward bias in CPI growth, however, real median family income has increased more than 25 percent in the last two decades.

GDP Price Index

Price indexes are weighted sums of various prices. The consumer price index reflects the price of a market basket of consumer goods. Whereas the CPI focuses on just a sample of consumer purchases, a more complex and more comprehensive price index, the *GDP price index,* keeps track of price changes for *all production* in the economy. The **GDP price index,** first introduced in Chapter 5, includes the prices of *all* final domestically produced goods and services in a year, including newly produced capital goods. When we consider the spending of any particular item, we say

GDP price index A comprehensive price index of all goods and services included in the gross domestic product

$$\text{Spending} = \text{price} \times \text{quantity}$$

Similarly, with GDP

$$\text{Nominal GDP} = \text{price index} \times \text{quantity index}$$
$$= \text{GDP price index} \times \text{real GDP}$$

By rearranging terms, we can calculate the GDP price index as nominal GDP divided by real GDP.

If we know nominal GDP and real GDP, then finding the GDP price index is easy. The real challenge is finding real GDP. Any measure of real GDP is constructed as the weighted sum of thousands of different goods and services produced in the economy. The question is what weights, or prices, to use. Between World War II and 1995, the Bureau of Economic Analysis (BEA) used prices of a particular year (most recently, 1987) to estimate real GDP. In this case, the quantity of each output in, say, 1994 (or any other year) was valued by the 1987 price of each output. So real GDP in 1994 was the sum of 1994 outputs valued at 1987 prices.

Moving from Fixed Weights to Chain Weights

Using prices from a single base year yields an accurate measure of real GDP as long as the year considered is close to the base year. But prices that prevailed in 1987 were used to value production in years from 1929 to 1995. The problem with fixing prices in some base year is that relative prices in fact change over time, and this change motivates economic activity. The use of fixed prices can distort estimates of real GDP.

In early 1996 BEA moved from a *fixed-weighted system* to a *chain-weighted system* to estimate the index of real GDP and the GDP price index. The chain-weighted system makes use of the natural order of the march of time by computing indexes in real GDP and in prices using weights that change from year to year. The weights used are those from two adjacent periods. For example, the index of real GDP for 1993 is based on prices in 1992 and 1993; the index of real GDP for 1994 is based on prices in 1993 and 1994; and the index of real GDP for 1995 is based on prices in 1994 and 1995. Thus, the index of real GDP for 1995 is not obtained from a direct comparison with 1992 prices but rather by moving along links in the chain. This approach is spelled out in Appendix B. All you need to know now is that the chain-weighted real GDP index adjusts the price weights more or less continuously, getting rid of much of the bias caused by a fixed-price weighting system. A good example of that bias involves computers, as discussed in the following case study.

As noted already, until 1996 BEA based its real GDP estimates on 1987 prices. Based on these estimates, most observers believed that the economic recovery that began in the spring of 1991 was driven primarily by investment, especially spending on computers. In this case study, we reconsider the role of computer spending as an economic stimulus.

Computer prices have fallen an average of 13 percent per year since 1982. Based on this rate of decline, a computer that cost, say, $10,000 in 1982 cost about $5,000 in 1987 and about $1,650 in 1995. According to these prices, that computer cost about the same in 1982 as a minivan; it cost about the same in 1995 as a 42-inch TV. So computers became dramatically less expensive between 1982 and 1995.

The sharp decline in the price of computers spurred computer purchases both in the office and in

CASE STUDY

Computer Prices and GDP Estimation

Location:

How do computer prices and sales compare in Europe? Context: European Computer Information Service, headquartered in London, specializes in tracking sales and prices across a range of computer products in all major European countries. Visit Context (http://www.context-ecis.co.uk/).

Computer Prices and GDP Estimation
continued

the home. Suppose the number of computers sold jumped from 200,000 in 1982 to 1,000,000 in 1995. In current, or nominal, dollars, spending on these computers declined from $2 billion in 1982 to $1.6 billion in 1995, a drop of 20 percent. When computer purchases are valued at the 1987 price of $5,000, however, computer spending increased from $1 billion in 1982 to $5 billion in 1995, a five-fold jump. Using the 1987 price understates computer spending in 1982 and overstates computer spending in 1995. Using the 1987 price also exaggerates the growth in computer spending between 1982 and 1995.

The chain-weighted measure of prices shows a sharply lower growth in computer spending compared to the fixed-weight approach. Based on the chain-weighted approach, investment grew less rapidly during the recovery that began in 1991 than during the four previous recoveries, so investment turned out to be less of a factor in stimulating economic expansion than it had been in the last two decades. The chain-weighting system, although it is more complicated than the fixed-weighted system, provides a more reliable picture of the economy.

Sources: "Improved Estimates of the National Income and Product Accounts for 1959–95: Results of the Comprehensive Revision," *Survey of Current Business,* Vol. 76 (Jan./Feb. 1996), pp. 1–31; and Robert Hershey, "Counting the Wealth of Nations: GDP's Accuracy Is Under Attack from All Sides," *New York Times,* 19 Dec. 1995.

Real GDP Estimates

Even though the chain-type index adjusts the weights from year to year, any index, by definition, must use some year as a reference point—that is, any index must answer the question "compared to what?" To provide such a reference point, the BEA set its quantity and price indexes equal to 100 in 1992. BEA also measures real GDP and its components in *"chained (1992) dollars,"* which are computed by multiplying the 1992 current-dollar value of GDP by the corresponding real GDP index for the year in question. For example, the real GDP index increased from 100 in 1992 to 105.8 in 1994. To determine the chained (1992) dollar estimate of real GDP in 1994, we multiply the current-dollar GDP in 1992, which is $6,244.4 billion, by 1.058 to get $6,604.2 billion.

There is one minor problem with the chain-weighting approach. Because the new formula uses chained weights and because each component of GDP is estimated separately, the chained (1992) dollar estimates for the detailed GDP components do not add up to the chained (1992) dollar estimates of GDP. Consequently, BEA also reports a *residual,* which is the difference between real GDP and the sum of component estimates. For years close to 1992, this residual is tiny. The residual grows as the year moves farther from 1992 (for example, in 1959 it was 3.1 percent of GDP). Not only is the residual relatively small, it changes in a smooth way over time. For the practical purposes of our analysis in subsequent chapters, we will assume that the residual is small enough to be ignored.

Exhibit 5 presents current-dollar estimates of GDP as well as chained (1992) dollar estimates of real GDP. The blue line indicates current-dollar GDP, or nominal GDP, since 1959. The red line indicates real GDP since 1959, or GDP measured in chained (1992) dollars. The two lines intersect in 1992, when real GDP equals nominal GDP. Current-dollar GDP is below real GDP in years prior to 1992 because real GDP is based on chained (1992) prices, which are

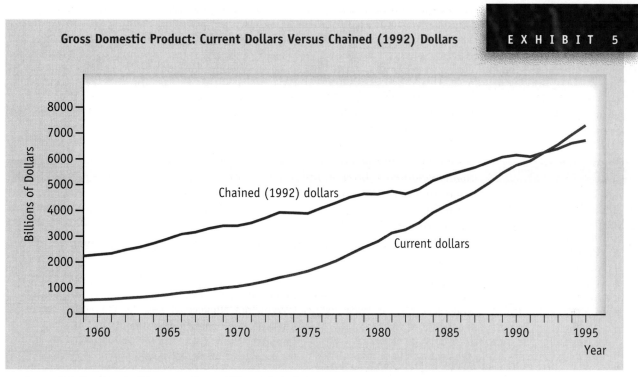

Gross Domestic Product: Current Dollars Versus Chained (1992) Dollars   E X H I B I T   5

Source: U.S. Department of Commerce, Bureau of Economic Analysis.

above current prices during years prior to 1992. Current-dollar GDP grows faster than real GDP because the growth in current-dollar GDP reflects growth in both real GDP and the price level.

CONCLUSION

This chapter explained how to measure GDP and how to adjust it for changes in the economy's price level. In subsequent chapters we will often refer to distinctions between real and nominal values. Though no price index is perfect, the price indexes now in use provide reasonably good measures of the trend in price levels over time. The national income accounts have limitations, but they do offer a reasonably accurate measure of year-to-year movements in the economy. The national income accounts are published in much greater detail than the preceding discussion suggests. Appendix A to this chapter provides additional detail regarding the national income accounts. Appendix B shows how to derive chain-weighted indexes.

S U M M A R Y

1. Gross domestic product measures the market value of all final goods and services produced during the year by resources located in the United States, regardless of who owns those resources.

2. The expenditure approach to GDP adds up the market value of all final goods and services produced in the economy during the year. The income approach to GDP adds up all the income generated as a result of that production during the year.

3. GDP reflects market production that is recorded; household production and the underground economy are not recorded and are therefore excluded from GDP. Improvements in the quality and variety of goods are generally not reflected in GDP either. In other ways GDP may overstate the true amount of production that occurs. GDP fails to account for depreciation of the capital stock or for any negative externalities arising from production.

4. Nominal GDP in a particular year values output based on market prices prevailing that year. To determine real GDP, nominal GDP must be adjusted for the effects of changes in the price level. Two indexes used to track the price level are the consumer price index, or CPI, and the GDP price index. No adjustment for changes in the price level is perfect.

QUESTIONS AND PROBLEMS

1. **(National Income Accounting)** Identify the component of aggregate expenditure to which each of the following belongs:
   a. Purchase of a new automobile manufactured in Japan.
   b. Purchase of one hour of legal counsel by a household.
   c. Construction of a new house.
   d. An increase in semiconductor inventories over last year's level.
   e. Acquistion of 10 new police cars for a city.

2. **(National Income Accounts)** Define gross domestic product. Indicate whether each of the following would be included in the 1996 U.S. measure of gross domestic product:
   a. Profits earned by Ford on automobile production in Ireland.
   b. Automobile parts manufactured in the United States in 1996 but not used until 1997.
   c. Social Security benefits paid by the U.S. government in 1996.
   d. Ground beef purchased and used by McDonald's in 1996.
   e. Ground beef purchased and consumed by a private U.S. household in 1996.
   f. Goods and services purchased in the United States in 1996 by a Canadian tourist.

3. **(Nominal GDP)** Indicate which of the following *must* have occurred in order for nominal GDP to rise. Explain your answers.
   a. Actual production must have increased.
   b. Prices must have increased.
   c. Real GDP must have increased.
   d. Both prices and actual production must have increased.

4. **(Expenditure Approach to GDP)** Consider the following annual information about a hypothetical country:

	Billions of Current Dollars
Personal consumption expenditures	200
Personal taxes	50
Exports	30
Depreciation	10
Government purchases	50
Gross private domestic investment	40
Imports	40
Government transfer payments	20

   a. What is the value of nominal GDP?
   b. What is the value of nominal net domestic product?
   c. What is the value of net investment?
   d. What is the value of net exports?

5. **(Investment)** In the national income accounts, one part of measured investment is net changes in inventories. Last year's inventories are subtracted from this year's inventories to obtain a net change. Explain why this variable is considered part of the national income. Also, discuss why it is not sufficient to measure inventories only for the current year. (Remember the difference between stocks and flows.)

6. **(Income Approach to GDP)** How does the income approach to measuring GDP differ from the expenditure approach? Explain the meaning of value added and its importance in using the income approach. Consider the following data for each stage in the production of a 5 pound bag of flour sold by your local grocery. Calculate the final market value of the flour.

Stage of Production	Sale Price
Farmer	$0.30
Miller	0.50
Wholesaler	1.00
Grocery	1.50

7. **(Price Index)** Home computers and video cassette recorders have not been part of the U.S. economy for very long, and both goods have been decreasing in price and improving in quality. What problems does this situation pose for people who are responsible for computing a price index?

8. **(Price Index)** Calculate a new price index for the data in Exhibit 4 in this chapter. Assume current year prices for the Twinkies, fuel oil, and cable TV of $0.45/package, $1.25/gallon, and $10.80 per month, respectively. Calculate the current year's cost of the market basket and the value of the current year's price index. What is the percentage change in the average price level?

9. **(Price Index)** The health expenditure component of the price index has been steadily rising. How might this index be biased by quality and substitution effects? Are there any substitutes for health care?

10. **(Consumer Price Index)** What is the value of the consumer price index in the base year? Calculate the annual rate of consumer inflation in each of the following situtations:
    a. The CPI equals 200 in 1996 and 240 in 1997.
    b. The CPI equals 150 in 1996 and 175 in 1997.
    c. The CPI equals 325 in 1996 and 340 in 1997.
    d. The CPI equals 325 in 1996 and 315 in 1997.

11. **(National Income Accounting)** Suppose a company produces something nobody wants. Since production of the good generates income to the resources employed, it is included in GDP on the income side. How would it be counted on the expenditure side?

12. **(National Income Accounts)** Explain why intermediate goods and services generally are not included directly in the measure of GDP. Are there any circumstances under which they would be included directly?

13. **(Price Index)** Consider the following data.

Good	Current Output Level (units)	Base Years Household Consumption Level (units)	Base Price (per unit)	Current Price (per unit)
Clothing	100,000	2	$10	$12
Food	120,000	3	2	4
Durables	6,000	1	50	40

a. Calculate the rate of price increase from the base period to the current period, using the consumer price index method.

b. Is the basket of goods used to calculate the CPI in the current year the same as the basket of goods that would be used to calculate the GDP price index?
c. What problems are associated with using the rate of change in the CPI as a measure of inflation?

14. **(Gross Domestic Product)** Explain why each of the following should be taken into account when GDP data are used to compare the "level of well-being" in different countries.
    a. Population levels.
    b. Distribution of income.
    c. The amount of production that takes place *outside* of markets (e.g., housekeeping by a family member).
    d. The length of the average work week.
    e. The degree of pollution in the environment.

15. **(Investment)** Answer the questions below on the basis of the following annual data:

	Billions of Current Dollars
New residential construction	$500
Purchases of existing homes	250
Sales value of newly issued stocks and bonds	600
New physical capital	800
Depreciation	200
Household purchases of new furniture	50
Net change in firms' inventories	100
Production of new intermediate goods	700

a. What is the value of gross private domestic investment?
b. What is the value of net investment?
c. Are any intermediate goods included in the measure of gross investment?

16. **(GDP Price Index)** What is the chain-weighted system to estimate the index of real GDP? What is meant by the *residual* reported by the Bureau of Economic Analysis in the chain-weighted system? What happens to the residual as the current year moves farther and farther from the base year? Calculate the chained (1992) dollar estimate of current-year real GDP for each of the following:
    a. The current-year's real GDP index equals 104.2.
    b. The current-year's real GDP index equals 107.8.
    c. The current-year's real GDP index equals 111.2.
    d. The current-year's real GDP index equals 98.5.

17. **(Consumer Price Index)** One form of the CPI that has been advocated by lobbying groups is a "CPI for the elderly." The Bureau of Labor Statistics currently pro-

duces only indexes for "all urban households" and "urban wage earners and clerical workers." Should the BLS produce such an index for the elderly?

18. **(GDP Price Index)** What is the relationship between a given year's real GDP and its nominal GDP? How does the method adopted in 1996 for measuring real GDP differ from the method used from 1929 to 1995?

19. **(Tracking a $7 Trillion Economy)** Explain why it has become increasingly difficult for the federal government to monitor economic activity in the United States.

20. **(Computer Prices and GDP Estimation)** Compared to the fixed-weighted system, how does the chain-weighted system better account for the economic incentives provided by price changes?

Using the Internet

21. Visit the Federal Reserve Bank of Chicago's "Economic Indicators" (**http://gopher.great-lakes.net:2200/1/partners/ChicagoFed/econind**). First look within "Nominal Gross Domestic Product, Historical." For the first quarter of 1956, record the amount of the GDP, consumption, investment, net exports, and government purchases. Next, look within "Nominal Gross Domestic Product, Current." Record the same information for the most recent quarter.

a. How much greater was the GDP in the most recent quarter?
b. For both quarters, calculate the percentage of the GDP for consumption, investment, net exports, and government purchases. Have these respective percentages changed greatly over time?

Appendix A

A CLOSER LOOK AT NATIONAL INCOME ACCOUNTS

This chapter has focused on gross domestic product, or GDP, the measure of output that will be of most interest in subsequent chapters. Other economic aggregates also convey useful information and receive media attention. One of these, *net domestic product,* has already been introduced. Exhibit 6 shows that net domestic product equals gross domestic product minus depreciation. In this appendix we examine other aggregate measures.

National Income

Thus far we have been talking about the value of production from resources located in the United States, regardless of who owns the resources. Sometimes we want to know how much American resource suppliers earn for their land, labor, capital, and entrepreneurial ability. **National income** captures all income earned by American-owned resources, whether those resources are located in the United States or abroad. National income results from several adjustments to net domestic product. First, net

production from American-owned resources abroad, and hence the net income earned from that production, must be added to net domestic product. To get net production, we add income earned by American resources abroad and subtract income earned by foreign-owned resources in the United States.

Second, the value of final goods and services is computed at market prices, but, because of **government subsidies,** such as payments to suppliers of low-income housing, some products sell for less than resource suppliers receive. Since subsidies are received as income, they should be included in national income, even though they are not part of the selling price.

Third, because of **indirect business taxes,** such as sales, excise, and property taxes, some products sell for more than resource suppliers receive. For example, a gallon of gasoline may sell for $1.25, but about $0.25 in taxes must be paid to the government before any resource supplier earns a penny. Since indirect business taxes are not received as income by any individual, they should not be included in national income, even though they are part of the selling price. Since indirect business taxes are about 20 times greater than government subsidies, we simplify the reporting by computing *indirect business taxes net of subsidies.*

National income therefore equals net domestic product plus net earnings from American resources abroad minus indirect business taxes (net of subsidies). Exhibit 6 shows how to go from net domestic product to national income. We have now moved from gross domestic product to net domestic product to national income. Next we peel back yet another layer to arrive at personal income, the income people actually receive.

Personal Income

Some of the income received this year was not earned this year, and some of the income earned this

EXHIBIT 6		
Deriving Net Domestic Product and National Income Using 1995 Data (in trillions of dollars)		
Gross domestic product (GDP)		$7.25
Minus depreciation		−0.82
Net domestic product		6.43
Plus net earnings of American resources abroad minus indirect business taxes (net of subsidies)		−0.64
National income		$5.79

Source: *Economic Report of the President,* February 1996; annual estimates based on figures from three quarters.

year was not actually received this year by those who earned it. By adding to national income the income received but not earned and subtracting the income earned but not received, we convert national income into all income *received* by individuals, which is termed **personal income.** Personal income, a widely reported measure of economic welfare, is computed by the federal government monthly.

The adjustment from national income to personal income is shown in Exhibit 7. Income *earned but not received* includes the employer's share of Social Security taxes, corporate income taxes, and undistributed corporate profits, which are profits the firm retains rather than pays as dividends. Income *received but not earned* in the current period includes government transfer payments, receipts from private pension plans, and interest paid by government and by consumers.

Disposable Income

Although several taxes have been considered so far, we have not yet discussed personal taxes. Personal taxes consist primarily of federal, state, and local personal income taxes and the employee's share of the Social Security tax. Subtracting personal taxes and other government charges from personal income yields **disposable income,** which is the amount

available for spending or saving—the amount that can be "disposed of" by the household. Think of disposable income as take-home pay. Exhibit 7 shows that personal income minus personal taxes and other government charges yields disposable income.

Summary of National Income Accounts

The income side of national income accounts can be summarized as follows. We begin with *gross domestic product,* or *GDP,* the market value of final goods and services produced during the year by resources located in the United States. We subtract depreciation from GDP to yield the *net domestic product.* From net domestic product we add net earnings from American resources abroad and subtract indirect business taxes (net of subsidies) to yield *national income.* We obtain *personal income* by subtracting from national income all income earned but not received (e.g., undistributed corporate profits) and adding all income received but not earned (e.g., transfer payments). By subtracting personal taxes and other government charges from personal income, we arrive at the bottom line: *disposable income,* the amount people are actually free either to save or to spend.

Summary Income Statement of the Economy

Exhibit 8 presents an annual income statement for the entire economy. The upper portion lists aggregate expenditure, which consists of consumption, gross investment, government purchases, and net exports. Because imports exceeded exports, net exports are negative. You might think of aggregate expenditure as the revenue of a giant firm. The income from this expenditure is broken down in the lower portion of Exhibit 8. After depreciation, net earnings from American resources abroad, and net indirect business taxes, the remaining forms of income make up national income. National income, which is the sum of all earnings from resources supplied by U.S. residents and firms, can be divided into its five components: employee compensation, proprietors' income, corporate profits, net interest, and rental income of persons.

Employee compensation, which is by far the largest source of income, includes both money wages and employer contributions to cover Social Security taxes, medical insurance, and other fringe benefits.

EXHIBIT 7

Deriving Personal Income and Disposable Income Using 1995 Data (in trillions of dollars)

National income	$5.79
Minus income earned but not received (Social Security taxes, corporate income taxes, undistributed corporate profits)	−1.65
Plus income received but not earned (government and business transfers, net personal interest income)	1.96
Personal income	6.10
Minus personal tax and nontax charges	−0.80
Disposable income	$5.30

Source: *Economic Report of the President,* February 1996; annual estimates based on figures for three quarters.

EXHIBIT 8

Expenditure and Income Statement for the U.S. Economy Using 1995 Data (in trillions of dollars)

Aggregate Expenditure

Consumption (C)	$4.94
Gross investment (I)	1.06
Government purchases (G)	1.36
Net exports (X − M)	−0.11
GDP	$7.25

Allocation of Income

Depreciation	$0.82
Net earnings of American resources abroad	−0.01
Net indirect business taxes	0.61
Compensation of employees	4.22
Proprietor's income	0.48
Corporate profits	0.59
Net interest	0.41
Rental income of persons	0.13
GDP	$7.25

Source: *Economic Report of the President,* February 1996; annual estimates based on figures for three quarters.

Proprietors' income includes the earnings of unincorporated businesses. **Corporate profits** are the net revenues received by incorporated businesses before subtracting corporate income taxes. **Net interest** is the interest received by individuals, excluding interest paid by consumers to businesses and interest paid by government.

Each family that owns its own home is viewed as a tiny firm that rents its home to itself. Since homeowners do not, in fact, rent homes to themselves, an *imputed* rental value is estimated based on what the market rent would be. **Rental income of persons** consists primarily of the imputed rental value of owner-occupied housing minus the cost of owning that property (such as property taxes, insurance, depreciation, and interest paid on the mortgage). From the totals in Exhibit 8, you can see that aggregate spending in the economy equals the income generated by that spending.

APPENDIX A QUESTIONS

1. **(National Income Accounts)** Use the following data to answer the questions below:

Net investment	110
Depreciation	30
Exports	50
Imports	30
Government purchases	150
Consumption	400
Indirect business taxes (net of subsidies)	35
Income earned but not received	60
Income received but not earned	70
Personal income taxes	50
Employee compensation	455
Corporate profits	60
Rental income	20
Net interest	30
Proprietor's income	40
Net earnings of U.S. resources abroad	40

a. Calculate GDP using the income-based and the expenditure methods.
b. Calculate gross investment.
c. Calculate NNP, NI, PI, and DI.
d. What percent of personal income is employee compensation?
e. What percent of personal income goes to personal income taxes?

2. **(National Income Accounting)** According to Exhibit 8, GDP can be calculated either by adding up final goods expenditures or by adding up the allocations of these expenditures to the various resources used to produce these goods. Why do you suppose the portion of final goods expenditures that goes to pay for intermediate goods and/or raw materials is excluded from the allocation of income method of calculation?

Appendix B

THE CHAIN-WEIGHTED INDEX

To compute the real GDP index, quantities of individual goods are weighted by their prices. To compute the GDP price index, prices of individual goods are weighted by their quantities. To derive these indexes, let's assume the economy produces only the three products discussed in the chapter—Twinkies, fuel oil, and cable TV. Exhibit 9 lists the output of these goods in year 1 and year 2. Also listed are the prices of each product in each year. Note that in our hypothetical economy the price of Twinkies declined, the price of fuel oil increased, and the price of cable TV was unchanged.

Column (5) lists the value of year 1 quantity based on year 1 prices. For example, 10,000 packages of Twinkies were produced at 49 cents per package, for a total value of $4,900. The value of each output in column (5) can be summed to yield year 1 output in year 1 prices, or nominal GDP in year 1—also known as year 1 output in current dollars. Nominal

output in year 1 is $13,900. Likewise, column (8) shows the value of year 2 output based on year 2 prices; nominal GDP in year 2, or output measured in current dollars, sums to $16,750. So nominal GDP increased from $13,900 in year 1 to $16,750 in year 2, an increase of 20.5 percent. This increase in nominal dollars reflects changes in both real output and the price level. We next sort out the change in real output from the change in the price level by developing indexes for output and prices.

Real GDP Index

Let's first consider the change in real output. We can't simply add 10,000 packages of Twinkies to 5,000 gallons of fuel oil and 200 months of cable TV to get 15,200 units of output. Such a sum makes no sense. Instead, each type of output must be valued, or weighted, based on prices of some year. But which year? Let's begin by valuing the output each

EXHIBIT 9					**Hypothetical Data Used to Develop Chain-Weighted Indexes**			
	(1)	(2)	(3)	(4)	(5) Year 1 Output at Year 1 Prices	(6) Year 2 Output at Year 1 Prices	(7) Year 1 Output at Year 2 Prices	(8) Year 2 Output at Year 2 Prices
	Units of Output		Price per Unit					
Good or Service	Year 1 (Q_1)	Year 2 (Q_2)	Year 1 (P_1)	Year 2 (P_2)	$(Q_1 \times P_1)$	$(Q_2 \times P_1)$	$(Q_1 \times P_2)$	$(Q_2 \times P_2)$
Packages of Twinkies	10,000	15,000	$0.49	$0.45	$ 4,900	$ 7,350	$ 4,500	$ 6,750
Gallons of Fuel Oil	5,000	4,000	1.00	1.50	5,000	4,000	7,500	6,000
Months of Cable T.V.	200	200	20.00	20.00	4,000	4,000	4,000	4,000
					$13,900	$15,350	$16,000	$16,750

year using year 1 prices. Column (5) values year 1 quantities based on year 1 prices, and column (6) values year 2 quantities based on year 1 prices. As you can see, based on year 1 prices, the value of output increased from $13,900 to $15,350—an increase of 10.4 percent. An index of output for year 2 using year 1 prices is found by dividing the sum of column (6) by the sum of column (5), then multiplying by 100. This real GDP index increased from 100 in year 1 to 110.4 in year 2.

What if we compute the quantity index using year 2 prices? Columns (7) and (8) show the value of output each year based on year 2 prices. The total value of output grew from $16,000 to $16,750, for an increase of 4.7 percent. An index of output increased from 100 in year 1 to 104.7 in year 2. Why did real output increase more based on year 1 prices than it did based on year 2 prices? Note that because the price of Twinkies declined, consumers increased their purchases, so quantity increased from 10,000 to 15,000. The dollar value of that increase is greater when Twinkies are valued at the year 1 price of 49 cents per pack rather than the year 2 price of 45 cents a pack. The opposite is true for fuel oil. The price increase from $1.00 to $1.50 per gallon resulted in a quantity reduction of 1,000 gallons. That drop in quantity is less significant relative to total GDP if oil is priced at $1.00 per gallon rather than at $1.50 per gallon. Using year 1 prices tends to exaggerate the expansion of output for products whose price declined and understate the reduction of output for products whose price increased.

So real GDP increased by 10.4 percent if computed in year 1 prices but only 4.7 percent if computed in year 2 prices. Which year's prices should be used? There is no right answer. The Bureau of Economic Analysis splits the difference by using a chain-weighted system based on a *geometric average* of the two quantity indexes. The geometric average is found by multiplying the quantity index in year 2 based on year 1 prices by the quantity index in year 2 based on year 2 prices, then taking the square root of that product. Specifically, the quantity index for year 2 based on year 1 prices is 110.4. The quantity index for year 2 based on year 2 prices is 104.7. So 110.4 times 104.7 equals 11,558.9, which has a square root of 107.5. Based on the chain-weighted formula, real GDP in year 2 is 7.5 percent greater than real GDP in year 1.

GDP Price Index

The GDP price index in year 2 based on year 1 quantities is found by dividing the sum of column (7) by the sum of column (5), then multiplying by 100. The GDP price index based on year 1 quantities increased from 100 in year 1 to 115.1 in year 2. The price index in year 2 based on year 2 quantities is 109.1, which is found by dividing the sum of column (8) by the sum of column (6), then multiplying by 100.

Notice that the price index is greater when computed based on year 1 quantities rather than year 2 quantities. Fixing quantities at year 1 levels ignores any quantity changes in response to a change in prices. For example, fixing quantities at year 1 levels prevents us from recognizing any increase in the quantity of Twinkies purchased in response to the drop in price or any decrease in the quantity of fuel-oil purchased in response to an increase in price. Thus fixing quantities at year 1 levels implies uneconomical behavior (just as the consumer price index implies uneconomical behavior).

The geometric average for the price index is found by multiplying the price index in year 2 based on year 1 quantities by the price index in year 2 based on year 2 quantities, then taking the square root of that product. The geometric average equals the square root of 115.1 times 109.1, or the square root of 12,557.4, which is 112.1. Based on this chain-weighted approach, the GDP price index increased by 12.1 percent between year 1 and year 2.

We have shown how to compute indexes for real GDP and the price level based on quantities and price for years 1 and 2. The Bureau of Economic Analysis likewise computes indexes for year 3 based on quantities and prices for years 2 and 3, and it computes indexes for year 4 based on quantities and prices for years 3 and 4. The resulting chain-type index remedies the bias of a fixed-weight index by taking the geometric average of two-fixed weighted indexes, one based in the previous period and the other based in the current period.

We began this appendix by focusing on the nominal change in GDP: The sum of column (8) is 1.205 times the sum of column (5). So nominal GDP grew by 20.5 percent between years 1 and 2. This nominal growth rate can be decomposed into the change in the quantity index and the change in the price index. Real GDP in year 2 is 1.075 times real GDP in year 1, and the GDP price index in year 2 is 1.121 times the GDP price index in year 1. The product of 1.075 multiplied by 1.121 is 1.205, which reflects the amount by which nominal GDP in year 2 exceeds nominal GDP in year 1.

APPENDIX B QUESTIONS

1. **(Real GDP Index)** Consider the impact on real GDP growth of a different set of year 2 prices in Exhibit 9 in this appendix. Assume that the prices in year 2 for Twinkies, fuel oil, and cable TV are now $0.40/package, $1.25/gallon, and $20.00/month, respectively.
   a. What is the percentage change in real GDP based on year 1 prices?
   b. What is the percentage change in real GDP based on year 2 prices?
   c. What is the percentage change in real GDP based on the chain-weighted formula?

2. **(GDP Price Index)** Again consider the new price data from question 1.
   a. Calculate the GDP price index for year 2 based on year 1 quantities.
   b. Calculate the GDP price index for year 2 based on year 2 quantites.
   c. What is the percentage change in the GDP price index according to the chain-weighted approach?
   d. Show that the nominal change in GDP can be decomposed into the change in the quantity index and the change in the price index.

Consumption and Aggregate Expenditure

9

Suppose a new college friend invited you home for the weekend. One thing you would learn from your visit is how well off the family is—you would get an impression of their standard of living. Is their home something you might see on *Lifestyles of the Rich and Famous* or is it more modest? Do they drive a new BMW or take the bus? What do they eat? What do they wear? The simple fact is that consumption tends to reflect income.

You can usually tell much about a family's economic status by observing their consumption pattern. Although you sometimes come across people who live well beyond their means or who still have the first nickel they ever earned, by and large consumption and income tend to be highly correlated. *The positive and stable relationship between consumption and income, both for the household and for the economy as a whole, is the central idea of this chapter.*

In this chapter we focus on the components of aggregate expenditure. Consumption is the most important, accounting for two-thirds of all spending, but we also discuss investment, government purchases, and net exports. You will learn whether and how each relates to the level of income in the economy. In Chapter 10, we combine these spending components to show how aggregate spending relates to the economy's level of income. We then use aggregate spending to derive the aggregate demand curve. In Chapter 11 we develop aggregate supply, then show how it interacts with aggregate demand to determine the economy's equilibrium levels of price and output. The role of government will be examined more explicitly in Chapter 12. Topics discussed in this chapter include:

- Circular flow of income and expenditure
- Consumption function
- Marginal propensities to consume and to save
- Shifts in the consumption function
- Investment
- Government purchases
- Net exports

EARLY VIEWS OF THE MACROECONOMY

We first consider some early views of the macroeconomy, which influenced modern-day thinking. In Chapter 8, we mentioned Quesnay's contribution to our understanding of the circular flow of income. He had other insights into the economy's performance that contributed to subsequent developments in macroeconomics. Quesnay argued that even though people were motivated by self-interest, the economy was ruled by natural laws, laws that government intervention would only distort. The French phrase *laissez-faire et laissez-passer*— roughly, "let it alone and let it flow"—came to be associated with the view that unfettered markets best promote national economic prosperity.

The Classical View

In 1776, Adam Smith (1723–1790) published *The Wealth of Nations*, the most famous book in economics. Smith established a school of thought that came to be called *classical economics*. During the previous 200 years, European countries had followed a mercantilist policy, which tried to regulate international trade in order to accumulate gold and silver in the public treasury. **Classical economists** criticized mercantilism and advocated *laissez-faire*, the view that unfettered markets best promote national economic prosperity. Classical economists did not deny the existence of depressions and high unemployment, but they argued that the sources of such crises lay outside the economic system, in the effects of wars, tax increases, poor growing seasons, and changing tastes. Such external "shocks" could reduce output and employment. The resulting downturn, however, was viewed as a short-run phenomenon that would be corrected by natural market forces, such as changes in prices, wages, and interest rates.

Simply put, classical economists argued that if the economy's price level was too high to sell all that was produced, prices would fall until the quantity supplied equaled the quantity demanded; if wages were too high to employ all who wanted to work, wages would fall until the quantity of labor supplied equaled the quantity demanded; and if interest rates were too high to channel the amount saved into the amount invested, the interest rate would fall until the amount saved equaled the amount invested.

Keynes and the Great Depression

Although classical economists acknowledged that capitalistic, market-oriented economies could experience temporary unemployment, the prolonged depression of the 1930s strained belief in the economy's ability to correct itself. As we discussed in Chapter 5, the Great Depression was marked by severe unemployment and much unused plant capacity. With abundant yet unemployed resources, output and income fell far short of the economy's potential.

The stark contrast between the natural market adjustments predicted by the classical theory and the years of high unemployment during the Great Depression represented a collision of theory and fact. In 1936, John Maynard Keynes, of Cambridge University in England, published *The General Theory of Employment, Interest, and Money*, a book that questioned the classical view of the economy and touched off what has come to be called the Keynesian revolution. *Keynesian theory and policy were developed to address the problem of unemployment arising from the Great Depression.* The main quarrel Keynes had with the classical

Net Bookmark

Adam Smith, political economist and philosopher, was born in Scotland in 1723. For more about Adam Smith, visit the biographies of famous Edinburghers, maintained by the City of Edinburgh District Council (http://www.efr.hw.ac.uk/EDC/edinburghers/biographies.html). For an overview of *The Wealth of Nations,* Smith's great work, visit "The Art Bin," maintained by Nisus Publishing (http://www.algonet.se/artbin/oweala.html).

Classical economists A group of 18th- and 19th-century economists who believed that recessions and depressions were short-run phenomena that corrected themselves through natural market forces; thus the economy was self-adjusting

economists was that prices and wages did not appear sufficiently flexible to ensure the full employment of resources. According to Keynes, prices and wages were relatively inflexible—they were "sticky"—so natural market forces would not, in a timely fashion, return the economy to full employment. Keynes also believed that business expectations might at times become so grim that even very low interest rates would not induce firms to invest all that consumers might save.

Though Keynes and the classical economists had differing views of how the economy works, there was still some agreement. Both talked about the economy in the context of the circular flow. To help clarify how the economy works, we next develop a circular flow model of the economy that reflects the flow of income and expenditure.

THE CIRCULAR FLOW OF INCOME AND EXPENDITURE

The accounting equality of aggregate income and aggregate expenditure introduced in the previous chapter can be expressed by the circular flows of income and spending in Exhibit 1. The main stream flows clockwise around the circle, first as income from firms to households (in the lower half of the circle), then as spending from households back to firms (in the upper half of the circle).

The Income Half of the Circular Flow

The circular flow is a continuous process, but the logic of the model is clearest if we begin at juncture (1), where firms in the U.S. make production decisions. After all, production must occur before income is earned and output is sold. Aggregate output, or GDP, gives rise to an equal amount of aggregate income. Households supply their land, labor, capital, and entrepreneurial ability to firms and get paid rent, wages, interest, and profit.

By assuming there is no capital depreciation and that firms pay out all profits to firms' owners (meaning that firms do not retain any earnings), we can say that GDP equals aggregate income, as noted at juncture (1). But not all income is available to households. At juncture (2) governments collect taxes. Some of these tax dollars are returned to the income stream as transfer payments at juncture (3). By subtracting taxes and adding transfers, we transform aggregate income into **disposable income,** or *DI,* which flows to households at juncture (4). Disposable income is take-home pay, which households can spend or save.

Disposable income (DI) The income households have available to spend or save after paying taxes and receiving transfer payments

The bottom half of this circular flow is the *income half* because it focuses on what happens to the income arising from production. Aggregate income is the total income from producing GDP, and disposable income is the income remaining after taxes are subtracted and transfers added. To simplify the discussion, we define **net taxes,** or *NT,* as taxes minus transfer payments. So *disposable income equals GDP minus net taxes.* To put it another way, we can say that aggregate income equals disposable income plus net taxes:

Net taxes (NT) Taxes minus transfer payments

$$\text{GDP} = \text{Aggregate income} = DI + NT$$

At juncture (4), firms have produced output and have paid resource suppliers; governments have collected taxes and made transfer payments. Households,

EXHIBIT 1   **The Circular Flow of Income and Expenditure**

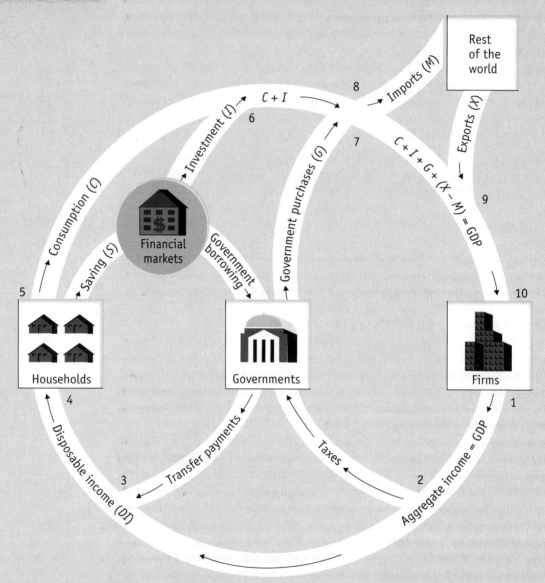

The circular flow diagram captures important relationships in the economy. The bottom half of the diagram depicts the income flow arising from production. At juncture (1) GDP equals aggregate income. Taxes leak out of the flow at point (2), but transfer payments augment the flow at point (3). Aggregate income minus taxes plus transfer payments equals disposable income, which flows to households at juncture (4).

The top half of the diagram shows the flow of expenditures on GDP. At juncture (5) households split their disposable income between consumption and saving. The saving stream flows into financial markets, where it is channeled to government borrowing and to business investment. At point (6) the injection of investment augments the spending stream. At juncture (7) government purchases represent another injection into the circular flow. At point (8) imports are a leakage of spending, and at point (9) exports are an injection of spending into the circular flow. Consumption plus investment plus government purchases plus exports minus imports, or net exports, equals the aggregate expenditure of GDP received by firms at point (10).

with disposable income in hand, must now decide how much to spend and how much to save. Since firms have already produced the output and have paid resource suppliers, firms are anxious to see how much consumers want to spend. Should any output go unsold, suppliers will be stuck with it; unsold goods must become part of firm inventories.

The Expenditure Half of the Circular Flow

Disposable income splits at juncture (5). Part flows to consumption, C, and the remainder to saving, S. Thus,

$$DI = C + S$$

Spending on consumption remains in the circular flow and represents the most important component of aggregate expenditure, about two-thirds of the total. Household saving flows to **financial markets,** which consist of banks and other financial institutions that provide a link between savers and borrowers. For simplicity, Exhibit 1 shows households as the only savers, although governments, firms, and the rest of the world could be savers, too. The primary borrowers are firms and governments, but households borrow as well, particularly for new homes, and the rest of the world also borrows. In reality, financial markets should be connected to all four economic actors, but we have simplified the flows to keep the exhibit from looking like a plate of spaghetti.

Since firms in our simplified model pay resource suppliers an amount equal to the entire value of output, firms have no revenue left for investment. They must borrow in financial markets to finance purchases of physical capital plus any increases in their inventories. Households also borrow from financial markets to purchase new homes. Therefore, investment, I, consists of spending on new capital by firms, including inventory increases, plus spending on residential construction. Investment spending enters the circular flow at juncture (6), so aggregate spending at that point totals $C + I$.

Governments must also borrow whenever they incur deficits, that is, whenever their total outlays—transfer payments plus purchases of goods and services—exceed their revenues. Government purchases of goods and services, represented by G, enter the spending stream in the upper half of the circular flow at juncture (7).

Some spending by households, firms, and governments goes for imports. Since spending on imports, M, flows to foreign producers, not U.S. producers, import spending leaks from the circular flow at juncture (8). But the rest of the world also buys U.S. products, so foreign spending on U.S. exports, X, enters the circular flow at juncture (9). The net impact of *the rest of the world* on aggregate expenditure equals exports minus imports, or net exports, $X - M$.

The upper half of the circular flow can be viewed as the expenditure half because it focuses on the components that make up aggregate expenditure: consumption, C; investment, I; government purchases, G; and net exports, $X - M$. Aggregate expenditure flows into firms at juncture (10). Total spending on U.S. output equals the market value of aggregate output in the economy, or GDP. In other words,

$$C + I + G + (X - M) = \text{aggregate expenditure} = \text{GDP}$$

Firms that cannot accurately anticipate how much consumers will spend on their products face the prospect of too much of the product left over—and hence extra inventory—or not enough available to satisfy consumer demand.

Financial markets Banks and other institutions that facilitate the flow of loanable funds from savers to borrowers

Leakages Equal Injections

Let's step back now and consider the big picture. In the lower half of the circular flow, aggregate income equals disposable income plus net taxes. In the upper half, aggregate expenditure equals the total spending on U.S. output. As we noted in Chapter 8, *the aggregate income arising from production equals the aggregate expenditure on that production*. This is the first accounting identity. Thus, aggregate income (disposable income plus net taxes) equals aggregate expenditure (spending by each sector), or

$$DI + NT = C + I + G + (X - M)$$
$$\text{Aggregate income} = \text{Aggregate expenditure}$$

Since disposable income equals consumption plus saving, we substitute $C + S$ for DI in the above equation to yield

$$C + S + NT = C + I + G + (X - M)$$

After subtracting C from both sides and adding M to both sides, the equation reduces to

$$S + NT + M = I + G + X$$

Leakage Any diversion of income from the domestic spending stream; includes saving, taxes, and imports

Injection Any payment of income other than by firms or any spending other than by domestic households; includes investment, government purchases, transfer payments, and exports

Note that at various points around the circular flow, some of the flow leaks from the main stream. Saving, S, net taxes, NT, and imports, M, are **leakages** from the circular flow. **Injections** into the main stream also occur at various points around the circular flow. Investment, I, government purchases, G, and exports, X, are *injections* into the circular flow. As you can see from the preceding equation, *leakages from the circular flow equal injections into that flow*. This leakages-injections equation demonstrates a second accounting identity based on the principles of double-entry bookkeeping.

Planned Investment Versus Actual Investment

As we have noted already, at juncture (1) in the circular flow, firms produce the aggregate output expected to meet the demand. But aggregate expenditure may not match production. Suppose, for example, that firms produce $7.0 trillion in output, but the spending components add up to only $6.8 trillion. Firms will end up with $200 billion in unsold products, which must be added to their inventories. Since increases in inventories are counted as investment, *actual* investment turns out to be $200 billion greater than firms had *planned*.

Planned investment The amount of investment firms plan to undertake during a year

Actual investment The amount of investment actually undertaken during a year; equals planned investment plus unplanned changes in inventories

Note the distinction between **planned investment,** the amount firms plan to invest before they know how much will be sold, and **actual investment,** which includes both planned investment and unplanned changes in inventories. Unplanned increases in inventories will cause firms to smarten up and decrease their production next time so as not to get stuck with more unsold goods. Only when there are no unplanned changes in inventories will the level of GDP be at what we will call an *equilibrium level*—that is, *a level that can be sustained*. Only in equilibrium will planned investment equal actual investment.

The relationship between actual and planned investment will be examined more closely in the next chapter. For now, you need only understand that the national income accounting system developed in the previous chapter reflects *actual* investment, not necessarily *planned* investment. *The national income accounts always look at economic activity after transactions have occurred—after the dust has settled.* Actual leakages must always equal actual injections.

CONSUMPTION

A key decision in the circular flow model is households' allocation of income between consumption and saving. How much households spend depends primarily on how much they have available to spend. Although this seems obvious, it is fundamental to an understanding of how the economy works. Let's look at this income-consumption link over time in the U.S. economy.

An Initial Look at Income and Consumption

The red line in Exhibit 2 depicts real disposable income in the United States since 1959, and the blue line depicts real consumer spending. *Disposable income,* remember, is the income actually available for spending and saving. (The use of the term "real" here and later indicates that the data have been adjusted for inflation so that dollars are of constant purchasing power, in this case 1992 dollars.)

Note in Exhibit 2 that consumer spending and disposable income tend to move together over time. Both are measured along the vertical axis in 1992 dollars. Consumer saving is the difference between disposable income and consumer spending; it is indicated in Exhibit 2 by the vertical distance between the two lines. Both real consumer spending and real disposable income increased nearly every year. Thus, the relationship between consumption and income has

Consumer Spending and Disposable Income in the United States Since 1959   E X H I B I T   2

Income and consumer spending move together over time. Consumer saving is the difference between disposable income and consumer spending and is shown by the blue shaded area on the graph.

Source: Developed from data found in U.S. Department of Commerce, *Survey of Current Business* 76 (Jan./Feb. 1996): Table 4.

EXHIBIT 3

Consumer Spending and Disposable Income in the United States since 1959

The clear, direct relationship between consumption and disposable income is apparent when the two variables are plotted against each other on the same graph.

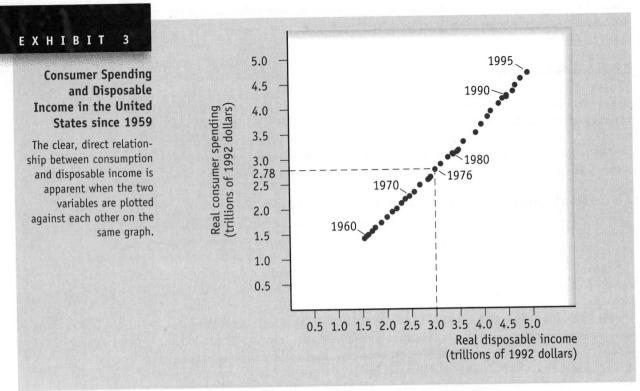

Source: Developed from data found in U.S. Department of Commerce, *Survey of Current Business* 76 (Jan./Feb. 1996): Table 4.

been relatively stable. Specifically, consumer spending averaged 93 percent of disposable income during the 1960s, 92 percent during the 1970s, 93 percent during the 1980s, and 94 percent during the 1990s. Put another way, saving averaged 7 percent of disposable income during the 1960s, 8 percent during the 1970s, 7 percent during the 1980s, and 6 percent during the 1990s.

Another way to graph the relationship between income and consumption over time is shown in Exhibit 3, where disposable income is measured along the horizontal axis and consumption along the vertical axis. Notice that each axis measures the same units: dollars of 1992 purchasing power. The exhibit focuses on the relationship between income and consumption in the United States since 1959. Each year is depicted by a point that reflects two values: disposable income and consumption. In 1976, for example, disposable income (read from the horizontal axis) was $3.0 trillion, and consumption (read from the vertical axis) was $2.78 trillion.

As you can see, there is a clear and direct relationship between consumption and disposable income, a relationship that should come as no surprise after Exhibit 2. You need little imagination to see that by connecting the points on the graph in Exhibit 3, you could trace a line relating consumption to income. Such a relationship has special significance in macroeconomics.

The Consumption Function

So far we have examined the link between consumption and income and have found it to be quite stable, particularly since World War II. Given their level of

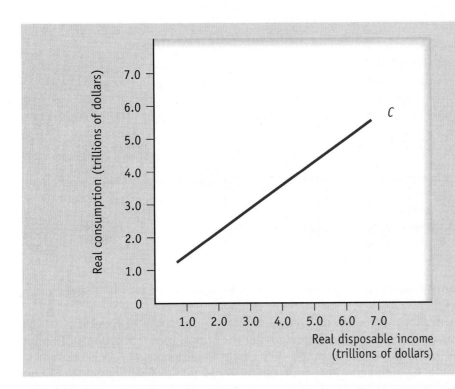

EXHIBIT 4

The Consumption Function

The consumption function, *C*, shows the relationship between consumption expenditure and disposable income, other things constant.

disposable income, households decide how much to consume and how much to save. So consumption depends on disposable income. *Disposable income is the independent variable, and consumption the dependent variable.*

Because consumption depends on income, we say that consumption is a *function* of income. Exhibit 4 presents a hypothetical **consumption function,** which shows a positive relationship between the level of disposable income in the economy and the amount spent on consumption, other determinants of consumption held constant. Again, both disposable income and consumption are measured in real terms, or in inflation-adjusted dollars. Notice that our hypothetical consumption function in Exhibit 4 looks similar to the actual historical relationship between consumption and disposable income, shown in Exhibit 3.

Consumption function The relationship between the level of income in an economy and the amount households spend on consumption, other things constant

Marginal Propensities to Consume and to Save

In Chapter 1, you learned that economic analysis focuses on activity at the margin. For example, what happens to consumption if income grows by a certain amount? To focus on such changes, we must apply marginal analysis to the relationship between changes in disposable income and changes in consumption. For example, suppose households receive another billion dollars in disposable income. Some of this additional income will be spent on consumption and some will be saved. The fraction of that additional income that is consumed is called the marginal propensity to consume. More precisely, the **marginal propensity to consume** equals the change in consumption divided by the change in income. Likewise, the fraction of that additional income that is saved is called the marginal propensity to save. Again, more precisely, the **marginal**

Marginal propensity to consume The fraction of a change in income that is spent on consumption; the change in consumption spending divided by the change in income that caused it

EXHIBIT 5	Marginal Propensity to Consume and Marginal Propensity to Save (trillions of dollars)

Income (real DI) (Y) (1)	Change in Income (ΔDI) (2)	Consumption (C) (3)	Change in C (ΔC) (4)	Saving (S) (5)	Change in Saving (ΔS) (6)	MPC = (4) ÷ (2) (ΔC/ΔDI) (7)	MPS = (6) ÷ (2) (ΔS/ΔDI) (8)
5.0	0.5	4.7	0.4	0.3	0.1	0.4/0.5 = 4/5	0.1/0.5 = 1/5
5.5	0.5	5.1	0.4	0.4	0.1	4/5	1/5
6.0	0.5	5.5	0.4	0.5	0.1	4/5	1/5
6.5	0.5	5.9	0.4	0.6	0.1	4/5	1/5
7.0		6.3		0.7			

Marginal propensity to save The fraction of a change in income that is saved; the change in saving divided by the change in income that caused it

propensity to save equals the change in saving divided by the change in income.

These propensities can be understood best by reference to Exhibit 5, which presents the hypothetical data underlying the consumption function of Exhibit 4. The table shows, for a range of possible incomes, how much consumers would like to spend and how much they would like to save. The first column presents alternative levels of disposable income, DI, beginning with $5.0 trillion and ranging up to $7.0 trillion in increments of $0.5 trillion.

As you can see from the table, if income increases from $5.0 trillion to $5.5 trillion, an increase of $0.5 trillion, consumption increases by $0.4 trillion and saving increases by $0.1 trillion. The marginal propensity to consume, or MPC, equals the change in consumption divided by the change in income. In this case, the change in consumption is $0.4 trillion and the change in income is $0.5 trillion, so the marginal propensity to consume is 0.4/0.5, or 4/5. Notice that each time income increases by $0.5 trillion, as indicated in column (2), consumption increases by $0.4 trillion, as indicated in column (4). Therefore, the MPC, listed in column (7), is 4/5 at all levels of income.

At each income level, the consumption decision also determines saving. Notice from column (6) that saving increases by $0.1 trillion with each $0.5 trillion increase in disposable income, so the marginal propensity to save, or MPS, equals 0.1/0.5, or 1/5, at all levels of income. The MPS is listed in column (8). Since disposable income is either spent or saved, the marginal propensity to consume plus the marginal propensity to save must add up to 1. In our example, 4/5 + 1/5 = 1. We can say more generally that MPC + MPS = 1.

MPC, MPS, and the Slope of the Consumption and Savings Functions

You may recall from the appendix to Chapter 1 that the slope of a straight line is equal to the vertical distance between any two points divided by the horizontal distance between those points—that is, the rise over the run. Consider, for example, the slope between points *a* and *b* on the consumption function in panel (a) of Exhibit 6. The horizontal distance between these points represents the change in disposable income (denoted (ΔDI)—in this case, $0.5 trillion.

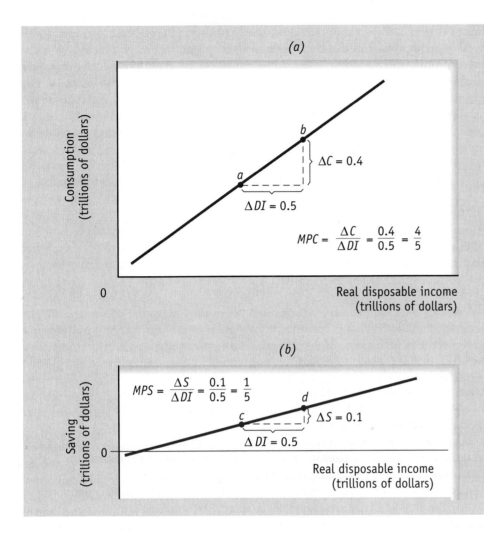

EXHIBIT   6

Marginal Propensities to Consume and to Save

The slope of the consumption function equals the marginal propensity to consume. For the straight-line consumption function of panel (a), the slope is the same at all levels of income and is given by the change in consumption divided by the change in disposable income that causes it. Hence, the marginal propensity to consume equals $\Delta C/\Delta DI$, or 0.4/0.5 = 4/5. The slope of the saving function equals the marginal propensity to save, $\Delta S/\Delta DI$, or 0.1/0.5 = 1/5.

The vertical distance represents the change in consumption (denoted ΔC)—in this case, $0.4 trillion. The slope equals the vertical distance divided by the horizontal distance, or 0.4/0.5, which equals the marginal propensity to consume of 4/5.

Thus, *the marginal propensity to consume is measured graphically by the slope of the consumption function.* After all, the slope is nothing more than the increase in consumption divided by the increase in income. *Because the slope of any straight line is constant everywhere along the line, the MPC for any linear, or straight-line, consumption function will be constant at all levels of income.* Our hypothetical data yield a consumption function that is linear, with a constant marginal propensity to consume. Note, however, that we make this constant-value assumption for simplicity and ease of exposition. In reality, the marginal propensity to consume will not necessarily be constant. The consumption function could be curved so that the MPC is greater at lower levels of income, meaning that the consumption function would flatten out as income increases.

Saving function The relationship between saving and the level of income in the economy, other things constant

Panel (b) of Exhibit 6 presents the **saving function,** *S,* which relates saving to the level of income, reflecting the hypothetical data presented in Exhibit 5. The saving function can be subjected to the same sort of graphical analysis as the consumption function. The slope between any two points on the saving function measures the change in saving divided by the change in income. For example, between points *c* and *d* in panel (b) of Exhibit 6, the change in income is $0.5 trillion and the resulting change in saving is $0.1 trillion. The slope between these two points therefore equals 0.1/0.5, or 1/5, which by definition equals the marginal propensity to save. Since the marginal propensity to consume and marginal propensity to save are simply different sides of the same coin, from here on we focus mainly on the marginal propensity to consume.

Nonincome Determinants of Consumption

Along a given consumption function, consumer spending depends on the level of disposable income in the economy, other things constant. Now let's see what factors are held constant and how changes in these factors could cause the entire consumption function to shift.

Net wealth The value of a household's assets minus its liabilities

Net Wealth and Consumption. Given the level of income in the economy, an important factor influencing consumption is each household's **net wealth**—that is, the value of all assets that each household owns minus any liabilities, or debts owed. Consider your own family. Your family's assets may include a home, cars, furniture, money in the bank, and the value of stocks, bonds, and pension funds. Your family's liabilities, or debt, may include a mortgage, car loans, credit card balances, and the like. To increase net wealth, your family can save or can pay off debts.

Household net wealth is assumed to be constant along a given consumption function. A decrease in net wealth would make consumers less inclined to spend rather than save at each level of income. To see why, suppose prices fall sharply on the stock market. Because of the decrease in wealth, households that own stock feel poorer so they spend less. Hence, a decrease in net wealth, other things held constant, encourages households to save more and spend less at each level of income. For example, when stock market prices fell sharply in October of 1987, the decrease in stockholders' net wealth prompted them to reduce consumption and increase saving at each level of income. Household saving as a percent of disposable income increased from 3.9 percent in the quarter before the crash to 5.7 percent in the quarter following the crash. Consumer spending on new housing, expensive cars, and jewelry declined.

Our original consumption function is depicted as line *C* in Exhibit 7. If net wealth declines, the consumption function shifts from *C* down to *C'*, because households now want to save more and spend less at every level of income.

Conversely, suppose stock prices on average increase sharply. This increase in net wealth increases the desire to spend. For example, stock prices increased sharply in 1995, increasing stockholders' net wealth; sales for luxury automobiles surged, as did sales of Tiffany jewelry and Mont Blanc pens (which sell for up to $6,000). As one market researcher observed at the time, "There's a sense of wealth and it's showing up in luxury goods."[1]

---

1   As quoted by Laura Bird, "Shoppers Return to Tiffany and Chanel," *The Wall Street Journal,* 6 September 1995

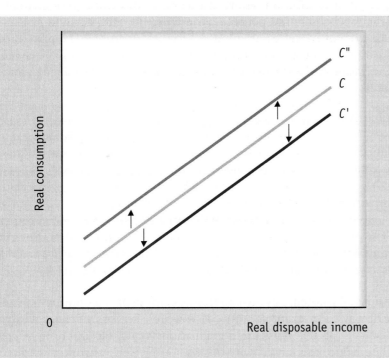

EXHIBIT 7

Shifts in the Consumption Function

A downward shift in the consumption function, such as from C to C', can be caused by a decrease in wealth, an increase in the price level, an unfavorable change in consumer expectations, or an increase in the interest rate. An upward shift, such as that from C to C'', can be caused by an increase in wealth, a decrease in the price level, a favorable change in expectations, or a decrease in the interest rate.

The consumption function shifts from C up to C'', reflecting households' desire to spend more at every level of income. Again, *it is a change in net wealth, not a change in income, that shifts the consumption function. A change in income, other things held constant, is reflected by a movement along a given consumption function, not a shift in the function.* Be mindful of the difference between a *movement along* the consumption function, which results from a change in income, and a *shift in* the consumption function, which results from a change in one of the nonincome determinants of consumption, such as net wealth.

The Price Level. Another variable that can affect the consumption function is the price level prevailing in the economy. As we have seen, households' net wealth is an important determinant of consumption. The greater the net wealth, other things constant, the greater consumption will be at each level of income. Much household wealth is held in dollar-denominated assets, such as savings accounts. When the price level changes, so does the real value of bank accounts and other dollar-denominated financial assets.

For example, suppose your wealth consists of $10,000 in a bank account. If the price level increases by 10 percent, your bank account will purchase about 10 percent fewer real goods and services. You feel poorer because you are poorer. The real value of your wealth has declined. To rebuild the real value of your wealth to some desired level, you decide to spend less and save more. An increase in the price level reduces the purchasing power of wealth held in fixed-dollar assets and, as a consequence, causes households to consume less and save more at each level of income. So the consumption function shifts down from C to C', as shown in Exhibit 7.

Conversely, should the price level ever fall, that would increase the real value of dollar-denominated assets. Since households are wealthier, they are willing and able to consume more at each level of income. For example, if the price level declines by 10 percent, your $10,000 bank account will now buy about 10 percent more real goods and services. A drop in the price level is reflected by a shift in the consumption function from C up to C''. *At each level of income, a change in the price level influences consumption by affecting the real value of net wealth.*

The Interest Rate. Interest is the reward paid to savers to defer consumption and the amount paid by borrowers for current spending power. When graphing the consumption function, we assume a given interest rate. If the rate of interest increases, other things constant, savers, or lenders, are rewarded more, and borrowers are charged more. The higher the interest rate, the less is spent on those items typically purchased on credit, such as homes and automobiles. Thus, at a higher rate of interest, households will save more, borrow less, and spend less. Greater saving at each level of income means less consumption. Simply put, *a rise in the interest rate, other things constant, will shift the consumption function down.* Conversely, *a drop in the interest rate will shift the consumption function up.*

Expectations. As noted earlier, expectations influence economic behavior in a variety of ways. For example, suppose you are a senior in college and you land a high-paying job that starts upon graduation. Your consumption will probably jump long before the job actually begins. Conversely, a worker who receives a layoff notice to take effect at the end of the year will likely reduce consumption immediately, well before the actual date of the layoff. If households grow concerned about employment, they reduce the amount consumed at each level of income.

Expectations about price levels and interest rates also affect consumption. For example, expectations of higher housing prices or higher interest rates in the future may prompt a household to purchase a home now. On the other hand, expectations of lower housing prices or lower interest rates make households defer major purchases. Thus, expectations affect spending at each level of income, and a change in expectations can shift the consumption function. This is why consumer confidence is monitored so closely by economic forecasters.

Again, keep in mind the distinction between *movements along a given consumption function* as a result of a change in income and *shifts in the consumption function* as a result of a change in another variable. We conclude our introduction to consumption with the following case study, which discusses consumption and saving patterns over people's lifetimes.

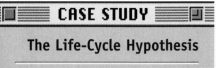

CASE STUDY

The Life-Cycle Hypothesis

Do rich people save a larger fraction of their incomes than poor people do? Both theory and evidence suggest that they do. The easier it is to make ends meet, the more likely it is that money will be left over for saving. Does it follow from this that richer economies save more than poorer ones—that economies save a larger fraction of total disposable income as they grow? In his famous book *The General Theory,* published in 1936, John Maynard Keynes drew that conclusion. But as later economists studied the data—such as that presented in Exhibit 3—it became clear that Keynes was wrong. For societies, the fraction of total disposable income saved seems to stay constant as income grows.

So how can it be that richer individuals save more than poorer individuals, yet richer countries do not necessarily save more than poorer countries? By the early 1950s, several answers had been proposed. One of the most important of these was the *life-cycle model of consumption*. According to this model, people tend to borrow when they are young to finance education and home purchases; in middle age, they pay off their debts and save more; in old age, they draw down their savings, or dissave. Some people still have substantial wealth at death, in part because of uncertainty regarding when death will occur and because some parents want to pass wealth to their children. But, net saving over a person's entire lifetime is small.

The life-cycle hypothesis suggests that the saving rate in an economy depends, among other things, on the relative number of savers and dissavers in the population. Other factors that influence the saving rate across countries include the manner in which saving is taxed, the convenience and reliability of saving institutions, and the relative cost of housing. In Japan, for example, 20,000 post offices nationwide offer savings accounts to more than half the country's population. In fact, Japan's postal savings system is the world's largest financial institution. Also, a home buyer in Japan must make a down payment that represents a relatively large fraction of the home's purchase price; this calls for substantial savings. Since saving in Japan is both necessary and convenient, the country has one of the highest saving rates in the world. In 1995, the Japanese saved 15 percent of disposable income, compared to only 4 percent for Americans.

Source: Paul Jessup and Mary Bochnak, "A Case for a U.S. Postal Savings System," *Challenge,* November/December 1992, pp. 57–59; and Malcolm Fisher, "Life Cycle Hypothesis," *The New Palgrave: A Dictionary of Economics* 3 (London: Macmillan Press, 1987), pp. 177-79. The Internet address for the Japanese Post Office is http://www.nttls.co.jp/POSTAL/guide.html.

The Life-Cycle Hypothesis
continued

Location:

For a profile of Japanese consumption and savings patterns, visit JETRO (Japan External Trade Organization), a nonprofit, Japanese government-related organization (http://www.jetro.go.jp/JETROINFO/CONSUMER/index.html).

We next consider the second component of aggregate expenditure: investment. Our objective is to develop the relationship between the total spending in the economy and the level of income.

INVESTMENT

The second component of aggregate expenditure is investment, or, more precisely, *gross private domestic investment*. By investment, we do not mean buying stocks, bonds, or other financial assets. Investment consists of spending on (1) new factories and new equipment such as computers, (2) new housing, and (3) net increases in inventories. Investment is undertaken because managers believe that such spending will increase the firm's profit.

An investment represents a commitment of current resources in expectation of a future stream of profit. Some machines, for example, are expected to last 3 years, others 30 years. Since the payoff occurs in the future, a potential investor must estimate how much profit a particular investment will yield this year, next year, the year after, and in all future years covered by the productive life of the investment. *Firms buy new capital goods only if they expect this investment to be more profitable than other possible uses of their funds.*

The Demand for Investment

To understand the investment decision, consider a simple example. The operators of the Hacker Haven Golf Club are contemplating buying solar-powered golf carts to rent to golfers. The model under consideration, called the Weekend Warrior, sells for $2,000, requires no maintenance or operating expenses, and is expected to last indefinitely. In this simplified example, the *expected rate of return* equals the annual dollar earnings expected from the investment divided by the purchase price. The first cart purchased is expected to earn a rental income of $400 per year. This income, divided by the cost of the cart, yields an expected rate of return on the investment of 400/2,000, or 20 percent per year. Additional carts will be used less. A second cart is expected to generate $300 per year in rental income, yielding a rate of return of 300/2,000, or 15 percent; a third cart, $200 per year, or 10 percent; and a fourth cart, $100 per year, or 5 percent. A fifth cart would not be used at all, so it has a zero expected rate of return.

Should the operators of Hacker Haven purchase any carts, and if so, how many? Suppose they plan to borrow the money to buy the carts. The number of carts they purchase will depend on the rate of interest they must pay to borrow money. If the market rate of interest exceeds 20 percent, their cost of borrowing exceeds the expected rate of return on even the first cart, so no carts will be purchased. What if the operators have enough money on hand to buy the carts? The market rate of interest also reflects what the club owners could earn on savings. If the interest rate paid on savings exceeds 20 percent, they could earn a higher rate of return by saving any funds on hand than by investing these funds in golf carts, so no carts would be purchased. *The market rate of interest represents the opportunity cost of investing in capital.*

Suppose the market rate of interest is 8 percent per year. At that rate of interest, the first three carts, with expected rates of return exceeding 8 percent, would more than pay for themselves. A fourth cart would lose money, since its expected rate of return is only 5 percent. Exhibit 8 measures the nominal interest rate along the vertical axis and the amount invested in golf carts along the horizontal axis. The step-like relationship shows the expected rate of return earned on additional dollars invested in golf carts. This relationship also indicates the amount invested in golf carts at each interest rate, so you can view this step-like relationship as Hacker Haven's demand for this type of investment. For example, the first cart costs $2,000 and earns a rate of return of 20 percent.

The horizontal line at 8 percent indicates the market rate of interest, which represents Hacker Haven's opportunity cost of investing. This line can be viewed as the supply of investment funds available to the course operators. Recall that the course operators' objective is to choose an investment strategy that maximizes profit. Profit is maximized when $6,000 is invested in the carts—that is, when three carts are purchased. The expected return from a fourth cart is 5 percent, which is below the opportunity cost of funds. Therefore, investing in four or more carts would lower total profit. The shaded area below the demand curve but above the supply curve indicates the amount by which the return on

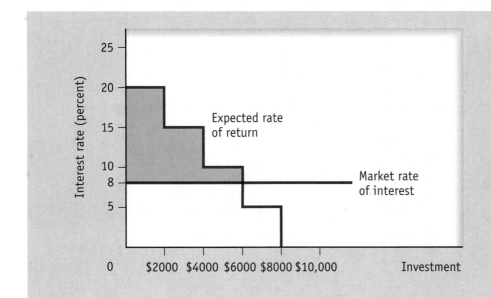

EXHIBIT 8

Rate of Return on Golf Carts and the Opportunity Cost of Funds

An individual firm will invest in any project whose rate of return exceeds the market interest rate. At an interest rate of 8 percent, Hacker Haven would purchase three golf carts, which represents investment spending of $6,000. The shaded area reflects the profitability of investing $6,000.

carts exceeds the opportunity cost of funds; this shaded area is a crude measure of the profit rate expected from investing in each cart.

From Micro to Macro

So far we have examined the investment decision for a single golf course, but there are about 13,000 golf courses in the United States. The industry demand for golf carts shows the relationship between the amount all course operators invest and the expected rate of return. Like the step-like relationship in Exhibit 8, the investment demand curve for the golf industry slopes downward.

Let's move beyond golf carts and consider the investment decisions in all industries: publishing, fast foods, apparel, and hundreds more. Individual industries generally have downward-sloping demands for investment. More is invested when the cost of borrowing is lower, other things constant. A downward-sloping investment demand curve for the entire economy can be derived, with some qualifications, from a horizontal summation of each industry's downward-sloping investment demand curve. The economy's *investment demand curve* is represented as *D* in Exhibit 9. It shows the negative relationship between the quantity of investment demanded and the market rate of interest, other things held constant, including business expectations. For example, in Exhibit 9, when the market rate of interest is 8 percent, the quantity of investment demanded is $0.6 trillion.

Planned Investment and the Economy's Level of Income

To integrate the discussion of investment with our earlier analysis of consumption, we need to know if and how planned investment varies with the level of income in the economy. Whereas we were able to present empirical evidence relating consumption to disposable income over time, there is less of a link between investment and disposable income. Since 1985, for example, investment shows little relation to the level of income. *Investment depends more on business*

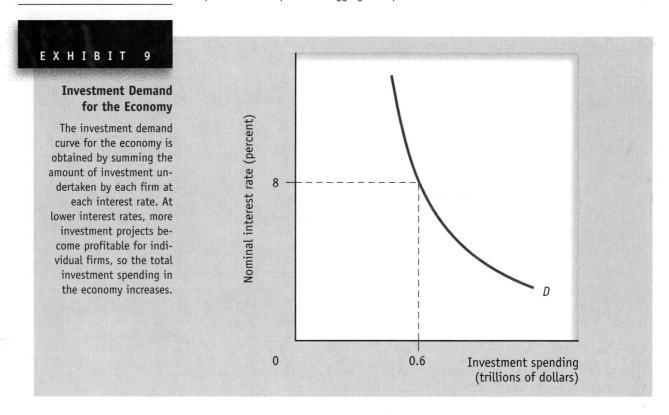

EXHIBIT 9

Investment Demand for the Economy

The investment demand curve for the economy is obtained by summing the amount of investment undertaken by each firm at each interest rate. At lower interest rates, more investment projects become profitable for individual firms, so the total investment spending in the economy increases.

Investment function The relationship between planned investment and the level of income, other things constant

Autonomous A term that means "independent"; autonomous investment is independent of the level of income

expectations and on interest rates than on the current level of income. Some investments may take years to complete, such as a new electric power plant. The investment decision is thus said to be "forward looking," based more on expected profit than on current levels of income and output.

So how does investment relate to disposable income? The simplest **investment function** assumes that planned investment is unrelated to the current level of disposable income; investment is said to be **autonomous** with respect to income. For example, suppose that given current business expectations and prevailing interest rates, firms plan to invest $0.6 trillion next year, regardless of the economy's income level. Exhibit 10 measures disposable income on the horizontal axis and *planned investment* on the vertical axis. Investment of $0.6 trillion is shown by the flat autonomous investment function, *I.* As you can see, along investment function *I,* planned investment does not vary even though real disposable income does.

Nonincome Determinants of Investment

The autonomous investment function isolates the relationship between the level of income in the economy and *planned investment*—the amount decision makers would like to invest, other things constant. We have already mentioned two important determinants that are held constant: the interest rate and business expectations. Now let's consider the effect of changes in these factors on investment.

Market Interest Rate. Investment, *I,* is based on a given interest rate. If the interest rate increases because of, say, some change in the nation's monetary policy that reduces the supply of loanable funds in the economy (as happened in

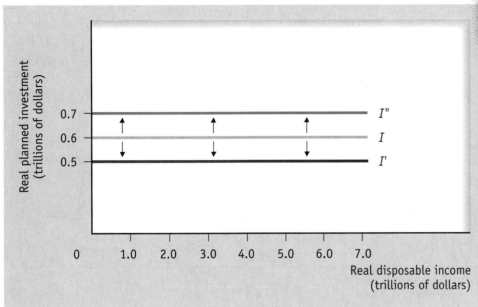

EXHIBIT 10

Autonomous Investment Function

Autonomous investment spending is assumed to be independent of income, as shown by the horizontal lines. An increase in the interest rate or declining business expectations can decrease autonomous investment, as shown by the downward shift from I to I'. A decrease in the interest rate or upbeat business expectations can shift the investment function up to I''.

1994), the cost of borrowing increases and this increases the opportunity cost of investment. The resulting decrease in planned investment is reflected in Exhibit 10 by a shift down in the autonomous investment function from I to I'. Conversely, a decrease in the rate of interest, other things held constant, will lower the cost of borrowing and will shift up the autonomous investment function from I to I''.

Business Expectations. As we noted in Chapter 5, investment depends primarily on business expectations, or on what Keynes called the "animal spirits" of business. If firms in general become more pessimistic about profit prospects, perhaps expecting a recession, their planned investment will decrease at every level of income, as reflected in Exhibit 10 by a decrease in the investment function from I down to I'. On the contrary, if profit expectations rise, firms will be more willing to invest, thereby increasing the investment function from I up to I''. *Factors that could affect business expectations, and hence investment, are wars, technological change, and changes in the tax structure.*

Now that we have examined consumption and investment individually, let's take a look at their year-to-year variability in the following case study.

CASE STUDY

Variability of Consumption and Investment

We already know that consumption makes up about two-thirds of GDP and that investment spending varies from year to year, averaging about one-eighth of GDP in the last decade. Now let's compare the year-to-year variability in consumption, investment, and GDP. Exhibit 11 shows the annual percentage change since 1960 in consumption, investment, and GDP, all measured in real terms.

Two points are obvious. First, fluctuations in consumption and in GDP are similar, though consumption varies slightly less than GDP. Second, investment

Annual Percentage Changes in U.S. Real GDP, Real Consumption, and Real Investment

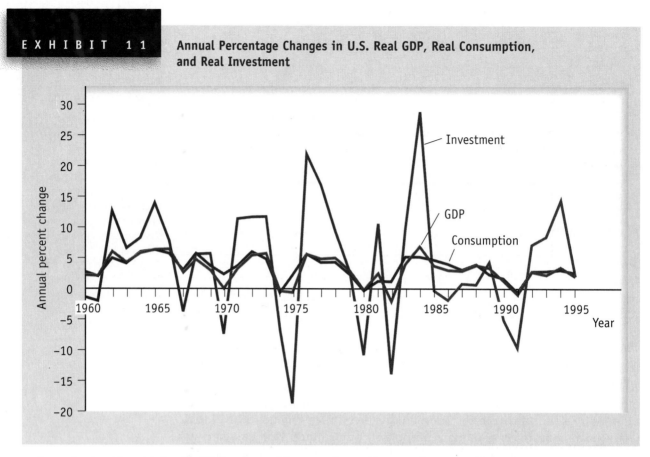

Source: Developed from data found in U.S. Department of Commerce, *Survey of Current Business* 76 (Jan./Feb. 1996): Table 2. Figures are based on chained (1992) dollars.

Variability of Consumption and Investment
continued

Location:

What is the latest measure of the GDP? What is the current economic forecast, as given by the National Association of Business Economists survey? What is the present status of consumer confidence, as measured by The Conference Board's "Consumer Confidence Index"? Visit *USA Today's* "Economy Track" to find out (**http://www.usatoday. com/money/economy/ econ0001.htm**).

fluctuates much more than either consumption or GDP. For example, in the recession year of 1982, GDP declined by 2.1 percent and investment declined by 14.4 percent; consumption actually increased by 1.1 percent. In 1984, GDP increased by 6.8 percent, investment increased 28.4 percent, and consumption increased 5.2 percent. And the recession that stretched into the first quarter of 1991 reduced GDP that year by 1.0 percent; investment declined by 9.7 percent, and consumption declined by 0.6 percent

During the 35 years since 1960, GDP declined during five years, with the decline averaging 0.9 percent annually during those recession years. Investment during those five years declined an average of 12.2 percent. On average, consumption increased 0.3 percent during the five recession years. So while consumption is the largest spending component, investment varies much more than consumption and accounts for much of the variability in real GDP. This is why economic forecasters pay special attention to investment plans.

Sources: *Economic Report of the President,* February 1996; and U.S. Department of Commerce, *Survey of Current Business* 76 (Jan./Feb. 1996).

GOVERNMENT

A third component of aggregate expenditure is government purchases of goods and services. The federal government purchases thousands of goods and services, ranging from weapon systems to White House lawn maintenance. State and local governments also purchase thousands of goods and services, ranging from road signs to education. In the United States, government purchases of goods and services account for about 20 percent of GDP. Most government purchases are made not by the federal government but by state and local governments.

Government Purchase Function

The **government purchase function** relates government purchases to the level of income in the economy, other things constant. Since decisions about government purchases are largely under the control of public officials, we assume these purchases do not depend directly on the level of income in the economy. We therefore assume that government purchases during a given year are *autonomous,* or independent of the level of income. *Autonomous government purchases, G,* do not vary with the level of income in the economy. Though not shown as an exhibit, an autonomous government purchase function would relate to income as a flat line similar to the autonomous investment function.

Government purchase function
The relationship between government purchases and the level of income in the economy, other things constant.

Net Taxes

As noted earlier, government purchases represent only one of the two components of government outlays; the other is *transfer payments,* such as Social Security and welfare benefits. Transfer payments are outright grants from governments to households. To fund government outlays, governments impose *taxes.* We saw from the discussion of the circular flow that by subtracting taxes and adding transfer payments, we transform real GDP into *disposable income.* Disposable income is take-home pay—the income households can spend or save.

Taxes and transfer payments affect aggregate spending indirectly by changing disposable income and thereby changing consumption. Taxes have a negative effect on consumption; transfer payments have a positive effect. In terms of consumption, what matters is the combined effect on disposable income of taxes and transfer payments: *net taxes,* or *NT,* defined already as taxes minus transfer payments. Net taxes, you may recall, are a leakage from the circular flow. For simplicity we will assume that net taxes are *autonomous,* so net taxes remain constant regardless of the level of real GDP. Hence, *autonomous net taxes* are independent of the level of income. We will examine the impact of net taxes in the next few chapters.

NET EXPORTS

In recent years, the rest of the world has had a growing influence on the U.S. economy. The rest of the world affects aggregate expenditure through imports and exports. The United States, with only one-twentieth of the world's population, accounts for about one-eighth of the world's exports and one-sixth of the world's imports.

Net Exports and Income

How do imports and exports relate to the level of income in the economy? When their income rises, Americans spend more, and some of this increased spending goes for imported goods. Higher incomes lead to more spending on Japanese automobiles, French wines, Korean VCRs, trips to Europe, and thousands of other foreign products.

How does the value of U.S. exports relate to the economy's level of income? The amount of U.S. exports purchased by the rest of the world depends on the income of foreigners, not on the U.S. level of income. The desire of the French to purchase U.S. computers or the desire of Saudi Arabians to purchase U.S. military hardware is not influenced by the level of disposable income in the United States.

Net export function **The relationship between net exports and the level of income in the economy, other things constant**

The **net export function** shows the relationship between net exports and the level of income in the economy, other things constant. Since our exports are relatively insensitive to the level of U.S. income but our imports tend to increase with income, *net exports,* which equal exports minus imports, tend to decline as income increases. Such an inverse relationship is developed graphically in the appendix to this chapter. For now, we simplify the analysis by assuming that net exports are *autonomous,* or independent of the level of disposable income. If exports exceed imports, net exports are positive; if imports exceed exports, net exports are negative; and if exports equal imports, net exports equal zero. U.S. net exports in nearly every year during the last three decades have been negative, so suppose net exports are autonomous and equal to −$0.1 trillion, or −$100 billion, as shown by the net export function $X - M$ in Exhibit 12.

Nonincome Determinants of Net Exports

Factors held constant along the net export function include the U.S. price level, the price levels in other countries, interest rates here and abroad, foreign income levels, and the exchange rate between the dollar and foreign currencies. Consider the effects of a change in one of these factors. Suppose the value of the dollar increases relative to foreign currencies, as it did in 1995. With the dollar worth more on world markets, foreign products become cheaper for Americans and U.S. products become more costly for foreigners. A rise in the dollar's value will increase imports and decrease exports, resulting in a decrease in net exports, shown in Exhibit 12 by a parallel drop in the net export function from $X - M$ down to $X' - M'$, a drop from −$100 billion to −$120 billion.

A decline in the value of the dollar, as occurred in 1994, will have the opposite effect, increasing exports and decreasing imports. An increase in autonomous net exports is shown in our example by a parallel increase in the net export function, from $X - M$ up to $X'' - M''$, reflecting an increase in autonomous net exports from −$100 billion to −$80 billion. Countries often devalue their currency in an attempt to increase their net exports and increase employment. The effect of changes in net exports on aggregate spending will be taken up in the next chapter.

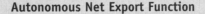

Autonomous Net Export Function   EXHIBIT 12

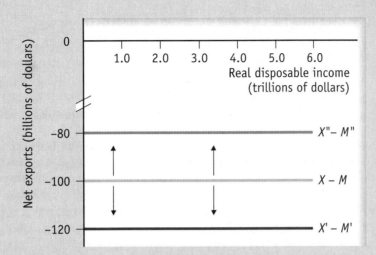

Autonomous net exports are assumed to be independent of disposable income, as shown by the horizontal lines. $X - M$ is the net export function if net exports are equal to −$100 billion. An increase in the value of the dollar relative to other currencies would cause net exports to decrease, as shown by the shift down to $X' - M'$. A decrease in the value of the dollar would cause net exports to increase, as shown by the shift up to $X'' - M''$.

CONCLUSION

This entire chapter has focused on the relationship between spending and income. We considered the four components of aggregate expenditure: consumption, investment, government purchases, and net exports. Consumption relates positively to the level of income in the economy. Investment relates more to such factors as the interest rate and business expectations than to income. Government purchases are also assumed to be autonomous, or independent of income. And net exports are assumed to be affected more by such factors as the exchange rate than by the level of domestic income. (In the appendix to this chapter, we develop a more realistic but also more complicated picture by showing how net exports decline as the level of income increases.) In the next chapter we show how consumption, investment, government purchases, and net exports add up to the aggregate expenditure function, which is then used to derive the equilibrium quantity of aggregate output demanded.

SUMMARY

1. Classical economists believed that external shocks to the economy could temporarily increase unemployment, but natural market forces, including adjustments in prices, wages, and interest rates, would reduce unemployment.

2. The Great Depression was so deep and so prolonged that belief in the natural recuperative powers of the economy was seriously challenged. Keynes argued that saving could exceed investment, so some goods would remain unsold. This would cause firms to cut production, creat-

ing unemployment. According to Keynes, wages and prices were relatively "sticky," so they would not adjust to ensure full employment.

3. The circular flow summarizes the flow of income and spending through the economy. Saving, net taxes, and imports represent leakages from the circular flow. In equilibrium these leakages equal the injections into the circular flow: investment, government purchases, and exports.

4. One of the most predictable and useful relationships in macroeconomics is that between consumption and disposable income. The consumption function indicates that the more income people have, the more they spend on consumption, other things constant.

5. The slope of the consumption function reflects the marginal propensity to consume, which equals the change in consumption divided by the change in income. The slope of the saving function reflects the marginal propensity to save, which equals the change in saving divided by the change in income.

6. Certain factors can cause the consumption function to shift. An increase in net wealth will reduce the need to save and hence increase consumption at every level of income. A higher price level will reduce the value of dollar-denominated assets, thereby reducing net wealth, which reduces consumption. An increase in the interest rate will make saving more rewarding and borrowing more costly and hence will decrease consumption. Finally, expectations about future income and price levels will also influence consumption.

7. Planned investment depends on the market rate of interest and on business expectations. Investment tends to be less related to the level of income in the economy.

8. Government purchases of goods and services make up about one-fifth of GDP, mostly by state and local governments. Government purchases are based on the public choices of elected officials and are assumed to be autonomous, or independent, of the level of income in the economy.

9. Net exports equal exports minus imports. Exports are unrelated to the level of income in this country. Imports tend to be positively related to income. Thus, net exports tend to decline as income increases. For simplicity, we initially assume that net exports are autonomous, or unrelated to domestic income.

QUESTIONS AND PROBLEMS

1. **(Classical Economic Theory)** It is sometimes said that the classical economic system assumed flexible prices, wages, and interest rates. Discuss how flexible prices and wages would eliminate excess production of goods, excess supply of labor, and excess supply of savings, all of which occur during a recession.

2. **(Classical Versus Keynesian Economics)** Why was the flexibility of wages, prices, and interest rates such an important issue between Keynesian and classical economists?

3. **(The Circular Flow)** What are the elements of the income half of the circular flow? Of the expenditure half?

4. **(Consumption Function)** How does an *increase* in each of the following variables affect the consumption function? The saving function?
   a. Autonomous net taxes
   b. Interest rates
   c. Consumer optimism, or confidence
   d. Price level
   e. Real wealth
   f. Disposable income

5. **(Leakages and Injections)** What are the components of the leakages and injections in the circular flow? How are leakages and injections related in the circular flow?

6. **(Planned Investment Versus Actual Investment)** Explain the distinction between planned investment and actual investment. Which is included in the circular flow?

7. **(MPC and MPS)** If real disposable income rises by $15 billion and consumption therefore rises by $12 billion, what is the value of the MPC? What is the relationship between the MPC and the MPS? If the MPC rises, what must happen to the MPS? What is the relationship between the MPC and the consumption function, between the MPS and the saving function?

8. **(Investment)** Consider Exhibit 8 in this chapter. If the owners of the golf course revised their estimates of the revenue from the golf carts so that each cart earned $100 less, how many carts would they buy when the interest rate was 8 percent? How many would they buy when the interest rate was 3 percent?

9. **(Investment)** Why would the following investment expenditures rise as interest rates fell?
   a. Purchase of a new plant and equipment
   b. Construction of new housing
   c. Accumulation of planned inventories

10. **(Government)** According to the textbook's model, how do changes in income affect government purchases and the government purchase function? How do changes in net taxes affect the consumption function?

11. **(Consumption)** Use the following data to answer the questions below.

Real Disposable Income	Consumption
$100	$150
200	200
300	250
400	300

   a. Graph the consumption function with consumption on the vertical axis and disposable income on the horizontal axis.
   b. If the consumption function is a straight line, what are its vertical intercept and slope?
   c. If investment is equal to $100, what level of disposable income causes savings to equal investment?

12. **(Consumption Function)** According to the discussion of the consumption function, a number of factors can cause this function to shift. What, if anything, happens to the savings function when the consumption function shifts? Explain.

13. **(Savings Function)** In Exhibit 6, the savings function crosses the horizontal axis. What does this mean and what can we say about the consumption function at this point?

14. **(Investment)** What are the components of gross private domestic investment? How does the investment demand curve differ from the investment function? Do they indicate actual or planned investment?

15. **(Net Exports)** What factors are held constant along the net export function? What would be the impact of a change in real disposable income, according to the model developed in the textbook?

16. **(Consumption and Savings)** Suppose that consumption equals $500 billion when disposable income is $0, and each increase of $100 billion in disposable income causes consumption to increase by $70 billion. Draw a graph of the saving function using this information.

17. **(Life-Cycle Hypothesis)** According to the life-cycle hypothesis, what is the pattern of savings for an individual over his or her lifetime? What impact does this behavior have on an individual's lifetime consumption pattern? What impact does the life-cycle behavior have on the saving rate in the overall economy?

18. **(Variability of Consumption and Investment)** Why do economic forecasters pay special attention to investment plans?

Using the Internet

19. Visit the Foreign Trade Division of the U.S. Census Bureau (**http://www.census.gov/ftp/pub/foreign-trade/www/**). Look under "Top Ten Trading International Partners" and, for the most recent month, record the following:

   a. The country with which the United States had the largest trade deficit, the amount of this deficit, and the trade balance with this country for the year to date.
   b. The country with which the United States has the largest trade surplus, the amount of the surplus, and the trade balance with this country for the year to date.

20. Visit the Foreign Trade Division of the U.S. Census Bureau (**http://www.census.gov/ftp/pub/foreign-trade/www/**). Look under "Press Release"— This is the U.S. International Trade in Goods and Services report, commonly known as the FT900. Write a summary of this information, including total imports, total exports, and the balance of trade.

Appendix
VARIABLE NET EXPORTS

In this appendix, we examine more closely the relationship between net exports and the U.S. level of income. We first look at exports and imports separately and then consider exports minus imports, or net exports.

Net Exports and Income

As we noted in the chapter, the amount purchased by foreigners depends not on the U.S. level of income but on income levels in their own countries. We therefore assume that U.S. exports do not vary with respect to the U.S. income level. Specifically, suppose the rest of the world spends $0.4 trillion per year on U.S. exports; the export function, X, would be as shown in panel (a) of Exhibit 13. On the other hand, when disposable income increases, U.S. consumers tend to spend more on all goods, including imported goods. Thus, the relationship between imports and income is positive, as expressed by the upward-sloping import function, M, in panel (b) of Exhibit 13. Imports are assumed to be 10 percent of disposable income, so when disposable income is $4.0 trillion, imports are $0.4 trillion.

So far we have considered imports and exports as separate functions of income. What matters in terms of total spending on U.S. products are exports, X, minus imports, M, or net exports, $X - M$. Since money spent on imports goes to foreign producers, not U.S. producers, imports are subtracted from the circular flow of spending. By subtracting the import function depicted in panel (b) from the export function in panel (a), we derive the *net export function*, depicted as $X - M$ in panel (c) of Exhibit 13. Note that when income is $4.0 trillion, *imports* in panel (b) equal $0.4 trillion. Since *exports* in panel (a) equal $0.4 trillion at all levels of income, net exports equal zero when U.S. disposable income equals $4.0 trillion. At levels of income below $4.0 trillion, net exports are positive because exports exceed imports. At levels of income greater than $4.0 trillion, net exports are neg-

EXHIBIT 13

Imports, Exports, and Net Exports

Exports are independent of the level of income, as shown in panel (a). Imports are positively related to income, as shown in panel (b). Net exports equal exports minus imports; net exports are negatively related to income, as shown in panel (c).

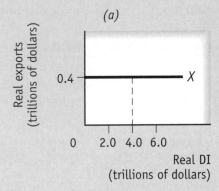

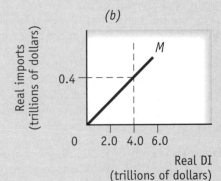

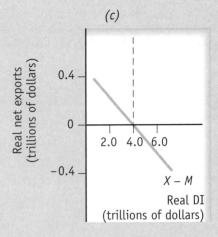

ative because imports exceed exports. The United States has experienced negative net exports during most of the last three decades. Our high trade deficit in recent years can be traced in part to the healthy level of economic expansion in the United States since 1983. Our trade deficit shrank during the economic recession of the early 1990s, but then increased again as the U.S. economy recovered.

Shifts in Net Exports

The net export function, $X - M$, shows the relationship between net exports and disposable income, other things constant. Suppose the value of the dollar increases relative to foreign currencies. With the dollar worth more on world markets, foreign products become cheaper for Americans and U.S. prod-

ucts become more expensive for foreigners. The impact of a rising dollar is to decrease exports but increase imports at each level of income. This decreases the net export function, as shown in Exhibit 14 by the shift from $X - M$ down to $X' - M'$. A decline in the dollar's value will have the opposite effect, increasing exports and decreasing imports, as reflected in Exhibit 14 by an upward shift in the net export function from $X - M$ to $X'' - M''$.

In summary, in this appendix we assumed that *imports relate positively to the level of income, whereas exports are independent of the domestic level of income. Net exports, which equal exports minus imports, therefore vary inversely with the level of income.* The net export function shifts up if the value of the dollar falls and shifts down if the value of the dollar rises.

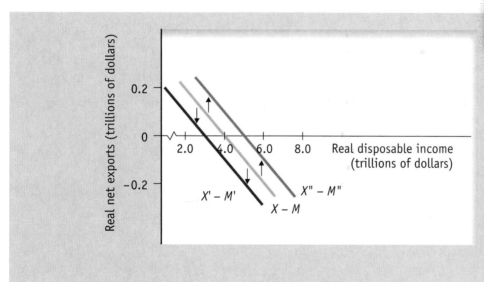

EXHIBIT   14

Shifts in Net Exports

A rise in the value of the dollar, other things held constant, will decrease exports and increase imports, thereby contributing to an decrease in net exports, as shown by the shift from $X - M$ down to $X' - M'$. A decrease in the value of the dollar will increase exports and decrease imports, causing net exports to fall, as shown by the shift from $X - M$ up to $X'' - M''$.

APPENDIX QUESTION

1. (Rest of the World) Using a graph of net exports ($X - M$) against disposable income, show the effects of the following:
   a. An increase in the foreign income level
   b. An increase in the U.S. income level
   c. An increase in U.S. interest rates
   d. An increase in the value of the dollar against foreign currencies

   Explain each of your answers.

Aggregate Expenditure and Demand-Side Equilibrium

Your economic success depends to a large extent on the overall performance of the economy. When the economy is expanding, jobs grow more abundant, so the chances of finding a good one increase. When the economy contracts, job opportunities shrink, as do job prospects. Thus, you should have a personal interest in the economy's level of output and the year-to-year changes in output. In this chapter we continue to build a model that will help us determine the economy's equilibrium level of output, or real GDP.

Chapter 9 considered the components of aggregate spending: consumption, investment, government purchases, and net exports. We discussed how each relates to the level of income in the economy. In this chapter, these components are added up to show how total spending, or aggregate expenditure, relates to the level of income. We use this information to derive the aggregate demand curve. Aggregate supply will be developed in Chapter 11; then, a fuller treatment of the effects of government spending and taxing will be examined in Chapter 12.

If we try to confront the economy head-on, it soon becomes a bewildering maze, which is why we often make progress only by making simplifying assumptions. In this chapter, we continue to assume there is no capital depreciation and no business saving, so we can say that *each dollar spent on production translates directly into a dollar of aggregate income*. Therefore, gross domestic product, or GDP, equals aggregate income. We also continue to assume that net exports are autonomous, or independent of the level of income. In Appendix A, we see what happens when imports increase with income. An algebraic approach to the aggregate expenditure framework is developed in Appendix B. Topics discussed in this chapter include:

- Aggregate expenditure function
- Equilibrium real GDP demanded
- Effect of changes in aggregate expenditure
- Simple spending multiplier
- Effect of changes in the price level
- Aggregate demand curve

10

CHAPTER

AGGREGATE EXPENDITURE AND INCOME

In the previous chapter, we examined the important link between income and consumption, a link that is the most stable in all of macroeconomics. In this section, we build on that relationship to uncover the link between aggregate spending and aggregate income, or real GDP.

The Components of Aggregate Expenditure

We begin developing the aggregate demand curve by asking how much aggregate output would be demanded at a given price level. By finding the quantity demanded at a given price level, we will identify a single point on the aggregate demand curve. We want to consider the relationship between aggregate spending and aggregate income, or real GDP, in the economy. By *real GDP,* we mean GDP measured in terms of real goods and services produced.

To get us started, suppose the price level in the economy is, say, 130, and we want to find out how much will be spent at various levels of real GDP, or real income. Exhibit 1 presents the hypothetical data that will serve as building blocks for constructing the aggregate expenditure function. This exhibit simply puts into tabular form relationssships that were introduced in the previous chapter—namely, consumption, saving, planned investment, government purchases, net taxes, and net exports.

The first column in Exhibit 1 lists a range of possible levels of real GDP in the economy, depicted as Y. The second column shows *net taxes,* or $NT,$ which are assumed to be $1.0 trillion at each level of real GDP. Subtracting net taxes from real GDP yields *disposable income,* listed in column (3) as $Y - NT$. Note that at all levels of real GDP, disposable income equals real GDP minus autonomous net taxes of $1.0 trillion. So each time real GDP increases by $0.5 trillion, disposable income also increases by $0.5 trillion.

Households have only two possible uses of disposable income: consumption and saving. Columns (4) and (5) show that the levels of *consumption, C,* and *sav-*

EXHIBIT 1	Table for Real GDP, with Net Taxes and Government Purchases (trillions of dollars)

Real GDP (Y) (1)	Net Taxes (NT) (2)	Disposable Income (Y − NT) (3) = (1) − (2)	Consumption (C) (4)	Saving (S) (5)	Planned Investment (I) (6)	Government Purchases (G) (7)	Net Exports (X − M) (8)	Planned Aggregate Expenditure [C + I + G + (X − M)] (9)
6.0	1.0	5.0	4.7	0.3	0.6	1.0	−0.1	6.2
6.5	1.0	5.5	5.1	0.4	0.6	1.0	−0.1	6.6
7.0	1.0	6.0	5.5	0.5	0.6	1.0	−0.1	7.0
7.5	1.0	6.5	5.9	0.6	0.6	1.0	−0.1	7.4
8.0	1.0	7.0	6.3	0.7	0.6	1.0	−0.1	7.8

ing, S, increase with disposable income. Each time real GDP and disposable income increase by $0.5 trillion, consumption increases by $0.4 trillion and saving increases by $0.1 trillion. Thus, as in the previous chapter, the marginal propensity to consume is 0.8 and the marginal propensity to save is 0.2.

Columns (6), (7), and (8) list three now-familiar injections of spending into the circular flow: *planned investment* of $0.6 trillion, *government purchases* of $1.0 trillion, and *net exports* of −$0.1 trillion. Note that since government purchases equal net taxes, the government budget is balanced. We want first to see how a balanced budget works before we look at the effects of budget deficits and budget surpluses, which we examine in Chapter 12. The sum of consumption, *C,* planned investment, *I,* government purchases, *G,* and net exports, *X − M,* is listed in column (9) as *planned aggregate expenditure,* which indicates the amount that households, firms, governments, and the rest of the world plan to spend on U.S. output at each level of income. Note that the only spending component that varies with the level of real GDP is consumption. As real GDP increases, so does disposable income, which increases the amount spent on consumption.

The equilibrium quantity of aggregate output demanded is achieved when the amount people plan to spend equals the amount produced. More precisely, the equilibrium quantity of real GDP demanded is achieved when planned aggregate expenditure equals real GDP. In Exhibit 1, this equality occurs where planned aggregate expenditure and real GDP equal $7.0 trillion.

Quantity of Real GDP Demanded

Some people find graphs easier to understand than tables. Graphs are also more general than tables and can show relationships between variables without focusing on particular numbers. The relationship between real GDP and planned aggregate expenditure in Exhibit 1 is graphed in panel (a) of Exhibit 2. Real GDP, measured along the horizontal axis, can be viewed in two ways—as the value of *aggregate output* and as the *aggregate income* generated by that level of output. Planned aggregate expenditure is measured on the vertical axis. Because real GDP, or income, is measured on the horizontal axis and expenditure is measured on the vertical axis, this graph is often called the **income–expenditure model.**

Note the focus of the horizontal axis shifts from disposable income in the previous chapter to real GDP in this chapter. This is not much of a transition since real GDP minus net taxes of $1.0 billion equals disposable income. So every level of real GDP implies a level of disposable income that is $1.0 billion lower. The link between real GDP and each spending component was spelled out in Exhibit 1.

The **aggregate expenditure function** shows, for a given price level, the amount economic actors plan to spend at each level of real GDP. The aggregate expenditure function is *C + I + G + (X − M). The equilibrium quantity of aggregate output demanded occurs where planned aggregate expenditure, measured along the vertical axis, equals real GDP, which is both the amount produced and the income arising from that production, measured along the horizontal axis.*

To gain perspective on the relationship between spending and real GDP, we use a handy analytical device—the 45-degree ray from the origin, first in-

Income-expenditure model A relationship between aggregate income and aggregate spending that determines, for a given price level, where income equals spending.

Aggregate expenditure function A relationship showing, for a given price level, the amount of planned spending for each level of income; the total of C + I + G + (X − M) at each level of income

EXHIBIT   2

Deriving the Equilibrium Output Demanded for a Given Price Level

The equilibrium quantity of aggregate output demanded, given the price level, is found where aggregate expenditure equals real GDP—that is, where desired spending equals the amount produced. In equilibrium, the leakages from the circular flow, in this case saving, S, plus net taxes, NT, equal the injections, in this case investment, I, plus government purchases, G, plus net exports, $(X - M)$.

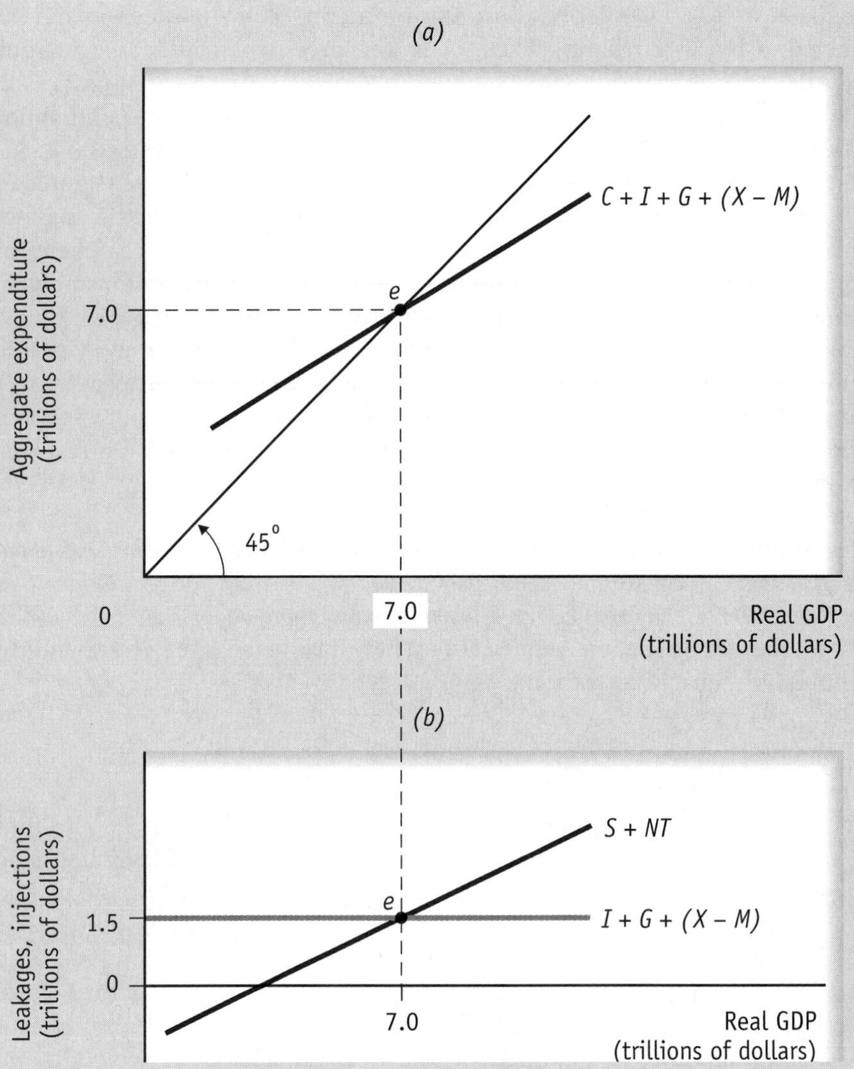

(a)

Aggregate expenditure (trillions of dollars)

$C + I + G + (X - M)$

7.0

e

45°

0   7.0   Real GDP (trillions of dollars)

(b)

Leakages, injections (trillions of dollars)

$S + NT$

e

1.5 $I + G + (X - M)$

0

7.0   Real GDP (trillions of dollars)

troduced in the appendix to Chapter 1. The special feature of this line is that any point along it is exactly the same distance from both axes. Since the line identifies all points where spending and real GDP are equal, it offers an easy way to find the point along the aggregate expenditure function that is exactly the same distance from each axis. The 45-degree line therefore can be used to find where planned aggregate expenditure equals real GDP—that is, where planned spending equals the amount produced.

The equilibrium quantity of aggregate output demanded occurs where the vertical sum of consumption, planned investment, government purchases, and net exports equals real GDP; in Exhibit 2, this occurs at point e, where the aggregate expenditure function intersects the 45-degree line. At point e, the amount people plan to spend, as measured along the vertical axis, equals the amount produced, as measured along the horizontal axis. We conclude that at the given price level, the equilibrium quantity of real GDP demanded equals $7.0 trillion.

When Output and Planned Spending Differ

To see how equilibrium is achieved, consider what happens when real GDP is initially less than the equilibrium amount. As you can see from panel (a) of Exhibit 2, at levels of real GDP less than the equilibrium amount, the aggregate expenditure function is above the 45-degree line. This means that planned spending exceeds real GDP. When the amount people plan to spend exceeds the amount firms produce, something has to give. Ordinarily what gives is the price level, but remember that we are seeking the equilibrium real GDP for a given price level, so the price level is assumed to be constant, at least for now. What gives in this model are firms' *inventories*.

If planned spending exceeds output, firms must dig into their inventories to make up the shortfall; firms thus experience *unintended inventory reductions*. Since firms cannot draw down inventories indefinitely, shortages prompt firms to increase production. As long as planned spending exceeds output, firms must increase production to make up the difference. As firms increase production, income rises as well. Production and income, both measured along the horizontal axis, will increase until planned spending just equals the amount produced. When output reaches $7.0 trillion, planned spending exactly matches output, so no unintended inventory adjustments occur. More importantly, when output reaches $7.0 trillion, planned spending just equals the amount produced and just equals the total income generated by that production. Therefore, $7.0 trillion is the equilibrium quantity of aggregate output demanded. Hence, we say that at a price level of 130, the equilibrium quantity of real GDP demanded is $7.0 trillion. In terms of the symbols introduced earlier, we say that *the equilibrium quantity of real GDP demanded equals aggregate expenditure—the sum of consumption, C, plus planned investment, I, plus government purchases, G, plus net exports, X − M.*

To reinforce the logic of the model consider what happens when real GDP exceeds the equilibrium level—that is, when the aggregate expenditure function is below the 45-degree line. Note in panel (a) of Exhibit 2 that, along that portion of the aggregate expenditure function to the right of point *e,* planned spending falls short of production. At levels of real GDP greater than the equilibrium level, the amount produced exceeds what people plan to buy, so unsold goods pile up. This swells inventories beyond the level that firms had planned to hold. As a result of these *unintended inventory increases,* firms reduce production, which reduces the income arising from production. Firms will continue to cut production until the amount they produce just equals aggregate expenditure, which occurs at a level of real GDP of $7.0 trillion.

Leakages Equal Planned Injections

We can draw on the circular flow model in Chapter 9 to focus on leakages and injections. We will see that, in equilibrium, the leakage of saving and net taxes must equal the injections of planned investment, government purchases, and net exports—that is, $S + NT = I + G + (X − M)$. The same equilibrium derived in the income-expenditure framework of panel (a) of Exhibit 2 can be found using the leakages-injections framework shown in panel (b).

Note that panel (b) has been placed under panel (a) so that levels of real GDP, measured along the horizontal axis, line up in the two panels. The upward-sloping saving function was introduced in the previous chapter. To that, we add autonomous net taxes to get an upward-sloping line, $S + NT$, reflecting leakages from the circular flow of saving plus net taxes. The horizontal line, $I + G + (X - M)$, drawn here at $1.5 trillion, is the sum of investment, government purchases, and net exports—the planned injections into the circular flow. The intersection occurs where real GDP equals $7.0 trillion, which is where leakages from the circular flow equal planned injections into the circular flow. This same equality can be derived from the table in Exhibit 1.

At levels of real GDP below $7.0 trillion, planned injections exceed leakages. Injections pump up real GDP, so real GDP tends to rise. At levels of real GDP above $7.0 trillion, leakages exceed planned injections; the excess leakages siphon off spending power, which reduces real GDP. To get some feel for how leakages and planned injections help establish equilibrium real GDP demanded, let's use the analogy of a bathtub that is partially filled with water. If the rate at which the faucet injects water into the tub exceeds the rate at which water leaks out the drain, the water level in the tub will rise. But if the leakage rate exceeds the injection rate, the water level will fall. Only when the injection rate equals the leakage rate will the water level remain unchanged, or be in equilibrium.

In summary, the equilibrium value of real GDP demanded can be found using either the income-expenditure approach illustrated in the upper panel of Exhibit 2 or the leakage-injection approach illustrated in the lower panel. Given the price level, the equilibrium level of aggregate output demanded is achieved only when the amount economic actors plan to spend equals the amount produced, which happens only when leakages from the circular flow equal planned injections into that flow. *Hence, for a given price level, there is only one point along the aggregate expenditure function at which planned spending equals real GDP.*

We have now discussed the forces that determine the equilibrium quantity of real GDP demanded for a given price level. In the next section, we examine the effect of a shift in the aggregate expenditure function.

THE SIMPLE SPENDING MULTIPLIER

In the previous section, we employed the aggregate expenditure function to determine the equilibrium level of aggregate output demanded for a particular price level. In this section, we continue to assume that the price level remains unchanged, as we trace the effects of shifts in the aggregate expenditure function on the equilibrium quantity of aggregate output demanded. Like a stone thrown into a still pond, the effect of any shift in the aggregate expenditure function ripples through the economy, generating changes in aggregate output that may far exceed the initial shift in spending.

Effects of an Increase in Aggregate Expenditure

We begin in equilibrium at point e in Exhibit 3. The equilibrium point shows where planned spending of $7.0 trillion equals real GDP. Now let's consider

Effect of an Increase in Autonomous Investment

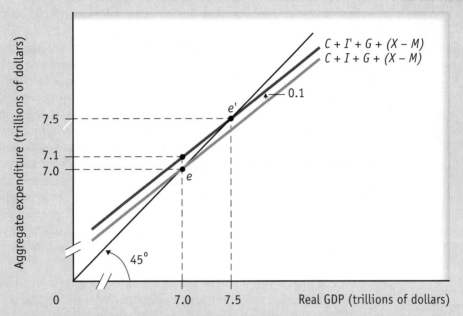

The economy is intially in equilibrium at point *e*, where spending and real GDP both equal $7.0 trillion. A $0.1 trillion increase in autonomous investment shifts the aggregate expenditure function vertically by $0.1 trillion from $C + I + G + (X - M)$ to $C + I' + G + (X - M)$. Real GDP rises until it equals spending at point *e'*. As a result of the $0.1 trillion increase in autonomous investment, real GDP demanded increases by $0.5 trillion, to $7.5 trillion.

the effect of an increase in one of the components of spending. Suppose firms become more optimistic about future profit prospects, so they increase their planned investment. Specifically, suppose planned investment increases from $0.6 trillion to $0.7 trillion per year, as reflected in Exhibit 3 by an increase in the aggregate expenditure function, which shifts up by $0.1 trillion, from $C + I + G + (X - M)$ to $C + I' + G + (X - M)$.

What happens to the equilibrium level of real GDP demanded? An instinctive response is to conclude that real GDP demanded will increase by $0.1 trillion, but in this case instinct is a poor guide. In Exhibit 3, you can see that as a result of the $0.1 trillion increase in the aggregate expenditure function, the equilibrium value shifts up to point *e'*, where the quantity of real GDP demanded equals $7.5 trillion. The $0.1 trillion increase in investment has somehow increased the equilibrium quantity of real GDP demanded by $0.5 trillion. Thus, each dollar of increased investment spending has multiplied fivefold. The **simple spending multiplier** is a number showing the multiple by which equilibrium real GDP changes for a given initial change in spending. The simple spending multiplier is computed as the ratio of the change in equilibrium output demanded to the initial expenditure change that caused it. In our example the multiplier equals 0.5/0.1, or 5. Soon we will provide a specific formula for the multiplier, but first we explore the source of the multiplier magic.

Simple spending multiplier The ratio of a change in equilibrium real GDP demanded to the initial change in expenditure that brought it about; the numerical value of the multiplier is 1/(1 − MPC)

The Spending Multiplier and the Circular Flow

The idea of the circular flow is central to an understanding of the process of adjustment from one equilibrium quantity of output demanded to another. As noted earlier, real GDP can be thought of as both the value of production and the income arising from that production. Recall that production yields income, which generates spending. We can think of each trip around the circular flow as a "round" of income and spending. A shift up in the aggregate expenditure function, as reflected in Exhibit 3, means that, at the initial equilibrium level of $7.0 trillion, planned spending now exceeds output by $0.1 trillion. Whenever planned spending exceeds output, production must increase. This increase in production increases income, which in turn increases planned spending. This increase in planned spending fuels yet another round of adjustments. *As long as planned spending exceeds output, production will increase, thereby creating more income, which will generate still more spending.*

We will describe what happens in each round when planned investment increases by $0.1 trillion, or $100 billion, assuming the price level remains constant. We will continue to assume that the marginal propensity to consume equals 4/5, or 0.8, though in the real world the MPC is not necessarily 0.8 or any other constant value.

Round One. Firms invest an additional $100 billion per year in new physical capital—new buildings, machines, trucks, computers, and the like. Firms that produce these capital goods respond by increasing production by $100 billion, which generates $100 billion in income to all those who supplied resources in the production of capital goods. Thus, total spending and total income increase by $100 billion in what is the first round of new spending arising from the increase in planned investment. The income-generating process does not stop there, however, because those who receive this additional income spend some of it and save some of it, laying the basis for round two of spending and income.

Round Two. Given a marginal propensity to consume of 4/5, or 0.8, those who receive the $100 billion as income will spend a total of $80 billion on toasters, movies, automobiles, and thousands of other goods and services. The other $20 billion of that $100 billion will be saved. Thus, the $100 billion in new income increases real GDP by $80 billion during the second round.

Round Three and Beyond. Focus now on the $80 billion that went toward consumption during round two. Production increases of $80 billion in the second round generate an equal amount of income to resource suppliers. Again, based on the marginal propensity to consume, we know that four-fifths of the additional income will be consumed and one-fifth will be saved. Thus, $64 billion will be spent on still more goods and services, and $16 billion will be saved. This spending continues to generate income, four-fifths of which is spent, thereby generating still more income.

When does the income-generating machine run out of fuel? At some point the new rounds of income and spending become so small that they disappear and the process stops. Looked at from another way, saving leaks from the circular flow during every round. *The more income that leaks as saving, the less that remains to fuel still more spending and income.* When the leakage to saving accu-

Round (1)	New Spending This Round (2)	Cumulative New Spending (3)	New Saving This Round (4)	Cumulative New Saving (5)
1	100	100	___	___
2	80	180	20	20
3	64	244	16	36
4	51.2	295.2	12.8	48.8
.	.	.	.	.
.	.	.	.	.
.	.	.	.	.
∞	0	500	0	100

EXHIBIT 4

Tracking the Rounds of Spending Following a $100 Billion Increase in Autonomous Spending (billions of dollars)

mulates to $100 billion, no new income or spending can be created, so the process stops.

Exhibit 4 summarizes the multiplier process in a more systematic way. The new spending generated in each round is shown in column (2) and the accumulation of new spending is shown in column (3). The new saving from each round is shown in column (4) and the accumulation of new saving in column (5). The first several rounds are listed, and subsequent rounds are summarized. For example, the new spending accumulated as of the third round is $244 billion—the sum of the first three rounds of spending. The new saving accumulated from the first three rounds is $36 billion. When the increase in spending has run its course, the cumulative effect has been to increase spending by $500 billion and to increase saving by $100 billion. Saving, a leakage from the circular flow, increases just enough to finance the $100 billion increase in investment, an injection into the circular flow.

Note that in our example planned investment increased by $100 billion, or $0.1 trillion, per year. *If this higher level of planned investment is not sustained in the following year, equilibrium spending will fall.* For example, if planned investment returns to $0.6 trillion, other things constant, equilibrium spending will return to $7.0 trillion.

As we will see, the equilibrium quantity of real GDP demanded would have increased by the same amount if consumers had decided to spend $100 billion more at each level of income—that is, if the consumption function rather than the investment function had shifted up by $100 billion. Equilibrium real GDP demanded would likewise have increased if government purchases or net exports had increased by $100 billion. *The change in the equilibrium quantity of aggregate output demanded depends on how much the aggregate expenditure function shifts, not on which spending component causes the shift.*

Numerical Value of the Spending Multiplier

Tracing the rounds of spending is one way to determine the effects of a particular change in spending, but this process is slow and tedious. What we need is a quick way of translating changes in planned spending into changes in the equilibrium level of real output demanded. Recall that the expansion stemming from an increase in autonomous spending depends on the marginal propensity to consume. The spending multiplier and the marginal propensity to consume are related in a way that proves useful in formulating the multiplier. *The larger the fraction of an increase in income that is respent, the greater the spending multiplier.* The marginal propensity to consume and the multiplier are directly related; the larger the MPC, the larger the multiplier. Thus, we can define the simple spending multiplier in terms of the MPC as follows:

$$\text{Simple spending multiplier} = \frac{1}{1 - \text{MPC}}$$

Since the MPC is 4/5, the denominator equals 1 − 4/5, or 1/5, and the simple spending multiplier equals the reciprocal of 1/5, which is 5. If the MPC were 3/4, the denominator would equal 1 − 3/4, or 1/4, and the simple spending multiplier would equal the reciprocal of 1/4, which is 4.[1]

Recall from Chapter 8 that the MPC and the MPS add up to 1, so 1 minus the MPC equals the MPS. With this information, we can define the simple multiplier in terms of the MPS as follows:

$$\text{Simple spending multiplier} = \frac{1}{1 - \text{MPC}} = \frac{1}{\text{MPS}}$$

The simple spending multiplier is the reciprocal of the MPS. When we express the equation this way, we can see that the smaller the MPS, the larger the fraction of each fresh round of income that is spent, so the larger the multiplier.

The focus of the spending multiplier thus far has been the national economy. The idea of the multiplier has some relevance for state and regional economies as well, as shown in the following case study.

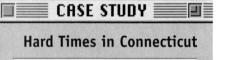

CASE STUDY

Hard Times in Connecticut

Because of a cutback in federal defense spending and a fall in worldwide orders for commercial aircraft, the United Technologies Corporation (UTC), a major producer of jet engines, announced in January of 1993 that by the end of 1994 it would eliminate 10,000 manufacturing jobs in Connecticut. UTC also planned to reduce its orders from dozens of Connecticut firms that supplied the company with everything from precision parts to janitorial services, thereby causing several thousand more job losses in the state. The direct layoffs, as well as expected layoffs by subcontractors, reflected an initial payroll loss exceeding $1 billion.

In a state with an expanding economy, job losses in one sector could be made up at least in part by job expansions in other sectors. But such losses proved especially painful in Connecticut, where a long recession had already re-

---

1   A more formal way of deriving the spending multiplier is to total the additions to spending arising from each new round of income and spending. For example, a $1 increase in investment generates $1 in spending in the first round. In the second round, it generates $1 times the MPC. In the third round, the new spending equals the spending that arose in the second round ($1 × MPC) times the MPC. This goes on round after round, with each new round equal to the spending from the previous round times the MPC. Mathematicians have shown that the sum of an infinite series of rounds, each of which is a constant fraction of the previous round, is 1/(1 − MPC) times the initial amount. In our context, 1/(1 − MPC) is the spending multiplier.

duced employment by 8 percent during the previous four years. Consequently, those who lost high-paying jobs making jet engines faced grim alternatives.

Hard Times in Connecticut
continued

This loss in employment and payroll rippled through the Connecticut economy, reducing the demand for housing, clothing, entertainment, restaurant meals, and other goods and services this income would have purchased. For example, the unemployed engine makers ate out less frequently, reducing the income of restaurant owners, workers, and suppliers. Those losing restaurant jobs reduced their own demand for goods and services.

So job losses had a multiplier effect in Connecticut. But the effect extended beyond the state's borders. For example, individuals who lost jobs demanded fewer automobiles, cutting incomes of auto workers living in places such as Detroit and San Diego. Thus, the number of job losses resulting from UTC's job cuts was greater for the nation as a whole than for Connecticut alone. Therefore, the spending multiplier is greater for the nation as a whole than for Connecticut.

Location:

United Technologies Corporation (UTC) provides technology products—including spacesuits—to customers in the aerospace, building, and automotive industries. To learn more, visit UTC (**http://www.utc.com/**). For information on the Connecticut state economy, browse *The Connecticut Economy,* published by the University of Connecticut (**http:www.lib.uconn.edu/Economics/review.htm**).

Sources: Michael Remez, "State Suppliers to Feel Big Sting from Pratt Cuts," *Hartford Courant,* 28 January 1993; and William McEachern, "Picking Up the Pieces After Connecticut's Great Recession," *The Connecticut Economy: A University of Connecticut Quarterly Review* (April 1993).

CHANGES IN THE PRICE LEVEL

Thus far in this chapter we have used the aggregate expenditure function to derive the equilibrium quantity of real GDP demanded *for a given price level*. But, as we shall see, for each price level there is a specific aggregate expenditure function, which yields a unique equilibrium quantity of real GDP demanded.

A Higher Price Level

What is the effect of a higher price level on the economy's aggregate expenditure function and, in turn, on the equilibrium quantity of real GDP demanded? Recall that consumers hold many assets, such as savings accounts, that are fixed in money terms, and a higher price level decreases the real value of these dollar-denominated assets. Consumers therefore feel poorer as a result of a decrease in their real wealth, so they are less willing to spend at every level of income. For reasons that will be more fully explained in Chapter 15, a higher price level also tends to increase the market rate of interest, and a higher interest rate reduces investment. Finally, a higher U.S. price level means that foreign goods are now relatively cheaper to U.S. consumers and U.S. goods are relatively more expensive abroad. So imports will rise and exports will fall, decreasing net exports. *A higher price level therefore reduces consumption, planned investment, and net exports, which all reduce aggregate spending.* This decrease in the aggregate expenditure function reduces the equilibrium quantity of real GDP demanded.

Each panel of Exhibit 5 represents a different way of expressing the effects of a change in the price level on the quantity of real GDP demanded. Panel (a) presents the income-expenditure model and panel (b) presents the aggregate

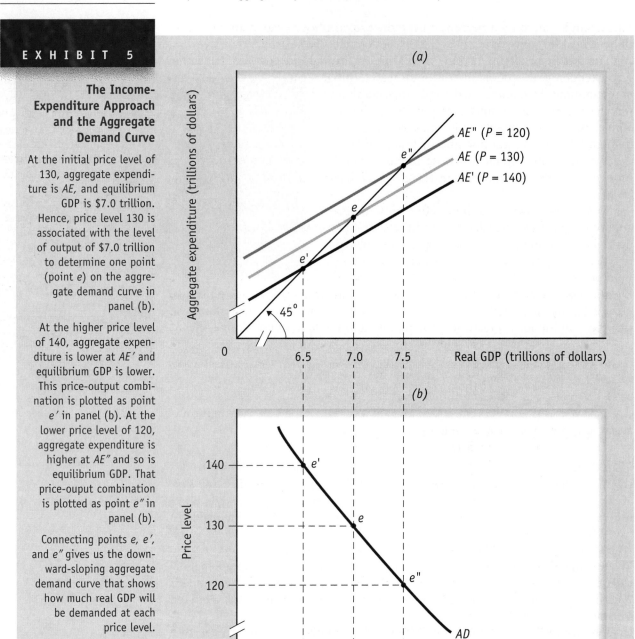

The Income-Expenditure Approach and the Aggregate Demand Curve

At the initial price level of 130, aggregate expenditure is *AE,* and equilibrium GDP is $7.0 trillion. Hence, price level 130 is associated with the level of output of $7.0 trillion to determine one point (point *e*) on the aggregate demand curve in panel (b).

At the higher price level of 140, aggregate expenditure is lower at *AE'* and equilibrium GDP is lower. This price-output combination is plotted as point *e'* in panel (b). At the lower price level of 120, aggregate expenditure is higher at *AE''* and so is equilibrium GDP. That price-ouput combination is plotted as point *e''* in panel (b).

Connecting points *e, e',* and *e''* gives us the downward-sloping aggregate demand curve that shows how much real GDP will be demanded at each price level.

demand model, which shows a relationship between the price level and output demanded. The idea is to show that the equilibrium aggregate expenditure for a given price level in panel (a) can be expressed as a point on the aggregate demand curve in panel (b). The two panels are aligned so that levels of real GDP on the horizontal axes correspond. At the initial price level of 130 in panel (a), the aggregate expenditure function, now denoted by *AE,* intersects the 45-degree line at point *e* to yield $7.0 trillion, the equilibrium quantity of real GDP demanded. Panel (b) shows more directly the link between the quantity of real GDP demanded and the price level. As you can see, when the price level is 130, the quantity demanded is $7.0 trillion. This combination of price level and real GDP is identified by point e on the aggregate demand curve.

Consider the effect of an increase in the price level from 130 to, say, 140. An increase in the price level reduces consumption, investment, and net exports. This reduction in planned spending is reflected in panel (a) by a decrease in the aggregate expenditure function from AE down to AE'. The increase in the price level affects each spending component except government purchases. As a result of this decrease in planned spending, the equilibrium quantity of real GDP demanded declines from $7.0 trillion to, say, $6.5 trillion. Panel (b) shows that an increase in the price level from 130 to 140 decreases the quantity of real GDP demanded from $7.0 trillion to $6.5 trillion, as reflected by point e'.

A Lower Price Level

The opposite holds if the price level is lower. At a lower price level, the value of assets fixed in dollars increases. Consumers on average are richer and so are more inclined to spend on consumption at each level of real GDP. A lower price level also tends to decrease the market rate of interest, which increases investment. Finally, a lower U.S. price level makes U.S. products relatively cheaper abroad and foreign products relatively more expensive to Americans, so exports increase and imports decrease. Thus, because of a decline in the price level, consumption, investment, and net exports increase at each level of real GDP. A lower aggregate expenditure function leads to a lower equilibrium quantity of real GDP demanded.

Refer again to Exhibit 5 and consider the effect of a decrease in the price level. Suppose the price level declines from 130 to, say, 120. As explained earlier, a decline in the price level causes consumption, planned investment, and net exports to increase, as reflected in panel (a) of Exhibit 5 by the shift up in the aggregate expenditure function from AE to AE''. An increase in planned spending at each level of income increases the equilibrium level of real GDP demanded from $7.0 trillion to $7.5 trillion, as indicated by the intersection of the top aggregate expenditure function with the 45-degree line at point e''. This same price increase can be viewed more directly in panel (b). As you can see, when the price level decreases to 120, the quantity of real GDP demanded increases to $7.5 trillion.

The aggregate expenditure function and the aggregate demand curve portray real output from different perspectives. The aggregate expenditure function shows, for a given price level, how planned spending relates to the level of real GDP in the economy. The aggregate demand curve shows, for various price levels, the quantity of real GDP demanded.

The Multiplier and Shifts in Aggregate Demand

Now that we have some idea how the aggregate expenditure function and the aggregate demand curve relate, we can trace the link between a change in autonomous spending and the resulting shift in the aggregate demand curve, at a given price level.

Suppose that an increase in business confidence spurs a $0.1 trillion increase in investment at each level of real GDP. Each panel of Exhibit 6 represents a

If the price level is lower, consumers typically are richer and are willing to spend more on consumption. However, a lower price level makes foreign products, like electronics, more expensive to Americans!

EXHIBIT 6

A Shift in the Aggregate Expenditure Function and a Shift in the Aggregate Demand Curve

A shift in the aggregate expenditure function that is not due to a change in the price level will cause a shift in the aggregate demand curve. In panel (a), an increase in investment, with the price level fixed at 130, causes aggregate expenditure to increase from $C + I + G + (X - M)$ to $C + I' + G + (X - M)$. As a result, the equilibrium level of real GDP demanded increases from $7.0 trillion to $7.5 trillion. In panel (b), the aggregate demand curve has shifted from AD to AD'. At the prevailing price level, the amount of output demanded has increased by $0.5 trillion.

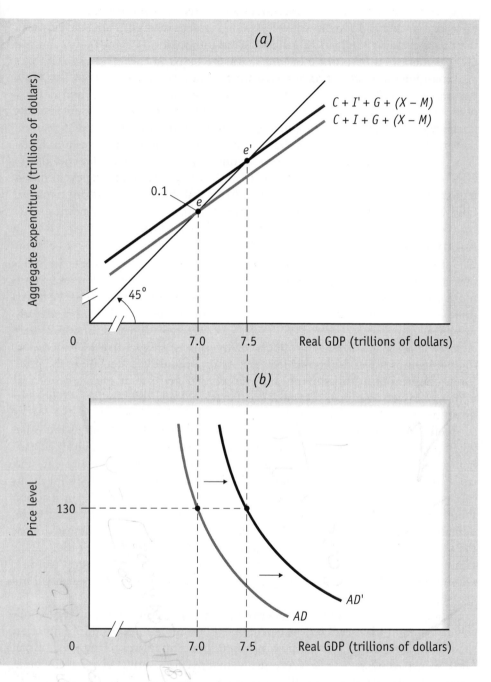

different way of expressing the effects of a change in planned spending on the quantity of real GDP demanded, assuming the price level remains unchanged. Panel (a) presents the income-expenditure model and panel (b) the aggregate demand model. Again, the two panels are aligned so that levels of real GDP on the horizontal axes correspond. At the price level of 130 in panel (a), the aggregate expenditure function, $C + I + G + (X - M)$, intersects the 45-degree line at point e to yield $7.0 trillion, the equilibrium quantity of real GDP demanded. Panel (b) shows more directly the link between the quantity of real

GDP demanded and the price level. As you can see, when the price level is 130, the quantity demanded is $7.0 trillion. This combination of price level and real GDP is identified by point *e* on the aggregate demand curve *AD*.

Exhibit 6 shows how shifts in the aggregate expenditure function and shifts in the aggregate demand curve are related. In panel (a), a $0.1 trillion increase in investment shifts the aggregate expenditure function up by $0.1 trillion, from $C + I + G + (X - M)$ to $C + I' + G + (X - M)$. As we have seen, because of the multiplier effect, such an increase in spending will raise the equilibrium quantity of real GDP demanded from $7.0 trillion to $7.5 trillion. Panel (b) shows the effects of the increase in spending on the aggregate demand curve, which shifts to the right, from *AD* to *AD'*. At the prevailing price level of 130, the quantity demanded has increased from $7.0 trillion to $7.5 trillion as a result of the $0.1 trillion increase in investment.

As we shall see, our discussion of the spending multiplier exaggerates the actual effect we might expect from a given shift in the aggregate expenditure function. For one thing, we assume that the price level remains constant. Incorporating aggregate supply into the analysis tends to reduce the impact of a given shift in aggregate expenditure because of resulting price changes. Moreover, as income increases there are other leakages in the circular flow in addition to saving, such as higher income taxes and increased spending on imports, and these leakages reduce the size of the multiplier. Finally, although we have presented the process in a timeless framework, the spending multiplier takes time to work itself out—perhaps as much as two years.

In summary, the aggregate expenditure function relates, for a given price level, planned spending with the level of income in the economy, or real GDP. A change in the price level will shift the aggregate expenditure function, leading to a new equilibrium quantity of real GDP demanded. These combinations of price levels and real GDP demanded are reflected as points along an aggregate demand curve. A shift in a spending component, such as planned investment, will shift the aggregate demand curve.

We close with a case study that considers the problem of too little saving in the U.S. economy.

Our approach so far has been to examine the impact of particular decisions on aggregate demand. For example, an increase in saving means a decrease in consumption and thus a reduction in aggregate demand. But in a more complete model of the economy, we must recognize that an increase in saving increases the supply of loanable funds in the economy, which stimulates investment, resulting in greater productivity and growth over time. Historically, nations that have saved the most also have invested the most, and investment is a key to a rising standard of living.

Thus, it is troubling that the saving rate in the United States is low today by international standards and has declined during the last two decades. During the 1960s and 1970s, gross saving in the United States, which includes saving by firms, households,

E X H I B I T   7   **Household Saving Rates (Percentage of Disposable Income)**

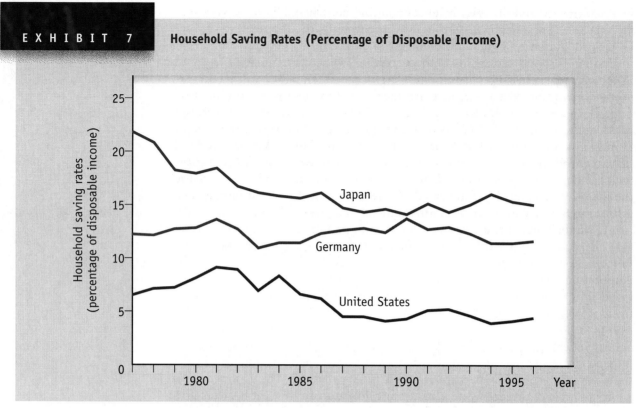

Sources: Developed from data appearing in *OECD Economic Outlook* 57 (June 1995): Annex Table 26, and U.S. Department of Commerce, *Survey of Current Business* 76 (Jan./Feb. 1996): Table 4; figures for 1995 and 1996 are projections.

Not Enough Saving
continued

and governments, averaged about 17 percent of GDP. Gross saving has since declined to about 12 percent of GDP in the 1990s.

Why has gross saving declined? First, growing federal budget deficits mean that the government sector as a whole is in deficit. The federal deficit has climbed from only 0.2 percent of GDP in the 1960s to about 3 percent in the 1990s. This government deficit subtracts from gross saving. Second, gross saving has declined because household saving has declined in recent years.

Exhibit 7 shows household saving as a percentage of disposable income since 1977 for the United States, Japan, and Germany. As you can see, the U.S. household saving rate is significantly below rates in the other two countries, and most recently was less than half the rates in Japan and Germany. The U.S. rate increased in the late 1970s but declined from 9.3 percent in 1981 to 4.8 percent in 1989. Since then it has bounced around, but has remained under 5.0 percent in most years. In Japan, the household saving rate dropped from a high of 21.8 percent in 1979 to about 15 percent of disposable income in 1984, where it has, more or less, remained. Germany's saving rate has stayed within a point or two of 12 percent of disposable income during the entire period. In the case study on the life-cycle hypothesis in Chapter 9, we offered some reasons why the saving rate is so much higher in Japan (e.g., saving is more convenient in Japan, housing is more expensive, and the fraction of the housing price required for a down payment is greater).

So the U.S. household saving rate has declined since 1981 and is now less than half the rates in our two major competing countries. The U.S. *gross* saving rate is also less than half that in Japan and is one quarter less than the rate in Germany.

To increase gross saving, the government can (1) increase public saving (that is, cut the deficit in the government sector) and (2) stimulate private saving. How can the government increase private saving? One possibility is to increase the after-tax return on saving, thereby providing households more incentive to save. For example, individual retirement accounts (IRAs) increase the rate of return on saving by allowing tax-free accumulation of funds held in qualified accounts until retirement. President Clinton proposed expanding IRAs and allowing for early withdrawals to pay for a first home or for a college education. Members of Congress have also tried to introduce measures that would promote saving. But saving patterns are not easily changed. Consider your own saving habit and what it would take to change it.

Sources: *Economic Report of the President,* February 1995, Chapter 3; and *OECD Economic Outlook* 57 (June 1995).

Not Enough Saving
continued

CONCLUSION

The central ideas of this chapter are the forces that determine the equilibrium quantity of aggregate output demanded at a given price level and the relationship between the spending multiplier and changes in the equilibrium level of aggregate output demanded. All this was aimed at developing the aggregate demand curve and how changes in spending components would shift the aggregate demand curve. The simple multiplier provides some intuition about the effect of a change in spending on real GDP, but the effect is exaggerated.

Our approach to calculating the simple multiplier is akin to determining the number of miles a car travels on a gallon of gasoline by testing the car on a treadmill, where it confronts no wind resistance, no hills, no potholes, and no bad drivers. Although the tests are obviously unrealistic, the results are still valuable for comparative purposes. We can say, for example, that a Honda Civic gets twice the fuel efficiency of a Lincoln Town Car. Similarly, we can examine the effects of various changes in the aggregate expenditure function to see which changes have the greatest impact on the quantity of real output demanded. The simple spending multiplier provides a first approximation of the effect of a shift in the aggregate expenditure function on the equilibrium quantity of real output demanded, just as mileage tests on a treadmill provide a first, albeit high, estimate of actual fuel efficiency.

This chapter focused on aggregate spending. A simplifying assumption used throughout was that net exports did not vary with the level of income. Appendix A adds more realism by looking at the effect of imports that increase with income. Since imports represent a leakage from the circular flow, this more realistic approach reduces the size of the spending multiplier.

Thus far we have determined the equilibrium quantity of aggregate output demanded using several approaches, including intuition, tables, and graphs. With the various approaches, we found that for each price level there is a specific quantity of aggregate output demanded, other things constant. Appendix B uses algebra to derive the equilibrium real GDP and the spending multiplier.

SUMMARY

1. By vertically summing the consumption, investment, government purchases, and net export functions, we derive the aggregate expenditure function, which indicates, for a given price level, planned spending at each level of income.

2. At a given price level, the equilibrium quantity of aggregate output demanded occurs where planned spending just equals the amount produced. And leakages from the circular flow equal planned injections, which means that saving and net taxes sum to planned investment, government purchases, and net exports.

3. The simple spending multiplier indicates the multiple by which a shift in planned spending changes the equilib-

rium level of aggregate output demanded. The simple spending multiplier examined in this chapter equals $1/(1 - MPC)$. The greater the MPC, the more of each dollar of income will be spent, and the greater the multiplier.

4. A higher price level results in a downward shift in the aggregate expenditure function, leading to a lower equilibrium quantity of aggregate output demanded. A lower price level results in an upward shift in the aggregate expenditure function, leading to a greater equilibrium quantity of aggregate output demanded. By tracing the equilibrium output demanded at alternative price levels, we can use the income-expenditure model to derive the aggregate demand curve.

QUESTIONS AND PROBLEMS

1. **(Aggregate Expenditure)** What are the components of aggregate expenditure? In the chapter's simplified model, which components vary with the level of real GDP? What determines the slope of the aggregate expenditure function?

2. **(Equilibrium)** What roles do inventories play in the establishment of equilibrium for aggregate output? To answer this question, suppose that firms are either overproducing or underproducing.

3. **(Simple Spending Multiplier)** Suppose that the MPC for the United States is about 0.90 and that a movie studio travels to Montana to make an adventure film. The production of the movie will inject $30 million into the Montana economy initially. One bright economics student claims this $30 million will generate $300 million in additional income for the state. However, some people believe this is an overestimate. What information is needed to decide who is correct?

4. **(Equilibrium)** What factors are equal at the equilibrium level of real GDP demanded? Answer in terms of both the income-expenditure framework and the leakages-injections framework. What is assumed about the price level when determining equilibrium in these frameworks? What is assumed about inventories?

5. **(Multiplier)** "A rise in planned investment spending in an economy will lead to a rise in consumer spending." Use the concept of the multiplier to verify this statement.

6. **(Simple Spending Multiplier)** Create a table similar to Exhibit 4 in this chapter, given that the marginal propensity to consume is equal to 0.90. Assuming the same $100 billion increase in autonomous spending, list the values for each of the first four rounds and determine the overall effect of the increase.

7. **(Simple Spending Multiplier)** For each of the following values for the MPC, determine the size of the multiplier and the total change in equilibrium real GDP demanded for an $8 billion decrease in autonomous spending:
   a. MPC = 0.9
   b. MPC = 0.75
   c. MPC = 0.6

8. **(Aggregate Expenditure Function)** Students often have trouble understanding why aggregate expenditure both depends on income and determines income. Use the economic concept of equilibrium to resolve this seeming paradox.

9. **(Equilibrium and the Simple Spending Multiplier)** Suppose that the MPC is 0.8, while the sum of planned investment, government purchases, and net exports is $500 billion.
   a. What is the level of saving plus net taxes at the equilibrium quantity of aggregate output demanded? Explain.
   b. Suppose that consumption equals $100 billion when real GDP is zero. Graph the $S + NT$ function and

the $I + G + (X - M)$ function, showing the equilibrium level of real GDP demanded.

c. What is the value of the multiplier?

d. Explain why the multiplier is related to the slope of the consumption function.

10. **(Multiplier and Aggregate Demand)** Suppose that at an average price level of 100, equilibrium output demanded is $1,000 billion, and that each point change in the price level causes the aggregate expenditure function to shift by $5 billion. Using a multiplier of 4, do the following:

a. Construct the aggregate demand curve.

b. Explain how a change in the multiplier would affect the slope of the aggregate demand curve.

c. State how much an increase in saving of $100 billion would affect the aggregate demand curve. Be specific.

11. **(Changes in the Price Level)** What is the effect of a lower price level, other factors constant, on the aggregate expenditure function and the equilibrium level of real GDP demanded? How does the multiplier interact with the price change to determine the new equilibrium?

12. **(Investment and the Multiplier)** The text assumes that all investment is autonomous. What would happen to the size of the multiplier if planned investment increased with the level of real GDP? Explain.

13. **(Shifts in Aggregate Demand)** Assume that the economy has a multiplier equal to 10. Indicate the size and direction of any shift in the aggregate expenditure function, equilibrium real GDP demanded, and the aggregate demand curve for each of the following changes in autonomous spending:

a. Autonomous spending rises by $8 billion.

b. Autonomous spending falls by $5 billion.

c. Autonomous spending rises by $20 billion.

14. **(Hard Times in Connecticut)** How would the scenario described in the case study "Hard Times in Connecticut" affect the aggregate expenditure function and the aggregate demand curve? Explain fully. How would the impact change if the size of the multiplier increased?

15. **(Not Enough Saving)** Why is it considered important to increase the gross saving rate in the United States? How might the federal government contribute to a higher gross saving rate?

Using the Internet

16. Visit the Federal Reserve Bank of St. Louis FRED (Federal Reserve Economic Data) Database and review the "FRED Database Index" (**http://www.stls.frb.org/fred/dataindx.html**). Look within "Gross Domestic Product in Current Dollars."

a. What is the GDP for the most recent quarter?

b. What is the last quarter to register a decrease in GDP?

Appendix A

VARIABLE NET EXPORTS

This chapter thus far has assumed that net exports do not vary with the level of income. A more realistic approach allows net exports to vary inversely with the level of income. Such a model of net exports was developed in the appendix to Chapter 9. This net export function is presented in panel (a) of Exhibit 8. The higher the income level in the economy, the more is spent on imports, so the lower are net exports. (If you need a reminder how this relationship was derived, review the appendix to Chapter 9.)

Panel (b) of Exhibit 8 shows what happens when variable net exports are added to consumption, government purchases, and investment. We add the variable net export function to the $C + I + G$ spending

EXHIBIT 8

Net Exports and the Aggregate Expenditure Function

In panel (a), net exports, $X - M$, equal exports minus imports. Net exports are added to consumption investment, and government purchases in panel (b) to yield $C + I + G + (X - M)$. The addition of net exports has the effect of rotating the spending function about the point where net exports are zero, which occurs where real GDP is $5.0 trillion.

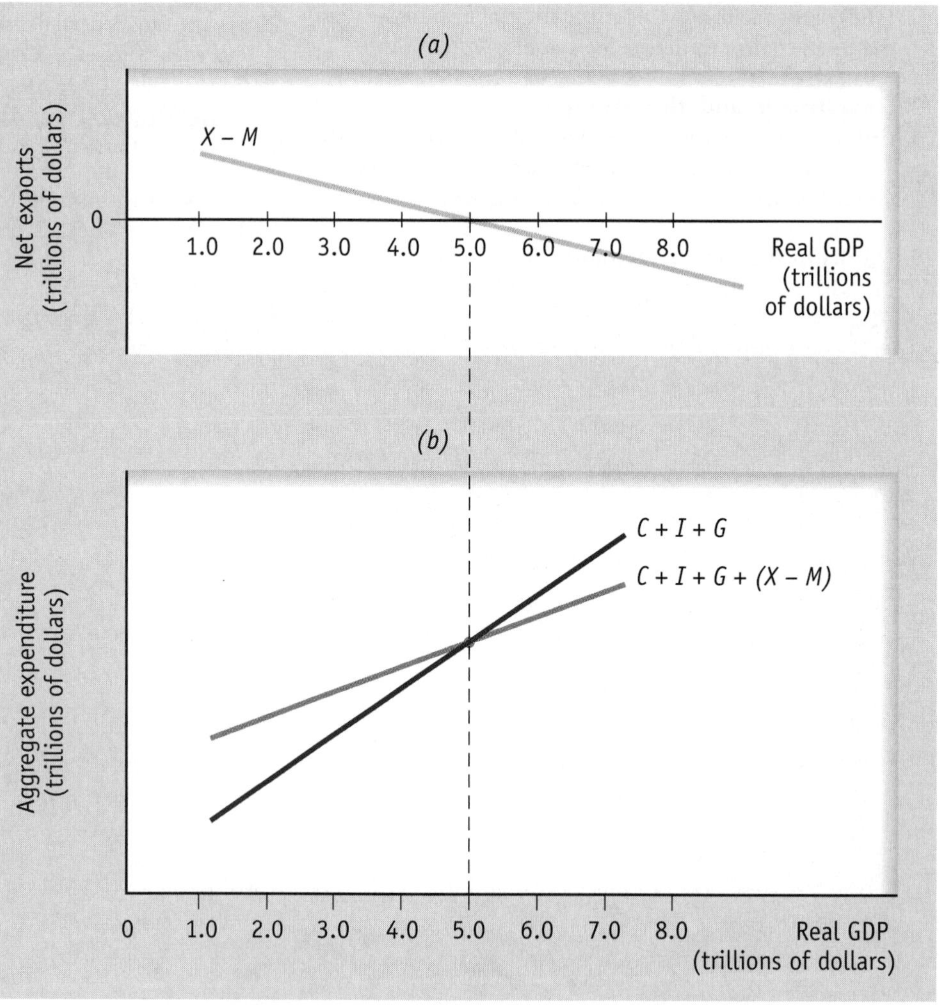

function to derive the $C + I + G + (X - M)$ spending function. Perhaps the easiest way to see how the addition of net exports affects aggregate expenditure is to begin where real GDP equals $5.0 trillion. Since net exports equal zero when real GDP equals $5.0 trillion (which is also where disposable income equals $4.0 trillion, as shown in the appendix to Chapter 9), the addition of net exports has no effect on the aggregate expenditure function when real GDP is $5.0 trillion. Therefore, $C + I + G$ and $C + I + G + (X - M)$ intersect where real GDP equals $5.0 trillion. At real GDP levels less than $5.0 trillion, net exports are positive, so the $C + I + G + (X - M)$ line is above the $C + I + G$ line. At income levels greater than $5.0 trillion, net exports are negative, so $C + I + G + (X - M)$ is below $C + I + G$. *Because net exports and real GDP are inversely related, the addition of variable net exports has the effect of flattening out, or reducing the slope of, the aggregate expenditure function.*

Net Exports and the Spending Multiplier

The inclusion of variable net exports makes the model more realistic but more complicated, and it requires a reformulation of the spending multiplier.

When net exports were autonomous, only the marginal propensity to consume determined how much would be spent and how much would be saved as income increased. The inclusion of variable net exports means that as income increases, U.S. residents spend more on imports. The **marginal propensity to import,** or **MPM,** is the fraction of each additional dollar of income that is spent on imported products. Imports are a leakage from the circular flow. Thus, there are now two leakages that grow with income: saving and imports. The introduction of this additional leakage changes the value of the multiplier from 1/MPS to the

Spending multiplier with net exports

$$= \frac{1}{MPS + MPM}$$

The larger the marginal propensity to import, the greater the leakage during each round of spending and the smaller the resulting spending multiplier. We assume that the MPM equals about 1/10, or 0.1. If the marginal propensity to save is 0.2 and the marginal propensity to import is 0.1, then only 70 cents of each additional dollar of disposable income is spent on output

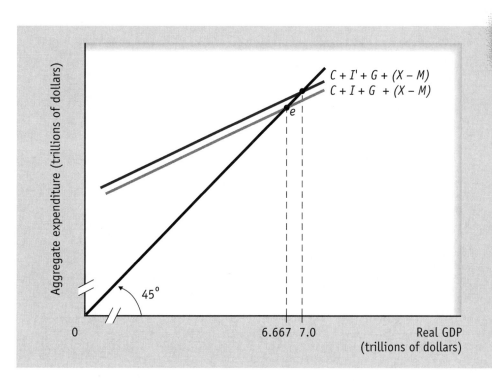

Effect of a Shift in Autonomous Spending on Equilibrium Income

An increase in planned investment, other things constant, shifts the spending function up from $C + I + G + (X - M)$ to $C + I' + G + (X - M)$, yielding a larger equilibrium quantity of real GDP demanded.

produced in the United States. We can compute the new multiplier as follows:

$$\text{Multiplier} = \frac{1}{\text{MPS} + \text{MPM}} = \frac{1}{0.2 + 0.1}$$

$$= \frac{1}{0.3} = 3.33$$

Thus, the inclusion of net exports reduces the spending multiplier in our hypothetical example from 5 to 3.33. *Because some of each additional dollar of income is spent on imports, less is spent on U.S. products, so any given shift in the aggregate expenditure function will have less of an impact on the equilibrium quantity of output demanded.*

A Change in Autonomous Spending

What is the level of equilibrium real GDP given the net export function described in the previous sec-tion, and how does equilibrium income change when there is a change in autonomous spending? Let's begin in Exhibit 9 with an aggregate expendi-ture function of $C + I + G + (X - M)$, where net exports depend on income. This aggregate expendi-ture function intersects the 45-degree line at point *e*, indicating an equilibrium value of real GDP de-manded of $6.667 trillion. Suppose now that invest-ment increases by $0.1 trillion at every level of in-come. This increase in investment will shift the entire aggregate expenditure function up by $0.1 trillion, from $C + I + G + (X - M)$ to $C + I' + G + (X - M)$, as shown in Exhibit 9. As you can see, equilibrium output demanded increases from $6.667 trillion to $7.0 trillion, representing an in-crease of $0.333 trillion, which is $0.1 trillion times the spending multiplier of 3.33. The derivation of these equilibrium values and the size of the multi-plier are explained in Appendix B.

Appendix B
ALGEBRA OF INCOME AND EXPENDITURE

This appendix will explain the algebra behind the material in the chapter, deriving the equilibrium value of aggregate output demanded. You should see some similarity between the presentation here and the circular-flow explanation of the national income accounts.

The Aggregate Expenditure Function
We will first determine where aggregate expenditure equals real GDP as found in this chapter and then derive the relevant spending multipliers assuming a given price level. Initially let's assume net exports are autonomous. Then we incorporate variable net exports into the framework.

The equilibrium quantity of aggregate output demanded occurs where aggregate expenditure equals real GDP. Aggregate expenditure is equal to the sum of consumption, C, investment, I, government purchases, G, and net exports, $X - M$. Algebraically, we can write the equilibrium condition as

$$Y = C + I + G + (X - M)$$

where Y equals income, or real GDP demanded. To flesh out the equilibrium aggregate expenditure, we begin with the heart of the income-expenditure model: the consumption function. The consumption function used throughout this chapter was a straight line; the equation for this line can be written as

$$C = 0.7 + 0.8(Y - 1.0)$$

The marginal propensity to consume is 0.8, Y is income, or real GDP demanded, and 1.0 is autonomous net taxes in trillions of dollars. Thus, $(Y - 1.0)$ is real GDP minus net taxes, which equals disposable income. The consumption function can be simplified to

$$C = -0.1 + 0.8Y$$

Consumption at each level of real GDP, therefore, equals −$0.1 trillion plus 0.8 times the level of income, or real GDP.

The second component of spending is investment, I, which we have assumed is autonomous and equal to $0.6 trillion. The third component of spending is autonomous government purchases, G, which we assumed to be $1.0 trillion. Net exports, $X - M$, the final spending component, we assumed to be −$0.1 trillion. Substituting the numerical values for each spending component in the aggregate expenditure function, we get

$$Y = -0.1 + 0.8Y + 0.6 + 1.0 - 0.1$$

Notice that there is only one variable in this expression: Y. If we rewrite the expression as

$$Y - 0.8Y = -0.1 + 0.6 + 1.0 - 0.1$$
$$0.2Y = 1.4$$

we can solve for the equilibrium level of real GDP demanded:

$$Y = 1.4/0.2$$
$$Y = \$7.0 \text{ trillion}$$

A More General Form of Income and Expenditure
The advantage of algebra is that it allows us to derive the equilibrium quantity of real GDP demanded in a more general way. Consider a consumption function of the general form

$$C = a + b(Y - NT)$$

where b is the marginal propensity to consume, and NT is net taxes. Consumption can be rearranged to

$$C = a - bNT + bY$$

where $a - bNT$ is *autonomous* consumption, that portion of consumption that is independent of the level of income, and bY is *induced* consumption, that portion of consumption generated by the level of income in the economy. In equilibrium, the quantity of GDP demanded equals the sum of consumption, C, autonomous investment, I, autonomous government purchases, G, and autonomous net exports, $X - M$, or

Income = Expenditure
$$Y = a - bNT + bY + I + G + (X - M)$$

Again, by rearranging terms and isolating Y on the left-hand side of the equation, we get

$$Y = \frac{1}{1 - b}(a - bNT + I + G + X - M)$$

The $(a - bNT + I + G + X - M)$ term represents autonomous spending—that is, the amount of spending that is independent of income. And $(1 - b)$ equals 1 minus the MPC. In the chapter we showed that $1/(1 - MPC)$ equals the simple spending multiplier. One way of viewing the forces that underlie the determination of equilibrium is to keep in mind that autonomous spending is *multiplied* through the economy until the equilibrium quantity of aggregate output is demanded.

The formula that yields the equilibrium quantity of aggregate output demanded can be used to focus on the origin of the spending multiplier. We can increase autonomous spending by, say, $1, to see what happens to the equilibrium real GDP demanded.

$$Y' = \frac{1}{1 - b}(a - bNT + I + G + X - M + \$1)$$

The difference between this expression and the initial equilibrium (that is, between Y' and Y) is $1/(1 - b)$. Since b equals the *MPC*, the simple multiplier equals $1/(1 - b)$. Thus, the change in equilibrium income equals the change in autonomous spending times the multiplier.

Introducing Variable Net Exports
Here we explain the algebra behind variable net exports, first introduced in the appendix to Chapter 9.

We begin by stating the equilibrium condition:

$$Y = C + I + G + (X - M)$$

Exports are assumed to equal $0.4 trillion at each level of income. Imports increase as disposable income increases and the marginal propensity to import has been assumed to be 0.1. Therefore, net exports equal

$$X - M = 0.4 - 0.1(Y - 1.0)$$

After incorporating the values for C, I, and G presented earlier, we can express the equilibrium condition as

$$Y = -0.1 + 0.8Y + 0.6 + 1.0 + 0.4 - 0.1(Y - 1.0)$$

which reduces to $0.3Y = \$2.0$ trillion, or $Y = \$6.667$ trillion.

Algebra can be used to generalize these results. If m represents the marginal propensity to import, net exports become $X - m(Y - NT)$. The equilibrium output can be found by solving for Y in the expression

$$Y = a + b(Y - NT) + I + G + X - m(Y - NT)$$

which yields

$$Y = \frac{1}{1 - b + m}(a - bNT + I + G + X + mNT)$$

The expression in parentheses represents autonomous spending. In the denominator, $1 - b$ is the marginal propensity to save and m is the marginal propensity to import. Appendix A demonstrates that $1/(MPS + MPM)$ equals the spending multiplier when net exports are included. Thus, equilibrium output equals the spending multiplier times autonomous spending. And an increase in autonomous spending times the multiplier gives us the resulting increase in the equilibrium quantity of aggregate output demanded.

1. **(The Spending Multiplier)** Suppose that the marginal propensity to consume (MPC) is 0.8 and the marginal propensity to import (MPM) is 0.05.
   a. What is the value of the multiplier?
   b. What would be the change in equilibrium output if investment increased by $100 billion?
   c. Using your answer to part b, calculate the change in the trade balance (net exports) caused by the change in aggregate output.

2. **(Equilibrium)** Suppose that when aggregate output equals zero, consumption equals $100 billion, autonomous investment equals $200 billion, govern-ment purchases equal $50 billion, and net exports equal $50 billion. Suppose also that MPC = 0.9 and MPM = 0.1.
   a. Construct a table showing the level of aggregate spending, net exports, and saving plus net taxes for aggregate output levels of zero, $500 billion, and $1,000 billion.
   b. Use autonomous spending and the multiplier to calculate the equilibrium quantity of real GDP demanded.
   c. What would the new equilibrium quantity of real GDP demanded be if an *increase* in U.S. interest rates caused net exports to change by $50 billion? Explain.

11

Aggregate Supply

Up to this point we have focused on the quantity of aggregate output demanded at a given price level. We have not yet introduced a theory of aggregate supply. Perhaps no area of macroeconomics is subject to more debate than that of aggregate supply. The debate surrounds the shape of the aggregate supply curve and the reasons for that shape. In this chapter, we will attempt to develop a single, coherent framework.

Although our focus continues to be on economic aggregates, you should keep in mind that aggregate supply reflects billions of individual production decisions made by millions of individual resource suppliers and firms in the economy. Each firm operates in its own little world, dealing with its own suppliers and customers and keeping a watchful eye on existing and potential competitors. Yet each firm also recognizes that success in part is linked to the performance of the economy as a whole. The theory of aggregate supply we describe here must be consistent with both the microeconomic behavior of individual suppliers and the macroeconomic behavior of the economy. In the appendix to this chapter, we will examine resource markets more closely to strengthen your understanding of the underpinnings of aggregate supply. Topics discussed in this chapter include:

- Expected price levels and long-term contracts
- Potential output
- Short-run aggregate supply

- Long-run aggregate supply
- Expansionary and contractionary gaps
- Changes in aggregate supply

AGGREGATE SUPPLY IN THE SHORT RUN

As you know, *aggregate supply* is the relationship between the price level in the economy and the quantity of aggregate output firms are willing and able to supply, other things held constant. The other things held constant along a given aggregate supply curve include the supply of resources to firms, the state of technology, and the set of formal and informal institutions that underpin the economic system. The greater the supply of resources, the better the technology, and the greater the production incentives provided by the economic institutions, the greater the aggregate supply. We begin by looking at the supply of the central resource: labor.

Net Bookmark

How strong is the labor market in your state? America's Labor Market Information System (ALMIS), a program sponsored by the Employment and Training Administration, U.S. Department of Labor (ETA), offers online labor market information through LMINet (**http://ecuvax.cis.ecu.edu/~lmi/lmi.html**), as well as links to state-specific sites (**http://ecuvax.cis.ecu.edu/~lmi/lmi_inet.html**).

Labor Supply and Aggregate Supply

Labor is the most important resource; it even has a holiday named after it: Labor Day. The supply of labor in an economy depends on the size and abilities of the adult population and household preferences for work versus leisure. Along a given labor supply curve—that is, for a given adult population and given preferences for work versus leisure—the quantity of labor supplied depends on the wage. At a higher wage, other things constant, more people are willing and able to work.

So far, so good. Things start getting complicated, however, when we recognize that the purchasing power of any given dollar wage depends on the economy's price level. The higher the price level, the less any given dollar wage will purchase, so the less attractive that dollar wage is to workers. Consider wages and the price level over time. Suppose a worker in 1970 was offered a job paying $20,000 per year. That salary may not impress you today, but at the time its real purchasing power would have exceeded $70,000 in 1996 dollars. Therefore, we must distinguish between the **nominal wage,** which measures the wage in current dollars (the number of dollars on your paycheck), and the **real wage,** which measures the wage in constant dollars—that is, dollars of constant purchasing power.

Both workers and employers care more about the real wage than the nominal wage. The problem is that most resource agreements must be negotiated in nominal wages because nobody knows for sure what price level will prevail during the life of the wage agreement. Workers as well as other resource suppliers must reach wage agreements based on the *expected* price level. Some resource prices, such as wages that are set by long-term contracts, remain in force for extended periods, sometimes for two or three years.

Even where there are no explicit labor contracts, there is often an implicit agreement that wages will be revised periodically. For example, in many firms the standard practice is to revise wages annually. So wage agreements may be either *explicit* (based on a labor contract) or *implicit* (based on the customs and conventions of the market). These explicit and implicit agreements make it difficult to revise the terms of the contract during the life of the agreement, even if the price level turns out to be higher or lower than expected. Some contracts may call for cost-of-living adjustments to be made annually during the life of the contract, but research shows that these adjustments only partially compensate for unexpected increases in the price level, and the wage adjustment occurs at the end of the period during which the unexpected price increase occurred.

Nominal wage The wage measured in terms of current dollars; the dollar amount on a paycheck

Real wage The wage measured in terms of dollars of constant purchasing power; hence, the wage measured in terms of the quantity of goods and services it will purchase

Potential Output and the Natural Rate of Unemployment

Here's the story. Firms and resource suppliers each begin the production period expecting a certain price level to prevail in the economy. Based on those expectations, they reach agreements on resource prices, such as wages. For example, firms and workers may expect the price level to increase 3 percent next year, so they agree on a nominal wage increase of 3 percent, which will leave the real wage unchanged. If their price-level expectations are realized, the agreed-upon nominal wage translates into the expected real wage, so everyone is satisfied with the way things work out. When the actual price level turns out as expected, we call the resulting level of output the economy's *potential output*. *Thus, the potential output is the amount produced when there are no surprises associated with the price level.* So, at the given real wage, workers are supplying just the quantity of labor they want to and firms are hiring just the quantity of labor they want to. Both parties are content with the arrangement.

Potential output The economy's maximum sustainable output level, given the supply of resources, technology, and the underlying economic institutions; the output level when there are no surprises about the price level

We can think of the **potential output** level as the economy's maximum *sustainable* output level, given the supply of resources, the state of technology, and the formal and informal institutions supporting the economy. Potential output is also referred to by other terms, including *natural rate of output, high-employment rate of output,* and *full-employment rate of output.* (Potential output is developed more fully in the appendix.)

If the economy is producing its potential output, does this mean that all resources in the economy—every worker, every machine, every acre of land—are employed? No. Remember from our discussion of unemployment that even in a vibrant, dynamic economy, some workers are unemployed. In a healthy economy, there are always both job openings and job seekers. Other resources may be periodically unemployed as well. To remain productive, farmland must at times lie fallow, machines must regularly be shut down for maintenance and repair, trucks must be serviced—even entire plants may be closed for retooling.

Natural rate of unemployment The unemployment rate that occurs when the economy is producing its potential level of output

The unemployment rate that occurs when the economy is producing its potential GDP is called the **natural rate of unemployment.** The natural rate of unemployment includes frictional, structural, and seasonal unemployment, but excludes cyclical unemployment. When the economy is producing its potential output, the number of job openings is equal to the number unemployed for frictional, structural, and seasonal reasons. During the 1960s, a widely accepted figure for the natural rate of unemployment was 4 percent of the labor force. Since then the rate has drifted up for reasons discussed in Chapter 6; today, estimates of 5 or 6 percent are most often mentioned.

Potential output depends largely on the supply of labor and on the productivity of that labor. The supply of labor, in turn, depends on household choices between labor and leisure. At the turn of the century, the average work week was about 62 hours.[1] Because human and physical capital and technology have improved during the century, worker productivity per hour has increased. The resulting higher real income has prompted many households to increase their consumption of leisure, so the average work week is now about 40 hours. Consequently, potential output is lower today than it would be if average hours worked had not fallen.

---

1   This estimate is from Stanley Lebergott, *Pursuing Happiness: American Consumers in the Twentieth Century* (Princeton, N.J.: Princeton University Press, 1993), p. 168.

In summary, potential output provides a reference point for the analysis in this chapter. *When the actual price level turns out as anticipated, the expectations of both workers and firms are fulfilled, and the economy produces its potential output.* Complications arise, however, when the actual price level that occurs in the economy differs from the expected price level. The *short run* is a period so brief that firms and those who supply resources to firms have insufficient time to adjust to an unexpected price level. In the *long run,* firms and resource suppliers have time to adjust completely to a price level that differs from their expectations.

Actual Price Level Higher Than Expected

As has been noted already, each firm's objective is to maximize profit. Profit equals total revenue minus total cost. In the short run, the prices of certain resources are fixed by contract. Suppose the economy's price level turns out to be higher than expected. What happens to the quantity of aggregate output supplied? Does it exceed the economy's potential, fall short of that potential, or equal that potential? Since the prices of many resources have been fixed for the duration of contracts, firms welcome a price level that is higher than expected. After all, in that situation the prices of their products, on average, are higher than expected, while the costs of at least some of the resources they employ remain constant.

Because a price level that is higher than expected results in higher profits in the short run, firms expand aggregate output beyond the economy's potential level. At first it might appear contradictory to talk about producing beyond the economy's potential, but remember that potential output implies not zero unemployment but the *natural rate* of unemployment. Even in an economy producing its potential output, there is some unemployed labor and some unused production capacity. If you think of potential GDP as the economy's normal capacity, you get a better understanding of how the economy can temporarily exceed that capacity. For example, during World War II, the United States pulled out all the stops to win the war. Factories operated around the clock. The unemployment rate fell below 2 percent—below the natural rate. Overtime was common. People worked longer and harder for the war effort than they normally would.

Consider your study habits. During most of the term, you probably display your normal capacity for academic work. As the end of the term draws near, however, you may shift into high gear, finishing term papers, studying late into the night for final exams, and generally running yourself ragged trying to pull things together. During those final frenzied weeks of the term, you study beyond your normal capacity, beyond the schedule you would prefer to follow on a regular or sustained basis. We often observe workers exceeding their normal capacity for short bursts: fireworks displayers around the Fourth of July, accountants during tax preparation time, farmers during harvest time, and elected officials during the last days of a campaign or a legislative session. Similarly, firms and their workers are able, for limited periods, to push output beyond the economy's potential.

Why Costs Rise When Output Exceeds Potential

The economy is flexible enough to expand output beyond potential GDP, just as you can extend yourself during final exams. You cannot, however, push

Unusual circumstances, such as the need to build aircraft around the clock during World War II, can cause the economy to exceed the potential GDP and drive unemployment rates below their natural rate.

Efficiency wage theory The idea that keeping wages above the level required to attract a sufficient pool of workers makes workers compete to keep their jobs and results in greater productivity

yourself for weeks without becoming exhausted—and the economy's resources cannot be stretched indefinitely without putting pressure on production costs. Even though many workers are bound by contracts, wage agreements may require overtime pay for extra hours or weekend work. Firms may have to spend more on recruiting, particularly to hire workers who had been frictionally unemployed. Some firms must resort to hiring workers who are not properly prepared for the available jobs—those who had been structurally unemployed. Retirees may need a bonus to draw them back into the labor force. If few additional workers are available, if available workers are less qualified, or if workers require additional pay for overtime, the nominal cost of labor will increase as output expands in the short run, even though most workers are bound by wage agreements.

The nominal cost of other resources may also increase as output is pushed beyond the economy's potential. As production expands, the demand for resources increases, so the prices of those resources purchased in markets where prices are flexible—such as the market for oil—will increase, reflecting their greater scarcity. Also, for the rate of production to expand, firms must use their machines and trucks more intensively, so this equipment wears out faster and is more subject to breakdown. Thus, the nominal cost per unit of output rises when production is pushed beyond the economy's potential output. But *because the prices of some resources are fixed in the short run by contracts, the cost of additional production rises less than does the revenue resulting from the higher price level, so profit-maximizing firms increase the quantity supplied.*

In summary, if the price level is greater than expected, firms have a profit incentive to increase the quantity of aggregate output supplied. At higher rates of output, however, the per-unit cost of additional output increases. When the price level is higher than expected, firms will maximize profits by expanding output as long as the revenue from additional production exceeds the cost of that production.

The Price Level, Real Wages, and Labor Supply

When the actual price level exceeds the expected price level, the real value of an agreed-upon nominal wage declines. We might ask why workers would be willing to increase the quantity of labor they supply when the price level is higher than expected. One answer is that since labor agreements require workers to offer their labor at the agreed-upon nominal wage, workers are simply complying with their contracts. Another possible explanation is that the contracted wage is higher than it needs to be to attract enough workers. The **efficiency wage theory** argues that by keeping wages above the level required to attract a sufficient number of workers, some firms ensure an abundant worker pool from which to hire. Wages that are higher than necessary also ensure that employees will be less likely to goof off or do anything that might jeopardize what is considered an attractive job. Since wages are higher than they need to be, workers gladly increase the quantity of labor supplied when firms expand output.

Actual Price Level Lower Than Expected

We have discovered that if the price level is greater than expected, firms expand output, but as they do, the per-unit cost of additional production increases. Now let's examine the effects of a price level that is lower than expected. Again, suppose that resource suppliers and firms are expecting a certain price level. If the price level turns out to be lower than expected, production is less attractive to firms. The price firms receive for their output is lower than they expected, but many of their production costs do not fall.

Since production is less profitable when the price level is lower than expected, firms reduce their quantity supplied, and the economy's output is below its potential. The result is that some workers are laid off, those who keep their jobs may work fewer hours, and unemployment exceeds its natural rate. Not only is less labor employed, but machines go unused and delivery trucks sit idle—even entire plants may shut down. For example, auto producers sometimes halt production for weeks if sales are slower than expected.

Just as some costs increase in the short run when output is pushed beyond the economy's potential, some costs decline when output falls below the economy's potential. As output falls below potential, some resources become unemployed, so the prices of resources purchased in markets where the price is flexible decline. Moreover, with an abundance of unemployed resources, firms can be more selective about which resources to employ, laying off the least productive first.

The Short-Run Aggregate Supply Curve

To review: If the price level turns out to be higher than expected, the quantity supplied increases beyond the economy's potential output. As output expands, the per-unit cost of additional production increases. If the price level turns out to be lower than expected, the quantity supplied shrinks below the economy's potential output. As output declines, the per-unit cost of production falls.

All of this is a long way of saying that *in the short run, there is a positive relationship between the actual price level and the quantity of aggregate output supplied.* What we have been describing is the **short-run aggregate supply (SRAS) curve,** which shows the relationship between the actual price level and the quantity of aggregate output producers in the economy are willing and able to supply, other things constant. The **short run** in this context is the period during which some resource prices, especially those for labor, are fixed by agreement. For simplicity, we can think of the short run as the duration of labor contracts.

Suppose the expected price level is 130. The short-run aggregate supply curve in Exhibit 1, $SRAS_{130}$, is based on that expected price level. If the price level turns out to be 130, as expected, producers supply the economy's potential level of output, which in Exhibit 1 is $7.0 trillion. This combination of price and quantity supplied is indicated by point *a*. If 130 turns out to be the actual price level, all firms and all resource suppliers will be content to supply that amount, because their supply and demand decisions were based on that expected price level. Unemployment is at the natural rate. Nobody is surprised. In Exhibit 1, levels of output that fall short of the economy's potential are shaded red and levels of output that exceed the economy's potential are shaded blue.

The slope of the aggregate supply curve depends on how quickly the cost of additional production rises as aggregate output expands. If, in the short run, increases in production costs per unit are relatively modest, the supply curve will be relatively flat. If these costs increase sharply with increased production,

Short-run aggregate supply (SRAS) curve A curve that shows the direct relationship between the price level and the quantity of aggregate output supplied in the short run, other things constant.

Short run A period during which some resource prices, especially those for labor, are fixed by agreement

Short-Run Aggregate Supply Curve When the Expected Price Level is 130

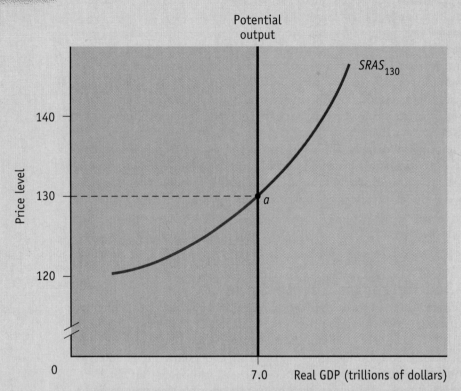

The short-run aggregate supply curve is drawn for a given expected price level of 130. Point *a* shows that if the actual price level equals the expected level, producers supply the potential level of output. If the price level exceeds 130, firms increase the quantity supplied. As they do, the cost per unit of producing additional output rises. With a price level below 130, firms decrease the quantity supplied. As they do, their cost per unit of producing additional output falls. Levels of output that fall short of the economy's potential are shaded red; levels of output that exceed the economy's potential are shaded blue.

the supply curve will be relatively steep. Notice that the short-run aggregate supply curve gets steeper as output increases, because resources become more scarce and hence more costly as output increases. Much of the controversy about the short-run aggregate supply curve involves its shape; shapes range from relatively flat to relatively steep.

EQUILIBRIUM IN THE SHORT RUN AND LONG RUN

A short-run equilibrium price level that is higher or lower than the expected price level will, in the long run, bring about additional adjustments. In the long run, firms and resource suppliers are able to renegotiate all agreements based on knowledge of the actual price level. In this section, we examine this long-run adjustment.

Actual Price Level Higher Than Expected

Let's begin in Exhibit 2 with an expected price level of 130. The short-run aggregate supply curve for that expected price level is $SRAS_{130}$. Given the short-run aggregate supply curve, the equilibrium levels of price and real GDP depend on the aggregate demand curve. The actual price level would equal the expected price level only if the aggregate demand curve intersects the aggregate supply curve, $SRAS_{130}$, at point *a*—that is, where the quantity equals potential output. Point *a* reflects a price level of 130, the expected price level, and potential output level of $7.0 trillion. Suppose, however, that the aggregate demand curve, *AD,* intersects $SRAS_{130}$ at point *b*. Point *b* is the short-run equilibrium point, reflecting a price level of 135 and a real GDP of $7.2 trillion. The actual price level in the short run is higher than expected, and the level of output exceeds the economy's potential of $7.0 trillion.

The amount by which equilibrium output in the short run exceeds the economy's potential is often referred to as the **expansionary gap;** in Exhibit 2, it is the short-run output of $7.2 trillion minus potential output of $7.0 trillion, or $0.2 trillion. As we will see, output exceeding potential GDP creates inflationary pressure. When real GDP exceeds potential output, the actual unemployment rate is below the natural rate of unemployment. Employees are working overtime, machines are being pushed to the limit, and farmers are sandwiching extra crops between usual plantings. *The more the short-run output exceeds the economy's potential, the larger the expansionary gap and the greater the upward pressure on the price level.*

The **long run** is a period during which firms and resource suppliers have the opportunity to renegotiate resource payments based on a knowledge of the actual market conditions—that is, based on knowledge of supply and demand. Simply put, in the long run, firms and resource suppliers can adjust resource prices based on knowledge of the aggregate demand curve. As workers and other resource suppliers negotiate higher resource payments, the short-run aggregate supply curve shifts up to the left to reflect the higher cost of resources. In Exhibit 2, the expansionary gap eventually causes the short-run aggregate supply curve to shift up to $SRAS_{140}$, which is based on an expected price level of 140. Notice that the short-run aggregate supply curve shifts up along the aggregate demand curve until the economy's potential output is the equilibrium quantity. *Actual output can exceed the economy's potential in the short run but not in the long run.*

As shown in Exhibit 2, the expansionary gap is closed by a reduction in the short-run aggregate supply curve from $SRAS_{130}$ back to $SRAS_{140}$. Whereas $SRAS_{130}$ was based on contracts reflecting an expected price level of 130, $SRAS_{140}$ is based on contracts reflecting an expected price level of 140. Because the expected price level and the actual price level are identical at point *c,* the economy at that point is not only in short-run equilibrium but also in *long-run equilibrium.* Consider all the equalities that hold at point *c:* (1) the actual price level equals the expected price level; (2) the quantity supplied in the short run equals potential output, which also equals the quantity supplied in the long run; and (3) the quantity supplied equals the quantity demanded. Point *c* will con-

Expansionary gap The amount by which actual output in the short run exceeds the economy's potential output

Long run A period during which wage contracts and resource price agreements can be renegotiated tinue to be the equilibrium point unless there is some change in aggregate supply or aggregate demand.

Note that in real terms the situation at point *c* is no different from what had been expected at point *a*. At both points, firms are willing and able to supply the economy's potential level of output of $7.0 trillion. The same amounts of labor and other resources are employed, and though the price level, the nominal wage rate, and other nominal resource payments are higher at point *c*, real wages and the real return to other resources are the same as they would have been at point *a*. For example, suppose the nominal wage rate was $10 per hour when the expected price was 130. If the expected price level increased from 130 to 140, an increase of 7.7 percent, the nominal wage rate would also increase by the same percentage to $10.77 per hour. With no change in the real wage between points *a* and *c*, firms demand enough labor to produce $7.0 trillion and workers supply enough labor to produce $7.0 trillion.

EXHIBIT 2   **Short-Run Equilibrium When the Price Level Exceeds Expectations**

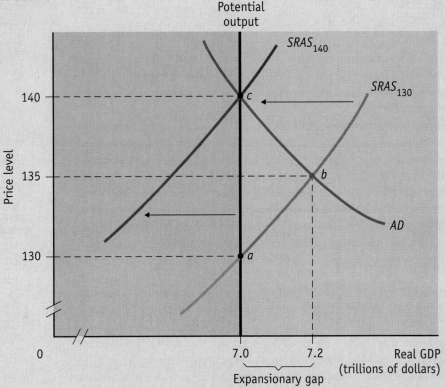

If the expected price level is 130, the short-run aggregate supply curve is *SRAS*₁₃₀. If the actual price level turns out as expected, the quantity supplied is the potential output, $7.0 trillion. If the price level is higher than expected, output exceeds potential, as shown by the short-run equilibrium at point *b*. The amount by which output of $7.2 trillion exceeds the economy's potential output is referred to as the expansionary gap. In the long run, price expectations will be revised upward. As costs rise, the short-run aggregate supply curve shifts upward to *SRAS*₁₄₀, and the economy moves to long-run equilibrium at point *c*.

If suppliers were continually surprised by higher-than-expected price levels, they would continue trying to expand output in the short run beyond the economy's potential level of output. As the economy adjusted in the long run to the higher-than-expected price levels, the short-run aggregate supply curve would shift to the left, creating an inflation spiral. Thus, in the short run, a higher-than-expected price level prompts an increase in the quantity of aggregate output supplied; in the long run, this higher-than-expected price level creates inflationary pressure that causes the short-run aggregate supply curve to shift to the left, reducing output and increasing the price level.

If a given increase in the price level came to be predicted with accuracy year after year, firms and resource suppliers would build these higher expected price levels into their agreements, raising resource prices enough to keep the real return to resources unchanged. The price level would move up each year by the expected amount, but the economy's output would remain at potential GDP, thereby skipping the round trip beyond the economy's potential and back.

Actual Price Level Lower Than Expected

Let's begin again with an expected price level of 130 as presented in Exhibit 3, where blue shading indicates output levels exceeding potential and red shading indicates output levels below potential. If the price level turned out as expected,

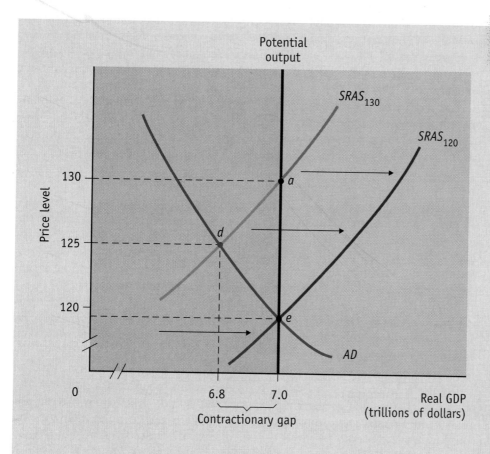

EXHIBIT 3

Short-Run Equilibrium When the Price Level Is Below Expectations

When the price level is below expectations, as indicated by the intersection of the aggregate demand curve *AD* with the short-run aggregate supply curve $SRAS_{130}$, short-run equilibrium occurs at point *d*. Production is below the economy's potential by the amount of the contractionary gap, $0.2 trillion. In the long run, resource suppliers will lower their price expectations. As resource costs fall, the short-run aggregate supply curve shifts out to $SRAS_{120}$, and the economy moves to long-run equilibrium at point *e*, with output at the potential level, $7.0 trillion.

Contractionary gap The amount by which actual output in the short run falls below the economy's potential output

the resulting equilibrium combination would occur at *a*. Suppose this time that aggregate demand intersects the short-run aggregate supply curve to yield a price level below expectations. The intersection of the aggregate demand curve, *AD,* with $SRAS_{130}$ establishes the short-run equilibrium point, *d*. Production of $6.8 trillion is below the economy's potential. The amount by which actual output falls short of potential GDP is called the **contractionary gap.** In this case, the contractionary gap is $0.2 trillion. The unemployment rate is greater than its natural rate.

Because the prevailing price level of 125 is lower than the expected level, the nominal wage based on an expected price level of 130 translates into a higher real wage in the short run. Since the price level is lower than expected, employers are no longer willing to negotiate as high a nominal wage. And with the unemployment rate higher than the natural rate, more workers are competing for jobs. If the price level and nominal wages are flexible, the combination of a high real wage and a pool of unemployed workers competing for jobs should make workers more willing to accept a lower nominal wage.

When firms and workers agree on a lower nominal wage, production costs decline, shifting the short-run aggregate supply curve outward. The short-run supply curve will continue to shift outward until it intersects the aggregate demand curve where the economy produces its potential output. This increase in supply is reflected in Exhibit 3 by a shift to the right in the short-run aggregate supply curve from $SRAS_{130}$ to $SRAS_{120}$. *If the price level and nominal wages are flexible, the short-run aggregate supply curve will move outward until the economy produces its potential output.* The new short-run aggregate supply curve is based on an expected price level of 120. Because the expected price level and the actual price level are now the same, the economy is in long-run equilibrium at point *e*.

Although the nominal wage is lower at point *e* than what was originally agreed upon when the expected price level was 130, the real wage is the same at point *e* as it was at point *a*. Since the real wage is the same, the amount of labor that workers supply is the same and real output is the same. All that has changed between points *a* and *e* is nominal variables—the price level, the nominal wage, and other nominal resource payments.

We conclude that when incorrect expectations cause firms and resource suppliers to overestimate the price level, output in the short run falls below the economy's potential. As long as wages and prices are flexible, however, firms and workers should be able to adjust their wage agreements in the long run when existing contracts expire; a drop in the nominal wage will shift the short-run aggregate supply curve to the right until the economy once again produces its potential level of output. *If wages and prices do not adjust very quickly to a contractionary gap, then shifts in the short-run aggregate supply curve may be slow to move the economy to its potential output. The economy can therefore appear to be stuck at an output and employment level below its potential.*

We are now in a position to provide an additional interpretation to the red and blue shaded areas of our exhibits. If a short-run equilibrium occurs in the blue shaded area, that is, the right or potential output, then the short-run aggregate supply curve will, in the long run, shift up and to the left. If a short-run equilibrium occurs in the red shaded area, then the short-run aggregate supply curve will, in the long run, shift down to the right. Only if a short-run equilibrium occurs at potential output will the short-run aggregate supply curve remain unchanged in the long run.

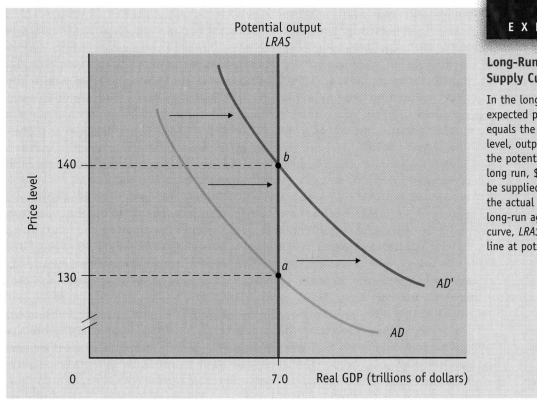

EXHIBIT 4

Long-Run Aggregate Supply Curve

In the long run, when the expected price level equals the actual price level, output will be at the potential level. In the long run, $7.0 trillion will be supplied regardless of the actual price level. The long-run aggregate supply curve, *LRAS,* is a vertical line at potential GDP.

Tracing Potential Output

If wages and prices are flexible enough, the economy will produce its potential level of output in the long run, as indicated in Exhibit 4 by the vertical line drawn at the economy's potential GDP, estimated here to be $7.0 trillion. The potential level of output depends on the supply of resources in the economy, on the level of technology, and on the production incentives provided by the formal and informal institutions of the economic system. The vertical line drawn at potential GDP is called the economy's **long-run aggregate supply (*LRAS*) curve.**

Note that as long as wages and prices are flexible, the economy's potential GDP is consistent with any price level. *In the long run, the actual price level depends only on the location of the aggregate demand curve.* In Exhibit 4, the initial price level of 130 is determined by the intersection of *AD* with the long-run aggregate supply curve. If the aggregate demand curve shifts out to *AD'*, then in the long run the equilibrium price level will increase to 140, and equilibrium output will return to the economy's potential GDP. Conversely, a fall in aggregate demand will, in the long run, lead only to a fall in the price level, with no change in output. *Note that these long-run movements are more like tendencies than smooth adjustments. The time required for resource prices to adjust may be quite long, particularly when the economy faces a contractionary gap.*

Long-run aggregate supply (LRAS) curve The vertical line drawn at potential output

Evidence on Aggregate Supply

What evidence is there that the long-run aggregate supply curve can be depicted by a vertical line drawn at the economy's potential GDP? Except during the Great Depression, unemployment over the last century has varied from year to year, but typically has returned to what would be viewed as the level that was consistent with potential GDP—about 4 or 5 percent. (Exhibit 2 in Chapter 7 graphs the unemployment rate since 1900.)

An expansionary gap creates labor shortages that in the long run result in a higher nominal wage and a higher price level. But a contractionary gap, as the Great Depression taught us, does not necessarily generate enough downward pressure to lower the nominal wage. Studies indicate that the nominal wage is slow to adjust to high unemployment. Nominal wages have declined in particular industries; during the 1980s, for example, nominal wages fell in airlines, steel, and trucking. But seldom have we observed actual declines across the economy in nominal wages, especially since World War II.

Hence, nominal wages do not adjust downward as quickly or as substantially as they do upward. The downward response that does occur tends to be slow and relatively weak. Consequently, we say that nominal wages tend to be "sticky" in the downward direction. *Since nominal wages fall slowly, if at all, the natural supply-side adjustments needed to return the economy to potential output may take so long as to seem ineffective.* Therefore, unemployment in excess of the natural rate can linger.

Even though the nominal wage seldom falls, a decline in the nominal wage is not necessary to close a contractionary gap. All that is needed is a fall in the real wage. And *the real wage will fall as long as the price level increases more than the nominal wage.* For example, if the price level increases by 4 percent and the nominal wage increases by 2 percent, the real wage falls by 2 percent. As long as the real wage falls enough, firms will be willing to demand enough additional labor to produce the economy's potential output. Since 1973, increases in nominal wage manufacturing have, on average, trailed increases in the consumer price index, but many economists feel that the CPI is biased up at least 1 percent per year. If we adjust nominal wages by a CPI adjusted to correct the upward bias, then the real manufacturing wage has increased by a total of about 5 percent since 1973.

In the following case study, we look more specifically at output gaps and discuss why wages are not more flexible.

Coordination failure A state in which workers and employers fail to achieve an outcome that all would prefer because they are unable to jointly choose strategies that would result in a preferred outcome

CASE STUDY

Output Gaps and Wage Flexibility

Let's look at the U.S. actual and potential GDP since 1980. Exhibit 5 measures the difference between actual and potential GDP as a percent of potential GDP. For example, in the recession year of 1982, actual output was 5.8 percent below potential output; this gap, incidentally, amounted to about $280 billion (in 1992 dollars). The economy need not be in recession for actual output to fall below potential output. For example, during the years 1983 through 1986, real GDP increased, yet actual output fell below potential output. In fact, actual output was below its potential in 10 of the 16 years shown, but only in the recession years of 1980, 1982, and 1991 did actual output decline.

So, actual output has been below potential output in the majority of years since 1980. Employers and employees clearly would have been better off if the gap had been reduced or eliminated. After all, more workers would have been employed and more goods and services would have been available. If workers and employers fail to reach an outcome that seems possible and that all would prefer, then they have failed to coordinate in some way. Contractionary gaps can thus be viewed as resulting from a **coordination failure.**

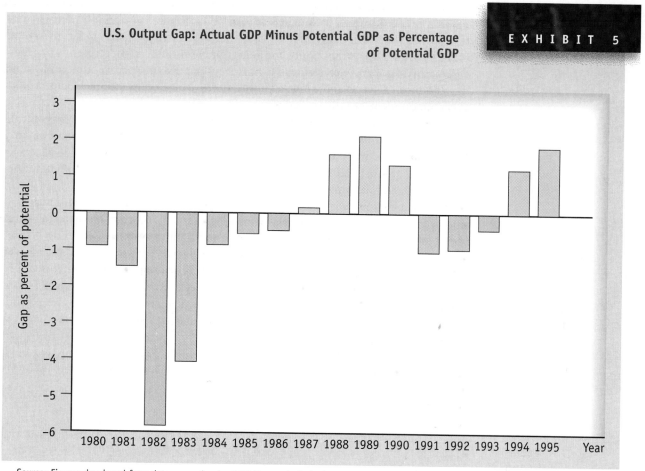

U.S. Output Gap: Actual GDP Minus Potential GDP as Percentage of Potential GDP

EXHIBIT 5

Source: Figures developed from data appearing in *OECD Economic Outlook* 57 (June 1995): Annex Table 11.

If employers and workers can increase output and employment by agreeing to lower nominal wages, why doesn't such a move occur quickly? First, as we have noted already, many workers are operating under long-term contracts, and wages fixed under such contracts are not very flexible, particularly in the downward direction. But why not negotiate short-term contracts if long-term contracts reduce the ability to achieve potential output? First, contract negotiations are costly, so a longer contract reduces the frequency of negotiations. Second, long-term contracts reduce the frequency of strikes, lockouts, and other settlement disputes that can arise in the course of contract negotiations. Thus, both workers and employers gain from long-term contracts, even though such contracts make wages more sticky and contractionary gaps more likely.

When unemployment is extensive, why do employers appear reluctant to cut nominal wages or to replace existing employees with lower-paid workers from the pool of the unemployed? One possible explanation has already been mentioned. Recall that the *efficiency wage theory* argues

Output Gaps and Wage Flexibility
continued

Location:

U.S. actual GDP has been below potential GDP in the majority of years since 1980, creating an output gap. To see how hourly wages have behaved over a similar period, visit LABSTAT, The Bureau of Labor Statistics' Public Access Server, and review "Employment, Hours and Earnings (Current Employment Statistics)" (gopher:// hopi2.bls.gov:70/11/ Formatted%20Tables).

that by keeping wages above the level required to attract enough workers, firms make workers compete to keep their jobs. This competition in job performance results in greater productivity. During recessions, these firms prefer to lay off workers and reduce the hours for remaining workers, rather than cut wages. Wage cuts may save payroll costs, but they can also reduce morale and could have negative effects on worker productivity, since workers may have a psychological resistance to wage cuts.

Workers also resist attempts to lower wages, despite the possibility of increased employment, because of the difficulty of coordinating a wage cut on a large scale. A worker might be willing to accept a wage cut only if all other workers do. But since wages are set by millions of individually negotiated contracts, a large-scale wage cut is nearly impossible to coordinate.

Another reason workers may be reluctant to accept lower nominal wages is unemployment benefits. When a worker is laid off, the incentive to accept a lower wage is reduced by the prospect of unemployment benefits. The greater these benefits and the longer their duration, the less the pressure to accept a lower wage. For example, in the latter part of the 1920s, unemployment benefits nearly tripled in Great Britain and eligibility requirements were relaxed. Despite record levels of unemployment, money wages remained unchanged during the period. Unemployment benefits had become a viable alternative to employment.

Sources: Laurence Ball and David Romer, "Sticky Prices and Coordination Failures," *American Economic Review* 81 (June 1991): pp. 539–52; *OECD Economic Outlook* 57 (June 1995): Annex Table 11; and Daniel Benjamin and Levis Kochin, "Searching for an Explanation of Unemployment in Interwar Britain," *Journal of Political Economy* 87 (June 1979): pp. 441–70.

CHANGES IN AGGREGATE SUPPLY

So far we have shown that, given the supply of resources in the economy, the state of technology, and the institutional structure of the economic system, the location of the short-run aggregate supply curve depends on the expected price level. When the actual price level differs from the expected price level, market forces shift the short-run aggregate supply curve until the economy again produces its potential level of output. In this section, we consider factors other than the expected price level that may affect aggregate supply. We distinguish between long-term trends in aggregate supply and **supply shocks,** which are unexpected events that affect aggregate supply, usually temporarily.

Supply shocks Unexpected events that affect aggregate supply, usually only temporarily

Increases in Aggregate Supply

The economy's potential output is based on the willingness and ability of households to supply resources to firms, the level of technology, and the institutional underpinnings of the economic system. Any change in these may affect the economy's potential output.[2] For example, labor supply may change over time because of a change in the size of the labor force or a change in

---

2   Changes in the economy's potential GDP over time are discussed in greater detail in Chapter 6, which examines U.S. productivity and economic growth.

household preferences for labor versus leisure. The U.S. labor force has doubled since 1948 as a result of a growth in population and a rising labor force participation rate, especially among women. At the same time, job training, education, and on-the-job experience have increased the quality of labor. Increases in both the quantity and the quality of the labor force have increased the economy's potential GDP, or long-run aggregate supply.

The quantity and quality of other resources also change over time. The capital stock—the amount of machines, buildings, and trucks—increases whenever the economy's gross investment exceeds the depreciation of capital. Even the quantity and quality of land can be increased—for example, by claiming land from the sea, as is done in the Netherlands, or by revitalizing soil that has lost its fertility. These increases in the quantity and quality of resources expand the economy's potential output. Institutional changes that define property rights more clearly or make contracts more easily enforced, such as the introduction of patent and copyright laws, will increase the incentives to undertake productive activity. *Changes in the labor force, in the supply of other key resources, and in the institutional arrangements of the economic system tend to occur gradually over time.* Exhibit 6 reflects a gradual shift in the economy's potential output from $7.0 trillion to $7.5 trillion. The long-run aggregate supply curve shifts from *LRAS* to *LRAS'*.

In contrast to the gradual, or long-term, changes that often occur in the supply of resources, *supply shocks* are unexpected events that change aggregate supply, often only temporarily. **Beneficial supply shocks** increase aggregate supply; examples include (1) abundant harvests that increase the supply of food, (2) discoveries of natural resources, such as the oil in Alaska and the North Sea, (3) changes in the economic system that promote more production, such as legislation that reduces the number of groundless lawsuits, and (4) technological breakthroughs that allow firms to combine resources more efficiently, such as the microchip, which has revolutionized the way information is gathered, processed, and transmitted.

Beneficial supply shocks Unexpected events that increase aggregate supply, usually only temporarily

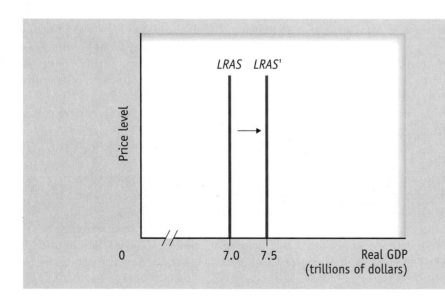

EXHIBIT 6

Effect of Gradual Change in the Supply of Resources

A gradual increase in the supply of resources increases the potential level of real GDP, in this case from $7.0 trillion to $7.5 trillion. The long-run aggregate supply curve shifts to the right.

EXHIBIT 7   **Effects of Supply Shocks on Aggregate Supply**

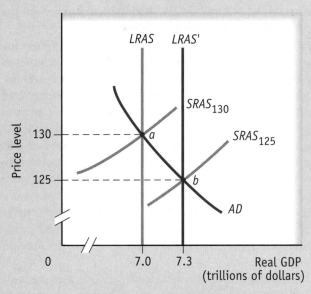

Given the aggregate demand curve, a supply shock may shift both the short-run aggregate supply curve and the long-run aggregate supply curve, or potential output. A beneficial supply shock lowers the price level and increases output, as reflected by the change in equilibrium from point *a* to point *b*. An adverse supply shock can be represented by a move from point *b* to point *a*, where the price level is higher but output is lower.

Exhibit 7 reflects the effect of a beneficial supply shock on short-run and long-run aggregate supply. The beneficial supply shock shown here increases both the short-run and long-run aggregate supply curves. Given the aggregate demand curve, *AD,* the equilibrium combination of price and output moves from point *a* to point *b*. *For a given aggregate demand curve, the happy outcome of a beneficial supply shock is an increase in output and a decrease in the price level.* For example, the per-barrel price of oil in 1986 dropped from over $30 to about $10, boosting output and lowering the inflation rate that year to only 1.9 percent, the lowest rate since the early 1960s. A beneficial supply shock may be only temporary. For example, oil prices have increased since 1986 from $10 to $20 per barrel. Favorable growing seasons also tend to boost short-run, but not long-run, aggregate supply.

Decreases in Aggregate Supply

A reduction in the supply of a key resource, other things constant, reduces potential output and long-run aggregate supply. Earlier, you learned that the average work week has become shorter, decreasing from about 62 hours at the turn of the century to about 40 hours today. This decline in the supply of labor has reduced potential output below what it would have been had hours not declined. A change in the composition of the work force toward younger, less experienced workers would also reduce aggregate supply. As we have noted already, changes in the supply of labor tend to occur gradually over time. In Exhibit 6, a gradual drop in the supply of labor would be reflected by a reduction in potential output (in this case, from $7.5 trillion to $7.0 trillion).

Adverse supply shocks are unexpected events that reduce short-run and long-run aggregate supply, usually only temporarily. For example, a drought could temporarily reduce the supply of a variety of products, including food, building materials, and raw materials, such as the cotton and flax used in textiles. A lack of rain could also affect water-powered energy sources. Or a government that had been stable could be toppled, destabilizing the economy. Such a change in the institutional underpinnings of the economic system would likely reduce production incentives. An adverse supply shock can be reflected by a shift to the left in the short-run and the long-run aggregate supply curves. Imagine starting at equilibrium point *b* in Exhibit 7, where the output level is $7.3 trillion and the price level is 125. Given the aggregate demand curve, the effect of an adverse supply shock is represented by a shift in the short-run and the long-run aggregate supply curves, moving the equilibrium combination from point *b* to point *a*, reducing output to $7.0 trillion and increasing the price level to 130.

The combination of reduced output and a higher price level is often referred to as stagflation. The United States encountered stagflation during the 1970s, when the economy was rocked by a series of adverse supply shocks, such as crop failures around the globe and the fourfold increase in oil prices achieved by OPEC in 1974. If the condition that reduces aggregate supply is only temporary, such as a drought, aggregate supply should increase when the source of the shock disappears. But some economists have begun to question an economy's ability to bounce back from swings in economic activity, as discussed in the following case study.

Adverse supply shocks Unexpected events that reduce aggregate supply, usually only temporarily

Hysteresis The argument that a long stretch of high (or low) unemployment can increase (or decrease) the natural rate of unemployment

Between World War II and the mid-1970s, unemployment in Western Europe was relatively low. Between 1960 and 1974, for example, the unemployment rate in France and Great Britain never reached as high as 4 percent. The worldwide recession of the 1970s, however, caused unemployment rates to drift up. The problem was that unemployment continued to climb in Europe long after the recession was over. The unemployment rates in France, Great Britain, and Italy remained above 10 percent for most of the 1980s. After a modest decline in the late 1980s, rates again topped 10 percent in the 1990s. In 1995, for example, the unemployment rate was 11.5 percent in France, 12 percent in Italy, and 23 percent in Spain.

Some observers argue that this increase in unemployment rates reflects an increase in the underlying natural rate of unemployment. Those economists who have studied the issue have borrowed a term from physics, *hysteresis* (pronounced *his-ter-eé-sis*), to explain what they believe happened to the natural rate of unemployment. When applied to the unemployment rate, the term **hysteresis** means that the natural rate of unemployment depends in part on the recent history of unemployment. *The longer the actual unemployment rate remains above what had been considered the natural rate, the more the natural rate itself will increase.*

Here are two possible explanations for this phenomenon. Those who are out of work can lose valuable job skills, thereby reducing their ability to find a

CASE STUDY

Why Is Unemployment So High in Europe?

Location:

For a relevant comparison of unemployment rates in Eastern and Central Europe, visit the Macroeconomic Policy and Management Division (ED-IMP), an organization of the World Bank's Economic Development Institute (http://www.worldbank.org/html/edi/edimp/unemp/unemp.html). For statistical data, visit the Division for Economic Analysis and Projections (DEAP), part of the United Nations Economic Commission for Europe (UN/ECE), and browse, under "Publications," the *Economic Bulletin for Europe* and the *Economic Survey of Europe* (http://www.unicc.org/unece/deap/).

job even after the economy recovers. Or, as weeks of unemployment turn into months, the shock and stigma of being unemployed may diminish, so the work ethic weakens, as does the desire to find a job. What's more, some European countries offer relatively generous unemployment benefits indefinitely, reducing the hardship of unemployment. Some people have collected unemployment benefits for more than a decade.

Keep in mind that hysteresis remains just a theory to explain high unemployment rates in Western Europe. The theory seems to have less relevance to the United States, where rates dropped throughout most of the 1980s and declined again after the recession of 1990–91. Still, as noted earlier, some economists argue that the natural rate of unemployment seems to have drifted up in the United States from about 4 percent in the 1960s to 5 or 6 percent today.

Sources: Olivier Blanchard and Lawrence Summers, "Beyond the Natural Rate Hypothesis," *American Economic Review* 78 (May 1988): pp. 182–87; "Economic and Financial Indicators," *The Economist,* 19 November–25 November 1994, p. 118.

CONCLUSION

Perhaps no subject in macroeconomics remains more debated than aggregate supply. The debate involves the slope of the aggregate supply curve and the reasons for that slope. No two introductory economics books are likely to discuss the topic in exactly the same way. This chapter calls attention to the expected price level as a key determinant of the nominal resource prices that shape aggregate supply in the short run. If firms and resource suppliers can fully adjust to unexpected changes in the price level, the economy will produce its potential output.

The appendix to this chapter takes a closer look at the relationship between resource markets and potential output. The next chapter will consider if and how public policy might be instrumental in moving the economy toward its potential GDP.

SUMMARY

1. Short-run aggregate supply is based on resource supply and demand decisions that reflect the expected price level. If the expected price level actually occurs, the economy produces its potential level of output. If the actual price level exceeds the expected price level, short-run equilibrium output exceeds the economy's potential, opening up an expansionary gap. If the actual price level is below the expected price level, short-run equilibrium output falls short of the economy's potential, opening up a contractionary gap. The short-run aggregate supply curve slopes upward.

2. Output can exceed the economy's potential in the short run, but in the long run a higher nominal wage will be

negotiated at the first opportunity. This higher nominal wage increases the cost of production, shifting the short-run aggregate supply curve back until equilibrium output equals the economy's potential.

3. If output in the short run falls short of the economy's potential, and if wages and prices in the economy are flexible, then a lower nominal wage will reduce production costs, shifting the short-run aggregate supply curve outward until equilibrium output equals the economy's potential.

4. Empirical evidence suggests that when output exceeds the economy's potential, wage and price levels increase.

But there is less evidence to support a downward movement of wage and price levels when output is below the economy's potential. Wages appear to be somewhat "sticky" in the downward direction.

5. The long-run aggregate supply curve, or the economy's potential level of output, depends on the amount and quality of resources available in the economy, the state of technology, and formal and informal institutions, such as patent laws and business practices that support the eco-nomic system. Increases in resource availability, improvements in technology, or institutional changes that provide greater production incentives increase aggregate supply and potential output.

6. Supply shocks are unexpected and usually temporary changes in aggregate supply. Beneficial supply shocks lead to increased output and a lower price level. Adverse supply shocks result in stagflation—reduced output and a higher price level.

QUESTIONS AND PROBLEMS

1. **(Short Run)** In the short run, prices may go up faster than costs do. The chapter discusses why this might happen. Suppose that labor and management agree to adjust wages for changes in the price level. How would such adjustments affect the slope of the aggregate supply curve?

2. **(Nominal and Real Wages)** Complete each of the following sentences:
   a. The _____ wage measures the wage in current dollars, while the _____ wage measures the wage in constant dollars.
   b. Wage agreements are based on the _____ price level and negotiated in _____ wages, while real wages are determined by the _____ price level.
   c. The higher the actual price level, the _____ is the real wage for a given nominal wage.
   d. If nominal wages are growing at 2 percent per year while annual inflation is 3 percent, then real wages are _____.

3. **(Potential Output)** Define the potential output level of the economy. What factors affect the potential output?

4. **(Natural Rate of Unemployment)**
   a. What is the relationship between potential output and the natural rate of unemployment?
   b. If the economy currently has frictional unemployment of 1 percent, structural unemployment of 2 percent, seasonal unemployment of 0.5 percent, and cyclical unemployment of 2 percent, what is the natural rate of unemployment? Where is the economy operating relative to its potential GDP?
   c. What happens to the natural rate of unemployment and potential GDP if cyclical unemployment rises to 3 percent with other types of unemployment unchanged from Part b?
   d. What happens to the natural rate of unemployment and potential GDP if structural unemployment falls to 1.5 percent with other types of unemployment unchanged from Part b?

5. **(Short-Run Aggregate Supply)** In constructing the short-run aggregate supply curve, what is meant by the term "short run"? Explain the role of labor contracts along the *SRAS*.

6. **(Contractionary Gaps)** After reviewing Exhibit 3 in this chapter, explain why contractionary gaps occur only in the short run and only when the actual price level is below what was expected.

7. **(Expansionary and Contractionary Gaps)** Answer the following questions on the basis of the graph below:

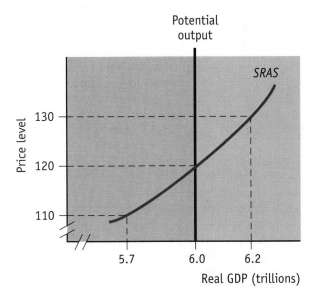

a. If the actual price level exceeds the expected price level reflected in long-term contracts, real GDP equals _____ and the actual price level equals _____ in the short run.

b. This situation results in a(n) _____ gap equal to _____.

c. If the actual price level is lower than the expected price level reflected in long-term contracts, real GDP equals _____ and the actual price level equals _____ in the short run.

d. This situation results in a(n) _____ gap equal to _____.

e. If the actual price level equals the expected price level reflected in long-term contracts, real GDP equals _____ and the actual price level equals _____ in the short run.

f. This situation results in _____ _____ _____ gap equal to _____.

8. **(Long Run)** The long-run aggregate supply curve is vertical at the economy's potential output level. Why would the long-run aggregate supply curve have to be centered at this level of output rather than below or above the potential level?

9. **(Long-Run Adjustment)** In the long run, why does an actual price that exceeds the expected price level lead to changes in the level of nominal wages? Why do these changes cause shifts in the short-run aggregate supply curve?

10. **(Wages)** In Exhibit 2 in this chapter, how does the real wage rate at point *a* compare with the real wage rate at point *c*? How do nominal wages compare? Explain your answers.

11. **(Long-Run Aggregate Supply)** Indicate whether each of the following, other things held constant, would lead to an increase, a decrease, or no change in long-run aggregate supply.
a. An increase in the level of technology.
b. A permanent decrease in the size of the capital stock.
c. An increase in the actual price level.
d. An increase in the expected price level.
e. A permanent increase in the size of the labor force.

12. **(Long-Run Adjustment)** The ability of the economy to eliminate any imbalances between actual output and potential output is sometimes called "self-correction." Using an aggregate supply and aggregate demand diagram, show why this self-correction process involves only *temporary* periods of inflation or deflation.

13. **(Short-Run Aggregate Supply)** Suppose you own a business and you observe an increase in the industry

price level for the product you produce. If you think that this price increase is strictly for your industry and not for the economy as s whole, what will your likely output response be? Explain.

14. **(Contractionary Gap)** What does a contractionary gap imply about the rate of unemployment? About the actual price level relative to the expected price level? What must happen to real and nominal wages in order to close a contractionary gap?

15. **(Efficiency Wage)** According to the efficiency wage theory, employers are reluctant to cut nominal wages when faced with a reduction in output demand and price, preferring instead to lay off workers and thereby create cyclical unemployment. Is there anything in the efficiency wage model that might explain an increase in the natural rate of unemployment?

16. **(Expansionary Gap)** How does an economy that is experiencing an expansionary gap in the short-run adjust in the long run?

17. **(Changes in Aggregate Supply)** What are supply shocks? Distinguish between beneficial and adverse supply shocks. Do such shocks affect the short-run supply curve, the long-run supply curve, or both? What is the resulting impact on potential GDP?

18. **(Output Gaps and Wage Flexibility)** What are the various reasons that nominal wages may be reluctant to fall during a contractionary gap?

19. **(Unemployment in Europe)** Is it possible that hysteresis could actually contribute to the reduction in the natural unemployment rate? Explain.

Using the Internet

20. Review the "NBER Official Business Cycle Dates," maintained by the National Bureau of Economic Research (NBER) (**gopher://nber.harvard.edu/**). Using the data in the table provided, answer the following:
a. What was the longest period of expansion from 1854–1991?
b. What was the longest period of contraction from 1854–1991?
c. What was the average duration of expansion from 1854–1991?
d. What was the average duration of business cycles from 1854–1991?

Appendix

THE MARKET FOR RESOURCES

So far we have not discussed in detail the pricing and output decisions of individual firms and resource suppliers. Resource markets play a key role in shaping aggregate supply. This appendix describes the behavior of resource markets, particularly the market for labor, the most important resource.

The key actors on the supply side are households and firms. We already know that (1) households supply resources and demand goods and services in order to maximize utility and (2) firms demand resources and supply goods and services in order to maximize profit. The willingness and ability of households to supply resources to firms depend on the expected earnings of these resources. The higher the expected earnings, other things constant, the greater the quantity of resources supplied to firms. Suppose initially that resource suppliers and demanders, when they formulate their wage agreements, know what the price level will be and are able to adjust their supply and demand based on that price level.

The Market for Labor

Although many resources are required for production, we focus primarily on labor because it accounts for most of the cost. What's more, aggregate employment is a key measure of the economy's performance and is thus of special interest to public policymakers. The interaction between the supply of labor by households and the demand for labor by producers determines the equilibrium wage rate and employment level in the economy. The level of employment, in turn, determines the quantity of aggregate output supplied in the economy. Even without a full-scale discussion of the market for labor, we can get some idea of the forces shaping the supply and demand for labor.

Supply of Labor. Individuals can use their time in two ways: for labor or for leisure. For simplicity, let's define *leisure* as all noncompensated uses of time, including watching TV, sleeping, studying, and making a sandwich. The wage rate is the reward per unit of time for supplying labor to the market. The higher the wage rate, other things constant, the greater the reward for working—that is, the more goods and services that can be purchased with the earnings from each hour of market work. One of the factors held constant when we compare alternative wage rates is the expected price level. For a given expected price level, any change in the nominal wage (the wage measured in terms of nominal dollars) is also a change in the expected real wage (the wage measured in real dollars)—that is, in terms of the quantity of goods and services it will purchase. *For a given expected price level, workers believe they can buy more goods and services as the nominal wage increases.*

The higher the nominal wage, the more goods and services that can be exchanged for an hour of work. Hence, the higher the nominal wage, the higher the opportunity cost of leisure, so the more labor households will supply. *The supply curve for labor by households therefore slopes upward, indicating that the quantity of labor supplied increases as the nominal wage rate increases, other things constant.*

Exhibit 8 presents such an upward-sloping market supply curve for labor, S_{130}. The nominal wage rate is measured on the vertical axis and the quantity of labor on the horizontal axis. This market supply curve for labor is the horizontal sum of all individual workers' supply-of-labor curves. Because the market supply curve is drawn for a given expected price level (in this case, 130), increases in the nominal wage along the supply curve also represent increases in the expected real wage.

Demand for Labor. What determines how much of a particular resource a producer will employ? A firm values resources because they are used to make goods and services that can be sold for a profit. A firm em-

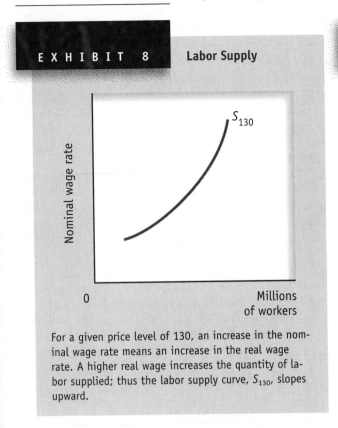

EXHIBIT 8   Labor Supply

For a given price level of 130, an increase in the nominal wage rate means an increase in the real wage rate. A higher real wage increases the quantity of labor supplied; thus the labor supply curve, S_{130}, slopes upward.

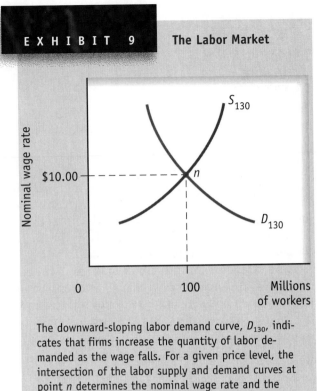

EXHIBIT 9   The Labor Market

The downward-sloping labor demand curve, D_{130}, indicates that firms increase the quantity of labor demanded as the wage falls. For a given price level, the intersection of the labor supply and demand curves at point n determines the nominal wage rate and the equilibrium level of employment.

ploys additional labor as long as doing so adds more to revenue than to cost. So each unit of labor (as well as each unit of other resources) must at least pay for itself. The most a firm is willing to pay for an additional unit of labor is that unit's *marginal* value to the firm: the increase in total revenue resulting from each additional unit of labor's production. The question is, what happens to the marginal value as additional units of labor are employed? Does it go up, go down, or remain the same?

The *law of diminishing marginal returns* says that as additional units of labor are employed along with fixed quantities of other resources, at some point the quantity of additional output produced begins to decline. This law tells us that the more labor employed, the lower the marginal product of each additional unit of labor. Remember, a producer will pay no more for each additional unit of labor than the value of that unit of labor's output.

The demand for labor in the economy is reflected by the downward-sloping market demand curve for labor, D_{130}, in Exhibit 9. The market demand curve for labor is the horizontal sum of each firm's demand for labor. This downward-sloping demand curve

shows that, given the expected price level of 130, the lower the nominal wage, the greater the quantity of labor firms demand. Because the market demand curve is drawn assuming a given expected price level, decreases in the nominal wage along the demand curve also represent decreases in the expected real wage. The supply and demand curves for labor intersect at the equilibrium point, *n,* to yield the equilibrium wage rate of $10.00 and the equilibrium quantity of labor of 100 million workers. In equilibrium, the wage equals labor's marginal value.

Changes in the Expected Price Level

What will happen to the wage and employment level if the price level expected to prevail in the economy is higher than 130? Suppose it is 140.

Supply Response. With a higher expected price level, workers expect that a given nominal wage will be worth less in real terms, because each dollar is expected to purchase less in real goods and services. Under these conditions, an increase in the nominal wage will be required to coax workers to give up the

Effect of a Higher Expected Price Level on Nominal Wage and Employment

EXHIBIT 10

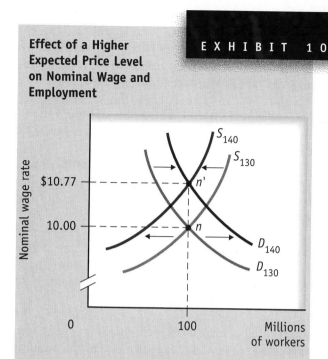

A higher price level reduces the quantity of labor supplied at any given nominal wage rate; the labor supply curve shifts from S_{130} to S_{140} as the price level rises from 130 to 140. At the same time, the higher price level increases the quantity of labor firms demand at any given nominal wage rate; the labor demand curve shifts from D_{130} to D_{140}. These two effects of a higher price level offset each other, so the equilibrium level of employment is unchanged at 100 million workers. The real wage at point n' is the same as at point n.

A higher expected price level means that the nominal value of labor's output is expected to be greater because product prices are expected to be higher. Since an increase in the expected price level from 130 to 140 increases the marginal revenue generated by each additional unit of labor, producers will be willing to pay a higher nominal wage for each additional unit of labor. This increase in labor demand is reflected in Exhibit 10 by a shift of the labor demand curve up and to the right, from D_{130} to D_{140}. This increased demand for labor indicates that producers are willing to hire more workers at each nominal wage, or are willing to pay a higher nominal wage for a given quantity of labor. Specifically, if the expected price level increases by 7.7 percent, producers are willing to pay a nominal wage that is 7.7 percent higher than before.

New Equilibrium. As a result of the higher expected price level, the new supply and demand curves intersect at point n', which corresponds to a nominal wage rate of $10.77. Notice that the increased demand for labor just offsets the decreased supply of labor, leaving the equilibrium quantity of labor unchanged at 100 million workers. The nominal wage has increased, but the increase in the expected price level has left the real wage unchanged. As we noted earlier, to derive the expected real wage, we can divide the nominal wage by the expected price level. Specifically, the higher wage rate, $10.77, divided by the higher expected price level, 140, is equal to the original wage rate, $10.00, divided by the original expected price level of 130. In each case the real wage is $7.69. If prices and nominal wages both go up by the same percentage, the real wage remains unchanged. Because the expected real wage is the same, the equilibrium quantity of labor remains unchanged.

If we traced the effects of a lower expected price level on the market for resources, we would find that the equilibrium nominal wage falls by the same percentage as the expected price level. Whenever nominal wages and expected prices fall by the same percentage, the expected real wage remains unchanged, so equilibrium employment also remains unchanged.

same amount of leisure as they did when the expected price level was lower.

The labor supply curve therefore shifts up and to the left, from S_{130} to S_{140}, as shown in Exhibit 10, indicating that workers have reduced the quantity of labor they will supply at each nominal wage, or that they now require a higher nominal wage for each quantity of labor supplied. Workers must be paid a nominal wage that increases by the same percentage as the increase in the price level. In this case, the price level increases by 7.7 percent, so the wage required to attract 100 million workers increases from $10 to $10.77.

Demand Response. The demand for labor, like the demand for other resources, is based on the value of output produced by each additional unit of that resource.

Potential GDP

Point a in Exhibit 11 indicates that when the expected price level is 130, the level of real GDP in the economy is $7.0 trillion. As we have seen, if the expected price level is higher or lower than 130, and if

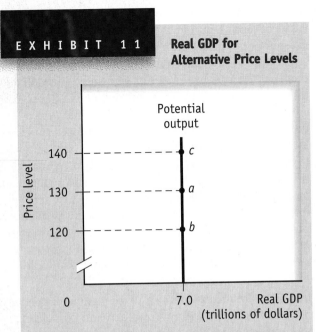

EXHIBIT 11 **Real GDP for Alternative Price Levels**

In the long run, changes in the price level will be matched by changes in the nominal wage rate. With the real wage unchanged, the level of employment is unchanged. With employment unchanged, potential output does not vary. So regardless of the price level, the long-run quantity of output supplied is potential output, which in this example equals $7.0 trillion.

producers and resource suppliers can adjust their demand for and supply of resources to reflect those expectations, then the quantities of resources employed do not change. If resource employment remains unchanged, real GDP also remains unchanged. Point c in Exhibit 11 shows that when the expected price level is 140, real GDP is $7.0 trillion. Point *b* shows that when the expected price level is lower, say 120, the economy's output is still $7.0 trillion.

The vertical line at a real GDP level of $7.0 trillion in Exhibit 11 traces the long-run relationship between alternative price levels and the quantity of output produced. The economy's potential GDP is $7.0 trillion, the amount produced when all resource owners and firms have *fully adjusted* to the actual price level in the economy; in other words, the quantity supplied equals the quantity demanded in each resource market, and the expected price level equals the actual price level. For example, the amount of labor that workers are willing and able to supply at the prevailing wage just equals the amount of labor firms are willing and able to demand. Notice that potential GDP is the same regardless of the price level. The amount of output produced in the economy is independent of the expected price level. *Potential output is determined by real factors: the quantity and quality of resources available, the level of technology, and the formal and informal institutions supporting the economic system.*

APPENDIX QUESTIONS

1. **(Labor Supply and Demand)** What important factor is held constant along a given labor supply curve and a given labor demand curve? Explain why the supply curve slopes upward and the demand curve slopes downward.

2. **(Equilibrium Level of Employment)** Use labor supply and labor demand curves to show the impact on the equilibrium level of employment, the nominal wage, and the expected real wage of each of the following events:
   a. An increase in the expected price level.
   b. An increase in labor productivity.
   c. A reduction in the size of the labor force.

Fiscal Policy

12

During the 1992 presidential campaign, the candidates argued over the best way to revive the ailing economy, which at the time was barely recovering from the 1990–1991 recession. George Bush proposed tax cuts and a relatively smaller role for government. Bill Clinton proposed increases in government spending to be financed by tax increases on high-income earners. And Ross Perot wanted to reduce the huge federal budget deficits that had become a part of the fiscal landscape since the early 1980s. All were talking about *fiscal policy*—the use of government purchases, transfer payments, taxes, and borrowing to influence aggregate economic activity.

In this chapter, we first explore the effects of fiscal policy on aggregate demand. Next, we bring aggregate supply into the picture to consider the impact of taxing and government spending on the level of income and employment in the economy. We then examine the role of fiscal policy in moving the economy to its potential level of output. Finally, we review fiscal policy as it has been practiced since World War II.

Throughout the chapter, we use relatively simple tax and spending programs to convey an intuitive idea of fiscal policy. A more realistic treatment, along with the algebra behind the numbers, appears in the appendix to the chapter. Topics discussed in this chapter include:

- Fiscal policy
- Discretionary fiscal policy
- Automatic stabilizers
- Lags in fiscal policy
- Limits of fiscal policy

THEORY OF FISCAL POLICY

Thus far, government has been viewed as relatively passive actor in our macro-economic model. In fact, government purchases and transfer payments at all levels now top $2.6 trillion per year, making government an important player in the economy. From federal deficits to welfare reform to the possible adoption of a flat tax, fiscal policy affects the economy in myriad ways. We now move fiscal policy to center stage.

As introduced in Chapter 4, *fiscal policy* is the deliberate manipulation of government purchases, transfer payments, taxes, and borrowing in order to influence macroeconomic variables such as employment, the price level, and the level of GDP. Fiscal policy is carried out explicitly at the federal level, though governments at all levels have an impact on the economy.

Using the aggregate expenditure framework developed earlier, we will initially focus on the demand side to consider the effect of changes in government purchases, transfer payments, and taxes on the quantity of real GDP demanded. The short story is that *at any given price level, an increase in government purchases or transfer payments increases the amount of real GDP demanded and an increase in taxes decreases the amount of real GDP demanded, other things constant.* In this section, we show how and why.

Changes in Government Purchases

Let's begin in Exhibit 1 with real GDP demanded of $7.0 trillion, as reflected at point *a*, where the aggregate expenditure function crosses the 45-degree line. This equilibrium was determined in Chapter 10, where government purchases and net taxes each equaled $1.0 trillion and were *autonomous*—that is, did not vary with income. Since government purchases equal net taxes, the government budget is in balance.

Now suppose government purchases increase by $0.1 trillion, or by $100 billion, assuming other things, including net taxes, remain constant. This additional spending shifts the aggregate expenditure function up by $0.1 trillion, to $C + I + G' + (X - M)$. Since planned spending now exceeds output, production must increase. This increase in production increases income, which in turn increases planned spending, and so it goes through a series of rounds.

The initial increase of $0.1 trillion in government purchases eventually increases the quantity of real GDP demanded at the given price level from $7.0 trillion to $7.5 trillion, shown as point *b*. Since output demanded increases by $0.5 trillion as a result of an increase of $0.1 trillion in government purchases, the government-purchases multiplier in our example is equal to 5. *As long as consumption is the only source of spending that varies with income, the multiplier for a change in government purchases, other things constant, equals* $1/(1 - MPC)$, or $1/(1 - 0.8)$ in our example. Thus, we can say that for a given price level, and given that only consumption varies with income, the

$$\text{Change in } Y = \text{Change in G} \times \frac{1}{1 - \text{MPC}}$$

where Y is the quantity of real GDP demanded.

Military spending decisions—such as how many multimillion dollar Air Force jets to purchase—are made first to ensure national security. Where and when this money is spent, however, and to what suppliers, typically are matters of fiscal policy.

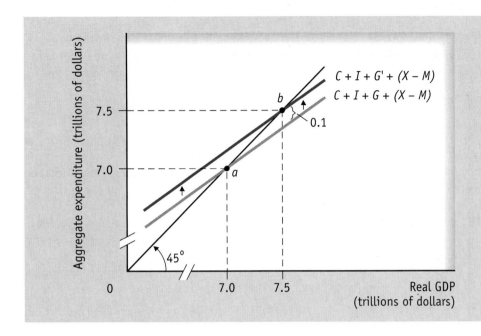

EXHIBIT 1

Effect of a $0.4 Trillion Increase in Government Purchases on Aggregate Expenditure and Real GDP Demanded

As a result of a $0.1 trillion increase in government purchases, the aggregate expenditure function shifts up by $0.1 trillion, increasing the level of real GDP demanded by $0.5 trillion.

This same multiplier was discussed in Chapter 10, where we focused on shifts in consumption, investment, and net exports.

Changes in Net Taxes

A change in net taxes will also affect the quantity of real GDP demanded, but the effect is less direct. A *decrease* in net taxes, other things constant, *increases* disposable income at each level of real GDP, so consumption increases. Suppose in Exhibit 2 we begin again at equilibrium point *a,* with real GDP equal to $7.0 trillion. Suppose, to stimulate aggregate demand, government cuts net taxes by $0.1 trillion, or by $100 billion, other things constant. We continue to assume that net taxes do not vary with income, or are autonomous. A $100 billion decrease in net taxes could result from a decrease in taxes, an increase in transfer payments, or some combination of the two. The $100 million decrease in net taxes increases disposable income by $100 million at each level of real GDP. Because households now have more disposable income, they spend more and save more at each level of real GDP.

Specifically, *consumption spending at each level of real GDP rises by the decrease in net taxes times the marginal propensity to consume.* In our example, desired consumption spending at each level of real GDP increases by $100 billion × 0.8, or $80 billion. Decreasing net taxes by $100 billion causes the aggregate expenditure function to shift up by $80 billion at all levels of income, as shown in Exhibit 2. This increase in spending triggers subsequent rounds of spending following a now-familiar pattern in the income-consumption cycle based on the marginal propensities to consume and to save. For example, the $80 billion increase in consumption initially increases income by $80 billion, which leads to $64 billion in consumption and $16 billion in saving, and so on through successive rounds. As a result, the equilibrium point moves from *a* to *c,* and real

Effect of a $0.1 Trillion, or $100 Billion, Decrease in Autonomous Net Taxes on Aggregate Expenditure and Real GDP Demanded

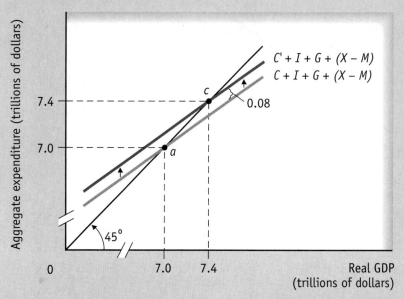

As a result of a decrease in autonomous net taxes of $0.1 trillion, or $100 billion, the consumption function shifts up by $80 billion, as does the aggregate expenditure function. An $80 billion increase in aggregate expenditure increases the level of real GDP demanded by $0.4 trillion. Keep in mind that the price level is assumed to be constant.

GDP demanded increases from $7.0 trillion to $7.4 trillion per year, or by $400 billion.

The effect of a change in net taxes on the quantity of real GDP demanded equals the resulting shift in the consumption function times the simple spending multiplier. Thus, we can say that the effect of a change in net taxes is

$$\text{Change in } Y = (-\text{MPC} \times \text{Change in } NT) \times \frac{1}{1 - \text{MPC}}$$

Here, the simple spending multiplier is applied to the shift in consumption that results from the change in the net tax. This equation can be rearranged as

$$\text{Change in } Y = \text{Change in } NT \times \frac{-\text{MPC}}{1 - \text{MPC}}$$

Autonomous net tax multiplier
The ratio of a change in equilibrium real GDP demanded to the initial change in autonomous net taxes that brought it about; the numerical value of the multiplier is −MPC/(1 − MPC)

where $-\text{MPC}/(1 - \text{MPC})$ becomes the **autonomous net tax multiplier,** which can be applied directly to the change in net taxes to yield the change in the quantity of real GDP demanded. For example, with an MPC of 0.8, the autonomous net tax multiplier equals −4. In our example, a *decrease* of $0.1 trillion in net taxes results in an *increase* in real GDP demanded of $0.4 trillion, assuming a given price level. As another example, an *increase* in net taxes of $0.2 trillion would, other things constant, *decrease* real GDP demanded by $0.8 trillion.

Changes in Net Taxes and Government Purchases Combined

It may prove useful at this point to compare the simple spending multiplier applying to changes in government purchases with the autonomous net tax multiplier. First, changes in government purchases and in net taxes have opposite effects on the level of real GDP demanded. Second, the absolute value of the multiplier is greater for a given change in government purchases than for an identical change in net taxes. This holds because changes in government purchases affect aggregate spending directly—each $100 increase in government purchases increases spending in the first round by $100. In contrast, each $100 change in net taxes affects consumption indirectly by way of a change in disposable income. Thus, each $100 decrease in taxes or each $100 increase in transfer payments increases disposable income by $100, which, with an MPC of 0.8, increases consumption in the first round by $80.

We are now in a position to consider the combined effects of changes in government purchases and in net taxes. The effect of a change in G on Y equals the change in G times $1/(1 - MPC)$. The effect of a change in NT on Y equals the change in NT times $-MPC/(1 - MPC)$. *The combined effect of changing government purchases and net taxes can be determined by adding their individual effects:*

$$\text{Change in } Y = \left(\text{Change in } G \times \frac{1}{1 - MPC}\right) + \left(\text{Change in } NT \times \frac{-MPC}{1 - MPC}\right)$$

For example, suppose that government purchases increase by $0.2 trillion and net taxes increase by only $0.1 trillion:

$$\text{Change in } Y = \left(\$0.2 \text{ trillion} \times \frac{1}{0.2}\right) + \left(\$0.1 \text{ trillion} \times \frac{-0.8}{0.2}\right)$$
$$= \$1.0 \text{ trillion} - \$0.4 \text{ trillion} = \$0.6 \text{ trillion}$$

The resulting budget deficit has a stimulative effect, increasing real GDP demanded at a given price level by $0.6 trillion. As another example, suppose government purchases and net taxes each increase $0.1 trillion:

$$\text{Change in } Y = \left(\$ 0.1 \text{ trillion} \times \frac{1}{0.2}\right) + \left(\$0.1 \text{ trillion} \times \frac{-0.8}{0.2}\right)$$
$$= \$0.5 \text{ trillion} - \$0.4 \text{ trillion} = \$0.1 \text{ trillion}$$

Here, real GDP demanded increases by $0.1 trillion, the same amount by which government purchases and net taxes increased. Throughout these examples, the multiplier for government purchases has been 5, but the net tax multiplier has been −4. Adding these two multipliers together yields a net multiplier of 1, what we call the balanced budget multiplier. The **balanced budget multiplier** shows that if government purchases and net taxes change by the same amount, other things constant, the quantity of aggregate output de-

Balanced budget multiplier A factor that shows that identical changes in government purchases and net taxes change real GDP demanded by that same amount; the numerical value of the muliplier is 1 manded at a given price level also changes by that amount. (The appendix offers a more general derivation of the balanced budget multiplier.) Incidentally, the balanced budget multiplier suggests that if net tax cuts are "paid for" by matching cuts in government purchases, other things constant, the effect will be to reduce aggregate output demanded by the amount of the tax cuts.

To summarize, the impact of fiscal policy depends on the combined effect of government purchases and net taxes. Generally, *an increase in government purchases or a reduction in net taxes, other things constant, increases real GDP demanded.* Thus far in this chapter, we have focused on the amount of real GDP demanded at a given price level. We are now in a position to bring aggregate supply into the picture.

INCLUDING AGGREGATE SUPPLY

In Chapter 11 we introduced the possibility that natural market forces may take a long time to close a contractionary gap. Let's consider the possible remedial effect of fiscal policy in such a situation.

Fiscal Policy with a Contractionary Gap

Let's begin with a short-run aggregate supply curve as indicated by $SRAS_{130}$ in Exhibit 3. This supply curve implies that if the price level turns out to be 130, the economy will produce the economy's potential level of output of $7.0 trillion. Suppose, however, that the aggregate demand curve, *AD,* intersects aggregate supply at point *e,* yielding the short-run output of $6.5 trillion and price level of 125. Since output falls short of the economy's potential, there is a contractionary gap of $0.5 trillion, as Exhibit 3 shows.

If markets adjust naturally to the resulting increase in unemployed resources, the money prices of resources would drop enough in the long run that the short-run aggregate supply curve would shift out enough to achieve an equilibrium at the economy's potential output. History suggests, however, that wages and other resource prices may be slow to adjust to a contractionary gap. Suppose policymakers believe that the move to potential output will take too long. If the policymakers introduce just the right fiscal policy, they could stimulate aggregate demand enough to return the economy to its potential level of output. Suppose a $0.2 trillion increase in government purchases provides just enough fiscal stimulus to shift the aggregate demand curve to the right, as shown in Exhibit 3 by the shift from *AD* to *AD**. If the price level remains at 125, this injection of additional spending will increase the quantity demanded from $6.5 to $7.5 trillion. This increase of $1.0 trillion reflects the multiplier effect, given a constant price level.

Because the aggregate supply curve slopes upward, however, more output will be supplied only if the price level rises. There is an excess quantity demanded at a price level of 125. This excess quantity demanded causes the price level to rise. As the price level rises, the quantity of real GDP supplied increases but the quantity of real GDP demanded decreases. The price level will rise until the quantity demanded equals the quantity supplied. In Exhibit 3, the new aggregate demand curve intersects the aggregate supply curve at *e*,* where the price level is the one originally expected and output equals potential GDP of $7.0 trillion.

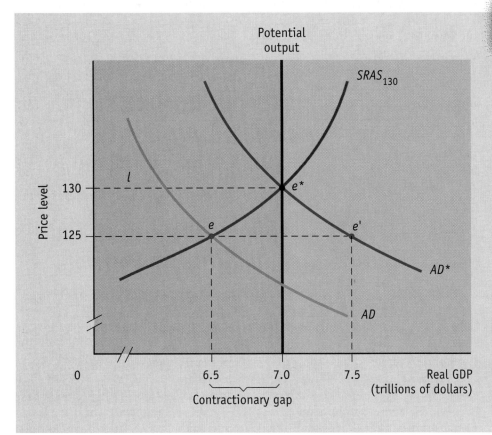

EXHIBIT   3

Fiscal Policy and a Contractionary Gap

The aggregate demand curve, *AD*, and the short-run aggregate supply curve, *SRAS*$_{130}$, intersect at point *e*. Because the price level of 125 is below the expected price level of 130, the level of output falls short of the economy's potential. The resulting contractionary gap is $0.5 trillion. This gap can be closed by an expansionary fiscal policy. An increase in government purchases, a decrease in net taxes, or some combination of the two could shift aggregate demand to *AD**, moving the economy to its potential level of output at *e**.

Since 130 was the price level on which producers originally based their production plans, the intersection at point *e** is not only a short-run equilibrium but also a long-run equilibrium. If fiscal policymakers are accurate enough (or lucky enough), they can provide the appropriate fiscal stimulus to close the contractionary gap and foster a long-run equilibrium at the economy's potential GDP. Note, however, that the increase in output is accompanied by a rise in the price level. What's more, if the federal budget was in balance before the fiscal stimulus, the increase in government spending creates a budget deficit. In fact, the federal government has been running substantial deficits since the tax cut of 1981.

What if policymakers overshoot the mark, and aggregate demand turns out to be greater than needed to achieve potential GDP? In the short run, the economy will produce beyond its potential level of output. In the long run, however, we expect that firms and resource owners will adjust to the unexpectedly high price level. The short-run supply curve will shift back until it intersects the aggregate demand curve at potential output, increasing the price level further but reducing the level of output back to $7.0 trillion.

Fiscal Policy with an Expansionary Gap

Suppose the short-run equilibrium price level exceeds the level on which long-term contracts are based, so output exceeds potential GDP. In Exhibit 4, the short-run aggregate supply curve is again based on an expected price level of

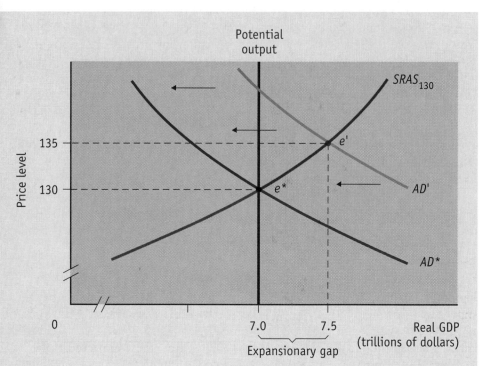

Fiscal Policy and an Expansionary Gap

With the price level above the expected level of 130, there is an expansionary gap equal to $0.5 trillion. The gap can be eliminated by a contractionary fiscal policy. An increase in net taxes, a decrease in government purchases, or some combination of the two could shift the aggregate demand curve back to AD^* and return the economy to potential output at point e^*.

130, but the aggregate demand curve, AD', implies a higher actual price level. So the short-run level of equilibrium output is initially $7.5 trillion, an amount exceeding the economy's potential output of $7.0 trillion. The economy therefore faces an expansionary gap of $0.5 trillion. Ordinarily, this gap would be closed by an upward shift in the short-run aggregate supply curve, which would return the economy to the potential level of output but at a higher price level.

But the use of fiscal policy opens the door to another possibility. By increasing net taxes, reducing government purchases, or using some combination of these, the government can reduce aggregate demand, thereby returning the economy to its potential level of output while avoiding an increase in the price level. If this fiscal policy is successful, the aggregate demand curve in Exhibit 4 will shift to the left from AD' to AD^*, and equilibrium will move from point e' to point e^*. Again, with just the right reduction in aggregate demand, the price level will fall to 130, the level implied by the long-run aggregate supply curve, and output will fall to $7.0 trillion, the potential GDP. Closing an expansionary gap through fiscal policy rather than through natural market forces results in a lower price level, not a higher one. Increasing net taxes or reducing government purchases would also reduce the government deficit or increase the surplus.

Such precisely calculated fiscal policies as described here are hard to accomplish, for their proper execution assumes that (1) the relevant spending multipliers can be predicted accurately, (2) aggregate demand can be shifted by the appropriate amount, (3) the potential level of output is accurately gauged, (4) various government entities can somehow coordinate their fiscal efforts, and (5) the shape of the short-run aggregate supply curve is known and will remain unchanged by the fiscal policy itself.

The Multiplier and the Time Horizon

In the short run, the aggregate supply curve slopes upward, so a shift in aggregate demand changes both the price level and the level of output. When aggregate supply gets in the act, the multiplier overstates the amount by which equilibrium output changes, assuming a constant price level. The exact change in equilibrium output in the short run depends on the steepness of the aggregate supply curve. *The steeper the short-run aggregate supply curve, the less impact a given shift in the aggregate demand curve will have on output and the more impact it will have on the price level.* If the economy is already producing its potential output, then in the long run any change in fiscal policy aimed at stimulating demand will increase the price level but will not affect the output level.

We now have some idea of how fiscal policy can work in theory. Let's step back to see how fiscal policy has been applied over the years.

FISCAL POLICY IN PRACTICE

Before the 1930s, fiscal policy was not explicitly used to influence the performance of the macroeconomy. Recall that the classical approach implied that natural market forces, by way of flexible prices, wages, and interest rates, would move the economy toward its potential GDP. Thus, there appeared to be no need for government intervention in the economy. Before the onset of the Great Depression, most economists believed that an active fiscal policy would do more harm than good.

The Great Depression and World War II

It is said that geologists learn more about the nature of the earth's crust from one major upheaval, such as an earthquake or a volcanic eruption, than from a dozen more common events. Likewise, economists learned more about the economy from the Great Depression than from many more modest economic fluctuations. Even though the depression occurred some six decades ago, economists continue to sift through the data from that economic calamity, looking for hints about how the economy really works.

Three developments in the years following the onset of the Great Depression bolstered the use of fiscal policy in the United States. The first was the influence of Keynes's *General Theory,* which argued that natural forces would not necessarily move the economy toward potential output. Keynes thought the economy could get stuck at a level of output that was well below its potential, requiring government to increase aggregate demand so as to stimulate output and employment. The second development was the impact of World War II on output and employment. The demands of war greatly increased expenditures and in the process virtually eliminated unemployment, pulling the U.S. economy out of the depression. The third development, largely a consequence of the first two, was the passage of the Employment Act of 1946, which gave the federal government responsibility for promoting full employment and price stability.

Prior to the Great Depression, the dominant fiscal policy was pursuing a balanced budget. Indeed, to head off a modest federal deficit in 1932, a tax increase

Net Bookmark

The influential economist John Maynard Keynes was born in 1883. Keynes's writings, including his May 1932 *Atlantic Monthly* article "The World's Economic Outlook" (**http://www. theAtlantic.com/atlantic/ atlweb/flashbks/budget/ keynesf.htm**), greatly influenced U.S. fiscal policy during and after the Great Depression.

was approved, an increase that deepened the depression. In the wake of Keynes and World War II, however, economists and policymakers grew more receptive to the idea that fiscal policy could be used to influence aggregate demand and thereby improve economic stability. No longer was the objective of fiscal policy to balance the budget but to promote full employment with price stability.

Automatic Stabilizers

Automatic stabilizers Structural features of government spending and taxation that smooth fluctuations in disposable income over the business cycle

The tools of fiscal policy can be divided into two categories: automatic stabilizers and discretionary fiscal policy. **Automatic stabilizers,** such as the federal income tax and unemployment insurance, are stabilization measures that, once adopted, require no congressional action to operate year after year. **Discretionary fiscal policy** requires ongoing decisions about government spending and taxation to promote full employment and price stability. So far this chapter has focused mostly on discretionary fiscal policy: conscious decisions to change taxes and government spending. Now let's get a clearer picture of automatic stabilizers.

Discretionary fiscal policy The deliberate manipulation of government spending or taxation in order to promote full employment and price stability

Automatic stabilizers smooth fluctuations in disposable income over the business cycle, thereby boosting aggregate demand during periods of recession and dampening aggregate demand during periods of expansion. Consider the federal income tax. For simplicity, we earlier assumed net taxes to be independent of the level of income. In fact, the federal income tax system is progressive, meaning the fraction of income paid in taxes increases as income increases. With a growing share of income going to taxes during expansions, there is proportionately less available for consumption. So the progressive income tax relieves some of the inflationary pressure that might otherwise arise during economic expansions. Conversely, when the economy is in recession, real GDP declines but taxes decline faster, so disposable income does not fall as much as real GDP. Thus, the progressive income tax cushions declines in disposable income, in consumption, and in aggregate demand.

Another automatic stabilizer is unemployment insurance. During an economic expansion, the unemployment insurance system automatically increases the flow of unemployment insurance premiums from the income stream into the unemployment insurance fund, thereby moderating aggregate demand. During a recession, unemployment increases and the system reverses itself: unemployment payments automatically flow from the insurance fund to those who become unemployed, thereby increasing their disposable income and propping up consumption and aggregate demand. Likewise, welfare spending automatically increases as more people become eligible during hard times. *As a result of these automatic stabilizers, during economic fluctuations disposable income varies proportionately less than does real GDP.*

Unemployment insurance, welfare benefits, and the progressive income tax were designed not so much as automatic stabilizers but as income redistribution programs. Their beneficial roles as automatic stabilizers are secondary effects of the legislation. Automatic stabilizers do not eliminate economic fluctuations, but they do reduce their magnitude. The stronger and more effective the automatic stabilizers are, the less need there is for discretionary fiscal policy.

Because of the greater influence of automatic stabilizers, the economy is more stable today than it was in 1929. Increases in federal income tax rates plus the introduction of payroll taxes and state sales taxes and state income taxes created more leakages in the circular flow, which reduced the size of the spending multipliers.

From the Golden Age to Stagflation

The decade of the 1960s was the Golden Age of fiscal policy. John F. Kennedy was the first U.S. president to argue that a federal budget deficit could stimulate an economy experiencing a contractionary gap. He expanded the goals of fiscal policy from simply moderating business fluctuations to promoting long-term economic growth, and he set numerical targets of no more than 4 percent unemployment and no less than a 4.5 percent annual growth rate of output. Fiscal policy was also used on occasion to provide an extra kick to an expansion, as in 1964, when income tax rates were cut to keep an expansion alive. *This tax cut, introduced to stimulate business investment, consumption, and employment, was perhaps the shining example of the successful use of fiscal policy during the 1960s.* The tax cut seemed to work wonders, increasing disposable income and consumption. The unemployment rate dropped below 5 percent for the first time in seven years, the inflation rate was under 2 percent, and the federal budget deficit in 1964 equaled only about 1 percent of GDP (compared to an average of more than 4 percent since 1982).

Fiscal policy is a type of demand-management policy because the idea is to increase or decrease aggregate demand to smooth business fluctuations. Demand-management policies were applied during much of the 1960s. But the 1970s were different. During much of the 1970s, the problem was stagflation—the double trouble of higher inflation and higher unemployment resulting from a decrease in aggregate supply caused by sharply increased oil prices, crop failures around the world, and other supply shocks. Demand-management policies were ill-suited to solving the problem of stagflation because an increase in aggregate demand would worsen inflation, whereas a decrease in aggregate demand would worsen unemployment.

Other concerns also caused economists and policymakers to question the effectiveness of discretionary fiscal policy: the difficulty of estimating the natural rate of unemployment, the time lags involved in implementing fiscal policy, the distinction between current and permanent income, and possible feedback effects of fiscal policy on aggregate supply. We will consider each of these concerns in turn.

Fiscal Policy and the Natural Rate of Unemployment

As we have seen, the unemployment rate that occurs when the economy is producing its potential GDP is called the *natural rate of unemployment*. For discretionary policy purposes, public officials must correctly estimate this natural rate. Suppose the economy is producing its potential output, and the natural rate of unemployment is 6 percent. What if government officials believe the natural rate is 5 percent and attempt to increase output and reduce unemployment through fiscal policy? Fiscal policy that increases aggregate demand will appear to succeed in the short run because output and employment will both expand. But stimulating aggregate demand will, in the long run, result only in a higher price level, while the level of output falls back to the economy's potential. Thus, temporary increases in output may persuade policymakers that their plan was a good one, even though attempts to increase production beyond potential GDP in the long run lead only to inflation.

Lags in Fiscal Policy

The time required to approve and implement fiscal legislation may hamper its effectiveness and weaken fiscal policy as a tool of economic stabilization. Even if the fiscal prescription is appropriate for the economy at the time it is proposed, the months and sometimes years required to approve legislation and to implement the change means the medicine could do more harm than good, taking effect only after the economy has already turned itself around. Since a recession is not usually identified as such until at least six months after it begins, and since the average recession lasts little more than a year, this leaves a narrow window of time to execute discretionary fiscal policy. (More will be said about timing problems in Chapter 16.)

Discretionary Policy and Permanent Income

It was once thought that discretionary fiscal policy could be turned on and off like a faucet, stimulating the economy by just the right amount. Given the marginal propensity to consume, a tendency that is among the most stable in macroeconomics, tax changes could increase or decrease disposable income to bring about the desired change in consumption. A more recent view is that people base their consumption decisions not merely on changes in their current income, but on changes in their permanent income.

Permanent income Income that individuals expect to receive on average over the long term

Permanent income is the income a person expects to receive on average over the long term. If people base consumption decisions more on their permanent incomes, consumption will be less responsive to *temporary* changes in income than to permanent ones. The short-term manipulation of tax rates to influence consumption will not yield the desired effects as long as people view the tax changes as only temporary. In 1967, for example, at a time when the U.S. economy was producing its potential level of output, the escalating war in Vietnam increased military spending, pushing the economy beyond its potential. The combination of a booming domestic economy and a widening war produced an expansionary gap by 1968. That year, Congress approved a temporary tax *surcharge,* which raised income tax rates for 18 months. The idea behind this fiscal policy was to reduce disposable income, thereby reducing consumption and aggregate demand as a way of relieving inflationary pressure in the economy. But the reduction in aggregate demand turned out to be disappointingly small, and inflation was hardly affected. Although several factors help explain why higher taxes failed to reduce consumption, most economists agree that the *temporary* nature of the tax increase meant that consumers faced only a small downward revision in their permanent income. Since permanent income changed little, consumption spending changed little. Consumers simply saved less. As another example, U.S. veterans of World War II received an unanticipated, one-time insurance dividend in 1950 of about $175, an amount that at the time represented about 4 percent of average family income. The marginal propensity to consume from this windfall was only about 0.3—much lower than the MPC expected from a permanent change in income. *To the extent that consumers base spending decisions on their permanent income, attempts to fine-tune the economy during business fluctuations with temporary tax-rate adjustments will be less effective.*

Feedback Effects of Fiscal Policy on Aggregate Supply

So far we have limited our discussion of fiscal policy to its effect on aggregate demand. Fiscal policy may also affect aggregate supply, though often the effect is unintentional. For example, suppose the government increases transfer payments to the jobless and finances these transfers with higher income taxes. Since the increase in transfers is offset by an increase in taxes, net taxes remain unchanged, as does disposable income. If the marginal propensity to consume is the same for both groups, the reduction in spending by those whose taxes increase should be just offset by the increase in spending by transfer recipients. Thus, according to a theory of fiscal policy focusing on aggregate demand, there should be no change in aggregate demand and hence no change in equilibrium real GDP.

But consider the possible effects of these changes on the supply of labor. The unemployed, who benefit from increased transfers, may stop looking for work or may search at a more leisurely pace. Conversely, workers who find their after-tax wage reduced by the higher tax may be less willing to work extra hours or to work a second job since the opportunity cost of leisure has decreased. In short, the supply of labor could fall as a result of the changes in taxes and transfers. A decrease in the supply of labor would decrease aggregate supply, reducing the economy's potential GDP.

Both automatic stabilizers and discretionary fiscal policy may affect individual incentives to work, spend, save, and invest, though these effects are usually unintended. We should keep these secondary effects in mind when we evaluate fiscal policies. It was concern about the effects of taxes on the supply of labor that served as a basis for tax cuts introduced in 1981, as we will see next.

Giant U.S. Budget Deficits of the 1980s and 1990s

In 1981, President Reagan and Congress agreed on a 23 percent tax reduction in average income tax rates and a major buildup in defense spending, with no substantial offsetting reductions in domestic programs. This tax cut reflected a supply-side philosophy that reductions in tax rates would make people willing to work harder because they could keep more of what they earned. Lower taxes would increase the supply of labor and other resources in the economy, thereby increasing aggregate supply and the economy's potential GDP. In its strongest form, the supply-side theory held that enough additional real GDP would be generated by the tax cuts that total tax revenue would actually increase. What has transpired since the tax cut? Let's look at events during the 1980s in the following case study.

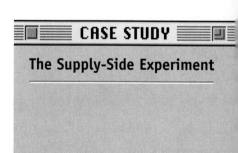

CASE STUDY

The Supply-Side Experiment

Taking the 1981–1988 period as the time frame for the examination, we can make some tentative observations about the effects of the federal income tax cut of 1981, which was implemented over three years. Before the tax cut went into effect, recession hit the economy and the unemployment rate climbed to nearly 10 percent of the work force in 1982.

Although it is difficult to untangle the growth generated by the tax cuts from the cyclical upswing following the recession of 1981–1982, we can say that between 1981 and 1988 employment climbed by 15 million and unemployment fell by 2 million. Output per capita increased by about 2.0 percent

The Supply-Side Experiment
continued

Location:

David Stockman, President Reagan's Director of the Office of Management and Budget, played a major role in creating a fiscal policy based on supply-side economic theory. To learn more about Stockman, browse a December 1981 *Atlantic Monthly* article and interview entitled "The Education of David Stockman," written by William Greider (http://www.theAtlantic.com/atlantic/atlweb/flashbks/classics/stockman.htm).

per year between 1981 and 1988. This rate was higher than the 1.1 percent average annual increase between 1973 and 1981 but lower than the 2.2 percent rate between 1948 and 1973.

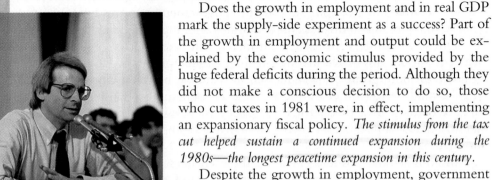

Does the growth in employment and in real GDP mark the supply-side experiment as a success? Part of the growth in employment and output could be explained by the economic stimulus provided by the huge federal deficits during the period. Although they did not make a conscious decision to do so, those who cut taxes in 1981 were, in effect, implementing an expansionary fiscal policy. *The stimulus from the tax cut helped sustain a continued expansion during the 1980s—the longest peacetime expansion in this century.*

Despite the growth in employment, government revenues did not expand enough to offset the combination of tax cuts and increased government spending. Between 1981 and 1988, federal spending grew at an average rate of 6.8 percent per year, and federal revenue grew at an average rate of 5.2 percent per year. So real GDP did not grow fast enough following the tax cut to generate the revenue required to fund growing government spending. Until 1981, deficits had been relatively small compared to, say, GDP—typically less than 1 percent of GDP. But deficits grew to about $200 billion a year by the middle of the 1980s; relative to GDP, that was about 5 percent. These deficits were the greatest ever experienced during peacetime. The recession of the early 1990s pushed the federal deficit up to 6 percent of GDP by 1992. The federal debt has more than quadrupled since 1981.

One surprising result of the supply-side experiment was that despite the huge federal deficits, which were expected to "crowd out" private investment, the proportion of national income that went to business investment during the years following the recession of 1982 was about the same as the average during the five expansionary periods between 1954 and 1980. Investment did not decline because there was an unusually large inflow of saving from abroad during the 1980s. High real U.S. interest rates, a strong dollar during the first half of the decade, and a stable political climate combined to make the United States an attractive place for foreigners to put their savings.

Sources: Some data are from the *Economic Report of the President,* February 1996; and Herbert Stein, *The Fiscal Revolution in America,* 2nd ed. (Washington, D.C.: The AIE Press, 1996).

During years of large federal deficits, the sum of U.S. consumption, investment, and government purchases exceed U.S. income and output. How could this occur? Domestic spending can exceed domestic output because U.S. households, firms, and governments borrow from abroad to help buy foreign production. Since the early 1980s, U.S. imports exceeded exports, and the resulting trade deficit has been financed in part by borrowing from abroad.

Given the potential effects of fiscal policy, particularly in the short run, we should not be surprised that elected officials might use fiscal policy to enhance their reelection prospects. We close the chapter with a look at how political considerations may shape fiscal policies.

After the recession of 1990–1991, the economy was slow to recover. At the time of the presidential election in 1992, the unemployment rate still languished at 7.5 percent, up two percentage points from where it stood in 1988, when President Bush was elected. The higher unemployment rate was too much of a hurdle to overcome and Bush lost to Clinton.

The link between economic performance and re-election success goes back a long way. Ray Fair of Yale University examined presidential elections dating back to 1916 and found that the state of the economy had a clear impact on the elections' outcomes. Specifically, he found that a declining unemployment rate and strong growth of real GDP per person during an election year increased the chances of election for the candidate of the incumbent party.

Another Yale economist, William Nordhaus, developed a theory of **political business cycles** to argue that incumbent presidents use expansionary policies to stimulate the economy, often only temporarily, during an election year. Their objective is to increase the chances of reelection by causing a reduction in the unemployment rate and an increase in output. For example, observers claim that President Nixon used expansionary policies to increase his chances for reelection in 1972.

The evidence to support the theory of political business cycles is not persuasive. One problem is that the theory limits presidential motivation to reelection, when in fact presidents may have other policy objectives. In the spring of 1992, for example, President Bush passed up an opportunity to stimulate the economy with a middle-class tax cut because the measure also called for tax increases on a much smaller group—upper-income taxpayers.

An alternative theory is that Democrats care relatively more about unemployment and relatively less about inflation than do Republicans. This theory is supported by evidence indicating that during a Democratic administration, unemployment is more likely to fall and inflation is more likely to rise than during a Republican administration. Republican presidents tend to pursue contractionary policies soon after coming into office and are more willing to endure a recession in order to reduce inflation. (The country suffered a recession in the second year of each of the last four Republican administrations.) Democratic presidents tend to pursue expansionary policies to reduce unemployment and are willing to put up with higher inflation to do so.

Sources: *Economic Report of the President,* February 1996; Ray Fair, "The Effects of Economic Events on Votes for President," *Review of Economics and Statistics* (May 1978): pp. 159–72; William Nordhaus, "Alternative Approaches to the Political Business Cycle," *Brookings Papers on Economic Activity,* No. 2 (1989): pp. 1–49.

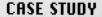

CASE STUDY

Discretionary Policy and Presidential Elections

Location :

Is there a link between economic performance and presidential reelection? The failure of President Bush to take action to end the recession of 1990–1991, for example, seems to have cost him the 1992 presidential election to Bill Clinton. Clinton, in an April 1992 campaign speech, critcized Bush's "do nothing" economic policies, instead advocating major government spending initiatives. Browse the contents of this speech, maintained by the U.S. Geological Survey (http://www. usgs.gov/public/nii/ econ-posit.html#).

Political business cycles Economic fluctuations that result when discretionary policy is manipulated for political gain

CONCLUSION

Because of huge federal budget deficits, the explicit use of discretionary fiscal policy as a tool for economic stabilization has been in decline. Since deficits were already large during economic expansions, it was hard to justify increasing deficits even more during a recession. President Clinton proposed a modest stimulus package in early 1993 to boost the recovery that was underway. His opponents blocked the measure, arguing that it would increase the deficit.

Another important tool of economic stabilization is monetary policy, which is the regulation of the money supply by the Federal Reserve System. In the next three chapters we will introduce money and financial institutions, examine monetary policy, and discuss the impact of monetary and fiscal policy on economic stability and growth.

SUMMARY

1. The effect of a change in government purchases on aggregate demand is the same as that of a change in any other type of spending. The simple multiplier for government purchases equals $1/(1 - MPC)$.

2. A change in net taxes (taxes minus transfer payments) affects consumption by changing disposable income. A given change in net taxes does not affect spending as much as would an identical change in government purchases. The multiplier for a change in autonomous net taxes equals $-MPC/(1 - MPC)$.

3. At a given price level, the combined effect of changes in government purchases and in net taxes is found by adding their individual effects. If both taxes and government purchases change by the same amount, the quantity of aggregate output demanded will also change by that amount, so the balanced budget multiplier equals 1.

4. An expansionary fiscal policy can close a contractionary gap by increasing government purchases or transfer payments or by reducing taxes. Because the short-run aggregate supply curve slopes upward, an increase in aggregate demand will raise both output and the price level

in the short run. Fiscal policy aimed at reducing aggregate demand in order to close an expansionary gap will reduce both output and the price level.

5. The tools of fiscal policy are automatic stabilizers and discretionary fiscal measures. Automatic stabilizers, such as the federal income tax, once implemented, require no congressional action to operate year after year. Discretionary fiscal measures require ongoing decisions about government spending and taxation.

6. Fiscal policy focuses primarily on the demand side, not the supply side. The problems of the 1970s, however, resulted more from a decline in aggregate supply than from a decline in aggregate demand.

7. The tax cuts of the early 1980s were introduced as a way of increasing aggregate supply. But government spending grew faster than revenue, and the result was huge deficits that stimulated aggregate demand, resulting in the longest peacetime expansion in this century. The huge federal deficits have discouraged additional discretionary fiscal policy as a way of stimulating aggregate demand further.

QUESTIONS AND PROBLEMS

1. **(Fiscal Policy)** Define fiscal policy. Indicate whether each of the following, other factors held constant, would lead to an increase, a decrease, or no change in the level of real GDP demanded:
   a. A decrease in government purchases.
   b. An increase in government purchases matched by an equal increase in autonomous net taxes.
   c. A decrease in transfer payments.
   d. A decrease in the marginal propensity to consume.
   e. An increase in autonomous transfer payments matched by an equal increase in autonomous taxes.

2. **(Fiscal Policy and the Simple Multiplier)** Assume that government purchases decrease by $10 billion, other

factors held constant. Calculate the change in the equilibrium level of real GDP demanded for each of the following values for the MPC. Then calculate the change if the government increased autonomous net taxes by $10 billion instead of reducing its purchases.
   a. 0.9
   b. 0.8
   c. 0.75
   d. 0.6

3. **(Tax Multiplier)** Explain why the tax multiplier for autonomous net taxes is equal to the government purchases multiplier times minus the marginal propensity to consume. If the MPC falls, what happens to the tax multiplier?

4. **(Automatic Stabilizers)** Often during recessions there is a large increase in the number of young people who volunteer for military service. Would this rise be considered a type of automatic stabilizer? Why or why not?

5. **(Change in Net Taxes)** Using the income-expenditure model, graphically illustrate the impact of a drop in autonomous government transfer payments of $15 billion on aggregate expenditure if the MPC equals 0.75. Explain why it has this impact. What is the impact on the equilibrium level of real GDP demanded?

6. **(Permanent Income)** "If the federal government wants to stimulate consumption by means of a tax cut, it should set up tax cuts that last a long time. If the government wants to stimulate savings in the short run, it should create a one-year tax cut." Evaluate these statements.

7. **(Fiscal Policy)** Will a 10-percent cut in a proportional income tax rate reduce government revenues by 10 percent? Why or why not? What would happen if there were a 10 percent cut in autonomous net taxes?

8. **(Fiscal Policy)** The chapter shows that increased government purchases, with taxes held constant, can eliminate a contractionary gap. How might a tax cut achieve the same results? Must the tax cut be larger than the earlier increase in government purchases? Why or why not?

9. **(Fiscal Policy with an Expansionary Gap)** Using the aggregate-demand/aggregate-supply model, graphically illustrate an economy with an expansionary gap. If the government closes the gap with a change in government purchases, do purchases rise or fall? In the long run, what happens to the level of real GDP? To the price level? Illustrate this on the AD/AS graph, assuming that the government changes its purchases by exactly the amount necessary to close the gap.

10. **(The Multiplier and the Time Horizon)** Explain the impact of the steepness of the short-run aggregate supply curve on the government's ability to use fiscal policy to change real GDP.

11. **(Fiscal Policy)** Suppose that the economy is experiencing a contractionary gap of $500 billion. Answer questions a through e, assuming that autonomous spending equals $400 billion, all net taxes are autonomous, the MPC equals 0.9, and the price level remains constant.
    a. What is the level of potential output?
    b. What change in government purchases would eliminate this contractionary gap?
    c. What change in autonomous net taxes, other factors constant, would eliminate this gap?

d. What "balanced budget" change in government spending would eliminate this gap?
e. How would your answers change if the price level changed?

12. **(Fiscal Policy)** Explain why effective discretionary fiscal policy requires information about each of the following:
    a. The slope of the short-run aggregate supply curve
    b. The natural rate of unemployment
    c. The size of the multiplier
    d. The speed with which self-correcting forces operate

13. **(Consumption)** Answer the questions below, using the following data. Assume an MPC of 0.8.

Disposable Income	Consumption
$ 0	$ 500
500	900
1,000	1,300
1,500	1,700

a. Assuming that net taxes are equal to $200 regardless of the the level of income, graph consumption against income (as opposed to disposable income).
b. How would an increase in net taxes to $300 affect your consumption function?
c. If the level of taxes were related to the level of income (i.e., income taxes were proportional), how would this affect your consumption function?

14. **(Automatic Stabilizers)** Distinguish between discretionary fiscal policy and automatic stabilizers. Provide some examples of automatic stabilizers. What is the impact of automatic stabilizers on disposable income as the economy moves through the business cycle?

15. **(Lags in Fiscal Policy)** Explain the effect of the lags in fiscal policy on the ability of the government to use discretionary fiscal policy to stabilize the economy.

16. **(Fiscal Policy Effectiveness)** Indicate whether each of the following would make fiscal policy more or less effective:
    a. A decrease in the marginal propensity to consume.
    b. Reduced lags in fiscal policy.
    c. Increased influence of fiscal policy on permanent income.
    d. Greater ability of the government to accurately determine the natural rate of unemployment.
    e. Greater feedback effects of fiscal policy on aggregate supply.

17. **(Multipliers)** Suppose that investment, in addition to having an autonomous component, also had a compo-

nent that varied directly with the level of real GDP. How would this affect the size of the government purchases and net taxes multipliers?

18. **(The Supply-Side Experiment)** Explain why it is difficult to determine whether or not the supply-side experiment was a success.

19. **(Discretionary Policy and Presidential Elections)** Suppose that fiscal policy creates changes in output faster than changes in prices. How might such timing play a role in the theory of political business cycles?

Using the Internet

20. The fiscal policy of the federal government manipulates, among other variables, the taxes Americans pay in order to influence variables in the economy. Visit "The Digital Daily," an electronic publication of the Internal Revenue Service (**http://www.irs.ustreas. gov/prod/cover.html**), and summarize the latest changes to the federal government's tax policy (it may be helpful to look within "Tax Info for You"). Who will benefit from these changes? What effect might these changes have on the economy?

Appendix

THE ALGEBRA OF DEMAND-SIDE FISCAL POLICY

In this appendix, we continue to focus on aggregate demand, using algebra. In Appendix B to Chapter 10, we solved for GDP demanded at a particular price level, then derived the simple spending multiplier for changes in spending, including government purchases. The change in GDP demanded resulting from a change in G, as derived in Appendix B to Chapter 10, is

Change in Y = Change in $G \times 1/(1 - MPC)$

The government spending multiplier is $1/(1 - MPC)$. In this appendix, we first derive the multiplier for net taxes that do not vary with income. Then we incorporate variable net exports and proportional income taxes into the framework. *Note that multiplier effects assume a given price level, so we limit the analysis to shifts in the aggregate demand curve.*

Net-Tax Multiplier

Consider the effects on the quantity of GDP demanded of a $1 increase in net taxes that do not vary with income. We begin with Y, the equilibrium derived in Appendix B to Chapter 10:

$$Y = \frac{1}{1 - b} (a - bNT + I + G + X - M)$$

where b is the marginal propensity to consume and $a - bNT$ is that portion of consumption that is independent of the level of income (review Appendix B to Chapter 10 if you need a refresher).

Now let's increase net taxes by $1 to see what happens to the level of real GDP demanded. Increasing net taxes by $1 yields

$$Y' = \frac{a - b(NT + \$1) + I + G + X - M}{1 - b}$$

The difference between Y' and Y is

$$Y' - Y = \frac{\$1(-b)}{1 - b}$$

Since b is the marginal propensity to consume, this difference can be expressed as $1 times $-MPC/(1 - MPC)$, which is the net-tax multiplier discussed in this chapter. With the MPC equal to 0.8, the net-tax multiplier equals $-0.8/0.2$, or -4, so the effect of increasing the net taxes by $1 is to reduce income by $4. If the MPC equals 0.75, the net-tax multiplier equals $- 0.75/0.25$, or -3.

The Multiplier When Both *G* and *NT* Change

In this chapter, we discussed the combined effects of government purchases and net taxes. Suppose that both increase by $1. We can bring together the two changes in the following equation:

$$Y^\star = \frac{a - b(NT + \$1) + I + G + \$1 + X - M}{1 - b}$$

The difference between this equilibrium and Y (the income level before introducing any changes in G or NT) is

$$Y^\star - Y = \frac{\$1(-b) + \$1}{1 - b}$$

which can be simplified to

$$Y^\star - Y = \frac{\$1(1 - b)}{1 - b} = \$1$$

Equilibrium aggregate output demanded increases by $1 as a result of $1 increases in both government purchases and net taxes. The *balanced budget multiplier* is equal to 1. More generally, we can say that if ΔG represents the change in government purchases and ΔNT represents the change in net taxes, the resulting change in aggregate output demanded, ΔY, can be expressed as

$$\Delta Y = \frac{\Delta G - b\Delta NT}{1 - b}$$

The Multiplier with a Proportional Income Tax

A net tax of a fixed amount is relatively easy to manipulate, but it is not very realistic. Instead, suppose we introduce a **proportional income tax** equal to t, where t lies between zero and 1. Incidentally, the proportional income tax is also the so-called *flat tax* that has been discussed in Congress lately as an alternative to the existing progressive income tax. Tax collections under a proportional income tax equal real GDP, Y, times the tax rate, t. With tax collections of tY, disposable income equals

$$Y - tY = (1 - t)Y$$

We plug this value for disposable income into the consumption function to yield

$$C = a + b(1 - t)Y$$

To consumption, we add the other components of aggregate expenditure, I, G, and $X - M$, to get

$$Y = a + b(1 - t)Y + I + G + (X - M)$$

Moving all the Y terms to the left-hand side of the equation yields

$$Y - b(1 - t)Y = a + I + G + (X - M)$$

or

$$Y[1 - b(1 - t)] = a + I + G + (X - M)$$

By isolating Y on the left-hand side of the equation, we get

$$Y = \frac{a + I + G + (X - M)}{1 - b(1 - t)}$$

The numerator on the right-hand side consists of the spending components. A $1 change in any of these components would change income by

$$\Delta Y = \frac{\$1}{1 - b(1 - t)}$$

Thus, the spending multiplier when there is a proportional income tax equals $1/[1 - b(1 - t)]$. Note that as the tax rate increases, the denominator increases, so the multiplier gets smaller. *The higher the proportional tax rate, other things constant, the smaller the multiplier.* Because a higher tax rate means a bigger reduction in disposable income, a higher tax rate reduces spending during each round of the expansion process.

Including Variable Net Exports

The previous section assumed that net exports did not change with income. If you have been reading the appendixes along with the chapters, you are already acquainted with how variable net exports fit into the picture. *The addition of variable net exports causes the aggregate expenditure function to flatten out, because net exports decrease as real income increases.* Real GDP demanded with variable net exports and a proportional income tax is

$$Y = a + b(1 - t)Y + I + G + X - m(1 - t)Y$$

This equation reduces to

$$Y = \frac{a + I + G + X}{1 - b + m + t(b - m)}$$

The higher the proportional tax rate, t, or the higher the marginal propensity to import, m, the larger the denominator, so the smaller the spending multiplier. If the marginal propensity to consume is 0.8, the marginal propensity to import is 0.1, and the proportional income tax rate is 0.2, the spending multiplier would be about 2.3—less than half the simple spending multiplier of 5.

Since we first introduced the simple spending multiplier, we have examined some considerations that reduce that simple multiplier—namely, (1) a marginal propensity to consume that responds primarily to permanent changes in income, not transitory changes, (2) a marginal propensity to import, and (3) a proportional income tax. The upward-sloping supply curve also reduces the affect on any given change in aggregate demand on equilibrium real GDP. After we introduce money in the next two chapters, we will consider other factors that reduce the size of the multiplier.

APPENDIX QUESTIONS

1. **(Equilibrium)** Suppose that the autonomous levels of consumption, investment, government purchases, and net exports are $500 billion, $300 billion, $100 billion, and $100 billion, respectively. Suppose further that the MPC is 0.85, the marginal propensity to import is 0.05, and income is taxed at a proportional rate of 0.25.
   a. What is the level of real GDP demanded?
   b. What is the size of the government deficit (or surplus) at this equilibrium output?
   c. What is the size of net exports at this output?
   d. What is the level of savings at this output?
   e. What change in autonomous spending is required to change equilibrium real GDP demanded by $500 billion?

2. **(Spending Multiplier)** If the marginal propensity to consume equals 0.8, the marginal propensity to import equals 0.2, and the proportional income tax rate is 0.25, what is the value of the spending multiplier? Indicate whether each of the following would increase the value of the spending multiplier, decrease it, or leave it unchanged:
   a. An increase in the marginal propensity to import.
   b. An increase in the marginal propensity to consume.
   c. An increase in the proportional tax rate.
   d. An increase in autonomous net taxes.

13

Money and the Financial System

Money has been a source of much fascination since earliest times. It has come to symbolize all personal and business finance. There is *Money* magazine, the "Money" section of *USA Today,* and cable TV shows such as *Moneyline, Moneyweek,* and *Your Money.* With money, you can articulate your preferences clearly—after all, money talks.

Money is the oil that lubricates the wheels of commerce. Just as oil makes for an easier fit among interacting gears, money reduces the friction of voluntary exchange. Too little oil can leave some parts creaking; too much oil can gum up the works. Similarly, too little or too much money in circulation makes exchange more difficult and creates economic problems.

First, a few words again about the distinction between stocks and flows. Recall that a stock is an amount measured at a particular point in time, such as the amount of food in your refrigerator, the amount of money you have with you right now, or the amount of gasoline in your car's tank. In contrast, a flow is an amount per unit of time, such as the calories you consume per day, the income you earn per week, or the miles you drive per month. *Money* is a stock and *income* is a flow. Don't confuse money with income.

In this chapter, we first discuss the evolution of money, moving from the most primitive economy to our own. Then we review monetary developments in the United States, focusing primarily on the 20th century. Topics discussed in this chapter include:

- Barter
- Functions of money
- Commodity and fiat moneys
- Federal Reserve System
- Depository institutions
- Banking problems of the 1990s

THE EVOLUTION OF MONEY

In the beginning there was no money. The earliest families were largely self-sufficient. Each family produced all it consumed and consumed all it produced, so there was little need for exchange. Without exchange, there was no need for money. When specialization first emerged, as some people went hunting and others took up farming, hunters and farmers had to trade. Thus, the specialization of labor resulted in exchange, but the kinds of goods traded were limited enough that people could easily exchange their products directly for other products—a system called *barter*.

Barter and the Double Coincidence of Wants

Barter depends on a **double coincidence of wants,** which occurs only when a trader is willing to exchange his or her product for what another offers. If the hunter is willing to exchange hides for the farmer's corn, that's a coincidence. But if the farmer is also willing to exchange corn for the hunter's hides, that's a double coincidence—hence, the expression *double coincidence of wants*. As long as specialization was limited, say to two or three goods, mutually beneficial trades were relatively easy to discover. As the economy developed, however, greater specialization in the division of labor increased the difficulty of finding goods that each trader wanted to exchange. Rather than just two possible types of producers, there were, say, a hundred types of producers.

Double coincidence of wants A situation in which two traders are willing to exchange their products directly

In a barter system, traders must not only discover a double coincidence of wants; they must also agree on a rate of exchange—that is, how many hides should be exchanged for a bushel of corn. When only two goods are produced, only one exchange rate must be determined, but as the number of goods produced in the economy increases, the number of exchange rates grows sharply. For example, if there are one hundred different goods, then 4,950 exchange rates must be determined. Increased specialization made the barter system of exchange more time-consuming and more cumbersome.

Sometimes differences between values of the units to be exchanged make barter difficult. For example, suppose the hunter wants to buy a home, which exchanges for 2,000 hides. The hunter will be hard-pressed to find a home seller in need of that many hides. These difficulties with barter have led people in even simple economies to use money.

Earliest Money and Its Functions

Nobody actually recorded the emergence of money. Thus, we can only speculate about how it first came into use. Through the experience accumulated from repeated exchanges, traders may have found that there were certain goods for which there was always a ready market. If a trader could not find a good that he or she desired personally, some good with a ready market could be accepted instead. So traders began to accept certain goods, not for immediate consumption, but because these goods would be accepted by others and therefore could be retraded later. For example, corn might become accepted because traders knew corn was always in demand. As one good became generally accepted in return for all other goods, that good began to function as **money.** *Any commodity that acquires a high degree of acceptability throughout an economy thereby becomes money.*

Money Anything that is generally acceptable in exchange for goods and services

Medium of exchange Anything that facilitates trade by being generally accepted by all parties in payment for goods or services

Commodity money Anything that serves both as money and as a commodity

Unit of account A common unit for measuring the value of every good or service

Money fulfills four important functions. Most importantly, money serves as a medium of exchange. Its function as a medium of exchange is what distinguishes it from other assets such as stocks, bonds, or real estate. Money also serves as a unit of account, a store of value, and a standard of deferred payment. Let's consider these functions in turn.

Medium of Exchange. Separating the sale of one good from the purchase of another requires an item acceptable to all parties involved in the transaction. If a community, by luck or by design, can find one commodity that everyone will accept in exchange for whatever is sold, traders can save much time, disappointment, and sheer aggravation. Suppose corn plays this role, a role that clearly goes beyond its usual function as food. We then call corn a medium of exchange because it is accepted in exchange by all buyers and sellers, whether or not they want corn to eat. A **medium of exchange** is anything that is generally accepted in payment for goods and services sold. The person who accepts corn in exchange for some product believes corn can be used later to purchase whatever is desired.

In this example, corn both is a commodity and serves as money, so we call it a **commodity money.** The earliest money was commodity money. Consider some commodities used as money over the centuries. Cattle served as money, first for the Greeks and then for the Romans. In fact, the word *"pecuniary"* ("of or relating to money") derives from the Latin word *pecus,* meaning "cattle." The so-called precious metals—gold and silver—were long popular as commodity moneys. Other commodity moneys used at various times include tobacco and wampum (polished strings of shells) in colonial America, tea pressed into small cakes in Russia, and dates in North Africa. Whatever serves as a medium of exchange is called money—no matter what it is, no matter how it first came to serve as a medium of exchange, and no matter why it continues to serve this function.

Corn, wampum (polished strings of shells), metals, and similar goods are commodities. In addition, these goods serve, or have served, as money.

Store of value Anything that retains its purchasing power over time

Unit of Account. As one commodity, such as corn, becomes widely accepted, the prices of all other goods come to be quoted in terms of that good. The chosen commodity becomes a common **unit of account,** a standard unit for quoting prices. The price of shoes or pots is expressed in terms of bushels of corn. Thus, not only does corn serve as a medium of exchange, it also becomes a yardstick for measuring the value of all goods and services. Rather than having to quote the rate of exchange for each good in terms of every other good, as is the case in a barter economy, people can measure the price of everything in terms of corn. For example, if a pair of shoes sells for two bushels of corn and a 5-gallon pot sells for one bushel of corn, then one pair of shoes has the same value in exchange as two 5-gallon pots.

Store of Value. Because people often do not want to make purchases at the time they sell an item, the purchasing power acquired through sales must somehow be preserved. Money serves as a **store of value** when it retains purchasing power over time. For example, corn serves as a store of value if it conserves purchasing power over time. The better money is at preserving purchasing power, the better it serves as a store of value.

Standard of Deferred Payment. People often borrow money to buy a home or a car, and they save for college or for retirement. These commitments to pay an amount in the future or receive payment in the future are specified in dollars. Money thereby serves as a **standard of deferred payment** to specify a future amount, enabling people to contract for future payments and receipts. So money is a yardstick not only for current payments and receipts, but future payments and receipts.

Standard of deferred payment An agreed unit of measure that enables people to contract for future payments and receipts

Problems with Commodity Money

There are problems with most commodity moneys, including corn. First, corn must be properly stored or its quality deteriorates; even then, it will not maintain its quality for long. Second, corn is bulky, so exchanges for major purchases become unwieldy. For example, if a new home cost 50,000 bushels of corn, many truckloads of corn would be involved in its purchase. Third, commodity money may not be easily divisible into smaller units. For example, when cattle served as money, any price that amounted to a fraction of a cow posed an exchange problem. Fourth, if all corn is valued equally in exchange, people will tend to keep the best corn and trade away the rest. The quality of corn in circulation will therefore decline, reducing its acceptability. Sir Thomas Gresham noted back in the 16th century that "bad money drives out good money," and this has come to be known as **Gresham's Law.** People tend to trade away inferior money and hoard the best. Fifth, commodity money usually ties up otherwise valuable resources as money, so commodity money has a relatively high opportunity cost, compared to, say, paper money.

Gresham's Law People tend to trade away inferior money and hoard the best

A final problem with corn, as with other commodity money, is that the value of corn depends on its supply and demand, which may vary unpredictably. If a bumper crop increased the supply of corn, corn would become less valuable, so more corn would be exchanged for all other goods. Any change in the demand for corn *as food,* such as occurred with the invention of corn chips, would alter the amount available as a medium of exchange, and this, too, would influence the value of corn. Erratic fluctuations in the market for corn limit its usefulness as money, particularly as a store of value and standard of deferred payment.

If people cannot rely on the value of corn over time, they will be reluctant to hold it or specify contracts for future payment or receipt. More generally, *since the value of money depends on its limited supply, anything that can be easily gathered or produced does not serve well as a commodity money.* For example, leaves would not serve well as a commodity money. What all this boils down to is that the best commodity money is durable, divisible, of uniform quality, and in limited supply.

Coins

The division of commodity money into units was often quite natural, as in bushels of corn or heads of cattle. When rock salt was used as money, it was cut into uniform bricks. Since salt was usually of consistent quality, a trader had only to count the bricks to determine the amount of money. When silver and gold were used as commodity money, both the quantity and the quality were open to question. Because precious metals could be debased with cheaper metals, the quantity and the quality of the metal had to be ascertained with each exchange.

This quality-control problem was addressed by coining the metal. *Coinage determined both the amount and quality of the metal.* The use of coins allowed payment

by count rather than by weight. A table on which this money was counted came to be called the *counter*—a term still used today. Initially, coins were stamped on only one side, but undetectable amounts of the metal could be shaved from the smooth side of the coin. To prevent such shaving, coins were stamped on both sides. But another problem arose: small amounts of the metal could be clipped from the edges. To prevent clipping, coins were bordered with a well-defined rim and were milled around the edges. If you have a dime or a quarter, notice the tiny serrations on the edge and the words along the border. These features, throwbacks from the time when these coins were silver rather than cheaper metals, prevented the recipient from "getting clipped."

The power to coin was vested in the *seignior*, or feudal lord. The power to coin money was considered an act of sovereignty, and counterfeiting was an act of treason. If the face value of the coin exceeded the cost of coinage, the minting of coins became a source of revenue to the seignior. **Seigniorage** (pronounced *seen'-your-edge*) refers to the revenue earned from coinage by the seignior. **Token money** is money whose face value exceeds the value of the material from which it is made. Coins (and paper money) now in circulation in the United States are token money. For example, the 25-cent coin costs the U.S. Mint only about three cents to make. The U.S. Mint earns about $500 million per year from coin production. Paper money is something else, as we will see next.

Money and Banking

The word *bank* comes from the Italian word *banca,* meaning "bench," since Italian money changers originally conducted their business on benches. Banking spread from Italy to England, where London goldsmiths offered the community "safekeeping" for money and other valuables. The goldsmiths had to give depositors their money back on request, but since withdrawals by some tended to be offset by deposits by others, the amount of idle cash, or gold, in the vault tended to remain relatively constant over time. Goldsmiths found that they could earn interest by making loans from this pool of idle cash.

Keeping one's money on deposit with a goldsmith was safer than leaving the money where it could be easily stolen, but it was a nuisance to have to visit the goldsmith each time money was needed. For example, a farmer might visit the goldsmith to withdraw enough money to buy a horse. The farmer would then pay the horse trader, who would promptly deposit the receipts with the goldsmith. Thus, money took a round trip from goldsmith to farmer to horse trader and back to goldsmith. Because depositors grew tired of going to the goldsmith every time they needed to make a purchase, goldsmiths instituted a practice whereby a purchaser, such as the farmer, could write the goldsmith instructions to pay someone else, such as the horse trader, a given amount from the purchaser's account. The payment amounted to having the goldsmith move gold from one stack (the farmer's) to another (the horse trader's). *These written instructions to the goldsmith were the first checks.* Checks have since become official-looking instruction forms, but they need not be, as evidenced by the actions of a Montana man who paid a speeding fine with a check written on a clean but frayed pair of underpants. The Western Federal Savings and Loan of Missoula honored the check.[1]

Founded in 1792, the United States Mint continues to serve its primary mission to produce sufficient coinage to meet the demands of commerce. The U.S. Mint has headquarters in Washington, DC, with production facilities in Philadelphia, Denver, San Francisco, and West Point (NY). The Mint is also responsible for the famed U.S. Bullion Depository at Fort Knox (KY). To learn more about the U.S. Mint, visit the Department of the Treasury (http://www.ustreas.gov/treasury/bureaus/mint/mint.html).

Seigniorage The difference between the face value of money and the cost of supplying it; the "profit" from issuing money

Token money The name given to money whose face value exceeds the cost of producing it

---

1   As reported in "Legal Briefs," *Newsweek,* 3 February 1992, p. 7.

By combining the two ideas of cash loans and checks, the goldsmith soon discovered how to make loans by check. Rather than lend idle cash, the goldsmith could create a checking account for the borrower. *The goldsmith could extend a loan by creating an account against which the borrower could write checks. In this way goldsmiths, or banks, were able to create a medium of exchange, or "create money."* This money, though based only on an entry in the goldsmith's ledger, was accepted because of the public's confidence that these claims would be honored.

The total claims against the goldsmith consisted of customer deposits plus deposits created through loans. Because these claims exceeded the value of gold on reserve, this was the beginning of a **fractional reserve banking system,** a system in which bank reserves amount to only a fraction of deposits. The *reserve ratio* measures reserves as a proportion of total claims against the goldsmith, or total deposits. For example, if the goldsmith had gold reserves valued at $5,000 but deposits totaling $10,000, the reserve ratio would be 50 percent.

Fractional reserve banking system A banking system in which only a portion of deposits is backed by reserves

Paper Money

Another way a bank could create money was to issue bank notes. **Bank notes** were pieces of paper promising the bearer specific amounts of gold or silver when the notes were presented to the issuing bank for redemption. In London, goldsmith bankers introduced bank notes about the same time they introduced checks. *Whereas checks could be redeemed only if endorsed by the payee, notes could be redeemed by anyone who held them.* Paper money was often "as good as gold," since the bearer could redeem the note for gold. Paper money was more convenient than gold because it took up less space and was easier to carry.

Bank notes Papers promising a specific amount of gold or silver to bearers who presented them to issuing banks for redemption; an early type of money

The amount of paper money issued depended on the bank's estimate of the proportion of notes that would be redeemed. The greater the redemption rate, the fewer notes that could be issued based on a given amount of reserves. Initially, these promises to pay were issued by private individuals or banks, but over time, governments took a larger role in printing and circulating notes.

Once paper money became widely accepted, it was perhaps inevitable that governments would begin issuing **fiat money,** which consists of paper money that derives its status as money from the power of the state, or by *fiat.* Fiat money is money because the government says it is money. It is not redeemable for anything other than more fiat money; it is not backed by a promise to pay something of intrinsic value. You can think of fiat money as mere paper money. It is acceptable not because it is intrinsically useful or valuable—as corn or gold is—but because the government requires that it be accepted as payment. Fiat money is declared **legal tender** by the government, meaning that creditors must accept it as payment for debts. *Gradually, people came to accept fiat money because they believed that others would accept it as well.* The money issued in the United States today, and indeed paper money throughout most of the world, is fiat money.

Fiat money Money not redeemable for any commodity; its status as money is conferred by the government

Legal tender Anything that creditors are required to accept as payment for debts

In a way, a well-regulated system of fiat money is more efficient for an economy than commodity money. Fiat money uses only paper, whereas commodity money requires that valuable commodities be used directly or held in reserve to support the system. As we shall see in the next chapter, paper money now makes up only a small fraction of the total money supply. Most modern money consists of checking accounts, which amount to little more than electronic entries in the computers of the nation's banking system.

The Value of Money

Money has grown increasingly more abstract—from a physical commodity, to a piece of paper representing a claim on a physical commodity, to a piece of paper of no intrinsic value, to an electronic entry representing a claim on a piece of paper of no intrinsic value. So why does money have value? The commodity feature of early money bolstered confidence in its acceptability. Commodities such as corn and tobacco had value in use even if for some reason they became less acceptable in exchange. When paper money came into use, its acceptability was initially fostered by the promise to redeem it for gold, silver, or other items of value. But since most paper money throughout the world is now fiat money, there is no promise of redemption. So why can a piece of paper bearing the image of Alexander Hamilton and the number 10 in each corner be exchanged for a large pepperoni pizza or anything else selling for $10? *People accept these pieces of paper because they believe others will do so.*

The value of money is reflected in its *purchasing power:* the rate at which money is exchanged for goods and services. The higher the price level, the fewer goods and services that can be purchased with each dollar, so the less each dollar is worth. Changes in the purchasing power of each dollar over time vary inversely with changes in the price level. As the price level increases, the purchasing power of money falls. To measure the purchasing power of the dollar in a particular year, first compute the price index for that year, then divide 100 by that price index. For example, relative to the base period of 1982–1984, the consumer price index for January 1996 was 154.4. The purchasing power of a dollar was therefore 100/154.4, or about $0.65, measured in 1982–1984 dollars. Exhibit 1 chronicles the steady decline since 1960 in the value of the dollar measured in terms of its average value in 1982–1984.

When Money Performs Poorly

One way to understand the functions of money is to look at situations in which money did not perform these functions well. In Chapter 7, we examined hy-

EXHIBIT 1

Purchasing Power of a Dollar Measured in 1982–1984 Constant Dollars

An increase in the price level reduces the amount of goods and services that can be purchased with a dollar. Since 1960, the price level has risen every year, so the purchasing power of the dollar has fallen continually.

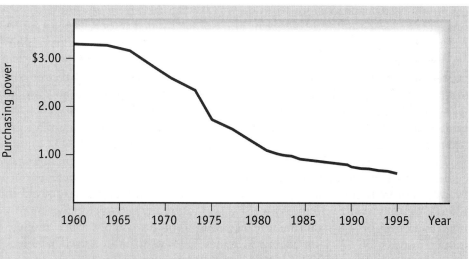

Source: *Economic Report of the President,* February 1996.

perinflation in Brazil. With prices growing by the hour, money no longer represented a stable store of value, so people couldn't wait to exchange rapidly inflating money for goods or for a "harder" currency. And with the price level rising rapidly, some merchants were quicker to raise their prices than others, so relative prices became distorted. Thus, money became less useful as a unit of account—that is, as a way of comparing the price of one good to that of another.

At some point, inflation may become so great that people will no longer accept the nation's money and will resort to barter. Likewise, if the supply of money dries up or if the price system is not allowed to function properly, barter may be the only remaining alternative. The following case study discusses instances when money performed poorly.

CASE STUDY

When the Monetary System Breaks Down

After Germany lost World War II, money in that country became almost useless because, despite tremendous inflationary pressure in the economy, the occupation forces imposed strict price controls. Since prices were set well below what people thought they should be, sellers stopped accepting money, and this forced people to use barter. Experts estimate that because of the lack of a viable medium of exchange, the German economy produced only half the output that it would have produced with a smoothly functioning monetary system. The "economic miracle" that occurred in Germany immediately after 1948 can be credited in large part to that country's adoption of a reliable monetary system.

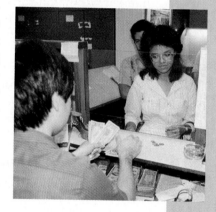

Location:

To learn more about the economies of Panama and Russia, explore "The World Factbook," a comprehensive publication of the U.S. Central Intelligence Agency (CIA) (http://www.odci.gov/cia/publications/pubs.html). While there, also browse "The Handbook of International Economic Statistics," a compilation of global economic statistics, including data for all of the republics of the former Soviet Union.

Money became extremely scarce during the 19th century in Brazil because of a copper shortage. Money-financed transactions became difficult because copper coins could no longer be minted, and people hoarded rather than traded the limited supply of coins. In response to this crisis, some merchants and tavernkeepers printed vouchers redeemable in goods and services. These vouchers circulated as money until copper coins returned to circulation. Similarly, there was often a shortage of money in the early American colonies. One way people dealt with the problem was by keeping careful records, showing who owed what to whom.

For a more recent example, consider Panama, a Central American country that relies on the U.S. dollar as a medium of exchange. In 1988, the United States, in response to charges that the leader of Panama was involved in drug dealing, froze Panamanian assets in the United States, precipitating a run on Panama's banks. Those banks were forced to close for nine weeks. Dollars in circulation dried up, so people resorted to barter. Because barter is much less efficient than a smoothly functioning monetary system, Panama's GDP reportedly fell by 30 percent in 1988.

In Russia, the hyperinflation of the ruble following the breakup of the Soviet Union increased Russian demand for so-called hard currencies, especially the dollar. A Russian central banker estimated that in 1995 the value of Russians' dollar holdings exceeded the value of their ruble holdings. In keeping with Gresham's Law, Russians preferred to trade their rubles and hoard their dollars.

Sources: Peter White, "The Power of Money," *National Geographic*, January 1993, pp. 80–107; and Frederic Dannen and Ira Silverman, "The Supernote," *The New Yorker*, 23 October 1995, pp. 50–55.

Thus, when the supply of money shrinks or when the official money fails to serve as a medium of exchange, some other mechanism may arise to facilitate exchange. But this second-best alternative is seldom as efficient as a smoothly functioning monetary system, because more resources must be diverted from production to exchange. A poorly functioning monetary system results in higher transaction costs. It has been said that no machine increases the economy's productivity as much as properly functioning money. Indeed, it seems hard to overstate the value of a reliable monetary system.

This concludes our introduction to money. We now consider the historical development of money and banking in the United States.

FINANCIAL INSTITUTIONS IN THE UNITED STATES

You have already learned about the origin of modern banks: goldsmiths lent money from deposits held for safekeeping. So you already have some idea of how banks operate. Recall from the circular flow model discussed earlier that household saving flows into financial markets and is lent to investors. Financial institutions attract the funds of savers and lend these funds to borrowers, serving as intermediaries between savers and borrowers. Financial institutions, or **financial intermediaries,** earn a profit by "buying low and selling high"—that is, by paying a lower interest rate to savers than they charge borrowers.

Financial intermediaries Institutions that serve as go-betweens, accepting funds from savers and lending them to borrowers

Commercial Banks and Thrifts

A wide variety of financial intermediaries respond to the economy's demand for financial services. **Depository institutions,** such as commercial banks, savings and loan associations, mutual savings banks, and credit unions, obtain funds primarily by accepting *deposits* from the public—hence their name. Other financial intermediaries, such as finance companies and insurance companies, acquire funds not through customer deposits but by collecting premiums or by borrowing. Our emphasis will be on depository institutions because they play a key role in providing the nation's money supply. Depository institutions can be classified broadly into two types: commercial banks and thrift institutions.

Depository institutions Commercial banks and other financial institutions that accept deposits from the public

Commercial banks are the oldest, largest, and most diversified of depository institutions. They are called **commercial banks** because historically they made loans primarily to *commercial* ventures, or businesses, rather than to households. Commercial banks hold two-thirds of all deposits of depository institutions. Until recently, commercial banks were the only depository institutions that offered demand deposits, or checking accounts. **Demand deposits** are so named because a depositor with such an account can write a check to *demand* those deposits at any time.

Commercial banks Depository institutions that make short-term loans primarily to businesses

Thrift institutions, or **thrifts,** include savings and loan associations, mutual savings banks, and credit unions. Historically, savings and loan associations and mutual savings banks specialized in making mortgage loans, which are loans to finance real estate purchases. Credit unions extend loans only to their "members" to finance homes or other major consumer goods such as cars.

Demand deposits Accounts at financial institutions that pay no interest and on which depositors can write checks to obtain their deposits at any time

Thrift institutions, or thrifts Depository institutions that make long-term loans primarily to households

Development of the Dual Banking System

Before 1863, commercial banks in the United States were chartered by the states in which they operated, so they were called *state banks*. These banks, like the English goldsmiths, issued bank notes. More than 10,000 different kinds of notes circulated and nearly all were redeemable for gold. The National Banking Act of 1863 and its later amendments created a new system of federally chartered banks called *national banks*. National banks were authorized to issue notes and were regulated by the Office of the Comptroller of the Currency, part of the U.S. Treasury. At this time, a tax was introduced on the notes issued by state-chartered banks, the idea being to tax state bank notes out of existence. But state banks survived by substituting checks for notes. Borrowers were issued checking accounts rather than bank notes. State banks thereby held on, and to this day the United States has a *dual banking system* consisting of both state banks and national banks.

Birth of the Federal Reserve System

During the 19th century, the economy experienced a number of panic "runs" on banks by depositors seeking to withdraw their funds. A panic was usually set off by the failure of some prominent financial institution. Following such a failure, other banks were besieged by fearful customers. Borrowers wanted additional loans and extensions of credit, and depositors wanted their money back. The failure of the Knickerbocker Trust Company in New York set off the Panic of 1907. This financial calamity underscored the lack of banking stability and so aroused the public that in 1908 Congress established the National Monetary Commission to study the banking system and make recommendations. That group's deliberations led to the Federal Reserve Act, passed in 1913 and implemented in 1914, which established the **Federal Reserve System** as the central bank and monetary authority of the United States.

Federal Reserve System **The central bank and monetary authority of the United States; known as "the Fed"**

Nearly all industrialized countries had formed central banks by 1900—the Bundesbank in Germany, the Bank of Japan, the Bank of England. The American public's suspicion of such monopoly power led to the establishment of not one central bank but 12 separate banks in 12 Federal Reserve districts around the country. The new banks were named after the cities in which they were located—the Federal Reserve Bank of Boston, New York, Chicago, San Francisco, and so on. *Throughout most of its history, the United States had what is called a decentralized banking system. The Federal Reserve Act moved the country toward a system that was partly centralized and partly decentralized.* All national banks were required to become members of the Federal Reserve System and became subject to new regulations issued by *the Fed,* as it came to be known. For state banks, membership was voluntary; most state banks did not join because they did not want to comply with the new regulations.

Powers of the Federal Reserve System

According to the 1913 act, the Federal Reserve System was to be directed by the Federal Reserve Board. This board was authorized "to exercise general supervision" over the 12 Reserve banks. The Federal Reserve's task was to ensure the availability of enough money and credit in the banking system to support a growing economy. The power to issue bank notes was taken away from national banks and turned over to the Federal Reserve banks. (Take out a dollar and notice what it says across the top: FEDERAL RESERVE NOTE. The seal to the left of George Washington's picture identifies which Reserve bank issued the note.) The Federal Reserve was also given other powers: *to buy and sell government securities, to extend loans to member banks, to clear checks, and to re-*

quire that member banks hold reserves equal at least to a specified fraction of their deposits.

Federal Reserve banks typically do not deal with the public directly. Each may be thought of as a bankers' bank. Reserve banks hold deposits of member banks, just as depository institutions hold deposits of the public. Reserve banks extend loans to member banks just as depository institutions extend loans to the public. In addition to serving as bankers' banks, Reserve banks serve as bankers to the federal government, holding government deposits and lending money to the government by purchasing federal securities.

Federal Reserve banks get their name from the fact that they hold member bank *reserves* on deposit. **Reserves** are funds that banks have on hand or on deposit with the Fed to promote banking safety, to facilitate interbank transfers of funds, to satisfy the cash demands of their customers, and to comply with Federal Reserve regulations. These reserves allow Reserve banks to clear checks written by a depositor in one commercial bank and deposited in another commercial bank. This check clearance is, on a larger scale, much like the goldsmith's moving of gold reserves from the farmer's account to the horse trader's account. Reserve banks also make loans to member banks. The interest rate charged to banks for these so-called *discount loans* is called the **discount rate.** By making discount loans to banks, the Fed can increase reserves in the banking system.

Member banks are required to own stock in the Federal Reserve bank in their district, and this stock ownership entitles them to a specified dividend and to vote for the Board of Directors of their district Federal Reserve bank. Any additional profit earned by the Reserve banks is turned over to the U.S. Treasury. Twelve commercial bankers, one representing each Federal Reserve district, also make up the *Federal Advisory Council,* which advises the Fed.

Reserves Funds that banks use to satisfy the cash demands of their customers and the reserve requirements of the Fed; reserves consist of deposits at the Fed plus currency physically held by banks

Discount rate Interest rate charged to member banks by Federal Reserve banks for discount loans

Banking During the Great Depression

From 1913 to 1929, both the Federal Reserve System and the national economy performed relatively well. But the stock market crash of 1929 was followed by the Great Depression, bringing a new set of problems for the Federal Reserve System. Frightened depositors wanted their money back, precipitating bank runs. But the Fed failed to respond to the crisis; it failed to act as a lender of last resort—that is, it did not lend banks the money they needed to satisfy deposit withdrawals in cases of runs on otherwise sound banks. Between 1930 and 1933, about 9,000 banks failed—roughly half the banks in existence.

The Federal Reserve System was established precisely to prevent such panics and to add stability to the banking system. What went wrong? In a word, everything. Between 1930 and 1933, the support offered by the Federal Reserve System seemed to crumble in stages. As businesses failed, they were unable to repay their loans. These defaults on loans led to the initial bank failures. As the crisis deepened, the public grew more concerned about the safety of deposits, so cash withdrawals increased. To satisfy the increased demand for currency, banks were forced to sell their holdings of stocks and bonds. But with many banks trying to sell and with few buyers, securities markets collapsed, sharply reducing the market value of these bank assets. Many banks did not have the resources to survive.

The Fed should have extended loans on a large scale to banks experiencing short-run shortages of cash, much as it did a half century later during the stock market crash of 1987. The Fed failed to act because it did not understand either the gravity of the situation or its own power to assist troubled banks. The Fed viewed bank failure as a regrettable but inevitable consequence of poor management or prior speculative excesses, or simply as the effect of a collapsing economy. The Fed did not seem to understand that the banking system's instability was contributing to the deterioration of the economy. For example, the stock market collapsed between 1929 and 1933 in part because many banks were trying to sell their securities at the same time. And the collapse came just when banks were badly in need of cash. Fed officials appeared concerned primarily with the solvency of the Federal Reserve banks. They did not realize that because Federal Reserve banks had unlimited money-creating power, they could not fail.

Roosevelt's Reforms

In his first inaugural address, President Franklin D. Roosevelt said, "The only thing we have to fear is fear itself," a view that was especially applicable to a fractional reserve banking system. Most banks were sound as long as people had confidence in the safety of their deposits. *But if many people became frightened and tried to withdraw their money, they could not do so because each bank held reserves amounting to only a fraction of its deposits.*

Upon taking office in March of 1933, President Roosevelt attempted to soothe prevailing fears by declaring a "banking holiday," which closed all banks for a week. A national suspension of banking business for a week was unprecedented, yet it was welcomed as a sign that something would be done. Roosevelt also proposed the Banking Acts of 1933 and 1935 and other measures as reforms aimed at shoring up the banking system and centralizing the power of the Federal Reserve in Washington. Let's consider the most important features of this legislation.

Board of Governors. The Federal Reserve Board was renamed the Board of Governors, and it became responsible for setting and implementing the nation's monetary policy. *Monetary policy* is the regulation of the economy's money supply to promote macroeconomic objectives. All 12 Reserve banks came under the authority of the Board of Governors, which consists of seven members appointed by the president and confirmed by the Senate. Each governor serves a 14-year term, and the terms are staggered so that one governor is appointed every two years. The president also appoints one of the governors to chair the board for a 4-year term. A president bent on changing the direction of monetary policy could be sure of changing only two members in a single presidential term and four members in two terms. Thus, board membership is relatively stable, and in one four-year term a president has only limited control over the board's monetary policy. *The idea was to insulate monetary authorities from short-term political pressures.*

Federal Open Market Committee. Originally, the power of the Federal Reserve was vested in each of the 12 Reserve banks. The Banking Acts established the *Federal Open Market Committee (FOMC)* to consolidate decisions about the most important tool of monetary policy—**open-market operations,** which are purchases and sales of U.S. government securities by the Fed. (Open-market

Open-market operations *Purchases and sales of government securities by the Federal Reserve in an effort to influence the money supply*

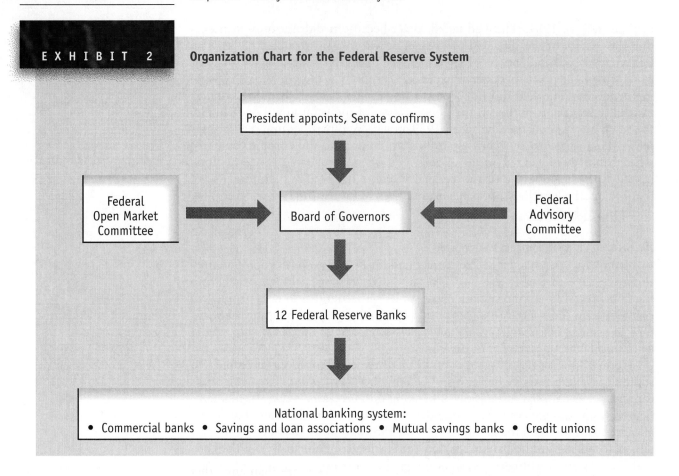

EXHIBIT 2

Organization Chart for the Federal Reserve System

President appoints, Senate confirms

Federal Open Market Committee → Board of Governors ← Federal Advisory Committee

12 Federal Reserve Banks

National banking system:
• Commercial banks • Savings and loan associations • Mutual savings banks • Credit unions

operations will be examined in the next chapter.) The FOMC consists of the seven board governors plus five presidents from the Reserve banks. Open-market operations are carried out in New York, and the president of the New York Fed is always on the FOMC. The organizational structure of the Federal Reserve System as it now stands is presented in Exhibit 2.

Reserve Requirements. As noted earlier, because reserves amount to only a fraction of deposits, we have a *fractional reserve* banking system. Specific reserve requirements had been established by the Federal Reserve Act of 1914. Member banks were required to hold in reserves a certain percentage of their deposits. The Banking Acts of 1933 and 1935 authorized the Board of Governors to vary reserve requirements within a range, thereby giving the Fed an additional tool of monetary policy.

Thus, as of 1935, the Federal Reserve System had a variety of tools to regulate the money supply, including *(1) conducting open-market operations—buying and selling U.S. government securities; (2) setting legal reserve requirements for member banks; and (3) setting the discount rate—the interest rate charged by the Reserve banks for loans to member banks.* We will explore these tools in greater detail in the next chapter.

FDIC. One cause of bank failures during the depression was the lack of confidence in the safety of bank deposits. The Federal Deposit Insurance Corporation (FDIC) was established in 1933 to insure the first $2,500 of each deposit account. Today the ceiling is $100,000 per account. Members of the Federal Reserve System are required to purchase FDIC insurance; the program is voluntary for other banks. About 97 percent of commercial banks and about 90 percent of savings and loan associations are insured by the FDIC. The rest are insured by private companies or state reserve funds. *Deposit insurance worked wonders to reduce bank runs by calming fears about bank safety.*

Restricting Bank Investment Practices. As part of the Banking Act of 1933, commercial banks were forbidden to buy and sell corporate stocks and bonds. The belief was that when commercial banks hold assets that fluctuate widely in value, the stability of the banking system is endangered. *The act limited bank assets primarily to loans and government securities.* Also, bank failures were thought to have resulted in part from interest-rate competition among banks for customer deposits. To reduce such competition, the Fed was empowered to set the maximum interest rates that could be paid on commercial bank deposits.

Goals of the Fed. Over the years, the Fed has accumulated additional responsibilities. Six goals are frequently mentioned as objectives of the Fed's policies: (1) a high level of employment in the economy, (2) economic growth, (3) price stability, (4) stability in interest rates, (5) stability in financial markets, such as the stock market, and (6) stability in foreign-exchange markets. *We can boil these goals down to high employment; economic growth; and stability in prices, interest rates, and exchange rates.*

Branch Banking Restrictions

The United States has about 10,000 commercial banks—more than any other country, but down from about 14,000 in 1985. Japan has only 150 commercial banks and other industrial countries have fewer than 1,000. The 10 largest U.S. commercial banks hold less than 40 percent of banking industry assets. In contrast, as few as a half dozen banks hold over half the assets in other developed countries, such as Australia, Canada, and the United Kingdom. Nine of the world's 10 largest banks are Japanese. *So, the United States has more banks than other countries, and bank assets are distributed more evenly across banks.*

The large number of banks in this country reflects government restrictions on *branches,* which are additional offices that carry out banking operations. Each state controls the type and number of branches that a bank can open. States on the East Coast and West Coast tend to be more lenient about branches than are the states in between. Until 1994, federal legislation prohibited interstate branching. The combination of intrastate and interstate restrictions on branching spawned the many commercial banks that exist today, most of which are relatively small. *Restrictions on interstate banking created inefficiencies, since banks could not achieve optimal size and could not as easily diversify their portfolio of loans among different regions.*

In recent years, three developments have allowed banks to get around branching restrictions: bank holding companies, automatic teller machines, and mergers. A **bank holding company** is a corporation that may own several different banks. Many states now permit holding companies to cross state lines, thereby skirting federal prohibitions against interstate banking. Moreover, a holding company can provide other services that banks are not authorized to

Bank holding company A corporation that owns banks

offer, such as financial advising, leasing, and issuing credit cards. Holding companies have blossomed in recent years, and the nation's major banks are all owned by holding companies. More than three-quarters of the nation's checking deposits are in banks owned by holding companies.

Another important development that has allowed banks to extend their presence is the automatic teller machine. In some states, banks have bypassed branching restrictions by having several banks share the same machine. Thus, *holding companies and automatic teller machines have allowed banks to avoid branching restrictions and thereby cover more territory.*

As we shall see, recent financial weakness of some banks has forced them to merge with stronger banks, and these mergers have spread the presence of the merged bank within states and across the country. For example, the recent mergers between Chase Manhattan and Chemical Bank and between BankAmerica and Security Pacific have resulted in larger banks with a broader geographical presence. More generally, federal legistation now allows bank mergers across states and allows interstate branching as long as the "host" state approves.

The Quiet Life of Depository Institutions

Restrictions imposed on depository institutions during the 1930s made banking a heavily regulated industry, something like a public utility. The federal government insured most deposits. Depository institutions, in turn, surrendered much of their freedom to wheel and deal. The assets they could acquire were carefully limited, as were the interest rates they could offer depositors. Households typically left their money in savings deposits earning 5 percent or less; checking deposits earned no interest. Banks and thrifts quietly accepted these deposits and made loans, earning their profit on the interest differential. The banking business became comfortable—largely insulated from the rigors of competition. As the expression "banker's hours" suggests, banks closed at 2:00 or 3:00 in the afternoon and remained closed on weekends. Banking was considered stuffy, even boring. In this staid business climate, offering a "free" toaster as a deposit bonus was considered state-of-the-art marketing.

Savings and loan associations and mutual savings banks were even more sheltered than commercial banks. They might pay 4 percent interest on deposits that were loaned out at 7 percent interest for 30-year home mortgages. If the loan went into default and the mortgage had to be foreclosed, rising postwar housing values made the house worth more than the unpaid loan. Under the circumstances, it was difficult to make a bad mortgage loan. But the quiet world of banking was shaken by developments in the 1970s that ultimately led to the elimination of many restrictions introduced during the 1930s. Let's look at what happened.

RECENT PROBLEMS WITH DEPOSITORY INSTITUTIONS

Money market mutual fund A collection of short-term interest-earning assets purchased with funds collected from many shareholders

The surge of inflation during the 1970s increased interest rates in the economy, and the world of the banker has not been the same since. In October 1972, Merrill Lynch, a major brokerage house, introduced an account combining a **money market mutual fund** with check-writing privileges. Money market mutual fund shares represent claims on a portfolio, or collection, of short-term interest-earning assets. By pooling the funds of many shareholders, the managers of a mutual fund can acquire a diversified portfolio of assets offering shareholders higher rates of interest than those available at most depository institutions. Money market mutual funds proved to be stiff competition for bank deposits, especially demand deposits, which paid no interest.

Depository Institutions Were Losing Deposits

Federal Reserve ceilings on the interest rates that depository institutions could offer their depositors reduced interest-rate competition for deposits *among* depository institutions. Depository institutions still competed for deposits in other ways, such as by offering free toasters or providing drive-through windows. As long as the interest-rate ceilings were at or above prevailing market rates of interest, the banking system as a whole did not have to worry about outside competition for customer deposits. When market interest rates rose above the ceiling that banks and thrifts could offer, however, many savers withdrew their deposits from banks and thrifts and put them into higher-yielding alternatives, such as money market mutual funds. The banks had used savers' deposits to make loans; when savers withdrew their deposits, banks and thrifts had to replace the funds needed to support their loans by borrowing at prevailing interest rates, which were typically higher than banks and thrifts earned on their existing loans.

Because their loans were typically for short periods, commercial banks got in less trouble than thrifts when interest rates rose. But thrifts had made loans for long-term mortgages, loans that would not be paid back for decades. *Because thrifts had to pay more interest to borrow funds than they were earning on these mortgages, they were in big trouble and many failed.*

Bank Deregulation

In response to the loss of deposits and other problems of depository institutions, Congress tried to ease regulations, thereby giving banks and thrifts greater discretion in their operations. For example, the interest-rate ceilings for deposits were eliminated and all depository institutions were authorized to offer checking accounts. Thrifts were given wider latitude in making loans and in the kinds of assets they could acquire. Additionally, all depository institutions were allowed to offer money market deposit accounts, which grew from only $8 billion in 1978 to $200 billion in 1982.

Some states, such as California and Texas, largely deregulated state-chartered savings and loan associations. The combination of deposit insurance, unregulated interest rates, and a wider latitude in the kinds of assets that could be purchased gave savings and loan associations a green light to compete for large sums of money in national markets and to acquire assets as they pleased. Once-staid financial institutions moved into the fast lane.

Thus, with deregulation, thrifts could wheel and deal, but with the benefit of deposit insurance. But deposit insurance encouraged some thrifts already in financial trouble to take big risks, to "bet the bank," because their depositors would be protected by deposit insurance. Banks that were already virtually bankrupt—so-called "zombie" banks—were able to attract additional deposits because of deposit insurance.

Meanwhile, since deposits were insured, most depositors paid little attention to their bank's health. *Thus, deposit insurance, originally introduced during the Great*

Depression to prevent bank panics, caused depositors to become complacent about the safety of their deposits. More important, it caused those who ran the banks and thrifts to take unwarranted risks because they were gambling with other people's money.

The result was a disaster, and depository institutions, particularly thrifts, failed at record rates. The number of thrifts has dropped by more than half since 1980, and more could still disappear through mergers or failures. When the dust settles, failures and mergers could reduce the number of thrifts well below the current level of 2,000.

Bailing Out the Thrifts

The insolvency and collapse of a growing number of thrifts prompted Congress, in August 1989, to approve the largest financial bailout of any industry in history—a measure expected to cost about $200 billion, a cost that contributes to current federal deficits. Taxpayers are expected to pay nearly two-thirds of the total cost, with the thrift industry paying the remaining third through higher deposit insurance premiums. The money has been spent to shut down failing thrifts and pay off insured depositors.

Part of the cleanup involved selling the office buildings, shopping malls, apartment buildings, land, and other assets formerly taken over by insolvent thrifts. A glut of such properties dragged down market values and reduced the federal government's ability to recoup its losses from deposit insurance. The problem is discussed in the following case study.

CASE STUDY

Easy Money, Empty Buildings

Location:

During the 1980s, banks and thrifts provided real estate developers with a ready supply of financing, even for admittedly shaky projects. Why? Among other reasons, deposit insurance provided unmerited confidence in depositors and consequently allowed banks and thrifts to take unwarranted risks. To learn more about deposit insurance, and banks in general, visit the Federal Deposit Insurance Corporation (FDIC) (http://www.fdic.gov/).

During the 1980s, a ready supply of financing from banks and thrifts, coupled with generous 1981 tax law provisions for developers, made new buildings look like sure-fire investments. The one-two punch of easy financing and tax incentives turned office-building construction into a growth industry. Office buildings shot up like weeds. But the growth in office-building construction occurred just as the financial service sector, the sector that was expected to fill those buildings with office workers, was starting to contract.

The increased supply of office buildings and decreased demand left many new buildings only partially filled or even empty. The office vacancy rates in U.S. downtown districts increased from an average of 7 percent in 1982 to 18 percent in 1992. The surplus depressed rents, which in real terms by 1992 were only half what they were in 1987. Building developers were not earning enough in rent to pay off their loans, so they defaulted on those loans. The banks and thrifts that financed construction became reluctant owners of these failed properties. They tried to sell the properties, but with many buildings for sale and few buyers, market values fell sharply. Many banks could not hang on and were dragged under by these bad loans.

A lot of investors lost money, especially developers and those who bankrolled the construction. The sad part for the economy as a whole is that money that could have gone to advancing technology, to more efficient machines, to better education, or to improved highways and airports instead went to finance unused or underused buildings. U.S. workers in the 1990s are less productive because much investment during the 1980s went not into productive capital but into what turned out to be gleaming office buildings that were not needed.

Sources: "Still Flat on Its Back," *The Economist,* 16 May 1992; and J.S. Cummins, K.A. Hassett, and R.G. Hubbard, "A Reconsideration of Investment Behavior Using Tax Reforms as Natural Experiments," *Brookings Papers on Economic Activity* No. 2, 1994: pp. 1–60.

Commercial Banks Were Also Failing

The U.S. banking system experienced more change and upheaval during the 1980s and early 1990s than at any other time since the Great Depression. As they had in the case of thrifts, risky decisions based on deposit insurance and the slump in property values also hastened the demise of many commercial banks. Hundreds of troubled banks such as Continental Illinois, First Republic Bank of Dallas, and the Bank of New England were taken over by the FDIC or forced into shotgun mergers with healthier competitors. Banks in Texas and Oklahoma failed because loans to oil drillers and farmers went sour. Banks in the Northeast failed because falling real estate values caused borrowers to default. Exhibit 3 shows the number of bank failures per year since 1935. The rising tide of failures during the 1980s is clear. Equally clear is the decline in fail-

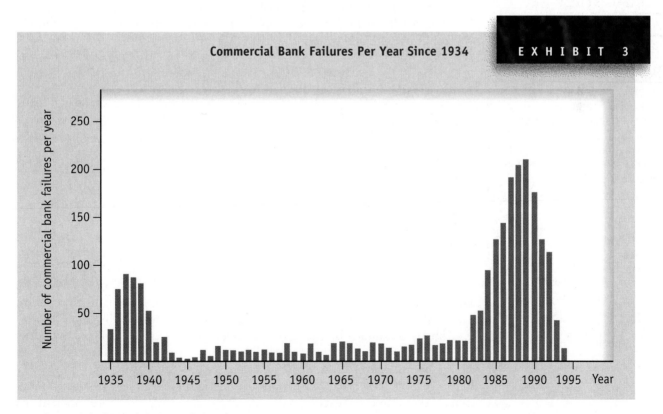

Commercial Bank Failures Per Year Since 1934

EXHIBIT 3

Source: Federal Deposit Insurance Corporation.

ures beginning in 1990. During the 1990s, bank profits also increased—to a record $44.5 billion in 1994,—so the industry has turned around.

CONCLUSION

Money has grown increasingly more abstract over time, moving from commodity money to paper money that represented a claim on some commodity such as gold, to paper money with no intrinsic value. As you will see, paper money reflects only a fraction of the money supply. Most modern money consists of little more than electronic entries in the banking system's computers. So, money has moved from a physical commodity to an electronic entry. Money today not so much changes hands as changes computer accounts.

Money and banking have been intertwined ever since the early goldsmiths offered to hold customers' valuables for safekeeping. Banking has since evolved from one of the most staid industries to one of the most competitive. Deregulation and branching innovations have made it easier to enter the industry and have increased the types of bank deposits. Reforms have given the Fed more uniform control over all depository institutions and have given the institutions greater access to the services provided by the Fed. Thus, all depository institutions can compete on more equal footing.

Deregulation provides greater freedom not only to prosper but also to fail. In the Darwinian world of deregulated banking, only the fittest will survive. Failures of depository institutions create a special problem, however, because these institutions provide the financial underpinning of the nation's money supply, as you will see in the next chapter. There we will examine more closely how banks operate and supply the nation's money.

SUMMARY

1. Barter was the first form of exchange. As specialization grew, it became more difficult to discover the double coincidence of wants required for barter. The time and inconvenience associated with barter led even simple economies to introduce money.

2. Anything that acquires a high degree of acceptability throughout an economy as a medium of exchange thereby becomes money. The first money was commodity money, where a good such as salt or gold also served as money. Eventually, what changed hands was a piece of paper that could be redeemed for something of value, such as gold. As paper money became widely accepted, governments eventually introduced fiat money, which is paper money that cannot be redeemed for anything other than more paper money. Fiat money is given its status as money by law. Most currencies throughout the world today are fiat money.

3. People accept fiat money because they believe others will do so as well. The value of money depends on how much it will buy. If money fails to serve as a medium of exchange, traders will resort to some second-best means of exchange, such as barter, a careful system of record-keeping, or some informal commodity money. When the monetary system breaks down, more time must be devoted to exchange, leaving less time for production, so the economy's efficiency suffers.

4. The Federal Reserve System was established in 1914 to stabilize the banking system. After many banks failed during the Great Depression, the Fed's powers were increased and centralized. Its control over all depository institutions was extended by legislation passed during the 1980s. The primary powers of the Fed are to (1) conduct open-market operations (buying and selling U.S. government securities to control the money supply), (2) establish and enforce reserve requirements for depository institutions, and (3) set the discount rate (the rate at which depository institutions can borrow from the Fed).

5. Regulations introduced during the Great Depression turned banking into a closely regulated and largely predictable industry. But high interest rates during the 1970s disturbed the quiet life of depository institutions. Reforms in the 1980s were designed to give depository institutions greater flexibility in competing with other kinds of financial intermediaries. Many thrifts used this flexibility to gamble on investments, but these gambles often failed, causing hundreds of thrifts to go bankrupt. In 1989, Congress approved a measure to close failing thrifts, pay off insured deposits, and regulate more closely the operations of remaining thrifts. Commercial banks also experienced record numbers of failures during the 1980s, but their problems were not as serious as those affecting the thrifts. By the mid-1990s, commercial banks were thriving once again.

QUESTIONS AND PROBLEMS

1. **(Barter)** Define a double coincidence of wants and explain its role in a barter system.

2. **(Commodity Money)** In medieval Japan rice was used for money. Why do you think this commodity was chosen to serve as money? What would happen to prices in general if there was a particularly good harvest one year?

3. **(Functions of Money)** "If an economy had only two goods (both *nondurable*), there would be no need for money because exchange would always be between those two goods." Does this statement disregard some important functions of money?

4. **(Gresham's Law)** Early in the history of the United States, tobacco was used as money. If you were a tobacco farmer and you had two loads of tobacco that were of different qualities, which would eventually be used for money and which for smoking? Under what conditions would both types of tobacco be used for money?

5. **(Types of Money)** Complete each of the following sentences:
   a. If the face value of a coin exceeds the cost of coinage, the resulting revenues to the issuer of the coin are known as _____.
   b. A product that serves both as money and as a commodity is _____ _____.
   c. Coins and paper money circulating in the United States have face values that exceed the value of the material from which they are made. Therefore, they are forms of _____ _____.
   d. If the government declares that creditors must accept a form of money as payment for debts, the money becomes _____ _____.
   e. A common unit for measuring the value of every good or service in the economy is known as a(n) _____ _____ _____.

6. **(Fiat Money)** Most economists believe that fiat money has value only to the extent that people believe it will retain its value. What does this statement mean? How could people lose faith in that money?

7. **(Savings and Loans)** In the early 1980s, the number of savings and loan institutions in the United States decreased drastically. Why? How did the government deal with the situation?

8. **(Depository Institutions)** Define depository institutions and list the various types found in the United States. How do they act as intermediaries between savers and borrowers? Why do they play this role?

9. **(Functions of Money)** What are the four important functions of money? Define each one.

10. **(Creation of Banking)** Discuss the various ways in which London goldsmiths functioned as early banks.

11. **(Money Versus Barter)** "Without money, everything would be more expensive." Explain this statement.

12. **(Money Versus Barter)** A barter system in which n goods are traded has $\{n(n-1)\}/2$ exchange rates, while a money system would have only n exchange rates. What number of exchange rates would be needed in a barter system and a money system for each of the following number of traded goods? What significance does this have for the transaction costs associated with trade?
   a. 100.
   b. 1,000.
   c. 10,000.

13. **(Money)** When monetary systems were based on monetary units whose values were determined by their gold content, new discoveries of gold were frequently followed by periods of inflation. Explain.

14. **(Banks and Interest Rates)** Banks and other financial intermediaries typically borrow short (e.g., accept short-maturity deposits) and lend long (e.g., offer thirty-year mortgages). Because long-term interest rates generally are higher than short-term rates, banks can "live off the spread." Why do you think that rising rates can create profit problems for banks?

15. **(Deregulation)** Some economists argue that deregulated deposit rates combined with deposit insurance have led to depository institution insolvencies. Why do you think they make such an argument?

16. **(Federal Reserve System)** What were the key reforms to the Federal Reserve System by President Roosevelt in the 1930s?

17. **(Goals of the Fed)** What is meant by *monetary policy?* What goals does the Fed try to achieve through monetary policy?

18. **(Branching Restriction)** As noted in the text, the United States is one of the few industrialized countries with restrictions on bank branching. These restrictions are applied both within states and across state lines. How have banks circumvented these restrictions?

19. **(Money)** Why is universal acceptability such an important characteristic of money? What other characteristics can you think of that might be important?

20. **(Federal Reserve System)** What powers were given to the Federal Reserve when it was first established? What types of banks were required to become members of the Fed? What types were not so required?

21. **(When the Monetary System Breaks Down)** In countries where the monetary system has broken down, to what various alternatives have the people resorted to maintain exchanges?

22. **(Easy Money, Empty Buildings)** The collapse of the commercial property market has had a decidedly regional flavor. The result has been a banking industry also characterized by regional failure. Do you think that branching restrictions could have contributed to the problem? What impact did the real estate collapse have on productivity?

Using the Internet

23. E-money, or electronic money, will change the way financial transactions occur in the future. Whether this change is for the better or worse is a matter of debate. Browse "E-Money (That's What I Want)," by Steven Levy, a fellow at the Freedom Forum Media Studies Center (originally published in *Wired!,* vol. 2, no. 12, 1994) (**http://www.hotwired.com/wired/2.12/features/emoney.html**) and "The Trouble with E-Cash," by David S. Bennahum (originally published in *Marketing Computers,* vol. 15, no. 4, April 1995) (**http://www.reach.com/matrix/troublewithecash.html**). Compare and contrast these positions. Who has the stronger argument? Why?

Banking and the Money Supply

14

In this chapter, we take a closer look at the role banks play in the economy. Why are we so interested in banks? After all, isn't banking a business like any other—dry cleaning, auto manufacturing, or home re-modeling? Why not devote the chapter to the home-remodeling business? Banks are special in macroeconomics because, like the London goldsmith, banks can convert a bor-rower's IOU into money, and money is a key ingredient in a healthy economy.

Since regulatory reforms have eliminated many of the distinctions between commercial banks and thrift institutions, and since thrifts represent a dwindling share of depository institutions, from here on, all depository institutions will usually be referred to more simply as *banks*. We first consider the role of banks in the economy and the types of deposits they hold. We then examine how banks work and show how the money supply expands through the creation of deposits. We also consider the operation of the Federal Reserve System in more detail. As we will see, the Federal Reserve, or the "Fed," attempts to control the growth of the money supply by controlling bank reserves. Topics discussed in this chapter include:

- Checkable deposits
- Monetary aggregates
- Balance sheets
- Money creation process
- Money multiplier

BANKS, THEIR DEPOSITS, AND THE MONEY SUPPLY

Banks attract their funds from savers and lend these funds to borrowers. Savers need a safe place for their money and borrowers need credit; banks try to earn a profit by serving both groups. To inspire depositor confidence, banks present an image of sober dignity—an image meant to foster assurance. For example, banks are more apt to be called First Trust, Security National, or Federal Savings than Benny's Bank, Easy Money Bank and Trust, or Last Chance Savings and Loan. In contrast, *finance companies* are financial intermediaries that do not get their funds from depositors, so they can choose names aimed more at borrowers—names such as Household Finance and The Money Store.

Banks Are Financial Intermediaries

By bringing together the two sides of the market, banks serve as financial intermediaries, or go-betweens. They gather various amounts from savers and package these funds into the amounts demanded by borrowers. Usually savers want to save relatively small amounts, while borrowers want to borrow relatively large amounts, so banks repackage the various small savings into larger amounts for borrowers. Banks also match up the preferred durations of savers with those of borrowers. Some savers need their money back next week, some next year, some only after retirement. Likewise, different borrowers want to borrow for different durations.

Coping with Asymmetric Information. Banks, as lenders, try to identify borrowers who are willing to pay interest and are able to repay the loans. But borrowers have more reliable information about their own credit history and financial plans than do lenders. Thus, in the market for loans there is **asymmetric information:** an inequality in the information known by each party to the transaction. This asymmetry would not create a problem if borrowers could be trusted to report relevant details to lenders. Some borrowers, however, have an incentive to suppress critical information, such as other debts, a troubled financial history, or plans to invest the borrowed funds in a risky venture. Because banks have experience and expertise in evaluating the creditworthiness of loan applicants, banks have a greater ability to cope with asymmetric information than would an individual saver. Moreover, because banks have experience in drawing up and enforcing contracts with borrowers, they can do so more cheaply than could an individual saver. Thus, savers are better off dealing with banks than making loans directly to the ultimate borrower. *The economy is more efficient because banks develop expertise in evaluating borrowers, structuring loans, and enforcing loan contracts.*

Asymmetric information Unequal information known by each party to a transaction

Reducing Risk through Diversification. By creating a diversified portfolio of assets rather than lending funds to a single borrower, banks reduce the risk to each individual saver. A bank lends a tiny fraction of each saver's deposits to each of its many borrowers. If one borrower fails to repay the loan, this failure will hardly affect a large, diversified bank. Certainly, such a default does not represent the personal disaster it would if one saver's entire nest egg had been loaned directly to that defaulting borrower.

Money and Liquidity

When a bank accepts a deposit, it promises to repay the depositor that amount. The deposit therefore is an amount the bank owes—it is a **liability** of the bank. When the bank lends these funds to a borrower, the borrower's promise to repay the loan is an amount owed to the bank—it is an **asset** of the bank.

Suppose you have some cash in your pocket. If you deposit this cash in a checking account, you can then write checks directing your bank to pay someone from your account. When you think of money, what most likely comes to mind is currency—dollar bills and coins. Indeed, dollar bills and coins are money, but money consists primarily of a particular class of bank liabilities—**checkable deposits,** or deposits against which checks can be written. Banks hold a variety of checkable deposits. The most important checkable deposits over the years have been *demand deposits,* which are held by commercial banks and do not earn interest. In recent years, financial institutions have developed other kinds of accounts that carry check-writing privileges but also earn interest, such as negotiable order of withdrawal (NOW) accounts.

Monetary aggregates are various measures of the money supply defined by the Federal Reserve. The most narrowly defined money supply is **M1,** which consists of currency (including coins) held by the nonbanking public, checkable deposits, and travelers checks. (Note that currency sitting in bank vaults is not included as part of the money supply, because it is not at the time being used as a medium of exchange.)

Currency has been declared legal tender by the federal government; this means that if currency is offered as payment, it must be accepted or the debt is canceled. Checkable deposits are the liabilities of the issuing banks, which stand ready to convert these deposits into currency. Checks are *not* legal tender, so sellers need not accept them, as signs that say "No Checks!" attest. Yet checks are so widely accepted as a medium of exchange that checkable deposits are counted as part of M1, the narrow definition of the money supply.

The primary currency circulating in the United States consists of Federal Reserve notes, which are issued by, and are liabilities of, the Federal Reserve banks. Federal Reserve notes are IOUs from the Fed to the bearer. Since Federal Reserve notes are redeemable for nothing other than more Federal Reserve notes, U.S. currency is *fiat money,* as we noted in Chapter 13. The other component of currency is coins, manufactured and distributed by the U.S. Mint. Our coins are token coins because their metal value is less—often much less—than their face value.

Liquidity describes the ease with which an asset can be converted into the medium of exchange without a significant loss of value. The most liquid asset is M1, which consists of (1) currency held by the nonbanking public, (2) checkable deposits, and (3) travelers checks, with currency being the most liquid of the three. In contrast, assets such as automobiles, real estate, and rare stamps rank low in liquidity. True, you could sell your automobile in minutes if you were willing to sell it for peanuts, but selling it for its market value would take time and involve some inconvenience.

Money consists primarily of checkable deposits, or deposits against which checks can be written. However, with many banks allowing depositors to easily shift funds from savings accounts to checking accounts by way of Automatic Teller Machines (ATMs), the strict definition of money becomes blurred.

Liability Anything that is owed to another individual or institution

Asset Anything of value that is owned

Checkable deposits Deposits in financial institutions against which checks can be written

Monetary aggregates Measures of the economy's money supply

M1 A measure of the money supply consisting of currency and coins held by the nonbank public, checkable deposits, and travelers checks

Liquidity A measure of the ease with which an asset can be converted into money without significant loss in its value

Other Deposits

We regard currency and checkable deposits as money because each serves as a medium of exchange; each is also a unit of account, a store of value, and a standard of deferred payment. Some other kinds of assets perform the store-of-value function and sometimes can be readily converted into currency or to checkable deposits. Because these financial assets are so close to money, under certain definitions we call them money.

Savings deposits Deposits that earn interest but have no specific maturity date

Savings deposits earn interest but have no specific maturity date. Banks often allow depositors to shift funds from savings accounts to checking accounts by simply making a phone call or pressing a few buttons on an automatic teller machine, so distinctions between the narrower and broader definitions of money have become blurred. **Time deposits** (also called *certificates of deposit,* or *CDs*) earn a fixed rate of interest if held for the specified period, which can range from several months to several years. Premature withdrawals are penalized by forfeiture of several months' interest. Neither savings deposits nor time deposits serve directly as a medium of exchange, so they are not included in M1, the narrowest definition of money.

Time deposits Deposits that earn a fixed rate of interest if held for the specified period, which can range anywhere from several months to several years

Money market mutual fund accounts, discussed in Chapter 13, represent another component of money, more broadly defined. Because of restrictions on the minimum balance, on the number of checks that can be written per month, and on the minimum amount of each check, these popular accounts are not viewed as money, based on the narrowest definition.

M2 A monetary aggregate consisting of M1 plus savings deposits, small time deposits, and money market mutual funds

Recall that M1 consists of currency (including coins) held by the nonbanking public, checkable deposits, and travelers checks. **M2** is a monetary aggre-

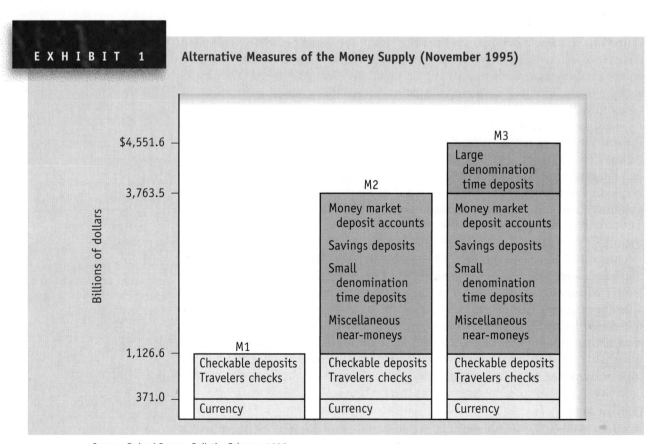

EXHIBIT 1   **Alternative Measures of the Money Supply (November 1995)**

Source: *Federal Reserve Bulletin,* February 1996.

gate that includes M1 as well as savings deposits, small-denomination time deposits, and money market mutual fund accounts. **M3** includes M2 plus large-denomination time deposits. In subsequent discussions, when we refer to the "money supply," we will usually be talking about M1, the narrow definition of money.

The size and relative importance of each monetary aggregate are presented in Exhibit 1. As you can see, M2 is more than three times as large as M1, and M3 is about four times as large. Thus, *the narrow definition of money describes only a fraction of broader aggregates.* And distinctions between M1 and M2 become less meaningful as banks allow depositors to transfer funds from one account to another.

You may be curious why the definitions of money did not include credit cards, such as VISA and MasterCard. After all, most sellers accept credit cards as readily as they accept cash or checks (some even prefer credit cards to checks). Shouldn't credit cards be included in any definition of money? Credit cards themselves are not money; they are simply a means of obtaining a short-term loan from the card issuer. If you use a credit card to purchase plane tickets from a travel agent, the transaction is not complete until the card issuer pays for the tickets. The credit card has not eliminated the use of money; it has merely postponed the travel agent's receipt of money.

HOW THE BANKING SYSTEM WORKS

Banks are profit-making institutions in the business of taking people's money on deposit, lending out a large portion of that money, and earning a profit on the difference between the interest paid on deposits and the interest received from loans. We could consider the operation of any type of depository institution (commercial bank, savings and loan, mutual savings bank, or credit union), but we will focus on commercial banks because they are the most important in terms of total assets. Moreover, the operating principles that apply to money creation in commercial banks generally apply to other depository institutions as well.

Starting a Bank

Let's begin with the formation of a bank. Suppose some business leaders in your hometown decide to form a commercial bank called Home Bank. To obtain a *charter,* or the right to operate, they must apply to the state banking authority, in the case of a state bank, or to the U.S. Comptroller of the Currency, in the case of a national bank. When the chartering agency reviews the application, it considers the quality of the bank's management, the amount of money the owners plan to invest, the need for an additional bank in the region, and the likely success of the bank.

Suppose the founders plan to invest $100,000 in the bank, and they so indicate on their application for a national charter. If their application is approved, they issue themselves shares of stock—certificates indicating ownership. Thus, they exchange $100,000 in cash for shares of stock in the bank. These shares are called the *owners' equity,* or the **net worth,** of the bank. Part of the $100,000, say $20,000, is used to buy shares in their district Federal Reserve bank. So Home Bank is now a member of the Federal Reserve System. With the remaining $80,000, the owners acquire and furnish the bank building.

EXHIBIT 2

Home Bank's Balance Sheet

Assets		Liabilities and Net Worth	
Building and furniture	$ 80,000	Net worth	$100,000
Stock in district Fed	20,000		
Total	$100,000	Total	$100,000

Balance sheet A financial statement that shows assets, liabilities, and net worth at a given point in time

To focus our discussion, we will examine the bank's **balance sheet,** presented in Exhibit 2. As the name implies, a balance sheet shows a balance between the two sides of the bank's accounts. The left-hand side lists the bank's assets. An asset is any physical property or financial claim owned by the bank. At this early stage, assets include the building and equipment owned by Home Bank plus its stock in the district Federal Reserve bank. The right-hand side lists the bank's liabilities and net worth. So far the right-hand side includes only the net worth of $100,000, an amount that also equals the bank's assets to this point. The two sides of the ledger must always be equal, or in *balance*—hence the name *balance sheet.* Since the two sides must be in balance, assets must equal liabilities plus net worth:

$$\text{Assets} = \text{Liabilities} + \text{Net worth}$$

The bank is now ready to open. Opening day is the bank's lucky day, because its first customer comes in with a briefcase full of $100 bills and puts $1,000,000 into a checking account. As a result of this deposit, the bank's assets increase by $1,000,000 in cash, and its liabilities increase by $1,000,000 in checkable deposits. Exhibit 3 shows the effects of this transaction on Home Bank's balance sheet. The customer has deposited $1,000,000 in the bank, so the bank owes the customer the amount deposited. On the right-hand side there are now two kinds of claims on the bank's assets: claims by the owners, called net worth, and claims by nonowners, called liabilities, which at this point consist of checkable deposits.

Reserve Accounts

Required reserve ratio The ratio of reserves to deposits that banks are required, by regulation, to hold

Where do we go from here? As was mentioned in Chapter 13, banks are required by the Fed to set aside, or to hold in reserve, a certain percentage of their deposits. The **required reserve ratio** dictates the minimum *proportion* of deposits the bank must hold in reserve. Suppose the required reserve ratio on

EXHIBIT 3

Home Bank's Balance Sheet After $1,000,000 Deposit

Assets		Liabilities and Net Worth	
Cash	$1,000,000	Checkable deposits	$1,000,000
Building and furniture	80,000	Net worth	100,000
Stock in district Fed	20,000		
Total	$1,100,000	Total	$1,100,000

checkable deposits is 10 percent. Home Bank must therefore hold in reserve 10 percent of its checkable deposits. The dollar amount that must be held in reserve is called **required reserves**—deposits multiplied by the required reserve ratio. All depository institutions are subject to the reserve requirements established by the Fed. Home Bank must therefore hold $100,000 as required reserves, which equals checkable deposits of $1,000,000 multiplied by 0.10. A bank must hold reserves either as cash in its vault or as deposits at the Fed, but neither earns the bank any interest income.

Required reserves The dollar amount of reserves a bank is legally required to hold

Suppose Home Bank opens a reserve account with the district Federal Reserve bank and deposits $100,000 in cash. Home Bank's reserves are now divided between $100,000 in required reserves on deposit with the Fed and $900,000 in **excess reserves** as cash in the vault. So far Home Bank has not earned a penny. Excess reserves, however, can be used to make loans or to purchase other interest-bearing assets, such as government securities.

Excess reserves Bank reserves in excess of required reserves

Liquidity Versus Profitability

Like the early goldsmiths, modern-day banks must be prepared to satisfy depositors' requests for funds. A bank loses reserves whenever a depositor demands cash or writes a check that gets deposited in another bank. The bank wants to be in a position to satisfy all depositor demands, even if many depositors ask for their money at the same time or even if many checks are written against its checkable deposits. A bank could fail if it lacked sufficient reserves to meet all depositor requests for funds. Required reserves are not meant to be used to meet depositor requests for funds, so banks often hold excess reserves or hold some assets that can be easily liquidated to satisfy any unexpected demand for funds. Banks may also want to have excess reserves on hand in case a valued customer needs an immediate loan.

The bank manager must therefore structure the portfolio of assets with an eye toward liquidity, but must not forget that the bank's survival also depends on profitability. *The two objectives of liquidity and profitability are at odds.* For example, the bank will generally find that the assets offering the highest interest rate tend to be less liquid than other assets of comparable risk. The most liquid asset is bank reserves, either in the bank's vault as cash or on account with the Fed, but reserves earn no interest. At one extreme, consider a bank that is completely liquid, holding all its assets as cash reserves. Such a bank would clearly have no difficulty meeting depositors' demands for funds. The bank is playing it safe—too safe. Since it holds no interest-earning assets, the bank will earn no income and will go bankrupt. At the other extreme, imagine a bank that uses all its excess reserves to acquire high-yielding but less liquid assets, such as long-term loans. Such a bank will run into liquidity problems whenever withdrawals exceed new deposits. The bank portfolio manager's task is to strike just the right balance between liquidity, or safety, and profitability. By law, the bank's choice of assets is limited primarily to loans and government securities.

Since reserves earn no interest, banks usually try to keep their excess reserves at a minimum. Banks continuously "sweep" their accounts to find excess reserves that can be put to some interest-bearing use. They do not let excess reserves remain idle even overnight. The **federal funds market** provides for day-to-day lending and borrowing among banks of excess reserves on account at the Fed. For example, suppose that at the end of the business day Home Bank has excess re-

Federal funds market A market for day-to-day lending and borrowing of reserves among financial institutions

EXHIBIT 4

Consolidated Balance Sheet of U.S. Commercial Banks as of November 29, 1995 (billions of dollars)

Assets		Liabilities and Net Worth	
Deposits with Fed	$ 24.0	Checkable deposits	$ 740.1
Cash	194.6	Savings deposits	761.3
Loans	2,586.7	Time deposits	916.6
U.S. government securities	716.3	Borrowings	652.2
Other securities	261.0	Other liabilities	660.8
Other assets	332.8	Net worth	384.4
Total	$4,115.4	Total	$4,115.4

Source: *Federal Reserve Bulletin,* February 1996.

serves of $50,000 on account at the Fed and is willing to loan that amount to another bank that finished the day with a reserve deficiency of $50,000. These two banks are brought together by a broker who specializes in the market for federal funds—that is, the market for excess reserves at the Fed. The interest rate paid on this loan is called the **federal funds rate,** which is determined by the supply and demand for federal funds.

Federal funds rate The interest rate prevailing in the federal funds market

To get some feel for the financial status of banks in the United States, consider the consolidated balance sheet for all U.S. commercial banks shown in Exhibit 4. Assets consist primarily of loans, with government securities second. On the liabilities side, bank deposits are sorted into three types: checkable deposits, savings deposits, and time deposits. Only checkable deposits have reserve requirements.

Before we discuss how Home Bank can create money, we must bring into the picture another important institution: the Federal Reserve. We will take a closer look at how the Fed operates, beginning with a simplified version of the Fed's balance sheet.

The Fed's Balance Sheet

In its capacity as a bankers' bank, the Fed clears checks for, extends loans to, and holds deposits of banks. In its capacity as banker to the federal government, the Fed holds deposits of the U.S. Treasury. The operation of Federal Reserve

EXHIBIT 5

Consolidated Balance Sheet of Federal Reserve Banks as of November 30, 1995 (billions of dollars)

Assets		Liabilities and Net Worth	
U.S. government securities	$380.8	Federal Reserve notes in circulation	$393.5
Discount loans to banks	0.2	Deposits of depository institutions	24.4
Coins	0.4	U.S. Treasury deposits	5.7
Other assets	59.2	Other liabilities	8.9
		Net worth	8.1
Total	$440.6	Total	$440.6

Source: *Federal Reserve Bulletin,* February 1996.

banks, like that of other banks, can be best studied by reviewing their balance sheet. Exhibit 5 presents a consolidated balance sheet for all Federal Reserve banks. Let's look at the Fed's assets. Note that *over three-fourths of the Federal Reserve's assets are U.S. government securities*. These securities are assets of the Fed because they are IOUs from the federal government. Another asset, though relatively tiny, is discount loans made by the Fed to banks. These loans are assets of the Fed because they are IOUs from the borrowing institutions.

Turning now to the other side of the balance sheet, we can see that *Federal Reserve notes in circulation account for over three-fourths of the Fed's liabilities*. Just as the goldsmiths issued notes, the Fed issues financial claims on itself. Bank deposits are another liability of the Fed, since these reserves can be requested by the banks at any time. These deposits facilitate the check-clearing process, which will be examined shortly. The deposits of the U.S. Treasury are also a liability of the Fed.

What the balance sheet does not reflect is the Fed's responsibility for the stability of financial markets. The Fed, through its regulation of financial markets, tries to prevent major disruptions and widespread panics. For example, during the stock market crash of 1987, Fed Chairman Alan Greenspan worked behind the scenes to ensure that banks had sufficient liquidity to calm the panic. In 1989, when a similar crash threatened, the Fed again stepped in to ensure the necessary liquidity.

The Fed is also an active trader in foreign exchange markets. Foreign currency operations are carried out by the New York Fed's foreign trading desk in cooperation with the U.S. Treasury. Some of the "other" Fed assets listed in Exhibit 5 are securities issued by foreign governments. For example, in order to influence foreign exchange rates, the Fed can sell German securities and receive marks in exchange. The marks can then be used to buy dollars from a U.S. bank. These transactions increase both the supply of marks and the demand for dollars, thereby affecting the exchange rate between the two currencies.

Two kinds of assets held by the Federal Reserve banks—U.S. securities and discount loans—earn interest for Reserve banks, whereas their two primary liabilities—Federal Reserve notes and reserves deposited by banks—require no interest payments by Reserve banks. *The Fed is therefore both literally and figuratively a money machine. It is literally a money machine because it provides the economy with Federal Reserve notes, and it is figuratively a money machine because its assets earn interest but its liabilities require no interest payment.* The Fed also earns revenue from various charges for bank services. After financing its operating cost, the Fed turns over any remaining income to the U.S. Treasury.

So the Fed supplies the nation's currency. The existence of paper money attracts counterfeiters. The following case study discusses recent trends in counterfeiting Federal Reserve notes.

Net Bookmark

The Federal Reserve Bank of New York is one of 12 regional Reserve Banks that, along with the Board of Governors in Washington, D.C., comprise the Federal Reserve System. Among other responsibilities, the New York Fed engages in currency market transactions on behalf of the U.S. monetary authorities and the customers of the Federal Reserve Bank of New York (foreign central banks and international agencies). The New York Fed also stores about $115 billion in monetary gold for about 60 foreign central banks, governments, and international agencies. Visit the Federal Reserve Bank of New York (http://www.ny.frb.org/welcome.html).

CASE STUDY

Tracking the Supernote

Until recently, U.S. currency had changed little—so little, in fact, that on the back of a $10 bill the car driving by the Treasury building is of Model T vintage. Since 1879, Crane & Company, of Dalton, Massachusetts, has been the exclusive supplier of U.S. currency paper. That paper is 75 percent cotton and 25 percent linen, with embedded red and blue fibers. In 1990, $100 and $50

Tracking the Supernote
continued

Location:

Where does our money come from? Visit the Bureau of Engraving and Printing (http:// www.ustreas.gov/treasury/ bureaus/bep/bep.html) for more information. What is the latest news about counterfeit protection and currency redesign? Visit "Our Money," a service of the Federal Reserve Bank of Minneapolis (http://woodrow. mpls.frb.fed.us/econed/ curric/money.htm). Test your knowledge with the online "Review Questions."

bills had two features added to make reproduction in copying machines more difficult: a translucent polymer thread embedded in the paper and microprinting around the portrait repeating the phrase THE UNITED STATES OF AMERICA. In 1993, these features were added to twenties, tens, and fives.

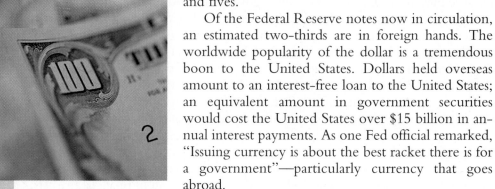

Of the Federal Reserve notes now in circulation, an estimated two-thirds are in foreign hands. The worldwide popularity of the dollar is a tremendous boon to the United States. Dollars held overseas amount to an interest-free loan to the United States; an equivalent amount in government securities would cost the United States over $15 billion in annual interest payments. As one Fed official remarked, "Issuing currency is about the best racket there is for a government"—particularly currency that goes abroad.

On U.S. soil, the Secret Service, by tracking suspicious purchases of paper and ink, has been able to seize 90 percent of counterfeit money before it gets into circulation. But foreign counterfeiting poses a problem for the Secret Service, which is primarily a domestic police force (only a small fraction of its 2,000 agents are stationed abroad). Of the counterfeit money seized in the United States in 1994, 72 percent was printed abroad. The volume of seizures outside the United States has been growing. For example, in Bogota, Colombia, counterfeiters print $100 and $20 bills on bleached paper from actual dollar bills. In 1995, the Canadian Mounties confiscated $112 million in fake $100 bills in Quebec.

By far the biggest threat to the integrity of U.S. currency is the so-called "supernote," which is a counterfeit $100 bill of extremely high quality that began showing up around 1990. It is reportedly printed in a Middle Eastern country unfriendly to the United States. It remains unclear whether this crime is motivated by profit alone or by a desire to destabilize U.S. currency around the world, a kind of economic terrorism. The supernote is a remarkable forgery, including sequential serial numbers and the polymer security thread that had taken Crane years to develop. The supernote can fool currency scanning machines at the nation's 12 Federal Reserve banks by perfectly emulating the magnetic field generated by ferrous oxide in the portrait's ink.

Supernotes are ubiquitous abroad, especially in Europe. Up to one-fifth of the $100 bills circulating in Russia in 1995 were believed to be supernotes. German banks reportedly would no longer accept $100 bills from Russian citizens. More generally, because of the supernote, merchants and bank tellers in Europe and the Far East have grown more reluctant to accept $100 bills.

In September 1995, the Secretary of the Treasury announced the first major redesign of U.S. currency since 1929. Production on a new $100 bill began in January 1996. The new bill remains the same size as before and is printed on the same Crane paper in the same green and black ink. Modifications to the $100 bill include a new off-center portrait of Franklin, a watermark, and a figure that shifts from green to black when viewed from different angles.

There are no plans to recall existing currency (the Treasury has a policy of never recalling existing currency for fear that the world's hoarders of dollars might switch to Deutsche marks or yen). Over time, preference for the new currency and the replacement of old bills as they pass through the Fed will eventually eliminate the old bills. Since the process could take years, there will be two types of currency in circulation for some time.

Sources: Frederic Dannen and Ira Silverman, "The Supernote," *The New Yorker,* 23 October 1995, pp. 50–55; and Michael Specter, "Forget the Ruble! Russians Obsessed with U.S. $100 Bill," *New York Times,* 4 November 1995.

Tracking the Supernot
continue

HOW BANKS CREATE MONEY

We are now in a position to examine how an individual bank and the banking system as a whole can create money. Our discussion will focus on the behavior of commercial banks because these are the largest and most important depository institutions, though thrifts can carry out similar activities.

Creating Money Through Excess Reserves

As we shall see, excess reserves are the raw material the banking system employs to support the creation of money. The Fed can influence the amount of excess reserves by (1) buying or selling U.S. government securities, (2) lending to banks through the "discount window," and (3) changing the required reserve ratio. By far the most important of these is buying or selling U.S. government securities, an activity called *open-market operations* because the Fed buys or sells these securities in the open market.

Assume there are no excess reserves in the banking system initially and that the reserve requirement on checkable deposits is 10 percent. To get our analysis rolling, suppose the Federal Reserve buys a $1,000 U.S. security from Home Bank. To pay for the security, the Fed simply increases Home Bank's reserve account with the Fed by $1,000. Where does the Fed get these reserves? It makes them up—creates them out of electronic ether, out of thin air! Home Bank has exchanged one asset, U.S. securities, for another asset, reserves on deposit with the Fed. So far the money supply has not changed, because neither U.S. securities nor Home Bank's reserves are part of the money supply. But the increase in excess reserves fuels an increase in the money supply.

The story, in brief, is this. A bank's lending is limited to the amount of its excess reserves. Suppose the bank extends a loan by increasing the borrower's checkable deposits. Since checkable deposits are money, the bank, by extending the loan, has created money. These borrowed funds eventually get spent and get deposited in a bank. That bank, after setting aside required reserves, can lend out a maximum of its excess reserves. Again the borrowed funds are spent and deposited in a bank, where they generate still more excess reserves. The money supply continues to expand in this fashion until no excess reserves are left in the banking system. Let's look at the credit creation process in greater detail in the following series of rounds.

Round One. After selling the $1,000 U.S. security to the Fed, Home Bank has $1,000 in excess reserves. Rather than sit on these reserves and earn no interest, Home Bank can make loans for the full amount of excess reserves. Suppose Home Bank is your regular bank and you apply for a $1,000 student loan. Home Bank approves your loan and consequently increases your checking ac-

| EXHIBIT 6 | Changes in Home Bank's Balance Sheet after Home Bank Lends You $1,000 |

Home Bank's Balance Sheet

Assets		Liabilities and Net Worth	
Loans	+ 1,000	Checkable deposits	+ 1,000

count by $1,000. *Home Bank has converted your promise to repay the loan, your IOU, into a $1,000 checkable deposit. Because checkable deposits are part of M1, this action increases the money supply by $1,000.* In the process, Home Bank's excess reserves have become required reserves. As shown in Exhibit 6, Home Bank's assets increase by $1,000, as do its liabilities. On the asset side, loans increase by $1,000 because your IOU becomes an asset to the bank. On the liability side, checkable deposits increase by $1,000 because Home Bank has increased your account by that amount. Home Bank has created money based on your promise to repay the loan.

Round Two. When you write a $1,000 check for tuition, your college promptly deposits this check in its checking account at College Bank. College Bank then increases the college's account by $1,000 and presents your check to the Fed. The Fed reduces Home Bank's reserve account by $1,000 and increases College Bank's reserve account by the same amount. The Fed then sends the check to Home Bank, which reduces your checkable deposits by $1,000. The Fed has "cleared" your check by settling the claim that College Bank had on Home Bank. So far, the $1,000 in checkable deposits has simply shifted from Home Bank to College Bank. Home Bank, by selling U.S. securities to the Fed, then lending you $1,000, has exchanged one asset, U.S. securities, for another asset, your IOU. In the process, the money supply has increased by $1,000, for College Bank's reserves and checkable deposits are now up by $1,000, and checkable deposits are money.

So College Bank has $1,000 more in reserves on deposit with the Fed. After setting aside $100, or 10 percent of your college's increase in deposits, as required reserves, College Bank has $900 in excess reserves. College Bank can thus make loans or purchase some other interest-bearing asset. Suppose the bank lends $900 to an enterprising business student who plans to open an all-night bait-and-bagel shop to lure early morning anglers on their way to a nearby fishing spot. College Bank extends the loan by providing this student

| EXHIBIT 7 | Changes in College Bank's Balance Sheet After the Bank Makes a $900 Loan |

Assets		Liabilities and Net Worth	
Loans	+ 900	Checkable deposits	+ 900

with a checking account balance of $900. As shown in Exhibit 7, College Bank's assets are up by the $900 loan, and its liabilities are up by the $900 increase in checkable deposits extended as a loan to the business student. *College Bank has converted the student's promise to repay the loan into money.*

Suppose the student writes a $900 check for equipment at a hardware store, which deposits the check into an account at Merchants Trust. Merchants Trust increases the hardware store's checkable deposits by $900 and sends the check to the Fed, which increases Merchants Trust's reserves by $900 and decreases College Bank's reserves by the same amount. The Fed then sends the check to College Bank, which reduces the borrower's checkable deposit account by $900.

So deposits at the Fed and checkable deposits are down by $900 at College Bank and up by that amount at Merchants Trust. Checkable deposits in the banking system at this point are $1,900 over what they were before we started: your college still has $1,000 more in checkable deposits at College Bank because you paid tuition, and the hardware store has $900 more in its account at Merchants Trust because of the enterprising student's equipment purchase.

Round Three and Beyond. Merchants Trust holds $90 of the $900 deposited as required reserves, which leaves $810 in excess reserves. Suppose $810 is loaned to an unscrupulous English major who is starting a new venture called "Term Papers 'R' Us." The English major hopes to sell research to students who have more money than brains. Exhibit 8 shows that Merchants Trust's assets are up by $810 in loans, and its liabilities are up by the same amount in checkable deposits.

The loan of $810 is spent at the college bookstore for a complete set of *Cliffs Notes*. The bookstore then deposits the check in its account at Fidelity Bank. Fidelity Bank credits the bookstore's checkable deposits with $810 and sends the check to the Fed for clearance. The Fed reduces Merchants Trust's reserves by $810 and increases Fidelity Bank's by the same amount. The Fed then sends the check to Merchants Trust, which reduces the English major's checkable deposits by $810. So deposits at the Fed and checkable deposits are down by $810 at Merchants Trust and up by the same amount at Fidelity Bank.

At this point checkable deposits in the banking system, and the money supply in the economy, are up by $2,710: your college's $1,000 checkable deposit at College Bank, plus the hardware store's $900 checkable deposit at Merchants Trust, plus the bookstore's $810 checkable deposit at Fidelity Bank. We could continue the credit expansion process with Fidelity Bank, which sets aside $81 in required reserves and uses the $729 in excess reserves as a basis for additional loans, but by now you get the idea.

Notice the pattern of deposits and loans emerging from the analysis. Each time a bank receives a new deposit, 10 percent is set aside to satisfy the reserve

Changes in Merchants Trust's Balance Sheet After an $810 Loan to English Major		EXHIBIT 8

Assets		Liabilities and Net Worth	
Loans	+ 810	Checkable deposits	+ 810

requirement. The rest becomes excess reserves, which can be left idle or can serve as a basis to extend loans or purchase government securities. In our example, excess reserves support loans that were then spent by the borrower. This spending became another bank's checkable deposits, thereby generating excess reserves to support still more loans. Thus, the excess reserves created initially by the Federal Reserve's purchase of U.S. securities were passed from one bank to the next in the chain. Each bank set aside 10 percent of new deposits as required reserves, then used the remaining 90 percent to support additional lending.

An individual bank in a banking system can lend no more than its excess reserves, because borrowers usually spend the amount borrowed. When a check clears, reserves at one bank usually fall but reserves in the banking system do not. A check drawn against one account will typically be deposited in another account—if not in the same bank, then in another. Thus, when a bank makes a loan and creates checkable deposits, the excess reserves on which that loan was based usually find their way back into the banking system. The recipient bank uses the new deposit to extend more loans and create more checkable deposits. The potential expansion of checkable deposits in the banking system therefore equals some multiple of the initial increase in excess reserves. Our example assumes that banks do not allow excess reserves to sit idle and that the public does not choose to hold some of the newly created money as cash.

Summary of Rounds

To review: *The initial and most important step in the process described in the preceding section is the Fed's injection of $1,000 in new reserves into the banking system.* In our example, this resulted from the Fed's $1,000 purchase of U.S. securities, but Home Bank's excess reserves would also increase if it borrowed $1,000 in the form of a discount loan from the Fed, or if the Fed freed up $1,000 in excess reserves by lowering the reserve requirement.

Home Bank uses this $1,000 in excess reserves to support its loan to you. You pay your tuition bill, and your college deposits the check in its bank. This deposit precipitates a series of rounds that expand the money supply. These rounds are summarized in Exhibit 9, where the banks are listed along the left-hand margin. Column (1) lists the increase in checkable deposits at each bank, column (2) lists the increase in required reserves resulting from the increase in checkable deposits, and column (3) lists the increase in loans each bank extends as a result of the increase in excess reserves. As you can see, the change in loans equals the change in checkable deposits minus the change in required reserves. Each bank loans out an amount equal to its excess reserves.

The increase in College Bank's checkable deposits is the change in the money supply arising from the first round. This $1,000 deposit translates into $100 in required reserves, leaving $900 in new loans. The $900 lent by College Bank ends up as checkable deposits in Merchants Trust, which sets aside $90 in required reserves and lends the balance of $810. The loan is spent and is deposited in an account at Fidelity Bank, which sets aside $81 as reserves and lends the balance. Theoretically, the process will continue until there are no more excess reserves in the system to serve as a basis for additional loans.

The banking system increases the money supply by a multiple of new reserves. Since people borrow money not to hold idle checkable deposits but to spend the borrowed funds, banks must have enough excess reserves to back up

Bank	Increase in Checkable Deposits (1)	Increase in Required Reserves (2)	Increase in Loans (3) = (1) − (2)
1. College Bank	$ 1,000	$ 100	$ 900
2. Merchants Trust	900	90	810
3. Fidelity Bank	810	81	729
All remaining rounds	7,290	729	6,561
Totals	$10,000	$1,000	$9,000

EXHIBIT 9

Summary of the Credit Expansion Process Resulting from the Fed's Purchase of $1,000 in U.S. Securities from Home Bank

their loans. Money expansion stops when the new reserves introduced into the banking system have been converted into required reserves. In our example, $1,000 in new reserves was introduced when the Fed purchased U.S. securities from Home Bank. The money expansion process stops when the increase in required reserves resulting from money expansion totals $1,000. Because the entire process begins with the Fed creating $1,000 in reserves, the Fed can rightfully claim that "The buck starts here," which is a slogan on New York Fed T-shirts.

For a change of pace, consider in the following case study some new developments in banking sparked by the revolution in personal computers and the Internet.

CASE STUDY

Banking on the Net

The Security First Network Bank (SFNB) never closes. It's open 24 hours a day, 365 days a year. Bank customers can pay bills, check account balances, and buy financial services from anywhere in the world—anywhere there is a personal computer and Internet access. SFNB is the nation's first "virtual" bank authorized by regulators to offer full banking services on the Internet. Accounts are insured by the Federal Deposit Insurance Corporation. Those opening a new account get a "virtual" toaster (actually, a screen saver). The bank can accept deposits from customers in all 50 states. Deposits are accepted through the mail or from wire transfers. Depositors can also use ATM cards to carry out transactions or get cash at thousands of cash machines.

Many more banking connections are in the works. As of 1995, around 40 banks worldwide had signed partnerships with software companies to develop Internet services. Some banks, such as Wells Fargo, have joined with retailers to create "virtual shopping malls," where customers can use credit cards to buy a variety of products. Also, bank customers are increasingly using software like Microsoft's *Money* (with over 1 million users) and Intuit's *Quicken* (with over 7 million users) as software interfaces to shop nationwide, even worldwide, for the best rates for deposits, credit cards, or loans. So a customer in St. Louis can get a housing

Location:

To explore banking on the Internet, visit First Security National Bank (**http://www.sfnb.com/**) or Wells Fargo's "On-Line Banking" (**http://www.wellsfargo.com/**). For more about banking software, such as Microsoft's *Money* and Intuit's *Quicken*, browse the "Microsoft Product Catalog" (**http://www.microsoft.com/Catalog/**) and the "Quicken Financial Network" (**http://www.intuit.com/**). To learn more about security on the Internet, visit "World Wide Web Security," maintained by Rutgers University Network Services (**http://www-ns.rutgers.edu/www-security/index.html**).

Banking on the Net
continued

mortgage in Atlanta, a car loan in Phoenix, a credit card in Boston, and a checking account in Chicago.

The Internet could become the biggest market in history, and banks want to become part of the picture. The Net already has hundreds of thousands of shops, all no more than a few keystrokes away. By the end of 1995, there were 40 million people on the Internet, with the total rising by an estimated 10 percent per month (U.S. consumers now buy more computers than televisions).

One limit to commerce over the Internet is security. The Internet has been likened to the high seas of old, vital to trade but owned by no one. Today's pirates are the hackers that try to crack communications codes. For example, in 1995, Netscape introduced what the company thought was a secure standard for Internet commerce. But two graduate students from Berkeley showed how to crack it in less than a minute.

Security problems will eventually be resolved. Over the long run, the Internet offers convenience for customers and potential cost savings for banks. Like telephone banking, which now accounts for one-fourth of bank transactions, on-line banking reduces the need for branches and branch personnel. Citibank, for example, has tried to encourage on-line use by eliminating fees for those who bank via computer. On-line banking seems to be here to stay. By 2005, three-quarters of U.S. households are expected to be doing some form of home banking.

Sources: Timothy O'Brien, "On-Line Banking Has Bankers Fretting PCs May Replace Branches," *The Wall Street Journal,* 25 October 1995; Steven Levy, "The End of Money?" *Newsweek,* 30 October 1995; and "Surf's Up for New-Wave Bankers," *The Economist,* 7 October 1995.

Another Possibility

Suppose that instead of buying the $1,000 worth of U.S. securities from Home Bank, the Fed buys them from a securities dealer and pays by issuing $1,000 in Federal Reserve notes. The Fed has increased the money supply by $1,000 by exchanging Federal Reserve notes, which become part of the money supply when in the hands of the public, for U.S. securities, which are not part of the money supply. Once the securities dealer puts this cash into a checkable deposit—or spends the cash, so the money ends up in someone else's checkable deposit—the banking system's money expansion process will be off and running.

Since the Fed is the only bank with the authority to print money, it is the only bank not constrained by reserve requirements. Indeed, the expressions "required reserves" and "excess reserves" do not apply to the Fed. The Fed can issue however much money the economy needs.

Excess Reserves, Reserve Requirements, and Money Expansion

One way the banking system as a whole eliminates excess reserves is by expanding the money supply. With a 10 percent reserve requirement, an initial injection of $1,000 in new reserves by the Fed could support, at most, $10,000 in new checkable deposits in the banking system as a whole, *assuming no bank holds excess reserves and nobody withdraws cash.* We can think of the $1,000 injection as the source of the $1,000 in reserves required to support the expansion of $10,000 in new checkable deposits.

The multiple by which the money supply increases as a result of an increase in the banking system's excess reserves is called the **money multiplier.** The **simple money multiplier** equals the reciprocal of the required reserve ratio, or $1/r$, where r is the reserve ratio. In our example the reserve ratio was 10 percent, or 0.10, so the reciprocal is $1/0.10$, which equals 10. The formula for the multiple expansion of checkable deposits can be written as

$$\text{Change in checkable deposits} = \text{Change in excess reserves} \times 1/r$$

The simple multiplier assumes that banks hold no excess reserves and the public withdraws no cash. The higher the reserve requirement, the more must be held as reserves, so the less that is available in excess reserves, and the smaller the money multiplier. If the reserve requirement were 20 percent instead of 10 percent, each bank would have to set aside twice as much for required reserves. The simple money multiplier in this case would be $1/0.20 = 5$, and the maximum possible increase in checkable deposits resulting from an initial $1,000 increase in excess reserves would therefore be $1,000 \times 5 = \$5,000$. Deposits in the banking system could be expanded by only half as much as when the reserve requirement was 10 percent. *Excess reserves fuel the deposit expansion process, and a higher reserve requirement drains this fuel from the banking system, thereby reducing the amount of new money that can be created.*

On the other hand, with a reserve requirement of only 5 percent, banks need to set aside less for required reserves and would consequently be able to make more loans because they would have greater excess reserves. The simple money multiplier in that case would be $1/0.05 = 20$. With $1,000 in new reserves and a 5 percent reserve requirement, the banking system could increase the money supply by a maximum of $1,000 \times 20 = \$20,000$.

In summary, money creation begins with an injection of new reserves into the banking system by the Fed. An individual bank loans an amount no greater than its excess reserves. The proceeds of this loan are spent and redeposited in the banking system, where the reserves thereby created serve as a basis for additional loans. An increase in bank reserves gives rise to a multiple expansion of checkable deposits, and checkable deposits are money. *The fractional reserve requirement is the key to the multiple expansion of checkable deposits in the banking system.* If each deposit had to be backed by 100 percent reserves, each $1 injected into reserves could create at most a $1 expansion of the money supply; the Fed, by purchasing securities or reducing the discount rate, could still help create excess reserves to expand the money supply, but that expansion would not exceed the initial excess reserves.

Now that we have been through the entire money expansion process, we can return to the beginning and consider what would happen if Home Bank, instead of extending loans, used its excess reserves to purchase U.S. securities. If Home Bank purchased U.S. securities from the public, at least some of the payment would eventually get deposited in a bank, and these new deposits would fuel the money creation process. For the money multiplier to operate, the bank need not use excess reserves in a specific way; the bank could use them to pay all its employees a Christmas bonus, for that matter. *As long as the bank's*

Money multiplier *The multiple by which the money supply increases as a result of an increase in excess reserves in the banking system*

Simple money multiplier *The reciprocal of the required reserve ratio, or $1/r$*

M_p

excess reserves serve as a basis for some action (other than to simply buy government securities from the Fed), these excess reserves can fuel an expansion of the money supply.

Limitations on Money Expansion

Various leakages from the multiple expansion process tend to reduce the size of the money multiplier, which is why 1/r is called the *simple* money multiplier. Let's consider leakages into cash and into excess reserves. Our example assumed that people do not choose to hold cash. *To the extent that people prefer to hold cash, the actual money multiplier is less than the simple money multiplier because cash withdrawals reduce reserves in the banking system.* With a reduction in reserves, banks have less ability to extend loans or buy securities. Likewise, if banks chose to do nothing with excess reserves, these reserves would not fuel expansion of the money supply.

Multiple Contraction of Money

We have already outlined the mechanics of the banking system, so the story of how the Federal Reserve System can reduce bank reserves, thereby reducing banks' ability to increase loans, can be a brief one. Again, we begin with no excess reserves and a reserve requirement of 10 percent. Suppose that rather than buy U.S. securities, the Fed *sells* Home Bank $1,000 worth of U.S. securities. Home Bank buys U.S. securities because they pay interest and are considered among the safest of investments. Home Bank pays with a check written against its reserve account at the district Federal Reserve bank. The Fed therefore reduces Home Bank's reserve account by $1,000. So Home Bank's deposits with the Fed are down by $1,000, and its securities are up by that amount.

Since Home Bank had no excess reserves at the outset, something has to give. To replenish reserves, Home Bank must recall loans (ask for repayment before the due date), sell some other asset, or borrow additional reserves. Suppose the bank calls in loans amounting to $1,000, and those who repay the loans do so with checks written against College Bank. When the checks clear, Home Bank's reserves are up by $1,000, just enough to satisfy its reserve requirement, but College Bank's reserves are down by $1,000. Since we assumed that there were no excess reserves at the outset, the loss of $1,000 in reserves leaves College Bank short of its required level of reserves. Specifically, in keeping with the legal reserve requirement, College Bank had $100 in required reserves supporting the $1,000 checkable deposits, so its reserves are now $900 below the required level. College Bank must therefore recall $900 in loans or otherwise try to replenish the $900 in required reserves.

And so it goes down the line. The Federal Reserve's sale of U.S. securities reduces bank reserves, forcing banks to recall loans or to replenish reserves somehow. *The maximum possible effect is to reduce the money supply by the amount of the original reduction in bank reserves times the simple money multiplier, which again equals 1 divided by the reserve requirement, or 1/r.* In our example, the Fed's sale of $1,000 in U.S. securities to Home Bank could conceivably reduce the money supply by as much as $10,000.

Change in the Discount Rate

The focus thus far has been on open-market operations, because this activity represents the primary tool of monetary policy. But there are other tools. The discount rate is the interest rate the Fed charges on loans to banks. The Fed can decrease or increase the discount rate as a way to encourage or discourage borrowing from the Fed. When the Fed decreases the discount rate, other things constant, borrowing from the Fed becomes cheaper, so the quantity of discount loans demanded increases. As borrowing increases, excess reserves in the banking system increase. These excess reserves serve as fuel for an expansion of the money supply. Thus, *a lower discount rate tends to expand the money supply.*

On the other hand, an increase in the discount rate makes borrowing from the Fed less attractive, so the quantity of discount loans demanded decreases. As loans decrease, reserves in the banking system decrease. As reserves decrease, so do excess reserves, reducing the banking system's ability to expand the money supply. Thus, *a higher discount rate tends to decrease the money supply.*

Federal law requires the Fed "to promote effectively the goals of maximum employment, stable prices, and moderate long-term interest rates." The law leaves it up to the Fed how best to pursue these goals. The Fed does not rely on congressional appropriations, so Congress cannot attempt to influence the Fed by withholding funds. In fact, the Fed makes a "profit" of about $20 billion a year, which it turns over to the U.S. Treasury. Thus, although the U.S. president appoints members of the Board of Governors, and these appointments must be approved by the Senate, the Fed operates with some independence from the president and Congress.

CONCLUSION

Banks play a unique role in the economy because they can transform someone's IOU into a checkable deposit, and a checkable deposit is money. The banking system's ability to expand the money supply depends on the amount of excess reserves in the banking system. Note the control that the Fed exerts over the money creation process. Through open-market operations, the Fed can vary the supply of new reserves by buying or selling U.S. securities. In our example, it was the purchase of $1,000 worth of U.S. securities that started the ball rolling. The Fed can also increase reserves by lowering the discount rate enough to stimulate bank borrowing from the Fed (though the Fed uses changes in the discount rate more as a signal of its policy goals than as a means of altering the money supply). And by reducing the required reserve ratio, the Fed can not only create excess reserves in the banking system but also increase the money multiplier. In practice, the Fed rarely changes the reserve requirement because of the disruptive effect of such a change on the banking system. *To control the money supply, the Fed relies primarily on open-market operations.* In the next chapter, we will consider the effects of the money supply on the economy.

SUMMARY

1. Banks are unlike other businesses in that they can turn a borrower's IOU into money—they can create money. Banks match the different desires of savers and borrowers. Banks also evaluate loan applications and diversify portfolios of assets to reduce the risk to any one saver.

2. The money supply is most narrowly defined as M1, which consists of currency held by the nonbanking public plus checkable deposits and travelers checks. Broader monetary aggregates include other kinds of deposits. M2 includes M1 plus savings deposits, small time deposits,

and money market mutual funds. M3 includes M2 plus large time deposits.

3. In acquiring portfolios of assets, banks attempt to maximize profits while simultaneously maintaining enough liquidity to satisfy depositors' demands for funds.

4. Any single bank can expand the money supply by the amount of its excess reserves. For the banking system as a whole, the maximum expansion of the money supply equals a multiple of excess reserves. The simple money multiplier equals the reciprocal of the reserve ratio. The money multiplier is reduced to the extent that banks

choose to hold some excess reserves as idle cash balances or the public wishes to withdraw cash from the banking system.

5. The key to changes in the money supply is the effect of the Fed's actions on excess reserves in the banking system. To increase the money supply, the Fed can buy U.S. government securities, reduce the discount rate, or lower the reserve requirement. To reduce the money supply, the Fed can sell U.S. government securities, increase the discount rate, or increase the reserve requirement. By far, the most important monetary tool for the Fed is open-market operations—buying or selling U.S. securities.

QUESTIONS AND PROBLEMS

1. **(Financial Intermediation)** In acting as financial intermediaries, what are the various needs or desires of savers and borrowers that banks must consider?

2. **(Types of Money)** Coca-Cola is a good substitute for Pepsi. Coffee is probably a poor substitute. How can the same principle be applied to the various types of money? Are a hundred pennies a perfect substitute for a dollar bill?

3. **(Bank Balance Sheets)** Show how each of the following *initially* affects bank assets, liabilities, and reserves. Do *not* include the results of bank behavior resulting from the Fed's action. Assume a required reserve ratio of 0.05.
   a. The Fed purchases $10 million worth of securities from banks.
   b. The Fed loans the banking system $5 million.
   c. The required reserve ratio is raised to 0.10.

4. **(Monetary Aggregates)** Indicate whether each of the following is included in any of the M1, M2, and/or M3 measures of the money supply:
   a. Currency held by the nonbanking public.
   b. Available credit on credit cards held by the nonbanking public.
   c. Savings deposits.
   d. Large-denomination time deposits.
   e. Money market mutual fund accounts.

5. **(Bank Reserves)** Explain why a reduction in the required reserve ratio cannot increase total reserves in the banking system. Is the same true of lowering the discount rate? What would happen if the Fed bought securities from or sold securities to the banking system?

6. **(Monetary Aggregates)** Calculate M1, M2, and M3 from the following information:

Large-denomination time deposits	$304 billion
Currency and coin held by nonbanking public $438 billion	
Checkable deposits $509 billion	
Small-denomination time deposits	$198 billion
Travelers checks $18 billion	
Savings deposits $326 billion	
Money market mutual fund accounts $637 billion	

7. **(Monetary Aggregates)** Suppose that $1,000 is moved from a savings account at a commercial bank to a checking account at the same bank. Which of the following statements will be true and which will be false?
   a. The level of currency will initially fall.
   b. The level of M1 will initially rise.
   c. The level of M2 will initially rise.

8. **(Creating Money)** Often it is claimed that banks create money by making loans. How can private banks create money? Isn't the government the only institution that can legally create money?

9. **(Bank Deposits)** Explain the differences among checkable deposits, demand deposits, savings deposits, and time deposits. Do they represent bank assets or bank liabilities?

10. **(Money Multiplier)** Suppose that the Federal Reserve lowers the required reserve ratio from 0.10 to 0.05. How will this affect the money multiplier, assuming that excess reserves are held to zero and there are no currency leakages? What are the money multipliers for required reserve ratios of 0.15 and 0.20?

11. **(Bank Balance Sheet)** Show how each of the following initially would affect a bank's assets and liabilities.

a.   Someone makes a $10,000 deposit.

b.   The bank makes a loan of $1,000 by establishing a checking account for $1,000.

c.   The loan gets spent.

d.   The bank has to write off a loan because the borrower defaults.

12. **(Bank Management)** Explain why a bank's manager must strike a balance between liquidity and profitability on the bank's balance sheet.

13. **(Money Creation)** Suppose Bank A, which faces a reserve requirement of 10 percent, receives a $1,000 currency deposit from its customer.

a.   Assuming it wishes to hold no excess reserves, determine how much the bank should lend. Show your answer on Bank A's balance sheet.

b.   Assuming that the loan shown in Bank A's balance sheet is redeposited in Bank B, show the changes in Bank B's balance sheet as it lends out the maximum possible.

c.   Repeat this process for Banks C, D, and E.

d.   Using the simple money multiplier, calculate the total change in the money supply resulting from the $1,000 initial deposit.

e.   Assume Banks A, B, C, D, and E each wished to hold 5 percent excess reserves. How would holding this level of excess reserves affect the total change in the money supply?

14. **(Federal Funds Market)** What is the federal funds market? How does it help banks strike a balance between liquidity and profitability?

15. **(Discount Rate)** Distinguish between the federal funds rate and the discount rate. What is the impact of raising the discount rate on the money supply?

16. **(Money Expansion and Contraction)** Assume that the banking system has total reserves of $225 billion, there are no excess reserves, and the required reserve ratio is 0.20. What is the initial size of the money supply?

What is the maximum change to the money supply if the Fed sells $10 billion in government securities on the open market? What is the maximum change to the money supply if the Fed buys $15 billion in government securities on the open market? What is the maximum change to the money supply if the Fed lowers the discount rate to 0.15 while total reserves remain at $225 billion?

17. **(Fed Balance Sheet)** Exhibit 5 shows the Fed's balance sheet. According to the balance sheet, what are the Fed's sources of income? Which source is most important?

18. **(Reserve Accounts)** Suppose that a bank's customer deposits currency equal to $4,000 in his or her checking account. The required reserve ratio is 0.25. If the bank wishes to hold no excess reserves, what will reserves on this new deposit equal? What does the maximum loan that the bank can make on the basis of the new deposit equal? If the bank chooses to hold reserves of $3,000 on the new deposit, what is the level of excess reserves on the deposit?

19. **(Tracking the Supernote)** Why did the U.S. government consider it important to redesign the $100 bill in order to combat the effects of the "supernote"?

20. **(Banking on the Net)** What impact is increased banking on the Internet likely to have on money to function as a medium of exchange?

Using the Internet

21. Banking systems are specific to each country. The rules governing bank formation, operation, and regulation in the United States, for instance, greatly differ from those in Switzerland. Visit "Swiss Banking," a service of JML Swiss Investment Counsellors (**http://www.jml.ch/jml/banking.html**), and "Frequently Asked Questions about Swiss Banks," maintained by SW Consulting SA (**http://www.swconsult.ch/chbanks/**). List three major differences between the Swiss and the U.S. banking system.

15

Monetary Theory and Policy

Thus far we have focused on how the banking system creates money. We showed that the Federal Reserve can influence the supply of money mainly through its control over excess reserves. How does the supply of money in the economy affect your chances of finding a job, your ability to finance a new car, the interest rate you pay on credit cards, or the ease of securing a student loan and the interest on that loan? The supply of money in the economy affects you in a variety of ways, but to understand those effects we must dig a little deeper.

The Fed's role in supplying money to the economy is called monetary policy. The study of the effect of money on the economy is called monetary theory. A central concern of monetary theory is the effect of the quantity of money on the economy's price level and on the level of output. What have economic theory and the historical record taught us about the relationship between the quantity of money in the economy and other macroeconomic variables?

Until now, we have not emphasized differences among competing theories of how the economy works. Traditionally, economists have maintained that there are two channels through which a change in the money supply may affect aggregate demand: an indirect channel, working through changes in the interest rate, and a direct channel. There was a time when the major debate among macroeconomists involved the relative importance of each channel. One group of economists believed the indirect channel was more important and the other group believed the direct channel was more important. Most economists now find some validity with each channel.

In this chapter, we consider the theory behind each channel. Note that although these two theories are different, they are not mutually exclusive. Each traces a different path between changes in the money supply and changes in aggregate demand, and both paths could operate at the same time. Topics discussed in this chapter include:

- Demand and supply of money
- Indirect channel to aggregate demand
- Direct channel to aggregate demand
- Equation of exchange
- Velocity of money
- Monetary targets

MONEY AND THE ECONOMY: THE INDIRECT CHANNEL

Let's review the important distinction between the stock, *money,* and the flow, *income.* How much money do you have with you right now? That amount is a *stock.* Income, in contrast, is a *flow,* indicating how much money you receive per period of time. Income has little meaning unless the time period is specified. You would not know whether to be impressed that a friend earned $100 unless you knew whether this was earnings per week, per day, or per hour.

The demand for money is a relationship between how much money people desire to hold and the interest rate. It may seem odd at first to be talking about the demand for money. You might think people would demand all the money they could get their hands on. But remember that money, the stock, is not the same as income, the flow. People express their demand for income by selling their labor and other resources. People express their demand for money by holding some of their wealth as money rather than holding some other assets that would earn a higher rate of return. But we are getting ahead of ourselves. The question we want to ask initially is why people demand money. Why do people maintain checking accounts and have cash in their pockets, purses, wallets, desk drawers, coffee cans, and wherever? The most obvious reason people demand money is because it is a convenient medium of exchange. *People demand money to carry out transactions.*

The Demand for Money

Because barter represents an insignificant portion of exchange in the modern industrial economy, households, firms, governments, and foreigners need money to conduct their daily transactions. Consumers need money to buy products, and firms need money to buy resources. *Money allows people to carry out their economic transactions more easily.* When credit cards are involved, the payment of money is delayed briefly, but all accounts must eventually be settled with money.

The demand for money needed to support exchange is called the **transactions demand for money.** The greater the value of transactions to be financed in a given period, the greater the quantity of money demanded for transactions. So the more active the economy is—that is, the greater the volume of exchange as reflected by the level of real output—the greater the transactions demand for money. Also, the higher the price level, the greater the transactions demand for money. The more things cost on average, the more money is required to purchase them.

Your transactions demand for money supports both expenditures you expect in the course of your normal economic affairs plus various unexpected expenditures. If you plan to buy lunch tomorrow, you will carry enough money to pay for it. But you also want to be able to pay for other possible contingencies. For example, you could have car trouble or you could come across an unexpected sale on a favorite item. You may have a little extra money with you right now for who knows what. Even *you* don't know.

The transactions demand for money is rooted in money's role as a medium of exchange. As we have seen, however, money is more than a medium of exchange; it is also a store of value. Because a household's income and expenditures are not perfectly matched each period, purchasing power is often saved to

Transactions demand for money The demand for money to support the exchange of goods and services

Money, in comparison to barter, simplifies the everyday transactions of consumers and businesses.

finance future expenditures. People save for a new home, for college, for retirement. The view of money that emphasizes the indirect channel focuses on two ways in which people can store their purchasing power: (1) in the form of money, and (2) in the form of other financial assets, such as private and government securities. When people purchase bonds and other financial assets, they are lending their money and are paid interest for doing so.

The demand for any asset is based on the flow of services it provides. The big advantage of money as a store of value is its liquidity: money can be immediately exchanged for whatever is for sale. In contrast, other financial assets, such as private and government bonds, must first be *liquidated,* or exchanged for money, which can then be used to buy goods and services. Money, however, has one major disadvantage when compared to other types of financial assets. Money in the form of currency and travelers checks earns no interest, and the interest rate earned on checkable deposits is typically below that earned on other financial assets. So those who hold their wealth in the form of money forgo some interest that could be earned by holding some other financial asset. For example, suppose a corporation could earn 3 percent more by holding financial assets other than money. The opportunity cost of holding $10 million as money rather than as some other financial asset would amount to $300,000 per year. *The interest forgone represents the opportunity cost of holding money.*

Money Demand and Interest Rates

When the market rate of interest is low, other things constant, the cost of holding money—the cost of maintaining liquidity—is low, so people hold a larger fraction of their wealth in the form of money. When the market rate of interest is high, the cost of holding money is high, so people hold less of their wealth in money and more of their wealth in other financial assets that pay more interest. Thus, other things constant, the quantity of money demanded varies inversely with the market rate of interest.

The money demand curve, D_m, in Exhibit 1 shows the quantity of money people in the economy demand at alternative interest rates, other things con-

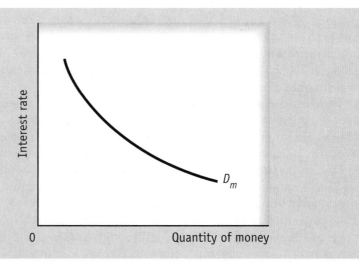

EXHIBIT 1

Demand for Money

The demand for money curve, D_m, slopes downward. As the interest rate falls, so does the opportunity cost of holding money; the quantity of money demanded increases.

Interest rate

D_m

0   Quantity of money

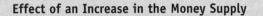

Effect of an Increase in the Money Supply   E X H I B I T   2

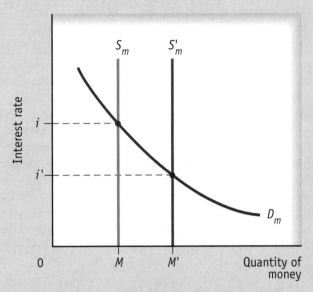

Since the supply of money is determined by the Federal Reserve, it can be represented by a vertical line. The intersection of the supply of money, S_m, and the demand for money, D_m, determines the equilibrium interest rate, i. Following an increase in the money supply to S'_m, the quantity of money supplied exceeds the quantity demanded at the original interest rate, i. People who are holding more money than they would like attempt to exchange money for bonds or other financial assets. In doing so, they drive the interest rate down to i', where quantity demanded equals the new quantity supplied.

stant. Both the quantity of money and the interest rate are in nominal terms. *The money demand curve slopes downward because the lower the interest rate, the lower the opportunity cost of holding assets as money.* Movements along the curve reflect the effects of changes in the interest rate on the quantity of money demanded, other things constant. *Held constant along the curve are the price level and real GDP. If either increases, the transactions demand for money increases, which shifts the money demand curve to the right.*

Supply of Money and the Equilibrium Interest Rate

The supply of money—the stock of money available in the economy at a particular time—is determined primarily by the Fed through its control over excess reserves in the banking system. The supply of money, S_m, is depicted as a vertical line, as in Exhibit 2. *A vertical supply curve implies that the quantity of money supplied is independent of the interest rate.* This vertical supply is a simplifying assumption. In reality, as the interest rate rises, banks grow more inclined to lend, so the money supply curve tends to slope upward.

The intersection of the supply of money, S_m, and the demand for money, D_m, determines the equilibrium rate of interest, i: the interest rate that equates the quantity of money supplied in the economy with the quantity of money demanded. At interest rates above the equilibrium level, the opportunity cost of holding money is higher, so the quantity of money people want to hold is less than the fixed quantity supplied. At interest rates below the equilibrium level, the opportunity cost of holding money is lower, so the quantity of money people want to hold is greater than the quantity supplied.

If the Fed increases the money supply, the money supply curve shifts to the right, as shown by the movement from S_m to S'_m in Exhibit 2. The quantity supplied now exceeds the quantity demanded at the original interest rate, i. Because of the increased supply of money, there is now more money in the hands of the public, so people are *able* to hold a greater quantity of money. But at interest rate i they are *unwilling* to hold that much. Since people are now holding more of their wealth as money than they would like, they exchange money for other financial assets, such as securities.

As people attempt to exchange money for other financial assets, the market rate of interest falls. "Other financial assets" includes bonds. As the demand for bonds increases, bonds can pay less interest yet still attract enough buyers. The interest rate falls until the quantity demanded just equals the quantity supplied. With the decline in the rate of interest to i' in Exhibit 2, the opportunity cost of holding money falls enough so the public is willing to hold the now-larger stock of money. *For a given demand for money, increases in the supply of money drive down the rate of interest, and decreases in the supply of money drive up the rate of interest.*

Now that you have some idea how money demand and supply determine the market rate of interest, you are ready to see how money fits into the model of the macroeconomy developed thus far. Specifically, you will observe how changes in the supply of money affect aggregate demand and equilibrium output.

MONEY AND AGGREGATE DEMAND

Monetary policy influences the market rate of interest, which, in turn, affects the level of planned investment, a component of aggregate demand. Let's work through the chain of causation in a specific economic setting.

Interest Rates and Planned Investment

Suppose the Federal Reserve believes that the economy is operating well below its potential level of output and decides to increase the money supply to stimulate output and employment. Recall that the Fed can expand the money supply by (1) purchasing U.S. government securities, (2) lowering the interest rate at which banks can borrow from the Fed, or (3) lowering reserve requirements.

The four panels of Exhibit 3 trace the links between changes in the money supply and changes in aggregate demand. We begin with the equilibrium rate of interest i, which is determined in panel (a) by the intersection of the demand for money, D_m, with the supply of money, S_m. Suppose the Fed purchases U.S. government securities and thereby increases the money supply, as shown in panel (a) by the shift to the right in the money supply curve from S_m to S'_m. After the increase in the supply of money, people are holding more of their wealth in money than they would prefer at the initial interest rate i, so they try to exchange one form of wealth, money, for other financial assets. This greater willingness to lend has no direct effect on aggregate demand, but it does reduce the market rate of interest.

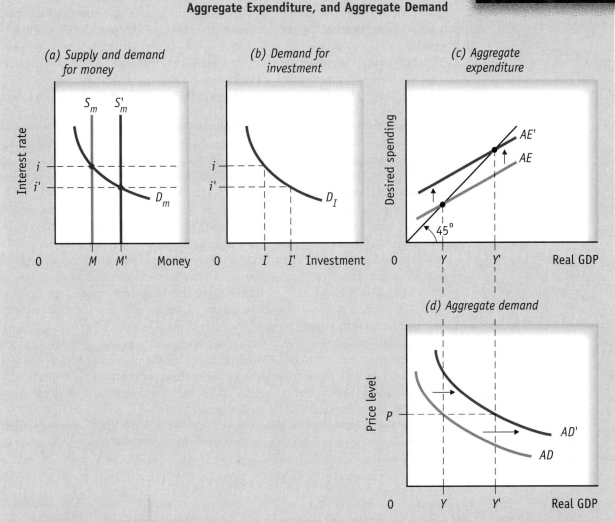

Effects of an Increase in the Money Supply on Interest Rates, Investment, Aggregate Expenditure, and Aggregate Demand

(a) Supply and demand for money

(b) Demand for investment

(c) Aggregate expenditure

(d) Aggregate demand

In panel (a), an increase in the money supply drives the interest rate down to i'. With the cost of borrowing now lower, the level of investment spending increases from I to I', as shown in panel (b). More investment spending drives aggregate expenditure up from AE to AE', as shown in panel (c). The increased expenditure sets off the multiplier process, so the quantity of aggregate output demanded increases from Y to Y'. The increase is shown by the shift to the right in the aggregate demand curve in panel (d).

A decline in the interest rate, other things constant, reduces the opportunity cost of financing new plants and equipment, thereby making new business investment more profitable. Likewise, a lower interest rate reduces the cost of mortgages on new housing, so housing investment increases. Thus, the decline in the rate of interest increases the quantity of investment demanded. Panel (b) shows the demand for investment, D_I, first introduced in Chapter 9. When the interest rate falls from i to i', the quantity of investment spending increases from I to I'.

The aggregate expenditure function in panel (c) shifts up by the increase in planned investment, from AE to AE'. The spending multiplier magnifies this increase in investment, leading to a greater increase in the quantity of real GDP demanded at each price level. The quantity demanded increases from Y to Y', as reflected in panel (c) by the intersection of the new aggregate expenditure function with the 45-degree line. This same increase is also reflected in panel (d), given price level P, by the horizontal shift in the aggregate demand curve from AD to AD'.

The sequence of events can be summarized as follows:

$$M\uparrow \;\rightarrow\; i\downarrow \;\rightarrow\; I\uparrow \;\rightarrow\; AE\uparrow \;\rightarrow\; AD\uparrow$$

An increase in the money supply, M, reduces the interest rate, i. The lower interest rate stimulates investment spending, I, which shifts up the aggregate expenditure function. This increase in the quantity of real GDP demanded at a particular price level is reflected by a shift to the right in the aggregate demand curve, from AD to AD'.[1]

We will now trace the same sequence in reverse, but we will dispense with the graphs. (Why not draw them yourself?) Suppose the Federal Reserve decides to reduce the money supply to cool down an overheated economy. The excess demand for money at the initial interest rate means that people will attempt to exchange other financial assets for money. These efforts to get more money raise the market rate of interest, or the opportunity cost of holding money. The interest rate increases until the quantity of money demanded declines just enough to equal the now-lower quantity of money supplied.

At the higher interest rate, businesses find it more costly to finance plants and equipment, and households find it more costly to finance new homes. Hence, a higher rate of interest reduces planned investment. The resulting decline in planned investment is magnified by the autonomous spending multiplier, leading to a greater decline in aggregate demand.

As long as the interest rate is sensitive to changes in the quantity of money supplied, and as long as investment is sensitive to changes in the interest rate, then changes in the supply of money affect planned investment. The extent to which a given change in planned investment affects aggregate demand depends on the size of the spending multiplier.

Money and the Slope of the Aggregate Demand Curve

When the aggregate demand curve was introduced, two reasons were offered for its downward slope: the first had to do with the effect of changes in the price level on the value of dollar-denominated wealth, and the second had to do with the effect of the price level on net exports. Based on the discussion of money and the interest rate, an additional reason for the shape of the aggregate demand curve can be introduced.

Money is demanded primarily to carry out transactions—to pay for goods and services. The amount of money required to finance transactions depends, among other things, on the price level. The higher the price level, the higher

---

1   The graphs are actually more complicated than those presented here. Since the demand for money depends on the level of real GDP, an increase in the quantity of real GDP demanded would shift the money demand curve to the right in panel (a). For simplicity, we have not shown a shift in the money demand curve. If we had shifted the money demand curve, the equilibrium interest rate would still have fallen, but not by as much, so investment and aggregate demand would not have increased by as much.

the dollar cost of each transaction, and the more money it takes to pay for a given level of real GDP. So the demand for money increases as the price level increases, other things constant. For a given supply of money, an increase in the demand for money leads to a higher interest rate. An increase in the interest rate reduces the quantity of planned investment. This decline in investment reduces the quantity of real GDP demanded.

The two panels of Exhibit 4 represent this relationship graphically. Panel (a) shows the economy's supply and demand for money, and panel (b) shows the aggregate demand curve. Let's begin with an interest rate of i in panel (a) and a price level of P in panel (b). The equilibrium interest rate is determined by the intersection of the money supply curve, S_m, and the money demand curve, D_m; this intersection occurs at point a in panel (a). Note that D_m is the demand for money when the price level is P. Point a in panel (b) indicates that when the price level is P, the quantity of real GDP demanded is Y.

If the price level increases to P', the amount of money needed to support a given level of transactions increases, so the demand for money shifts to the right, from D_m to D'_m in panel (a). People demand more money at every interest rate. People try to get more money to support transactions at the higher price level by exchanging some of their other financial assets for money. But the existing money stock is fixed at S_m; there is no more. As people try to sell other financial assets, such as bonds, for money, bond buyers require a higher rate of inter-

Effect of a Change in the Price Level on Quantity Demanded   **E X H I B I T   4**

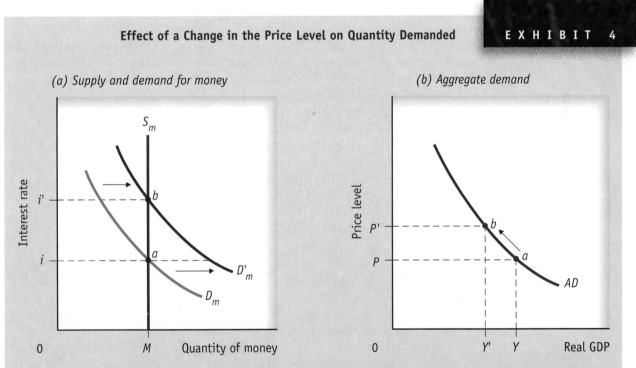

An increase in the price level from P to P' increases the transactions demand for money from D_m to D'_m and drives the interest rate up from i to i'. The rise in the interest rate reduces investment spending and aggregate expenditure. Through the multiplier process, the quantity of aggregate output demanded falls from Y to Y'. Panel (b) shows that higher price levels are associated with lower quantities of real output demanded. Changes in the price level lead to movements along the aggregate demand curve.

est. The interest rate rises until the quantity of money demanded just equals the given supply of money, as shown by equilibrium point *b* in panel (a).

An increase in the interest rate has a now-familiar effect on the quantity of aggregate output demanded. When the interest rate increases, investment becomes more costly, so investment spending declines. Thus, as the price level increases from *P* to *P'* in panel (b), the higher demand for money drives up the interest rate and reduces the quantity of planned investment. This decline in investment reduces the quantity of aggregate output demanded from *Y* to *Y'*, reflected by the movement along the aggregate demand curve in panel (b) from point *a* to point *b.*

In summary, the aggregate demand curve is drawn assuming a given supply of money in the economy. Changes in the price level alter the amount of money needed to carry out transactions, thereby shifting the money demand curve. A higher price level leads to a higher interest rate, which results in less investment and a decrease in the quantity of aggregate output demanded. A lower price level leads to a lower interest rate, resulting in more investment and an increase in the quantity of aggregate output demanded. This relationship between the price level and the interest rate provides another reason why the aggregate demand curve slopes down to the right.

Adding Aggregate Supply

Even after tracing the effect of a change in the money supply on aggregate demand, we still have only half the story. To determine the effects of monetary policy on the equilibrium level of real GDP in the economy, we need the supply side. An aggregate supply curve can help show how a given shift in aggregate demand affects real GDP and the price level. In the short run, the aggregate supply curve slopes upward, so the quantity supplied will expand only if the price level increases. *For a given shift in the aggregate demand curve, the steeper the short-run aggregate supply curve, the smaller the increase in real GDP and the larger the increase in the price level.*

Assume the economy is producing at point *a* in Exhibit 5, where the aggregate demand curve, *AD,* intersects the short-run aggregate supply curve, $SRAS_{130}$, yielding a short-run equilibrium output of $6.8 trillion and a price level of 125. As you can see, the actual price level of 125 is below the expected price level of 130, so the short-run equilibrium output of $6.8 trillion is below the economy's potential of $7.0 trillion, yielding a contractionary gap of $0.2 trillion. (Note that price and output levels below the economy's potential are shaded in red, and those above that potential are shaded in blue.)

The Fed can wait to see whether natural market forces close the gap as the short-run aggregate supply curve shifts to the right, or it can intervene and attempt to close the gap with an expansionary monetary policy. For example, in 1992 and 1993 the Fed aggressively increased the money supply in order to stimulate aggregate demand. If the Fed increases the money supply by exactly the appropriate amount, the new equilibrium is achieved at point *b,* where the economy is producing its potential output. Given all the connections in the chain of causality between changes in the money supply and changes in equilibrium output, however, it would actually be quite difficult for the Fed to execute such a precise monetary policy—but more on that later.

To review: *An increase in the money supply reduces the market rate of interest, resulting in an increase in investment and a consequent increase in aggregate demand. As*

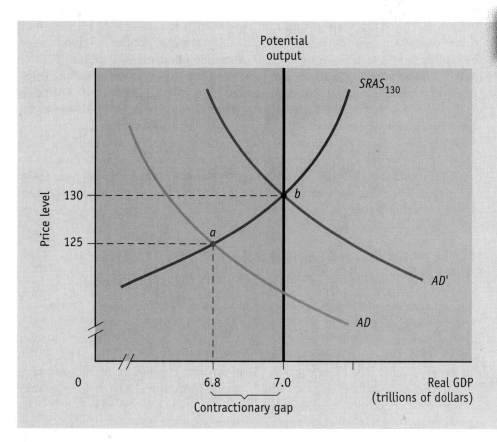

EXHIBIT 5

Expansionary Monetary Policy to Correct a Contractionary Gap

At point *a,* the economy is producing below potential. There is a contractionary gap equal to $0.2 trillion. If the Federal Reserve increases the money supply, the aggregate demand curve shifts to *AD'.* Equilibrium will be reestablished at point *b,* with price level 130 and output at the potential level of $7.0 trillion.

aggregate demand increases along a given short-run aggregate supply curve, both the equilibrium price and output increase. *As long as the short-run aggregate supply curve slopes upward, the short-run effect of an increase in the money supply is an increase in both real output and the price level.*

Fiscal Policy with Money

Now that we have considered the indirect effect that money has on aggregate demand and equilibrium output, we can take another look at fiscal policy. Suppose there is an increase in government purchases, other things constant. In Chapter 12, we found that an increase in government purchases increases aggregate demand and, in the short run, leads to both a greater output and a higher price level. Once money enters the picture, however, we must recognize that an increase in either real output or the price level increases the demand for money.

Thus, an increase in government purchases increases money demand. For a given supply of money, an increase in money demand leads to a higher interest rate. But a higher interest rate *reduces* the quantity of investment demanded. We therefore say that the fiscal stimulus of government purchases *crowds out* some investment. This reduction in investment will, to some extent, dampen the expansionary effects of fiscal policy on real output. Hence, *the inclusion of money in the fiscal framework introduces yet another reason why the simple spending multiplier overstates the increase in real output arising from any given fiscal stimulus.*

Likewise, any fiscal policy designed to reduce aggregate demand will be tempered by monetary effects. Suppose that, in an attempt to cool inflation, government purchases are reduced. As aggregate demand declines, equilibrium output and the price level fall in the short run. With a lower level of output and a lower price level, less money is needed to carry out transactions, so the demand for money falls. Again, with the supply of money unchanged, a drop in the demand for money leads to a lower interest rate. This drop in the interest rate stimulates investment spending, to some extent offsetting the effects of the drop in government purchases. Thus, *given the supply of money, the impact of changes in the demand for money on interest rates reduces the effectiveness of fiscal policy.*

When we look at the impact of money on the economy through the indirect channel, we see that money influences aggregate demand and equilibrium output through its effect on the interest rate. Another framework focuses more directly on the effects of changes in the money supply on aggregate demand. We next examine this direct channel.

MONEY AND THE ECONOMY: THE DIRECT CHANNEL

The indirect channel assumes that the only alternative to holding money as a store of value is holding other *financial* assets. In this view, an increased supply of money makes people want to exchange money for other financial assets, which lowers the rate of interest and stimulates investment. Thus, changes in the money supply affect aggregate demand through changes in the interest rate.

Another view of the effect of money sees a more direct channel for money in aggregate spending. In the more direct channel, money is just one asset among many that can serve as a store of value. In addition to other financial assets, people hold *real* assets, such as real estate and automobiles. An increase in the money supply means that, at the initial interest rate, the quantity of money supplied exceeds the quantity demanded. People are therefore holding more of their wealth in the form of money than they would like. As they attempt to reduce their money holdings, people increase their demand for all kinds of assets, including homes and other durable goods. So in the direct channel, an increase in the supply of money increases the demand for both other financial assets and real assets. This increased desire to buy real assets increases aggregate demand directly. The direct channel relies on a framework called the equation of exchange, which we will examine next.

The Equation of Exchange

Equation of exchange The quantity of money, M, multiplied by its velocity, V, equals nominal income, which is the product of the price level, P, and real GDP, Y.

Every transaction in the economy involves a two-way swap: the seller surrenders goods and services for money, and the buyer surrenders money equal in value to the asking price. One way of expressing this relationship among key variables in the economy is the **equation of exchange,** first developed by the classical economists. Although this equation can be arranged in different ways depending on the variables to be emphasized, the basic version is

$$M \times V = P \times Y$$

Velocity of money The average number of times per year a dollar is used to purchase final goods and services

where M is the quantity of money in the economy; V is the **velocity of money,** or the average number of times per year each dollar is used to purchase final goods and services; P is the price level; and Y is real national output, or real GDP. The equation of exchange says that the quantity of money in circulation, M, multiplied by the number of times that money turns over (changes hands), V, equals the average price level of products sold, P, times real output, Y. The price level, P, times real output, Y, equals the economy's nominal income and output.

Consider a simple economy in which total sales during the year consist of 1,000 bags of popcorn priced at $1 each and 1,000 six-packs of Pepsi priced at $3 each. The total output, Y, equals 2,000 units, and the average price level, P, is $2 per unit. The nominal value of output, $P \times Y$, equals $2 \times 2,000$, or $4,000, which also equals the income received by resource suppliers. Suppose the total money supply in this economy is $500. How often is each dollar used on average to pay for final goods and services during the year? In other words, what is the velocity of money? We can derive the velocity by rearranging the equation of exchange to yield

$$V = \frac{P \times Y}{M} = \frac{\$4,000}{\$500} = 8$$

Given the value of total output and the money supply, each dollar on average must have turned over eight times to finance final goods and services. There is no other way these market transactions could occur. The specific value of velocity is implied by the values of the other variables. Incidentally, velocity reflects spending only on final goods and services—not intermediate goods, secondhand goods, or financial assets, even though such spending also takes place in the economy. Thus, each dollar, in fact, works harder than is implied by velocity.

Classical economists developed the equation of exchange as a way of explaining the economy's price level. The equation says that total spending ($M \times V$) is always equal to total receipts ($P \times Y$), as was the case in our circular flow analysis. As described thus far, however, the equation of exchange is simply an *identity*—a relationship expressed in such a way that it is true by definition. Another example of an identity would be a relationship equating miles per gallon to the distance driven divided by the gasoline required.

The Quantity Theory of Money

Those who point to the direct channel of money on aggregate demand, a group called *monetarists,* claim that velocity is relatively stable, at least in the near term. To the extent that velocity varies over time, monetarists claim it varies in a predictable manner unrelated to changes in the money supply. By arguing that velocity is predictable, monetarists transform the equation of exchange from an identity into a theory—the quantity theory of money. The **quantity theory of money** states that if the velocity of money is stable or at least predictable, then the equation of exchange can be used to predict the effects of changes in the money supply on nominal income, $P \times Y$. For example, if M is increased by 10 percent and if V remains constant, then $P \times Y$, which measures nominal income, *must* also increase by 10 percent.

Thus, an increase in the money supply increases aggregate demand, and the increase in aggregate demand results in a higher nominal income. How is this increase in nominal income ($P \times Y$) divided between changes in the price level and changes in real GDP? The answer does not lie in the quantity theory, for

*Quantity theory of money **If the velocity of money is stable or at least predictable, then changes in the money supply have predictable effects on nominal income***

that theory is stated only in terms of nominal income. The answer lies in the shape of the aggregate supply curve. In the short run, the aggregate supply curve slopes upward, so a shift to the right in the aggregate demand curve will increase both real output and the price level. If there is much unemployment and much idle capacity, short-run changes in the price level may be relatively small. If the economy is already producing its potential output, short-run changes in the price level will be relatively large. So, *in the short run, changes in nominal output are divided between changes in real GDP and changes in the price level.*

In the long run, the aggregate supply curve is vertical at the economy's potential level of output. If the economy is already operating at its potential output, then a shift to the right in the aggregate demand curve will in the long run increase only the price level, leaving output unchanged at potential GDP. Note that the economy's potential level of output is not affected by changes in the money supply. Thus, *in the long run, increases in the money supply result only in higher prices.*

What is the long-run relationship between increases in the money supply and inflation? Since the Federal Reserve System was established in 1914, the United States has suffered three major episodes of high inflation, and each was preceded and accompanied by a corresponding increase in the rate of growth in the money supply. These inflation episodes occurred from 1914 to 1920, 1939 to 1948, and 1967 to 1980. The following case study examines evidence linking increases in the money supply with inflation across countries.

CASE STUDY

The Money Supply and Inflation

Location:

Argentina, Bolivia, and Israel all have been able to tame hyperinflation in the 1990s. To learn more about the Argentinean economy, visit Argentina's Ministry of Economy and Public Works and Services (http://www.mecon.ar/). For more about the Bolivian economy, visit the "Bolivia Reference Desk," published by the University of Texas—Latin American Network Information Center (http://lanic.utexas.edu/la/sa/bolivia/). To learn more about the Israeli economy, visit the Economic Affairs Department of the Consulate General of Israel to the Mid-Atlantic States (http://www.israphl.org/econ.html).

What is the experience across countries between increases in the money supply and inflation? Panel (a) in Exhibit 6 illustrates the relationship between the average annual growth rate in M2 from 1980 to 1990 and the average annual rate of inflation from 1980 to 1990 for the 85 countries for which complete data are available. As you can see, the points fall rather neatly along the trend line, showing a positive relation between money growth and inflation. Since most countries are bunched below an inflation rate of 20 percent, these points are broken out in finer detail in panel (b). Countries with low rates of money growth also experienced low rates of inflation.

In panel (a), Argentina, Bolivia, and Israel—three countries that experienced annual inflation exceeding 100 percent—also had an annual growth in the money supply exceeding 100 percent. Hyperinflation is largely a 20th-century phenomenon, and in every case it was accompanied by extremely rapid growth in the supply of paper money. For example, Argentina, which had the highest average annual inflation rate over the 10-year period in the sample, at 395 percent, also had the highest average annual rate of growth in the money supply, at 369 percent.

How do hyperinflations end? Monetary authorities must convince the public they are committed to halting the rapid growth in the money supply. The most famous hyperinflation was in Germany between August of 1922 and November 1923, when inflation averaged 322 percent *per month.* Inflation was halted when the German government created an independent central bank that

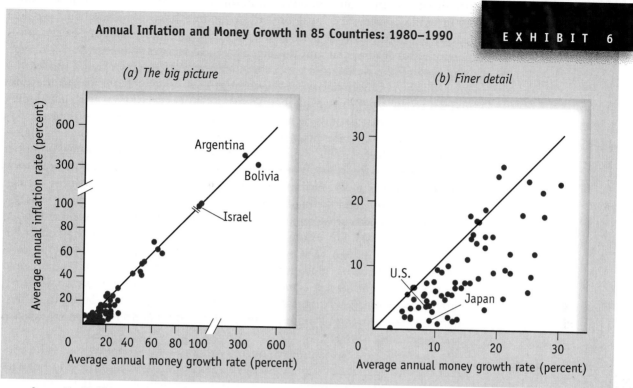

Annual Inflation and Money Growth in 85 Countries: 1980–1990

EXHIBIT 6

(a) The big picture

(b) Finer detail

Source: The World Bank, *World Development Report 1992* (New York: Oxford University Press, 1992), Table 13.

issued a new currency convertible on demand into gold. Argentina, Bolivia, and Israel all managed to tame inflation during the 1990s; for each country, the inflation rate in 1995 was well under 10 percent per year.

Sources: Michael Salemi, "Hyperinflation," *The Fortune Encyclopedia of Economics*, D.R. Henderson, ed. (New York: Warner Books, 1993), pp. 208–11; and Central Intelligence Agency, *The World Factbook: 1995–96*, (Washington, D.C.: Brassey's, 1995).

The Money Supply and Inflation
continued

To review, *what turns the equation of exchange from an identity into a theory is the monetarist assertion that velocity is relatively stable, or at least predictable.* If velocity *is* predictable, changes in the money supply affect nominal income in a predictable way. Velocity is therefore a key component of the quantity theory of money. Let's consider some factors that might influence velocity.

What Determines the Velocity of Money?

Velocity depends on the customs and conventions of commerce. In colonial times, money might be tied up in transit for days as a courier on horseback carried a payment from a merchant in Boston to one in Baltimore. Today the electronic transmission of funds takes only seconds, so the same stock of money can move around much more quickly to finance many more transactions. *The velocity of money has also been increased by a variety of commercial innovations that have facilitated exchange.* For example, a wider use of charge accounts and credit cards has reduced the need for shoppers to carry cash. Likewise, automatic teller machines have made cash more accessible any time and ATM cards can be used at a growing number of retail outlets, so people have reduced their "walking around" money. Monetarists argue that although such changes can affect velocity, financial innovations do not occur suddenly or frequently. Moreover, their effects are predictable, so the quantity theory remains a useful model.

Another institutional factor that determines velocity is the frequency with which workers get paid. If workers are paid $1,000 every two weeks, which they spend during that period, each worker's average money balance during the pay period is $500. If, on the other hand, workers are paid $500 every week, their average money balance falls to $250. Thus, the more often workers are paid, other things constant, the lower their average money balances, so the more active the money supply and the greater its velocity. Again, payment practices change slowly over time, and the effects of these changes on velocity are predictable.

The better money serves as a store of value, the more money people want to hold, so the lower its velocity. For example, the introduction of interest-bearing checking accounts made money a better store of value. When inflation is high, money is not as good a store of value; people become more reluctant to hold money, and try to exchange it for some asset that retains its value during inflation. This reduction in people's willingness to hold money during periods of high inflation increases the velocity of money. Thus, *velocity increases with a rise in the inflation rate, other things constant.*

The usefulness of the modern quantity theory hinges on how stable and predictable the velocity of money is. Even a small unexpected change in velocity could undermine the ability of the equation of exchange to predict nominal income. For example, if velocity turned out to be 5 percent less than expected, then nominal GDP would also be 5 percent less than expected. Let's examine the stability of velocity over the years.

How Stable Is Velocity?

Exhibit 7 graphs velocity since 1915, measured both as nominal GDP divided by M1 and as nominal GDP divided by M2. Let's first consider the velocity of M1. Based on this exhibit, is it reasonable to conclude that the velocity of M1 is relatively stable? That depends on the time period we consider and what we mean by "relatively stable." As you can see, from 1915 to 1947 velocity of M1 fluctuated a fair amount, but the trend was downward. From 1947 to 1979 the trend was upward, with less variability than before. In fact, between 1973 and 1979 velocity grew each year at a rate of between 3.0 and 4.3 percent. *Velocity growth appeared so relatively stable during this 6-year stretch that some economists began to talk about an economic law relating the money supply to nominal GDP.* More attention was thus accorded the direct channel of money during the latter part of the 1970s. Whereas the decade of the 1960s was the high point for supporters of the indirect channel, which worked through changes in interest rates, the period of the late 1970s was perhaps the high point for supporters of the direct channel.

After 1979, however, the velocity of M1 became more erratic. For example, after jumping 4.2 percent in 1981, it dropped 2.5 percent during the recession year of 1982, the largest decline since 1946. That swing meant that nominal GDP was 6.7 percent lower in 1982 than it would have been had velocity continued to grow in 1982 as it had in 1981. The decline in velocity, coupled with a slower growth in the money supply, has been viewed by some economists as causing the deepest recession since the Great Depression.

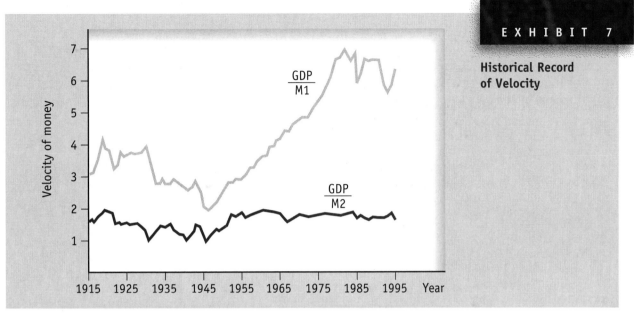

EXHIBIT 7

**Historical Record
of Velocity**

Sources: *Long-Term Economic Growth, 1860–1970* (Washington, D.C.: U.S. Government Printing Office, 1973); and *Economic Report of the President,* February 1996.

The velocity of M1 has continued to be volatile in the 1990s, dropping by 7.4 percent in 1992 and by 4.9 percent in 1993, but increasing by 4.0 percent in 1994 and by 7.0 percent in 1995. The equation of exchange has consequently become less reliable as a short-run predictor of the effects of a change in M1 on nominal GDP. There is less talk now about economic laws relating money supply to nominal GDP. Some economists believe that the link between the money supply and nominal GDP has been disturbed only temporarily. Others aren't so sure.

The deregulation of the interest paid on checkable deposits is a possible source of the demise of a predictable relation between M1 and nominal income. Prior to 1980, with minor exceptions, interest was not paid on checkable deposits. Since people can now earn interest on their checking accounts, they choose to hold more money in checking accounts, thus reducing the velocity of M1.

The velocity of M2 has been more stable than the velocity of M1, especially since the mid-1950s, as you can see in Exhibit 7. In setting objectives for monetary growth, the Fed in 1987 switched from a focus on M1 to a focus on M2. But even M2 velocity has become more volatile lately, growing by 3.6 percent in 1992, 3.5 percent in 1993, and 5.0 percent in 1994. The Fed announced in July 1993 that monetary aggregates, including M2, were no longer considered reliable guides for monetary policy.

MONEY SUPPLY VERSUS INTEREST RATE TARGETS

According to the indirect channel, monetary policy affects the economy largely by influencing the market interest rate. Monetarists think the linkage is more direct—that changes in the growth of the money supply affect how much peo-

EXHIBIT 8

Targeting Interest Rates Versus the Supply of Money

An increase in the price level or in real GDP increases the demand for money from D_m to D'_m. If the Federal Reserve holds the money supply at S_m the interest rate will rise from i (at point e) to i' (at point e'). Alternatively, the Fed could hold the interest rate constant by increasing the supply of money to S'_m. The Fed may choose any point along the money demand curve, D'_m.

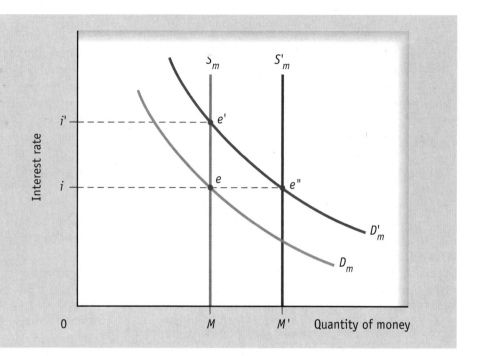

ple want to spend. The indirect channel suggests that monetary authorities should worry about interest rates; the direct channel suggests authorities should focus on the money supply. Thus, there is a debate over whether monetary authorities should focus on keeping interest rates stable or on keeping the money stock stable. As we will see, the Fed lacks the tools to do both at the same time.

Contrasting Policies

To demonstrate the effects of different policies, we begin with the money market in equilibrium at point e in Exhibit 8. The interest rate is i and the money stock is M, values the monetary authorities find appropriate. Suppose there is an increase in the demand for money in the economy, perhaps because of an increase in aggregate demand. The money demand curve shifts to the right, from D_m to D'_m.

When confronted with an increase in the demand for money, monetary authorities can do nothing, allowing the interest rate to rise, or they can increase the supply of money in an attempt to keep the interest rate constant. If monetary authorities do nothing, the quantity of money in the economy will remain at M, but the interest rate will rise because the greater demand for money will shift the equilibrium up from point e to point e'. Alternatively, monetary authorities can try to keep the interest rate at its initial level by increasing the supply of money from S_m to S'_m. In terms of possible combinations of the money stock and the interest rate, monetary authorities must choose from points lying along the new money demand curve.

A growing economy usually needs a growing money supply. If monetary authorities maintain a constant growth in the money supply, the interest rate will probably fluctuate unless the growth in the supply of money each period just happens to match the growth in the demand for money. Alternatively, monetary authorities could try to adjust the money supply each period by the amount needed to keep the interest rate stable. With this approach, changes in the money supply would have to offset any changes in the demand for money.

Interest rate fluctuations could be harmful if they create undesirable fluctuations in investment. For interest rates to remain stable during economic expansions, the money supply should grow at the same rate as the demand for money. Likewise, for interest rates to remain stable during economic contractions, the money supply should shrink by the same rate as the demand for money. Hence, for monetary authorities to maintain the interest rate at some specified level, the money supply must increase during periods of economic expansion and decrease during periods of economic contraction. Unfortunately, *such changes in the money supply would tend to reinforce fluctuations in economic activity, thereby adding more instability to the economy.* Let's examine monetary policy in recent years.

Targets Until 1982

Between World War II and October 1979, the Fed attempted to stabilize interest rates. Stable interest rates were viewed as a prerequisite for an attractive investment environment and, thus, for a stable economy. Milton Friedman, the Nobel Prize winner and father of modern monetarism, argued that this exclusive attention to interest rates made monetary policy a major source of instability in the economy because changes in the money supply reinforced fluctuations in the economy. Monetarists said that the Fed should pay less attention to interest rates and instead focus on a steady and predictable growth in the money supply.

The debate raged during the 1970s, and monetarists made some important converts. Amid growing concern about the rising inflation rate, the Fed, under its new chairman, Paul Volcker, announced in October 1979 that it would deemphasize interest rates and would instead target the growth in specific monetary aggregates. Not surprisingly, the interest rate became much more volatile.

But many observers believe that a sharp reduction in money growth in the latter half of 1981 caused the recession of 1982. Inflation declined rapidly, but the unemployment rate jumped to over 10 percent. People got worried. As you might expect, the Fed was widely criticized for its monetary policy. Volcker was denounced by farmers, politicians, and businesspeople. Emotions ran high. Volcker was reportedly even given Secret Service protection. In October 1982, three years after the focus on interest rates was dropped, Volcker announced that the Fed would pay attention to both interest rates *and* money growth. In effect, the Fed returned to a policy of smoothing interest rates.

Monetarists do not acknowledge that the attempt to focus on the money supply was a failure. Rather, they argue that the Fed never really implemented a policy of steady, predictable growth in the money supply, so the 3-year period should not be viewed as a test of the effectiveness of monetarism. Some monetarists even believe that the Fed espoused monetarism simply as a smoke screen for putting the brakes on inflation rates that exceeded 12 percent in 1979 and 1980. According to this argument, Congress would have objected if the Fed had announced an explicit policy of raising interest rates to cool inflation.

Targets after 1982

The Fed is always feeling its way, looking for signs about the direction of the economy. The rapid pace of financial innovations and deregulation made the

Net Bookmark

Alan Greenspan became Chairman of the Board of Governors of the Federal Reserve System in 1987. To browse speeches by Alan Greenspan, visit "Speeches by Federal Reserve Officials," a service of the Federal Reserve Bank of Minneapolis (http:// woodrow.mpls.frb.fed.us/ info/speeches/).

definition and measurement of the money supply more difficult. What's more, as we have seen, the relationship between M1 and economic activity began to break down in the 1980s. In 1987, the Fed announced it would no longer set targets for M1 growth. The Fed switched the focus to M2, which appeared to have a more stable link to economic activity. But, by the early 1990s, the link between M2 and economic activity also deteriorated.

Alan Greenspan, who became the Fed chairman in 1987, said that in the short run changes in the money supply "are not linked closely enough with those of nominal income to justify a single-minded focus on the money supply."[2] In 1993, he testified in Congress that the Fed would no longer target monetary aggregates as a guide to monetary policy. The Fed's focus in the last few years has been on short-term interest rates as the instrument of monetary policy. For example, in 1992 and 1993 the Fed reduced interest rates to stimulate the economy. But in 1994, fears of inflation prompted the Fed to raise interest rates to slow the economy down.

Thus far we have confined the discussion of monetary policy to domestic issues. But international transactions complicate the picture, as is discussed in the following case study.

CASE STUDY

International Finance

Location:

How much is the U.S. dollar currently worth? Browse the latest values of foreign currencies versus the U.S. dollar, as certified by the Federal Reserve Bank of New York and published by the University of Michigan's Gopher System (gopher://una.hh.lib.umich.edu/00/ebb/monetary/noonfx.frb).

Savers throughout the world have a financial incentive to seek out the highest interest rate they can earn. For a Japanese saver, for example, the alternatives might be buying Japanese corporate bonds paying, say, 4 percent or buying U.S. corporate bonds paying, say, 7 percent. To purchase U.S. corporate bonds, that Japanese saver would first have to purchase U.S. dollars with Japanese yen. Therefore, relatively high interest rates in the United States cause foreigners to exchange their own currencies for dollars. This increase in the demand for dollars causes the dollar to appreciate relative to other currencies.

Between 1980 and 1985, real interest rates in the United States were higher than foreign interest rates, and the U.S. dollar appreciated by about 55 percent relative to other currencies. Interest rates, therefore, affect not only domestic investment but the value of the dollar on world currency markets. A higher-valued dollar means that U.S. residents find foreign goods cheaper and foreigners find U.S. goods more expensive, so imports increase and exports decrease. The result is a reduction in the demand for U.S. output. A stronger dollar contributed to a decline in American competitiveness in world markets.

At the time, Chairman Volcker said the dollar was too high on world markets. In 1985 and 1986, the Fed pursued an expansionary monetary policy, one aimed at reducing real interest rates. Real interest rates in the United States began a sharp decline in early 1985, a decline that continued until 1987. When U.S. interest rates fall relative to foreign interest rates, the foreign demand for

---

2   As quoted in "Greenspan Asks That Fed Be Allowed to Pay Interest," *The Wall Street Journal*, 11 March 1992.

U.S. dollars also falls and the dollar tends to depreciate. By 1987, the value of the dollar had fallen nearly to its 1980 level. A lower value of the dollar means that U.S. residents find foreign goods more expensive and foreigners find U.S. goods cheaper, so imports decrease and exports increase. The result is an increase in net exports and thus an increase in the demand for U.S. output. The Fed's actions were coordinated with central banks in other countries. Such *international policy coordination* has become of growing importance in U.S. monetary policy.

Sources: "1995 Monetary Objectives," *Summary Report of the Federal Reserve Board,* 19 July 1995; and *OECD Outlook* 57 (June 1995).

CONCLUSION

This chapter has described two ways of viewing the effects of money on the economy's performance, but we should not overstate the differences. In the model that focuses on the indirect channel, an increase in the money supply means that people are holding more money than they would like at prevailing interest rates, so they exchange one form of wealth, money, for other financial assets, such as private or government securities. This increased demand for other financial assets has no direct effect on aggregate demand, but it does reduce the interest rate, and this lower interest rate stimulates investment. The increase in planned investment is magnified by the spending multiplier, increasing aggregate demand. The ultimate effect of this increase in demand on real output and the price level depends on the shape of the aggregate supply curve.

In the model that focuses on the direct channel, changes in the money supply act more directly on both output and prices. If velocity is relatively stable or at least fairly predictable, then changes in the money supply will have a predictable effect on nominal income and output in the economy. The mechanism through which changes in money translate into changes in nominal income is no more complicated than the equation of exchange. Increase the supply of money in the economy, and people try to reduce their money balances to the desired level by exchanging money for other assets, including houses and cars. This greater spending leads to an increase in aggregate demand and to a greater nominal output.

Each model employs a different perspective to examine the way the economy works. The indirect approach uses the income-expenditure model, with the components of aggregate spending as basic building blocks. The direct approach uses the equation of exchange, with the elements of that equation as basic building blocks. To understand why these are alternative ways of viewing the same thing, consider the following analogy.

Suppose city officials, concerned about traffic congestion, ask their engineers and planners to estimate the total number of trips made from the suburbs to the city each month. The city engineers check with the state department of motor vehicles and find that 100,000 cars are registered to suburban residents. The engineers then estimate that each car makes an average of 15 trips to the city per month, for a total of 1.5 million trips. In contrast, the city planners consider the number of trips to the city by suburban residents. They estimate that those suburbanites who commute to work make 700,000 trips per month, shoppers make 500,000 trips per month, and joyriders make 300,000 trips per month, for a total of 1.5 million trips.

The engineers focus on the number of cars and the average number of trips taken by each. Likewise, to arrive at total spending, the direct channel focuses on the money supply and the average number of "trips" each dollar takes—that is, the average number of times each dollar is spent. Note that the engineers count all registered vehicles, even though some may sit in garages. Similarly, the direct channel counts all dollars, even though some remain idle in checking accounts or piggy banks. In contrast, the city planners focus not on the number of cars but on the different sources of trips to the city by suburban residents. Likewise, the indirect channel focuses not on the money stock but on the spending by various sectors in the economy.

SUMMARY

1. The opportunity cost of holding money is the higher interest that could be earned by holding other financial assets. Along a given money demand curve, the quantity of money demanded is inversely related to the interest rate. The demand for money itself increases with an increase in the price level or in real GDP.

2. The supply of money is determined by the Fed. The intersection of the supply and demand for money determines the equilibrium interest rate. According to the approach that emphasizes the indirect channel, an increase in the supply of money reduces the interest rate, which increases investment spending. This increase in investment increases aggregate demand, which increases real output and the price level.

3. The approach that emphasizes the direct channel, also called monetarism, focuses on the role of money through the equation of exchange, which states that the money stock, M, multiplied by the average number of times, V, each dollar is used to pay for final output

equals the price level, P, multiplied by real GDP, Y. So, $M \times V = P \times Y$.

4. The two approaches agree that an increase in the supply of money results in a lower interest rate and greater investment. But the direct-channel approach also claims that when the supply of money increases, people exchange money for other assets, including real assets, such as homes and cars. If velocity is stable enough, the effect of changes in the money supply on nominal output can be predicted.

5. During most of the 1970s, velocity appeared relatively stable, but since 1979 the velocity of M1 has been so variable that economists began to question the usefulness of the quantity theory, at least in the short run. Velocity has been more stable for M2 than for M1, but in the 1990s even M2 velocity grew more volatile. As a result of the increased volatility of investment, the Fed no longer focuses on growth in monetary aggregates and instead pays more attention to short-term interest rates.

QUESTIONS AND PROBLEMS

1. **(Transactions Demand for Money)** Indicate whether each of the following would lead to an increase, a decrease, or no change in the quantity of money people want to hold. Also indicate whether there is a shift in the money demand curve or a movement along a given money demand curve.
   a. A decrease in the price level.
   b. An increase in real output.
   c. An improvement in money's ability to act as a store of value.
   d. An increase in the market rate of interest

2. **(Opportunity Costs)** How has lifting the prohibition against paying interest on checkable deposits affected the

opportunity cost of holding currency? What has the effect been on the opportunity cost of holding checkable deposits? Will currency leakages and thus the money multiplier also be affected?

3. **(Indirect Channel for Monetary Policy)** According to the indirect channel for monetary policy, what is the impact of a decrease in the required reserve ratio on aggregate demand? Explain each step by which aggregate demand is affected.

4. **(Demand for Money)** If money is so versatile and can buy anything, why don't people demand an *infinite* amount of money?

5. **(Demand for Money)** Would the quantity of money demanded be less sensitive to changes in interest rates if we defined money as M2 instead of M1? Would the same hold true if there was a ceiling on interest paid on money market mutual funds?

6. **(Fiscal Policy with Money)** Explain why incorporating money into our macroeconomic framework moderates the effects of fiscal policy. That is, how does the existence of the supply and demand for money diminish the effects of increased government spending?

7. **(Money and Aggregate Demand)** Consider the indirect channel for the impact of monetary policy on aggregate demand. Explaining each answer, indicate whether each of the following would increase, decrease, or have no impact on the ability of open-market operations to affect aggregate demand:
   a. Investment demand becomes less sensitive to changes in the interest rate.
   b. The marginal propensity to consume rises.
   c. The money multiplier rises.
   d. Banks' desire to hold excess reserves rises.
   e. The demand for money becomes more sensitive to interest rate changes.

8. **(Equation of Exchange)** Define the velocity of money. Calculate the velocity of money if real GDP is 3,000 units, the average price level is $4 per unit, and the quantity of money in the economy is $1,500. What is the velocity if the average price level drops to $3 per unit? What is the velocity if the average price level is still $4 per unit but the money supply rises to $2,000? What is the velocity if the average price level is $2 per unit, the money supply is $2,000, and real GDP is 4,000 units?

9. **(Velocity)** Why do some economists believe that higher expected inflation will generally lead to a rise in velocity?

10. **(Monetary Policy and Aggregate Supply)** Assume that the economy is initially in long-run equilibrium. Using an *AD-AS* diagram, graphically illustrate and explain the short-run and long-run impacts of an increase in the money supply.

11. **(Quantity Theory of Money)** What basic assumption about the velocity of money transforms the equation of exchange into the quantity theory of money? (a) According to the quantity theory, what happens to nominal income if the money supply increases by 5% and velocity does not change? (b) What happens to nominal income if the money supply decreases by 8% and velocity does not change? (c) What happens to nominal income if the money supply increases by 5% and velocity increases by 5%? (d) What happens to the price level in the short run in each situation?

12. **(Money Demand)** Suppose the amount of money you hold for transactions purposes equals your average checking account balance (i.e., you never carry cash). Assume that your paycheck of $1,000 per month is deposited directly into your account and you spend your money at a uniform (constant) rate such that at the end of each month your checking balance is zero.
   a. What is your transactions demand for money?
   b. How would each of the following affect your money demand level?
      i. You are paid $500 twice a month instead of $1,000 once a month.
      ii. You are uncertain about your total spending each month.
      iii. You spend a lot in the beginning of each month (e.g., for rent) and little at the end of each month.
      iv. Your monthly income increases.

13. **(Money and Aggregate Demand)** How does the addition of money to the macroeconomic model help explain the downward slope of the *AD* curve? What happens to the *AD* curve if the money supply changes?

14. **(Equation of Exchange)** Using the equation of exchange, show why fiscal policy alone cannot increase *nominal* GDP if the velocity of money is constant.

15. **(Indirect Channel Versus Direct Channel)** A main difference between the indirect and direct channels for monetary policy is their underlying assumptions about what people consider as alternatives to holding money as a store of value. Explain this difference. What do the different assumptions imply about how changes in the money supply influence aggregate demand?

16. **(Monetary Policy and an Expansionary Gap)** Consider the appropriate direction for monetary policy to close an expansionary gap, assuming the indirect channel. (a) Should the Fed increase or decrease the money supply? (b) If the Fed uses open-market operations, should it buy or sell government securities? (c) Indicate whether each of the following increases, decreases, or remains unchanged in the short run: the market rate of interest, quantity demanded of money, investment, aggregate demand, potential output, the price level, and equilibrium real GDP.

17. **(Monetary Equilibrium)** Exhibit 2 shows the impact on interest rates of an increase in the supply of money.

Considering the transactions demand for money and the impact of money on aggregate demand as illustrated in Exhibit 3, why is the new interest rate shown in Exhibit 2 likely to be too low to be a new short-run equilibrium rate?

18. **(Quantity Theory of Money)** The quantity theory, in explaining the short-run impact of a change in the money supply on the economy, states that the impact on nominal GDP can be determined without any information on the *AD* curve, so long as the velocity of money is predictable. Discuss this assertion.

19. **(Velocity of Money)** Indicate whether each of the following would lead to an increase or a decrease in the velocity of money:
    a. Increasing the speed of electronic funds transfers.
    b. Decreased use of credit cards.
    c. Decreasing the frequency with which workers are paid.
    d. Higher inflation.

20. **(Money Supply Versus Interest Rate Targets)** Assume that the economy's real GDP is growing. What will happen to money demand? If the Fed leaves the money supply unchanged, what will happen to the interest rate? If the Fed changes the money supply to match the change in money demand, what will happen to the interest rate? What effect would the second type of action likely have on the economy's stability through the course of economic fluctuations?

21. **(The Money Supply and Inflation)** According to Exhibit 6, what is the relationship between rates of money growth and inflation? How does this explain the problem of hyperinflation experienced in some 20th century economies?

22. **(International Finance)** What was the relationship between real interest rates in the United States and the international value of the U.S. dollar during the 1980s? Explain this relationship.

Using the Internet

23. The Federal Reserve Bank of Minneapolis, through "Woodrow," its online service, publishes a historical table of discount rates, or the interest rate charged by Reserve Banks when they extend credit to depository institutions (**http://woodrow.mpls.frb.fed.us/ economy/index.html**).

    a. What is the current discount rate? In general, how does the current rate compare to historical rates?
    b. Graph the rates for the first period of each year from 1976–1996. What trends are apparent over this time period?
    c. Look in particular at the rates from 1979 to 1984. What type of monetary policy was the Fed pursuing over this period? What do you suppose the economic effect of this policy was on consumers? Investors? Builders?

The Policy Debate: Active or Passive?

16

We have now considered both fiscal and monetary policies and are in a position to take a broader view of the impact of government policy on the U.S. economy. A policy distinction emphasized in this chapter is between the *active approach* and the *passive approach*. The active approach views the private sector as relatively unstable and unable to absorb shocks when they occur. According to advocates of an active approach, economic fluctuations arise primarily from the private sector, particularly investment, and natural market forces may not be much help when the economy gets off track. In other words, "The economy has fallen, and it can't get up." To move the economy to its potential output, the active approach calls for the use of discretionary policy. The passive approach, on the other hand, considers the private sector to be relatively stable and able to absorb shocks when they occur. According to advocates of a passive approach, when the economy gets off track, natural market forces move it back on track.

In this chapter, we consider the pros and cons of *active* government intervention in the economy along with those of *passive* reliance on natural market forces. We also examine the role that expectations play in determining the effectiveness of stabilization policy. We will learn why unanticipated stabilization policies have more impact on employment and output than do anticipated policies. Finally, the chapter explores the trade-off between unemployment and inflation. As you read, keep in mind that issues of macroeconomic policy remain the most widely debated of economic questions. Topics discussed in this chapter include:

- Active versus passive policies
- Self-correcting mechanisms
- Rational expectations
- Policy rules and policy credibility

- The time inconsistency problem
- The short-run and long-run Phillips curves
- Natural rate hypothesis

ACTIVE POLICY VERSUS PASSIVE POLICY

According to the *active approach,* discretionary government policy can reduce the costs imposed by an unstable private sector. According to the *passive approach,* discretionary policy is part of the problem, not part of the solution. The two approaches differ in their assumptions about how quickly natural market forces operate.

Closing a Contractionary Gap

Perhaps the best way to describe each approach is by examining a particular macroeconomic problem. Suppose the economy is in short-run equilibrium at point *a* in panel (a) of Exhibit 1, with a real GDP of $6.8 trillion, which is below the economy's potential of $7.0 trillion. The contractionary gap of $0.2 trillion results in unemployment that exceeds its natural rate (the rate of unemployment when the economy is producing its potential output). What should public officials do when confronted with this situation?

Those who subscribe to the passive approach, like their classical predecessors, have more faith in the self-correcting mechanisms of the economy than do

EXHIBIT   1   **Closing a Contractionary Gap**

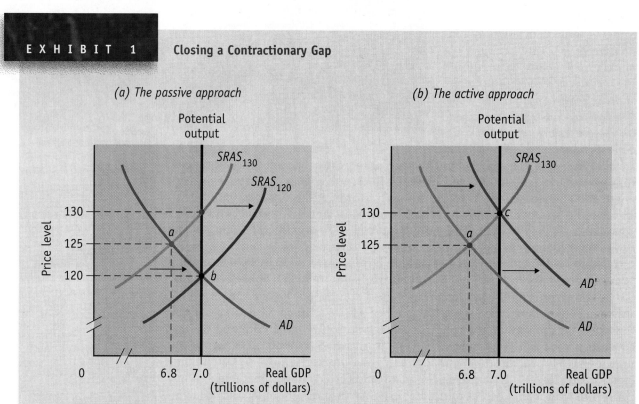

At point *a* in both panels, the economy is in short-run equilibrium, with unemployment above the natural rate. According to the passive approach, that high unemployment will eventually cause wages to fall, reducing firms' cost of doing business. The decline in costs will cause the short-run aggregate supply curve to shift out to $SRAS_{120}$, moving the economy to its potential level of output at point *b* in panel (a). In panel (b), the government employs an active approach to shift the aggregate demand curve from *AD* to *AD'*. If the policy works, the economy moves to its potential level of output at point *c*.

those who subscribe to the active approach. In what sense is the economy self-correcting? According to the passive approach, wages and prices are flexible enough to adjust within a reasonable period to labor shortages or surpluses. The high unemployment in panel (a) will cause wages to fall, which will reduce production costs, which will increase short-run aggregate supply. (Though not shown in the exhibit, money wages need not actually fall; money wage increases may simply lag behind increases in the price level, so that real wages fall.) According to the passive approach, the short-run aggregate supply curve will, within a reasonable period, shift out from $SRAS_{130}$ to $SRAS_{120}$, moving the economy to its potential level of output at point b. *According to the passive approach, the economy is inherently stable, gravitating in a reasonable amount of time toward potential GDP. Consequently, advocates of passive policy see little reason for active government intervention.* The passive approach is to let natural market forces close the contractionary gap. So passive policy is to do nothing special.

Advocates of an active approach, on the other hand, believe that prices and wages are not very flexible, particularly in the downward direction. They believe that when supply shocks or sagging demand result in unemployment that exceeds the natural rate, the economy does not quickly adjust to eliminate this unemployment. Advocates of the active approach argue that even when there is much unemployment in the economy, the renegotiation of long-term wage contracts in line with a lower expected price level may take a long time. Thus, the wage reductions required to shift the short-run aggregate supply curve out may also take a long time, even years. The longer natural market forces take to lower unemployment to the natural rate, the greater the forgone output during the adjustment period and the greater the economic and psychological costs to those unemployed during that period. Because advocates of an active policy associate a high cost with the passive approach, they believe that the economy needs an active stabilization policy to alter aggregate demand to achieve the natural rate of output and price stability.

A decision by the government to intervene in the economy to speed the return to potential output—that is, a decision to use discretionary policy—reflects an active approach. In panel (b) of Exhibit 1, we begin at the same point a as in panel (a). At point a, short-run equilibrium output is below potential output, so the economy is experiencing a contractionary gap. Through monetary policy, fiscal policy, or some mix of the two, active policy attempts to increase aggregate demand from AD to AD', moving equilibrium from point a to point c and closing the contractionary gap. One cost of such a policy is an increase in the price level. To the extent that the stimulus to aggregate demand worsens the federal budget deficit, another cost of active policy is an increase in the national debt, a cost that will be examined more closely in the next chapter.

Closing an Expansionary Gap

Let's consider the situation in which the short-run equilibrium output exceeds the economy's potential. Suppose that the actual price level of 135 exceeds the expected price level of 130, causing an expansionary gap of $0.2 trillion, as shown in Exhibit 2. The passive approach argues that natural market forces will prompt firms and workers to negotiate higher wage agreements. These higher nominal wages will increase production costs, shifting the short-run supply curve up and to the left, from $SRAS_{130}$ to $SRAS_{140}$, as shown in panel (a), lead-

EXHIBIT 2   **Policy Responses to an Expansionary Gap**

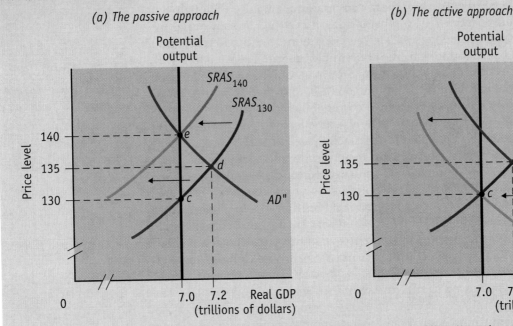

At point *d* in both panels, the economy is in short-run equilibrium, producing $7.2 trillion. Unemployment is below the natural rate. In the passive approach reflected in panel (a), the government makes no change in policy, so natural market forces will eventually bring about a higher negotiated wage, shifting the short-run supply curve up to $SRAS_{140}$. The new equilibrium at point *e* will result in a higher price level and a lower level of output and employment. An active policy might be able to reduce aggregate demand, shifting the equilibrium from point *d* to point *c* in panel (b), thus closing the expansionary gap without increasing the price level.

ing to a higher price level and reducing output to the economy's potential. So the natural adjustment process will result in a higher price level, or inflation.

An active approach sees discretionary policy as a way of returning the economy to its potential output without an increase in the price level, or inflation. Advocates of active policy believe that if aggregate demand can be reduced from AD'' to AD', as shown in panel (b) of Exhibit 2, then the equilibrium point will move down along the initial aggregate supply curve from *d* to *c*. *Whereas the passive approach relies on natural market forces to close an expansionary gap through a decrease in short-run aggregate supply, an active approach relies on just the right discretionary policy to close the gap through a decrease in aggregate demand.* The passive approach results in a higher price level, but the passive approach results in a lower price level. Thus, the correct discretionary policy can relieve the inflationary pressure associated with an expansionary gap. Whenever the Fed attempts to cool an overheated economy, as it did in 1994, this reflects an active monetary policy to close an inflationary gap. The economy was flying high, with output presumably exceeding potential, and the Fed was trying to orchestrate a so-called "soft landing."

Problems with Active Policy

The timely adoption and implementation of an appropriate active policy is not easy. One problem confronting policymakers is the difficulty of identifying the economy's potential level of output and the amount of unemployment associated with that level of output. Suppose the natural rate of unemployment is 6 percent, but policymakers believe it is 5 percent. As they pursue their elusive objective of 5 percent unemployment, they will find that output is constantly pushed beyond its potential, creating higher prices in the long run with no permanent reduction in unemployment. Recall that in the short run, if output is pushed beyond the economy's potential, an expansionary gap will open up, which will cause an upward shift in the short-run aggregate supply curve until the economy returns to its potential level of output at a higher price level.

Even if policymakers can accurately estimate the economy's potential level of output, formulating an effective policy requires abundant knowledge of current and future economic conditions. To pursue an effective active policy, policymakers must *first* be able to forecast what aggregate demand and aggregate supply would be without government intervention. Simply put, they must be able to predict what would happen with a passive policy. *Second,* policymakers must have in their discretionary arsenal the tools necessary to achieve the desired result relatively quickly. *Third,* policymakers must be able to forecast the effects of an active policy on the economy's key performance measures. *Fourth,* policymakers must work together. Fiscal policy and monetary policy are pursued by separate bodies that often fail to coordinate their efforts. To the extent that an active policy requires such coordination, the policy may not work as desired. In 1995, for example, Congress considered an expansionary tax cut at the same time the Fed was pursuing a contractionary monetary policy. *Fifth,* policymakers must be able to implement the appropriate policy, even if that policy involves short-term political costs. For example, during inflationary times the optimal policy may call for a tax increase or a tighter monetary policy, policies that may not be popular because they increase unemployment. *Finally,* policymakers must be able to deal with a variety of lags. As we will see next, these lags compound the problems of pursuing an active policy.

Separate bodies often fail to coordinate fiscal and monetary policies. For example, Congress in 1995 pursued an aggressive fiscal policy of tax and budget cuts while the Fed pursued a contractionary monetary policy.

The Problem of Lags

So far we have ignored the time required to implement policy. That is, we have assumed that the desired policy was selected and implemented instantaneously. We have also assumed that, once implemented, the policy would work as advertised—again, in no time. Actually, there may be long, sometimes unpredictable, lags at several stages in the process. These lags reduce the effectiveness of active policies.

First, there is a **recognition lag,** which is the time it takes to identify a problem and determine how serious it is. For example, time is required to accumulate data indicating that the economy is indeed performing below its potential. Even if initial data seem to provide early warning signals, these data are often subsequently revised. Therefore, policymakers must await additional evidence of trouble rather than risk responding to what may turn out to be a false alarm. One problem is that a recession is not recognized as such until more than six months after it begins. Since the average recession lasts about a year, the recession may be more than half over before it is officially recognized as such.

Even after enough evidence has accumulated, policymakers usually take additional time deciding what to do, so there is a **decision-making lag.** In the case of fiscal policy, Congress and the president must develop and agree upon an appropriate course of action. Fiscal legislation usually takes months to approve; it could take more than a year. On the other hand, the Fed can decide

Recognition lag The time needed to identify a macroeconomic problem and assess its seriousness

Decision-making lag The time needed to decide what to do after a macroeconomic problem is identified on the appropriate monetary policy more quickly than can those in charge of fiscal policy, so the decision-making lag is shorter for monetary policy.

Once a decision has been made, the new policy must be introduced, which often involves an **implementation lag.** Again, monetary policy has the advantage: after a policy has been adopted, the Fed can buy or sell U.S. securities, change the discount rate, or alter reserve requirements relatively quickly. The implementation lag is longer for fiscal policy. For example, if tax rates change, new tax forms may need to be printed and distributed (though in 1992, President Bush was able to increase disposable income by temporarily reducing payroll withholding taxes). If government spending changes, the appropriate government agencies must get involved. The implementation of fiscal policy can take more than a year. For example, in February 1983 the nation's unemployment rate reached 10.3 percent, with 11.5 million unemployed. The following month, Congress passed the Emergency Jobs Appropriation Act, providing $9 billion to create what supporters of the measure claimed would be hundreds of thousands of new jobs. Fifteen months later, only $3.1 billion had been spent and only 35,000 new jobs had been created because of the measure, according to a U.S. General Accounting Office study. By that time, the economy had recovered on its own, reducing the unemployment rate to 7.1 percent and increasing the number employed by 6.2 million! This public spending program was implemented only after the recession had bottomed out. Likewise, in the spring of 1993, President Clinton proposed a $16 billion stimulus package to help boost what appeared to be a sluggish recovery. The measure was defeated because it would have increased the deficit, yet the economy still gained 5.6 million jobs between January of 1993 and December of 1994.

Once a policy has been implemented, there is an **effectiveness lag** before the full impact of the policy registers on the economy. One problem with monetary policy is that the lag between a change in the money supply and its effect on aggregate demand and output is long and variable, ranging from several months up to 3 years. Fiscal policy, once enacted, usually requires 3 to 6 months to take effect and between 9 and 18 months to register its full effect.

These various lags make an active policy difficult to execute. The more variable the lags, the harder it is to predict when a particular policy will take effect and what the state of the economy will be at that time. To advocates of passive policy, these lags are reason enough to avoid discretionary policy. *Advocates of a passive approach argue that an active stabilization policy imposes troubling fluctuations in the price level and in the level of output because it often takes hold only after market forces have already returned the economy to its potential level of output.*

Talk in the media about "jump-starting" the economy reflects the active approach, which views the economy as a sputtering machine that can be fixed by an expert mechanic. The passive approach views the economy as more like a supertanker on automatic pilot. The policy question then becomes whether to trust that automatic pilot (i.e., the self-correcting tendencies of the economy) or to try to override the mechanism with active discretionary policies.[1]

Review of Policy Perspectives

The active and passive approaches embody different views about the natural stability of the economy and the ability of the government to implement appro-

Implementation lag The time needed to introduce a change in monetary or fiscal policy

Effectiveness lag The time necessary for changes in monetary or fiscal policy to have an effect on the economy

---

1   This analogy was contributed by J. W. Mixon, Jr. to *The Teaching Economist* 4 (Spring 1992): 3, edited by W. A. McEachern.

priate discretionary policies. Hence, they disagree about the role of government in the economy. As we have seen, advocates of an active approach think that the natural adjustments of wages and prices can be excruciatingly slow, particularly when unemployment is high, as it was during the Great Depression. Prolonged high unemployment means that much output must be sacrificed, and the unemployed must suffer personal hardship during the slow adjustment period. If high unemployment lasts a long time, labor skills may grow rusty and some long-term unemployed workers may drop out of the labor force. Therefore, prolonged unemployment may cause the economy's potential GDP to fall, as the case study of hysteresis in Chapter 11 suggested.

Thus, active policy associates a high cost with the failure to pursue a discretionary policy. And, despite the lags involved, advocates of active policy prefer action—whether through fiscal policy, monetary policy, or some combination of the two—to inaction. Passive policy advocates, on the other hand, believe that uncertain lags and ignorance about how the economy works prevent the government from accurately determining or effectively implementing the appropriate active policy. Therefore, the passive approach, rather than pursuing a misguided activist policy, relies more on the economy's natural ability to correct itself and on the government's automatic stabilizers.

Differences between active and passive approaches emerged during the presidential campaign of 1992, as the economy emerged sluggishly from a recession, as is discussed in the following case study.

CASE STUDY

Presidential Economics

In the third quarter of 1990, after the longest peacetime expansion this century, the U.S. economy slipped into a recession, touched off by Iraq's invasion of Kuwait. Because of huge federal deficits, policymakers were reluctant to turn to discretionary fiscal policy to stimulate the economy. That task was left to monetary policy. The Fed supplied additional reserves to the banking system and cut the discount rate several times—moves aimed at stimulating spending. The recession lasted only nine months, but the recovery was sluggish, with a growth rate slower than usual.

That sluggish recovery was the economic setting for the presidential election of 1992 between Democratic challenger Bill Clinton and Republican President George Bush. Since monetary policy did not seem to be providing a sufficient kick, was additional fiscal stimulus a viable option? With the federal budget deficit in 1992 already approaching $300 billion, a record level, would a higher deficit do more harm than good?

Bush's biggest liability during the campaign was the sluggish recovery and mounting federal debt; these were Clinton's biggest assets. Clinton's economic positions were that (1) Bush had not done enough to revive the economy; (2) Bush and his predecessor, President Reagan, were responsible for the jump in federal deficits; and (3) Bush could not be trusted because he broke his 1988 campaign pledge of no new taxes by signing a tax increase in 1990. Clinton called for raising the marginal tax rate on the top 2 percent of taxpayers and cutting taxes for the middle class. He also promised to create jobs through government spending that would "invest in America."

Location:

Presidents Bill Clinton and George Bush approached the 1992 presidential campaign with different ideas for how the government should manage fiscal and monetary policy. For more information about the economic views of each, browse their respective inaugural addresses, compiled by the Congressional Research Service of the Library of Congress and maintained by Columbia University's Bartleby Library (http:// www.columbia.edu/acis/ bartleby/inaugural/index. html).

Presidential Economics
continued

Bush tried to point out that technically the recession was over and the economy was on the right track. He blamed a Democratic Congress for blocking his recovery proposals, and he renewed his pledge of no new taxes (saying he really meant it this time). In fact, Bush promised to cut taxes by 1 percent, arguing that this would reallocate spending from government back to households.

Though both candidates were short on specifics, Clinton saw a stronger role for government, and Bush saw a stronger role for the private sector. Clinton's approach was more *active,* and Bush's approach was more *passive.* Neither candidate proposed aggressive deficit-reducing measures. Both apparently recognized that there were few votes to be gained by raising taxes or cutting government programs. Only third-party candidate Ross Perot said much about the deficit. In the end, the negative economic reports that dominated the news made people willing to gamble on Clinton. Evidently, during hard times an active policy has more voter appeal than a passive policy.

Sources: David Wessel, "Wanted: Fiscal Stimulus without Higher Taxes," *The Wall Street Journal,* 5 October 1992; and Herbert Stein, "The Inane Campaign Gives Me a Pain," *The Wall Street Journal,* 7 October 1992.

ROLE OF EXPECTATIONS

The effectiveness of a particular government policy depends in part on what people expect. As we observed in Chapter 11, the short-run aggregate supply curve is drawn for a given expected price level reflected in long-term wage contracts. If workers and firms expect more inflation, their labor agreements will reflect these inflationary expectations. An influential approach in macroeconomics, called the **rational expectations** school, argues that people form expectations on the basis of all available information, including information about the probable future actions of policymakers. Thus, aggregate supply depends on what sort of macroeconomic course policymakers are expected to pursue. For example, if people observe that the government tries to stimulate aggregate demand every time real output falls below the economy's potential, they will come to anticipate the effects of this policy on the levels of price and output. Robert Lucas, of the University of Chicago, won the 1995 Nobel Prize for his work in rational expectations.

Rational expectations A school of thought that claims people form expectations based on all available information, including the probable future actions of government policymakers

Monetary authorities are required to testify before Congress regularly, indicating the monetary policy they plan to pursue. We will consider the role of expectations in the context of monetary policy by examining the relationship between policy pronouncements and equilibrium output. We could employ a similar approach with fiscal policy, but active discretionary fiscal policy over the last decade has been viewed as less of an option because of huge federal deficits. To be sure, there are still tax increases, as in 1993, and proposed tax cuts, as in 1995, but monetary policy has been at center stage for the past decade.

Monetary Policy and Expectations

Suppose the economy is producing the potential rate of output. At the beginning of the year, firms and employees must negotiate wage agreements. While labor negotiations are under way, the Fed announces that throughout the year its monetary policy will aim at serving the money needs of an economy producing at the potential level. Thus the Fed plans to hold the price level con-

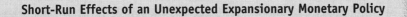

Short-Run Effects of an Unexpected Expansionary Monetary Policy

EXHIBIT 3

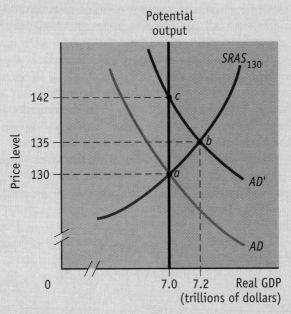

At point *a*, firms and workers expect the price level to be 130; supply curve $SRAS_{130}$ reflects those expectations. If the Federal Reserve unexpectedly pursues an expansionary monetary policy, the aggregate demand curve will be *AD'* rather than *AD*. Output will temporarily rise above the potential rate (at point *b*), but in the long run it will fall back to the potential rate at point *c*. The short-run effect of monetary policy is a higher level of output, but the long-run effect is just an increase in the price level.

stant. This seems to be the appropriate policy since the level of unemployment is already at the natural rate. Until the year is under way and monetary policy is actually implemented, however, the public cannot be sure what the Fed will do. Firms and workers understand that the Fed's plans appear optimal under the circumstances, since an expansionary monetary policy would, in the long run, simply result in inflation.

If workers limit their wage demands to the growth in labor productivity, this would be consistent with the Fed's announced policy of a constant price level. Alternatively, workers could try for higher wages, but that option would ultimately lead to inflation. Suppose workers and firms believe the Fed's pronouncements and agree on wage settlements based on expectations of a constant price level. If the Fed follows through, as promised, then the price level will be constant, output will remain at the economy's potential, and unemployment will remain at the natural rate. The situation is depicted in Exhibit 3, where the short-run aggregate supply curve, $SRAS_{130}$, is based on wage contracts reflecting an expected price level of 130. If the Fed follows the announced course, aggregate demand will be *AD* and equilibrium will be at point *a*, where the price level is as expected and the economy is producing $7.0 trillion, the potential level of output.

Suppose, however, that after workers and firms have signed labor pacts—that is, after the short-run aggregate supply curve has been determined—public officials become dissatisfied with the prevailing level of unemployment. Perhaps election-year concerns about unemployment or a false alarm about the onset of a recession prompts officials to pressure the Fed into stimulating aggregate demand and lowering unemployment in the short run through an expansionary monetary policy.

An expansionary monetary policy increases aggregate demand beyond *AD,* the level anticipated by firms and employees, to *AD'*. This unexpected policy stimulates output and employment in the short run to equilibrium point *b.* Output increases to $7.2 trillion, and the price level increases to 135. This temporary boost in output and reduction in unemployment lasts perhaps long enough to help public officials get reelected.

In the short run, workers are locked into wage levels that, because of the higher price level, are lower in real terms than they had bargained for. At their next opportunity, however, they will negotiate higher wages. These higher wage agreements will eventually cause the short-run aggregate supply curve in Exhibit 3 to shift up, intersecting *AD'* at point *c,* the economy's potential output. (To keep the diagram less cluttered, the shifted short-run aggregate supply curve is not shown.) So output once again returns to the economy's potential GDP, but in the process the price level rises to 142.

Thus, the unexpected expansionary monetary policy causes a short-run increase in output and employment, but in the long run the increase in the aggregate demand results only in a higher price level, or inflation. After a short-run surge in output, the short-run aggregate supply curve shifts to the left, the price level climbs, and output returns once again to the economy's potential.

Time inconsistency problem The problem that arises when policy-makers have an incentive to announce one policy to influence expectations but then to pursue a different policy once those expectations have been formed and acted upon

The **time inconsistency problem** arises when policymakers have an incentive to announce one policy to influence expectations but then to pursue a different policy once those expectations have been formed and acted upon. As we shall see in the next section, one solution to the time inconsistency problem is to take discretion away from the policymakers so that once a policy is announced, it cannot be changed.

Anticipating Monetary Policy

Suppose Fed policymakers grow alarmed by the resulting inflation. The next time around, the Fed once again announces that it plans a monetary policy that will hold the price level constant at 142, a policy aimed at keeping the economy's output at its potential. From their previous experience, however, workers and firms have learned that the Fed is willing to accept higher inflation for a temporary reduction in unemployment. Consequently, they take the Fed's announcement with a grain of salt. Workers, in particular, do not want to get caught again with their real wages down should the Fed implement a stimulative monetary policy, so a high-wage-increase settlement is reached.

In effect, workers and firms are betting that when the chips are down, monetary authorities will pursue an expansionary monetary policy regardless of their pronouncement to the contrary. The short-run aggregate supply curve reflecting these high-wage-increase agreements is depicted by $SRAS_{152}$ in Exhibit 4, where 152 is the expected price level. Note that *AD'* is the aggregate demand that would result if the Fed's announced constant-price-level policy were pursued; that demand curve intersects the potential output line at point *c,* where

Short-Run Effects of the Fed Pursuing a More Expansionary Policy than Announced

EXHIBIT 4

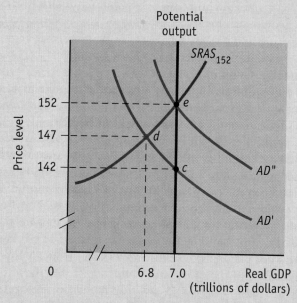

The Fed announces a monetary policy that will keep the price level at 142. Firms and workers, however, do not believe the announcement; they think the monetary policy will be expansionary. The short-run aggregate supply curve, $SRAS_{152}$, reflects their forecasts of the price level. The Fed must then decide what to do. If it follows the noninflationary policy, aggregate demand will be AD', and output will fall below potential to point d. To keep the economy performing at its potential, the Fed must increase the money supply by as much as workers and firms expected.

the price level is 142. But AD'' is the aggregate demand that firms and workers expect based on an expansionary policy. Firms and workers have agreed to wage settlements that will produce the economy's potential level of output if the Fed behaves as *expected*, not as *announced*.

Monetary authorities must now decide whether to stick with their announced plan of holding the price level constant or follow a more expansionary monetary policy. If they pursue the constant-price-level policy, aggregate demand will turn out to be AD' and short-run equilibrium will occur at point d. Short-run output will fall below the economy's potential, resulting in unemployment above the natural rate. If the monetary authorities want to keep the economy performing at its potential, they have only one alternative—to match expectations. Monetary authorities *must* pursue an expansionary monetary policy, a course of action that reinforces public skepticism of policy announcements. This expansionary policy will result in an aggregate demand of AD'', leading to an equilibrium at point e, where the price level is 152 and the economy produces its potential output. The economy moves directly from point c to point e.

Thus, firms and workers enter their negotiations with the realization that the Fed has an incentive to pursue an expansionary monetary course. Therefore, workers and firms agree to high wage increases, and the Fed follows with an expansionary policy, a policy that results in more inflation. Once workers and firms come to expect an expansionary monetary policy and the resulting inflation, such a policy does not spur even a temporary boost in output beyond the economy's potential. *Economists of the rational expectations school believe that an expansionary monetary policy, if fully and correctly anticipated, has no effect on output or employment. Only unanticipated or incorrectly anticipated changes in policy can influence output and employment.*

Policy Credibility

If the economy is already producing its potential output, an unexpected expansionary monetary policy would increase output and employment temporarily. The costs, however, are not only inflation in the long term but also a loss of credibility the next time around. Is there any way out of this? For the Fed to pursue a policy consistent with a constant-price-level course, its announcements must somehow be *credible,* or believable. Firms and workers must believe that when the time comes to make a hard decision, the Fed will follow through as promised. Perhaps the Fed could offer some sort of insurance policy to make everyone believe that policymakers who deviate from the set course will pay dearly—for example, the chairman of the Fed could promise to resign if the Fed does not pursue the announced course. Ironically, policymakers are often more credible and therefore more effective if they have their discretion taken away. In this case, a hard-and-fast rule could be substituted for a policymaker's discretion. Policy rules will be considered in the next section.

Consider the problems facing central banks in countries that have experienced hyperinflation. For an anti-inflation policy to succeed at the least possible cost in forgone output, the public must believe the announcements of central bankers. How do they establish credibility? Some economists believe that the most efficient anti-inflation policy is **cold turkey,** which is to announce and execute tough measures to stop inflation, such as halting the growth in the money supply. For example, in 1985 the annual rate of inflation in Bolivia was running at 20,000 percent when the new government announced a stern new policy. The restrictive new measures worked and inflation was stopped within a month, with only a 5 percent loss on output. Around the world, credible anti-inflation policies have been successful.[2] Drastic measures may involve costs. For example, some economists argue that the Fed's drastic measures to curb high U.S. inflation during the early 1980s precipitated the worst recession since the Great Depression. Some say that the Fed's pronouncements were not credible and therefore resulted in a recession.

Much depends on the Fed's time horizon. If policymakers take the long view of their duties, they will be reluctant to risk their long-run policy effectiveness for a temporary reduction in unemployment. If Fed officials realize that their credibility is hard to develop but easy to undermine, they will carefully weigh the effects of their actions on their reputations and follow what advocates of passive policy believe is the optimal policy: slow, steady growth in the

Cold turkey The announcement and execution of tough measures to reduce high inflation

---

2   For a discussion about how four hyperinflations in the 1920s ended, see Thomas Sargent, "The Ends of Four Big Inflations," *Inflation: Causes and Consequences,* Robert Hall, ed. (Chicago: University of Chicago Press, 1982), pp. 41–98.

money supply. Often Congress tries to pressure the Fed to stimulate the economy. Consider central bank independence around the world in the following case study.

Some economists argue that the Fed would do better in the long run if it were committed to the single goal of price stability. For instance, look at the German experience. By law, the Bundesbank, the German central bank, is not subject to instructions from the government or from any other authority. And, by law, the goal of price stability is given the highest priority. Since 1960, the German inflation rate has been only half the U.S. rate. The story is similar in Japan. Since 1975, there has been a strong commitment by the Japanese central bank to low inflation, and inflation in Japan since 1975, has averaged only half the U.S. rate.

Some economists argue that to focus on price stability, a central bank should be insulated from political influence. When the Fed was established, several features insulated the Fed from the ordinary political process—the 14-year terms with staggered appointments, for example. Also, the Fed is prohibited from purchasing securities directly from the U.S. Treasury. What's more, since the Fed has its own source of income (interest on government securities), it does not rely on Congress for a budget.

Does this independence affect performance? When central banks for 17 advanced industrial countries are ranked from least independent to most independent, inflation is the lowest in countries with the most independent central banks and highest in countries with the least independent central banks. For example, the most independent central banks are in Germany and Switzerland, and their average inflation rate from 1973 to 1988 was about 3 percent per year. The least independent banks during that period were in Spain, New Zealand, Australia, and Italy, where the rate of inflation averaged 11.5 percent per year. The U.S. central bank is considered relatively independent; our inflation rate, which averaged 6.5 percent per year between 1973 and 1988, was between the average rates for the most independent and least independent groups.

The tendency around the world is toward greater central bank independence. Since 1988, for example, Australia and New Zealand have amended the laws governing their central banks to make price stability the primary goal. The Maastricht agreement, which defines the framework for establishing a single European currency in 1999, identifies price stability as the main objective and requires member countries to give their central banks greater independence. And Chile and Argentina, developing countries that recently experienced hyperinflation, have legislated more central bank independence.

Sources: Alberto Alesina and Lawrence Summers, "Central Bank Independence and Macroeconomic Performance: Some Comparative Evidence," *Journal of Money, Credit and Banking*, 25 (May 1993): pp. 151–62; and Patricia Pollard, "Central Bank Independence and Economic Performance," *Federal Reserve Bank of St. Louis*, July/August 1993, pp. 21–36.

CASE STUDY

Central Bank Independence and Price Stability

Location:

The Bundesbank, the German central bank, is located in Frankfurt, Germany. By law, the Bundesbank is autonomous and has as its primary responsibility the goal of price stability. To discover more, visit the *Frankfurt Money Strategist*, a research report that, in its words, is "the eyes and ears on the European Continent for private investors, the money management industry, diverse financial professionals, government officials, and others needing to understand the Bundesbank, German interest rates, and macro-economic trends . . . ." (http://www.helix.net/fms/).

Aggregate demand and aggregate supply provide a way of picturing how output and the price level adjust to a new equilibrium, but this picture says little about how fast this adjustment occurs. The speed of adjustment is an empirical question; an empirical tool, the *Phillips curve,* has been developed to focus on the issue of timing. We next examine the Phillips curve.

THE PHILLIPS CURVE

At one time, policymakers thought they faced a fairly stable long-run tradeoff between inflation and unemployment. This view was suggested by the research of New Zealand economist A. W. Phillips, who in 1958 published an article that examined the historical relation between inflation and unemployment in the United Kingdom.[3] Based on about 100 years of evidence, his data suggested an inverse relationship between the unemployment rate and changes in money wages (serving as a measure of inflation). This relationship implied that the opportunity cost of reducing unemployment was higher inflation, and the opportunity cost of reducing inflation was higher unemployment.

Phillips curve A curve showing possible combinations of the inflation rate and the unemployment rate

The possible options with respect to unemployment and inflation are illustrated by the **Phillips curve** in Exhibit 5. The unemployment rate is measured along the horizontal axis and the inflation rate along the vertical axis. Let's begin at point *a*, which depicts one possible combination of unemployment and inflation. Fiscal or monetary policy could be used to stimulate output and thereby reduce unemployment, moving the economy from point *a* to point *b*.

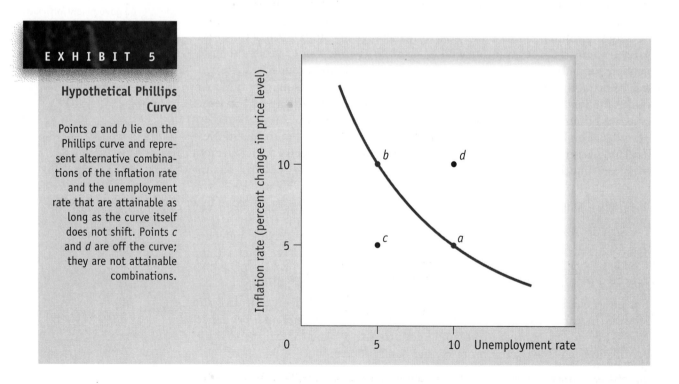

EXHIBIT   5

Hypothetical Phillips Curve

Points *a* and *b* lie on the Phillips curve and represent alternative combinations of the inflation rate and the unemployment rate that are attainable as long as the curve itself does not shift. Points *c* and *d* are off the curve; they are not attainable combinations.

---

3   A.W. Phillips, "Relation Between Unemployment and the Rate of Change in Money Wage Rates in the United Kingdom, 1861–1957," *Economica* 25 (November 1958): pp. 283–299.

Notice, however, that the reduction in unemployment comes at the cost of higher inflation. A reduction in unemployment with no change in inflation would be represented by point *c*. But as you can see, this alternative is not an option available on the curve. Thus, policymakers were thought to face a difficult trade-off: they could choose either lower inflation or lower unemployment, but not both.

Not everyone accepted the implications of the Phillips curve, but during the 1960s, policymakers increasingly came to believe that they faced a stable, long-run trade-off between unemployment and inflation. The Phillips curve was based on an era when inflation was low and the primary disturbances in the economy were to aggregate demand. Changes in aggregate demand can be viewed as movements along a given short-run aggregate supply curve. If aggregate demand increased, the price level increased, but unemployment decreased. If aggregate demand decreased, the price level decreased, but unemployment increased. Many economists therefore assumed that there was a trade-off between inflation and unemployment. Hence, with appropriate demand-management policies, government policymakers could choose any point along the Phillips curve.

The 1970s proved this view wrong for two reasons. First, some of the biggest disturbances were adverse *supply* shocks, such as the shocks created by the oil embargoes and worldwide crop failures. These shocks shifted the aggregate supply curve to the left. A reduction in aggregate supply led to both higher inflation *and* higher unemployment. This stagflation was at odds with the Phillips curve. Second, economists learned that when short-run equilibrium output exceeds potential output, the economy opens an expansionary gap. As this gap is closed by the upward movement of the short-run aggregate supply curve, the results are greater inflation *and* higher unemployment—results inconsistent with a given Phillips curve.

The combination of high inflation and high unemployment resulting from stagflation and expansionary gaps is represented by an outcome such as point *d* in Exhibit 5. By the end of the 1970s, increases in inflation and unemployment suggested either that the Phillips curve had shifted out or that it no longer described economic reality. The situation called for a reexamination of the Phillips curve, a reexamination that led economists to distinguish between short-run Phillips curves and the long-run Phillips curve.

Short-Run Phillips Curve

To discuss the underpinnings of the Phillips curve, we must return to the short-run aggregate supply curve. We begin by assuming that the price level this year is reflected by a price index of, say, 100. Suppose that people expect prices to be about 4 percent higher next year. So the expected price level next year is 104. Workers will therefore negotiate labor contracts based on an expected price level of 104, which is 4 percent higher than the current price level. As the short-run aggregate supply curve in panel (a) of Exhibit 6 indicates, if *AD* is the aggregate demand curve and the price level is 104, as expected, output will equal the economy's potential GDP, shown here to be $7.0 trillion. Recall that when the economy produces its potential GDP, unemployment is equal to the natural rate.

The short-run relationship between inflation and unemployment is presented in panel (b) of Exhibit 6 under the assumption that people expect the inflation rate to be 4 percent. The unemployment rate is measured along the horizontal axis and the inflation rate along the vertical axis. Panel (a) shows that when the inflation rate is 4 percent, the economy produces its potential GDP. When the economy produces its potential GDP, unemployment is at the natural rate, which we assume to be 6 percent in panel (b). The combination of 4 percent inflation and 6 percent unemployment is reflected by point *a* in panel (b), which corresponds to point *a* in panel (a).

What if aggregate demand turns out to be greater than expected, as indicated by curve *AD'* in panel (a)? In the short run, the greater demand results in equilibrium at point *b*, with a price level of 106 and an output level of $7.1 trillion. Since the price level is greater than the expected level reflected in wage contracts, the inflation rate is also greater than expected. Specifically, the infla-

EXHIBIT 6

Relationship Between the Short-Run Aggregate Supply Curve and the Short-Run Phillips Curve

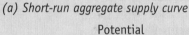

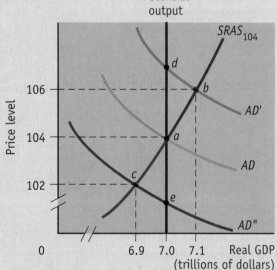

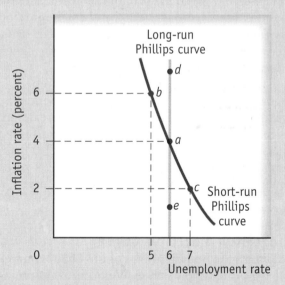

(a) Short-run aggregate supply curve

(b) Short-run and long-run Phillips curves

If people expect a price level of 104, which is 4 percent higher than the current level, and if *AD* is the aggregate demand curve, then the price level will actually be 104 and output will be at the potential rate. Point *a* in both panels represents this situation. Unemployment will be at the natural rate, 6 percent.

If aggregate demand is higher than expected (*AD'* instead of *AD*), the economy will be at point *b* in both panels. If aggregate demand is less than expected (*AD''* rather than *AD*), short-run equilibrium will be at point *c*; the price level, 102, will be lower than expected, and output will be below the potential rate. The lower inflation rate and higher unemployment rate are shown as point *c* in panel (b). In panel (b), points *a*, *b*, and *c* trace the short-run Phillips curve.

In the long run, the actual price level equals the expected price level and output is at the potential level, $7.0 trillion, in panel (a), and unemployment is at the natural rate, 6 percent, in panel (b). Points *a*, *d*, and *e* represent that situation; they lie on the vertical long-run Phillips curve.

tion rate turns out to be 6 percent, not 4 percent. Output now exceeds the economy's potential, so the unemployment rate falls below the natural rate to 5 percent. This combination of a higher inflation rate and a lower level of unemployment is depicted by point *b* in panel (b), which corresponds to point *b* in panel (a).

What if aggregate demand turns out to be less than expected, as indicated by *AD"* in panel (a)? In the short run, the lower demand results in equilibrium at point *c,* where the price level of 102 is lower than the expected level reflected in labor contracts, and output of $6.9 trillion is below potential GDP. With a lower-than-expected price level, the inflation rate is 2 percent rather than the expected 4 percent. With output below the economy's potential, the unemployment rate is 7 percent, which exceeds the natural rate. This combination of lower-than-expected inflation and higher-than-expected unemployment is reflected by point *c* on the curve in panel (b).

Note that the short-run aggregate supply curve in panel (a) can be used to establish the inverse relationship between the inflation rate and the level of unemployment illustrated in panel (b). This latter curve is called a **short-run Phillips curve,** and it is generated by the intersection of alternative aggregate demand curves with a given short-run aggregate supply curve. *The short-run Phillips curve is therefore based on labor contracts reflecting a given expected price level, which implies a given expected rate of inflation.* The short-run Phillips curve in panel (b) is based on an expected inflation rate of 4 percent. If inflation turns out as expected, unemployment will equal the natural rate. If inflation is higher than expected, unemployment in the short run will fall below the natural rate. If inflation is lower than expected, unemployment in the short run will exceed the natural rate.

Short-run Phillips curve A curve, based on an expected price level, that reflects an inverse relationship between the inflation rate and the level of unemployment

Long-Run Phillips Curve

If inflation is higher than was expected when long-term labor contracts were negotiated, output can exceed the economy's potential in the short run, but not in the long run. Labor shortages and worker dissatisfaction with shrinking real wages will lead to higher wage agreements during the next round of negotiations. The short-run aggregate supply curve will shift up to the left until it passes through point *d* in panel (a) of Exhibit 6, returning the economy to its potential level of output. Point *d* represents a higher price level, and hence a higher rate of inflation. But notice that the higher inflation is no longer associated with reduced unemployment.

The economy, in closing the expansionary gap, thus experiences both higher unemployment and a higher inflation. At point *d* in panel (a), the economy is producing its potential GDP, which means that unemployment equals the natural rate. This combination of the natural rate of unemployment and higher inflation is depicted by point *d* in panel (b). The unexpectedly higher aggregate demand has no lasting effect on output or unemployment. Note that whereas points *a, b,* and *c* are on the same short-run Phillips curve, point *d* is not.

To trace the long-run effects of a lower-than-expected price level, let's return again to point *c* in panel (a) of Exhibit 6. At this point, the actual price level is below the expected level reflected in long-term contracts, so output is below potential GDP. If firms and workers negotiate lower money wages (or if the growth in nominal wages trails inflation), the short-run aggregate supply curve will shift to the right until it passes through point *e*, where the economy returns once again to its potential level of output. Both inflation and unemployment will fall, as reflected by point *e* in panel (b).

Note that points *a, d,* and *e* in panel (a) depict long-run equilibrium points, so the expected price level equals the actual price level. At those same points in panel (b), the expected inflation rate equals the actual rate, so unemployment equals the natural rate. We can connect points *a, d,* and *e* in panel (b) to form what is called the **long-run Phillips curve.** *When employers and workers have the time and the ability to adjust fully to any unexpected change in aggregate demand, the long-run Phillips curve is a vertical line drawn at the economy's natural rate of unemployment, as shown in panel (b).* As long as prices and wages are flexible, the rate of unemployment, in the long run, is independent of the rate of inflation. *Thus, according to proponents of this type of analysis, in the long run policymakers cannot choose between unemployment and inflation. They can choose only among alternative levels of inflation.*

The Natural Rate Hypothesis

As defined in Chapter 11, the natural rate of unemployment is the rate that is consistent with the economy's potential level of output, which we have discussed extensively already. An important idea to emerge from this reexamination of the Phillips curve is the **natural rate hypothesis,** which states that in the long run the economy tends toward the natural rate of unemployment. This natural rate is largely independent of the level of the *aggregate demand* stimulus provided by monetary or fiscal policy. Policymakers may be able to push the economy beyond its natural, or potential, rate of production temporarily, but only if the public does not anticipate the resulting level of aggregate demand and the resulting price level.

Weak Version. The **weak version of the natural rate hypothesis** states that policymakers can influence the trade-off between unemployment and inflation in the short run but not in the long run. Unemployment could be maintained below the natural rate, but only at the cost of ever-increasing inflation. For example, if the Fed unexpectedly increased the money supply at a faster and faster rate, actual inflation would rise faster and faster, continually exceeding expected inflation. Unemployment would fall, but such a policy is clearly self-limiting. In the long run, monetary or fiscal policy affects only the rate of inflation, not the rate of unemployment; in the long run, there is no trade-off between inflation and unemployment.

Strong Version. In the **strong version of the natural rate hypothesis,** even this short-run kick becomes smaller and smaller over time. According to rational expectations theory, market participants gain experience as time goes by, so they adjust more and more quickly to policy decisions that are expected to affect the price level. As market participants learn more about the behavior of policymakers, the cycles generated by short-run fluctuations in inflation and unemployment arising from discretionary policy get smaller and smaller. People become more adept not only at predicting the effects of a policy on the economy but also at predicting the policy itself. It becomes more and more difficult for policymakers to surprise the public. Therefore, the short-run gains in employment resulting from monetary or fiscal surprises diminish as the public comes to expect as much. An implication of the natural rate hypothesis is that

Long-run Phillips curve A vertical line drawn at the economy's natural rate of unemployment that traces equilibrium points that can occur when employers and workers have the time to adjust fully to any unexpected change in aggregate demand

Natural rate hypothesis The natural rate of unemployment is largely independent of the stimulus provided by monetary or fiscal policy

Weak version of the natural rate hypothesis Policymakers can trade off between unemployment and inflation in the short run but not in the long run

Strong version of the natural rate hypothesis The short-run gains in employment resulting from monetary or fiscal surprises diminish as the public comes to expect as much

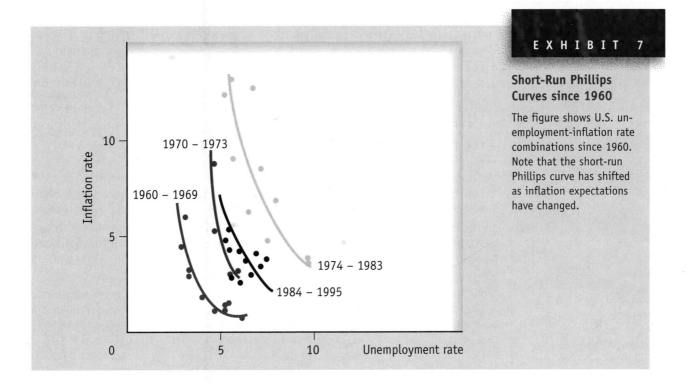

EXHIBIT 7

Short-Run Phillips Curves since 1960

The figure shows U.S. unemployment-inflation rate combinations since 1960. Note that the short-run Phillips curve has shifted as inflation expectations have changed.

regardless of policymakers' concerns about unemployment, the policy that results in low inflation is generally going to be the optimal policy in the long run.

Evidence of the Phillips Curve

What has been the actual relationship between unemployment and inflation in the United States? In Exhibit 7, each year since 1960 is represented by a point, with the unemployment rate measured along the horizontal axis and the inflation rate measured along the vertical axis. Superimposed on these points is a series of short-run Phillips curves showing patterns of unemployment and inflation during four distinct periods since 1960. Remember, each short-run Phillips curve is drawn for a given expected rate of inflation. A change in inflationary expectations results in a shift in the short-run Phillips curve.

The clearest trade-off between unemployment and inflation seems to have occurred between 1960 and 1969; the points for those years fit neatly along the curve. In the early part of the decade, inflation was low but unemployment was high; as the 1960s progressed, unemployment declined but actual inflation increased. The average inflation rate during the decade was only 2.5 percent, and the average unemployment rate was 4.8 percent.

The short-run Phillips curve appears to have shifted up to the right for the period 1970–1973, when inflation and unemployment both climbed to an average of 5.2 percent. In 1974, sharp increases in oil prices and crop failures around the world sparked another shift in the curve. Though points for the decade between 1974 and 1983 do not lie as neatly along the curve as points for earlier periods do, a trade-off between inflation and unemployment is still evident. During the 1974–1983 period, inflation rose on average to 8.2 percent and unemployment climbed on average to 7.5 percent.

Milton Friedman, a Nobel prize winning economist, is perhaps the best known advocate of fixed-growth-rate monetary policy. For information about Friedman, visit "Nobel Laureates in Economic Sciences," a service of the Ohio State University's Fisher College of Business (http://www.cob.ohio-state.edu/facstf/homepage/tomassini/nobel/friedman.html). To learn more about his ideas, browse a June 1992 interview with Friedman conducted by *The Region,* published by the Federal Reserve Bank of Minneapolis (http://woodrow.mpls.frb.fed.us/pubs/region/int692.html).

Finally, after recessions in the early 1980s, the short-run Phillips curve seems to have shifted down since 1983; average inflation for 1984–1995 fell to 3.7 percent and average unemployment fell to 6.2 percent. Changes in the average unemployment rate across periods since 1960 suggest that the underlying natural rate of unemployment may have shifted as well. (You'll recall that earlier we discussed the possibility that the natural rate has drifted higher since the 1960s.)

POLICY RULES VERSUS DISCRETION

As noted earlier, the active approach views the economy as inherently unstable and in need of discretionary policy to eliminate excessive unemployment when it arises. The passive approach views the economy as so stable that discretionary policy is not only unnecessary but may itself cause destabilizing swings in aggregate demand that ultimately lead to more inflation. In place of discretionary policy, the passive approach often calls for predetermined rules to guide the actions of policymakers. In the context of fiscal policy, these predetermined rules may take the form of automatic stabilizers, such as unemployment insurance, a progressive income tax, and transfer payments, all of which are aimed at offsetting the effects of business fluctuations. In this section, we examine the arguments for rules versus discretion in the context of monetary policy.

Rationale for Rules

The rationale for passive rules rather than the use of active discretion arises from different views of how the economy works. One view holds that *the economy is so complex and economic aggregates interact in such obscure ways and with such varied lags that policymakers cannot comprehend what is going on well enough to pursue an active monetary or fiscal policy.* With regard to monetary policy, Milton Friedman is perhaps the best-known advocate of this position. He argues that although there is a link between money growth and the growth in nominal GDP, the exact relationship is hard to pin down because of long lags in the response of economic activity to changes in money growth. If the central bank adopts a discretionary policy that is based on an incorrect estimate of the lag, money may expand just when a tighter monetary policy is more appropriate. To avoid the timing problem, Friedman recommends that the Fed follow a fixed-growth-rate monetary policy year after year, such as an annual growth rate of 3 percent in the money supply.

A comparison of economic forecasters and weather forecasters may help shed light on the position of those who advocate the use of a passive rule. Suppose you are in charge of the heating and cooling system at a major shopping mall. You realize that weather forecasters have a poor record in your area, particularly in the early spring, when days can be either warm or cold. Each day you must guess what the temperature will be and, based on that guess, decide whether to fire up the heater or turn on the air conditioner. Because the ventilation system and the mall are so large, you must start up the system long before you know for sure what the weather will be. Once the system has been turned on, it cannot be turned off until later in the day.

Suppose you guess the day will be cold, so you turn on the heat. If the day turns out to be cold, your policy is correct and the mall temperature will be just right. But if the day turns out to be warm, the heater will make the mall unbearable. You would have been better off with no heat. In contrast, if you turn on the air conditioner expecting a warm day but the day turns out to be cold, the mall will be freezing. The lesson is that if you have little ability to predict the weather, you should use neither heat nor air conditioning. Similarly, if monetary officials cannot predict the course of the economy, they should not try to fine-tune monetary policy. Complicating the prediction problem is the fact that monetary officials are not sure about the lags involved with monetary policy. The situation is comparable to your not knowing for sure when you turn the switch to "on" how long the system will actually take to come on.

This analogy applies only if the cost of doing nothing—using neither heat nor air conditioning—is relatively low. In the early spring, you can assume that there is little risk of the weather being so cold that water pipes will freeze or so hot that the walls will sweat. This assumption is like the passive view that the economy is inherently stable and periods of prolonged unemployment are unlikely. In such an economy, the costs of *not* intervening are relatively low. In contrast, advocates of active policy believe that there can be wide and prolonged swings in the economy (analogous to wide and prolonged swings in temperature), so doing nothing involves significant risks.

Rules and Rational Expectations

Another group of economists also advocates passive rules, but not because they believe we know too little about how the economy works. Proponents of the *rational expectations approach* claim that people on average have a pretty good idea about how the economy works and what to expect from government policy-makers. Individuals and firms know enough about the monetary and fiscal policies pursued in the past to anticipate, with reasonable accuracy, future policies and the effects of these policies on the economy. Some individuals will forecast too high and some too low, but on average forecasts will turn out to be about right. *To the extent that monetary policy is fully anticipated by workers and firms, it has no effect on the level of output; it affects only the level of prices.* Thus, only unexpected changes in policy can bring about short-run changes in output.

Since, in the long run, changes in the money supply affect only the rate of inflation, not real output, followers of the rational expectations theory believe that the Fed should not try to pursue a discretionary monetary policy. Instead, they believe the Fed should follow a predictable monetary rule. A monetary rule would reduce monetary surprises and would therefore reduce departures from the natural rate of output. *Whereas Friedman advocates a rule because of the Fed's ignorance about the lag structure of the economy, those who subscribe to the rational expectations theory advocate a predictable rule to avoid monetary surprises, which result in departures from the natural rate of output.*

Theory of Real Business Cycles

A new theory in the debate about the appropriate role for monetary policy is **real business cycle theory,** which holds that fluctuations in real GDP and employment are caused not by misguided monetary policy but by real shocks to the economy, such as changes in tastes and in technology. According to real business cycle theory, *real* factors, such as random shocks to the economy's real potential output, rather than nominal factors, such as the money supply and its rate of growth, are the most important sources of aggregate fluctuations.

Real business cycle theory Fluctuations in real GDP and employment are caused not by misguided monetary policy but by real shocks to the economy, such as changes in tastes and in technology

Real business cycle theory draws no distinction between the short-run aggregate supply curve and the long-run aggregate supply curve. According to this theory, wages are assumed to be so flexible that the labor market is always in equilibrium and unemployment is always at its natural rate. Therefore, the vertical long-run aggregate supply curve is also the short-run aggregate supply curve. Fluctuations in output and employment occur because of shifts in the aggregate supply curve—that is, shifts in the potential level of output. Usually, the long-run aggregate supply curve shifts to the right and the economy expands. But the growth rate in aggregate supply varies. Sometimes the long-run aggregate supply curve shifts to the left, resulting in a decrease in real GDP and an increase in unemployment. Because real business cycle theory views most business cycles as resulting from fluctuations in the economy's potential level of output, this theory sees little role for an active policy to reduce business fluctuations.

According to real business cycle theory, monetary policy that influences aggregate demand has no effect on real GDP, though it does affect the price level. Although real business cycle theory sees no role for money in the business cycle, it does identify money as an important determinant of inflation. Under the circumstances, the Fed should focus on keeping inflation low and forget about trying to offset business fluctuations.

Despite support by some economists for rules rather than discretion, central bankers appear reluctant to follow hard-and-fast rules about the course of future policy. Discretion appears to rule the day. As Paul Volcker, the former Fed chairman, argued:

The appeal of a simple rule is obvious. It would simplify our job at the Federal Reserve, make monetary policy easy to understand, and facilitate monitoring of our performance. And if the rule worked, it would reduce uncertainty. . . . But unfortunately, I know of no rule that can be relied on with sufficient consistency in our complex and constantly evolving economy.[4]

CONCLUSION

This chapter examined the implications of active versus passive policy. The important question is whether the economy is (1) essentially stable and self-correcting when it gets off track or (2) essentially unstable and in need of active policies. Advocates of active policy believe that the Fed and the federal government should reduce economic fluctuations by stimulating a sluggish economy when output falls below its potential level and by dampening an overheated economy when output exceeds its potential level. Active policy advocates argue that government attempts to insulate the economy from the ups and downs of the business cycle may be far from perfect but are better than nothing. Some activists also believe that high unemployment may be self-reinforcing, because some unemployed workers lose valuable job skills and grow to accept unemployment as a way of life, as has happened in Europe.

---

4   Statement of Paul Volcker, then chairman of the Board of Governors of the Federal Reserve System, before the Committee on Banking, Finance, and Urban Affairs, U.S. House of Representatives, August 1983.

Passive policy advocates, on the other hand, believe that discretionary policy may contribute to the cyclical swings in the economy, leading to higher inflation in the long run with no permanent effect on either output or employment. This group relies on passive rules for monetary policy and automatic stabilizers for fiscal policy.

The active-passive debate in this chapter has focused on monetary policy primarily because discretionary fiscal policy in recent years has been hampered by chronic federal deficits that have ballooned the national debt. In the next chapter, we will take a closer look at these deficits and the debt that has resulted.

SUMMARY

1. Advocates of active policy view the private sector—particularly fluctuations in investment—as the main source of economic instability in the economy. Because the return to potential output can be slow and painful, activists recommend that government intervene with monetary or fiscal policy to stimulate aggregate demand when actual output is below potential output.

2. Advocates of passive policy argue that the economy has a natural resiliency that will cause output to return to its potential level within a reasonable amount of time even if upset by some shock. They point to the variable and uncertain lags associated with discretionary policy as reason enough to steer clear of active intervention.

3. At one time, public officials were thought to face a stable trade-off between higher unemployment and higher inflation. Recent evidence suggests that if there is a trade-off, it exists only in the short run, not in the long run. Expansionary fiscal or monetary policies, if unexpected, can stimulate output and employment in the short run. But if the economy is already at or near its potential output, these expansionary policies will, in the long run, result only in higher inflation.

4. The passive policy approach suggests that the government should follow steady and predictable policies and avoid trying to stimulate or dampen aggregate demand over the business cycle. Passive policies are reflected in strict monetary rules, such as a fixed rate of growth in the money supply, and automatic fiscal stabilizers.

QUESTIONS AND PROBLEMS

1. **(Active Approach vs. Passive Approach)** Contrast the passive approach's view of the behavior of wages and prices during a contractionary gap to the active approach's view.

2. **(Aggregate Supply)** What is the variable that naturally adjusts in the labor market, shifting the short-run aggregate supply curve to guarantee employment at the natural rate? Why does the active approach assume that the short-run aggregate supply curve shifts up more easily and quickly than it shifts down? Why or why not?

3. **(Rational Expectations)** Can the government fool the public with erratic monetary and fiscal policy if the public has rational expectations? Suppose that the government uses a monetarist rule. How will rational expectations affect the impact of the rule?

4. **(Active Approach)** Explain why proponents of the active approach recommend government intervention to close an expansionary gap.

5. **(Macroeconomic Policy)** Some economists argue that only unanticipated increases in the money supply cause increases in real GDP. Explain why this may be the case.

6. **(Policy Lags)** Identify the lags in discretionary policy described by each of the following statements. Why would long lags make discretionary policy less effective?
   a. The time between the government determining that the economy is in the midst of a major recession and approving a tax cut to reduce unemployment.
   b. The time between the government increasing the money supply and the policy affecting the economy.
   c. The time between the start of a recession and the government identifying the existence and severity of the recession.

d. The time between the Fed deciding to reduce the money supply and the money supply actually falling.

7. **(Problems with Active Policy)** Use an *AD/AS* graph to illustrate and explain the short-run and long-run effects on the economy of the following situation: Both the natural rate of unemployment and the actual rate of unemployment are 5 percent. However, the government believes that the natural rate of unemployment is 6 percent and that the economy is overheating. Therefore, the government introduces a policy to reduce aggregate demand.

8. **(Phillips Curve)** Why does a movement up the short-run Phillips curve imply a declining real wage for workers? Would workers allow this decline to continue unabated? How would the short-run Phillips curve adjust to changes in workers' perceptions about their real wages?

9. **(Rational Expectations)** Define rational expectations. Using an *AD/AS* graph, illustrate the short-run impact on prices, output, and unemployment of an increase in the money supply that is correctly anticipated by the public. Assume that the economy is operating initially at potential output.

10. **(Potential GNP)** Why is it hard for policymakers to decide if the economy is operating at its potential output level? Why is this a problem?

11. **(Active Approach vs. Passive Approach)** Discuss the role each of the following should play in the debate between the active and passive approaches.
    a. The speed of adjustments in nominal wages.
    b. The speed of adjustments in expectations about inflation.
    c. The existence of lags in policy creation and implementation.
    d. Variability in the natural rate of unemployment over time.

12. **(Phillips Curve)** Describe the different Phillips curve trade-offs implied by the active approach to policy, the weak version of the natural rate hypothesis, and the strong version of the natural rate hypothesis.

13. **(Phillips Curve)** Indicate the impact on the short-run Phillips curve of each of the following:

a. An increase in actual inflation, but not in expected inflation.
b. An increase in expected inflation.
c. An unanticipated decrease in the money supply.
d. A decrease in expected inflation.

14. **(Phillips Curve)** What will shift the long-run Phillips curve?

15. **(Phillips Curve)** Suppose the economy is at point *d* on the long-run Phillips curve shown in Exhibit 6. If that inflation rate is unacceptably high, how can policy makers get the inflation rate down? Would rational expectations help or hurt their efforts?

16. **(Policy Rules)** Some economists call for predetermined rules to guide the actions of government policymakers. What are the two rationales given for such rules?

17. **(Real Business Cycles)** Define the real business cycle theory. According to this theory, how does the short-run aggregate supply curve compare to the long-run curve? Why?

18. **(Expectations and Policy)** Suppose that people in an election year believe that public policymakers are going to pursue expansionary policies to enhance their reelection chances. Why might such expectations put pressure on officials to pursue such policies even if they weren't planning to?

19. **(Presidential Economics)** During the 1992 campaign, both President George Bush and challenger Bill Clinton called for some tax cuts. The economy at the time was in the midst of a slow recovery from the 1990-1991 recession. Use the discussion of policy lags to analyze the potential danger of such tax cuts.

20. **(Central Bank Independence and Price Stability)** One source of independence for the Fed, as suggested in Chapter 13, is the length of term for members of the Board of Governors. Given that the Fed's annual operating expenses are less than $1.5 billion, is there anything in Chapter 14's Exhibit 5 that suggests another source for Fed independence?

21. The U.S. Government takes an active approach in not only domestic economic policy but, under certain circumstances, in the policies of foreign countries as well. For example, in 1995 the U.S. government promised Mexico approximately $20 billion to support the falling Mexican Peso. Why would the U.S. government pursue such a policy in Mexico? For differing views on this issue, review the "Treasury Secretary's Report to Congress on Mexico," maintained by the Department of the Treasury (**http://www. ustreas.gov/treasury/mexico/top.html**) and "The proposed Bailout of Mexico," a January 26, 1995, speech made before Congress by Rep. Marcy Kaptur (D, OH). To find the speech, recorded in the *Congressional Record*, visit the Government Printing Office's "GPO Gate" (**http://ssdc.ucsd.edu/ gpo/**) and search within the 1995 *Congressional Record* for "The Proposed Bailout in Mexico." In general, should the U.S. government take an active approach in foreign economic policy?

Budgets, Deficits, and Public Policy

T he word *budget* derives from the Old French word *bougette,* which means "little bag." The annual federal budget is now over $1,600,000,000,000—over $1.6 trillion dollars. Big money! If this "little bag" contained $100 bills, it would weigh over 17,000 *tons!* These $100 bills would fill over 600 trailer trucks. These $100 bills could paper over a 10-lane highway stretching from Bangor, Maine, to Los Angeles, California. This budget could buy every U.S. household a new Mercedes every other year. If the president's sole function were to pay the bills by writing million-dollar checks, he would have to write 3 checks a minute, 24 hours a day, 365 days a year to keep up with federal spending.

In this chapter, we first examine the federal budget process, then turn to the major budget concern today: the giant budget deficits of the 1980s and 1990s and the resulting explosion of national debt. We look at the source of deficits over the years and the immediate effects of deficits on the economy. We then examine the short-run and long-run effects of the national debt. Topics discussed in this chapter include:

- The budget process
- The burden of the debt
- Rationale for deficits
- Measures to reduce deficits
- Impact of deficits

17

THE FEDERAL BUDGET PROCESS

Government budget A plan for government expenditures and revenues for a specified period, usually a year

The **government budget** is a plan for government expenditures and revenues for a specified period, usually a year. The period covered by the federal budget is called the *fiscal year,* and it runs from October 1 of one year to September 30 of the following year. Social Security and Medicare made up 32.7 percent of the budget in fiscal year 1995, and welfare accounted for 14.5 percent. So about half the federal budget consists of cash and in-kind payments to individuals. National defense accounted for 18.0 percent of the budget (down from 28.1 percent in 1987). Interest payments on the debt soaked up 15.3 percent, or nearly one in six federal dollars, up from 7.0 percent in 1975. Exhibit 1 provides a breakdown of federal spending by major category. (For the breakdown during the past 50 years, see Exhibit 4 in Chapter 4.)

The Presidential Role in the Budget Process

Before 1921, the federal budget played a minor role in the economy, with federal spending, except during wartime, amounting to less than 3 percent relative to GDP (versus 22 percent today). Federal agencies made budget requests directly to Congress, bypassing the president entirely. Legislation in 1921 created the Office of Management and Budget (OMB) to examine agency budget requests and to help the president develop a budget proposal. The Employment Act of 1946 created the Council of Economic Advisers to forecast economic activity and assist the president in formulating an appropriate fiscal policy. During the 1960s and 1970s, various measures were introduced by the executive

EXHIBIT 1

Composition of Federal Expenditures: Fiscal Year 1995

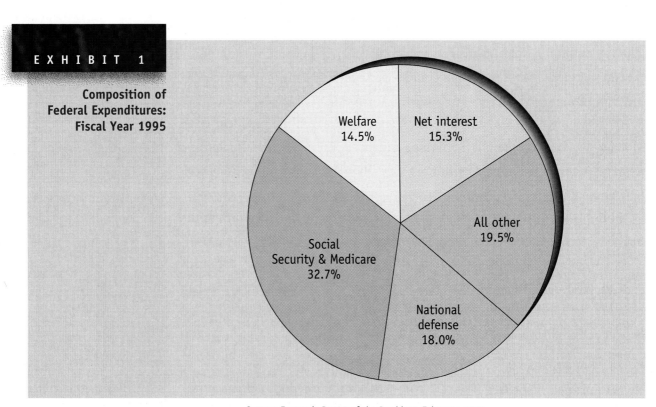

Source: *Economic Report of the President,* February, 1996.

branch to improve the evaluation of government programs. By the mid-1970s, the president had in place the staff and the procedures to translate policy into a budget proposal to be presented to Congress.

Development of the president's budget begins a year before it is submitted to Congress, with each agency preparing a budget request. The formal budget process begins in January, when the president submits to Congress a fat book called *The Budget of the United States Government* (the 1996 budget took up five volumes). This document details the president's proposals about what should be spent in the upcoming year and how this spending should be financed. At this stage, however, the president's budget is little more than detailed suggestions for congressional consideration. Soon after a budget is proposed, the *Economic Report of the President* is also transmitted to Congress. This report, required under the Employment Act of 1946 and written by the Council of Economic Advisers, reflects the administration's views about the state of the economy and includes fiscal policy recommendations for fostering "maximum employment, production, and purchasing power."

The Congressional Role in the Budget Process

The Congressional budget cycle begins in January, when the president's budget is delivered to Congress. Budget committees in the House and the Senate then work over the President's budget and eventually agree on the size of the budget, spending by major category, and expected revenues. Once an overall budget outline has been approved by Congress as a *budget resolution,* this resolution is supposed to discipline the many congressional committees and subcommittees that authorize spending by establishing a framework to guide spending and revenue decisions. The budget cycle supposedly ends on October 1, when the new fiscal year begins. Thus, the federal budget has a congressional gestation period of about nine months, though, as we have noted, the president's budget begins taking shape a year before the January submission.

The spending side of the budget is usually outlined in much greater detail than the revenue side. Most taxes are collected on the basis of certain rules and schedules that change infrequently. Of special interest is the bottom line, the relationship between *budgeted* expenditures and *projected* revenues. The difference between expenditures and revenues is one measure of the budget's fiscal impact. *When expenditures exceed revenues, the budget is projected to be in deficit. A larger deficit is expected to stimulate aggregate demand.* Alternatively, *when revenues exceed expenditures, the budget is projected to be in surplus. A larger surplus is expected to dampen aggregate demand.*

Problems with the Budget Process

The federal budget process sounds good on paper, but it does not work well in practice. There are several problems.

Continuing Resolutions Instead of Budget Decisions. The budget timetable discussed in the preceding section is often ignored by Congress. Because deadlines are often missed, budgets typically run from year to year based on **continuing resolutions,** which are agreements to allow agencies, in the absence of an approved budget, to spend at the rate of the previous year's budget. Poorly conceived programs continue through sheer inertia; successful programs cannot be expanded.

Continuing resolutions Budget agreements that allow agencies, in the absence of an approved budget, to spend at the rate of the previous year's budget

On occasion, the president must shut down some government functions temporarily because not even the continuing resolution can be approved in time.

Overlapping Committee Authority. An overlap in budget authority across the many congressional committees and subcommittees requires the executive branch of government to defend the same section of the president's budget before several committees in both the House and the Senate. Those responsible for running the federal government end up spending much of their time testifying before assorted congressional committees. Because several committees have jurisdiction over the same area, no committee really has final authority, so matters often remain unresolved even after extensive committee deliberations.

Lengthy Budget Process. You can imagine the difficulty of using the budget as a tool of fiscal policy when the budget process takes so long. Given that the average recession lasts only about a year and that budget preparations begin more than a year and a half before the budget goes into effect, planning discretionary fiscal measures to address economic fluctuations is difficult. That's one reason why congressional attempts to stimulate an ailing economy often seem so half-hearted; by the time Congress agrees on a fiscal remedy, the economy has often taken a turn for the better on its own.

Entitlement programs Guaranteed benefits for those who qualify under government transfer programs such as Social Security and Aid to Families with Dependent Children

Uncontrollable Budget Items. Congress has only limited control over much of the budget. Some budget items, such as interest on the national debt, cannot be changed in the near term. *About three-quarters of the budget falls into expenditure categories that are determined by existing laws.* For example, once Congress establishes eligibility criteria, **entitlement programs,** such as Social Security, Medicare, and Aid to Families with Dependent Children, take on a life of their own, with each annual appropriation simply reflecting the amount required to support the expected number of entitled beneficiaries. Congress has no say in such appropriations unless it chooses to change the eligibility criteria or the level of benefits. In 1995, Congress voted to turn responsibility for some entitlement programs over to the states along with block grants to fund the programs.

By budgeting in great detail, Congress, with precision, may reward friends with gifts—like a $2.7 catfish farm—and punish enemies.

Overly Detailed Budget. The federal budget is divided into thousands of accounts and subaccounts. Congress tends to budget in such minute detail that the big picture often gets lost. To the extent that the budget is a way of making political payoffs, such micromanagement allows Congress to reward friends and punish enemies with great precision. For example, though a huge deficit was projected, Congress still found room in a recent budget for $2.7 million to build a freshwater catfish farm in Arkansas, $2.5 million to remove asbestos from a meat-packing plant in Iowa, and $10 million to build a ramp to the Milwaukee Brewers stadium parking lot. Moreover, before the line-item veto was approved in April 1996, the president had little control over the specifics of the budget and had to either accept or veto the entire budget as is. Since the president usually receives the budget at the 11th hour, a veto would shut down the federal government, so budget vetoes were rare. *This detailed budgeting is not only time-consuming, but it also reduces the flexibility of fiscal policy.* When economic conditions change or when there is a shift in the demand for certain kinds of publicly provided goods, the federal government cannot easily reallocate funds from one account to another.

Suggested Budget Reforms

Several reforms have been suggested to improve the budget process. First, the annual budget could be converted into a two-year budget, or *biennial budget*. As it is, Congress spends nearly all of the year working on the budget. The executive branch is always dealing with three budgets: administering an approved budget, defending a proposed budget before congressional committees, and preparing the next budget for submission to Congress. If decisions were made for two years at a time, Congress would not continually be involved with budget deliberations, and executive branch heads could run their agencies rather than marching from committee hearing to committee hearing. Two-year budgets, however, would require longer-term economic forecasts of the economy and would be even less useful than one-year budgets as a tool of discretionary fiscal policy.

Another possible reform would be for Congress to simplify the budget document by concentrating on major groupings and eliminating line items. Each agency head could then be given an overall budget, along with the discretion to allocate funds in a manner consistent with the perceived demands for agency services. The drawback is that agency heads may have different priorities than elected representatives. We will consider other reforms later in the chapter after we discuss the federal deficit.

FEDERAL BUDGET DEFICITS

The big budget story in recent years has been the giant federal deficits. When government spending—that is, government purchases plus transfer payments—exceeds government revenue, the result is a *budget deficit,* a term first introduced in Chapter 5. Since 1960, the federal government has experienced a budget deficit in every year but one. To place deficits in perspective, we will first examine the economic rationale for deficit financing.

Rationale for Deficits

Deficit financing has been justified for outlays that increase the economy's productivity—outlays for investments such as highways, waterways, and dams. The cost of these capital projects should be borne in part by future taxpayers, who will also benefit from these investments. Hence, there is some justification for borrowing to finance capital projects so that future taxpayers can help pay for them. This rationale is used to fund capital projects at the state and local level, but the federal budget does not break out capital expenditures.

Until the Great Depression, federal deficits occurred only during wartime. Because wars involved much hardship, public officials were understandably reluctant to increase taxes much to finance war-related expenditures. Deficits arising during wars were largely self-correcting, however, because after each war government expenditures dropped faster than did government revenues.

The depression led John Maynard Keynes to develop an expanded role for the federal budget. As you know, the Keynesian prescription for fighting an economic slump is for the federal government to stimulate aggregate demand through deficit spending. As a result of the depression, automatic stabilizers were also introduced; these increase government spending during recessions and decrease it during expansions. The federal deficit increases during recessions because, as economic activity slows down, unemployment rises, increasing government outlays for unemployment benefits and other transfer payments. Furthermore, tax revenues decline during recessions. For example, as a result of the 1990–1991 recession, annual tax revenues from corporations fell by $14 billion between 1989 and 1992, while payments for "income security" jumped by $60 billion. An economic recovery is the other side of the coin. As business activity expands, so do jobs, personal income, and corporate profits, causing federal revenue to swell. With reduced joblessness, transfer payments decline. Thus, the federal deficit falls. Thanks largely to a recovering economy, the federal deficit dropped from $290.4 billion in 1992 to $163.8 billion in 1995. Federal spending grew by only 3.7 percent in 1995; receipts grew by 7.4 percent.

Budget Philosophies and Deficits

Annually balanced budget Budget philosophy prior to the Great Depression; aimed at equating revenues with expenditures, except during times of war

Several budget philosophies have emerged over the years. Fiscal policy prior to the Great Depression aimed at maintaining an **annually balanced budget,** except during times of war. Since tax revenues rise during expansions and fall during recessions, the annually balanced budget calls for the federal government to increase spending during expansions and reduce spending during recessions. But such spending will worsen fluctuations in the business cycle, overheating the economy during expansions and increasing unemployment during recessions.

Cyclically balanced budget A budget philosophy calling for budget deficits during recessions to be financed by budget surpluses during expansions

A second budget philosophy is to have a **cyclically balanced budget,** which calls for budget deficits during recessions and budget surpluses during expansions. Fiscal policy is thereby able to dampen swings in the business cycle, yet not, on balance, increase budget debt over the cycle. Many state governments have established "rainy day" funds to build up budget surpluses during the good times for use during hard times.

Functional finance A budget philosophy aiming fiscal policy at achieving potential GDP rather than balancing budgets either annually or over the business cycle

A third budget philosophy is **functional finance,** which says that policymakers should be less concerned with balancing the budget annually or even over the business cycle than with seeing that the economy produces its potential output. The functional finance philosophy argues that one of the federal government's primary responsibilities is to promote economic stability at the potential level of output. If the budget needed to keep the economy operating at its potential involves chronic deficits, so be it.

Since the Great Depression, budgets in this country have been neither annually nor cyclically balanced. *Although budget deficits have been greater during recessions than during expansions, the federal budget has been in deficit in all but eight years since 1931.* In fact, the budget has been in deficit in all but one year since 1960.

Deficits in the 1980s

In 1981, President Reagan secured a 3-year budget resolution that included a historic tax cut along with increases in defense spending. Some so-called *supply-side* economists argued that tax cuts would stimulate enough economic activity to keep tax revenues from falling. The congressional budget resolution adopted in 1981 was based on an assumption that unspecified spending cuts would bring the two sides of the budget into balance, but the promised cuts in spending were never made.

Moreover, overly optimistic revenue projections—so-called "rosy scenarios"—were built into the budget. The budget projected that real GDP would grow by 5.2 percent in 1982, but the economy fell into a recession and instead output dropped by 2.1 percent. The recession caused the automatic stabilizers in the budget to take over, thereby reducing revenues and increasing spending still more. Since spending was underestimated and revenue was overestimated, the deficit in 1982 amounted to about 4 percent relative to GDP, at the time one of the largest peacetime deficits in history.

The deficit served as a backdrop for budget debates in the early 1980s. President Reagan's budget strategy called for increases in defense spending, but he promised to veto any new taxes or any cuts in Social Security. The deficit climbed to 6.1 percent of GDP in 1983. During the presidential campaign of 1984, Democratic candidate Walter Mondale warned that taxes would have to be increased to reduce the deficits. President Reagan, however, blamed the deficits on the recession and predicted that as the economy improved, the deficit would disappear even without tax increases; he claimed the country would "grow out of" the deficits.

Reagan won the 1984 election but he lost the argument about the deficit. The federal government had cut tax rates but did not cut expenditures. *Although federal revenues relative to GDP declined, federal spending rose relative to GDP, from 22.5 percent in 1980 to 24.4 percent in 1986.* Exhibit 2 presents the federal budget deficit relative to GDP since 1970. As you can see, the deficit as a percentage of GDP climbed in the early 1980s, declined somewhat as the economy improved after the recession of 1982, increased in 1990 with the onset of another recession, then declined after 1992 because of President Clinton's 1993 tax increase and a recovering economy. Note that the deficit relative to GDP was lower in 1995 than it was in the mid-1970s.

Deficit Reduction Measures

Deficit reduction laws adopted in the mid-1980s had limited effect. During the 1988 presidential campaign, both major candidates largely ignored the issue of the deficit, since to make much of it would only raise the question of what was to be done, and neither candidate wanted to talk about taxes.

With concern about the deficit growing, Congress and President Bush agreed to the 1990 Budget Enforcement Act (BEA), a package of spending cuts and tax increases aimed at trimming the projected deficit. Rather than relying exclusively on a deficit cap, as did earlier measures, the new law applied spending caps to three broad areas of discretionary spending (defense, international programs, and domestic programs). If the caps were exceeded, automatic across-the-board cuts would be applied to that area of spending. The BEA also had a pay-as-you-go feature requiring that any proposals to increase spending or decrease revenues had to be offset by new spending cuts or revenue increases. Some cynics viewed the new law simply as a way to put off hard decisions about the federal deficit until after the 1992 presidential election.

In the spring of 1993, President Clinton proposed and Congress approved a tax increase on high-income earners. This tax increase combined with a recovering economy to reduce the budget deficit in 1993, 1994, and 1995. But the deficit was expected to start climbing once again in the latter half of the

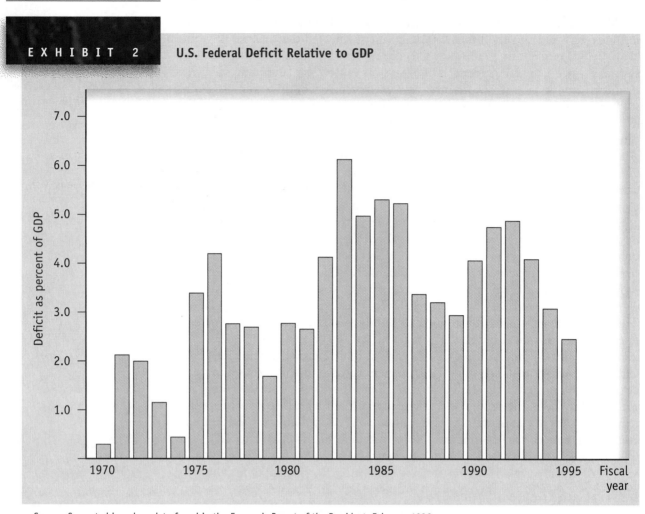

EXHIBIT 2

U.S. Federal Deficit Relative to GDP

Source: Computed based on data found in the *Economic Report of the President,* February 1996.

decade. In 1995, the Republican Congress proposed eliminating the deficit by the year 2002, as is discussed in the following case study.

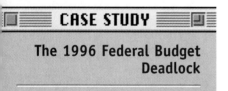

CASE STUDY

The 1996 Federal Budget Deadlock

In the fall of 1995, both President Clinton and the Republican Congress said they wanted a 1996 budget that would be part of a long-range plan to balance the federal budget within 7 years, or by the year 2002. But they disagreed about how to do this. Republicans wanted to revamp Medicaid and welfare, turning responsibility for these programs over to the states. They also proposed a 7-year $200 billion tax cut as part of the deal, including a $500 per child tax credit and lower capital gains tax rates. On December 6, 1995, Clinton vetoed the Republican plan, saying the proposed spending cuts would hurt the poor and the proposed tax cut would benefit the rich.

The day after his veto, he offered his own budget plan—a 1,000-page document that he said would eliminate the deficit in 7 years by cutting 20 percent from lower-priority domestic programs. Most of the spending cuts would occur in the later years. Education, the environment, Medicare, and Medicaid would be least affected. Clinton also proposed a $98 billion tax cut. Republicans claimed that Clinton's budget would fall far short of balancing in 7 years, and Congress rejected the proposal. The budget standoff meant that most agencies were without budgets, resulting in two government shutdowns that closed many federal agencies for a total of 27 days. To avoid yet another shutdown, President Clinton in April 1995 signed the eighth stopgap-funding bill enacted since the fiscal year began October 1, 1995. Thus, the fiscal year was half over, but many agencies were still without a budget.

The 1996 Federal Budget Deadlock
continued

Location:

In 1995, the Republican Congress held sharply different views for balancing the budget than did Democrats in Congress or President Clinton. To learn more about these views, visit The Concord Coalition, a nonpartisan, grassroots movement founded by former Senators Warren B. Rudman and Paul E. Tsongas to eliminate the deficit and manage entitlements (**http://sunsite.unc. edu/concord/**).

Much of the debate about efforts to balance the federal budget in 7 years focused on whether to use the economic assumptions of the Office of Management and Budget (OMB), an executive agency, or those of the Congressional Budget Office (CBO), a congressional agency. The OMB projected an average annual growth rate in real GDP of 2.5 percent over the 7 years; the CBO estimate averaged 2. 3 percent. Clinton used OMB estimates; Congress used CBO estimates.

How does this small difference affect the deficit projected in 2002? First, slower growth affects the deficit by directly lowering projected GDP and hence, federal revenues, in 2002. Suppose that federal revenues remain a constant 18.45 percent of GDP, which was the average for 1990 to 1994. In this case, GDP in 2002 would be $143 billion lower with a real growth rate of 2.3 percent instead of 2.5 percent. The GDP shortfall would create a federal revenue shortfall of about $26 billion.

What's more, lower growth would also decrease revenues in each of the years 1996 to 2001, increasing the federal debt by the end of 2001 by about $75 billion more than it would be with the 2.5 percent growth rate. Interest costs on this additional debt would raise the deficit another $3 billion, for a total increase in the projected 2002 deficit of $29 billion. And the additional debt by the end of 2002 would amount to $29 billion plus $75 billion, or $104 billion. These calculations likely understate the actual increase in the projected deficit because they ignore any increased federal spending that would result from a lower growth rate in real GDP.

This simple comparison shows how sensitive deficit projections are to relatively small changes in economic assumptions. In view of the great uncertainty surrounding most economic forecasts, deficit projections are a tricky business.

Sources: Christopher Georges, "Congress Passes Debt-Ceiling Measure, Agrees to Spend More on Social Security," *The Wall Street Journal*, 29 March 1996; Christopher Neely, "The Devil Is in the Budget Details, *National Economic Trends*, January 1996; Peter Brimlow, "Fuzzy Numbers," *Forbes*, 25 March 1995; and David Rogers, "Government Begins Second Fiscal Half Still Deadlocked Over Spending Bills," *The Wall Street Journal*, 1 April 1996.

Why Deficits? Why Now?

Why did federal budget deficits become the status quo? The most obvious answer is that Congress is not required to balance the budget. In contrast, 49 states now require that their own budgets be balanced. As we have mentioned already, current deficits have been caused by a combination of tax cuts and spending increases. But why has the budget been in deficit for all but eight years since 1931?

As an explanation, let's consider one widely accepted model of the public sector. Elected officials attempt to maximize political support, including votes and campaign contributions. Voters like public spending programs but dislike taxes, so spending programs win support and taxes lose support. Because of this asymmetry, candidates attempt to maximize their chances of getting elected by offering a budget that is long on benefits but short on taxes. Moreover, the many fragmented congressional committees push their favorite programs with little concern about the overall budget. For example, a defense bill recently included eighteen F-14D fighter jets and thirty-six V-22 Osprey aircraft because the planes were produced by firms located in key congressional districts. The Pentagon did not want the planes.

The Relationship between Deficits and Other Aggregate Variables

There is much talk in the news media about the relationships among deficits, interest rates, and inflation. To develop a clearer understanding of these relationships, let's consider the following simplification. We begin with the federal budget in balance and the economy producing its potential GDP (point *a* in Exhibit 3). The short-run aggregate supply curve is based on long-term labor contracts reflecting an expected price level of 130.

Suppose an unexpected decline in private-sector spending reduces aggregate demand. Recent research suggests that each percentage point added to the unemployment rate cuts output by two percentage points. As employment and output decline, the automatic stabilizers kick in, reducing tax revenues and increasing transfer payments. These stabilizers keep aggregate demand from falling as much as it would without them. Still, the aggregate demand curve drops from AD to AD', resulting in a short-run equilibrium at output level of $6.8 trillion. This combination of reduced tax revenues and increased government outlays results in a budget deficit. According to research, every 1 percent increase in the unemployment rate increases the federal deficit by over $30 billion.

Now let's consider the association between this deficit and what happens to real output, the price level, and interest rates. The first two are easy to predict: the deficit resulting from the automatic stabilizers occurs with falling real output and a falling price level, or reduced inflation. With regard to the interest rate, when output and the price level decline, the transactions demand for money declines as well, so the interest rate tends to fall. Thus, *a deficit resulting from automatic stabilizers will be associated with a lower level of prices, output, and interest rates.*

At point *b,* the economy is in recession, with a short-run equilibrium output that is below the economy's potential. Policymakers can either do nothing, waiting for natural market forces to correct the problem of unemployment, or they can intervene in some way. Recall that activists believe that if government takes no action, the adjustment to potential output could be long and painful, with much unemployment and much forgone output. Advocates of passive pol-

Deficits and Other Measures of the Economy's Performance

EXHIBIT 3

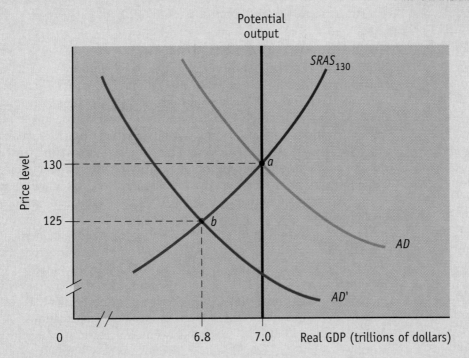

At point *a*, the federal budget is in balance and output is at potential. A decline in aggregate demand to *AD'* triggers automatic stabilizers. Tax revenues fall, transfer payments increase, and the budget moves to a deficit position. In this case, the deficit is associated with falling output and a falling price level.

With the economy now at point *b*, suppose policymakers stimulate aggregate demand through expansionary fiscal policy. Tax revenues fall, government expenditures increase, and the deficit grows larger. Here the deficit is associated with rising output and a rising price level.

icy believe that government intervention involves unpredictable lags and may affect aggregate demand only after the economy has naturally returned to its potential.

Suppose the government increases its spending, financing this increase by selling government securities to the public, a move that tends to put upward pressure on interest rates. According to the activist view, the appropriate increase in government spending could stimulate aggregate demand just enough to return the economy to its potential GDP. The effects of this policy would be represented in Exhibit 3 by a movement from point *b* back to point *a*. In essence, increased government demand offsets the decline in private sector demand.

What is the relationship between the deficit that results from this discretionary fiscal policy and the other macroeconomic aggregates of concern? This deficit is associated with a greater output and a higher price level. The interest rate rises not only because the Treasury sells bonds to finance the deficit but also because the higher price and output levels increase the demand for money.

Thus, *the deficit that arises from discretionary fiscal policy is associated with a higher real output, a higher price level, and a higher interest rate*. Consequently, there is no necessary relationship between deficits and various measures of economic performance. In both cases there are deficits, but the results of the deficits on real output, the price level, and interest rates differ.

Crowding Out and Crowding In

Crowding out The displacement of interest-sensitive private investment that occurs when increased government spending drives up interest rates

Suppose the federal government decides to expand the interstate highway system with a program that will cost $10 billion this year. To pay for the new system, the U.S. Treasury sells securities, or IOUs. The government's increased demand for credit raises interest rates in the market for loans. Higher interest rates in turn discourage, or crowd out, some private investment, reducing the expansionary effect of the deficit. The extent of **crowding out** is a matter of debate. Some argue that although borrowing from the public may displace some private-sector borrowing, discretionary fiscal policy will result in a net increase in aggregate demand, leading to greater output and employment. Others believe the crowding out is more extensive, so borrowing from the public in this way could result in little or no increase in aggregate demand and output.

Although crowding out is likely to occur to some degree, there is another possibility. If the economy is operating well below its potential, the additional fiscal stimulus provided by deficit spending could encourage firms to invest more and could thus result in a higher level of investment. Recall that an important determinant of investment is business expectations. A government deficit could stimulate a weak economy, increasing aggregate demand and putting a sunny face on business expectations. As business expectations grow more favorable, firms could become more willing to invest. This ability of government deficits to stimulate private investment is sometimes called **crowding in,** to distinguish it from crowding out.

Crowding in The potential for government spending to stimulate private investment in an otherwise sluggish economy

Were you ever unwilling to patronize a restaurant because it was too crowded? You simply did not want to put up with the hassle and long wait and were thus "crowded out." Similarly, large government deficits may "crowd out" some investors by driving up interest rates. On the other hand, did you ever pass up a restaurant because the place seemed dead—it had few customers? Perhaps you wondered why so few people chose to eat there. With just a few more customers, you might have stopped in—you might have been willing to "crowd in." Similarly, businesses may be reluctant to invest in a lifeless economy. The economic stimulus resulting from deficit spending could encourage some investors to "crowd in."

The Twin Deficits

To finance the huge deficits of the early 1980s, the U.S. Treasury had to sell securities, driving up the market rate of interest. With U.S. interest rates relatively high, foreigners were more willing to save by investing in dollar-denominated assets. To buy such assets, foreigners had to exchange their currencies for dollars. This greater demand for dollars caused the dollar to appreciate relative to foreign currencies during the first half of the 1980s. The rising value of the dollar made foreign goods cheaper in the United States and U.S. goods more expensive abroad. Thus, U.S. imports increased and U.S. exports decreased, so the foreign trade deficit increased.

The higher trade deficits meant that foreigners were accumulating dollars. Foreigners invested these dollars in U.S. assets, including U.S. government securities, and thereby helped fund the giant federal deficits. The increase in funds from abroad in the 1980s was both good news and bad news for the U.S. economy. The good news was that the supply of foreign funds increased investment in the United States over what it would have been in the absence of these funds. Ask residents what they think of foreign investment in their town; they will likely say it's great. Still, investment as a percent of GDP declined more or less steadily from 18.8 percent in 1979 to 13.0 percent in 1992.

But the foreign supply of funds reflected the fact that the saving rate in the United States is now about the lowest it has been since the Great Depression, and the United States is now the largest borrower in the world. Such a pattern could pose problems in the long run. The United States has surrendered a certain amount of control over its economy to foreign investors. The return on foreign investments in the United States flows abroad.

Deficits in Other Countries

In sheer size, the U.S. federal government has had the largest government deficits in the world. When we include all levels of government, however, the deficit does not look so bad because state and local governments typically run a budget surplus. Exhibit 4 shows the deficits for 13 industrial countries for all levels of government, measured as a percentage of potential GDP. As you can see, the U.S. government deficit at all levels relative to potential GDP is among the lowest of the countries listed. The largest deficit was in Greece, at 11.1 percent of potential GDP.

THE BALLOONING NATIONAL DEBT

Whereas the federal deficit is a flow variable measuring the amount by which expenditures exceed revenues in a particular year, the federal debt, or the **national debt,** is a stock variable measuring the accumulation of past deficits. Federal deficits add up. It took 39 presidents, 6 wars, the Great Depression, and more than 200 years for the federal debt to reach $1 trillion, as it did in 1981. It took only 3 presidents and another 15 years for that debt to reach $5 trillion, as it did in 1995. (In constant 1995 dollars, the national debt in 1981 was about $1.5 trillion.) Ironically, the biggest growth occurred primarily under President Reagan, who was first elected on a promise to balance the budget.

National debt The net accumulation of federal budget deficits

In talking about the national debt, we distinguish between the gross debt and debt held by the public. The *gross debt* includes U.S. Treasury securities purchased by various federal agencies, such as the Social Security trust fund. Since this is debt the federal government owes to itself, we often ignore such debt to focus on *debt held by the public,* which includes debt held by banks (including Federal Reserve banks), firms, households, and foreign entities. As of 1995, the gross federal debt stood at about $5.0 trillion and the debt held by the public stood at $3.6 trillion.

The National Debt since World War II

The top line in panel (a) of Exhibit 5 represents the debt held by the public since World War II, as measured in current dollars. At the end of World War

EXHIBIT 4   **Government Deficits as a Percentage of Potential GDP**

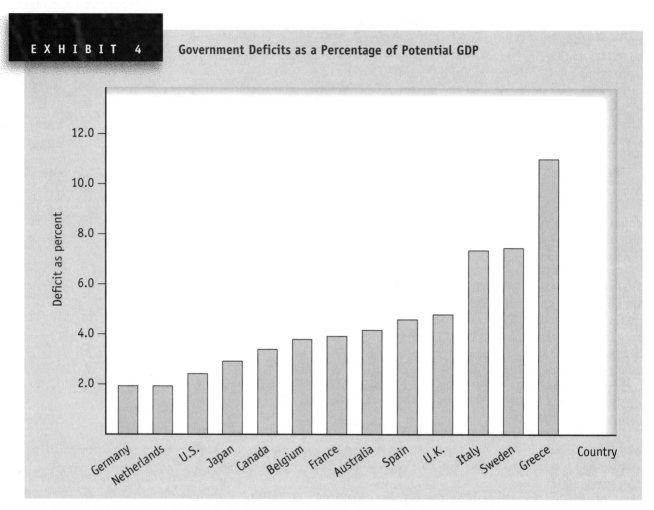

Source: Based on estimates developed by the Organization of Economic Cooperation and Development, *OECD Economic Outlook* 57 (June 1995): Annex Table 31.

II, the federal debt held by the public was $242 billion, about $200 billion of which resulted from financing the war. Between 1946 and the mid-1970s, the national debt grew slowly. By 1974, the national debt had increased to only $344 billion; by 1995, however, the debt held by the public jumped to over $3.6 trillion.

Because of inflation, a 1995 dollar purchases far less than did the 1946 dollar. Thus, a dollar's worth of debt in 1995 does not represent as great a liability as a dollar's worth of debt in 1946. To adjust for inflation, we can measure the federal debt in constant dollars. As the lower line in panel (a) of Exhibit 5 shows, in 1946 constant dollars, the national debt actually declined from $242 billion in 1946 to $165 billion in 1980 but then climbed to $470 billion in 1995. Hence, when figures are adjusted for inflation, the growth of the national debt is not nearly as dramatic. Measured in *constant dollars,* the federal debt declined between 1946 and 1980, but grew at an average annual rate of 7.2 percent between 1980 and 1995.

Postwar Measures of Federal Debt Held by the Public

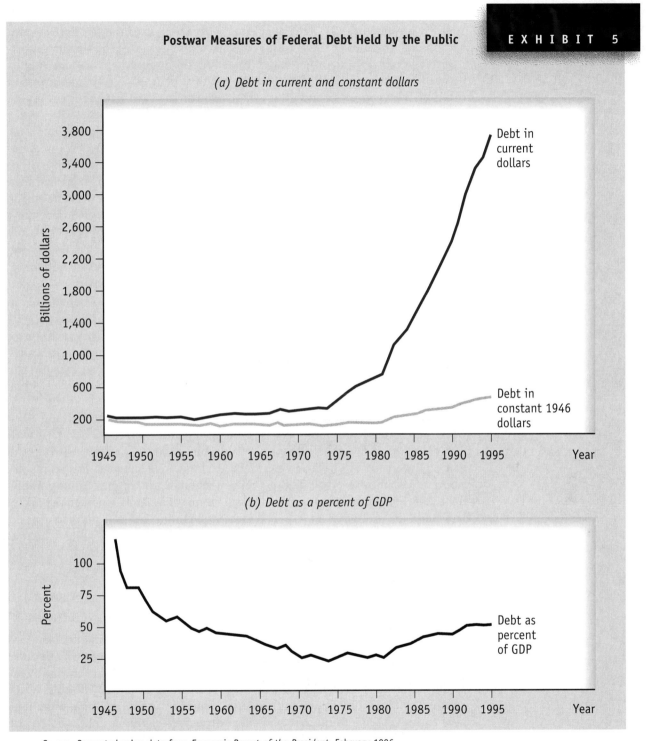

(a) Debt in current and constant dollars

(b) Debt as a percent of GDP

Source: Computed using data from *Economic Report of the President,* February 1996.

Debt Relative to GDP

Another way to measure debt over time is to relate it to the economy's production and income, or GDP (just as a bank might compare the size of a mortgage to a borrower's income). Panel (b) of Exhibit 5 shows federal debt held by the public relative to GDP. In 1946, the national debt was 114 percent relative to GDP. Between 1946 and 1980, debt relative to GDP declined to only 26 percent, but then climbed to 51 percent by 1995.

Let's consider briefly why debt has changed relative to GDP. For debt as a percentage of GDP to decline, GDP must grow faster than debt. Nominal national debt grew by only 3.2 percent per year between 1946 and 1980, a period during which nominal GDP grew by 7.8 percent per year. National debt as a percentage of GDP therefore fell between 1946 and 1980, as reflected in panel (b) of Exhibit 5. Between 1980 and 1995, however, nominal debt grew by a whopping 11.5 percent per year, whereas nominal GDP grew by only 6.6 percent per year, so debt as a percentage of GDP increased.

An International Perspective on National Debt

How does public-sector debt in the United States compare to debt levels in other countries? Exhibit 6 compares the U.S. public-sector debt levels in 1994 as a percentage of GDP with 11 other industrial countries. Two measures of debt are used: total debt and net debt. *Total debt* includes all outstanding liabilities of federal, state, and local governments. *Net debt* is calculated by subtracting the governments' financial assets, such as loans to students and farmers, stock shares, cash on hand, and foreign exchange on reserve.

As you can see in Exhibit 6, despite the huge increase in federal debt since 1980, the United States ranks about in the middle for industrial countries, with total debt for all levels of government combined amounting to a little more than 63.2 percent of GDP and net debt at about 37.7 percent. Belgium's net debt in 1994 amounted to 127.8 percent of its GDP, the highest among industrial countries. Italy ranked second highest in net debt, at 121 percent of GDP. Because political support in Italy is fragmented among a dozen political parties, a government can be formed only through coalitions among several parties. That resulting coalition is so fragile that it cannot easily withstand the fallout from raising taxes or cutting spending; hence deficit spending persists.

Interest Payments on the Debt

Purchasers of government securities range from individuals who buy a $25 savings bond to institutions that buy $1 million Treasury notes. When these securities mature, the government issues more securities to pay them off. Because most government securities are short term, the national debt "turns over" rapidly—about 45 percent of the debt is refinanced every 12 months. With over $150 billion coming due each month, debt service payments are quite sensitive to movements in interest rates. Based on a $4.0 trillion debt held by the public, a 1-percentage-point increase in the nominal interest rate increases annual interest costs by $40 billion.

As a percentage of the federal budget, interest payments grew from 7.0 percent in 1975 to 15.3 percent in 1995. Interest payments as a percentage of federal personal income tax collections have doubled from about 20 percent in 1980 to 40 percent in 1995. Part of the problem of the debt is that it is an abstraction. To put interest payments in context, consider this: In 1995, interest

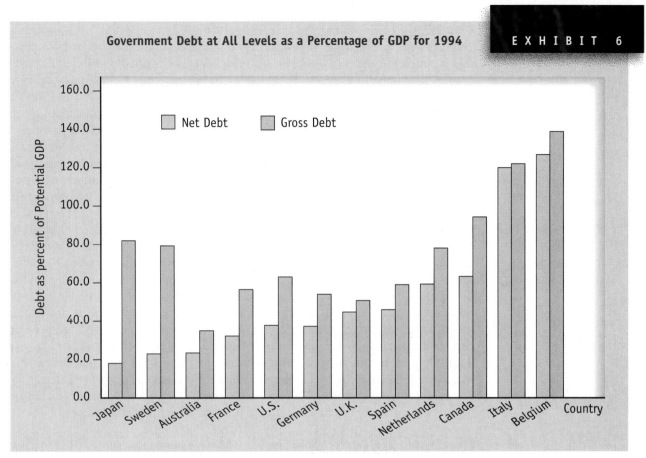

Government Debt at All Levels as a Percentage of GDP for 1994   E X H I B I T   6

Source: Developed from data found in *OECD Economic Outook* 57 (June 1995):Annex Tables 34 and 35.

payments on the national debt amounted to about $275 per month for each of the 70 million U.S. families; that's equivalent to a car payment.

Interest Payments and Seigniorage

One factor that influences interest payments is *seigniorage*. You'll recall that this term was originally used to refer to the profit the "lord of the manor" derived from issuing coins whose metallic value was less than their face, or exchange, value. In the modern setting, seigniorage refers to the revenue that the U.S. Treasury gets every year from the Federal Reserve System. As you know, the Fed adds money to the economy by purchasing Treasury securities from the public. Although the Fed earns interest on these securities, it pays no interest on the money it creates. Some of the interest received by the Fed is used to cover its operating expenses. The rest is returned to the U.S. Treasury. Since 1913, the Fed has returned an average of 87 percent of its earnings to the Treasury. In 1995, for example, the Federal Reserve System returned about $25 billion to the Treasury. *Seigniorage, a by-product of monetary policy, reduces the deficit.*

Who Bears the Burden of the Debt?

Deficit spending is a way to increase current expenditures without raising taxes. The national debt raises moral questions about the right of one generation of taxpayers to bequeath to the next generation the burden of its own borrowing. The director of the Congressional Budget Office argued before Congress that "by running up large federal deficits, the current generation is lowering the living standard for its children and grandchildren." Similarly, Nobel laureate Franco Modigliani believes that deficit spending amounts to "enjoying it now and paying it later" by pushing the bill on to future generations in the form of the higher taxes that will be required to cover interest and principal. And Benjamin Friedman of Harvard University says, "America has thrown a party and billed the tab to the future. The costs, which are only beginning to come due, will include a lower standard of living for individual Americans and reduced American influence and importance in world affairs."[1] To what extent do budget deficits shift the burden to future generations? Let's consider arguments about the burden of the debt.

Foreign Ownership of Debt. It is often argued that the debt is not a burden to future generations because, although future generations must service the debt, those same generations will receive the debt service payments. It's true that if U.S. citizens forgo present consumption to buy bonds, they or their heirs will receive the interest payments, so debt service payments will stay in the country. But foreigners who purchase U.S. government securities forgo the present consumption and receive the future benefits. An influx of foreign capital reduces the amount of current consumption that Americans must sacrifice to finance the national debt. *A reliance on foreigners, however, increases the burden of the debt on future generations because future debt service payments no longer remain in the country.* Foreigners now hold about 18 percent of debt held by the public.

Crowding Out and Capital Formation. As we have said, government borrowing drives up interest rates, crowding out some private investment by making it more costly. The long-run opportunity cost of crowding out will depend on how the government spends the borrowed dollars. If additional federal outlays are oriented toward investments such as improving interstate highways or educating the workforce, the public investment may be as productive as any private investment forgone. Hence, there should be no harmful effects on the economy's long-run productive capability. If, however, the additional borrowed dollars go toward current consumption, such as farm subsidies or retirement benefits, the economy's capital formation will be less than it would otherwise be. With less investment today, there is less of an endowment of capital equipment and technology for future generations.

Ironically, as we mentioned in Chapter 6, despite the growing federal deficits, government investments in roads, bridges, and airports—so-called *public capital*—has declined. In 1970, the value of the nation's public capital stock was about 50 percent relative to GDP; this figure has declined to about 40 percent today. So public investment has declined. Some argue that declining investment in the public infrastructure serves as a drag on productivity growth. For example, the failure to invest sufficiently in airports and in the air traffic control system has resulted in congested airports and flight delays.

Private investment has also declined since 1979 relative to GDP. U.S. in-

1   Benjamin Friedman, *Day of Reckoning* (New York: Random House, 1988), p. 4.

vestment as a percentage of GDP is much lower than in Japan. Over time, a decline in the rate of investment slows the rate of growth in productivity and the overall rate of economic growth. Thus, government deficits of one generation can affect the standard of living for the next. In this sense, the deficit of one generation imposes a burden on future generations. And the problem is worse than that because the deficit does not now capture all burdens passed on to future generations. For example, the Social Security program transfers resources from one generation to the next. Martin Feldstein, a Harvard economist, argues that unfunded liabilities of government retirement programs, such as Social Security, should be included in the deficit. Such an inclusion would triple the measure of the national debt. A model that considers some intergenerational effects is discussed in the following case study.

Robert Barro has developed a model that assumes parents are concerned about the welfare of *their* children, who, in turn, are concerned about the welfare of their children, and so on for generations. Thus the welfare of all generations is tied together. According to Barro, parents concerned about future generations will reduce the burden of federal debt on future generations and reduce the stimulative effect of deficit spending.

Here's his argument. When the government incurs deficits to finance higher spending, this keeps current taxes lower than they would otherwise be, but taxes in the future must be increased to service the resulting debt. If there is no regard for the welfare of future generations, then the older people are, the more attractive debt becomes relative to taxes. Older people can enjoy the benefits of public spending now, but will not live long enough to finance the debt through higher taxes or lower benefits. If people are concerned about their children's welfare, however, they will be more reluctant to run deficits now and thereby raise future taxes.

Parents can undo the harm that deficit financing imposes on their children by consuming less now and saving more for their children. As governments substitute deficits for taxes, parents will consume less and save more to increase gifts and bequests to their children. If increases in household saving just offset increases in federal deficits, fiscal policy will not increase aggregate demand, because the decline in consumption will negate the fiscal stimulus provided by deficits. This intergenerational transfer of income within the family offsets the future burden of higher debt and neutralizes the effect of deficit spending on aggregate demand, output, and employment.

The large budget deficits since the early 1980s, caused in part by tax cuts, seem to provide a natural experiment for testing Barro's theory of government debt. The evidence fails to support his theory, since the large federal deficits coincided with a low national savings rate. Yet those who hold Barro's view interpret events of the period differently. They say that maybe the saving rate was low because people were optimistic about future economic growth, an optimism that was reflected by a huge increase in the stock market. Or maybe the

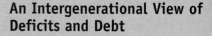

CASE STUDY

An Intergenerational View of Deficits and Debt

Location:

Many young people are aware that a high federal deficit will result in higher taxes and/or fewer public benefits in the future, and their voices are now being heard. For example, visit Third Millennium, a national, non-partisan, non-profit organization launched by young adults to "redirect our country's attention from the next election cycle to the next generational cycle" (**http://www.thirdmil.org/index.shtml**). Also visit Conservative Generation X, an organization and NewsLetter started by ex-alternative radio DJs Ehren Filippello and Paul Colligan (**http://www.cgx.com/**).

An Intergenerational View of Deficits and Debt
continued

savings rate was low because people believed the tax cuts would result not in higher future taxes but in a lower government spending, as President Reagan promised.

But there are other reasons to be skeptical about Barro's theory. First, individuals without children may not be concerned about the welfare of future generations. Second, the theory assumes that people are well informed about current spending and tax policies and about the future consequences of current policies; many people are in fact poorly informed about such matters. One survey found that only one in ten adults polled had any idea about the size of the federal deficit (only one in ten adults said correctly that the deficit was between $100 billion and $400 billion).

Yet we cannot dismiss the model. Many young people recognize that a high federal deficit will raise taxes and/or diminish public benefits in the future. Some have even organized to oppose federal deficits.

Sources: Robert J. Barro, "Are Government Bonds Net Worth?", *Journal of Political Economy* 82 (Novenber/December 1974): pp. 1095–1117; Robert J. Barro, "The Ricardian Approach to Budget Deficits," *Journal of Economic Perspectives* 3 (Spring 1989): pp. 37; and Jay Mathews, "How High Is the Deficit, the Dow? Most in Survey Didn't Know," *The Hartford Courant,* 19 October 1995.

REDUCING THE DEFICIT

Among economists, there is some disagreement over whether the current deficits pose a major problem for the country. Most agree that chronic deficits are undesirable. As we have seen, recent legislation and the Budget Enforcement Act of 1990 have not done the job. One way of eliminating the deficit is to raise taxes enough to cover it, but some economists believe that higher taxes could substantially slow the economy. Some also believe that the giant deficits, while undesirable in themselves, have at least slowed the growth in federal spending (federal spending as a percentage of GDP fell slightly from 24.0 percent in 1986 to 22.5 percent in 1995). According to this view, a tax hike would simply support higher government spending and do little for the deficit.

As mentioned earlier, elected officials pay a political price for increasing taxes and are thus understandably reluctant to do so. A promise to raise taxes could prove hazardous to a politician's career. Instead, members of Congress pursue reelection by supporting innumerable programs for special-interest constituencies. Individual members of Congress tend to spend for narrow purposes and in so doing tend to overspend in total.

Line-Item Veto

Line-item veto A provision to allow the president to reject particular portions of the budget rather than simply accept or reject the entire budget

One proposal designed to reduce the impact of special interests on the budget and at the same time provide the executive branch with more flexibility is to give the president a line-item veto. The **line-item veto,** passed as part of the Republican Congress's "Contract with America," allows the president to reject particular portions of the budget rather than simply accept or reject the entire budget. President Clinton signed the measure into law in April 1996. An argument for the line-item veto is that the president is the only elected representative with a broad enough constituency to reject the special-interest programs often embedded in the budget. To approve a vetoed item, Congress must demonstrate a strong preference for the project by coming up with a two-thirds majority. But even a line-item veto cannot reduce certain spending commitments such as interest payments or Social Security benefits, which account for more than half of the budget. The governors of 43 states also have the line-item veto for their state budgets, but this power does not seem to affect the level of total spending.[2]

Balanced Budget Amendment

Another attempt to force the government to control spending is a proposed amendment to the U.S. Constitution requiring a balanced federal budget. There have been two kinds of criticism of a **balanced budget amendment.** The first stems from the belief that the amendment would work too well. Both automatic and discretionary fiscal policies use deficits and surpluses as policy tools to stimulate the economy during recessions and to dampen the economy during expansions. A balanced budget requirement would reduce the government's ability to employ fiscal policy to cope with business fluctuations, particularly recessions. Another problem with requiring a balanced budget is that tax rates would have to be raised during recessions. The higher rates would not only reduce disposable income but might reduce incentives to work and to invest. To allow some room for fiscal policy, proposed balanced budget amendments typically allow Congress the ability to override this restriction with a greater-than-majority vote, such as two-thirds or three-fifths. Despite this escape clause, some policymakers remain concerned that fiscal policy would be undermined by a balanced budget amendment. But discretionary fiscal policy has been largely undermined anyway by large chronic deficits (though automatic stabilizers still operate).

A second kind of criticism of a balanced budget amendment is that any budget restriction would probably be difficult to specify and easy to bypass. Even if such a measure held down spending by the federal government, authority for certain types of spending could simply be pushed down to lower levels of government through unfunded *mandates,* which are federal laws and regulations that require state and local governments to carry out certain functions. Another fear is that the federal government would use greater regulation of the private sector to achieve what it could not fund directly through the budget. For example, rather than subsidize an employment training program for unskilled workers, the federal government might simply require employers to hire and train such workers. Or the federal budget might require banks to grant low-interest loans for inner-city development. Some people think that such government intervention in the market might ultimately prove to be less efficient than using the budget to achieve the desired outcome. In early 1995, the U.S. House of Representatives approved a balanced budget amendment, but the measure failed in the Senate.

CONCLUSION

Keynes introduced the idea that federal deficit spending is an appropriate fiscal policy when private aggregate demand is insufficient to achieve potential out-

Balanced budget amendment Proposed amendment to the U.S. Constitution requiring a balanced federal budget

Net Bookmark

In an attempt to control federal spending, the U.S. House of Representatives in 1995 approved a balanced-budget amendment to the U.S. Constitution, but the measure failed in the Senate. For the latest status on a balanced budget amendment, visit "The Legislative Process," a service of the U.S. House of Representatives (**http://www.house. gov/Legproc.html**). To browse the current budget, visit "The Budget of the United States Government", as provided by STAT-USA of the Department of Commerce (**http://www. doc.gov/in query/ BudgetFY96/BudgetFY96. html**).

---

2   See John Carter and David Schap, "Line-Item Veto: Where Is Thy Sting," *Journal of Economic Perspectives* (Spring 1990).

put. The federal budget has not been the same since. The budget has been in deficit every year but one since 1960. Since the early 1980s, giant federal deficits have dominated the fiscal policy debate. One reason budget deficits are hard to reduce is that the pain of such reduction comes in the near term, but the benefits are off in the future (anyone trying to lose weight can relate to this problem). As people get used to huge deficits, the numbers seem less scary, and politicians grow more reluctant to incur the political cost of fixing the problem. Italy experienced huge federal deficits for years; they became standard practice. But these huge deficits eventually bore the bitter fruit of political and economic crisis in that country.

SUMMARY

1. The federal budget process suffers from a variety of problems, including overlapping committee jurisdictions, lengthy budget deliberations, extensive use of continuing resolutions, budgeting in too much detail, and a lack of year-to-year control over most of the budget. Suggested improvements include instituting a biennial budget and budgeting in less detail.

2. Deficits usually rise during wars and severe recessions, but huge deficits also occurred during the economic expansion of the 1980s. The deficits arose from a combination of tax cuts during the early 1980s and growth in federal spending. As a percentage of GDP, the national debt has doubled since 1980.

3. There is no clear, consistent relation between deficits and other measures of macroeconomic performance, such as output, the price level, and interest rates. If a fall in aggregate demand results in a recession, deficits increase because of automatic stabilizers, but output, the

price level, and the interest rate all decline. If discretionary fiscal policy is used to rekindle aggregate demand, deficits increase; so do output, the price level, and the interest rate.

4. To the extent that deficits crowd out private capital formation, this decline in investment reduces the economy's ability to grow. Foreign holdings of debt also impose a burden on future generations because future payments to service this debt are paid to foreigners and are consequently not available to U.S. citizens. Thus, the deficits of one generation can reduce the standard of living of the next.

5. Several congressional measures have been aimed at reducing the deficit, and the deficit relative to GDP has declined in the 1990s. Additional remedies include tax increases, expenditure reductions, the line-item veto, and most recently the proposed balanced budget amendment.

QUESTIONS AND PROBLEMS

1. **(The Federal Budget Process)** The budget resolution passed by Congress and signed by the president shows the relationship between *budgeted* expenditures and *projected* revenues. Why does this require forecasts of the state of the economy? Under what circumstances would the actual budget fail to match the budget resolution?

2. **(Problems with the Budget Process)** In terms of the policy lags described in Chapter 16, discuss the following problems with the budget process: (a) continuing resolutions, (b) overlapping committee authority, (c) uncontrollable budget items, and (d) an overly detailed budget.

3. **(Government Budget Deficits)** During the 1984 presidential campaign, President Reagan claimed that the

country would grow out of the deficit it was experiencing. What was the reasoning behind his statement? Did the economy in fact grow out of the deficit?

4. **(Crowding Out)** Is it possible for U.S. federal budget deficits to crowd out investment spending in other countries? How could German or British investment be hurt by large U.S. budget deficits?

5. **(Budget Reform)** What is a biennial budget, and what do its advocates claim is its advantage? What are the drawbacks to a biennial budget?

6. **(Seigniorage)** Earlier in the text we noted that the Fed pays no interest to commercial banks that hold reserves

with the Fed. If the Fed were forced to pay interest, how would this affect the level of seigniorage returned to the U.S. Treasury? How might this complicate attempts to reduce federal budget deficits?

7. **(Budget Philosophies)** Explain the differences among an annually balanced budget, a cyclically balanced budget, and function finance. How does each affect economic fluctuations?

8. **(Budget Deficits)** One alternative to balancing the budget annually or cyclically is to produce a government budget that would be balanced if the economy were at full-employment output. Given the cyclical nature of government tax revenues and spending, how would the budget deficit or surplus vary over the business cycle?

9. **(Crowding Out)** One kind of crowding out caused by government budget deficits is called *international* crowding out. Explain why a reduction is net exports is likely to occur.

10. **(Deficits and Other Aggregate Variables)** Distinguish between the short-run changes in real output, the price level, and interest rates associated with deficits caused by automatic stabilizers and the short-run effects associated with deficits caused by discretionary fiscal policy. Assume that the budget is initially in balance.

11. **(Debt Burden)** Suppose that government budget deficits are financed to a considerable extent by foreign sources. How does this create a potential burden for the domestic economy in the future?

12. **(Balanced Budget Amendment)** Some members of Congress have been pushing for a balanced budget amendment as a tool to control federal spending. What are the major criticisms of such an amendment?

13. **(Crowding Out)** How might federal deficits crowd out private domestic investment? How might this affect future standards of living?

14. **(Debt Service)** According to the text, the percentage of federal income tax revenues necessary to service the debt has more than doubled since 1975. What problems does this create for public officials and spending programs? Do you need to run a budget surplus to "solve" the problem?

15. **(The Budget Process and the Executive Branch)** Explain why the executive branch of the U.S. government is always dealing with three budgets.

16. **(The National Debt)**
   a. Assume that the national debt initially is equal to $3 trillion and the federal government then runs a deficit of $300 billion:
      (i).   What is the new level of national debt?
      (ii.) If 100 percent of the deficit is financed by the sale of securities to federal agencies, what happens to the level of debt held by the public? To the level of gross debt?
      (iii.) If GDP increased by 5 percent in the same year, what happens to gross debt as a percentage of GDP? To the level of debt held by the public as a percentage of GDP?
   b. Assume that the national debt initially is equal to $2.5 trillion and the federal government then runs a deficit of $100 billion:
      (i).   What is the new level of national debt?
      (ii.) If 100 percent of this deficit is financed by the sale of securities to the public, what happens to the level of debt held by the public? To the level of gross debt?
      (iii.) If GDP increases by 6 percent in the same year, what happens to gross debt as a percentage of GDP? To the level of debt held by the public as a percentage of GDP?

17. **(Functional Finance)** The functional finance approach to budget deficits would have the federal budget set so as to promote an economy operating at potential output levels. What operational problems might you expect if the country were to use this kind of budgetary philosophy?

18. **(An Intergenerational View of Deficits and Debt)** Explain why Robert Barro argues that, if parents are concerned about the future welfare of their children, the effects of deficit spending will be neutralized.

Using the Internet

19. Try your hand at balancing the federal budget. Visit the "National Budget Simulation," a project developed by UC-Berkeley's Center for Community Economic Research **(http://garnet.berkeley.edu:3333/ budget/budget.html)**.

   a. Tabulate the changes you make in the budget. Are you successful in balancing the budget? How much of a deficit/surplus are you left with? What does this exercise suggest about the process of creating a balanced budget?
   b. Examine again the budget cuts and/or increases you made. What problems would such changes pose for a politician facing reelection?
   c. This budget simulator allows you only to change spending and tax expenditures over a one year period. What problems does this pose to finding a realistic economic solution for balancing the budget?

Elasticity of Demand and Supply

18

As we noted in Chapter 1, macroeconomics focuses on aggregate markets—on the big picture. But the big picture is a mosaic pieced together from individual decisions made by U.S. households, firms, governments, and the rest of the world. To understand how the economy works, we must take a closer look at these individual decisions. In market economies, the price system guides production and consumption decisions. Prices inform consumers and producers about the relative scarcity of goods and resources.

A downward-sloping demand curve and an upward-sloping supply curve combine to form a powerful analytical tool. To harness the energy of this tool, you must learn more about the shapes of the demand and supply curves. The more you know about the shapes of the curves, the more you can say about the effects of, say, a change in price on the quantity demanded. Firms and governments are willing to pay dearly for predictions about the effect of economic changes on the amount purchased. For example, Taco Bell would like to know what will happen to taco sales if the price of tacos changes. Tax officials would like to know the impact of a change in cigarette taxes on tax receipts. College officials would like to know the impact of a hike in tuition on enrollment. Subway officials would like to know the impact of fare hikes on ridership. And Microsoft would like to know what happens to software sales when consumer incomes grow. To answer such questions, we must consider how *responsive* people are to economic changes such as a change in price or a change in consumer income. *Elasticity* is a tool used to measure such responsiveness. Topics discussed in this chapter include:

- Price elasticity of demand
- Determinants of price elasticity
- Price elasticity of supply
- Income elasticity of demand
- Cross-price elasticity

PRICE ELASTICITY OF DEMAND

Just before Thanksgiving of 1995, Delta Airlines, in an attempt to boost holiday sales, announced fare cuts of up to 50 percent. Was this a good idea for Delta? For Delta's total revenue to increase, the growth rate in ticket sales would have to more than offset the decline in ticket fares. A firm's success or failure often depends on how much it knows about the market for its product. For example, Delta would have liked to know how many more tickets it would sell by cutting prices.

Similarly, the operators of Taco Bell would like to know what would happen to sales if the price of a taco increased from, say, $0.90 to $1.10. The law of demand says that a higher price will reduce quantity demanded, but by how much? How sensitive is quantity demanded to a change in price? Would the number of tacos sold decline only a little or a lot? After all, if quantity demanded declined just a little, a price increase might be a profitable move for Taco Bell.

Let's get more specific about the sensitivity of changes in quantity demanded to changes in price. Consider the alternative demand curves in Exhibit 1; in each panel, we begin with a price of $0.90 per taco and a quantity demanded of 105,000 tacos per day. Now suppose the taco price increases to $1.10. Note that quantity demanded drops to 95,000 tacos per day in panel (a), but to 75,000 tacos per day in panel (b). In response to the price increase, consumers in panel (b) cut their quantity demanded more than do consumers in panel (a). The numerical measure of this responsiveness is called the *price elasticity of demand*. *Elasticity* is simply another word for *responsiveness*.

Calculating Price Elasticity of Demand

In simplest terms, the **price elasticity of demand** is the percent change in the quantity demanded divided by the percent change in price, or

$$\text{Price elasticity of demand} = \frac{\text{Percent change in quantity demanded}}{\text{Percent change in price}},$$

Recall that the law of demand states that price and quantity demanded are inversely related, so the change in price and the change in quantity demanded will be in opposite directions. Hence, in the elasticity formula the numerator and the denominator have opposite signs, so the price elasticity of demand has a negative sign.

To compute the percent change in price or in quantity demanded, we use as a base the average of the initial value and the new value. For example, in Exhibit 1, the price increases from $0.90 to $1.10, an increase of $0.20. The base used to calculate the percent change is the average of $0.90 and $1.10, which is $1.00. The percent change in price is therefore $0.20/$1.00, or 20 percent.

The same holds for changes in quantity demanded. In panel (a), the quantity demanded falls from 105,000 to 95,000 tacos per day, so the base used to calculate the percent change is the average, or 100,000. The percent change in quantity demanded is therefore −10,000/100,000, or −10 percent. The resulting *price elasticity of demand* is the percent change in quantity demanded, −10 percent, divided by the percent change in price, 20 percent, or −10%/20%,

Net Bookmark

Why would Delta Air Lines cut airline fares right before the busy holiday season? Delta is betting that the demand for airline tickets is price elastic. Specifically, Delta believes that if prices are lower, the quantity of tickets demanded will more than offset the decline in price. To discover more about Delta Air Lines and its air fare strategies, visit Delta Air Lines "Skylinks" (**http://www. delta-air.com/**).

Price elasticity of demand A measure of the responsiveness of quantity demanded to a price change; the percent change in quantity demanded divided by the percent change in price

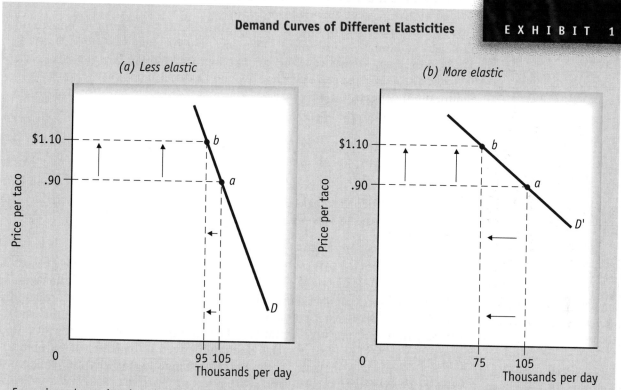

Demand Curves of Different Elasticities   EXHIBIT 1

For a given change in price, the less elastic the demand, the smaller the change in quantity demanded. In panel (a), a 20 percent increase in price leads to a 10 percent decrease in quantity demanded. In panel (b), with more elastic demand D', the same 20 percent price increase leads to a 33 percent decrease in quantity demanded.

which is -0.5. So the price elasticity of demand between points a and b in panel (a) is -0.5.

If the quantity demanded falls from 105,000 to 75,000 tacos per day, as it does in panel (b), the base used for computing the percent change is 90,000, which is the average of 105,000 and 75,000. So the percent change in quantity demanded is $-30,000/90,000$, or -33 percent. The resulting price elasticity of demand is $-33\%/20\%$, or -1.65. So demand in panel (b) is about three times more responsive to the price increase than is demand in panel (a).

Note that elasticity expresses a relationship between two amounts: the percent change in quantity demanded and the percent change in price. Since the focus is on the percent change, we need not be concerned with how output or price is measured. For example, suppose the good in question is apples. It makes no difference in the elasticity formula whether the measure of apples is in pounds, bushels, or even tons. All that matters is the percent change in quantity demanded, not how quantity demanded is measured. Nor does it matter whether we measure the price in U.S. dollars, Mexican pesos, French francs, or Botswanan thebes. All that matters is the percent change in price.

Let's develop a more general price elasticity formula. Suppose that if the price increases from p to p', the quantity demanded decreases from q_D to q'_D. The **price elasticity formula** for calculating the price elasticity of demand,

Price elasticity formula Percent change in quantity divided by the percent change in price; the average quantity and the average price are used as bases for computing percent changes in quantity and in price

E_D, between the two points is the percent change in quantity demanded divided by the percent change in price, or

$$E_D = \frac{q'_D - q_D}{(q'_D + q_D)/2} \div \frac{p' - p}{(p' + p)/2}$$

The 2s cancel out to yield

$$E_D = \frac{q'_D - q_D}{q'_D + q_D} \div \frac{p' - p}{p' + p}$$

Incidentally, because the average quantity and average price are used as a base for computing percent change, the same elasticity measure results whether the change is from the higher price to the lower price or the other way around.

Categories of Price Elasticity of Demand

Inelastic demand The type of demand that exists when a change in price has relatively little effect on quantity demanded; the percent change in quantity demanded is less than the percent change in price

Price elasticity of demand can be divided into three general categories, based on how responsive quantity demanded is to a change in price. If the percent change in quantity demanded is smaller than the percent change in price, the resulting price elasticity has a value between 0 and -1.0, and demand is said to be **inelastic,** meaning that quantity demanded is relatively unresponsive to a change in price. For example, the elasticity derived in panel (a) of Exhibit 1 is -0.5, so demand is inelastic. If the percent change in quantity demanded just equals the percent change in price, the resulting price elasticity has a value of -1.0, and demand is said to be **unit elastic.** Finally, if the percent change in quantity demanded exceeds the percent change in price, the resulting price elasticity is more negative than -1.0, and demand is said to be **elastic.** For example, the elasticity derived in panel (b) of Exhibit 1 was -1.65, so demand is elastic. In summary, *the price elasticity of demand is inelastic if between 0 and -1.0, unit elastic if equal to -1.0, and elastic if more negative than -1.0.*

Unit-elastic demand The type of demand that exists when a percent change in price causes an equal (but of opposite sign) percent change in quantity demanded; the elasticity value is minus one

Elastic demand The type of demand that exists when a change in price has a relatively large effect on quantity demanded; the percent change in quantity demanded exceeds the percent change in price

Elasticity and Total Revenue

Knowledge of price elasticity is especially valuable to producers because it tells them what happens to their total revenue when the price changes. **Total revenue** *(TR)* is the price multiplied by the quantity sold at that price, or $TR = p \times q$. What happens to total revenue when the price decreases? Well, according to the law of demand, if the price falls, the quantity demanded increases. The lower price means producers get less per unit, which tends to decrease total revenue. But the increased quantity demanded that results from a lower price tends to increase total revenue. The overall change in total revenue resulting from a lower price is the net result of these opposite effects. If the positive effect of a greater quantity demanded exceeds the negative effect of a lower price, total revenue will rise. More specifically, when demand is *elastic,* the percent increase in quantity demanded exceeds the percent decrease in price, so total revenue increases. When demand is *unit elastic,* the percent increase in quantity demanded just offsets the percent decrease in price, so total revenue remains unchanged. Finally, when demand is *inelastic,* the percent increase in quantity demanded is less than the percent decrease in price, so total revenue decreases.

Total revenue Price multiplied by the quantity sold at that price

Price Elasticity and the Linear Demand Curve

The price elasticity of demand usually varies along a demand curve. An examination of the elasticity of a particular type of demand curve, the linear demand curve, will tie together the concepts examined thus far. A **linear demand curve** is simply a straight-line demand curve. Panel (a) of Exhibit 2 presents a linear demand curve, and panel (b) shows the total revenue generated at each price-quantity combination along the demand curve. Recall that total revenue equals price times quantity.

Linear demand curve A straight-line demand curve

Since the demand curve in panel (a) is linear, the slope is constant, so a given decrease in price always causes the same unit increase in quantity demanded. For example, a $10 drop in price always increases quantity demanded by 100 units. But *the price elasticity of demand is greater on the higher-price end of the demand curve than on the lower-price end.* Here is why. Because quantity demanded is smaller at the upper end of the demand curve than at the lower end, a 100-unit increase in quantity demanded represents a greater percent change at the upper

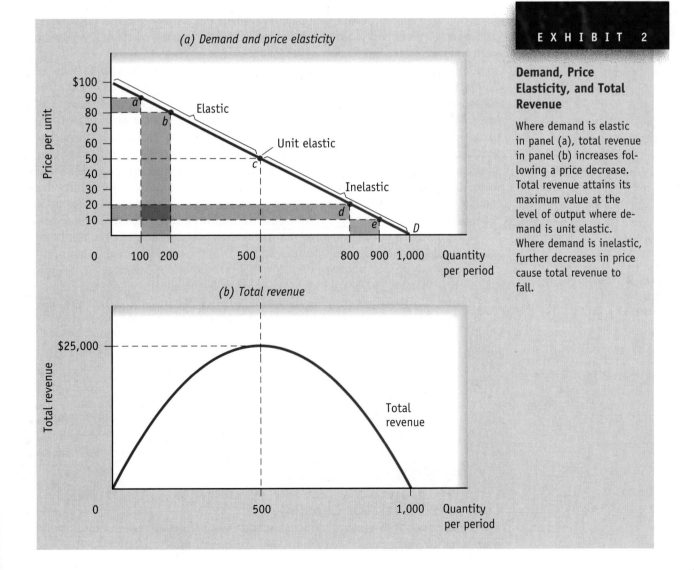

(a) Demand and price elasticity

(b) Total revenue

EXHIBIT 2

Demand, Price Elasticity, and Total Revenue

Where demand is elastic in panel (a), total revenue in panel (b) increases following a price decrease. Total revenue attains its maximum value at the level of output where demand is unit elastic. Where demand is inelastic, further decreases in price cause total revenue to fall.

end than at the lower end. But, because the price *level* is higher at the upper end than at the lower end of the curve, a $10 decrease in price represents a smaller percent change in price at the upper end than at the lower end. Thus, at the upper end of the demand curve, the percent increase in quantity demanded is relatively large and the percent decrease in price is relatively small, so the price elasticity of demand is relatively large. At the lower end of the demand curve, the percent increase in quantity demanded is relatively small and the percent decrease in price is relatively large, so the price elasticity of demand is relatively small.

Consider a movement from point *a* to point *b* on the upper end of the demand curve in Exhibit 2. The 100-unit increase in quantity demanded is a percent change of 100/150, or 67 percent. The $10 price drop is a percent change of −10/85, or about −12 percent. Therefore, the price elasticity of demand between points *a* and *b* is 67/−12, which equals −5.6. Between points *d* and *e* on the lower end, however, the 100-unit quantity increase is a percent change of 100/850, or only 12 percent, and the $10 price decrease is a percent change of −10/15, or −67 percent. The price elasticity of demand thus falls to 12/−67, or −0.18. In other words, *if the demand curve is linear, consumers are more responsive to a given price change when the initial price of a product is relatively high than when the price is relatively low.*

Demand becomes less elastic as we move down the curve. At a point halfway down the linear demand curve in Exhibit 2, the elasticity is equal to −1.0. *This halfway point divides a linear demand curve into an elastic upper half and an inelastic lower half.* You can observe the clear relationship between the elasticity of demand in the upper diagram and total revenue in the lower diagram. Note that where demand is elastic, a decrease in price increases total revenue because the gain in revenue from selling more units (represented by the large blue rectangle in the top panel) exceeds the loss in revenue from selling at the lower price (the small red rectangle). Where demand is inelastic, a price decrease reduces total revenue because the gain in revenue from selling more units (the small blue rectangle) is less than the loss in revenue from selling at the lower price (the large red rectangle). Where demand is unit elastic, the gain and loss of revenue exactly cancel each other out, so total revenue at that point remains constant (hence, total revenue "peaks out" in the lower portion of the exhibit).

In summary, total revenue increases as the price declines until the midpoint of the linear demand curve is reached, where total revenue peaks. In Exhibit 2, total revenue peaks at $25,000 when quantity demanded equals 500 units. Below the midpoint of the demand curve, total revenue declines as the price falls. More generally, regardless of whether the demand curve is a straight line or a curve, there is a relationship between the price elasticity of demand and total revenue: a price decrease *increases* total revenue if demand is elastic, *decreases* total revenue if demand is inelastic, and *has no effect* on total revenue if demand is unit elastic. Finally, note that a downward-sloping linear demand curve has a constant slope but a varying elasticity, so *the slope of a demand curve is not the same as the price elasticity of demand.*

Constant-Elasticity Demand

Price elasticity varies along a linear demand curve unless the demand curve is horizontal or vertical, as in panels (a) and (b) of Exhibit 3. These two demand

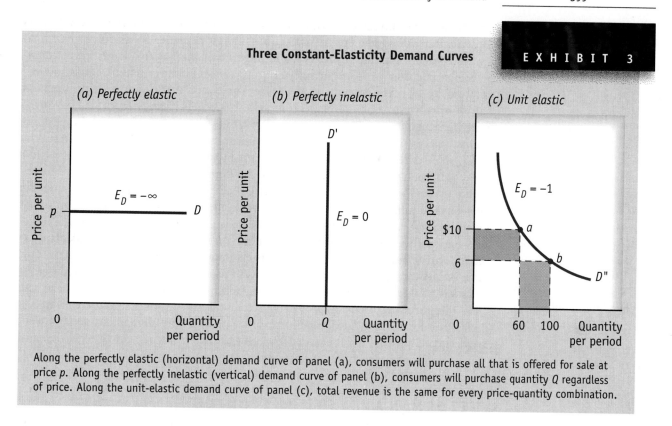

Three Constant-Elasticity Demand Curves   E X H I B I T   3

Along the perfectly elastic (horizontal) demand curve of panel (a), consumers will purchase all that is offered for sale at price *p*. Along the perfectly inelastic (vertical) demand curve of panel (b), consumers will purchase quantity *Q* regardless of price. Along the unit-elastic demand curve of panel (c), total revenue is the same for every price-quantity combination.

curves, along with the special demand curve in panel (c), are called *constant-elasticity demand curves* because the elasticity does not change along the curves.

Perfectly Elastic Demand. The horizontal demand curve in panel (a) indicates that consumers will demand all that is offered for sale at the given price *p*. If the price rises above *p*, however, the quantity demanded drops to zero. This demand curve is said to be **perfectly elastic,** and its numerical elasticity value is minus infinity, a number too negatively large to be defined. You may think this is an odd sort of demand curve: consumers, as a result of a small increase in price, go from demanding as much as is available to demanding nothing. As you will see later, this reflects the demand for the output of any individual producer when many producers are selling identical products.

Perfectly elastic demand curve A horizontal line reflecting a situation in which any price increase reduces quantity demanded to zero; the elasticity value is minus infinity

Perfectly Inelastic Demand. The vertical demand curve in panel (b) of Exhibit 3 represents the situation in which quantity demanded does not vary at all when the price changes. This demand curve expresses consumers' sentiment that "price is no object." For example, if you were very rich and needed insulin injections to stay alive, price would be no object. No matter how high the price of insulin, you would continue to demand the amount necessary to stay alive. Likewise, if the price of insulin drops, you would not increase the quantity demanded. Vertical demand curves are called **perfectly inelastic** because price changes do not affect quantity demanded, at least not over the range of prices shown by the demand curve. Since the percent change in quantity is zero for any given percent change in price, the numerical value of the elasticity is zero.

Perfectly inelastic demand curve A vertical line reflecting a situation in which price change has no effect on the quantity demanded; the elasticity value is zero

Unit Elastic. Panel (c) in Exhibit 3 presents a demand curve that is unit elastic everywhere along the curve. This means that a percent change in price will always result in an identical percent change in quantity demanded but of opposite sign. Because percent changes in price and in quantity will be equal and offsetting, total revenue will be the same for every price-quantity combination along the curve. For example, when the price falls from $10 to $6, the quantity demanded increases from 60 to 100 units. The red shaded rectangle represents the loss in total revenue because all units are sold at the lower price; the blue shaded rectangle represents the gain in total revenue because more units are sold when the price drops. Because the demand curve is unit elastic, the revenue gained by selling more units just equals the revenue lost by lowering the price on all units, so total revenue is unchanged at $600. A demand curve that is unit elastic all along the curve would actually be quite rare.

Each of the demand curves in Exhibit 3 is called a **constant-elasticity** demand curve because the elasticity is the same all along the curve. In contrast, the downward-sloping linear demand curve examined earlier had a different elasticity value at each point along the curve. Exhibit 4 lists the values of the five categories of price elasticity we have discussed, summarizing the varying effects of a 10 percent increase in the price on quantity demanded and on total revenue. Give this exhibit some thought, and see if you can draw a demand curve to reflect each type of elasticity.

Constant elasticity of demand
The type of demand that exists when price elasticity is the same everywhere along the curve; the elasticity value is constant

DETERMINANTS OF THE PRICE ELASTICITY OF DEMAND

Thus far, we have explored the technical properties of demand elasticity. We have not yet considered why the price elasticities of demand vary for different goods. Several characteristics influence the price elasticity of demand for a good. We will examine each of these in detail.

Availability of Substitutes

As we noted in Chapter 3, your particular wants can be satisfied in a variety of ways. If the price of pizza increases, that makes other foods relatively cheaper.

EXHIBIT 4

Summary of Price Elasticity of Demand

	Effects of a 10 Percent Increase in Price		
Price Elasticity Value	**Type of Demand**	**What Happens to Quantity Demanded**	**What Happens to Total Revenue**
$E_D = 0$	Perfectly inelastic	No change	Increases by 10 percent
$-1 < E_D < 0$	Inelastic	Drops by less than 10 percent	Increases by less than 10 percent
$E_D = -1$	Unit elastic	Drops by 10 percent	No change
$-\infty < E_D < -1$	Elastic	Drops by more than 10 percent	Decreases
$E_D = -\infty$	Perfectly elastic	Drops to 0	Drops to 0

If close substitutes are available, an increase in the price of pizza will encourage consumers to shift to these substitutes and to lower the quantity of pizza demanded. But if nothing else satisfies like pizza, the quantity of pizza demanded will not decline as much. *The greater the availability of substitutes for a good and the closer these substitutes, the greater the price elasticity of demand.*

The number and similarity of substitutes depend on how we define the good. *The more broadly we define a good, the fewer substitutes there will be and the less elastic the demand will be.* For example, the demand for shoes is less elastic than the demand for running shoes because there are few substitutes for shoes but several substitutes for running shoes, such as sneakers, tennis shoes, cross-trainers, walking shoes, and the like. The demand for running shoes, however, is less elastic than the demand for Nike running shoes because the consumer has more substitutes for Nikes, including Reeboks, New Balance, and so on. Finally, the demand for Nike running shoes is less elastic than the demand for a specific model of Nikes, such as Nike Air Max[2] Lite.

For some goods, such as insulin, there are simply no close substitutes. The demand for such goods tends to be less elastic than for goods with close substitutes. Because a producer would like to be able to increase price without having consumers switch to substitutes, the producer would like consumers to believe there are no substitutes for that particular product. Much advertising is aimed at establishing in the consumer's mind the uniqueness of a particular product. For example, each manufacturer of running shoes spends millions trying to create a niche in the consumer's mind.

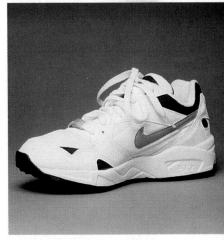

The demand for running shoes is less elastic than the demand for Nike running shoes because consumers have more substitutes for Nike shoes—Reebok, New Balance, and similar brands—than for running shoes in general.

Proportion of the Consumer's Budget Spent on the Good

Recall that a higher price reduces quantity demanded in part because a higher price causes the real spending power of consumer income to decline. A demand curve reflects both the *willingness* and *ability* to purchase a good at alternative prices. Because spending on some goods represents a large share of the consumer's budget, a change in the price of such goods has a substantial impact on the quantity that consumers are *able* to purchase. An increase in the price of housing, for example, reduces the ability to purchase housing. The income effect of a higher price is to reduce the quantity demanded. In contrast, the income effect of an increase in the price of, say, paper towels is trivial because paper towels represent such a small proportion of any budget. *The more important the item is as a proportion of the consumer's budget, other things constant, the greater will be the income effect of a change in price, so the more elastic will be the demand for the item.* The smaller the spending on the item as a proportion of the budget, other things constant, the smaller the income effect of a change in price, so the less elastic the demand for the item. Hence the demand for housing, automobiles, or college will tend to be more elastic at the prevailing price than the demand for paper towels, pencils, or flashlight batteries.

A Matter of Time

Consumers can substitute lower-priced goods for higher-priced goods, but this usually takes time. Suppose your college announces a substantial increase in room and board fees, effective immediately. Some students will move off campus as soon as they can; others will wait until the end of the school year. And, over time, fewer students may apply for admission, and more incoming students will choose off-campus housing. Thus, *the longer the adjustment period considered, the greater the ability to substitute away from relatively higher-priced products toward lower-priced alternatives, so the more responsive the change in quantity demanded is to a given change in price.* As another example, between 1973 and 1974, the price of gasoline increased 45 percent, but the quantity demanded decreased by only 8 percent. As more time passed, however, people purchased smaller cars and made more use of public transportation. And since the price of oil used to heat homes and to fire electric generators had increased as well, people bought more energy-efficient appliances, and added more insulation to their homes. Again, the change in quantity demanded was greater the more time consumers had to respond to the price increase.

Exhibit 5 demonstrates how demand becomes more elastic over time. Given an initial price of $1.00, let D_w be the demand curve one week after a price change; D_m, one month after; and D_y, one year after. If the price increases from $1.00 to $1.25, the more time consumers have to respond to the price increase, the greater reduction in quantity demanded. For example, the demand curve D_w shows that one week after the price increase, the quantity demanded has not declined much—in this case, from 100 to 95. The demand curve D_m indicates a greater reduction in quantity demanded after one month, and demand curve D_y shows the greatest reduction in quantity demanded after one year. Notice that *among these demand curves and over the range starting from the point of intersection, the flatter the demand curve, the more price elastic the demand.*

Elasticity Estimates

Let's consider some estimates of the price elasticity of demand for particular goods and services. As we have noted, the substitution of relatively lower-priced goods for a good whose price has just increased often takes time. Thus,

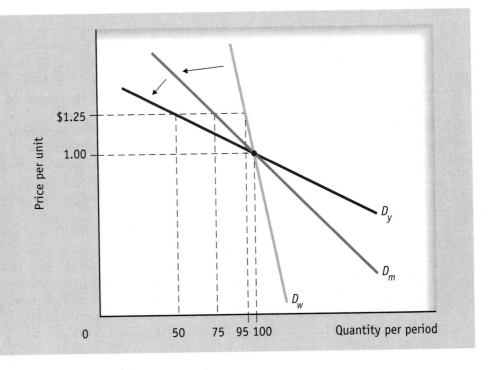

EXHIBIT 5

Demand Becomes More Elastic over Time

D_w is the demand curve one week after a price increase from $1.00 to $1.25. Along this curve, quantity demanded falls from 100 to 95. One month after the price increase, quantity demanded has fallen to 75 along D_m. One year after the price increase, quantity demanded has fallen to 50 along D_y. At any given price, D_y is more elastic than D_m, which is more elastic than D_w.

EXHIBIT 6

Selected Price
Elasticities of Demand

Product	Short Run	Long Run
Cigarettes	—	−0.4
Electricity (residential)	−0.1	−1.9
Air travel	−0.1	−2.4
Medical care and hospitalization	−0.3	−0.9
Gasoline	−0.4	−1.5
Milk	−0.4	—
Wine	−0.7	−1.2
Movies	−0.9	−3.7
Natural gas (residential)	−1.4	−2.1
Automobiles	−1.9	−2.2
Chevrolets	—	−4.0

Sources: F. Chaloupka, "Rational Addictive Behavior and Cigarette Smoking," *Journal of Political Economy*, (August 1991); J. Johnson et al., "Short-Run and Long-Run Elasticities for Canadian Consumption of Alcoholic Beverages," *Review of Economics and Statistics* (February 1992); R. Archibald and R. Gillingham, "The Review of the Short-Run Consumer Demand for Gasoline Using Household Survey Data," *Review of Economics and Statistics* 62 (November 1980); J. Griffin, *Energy Conservation in the OECD, 1980-2000* (Cambridge, Mass.: Balinger, 1979); H. Houthakker and L. Taylor, *Consumer Demand in the United States: Analysis and Projections,* 2d ed. (Cambridge, Mass.: Harvard University Press, 1970); and G. Lakshmanan and W. Anderson, "Residential Energy Demand in the United States," *Regional Science and Urban Economics* 10 (August 1980).

when estimating price elasticity, economists often distinguish between a period during which consumers have little time to adjust—let's call it the *short run*—and a period during which consumers can fully adjust to a price change—let's call it the *long run*. Exhibit 6 provides some short-run and long-run price elasticity estimates for selected products.

The price elasticity is greater in the long run because consumers have more time to adjust. For example, if the price of electricity rose today, consumers in the short run might cut back a bit in their use of electrical appliances and those with electric heat might turn the thermostat down in winter. Over time, however, consumers would switch to more energy-efficient appliances and might convert from electric heat to oil or natural gas. So demand is more elastic in the long run than in the short run, as is reflected in Exhibit 6. In fact, in every instance where values for both the short run and the long run are listed, the long run is more elastic than the short run. Notice also that the long-run price elasticity of demand for Chevrolets exceeds the price elasticity for automobiles in general. There are many more substitutes for Chevrolets than for automobiles. There are no close substitutes for cigarettes, even in the long run, so the demand for cigarettes is price inelastic. The following case study looks more closely at the demand for medicinal drugs, using cross-sectional data from six countries.

CASE STUDY

Pharmaceutical Prices across Countries

A study of medicinal drugs across six industrial countries attempted to uncover the effect of price on per-capita drug consumption. On average, prices of the 167 drugs examined were highest in the United States and lowest in France. Exhibit 7 shows the relationship between the average price, shown as an index on the vertical axis, and per-capita drug consumption, shown on the horizontal axis. Each point reflects a price-quantity combination for one of the six countries examined.

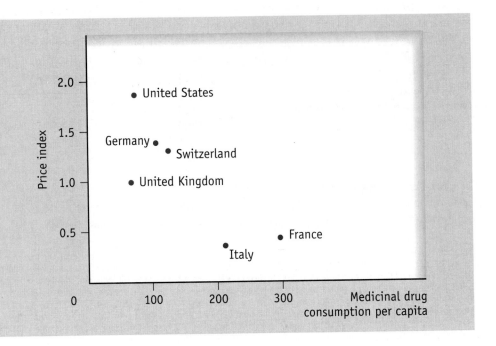

EXHIBIT 7

Medicinal Drug Prices and Per-Capita Consumption in Six Countries
Source: Data from Tadeusz Szuba, "International Comparisons of Drug Consumption: Impact of Prices." *Social Science and Medicine* 22 (1986): pp. 1019–25; figures are for 1983.

Pharmaceutical Prices across Countries
continued

Location:

To learn more about the pharmaceutical industry, visit PhARMA: America's Pharmaceutical Research Companies (http://www.phrma.org/index.html). Also browse "Preparing for Change: The Parmaceutical Industry," a study by E.B. Baatz and published by *CIO Magazine* (http://www.cio.com/CIO/0901_pharm.html).

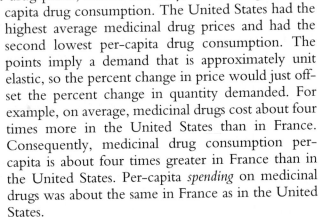

You would need little imagination to see that the six points reflect a rough, though familiar, pattern between price and quantity demanded. In accordance with the law of demand, price and quantity are inversely related. The two countries with the lowest drug prices, France and Italy, had the highest per-capita drug consumption. The United States had the highest average medicinal drug prices and had the second lowest per-capita drug consumption. The points imply a demand that is approximately unit elastic, so the percent change in price would just off-set the percent change in quantity demanded. For example, on average, medicinal drugs cost about four times more in the United States than in France. Consequently, medicinal drug consumption per-capita is about four times greater in France than in the United States. Per-capita *spending* on medicinal drugs was about the same in France as in the United States.

Another line of research involves the pricing of new drugs; the results support the proposition that the greater the availability of substitutes and the closer these substitutes, the greater the price elasticity of demand. For example, one study examined the amount by which new drugs are priced above their existing substitutes. The study found that the greater the number of substitutes available, the lower the introductory price of a new drug. And the average price premium for a new drug that is more therapeutically advanced than existing substitutes is substantially greater than the price premium for a new drug that offers a more modest improvement over existing products. Finally, a new drug that performs about the same as existing products is priced at or below the level of existing products. The point is that new drugs with less price-elastic demand (because of superior performance and the lack of substitutes) exhibit a greater price premium over existing products than do new drugs that are more price elastic.

Sources: Tadeusz Szuba, "International Comparisons of Drug Consumption: Impact of Prices," *Social Science and Medicine* 22 (1986): pp. 1019–25; William Comanor and Stuart Schweitzer, "Pharmaceuticals," *The Structure of American Industry*, 9th ed., Walter Adams and James Brock, eds. (Englewood Cliffs, N.J.: Prentice Hall, 1995), pp. 177–96; and Zvi Griliches and Iain Cockburn, "Generic and New Goods in Pharmaceutical Price Indexes," *American Economic Review* 84 (December 1994): pp. 1213–32.

Pharmaceutical Prices across Countries
continued

PRICE ELASTICITY OF SUPPLY

Prices signal both sides of the market about the relative scarcity of products; high prices discourage consumption but encourage production. The price elasticity of demand measures how responsive consumers are to a price change. Similarly, the **price elasticity of supply** measures how responsive producers are to a price change. This elasticity is calculated in the same way as demand elasticity, but using the percent change in quantity supplied instead of the percent change in quantity demanded. In simplest terms, the price elasticity of supply equals the percent change in quantity supplied divided by the percent change in price.

Price elasticity of supply A measure of the responsiveness of quantity supplied to a price change; the percent change in quantity supplied divided by the percent change in price

Let's look at the elasticity formula for an upward-sloping supply curve. If the price increases from p to p', the quantity supplied increases from q_S to q'_S. The price elasticity of supply, E_s, is

$$E_S = \frac{q'_s - q_s}{(q'_s + q_s)/2} \div \frac{p' - p}{(p' + p)/2}$$

Again, the 2s cancel out, so the formula reduces to

$$E_S = \frac{q'_s - q_s}{q'_s + q_s} \div \frac{p' - p}{p' + p}$$

Since a higher price usually results in an increased quantity supplied, the percent change in price and the percent change in quantity supplied move in the same direction, so the price elasticity of supply is usually positive.

Categories of Supply Elasticity

The terminology for supply elasticity is the same as for demand elasticity: If supply elasticity is less than 1.0, supply is *inelastic*; if its value is equal to 1.0, supply is *unit elastic*; and if its value is greater than 1.0, supply is *elastic*. There are also some special values of supply elasticity to consider.

Perfectly Elastic Supply. At one extreme is the horizontal supply curve, such as supply curve S in panel (a) of Exhibit 8. In this case, producers will supply none of the good at a price below p but will supply any amount at a price of p. The quantity actually supplied at price p will depend on the amount demanded at that price. Because a tiny increase from a price just below p to a price of p will

Perfectly elastic supply curve *A horizontal line reflecting a situations in which any price decrease reduces the quantity supplied to zero; the elasticity value is infinity*

result in an unlimited supply, this curve is said to reflect **perfectly elastic supply,** with a mathematical elasticity value of infinity. As individual consumers, we typically face perfectly elastic supply curves. When we go to the supermarket, we usually can buy as much as we want at the prevailing price. This is not to say that all consumers together could buy an unlimited amount at the prevailing price. (Recall the fallacy of composition: What is true for any individual consumer is not necessarily true for all consumers as a group.)

Perfectly inelastic supply curve *A vertical line reflecting a situation in which a price change has no effect on the quantity supplied; the elasticity value is zero*

Perfectly Inelastic Supply. The most unresponsive relationship between price and quantity supplied is the one in which there is no change in the quantity supplied regardless of the price. Such a case is represented by the vertical supply curve S' in panel (b) of Exhibit 8. Because the percent change in quantity supplied is zero, regardless of the change in price, the value of the supply elasticity equals zero. This curve reflects **perfectly inelastic supply.** Any good that is in fixed supply, such as Picasso paintings or 1978 Dom Perignon champagne, will have a perfectly inelastic supply curve.

Unit-elastic supply *A percent change in price causes an identical percent change in quantity supplied; depicted by a supply curve that is a straight line through the origin; the elasticity value is one*

Unit Elastic Supply. Any supply curve that can be represented as a straight line from the origin, such as S'' in panel (c) of Exhibit 8—is **unit elastic.** This means that a percent change in price will always result in an identical percent change in quantity supplied. For example, along S'' a doubling of the price results in a doubling of the quantity supplied.

EXHIBIT 8   Three Constant-Elasticity Supply Curves

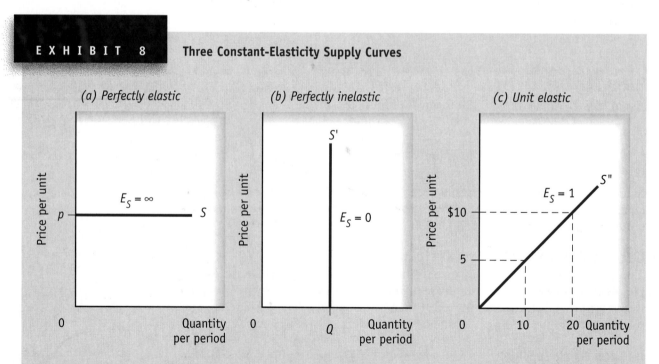

Supply curve S in panel (a) is perfectly elastic (horizontal). Along S, firms will supply any amount of output demanded at price p. Supply curve S' is perfectly inelastic (vertical). S' shows that the quantity supplied is independent of the price. In panel (c), S'' is a ray, which has a unit-elastic price elasticity of supply. Any percentage change in price will result in the same percentage change in quantity supplied.

Determinants of Supply Elasticity

The elasticity of supply indicates how responsive producers are to a change in price. Their responsiveness depends on how easy or difficult it is to alter output as a result of a change in price. If the cost of supplying each additional unit rises sharply as output expands, then a higher price will elicit little increase in quantity supplied, so supply will tend to be inelastic. But if the additional cost rises slowly as output expands, the lure of a higher price will prompt a large increase in output. In this case supply will tend to be more elastic.

An important determinant of supply elasticity is the length of the adjustment period under consideration. Just as demand becomes more elastic over time as consumers adjust to price changes, supply also becomes more elastic over time as producers adjust to price changes. The longer the time period under consideration, the more able producers are to adjust to changes in relative prices. Exhibit 9 presents a different supply curve for each of three time periods. S_w is the supply curve when the period of adjustment is a week. As you can see, a higher price will not elicit much of a response in quantity supplied because firms have little time to adjust. Thus, such a supply curve will tend to slope steeply, reflecting inelastic supply.

S_m is the supply curve when the adjustment period under consideration is a month. In that time, firms can more easily adjust the rate at which they employ some resources. As a result, firms have a greater ability to vary output. Thus, supply is more elastic when the adjustment period is a month than when it is a week. Supply is still more elastic when the adjustment period is a year, as is shown by S_y. If firms can vary all inputs in a year, a higher price will draw new firms into the market.

So a given price increase will elicit a greater quantity supplied, the longer

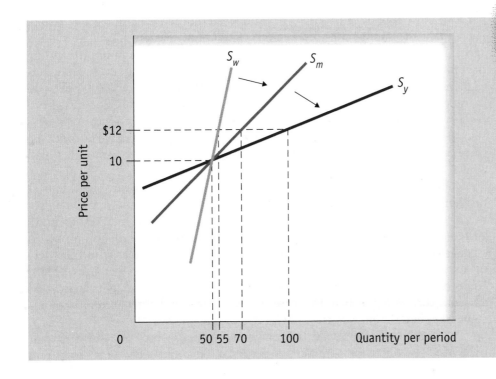

EXHIBIT 9

Market Supply Becomes More Elastic over Time

The supply curve one week after a price increase, S_w, is less elastic, at a given price, than the curve one month later, S_m, which is less elastic than the curve one year later, S_y. Given a price increase from $10 to $12, quantity supplied increases to 55 units after one week, to 70 units after one month, and to 100 units after one year.

the adjustment period. For example, if the price of oil increases, oil producers in the short run can try to pump more from existing wells, but in the long run they can try to discover more oil in the remote jungles of the Amazon or the stormy waters of the North Sea. Empirical estimates confirm the positive link between the price elasticity of supply and the length of the adjustment period. *The elasticity of supply is therefore greater the longer the period of adjustment.* Firms' ability to alter supply in response to price changes differs across industries. The response time will be slower for producers of electricity, oil, and timber than for window washing, lawn maintenance, and hot-dog vending.

Now that you have been introduced to the elasticities of demand and supply, your understanding of elasticity will be reinforced by working through an example involving both demand and supply. In the next section, we consider the effects of a sales tax on equilibrium price and quantity, and link these effects to price elasticities.

ELASTICITY AND TAX INCIDENCE: AN APPLICATION

Suppose a tax of $0.40 is imposed on each pack of cigarettes sold. There is much confusion about who exactly pays the tax. Is it paid by producers or by consumers? As you will see, the *tax incidence*—that is, who ultimately pays the tax—depends on the elasticities of demand and supply.

Demand Elasticity and Tax Incidence

Panel (a) in Exhibit 10 depicts the demand, *D,* and supply, *S,* for cigarettes. Before the tax is imposed, the intersection of demand and supply yields an equilibrium price of $2 per pack and an equilibrium quantity of 10 million packs per day. Now suppose a tax of $0.40 is imposed on each pack of cigarettes sold. Recall that the supply curve represents the amount that producers are willing and able to supply at each price. Since producers are now required to pay the government $0.40 for each pack of cigarettes they sell, the tax causes suppliers to increase the amount they must be paid to supply cigarettes by $0.40 per pack. This decrease in supply is reflected by a vertical shift in the supply curve, from *S* up to S_t. *The effect of the tax is to shift up the supply of cigarettes by the vertical amount of $0.40—the amount of the tax.* The demand curve remains the same since nothing has happened to demand; only the quantity demanded will change.

Since suppliers are the ones who collect the tax for the government, they at first appear to be the ones who pay the tax. But let's take a closer look. The result of the tax in panel (a) is to raise the equilibrium price from $2.00 to $2.30 and to decrease the equilibrium quantity from 10 million to 9 million packs. As a result of the tax, consumers pay $2.30, or $0.30 more per pack, and the net-of-tax amount that producers receive is $1.90, or $0.10 less per pack. Thus, $0.30 of the $0.40 tax is paid by consumers in the form of a higher price, and $0.10 is paid by suppliers in the form of a reduction in the net amount they receive per pack.

The shaded area represents the total tax collected, which equals the tax per pack of $0.40 times the 9 million packs sold, for a total of $3.6 million. You

Effects of Different Demand Elasticities on Sales Tax Incidence

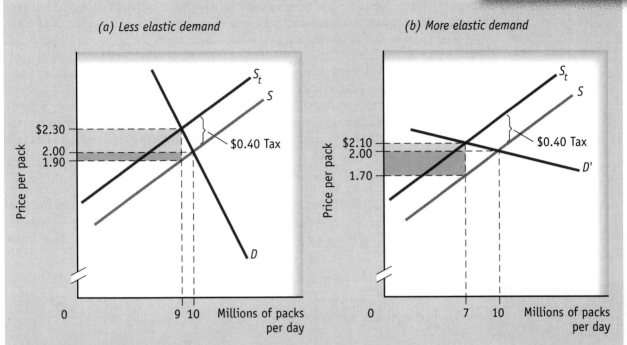

(a) Less elastic demand   *(b) More elastic demand*

The imposition of a $0.40-per-pack tax shifts the supply curve vertically from S to S_t. In panel (a), with less elastic demand, the market price rises from $2.00 to $2.30 per pack and the quantity demanded and supplied falls from 10 million packs to 9 million. In panel (b), with more elastic demand, the same tax leads to an increase in price from $2.00 to $2.10 per pack; the quantity demanded and supplied falls from 10 million packs to 7 million. The more elastic the demand, the more the tax is paid by producers in the form of a lower price net of taxes.

can see that the original price line at $2 divides the shaded area into two portions—the portion of the tax paid by consumers through a higher price (the lighter shading) and the portion paid by producers through a lower after-tax price (the darker shading).

The same situation is depicted in panel (b) of Exhibit 10, with the single difference being that demand is more price elastic than in panel (a). In panel (b), consumers cut quantity demanded more sharply in response to a change in price, so the suppliers cannot as easily pass the tax along as a higher price. Hence, the price increases by only $0.10, to $2.10, and the after-tax receipts of producers decline by $0.30 per pack, to $1.70. Total tax revenues equal $0.40 per pack times 7 million packs sold, or $2.8 million. Again, the light blue rectangle shows the portion of the total taxes paid by consumers through a higher price, and the dark blue rectangle shows the portion of the total taxes paid by producers through a lower after-tax price. Note that the amount by which the price increases and the amount by which the producers' after-tax receipt declines must always sum to $0.40, the amount of the tax per unit.

Thus, the tax is the difference between the amount consumers pay and amount producers receive. More generally, as long as the supply curve slopes upward, *the more elastic the demand, the less the tax is passed on to consumers as a higher price and the more the tax is levied on producers, who receive a lower after-tax price for their product.* Also note that the amount sold falls more in panel (b) than in panel (a); other things constant, the total tax revenue is lower when demand is more elastic. Because tax revenue falls as demand elasticity increases, governments tend to tax those products, such as cigarettes, alcohol, gasoline, and gambling, for which demand is relatively inelastic.

Supply Elasticity and Tax Incidence

The effect of the elasticity of supply on the tax incidence is shown in Exhibit 11. In both panels the demand curve is the same, but the supply curve is more elastic in panel (a) than in panel (b). Again, we begin with an equilibrium price of $2.00 per pack and equilibrium quantity of 10 million packs per day. Because a sales tax of $0.40 per pack is imposed on cigarettes, the supply curve shifts vertically by $0.40. Notice that in panel (a), the equilibrium price rises to $2.30— a $0.30 increase over the pretax price of $2.00. But in panel (b), the price increases by only $0.10. Thus, more of the tax is passed on to consumers in panel (a), where supply is more elastic, than in panel (b), where supply is less elastic. More generally, as long as the demand curve slopes downward, *the more elastic*

E X H I B I T   1 1   **Effects of Different Supply Elasticities on Sales Tax Incidence**

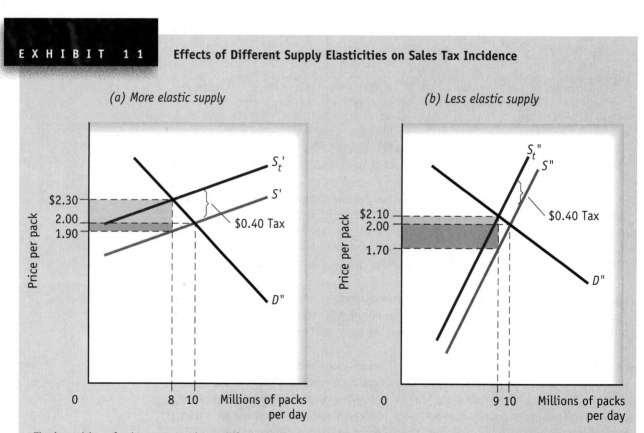

The imposition of a $0.40-per-pack tax shifts both the more elastic supply curve of panel (a) and the less elastic curve of panel (b) vertically by $0.40. In panel (a), the market price rises from $2.00 per pack to $2.30; in panel (b), the price rises to $2.10 per pack. Thus, the more elastic the supply, the more the tax is paid by consumers.

the supply, the more the tax is passed on to consumers and the less it is levied on producers. We conclude that *the less elastic the demand and the more elastic the supply, the higher the proportion of the tax paid by consumers.*

OTHER ELASTICITY MEASURES

The price elasticities of demand and supply are frequently used in economic analysis, but other elasticities also provide useful information, such as how demand responds to a change in consumer income or to a change in the price of a related good.

Income Elasticity of Demand

What happens to the demand for new cars, garden supplies, or computer software if consumer income increases by, say, 10 percent? The answer to this question is of great interest to producers of these and other goods because it helps producers to predict the effect of rising incomes on quantity sold and on total revenues. The **income elasticity of demand** measures how demand changes in response to a change in income. Whereas the price elasticity of demand measures the sensitivity of a change in quantity demanded to a change in price along a given demand curve, *the income elasticity of demand measures the sensitivity of a change in demand to a change in income.* More specifically, the income elasticity of demand measures, at a given price, the percent change in demand divided by the percent change in income that caused it.

Income elasticity of demand **The percent change in demand (at a given price) divided by the percent change in income**

As we noted in Chapter 3, the demand for some products, such as bus rides and laundromat services, actually declines as income increases. Thus, the income elasticity of demand for such products will be negative. Goods with an income elasticity less than zero are called *inferior goods.* The demand for most goods increases as income increases. These goods are called *normal goods,* and they have an income elasticity greater than zero.

Let's take a closer look at normal goods. Suppose demand increases with income but by a smaller percent than income increases. In such cases the value of income elasticity is greater than zero but less than 1. For example, people buy more food as their incomes rise, but the percent increase in demand is less than the percent increase in income. Normal goods with an income elasticity less than 1 are said to be *income inelastic. Necessities* such as food, housing, and clothing often have an income elasticity of less than 1.

Goods with an income elasticity greater than 1 are said to be *income elastic.* Luxuries, such as fine cars, vintage wine, and meals at fancy restaurants, often have an income elasticity greater than 1. For example, during 1990 and 1991, the U.S. economy experienced a recession, meaning that national income declined; as a result, the demand for meals at fancy restaurants declined, and some restaurants went out of business. During the same period, the demand for basic foods such as bread, sugar, and cheese changed very little. Incidentally, the terms *necessities* and *luxuries* are not meant to imply some value judgment about the merit of particular goods; they are simply convenient definitions economists use to classify economic behavior.

Exhibit 12 presents some income elasticity estimates for various goods and

EXHIBIT 12

Selected Income Elasticities of Demand

Product	Income Elasticity	Product	Income Elasticity
Private education	2.46	Physicians' services	0.75
Automobiles	2.45	Coca Cola	0.68
Wine	2.19	Beef	0.62
Owner-occupied housing	1.49	Food	0.51
Furniture	1.48	Coffee	0.51
Dental service	1.42	Cigarettes	0.50
Restaurant meals	1.40	Gasoline and oil	0.48
Shoes	1.10	Rental housing	0.43
Chicken	1.06	Beer	0.27
Spirits ("hard" liquor)	1.02	Pork	0.18
Clothing	0.92	Flour	−0.36

Sources: F. Gasmi et al., "Econometric Analyses of Collusive Behavior in a Soft-Drink Market," *Journal of Economics and Management Strategy* (Summer 1992); J. Johnson et al., "Short-Run and Long-Run Elasticities for Canadian Consumption of Alcoholic Beverages," *Review of Economics and Statistics* (February 1992); H. Houthakker and L. Taylor, *Consumer Demand in the United States: Analyses and Projections,* 2d ed. (Cambridge, Mass.: Harvard University Press, 1970); C. Huang et al., "The Demand for Coffee in the United States, 1963–77," *Quarterly Review of Economics and Business* (Summer 1980); and G. Brester and M. Wohlgenant, "Estimating Interrelated Demands for Meats Using New Measures for Ground and Table Cut Beef," *American Journal of Agricultural Economics* (November 1991).

services. The figures indicate that as income increases, consumers spend proportionately more on items such as private education, automobiles, wine, owner-occupied housing, furniture, dental service, and restaurant meals. As income increases, consumer spending increases, but less than proportionately, for items such as food, cigarettes, gasoline, rental housing, and beer. So as income rises, the demand for owner-occupied housing increases more than the demand for rental housing and the demand for wine increases more than the demand for beer. Flour has negative income elasticity, indicating that the demand for flour declines as income increases. As income increases, consumers switch from home baking to purchasing baked goods.

As we have noted, the demand for food is income inelastic. The demand for food also tends to be price inelastic. This combination of income inelasticity and price inelasticity creates special problems in agricultural markets, as described in the following case study.

CASE STUDY

The Demand for Food and "The Farm Problem"

Despite decades of federal support through various farm assistance programs, the number of farmers continues to drop. By the early 1990s, the United States had only 4.6 million farms, down from 23 million in 1950. The demise of the family farm can be traced to the price and income elasticities of demand for farm products and to technological breakthroughs that made larger farms more efficient.

Many of the forces that determine farm production are beyond the farmer's control. Temperature, rain, insects, and other external forces affect crop size and quality. For example, the summer of 1988 was hot and dry, cutting crop production by 14 percent compared to 1987. Such swings in production create special problems for farmers because the demand for most farm crops, such as milk, eggs, corn, potatoes, oats, sugar, and beef, is price inelastic.

The effect of inelastic demand on farm revenue is illustrated in Exhibit 13. Suppose in a normal year, farmers supply 10 billion bushels of grain at a market price of $5 per bushel. Total revenue, which is price times quantity, comes to $50 billion in our example. Suppose that more favorable growing conditions increase crop production to 11 billion bushels, an increase of 10 percent. Because demand is price inelastic, the average price in our example must fall by more than 10 percent to, say, $4 per bushel, in order to clear the market of the additional billion bushels. Thus, the 10 percent increase in farm production can be sold only if the price drops by 20 percent.

Because, in percentage terms, the drop in price exceeds the increase in output, total revenue declines from $50 billion to $44 billion. So, farm revenue drops by over 10 percent, despite the 10 percent increase in production. *Since demand is price inelastic, an increase in output reduces total revenue.* Of course, the up side of inelastic demand for farmers is that a lower-than-normal crop results in a proportionately higher price and a higher total revenue. For example, because of the drought of 1988, corn prices rose by more than 50 percent and net farm income was up sharply. So weather-generated changes in farm production create substantial year-to-year swings in farm revenue.

Problems created by fluctuations in farm revenue are compounded in the long run by the *income inelasticity* of demand for grain and, more generally, food. As household incomes grow over time, the food budget may increase because people substitute prepared foods and restaurant meals for home cooking. But

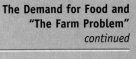

The Demand for Food and "The Farm Problem"
continued

Location:

To discover more about the economics of farming, visit the Economic Research Service (ERS), an agency of the U.S. Department of Agriculture (http://www.econ.ag.gov/). Also visit "Economy," a service of the Bureau of the Census (http://www.census.gov/), and "Agricultural Economics," a service of Cornell University's Mann Library (http://www.mannlib.cornell.edu/catalog/subject/ag-econ.html). For global economic information about farming, visit the World Agricultural Information Center (WAICENT), a service of the Food and Agriculture Organization of the United Nations (FAO) (http://www.fao.org/waicent/waicent.htm).

EXHIBIT 13

The Demand for Grain

The demand for grain tends to be price inelastic. As the market price falls, total revenue also falls.

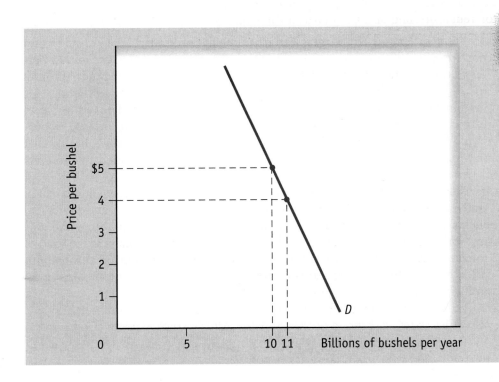

EXHIBIT 14

The Effect of Increases in Supply and Demand on Farm Revenue

Over time, technological advances in farming have sharply increased the supply of grain. In addition, increases in household income over time have increased the demand for farm products. But because increases in the supply of grain have exceeded increases in demand, the combined effect has been a drop in the market prices and a fall in total farm revenue.

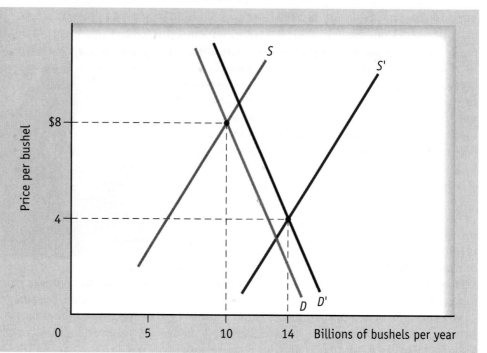

The Demand for Food and "The Farm Problem"
continued

this switch has little effect on their total demand for farm products. Thus, as the economy grows over time and real incomes rise, the demand for farm products tends to increase by less than the increase in real income, as reflected by the shift in the demand curve from D to D' in Exhibit 14.

Because of technological improvements in production, the supply of farm products has increased sharply. Farm output per worker is *seven times* greater now than in 1950 because of such factors as more sophisticated machines, better fertilizers, and healthier seed strains. Exhibit 14 shows the supply of grain increasing from S to S'. Since the increase in supply has exceeded the increase in demand, the price of grain has declined. And because the demand for grain is price inelastic, the percent drop in price exceeds the percent increase in output. The combined effect in our example is lower total farm revenue. In fact, net income (adjusted for inflation) to all U.S. farmers combined in the early 1990s was only half what it had been in the early 1950s.

Another wild card in the farm-revenue equation is unstable foreign demand. Foreign demand for U.S. crops depends on foreign production and prices, on the exchange rate between the dollar and foreign currencies, and on public policy with regard to foreign trade. Thus, many of the forces shaping the market for farm products are beyond the farmer's control. And demand that is both price inelastic and income inelastic means that greater farm output may result in lower total revenue.

Sources: Bruce L. Gardner, "Changing Economic Perspective on the Farm Problem," *Journal of Economic Literature* 30 (March 1992): pp. 62–105; Ching-Fun Cling and James Peale, "Income and Price Elasticities," *Advances in Econometrics Supplement,* Henri Theil, ed. (Greenwich,Conn.: JAI Press, 1989); and *Economic Report of the President,* February 1995, Tables B-98 to B-103.

Cross-Price Elasticity of Demand

The responsiveness of demand for one good to changes in the price of another good is called the **cross-price elasticity of demand.** It is defined as the percent change in the demand of one good (holding the price constant) divided by the percent change in the price of another good. Its numerical value can be positive, negative, or zero, depending on whether the two goods in question are substitutes, complements, or unrelated, respectively.

Cross-price elasticity of demand The percent change in the demand of one good (at a given price) as a result of the percent change in the price of another good

Substitutes. If an increase in the price of one good leads to an increase in the demand for another good, the value of their cross-price elasticity is positive, and the goods are considered *substitutes*. For example, an increase in the price of Coke, other things constant, will increase the demand for Pepsi, reflecting the fact that the two are substitutes. In fact, the cross-price elasticity between Coke and Pepsi is about 0.7, indicating that a 10 percent increase in the price of one will increase the demand for the other by 7 percent.[1]

Complements. If an increase in the price of one good leads to a decrease in the demand for another good, the value of their cross-price elasticity is negative, and the goods are considered *complements*. For example, an increase in the price of gasoline, other things constant, will reduce the demand for tires because people will drive less and so will replace their tires less frequently. Gasoline and tires have a negative cross-price elasticity and are complements.

In summary, when the change in demand for one good has the same sign as the change in price of another good, the two goods are substitutes; when the change in demand for one good has the opposite sign from the change in price of another good, the goods are complements. Most pairs of goods selected at random are *unrelated,* so the value of their cross-price elasticity is approximately zero.

CONCLUSION

Because this chapter has tended to be more quantitative than earlier chapters, you may have been preoccupied with the mechanics of the calculations and thus may have overlooked the intuitive appeal and the neat simplicity of the notion of elasticity. *An elasticity measure represents the willingness and ability of buyers and sellers to alter their behavior in response to a change in their economic circumstances.* For example, if the price of a good falls, consumers may be able but not willing to increase their consumption of the good. In that case, the demand would be inelastic.

Firms try to estimate the price elasticity of demand for their products. Since a corporation often produces an entire line of products, it also has a special interest in certain cross-price elasticities. For example, the Coca-Cola Corporation needs to know how changing the price of Cherry Coke will affect sales of Classic Coke. Similarly, Procter and Gamble wants to know how changing the price of Safeguard soap will affect sales of Ivory soap. Governments, too, have

---

1   This estimate was reported in F. Gasmi, J. Laffont, and Q. Vuong, "Econometric Analysis of Collusive Behavior in a Soft-Drink Market," *Journal of Economics and Management Strategy* (Summer 1992).

an ongoing interest in various elasticities. For example, state governments want to know the effect of a 1 percent increase in the sales tax on total tax receipts, and local governments want to know how an increase in income will affect the demand for real estate and, hence, the revenue generated by a property tax. And international groups are interested in elasticities; for example, the Organization of Petroleum Exporting Countries (OPEC) is concerned about the price elasticity of demand for oil. Many questions can be answered by referring to particular elasticities. Some corporate economists estimate elasticities for a living.

SUMMARY

1. The price elasticities of demand and supply show how sensitive buyers and sellers are to changes in the price. More elastic means more responsive, and less elastic means less responsive.

2. If demand is elastic—that is, if the percent change in quantity exceeds the percent change in price, a price increase will reduce total revenue and a price decrease will increase total revenue. If demand is inelastic—that is, if the percent change in quantity is less than the percent change in price, then a price increase will increase total revenue and a price decrease will reduce total revenue. And if demand is unit elastic—that is, if the percent change in quantity just equals the percent change in price, a price change will leave total revenue unchanged.

3. Along a linear, or straight-line, demand curve, the elasticity of demand falls steadily as the price falls. Constant-elasticity demand curves have the same elasticity everywhere along the curve.

4. Demand will be more elastic (1) the greater the availability of substitutes and the more closely they resemble the good demanded, (2) the more narrowly the good is defined, (3) the larger the proportion of the consumer's budget spent on the good, and (4) the longer the time available to adjust to a change in price.

5. We use the same kind of calculations and the same terminology for the price elasticity of supply as for the price elasticity of demand, except the price elasticity of demand is negative whereas the price elasticity of supply is positive. If marginal production costs rise sharply as output expands, supply will be less elastic. Also, the longer the time period under consideration, the more elastic the supply.

6. The income elasticity of demand measures the responsiveness of demand to changes in consumer income. This elasticity is positive for normal goods and negative for inferior goods.

7. The cross-price elasticity of demand measures the responsiveness of demand to changes in the price of another product. Two goods are defined as substitutes, complements, or unrelated, depending on whether the value of their cross-price elasticity of demand is positive, negative, or equal to zero, respectively.

QUESTIONS AND PROBLEMS

1. **(Demand Elasticity)** How is it possible for many price elasticities to be associated with a single linear demand curve?

2. **(Demand Elasticity)** Suppose that a company is concerned only with maximizing its total revenue. What pricing policy should it follow?

3. **(Calculating Price Elasticity of Demand)** Suppose the initial price and quantity demanded of a good are $1 per unit and 50 units, respectively. A reduction in price to $0.20 results in an increase in quantity demanded to 70 units. Show that these data yield an elasticity of −0.25. A 10 percent rise in the price can be expected to reduce the quantity demanded by what percentage?

4. **(Categories of Price Elasticity of Demand)** For each of the following measures of price elasticity of demand, indicate whether demand is elastic, inelastic, perfectly elastic, perfectly inelastic, or unit elastic. In addition, indicate what would happen to the firm's total revenue if it raised its price in each elasticity range identified.

a. $E_D = -2.5$
b. $E_D = -1.0$
c. $E_D = -\infty$
d. $E_D = -0.8$

5. **(Price Elasticity of Supply)** Calculate the price elasticity of supply for each of the following combinations of prices and quantities supplied. Indicate whether supply is elastic, inelastic, perfectly elastic, perfectly inelastic, or unit elastic for each combination.
   a. Price falls from \$2.25 to \$1.75; quantity supplied falls from 600 units to 400 units.
   b. Price falls from \$2.25 to \$1.75; quantity supplied falls from 600 units to 500 units.
   c. Price falls from \$2.25 to \$1.75; quantity supplied remains at 600 units.
   d. Price falls from \$2.25 to \$1.75; quantity supplied falls from 600 units to 466.67 units.

6. **(Determinants of Price Elasticity)** What situations are likely to increase the price elasticity of demand for a product? The price elasticity of supply?

7. **(Constant-Elasticity Curves)**
   a. What is the price elasticity of demand for the curve in panel (a) below? What do you call this type of demand curve? What is the value of its slope? What would happen to the quantity demanded if the price rose by 10 percent?
   b. What is the price elasticity of demand for the curve in panel (b)? What do you call this type of demand curve? What is the value of its slope? What would happen to the quantity demanded if the price rose by 10 percent?
   c. What is the price elasticity of supply for the curve in panel (c)? What do you call this type of supply curve? What is the value of its slope? What would happen to the quantity supplied if the price rose by 10 percent?

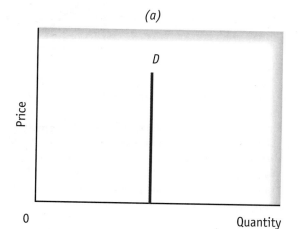

(a)

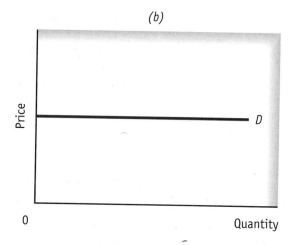

(b)

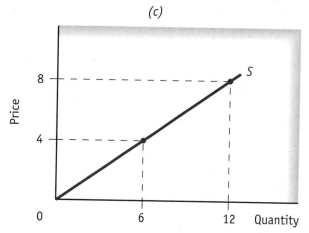

(c)

8. **(Tax Incidence)** Often it is claimed that a tax on the sale of a specific good will simply be passed on to consumers. What is necessary for this to happen? In what cases might very little of the tax be passed on to consumers?

9. **(Cross-Price Elasticity)** Rank the following in order of increasing cross-price elasticity (from negative to positive) with coffee. Explain your reasoning.
   a. Bleach
   b. Tea
   c. Cream
   d. Cola

10. **(Price Elasticity of Demand)** Explain why the price elasticity of demand for Coke is greater than that for soft drinks generally.

11. **(Price Elasticity of Demand)** Fill in values for each point listed in the following table. What relationship is highlighted?

P	Q	Price Elasticity	Total Revenue
$10	0	___	___
9	1	___	___
8	2	___	___
7	3	___	___
6	4	___	___
5	5	___	___
4	6	___	___
3	7	___	___
2	8	___	___
1	9	___	___
0	10	___	___

12. **(Taxes and Elasticity)** Suppose a tax is imposed on a good that has a perfectly elastic suppy curve.
   a. Who pays the tax?
   b. Using supply and demand curves, show how much tax revenue is collected.
   c. How would this tax revenue change if the supply curve became less elastic?

13. **(Income Elasticity)** Calculate the income elasticity of demand for each of the following goods.

	Income = $10,000	Income = $20,000
Good 1	10	25
Good 2	4	5
Good 3	3	2

Indicate whether each good is inferior or normal; if normal, whether it is a necessity or a luxury.

14. **(Substitutes and Complements)** Using supply and demand curves, predict the impact on the price and quantity of Good 1 (above) of an increase in the price of Good 2 if
   a. they are substitutes.
   b. they are complements.

15. **(Tax Incidence)** According to the text, the incidence of an excise tax (for buyers versus sellers) depends upon the relative sizes of the supply and demand elasticities. Can you think of any other people who might be hurt and therefore bear some of the tax burden, if such a tax were imposed? Explain.

16. **(Other Elasticity Measures)** Complete each of the following sentences:
   a. The income elasticity of demand measures, for a given price, the ___ ___ in demand divided by the ___ ___ in income from which it resulted.
   b. ___ are also said to be income inelastic; ___ are also said to be income elastic.
   c. The responsiveness of demand for one good to a change in the price of another good is known as the ___ ___ ___ ___.
   d. If a decrease in the price of one good causes a decrease in demand for another good, the two goods are ___.
   e. If the value of the cross-price elasticity is approximately zero for two goods, the two goods are considered ___.

17. **(Cross-Price Elasticities)** Suppose that the cross-price elasticity of compact disks to cassettes is 0.8. What would happen to the revenues to cassette producers if compact disk prices were increased by 10 percent, assuming that cassette prices did not change? Be specific in your answer.

18. **(Pharmaceutical Prices Across Countries)** Given the case study's discussion of the pricing of new drugs, what would you expect the pricing strategy to be for generic drugs? What would tend to happen to the prices of the brand-name drugs that generic drugs imitate?

Use the diagram to answer the next two questions.

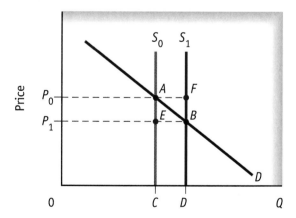

19. **(The Demand for Food and "The Farm Problem")** Suppose that this diagram represents the supply and demand curves for the farm industry. Show on the diagram how you would determine the change in farm revenues that would occur when the supply increased from S_0 to S_1. If demand is inelastic, what must be true of the relative size of the geometric areas illustrating this change?

20. **(The Demand for Food and "The Farm Problem")** Suppose that to aid farmers, government decided to stablize prices at P_0 by buying up the surplus farm products. Show on the diagram how much this would cost the government. How much would farm income change from what it would have been without the government intervention?

Using the Internet

21. Using the principle of elasticity of demand, consider the following:

a. Tap water is readily available and usually inexpensive. Why, then, does relatively expensive bottled water find success with consumers? In pursuit of an answer, visit Fountainhead Water Company (http://www.firstunion.com/ftnhead/) and Pure Spring Water Company, producer of "Virgin Pure Spring Water" (http://www.mindspring.com/~pure/pure.html). Consider how these products are being marketed.

b. Jolt Cola Company, founded in 1985, initially marketed Jolt Cola, with "Twice the Caffeine," as a different product from Coca-Cola or Pepsi-Cola. Recently, however, Jolt has been challenging the other cola companies to "taste tests"—visit "Jolt Bolt" (http://www.joltcola.com/). Why would Jolt initiate these taste tests?

19

Consumer Choice and Demand

The law of demand is a key building block in economics. You have already learned two reasons why demand curves slope downward. The first is the *substitution effect* of a price change. When the price of a good falls, consumers substitute that now-cheaper good for other goods. The second reason demand curves slope downward is the *income effect* of a price change. When the price of a good falls, the real incomes of consumers increase, so more of the good will be purchased as long as the good is normal.

Demand is so important that you must know more about it. In this chapter, we derive the law of demand, focusing on the logic of consumer choice in a world of scarcity. The objective of this chapter is not to tell you how to maximize utility. That comes naturally. But you do need a theory to understand your behavior and the implications of that behavior. Topics discussed in this chapter include:

- Total and marginal utility
- The law of diminishing marginal utility
- Measuring utility
- Utility-maximizing conditions
- Consumer surplus
- The role of time in demand

UTILITY ANALYSIS

Suppose you and a friend dine together. After dinner, your friend asks how you enjoyed your meal. You might say, "It was delicious," or "I liked it better than my last meal here." You would not say, "I liked mine twice as much as you liked yours." Nor would you say, "It deserves a rating of 86 on the consumer satisfaction index." The utility, or satisfaction, you derived from that meal cannot be measured objectively. You cannot give your meal an 86 satisfaction rating and your friend's meal a 43. You can say whether one of your personal experiences was more satisfying than another, but you can't make comparisons with other people's experience. What we *can* do is infer that a person likes apples more than oranges if, when the two are priced the same, that person always buys apples.

Tastes and Preferences

As was mentioned in Chapter 4, *utility* is the sense of pleasure or satisfaction that comes from consumption. Utility is subjective. The utility you derive from consuming a particular good depends on your **tastes,** which are your attitudes toward and preferences for different goods and services—your likes and dislikes in consumption. Some goods are extremely appealing to you, and others are not. You may not understand, for example, why someone would pay good money for raw oysters, chicken livers, polka music, martial arts movies, or the Psychic Friends Network. Economists actually have little to say about the origin of tastes or why tastes seem to differ across individuals. *Economists assume simply that tastes are given and are relatively stable—that is, different people may have different tastes but an individual's tastes are not changing all the time.* To be sure, tastes for some products change over time (for example, U.S. sales of mountain bikes have increased from 1 million in 1985 to 10 million today), but tastes are thought to be stable enough to make it possible to study such matters as the relationship between price and quantity demanded. If tastes were not reasonably stable, then we could not make the assumption in demand analysis that "other things remain constant."

Tastes A consumer's preferences for different goods and services

The Law of Diminishing Marginal Utility

Suppose it's a hot day and you are extremely thirsty after jogging four miles. You pour yourself a glass of cold water. That first glass is wonderful, and it puts a serious dent in your thirst; the next one is not quite as wonderful, but it is still pretty good; the third is just fair; and the fourth glass you barely finish. Let's talk about the *utility,* or satisfaction, you get from consuming water.

We distinguish between total utility and marginal utility. **Total utility** is the total satisfaction a consumer derives from consumption. For example, total utility is the total satisfaction you get from consuming four glasses of water. **Marginal utility** is the change in total utility resulting from a one–unit change in consumption of a good. For example, the marginal utility of the third glass of water is the change in total utility resulting from consuming that third glass of water.

Your experience with water reflects a basic principle of utility analysis: the **law of diminishing marginal utility.** This law states that the more of a good an individual consumes per time period, other things constant, the smaller the

Total utility The total satisfaction a consumer derives from consumption

Marginal utility The change in total utility derived from a one-unit change in consumption of a good

Law of diminishing marginal utility The more of a good consumed per period, the smaller the increase in total utility from consuming one more unit, other things constant

increase in total utility—that is, the smaller the marginal utility of each additional unit consumed. The marginal utility you derive from each glass of water declines as your consumption increases. You enjoy the first glass a lot, but each additional glass provides less and less marginal utility. If someone forced you to drink a fifth glass, you probably would not enjoy it; your marginal utility from a fifth glass would likely be negative.

Diminishing marginal utility is a feature of all consumption. A second Big Mac may provide some marginal utility, but the marginal utility of a third one during the same meal would be slight or even negative. You may still enjoy a second video movie on Friday night, but a third and fourth video would be numbing. That first Vat O'Slurpee may be just what you needed on a hot day, but a second one is too much. More generally, the expression "Been there, done that" conveys the idea that, for many activities, things start to get old after the first time.

Marginal utility does not always decline right away or very quickly. For example, you may eat many potato chips before the marginal utility of additional chips begins to fall. After a long winter, that first warm day of spring is something special and is the cause of "spring fever." The fever is cured, however, by many warm days like the first. By the time August arrives, people attach much less marginal utility to yet another warm day. For some goods the drop in marginal utility with additional consumption is more dramatic. A second copy of the same daily newspaper would likely provide you with no marginal utility (in fact, the design of newspaper vending machines relies on the fact that you will not want to take more than one paper).[1] Likewise, a second viewing of the same movie at one sitting usually yields no additional utility. A second day at Orlando's Universal Studios may provide few additional thrills, which is why the theme park often offers the second day free.

MEASURING UTILITY

So far our descriptions of utility have used such words as "wonderful," "good," and "fair." We cannot push the analysis very far if we are limited to such subjective language. If we want to predict behavior based on changes in the economic environment, we must develop a consistent way of viewing utility.

Units of Utility

Let's go back to the water example. Although there really is no objective way of measuring utility, if pressed you might be able to be more specific about how much you enjoyed each glass of water. For example, you might say the first glass was twice as good as the second, the second was twice as good as the third, the third was twice as good as the fourth, but a fifth glass would have been a chore to finish. In order to get a handle on this description of your satisfaction, let's assign arbitrary numbers to the amount of utility from each quantity consumed, so the pattern of numbers reflects the pattern of your satisfaction. The

Net Bookmark   Universal Studios Florida in Orlando claims that guests who visit for one day will want "just one more day"—or two more days, or even a year's worth of fun." The law of diminishing marginal utility, however, states that, although a guest may think that a year's stay at the park would be fun, by year's end the guest probably would no longer find the stay enjoyable. Discover for yourself; visit Universal Studios Florida, part of the "MCA/Universal Cyberwalk" (http://www.usf.com/).

---

1   This example appeared in Marshall Jevons, *The Fatal Equilibrium* (Cambridge, Mass.: MIT Press, 1985).

numbers themselves are not important; only the relationship among the numbers matters. Let's say the first glass of water provides you with 40 units of utility, the second glass yields 20, the third yields 10, and the fourth yields 5. A fifth glass would yield negative utility, in this case, say, −2 units of utility. *Developing numerical values for utility allows us to be more specific about the relative weights you attach to the utility derived from consumption.*

Although we have assigned some numerical measure to utility, economists have developed another, more general, approach to utility, one that does not require that numbers be attached to specific levels of utility. All the new approach requires is that consumers be able to rank their preferences for goods. This approach is more general and more flexible and will be taken up in the appendix. So keep in mind that although we have attached numbers to a subjective measure of utility, numbers are not really required. Numbers at this point simply make utility less abstract and easier to analyze.

If it would help, you could think of units of utility more playfully as kicks, thrills, or jollies—as in, getting your jollies from consumption. By attaching a numerical measure to utility, we can compare the total utility a particular consumer gets from different goods as well as the marginal utility that a consumer gets from additional consumption. Thus, we can employ units of utility to evaluate a consumer's preferences for various goods. Note, however, that we should not try to compare units of utility across consumers. *Each individual has a uniquely subjective utility scale.*

The first column of Exhibit 1 lists possible quantities of water you might consume after running four miles; the second column presents the total utility derived from that consumption; and the third column shows the marginal utility of each additional glass of water consumed. Recall that marginal utility is the change in total utility that results from consuming an additional unit of the good. You can see from the second column that total utility increases with each of the first four glasses, but by smaller and smaller amounts. The third column shows that the first glass of water yields 40 units of utility, the second glass yields 20 units, and so on. Marginal utility declines after the first glass of water, becoming negative with the fifth glass. Total utility is the sum of the marginal utilities; it is graphed in panel (a) of Exhibit 2. Again, because of diminishing marginal utility, each glass adds less to total utility, so total utility increases but at a decreasing rate. Marginal utility is presented in panel (b).

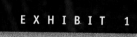

Units of Water Consumed (8-ounce glass)	Total Utility	Marginal Utility
0	0	—
1	40	40
2	60	20
3	70	10
4	75	5
5	73	−2

EXHIBIT 1

Utility You Derive from Water After Jogging Four Miles

EXHIBIT 2

Total Utility and Marginal Utility You Derive from Water after Jogging Four Miles

Total utility increases with each of the first four glasses of water consumed (panel [a]), but by smaller and smaller amounts (panel [b]). The fifth glass causes total utility to fall, implying that marginal utility is negative in panel (b).

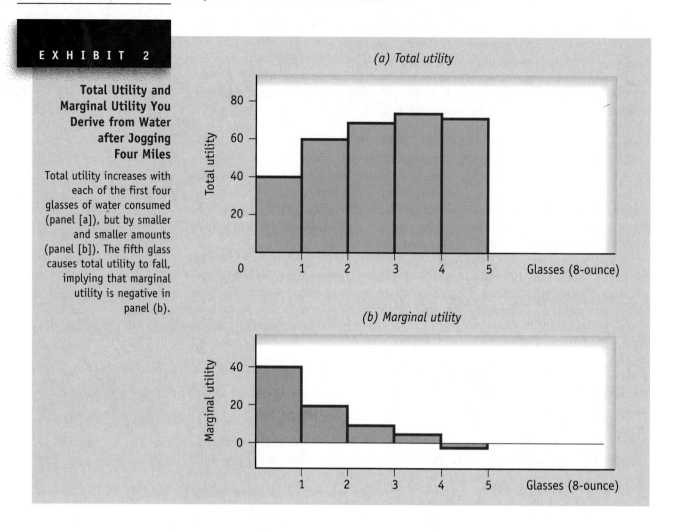

(a) Total utility

(b) Marginal utility

Utility Maximization in a World without Scarcity

Economists assume that your objective in the consumption of water, as in all consumption, is to *maximize total utility*. So how much water do you consume? If the price of water is zero, you drink water as long as each additional glass increases total utility, which means you consume four glasses of water. *So when a good is free, you increase consumption as long as additional units provide positive marginal utility.*

Let's extend the analysis of utility to discuss the consumption of food and clothing. We will continue to translate the relative satisfaction you receive from consumption into units of utility. Suppose the total utility and the marginal utility for alternative rates of consumption of these goods, given your tastes and preferences, are as presented in Exhibit 3. Spend a little time looking at it. You can see from columns (3) and (7) that both goods exhibit diminishing marginal utility. Given this set of preferences, how much of each good would you consume? If the price of each good was zero, you would increase consumption as long as you derived positive marginal utility from additional units of each good. Thus, you would consume at least the first six units of each good because both goods generate positive marginal utility at that level of consumption. Did you ever go

Total and Marginal Utility from Food and Clothing

EXHIBIT 3

Units of Food Consumed per Period (1)	Total Utility of Food (2)	Marginal Utility of Food (3)	Marginal Utility of Food per Dollar Expended (price = $4) (4)	Units of Clothing per Period (5)	Total Utility of Clothing (6)	Marginal Utility of Clothing (7)	Marginal Utility of Clothing per Dollar Expended (price = $2) (8)
0	0	—	—	0	0	—	—
1	25	25	$6\frac{1}{4}$	1	20	20	10
2	41	16	4	2	34	14	7
3	53	12	3	3	44	10	50
4	62	9	$2\frac{1}{4}$	4	50	6	3
5	68	6	$1\frac{1}{2}$	5	54	4	2
6	72	4	1	6	57	3	$1\frac{1}{2}$

to a party where the food and drinks were free to you? How much did you eat and drink? You probably ate and drank until you didn't want any more—that is, until the marginal utility of each good consumed declined to zero.

Utility Maximization in a World of Scarcity

Alas, scarcity is our lot, so we should focus on how a consumer chooses in a world shaped by scarcity. Suppose the price of food is $4 per unit, the price of clothing is $2 per unit, and your income is $20 per period. Under these conditions, the utility you receive from different goods relative to their prices determines how you allocate your income. In the real world, consumption depends on tastes (as reflected by the marginal utilities), prices, and your income.

How do you allocate income between the two goods so as to maximize utility? Suppose you start off with some bundle of food and clothing. If you can increase your utility by reallocating expenditures, you will do so, and you will continue to make adjustments as long as you can increase your utility. There may be some trial and error involved in your consumption decisions at first, but as you learn from your mistakes you move toward the utility-maximizing position. When no further utility-increasing moves are possible, you have settled on the bundle that maximizes your utility, given your tastes, prices, and your income—*you have arrived at the equilibrium combination.* Once you achieve this equilibrium, you will maintain this consumption pattern unless there is a change in your tastes, prices, or your income.

To get the allocation process rolling, suppose you start off spending your entire budget of $20 on food, purchasing 5 units, which yield a total of 68 units of utility per period. You soon realize that if you reduce food consumption by 1 unit, you can buy the first 2 units of clothing. You thus give up 6 units of utility, the marginal utility of the fifth unit of food, to gain a total of 34 units of utility from the first 2 units of clothing. Total utility thereby increases from 68 to 96 units of utility per period. Then you notice that if you reduce your food consumption to 3 units, you give up 9 units of utility from the fourth unit of food but gain 16 units of utility from the third and fourth units of clothing. This is another utility-increasing move. Further reductions in food, however, would reduce your total utility because you would give up 12 units of utility from the third unit of food but gain only 7 units of utility from the fifth and sixth units of clothing. Thus, by trial and error, you find that the utility-maximizing equilibrium bundle is 3 units of food and 4 units of clothing, for a total utility of 103. This involves an outlay of $12 on food and $8 on clothing. *You are in equilibrium when consuming this bundle because any change would lower your total utility.*

The Utility-Maximizing Conditions

When a consumer is in equilibrium, there is no way to increase utility by reallocating the budget. In fact, as you can see from the previous example, once equilibrium has been achieved, any shift in spending from one good to another will decrease utility. We will now examine a special property of the utility-maximizing combination: In equilibrium, the last dollar spent on each good yields the same utility. More specifically, *utility is maximized when the budget is completely spent and the marginal utility of a good divided by its price is identical for the last unit of each good purchased.* In short, the consumer gets the same bang per last buck spent on each good. Let's see how this works.

Columns (4) and (8) in Exhibit 3 indicate the marginal utility of each dollar's worth of food and clothing. Column (4) is derived by dividing the marginal utility of food by its price of $4. Column (8) is derived the same way, using the marginal utility of clothing and its price of $2. You can see that the equilibrium choice of 3 units of food and 4 units of clothing exhausts the $20 budget and yields 3 units of utility for the last dollar spent on each good. **Consumer equilibrium** is achieved when the budget is completely spent and the last dollar spent on each good yields the same utility, or the marginal utility of food divided by the price of food equals the marginal utility of clothing divided by the price of clothing.

Although we have considered only two goods, the logic of utility maximization applies to any number of goods. The consumer reallocates spending until the last dollar spent on each product yields the same marginal utility. *In equilibrium, higher-priced goods must yield more marginal utility than lower-priced goods—enough additional utility to compensate for their higher price.* In our example, since food costs twice as much as clothing, the marginal utility of the final unit of food consumed must, in equilibrium, be twice that of the final unit of clothing consumed. In fact, 12 units of utility, the marginal utility of the third unit of food, is twice as much as 6 units of utility, the marginal utility of the fourth unit of clothing. Economists do not claim that you consciously equate the ratios of marginal utility to price, but they do claim that you act as if you had made such calculations. *Thus, you decide how much of each good to purchase by considering your relative preferences for the alternative goods, the prices of the alternative goods, and your income.*

Consumer equilibrium The condition in which an individual consumer's budget is completely spent and the last dollar spent on each good yields the same marginal utility; utility is maximized

Deriving the Law of Demand from Marginal Utility

The purpose of utility analysis is to provide information about demand. How does the previous analysis relate to your demand for food? It yields a single

point on your demand curve for food: at a price of $4 per unit, you will de-
mand 3 units of food per period. This point is based on a given income of $20
per period, a given price for clothing of $2 per unit, and the tastes reflected in
your utility schedules.

This single point, in itself, gives us no idea about the shape of your demand
curve. To generate another point, let's change the price of food, keep other
things constant, and see what happens to the quantity demanded. Suppose the
price of food drops from $4 to $3 per unit. What will happen to your consumption decision, given the preferences already outlined in the discussion of
Exhibit 3? Exhibit 4 is the same as Exhibit 3, except the price of food has been
changed from $4 to $3 per unit. Your original consumption choice was 3 units
of food and 4 units of clothing. At that combination, the marginal utility per
dollar expended on the third unit of food is 4 but the marginal utility per dollar spent on the fourth unit of clothing is 3. The marginal utility of the last dollar spent on each good is no longer equal across goods. What's more, if you
maintained the original combination of food and clothing, you would have $3
left over in your budget because you would be spending only $9 on food. You
can increase your utility by consuming a different bundle. Take a moment to
see if you can determine what the new equilibrium bundle should be.

In light of your utility schedules in Exhibit 4, you would increase your consumption of food to 4 units per period. This increase exhausts your budget and
equates the marginal utility of the last dollar expended on each good. Your
consumption of clothing in this example remains the same (though it could
have changed due to the income effect of a price change). But as your consumption of food increases to 4 units, the marginal utility of the fourth unit, 9,
divided by the price of $3 yields 3 units of utility per dollar of expenditure,
which is the same as for the fourth unit of clothing. You are in equilibrium
once again. Your total utility increases by the 9 units of utility you receive from

Total and Marginal Utility from Food and Clothing After Price of Food Decreases from $4 to $3   EXHIBIT 4

Units of Food Consumed per Period (1)	Total Utility of Food (2)	Marginal Utility of Food (3)	Marginal Utility of Food per Dollar Expended (price = $3) (4)	Units of Clothing per Period (5)	Total Utility of Clothing (6)	Marginal Utility of Clothing (7)	Marginal Utility of Clothing per Dollar Expended (price = $2) (8)
0	0	—	—	0	0	—	—
1	25	25	$8\frac{1}{3}$	1	20	20	10
2	41	16	$5\frac{1}{3}$	2	34	14	7
3	53	12	4	3	44	10	5
4	62	9	3	4	50	6	3
5	68	6	2	5	54	4	2
6	72	4	$1\frac{1}{3}$	6	57	3	$1\frac{1}{2}$

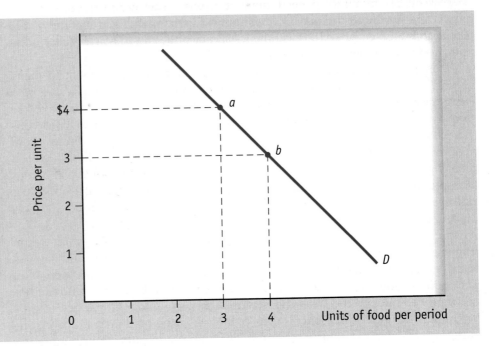

**Demand for Food
Generated from
Marginal Utility**

At a price of $4 per unit
of food, the consumer is
in equilibrium when con-
suming 3 units of food
(point *a*). Marginal utility
per dollar is the same for
all goods consumed. If
the price falls to $3, the
consumer will increase
consumption to 4 units of
food (point *b*). Points *a*
and *b* are two points on
this consumer's demand
curve for food.

the fourth unit of food; hence, you are clearly better off as a result of the price
decrease.

We now have a second point on your demand curve for food—when the
price of food is $3 per unit, 4 units are demanded. The two points are presented
as *a* and *b* in Exhibit 5. We could continue to change the price of food and
thereby generate additional points on the demand curve, but we get some idea
of the demand curve's slope from these two points. It slopes downward. The
shape of the demand curve for food conforms to our expectations based on the
law of demand: Price and quantity demanded are inversely related. (Try to determine the price elasticity of demand between points *a* and *b*. Hint: what does
total revenue tell you?)

Even animals seem to behave in a way that appears consistent with the law
of demand, as we'll see in the following case study.

CASE STUDY

Demand in the Animal World

To examine implications of the law of demand, researchers have experimented
with animals who must perform specific tasks in exchange for a portion of food
or drink. "Prices" are determined by the tasks performed. Relative prices are
then changed by varying the amount of "work" required per portion. For example, several researchers at Texas A&M University have shown that consumption choices among rats seem to be consistent with the law of demand.
Each rat confronted a set of relative prices between root beer and Tom Collins
mix. The "price" of each was based on the number of times the rat had to press
a lever to get a small amount of the beverage.

With identical prices for root beer and Collins mix, the rats expressed a clear
preference for root beer. There is nothing special about such a finding, but to
observe the effects of change in the price on quantity demanded, the number

of lever pushes required to get Collins mix was reduced and the number of lever pushes to get root beer was increased. The law of demand predicts that consumption of Collins mix would increase and root beer would fall. As expected, the rats consumed much less root beer and much more Collins mix. Similar experiments have been carried out using other animals and other combinations of goods. Typically, when relative "prices" changed—that is, when the efforts required to secure the goods changed—the animals changed their desired consumption mix in a manner consistent with the law of demand.

Certain animal behavior in the wild also appears consistent with the idea that resources are valued more when they are relatively scarce. For example, when food is naturally abundant in the environment, some species devote little or no energy to establishing and defending food sources. For example, wolves exhibit no territorial concerns when game is plentiful. But when game is scarce, wolves carefully mark their territory and defend it against interlopers.

Demand in the Animal World
continued

Location:

Studies have shown that animal behavior often reflects economic laws, such as the law of demand. *The Journal of the Experimental Analysis of Behavior,* for example, often publishes studies of this nature. To browse recent articles, visit "The Journal of the Experimental Analysis of Behavior" (http://www.envmed.rochester.edu/wwwrap/behavior/jeab/jeabhome.htm).

Sources: John Kagel et al., "Experimental Studies of Consumer Demand Behavior Using Laboratory Animals," *Economic Inquiry* 13 (March 1975): pp. 22–38; D. MacDonald, J. Kagel, and R. Battalio, "Animals' Choices over Uncertain Outcomes: Further Experimental Results," *Economic Journal* 101 (September 1991): pp. 1067–84; Richard Foltin, "An Economic Analysis of 'Demand' for Food in Baboons," *Journal of Experimental Analysis and Behavior* 56 (November 1991): pp. 445–54.

We have gone to some length to explain how you (or any consumer) maximize utility. Your tastes and preferences naturally guide you to the most preferred bundle, given your income and the relative prices of goods and services. You are not even conscious of your behavior. The urge to maximize utility is like the force of gravity: both work whether or not you understand them. Now that you have some idea of utility, let's consider an application of utility analysis.

Consumer Surplus

In our example, total utility increased when the price per unit of food fell from $4 to $3. In this section, we take a closer look at how consumers benefit from a lower price. Suppose your demand for pizza is as shown in Exhibit 6, which measures on the horizontal axis the number of medium-size pizzas demanded per month. Recall that in constructing a demand curve, we hold tastes, income, and the prices of related goods constant; only the price of pizza varies.

At a price of $8 or above, you find that the marginal utility of other goods that you could buy for $8 is higher than the marginal utility of a pizza. Consequently, you buy no pizza. At a price of $7, you buy one pizza per month, so the marginal utility of the first pizza exceeds what you could have received by spending that money on your best alternative—say, a movie and a Coke. A price of $6 prompts you to buy two pizzas a month. The second pizza is worth at least $6 to you. At a price of $5, you buy three pizzas a month, and at $4, you buy four pizzas a month. *In each case, the value to you of the last unit purchased must at least equal the price; otherwise, you would not have purchased that unit.* Along

30

EXHIBIT 6   **Consumer Surplus**

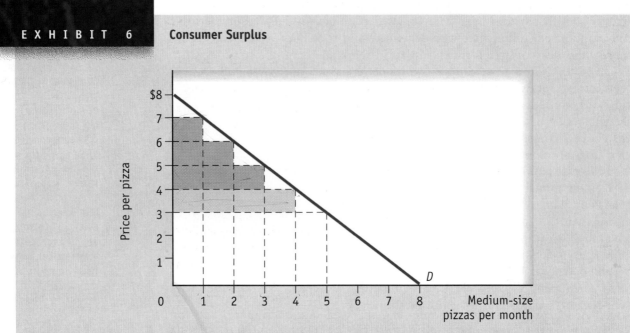

At a given quantity of pizza, the height of the demand curve shows the value of the last unit purchased. The area under the demand curve up to a specific quantity shows the total value the consumer places on that quantity. At a price of $4, the consumer purchases four pizzas. The first pizza is valued at $7, the second at $6, the third at $5, and the fourth at $4; the consumer values four pizzas at $22. Since the consumer pays $4 per pizza, all four can be obtained for $16. The difference between what the consumer would have been willing to pay ($22) and what the consumer actually pays ($16) is called consumer surplus. When the price is $4, the consumer surplus is represented by the dark shaded area under the demand curve above $4. When the price of pizza falls to $3, consumer surplus increases by $4, as is reflected by the lighter shaded area.

Marginal valuation The dollar value of the marginal utility derived from consuming each additional unit of a good

the demand curve, therefore, the price reflects your **marginal valuation** of the good, or the dollar value of the marginal utility derived from consuming each additional unit.

Notice that when the price is $4, you purchase each of the four pizzas for that price even though you would have been willing to pay more than $4 apiece for the first three pizzas. The first pizza provides marginal utility that you value at $7; the second, marginal utility valued at $6; and the third, marginal utility valued at $5. In fact, if you had to you would have been willing to pay $7 for the first, $6 for the second, and $5 for the third. The value of the total utility of the first four pizzas is $7 + $6 + $5 + $4 = $22. But when the price is $4, you get all four pizzas for $16. Thus, a price of $4 confers a **consumer surplus,** or a consumer bonus, equal to the difference between the maximum amount you would have been willing to pay ($22) and what you actually paid ($16). When the price is $4 per pizza, your consumer surplus is $6, as shown by the six darker shaded blocks in Exhibit 6. The consumer surplus is equal to the value of the total utility you receive from consuming the pizza minus your total spending on pizza.

Consumer surplus The difference between the maximum amount that a consumer is willing to pay for a given quantity of a good and what the consumer actually pays

If the price falls to $3, you purchase five pizzas a month. Evidently you feel that the marginal benefit you receive from the fifth one is worth at least $3. The lower price means that you get to buy all the pizzas for $3 even though most are worth more than $3 to you. Your consumer surplus when the price is $3 is the value of the total utility conferred by the first five pizzas, which is $7 + $6 + $5 + $4 + $3 = $25, minus the cost, which is $3 × 5 = $15. Thus, the consumer surplus is $25 − $15 = $10, as indicated by both the dark and the light shaded blocks in Exhibit 6. When the price declines to $3, you are able to purchase all units for less, so your consumer surplus increases by $4, as reflected by the four lighter shaded blocks in Exhibit 6. You can see why consumers benefit from lower prices.

Market Demand and Consumer Surplus

Let's talk more generally now about the market demand for a good, assuming the market consists of you and two other consumers. *The market demand curve is simply the horizontal sum of the individual demand curves for all consumers in the market.* Exhibit 7 shows how the demand curves for three consumers in the market for pizza are summed horizontally to yield the market demand curve (you are consumer A in this example). At a price of $4 per pizza, for example, consumer A demands 4 pizzas, consumer B demands 2, and consumer C demands none. The market quantity demanded at a price of $4 is therefore 6 pizzas. At a price of $2 per pizza, A's quantity demanded is 6 pizzas, B's is 4, and C's is 2, for a total quantity demanded of 12 pizzas. The market demand curve shows the total quantity demanded by all consumers at various prices.

With certain qualifications that we need not go into here, the idea of consumer surplus can be used to examine market demand as well as individual de-

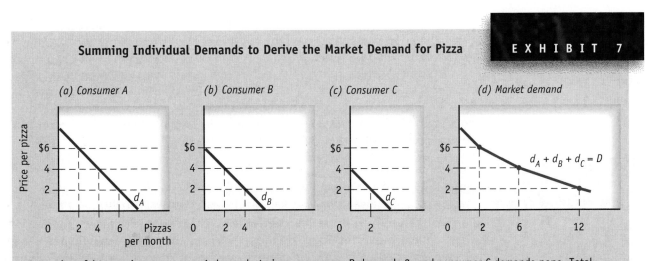

Summing Individual Demands to Derive the Market Demand for Pizza   **EXHIBIT 7**

At a price of $4 per pizza, consumer A demands 4 pizzas, consumer B demands 2, and consumer C demands none. Total market demand at a price of $4 is 4 + 2 + 0 = 6 units. At a lower price of $2 per pizza, consumer A demands 6 pizzas, B demands 4, and C demands 2. Market demand at a price of $2 is 12 units. The market demand curve D is the horizontal sum of individual demand curves d_A, d_B, and d_C.

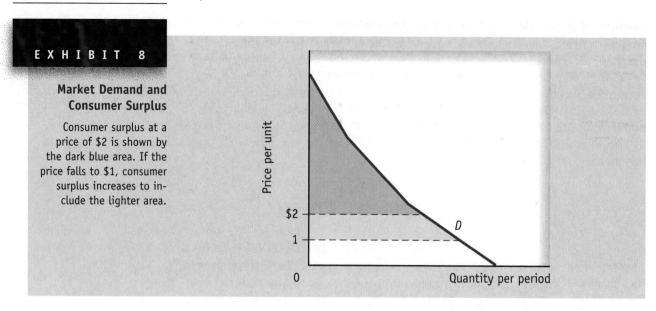

EXHIBIT 8

Market Demand and Consumer Surplus

Consumer surplus at a price of $2 is shown by the dark blue area. If the price falls to $1, consumer surplus increases to include the lighter area.

mand. We can sum each consumer's surplus to arrive at the market consumer surplus. *As with individual demand curves, consumer surplus for the market demand curve is measured by the difference between the value of the total utility received from consumption and the total amount paid for that consumption.*

Instead of considering just three consumers, we could consider the market demand when there are many consumers. In Exhibit 8, we present the market demand for pizza when there are thousands of consumers in the market. If the price per pizza in Exhibit 8 is $2, each person adjusts quantity demanded until the marginal valuation of the last pizza each purchases equals $2. But each consumer gets to buy all the other units for $2 as well. In Exhibit 8, the dark shading, bounded below by the price of $2 and above by the demand curve, depicts the market consumer surplus when the price is $2. The light shading represents the increase in consumer surplus if the price drops to $1 per unit. Note that if the good was given away, the consumer surplus would not be that much greater than when the price is $1.00.

Consumer surplus reflects the net benefit consumers get from market exchange. Consumer surplus is a useful measure of economic welfare and can be used to compare the effects of different market structures, different tax structures, and different public expenditure programs, such as free medical care, as is discussed in the following case study.

CASE STUDY

The Marginal Value of Free Medical Care

Certain Americans, such as the elderly and those on welfare, are provided government-financed medical care. State and federal taxpayers spent over $300 billion in 1995 on over 75 million Medicare and Medicaid recipients, for an average annual outlay of about $4,000 per beneficiary. The cost to Medicaid beneficiaries is usually little or nothing. The problem with giving something away is that beneficiaries consume it up to the point where their marginal benefit from the final unit is zero, though the cost to taxpayers can be substantial.

This is not to say that beneficiaries derive no benefit from free medical care. Even though they may attach little or no value to marginal units, they likely derive a substantial consumer surplus from the other units they consume. For example, suppose that the previous exhibit, Exhibit 8, represents the demand for medical care by beneficiaries of Medicare and Medicaid. If the price to them is zero, they consume up to the point where the demand curve intersects the horizontal axis, so their consumer surplus is reflected by the entire area under the demand curve.

One way to reduce the taxpayer cost of such programs without significantly harming beneficiaries is to charge a nominal fee—say $1 per physician visit. As a result, beneficiaries would eliminate visits they valued less than $1. This would yield significant savings to taxpayers, yet would still leave beneficiaries with adequate health care and with a substantial consumer surplus (measured in Exhibit 8 as the area under the demand curve but above the $1 price). As a case in point, one Medicaid experiment in California required a group of beneficiaries to pay $1 per visit for their first two office visits per month (after two visits, the price reverted to zero). Few could argue that a cost of at most $2 per month represents a substantial burden on recipients. A control group continued to receive completely free medical care. The $1 charge reduced office visits by 8 percent.

Medical care, like other goods and services, is also sensitive to the time component of the cost (a topic to be examined in the next section). For example, a 10 percent increase in the travel time required to visit a free outpatient clinic resulted in a 10 percent reduction in visits. Similarly, when the relocation of a free clinic at one college increased students' walking time by ten minutes, student visits declined by 40 percent.

This discussion does not mean that certain groups do not deserve low-cost medical care. The point is that when something is free, people consume it until their marginal benefit is zero. Even a modest money or time cost will reduce consumption yet will still leave beneficiaries with a substantial consumer surplus. A second problem with giving something away is that beneficiaries are less sensitive about getting honest value for their money since they pay little or nothing for the good. This opens the possibility for fraud and abuse by health care providers. According to experts, about 10 percent of government spending on health care is wasted because of padded bills, fake claims, and other activities that would not be tolerated if the beneficiaries were paying their own bills. Those same beneficiaries who express little concern when the government is overcharged would strongly object if, say, Sears, Wal-Mart, or McDonald's tried overcharging them.

Sources: Steven Rhoads, "Marginalism," *The Fortune Encyclopedia of Economics*, D.R. Henderson, ed. (New York: Warner Books, 1993), pp. 31–33; Joseph White, "Paying the Right Prices: What the United States Can Learn from Health Care Abroad," *Brookings Review* (Spring 1994) pp. 6–11; and L. J. Davis, "Medscam," *Mother Jones*, March/April 1995. Health care fraud is discussed at Internet site http://www.whistleblowers.com/heal.html.

The Marginal Value of Free Medical Care
continued

Location:

The Health Care Financing Administration (HCFA), a federal agency, administers the Medicare and Medicaid program that help pay the medical costs of over 75 million Americans. To learn more about the HCFA, and for an overview of the Medicare and Medicaid programs, visit "HCFA: The Medicare and Medicaid Agency" (http://www.hcfa.gov/).

THE ROLE OF TIME IN DEMAND

Because consumption does not occur instantaneously, time also plays an important role in demand analysis. Consumption takes time and, as Benjamin Franklin said, time is money—time has a positive value for most people. Con-

Consumers naturally want to buy goods on sale. However, if shoppers must miss work to take advantage of the sale, the cost of time likely will outweigh the benefits of the sale.

sequently, the cost of consumption has two components: the *money price* of the good and the *time price* of the good. Goods are demanded because of the services they offer. Your demand for medicine is based on its ability to cure you; your interest is not in the medicine itself but in the service it provides. Thus, you may be willing to pay more for medicine that works more quickly. Similarly, it is not the microwave oven, personal computer, or airline trip that you demand, but the services they provide. Other things held constant, the good that provides the same service in less time is preferred.

The money price of a good is usually the same for all consumers in the market, but since their opportunity costs of time differ, the time price of consuming that good differs among consumers. Your willingness to pay a premium for time-saving goods and services depends on the opportunity cost of your time. Differences in the value of time among consumers explains differences in the consumption patterns observed in the economy.

Consider the alternative ways to get to Europe. You could, for example, take the Concorde or a regular airline. Your mode of travel will depend in part on your opportunity cost of time, because goods with lower time costs tend to have higher money costs. The Concorde takes less than half the time of other flights, but because the Concorde is much more expensive, only travelers with an extremely high opportunity cost of time, such as busy corporate executives and celebrities, will pay such a premium for faster service. Students on their summer vacations may be more inclined to opt for some discount excursion fare or even standby status; for them, the lower money cost more than compensates for the higher time cost.

A retired couple is likely to have a lower opportunity cost of time and so will purchase fewer time-saving goods, such as microwave ovens and frozen dinners, than, say, a working couple in the fast lane. The retired couple may clip coupons and search the newspapers for bargains, sometimes going from store to store for particular grocery items on sale that week. The working couple will usually ignore the coupons and sales and will often eat out or purchase items at the more expensive convenience stores. The retired couple will be more inclined to drive across the country on vacation, whereas the working couple will fly to a vacation destination. Differences in the opportunity cost of time shape your consumption patterns and add another dimension to our analysis of demand.

CONCLUSION

Rather than relying on the substitution and income effects of a price change, we have developed a utility-based analysis of consumer choice. The focus is on the utility, or enjoyment, that consumers receive from consumption. In observing consumer behavior, we assume that for a particular individual, utility can be measured in some systematic way, even though different consumers' utility levels cannot be compared. Our ultimate objective is to predict how consumer choice is affected by such variables as a change in price. We judge a theory not by the realism of its assumptions but by the accuracy of its predictions. Based on this criterion, the theory of consumer choice presented in this chapter has proven to be quite useful.

Again, we stress that consumers do not have to understand the material presented in this chapter in order to maximize utility. Economists assume that rational consumers attempt to maximize utility naturally and instinctively. In this chapter, we simply tried to analyze that process using a model of consumer choice based on utility analysis. A more general approach to consumer choice, an approach that does not require a specific measure of utility, is developed in the appendix to this chapter.

SUMMARY

1. Utility is the sense of pleasure or satisfaction that comes from consumption; it is the want-satisfying power of goods and services. The utility you receive from consuming a particular good depends on your tastes. We distinguish between the total utility derived from consuming a good and the marginal utility derived from consuming one more unit of that good. The law of diminishing marginal utility says that the greater the amount of a particular good consumed per time period, other things constant, the smaller the increase in total utility received from each additional unit consumed.

2. Any assessment of the want-satisfying power of consumption must be made by each individual consumer, so utility is a subjective notion. By translating an individual's subjective measure of satisfaction into units of utility, we can predict the effect of a change in price on quantity demanded.

3. The consumer's objective is to maximize utility within the limits imposed by income and prices. In a world without scarcity, utility would be maximized by consuming goods until the marginal utility of the last unit of each good consumed was zero. In the real world, a world shaped by scarcity, utility is maximized when the final unit of each good consumed yields the same utility per dollar spent. Put another way, utility is maximized when the marginal utility divided by the price is identical for each good consumed.

4. Utility analysis can be used to construct an individual consumer's demand curve. By changing the price and observing the utility-maximizing levels of consumption, we can generate points along the demand curve.

5. When the price of a good drops, other things constant, the consumer is able to buy all units of the good at the lower price. Thus, we say that consumers typically receive a surplus, or a bonus, from consumption, and this surplus increases as the price falls.

6. The market demand curve is simply the horizontal sum of the individual demand curves for all consumers in the market. With some qualifications, consumer surplus for the market demand curve can be measured as the difference between the value of the total utility received from consumption and the total amount paid for that consumption.

7. There are two components to the cost of consumption: the money price of the good and the time price of the good. People with a higher opportunity cost of time are willing to pay a higher money price for goods and services that save time.

QUESTIONS AND PROBLEMS

1. **(Diminishing Marginal Utility)** Some restaurants offer "all you can eat" meals. How is this practice related to diminishing marginal utility? What restrictions must the restaurant impose on the customer in order to make a profit?

2. **(Consumer Equilibrium)** These two tables illustrate Eileen's total utilities from watching first-run movies in a theater (t) and renting movies on video (v). Suppose that Eileen has a monthly entertainment budget of $36, each movie in a theater costs $6, and each video rental is $3.

Q(t)	TU(t)	MU(t)	MU(t)/P(t)
0	0	——	——
1	200	——	——
2	290	——	——
3	370	——	——
4	440	——	——
5	500	——	——
6	550	——	——
7	590	——	——

Q(v)	TU(v)	MU(v)	MU(v)/P(v)
0	0	——	————
1	250	——	————
2	295	——	————
3	335	——	————
4	370	——	————
5	400	——	————
6	425	——	————
7	445	——	————

a. Complete the tables.
b. Does Eileen's response to both goods obey the law of diminishing marginal utility? Explain your answer.
c. How much of each good will Eileen consume in equilibrium?
d. Suppose the prices of both types of movies drops to $1 while Eileen's entertainment budget shrinks to $10. How much of each good will Eileen consume in equilibrium?

3. **(Marginal Utility)** Is it possible for marginal utility to be negative and yet total utility to be positive? Why or why not?

4. **(Consumer Equilibrium)** Suppose that a consumer has a choice between two goods, X and Y. If the price of X is $2 per unit and the price of Y is $3 per unit, how much of X and Y will the consumer purchase, given an income of $17? Use the following information on marginal utility:

Units	MU_X	MU_Y
1	10	5
2	8	4
3	2	3
4	2	2
5	1	2

5. **(Consumer Equilibrium)** Consider two goods, X and Y. Suppose that $MU_X = MU_Y$ and the price of X is less than the price of Y. Is the consumer in equilibrium? Why or why not? If not, what should the consumer do to attain equilibrium?

6. **(Consumer Allocation)** Suppose that $MU_X = 100$ and that the price of X is $10 and the price of Y is $5. Assuming that the consumer is in equilibrium, what must the marginal utility of Y be?

7. **(Time Price and Money Price)** In many amusement parks, you pay an admission fee to the park and then you need not pay for each ride. How are rides allocated in such parks?

8. **(Utility Maximization)** Suppose that the price of X is twice as high as the price of Y. You are a utility maximizer who allocates your budget between each good.
   a. What must be true about the relationship between the marginal utility levels of the last unit consumed of each good?
   b. What must be true about the relationship between the marginal utility levels of the last dollar spent on each good?

9. **(Consumer Surplus)** Suppose that consumers buy 500 shirts per year when the price of shirts is $30 and 1,000 shirts per year when their price is $25.
   a. What can you say about the marginal valuation consumers place on the 300th shirt, the 700th shirt, and the 1,200th shirt they might buy each year?
   b. With diminishing marginal utility, are consumers deriving any consumer surplus? Explain.
   c. Use a market demand curve to illustrate the change in consumer surplus when the price drops to $25.

10. **(Marginal Utility and the Law of Demand)** Assume that Daniel allocates his budget of $24 per week among three goods. Use the following table of the marginal utilities for good A, good B, and good C to answer the questions below:

Q(A)	MU(A)	Q(B)	MU(B)	Q(C)	MU(C)
1	50	1	75	1	25
2	40	2	60	2	20
3	30	3	40	3	15
4	20	4	30	4	10
5	15	5	20	5	7.5

   a. If the price of A is $2, the price of B is $3, and the price of C is $1, how much of each will Daniel purchase in equilibrium?
   b. If the price of A rises to $4 while other prices and Daniel's budget remain unchanged, how much of each will Daniel purchase in equilibrium?
   c. Using the information from parts (a) and (b), draw a demand curve for good A. Be sure to indicate the price and quantity for each point on the curve labeled.

11. **(Tastes and Utility)** Complete each of the following sentences:
   a. Your tastes determine the _____ you derive from consuming a particular good.
   b. _____ utility is the change in _____ _____ utility resulting from a _____ change in the consumption of a good.
   c. As long as marginal utility is positive, total utility is _____.

d. The law of diminishing marginal utility states that as an individual consumes more of a good during a given time period, other things constant, total utility _____ _____ _____ _____.

12. **(Marginal Valuation)** The height of the demand curve reflects the marginal valuation of a given unit of the good demanded. An increase in income will, if the good is normal, shift the demand curve to the right and therefore increase the height of the demand curve. Does this mean that consumers get greater marginal utility from each unit of this good than they did before? Explain.

13. **(Consumer Surplus)** Suppose that a good is in perfectly elastic supply at a price of $5. The demand for this good is linear, with the quantity demanded falling to zero when the price rises to $25. If the slope of this linear demand curve is −0.25, draw a supply and demand graph to illustrate the consumer surplus that occurs when the market is in equilibrium.

14. **(Utility Maximization and Scarcity)** Explain how a consumer maximizes utility differently in a world without scarcity than in a world with scarcity.

15. **(Demand in the Animal World)** As discussed in the chapter, the cost of consumption has two components: the money price and the time price. How does this relate to the rat experiment in the case study "Demand in the Animal World"?

16. **(The Marginal Value of Free Medical Care)** Medicare recipients pay a monthly premium for coverage, must meet an annual deductible, and have a copayment for doctor's office visits. There is no coverage for prescription medications. What impact would an increase in the monthly premium have on their consumer surplus? What would be the impact of a reduction in their co-payments? What would be the impact on the quantity demanded and consumer surplus if Medicare started providing coverage for prescription medications?

Using the Internet

17. USADATA, a market research company, compiles data on consumer choices and preferences. Review the "National Reports" from USADATA (**http://www.usadata.com/usadata/demo/**).

a. Look within the reports titled "Grocery Stores." What is the most common amount consumers spend on groceries per week? What percentage of consumers use coupons at least once a week? Why might consumers fail to use coupons?

b. Look within "Beverages Consumed." Examine "Any Beverage." What percentage of consumers drank domestic beer in the last week? What percentage drank imported beer? Why is domestic beer consumption higher?

Appendix
INDIFFERENCE CURVES AND UTILITY MAXIMIZATION

The approach used in the main part of the chapter, marginal utility analysis, requires some numerical measure of utility in order to determine the optimal bundle of goods and services. Economists have developed another, more general, approach to utility and consumer behavior, one that does not require that numbers be attached to specific levels of utility. All the new approach requires is that consumers be able to rank their preferences for various combinations of goods. For example, the consumer should be able to say whether combination A is preferred to combination B, combination B is preferred to combination A, or both combinations are equally preferred. This approach is more general and more flexible. We begin with an examination of consumer preferences.

Consumer Preferences

Indifference curve analysis is an approach to the study of consumer behavior that requires no numerical measure of utility. An indifference curve shows all combinations of goods that provide the consumer the same satisfaction, or the same utility. Thus the consumer finds all combinations equally preferred. Since each of the alternative bundles of goods yields the same level of utility, the consumer is *indifferent* about which combination is actually consumed. We can best explain the use of indifference curves through the following example.

In the real world consumers choose from among thousands of goods and services, but to keep the analysis manageable, suppose there are only two goods available: food and clothing. In Exhibit 9, the horizontal axis measures the quantity of food an individual consumes per period. The vertical axis measures the quantity of clothing the individual consumes per period. At point *a*, the individual consumes 8 units of clothing and 1 unit of food. The question is: Holding the consumer's total utility constant, how

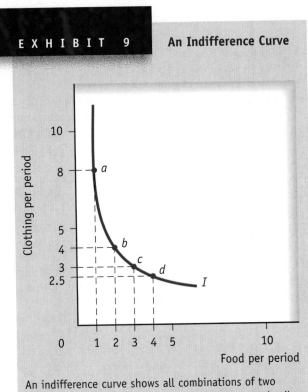

EXHIBIT 9   An Indifference Curve

An indifference curve shows all combinations of two goods that provide a consumer with the same total utility. Points *a* through *d* depict four such combinations. Indifference curves have negative slopes and are convex to the origin.

much clothing would the consumer be willing to give up to get a second unit of food? As you can see, in moving from point *a* to point *b*, the consumer is willing to give up 4 units of clothing to get 1 more unit of food. Total utility is the same at points *a* and *b*. The marginal utility of that additional unit of food is just sufficient to compensate the consumer for decreasing clothing consumption by 4 units. Thus, at point *b*, the person is consuming 4 units of clothing and 2 units of food and is indifferent between this combination and the combination reflected by point *a*, since total utility is the same at both points.

In moving from point *b* to point *c*, again the total utility is constant; the consumer is now willing to give up only 1 unit of clothing to get another unit of food. At point *c*, the consumption bundle consists of 3 units of clothing and 3 units of food. Once at point *c*, the individual is willing to give up only one-half unit of clothing to get another unit of food. Combination *d* therefore consists of 2.5 units of clothing and 4 units of food.

We can connect points *a*, *b*, *c*, and *d* to form an indifference curve, *I*, which represents possible combinations of food and clothing that would keep the consumer at the same level of total utility. Since points on the curve offer the same total utility, the consumer is indifferent among them—hence the name *indifference curve*. Note that we don't know, nor do we need to know, the value of that total utility—that is, there is no particular number attached to it. *Combinations of goods along the indifference curve reflect some constant, though unspecified, level of total utility.*

For the consumer to remain indifferent among bundles of goods, the decrease in utility from consuming less of one good must be just offset by the increase in utility from consuming more of another good. Thus, along an indifference curve, there is an inverse relationship between the quantity of one good consumed and the quantity of another consumed. Because of this inverse relationship, *indifference curves slope downward.*

Indifference curves are also *convex to the origin*, which means that they are bowed inward toward the origin: the curve gets flatter as we move down it. Here is why. A consumer's willingness to substitute food for clothing depends on how much of each the individual is currently consuming. At combination *a*, for example, the individual is consuming 8 units of clothing and only 1 unit of food, so there is much clothing relative to food. Because food is relatively scarce in the consumption bundle, another unit of food has a high marginal value and the consumer would be willing to give up 4 units of clothing to get it. Once the consumer reaches point *b*, the amount of food consumed has doubled, so the consumer is not quite so willing to surrender clothing to get another unit of food. In fact, the consumer will forgo only 1 unit of clothing to get 1 more unit of food. This moves the consumer from point *b* to point *c*. At point *c*, the consumer has 3 units of food and so is willing to give up only one-half unit of clothing to get a fourth unit of food.

The **marginal rate of substitution,** or **MRS,** between food and clothing indicates the maximum amount of clothing that the consumer is willing to give up to get one more unit of food, neither gaining nor losing utility in the process. Because the MRS measures the willingness to trade clothing for food, it depends on the amount of each good the consumer already has at the time. Mathematically, the MRS is equal to the absolute value of the slope of the indifference curve. Recall that the slope of any line is the vertical change between two points on the line divided by the corresponding horizontal change. For example, in moving from combination *a* to combination *b* in Exhibit 9, the consumer is willing to give up 4 units of clothing to get 1 more unit of food; the slope between those two points equals −4, so the MRS is 4. In the move from *b* to *c*, the slope is −1, so the MRS is 1. And from *c* to *d*, the slope is −0.5, so the MRS is 0.5.

The **law of diminishing marginal rate of substitution** says that as the consumption of food increases, the amount of clothing that the consumer is willing to give up to get another unit of food declines. With minor exceptions, this law applies more generally to all pairs of goods. Because the marginal rate of substitution of clothing for food declines with an increase in food consumption, the indifference curve has a diminishing slope, meaning that it is convex when viewed from the origin. Suppose that "food per period" measures meals per day. The consumer is willing to give up 4 units of clothing to get a second meal per day and 1 unit of clothing to get a third meal per day, but only one-half unit of clothing to get a fourth meal per day. As we move down the indifference curve, the amount of food consumed increases, so the marginal utility of additional units of food decreases. Conversely, the amount of clothing consumed decreases and its marginal utility increases. Thus, in moving down the indifference curve, the consumer is willing to give up smaller and smaller amounts of clothing to get additional units of food.

We have focused on a single indifference curve, which indicates some constant but unspecified level

An Indifference Map

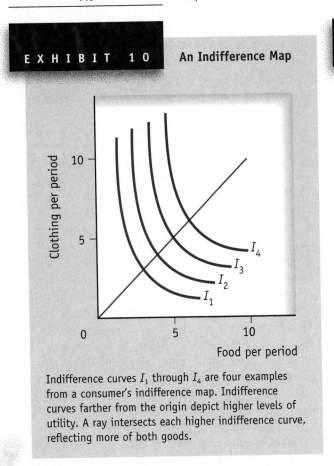

Indifference curves I_1 through I_4 are four examples from a consumer's indifference map. Indifference curves farther from the origin depict higher levels of utility. A ray intersects each higher indifference curve, reflecting more of both goods.

Indifference Curves Do Not Intersect

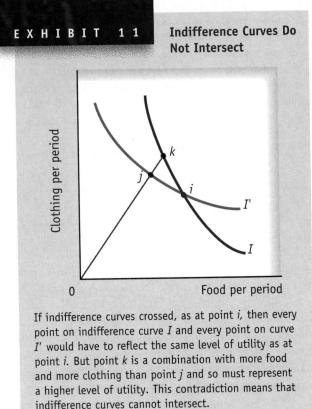

If indifference curves crossed, as at point i, then every point on indifference curve I and every point on curve I' would have to reflect the same level of utility as at point i. But point k is a combination with more food and more clothing than point j and so must represent a higher level of utility. This contradiction means that indifference curves cannot intersect.

of utility. We can use the same approach to generate a series of indifference curves, called an **indifference map,** for a particular consumer's consumption of the two goods in question. An indifference map is a graphical representation of a consumer's tastes. Each curve in the indifference map reflects a different level of utility. Part of such a map is shown in Exhibit 10, where indifference curves for a particular consumer are labeled I_1, I_2, I_3, and I_4. Each consumer will have a unique indifference map based on that consumer's preferences.

Because both goods yield utility, the consumer prefers more of each, rather than less. Thus, curves farther from the origin represent greater consumption levels and, therefore, higher levels of total utility. The total utility level along I_2 is greater than that along I_1, I_3 is greater than I_2, and so on. We can see this best if we draw a ray from the origin and follow it to higher indifference curves. Such a ray has been included in Exhibit 10. By following that ray to

higher and higher indifference curves, we see that the combination on each successive indifference curve reflects greater amounts of *both* goods. Since the consumer values both goods, the greater amounts of each good reflected on higher indifference curves represent higher levels of utility.

Note that indifference curves are not necessarily parallel as Exhibit 10 may suggest. Although they are not necessarily parallel, indifference curves in a consumer's indifference map do not intersect. Exhibit 11 shows why. If indifference curves I and I' intersect at point i, then that combination of goods lies on both indifference curves. Since the consumption of the bundle at point i reflects some specific level of utility and since point i lies on both curves, both curves must have this same level of utility. A ray from the origin intersects the curves at points j and k. Combination k has more of both goods than does combination j. Because more is preferred to less, k must provide greater utility than j. Since the utility at point k exceeds the utility at point j, the utility along I must exceed the utility along I'. But we already said that if the two indifference curves intersect at i, they must have equal utility. *Because the curves cannot reflect both an identical utility level and different utility levels, we conclude that the curves cannot intersect.*

Let's summarize the properties of indifference curves.

1. *An indifference curve reflects a constant level of utility, so the consumer is indifferent among consumption combinations along a given curve.*
2. *If total utility is to remain constant, an increase in the consumption of one good must be offset by a decrease in the consumption of the other good, so indifference curves slope downward.*
3. *Because of the law of diminishing marginal rate of substitution, indifference curves are bowed in toward the origin.*
4. *Indifference curves do not intersect.*

Given a consumer's indifference map, how much of each good will be consumed? To determine that, we must consider the relative prices of the goods and the consumer's income. In the next section we focus on the consumer's budget.

The Budget Line

The **budget line** reflects all possible combinations of clothing and food that could be purchased, given the prices and the consumer's budget. Suppose the price of clothing is $2 per unit, the price of food is $4 per unit, and the consumer's budget is $20 per period. If the entire $20 is spent on clothing, the consumer can afford to buy 10 units. Alternatively, if the entire $20 is spent on food, the consumer can afford 5 units. In Exhibit 12, the consumer's budget line meets the vertical axis at 10 units of clothing and meets the horizontal axis at 5 units of food. We can connect the axis intercepts to form the budget line. The consumer can afford any combination of goods on the budget line, or the budget constraint. You might think of the budget line as the individual's *consumption possibilities frontier.*

Let's find the slope of the budget line. At the point where the budget line meets the vertical axis, the quantity of clothing that can be purchased equals the consumer's income divided by the price of clothing, or I/p_C, where I is income and p_C is the price of clothing. At the point where the budget line meets

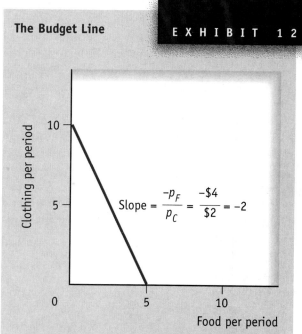

The Budget Line

EXHIBIT 12

$$\text{Slope} = \frac{-p_F}{p_C} = \frac{-\$4}{\$2} = -2$$

The budget line shows all combinations of food and clothing that can be purchased at fixed prices with a given amount of income. If all income is spent on clothing, 10 units can be purchased. If all income is spent on food, 5 units can be purchased. Points between the vertical intercept and the horizontal intercept represent combinations of some food and some clothing. The slope of the budget line is -2, illustrating that the cost of 1 unit of food is 2 units of clothing.

the horizontal axis, the quantity of food that can be purchased equals the consumer's income divided by the price of food, or I/p_F, where p_F is the price of food. The slope of the budget line in Exhibit 12 can be calculated by the movement from the vertical intercept to the horizontal intercept (the rise over the run). That is, we divide the vertical change $(-I/p_C)$ by the horizontal change (I/p_F) as follows:

$$\text{Slope of budget line} = -\frac{I/p_C}{I/p_F} = -\frac{p_F}{p_C}$$

Along the budget line, the vertical value falls as the horizontal value increases, so the slope is negative. The slope of the budget line equals minus the food price divided by the clothing price; in our example it is $-\$4/\$2$, which equals -2. The slope of the budget line indicates what it costs the consumer in terms of forgone clothing to get another unit of food. The consumer must give up 2 units of clothing for each additional unit of food. *Note that the income term cancels out, so the slope of a line depends only on relative prices, not on the level of income.*

As you know, the demand curve shows the quantity that the consumer is willing and able to buy at alternative prices. The indifference curve indicates what the consumer is *willing* to buy. The budget line shows what the consumer is *able* to buy. We must therefore bring together the indifference curve and the budget line to find out what quantity the consumer is both willing and able to buy.

Consumer Equilibrium at the Tangency

As always, the consumer's objective is to maximize utility. We know that indifference curves farther from the origin represent higher levels of utility. The utility-maximizing consumer therefore will select that combination along the budget line in Exhibit 13

| EXHIBIT 13 | Utility Maximization |

The consumer's utility is maximized at point e, where indifference curve I_2 is just tangent to the budget line.

that lies on the highest attainable indifference curve. Combination *a* consists of 8 units of clothing, costing a total of $16, and 1 unit of food for $4, for a total outlay of $20. Point *a* is on the budget line and thus is a combination the consumer is *able* to consume, but *a* is not on the highest attainable indifference curve. Given prices and income, the consumer maximizes utility at the combination of food and clothing depicted by point *e* in Exhibit 13, where indifference curve I_2 just touches, or *is tangent to,* the budget line. This utility-maximizing consumption bundle consists of 4 units of clothing totaling $8 and 3 units of food totaling $12; this combination exhausts the $20 budget. Other, "better," indifference curves, such as I_3, lie completely above the budget line and are thus unattainable.

Since the consumer is maximizing utility at point *e,* this is an equilibrium outcome. Note that the indifference curve is tangent to the budget line at the equilibrium point, and the slope of a curve equals the slope of a line drawn tangent to that curve. At point *e,* therefore, the slope of the indifference curve equals the slope of the budget line. Recall that the absolute value of the slope of the indifference curve is the consumer's marginal rate of substitution, and the absolute value of the slope of the budget line equals the price ratio. In equilibrium, therefore, the marginal rate of substitution between clothing and food, MRS, must equal the ratio of the price of food to the price of clothing, or

$$MRS = \frac{p_F}{p_C}$$

What is the relationship between indifference curve analysis and the marginal utility theory introduced in the chapter? The marginal rate of substitution of clothing for food can also be revealed by the marginal utilities of clothing and food presented in the chapter. Exhibit 3 indicated that the marginal utility provided by the third unit of food was 12, and the marginal utility provided by the fourth unit of clothing was 6. Since the marginal utility of food (MU_F) is 12 and the marginal utility of clothing (MU_C) is 6, the consumer is willing to give up 2 units of clothing to get 1 more unit of food. Thus, the marginal rate of substitution of clothing for food equals the ratio of food's marginal utility (MU_F) to clothing's marginal utility (MU_C), or

$$\text{MRS} = \frac{\text{MU}_F}{\text{MU}_C}$$

In fact, the slope of the indifference curve equals $-\text{MU}_F/\text{MU}_C$. Therefore, *in equilibrium, the slope of the indifference curve equals the slope of the budget line.* Since the slope of the budget line equals $-p_F/p_C$, the equilibrium condition for the indifference curve approach can be written as

$$-\frac{\text{MU}_F}{\text{MU}_C} = -\frac{p_F}{p_C}$$

which can be easily rearranged to show that

$$\frac{\text{MU}_F}{p_F} = \frac{\text{MU}_C}{p_C}$$

This equation is the same equilibrium condition for utility maximization presented in the chapter using marginal utility analysis. The equality says that in equilibrium—that is, when the consumer maximizes total utility—the last dollar spent on each good yields the same marginal utility. If this equality does not hold, the consumer can increase total utility by adjusting consumption until the equality occurs.

Effects of a Change in Income

We have established the equilibrium consumption bundle for a particular consumer, given the consumer's income and product prices. What happens if the consumer's income changes? For example, suppose that the consumer's income is cut in half, from $20 to $10 per period, yet prices remain as before. Exhibit 14 shows the effects of this reduction in income on the equilibrium bundle consumed. Since income falls but prices remain the same, the new budget line is below, but parallel to, the old budget line. Because of the decrease in income, the budget now buys less of each good. If the entire budget is devoted to clothing, only 5 units can be purchased; if it is devoted to food, only 2.5 units can be purchased. The consumer once again maximizes utility by consuming that combination of goods that is on the highest attainable indifference curve—in this case point e' on indifference curve I'. The drop in income reduces the consumer's purchasing power, re-

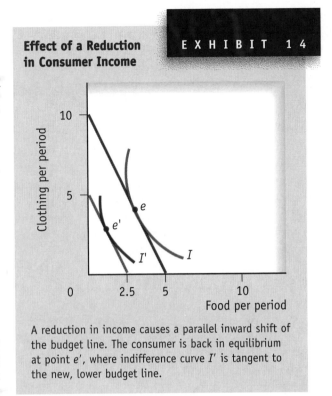

Effect of a Reduction in Consumer Income

EXHIBIT 14

A reduction in income causes a parallel inward shift of the budget line. The consumer is back in equilibrium at point e', where indifference curve I' is tangent to the new, lower budget line.

sulting in a lower level of utility. (Note that food and clothing are both normal goods, since a drop in income results in reduced consumption of both.)

Effects of a Change in Price

What happens to equilibrium consumption if there is a change in price? The answer can be found by deriving the demand curve. We begin at point e, our initial equilibrium, in panel (a) of Exhibit 15. At point e, the person consumes 4 units of clothing and 3 units of food. Suppose that the price of food falls from $4 per unit to $3 per unit, other things constant. The price drop means that if the entire budget were devoted to food, the consumer could purchase 6.67 units of food (20/3). Since the price of clothing has not changed, however, 10 units of clothing remains the maximum amount that can be purchased. Thus, the budget line's vertical intercept remains fixed at 10 units, but the lower end of the budget line rotates out.

After the price change, the new equilibrium position occurs at e'', where the quantity of food in-

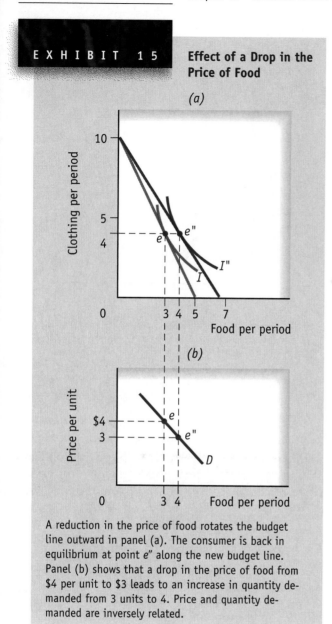

EXHIBIT 15

Effect of a Drop in the Price of Food

(a)

(b)

A reduction in the price of food rotates the budget line outward in panel (a). The consumer is back in equilibrium at point e'' along the new budget line. Panel (b) shows that a drop in the price of food from $4 per unit to $3 leads to an increase in quantity demanded from 3 units to 4. Price and quantity demanded are inversely related.

creases from 3 units to 4 units. Since the consumer is on a higher indifference curve at e'', the consumer is clearly better off after the price reduction (consumer surplus has increased).

Income and Substitution Effects

We originally explained the law of demand in terms of an income effect and a substitution effect. We have now developed the analytical tools to examine these two effects more precisely. Suppose the price of food falls from $4 to $2, other things constant. The maximum amount of food that can be purchased with a budget of $20 per period is 10 units, as shown in Exhibit 16, so the budget line rotates out from 5 to 10 units of food. As you can see, after the price change, the quantity of food demanded increases from 3 units to 5 units. The increase in utility shows that the consumer benefits from the price drop.

The increase in the quantity of food demanded can be broken down into the substitution effect and the income effect of a price change. When the price of food falls, the change in the ratio of the price of food to the price of clothing is reflected by the change in the slope of the budget line. In order to derive the substitution effect, let's assume the consumer must maintain the same level of utility after the price change as before. Given the new set of relative prices, the consumer would increase the quantity of food demanded to the point on indifference curve I where the indifference curve is just tangent to *CF*, the dashed budget line. That tangency keeps utility at the initial level but reflects the new set of relative prices. Thus, we adjust the consumer's budget line to correspond to the new relative prices, but at an income level that keeps the consumer on the same indifference curve.

The consumer moves down along indifference curve I to point e', purchasing less clothing and more food. This change in quantity demanded reflects the *substitution effect* of the lower price of food. The substitution effect always increases the quantity demanded of the good whose price has dropped. Since consumption bundle e' represents the same level of utility as consumption bundle e, the consumer is neither better off nor worse off at point e'.

But at point e', the consumer is not spending all the income available. The drop in the price of food

creases from 3 units to 4 units, and, as it happens, the quantity of clothing consumed remains at 4 units. Thus, price and quantity demanded are inversely related, other things constant, and we have again derived the law of demand. The demand curve in panel (b) of Exhibit 15 reflects how price and quantity demanded are related. Specifically, when the price of food falls from $4 per unit to $3 per unit, other things constant, the quantity of food demanded in-has increased the amount of food that can be purchased, as shown by the expanded budget line that runs from 10 units of clothing to 10 units of food. The consumer's *real income* has increased because of the lower price of food. As a result, the consumer is able to attain point *e** on indifference curve *I**. At this point, the person consumes 5 units each of food and clothing. Because prices are held constant during the move from *e'* to *e**, the change in consumption is due solely to a change in real income. Thus, the change in the quantity of food demanded reflects the *income effect* of the lower food price.

We can now distinguish between the substitution effect and the income effect of a drop in the price of food. The substitution effect is shown by the move from point *e* to point *e'* in response to a change in the relative price of food, with the consumer's utility held constant along *I*. The income effect is shown by the move from *e'* to *e** in response to an increase in real income, with relative prices held constant.

The overall effect of a change in the price of food is the sum of the substitution effect and the income effect. In our example, the substitution effect accounts for a 1-unit increase in the quantity of food demanded, as does the income effect. Thus, the income and substitution effects combine to increase the quantity of food demanded by 2 units when the price falls from $4 to $2. The income effect is not always positive. For inferior goods, the income effect is negative, so as the price falls, the income effect can cause consumption to fall, offsetting part or even all of the substitution effect. Incidentally, notice that as a result of the increase in real income, clothing consumption increases as well—from 4 units to 5 units in our example.

Conclusion

Indifference curve analysis does not require us to attach numerical values to particular levels of utility, as marginal utility theory does. The results of indifference curve analysis confirm the conclusions drawn from our simpler models. Indifference curves provide a logical way of viewing consumer choice, but consumers need not be aware of this approach to make rational choices. The purpose of the analysis in this chapter is to predict consumer behavior—not to advise consumers how to maximize utility.

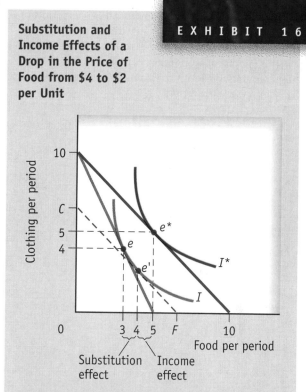

Substitution and Income Effects of a Drop in the Price of Food from $4 to $2 per Unit

EXHIBIT 16

A reduction in the price of food moves the consumer from point *e* to point *e**. This movement can be decomposed into a substitution effect and an income effect. The substitution effect (from *e* to *e'*) reflects a reaction to a change in relative prices along the original indifference curve. The income effect (from *e'* to *e**) moves the consumer to a higher indifference curve at the new relative price ratio.

1. **(Slope of Indifference Curve)** The slope of an indifference curve equals the marginal rate of substitution. If two goods were *perfectly* substitutable, what would the indifference curves look like? Explain.

2. Consider a consumer with an income of $90 that is allocated between goods A and B. Initially, the price of A is $3, and the price of B is $4.

a. Draw the consumer's budget line, indicating its slope if units of A are on the horizontal axis and units of B are on the vertical axis.

b. Add an indifference curve to your graph and label the point of consumer equilibrium. Indicate the consumption levels of A and B. Explain why this is consumer equilibrium.

c. Now assume that the price of A rises to $4. Draw the new budget line, the new point of consumer equilibrium, and the consumption levels of goods A and B. What is the marginal rate of substitution at the new equilibrium point?

d. Draw the demand curve for good A, labeling the different price and quantity demand combinations determined in parts (b) and (c).

Production and Cost in the Firm

20

Each year throughout the world, millions of new firms enter the marketplace, and almost as many leave. The firm's decision makers must choose what goods and services to produce and what resources to employ. They must make plans while confronting uncertainty about consumer demand, resource availability, and the intentions of other firms in the market. *The lure of profit is so strong, however, that eager entrepreneurs are ever ready to pursue their dreams.*

The previous chapter explored the consumer behavior underlying the demand curve. This chapter examines the producer behavior underlying the supply curve. More specifically, we examine a firm's production and cost of operation as a prelude to the analysis of supply. In the previous chapter, you were asked to think like a consumer, or demander. In this chapter, you must think like a producer, or supplier. You may feel more natural as a consumer (after all, you *are* a consumer), but you know more about suppliers than you may realize. You have been around suppliers all your life—bookstores, video stores, department stores, grocery stores, convenience stores, dry cleaners, gas stations, auto dealers, restaurants, and hundreds of other types of suppliers listed in the Yellow Pages. Although you may not yet have been a supplier, you already have some idea how suppliers operate. Topics discussed in this chapter include:

- Explicit and implicit costs
- Economic and normal profit
- Increasing and diminishing returns

- Short-run costs
- Long-run costs
- Economies and diseconomies of scale

COST AND PROFIT

When we examined consumer demand, we assumed that consumers try to maximize utility, a goal that provides the motivation for consumer behavior. When we turn to production, we assume that producers try to maximize *profit*—that is, the difference between the total revenue from the sale of output and the opportunity cost of attracting resources to the firm. Over time, the firms that survive and grow are those that are the most profitable. Firms that are unprofitable year after year eventually fail.

Explicit cost *Opportunity cost of a firm's resources that takes the form of cash payments*

Explicit and Implicit Costs

To hire resources, producers must pay resource owners at least their *opportunity cost*—what the resources could earn in their best alternative use. For resources purchased in resource markets, the corresponding cash payments approximate the opportunity cost. For example, the $3 per pound that Domino's Pizza pays for cheese reflects a price the cheese supplier could get elsewhere. Some resources, however, are owned by the firm (or, more precisely, are owned by the firm's owners), so there are no direct cash payments for their use. For example, the firm pays no rent to operate in a company-owned building. Similarly, the owner and operator of the corner grocery usually does not pay himself or herself an hourly wage. But these resources are not free. *Whether resources are hired in resource markets or owned by the firm, resources have an opportunity cost.* The company-owned building could likely be sold or rented to another user; the store owner and operator could find another job.

Implicit cost *A firm's opportunity cost of using its own resources or those provided by its owners without a corresponding cash payment*

A firm's **explicit costs** are the actual cash payments for resources purchased in resource markets: wages, rent, interest, insurance, taxes, and the like. In addition to these direct cash outlays, or explicit costs, the firm also faces **implicit costs,** which are the opportunity costs of using resources owned by the firm or provided by the firm's owners. Examples include the use of a company-owned building, use of company funds, or the time of the firm's owners. Like explicit costs, implicit costs reflect an opportunity cost. But unlike explicit costs, implicit costs require no cash payment and no entry in the firm's *accounting statement,* which records the firm's revenues, explicit costs, and accounting profit.

Alternative Measures of Profit

A particular example may help clarify the distinction between implicit and explicit costs. Meet Wanda Wheeler, an aeronautical engineer who earns $40,000 a year working for the Skyhigh Aircraft Company. On her way home from work one day, she gets an idea for a rounder, more friction-resistant airplane wheel. She decides to quit her job and start a business she calls The Wheeler Dealer. To buy the necessary machines and equipment, she withdraws her savings of $20,000 from her bank account, where it had been earning interest of $1,000 per year. She hires an assistant and starts producing the wheel in her garage, which she had been renting to a neighbor for $100 per month.

Sales are slow at first—people keep telling her she is just trying to reinvent the wheel—but her wheel eventually gets rolling. When Wanda and her accountant examine the firm's performance for the year, they are quite pleased. As you can see in the top part of Exhibit 1, total revenue in 1996 was $90,000.

Economic profits for entrepreneurs who quit full-time work reflect not only accounting profits—total revenue minus explicit costs—but also the opportunity costs of all resources used in production.

Total revenue	$90,000	**EXHIBIT 1**
Less explicit costs:		
Assistant's salary	−15,000	**Accounts of The**
Material and equipment	−20,000	**Wheeler Dealer, 1996**
Equals accounting profit	$55,000	
Less implicit costs:		
Wanda's forgone salary	−$40,000	
Forgone interest on savings	−1,000	
Forgone garage rental	−1,200	
Equals economic profit	$12,800	

After paying the assistant's salary and covering the cost of materials, the firm shows an accounting profit of $55,000. **Accounting profit** equals total revenue minus explicit costs. This is the profit used by accountants to determine a firm's taxable income.

But accounting profit ignores the opportunity cost of Wanda's own resources used in the firm. First is the opportunity cost of her time. Remember that she quit a $40,000-a-year job to work full time on her business, thereby forgoing that salary. Second is the $1,000 in interest she forgoes by using her savings. And, third, by using her garage for the business, she forgoes $1,200 per year in rental income. The forgone salary, interest, and rental income are implicit costs because, although Wanda makes no explicit payment for the resources, she gives up income generated from their best alternative uses. **Economic profit** equals total revenue minus all costs, both implicit and explicit; *economic profit takes into account the opportunity cost of all resources used in production.* In Exhibit 1, accounting profit of $55,000 less implicit costs of $42,200 equals economic profit of $12,800.

What would happen to the accounting statement if Wanda decided to pay herself a salary of, say, $40,000 per year? Explicit costs would increase by $40,000, implicit costs would decrease by $40,000, and accounting profit would decrease by $40,000. Economic profit would not change, however, since it already takes into account both implicit and explicit costs.

There is one other important profit measure to consider: the accounting profit required to induce the firm's owners to employ their resources in the firm. The level of accounting profit just sufficient to ensure that *all* resources used by the firm earn their opportunity cost is called a **normal profit.** Wanda's firm earns a normal profit when the accounting profit equals the sum of the salary she gave up at her regular job ($40,000), the interest she gave up by using her own savings ($1,000), and the rent she gave up on her garage ($1,200). Thus, if the accounting profit is $42,200 per year—the opportunity cost of resources Wanda supplies to the firm—the company earns a normal profit. *Any accounting profit in excess of a normal profit is economic profit.*

If accounting profit is large enough, it can be divided into normal profit and economic profit. The $55,000 in accounting profit earned by Wanda's firm consists of (1) a normal profit of $42,200, which just covers the opportunity

Accounting profit A firm's total revenue minus its explicit cost

Economic profit A firm's total revenue minus its explicit and implicit costs

Normal profit The accounting profit required to induce a firm's owners to employ their resources in the firm; the accounting profit earned when all resources used by the firm earn their opportunity cost

cost of Wanda's resources supplied to the firm, and (2) an economic profit of $12,800, which is over and above what these resources could earn in their best alternative use. As long as economic profit is positive, Wanda is better off running her own firm than working for the Skyhigh Aircraft Company. If total revenue had been only $50,000, accounting profit of only $15,000 would cover less than half of Wanda's salary, to say nothing of her forgone rent and interest. Since Wanda would not be earning even a normal profit, she would be better off back in her old job.

To understand profit maximization, which is total revenue minus total cost, we must develop an understanding of cost, and cost is determined by production. In the next section, we begin to consider production—the relationship between inputs and outputs.

PRODUCTION IN THE SHORT RUN

We shift now from a discussion of profit to a discussion of how firms operate. Suppose a new McDonald's has just opened in your neighborhood, and its business is booming far beyond expectations. The manager responds to the unexpected demand by quickly hiring more workers. But suppose that cars are still backed up into the street waiting for a parking space. The solution is to add a drive-through window, but such an expansion takes time.

Variable resource Any resource that can be varied in the short run to increase or decrease the level of output

Fixed resource Any resource that cannot be varied in the short run

Short run A period during which at least one of a firm's resources is fixed

Long run A period during which all resources under the firm's control are variable

Fixed and Variable Resources

Some resources, such as labor, are called **variable resources** because they can be varied quickly to change the output level. Adjustments in some other resources, however, take more time; the size of the building, for example, cannot easily be altered. Such resources are therefore called **fixed resources.** When considering the time required to alter the quantity of resources employed, economists distinguish between the short run and the long run. In the **short run,** at least one resource is fixed. In the **long run,** no resource is fixed.

Output can be changed in the short run by adjusting variable resources, but the size, or *scale,* of the firm is fixed in the short run. In the long run, however, all resources can be varied. The length of the long run differs from industry to industry because the nature of the production process differs. For example, the size of a McDonald's restaurant can be increased more quickly than can the size of an electric power plant. Thus, the long run for McDonald's is shorter than the long run for an electric company. As the length of time required to plan and construct a new building increases, so does the length of the long run.

The Law of Diminishing Marginal Returns

Let's focus on the short-run link between resource use and the rate of production by considering a hypothetical moving company called The Smoother Mover. Suppose the company's fixed resources are already in place and consist of a warehouse, a moving van, and moving equipment. In this example, labor will be the only variable resource of significance.

Exhibit 2 relates the amount of labor employed to the amount of output produced. Labor is measured in workers per day, and output is measured in tons of furniture moved per day. The column on the left shows the amount of la-

EXHIBIT 2

The Short-Run
Relationship between
Units of Labor and
Tons of Furniture
Moved

Units of the Variable Resource (labor per day)	Total Product (tons moved per day)	Marginal Product (tons moved per day)
0	0	———
1	2	2
2	5	3
3	9	4
4	12	3
5	14	2
6	15	1
7	15	0
8	14	−1

bor employed, which ranges from 0 to 8. The center column shows the tons of furniture moved, or the **total product,** at each level of employment. The relationship between the amount of resources employed and total product is called the firm's *production function.* The right column shows the **marginal product** of each worker—that is, the amount by which the total product changes with each additional unit of labor, assuming all other resources remain unchanged.

Increasing Marginal Returns. Without labor, nothing gets moved, so when the quantity of labor is 0, the total product is 0. Consider what happens when labor enters the picture. If only one worker is employed, that worker alone must do all the driving, packing, crating, and moving. Some of the larger pieces of furniture, such as couches and beds, cannot easily be moved by one person. Still, in our example one worker manages to move 2 tons of furniture per day.

When a second worker is employed, some division of labor in packing is possible and two workers can handle the larger household items much more easily than could just the one worker, so total production more than doubles, reaching 5 tons per day. The marginal product resulting from adding a second worker is 3 tons per day. Adding a third worker allows for a better division of labor, which contributes to increased output. For example, one worker can specialize in packing fragile objects while the other two do the heavy lifting. The total product of three workers is 9 tons per day, which is 4 tons more than that of two workers. Because the marginal product increases, the firm experiences **increasing marginal returns** as each of the first three workers is added. Marginal returns increase because additional workers can specialize and can thereby make more efficient use of the fixed resources.

Diminishing Marginal Returns. The addition of a fourth worker adds to the total product, but not as much as was added by the third worker. Adding still more workers increases total product by successively smaller amounts, so the marginal product in Exhibit 2 declines. Indeed, with eight workers, the working area becomes so crowded that workers get in each other's way. Transporting workers to and from moving sites cuts into production because workers take up valu-

Total product The total output produced by a firm

Marginal product The change in total product that occurs when the usage of a particular resource increases by one unit, all other resources constant

Increasing marginal returns Marginal product increases experienced by a firm when another unit of a particular resource is employed, all other resources constant

Law of diminishing marginal returns *When more and more of a variable resource is added to a given amount of a fixed resource, the resulting change in output will eventually diminish and could become negative*

able space on the moving van. As a result, the total product actually declines when an eighth worker is added, so the marginal product turns negative.

Beginning with the fourth worker, the **law of diminishing marginal returns** takes hold. This law states that as additional quantities of the variable resource are combined with a given amount of fixed resources, a point is eventually reached where each additional unit of the variable resource yields a smaller marginal product. *The law of diminishing marginal returns is the most important feature of production in the short run.* Evidence of diminishing returns is abundant. For example, McDonald's can add only so many workers before growing congestion in the work area causes marginal product to decline; as more workers are added, marginal product will at some point turn negative.

EXHIBIT 3

The Total and Marginal Product of Labor

When marginal product is rising, total product is increasing by increasing amounts. When marginal product is decreasing but is still positive, total product is increasing by decreasing amounts. When marginal product equals 0, total product is at a maximum. Finally, when marginal product is negative, total product is falling.

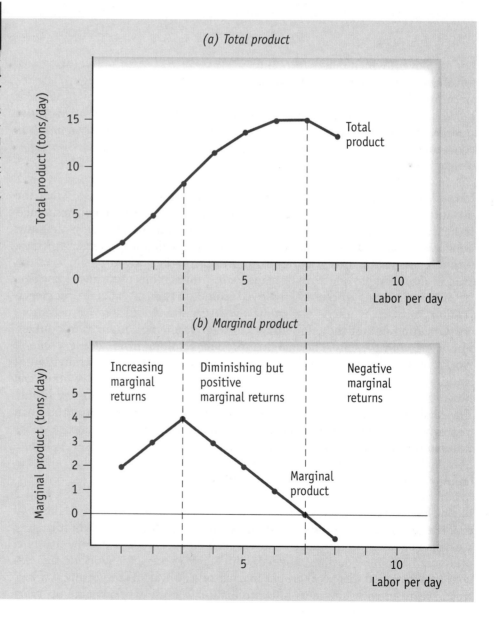

("Too many cooks spoil the broth.") In your studies, the productivity of the first hour of studying is likely to be greater than that of your fifth hour at one sitting. In agriculture, if marginal product continued to increase indefinitely, the world's supply of vegetables could be grown in a backyard simply by adding more labor and fertilizer to the fixed plot of land.

The Total and Marginal Product Curves

Panels (a) and (b) of Exhibit 3 illustrate the relationship between total product and marginal product, using the data from Exhibit 2. Note that as long as the marginal-product curve is rising—that is, as long as marginal returns are increasing—the total product increases by increasing amounts. But as the marginal-product curve begins to decline—that is, when marginal returns start to diminish—total product still increases, but at a decreasing rate. As long as marginal product is positive, total product is increasing. At the output level where marginal product becomes negative, the total product curve begins to turn down.

COSTS IN THE SHORT RUN

Now that we have examined the relationship between the amount of resources used and the level of output, we can consider how the firm's cost of production varies as its level of output varies. Short-run cost is divided into two categories: fixed cost and variable cost. Simply put, fixed cost is paid for fixed resources and variable cost is paid for variable resources. A firm must pay a **fixed cost** even if no output is produced. Even if The Smoother Mover hires no labor and moves no furniture, this firm must pay for property taxes, insurance premiums, vehicle registration, maintenance, plus principal and interest on any loans for its warehouse, van, and equipment. By definition, fixed cost is just that: fixed—it does not vary with output in the short run. Another name for fixed cost is *sunk cost* because these costs are incurred in the short run even if the firm decides to produce nothing. Let's assume that the firm's *fixed cost* comes to $200 per day.

Fixed cost Any production cost that is independent of the firm's rate of output

   Variable cost, as the name implies, is the cost of variable resources. When output is 0, variable cost is $0 because no variable resource is employed. When output increases, more variable resources are employed, so variable cost increases. The amount by which variable cost increases depends on the amount of variable resources employed and the prices of those resources. In our example, variable cost consists of labor costs. Suppose labor costs the firm $100 per worker per day. The *variable cost* in this example can be found, therefore, by multiplying the amount of labor employed by $100.

Variable cost Any production cost that increases as output increases

Total Cost and Marginal Cost in the Short Run

Exhibit 4 presents daily cost data for The Smoother Mover. The table lists the cost of production associated with alternative levels of output. Column (1) shows possible levels of output in the short run, measured in tons of furniture per day.

Total Cost. Column (2) indicates the fixed cost (*FC*) for each level of output. Note that fixed cost remains constant at $200 per day regardless of the level of

EXHIBIT 4

Short-Run Cost Data for The Smoother Mover

Tons Moved per Day (q) (1)	Fixed Cost (FC) (2)	Workers per Day (3)	Variable Cost (VC) (4)	Total Cost (TC = FC + VC) (5)	Marginal Cost $\left(MC = \dfrac{\Delta TC}{\Delta q} \right)$ (6)
0	$200	0	$ 0	$200	——
2	200	1	100	300	$ 50.00
5	200	2	200	400	33.33
9	200	3	300	500	25.00
12	200	4	400	600	33.33
14	200	5	500	700	50.00
15	200	6	600	800	100.00

output. Column (3) shows the amount of labor required to produce each level of output and is based on the productivity measures reported in the previous two exhibits. (Only the first 6 units of labor are listed because units 7 and beyond added nothing to total product.) For example, moving 2 tons requires one worker, 5 tons requires two workers, and so on. Column (4) lists the variable cost (VC) per day, which equals the cost of $100 per unit of labor times the quantity of labor employed. For example, the variable cost of moving 9 tons of furniture per day is $300, since three workers are employed. Column (5) lists the **total cost** (TC) of each level of output, which is the sum of fixed cost and variable cost: $TC = FC + VC$. Note that at 0 units of output, variable cost is $0, so total cost equals only the fixed cost of $200. Note also that *total cost reflects the opportunity cost of all resources employed by the firm, so total cost includes a normal profit.*

Total cost The sum of fixed cost and variable cost; the opportunity cost of all resources employed by the firm

Marginal Cost. Of major interest to the firm is how total cost changes as output changes. More specifically, what is the marginal cost of producing another unit? The **marginal cost** of production listed in column (6) is simply the change in total cost divided by the change in output, or $MC = \Delta TC/\Delta q$, where Δ means change. For example, increasing output from 0 to 2 tons increases total cost by $100 ($300 − $200). The marginal cost of each of the first 2 tons is the change in total cost, $100, divided by the change in output, 2, or $100/2, which equals $50. The marginal cost of each of the next three tons equals $100/3, or $33.33.

Marginal cost The change in total cost resulting from a 1-unit change in output; the change in total cost divided by the change in output

Notice in column (6) that marginal cost first decreases, then increases. *Changes in marginal cost reflect changes in the productivity of the variable resources employed.* Recall from Exhibit 2 that the first three workers contributed to increasing marginal returns, with each worker producing more than the last. This greater productivity of labor results in a falling marginal cost for the output produced by the first three workers. As more labor is added beyond three workers, however, the firm experiences diminishing marginal returns to labor, so the marginal cost of output increases. *When the firm experiences increasing marginal returns, the marginal cost of output decreases; when the firm experiences diminishing marginal returns, the marginal cost of output increases.*

Thus, the marginal cost in Exhibit 4 first falls and then rises, because of first increasing and then diminishing marginal returns. Specifically, the labor employed by The Smoother Mover shows increasing marginal returns for the first 9 tons of furniture moved and decreasing marginal returns thereafter.

Total and Marginal Cost Curves. Exhibit 5 shows the cost curves for the data in Exhibit 4. Since fixed cost does not vary with output, the *fixed cost curve* is a horizontal line at the $200 level in panel (a). Variable cost is $0 when output is 0, so the *variable cost curve* starts from the origin. Initially, the variable cost increases slowly as output increases because of increasing marginal returns to labor. As soon as labor reaches the point of diminishing marginal returns, however, variable cost begins to climb more sharply as output expands. So variable

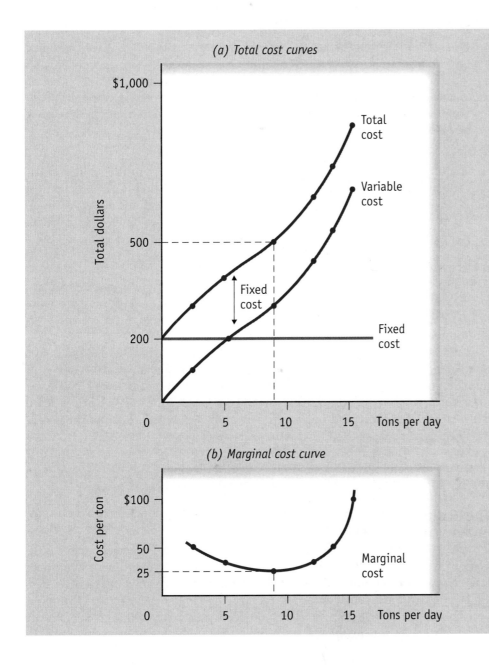

(a) Total cost curves

(b) Marginal cost curve

EXHIBIT 5

Total and Marginal Cost Curves

In panel (a), fixed cost is constant at all levels of output. Variable cost starts from the origin and increases slowly at first as output increases. When the variable resources generate diminishing marginal returns, variable cost begins to increase more rapidly. Total cost is the vertical sum of fixed cost and variable cost. In panel (b), marginal cost first declines, reflecting increasing marginal returns, and then increases, reflecting diminishing marginal returns.

cost increases slowly at first, then increases sharply. The *total cost curve* is derived by *vertically* summing the variable cost curve and the fixed cost curve. Because a constant amount of fixed cost is added to variable cost, the total cost curve is the variable cost curve shifted vertically by the amount of fixed cost.

We have already discussed the reasons for the pattern of marginal cost. In panel (b) of Exhibit 5, the marginal cost curve at first declines and then increases, reflecting labor's increasing and then diminishing marginal returns. There is a geometric relationship between panels (a) and (b) because the change in total cost resulting from a 1-unit change in production equals the marginal cost. With each successive unit of output, the total cost increases by the marginal cost of that unit. Thus, *the slope of the total cost curve at each level of output equals the marginal cost at that level of output.* The total cost curve can be divided into two sections, based on what happens to marginal cost:

1. Because of increasing marginal returns from the variable resource, marginal cost at first declines, so total cost initially increases by successively smaller amounts and the slope of the total cost curve gets flatter.
2. Because of diminishing marginal returns from the variable resource, marginal cost begins to increase after the ninth unit of output, leading to a steeper and steeper total cost curve.

Keep in mind that economic analysis is marginal analysis. Marginal cost is a key to economic decisions made by firms. The firm operating in the short run has no control over its fixed cost, but, by varying output in the short run, the firm alters its variable cost and hence its total cost. Marginal cost indicates how much total cost will increase if one more unit is produced or how much total cost will drop if production is reduced by one unit.

Average Cost in the Short Run

Although total cost and marginal cost are of the most analytical interest, the average cost per unit of output also is useful. There are average cost measures corresponding to fixed cost, variable cost, and total cost. These three average costs are shown in columns (5), (6), and (7) of Exhibit 6.

Average fixed cost Fixed cost divided by output

Let's begin with the **average fixed cost,** or *AFC,* which equals fixed cost divided by output, or $AFC = FC/q$. In our example, average fixed cost equals the fixed cost of $200 divided by the level of output. As the data in column (5) indicate, average fixed cost declines steadily as output increases, because $200 is averaged over more and more units of output. Column (6) lists the **average variable cost,** or *AVC,* which equals variable cost divided by output, or $AVC = VC/q$. The final column lists **average total cost,** or *ATC,* which is total cost divided by output, or $ATC = TC/q$. Both average variable cost and average total cost first decline as output expands, and then increase.

Average variable cost Variable cost divided by output

Average total cost Total cost divided by output; the sum of average fixed cost and average variable cost

The Relationship between Marginal Cost and Average Cost

To understand the relationship between marginal cost and average variable cost, perhaps we can begin with an analogy of college grades. Consider a hypothetical example of how your grades for the term, which are your marginal grades, affect your cumulative grade point average, or your average grades. Suppose you do well your first term, starting your college career with a grade point of 3.0. Your grades for the second term slip to 2.4, reducing your average to 2.7.

Short-Run Cost Data for a Hypothetical Firm

EXHIBIT 6

Total Output (q) (1)	Variable Cost (VC) (2)	Total Cost $(TC = FC + VC)$ (3)	Marginal Cost $\left(MC = \dfrac{\Delta TC}{\Delta q}\right)$ (4)	Average Fixed Cost $\left(AFC = \dfrac{FC}{q}\right)$ (5)	Average Variable Cost $\left(AVC = \dfrac{VC}{q}\right)$ (6) = (2)/(1)	Average Total Cost $\left(ATC = \dfrac{TC}{q}\right)$ (7) = (3)/(1)
0	$ 0	$200	$ 0	∞	——	∞
2	100	300	50.00	$100.00	$50.00	$150.00
5	200	400	33.33	40.00	40.00	80.00
9	300	500	25.00	22.22	33.33	55.55
12	400	600	33.33	16.67	33.33	50.00
14	500	700	50.00	14.29	35.71	50.00
15	600	800	100.00	13.33	40.00	53.33

You slip again in the third term to 2.1, lowering your average to 2.5. Your grades for the fourth term improve to 2.5, but since your average was already 2.5, it remains unchanged at 2.5. The next term you improve to a 3.0, which pulls up your average to 2.6. Notice that as long as your term grades are below your average grade, your average falls. When your term performance improves, your average does not improve until your term grades exceed your average grades. Think of your term grades as first pulling down your average and then pulling up your average.

In Exhibit 6, marginal cost has the same relationship to average cost as your term grades have to your grade point average. Consider the relationship between the marginal cost in column (4) and the average variable cost in column (6). Because of increasing marginal returns to the first three workers, the marginal cost falls for the first 9 tons of furniture moved. Since marginal cost is below the average variable cost for the first 9 tons, marginal cost pulls down the average variable cost. The marginal cost of the ninth ton is $25, which is below its average variable cost of $33.33. Diminishing marginal returns set in with the fourth worker, raising the marginal cost of the twelfth ton to $33.33. But because the average variable cost had already been $33.33 for the ninth ton, the average variable cost for the twelfth ton remains unchanged at $33.33. The marginal cost for the fourteenth ton jumps to $50, pulling up the average variable cost to $35.71.

The average cost data from Exhibit 6 are graphed as average cost curves in Exhibit 7, along with the marginal cost curve already introduced in Exhibit 5. Average fixed cost falls continually as output expands. Average variable and average total cost first fall and then, after reaching a low point, rise; overall, each curve has a U shape. The shape of the average variable cost curve is determined by the shape of the marginal cost curve, and each in turn is shaped by increasing and diminishing marginal returns. At low levels of output, marginal cost de-

EXHIBIT 7   **Average and Marginal Cost Curves**

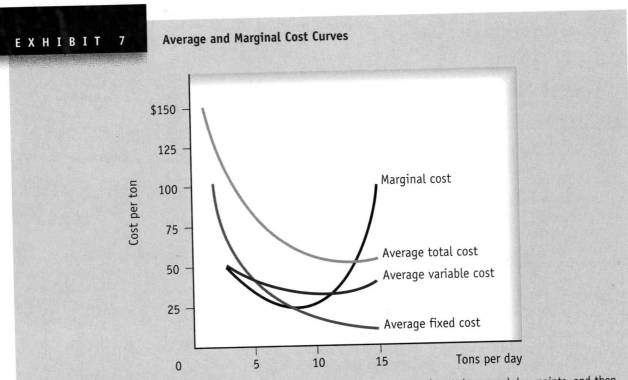

Average fixed cost drops as output expands. Average variable cost and average total cost drop, reach low points, and then rise; overall, they take on U shapes. When marginal cost is below average variable cost, average variable cost is falling. When marginal cost equals average variable cost, average variable cost is at its minimum value. When marginal cost is above average variable cost, average variable cost is increasing. The same relationship holds between marginal cost and average total cost.

clines as output expands because of increasing marginal returns. As long as marginal cost is below average variable cost, average variable cost falls as output expands. The marginal cost curve and the average variable cost curve intersect where output is 12 tons per day and the cost is $33.33 per ton. At higher rates of output, marginal cost exceeds average variable cost, so average variable cost starts to rise as output expands—the higher marginal cost begins to pull up the average. Thus, the marginal cost curve explains why the average variable cost curve has a U shape.

The average total cost curve is the vertical sum of the average fixed cost curve and the average variable cost curve. Therefore, the shape of the average total cost curve reflects the shapes of the underlying average cost curves. Note that as output increases, the average variable cost and the average total cost curves grow closer together because average fixed cost, which is the vertical difference between the two, becomes smaller.

The marginal cost curve has the same relationship to the average total cost curve as to the average variable cost curve, and for the same reasons. When marginal cost is below average total cost, average total cost declines as output expands. The two curves intersect at 14 units of output. At higher levels of output, marginal cost is above average total cost, so average total cost increases as output expands. Because of these relationships, *the rising marginal cost curve inter-*

sects both the average variable cost curve and the average total cost curve where these average curves are at a minimum. Note that the minimum point on the average total cost curve occurs at a greater level of output than does the minimum point on the average variable cost curve because a falling average fixed cost continues to pull the average total cost curve down even after the average variable cost has begun to rise.

Summary of Short-Run Cost Curves

The level of the firm's fixed costs, the price of variable inputs, and the law of diminishing marginal returns determine the shape of all the short-run cost curves. The shape of the marginal product curve discussed earlier in the chapter determines the shape of the marginal cost curve. And the shape of the marginal product curve is determined by the production function, which is the relationship between the variable resource and output. Thus, the marginal cost curve depends ultimately on how much each unit of the variable resource, labor, produces. When the marginal product of labor increases, the marginal cost of output must fall. Conversely, as diminishing marginal returns set in, the marginal cost of output must rise. Thus, marginal cost first falls, then rises. And the marginal cost curve dictates the shapes of the average variable cost and average total cost curves. When marginal cost is less than average cost, average cost is falling; when marginal cost is above average cost, average cost is rising.

COSTS IN THE LONG RUN

Thus far, our analysis has focused on how costs vary as the rate of output expands in the short run for a firm of a given size. In the long run, all inputs that are under the firm's control can be varied, so there are no fixed costs. The long run is not just a succession of short runs. The long run is best thought of as a *planning horizon*, the years in the future for which the firm tries to plan. In the long run, the choice of input combinations is flexible, but this flexibility is valid only for a firm that has not yet acted on its plans. Firms plan in the long run, but they produce in the short run. Once the size of the plant has been selected and resources have been committed, the firm has fixed costs and is once again back in the short run. We turn now to the long-run cost curve.

The Long-Run Average Cost Curve

Suppose that, because of the special nature of technology in the industry, a firm's plant can be one of only three possible sizes: small, medium, or large. Exhibit 8 presents this simple case. The short-run average total cost curves for the three plant sizes are SS', MM', and LL'. Which size plant should the firm build to minimize the average cost of production? The appropriate size, or scale, for the plant depends on how much the firm wants to produce. For example, if q is the desired production rate in the long run, the average cost per unit will be lowest with a small plant. If the desired output level is q', the medium plant size ensures the lowest average cost.

More generally, for any output less than q_a, the average cost of output is lowest when the plant is small. For output levels between q_a and q_b, the average cost is lowest when the plant is of medium size. And for output levels that exceed q_b, the average cost is lowest when the plant is large. The **long-run**

Long-run average cost curve A curve that indicates the lowest average cost of production at each level of output when the firm's size is allowed to vary; also called the planning curve and the envelope curve

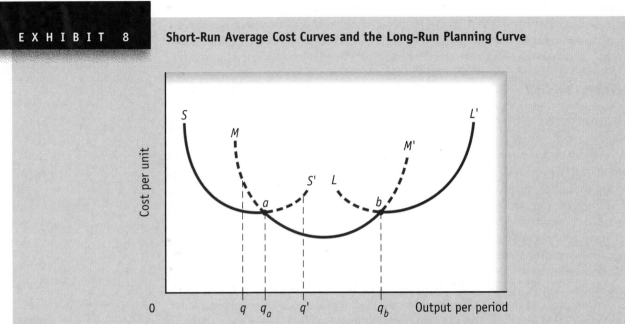

EXHIBIT 8

Short-Run Average Cost Curves and the Long-Run Planning Curve

Curves *SS'*, *MM'*, and *LL'* show short-run average total costs for small, medium, and large plants, respectively. For output less than q_a, average cost is lowest when the plant is small. Between q_a and q_b, cost is lowest with a medium-size plant. If output exceeds q_b, the large plant is best. The long-run average-cost curve is *SabL'*.

average cost curve connects portions of the three short-run average cost curves that are lowest for each output level. In Exhibit 8, that curve consists of the line segments connecting *S, a, b,* and *L'*.

Now suppose that the number of possible plant sizes is large. Exhibit 9 presents a sample of possible short-run average total cost curves. The long-run average cost curve is created by connecting the points on the various short-run average cost curves that represent the lowest per-unit cost for each level of output. Each of the short-run cost curves is tangent to the long-run average cost curve, which is sometimes called the firm's *planning curve,* or *envelope curve.* An envelope curve is the long-run curve tangent to each of a family of short-run curves. If we could display enough cost curves, we would have a different plant size for each level of output. These points of tangency represent the least-cost way of producing each particular level of output, given the technology and resource prices. For example, the short-run average cost curve ATC_1 is tangent to the planning curve at point *a,* indicating that the least-cost way of producing output level *q* is with the plant size associated with ATC_1. No other size plant would produce output level *q* at as low a cost per unit. Note, however, that other output levels along ATC_1 have a lower average cost of production. In fact, for output level *q'* at point *b,* the average cost per unit is only $10, compared to an average cost per unit of $11 for producing *q* at point *a.* Point *b* depicts the lowest average cost along ATC_1. So although the point of tangency represents the least-cost way of producing a particular level of output, it does not in this case represent a least-cost output level for this particular plant size.

If the firm decides to produce output level *q',* which size plant should it choose to minimize the average cost of production? Output level *q'* could be

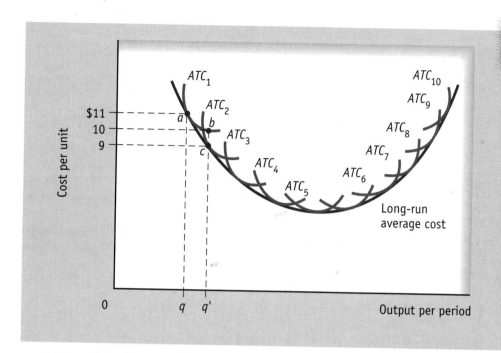

EXHIBIT 9

Family of Many Short-Run Cost Curves Forming a Firm's Long-Run Planning Curve

With many possible plant sizes, the long-run average cost curve is the envelope of portions of the short-run average cost curves. Each short-run curve is tangent to the long-run average cost curve, or long-run planning curve. Each point of tangency represents the least-cost way of producing a particular level of output.

produced at point b, which represents the minimum average cost along ATC_1. The firm, however, could achieve a lower average cost with a larger plant. Specifically, if the firm built a plant of the size associated with ATC_2, the average cost of producing q' would be minimized at point c. *Each point of tangency between a short-run average cost curve and the long-run average cost curve, or planning curve, represents the least-cost way of producing that particular level of output.*

Economies of Scale

Like short-run average cost curves, the long-run average cost curve appears to be U-shaped. Recall that the shape of the short-run average total cost curve is determined primarily by the law of diminishing marginal returns. A different principle shapes the long-run cost curve. A firm experiences **economies of scale** when long-run average cost falls as output expands. Consider some sources of economies of scale. *A larger size often allows for larger, more specialized machines and greater specialization of labor.* For example, compare the household-size kitchen of a small restaurant with the kitchen at McDonald's. At low levels of output, say 15 meals a day, the smaller kitchen produces meals at a lower average cost than does McDonald's. But if production in the smaller kitchen increases beyond, say, 100 meals per day, a kitchen on the scale of McDonald's would have a lower average cost. Thus, because of economies of scale, the long-run average cost curve for a restaurant falls as firm size increases. So a larger scale of operation allows firms to employ larger, more efficient, machines and to allow workers a greater degree of specialization.

Diseconomies of Scale

Often another force, called **diseconomies of scale,** is eventually set in motion as the firm expands. With diseconomies of scale, the long-run average cost increases as output expands. As the amount and variety of resources employed

Net Bookmark

IBM, the World's largest computer company with almost $72 billion in sales in 1995 and 220,000 employees, found that its size was as much a hindrance as a help to generating profits. To avoid the diseconomies of scale inherent in its corporate structure, IBM restructured and decentralized into six smaller decision-making groups. For more, visit IBM (http://www.ibm.com/).

Economies of scale Forces that cause reduction in a firm's average cost as the scale of operations increases in the long run

Diseconomies of scale Forces that cause a firm's average cost to increase as the scale of operations increases in the long run

increase, so does the management task of coordinating all these inputs. As the work force grows, additional layers of management are needed to monitor production. In the thicket of bureaucracy that develops, communication may become garbled. The top executives have more difficulty keeping in touch with the shop floor because information is distorted as it passes through the chain of command. Indeed, in very large organizations, rumors may become a primary source of information, thereby reducing the efficiency of the organization and increasing average cost. For example, IBM reportedly has undertaken a massive restructuring program because the firm was experiencing diseconomies of scale, particularly in management. IBM's solution was to decentralize into six smaller decision-making groups. Note that diseconomies of scale result from a larger firm size, whereas diminishing marginal returns result from using more variable resources in a firm of a given size.

In the long run, the firm can vary the inputs under its control. Some inputs, however, are not under the firm's control, and the inability to vary these inputs may be a source of diseconomies of scale. Consider economies and diseconomies of scale at the movies in the following case study.

CASE STUDY

At the Movies

Location:

In most movie theaters, employees and advertising account for a significant amount of costs. As a result, theater owners take advantage of economies of scale by increasing the number of screens per theater. "Movie-Fone," and its Internet version "MovieLink," take advantage of economies of scale on a nationwide level, allowing moviegoers to view showtimes for all theaters in most major cities and to purchase tickets in advance for many of these theaters using a credit card. Visit MovieLink (http://www.movielink.com/).

Movie theaters reflect both economies and diseconomies of scale. A movie theater with one screen needs someone to sell tickets, someone to operate the concession stand (concession stand sales, incidentally, account for well over half the profits at most theaters), and someone to operate the projector. If another screen is added, the same staff can perform these tasks for both screens. Thus, the ticket seller becomes more productive because he or she sells tickets for both movies. Furthermore, construction costs per screen are reduced because only one lobby and one set of restrooms are required. This is why we see theater owners adding more and more screens at the same location; they are taking advantage of economies of scale.

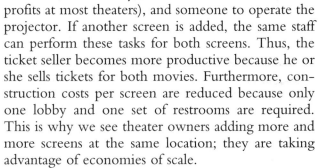

But why stop at, say, 12 screens? Why not 20 or 30, particularly in thickly populated urban areas, where sufficient demand would warrant such a high level of output? One problem with expanding the number of screens is that the public roads leading to the theaters are a resource that theaters cannot control. The congestion around the theater grows with the number of screens at that location. Also, the supply of popular films may not be sufficient at any one time to fill so many screens.

Finally, time itself is a resource that the firm cannot easily control. Only certain hours are popular with moviegoers. Scheduling becomes more difficult because the manager must space out starting and ending times to avoid having too many customers arrive and depart at once. No more additional "prime time" can be created. Thus, theater owners lack control over such inputs as the size of public roads, the supply of films, and the amount of "prime time" in the day, and this lack of control may contribute to an increase in the long-run average cost as output expands, or to diseconomies of scale. Incidentally, theaters do not like to book long movies because they claim more scarce time, yet owners cannot charge more for a movie that takes two hours instead of an hour and a half.

Sources: Leonard Klady, "Theaters Scramble to Fit in Summer Pix," *Variety,* 6 August 1995; Kurt Eichenwald, "Deal to Combine Two Theater Chains Is Called Off," *New York Times,* 13 May 1995; and Norihiko Shirouzu, "Japan's Film Fans Marvel at Multiplexes," *The Wall Street Journal,* 8 March 1995.

It is possible for average cost to neither increase nor decrease with changes in firm size. If neither economies of scale nor diseconomies of scale are apparent in the production process, the firm experiences *constant average costs.* Perhaps economies and diseconomies of scale exist simultaneously but have offsetting effects.

Exhibit 10 presents a firm's long-run average cost curve, which is divided into segments reflecting economies of scale, constant long-run average cost, and diseconomies of scale. The rate of production must reach quantity *A* for the firm to achieve the **minimum efficient scale,** which is the lowest rate of output at which long-run average cost is at a minimum. From output level *A* to level *B,* average cost is constant. Beyond output level *B,* diseconomies of scale increase long-run average cost.

Minimum efficient scale The lowest rate of output at which a firm takes full advantage of economies of scale

Economies and Diseconomies of Scale at the Firm Level

The discussion of firms thus far has referred to a particular plant—a movie theater or a restaurant, for example. But a firm could also be a collection of plants, such as the thousands of McDonald's restaurants. More generally, we can dis-

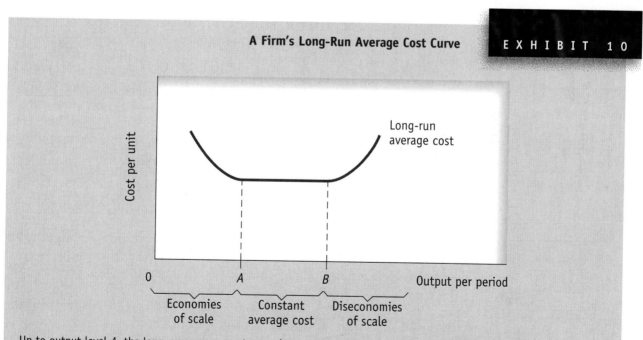

A Firm's Long-Run Average Cost Curve   **E X H I B I T   1 0**

Up to output level *A,* the long-run average cost curve has a negative slope; the firm is experiencing economies of scale. Output level *A* is the minimum efficient scale—the lowest rate of output at which the firm takes full advantage of economies of scale. Between *A* and *B,* the average cost is constant. Beyond output level *B,* the long-run average cost curve slopes upward, reflecting diseconomies of scale.

tinguish between economies and diseconomies of scale at the *plant level*—that is, at a particular location—and at the *firm level,* where the firm is a collection of plants. We discuss these issues in the following case study.

McDonald's experiences economies of scale at the plant, or restaurant, level because of its specialization of labor and machines, but it also benefits from economies of scale at the company level. Operating at many locations allows the company to standardize menus and operating procedures, to centralize its management training program at Hamburger University (McDonald's school for restaurant operators), and to spread the cost of its advertising over thousands of individual "plants."

The menu at a local fast-food outlet is the result of intense planning. Every stage of food preparation is timed and evaluated. Each of the major chains calculates how long it takes employees to do everything from flipping burgers to putting pickles on buns. Before any new product is introduced, labor requirements are monitored closely. For example, before Burger King decided to switch from one cola to another, the company spent more than two years on market research. Reportedly, undercover researchers were sent to competitors' sites to track the time required to inform customers who had asked for one brand of cola that only the other brand was available.

Some diseconomies arise in such large-scale operations. The fact that the menu must be uniform around the country means that if customers in some parts of the country do not like a product, it usually does not get on the menu regardless of its popularity elsewhere. McDonald's McRib sandwich never quite caught on in some parts of the country and had to be dropped. Wendy's plans for a gourmet hamburger had to be scrapped because most customers in two states were not familiar with such ingredients as alfalfa sprouts and guacamole. Another problem with a uniform menu is that the ingredients must be available around the country and cannot be subject to droughts or sharp swings in price. One chain decided not to add bacon strips as an option on its burgers because the price of pork bellies fluctuated so much.

McDonald's has become more flexible by putting mini-restaurants in airports, gas stations, and Wal-Marts; these so-called satellite restaurants accounted for half of the company's new U.S. outlets opened in 1995. McDonald's has also moved aggressively overseas and is now in more than 80 countries around the world, so menu planning has become increasingly complex. For example, when McDonald's went into Russia, the company had to develop supply sources for beef, potatoes, lettuce, and other ingredients. In some cases, the company had to train farmers how to grow their products to specifications. Thus, when a firm expands to multiple firms and to multiple countries, it experiences economies of scale and diseconomies of scale.

Sources: Harlan Byrne, "Big Mac, on the Attack," *Barron's,* 6 February 1995; Richard Gibson, "At McDonald's, New Recipes for Buns, Eggs," *The Wall Street Journal,* 13 June 1995; and Greg Burns, "French Fries with a Quart of Oil," *Business Week,* 27 November 1995. An Internet site featuring McDonald's restaurants in Austria is at http://www.mcdonalds.co.at/mcdonalds/.

CONCLUSION

In this chapter, by considering the relationship between production and cost, we have developed the foundations for a theory of firm behavior. In the appendix, we present an alternative way of determining a firm's most efficient combination of resources. Despite what may appear to be a tangle of short-run and long-run cost curves, *only two relationhips between resources and outputs underlie all the curves. In the short run, it is increasing and diminishing returns to the variable resource. In the long run, it is economies and diseconomies of scale.* If you understand the sources of these two phenomena, you have grasped the central ideas of this chapter. Our examination of the relationship between resource use and the amount produced in both the short run and the long run will help us derive an upward-sloping supply curve in the next chapter.

SUMMARY

1. Explicit costs are opportunity costs of a firm's resources that take the form of cash payments. Implicit costs are the opportunity costs of using resources owned by the firm or provided by the firm's owners. A firm is said to be earning a normal profit if total revenue just covers all implicit and explicit costs. Economic profit equals total revenue minus both explicit and implicit costs.

2. Resources that can quickly be varied to increase or decrease the output level are called variable resources. Other resources, such as capital, are called fixed resources because of the time required to alter the amount of the resource used. In the short run, at least one resource is fixed. In the long run, all resources are variable.

3. Short-run increases in the variable resource initially may result in increasing marginal returns as the firm takes advantage of increased specialization of the variable resource. The law of diminishing marginal returns indicates that a point is eventually reached where additional units of the variable resource, combined with the fixed resources, yield a smaller marginal product.

4. The law of diminishing marginal returns is the most important feature of firm production in the short run, and is the reason why the marginal cost curve eventually slopes upward as output expands. The law of diminishing marginal returns also explains why average cost eventually increases as output increases in the short run.

5. In the long run, all inputs under the firm's control are variable, so there are no fixed costs. The firm's long-run average cost curve is an envelope formed by a series of short-run average total cost curves. The long run is best thought of as a planning horizon.

6. In the long run, the firm selects the most efficient size for the desired level of output. Once the size of the firm has been selected and resources have been committed, some resources become fixed, so the firm is back in the short run. Thus, the firm plans for the long run but produces in the short run.

7. The long-run average cost curve, like the short-run average total cost curve, tends to be U-shaped. As output expands, average cost at first declines because of economies of scale—a larger plant size allows for more specialized machinery and a more extensive division of labor. Eventually, average cost stops falling. Average cost may be constant over some range. As output expands still further, the plant may encounter diseconomies of scale as the cost of coordinating resources grows.

QUESTIONS AND PROBLEMS

1. **(Explicit Versus Implicit Costs)** Old MacDonald is currently raising corn on his 100-acre farm. He can make an accounting profit of $100 per acre. However, if he raised soybeans, he could make $200 per acre. Is the farmer currently earning an economic profit? Why or why not?

2. **(Explicit Versus Implicit Costs)** Identify each of the following as an explicit or implicit cost:
   * Payments for labor purchased in the outside market.
   * The use by a firm of a warehouse owned by the firm which could be rented to another firm.
   * Rent paid for the use of a warehouse not owned by the firm.

- The wages that owners could earn if they did not work for themselves. Calculate the accounting and economic profit or loss in each of the situations below:
  a. A firm with total revenues of $150 million, explicit costs of $90 million, and implicit costs of $40 million.
  b. A firm with total revenues of $125 million, explicit costs of $100 million, and implicit costs of $30 million.
  c. A firm with total revenues of $100 million, explicit costs of $90 million, and implicit costs of $20 million.
  d. A firm with total revenues of $250,000, explicit costs of $275,000, and implicit costs of $50,000.

3. **(Normal Profits)** Why is it reasonable to think of normal profits as a type of cost to the firm?

4. **(Short-Run Versus Long-Run)** What distinguishes a firm's short-run period from its long-run period?

5. **(Diminishing Returns)** Suppose that you have some farmland. You must decide how many times during the year you will grow your crops. Also, you must decide how to space each plant (or seedling). Will diminishing returns be a factor in your decision making?

6. **(Marginal Cost and Average Costs)** Explain why the marginal cost curve must intersect the average total cost and the average variable cost curves at their minimum points. Why must average total cost and average variable cost approach each other as output increases?

7. **(Total and Marginal Product)**
   a. Define the law of diminishing marginal returns.
   b. Complete the table below:

Units of the Variable Resource	Total Product	Marginal Product
0	0	—
1	10	___
2	22	___
3	___	9
4	___	4
5	34	___

   c. At what point do diminishing marginal returns set in?

8. **(Short-Run Costs)** What effect would each of the following have on the short-run marginal cost curve or the fixed cost curve?

   a. An increase in wage rates
   b. A decrease in property taxes
   c. A rise in the purchase price of new captial
   d. A rise in oil prices (or energy prices)

9. **(Long-Run Average Cost)** What factors would shift the long-run average cost curve? How would these changes also affect the short-run average total cost curves?

10. **(Fixed and Variable Costs)** Distinguish between fixed and variable costs. Do both types of costs affect short-run marginal cost? Why or why not?

11. **(Marginal Product and Costs)** Let L equal units of labor. Q equal units of output, and MP equal the marginal product of labor.
    a. Fill in the table.

L	Q	MP	VC	TC	MC	ATC
0	0	___	$ 0	$12	___	___
1	6	___	3	15	___	___
2	15	___	6		___	___
3	21	___	9		___	___
4	24	___	12		___	___
5	26	___	15		___	___
6	27	___	18		___	___

    b. At what level of labor do the marginal returns of labor diminish?
    c. What is the implication for marginal cost of the answer to part b?
    d. What is the average variable cost when $Q = 24$?
    e. What is the level of fixed cost?
    f. What is the price of a unit of labor?

12. **(Average and Marginal Costs)** Assume that labor and capital are the only inputs used by the firm for the cost table below. Capital is fixed at 5 units, which cost $100 each. Workers can be hired for $200 each. Fill in the table to show average fixed cost (AFC), average variable cost (AVC), average total cost (ATC), and marginal cost (MC).

Quantity of Labor	Total Output	AFC	AVC	ATC	MC
0	0	___	___	___	___
1	100	___	___	___	___
2	250	___	___	___	___
3	350	___	___	___	___
4	400	___	___	___	___
5	425	___	___	___	___

13. **(Short- and Long-Run Costs)** Suppose that a firm has only three possible scales of production, with the middle scale of production achieving the lowest average cost of any of the three scales. Let the three short-run average total cost curves be U-shaped and intersect each other as shown below.

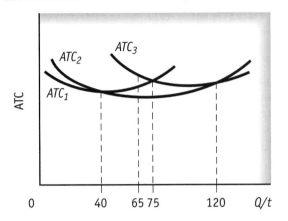

a. Which scale of production is best when Q = 65?
b. Which scale of production is best when Q = 75?
c. Indicate on the diagram the long-run average cost curve.

14. **(Short-Run Production and Costs)**

a. Complete the table below, assuming that each unit of labor costs $75 per day:

Quantity of Labor per Day	Output per Day	Fixed Cost	Variable Cost	Total Cost	Marginal Cost
0	___	$300	___	___	___
1	5	___	75	___	15
2	11	___	150	450	12.5
3	15	___	___	525	___
4	18	___	300	600	25
5	20	___	___	___	37.5

b. Graph the fixed cost, variable cost, and total cost curves for the above data.
c. What is the marginal product of the third unit of labor?
d. What is average total cost when output is 18 units per day?

15. **(Diminishing Marginal Product)** Explain why the marginal cost of production *must* increase if the marginal product of the variable resource is decreasing.

16. **(Long-Run Average Cost Curve)** Explain the shape of the long-run average cost curve. What is meant by the minimum efficient scale?

17. **(Short-Run Cost)** In Exhibit 7, the output level where average total cost is at a minimum is greater than the output level where average variable cost is at a minimum. Why do you suppose this is true?

18. **(Short-Run Costs)** Identify each of the curves in the following graph:

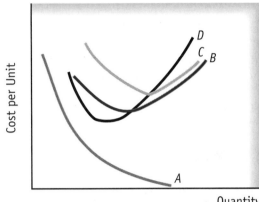

19. **(At the Movies)** (a) The case study states that the concession stand accounts for well over half the profits at most theaters. Given this, what are the benefits of the staggered movie times allowed by multiple screens? (b) What is the benefit to a multiscreen theater of locating at a shopping mall?

20. **(Billions and Billions of Burgers)** How does having a menu that is uniform around the country provide McDonald's with economies of scale? Why is menu planning made more complex by expanding into other countries?

=== **Using the Internet** ===

21. Using the Hoover Institution's "Hoover's Online Corporate Directory" (**http://www.hoovers.com/**), compare the structure and financial status of McDonald's Corporation and Wendy's International, Inc. Recall the case study "Billions and Billions of Burgers." In your opinion, which firm is more successful? What does this comparison illuminate about company size in relation to cost and production?

Appendix
A CLOSER LOOK AT PRODUCTION AND COSTS

In this appendix, we develop a model to determine how a profit-maximizing firm will combine resources to produce a particular amount of output. The quantity of output that can be produced with a given amount of resources depends on the existing *state of technology,* which is the prevailing knowledge of how resources can be combined. Therefore, we will begin by considering the technological possibilities available to the firm.

The Production Function and Efficiency

The ways in which resources can be combined to produce output are summarized by a firm's production function. The *production function* identifies the maximum quantities of a particular good or service that can be produced per time period with various combinations of resources, for a given level of technology. The production function can be presented as an equation, a graph, or a table.

The production function summarized in Exhibit 11 reflects, for a hypothetical firm, the output resulting from particular combinations of resources. This firm uses only two resources: capital and labor. The amount of capital used is listed in the left-hand column of the table, and the amount of labor employed is listed across the top. For example, if 1 unit of capital is combined with 7 units of labor, the firm can produce 290 units of output per period.

We assume that the firm produces the maximum possible output given the combination of resources employed, and that the same output could not be produced with fewer resources. Since we assume that the production function combines resources efficiently, 290 units is the most that can be produced with 7 units of labor and 1 unit of capital. Thus, we say that production is **technologically efficient.**

We can examine the effects of adding additional labor to an existing amount of capital by starting with some level of capital and reading across the table. For example, when 1 unit of capital and 1 unit of labor are employed, the firm produces 40 units of output per period. If the amount of labor is increased by 1 unit and the amount of capital employed is held constant, output increases to 90 units, so the marginal product of labor is 50 units. If the amount of labor employed increases from 2 to 3 units, other things constant, output goes to 150 units, yielding a mar-

EXHIBIT 11	Units of Capital Employed per Period	Units of Labor Employed per Period						
A Firm's Production Function Using Labor and Capital: Production per Period		**1**	**2**	**3**	**4**	**5**	**6**	**7**
	1	40	90	150	200	240	270	290
	2	90	140	200	250	290	315	335
	3	150	195	260	310	345	370	390
	4	200	250	310	350	385	415	440
	5	240	290	345	385	420	450	475
	6	270	320	375	415	450	475	495
	7	290	330	390	435	470	495	510

ginal product of 60 units. By reading across the table, you will discover that the marginal product of labor first rises, showing increasing marginal returns from the variable resource (labor), and then declines, showing diminishing marginal returns. Similarly, by holding the amount of labor employed to 1 unit and following down the column, you will find that the marginal product of capital also reflects first increasing marginal returns, then diminishing marginal returns.

Isoquants

Notice from the tabular presentation of the production function in Exhibit 11 that different combinations of resources may yield the same level of output. For example, several combinations of labor and capital yield 290 units of output. Some of the information provided in Exhibit 11 can be presented more clearly in graphical form. In Exhibit 12, the quantity of labor employed is measured along the horizontal axis and the quantity of capital is measured along the vertical axis. The combinations that yield 290 units of output are presented in Exhibit 12 as points *a, b, c,* and *d.* These points can be connected to form an *isoquant,* Q_1, which shows the possible combinations of the two resources that produce 290 units of output. Likewise, Q_2 shows combinations of inputs that yield 415 units of output, and Q_3 shows combinations that yield 475 units of output. (The colors of the isoquants match those of the corresponding entries in the production function table in Exhibit 11.)

An isoquant, such as Q_1 in Exhibit 12, is a curve that shows all the technologically efficient combinations of two resources, such as labor and capital, that produce a certain amount of output. *Iso* is from the Greek word meaning "equal," and *quant* is short for "quantity"; so *isoquant* means "equal quantity." Along a particular isoquant, such as Q_1, the amount of output produced remains constant, in this case 290 units, but the combination of resources varies. To produce a particular level of output, the firm can use resource combinations ranging from much capital and little labor to much labor and little capital. For example, a paving contractor can put in a new driveway with 10 workers using shovels and hand rollers; the same job can also be done with only 2 workers, a road grader, and a paving machine. A Saturday-afternoon charity car wash to raise money to send the school band to Disney World is labor-intensive, involving perhaps a dozen workers per car.

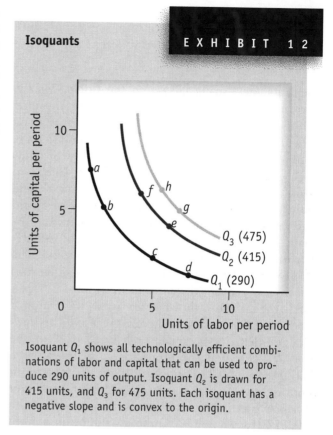

Isoquants   EXHIBIT 12

Isoquant Q_1 shows all technologically efficient combinations of labor and capital that can be used to produce 290 units of output. Isoquant Q_2 is drawn for 415 units, and Q_3 for 475 units. Each isoquant has a negative slope and is convex to the origin.

In contrast, a professional car wash is fully automated, requiring only one worker to turn on the machine and collect the money. An isoquant shows such alternative combinations of resources that produce the same level of output. Let's consider some properties of isoquants.

Isoquants Farther from the Origin Represent Greater Output Levels. Although we have included only three isoquants in Exhibit 12, there is a different isoquant for every quantity of output depicted in Exhibit 11. Indeed, there is a different isoquant for every output level the firm could possibly produce, with isoquants farther from the origin indicating higher levels of output.

Isoquants Slope Down to the Right. Along a given isoquant, the quantity of labor employed is inversely related to the quantity of capital employed, so isoquants have negative slopes.

Isoquants Do Not Intersect. Since each isoquant refers to a specific level of output, no two isoquants intersect, for such an intersection would indicate that the same combination of resources could, with equal efficiency, produce two different amounts of output.

Isoquants Are Usually Convex to the Origin. Finally, isoquants are usually convex to the origin, meaning that the slope of the isoquant gets flatter down along the curve. To understand why, keep in mind that the slope of the isoquant measures the ability of additional units of one resource—in this case, labor—to substitute in production for another—in this case, capital. As we said, the isoquant has a negative slope. Take away the minus sign and the slope of the isoquant is the **marginal rate of technical substitution,** or **MRTS,** between two resources. The MRTS indicates the rate at which labor can be substituted for capital without affecting output. When much capital and little labor are used, the marginal productivity of labor is relatively great and the marginal productivity of capital is relatively small, so one unit of labor will substitute for a relatively large amount of capital. For example, in moving from point a to b along isoquant Q_1 in Exhibit 12, 1 unit of labor substitutes for 2 units of capital, so the MRTS between points a and b equals 2. But as more units of labor and fewer units of capital are employed, the marginal product of labor declines and the marginal product of capital increases, so it takes more labor to make up for a reduction in capital. For example, in moving from point c to point d in Exhibit 12, 2 units of labor substitute for 1 unit of capital; hence, the MRTS between points c and d equals 1/2.

The extent to which one input substitutes for another, as measured by the marginal rate of technical substitution, is directly linked to the marginal productivity of each input. For example, between points a and b, 1 unit of labor replaces 2 units of capital, yet output remains constant. So labor's marginal product, MP_L—that is, the additional output resulting from an additional unit of labor—must be twice as large as capital's marginal product, MP_C. In fact, *all along the isoquant, the marginal rate of technical substitution of labor for capital equals the marginal product of labor divided by the marginal product of capital, which also equals the absolute value of the slope of the isoquant.* Thus, we can say that

$$|\text{Slope of isoquant}| = \text{MRTS} = MP_L/MP_C$$

where the vertical lines on either side of "Slope of isoquant" mean the absolute value. For example, between points a and b the slope equals -2, which has an absolute value of 2, which equals the marginal rate of substitution of labor for capital and the ratio of marginal productivities.

If labor and capital were perfect substitutes in production, the rate at which labor substituted for capital would remain fixed along the isoquant, so the isoquant would be a downward-sloping straight line. Since most resources are *not* perfect substitutes, however, the rate at which one substitutes for another changes along an isoquant. As we move down along an isoquant, more labor is required to offset each 1-unit decline in capital, so the slope of the isoquant gets flatter, yielding an isoquant that is convex to the origin.

Let's summarize the properties of isoquants.

1. *Isoquants farther from the origin represent greater levels of output.*
2. *Isoquants slope downward.*
3. *Isoquants never intersect.*
4. *Isoquants tend to be bowed toward the origin.*

Isocost Lines

Isoquants graphically illustrate a firm's production function for all quantities of output the firm could possibly produce. Given these isoquants, how much should the firm produce? More specifically, what is the firm's profit-maximizing level of output? The answer depends on the cost of resources and on the amount of money the firm plans to spend.

Suppose a unit of labor costs the firm $15,000 per year, and the cost for each unit of capital is $25,000 per year. The total cost (TC) of production is

$$TC = (w \times L) + (r \times C)$$
$$= \$15,000L + \$25,000C$$

where w is the annual wage rate, L is the quantity of labor employed, r is the annual cost of capital, and C is the quantity of capital employed. An **isocost line** identifies all combinations of capital and labor the firm can hire for a given total cost. Again, iso is from the Greek meaning "equal," so an isocost line is a line representing equal cost. In Exhibit 13, for example, the line $TC = \$150,000$ identifies all combinations of labor and capital that cost the firm a total of $150,000. The entire $150,000 could pay for 6 units of capital per year; if the entire budget is spent only on labor, 10 workers per year could be hired; or the firm can employ any combination of resources along the isocost line.

Recall that the slope of any line is the vertical change between two points on the line divided by the corresponding horizontal change (the rise over the run). At the point where the isocost line meets the vertical axis, the quantity of capital that can be purchased equals the total cost divided by the annual cost of capital, or TC/r. At the point where the isocost line meets the horizontal axis, the quantity of labor that can be hired equals the firm's total cost divided by the annual wage, or TC/w. The slope of any isocost line in Exhibit 13 can be calculated by considering a movement from the vertical intercept to the horizontal intercept. That is, we divide the vertical change $(-TC/r)$ by the horizontal change (TC/w), as follows:

$$\text{Slope of isocost line} = -\frac{TC/r}{TC/w} = -\frac{w}{r}$$

The slope of the isocost line equals minus the price of labor divided by the price of capital, or $-w/r$, which indicates the relative prices of the inputs. In our example, the absolute value of the slope of the isocost line equals w/r, or

$$\begin{aligned}\left|\text{Slope of isocost line}\right| &= w/r \\ &= 15{,}000/25{,}000 \\ &= 0.6\end{aligned}$$

The wage rate of labor is 0.6 of the annual cost of capital, so hiring one more unit of labor, without incurring any additional cost, implies that the firm must employ 0.6 unit less capital.

A firm is not confined to a particular isocost line. Thus, a firm's total cost depends on how much the firm plans to spend. This is why in Exhibit 13 we include three isocost lines, not just one, each corresponding to a different total budget. In fact, there is a different isocost line for every possible budget. *These isocost lines are parallel because each reflects the same relative resource price.* Resource prices are assumed to be constant regardless of the amount employed.

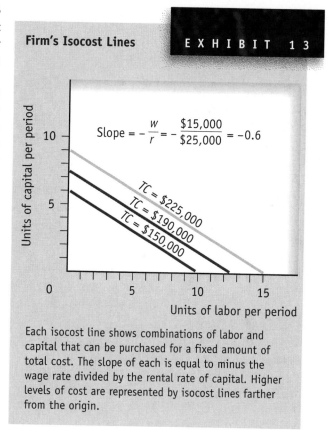

Firm's Isocost Lines   **E X H I B I T   1 3**

$\text{Slope} = -\dfrac{w}{r} = -\dfrac{\$15{,}000}{\$25{,}000} = -0.6$

$TC = \$225{,}000$
$TC = \$190{,}000$
$TC = \$150{,}000$

Units of capital per period (vertical axis, marked 5 and 10)

Units of labor per period (horizontal axis, marked 5, 10, 15)

Each isocost line shows combinations of labor and capital that can be purchased for a fixed amount of total cost. The slope of each is equal to minus the wage rate divided by the rental rate of capital. Higher levels of cost are represented by isocost lines farther from the origin.

The Choice of Input Combinations

We bring the isoquants and the isocost lines together in Exhibit 14. Suppose the firm has decided to produce 415 units of output and wants to minimize its total cost. The firm could select point f, where 6 units of capital are combined with 4 units of labor. This combination, however, would cost $210,000 at prevailing prices. Since the profit-maximizing firm wants to produce its chosen output at the minimum cost, it tries to find the isocost line closest to the origin that still touches the isoquant. Only at a point of tangency does a movement in either direction along an isoquant shift the firm to a higher cost level. So *the point of tangency between the isocost line and the isoquant shows the minimum cost required to produce a given output.*

Consider what is going on at the point of tangency. At point e in Exhibit 14, the isoquant and the isocost line have the same slope. As mentioned already, the absolute value of the slope of an isoquant equals the marginal rate of technical substitution between labor and capital, and the absolute value of the

E X H I B I T   1 4

EXHIBIT 14 **Optimal Combinations of Inputs**

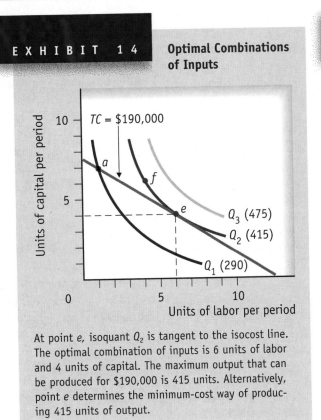

At point e, isoquant Q_2 is tangent to the isocost line. The optimal combination of inputs is 6 units of labor and 4 units of capital. The maximum output that can be produced for $190,000 is 415 units. Alternatively, point e determines the minimum-cost way of producing 415 units of output.

EXHIBIT 15 **The Long-Run Expansion Path**

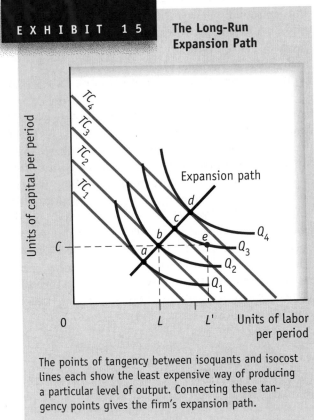

The points of tangency between isoquants and isocost lines each show the least expensive way of producing a particular level of output. Connecting these tangency points gives the firm's expansion path.

slope of the isocost line equals the ratio of the input prices. So when a firm produces output in the least costly way, the marginal rate of technical substitution must equal the ratio of the resource prices, or

$$\text{MRTS} = w/r = 15{,}000/25{,}000 = 0.6$$

This equality shows that the firm adjusts resource use so that the rate at which one input can be substituted for another in production—that is, the marginal rate of technical substitution—equals the rate at which one resource can be traded for another in resource markets, which is w/r. If this equality does not hold, it means that the firm could adjust its input mix to produce the same output for a lower cost.

The Expansion Path

Imagine a set of isoquants representing each possible level of output. Given the relative cost of resources, we could then draw isocost lines to determine the optimal combination of resources for producing each level of output. The points of tangency in Exhibit 15 show the least–cost input combinations for produc-

ing several output levels. For example, output level Q_2 can be produced most cheaply using C units of capital and L units of labor. The line formed by connecting these tangency points is the firm's expansion path. If the resources are capital and labor, we often refer to this path as the long-run expansion path. The expansion path need not be a straight line, though it will generally slope upward, implying that firms will expand the use of both resources in the long run as output increases. Note that we have assumed that the prices of inputs remain constant as the firm varies output along the expansion path, so the isocost lines at the points of tangency are parallel—that is, they have the same slope.

The expansion path indicates the lowest long-run total cost for each level of output. For example, the firm can produce output level Q_2 for TC_2, output level Q_3 for TC_3, and so on. Similarly, the firm's long-run average cost curve conveys, at each level of output, the total cost divided by the level of output. The firm's expansion path and the firm's long-run average cost curve represent alternative ways of portraying costs in the long run, given resource prices and technology.

We can use Exhibit 15 to distinguish between short-run adjustments in output and long-run adjustments. Let's begin with the firm producing Q_2 at point b, which requires C units of capital and L units of labor. Now suppose that in the short run, the firm wants to expand output to Q_3. Since capital is fixed in the short run, the only way to expand output to Q_3 is by expanding the quantity of labor employed to L', which requires moving to point e in Exhibit 15. Point e is not the cheapest way to produce Q_3 in the long run, for it is not a tangency point. In the long run, capital usage is variable, and if the firm wishes to produce Q_3, it should adjust capital and shift from point e to point c, thereby minimizing the total cost of producing Q_3.

One final point: If the relative prices of resources change, the least-cost combination of those resources will also change, so the firm's expansion path will change. For example, if the price of labor increases, capital becomes cheaper relative to labor. The effi-

cient production of any given level of output will therefore call for less labor and more capital. With the cost of labor higher, the firm's total cost for each level of output rises. Such a cost increase would also be reflected by an upward shift in the average total cost curve.

Summary

A firm's *production function* specifies the relationship between resource use and output, given prevailing technology. An *isoquant* is a curve that illustrates the possible combinations of resources that will produce a particular level of output. An *isocost* line presents the combinations of resources the firm can employ, given resource prices and the amount of money the firm plans to spend.

For a given level of output—that is, for a given isoquant—the firm minimizes its total cost by choosing the lowest isocost line that just touches, or is tangent to, the isoquant. The least-cost combination of resources will depend on the productivity of resources and the relative cost of resources.

APPENDIX QUESTION

1. **(Choice of Input Combinations)** Suppose that a firm's cost of labor is $10 per unit and its cost of capital is $40 per unit.
   a. Construct an isocost line such that total cost is constant at $200.
   b. If this firm is producing efficiently, what is the marginal rate of technical substitution between labor and capital?
   c. Prove your answer to part b using isocost lines and isoquant curves.
   d. How are the expansion path and the long-run average cost curve related?

21

Perfect Competition

I n the previous chapter, we examined the cost curves of individual firms in both the short run and the long run. We have not yet addressed how much a firm will produce and what price it will charge. What we can say for sure is that the answer to both questions will be guided by profit maximization. To answer these questions we revisit an old friend: demand. In this chapter we find that, given a firm's cost curves, the amount it produces and the price it charges will depend on the demand for its product. We bring together cost and demand to determine the profit-maximizing levels of price and output.

In the next few chapters we will examine how firms respond to their economic environments in deciding what to produce, in what quantities, and at what price. But, the assumption is that, no matter what the market structure, firms try to maximize profit. Topics discussed in this chapter include:

- Market structure
- Price takers
- Marginal revenue
- Golden rule of profit maximization
- Loss minimization

- Firm's short-run supply curve
- Industry's long-run supply curve
- Competition and efficiency
- Producer surplus

AN INTRODUCTION TO PERFECT COMPETITION

First, a few words about terminology. An industry consists of all firms that supply output to a particular market, such as the auto market or the shoe market. The terms *industry* and *market* are used interchangeably throughout the chapter. The decisions a firm makes depend on the structure of the market in which the firm operates. **Market structure** describes the important features of a market, such as the number of firms (are there many or few?), the product's degree of uniformity (do firms in the market supply identical products or are there differences?), the ease of firm entry into the market (is entry easy or is it blocked by natural or artificial barriers?), and the forms of competition among firms (do firms compete only through prices or are advertising and product differentiation common as well?). The various features will become clearer as we examine each type of market structure in the next few chapters.

Market structure Important features of a market, such as the number of firms, uniformity of product among firms, ease of entry, and forms of competition

Perfectly Competitive Market Structure

We begin with **perfect competition,** in some ways the most basic of market structures. A *perfectly competitive* market is characterized by the following: (1) there are many buyers and sellers, so many that each buys or sells only a tiny fraction of the total amount exchanged in the market; (2) firms produce a standardized, or *homogeneous,* product; (3) buyers and sellers are fully informed about the price and availability of all resources and products; and (4) firms and resources are freely mobile, with no obstacles, such as patents, licenses, high capital costs, or ignorance about available technology, to prevent new firms from entering or existing firms from leaving a market.

Perfect competition A market structure in which there are large numbers of fully informed buyers and sellers of a homogeneous product, with no obstacles to entry or exit of firms in the long run

If these conditions are present in a market, individual participants have no control over the price. Price is determined by market supply and demand. Once the market establishes the price, each individual firm is free to supply whatever amount maximizes the firm's profit. A perfectly competitive firm is so small relative to the size of the market that the firm's choice of what quantity to supply has no effect on the market price. A perfectly competitive firm is called a **price taker** because it must "take," or accept, the market price.

Price taker A firm that faces a given market price and whose actions have no effect on that market price

A model of perfect competition allows us to make a number of predictions that hold up when we examine the real world. Some markets, such as stock markets and world grain markets, closely approximate perfect competition. Perfect competition is also an important benchmark for evaluating the efficiency of production in other types of markets. Let's now look at demand under perfect competition.

Demand under Perfect Competition

In Exhibit 1, the market price of $5 per unit is determined in panel (a) by the intersection of the market demand curve, *D,* and the market supply curve, *S.* Once the market price is established, any firm can sell all it wants at that market price. The demand curve as it appears to an individual firm is therefore a horizontal line drawn at the market price. In our example, a firm's demand curve, identified as *d* in panel (b), is drawn at the market price of $5 per unit. This perfectly elastic demand curve indicates that the perfectly competitive firm can sell all it wants at the market price. Note that the firm's output is much smaller than the market's. For example, there could be a thousand firms in the market, so any particular firm produces only a tiny fraction of market output.

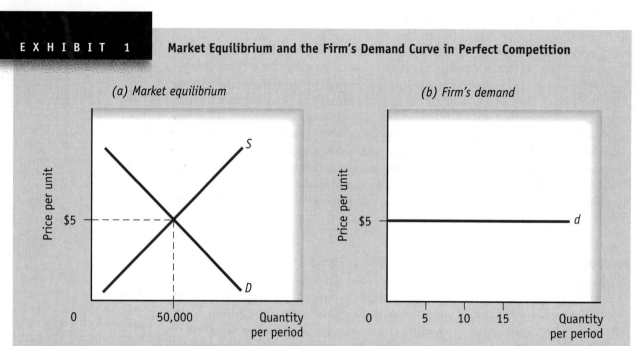

EXHIBIT   1   **Market Equilibrium and the Firm's Demand Curve in Perfect Competition**

In panel (a), the market price of $5 is determined by the intersection of the market demand and supply curves. The individual perfectly competitive firm can sell any amount at that price. The demand curve facing the competitive firm is horizontal at the market price, as shown by demand curve *d* in panel (b).

As we have seen, each firm is a *price taker* because its output is so small relative to market supply that the firm has no impact on the market price. Also, because all firms supply identical goods, any firm charging more than the market price will sell no output. For example, if a farmer charged $5.50 per bushel of grain, customers in this market would simply turn to other suppliers. Any firm is, of course, free to charge less than the market price, but why do that when the firm can sell all it wants at the market price? Firms are not stupid, or, if they are, they don't last long.

It has been said, "In perfect competition there is no competition." Ironically, two neighboring corn farmers in perfect competition are not really rivals. They both sell as much corn as they want to at the market price. The amount one sells has no effect on the price the other receives.

SHORT-RUN PROFIT MAXIMIZATION

We assume that firms try to maximize economic profit. Firms that ignore this strategy will not be around long. Economic profit equals total revenue minus total opportunity cost, including both explicit and implicit costs. Implicit cost, you will recall, is the opportunity cost of resources owned by the firm and includes a normal profit; economic profit is any profit above normal profit. How do firms maximize profit? As we have learned, the perfectly competitive firm has no control over price. What the firm does control is the amount produced, the rate of output. The question then boils down to this: What rate of output will maximize profit?

Short-Run Costs and Revenues for a Perfectly Competitive Firm

Quantity of Output per period (q) (1)	Marginal Revenue (Price) (p) (2)	Total Revenue (TR = q × p) (3) = (1) × (2)	Total Cost (TC) (4)	Marginal Cost $\left(MC = \dfrac{\Delta TC}{\Delta q}\right)$ (5)	Average Total Cost $\left(ATC = \dfrac{TC}{q}\right)$ (6) = (4) ÷ (1)	Economic Profit or Loss = TR − TC (7) = (3) − (4)
0	—	$ 0	$15.00	—	∞	−$15.00
1	$5	5	19.75	$ 4.75	$19.75	−14.75
2	5	10	23.50	3.75	11.75	−13.50
3	5	15	26.50	3.00	8.83	−11.50
4	5	20	29.00	2.50	7.25	−9.00
5	5	25	31.00	2.00	6.20	−6.00
6	5	30	32.50	1.50	5.42	−2.50
7	5	35	33.75	1.25	4.82	1.25
8	5	40	35.25	1.50	4.41	4.75
9	5	45	37.25	2.00	4.14	7.75
10	5	50	40.00	2.75	4.00	10.00
11	5	55	43.25	3.25	3.93	11.75
12	**5**	**60**	**48.00**	**4.75**	**4.00**	**12.00**
13	5	65	54.50	6.50	4.19	10.50
14	5	70	64.00	9.50	4.57	6.00
15	5	75	77.50	13.50	5.17	−2.50
16	5	80	96.00	18.50	6.00	−16.00

Total Revenue Minus Total Cost

The firm maximizes profit by finding the rate of output that makes total revenue minus total cost as large as it can possibly be. Columns (3) and (4) in Exhibit 2 list the firm's total revenue and total cost for each rate of output. Remember that total cost already includes a normal profit, so total cost includes all opportunity costs. Although Exhibit 2 does not distinguish between fixed and variable costs, fixed cost must equal $15, since total cost is $15 when output is zero. The fact that the firm incurs a fixed cost indicates that at least one resource must be fixed, so the firm must be operating in the short run.

Total revenue for a perfectly competitive firm is simply the price per unit ($5, in this example) times the rate of output. Total revenue in column (3) minus total cost in column (4) yields the economic profit or loss per period, which is presented in column (7). As you can see, at very low and very high rates of output, total cost exceeds total revenue, so the firm incurs an *economic loss*. Between 7 and 14 units of output, total revenue exceeds total cost, so the firm earns an economic profit. Economic profit is maximized at $12 when the firms produces 12 units per period (the 12 and 12 combination is just a coincidence).

These results are graphed in panel (a) of Exhibit 3, which shows the total revenue and total cost curves. As output increases by 1 unit, total revenue increases by $5, so the firm's total revenue curve is a straight line emanating from the origin, with a slope of 5. The short-run total cost curve has a backward S shape reflecting first increasing marginal returns, then diminishing marginal re-

EXHIBIT 3

Short-Run Profit Maximization

In panel (a), the total revenue curve for a competitive firm is a straight line with a slope equal to the market price of $5. Total cost increases with output, first at a decreasing rate and then at an increasing rate. Profit is maximized at 12 units of output, where total revenue exceeds total cost by the greatest amount. In panel (b), marginal revenue is a horizontal line at the market price of $5. Profit is maximized at 12 units of output, where marginal cost equals marginal revenue (point e). Profit is output (12 units) multiplied by the difference between price ($5) and average total cost ($4), as shown by the shaded rectangle.

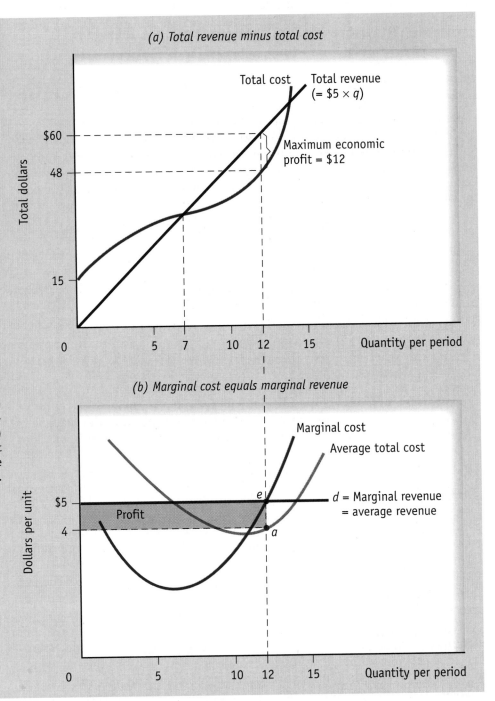

(a) Total revenue minus total cost

(b) Marginal cost equals marginal revenue

turns from changes in the amount of variable resource employed. Total cost increases, first at a decreasing rate and then at an increasing rate.

Comparing total revenue and total cost is one way to find the profit-maximizing rate of output. At rates of output less than 7 units or greater than 14 units, total cost exceeds total revenue, resulting in an economic loss, which is measured by the vertical distance between the two curves. Total revenue exceeds total cost between output rates of 7 units and 14 units; at these outputs the firm earns an economic profit. *Profit is maximized at the level of output where total revenue exceeds total cost by the greatest amount.* We already know that this distance is greatest when 12 units are produced.

Marginal Cost Equals Marginal Revenue in Equilibrium

A second and more revealing way to find the profit-maximizing rate of output is to focus on marginal revenue and marginal cost. Column (2) of Exhibit 2 presents the firm's marginal revenue. **Marginal revenue** is the change in total revenue divided by the change in output, or $MR = \Delta TR/\Delta q$. In perfect competition the firm is a price taker, so if one more unit is sold, total revenue increases by an amount equal to the market price. Thus, *in perfect competition, marginal revenue equals the market price.* In this example, marginal revenue is $5.

In the previous chapter you learned that *marginal cost* is the change in total cost divided by the change in output. Column (5) of Exhibit 2 presents the firm's marginal cost at each level of output. Marginal cost first declines, reflecting increasing marginal returns in the short run as more of the variable resource is employed. Marginal cost then increases, reflecting diminishing marginal returns.

The firm will expand output as long as each additional unit sold adds more to total revenue than to total cost—that is, as long as marginal revenue exceeds marginal cost. As long as marginal revenue exceeds marginal cost, the "marginal" profit is positive—that is, the sale of the additional units adds to the firm's total profit. Comparing columns (2) and (5) in Exhibit 2, we see that marginal revenue exceeds marginal cost for each of the first 12 units of output. The marginal cost of unit 13, however, is $6.50, compared to a marginal revenue of $5. Producing the 13th unit would reduce total profit by $1.50. Total profit is in the right-hand column. Since we assume that the firm will maximize profit, the firm will limit its output rate to 12 units per period.

A firm will expand output as long as marginal revenue exceeds marginal cost, and it will stop expanding if marginal cost rises above marginal revenue. A shorthand for this approach is the **golden rule of profit maximization,** which says the firm produces where marginal cost equals marginal revenue. The golden rule flows from our assumption about profit maximization. The market provides rewards and penalties that will lead firms to the golden-rule solution, even if a firm is unaware of that rule.

Measuring Profit in the Short Run

Per-unit cost and revenue data are graphed in panel (b) of Exhibit 3. Marginal revenue is a horizontal line at the market price of $5, which also represents the competitive firm's demand curve. At any point along the demand curve, marginal revenue equals the price. Marginal revenue for the competitive firm also equals the **average revenue,** which is the total revenue divided by the output. Average revenue is also the price. Regardless of the output, therefore, the following equality holds at all points on the competitive firm's demand curve:

Marginal revenue = Market price = Average revenue

The marginal-cost curve intersects the marginal-revenue (and demand) curve at point *e*, where the rate of output is about 12 units. At lower rates of output, marginal revenue exceeds marginal cost, so the firm could increase

Marginal revenue The change in total revenue resulting from a 1-unit change in sales; in perfect competition, marginal revenue equals the market price

Golden rule of profit maximization To maximize profit or minimize loss, a firm should produce at the level of output where marginal cost equals marginal revenue

Average revenue Total revenue divided by output; in all market structures, average revenue equals the market price

When market price is low enough that no level of output will cover costs, firms, such as auto manufacturers, can either produce at a loss or temporarily stop production.

profit by expanding output. At higher rates of output, marginal cost exceeds marginal revenue, so the firm could increase profit by reducing output. Profit appears as the shaded rectangle. The height of that rectangle, *ea*, equals the price (or average revenue), $5, minus the average total cost, $4, at that level of output. Thus, price minus average total cost yields an average profit per unit of $1. Total profit, $12, equals the average profit per unit, $1 (denoted by *ea*), times the 12 units produced.

Note that with total cost and total revenue curves, we measure total profit by the vertical *distance* between the two curves. But with per-unit curves, we measure total profit by an *area*—that is, by the two dimensions that result from multiplying the average profit per unit times the number of units sold.

MINIMIZING SHORT-RUN LOSSES

An individual firm in perfect competition has no control over the market price. Sometimes the price is so low that no level of output will yield a profit. Faced with losses at all levels of output, the firm can continue to produce at a loss or can temporarily shut down production, such as when an auto plant responds to slack demand by temporarily halting production for weeks or months. Note that even if the firm shuts down, it cannot go out of business in the short run. The short run is by definition a period too short to allow existing firms to leave the industry. In a sense, a firm is trapped in the industry in the short run.

Fixed Cost and Minimizing Losses

Your instincts probably tell you that the firm, rather than produce at a loss, should shut down. It's not that simple. Keep in mind that the firm has two types of costs in the short run: fixed cost, which must be paid in the short run even if the firm produces nothing, and variable cost, which depends on the level of output. If the firm shuts down, it must still pay property taxes, fire insurance, interest on any loans, and other overhead expenses incurred even when output is zero. *There may be some level of output greater than zero at which the firm's revenue will not only cover variable cost but also cover some portion of fixed cost.* A firm will produce if the revenue thus generated exceeds the variable cost of production.

Consider the same cost data presented earlier in Exhibit 2, but now suppose the market price has fallen from $5 to $3. This new situation is presented in Exhibit 4. Because of the lower price, total revenue and total profit are lower at all rates of output. Column (8) indicates that each output rate results in a loss. If the firm produces nothing, its loss is the fixed cost of $15. But if the firm produces between 6 and 12 units per period, it loses less than $15. From column (8), you can see that the loss is minimized at $10 when 10 units are produced, so the firm minimizes its loss by producing 10 units per period rather than shutting down. The firm's total cost increases from $15 at zero output to $40 when output is 10. So total cost increases by $25, which is the variable cost of producing 10 units. Since total revenue from selling 10 units is $30, the firm covers its variable cost of $25, leaving $5 toward paying fixed cost.

Panel (a) of Exhibit 5 presents the firm's total cost and total revenue curves

Minimizing Losses in the Short Run

EXHIBIT 4

Quantity of Output per period (q) (1)	Marginal Revenue (Price) (p) (2)	Total Revenue ($TR = q \times p$) (3) = (1) × (2)	Total Cost (TC) (4)	Marginal Cost $\left(MC = \dfrac{\Delta TC}{\Delta q}\right)$ (5)	Average Total Cost $\left(ATC = \dfrac{TC}{q}\right)$ (6) = (4) ÷ (1)	Average Variable Cost $\left(AVC = \dfrac{TVC}{q}\right)$ (7)	Total Profit or Loss = $TR - TC$ (8) = (3) − (4)
0	—	$ 0	$15.00	—	∞	—	−$15.00
1	$3	3	19.75	$ 4.75	$19.75	$4.75	−16.75
2	3	6	23.50	3.75	11.75	4.25	−17.50
3	3	9	26.50	3.00	8.83	3.83	−17.50
4	3	12	29.00	2.50	7.25	3.50	−17.00
5	3	15	31.00	2.00	6.20	3.20	−16.00
6	3	18	32.50	1.50	5.42	2.92	−14.50
7	3	21	33.75	1.25	4.82	2.68	−12.75
8	3	24	35.25	1.50	4.41	2.53	−11.25
9	3	27	37.25	2.00	4.14	2.47	−10.25
10	**3**	**30**	**40.00**	**2.75**	**4.00**	**2.50**	**−10.00**
11	3	33	43.25	3.25	3.93	2.57	−10.25
12	3	36	48.00	4.75	4.00	2.75	−12.00
13	3	39	54.50	6.50	4.19	3.04	−15.50
14	3	42	64.00	9.50	4.57	3.50	−22.00
15	3	45	77.50	13.50	5.17	4.17	−32.50
16	3	48	96.00	18.50	6.00	5.06	−48.00

from the data in Exhibit 4. The total cost curve has not changed and is the same as in Exhibit 3. The drop in price from $5 to $3 per unit changes the slope of the total-revenue curve from 5 to 3, so the total revenue curve is now flatter than in Exhibit 3. Notice that the total revenue curve now lies below the total cost curve at all output rates. The vertical distance between the two curves measures the firm's loss at each level of output. If the firm produces nothing, the loss is its fixed cost of $15. The vertical distance between the two curves is minimized at an output level of about 10 units, where the loss is $10.

Marginal Cost Equals Marginal Revenue

We get the same result using marginal analysis. The per-unit data from Exhibit 4 are presented in panel (b) of Exhibit 5. *The firm will produce rather than shut down if marginal cost equals marginal revenue at a level of output where the price exceeds the average variable cost.* In Exhibit 5, the marginal cost and marginal revenue curves intersect at point *e*, where the output level is about 10 units per period and the price of $3 exceeds the average variable cost of $2.50. The average total cost at this level of output is $4, and the average variable cost is $2.50. The difference of $1.50 is the average fixed cost.

Because the price of $3 exceeds the average variable cost, the firm is able to

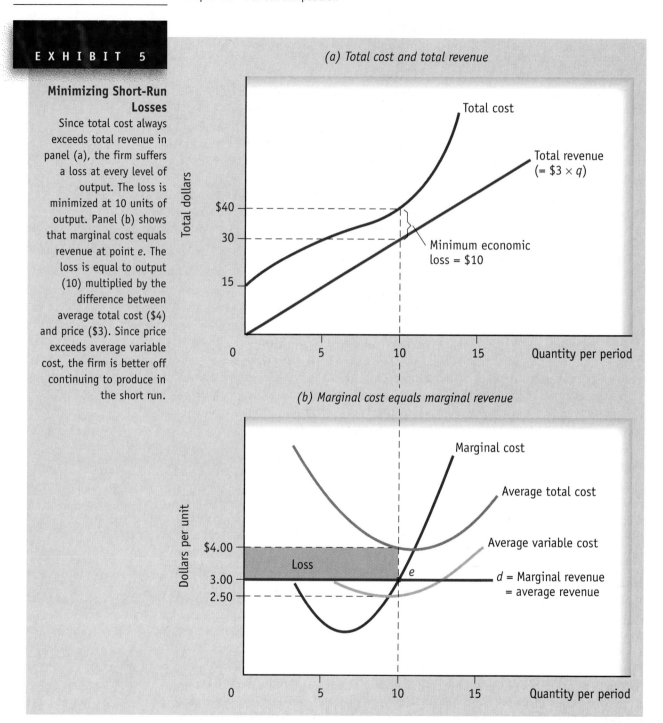

Minimizing Short-Run Losses
Since total cost always exceeds total revenue in panel (a), the firm suffers a loss at every level of output. The loss is minimized at 10 units of output. Panel (b) shows that marginal cost equals revenue at point e. The loss is equal to output (10) multiplied by the difference between average total cost ($4) and price ($3). Since price exceeds average variable cost, the firm is better off continuing to produce in the short run.

(a) Total cost and total revenue

Total dollars

Total cost

Total revenue
(= $3 × q)

$40
30

Minimum economic
loss = $10

15

0   5   10   15   Quantity per period

(b) Marginal cost equals marginal revenue

Dollars per unit

Marginal cost

Average total cost

Average variable cost

$4.00

Loss

3.00
2.50

e

d = Marginal revenue
= average revenue

0   5   10   15   Quantity per period

cover all its variable cost and a portion of its fixed cost. Specifically, $2.50 of the price pays the average variable cost, and $0.50 covers a portion of the average fixed cost. This leaves a loss of $1 per unit, which, when multiplied by 10 units, yields a total loss of $10 per period. This loss is identified in panel (b) by the shaded rectangle. If the firm were to shut down, the loss of $15 would exceed the $10 loss from producing.

Shutting Down in the Short Run

As long as the loss resulting from producing is less than the shutdown loss, the firm will produce in the short run. You may have read or heard about firms that report a loss; most firms reporting a loss continue to operate. But *if the average variable cost of production everywhere exceeds the price, the firm will shut down.* After all, why should the firm produce if doing so only increases its short-run loss? For example, suppose the price falls to $2 per unit. As you can see from column (7) of Exhibit 4, the average variable cost exceeds $2 at all levels of output. By shutting down, the firm suffers a loss equal only to its fixed cost—a loss that is clearly less than its fixed cost plus a portion of its variable cost.

From column (7) of Exhibit 4 you can also see that the lowest price at which the firm would cover its average variable cost is $2.47, which is the average variable cost when output is 9 units. At this price the firm will be indifferent between producing and shutting down, since either way its total loss will be the fixed cost of $15. Any price above $2.47 will allow the firm, by producing, to cover some portion of fixed cost.

Note that shutting down is not the same as going out of business. In the short run, a firm keeps its productive capacity intact—paying the rent, keeping trucks in working order, keeping water pipes from freezing in the winter, and so on. The firm therefore does not escape fixed cost by shutting down, since fixed cost is defined as that portion of cost that does not vary with output. Should prices rise enough or costs decline enough, the firm can easily resume operation. If market conditions look grim and are never expected to improve, operators will consider going out of business, but the firm cannot go out of business in the short run.

The Firm and Industry Short-Run Supply Curves

A firm will vary its output as the market price changes. If the price allows the firm to cover average variable cost and at least some fixed cost, the firm will produce where marginal cost equals marginal revenue. But if average variable cost is everywhere above the price, the firm will shut down. The effects of various prices on the firm's output are summarized in Exhibit 6. Points 1, 2, 3, 4, and 5 reflect intersections of the marginal cost curve with different demand, or marginal-revenue, curves.

At a price as low as p_1, the firm will shut down rather than produce at point 1 because no output level generates revenue sufficient to cover average variable cost; so output, q_1, is zero. At a price of p_2, the firm will be indifferent between producing q_2 and shutting down because either way the loss will equal fixed cost since the price just covers average variable cost. Point 2 is called the *shutdown point.* If the price is p_3, the firm will produce q_3 to minimize its loss. At p_4, the firm will produce q_4 to earn just a normal profit, since price equals average total cost. Point 4 is called the *break-even point.* If the price rises to p_5, the firm will earn a short-run economic profit by producing q_5.

The Short-Run Firm Supply Curve. *As long as the price is high enough to cover the firm's average variable cost, the firm will supply the quantity determined by the intersection of its upward-sloping marginal cost curve and its marginal-revenue, or demand, curve.* Thus, that portion of the firm's marginal cost curve that intersects and rises above the low point on its average variable cost curve becomes the **short-run**

Short-run firm supply curve *A curve that indicates the quantity a firm supplies at each price in the short run; that portion of a firm's marginal cost curve that intersects and rises above the low point on its average variable cost curve*

EXHIBIT 6

Summary of Short-Run Output Decisions

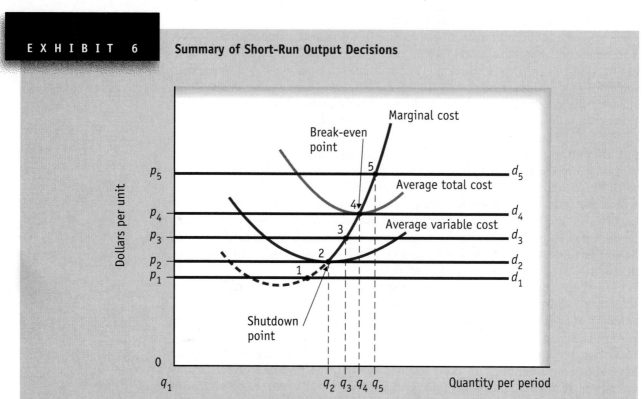

At price p_1, the firm produces nothing because p_1 is less than the firm's average variable cost. At price p_2, the firm is indifferent between shutting down and producing q_2 units of output, because in either case the firm would suffer a loss equal to its fixed cost. At p_3, it produces q_3 units and suffers a loss that is less than its fixed cost. At p_4, the firm produces q_4 and just breaks even, since p_4 equals average total cost. Finally, at p_5, the firm produces q_5 and earns an economic profit. The firm's short-run supply curve is that portion of its marginal cost curve at or rising above the minimum point of average variable cost (point 2).

firm supply curve. *In Exhibit 6, the short-run supply curve is the upward-sloping portion of the marginal cost curve, beginning at point 2.* The firm's short-run supply curve indicates the quantity the firm is willing and able to supply in the short run at each alternative price. The quantity supplied when the price is p_2 or higher is determined by the intersection of the firm's marginal cost curve and demand curve. The firm shuts down when the price is below p_2.

Short-run industry supply curve
A curve that indicates the quantity all firms in an industry supply at each price in the short run; the horizontal sum of each firm's short-run supply curve

The Short-Run Industry Supply Curve. Exhibit 7 presents an example of how supply curves for just three firms with identical marginal cost curves can be summed horizontally to form the short-run industry supply curve. (In perfectly competitive industries, there will obviously be many more firms.) The **short-run industry supply curve** is the horizontal sum of each firm's short-run supply curve. At a price below p, no output is supplied. At a price of p, 10 units are supplied by each of the three firms, for a market supply of 30 units. At a price above p, say p', 20 units are supplied by each firm, so the market supply is 60 units.

Firm Supply and Industry Equilibrium. Exhibit 8 shows the relationship between the short-run profit-maximizing output of the individual firm and the market

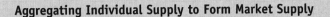

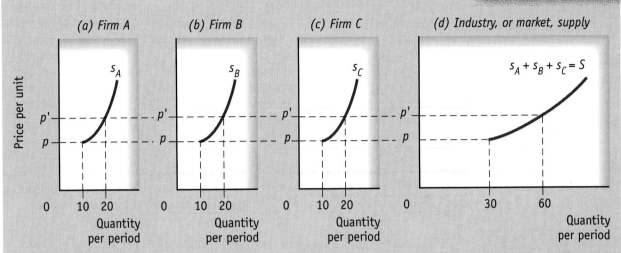

Aggregating Individual Supply to Form Market Supply

EXHIBIT 7

At price p, firms A, B, and C each supply 10 units of output. Total market supply is 30 units. In general, the market supply curve, panel (d), is the horizontal summation of the individual firm supply curves s_A, s_B, and s_C.

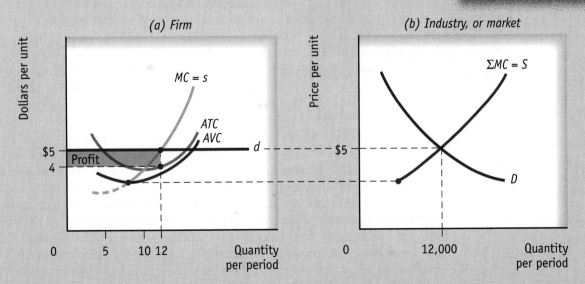

Relationship between Short-Run Profit Maximization and Market Equilibrium

EXHIBIT 8

The market supply curve S in panel (b) is the horizontal sum of the supply curves of all firms in the industry. The intersection of S with the market demand curve D determines the market price, $5. That price, in turn, determines the height of the perfectly elastic demand curve facing the individual firm in panel (a). That firm produces 12 units (where marginal cost equals marginal revenue of $5) and earns an economic profit of $1 per unit, or $12 in total.

equilibrium price and quantity. We assume there are 1,000 identical firms in this industry. Their individual supply curves (represented by the portion of the marginal cost curve at or rising above the average variable cost) are summed horizontally to yield the market, or industry, supply curve. At a price of $5 per unit, each firm supplies 12 units, for a total quantity supplied of 12,000 units. In the short run, each firm earns an economic profit of $12, represented by the shaded rectangle.

In summary, a perfectly competitive firm selects the short-run output rate that maximizes profit or minimizes loss. When confronting a loss, a firm will either produce an output that minimizes its loss or shut down temporarily.

Given the conditions for perfect competition, the market will converge toward equilibrium. But how is that equilibrium actually reached? In the real world, markets operate based on customs and conventions, which vary across markets. For example, the rules acceptable on the New York Stock Exchange are not the same as those followed in the market for flowers. In the following case study, we consider one of the oldest market mechanisms—auctions.

CASE STUDY

Auction Markets

Location:

Auctions held over the Internet are now quite common. For example, visit eBay's "Auction Web" to witness a Dutch auction (**http://www. ebay.com/aw/**). To see a live Internet auction, visit "ON-SALE Interactive Marketplace," a live Internet auction house offering computers and electronics (**http://www.onsale. com/**). For more about how auctions work, visit the Auction Marketing Institute (AMI), a nonprofit professional educational organization (**http://www.auctionweb. com/ami/**).

Five days a week in a huge building 10 miles outside Amsterdam, 2,500 buyers gather to participate in the world's largest flower auction. About 14 million blooms from 5,000 growers are auctioned off each day in the largest commercial building in the world, spread across the equivalent of 100 football fields. Flowers are grouped by type and auctioned off separately—long-stemmed roses, tulips, and so on. Hundreds of buyers are seated in the theater-type setting with their fingers on buttons. Once the flowers are presented, an electric clock with a hand that moves counterclockwise starts ticking off descending prices until a buyer stops it by pushing a button. The winning bidder gets to choose how many and which items to take. The clock starts ticking again until another buyer stops it, and so on. The clock continues until all flowers are sold. Flower auctions occur swiftly; on average a transaction occurs every four seconds.

This is an example of a *Dutch auction,* which starts at a high price and works down until a buyer stops the clock. Flowers have been auctioned off in Amsterdam for the last 400 years. Dutch auctions are more common when there are multiple lots of similar items to be sold, such as flowers in Amsterdam, tobacco in Canada, and fish in seaports around the world.

More common than the Dutch auction is the *English open outcry auction,* where bidding opens at a low price and moves up until only one buyer remains. Products sold this way include wine, art, antiques, livestock, and automobiles. The English system provides buyers with valuable information about what other buyers think the item is worth, which is why the best seats are toward the back of the room.

The word auction is from the Latin root *auctus,* meaning "to increase." Auctions were common in ancient Rome, where they were used to sell everything from the spoils of war to, on one occasion, the title of Roman emperor.

Auction Markets
continued

In some auctions, such as for art or for a foreclosed property, the item is not sold unless the bid reaches what is considered by the seller a suitable price. In other auctions, such as for cut flowers or fresh fish, the goods are perishable and must be sold as quickly as possible (one New England grocery chain guarantees that its seafood "is shipped from shore to store in 36 hours or less").

Auctions generate useful information to industry members. For example, during bidding at the Portland, Maine, fish auction, some buyers provide their fish processors a blow-by-blow account via cellular phones—information that processors use to revise their daily plans and identify profitable opportunities. One problem with auctions is that bidders may try to conspire to keep the price down. More than half of the criminal antitrust cases filed by the U.S. Justice Department during the 1980s involved bid rigging or price fixing in auction markets. Despite the potential problems of such bidding "rings," auctions will persist because they quickly determine a market-clearing price and are especially effective for unique items, such as works of art, or perishable items, such as flowers or fish.

Sources: Jane Katz, "High Bid," *Regional Review*, Federal Reserve Bank of Boston, (Spring 1995): pp. 18–24; Advertising circular for Shaw's Food and Drug, 12 November 1995; Richard Woodward, "Business Is Blooming," *New York Times Magazine*, 9 May 1993; Vernon L. Smith, "Auctions," *The New Palgrave Dictionary of Economics*, Vol. 1, J. Eatwell et al., eds. (New York: Stockton Press, 1987): pp. 138–44.

PERFECT COMPETITION IN THE LONG RUN

In the short run, variable resources can be altered, but other resources, which mostly determine firm size, are fixed. In the long run, however, firms have time to come and go and to adjust their size—that is, to adjust the scale of their operations. In the long run, there is no distinction between fixed and variable costs because all resources under the firm's control are variable.

Short-run economic profit will attract new entrants and encourage existing firms to expand the scale of their operations. Short-run economic profit attracts resources from industries where firms are earning only normal profit or are perhaps suffering losses. An increase in the number and/or size of firms will increase market supply in the long run, and an increase in market supply reduces the price. New firms will continue to enter a profitable industry and existing firms will continue to increase their size as long as economic profit is positive. Entry and expansion will stop only when the increase in supply has reduced the market price to the point where economic profit is zero. *So short-run economic profit will attract new entrants and may cause existing firms to expand; market supply will thereby expand until economic profit is eliminated.*

On the other hand, a short-run loss will prompt some firms to leave the industry or to reduce the scale of their operation. In the long run, departures and reductions in scale will reduce market supply and increase market price until remaining firms break even—that is, earn a normal profit.

Zero Economic Profit in the Long Run

Exhibit 9 shows the individual firm and the market in long-run equilibrium. In the long run, market supply adjusts as firms enter or leave the market or change the scale of their operations; *this process continues until the market supply curve intersects the market demand curve at a price that equals the lowest point on each firm's*

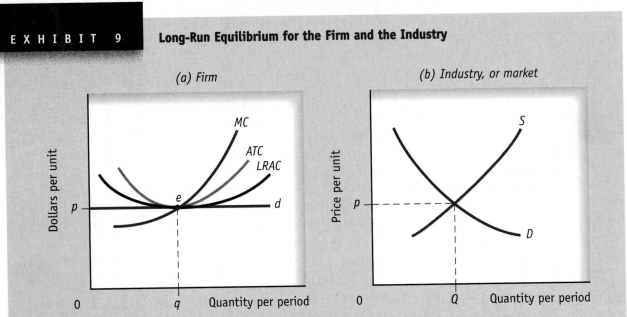

EXHIBIT 9   **Long-Run Equilibrium for the Firm and the Industry**

(a) Firm   *(b) Industry, or market*

In long-run equilibrium, the firm produces *q* units of output and earns a normal profit. At point *e*, price, marginal cost, short-run average total cost, and long-run average cost are all equal. There is no reason for new firms to enter or for existing firms to leave the market. Thus, the market supply curve, *S*, in panel (b) does not shift. As long as market demand, *D*, is stable, the industry will continue to produce a total of *Q* units of output at price *p*.

long-run average cost curve, or LRAC. A higher price would generate economic profit in the short run and would therefore attract new entrants in the long run. A lower price would result in a loss in the short run, causing some firms to leave the industry in the long run.

Perfect competition in the long run cuts economic profit to zero. Because the long run is a time period during which all resources under the firm's control are variable and because firms try to maximize profit, *firms in the long run will adjust their scale of operation until their average cost of production is minimized.* Firms that fail to minimize costs will not survive in the long run. At point *e* in Exhibit 9, the firm is in equilibrium, producing *q* units and earning only a normal profit. At point *e*, price, marginal cost, short-run average total cost, and long-run average cost are all equal. No firm in the market has any reason to alter its output and no outside firm has any incentive to enter this industry, since each existing firm in the market is earning normal, but not economic, profit.

The Long-Run Adjustment to a Change in Demand

To explore the long-run adjustment process, let's consider how a firm and an industry respond to an increase in market demand. Assume that the costs facing each individual firm do not depend on the number of firms in the industry (this assumption will be explained soon).

Effects of an Increase in Demand. Exhibit 10 shows a perfectly competitive market in long-run equilibrium, with the market supply curve intersecting the mar-

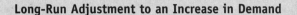

Long-Run Adjustment to an Increase in Demand   E X H I B I T   1 0

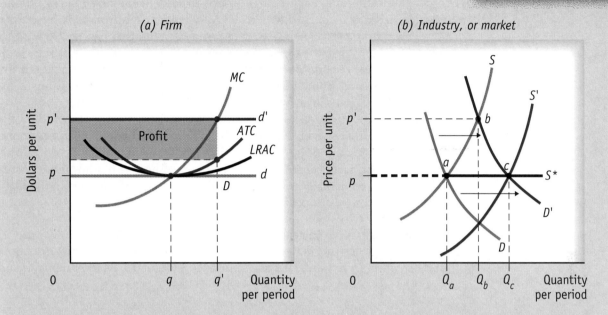

An increase in market demand from D to D' in panel (b) moves the short-run equilibrium point from a to b. Output rises to Q_b and price increases to p'. The rise in market price causes the demand curve facing the firm to rise from d to d' in panel (a). The firm responds by increasing output to q' and earns an ecomonic profit, identified by the shaded rectangle. With existing firms earning economic profits, new firms enter the industry in the long run. Market supply shifts out to S' in panel (b). Output rises further, to Q_c, and price falls back to p. In panel (a), the firm's demand curve shifts back to d, eliminating economic profits. The short-run adjustment is from point a to point b in panel (b), but the long-run adjustment is from point a to point c.

ket demand curve at point a in panel (b). The market–clearing price is p and the market quantity is Q_a. The individual firm, shown in panel (a), supplies q at that market price, earning a normal profit in this long-run equilibrium. Each firm earns a normal profit by producing at a point where price, or marginal revenue, equals marginal cost, short-run average total cost, and long–run average cost, as shown at output rate q in panel (a). (Remember, a normal profit is included in the firm's average total cost curve.)

Now suppose the market demand for this product increases from D to D', causing the market price to increase in the short run to p'. Each firm responds to the higher price by expanding output along its short–run supply, or marginal-cost, curve until quantity supplied is q'. At that rate of output, the firm's marginal cost intersects the new marginal revenue curve, which is also the firm's new demand curve, d'. Because all firms expand production, industry output increases to Q_b, where the change in industry quantity is the sum of the changes of all the individual firms in the industry. Note that in the short run, each firm is now earning an economic profit, shown by the shaded rectangle in panel (a).

In the long run, economic profit attracts new firms. Their entry adds additional supply to the market, shifting out the market supply curve, which causes the market price to fall. Firms continue to enter as long as they can earn an economic profit. The market supply curve eventually shifts out to S', where supply intersects D' at point c, returning the price to its initial equilibrium level, p. The decline in the market price has dropped the demand curve facing the individual firm from d' back down to d. As a result, each firm reduces output from q' back to q and once again each earns just a normal profit. Notice that although industry output increases from Q_a to Q_c, each firm's output returns to q. In our example, the additional output comes from new firms attracted to the industry rather than from greater output from existing firms. Existing firms could not expand without increasing their long-run average costs.

New firms are attracted to the industry by the short-run economic profits arising from the increase in demand. The resulting increase in market supply, however, decreases the price and drives the profits of new and existing firms down to the normal level. In Exhibit 10(b), the short-run adjustment in response to increased demand is from point a to point b; in the long run, the market equilibrium moves to point c.

Effects of a Decrease in Demand. Next, we consider the effect of a decrease in demand on the long-run market adjustment process. The initial long-run equilibrium situation in Exhibit 11 is the same as in Exhibit 10. Market demand and

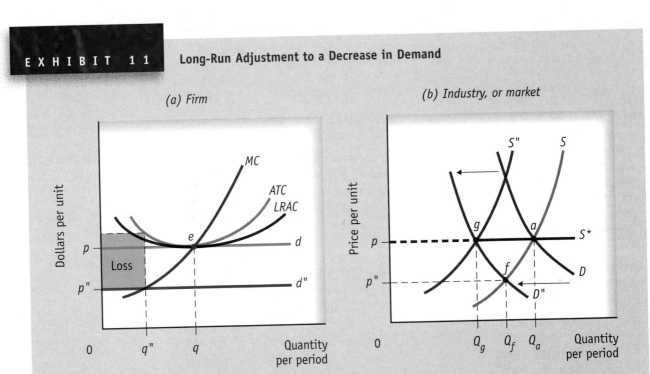

EXHIBIT 11   Long-Run Adjustment to a Decrease in Demand

(a) Firm

(b) Industry, or market

A decrease in demand to D'' in panel (b) disturbs the long-run equilibrium at point a. Prices are driven down to p'' in the short run; output falls to Q_f. In panel (a), the firm's demand curve shifts down to d''. Each firm reduces its output to q'' and suffers a loss. As firms leave the industry in the long run, the market supply curve shifts left to S''. Market prices rise to p as output falls further to Q_g. At price p, the remaining firms once again earn zero economic profit. Thus, the short-run adjustment is from point a to point f in panel (b); the long-run adjustment is from point a to point g.

supply intersect at point a in panel (b) to yield an equilibrium price of p and an equilibrium quantity of Q_a. The firm in panel (a) earns a normal profit in the long run by producing output level q, where price, or marginal revenue, equals marginal cost, short-run average cost, and long-run average cost.

Now suppose that the demand for this product declines, as reflected in panel (b) by the shift to the left in the market demand curve, from D back to D''. In the short run, this decline in demand reduces the market price to p''. As a result, the demand curve facing each individual firm drops from d to d''. Each firm responds in the short run by cutting its output to q'', where marginal cost equals the now-lower marginal revenue, or price. Market output falls to Q_f. Each firm operates at a loss, a loss reflected by the shaded rectangle in panel (a), because the lower market price is below short-run average total cost (though the price must still be above average variable cost, since the firm's short-run supply curve, MC, is defined as that portion of the firm's marginal-cost curve at or above its average variable cost curve).

In the long run, continued losses force some firms out of the industry. As firms leave, market supply decreases, or shifts to the left, so the market price increases. Firms continue to leave until the market supply decreases to S'', where supply intersects D'' at point g. Output has fallen to Q_g, and price has returned to p. With the price back up to p, the remaining firms once again earn a normal profit. At the conclusion of the adjustment process, each remaining firm produces q, the initial equilibrium quantity, but because some firms have left the industry, market output has fallen from Q_a to Q_g. Note that the adjustment process involves the departure of firms from the industry rather than a reduction in the scale of firms; a reduction in scale would have increased each firm's long-run average cost.

THE LONG-RUN SUPPLY CURVE

Thus far, we have looked at the industry and firm responses to changes in demand, distinguishing between a short-run adjustment and a long-run adjustment. In the short run, firms alter quantity supplied by moving up or down their marginal cost curves (that portion at or rising above average variable cost) until marginal cost equals marginal revenue, or price. If no price covers average variable cost, firms shut down in the short run. The long-run adjustment, however, involves the entry or exit of firms until the new short-run market supply curve generates an equilibrium price that provides remaining firms with normal profit.

In Exhibits 10 and 11, we began with an initial long-run equilibrium point and were able to identify two more long-run equilibrium points generated by the intersection of the shifted demand curve and the shifted short-run market supply curve. In each case, the price remained the same in the long run, but industry output increased in panel (b) of Exhibit 10 and decreased in panel (b) of Exhibit 11. Connecting these long-run equilibrium points yields the *long-run industry supply curve,* labeled S^* in Exhibits 10 and 11. The **long-run industry supply curve** shows the relationship between price and quantity supplied once firms have fully adjusted to any short-term economic profit or loss resulting from a shift in market demand.

Long-run industry supply curve A curve that shows the relationship between price and quantity supplied once firms fully adjust to any change in market demand

Constant-Cost Industries

The industry we have depicted thus far is called a **constant-cost industry** because the minimum average cost on the firm's long run average cost curve does not change as industry output changes. Resource prices and other production costs remain constant in the long run as industry output increases or decreases. In a constant-cost industry, each firm's production costs are independent of the number of firms in the industry, so minimum average cost remains constant in the long run as firms enter or leave the industry. *The long-run supply curve for a constant-cost industry is horizontal,* as is depicted in Exhibits 10 and 11.

A constant-cost industry is most often characterized as one that hires only a small portion of the resources available in the resource market. Firms need not increase the price paid for resources to draw them away from competing uses, because firms in this industry hire only a small share of the resources available. For example, output in the pencil industry can expand without bidding up the prices of wood, graphite, and synthetic rubber, since the pencil industry uses such a small share of the market supply of these resources.

Increasing-Cost Industries

Net Bookmark Firms in increasing-cost industries, such as housing construction, in the long run encounter increased production costs as output expands. To learn more about the economics of housing construction, visit the National Association of Home Builders (NAHB) (**http://www.nahb.com/**).

The firms in some industries encounter higher average costs as industry output expands in the long run. Firms in these **increasing-cost industries** find that expanding output bids up the prices of some resources or otherwise increases production costs, and these higher production costs shift each firm's cost curves upward. For example, an expansion of the oil industry could bid up the price of drilling equipment and the wages of petroleum engineers and geologists, raising production costs for each oil exploration firm. Likewise, an expansion of the housing-construction industry could bid up the price of lumber, roofing materials, and carpenters.

To illustrate the equilibrium adjustment process for an increasing-cost industry, we begin again in long-run equilibrium in panel (b) of Exhibit 12, where the industry demand curve, D, intersects the short-run industry supply curve, S, at equilibrium point a to yield the market price p_a and the market quantity Q_a. When the price is p_a, the demand (and marginal revenue) curve facing each firm is d_a in panel (a). The firm produces the rate of output at which marginal cost equals price, or marginal revenue, shown by point a in panel (a). At the firm's equilibrium rate of output, q, average total cost is at a minimum, so average total cost equals the price and the firm earns no economic profit in this long-run equilibrium.

Suppose an increase in the demand for this product shifts the market demand curve to the right from D to D' in panel (b). The new demand curve intersects the short-run market supply curve S at point b, yielding the short-run equilibrium price p_b and quantity Q_b. With an increase in the equilibrium price, each firm's demand curve shifts from d_a up to d_b in panel (a). The new equilibrium in the short run occurs at point b in panel (a), where the marginal cost curve intersects the new demand curve, which is also the marginal revenue curve. Each firm produces output q_b. In the short run, each firm earns an economic profit equal to q_b times the difference between the price, p_b, and the average total cost at that rate of output.

Economic profit attracts new entrants. So far, the sequence of events is the same as for a constant-cost industry. Because this is an increasing-cost industry,

Constant-cost industry An industry that can expand or contract without affecting the long-run per-unit cost of production; the long-run industry supply curve is horizontal

Increasing-cost industry An industry that faces higher per-unit production costs as industry output expands in the long run; the long-run industry supply curve slopes upward

An Increasing-Cost Industry   **E X H I B I T   1 2**

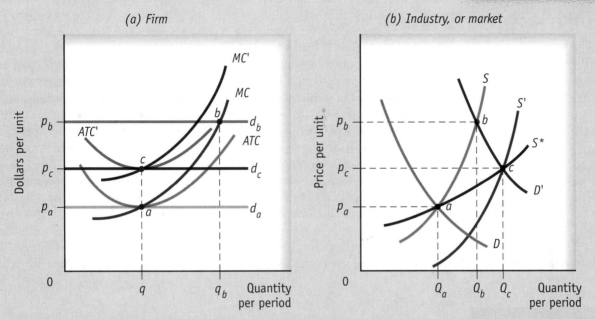

(a) Firm   *(b) Industry, or market*

An increase in demand to D' in panel (b) disturbs the initial equilibrium at point a. A short-run equilibrium is established at point b, where D' intersects the short-run market supply curve, S. At the higher price, p_b, the firm's demand curve shifts up to d_b, and its output increases to q_b in panel (a). At point b, the firm is earning an economic profit. New firms enter to try to capture some of the profits. As they do so, input prices are bid up, so each firm's marginal and average cost curves rise. The intersection of the new market supply curve, S', with D' determines the market price, p_c. At p_c, individual firms are earning zero economic profit. Point c is a point of long-run equilibrium. By connecting long-run equilibrium points a and c in panel (b), we obtain the upward-sloping long-run market supply curve, S^*, for this increasing-cost industry.

however, new entry and industry expansion drive up the cost of production, raising each firm's marginal and average cost curves. In panel (a) of Exhibit 12, MC and ATC shift up to MC' and ATC'. (For ease of exposition, we assume that the new cost curves are parallel to the old curves, so the minimum efficient plant size remains the same.)

The entry of new firms also shifts out the short-run industry supply curve, thus reducing the market price of output. *New firms enter the industry until the combination of a higher production cost and a lower output price squeezes economic profit to zero.* This equilibrium occurs when new entry has shifted the short-run industry supply curve out to S', which lowers the price until it equals the minimum on the firm's new average total cost curve. The market price does not fall to the initial equilibrium level, because each firm's average total cost curve has shifted up. The intersection of the new short-run market supply curve, S', and the increased market demand curve, D', determines the new long-run market equilibrium point, identified as point c. Points a and c are on the *upward-sloping* long-run supply curve, denoted as S^*, for this increasing-cost industry.

For firms in constant-cost industries, each firm's costs depend simply on the scale of its plant and its choice of output level. For firms in increasing-cost industries, costs depend also on the number of firms in the market. By bidding up the price of resources, long-run expansion increases each firm's production costs. The long-run supply curve for an increasing-cost industry slopes upward, like S^* in Exhibit 12.

Decreasing-Cost Industries

Decreasing-cost industry The rare case in which an industry faces lower per-unit production costs as industry output expands in the long run; the long-run industry supply curve slopes downward

Firms in some industries may experience lower production costs as output expands in the long run, *though this is extremely rare*. Firms in **decreasing-cost industries** find that as industry output expands, the cost of production falls, causing a downward shift in each firm's cost curves. For example, in the coal-mining industry, a major cost is pumping water out of the mine shafts. As more mines in the same area begin operating pumps, the water table in the area falls, so each mine's pumping costs go down.

An increase in market demand results in a higher price in the short run, so firms earn economic profit. This profit attracts new entrants in the long run, reducing production costs for all firms in the industry. Decreasing-cost industries have long-run supply curves like the one depicted in Exhibit 13, where point *a* is the initial equilibrium, point *b* is the short-run adjustment to an increase in demand, and point *c* is the long-run equilibrium adjustment as new firms are

E X H I B I T   1 3   **A Decreasing-Cost Industry Adjusts to an Increase in Demand**

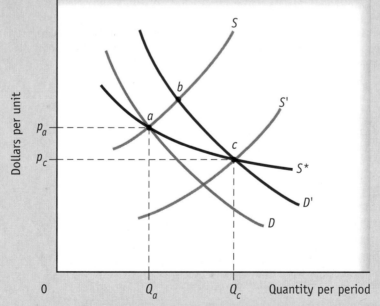

An increase in market demand moves the industry from starting point *a* to short-run equilibrium at point *b*. With each firm earning an economic profit, new firms begin to enter. If entry drives down the average cost of production, long-run equilibrium will be reestablished at point *c*, with a lower price than at point *a*. Connecting long-run equilibrium points *a* and *c* yields the downward-sloping long-run market supply curve, S^*, for this decreasing-cost industry.

attracted by short-run profits. In the long run, the price, p_c, falls below the initial price, p_a. Entry eliminates economic profit by driving down the price.

In summary, firms in perfect competition can earn an economic profit, a normal profit, or economic loss in the short run, but in the long run the entry or exit of firms drives economic profit to zero so that firms earn only a normal profit. This is true whether the industry in question exhibits constant costs, increasing costs, or decreasing costs. Notice that regardless of the nature of costs in the industry, the industry supply curve is less elastic in the short run than in the long run. In the long run, firms can adjust all their resources, so they are better able to respond to changes in price.

We mentioned at the outset that perfect competition serves as a useful benchmark for evaluating the efficiency of markets. Let's examine the qualities of perfect competition that make it so useful.

PERFECT COMPETITION AND EFFICIENCY

There are two concepts of efficiency used in judging market performance. The first, called *productive efficiency,* refers to the notion of efficiency developed in the production possibilities curve introduced in Chapter 2. The second, called *allocative efficiency,* emphasizes the choice of goods to be produced and the distribution of these goods among consumers.

Productive Efficiency

Productive efficiency occurs when the firm produces at the minimum point on its long-run average-cost curve. In the long run in perfect competition, the entry and exit of firms and any adjustment in the scale of each firm ensure that each firm produces at the minimum point on its long-run average cost curve. Firms whose size is not at the minimum efficient level must either alter their size or leave the industry to avoid continued losses. Thus, the long-run industry output in perfect competition is produced at the least possible cost per unit.

Productive efficiency The condition that exists when output is produced with the least-cost combination of inputs, given the level of technology

Allocative Efficiency

The fact that goods are produced at the least possible cost does not mean that the *allocation* of resources is the most efficient one possible. It may be that the goods being produced are not the ones consumers most prefer. This situation is akin to that of the airline pilot who informs the passengers that there is some good news and some bad news: "The good news is that we're making record time; the bad news is that we're lost!" Firms may be producing goods efficiently, yet producing the wrong goods. **Allocative efficiency** occurs when firms produce the output that is most preferred by consumers.

How do we know that perfect competition guarantees that the goods produced are those most preferred by consumers? The answer lies with the demand and supply curves. You'll recall that the demand curve reflects the marginal value that consumers attach to each unit, so the price is the amount of money that people are willing and able to pay for the final unit they consume. We also know that, in both the short run and the long run, the equilibrium price in perfect competition equals the marginal cost of supplying the last unit sold. Marginal cost measures the opportunity cost of using those resources in their best

Allocative efficiency The condition that exists when firms produce the output that is most preferred by consumers; the marginal cost of each good just equals the marginal benefit that consumers derive from that good alternative use. Thus, supply and demand intersect at the combination of price and quantity at which the opportunity cost of the resources employed to produce the last unit of output just equals the marginal value, or the marginal benefit, that consumers attach to that unit of output.

As long as marginal cost equals marginal benefit, the last unit produced is valued as much as, or more than, any other good that could have been produced using those same resources. There is no way to reallocate resources to increase the value of output. Thus, there is no way to reallocate resources to increase the total utility or total benefit consumers enjoy from output. *When the marginal cost of each good equals the marginal benefit that consumers derive from that good, the market is said to be allocatively efficient.*

Gains from Voluntary Exchange through Competitive Markets

If the marginal cost to firms of supplying the good just equals the marginal benefit to consumers, does this mean that market exchange confers no net benefits to participants? No! Market exchange usually benefits both consumers and producers. Recall that consumers garner a surplus from market exchange because the maximum amount they would be willing to pay for each unit of the good exceeds the amount they in fact pay. Exhibit 14 depicts a market in short-run equilibrium. The consumer surplus in this exhibit is represented by the blue shaded area, which is below the demand curve but above the market-clearing price of $10.

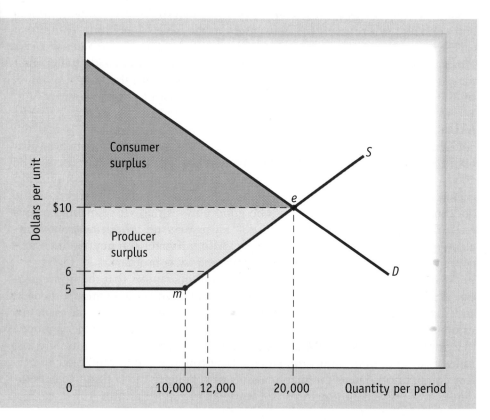

EXHIBIT 14

Consumer Surplus and Producer Surplus for a Competitive Market in the Short Run

Consumer surplus is represented by the area above the market-clearing price of $10 per unit and below the demand curve; it is shown as a blue triangle. Producer surplus is represented by the area above the short-run market supply curve and below the market-clearing price of $10 per unit; it is shown by the gold shading. At a price of $5 per unit, there is no producer surplus. At a price of $6 per unit, producer surplus is the shaded area between $5 and $6.

Producers in the short run also usually derive a net benefit, or a surplus, from market exchange, because the amount they receive for their output exceeds the minimum amount they would require to supply that amount of the good in the short run. Recall that the short-run market supply curve is the sum of that portion of each firm's marginal cost curve at or above the minimum point on its average variable cost curve. Point *m* in Exhibit 14 is the minimum point on the market supply curve; it indicates that at a price of $5, firms are willing to supply 10,000 units. At prices below $5, quantity supplied is zero. At point *m*, firms in this industry gain no net benefit from production in the short run, because the total industry revenue derived from selling 10,000 units at $5 each just covers the variable cost incurred by producing that amount of output.

If the price increases to $6, firms increase their quantity supplied until their marginal cost equals $6. Market output increases from 10,000 to 12,000 units. Total revenue increases from $50,000 to $72,000. Part of the increased revenue covers the higher marginal cost of production. But the balance of the increased revenue is a bonus to producers, who would have been willing to supply 10,000 units for only $5 each. When the price is $6, they get to sell these 10,000 units for $6 each rather than $5 each. Thus, the producer surplus is the shaded area between $5 and $6. At higher prices, the producer surplus is greater because firms get to sell all their output for the higher price even though they would have been willing to offer most of it for a lower price.

In the short run, **producer surplus** is the total revenue producers are paid for a commodity minus their total variable cost of producing the commodity. In Exhibit 14, the market-clearing price is $10 per unit, and the producer surplus is depicted by the area under the price but above the market supply curve. That area represents the market price minus the marginal cost of each unit produced. Allocative efficiency occurs at point *e*, which is the combination of price and quantity that maximizes the sum of consumer surplus and producer surplus.

Producer surplus The amount by which total revenue from production exceeds total variable cost

Note that producer surplus is not the same as economic profit. Any price that exceeds the average variable cost will result in a short-run producer surplus, even though that price could result in a short-run economic loss. The definition of producer surplus ignores fixed cost, because fixed cost is irrelevant to the firm's short-run production decision. Firms cannot avoid paying fixed cost in the short run, no matter what they do. Fixed costs are *sunk* in the short run because the firm must pay them whether or not the firm produces. Only variable cost matters. For each firm, the marginal cost is the increase in total variable cost as output increases, and the sum of the marginal costs for all units is the total variable cost.

Producer surplus is more easily observed in the short run than in the long run. If producer surplus is defined narrowly as total revenue minus total variable cost, producer surplus in the long run for perfectly competitive industries is zero. In long-run equilibrium, all costs are variable and total cost equals total revenue, so there is no producer surplus. But for increasing-cost industries, the definition of producer surplus is often broadened to include the higher incomes to those resource owners whose pay rates increase when industry demand increases. For example, suppose an increase in the world's demand for grain drives up the rental price of farm acreage. Owners of such land earn more as the rental price increases; they earn a producer surplus. Or suppose an increase in the popularity of professional sports drives up the pay of professional athletes. These pros could be thought of as earning producer surplus.

The combination of consumer surplus and producer surplus shows the gains from voluntary exchange. Even though marginal cost equals marginal benefit in equilibrium, both consumers and producers usually garner a bonus, or a surplus, from market exchange. The gains from market exchange have been examined in an experimental setting, as is discussed in the following case study.

CASE STUDY

Experimental Economics

Location:

The University of Iowa College of Business Administration runs the Iowa Electronic Markets (IEM), a computerized futures market operated over the Internet. Contract payoffs are based on real-world events such as political outcomes, companies' earnings per share (eps), and stock price returns. For example, participants around the globe bought and sold contracts concerning the nominee at the 1996 Republican national convention. Pictured here are two candidates for the Republican nomination for president, Malcolm Forbes, Jr., and Robert Dole. The IEM provide a valuable source of experimental economic data over the Internet. See for yourself—visit the "Iowa Electronic Markets" (http://www. biz.uiowa. edu/iem/index. html).

Economists have limited opportunities to carry out the kind of controlled experiments available in the physical and biological sciences. But about four decades ago, Professor Vernon Smith, now at the University of Arizona, began some experiments to see how quickly and how efficiently a group of test subjects could achieve market equilibrium. His original experiment involved 22 students, 11 of whom were designated as "buyers" and 11 as "sellers." Each buyer was given a card indicating the value of purchasing one unit of a hypothetical commodity; these values ranged downward from $3.25 to $0.75, forming a downward-sloping demand curve. Each seller was given a card indicating the cost of providing one unit of that commodity; these costs ranged upward from $0.75 to $3.25, forming an upward-sloping supply curve. Buyers and sellers knew only what was on their own cards.

To provide market incentives, participants were told they would receive a cash bonus at the end of the experiment based on the difference between their cost or their value and the price they negotiated in the open market. As a way of trading, Smith established a system in which any buyer or seller announced a bid or an offer to the entire group—a system called a *double continuous auction*—based on rules similar to those governing stock markets and commodity exchanges. A transaction occurred whenever any buyer accepted an offer or when any seller accepted a bid. *Smith found that the price quickly converged to the market-clearing level,* which in this experiment was $2.00.

Smith and his followers have since performed thousands of experiments testing the properties of markets. The experiments show that under most circumstances, markets are extremely efficient in moving goods from the lowest-cost producers to the consumers who place the highest value on the goods. This maximizes the sum of consumer and producer surplus and thus maximizes social welfare. One surprising finding is how few participants are required to establish a market price. Most such experiments use only four buyers and four sellers, each capable of trading several units. Some experiments use only two sellers, yet the competitive equilibrium model performs quite well under double-auction rules.

Incidentally, most U.S. retail markets, such as supermarkets and department stores, use *posted-offer pricing*—that is, the price is marked, not negotiated. Experiments show that posted pricing does not adjust to changing market conditions as quickly as does a double continuous auction. Despite their slow response times, posted prices may be the choice for large, stable markets, because posted pricing involves low transaction costs. In contrast, continuous-auction pricing involves high transaction costs, requiring in the case of stock and commodity markets thousands of people in full-time negotiations to maintain prices at an equilibrium level.

Experiments have provided an empirical foundation for economic theory and have yielded insights about how market rules affect market outcomes. They have also helped shape markets that did not exist, such as the market for pollution rights or for broadcast spectrum rights. Finally, experiments offer a safe and inexpensive way for those in emerging market economies, such as Poland, Russia, and Hungary, to learn how markets work.

Sources: Vernon Smith and Arlington Williams, "Experimental Market Economics," *Scientific American* (December 1992): pp. 116–21; Vernon Smith, "Experimental Methods in Economics," *The New Palgrave Dictionary of Economics,* Vol. 2, J. Eatwell et al., eds. (New York: Stockton Press, 1987), pp. 241–49; and Vernon Smith, "Economics in the Laboratory," *Journal of Economic Perspectives* 8 (Winter 1994): pp. 113–34.

CONCLUSION

Let's review the assumptions of a perfectly competitive market and see how they relate to ideas developed in this chapter. *First,* there must be many buyers and many sellers. This is necessary so that no individual buyer or seller is large enough to influence the price (though recent experiments show that the large-number assumption may be stronger than it needs to be). *Second,* firms must produce a homogeneous product. If consumers could distinguish among the output of different producers, they might prefer one firm's product even at a higher price, so different producers could sell at different prices. In that case, not every firm would be a price taker—that is, the firms' demand curves would no longer be horizontal. *Third,* all market participants must have full information about all prices and all production processes. Otherwise, some producers could charge more than the market price, and some uninformed consumers would pay that higher price. Also, through ignorance, some firms might select outdated technology or fail to recognize the opportunity for short-run economic profits. *Fourth,* all resources must be mobile in the long run, and there must be no obstacles preventing new firms from moving into profitable markets. Otherwise, some firms could earn economic profits in the long run.

Perfect competition is not the form of market structure most commonly observed in the real world. The markets for agricultural products, stocks, commodities such as gold and silver, and foreign exchange come close to being perfect. But even if no single example of perfect competition could be found, the model would be a useful tool for analyzing market behavior. As you will see in the next two chapters, perfect competition provides a valuable benchmark for evaluating the efficiency of other market structures.

SUMMARY

1. Market structure describes important features of the economic environment in which firms operate. These features include the number of competing firms, the ease or difficulty of entering the market, the similarities or differences in the output produced by each firm, and the forms of competition among firms. As we will see in the next two chapters, there are four types of market structure. This chapter examined perfect competition.

2. Perfectly competitive markets are characterized by (1) a large number of buyers and sellers; (2) production of a homogeneous product; (3) full information about the availability and price of all resources, goods, and technologies; and (4) free and complete mobility of resources. Firms in such markets are said to be price takers because no individual firm can influence the price. Individual firms can vary only the amount they choose to sell at the market price.

3. The market price in perfect competition is determined by the intersection of the market demand and market supply curves. Each firm then faces a demand curve that is a horizontal line drawn at the market price. Because this demand curve is horizontal, it represents the average revenue and the marginal revenue the firm receives at each level of output.

4. The perfectly competitive firm maximizes profits or minimizes losses by producing where marginal cost equals marginal revenue. That portion of the firm's marginal cost curve at or above the average variable cost curve is the firm's short-run supply curve. Fixed cost, or sunk cost, is irrelevant in the short-run production decision. The horizontal summation of all firms' supply curves forms the market supply curve.

5. Because firms are not free to enter or leave the market in the short run, economic profit or loss is possible in the short run. In the long run, however, some firms will adjust their scale of operations and other firms will enter or leave the market until economic profit or loss is driven to zero. In the long run, each firm will produce at the lowest point on its long-run average cost curve. At this level of output, the marginal cost, marginal revenue, price, and average total cost are all equal. Firms that fail to produce at this least-cost combination will not survive in the long run.

6. In the short run, a firm alters quantity supplied in response to a change in price by moving up or down its marginal cost curve. The long-run industry adjustment to a change in demand involves firms' entering or leaving the market until the remaining firms in the industry earn just a normal profit. As the industry expands in the long run, the industry supply curve reflects either increasing costs, constant costs, or decreasing costs.

7. Perfectly competitive markets reflect both productive efficiency, because output is produced using the most efficient combination of resources available, and allocative efficiency, because the goods produced are those most valued by consumers. In equilibrium, perfectly competitive markets allocate goods so that the marginal cost of the last unit produced equals the marginal value that consumers attach to that last unit purchased. Voluntary exchange in competitive markets maximizes consumer surplus and producer surplus.

QUESTIONS AND PROBLEMS

1. **(Market Structure)** Define market structure. What factors are considered in determining the market structure of a particular industry?

2. **(Demand in Perfect Competition)** What type of demand curve does a perfectly competitive firm face for its product? Why?

3. **(Perfect Competition)** Some people have claimed that there is strong competition in the U.S. auto market. Give some reasons why this market could not be considered perfectly competitive.

4. **(Short-Run Profit Maximization)** Assume that a perfectly competitive firm has the following fixed and variable costs in the short run. The market price for the firm's product is $150.
   a. Complete the following table:

Output	FC	VC	TC	TR	Profit/ Loss
0	$100	$ 0	____	____	_____
1	100	100	____	____	_____
2	100	180	____	____	_____
3	100	300	____	____	_____
4	100	440	____	____	_____
5	100	600	____	____	_____
6	100	780	____	____	_____

   b. At what output level does the firm maximize profit or minimize loss?
   c. What is the firm's marginal revenue at each positive level of output? Its average revenue?
   d. What do you know about the relationship between marginal revenue and marginal cost for output units below the profit-maximizing (or loss-minimizing) level? For units above the profit-maximizing (or loss-minimizing) level?

5. **(Total Revenue)** Consider Exhibit 3(a) in this chapter. Explain why the total revenue curve is a straight line from the origin, whereas the slope of the total cost curve changes.

6. **(Profit Maximization)** Consider Exhibit 3(b) in this chapter. Why doesn't the firm choose the output that maximizes average profits (i.e., the output for which average cost is the lowest)?

7. **(Price and Marginal Revenue)** Explain why price and marginal revenue are identical in the perfectly competitive model.

8. **(Short-Run Production Decision)** Each of the following situations could exist for a firm in the short run. In each case, indicate whether (a) the firm should produce in the short run, (b) the firm should shut down in the short run, or (c) additional information is needed to determine whether or not to produce in the short run.

_____ Total cost exceeds total revenue at all output levels.
_____ Total variable cost exceeds total revenue at all output levels.
_____ Total revenue exceeds total fixed cost at all output levels.
_____ Marginal revenue exceeds marginal cost at the current output level.
_____ Price exceeds average total cost at all output levels.
_____ Average variable cost exceeds price at all output levels.
_____ Average total cost exceeds price at all output levels.

9. **(Entry and Exit of Firms)** Why is it reasonable that the competitive model does not allow for the entry of firms in the short run?

10. **(Long-Run Industry Supply)** Why does the long-run industry supply curve for an increasing-cost industry slope upward? What causes the increasing costs in an increasing-cost industry?

11. **(Competitive Equilibrium)** Draw the short- and long-run cost curves of a competitive firm in long-run equilibrium. Indicate the equilibrium price and quantity.
   a. Discuss the firm's short-run response to a reduction in the price of a variable resource.
   b. Assuming that the industry is a constant-cost industry, describe the process by which the industry returns to long-run equilibrium.

12. **(Short-Run Competitive Supply)** An individual competitive firm's short-run supply curve is the portion of its marginal cost curve that equals or rises above the average variable cost. Explain why this is true.

13. **(Short-Run Competitive Supply)** Use the following data to answer the questions below:

Q	TVC	Q	TVC
1	$10	5	$31
2	16	6	38
3	20	7	46
4	25	8	55
		9	65

   a. Calculate the marginal cost for each level of production.
   b. Calculate the average variable cost for each level of production.
   c. How much would the firm produce if it could sell its product for $5? for $7? for $10? Explain your answers.
   d. Assuming that its fixed cost is $3, calculate the firm's profit at each of the production levels determined in part c.

14. **(Long-Run Competitive Behavior)** Suppose that a constant-cost industry consists entirely of firms with U-shaped long-run average cost curves. Explain why variation in industry output in response to changes in demand must, in the long run, come from variation in the number of firms rather than from variation in the scale of production by firms in the industry.

15. **(Gains from Exchange in Perfect Competition)** Use the data below to answer the following questions.

Quantity	Marginal Cost	Marginal Valuation
0	—	—
1	$ 2	$10
2	3	9
3	4	8
4	5	7
5	6	6
6	8	5
7	10	4
8	12	3
9	15	2
10	18	1

   a. For the product shown above, assume that the minimum point of the firm's average variable cost curve occurs at $2. Construct a supply and demand diagram for the product and indicate the equilibrium price and quantity.
   b. On the graph, label the area of consumer surplus as *f*. Label the area of producer surplus as *g*.
   c. If the equilibrium price were $2, what would be the amount of producer surplus?

16. **(Short-Run and Long-Run Equilibrium)** Consider a normal good that is produced in a constant-cost, perfectly competitive industry. Initially, the firm is in long-run equilibrium.

    a. Graphically illustrate and explain the short-run adjustments of the market and the firm to a decrease in consumer incomes. Be sure to discuss any changes in output levels, prices, profits, and/or the number of firms.

    b. Next, show on your graph and explain the long-run adjustment to the income change. Be sure to discuss any changes in output levels, prices, profits, and/or the number of firms.

17. **(Decreasing-Cost and Increasing-Cost Industries)**

    a. The graph below shows possible long-run market supply curves for a perfectly competitive industry. Identify which supply curve indicates a constant-cost industry, an increasing-cost industry, and a decreasing industry.

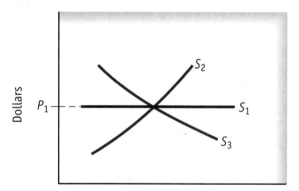

    b. Explain the difference between a decreasing-cost industry and an increasing-cost industry.

    c. Distinguish between the long-run impact of an increase in market demand in a decreasing-cost industry versus an increasing-cost industry.

18. **(Productive Efficiency and Allocative Efficiency)** Define productive efficiency and allocative efficiency. What conditions must be met in order to achieve them?

19. **(Auction Markets)** Which of the characteristics of the perfectly competitive market structure are found in the Amsterdam flower market?

20. **(Experimental Economics)** In the University of Arizona experiment, which "buyers" ended up with a surplus at the market-clearing price of $2? Which "sellers" had a surplus? Which "buyers" or "sellers" did not engage in a transaction?

Using the Internet

21. When the federal government, through the Federal Communications Commission (FCC), decided to auction licenses to use the radio spectrum for broadband communications services (cellular phones, wireless computer and faxes, and the like), it needed to ensure that the billion dollar auction ran effectively. The solution? Visit the FCC and look within "Auctions" (**http://www.fcc.gov/**). Also review "Historic FCC Auction Uses New Economic Design," by Mary E. Hanson and maintained by the National Science Foundation (**http://www.nsf.gov/nsf/press/pr9479.htm**) and "Access to the Airwaves: Going, Going, Gone," by Kathleen O'Toole and maintained by the Stanford School of Business (**http://gsb-www.stanford.edu/sbsm/sbsm62404a.html**). Briefly discuss the type of auction the FCC used. What is the economic effect of such an auction?

Monopoly

*M*onopoly is a Greek word meaning "one seller." Monopolists sell electricity, cable TV service, postage stamps, local phone service in most markets, food at sports arenas, and other products with no close substitutes. You have probably heard about the evils of monopoly. You may have even played the board game, Monopoly, on a rainy day. In this chapter, we will sort out fact from fiction.

Pure monopoly, like perfect competition, is not as common as other market structures. But by understanding monopoly, we will shed light on other market structures that lie between perfect competition and pure monopoly. Topics discussed in this chapter include:

- Barriers to entry
- Price elasticity and marginal revenue
- Economic profit in the short run and the long run
- Welfare cost of monopoly
- Price discrimination

Barrier to entry Any impediment that prevents new firms from competing on an equal basis with existing firms in an industry

Patent A legal barrier to entry that conveys to its holder the exclusive right to supply a product for a certain period of time

Innovation The process of turning an invention into a marketable product

Net Bookmark

Over 80 percent of the world's patents are granted by the U.S. Patent and Trademark Office (PTO) (http://www.uspto.gov/), the European Patent Office (http://www.epo.co.at/epo/), and the Japanese Patent Office (http://www.patent-jp.com/JPS.htm). In the United States, the Patent and Trademark Office, a noncommercial federal entity established over 200 years ago, processes patents and trademarks and disseminates patent and trademark information. The PTO also maintains the "U.S. Patent Database" (http://patents.cnidr.org:4242/).

BARRIERS TO ENTRY

Perhaps the single most important feature of a monopolized market is that, because of *barriers to entry,* new firms cannot profitably enter the market in the long run. **Barriers to entry** are restrictions on the entry of new firms into an industry. We will examine three types of barriers: legal restrictions, economies of scale, and the monopolist's control of an essential resource.

Legal Restrictions

One way to prevent new firms from entering a market is to make entry illegal. Patents, licenses, and other legal restrictions imposed by the government provide some producers with legal protection against market entry.

Patents and Invention Incentives. In the United States, a **patent** awards inventors the exclusive right to production for 17 years. Originally enacted in 1790, the patent laws encourage inventors to invest the time and money required to make new discoveries. If others could simply copy successful products, inventors would be less inclined to incur the up-front costs of developing new products and bringing them to the market. Patents also provide the stimulus to turn an invention into a marketable product, a process called **innovation.**

Licenses and Other Entry Restrictions. Governments often confer monopoly status by awarding a single firm the exclusive right to supply particular goods and services. Federal licenses give certain firms the right to broadcast radio and TV signals; state licenses are required to provide services such as medical care, haircuts, and legal assistance. A license is not a monopoly, but it often confers the ability to charge a price above what would be the competitive level. Governments confer monopoly rights to sell hot dogs at civic auditoriums, collect garbage, provide bus and cab service in and out of town, and supply services ranging from electricity to cable TV. The government itself may claim the right to provide certain products by outlawing competitors. For example, many states are monopoly sellers of liquor and lottery tickets, and the U.S. Postal Service has the exclusive right to deliver first-class mail.

Economies of Scale

A monopoly sometimes emerges naturally when a firm experiences *economies of scale* as reflected by a declining average cost curve. When this is the case, a single firm can satisfy the market demand at a lower average cost per unit than could two or more firms operating at smaller levels of output. Thus, a single firm will emerge from the competitive process as the sole seller in the market. Cable TV is an industry that exhibits economies of scale. Once the cable has been installed throughout the community—that is, once costs are sunk—the marginal cost of hooking up each additional household is relatively small. Consequently, the average cost per household declines as more and more households join the existing system.

Because such a monopoly emerges from the nature of production, it is called a *natural monopoly,* to distinguish it from the artificial monopolies created by government patents, licenses, and other legal barriers to entry. A new entrant cannot sell enough output to experience the economies of scale enjoyed by an established natural monopolist, so entry into the market is naturally blocked. We will have more to say about the regulation of natural monopolies in a later chapter, where we examine government regulation of markets.

Control of Essential Resources

Sometimes the source of monopoly power is a firm's control over some non-reproducible resource critical to production. For example, professional sports leagues try to block the formation of competing leagues by signing the best athletes to long-term contracts and by seeking the exclusive use of sports stadiums and arenas. Similarly, the world's diamond trade is operated primarily by De Beers Consolidated Mines, which controls the world's supply of rough diamonds, as is discussed in the following case study.

In 1866, a child walking along the Orange River in South Africa picked up an interesting looking stone that turned out to be a 21-carat diamond. That discovery sparked the development of the greatest diamond mine in history. That mine was owned by De Beers Consolidated Mines, which eventually expanded from mining to buying rough diamonds mined elsewhere around the world. By controlling the supply of rough diamonds, De Beers has attempted to maintain a worldwide monopoly for the last six decades.

De Beers now controls 80 percent of the world's diamond trade—not quite a monopoly, but close to it. The company keeps prices high by carefully limiting supply and promoting market demand. Several times a year, De Beers invites buyers to London, where they are offered a box of diamonds for a set price—no negotiating. If the box of diamonds is not purchased, the buyer may not be invited next time. Because De Beers tries to reduce market competition, the company cannot operate in the United States due to antitrust legislation (which is why U.S. buyers go to London).

It may surprise you that diamonds are not rare gems, either in nature or in jewelry stores. Nearly all jewelry stores offer more diamonds for sale than any other gem. Diamonds may be the most common natural cut gemstone. Jewelers are willing to hold large inventories of diamonds because they are confident that, because of De Beers' supply controls and marketing efforts, the price will not plummet tomorrow. De Beers' slogan is "Diamonds are forever," which implies both that diamonds retain their value and that diamonds should stay in the family. This keeps secondhand diamonds, which are good substitutes for newly cut diamonds, off the market, where they could otherwise increase supply and drive down the price.

The average price for rough diamonds declined in 1995 because of the leakage of rough diamonds from Russia, the world's largest supplier and a country suffering from falling output and triple-digit inflation. The Russian government agreed to sell 95 percent of its diamonds to De Beers, but Russia has apparently

CASE STUDY

Are Diamonds Forever?

Location:

For more than 60 years, De Beers Consolidated Mines has struggled to maintain a worldwide monopoly on the diamond trade. Visit De Beers (http://www.debeers.co.za/). For more about Russia's involvement in the diamond trade, visit "The Mystique of Diamonds," a service of the American Gem Society (http://www.ags.org/mystque.htm).

Are Diamonds Forever?
continued

been selling half its diamonds, and the better stones at that, to independent dealers, leaving the rest for De Beers. A monopoly that relies on the control of a key resource loses its monopoly status once that control slips away.

Sources: Neil Behrmann, "De Beers Diamond Cartel Shows Flaws," *The Wall Street Journal,* 31 October 1994; "Some Diamonds Are Not Forever," *The Economist,* 19 August 1995; and *The World Factbook: 1995–96,* Central Intelligence Agency (Washington: Brassey's, 1995).

Local monopolies are more common than national or international monopolies. In rural areas, monopolies include the only grocery store, movie theater, and restaurant for miles around. But long-lasting monopolies are rare because, as we will see, the economic profit often earned by a monopolist provides others with a powerful incentive to supply close substitutes. Also, over time, technological change tends to break down barriers to entry. For example, the development of wireless transmission of long-distance telephone calls gave rise to competitors for AT&T. Likewise, fax machines, e-mail, the Internet, and firms like Federal Express now compete with the U.S. Postal Service's monopoly on first-class mail, as we will see in a later case study. And the ability to produce synthetic diamonds will create more control problems for De Beers.

REVENUE FOR THE MONOPOLIST

Because the monopoly firm supplies the entire market, the demand curve for goods or services produced by a monopolist is also the market demand curve. The demand curve for the firm's output therefore slopes downward, reflecting the law of demand—price and quantity demanded relate inversely.

Demand and Marginal Revenue

Exhibit 1 shows the downward-sloping market demand curve for a typical monopolist. This monopolist can sell 4 units at a price of $6.75 per unit. That price-quantity combination yields a total revenue of $6.75 × 4, or $27. Total revenue divided by the quantity is the *average revenue per unit,* which in this case is $27/4, or $6.75. (All we have said is that price times quantity equals total revenue, so total revenue divided by quantity equals the price.) Hence, the average revenue per unit is equal to the price.

To sell 5 units, this monopolist must drop the price to $6.50 per unit, for a total revenue of $6.50 × 5, or $32.50 and an average revenue of $6.50. Again, the average revenue equals the price for any level of sales, so *the demand curve is also the monopolist's average-revenue curve,* just as the perfectly competitive firm's demand curve is also that firm's average-revenue curve.

The relationship between price and marginal revenue is different in monopoly than in perfect competition. Recall that for a perfectly competitive firm, marginal revenue is always equal to the market price because each firm can sell as much as it chooses at that price. Now consider the marginal revenue the monopolist receives from selling a fifth unit of the good. When the price drops from $6.75 to $6.50, total revenue goes from $27 to $32.50. Thus, marginal revenue, which is the change in total revenue resulting from selling one more

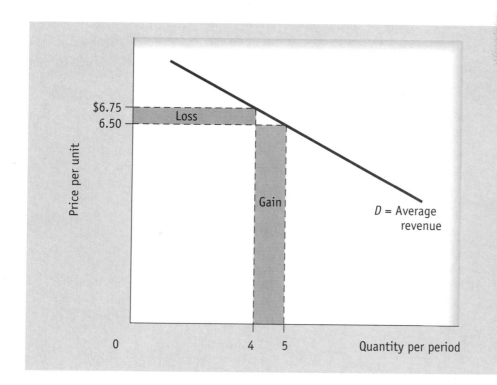

EXHIBIT 1

Monopoly Demand: Loss and Gain in Total Revenue from Selling One More Unit

If a monopolist increases production from 4 units to 5, the revenue for the fifth unit sold is $6.50. However, the monopolist loses $1 on the first 4 units, since each unit must now be priced at $6.50, rather than $6.75. Marginal revenue equals the gain minus the loss, or $6.50 − 1.00 = $5.50. Hence, marginal revenue is $5.50 and is less than the price ($6.50).

unit, is $5.50, which is less than the price, or average revenue, of $6.50. *For a monopolist, the marginal revenue is less than the price, or average revenue.*

The Gain and Loss from Selling One More Unit

A closer look at Exhibit 1 reveals why marginal revenue will be less than the price. The monopolist sells the fifth unit for $6.50, as shown by the vertical rectangle marked *Gain*. To sell a fifth unit, however, the monopolist must offer *all* five units for $6.50 each. Thus, by selling five units at $6.50 each, the firm forgoes the additional $0.25 per unit from selling the first four units for $6.75 each. This reduction in revenue from the first four units totals $1.00 ($0.25 × 4) and is identified in Exhibit 1 by the horizontal rectangle marked *Loss*. The net change in total revenue from selling a fifth unit—that is, the marginal revenue from a fifth unit—equals the *Gain* minus the *Loss*, which equals $6.50 minus $1.00, or $5.50.

As we move down a demand curve, marginal revenue declines for two reasons: (1) the amount received from selling another unit declines (since the price drops), and (2) the revenue forgone by selling all units at this lower price increases (since the quantity that had been sold at a higher price increases). Both factors reduce the marginal revenue as the price falls along a given demand curve.

The numbers behind the demand curve in Exhibit 1 are presented in the first two columns of Exhibit 2. The first column lists quantities of the good, and the second column lists the price, or average revenue, corresponding to each quantity demanded. The two columns together are the demand for the monopolist's good. The monopolist's *total revenue*, which equals price times quan-

EXHIBIT 2

Revenue for a
Monopolist

Quantity per period (Q) (1)	Price (average revenue) (p) (2)	Total Revenue (TR = Q × p) (3) = (1) × (2)	Marginal Revenue $\left(MR = \dfrac{\Delta TR}{\Delta Q} \right)$ (4)
0	$7.75	$ 0.00	——
1	7.50	7.50	$ 7.50
2	7.25	14.50	7.00
3	7.00	21.00	6.50
4	6.75	27.00	6.00
5	6.50	32.50	5.50
6	6.25	37.50	5.00
7	6.00	42.00	4.50
8	5.75	46.00	4.00
9	5.50	49.50	3.50
10	5.25	52.50	3.00
11	5.00	55.00	2.50
12	4.75	57.00	2.00
13	4.50	58.50	1.50
14	4.25	59.50	1.00
15	4.00	60.00	0.50
16	3.75	60.00	0.00
17	3.50	59.50	−0.50

tity, appears in column (3). *Marginal revenue,* the change in total revenue as a result of selling one more unit, is listed in column (4).

Note that only for the first unit sold does marginal revenue equal the price. For additional units of output, marginal revenue is below the price, and the difference between the two grows larger as the price declines. Marginal revenue is negative for prices below $3.75. This means that the revenue gained from selling one more unit is less than the revenue lost from selling all previous units at the lower price.

This analysis assumes that all units of the good sell for the same price; that is, when the price is $6.50, all 5 units must sell for $6.50 each. Although this is often true, later in this chapter we will consider the possibility that a monopolist may be able to charge different prices for different units of the good. At that time, we will revisit a monopolist's marginal revenue.

Revenue Curves

The data in Exhibit 2 are graphed in Exhibit 3, which shows the demand and marginal revenue curves in panel (a) and the total revenue curve in panel (b). Note that the marginal revenue curve is below the demand curve, and that the total revenue curve is at a maximum when marginal revenue is zero. Total revenue, recall, equals price times quantity. Take a minute to study these relationships—they are important.

Earlier you learned that the price elasticity for a straight-line demand curve decreases as you move down the curve. Where demand is elastic—that is,

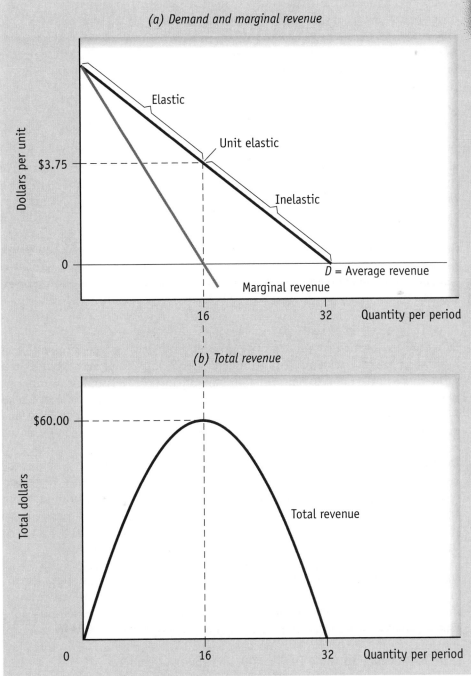

EXHIBIT 3

Monopoly Demand and Marginal and Total Revenue

Where demand is price elastic, marginal revenue is positive, so total revenue increases as the price falls and quantity increases. Where demand is price inelastic, marginal revenue is negative, so total revenue decreases as the price falls and quantity increases. Where demand is unit elastic, marginal revenue is zero, so total revenue is at a maximum, neither increasing nor decreasing.

(a) Demand and marginal revenue

Elastic

Unit elastic

Inelastic

$3.75

0

D = Average revenue

Marginal revenue

16   32   Quantity per period

(b) Total revenue

$60.00

Total revenue

0   16   32   Quantity per period

where the percent increase in quantity demanded more than offsets the percent decrease in price—a decrease in price will increase total revenue. On the other hand, where demand is inelastic, the increase in quantity is not enough to make up for the loss in revenue from a lower price, so total revenue will decline if the price falls. Therefore, *where demand is elastic, marginal revenue is positive, so total revenue increases as the price falls.* Demand is unit elastic at the price of $3.75.

At that price, marginal revenue is zero and total revenue is at a maximum. From Exhibit 3, you can see that marginal revenue becomes negative if the price drops below $3.75, indicating an inelastic demand at price levels below $3.75. *Where demand is inelastic, marginal revenue is negative, so total revenue decreases as the price falls.* Your understanding of elasticity will help later in determining the price and output combination that maximizes the monopolist's profit.

FIRM COSTS AND PROFIT MAXIMIZATION

Given the demand curve, the important question is: How will the monopolist choose among the price-quantity alternatives? We assume that the objective of the monopolist, like that of other firms, is to *maximize economic profit.* In the case of perfect competition, the firm must choose the profit-maximizing *quantity* because the price is already determined by the market. The perfect competitor is a *price taker.* The monopolist, however, can choose either the price or the quantity, but choosing one determines the other. Because the monopolist can select the price that maximizes profit, we say the monopolist is a *price searcher.* More generally, any firm that has some control over the price it charges is a **price searcher.**

Price searcher A firm that has some control over the price it charges because its demand curve slopes downward

Profit Maximization

What are the profit-maximizing price and output levels for a monopolist? Exhibit 4 repeats the revenue data from Exhibits 2 and 3 and also includes the short-run cost data developed in the previous chapter. We assume this monopolist faces the same costs as any other firm. For example, since total cost equals $15 when output is zero, fixed cost must equal $15. Given the cost and revenue data, there are two ways to find the price and quantity that maximize profit.

Total Revenue Minus Total Cost. The profit-maximizing monopolist employs the same decision rule as the competitive firm. *The monopolist must find the production level where total revenue exceeds total cost by the greatest amount.* Economic profit appears in the right-hand column of Exhibit 4. As you can see, the maximum profit is $12.50, which occurs at an output of 10 units and a price of $5.25. At that level of output, total revenue is $52.50 and total cost is $40.00.

Marginal Cost Equals Marginal Revenue. The profit-maximizing monopolist increases output as long as selling additional output adds more to total revenue than to total cost. So the monopolist expands output as long as marginal revenue exceeds marginal cost but must stop before marginal cost exceeds marginal revenue. Again, profit is maximized at $12.50 when output is 10 units. The marginal revenue for unit 10 is $3.00, and the marginal cost is $2.75. Because unit 11 has a marginal cost of $3.25 but a marginal revenue of only $2.50, producing that additional unit would lower profit from $12.50 to $11.75. As you can see, at output levels in excess of 10 units, marginal cost exceeds marginal revenue. For simplicity, we say that *the profit-maximizing output occurs where marginal cost equals marginal revenue.*

Graphical Solution. The cost and revenue data in Exhibit 4 are reflected in Exhibit 5, with per-unit cost and revenue curves in panel (a) and total-cost and

EXHIBIT 4

Short-Run Costs and Revenue for a Monopolist

Quantity per period (Q) (1)	Price (average revenue) (p) (2)	Total Revenue (TR = Q × p) (3) = (1) × (2)	Marginal Revenue ($MR = \frac{\Delta TR}{\Delta Q}$) (4)	Total Cost (TC) (5)	Marginal Cost ($MC = \frac{\Delta TC}{\Delta Q}$) (6)	Average Total Cost ($ATC = \frac{TC}{Q}$) (7)	Total Profit or Loss = TR − TC (8)
0	$7.75	$ 0.00	—	$ 15.00	—	—	−$15.00
1	7.50	7.50	$ 7.50	19.75	$ 4.75	$19.75	−12.25
2	7.25	14.50	7.00	23.50	3.75	11.75	−9.00
3	7.00	21.00	6.50	26.50	3.00	8.83	−5.50
4	6.75	27.00	6.00	29.00	2.50	7.75	−2.00
5	6.50	32.50	5.50	31.00	2.00	6.20	1.50
6	6.25	37.50	5.00	32.50	1.50	5.42	5.00
7	6.00	42.00	4.50	33.75	1.25	4.82	8.25
8	5.75	46.00	4.00	35.25	1.50	4.41	10.75
9	5.50	49.50	3.50	37.25	2.00	4.14	12.25
10	**5.25**	**52.50**	**3.00**	**40.00**	**2.75**	**4.00**	**12.50**
11	5.00	55.00	2.50	43.25	3.25	3.93	11.75
12	4.75	57.00	2.00	48.00	4.75	4.00	9.00
13	4.50	58.50	1.50	54.50	6.50	4.19	4.00
14	4.25	59.50	1.00	64.00	9.50	4.57	−4.50
15	4.00	60.00	0.50	77.50	13.50	5.17	−17.50
16	3.75	60.00	0.00	96.00	18.50	6.00	−36.00
17	3.50	59.50	−0.50	121.00	25.00	7.12	−61.50

total-revenue curves in panel (b). The intersection of the two marginal curves at point *e* in panel (a) indicate that profit is maximized when about 10 units are sold. At that level of output, we move up to the demand curve to find the profit-maximizing price of $5.25. The average total cost of $4.00 is identified by point *b*. The average profit per unit sold equals the price of $5.25 minus the average total cost of $4.00. Economic profit is the average profit per unit of $1.25 multiplied by the 10 units sold, for a total of $12.50, as identified by the shaded rectangle. So the profit-maximizing level of output is found where the rising marginal cost curve intersects the marginal revenue curve. Because no portion of the marginal cost curve will ever be less than zero, marginal cost will never intersect marginal revenue where marginal revenue is negative. Thus, *the monopolist will produce only where the demand curve is elastic.*

In the lower panel, the firm's profit or loss is measured by the vertical distance between the total revenue and total cost curves. The profit-maximizing firm will produce at the level of output where total revenue exceeds total cost by the greatest amount. Put another way, the firm will expand output as long as the increase in total revenue that results from selling one more unit exceeds the increase in total cost that results from producing that unit. The change in

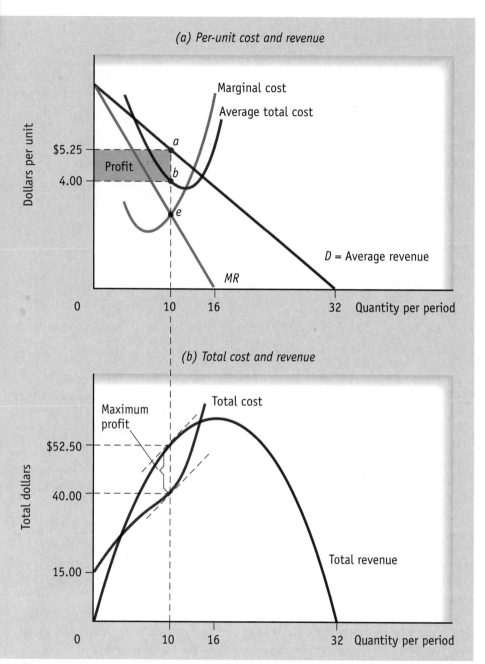

Monopoly Costs and Revenue

The monopolist produces 10 units of output and charges a price of $5.25. Total profit, shown by the blue rectangle in panel (a), is $12.50, the profit per unit multiplied by the number of units sold. In panel (b), profit is maximized where marginal revenue (the slope of the total revenue curve) equals marginal costs (the slope of the total cost curve), at 10 units of output. Profit is total revenue ($52.50) minus total cost ($40.00), or $12.50.

(a) Per-unit cost and revenue

(b) Total cost and revenue

total revenue as a result of a 1-unit change in output equals the marginal revenue, or the slope of the total revenue curve. Likewise, the change in total cost resulting from a 1-unit change in output equals the marginal cost, or the slope of the total cost curve. *The profit-maximizing quantity can be found where the slopes of the total revenue and total cost curves are equal, which is the same as finding the level of output at which marginal cost equals marginal revenue.* In panel (b), you can see that the slopes are equal where output is 10 units.

One common myth is that the monopolist will charge as high a price as possible. But the monopolist is interested in maximizing profit, not price. The amount the monopolist can charge is limited by consumer demand. The monopolist depicted here could have charged a price of $7.50, but only one unit would have been sold at that price. Indeed, the monopolist could have charged $8 per unit, but no output would have been sold. So charging the highest possible price is not consistent with maximizing profit.

Short-Run Losses and the Shutdown Decision

Being a monopolist does not guarantee economic profit. A monopolist is the sole producer of a particular good, but the demand for that good may not be great enough to generate profits in either the short run or the long run. After all, many new products are protected from direct competition by patents, yet many patented products fail to attract enough buyers to survive. And even a monopolist that is initially profitable may eventually suffer losses because of rising costs or falling demand. For example, Coleco, the original mass producer of Cabbage Patch dolls, went bankrupt after that craze died down. In the short run, the loss-minimizing monopolist, like the loss-minimizing perfect competitor, must decide whether to produce or to shut down. *If the price covers average variable cost, the firm will operate. If no price covers average variable cost, the firm will shut down, at least temporarily.*

Loss minimization is illustrated graphically in Exhibit 6, where the marginal cost curve intersects the marginal revenue curve at point *e*. At the equilibrium level of output, *Q*, the price, *p* (at point *b*), is above the average variable cost (at point *c*) but below the average total cost (at point *a*). Since the firm covers its variable cost and makes some contribution to fixed cost, it loses less by producing *Q* than by shutting down. The firm's loss per unit is *ab*, which is the av-

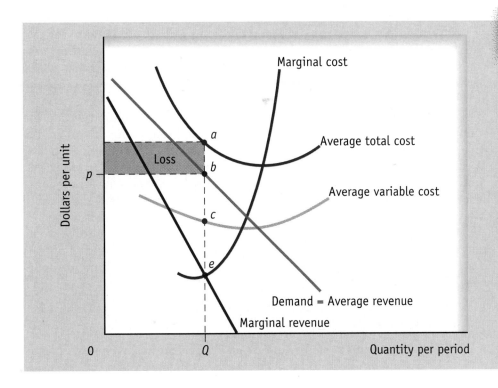

EXHIBIT 6

The Monopolist Minimizes Losses in the Short Run

Marginal cost equals marginal revenue at point *e*. At quantity *Q*, price *p* (at point *b*) is less than average total cost (at point *a*), so the monopolist is suffering a loss. The monopolist will continue to produce in the short run because price is greater than average variable cost (at point *c*).

erage total cost minus the average revenue, or price. The total loss, identified by the shaded rectangle, is the average loss per unit, *ab,* times the number of units sold, Q. The firm will shut down if the average variable cost curve is above the demand curve, or average revenue curve, at all output levels.

Recall that for the perfectly competitive firm, that portion of the marginal cost curve above the average variable cost curve shows how much the firm supplies at each price. Thus, that portion of the marginal cost curve represents a perfect competitor's supply curve. For the monopolist, there is no curve that reflects combinations of price and quantity supplied, so *there is no monopolist supply curve.* The intersection of a monopolist's marginal cost and marginal revenue curves identifies the profit-maximizing (or loss-minimizing) quantity, but the price must be read off the demand curve.

Long-Run Profit Maximization

With perfectly competitive firms, the distinction between the short run and the long run is important, for in the long run entry and exit of firms can occur. For the monopolist, the distinction between the short and long run is less important. *Since by definition, monopoly means only one seller, then monopoly profit can persist in the long run.*

A monopolist that earns economic profit in the short run may find that profits can be increased in the long run by adjusting the size of the firm. A monopolist that suffers a loss in the short run may be able to eliminate that loss in the long run by adjusting to a more efficient size or by increasing demand for the product. A monopolist unable to erase a loss in the long run will leave the market.

Contestable Markets

The key to monopoly power is barriers to entry and exit. Even though only one firm may now be serving the market, as long as there are no entry or exit barriers, other firms will enter to "contest" this market if the existing firm charges a price that yields an economic profit. A **contestable market** is one in which the potential entrant can serve the same market and has access to the same technology as the existing firm.

Contestable market One in which potential entrants can serve the same market and have access to the same technology as an existing firm

For example, suppose that you cut grass in your neighborhood during the summer. All you need is the family lawn mower and some time. If you are the only one in your neighborhood who offers these services, are you a monopolist? Well, you are a monopolist in the sense that you are the only seller of services in this particular market. But you are not necessarily a monopolist in the sense that you have market power. Because no special skills are required and because most homeowners already own lawn mowers, entry into this market is easy.

How high would the price you charge for cutting lawns have to be to attract rivals? Since the lawn mower in most households is underutilized, its opportunity cost is near zero. Only the opportunity cost of your time is important. Suppose the opportunity cost of your time is the same as that of potential competitors. If demand is such that you can charge a price that yields an economic profit—that is, that pays you more than the opportunity cost of your time—you may be undercut by new entrants.

This market is contestable because entry barriers are relatively low. No irreversible investments need to be made. An investment is said to be *irreversible* if, once made, the asset is dedicated to the production of a particular good and cannot easily be redirected toward producing another good. For example, auto manufacturers who invest in specialized machines and cosmetic surgeons who invest in specialized education are making irreversible investments. Entrepreneurs are less willing to risk entering a market if entry requires irreversible investments. Therefore, whenever irreversible investments in human or physical capital must be made in order to produce in a particular market, that market is not likely to be contestable. In our lawn-mowing example, we assumed that most households already owned mowers, so people from such households could easily enter the market.

Let's consider an example of contestability on a larger scale. Suppose only one airline offers passenger service between two cities. If, at the first sign of economic profit, other airlines can easily send planes into that market and can reassign these planes to different routes if profits disappear, the market is contestable. In summary, the sole producer in a market may not be able to earn economic profit if the market is contestable—that is, if there are no barriers to entry or exit.

MONOPOLY AND THE ALLOCATION OF RESOURCES

If monopolists are no more greedy than firms in perfect competition (since both maximize profit), if monopolists do not charge the highest possible price, and if monopolists are not guaranteed a profit, then what's the problem? Let's compare a monopoly with that benchmark established in the previous chapter: perfect competition.

Price and Output under Perfect Competition

Consider the long-run equilibrium price and output for the perfectly competitive market. Suppose the long-run supply curve in perfect competition is horizontal, as shown by S_c in Exhibit 7. Since this is a constant-cost industry, the horizontal long-run supply curve in perfect competition also equals marginal cost and average total cost at each level of output.

Long-run equilibrium occurs at point e, where market demand and market supply intersect to yield price p and quantity Q. Remember, the demand curve reflects the marginal benefit from each unit purchased. In competitive equilibrium, this marginal benefit equals the marginal cost to society of producing the final unit sold. Because consumers are able to purchase Q units at price p, they enjoy a net benefit from consumption, or a consumer surplus, which is measured by the entire shaded triangle aep.

Price and Output under Monopoly

When there is only one firm in the industry, the industry demand curve becomes the monopolist's demand curve, so the price the monopolist charges determines how much is sold. Because the monopolist's demand curve slopes downward, the marginal revenue curve also slopes downward, as is indicated by MR_m in Exhibit 7. Suppose the monopolist can produce at the same constant long-run average cost as can the competitive industry. The monopolist maximizes profit in the long run by finding the size firm that equates marginal

EXHIBIT 7   **Perfect Competition and Monopoly**

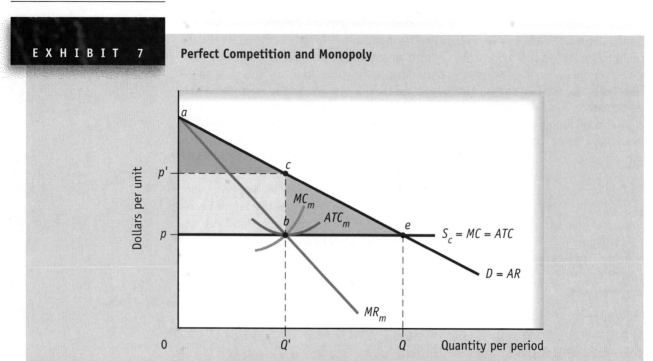

A perfectly competitive industry would produce output Q, determined at the intersection of market demand curve D and supply curve S_c. The price would be p. A monopoly that could produce output at the same minimum average cost would produce output Q', determined at point b, where marginal cost and marginal revenue intersect. It would charge price p'. Hence, output is lower and price is higher under monopoly than under perfect competition.

cost with marginal revenue; this firm size is reflected by ATC_m and MC_m in Exhibit 7. Marginal cost equals marginal revenue at point b, yielding equilibrium output Q' at price p'. The consumers' marginal benefit, identified as point c, exceeds the monopolist's marginal cost, identified as point b. Society would be better off if output were expanded beyond Q', because the marginal value consumers attach to additional units exceeds the marginal cost of producing those additional units.

Allocative and Distributive Effects

Consider the allocative and distributive effects of monopoly versus perfect competition. In Exhibit 7, the monopolist earns economic profit equal to the rectangle $p'cbp$. Consumer surplus under perfect competition was the large triangle *aep;* under monopoly, it shrinks to the smaller triangle *acp',* which in this example is only one-fourth as large. By comparing the situation under monopoly with that under perfect competition, you can see that monopoly profit comes entirely from what was consumer surplus under perfect competition. Because the profit rectangle reflects a transfer from consumers to the monopolist, this amount is not lost to society and so is not considered a welfare loss of monopoly.

Notice, however, that consumer surplus has been reduced by more than the profit rectangle. Consumers have also lost the triangle *ceb,* which was part of the consumer surplus under perfect competition. The *ceb* triangle is called the **deadweight loss,** or *welfare loss,* of monopoly because it is a loss to consumers

Deadweight loss A loss of consumer surplus and producer surplus that is not transferred to anyone else; it can result from monopolization of an industry

that is a gain to nobody. Thus, *if the monopolist can produce output at the same minimum average cost as the competitive firm, the triangle* ceb *measures the welfare loss arising from the higher price and reduced output of the monopolist.* This triangle is a deadweight loss because it represents consumer surplus forgone on units of output that are not produced. Empirical estimates of the U.S. annual welfare cost of monopoly have ranged from about 1 percent to about 5 percent of national income. Applied to 1996 national income data, these estimates imply a welfare cost that could range from about $70 billion to $350 billion.

PROBLEMS ESTIMATING THE WELFARE COST OF MONOPOLY

The actual cost of monopoly could differ from the welfare loss described in the previous section. We will first consider reasons why the welfare loss of monopoly might be smaller than that measured in Exhibit 7 and then consider reasons why it might be larger.

Monopolies do not always result in higher market prices. Prior to World War II, Alcoa, the only U.S. manufacturer of aluminum, kept prices relatively low to discourage competition.

Why the Welfare Loss of Monopoly Might Be Lower

If firms in an industry experience economies of scale, a monopolist may be able to produce output at a lower cost per unit than could competitive firms. Therefore, the price could be lower under monopoly than under competition. Even where there are no economies of scale, the monopolist may keep the price below the profit-maximizing level to avoid attracting new competitors. For example, before World War II, Alcoa was the only manufacturer of aluminum in the United States. Some observers claim the company kept prices low to discourage potential rivals from entering the industry.

The welfare loss shown in Exhibit 7 may also overstate the true cost of monopoly because monopolists may, in response to public scrutiny and political pressure, keep prices below what the market could bear. We speak here not about government-regulated monopolies, which will be addressed later, but about monopolies that keep prices down to avoid public attention and criticism. Although monopolists would like to earn as great an economic profit as possible, they realize that if the public outcry over high prices and high profits grows loud enough, some sort of government intervention could reduce or even eliminate profits. For example, the prices and profits of drug companies, which individually are monopoly producers of patented medicines, came under scrutiny by President Clinton, who threatened to regulate drug prices. Firms may try to avoid such treatment by keeping prices below the level that would maximize economic profit.

Why the Welfare Loss of Monopoly Might Be Higher

Another line of thinking suggests that the welfare loss of monopoly may, in fact, be greater than shown in our simple diagram. *If resources must be devoted to securing and maintaining a monopoly position, monopolies may involve more of a welfare loss than simple models suggest.* For example, consider radio and TV broadcasting rights, which confer on the recipient the exclusive right to use a particular band of the scarce broadcast spectrum. In the past, these rights have been given away by government agencies to the applicants deemed most deserving. Because these rights are so valuable, numerous applicants spend a bundle on lawyers' fees, lobbying expenses, and other costs associated with making themselves appear the most deserving. The efforts devoted to securing and maintaining a monopoly position are largely a social waste because they use up scarce resources but add not one unit to output. Activities undertaken by individuals or firms to influence public policy in a way that will directly or indirectly redistribute income to themselves are referred to as **rent seeking.**

The monopolist, insulated from the rigors of competition in the marketplace, may also grow fat and lazy—and become inefficient. Since some monopolies could still earn an economic profit even if output were not produced at the least possible cost, corporate executives may waste resources to create a more comfortable life for themselves. Long lunches, afternoon golf, Oriental carpets, and extensive employee benefits may make company life more enjoyable, but these additional expenses also increase the average cost of production.

Monopolists have also been criticized for being slow to adopt the latest production techniques, being reluctant to develop new products, and generally lacking innovativeness. Because monopolists are largely insulated from the rigors of competition, they may take it easy. As the Nobel Prize–winning British economist J. R. Hicks remarked, "The best of all monopoly profits is a quiet life." Consider, in the following case study, the performance of one of the oldest monopolies in the United States, the post office.

Rent seeking Activities undertaken by individuals or firms to influence public policy in a way that will directly or indirectly redistribute income to them

CASE STUDY

The Mail Monopoly

Location:

The U.S. Postal Service, with increased use of the Internet, has established a presence on the World Wide Web. Visit the U.S. Postal Service (http://www.usps.gov/). Private delivery services are on the Web as well. Visit "FedEx: The World on Time," maintained by the Federal Express Corporation (http://www.fedex.com/) and "United Parcel Service: Moving at the Speed of Business," maintained by United Parcel Service of America, Inc. (http://www.ups.com/).

The U.S. postal monopoly was established in 1775 and has operated since then under federal protection. In 1971, Congress converted the Post Office Department into an independent agency called the U.S. Postal Service. The Postal Service handles over half a billion pieces of mail a day—nearly half the world's total. It has a legal monopoly in delivering first-class letters; it also has the exclusive right to the use of the space inside people's mailboxes.

The Postal Service monopoly has suffered in recent years because of higher postal rates and new competition from emerging technologies. The price of a first-class stamp has climbed from 6 cents in 1970 to 32 cents by 1995, a price increase more than double the average rate of inflation and triple the average increase in telephone rates. Emerging technologies such as fax machines and electronic mail also compete with the Postal Service (e-mail messages now outnumber first-class letters).

United Parcel Service (UPS) is more mechanized and more containerized than the Postal Service, thus reducing costs and breakage. The Postal Service has tried to emulate UPS, but with only limited success. Postal employees are also paid more on average than UPS employees or those of other private-sector deliverers, such as Federal Express.

Despite threatened legal actions by the Postal Service, Federal Express and others have captured 90 percent of the overnight-mail business. Since the Postal Service has no monopoly beyond first class, it has lost huge chunks of the other classes to private firms offering lower rates and better service. For example, in the last 20 years, UPS and others have taken away 95 percent of fourth-class mail—parcel post business. When the Postal Service recently raised third-class ("junk" mail) rates, third-class mailers shifted to other forms of advertising, including cable TV and telemarketing. So the Postal Service is losing its monopoly in first class because of competition in overnight mail and competition from new technologies.

Source: Mark Lewyn, "The Check's Still Not in the Mail," *Business Week,* 28 March 1995; Randall Cronk, "The Net that Manages the Mail," *Byte,* March 1995; and Suneel Ratan, "Snail Mail Struggles to Survive," *Time,* Special Issue, Spring 1995.

The Mail Monopoly
continued

Not all economists believe that monopolists, especially private monopolies, manage their resources with any less vigilance than do perfect competitors. Economist Joseph Schumpeter argued that because monopolists are protected from rivals, they are in a good position to capture the fruits of any innovation and therefore will be more innovative than more competitive firms. Other economists argue that if a private monopolist strays from the path of profit maximization, the value of the firm's stock will drop. This lower stock price provides an incentive for outsiders to buy a controlling share of the firm's stock, shape up the operation, and watch profits—as well as the value of the firm's stock—grow. This *market for corporate control* is thus said to direct monopolists along the path of efficient production.

MODELS OF PRICE DISCRIMINATION

So far we have assumed that the monopolist charges all consumers the same price. Under certain conditions, the monopolist can increase profit through **price discrimination,** which is charging different prices to different groups of consumers for reasons unrelated to costs. For example, many firms offer senior-citizen discounts. Admissions to sporting events, movies, plays, and other shows are lower for children. You, as a student, also qualify for reduced prices for a variety of products. Firms offer certain groups reduced prices, because doing so enhances firm profits. Let's see how and why.

Price discrimination Selling the same good for different prices to different consumers as a way to increase profit

Conditions for Price Discrimination

To practice price discrimination, certain conditions must exist. First, the demand curve for the product must slope downward, indicating that the producer has some control over the price—some market power. This condition holds for the monopolist but not for perfect competitors. Second, there must be at least two classes of consumers, each with a different price elasticity of demand. Third, the producer must be able, at little cost, to identify and charge different prices to each class of consumers. Finally, the monopolist must be able to prevent those who pay the lower price from reselling the product to those who pay the higher price.

Examples of Price Discrimination

Let's consider some examples of price discrimination. Because expenses are paid by their companies, businesspeople generally are less sensitive to changes in the price of travel and communication than are householders. Therefore, businesspeople have a less elastic demand for travel and communication than do householders, so airlines and telephone services try to maximize profits by charging the business customers higher rates than residential customers.

But how do firms distinguish between classes of customers? Telephone companies are able to sort out their customers by charging different rates based on the time of day. Long-distance charges are higher during normal *business* hours than during evenings and weekends, when householders, who presumably have a higher price elasticity of demand, make social calls. The airlines try to distinguish between business customers and household customers based on the terms under which tickets are purchased. Householders plan their vacations well in advance and often stay over Saturday. They have more flexibility about when they travel and are more sensitive to price than are business travelers. Business travel, on the other hand, is more unpredictable, more urgent, and seldom involves a weekend stay. The airlines separate business travelers from vacationers by requiring purchasers of "super-saver" fares to buy tickets well in advance and to stay over Saturday.

Major amusement parks, such as Disney World, often think of customers as falling into two distinct groups with different elasticities: local residents and out-of-towners. Out-of-towners typically spend a substantial amount on airlines and lodging just to get to there, so they are less sensitive to the price of admission than are local residents, who can go any time. The problem is how to charge a lower price to local residents. The parks do this by making discount coupons available locally, such as through a shopping circular or through local businesses, such as dry cleaners, which tourists are not likely to visit.

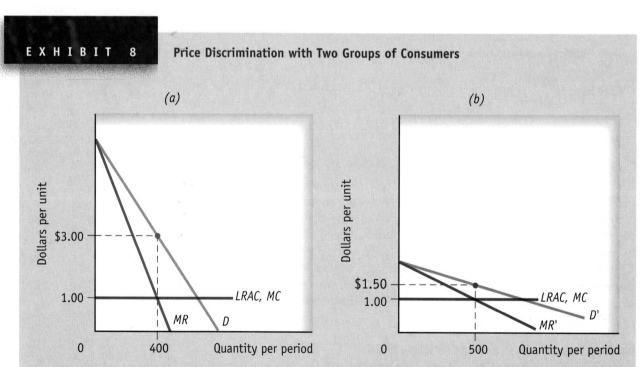

EXHIBIT 8

Price Discrimination with Two Groups of Consumers

A monopolist that faces two groups of consumers with different demand elasticities may be able to practice price discrimination. With marginal cost the same in both markets, the firm sells 400 units to the high-marginal-value consumers in panel (a) and charges them a price of $3 per unit. It sells 500 units to the low-marginal-value consumers in panel (b) and charges them a price of $1.50.

A Model of Price Discrimination

Exhibit 8 shows the effects of price discrimination. Consumers are divided into two groups with distinctly different demands. *At a given price level,* the price elasticity of demand in panel (b) is greater than that in panel (a). You may think of panel (b) as reflecting the demand of college students, senior citizens, or some other group that tends to be more sensitive to the price.

The exhibit also shows the marginal cost curve. For simplicity, we assume that the monopolist produces at a constant long-run average cost of $1, and that this cost is the same for both groups. The monopolist maximizes profit by finding the output in each market that equates marginal cost with marginal revenue. In panel (a), the resulting price is $3 per unit; in panel (b), that price is $1.50 per unit. So profit maximization results in charging a lower price to the group with more elastic demand.

Perfect Price Discrimination: The Monopolist's Dream

The demand curve conveys the marginal value of each unit consumed and reflects the maximum amount consumers would pay for each unit. If the monopolist could charge a different price for each unit sold, a price reflected by the demand curve, the firm's marginal revenue from selling one more unit would equal the price of that unit. Thus, the demand curve would become the firm's marginal revenue curve. The **perfectly discriminating monopolist** charges a different price for each unit of the good.

In Exhibit 9, the monopolist is assumed to produce at a constant average cost in the long run. A perfectly discriminating monopolist, like any producer, would maximize profit by finding the output level where marginal cost equals marginal revenue, as at point *e* in Exhibit 9. The perfectly discriminating monopolist's economic profit is defined by the area of the shaded triangle *aec*. Price

Perfectly discriminating monopolist A monopolist who charges a different price for each unit of the good

EXHIBIT 9

Perfect Price Discrimination

If a monopolist can charge a different price for each unit sold, it may be able to practice perfect price discrimination. By setting the price of each unit equal to the maximum amount consumers are willing to pay for that unit (shown by the height of the demand curve), the monopolist can achieve a profit equal to the area of the shaded triangle. Consumer surplus is zero.

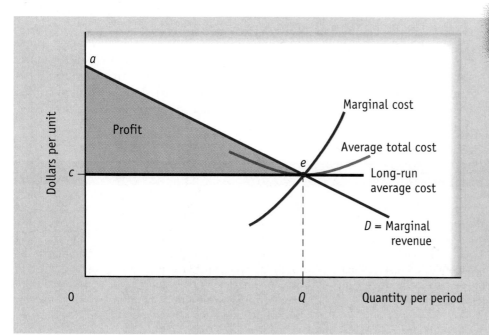

discrimination is a way of increasing firm profit; it could also allow a monopolist to survive in the long run even if its average cost curve lies completely above the demand curve. Put another way, even if no *single* price would cover average cost, charging different prices may cover average cost.

By charging a different price for each unit of output, the perfectly discriminating monopolist is able to convert every dollar of consumer surplus into economic profit. Although this might seem unfair to consumers, perfect price discrimination gets high marks based on allocative efficiency. In fact, because we have assumed that this is a constant-cost industry, Q is the same level of output that would result from perfect competition. As in the perfectly competitive outcome, the marginal cost of the last unit of output produced just equals the marginal benefit consumers attached to that unit. And although consumers reap no consumer surplus, the total benefits they received from consuming the good just equal the total amount they paid for the good. Note also that because the monopolist does not restrict output, there is no deadweight loss of monopoly—no welfare-loss triangle. Hence, perfect price discrimination enhances social welfare when compared with monopoly output in the absence of price discrimination.

CONCLUSION

Pure monopoly, like perfect competition, is not that common. Perhaps the best examples are firms producing a patented item with unique characteristics, such as certain prescription drugs. Still, not many firms sell a product for which there are no close substitutes. The lure of economic profit encourages rivals to hurdle even seemingly high barriers to entry. Changing technology also works against monopoly in the long run. The railroad monopoly was erased by the interstate highway system. AT&T's monopoly on long-distance phone service crumbled as microwave technology replaced copper wire. The U.S. Postal Service's monopoly is being eroded by express delivery, fax machines, and e-mail. And cable TV may soon lose its local monopoly status as fiber-optics technology gives local phone companies access to the market.

Though perfect competition and pure monopoly are relatively rare, our examination of them yields a framework that will help us view market structures that lie between the two extremes. As we will see, many firms have some degree of monopoly power—that is, they face downward-sloping demand curves. In the next chapter, we will consider two market structures in which firms have some monopoly power.

SUMMARY

1. A monopolist sells a product with no close substitutes. A monopoly can persist in the long run only if the entry of new firms into the market is blocked. Three barriers to entry are (1) legal restrictions, such as patents and operating licenses; (2) economies of scale, which lower average cost as output expands in the long run; and (3) control over a key resource.

2. Because a monopolist is the sole supplier, the market demand curve is also the monopolist's demand curve. Because the monopolist can sell more only if the price falls, the marginal revenue is less than the price. When demand is elastic, marginal revenue is positive and total revenue increases as the price falls. When demand is inelastic, marginal revenue is negative and total revenue decreases as the price falls.

3. If, at some positive rate of output, the monopolist can at least cover variable cost, profit is maximized or loss is minimized in the short run by finding the output rate that equates marginal cost with marginal revenue.

4. In the short run, the monopolist, like the perfect competitor, can earn economic profit but will shut down unless the price is at or above the average variable cost. In the long run, the monopolist, unlike the perfect competitor, can earn an economic profit as long as the entry of new firms is blocked. The sole producer in a market that is contestable will earn no economic profit in the long run.

5. Resources are not allocated as efficiently under unregulated monopoly as under perfect competition. If costs are similar for both types of firms, the monopoly price will be higher and monopoly output will be lower than under perfect competition. Monopoly usually results in a net welfare loss when compared to perfect competition because the loss in consumer surplus under monopoly exceeds the gain in monopoly profit.

6. To increase profit through price discrimination, the monopolist must have at least two identifiable types of consumers with different elasticities of demand and must be able to prevent those consumers charged the lower price from reselling to those charged the higher price. A perfect price discriminator charges a different price for each unit of the good, thereby capturing all consumer surplus as economic profit. Perfect price discrimination seems unfair because the monopolist "cleans up," but it gets high marks in terms of allocative efficiency.

QUESTIONS AND PROBLEMS

1. **(Barriers to Entry)** Complete each of the following sentences:
   a. Patents and licenses are examples of _____ _____ imposed by the government that prevent entry into an industry.
   b. A U.S. _____ awards inventors the exclusive right to production for 17 years.
   c. When economies of scale make it possible for a single firm to satisfy market demand at a lower cost per unit than could two or more firms, the single firm is considered a _____ _____.
   d. A potential barrier to entry is a firm's control of a(n) _____ resource critical to production in the industry.

2. **(Barriers to Entry)** Explain how economies of scale can be a barrier to entry.

3. **(Demand Facing a Monopolist)** Explain how the demand curve faced by a monopolist differs from the demand curve faced by a perfectly competitive firm. Why?

4. **(Revenue Maximization)** Suppose a UFO crashes in your backyard. Ignoring any costs that may be involved, what price would you charge people to come and view the site?

5. **(Monopoly)** Only one airline has flights to and from some of the South Sea islands. Would this airline qualify as a monopoly? How would such a company price its flights to the islands to maximize profits? Would it price cargo and mail at the same rate per pound as passengers? Why or why not?

6. **(Demand and Marginal Revenue)** Explain why the marginal revenue curve for a monopolist falls below its demand curve, rather than coinciding with the demand curve as occurs for a perfectly competitive firm. Is it ever possible for a monopolist's marginal revenue curve to coincide with its demand curve?

7. **(Monopoly)** Why is it impossible for a profit-maximizing monopolist to choose any price *and* any quantity it wishes?

8. **(Monopoly and Welfare)** Why is society worse off under monopoly than under perfect competition even if both market structures face the same constant long-run average cost? When might monopoly be more efficient?

9. **(Price Discrimination)** Explain how it may be profitable for Koreans to sell new autos at a cheaper price in the United States than in Korea, even with transportation costs.

10. **(Perfect Price Discrimination)** Why is the demand curve equal to the marginal revenue curve for the perfectly discriminating monopolist?

11. **(Monopoly)** Suppose that a certain manufacturer has a monopoly on the sorority and fraternity ring business (a constant-cost industry) because he has persuaded the "Greeks" to give him exclusive rights to their insignia.
    a. Using demand and cost curves, draw a diagram representing the company's profit-maximizing pricing-output decision.

b. Why is marginal revenue less than price for this company?

c. On your diagram, show the deadweight loss that occurs because the output level is determined by the monopoly situation rather than by a competitive market. Explain.

d. What would happen if the Greeks decided to charge the manufacturer a royalty fee of $3 per ring?

12. **(Price-Discriminating Monopoly)** Suppose that do-dads are sold to two types of people and that the long-run production costs are constant at $1 per do-dad. Use the following data to answer the questions below. Q_1 represents sales to type-1 people; Q_2 is sales to type-2 people.

p	Q_1	Q_2	$Q_1 + Q_2$	Short-run MC of total Q
$10	4	12	16	$ 1.50
9	6	14	20	2.00
8	8	16	24	3.00
7	10	18	28	7.00
6	12	20	32	12.00
5	14	22	36	20.00
3	18	26	44	40.00
1	22	30	52	80.00

a. Determine the short-run equilibrium price and quantity for this industry, assuming it is competitive.

b. Determine the long-run equilibrium price and quantity for this industry, assuming it is competitive.

c. If do-dads were produced by a nondiscriminating monopolist, what price and quantity would maximize short-run profits? long-run profits?

d. If this monopolist could practice price discrimination, what would be the long-run profit-maximizing price and quantity for each group of buyers?

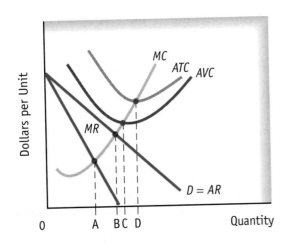

13. **(Short-Run Equilibrium for a Monopolist)** Consider the graph (lower left) showing the short-run situation of a monopolist. At what output level and price will the firm operate in the short run? Why?

14. **(Short-Run Equilibrium for a Monopolist)** Answer the following questions on the basis of the monopolist's situation illustrated in the graph below.

a. At what output level and price will the monopolist operate?

b. In equilibrium, what will be the firm's total cost and total revenue?

c. What will be the firm's profit or loss in equilibrium?

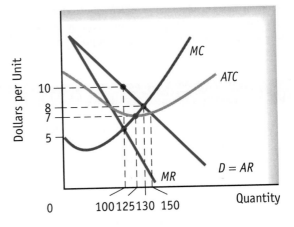

15. **(Contestable Markets)** Define a contestable market. What role does investment play in determining whether a market is contestable or not?

16. **(Monopoly and Elasticity)** Explain why a monopoly firm would never knowingly produce on the inelastic portion of its demand curve.

17. **(Price Discrimination)** What conditions must be met in order for a monopolist to price discriminate successfully?

18. **(Welfare Cost of Monopoly)** Explain why the welfare loss of a monopoly may be smaller or larger than the loss shown in Exhibit 7.

19. **(Are Diamonds Forever?)** How does the De Beers cartel maintain price control in the diamond market? How might this control be threatened?

20. **(The Mail Monopoly)** Consider the definition of a monopolist. Can the U.S. Postal Service be considered a monopoly in first-class postage? Why or why not? What has happened to the price elasticity of demand for first-class letters?

Using the Internet

21. Visit "Intellectual Value," an article by Esther Dyson originally published in the December 1994 newsletter *Release 1.0* (http://www.hotwired.com/wired/3.07/features/dyson.html), and "Steal This Article," an article by Paulina Borsook published in *Upside Magazine* (http://www.upside.com/resource/print/9603/ip.html),

   a. List three economic effects that the Internet will have on creators and distributers of intellectual property (books, music, computer software, and the like).

   b. What does Dyson mean by the following statement? "We are entering a new economic environment . . . where a new physical set of rules will govern . . . . Chief among the new rules is that 'content is free.' While not all content will be free, the new economic dynamic will operate as if it were."

   c. Why does Borsook title her article "Steal this Article"?

Monopolistic Competition and Oligopoly

P erfect competition and pure monopoly represent the two extreme market structures. Under perfect competition, many suppliers offer a homogeneous commodity to a market where firms can enter and leave the industry with ease. Monopoly involves only one seller of a product with no close substitutes; competitors are blocked from entering this market by natural or artificial barriers to entry. These polar market structures are logically appealing and are useful in describing the workings of some markets observed in the economy. But most firms operate in markets that are not well described by either model. Some firms are in markets that have many sellers producing goods that vary slightly, such as the many radio stations that vie for your attention or the video rental stores that abound. Other firms are in markets that consist of a small number of sellers who in some cases produce homogeneous goods (such as the markets for oil, steel, or aluminum) and in other cases produce differentiated goods (such as the markets for automobiles, breakfast cereals, or cigarettes). In this chapter, we examine the two additional markets that inhabit the vast gray area between perfect competition and pure monopoly. Topics discussed in this chapter include:

- Monopolistic competition
- Product differentiation
- Models of oligopoly
- Mergers

MONOPOLISTIC COMPETITION

During the 1920s and 1930s, economists began formulating models to fit between perfect competition and pure monopoly. Two models of *monopolistic competition* were developed independently. In 1933 at Harvard University, Edward Chamberlin published *The Theory of Monopolistic Competition*. Across the Atlantic that same year, Cambridge University's Joan Robinson published *The Economics of Imperfect Competition*. Although the theories differed, their underlying principles were similar. We will discuss Chamberlin's approach.

Characteristics of Monopolistic Competition

As the expression **monopolistic competition** suggests, the market contains elements of both monopoly and competition. Chamberlin used the expression to describe a market characterized by many producers offering products that are close substitutes but are not viewed as identical by consumers. Examples include the many convenience stores found throughout a metropolitan area. Because the products of different suppliers differ slightly—for example, some convenience stores are closer to you than others—the demand curve for each particular producer is not horizontal but rather slopes downward. Each producer therefore has some power over the price it charges. Thus, the firms that populate this market are not *price takers,* as they would be under perfect competition, but are *price searchers.*

Because barriers to entry are relatively low, firms in monopolistic competition can enter or leave the market with relative ease. Consequently, there are enough sellers that they behave competitively. There are also enough sellers that each tends to get lost in the crowd. For example, in a large metropolitan area, an individual restaurant, gas station, drugstore, video rental store, dry cleaner, or convenience store tends to act *independently*. In a small town, there may be only two or three sellers in each market, so they keep an eye on one another; they act *interdependently*. You will understand the significance of this independent versus interdependent behavior later in the chapter.

Monopolistic competition A market structure characterized by a large number of firms selling products that are close substitutes, yet different enough that each firm's demand curve slopes downward

Product Differentiation

Under perfect competition, the product is homogeneous, such as a bushel of wheat. Under monopolistic competition, the product differs across sellers, such as the difference between a Big Mac and a Whopper. Sellers can differentiate their products in four basic ways.

Physical Differences. The most obvious way products differ is by their physical appearance and their qualities. The ways that products can differ are seemingly endless: size, weight, color, taste, texture, and so on. Shampoos, for example, differ in color, scent, thickness, lathering ability, and bottle design. Particular brands aim at consumers with dandruff and those whose hair is normal, dry, or oily.

Location. The number and variety of locations where a product is available represent another means of differentiation. Some products seem to be available everywhere; finding others requires some search and travel. If you live in a metropolitan area, you are no doubt accustomed to a large number of convenience stores. Each wants to be closest to you when you need that half gallon of milk or bag of Doritos—hence the proliferation of stores. As the name says, these mini grocery stores are selling *convenience*. Their prices are higher and their selections are more limited than those of regular grocery stores, but they are likely to be nearer customers and they stay open later.

Services. Products also differ based on the accompanying services. For example, some pizza sellers deliver; others do not. Some retail stores offer helpful product demonstrations by a well-trained sales staff; other stores are essentially self-service. Some offer a money-back guarantee; others say "no returns."

Product Image. A final way that products differ is in the image the producer tries to foster in the consumer's mind. For example, a clothing manufacturer may try to persuade you that its jeans are special because some celebrity's name is on the back pocket. Some brand names may suggest high quality by the way they are promoted, the form of packaging, or the kind of stores in which they are sold. For example, some shampoos are sold only in beauty salons. Producers try to find a particular niche in the consumer's mind through product promotion and advertising.

Short-Run Profit Maximization or Loss Minimization

Because each monopolistic competitor offers a product that differs somewhat from other products in the industry, each seller has some control over the price charged. This *market power* means the product's demand curve slopes downward, though not as steeply as a monopolist's demand curve. Since many firms are selling close substitutes, any firm that raises its price can expect to lose some customers to rivals. In contrast, a monopolist has no rivals and so loses relatively fewer customers when the price increases. On the other hand, a perfect competitor who raises the price can expect to lose *all* customers. Therefore, a monopolistic competitor's demand tends to be more elastic than a monopolist's and less elastic than a perfect competitor's.

Recall that the number and similarity of available substitutes for a given product are important determinants of the price elasticity of demand. Therefore, the elasticity of the monopolistic competitor's demand depends on (1) the number of rival firms that produce a similar product and (2) the firm's ability to differentiate its product from those of its rivals. *A firm's demand will be more elastic the greater the number of competing firms and the less differentiated the firm's product.*

Marginal Cost Equals Marginal Revenue. From our study of monopoly, we know that the downward-sloping demand curve means the marginal revenue curve also slopes downward and lies below the demand curve. Exhibit 1 depicts demand and marginal revenue curves for a firm in monopolistic competition. The exhibit also presents cost curves. Remember that the forces that determine the cost of production are largely independent of the forces that shape demand, so there is nothing special about a monopolistic competitor's cost curves.

If a firm in the short run can at least cover its variable cost, it will increase output as long as marginal revenue exceeds marginal cost. A monopolistic competitor maximizes profit in the short run just as a monopolist does: *the profit-maximizing level of output occurs where marginal cost equals marginal revenue; the profit-maximizing price is found on the demand curve at that level of output.* Exhibit 1

Convenience stores target customers who live nearby, who need products at odd hours, or who are in a hurry—in other words, customers who are willing to spend more and limit their choice of selection.

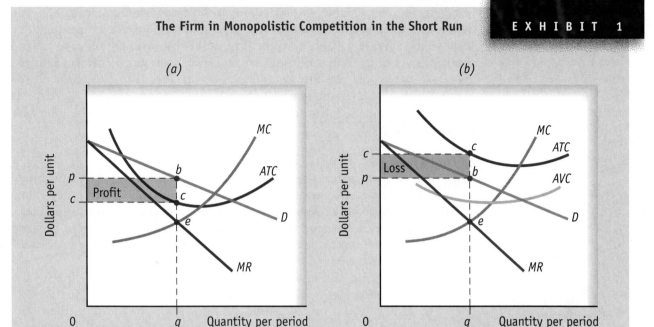

EXHIBIT 1

The Firm in Monopolistic Competition in the Short Run

The monopolistically competitive firm produces the level of output at which marginal cost equals marginal revenue (point e) and charges the price indicated by point b on the downward-sloping demand curve. In panel (a), the firm produces q units, sells them at price p, and earns a short-run profit equal to (p − c) multiplied by q, shown by the blue rectangle. In panel (b), the average total cost exceeds the price at the optimal level of output. Thus, the firm suffers a short-run loss equal to (c − p) multiplied by q, represented by the red rectangle.

shows the price and output combinations that maximize short-run profit in panel (a) and minimize short-run loss in panel (b). In each panel, the marginal cost and marginal revenue curves intersect at point e, yielding equilibrium output q, equilibrium price p, and average total cost c.

Maximizing Profit or Minimizing Loss in the Short Run. Recall that the short run is a period too brief to allow firms to enter or leave the market. The demand and cost conditions shown in panel (a) of Exhibit 1 indicate that this firm will earn an economic profit in the short run. At the firm's profit-maximizing level of output, average total cost, c, is below the price, p. As noted earlier, the difference between the two is the firm's profit per unit, which, when multiplied by the quantity sold, yields the economic profit, shown by the shaded rectangle in panel (a). Quantity supplied is determined by the intersection of the marginal cost and marginal revenue curves, and the price appears on the demand curve at that quantity. Incidentally, because the demand curve is above the marginal revenue curve, a monopolistic competitor, like a monopolist, has no supply curve—that is, there is no curve that uniquely relates price and quantity supplied.

The monopolistic competitor, like other firms, has no guarantee of economic profit. The firm's demand and cost curves could be as shown in panel (b), where the firm's average total cost curve lies above the demand curve, so no level of output would allow the firm to break even. In such a situation, the firm must decide whether to produce or to shut down temporarily. The rule here is the same as with perfect competition and monopoly: as long as the price is above the average variable cost, the firm in the short run should produce and thereby cover at least a portion of its fixed cost. If the price fails to cover the average variable cost, the firm should shut down. Recall that the halt in production may be only temporary; shutting down is not necessarily the same as going out of business. Firms that expect losses to persist may, in the long run, leave the industry.

Zero Economic Profit in the Long Run

Since there are no barriers to entry, short-run economic profit will attract new entrants in the long run. Because new entrants offer a product that is quite similar to those offered by existing firms, they draw customers from existing firms, thereby reducing the demand facing each firm. Entry will continue in the long run until economic profit disappears. *Because of the ease of entry, monopolistically competitive firms will earn no economic profit in the long run.*

If they incur short-run losses, some monopolistic competitors will leave the industry in the long run, redirecting their resources to activities that are expected to earn at least a normal profit. As firms leave the industry, their customers will switch to the remaining firms, increasing the demand for each remaining firm's product. Firms will continue to leave in the long run until the remaining firms have enough customers to earn normal profit, but not economic profit.

Exhibit 2 shows the long-run equilibrium for a typical monopolistic competitor. In the long run, entry and exit will alter each firm's demand curve until economic profit disappears—that is, until average total cost equals the price. In Exhibit 2, the marginal cost curve intersects the marginal revenue curve at point *a*. At the equilibrium level of output, *q*, the demand curve at point *b* is tangent to the average total cost curve. Since average total cost equals the price, *p*, the firm earns no economic profit.[1] At all other levels of output, the firm's average total cost is above its demand curve, so the firm would lose money if it reduced or expanded its output.

Thus, if entry is easy and if all firms are selling goods that are close, but not perfect, substitutes, short-run economic profit will draw new entrants into the industry in the long run. The demand curve facing each firm shifts left until the profit disappears. A short-run economic loss will prompt some firms to leave the industry in the long run until remaining firms earn just a normal profit. In summary, *monopolistic competition is like pure monopoly in the sense that firms in each industry face demand curves that slope downward. Monopolistic competition is like perfect competition in the sense that easy entry and exit eliminate economic profit or economic loss in the long run.*

---

1   You may wonder why average cost equals the price at the same level of output where marginal cost equals marginal revenue. An explanation relies on total-cost and total-revenue curves, which are not shown. Recall that the slope of the total-cost curve equals the firm's marginal cost, and the slope of the total-revenue curve equals the firm's marginal revenue. Where average cost equals price, the firm earns a normal profit but no economic profit. Where there is no economic profit, the total-cost curve is tangent to the total-revenue curve, so both total curves have the same slope at that level of output. Therefore, marginal cost must equal marginal revenue at that level of output.

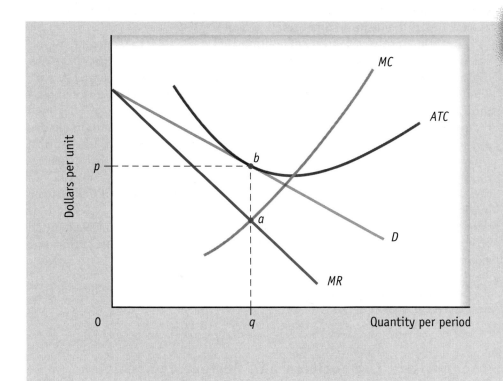

EXHIBIT 2

Long-Run Equilibrium in Monopolistic Competition

If existing firms are earning economic profits, new firms will enter the industry. The entry of such firms reduces the demand facing each firm. In the long run, demand is reduced until marginal revenue equals marginal cost (point *a*) and the demand curve is tangent to the average total cost curve (point *b*). Profit is zero at output *q*. With zero economic profit, no new firms enter, so the industry is in long-run equilibrium.

One way to understand how short-run economic profit can be competed away by new firms in the long run is to consider the evolution of a newly emerging industry, as is discussed in the following case study.

CASE STUDY

Fast Forward

Video recorders have now become standard equipment in the typical home. These recorders fueled demand for videotaped movies. The first videotape rental outlets required tape deposits, imposed membership fees of up to $100, and rented tapes for as much as $5 per day. Despite the high prices and high fees, the exploding number of VCRs allowed these early rental stores to thrive. What's more, part of the initial surge in rental demand came from consumers who were catching up on older movies they had missed at the theaters. In the beginning, most rental stores faced no competition in their area, and they likely earned short-run economic profits.

But these profits attracted competitors. Since market entry was relatively easy, new rental stores opened for business. Other types of stores—convenience stores, grocery stores, bookstores, even drug-stores—also began renting tapes as a sideline. The growth rate of new rental outlets soon outstripped the growth rate in VCRs. Between 1982 and 1987, for example, the number of outlets renting tapes increased fourfold. And once con-

Location:

While smaller video rental stores were forced to close in the wake of increased availability of substitute goods, such as cable television, Blockbuster Video has been able to increase its market share. Learn more about Blockbuster Video—visit "Blockbuster Entertainment," maintained by Viacom, Inc. (http://pwr.com/blockbuster/).

Fast Forward
continued

sumers caught up with the backlog of movies, that demand dried up and demand came to focus primarily on new releases.

Thus, the supply of rental movies increased faster than the demand. Worse yet for video stores, cable television with 40 to 50 channels, pay-per-view options, and direct video sales to consumers all substituted for video rentals. The greater supply of rentals along with the increased availability of substitutes had the predictable effect on market prices. Rental rates declined sharply—to as little as 99 cents per night—and membership fees and tape deposits disappeared. Some rental stores could not survive at such a low price, and they dropped out of the industry. In fact, so many failed that a market soon developed to buy and resell their tape inventories. The "shakeout" in the industry is still going on, and many existing rental stores will fail. As the market evolves, one large firm, Blockbuster, has increased its market share. If that firm comes to dominate the market, the movie rental market could change from monopolistic competition to oligopoly, a market structure to be examined later in the chapter.

Sources: Howard Rutinsky, "Curtains for the Video Stores?" *Forbes*, 12 April 1993; Gail DeGeorge, "Wayne's World: Busting Beyond Video," *Business Week*, 1 November 1993; and Matt Kopka, "Blockbuster Reconsiders Audio," *Publishers Weekly*, 6 March 1995.

Monopolistic Competition and Perfect Competition Compared

How does monopolistic competition compare with perfect competition in terms of efficiency? In the long run, neither a perfect competitor nor a monopolistic competitor can earn economic profit, so what's the difference? The difference arises because of the different demand curves facing individual firms in each of the two market structures. Exhibit 3 presents the long-run equilibrium price and quantity for firms in each of the two market structures, assuming each firm has identical cost curves. In each case, the marginal cost curve intersects the marginal revenue curve at the level of output where the average cost curve is tangent to the demand curve faced by the firm.

The demand curve for the firm in perfect competition is a horizontal line drawn at the market price, as shown in panel (a). The average cost curve is tangent to this demand curve at the lowest point of the average total cost curve. Thus, a perfect competitor in the long run produces at the lowest possible average cost. In panel (b), a monopolistic competitor faces a downward-sloping demand curve because its product differs somewhat from that of other producers. In the long run, the monopolistic competitor produces less than the amount necessary to achieve the lowest possible average cost. Thus, the price and average cost under monopolistic competition, identified in panel (b) as p', exceed the price and average cost under perfect competition, identified in panel (a) as p. *If firms have the same cost curves, the firm under monopolistic competition produces less and charges more than the firm under perfect competition.*

Firms in monopolistic competition are not producing at minimum average cost. They are said to have **excess capacity**, since production is short of the level that would achieve the lowest average cost. Excess capacity means that producers could easily serve more customers and in the process would lower the average cost of production. If the marginal value of production exceeds the

Excess capacity The difference between a monopolistic competitor's minimum average cost and its profit-maximizing level of output

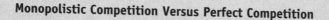

Monopolistic Competition Versus Perfect Competition

EXHIBIT 3

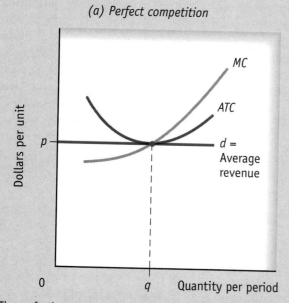

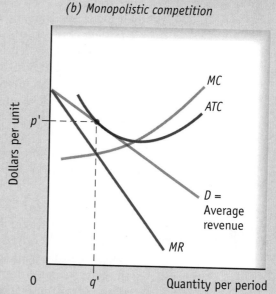

The perfectly competitive firm of panel (a) faces a demand curve that is horizontal at market price *p*. Long-run equilibrium occurs at output *q*, where the demand (average revenue) curve is tangent to the average total cost curve at its lowest point. The monopolistically competitive firm of panel (b) is in long-run equilibrium at output *q'*, where demand is tangent to average total cost. However, since the demand curve slopes downward, the tangency does not occur at the minimum point of average total cost. Hence the monopolistically competitive firm produces less output at a higher price than does a perfectly competitive firm facing the same cost conditions.

marginal costs of production, expanding output would increase marginal value more than marginal cost, thereby increasing economic welfare. Such excess capacity exists with gas stations, drugstores, convenience stores, restaurants, motels, bookstores, flower shops, and other firms in monopolistic competition. Consider the excess capacity in the funeral-home business. Industry analysts argue that the nation's 22,300 funeral homes could efficiently handle 4 million funerals a year, but only half that number of people die. So the industry on average operates at only 50 percent of capacity, resulting in a higher average cost per funeral.

There is another difference between perfect competition and monopolistic competition that does not show up in Exhibit 3. Although the cost curves drawn in each panel of Exhibit 3 are identical, firms in monopolistic competition in fact spend more on advertising and other promotional expenses to differentiate their products than do firms in perfect competition. These higher costs shift up their average cost curves.

Some economists, including Joan Robinson, have argued that monopolistic competition results in too many suppliers and in product differentiation that is often artificial. But Edward Chamberlin, in outlining his theory of monopolistic competition, argued that consumers are willing to pay a higher price for having a greater selection. According to this view, consumers benefit from the wider choice among gas stations, restaurants, convenience stores, clothing stores, drugstores, economics textbooks, and many other goods and services. For example, what if half of the restaurants were closed just so the remaining ones could operate at full capacity? Some consumers would be disappointed if their favorite restaurant went out of business.

Perfect competitors and monopolistic competitors are so numerous in their respective markets that the action of any one competitor has little effect on the behavior of others in the market. Another important market structure in the gray area between perfect competition and monopoly is *oligopoly,* a Greek word meaning "few sellers." We next focus on the market structure with few sellers.

AN INTRODUCTION TO OLIGOPOLY

Oligopoly A market structure characterized by a small number of firms whose behavior is interdependent

When you think of "big business," you are thinking of **oligopoly,** a market dominated by a few sellers. Perhaps three or four firms account for more than half the market output. Many industries, including steel, automobiles, oil, breakfast cereals, and tobacco, are *oligopolistic*. Oligopoly, however, also describes the market for groceries in regions where there might be only a few grocery stores, or the market for gasoline in regions where there are only a few gas stations. Because an oligopolistic market has only a few firms, each firm must consider the effect of its own policies on competitors' behavior. Oligopolists are therefore *interdependent*.

Varieties of Oligopoly

In some oligopolistic industries, such as steel and oil, the product is homogeneous. In other industries, such as automobiles and tobacco, the product is differentiated across producers. Where the products are homogeneous, there is greater interdependence among the few dominant firms in the industry. For example, because steel ingots are essentially identical, steel producers are quite sensitive to each other's pricing policies. A small rise in the price, will send customers to a rival supplier. But in markets where the product is differentiated, such as the auto industry, producers are not quite as sensitive about each other's pricing policies as are steel producers.

Because of this interdependence among firms in an industry, the behavior of a particular firm is difficult to analyze. *Each firm knows that any changes in its product quality, price, output, or advertising policy may prompt a reaction from its rivals. And each firm may react if the behavior of other firms changes.* Monopolistic competition is like a professional golf tournament, where each player is striving for a personal best; oligopoly is more like a tennis match, where each player's actions depend on how and where the opponent hits the ball.

Why have some industries evolved into an oligopolistic market structure, dominated by only a few firms, whereas other industries have not? Although the reasons are not always clear, *an oligopolistic market structure can often be traced to some form of barrier to entry, such as economies of scale, legal restrictions, brand names built up by years of advertising, or control over an essential resource.* In the previous chapter, we examined barriers to entry as they applied to monopoly. The same principles apply to oligopoly. In the following case study, we consider some barriers to entry in the airline industry.

The Unfriendly Skies

At one time, airline routes were straight lines from one city to another. Now they radiate like the spokes of a wagon wheel from a "hub" city. From 29 hub airports across the country, the airlines send out planes along the spokes to about 400 commercial airports, then quickly bring them back to the hubs. The major airlines dominate hub airports. For example, American and United dominate Chicago's O'Hare International, which is a big, centrally located airport. A new airline trying to enter the industry would have to secure a hub airport as well as landing rights at crowded airports around the country—not an easy task, since all the viable hubs are taken, as are the landing rights at those airports.

Six out of seven flight reservations are booked through travel agents. Another barrier to entry is the computerized reservation systems used by these agents. American has the Sabre system and United has the Apollo system. American and United offer their systems free to travel agents, provided the agents make a certain number of reservations with American or United, whichever is providing the system. Entering reservations for other airlines on the system requires more keystrokes. Thus, travel agents prefer to book with American if they use the Sabre system or with United if they use the Apollo system.

Still another barrier to entry is the frequent-flier mileage programs. The biggest airlines fly more national and international routes, so they offer greater opportunities both to accumulate frequent-flier miles and to use the accumulated mileage for free flights. So the biggest airlines have the most attractive programs.

These three factors—landing slots, reservation systems, and frequent-flier programs—create barriers to entry for new entrants and create barriers to expansion for smaller airlines already in the industry. Five airlines now dominate the market. American, United, Delta, USAir, and Northwest handle about 70 percent of all traffic and control 80 percent of the hubs.

Location:

Strong frequent flier programs help major airlines maintain a dominant position in the market and hinder smaller airlines from expanding their market share. To explore frequent flier programs offered by three major airlines, visit American Airlines (http://www.amrcorp. com/aa_home/), Delta Air Lines (http://www.delta-air. com/index.html), and United Airlines (http://www.ual. com/).

Sources: Edward Phillips, "USAir Unable to Stem Mounting Losses," *Aviation Week & Space Technology*, 6 February 1995; Bridget O'Brian, "Fare Wars Hurt Southwest Airlines and Continental," *The Wall Street Journal*, 27 January 1995; and Shlomo Reifman, "Jobs and Productivity," *Forbes*, 24 April 1995.

Economies of Scale

Perhaps the most significant barrier to entry is economies of scale. Recall that the minimum efficient scale is the lowest rate of output at which the firm takes full advantage of economies of scale. If a firm's minimum efficient scale is relatively large compared to industry output, then only a few firms are needed to produce the total output demanded in the market. A good example is the auto industry. Research shows that an automobile plant of minimum efficient scale can produce enough cars to supply nearly 10 percent of the U.S. market. If there were 100 auto plants, each would supply such a tiny portion of the market that the average cost per car would be higher than if only 10 plants manufactured autos.

In the automobile industry, economies of scale is a barrier to entry. To compete with existing producers, a new entrant must sell enough automobiles to reach a competitive scale of operation. Exhibit 4 presents the long-run average-cost curve for a typical firm in the industry. If a new entrant sells only S cars, the average cost per unit, c_a, far exceeds the average cost, c_b, facing firms that have reached the rate of output, M, achieved at the minimum efficient size. If autos sell for less than c_a, a potential entrant can expect to lose money, and this prospect will likely discourage entry.

High Cost of Entry

There is another aspect to the problem faced by potential entrants into oligopolistic industries. The total cost of reaching the minimum efficient size is often huge. For example, the cost of building a plant of minimum efficient size may be extremely high (an auto plant can cost over $1 billion). Promoting a product enough to compete with established brands may also require an enormous initial outlay. High start-up costs and established brand names can create substantial barriers to entry, especially since the fortunes of a new product are not certain. An unsuccessful attempt at securing a place in the market could result in crippling losses; the prospect of such losses turns away many potential entrants. For example, Unilever lost $160 million in 1995 because its new detergent, Power, failed to crack into the market.

Under perfect competition, all firms sell identical products. There is no incentive to advertise or to promote a particular product, since consumers know that all products are alike. Moreover, producers already can sell all they want at

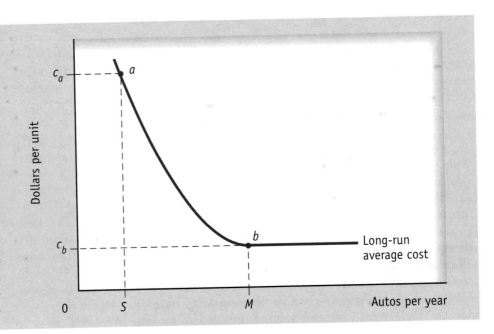

EXHIBIT 4

Economies of Scale as a Barrier to Entry

At point *b*, an existing firm can produce *M* automobiles at an average cost of c_b. A new entrant that can hope to sell only *S* automobiles will incur a much higher average cost of c_a at point *a*. If cars sell for less than c_a, the new entrant will suffer a loss. In this case, economies of scale serve as a barrier to entry, protecting the existing firms.

the prevailing market price, so why advertise? Under oligopoly, however, firms often pour resources into differentiating their products. Some of these expenditures have the beneficial effects of providing valuable information to consumers and offering them a wider array of products. Some forms of product differentiation, however, may be of little value. Slogans such as "Gotta have it!" or "Uh huh!" convey little information, yet Pepsi and Coke have spent millions on such messages. Product differentiation expenditures create barriers to entry. Oligopolies often compete by offering a variety of models or products. For example, several cereal makers offer more than a dozen products each. There are over 25 different laundry detergents. With the proliferation of brands, retail shelf space grows scarce, making new entry more difficult.

MODELS OF OLIGOPOLY

Since oligopolists are interdependent, analyzing their behavior gets complicated. Because of this interdependence, we should not expect any *one* model of oligopoly theory to explain all oligopoly behavior. The demand curve facing an individual firm cannot be specified until the behavior of competing firms has been determined. At one extreme, the firms in the industry may try to coordinate their behavior so they act collectively as a single monopolist, forming a cartel, such as the Organization of Petroleum Exporting Countries (OPEC). At the other extreme, oligopolists may compete so fiercely that price wars erupt, as with airfare warfare and cigarette price wars.

Many theories have been developed to explain oligopoly pricing behavior. We will consider five of the better-known models: (1) cartels, (2) price leadership, (3) game theory, (4) the kinked demand curve, and (5) cost-plus pricing. As you will see, each model has some relevance in explaining observed behavior, though none is entirely satisfactory as a general theory of oligopoly.

Collusion and Cartels

In an oligopolistic market there are few firms; hence, they may try to *collude,* or agree on price and output levels, in order to decrease competition and increase profit. A **cartel** is a group of firms that agree to coordinate their production and pricing decisions so that they act as a single monopolist to earn monopoly profits. Cartels are more likely when the good supplied is homogeneous, as with oil or steel. A cartel provides benefits to member firms—greater certainty about the behavior of "competitors," an organized effort to block new entry, and, as a result, increased profit. Colluding firms usually reduce output, increase price, and block the entry of new firms. Consumers suffer because prices are higher as a result of limited output, and potential entrants suffer because free enterprise is restricted. Collusion and cartels are illegal in this country; most other countries are more tolerant.

Cartel A group of firms that agree to coordinate their production and pricing decisions, thereby behaving as a monopolist

Monopoly profit can be so tempting that firms sometimes break the law. During the 1950s, for example, there was evidence of extensive collusion among electrical equipment producers, and some executives went to jail for their participation in the scheme. In many European countries, formal collusion among firms through cartels is not only legal but is sometimes encouraged by government. Some cartels are worldwide in scope, such as the now-familiar oil cartel OPEC. If OPEC held a meeting in the United States, its members would be arrested for price fixing. Cartels can operate worldwide (even though they are outlawed in some countries) because there are no international laws to stop them.

Suppose that the firms in an industry establish a cartel. The industry demand curve, D, appears in Exhibit 5. What price will maximize the cartel's profit, and how will market output be divided among participating firms? The first task of the cartel is to determine the marginal cost of production for the cartel as a whole. Since the cartel acts as if it were a single monopoly operating many plants, the marginal cost curve in Exhibit 5 sums the marginal cost curves of all firms in the cartel. The cartel's marginal cost curve intersects the marginal revenue curve to determine the price and output that maximize the cartel's profit. This intersection yields price p and industry output Q. So far, so good. *For cartel profit to be maximized, output must be allocated so that the marginal cost of production is identical across firms.* All this is easier said than done. Problems with maintaining a successful cartel are discussed below.

Differences in Cost. If all firms have identical costs, output and profit are easily allocated across firms (each firm produces the same output), but if costs differ, problems arise. The greater the differences in average cost across firms, the greater will be the differences in economic profit across firms. If cartel members try to equalize each firm's total profit, a high-cost firm would need to sell more than a low-cost firm. But this allocation scheme would violate the profit-maximizing condition for the cartel, which is that the marginal cost be identical across firms. Thus, *if average costs differ across firms, there is a conflict between maximizing the cartel profit and equalizing the profit of each cartel member.* If the cartel allocates high-cost firms less output than they want, they could drop out of

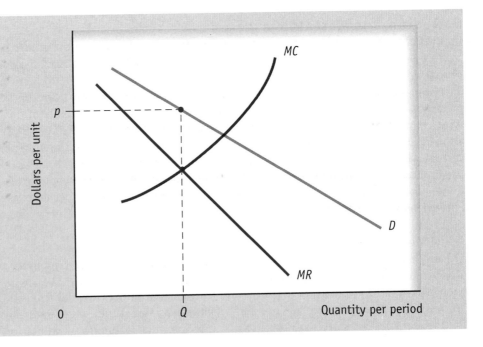

EXHIBIT 5

Cartel Model Where Firms Act as a Monopolist

A cartel acts like a monopolist. Here D is the market demand curve, MR the associated marginal revenue curve, and MC the horizontal sum of the marginal cost curves of cartel members. Cartel profits are maximized when the industry produces quantity Q and charges price p.

the cartel, thereby undermining it. In reality, the allocation of output is typically the result of haggling among cartel members. Firms that are more influential or more adept at bargaining will get a larger share of output. Allocation schemes are sometimes based on geography or on the historical division of output among firms.

Number of Firms in the Cartel. The greater the number of firms in the industry, the more difficult it is to negotiate an acceptable allocation of output among them. Consensus is harder to achieve as the cartel grows, because the chances increase that at least one member will become dissatisfied.

New Entry into the Industry. If a cartel cannot block the entry of new firms into the industry, new entry will eventually force the price down to where firms earn just a normal profit. The profits of the cartel attract entry, entry increases market supply, and increased supply forces the price down. A cartel's continued success therefore depends on barriers that block the entry of new firms.

Cheating. Perhaps the biggest problem in keeping the cartel running is the strong temptation to cheat on the agreement. By offering a price slightly below the established price, a firm can usually increase its sales and profit. Because oligopolists usually operate with excess capacity, some may cheat on the established price. They may attempt to sell more by offering extra services, rebates, or other concessions rather than lowering the price. The incentive to cut prices is particularly strong when industry sales are in a slump. Typically, when production is low, so is the marginal cost of producing more output. Cartel agreements collapse if cheating becomes widespread.

OPEC. The problems of establishing and maintaining a cartel are reflected in the spotty history of OPEC. In 1985, the average price of oil reached $34 a barrel. By 1995, because of competition among the world's oil producers, the price had dropped to half that, despite disruption of oil supplies because of the Persian Gulf war. Many OPEC member countries are poor and rely on oil as a major source of revenue, so they argue over the price and their market share. OPEC members also cheat on the cartel.

Like other cartels, OPEC has had difficulty with new entrants. The high prices resulting from OPEC's early success attracted new oil suppliers from the North Sea, Mexico, and elsewhere. Most observers doubt that OPEC will ever regain its former power. Efforts to cartelize the world supply of a number of products, including bauxite, copper, and coffee, have thus far failed.

In summary, *establishing and maintaining an effective cartel will be more difficult (1) if the product differs across firms, (2) if costs differ across firms, and (3) if entry barriers are relatively low.*

Price Leadership

An informal, or *tacit,* type of collusion occurs in industries that contain **price leaders,** who set the price for the rest of the industry. A dominant firm or a few firms establish the market price, and other firms in the industry follow that lead, thereby avoiding price competition. The price leader also initiates any change in the price, and others follow.

Price leader A firm whose price is adopted by the rest of the industry

Historically, the steel industry has been a good example of the price-leadership form of oligopoly. Typically, U.S. Steel, the largest firm in the industry, would set the price for various products, and other firms would follow. Congressional investigations into the pricing policy in this industry indicate that smaller steel producers relied on the price schedules of U.S. Steel. Public pressure on U.S. Steel not to raise the price shifted the price-leadership role onto smaller producers, resulting in a rotation of the leadership function among firms. Although the rotating price leadership did reduce price conformity among firms in the industry, particularly during the 1970s, prices were still higher than they would have been with no price leadership.

Like other forms of collusion, price leadership is subject to a variety of obstacles. First, the practice often violates antitrust laws. Second, there is no guarantee that other firms will follow the leader. If other firms in the industry do not follow a price increase, the leading firm must either roll back prices or lose sales to lower-priced competitors. Third, the more different the product across sellers, the less effective price leadership will be as a means of collusion. Finally, some firms will try to cheat on the agreement by cutting the price to increase sales and profits.

Cost-Plus Pricing

Cost-plus pricing A method of determining the price of a good by adding a percentage markup to average variable cost

Another model of oligopoly behavior relies on the observation that many oligopolists employ **cost-plus pricing** strategies. Each firm establishes a price by calculating the average variable cost per unit and then adding a percentage, called a *markup,* to cover "overhead" and generate a profit on the firm's investment. This approach seems to ignore the demand curve, since price is determined as a function of cost, not demand. But more on that later.

Cost-plus pricing appears attractive to producers for several reasons. First, it provides a way of coping with uncertainty about the exact shape and elasticity of the demand curve. Second, the very effort of calculating appropriate prices based on marginal analysis is costly, particularly if the firm produces a variety of products. Adopting a simple markup rule greatly simplifies the pricing process. Third, if firms in the industry have similar costs, their use of the same markup percentage will tend to yield similar prices across the industry, generating an implicit form of price collusion.

Choosing the Target Level of Output and the Markup. Because the average variable cost per unit varies with the level of output, the firm adopting a markup approach must project the amount sold. For example, the firm may project that output will be 75 percent of its capacity. If the firm's average variable cost at that level of output is, say, $80 per unit, a 50-percent markup would yield a retail price of $120. This markup is designed to cover those elements of cost that do not vary with output, such as outlays for research and development. Some producers also build into the price a target rate of profit. For example, General Motors has employed a markup policy aimed at earning a 15-percent after-tax rate of return on its investment. GM projects its output to be 80 percent of its capacity.

An Assessment of Cost-Plus Pricing. Cost-plus pricing has an appealing simplicity, and it grows more attractive as a firm's product line expands. A firm like General Electric sells hundreds of different products, so the firm is hard-pressed to allocate the cost of basic research and overhead to particular products. Or consider the problem faced by a grocery store trying to price the thousands of products it sells. The simplest approach is to use a percentage markup to determine the price of each product. There is abundant evidence that markup pricing is used extensively, particularly in retailing. Firms do not have to be oligopolistic to adopt a cost-plus pricing policy; firms in other types of industries may employ the policy as well.

Although cost-plus pricing appears to be inconsistent with marginal analysis, some observers argue that the cost-plus approach is, in fact, a profit-maximizing response to complicated and uncertain market conditions. When executives were interviewed about their companies' use of cost-plus pricing, most said that they did not believe profits could be increased by any change in pricing procedures. Apparently they believed they were charging the prices that maximized profits. Moreover, close scrutiny of actual policies indicates that *firms do not apply the same markup to all their products but vary the markup inversely with the price elasticity of demand for the product.* The greater the elasticity of demand, the lower the markup. This finding suggests that firms do take demand into account and do employ the markup rule in a way that is consistent with profit maximization.

Game Theory

How will firms act when they recognize their interdependence but either cannot or do not collude? Because oligopoly involves interdependence among a few firms, we can think of interacting firms as players in a poker game. This approach was developed by John von Neumann and Oskar Morgenstern in their classic book, *Theory of Games and Economic Behavior,* published in 1944. **Game theory** examines oligopolistic behavior as a series of strategic moves and countermoves among rival firms. It analyzes the behavior of decision makers, or players, whose choices affect one another. The focus is on the players' incentives either to cooperate or to compete.

As an example, consider the market for gasoline in a rural community with only two gas stations; let's call them *A* and *B*. Here we focus on an oligopoly consisting of two firms, or a **duopoly.** Suppose customers are indifferent between the two brands and consider only the price when choosing between stations. To keep the analysis manageable, suppose only two prices are possible: a high price or a low price. If both gas stations charge the high price, they split the total quantity demanded and each gas station earns a profit of $70 per day. If they both charge the low price, they also split the market, but profit drops to only $40 per day. If one charges the high price but the other charges the low price, the low-price station really cleans up, earning a profit of $100 per day. But the high-price station has few customers and loses $20 per day.

What price will each gas station charge? The answer depends on the assumptions about firm behavior—that is, what *strategy* each player pursues. A **strategy** reflects a player's operational plan. Exhibit 6 shows the *payoff matrix* for the two gas stations, with the price strategy that A pursues shown along the left-hand margin and the price strategy that B pursues shown along the top. A **payoff matrix** is a table listing the profits, or payoff, that each of the two rival firms can expect based on the strategy that each firm adopts. As we have noted already, each firm can charge either a "high price" or a "low price."

Net Bookmark

To learn more about game theory, visit the *International Journal of Game Theory,* a quarterly journal founded in 1971 by Oskar Morgenstern (http://www.tau.ac.il/ijgt/index.html). Why do rival firms sometimes agree to cooperate and other times insist on competing? Why do decision makers in businesses behave as they do? Game theory—the study of strategic moves and countermoves among rival firms—attempts to offer answers. To learn more about game theory, visit the *International Journal of Game Theory,* a quarterly journal founded in 1971 by Oskar Morgenstern (http://www.tau.ac.il/ijgt/index.html).

Game theory A model that analyzes oligopolistic behavior as a series of strategic moves and countermoves by rival firms

Duopoly A market with only two producers, who compete with each other; a type of oligopoly market structure

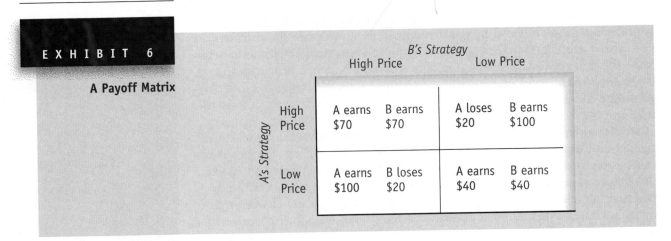

EXHIBIT 6

A Payoff Matrix

		B's Strategy	
		High Price	Low Price
A's Strategy High Price		A earns $70 B earns $70	A loses $20 B earns $100
A's Strategy Low Price		A earns $100 B loses $20	A earns $40 B earns $40

Each cell of the matrix reports each firm's earnings, depending on the strategy. For example, the upper left-hand cell indicates that, if both firms charge the high price, then each will earn $70 per day.

Given this payoff matrix, what does each firm do? Again, the answer depends on each firm's strategy. One common game-theory strategy is to avoid the worst outcome. The worst outcome is to lose $20 per day by being the only gas station charging the high price. The way each firm avoids that outcome is to charge the low price. So if each gas station tries to avoid the worst outcome, both will charge the low price and each will earn $40 per day, as is reflected by the cell in the lower right-hand corner. Note that this payoff is lower than the $70 each could earn if both charged the high price. However, each firm realizes that if it charges the high price, its rival could increase profits to $100 per day by dropping the price.

Avoiding the worst outcome is only one of several strategies we could consider to analyze oligopoly markets in terms of game theory. Outcomes can be as volatile as the personalities involved. Some players are more conservative, and some are more willing to take risks. Price wars sometimes break out among oligopolists. For example, just before Thanksgiving of 1995, American Airlines announced holiday discounts. A few days later, TWA cut fares even more; then Delta topped them with cuts of up to 50 percent in more than 19,000 markets. Within hours, American Airlines, United Airlines, and other major carriers said they would match Delta's reductions. More cuts were expected.[2] So goes the price war in the troubled airline industry.

Strategy In game theory, the operational plan pursued by a player; for example, one strategy is to avoid the worst outcome

Payoff matrix In game theory, a table listing the payoffs that each player can expect based on the strategy that each player pursues

The Kinked Demand Curve

Prices in some oligopolistic industries appear to be stable even during periods when altered cost conditions suggest that a price change would be appropriate. An often-cited case of price stability occurred in the sulfur industry, where the price remained at $18 per ton for a dozen consecutive years, despite major shifts in the cost of production. One oligopoly model sheds light on this apparent price stability. That model relies on the simple idea that if a firm cuts its price, other

---

2   Martha Brannigan, "Delta Air Slashes Fares Up to 50%; Other Carriers Will Match Prices," *The Wall Street Journal,* 14 November 1995.

firms will cut theirs as well to avoid losing customers to the price cutter. But if a firm raises its price, other firms will stand pat, hoping to attract customers away from the price raiser. If an oligopolist expects such responses from competitors, the **kinked demand curve** describes the oligopolist's pricing strategy.

To develop the kinked demand curve model, we start at point e in Exhibit 7, with the firm producing q units at price p. If the firm changes its price, its rivals may choose to imitate the price change or to ignore it. The firm's demand curve will depend on whether other firms follow price moves or ignore them. The firm's demand curve DD assumes that rivals will not follow a change in price. The firm's demand curve $D'D'$ assumes that rivals will match any change in price. As you can see, DD is flatter than $D'D'$. To see why, suppose that General Motors (GM) raises its prices, but other auto producers do not. In this situation, GM will lose far more sales than if other producers also raised their prices. Likewise, if GM cuts prices but others do not, GM will pick up more sales than if all producers cut prices. Thus, if rivals do not follow price changes, any price increase will drive away more customers and any price decrease will attract more customers than if rivals matched price changes. Therefore, each oligopolist's demand curve is flatter when rivals do not follow price changes than when they do.

If rivals follow a price decrease but do not follow a price increase, the oligopolist's demand curve is DeD'. That portion of the demand curve reflecting a price increase, De, is flatter than that portion of the demand curve reflecting a price decrease, eD'. Because rivals match a price decrease but not a price increase, this oligopolist's demand curve, DeD', has a *kink* at the firm's current price–quantity combination, point e.

Kinked demand curve A demand curve that illustrates price stickiness; if one firm cuts its prices, other firms in the industry will cut theirs as well, but if the firm raises its prices, other firms will not change theirs

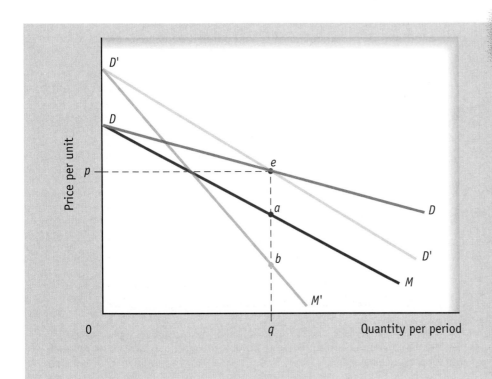

EXHIBIT 7

The Kinked Demand Model of Oligopoly

In the initial situation, an oligopolist is at point e, selling q units at price p. The firm's demand curve is DD if its competitors do not match its price changes; its demand curve is $D'D'$ if competitors do match price changes. Assuming that the firm's rivals match price cuts but not price increases, the relevant demand curve is DeD', with a kink at quantity q. $DabM'$ is the associated marginal revenue curve, with a gap at quantity q.

Marginal Revenue. To find the marginal revenue curve for the kinked demand curve, we simply piece together the relevant portions of the underlying marginal revenue curves. Segment *Da* is the marginal revenue curve applicable to portion *De* of the kinked demand curve. And segment *bM'* is the marginal-revenue curve associated with the portion *eD'* of the kinked demand curve. The marginal revenue curve is thus *DabM'*. Because there is a kink in the demand curve, the marginal revenue curve is not a single line; it has a gap at the currently produced quantity, *q*. The kinked demand curve and the corresponding marginal revenue curve appear in Exhibit 8.

Price Rigidity. Within the gap in the marginal revenue curve, *ab,* the firm will not respond to small shifts in the marginal cost curve. Suppose that curve *MC* in Exhibit 8 is the initial marginal cost curve. The point where *MC* crosses the gap in the marginal revenue curve identifies the profit-maximizing levels of quantity, *q,* and price, *p*. What happens to equilibrium price and quantity if the marginal cost curve drops to *MC'*? Nothing happens, because the oligopolist can do no better than to offer quantity *q* at price *p*. The same holds if marginal cost increases to *MC''*—again, there is no change in the equilibrium price and quantity. *Since changes in the marginal cost curve do not necessarily affect the price, the price tends to be rigid, or stable, in oligopolistic industries if firms behave in the manner described by the kinked demand curve.* It takes a greater shift in the marginal cost curve to produce a change in equilibrium price and quantity. Specifically, to change the equilibrium price and quantity, the marginal cost curve must change enough to intersect the marginal revenue curve above point *a* or below point *b* in Exhibit 8.

EXHIBIT 8   **Demand and Marginal Revenue Curves for the Kinked Demand Model**

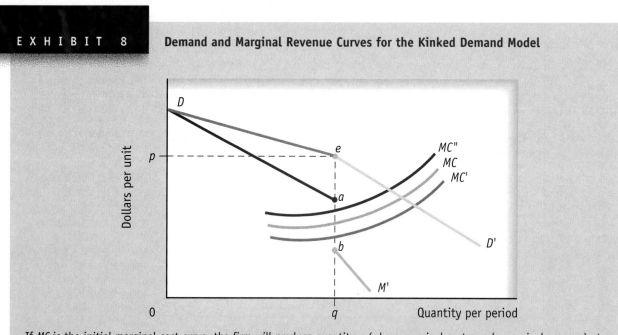

If *MC* is the initial marginal cost curve, the firm will produce quantity *q* (where marginal cost equals marginal revenue) at price *p*. Marginal cost could fall to *MC'* or increase to *MC''* without affecting the quantity produced. Likewise, price *p* will be rigid if marginal cost for output *q* varies between *a* and *b*.

Although the kinked demand model offers a possible explanation for price rigidities observed over the years, the model is silent about how the equilibrium price and quantity are initially determined. What's more, not all prices are rigid. For example, during the inflationary periods of the 1970s and early 1980s, some oligopolies increased prices frequently. In fact, some oligopolies change prices more often than some monopolies, even though the kinked demand model predicts just the opposite.

Summary of Models

Each of the oligopoly models we have considered helps explain certain phenomena observed in oligopolistic markets. The *cartel,* or *collusion,* model shows why oligopolists might want to cooperate to determine market price and output; that model also explains why cartels are hard to establish and maintain. The *price-leadership* model explains how and why firms may act in unison on prices without actually establishing a formal cartel. The *cost-plus pricing* model explains why a firm, in the face of complex costs and uncertain market conditions, may attempt to simplify pricing policy by adding a markup percentage to average variable cost. *Game theory* models show that, because of firm interdependence, market strategies can range from cooperation to price wars. Finally, the *kinked demand curve* explains why some oligopoly prices tend to remain unchanged even in the face of changing costs.

Comparison of Oligopoly and Perfect Competition

As we have seen, each oligopoly model explains a piece of the oligopoly puzzle. Each model has limitations, however, and none represents a complete depiction of all oligopoly behavior. Consequently, since there is no typical, or representative, model of oligopoly, "the" oligopoly cannot be compared with the competitive model. We might, however, imagine an experiment in which we took the hundreds of firms that populate a competitive industry and, through a series of giant mergers, combined them to form, say, a half-dozen firms. We would thereby transform the industry from perfect competition to oligopoly. How would the behavior of firms in this industry differ before and after the massive merger?

Price Is Usually Higher under Oligopoly. With fewer competitors, these firms would become more interdependent. Oligopoly models presented in this chapter suggest that the firms could conceivably act in concert in their pricing policies. Even cost-plus pricing could be a tool for tacit price collusion if firms faced similar costs and adopted similar markup rules. *If the oligopolists engaged in some sort of implicit or explicit collusion, industry output would be smaller and the price would be higher under oligopoly than under perfect competition.* Even if oligopolists did not collude but simply operated with excess capacity, the average cost of production in the long run would be higher with oligopoly than with perfect competition. The price could become temporarily lower under oligopoly compared to perfect competition if a price war broke out among oligopolists.

Higher Profits under Oligopoly. In the long run, easy entry prevents perfect competitors from earning more than a normal profit. With oligopoly, however, there are presumably barriers to entry, such as economies of scale or brand names, that allow firms in the industry to earn long-run economic profits. Such barriers could be insurmountable for a new entrant. Therefore, *we should expect profit rates in the long run to be higher under oligopoly than under perfect competition.* Profit rates do in fact appear to be higher in industries where a few firms account for a high proportion of industry sales. Some economists view these higher profit rates as troubling evidence of market power. But not all economists share this view. Some argue that since the largest firms in oligopolistic industries tend to earn the highest rates of return, higher profit rates in oligopolistic industries stem from the greater efficiency arising from economies of scale in these large firms.[3] Many of these issues will be examined later, when we explore government's role in regulating markets.

Mergers and Oligopoly

Because large firms are potentially more profitable than small ones, some firms have pursued rapid growth by merging with other firms. In some industries, the *merging,* or joining together, of two firms has created oligopolies. Over the last century, there have been four major merger waves in this country. The first occurred between 1887 and 1904. Some of today's largest firms, including U.S. Steel and Standard Oil, were formed during this first merger movement. These tended to be **horizontal mergers,** meaning that the merging firms produced the same products. For example, the firm that is today U.S. Steel was created in 1901 through a billion-dollar merger that involved dozens of individual steel producers and two-thirds of the industry's productive capacity. During this time, similar merger waves occurred in Canada, Great Britain, and elsewhere, creating dominant firms that remain today.

Horizontal merger A merger in which one firm combines with another firm that produces the same product

The second merger wave took place between 1916 and 1929, when vertical mergers were more common. A **vertical merger** is the merging of one firm with a firm that either supplies its inputs or demands its outputs. Thus, it is the merging of firms at different stages of the production process. For example, a steel firm might merge with a firm that mines iron ore.

Vertical merger A merger in which one firm combines with another from which it purchases inputs or to which it sells output

The third merger wave occurred during the 25 years following World War II. More than 200 of the 1,000 largest firms in 1950 had disappeared by 1963 as a result of mergers. In that period, many large firms were absorbed by other, usually larger, firms. The third merger wave culminated in the peak merger activity of 1964 to 1969, when **conglomerate mergers,** which join firms in different industries, accounted for four-fifths of all mergers.

Conglomerate merger A merger involving the combination of firms producing in different industries

The most recent merger boom, the fourth merger wave, began in the late 1970s and continues today. Corporate *takeovers* grew more common in the 1980s. In a takeover, one firm seizes another against its managers' will. Some of the mergers have been huge. The trend in the 1990s has been away from conglomerate mergers toward horizontal and vertical mergers and acquisitions—for example, among media giants, insurance companies, and computer and software makers. A record value of mergers occurred in 1995. Some of the big conglomerate mergers of the 1960s have been dissolved as the core firm sells off unrelated operations.

---

3   For this argument, see Harold Demsetz, "Industry Structure, Market Rivalry, and Public Policy," *Journal of Law and Economics* 16 (April 1973): pp. 1–10.

CONCLUSION

This chapter moves us from the extremes of perfect competition and pure monopoly to the gray area inhabited by most firms. Firms in monopolistic competition and firms in oligopoly face a downward-sloping demand curve for their products. In choosing the profit-maximizing price-output combination, the firm in monopolistic competition is not very concerned about the effects of this choice on the behavior of competitors. But oligopolistic firms are interdependent and therefore must consider the effects their pricing and output decisions will have on other firms. This interdependence complicates the analysis of oligopoly, leaving open a wide array of possible models.

The analytical results derived in this chapter are not as neat as those derived for the polar cases of perfect competition and pure monopoly, but we can still point to general conclusions, using perfect competition as our benchmark. Perfect competitors in the long run operate at minimum average cost, while the other types of firms usually operate with excess capacity. Therefore, given identical cost curves, monopolistic competitors and oligopolists tend to charge higher prices than perfect competitors, especially in the long run. In the long run, monopolistic competitors, like perfect competitors, earn only a normal profit because entry barriers are low. But oligopolists can earn economic profit in the long run if new entry is somehow restricted. In a later chapter, we will examine how government policy is often aimed at making firms more competitive. *Regardless of the market structure, however, profit maximization prompts firms to produce the output level at which marginal cost equals marginal revenue.*

SUMMARY

1. Whereas the pure monopolist produces output that has no close substitutes, a monopolistic competitor must contend with many rivals offering close substitutes. Because there are some differences among the products offered by different firms, even if the difference is based on the location of the seller, each monopolistic competitor faces a downward-sloping demand curve.

2. Sellers in monopolistic competition differentiate their products through (1) physical qualities, (2) sales locations, (3) services provided with the product, and (4) the image of the product established in the consumer's mind.

3. In the short run, monopolistic competitors that can at least cover their average variable costs will maximize profits or minimize losses by producing where marginal cost equals marginal revenue. In the long run, free entry and exit of firms ensure that monopolistic competitors earn only normal profit, which occurs where the average total cost curve is tangent to the firm's downward-sloping demand curve.

4. An oligopoly is a market dominated by a few sellers, some of which are large enough relative to the entire market to influence price. In some oligopolistic industries, such as steel or oil, the product is homogeneous; in other oligopolistic industries, such as automobiles or tobacco, the product differs.

5. Because an oligopolistic market consists of few firms, each firm may react to another firm's changes in quality, price, output, or advertising policy. Because of this interdependence among oligopolists, the behavior of producers is difficult to analyze. No single model of behavior characterizes oligopolistic markets.

6. In this chapter, we considered five models of oligopoly behavior: (1) the cartel, through which firms collude to behave like a monopolist; (2) price leadership, whereby one or a few firms set the price for the industry and other firms follow the leaders; (3) cost-plus pricing, whereby each firm determine prices by estimating average variable cost and adding a percentage markup to cover nonallocated costs and to earn a target rate of profit; (4) game theory, which focuses on each firm's strategy, based on the responses of rivals; and (5) the kinked demand curve, which assumes that a firm's rivals follow price decreases but do not follow price increases.

QUESTIONS AND PROBLEMS

1. **(Market Structures)** Indicate whether each of the following characteristics is true in perfect competition, monopolistic competition, oligopoly, and/or monopoly:
   a. A large number of sellers.
   b. A homogeneous product.
   c. Advertising by firms.
   d. Barriers to entry.
   e. Firms that are price searchers.

2. **(Monopolistically Competitive Demands)** Why does the monopolistically competitive firm's demand curve slope downward in the long run, even after the entry of new firms?

3. **(Monopolistic Competition Versus Perfect Competition)** Illustrated below are the marginal cost and long-run average total cost curves for a small firm. (a) Locate the long-run equilibrium price and quantity if the firm is perfectly competitive. Label the price and quantity P_1 and Q_1. (b) Draw in a demand and marginal revenue curve to illustrate long-run equilibrium if the firm is monopolistically competitive. Label the price and quantity P_2 and Q_2. (c) How do the monopolistically competitive firm's price and output compare to that of the perfectly competitive firm's? (d) How do long-run profits compare for the two types of firms? (e) Does the monopolistically competitive firm generate allocative and productive efficiency? Explain.

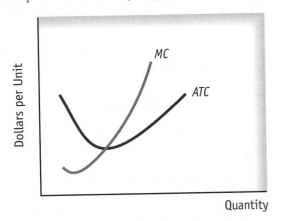

4. **(Short-Run Behavior)** Assume that a monopolistically competitive firm has the following demand and cost figures in the short run:

Output	Price	FC	VC	TC	TR	Profit/Loss
0	$100	$100	$ 0	___	___	___
1	90	___	50	___	___	___
2	80	___	90	___	___	___

Output	Price	FC	VC	TC	TR	Profit/Loss
3	70	___	150	___	___	___
4	60	___	230	___	___	___
5	50	___	330	___	___	___
6	40	___	450	___	___	___
7	30	___	590	___	___	___

   a. Complete the above table.
   b. What is the best profit or loss available to the firm?
   c. Should the firm operate or shut down in the short run? Why or why not?
   d. What is the relationship between marginal revenue and marginal cost as the firm increases output?

5. **(Kinked Demand)** Given a kinked demand curve, will oligopolists always experience economic profits, or could they have short-run losses? What significance does a kinked demand curve have for short-run losses?

6. **(Oligopoly)** "If the United Auto Workers union bargains for higher wages at Ford, Ford will simply pass on the additional costs to consumers in the form of higher prices." Must this statement be true? Why or why not?

7. **(Cartels)** Why would each of the following induce some members of OPEC to cheat on their cartel agreement?
   a. Some cartel members are less developed countries.
   b. There are a large number of members.
   c. International debts of some members grow.
   d. Expectations grow that some members will cheat.

8. **(Price Leadership)** Is it reasonable to assume that a price leader will always be the largest producer (that is, the firm with the largest scale)?

9. **(Cost-Plus Pricing)** How might a firm decide whether its markup was too high or too low? Is this determination governed by market conditions? How may cost-plus pricing be consistent with profit maximization?

10. **(Mergers)** Indicate whether each of the following would be a horizontal, vertical, or conglomerate merger:
    a. Disney Pictures and Sony Pictures.
    b. Sony Pictures and a chain of movie theaters.
    c. A chain of movie theaters and a popcorn machine manufacturer.
    d. A popcorn machine manufacturer and an automobile producer.
    e. Ford and General Motors.

11. **(Game Theory)** Suppose there are only two automobile companies, Ford and Chevy, and Ford believes that Chevy will match any price it sets. Use the following price and profit data to answer the questions below.

If Ford sells for	and Chevy sells for	Ford's profits (millions)	Chevy's profits (millions)
$ 4,000	$ 4,000	$ 8	$ 8
4,000	8,000	12	68
4,000	12,000	14	2
8,000	4,000	6	12
8,000	8,000	10	10
8,000	12,000	12	6
12,000	4,000	2	14
12,000	8,000	6	12
12,000	12,000	7	7

  a. What price will Ford set for its cars?
  b. What price will Chevy set, given Ford's price?
  c. What is Ford's profit after Chevy's response?
  d. If they collaborated to maximize joint profits, what prices would the two companies set?
  e. Given your answer to part d, how could undetected cheating on price cause each car maker's profits to rise?

12. **(Oligopoly)** Do the firms in an oligopoly act independently or interdependently? What effect does this have on the demand curve facing an individual firm? How might the oligopolist attempt to deal with this effect?

13. **(Monopolistic Competition)** In the long run, the monopolistically competitive firm earns zero economic profit, which is exactly what would occur if the industry were perfectly competitive. Assuming that the cost curve for each firm is the same whether the industry is perfectly or monopolistically competitive, answer the following questions.
  a. Why don't perfectly and monopolistically competitive firms produce the same industry output in the long run?
  b. Why is the monopolistically competitive industry said to be economically inefficient?
  c. What benefits might cause us to prefer the monopolistically competitive result over the perfectly competitive result?

14. **(Cartel)** Use a revenue and cost curve graph to illustrate and explain how a cartel behaves like a monopolist.

15. **(Product Differentiation)** What are the four basic ways in which a firm can differentiate its product? What role can advertising play in product differentiation? How can advertising become a barrier to entry?

16. **(Oligopoly)** What are the two types of products sold under oligopoly? Is the level of interdependence the same in both types? Why or why not?

17. **(Kinked Demand Curve)** If a firm believes that it is facing a kinked demand curve, what assumptions is it making about its rivals' reactions to price changes by the firm? What impact does this have on the shape of the firm's demand curve and marginal revenue curve? How does the firm react to changes in its production costs?

18. **(Oligopoly)** Many industries that appear to be monopolistically competitive turn out to be oligopolies, because one firm may actually produce many of the differentiated products that compete with each other. Why would firms in an industry pursue such a strategy?

19. **(Fast Forward)** Use a cost and revenue graph to illustrate and explain the short-run profits in the video rental business. Then use a second graph to illustrate the long-run situation. Explain fully.

20. **(The Unfriendly Skies)** One complaint frequently heard about air fares is that flying from a hub city airport is more expensive than flying from a nearby city that is not a hub. How may this reflect a different level of competition in hub city airports? How may it also be a form of product differentiation?

Using the Internet

21. Visit Paul Walker's "Outline of the History of Game Theory," maintained by the Department of Economics, University of Canterbury, New Zealand (**http://www.canterbury.ac.nz/econ/hist.htm**). How old are the roots of game theory? What is the most recent development?

Resource Markets

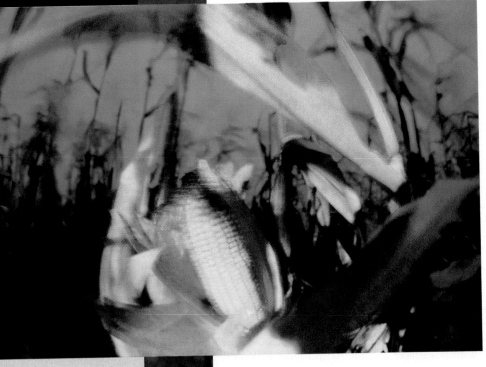

Why does Charles Schulz, the cartoonist, earn $25 million a year for drawing *Peanuts,* while Charles Schultze, the economist, earns peanuts, relatively speaking, for drawing conclusions about the economy? Demand and supply. Why do surgeons earn twice as much as general practitioners? Demand and supply. Why does prime Iowa corn acreage cost more than scrubland in the Texas panhandle? Demand and supply. Why are the buildings in downtown Chicago taller than those in the farm towns of southern Illinois? Demand and supply.

You say you've been through demand and supply already? True. But the earlier discussion focused on the product market—that is, the market for final goods and services. Goods and services, however, are produced by resources—land, labor, capital, and entrepreneurial ability. Demand and supply in the resource market determine the price and employment of resources. The distribution of resource ownership then determines the distribution of income throughout the economy.

Since your earnings depend on the market value of your resources, resource markets should be of particular interest to you. Certainly one key element in your career decision is the expected income associated with alternative careers. The next several chapters will examine how demand and supply interact to establish market prices for various resources. Topics discussed in this chapter include:

- Resource markets
- Opportunity cost and economic rent
- Marginal revenue product

- Marginal resource cost
- Shifts in resource demand
- Elasticity of resource demand
- Distribution of resource earnings

THE ONCE-OVER

You already know a lot more about resource markets than you think. See if you can answer the following questions.

Resource Demand

Consider first the demand for land. A neighbor offers Farmer Jones the opportunity to lease 100 acres of farmland. Jones figures that farming the extra land would cost $70 per acre but would yield $60 per acre in additional revenue. Should he lease the extra land? What do you think? Since the additional cost of farming that land would exceed the additional revenue, the answer is no.

Next, consider labor. The manager of Wal-Mart knows that hiring one more sales clerk would increase total cost by $400 per week but would increase total revenue by $500 per week. Should the additional worker be hired? Sure. The additional sales clerk would increase Wal-Mart's profit by $100 per week. As long as the additional revenue from employing another worker exceeds the additional cost, the firm should hire that worker.

What about capital? Suppose that you operate a lawn-and-garden service during the summer, earning an average of $20 per lawn. You mow about 15 lawns a week, for a total revenue of $300. You are considering upgrading to a larger, faster lawn mower called the Lawn Monster. The bigger mower would cut your time per lawn in half, enabling you to care for 30 lawns per week, so your total revenue would double to $600 per week. The mower would cost you an extra $200 per week. Should you make the switch? Since the additional revenue of $300 exceeds the additional cost of $200, you should move up to the Monster.

These examples show that *a firm demands additional units of a resource as long as the marginal revenue generated by each additional unit exceeds the marginal cost.*

Resource Supply

You likely also understand the economic logic behind resource supply. Suppose you are deciding between two jobs that are identical except that one pays more than the other. Is there any question which job you will take? If the working conditions of both jobs are equally attractive, you will choose the higher-paying job. Now consider your choice between two jobs that pay the same; one has normal nine-to-five hours, but the other starts at 5:00 A.M., an hour when your body tends to reject conscious activity. Which would you choose? You would select the job more in accord with your natural body rhythms.

Resource owners will supply their resources to the highest-paying alternative, other things constant. Since other things are not always constant, however, resource owners must often be paid more to supply their resources to certain uses. In the case of labor, the worker's utility depends on both pay and other nonmonetary aspects of the job. People must be paid more to work in jobs that are dirty, dangerous, dull, exhausting, of low status, and that involve inconvenient hours than to work in jobs that are clean, safe, stimulating, of high status, and involve convenient hours. *A resource owner will supply additional units of the resource as long as doing so increases his or her utility.*

THE DEMAND AND SUPPLY OF RESOURCES

In the market for goods and services—that is, in the product market—households are the demanders and firms are suppliers. Households demand the goods and services that maximize utility, and firms supply the goods and services that maximize profit. In the resource market, the roles of demand and supply are reversed: firms are demanders and households are suppliers. Firms demand the resources that maximize profit and households supply the resources that maximize utility. *Any differences between the profit-maximizing goals of firms and the utility-maximizing goals of households are reconciled through voluntary exchange in markets.*

Exhibit 1 presents the market for a particular resource—in this case, carpenters. As you can see, the demand curve slopes downward and the supply curve slopes upward. *Like the demand and supply for final goods and services, the demand and supply for resources depend on the willingness and the ability of buyers and sellers to participate in market exchange.* This market will converge to the equilibrium wage rate, or the market price, for this type of labor.

The Market Demand Curve

Why does a firm employ resources? Resources produce goods and services, which a firm tries to sell for a profit. The firm does not value the resources themselves but the resources' ability to produce goods and services. Because the value of any resource depends on the value of what it produces, the demand for a resource is a **derived demand**—derived from the demand for the final product. For example, a carpenter's pay derives from the demand for carpentry products, such as new homes; a movie star's pay derives from the demand for movies; and a professional baseball player's pay derives from the demand for ball games. The derived nature of resource demand explains why professional baseball players earn more on average than professional soccer players, and why CBS paid more than $1 billion for the rights to televise the men's NCAA bas-

Derived demand *The demand for a resource is derived from the demand for the product the resource produces*

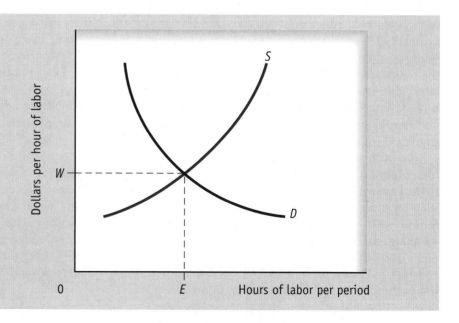

EXHIBIT 1

Resource Market for Carpenters

The intersection of the upward-sloping supply curve of carpenters with the downward-sloping demand curve determines the equilibrium wage rate, *W*, and the level of employment, *E*.

ketball tournament, whereas ESPN paid only $17 million for rights to the women's NCAA tournament.

The market demand for a resource is the sum of the demands for that resource in all its various uses. For example, the market demand for carpenters sums all the demands for this type of labor in residential and commercial construction, renovations, furniture making, and so on. Similarly, the market demand for lumber sums its demand in housing, paper products, railway ties, firewood, furniture, pencils, toothpicks, and so on. The demand curve for a resource, like the demand curve for the goods produced by that resource, slopes downward, as depicted in Exhibit 1. As the price of a resource falls, producers are more willing and more able to employ that resource.

Consider first the producer's greater *willingness* to hire resources as the price falls. In constructing the demand curve for a particular resource, we hold constant the prices of other resources. So if the price of a particular resource falls, it becomes relatively cheaper compared to other resources the firm could use to produce the same output. Firms therefore are more willing to hire this resource rather than hire other, now relatively more costly, resources. Thus, we observe *substitution in production*—coal for oil, security alarms for security guards, and backhoes for grave diggers, as the relative prices of coal, security alarms, and backhoes fall.

A lower price for a resource also increases a producer's *ability* to hire that resource. For example, if the resource price falls, a firm can hire more of the resource for the same total cost. The lower resource price means the firm is *more able* to buy the resource.

The Market Supply Curve

The market supply of a resource sums all the individual supply curves for that resource. Resource suppliers tend to be both more *willing* and more *able* to supply the resource as the resource price increases, so the market supply curve tends to slope upward. Resource suppliers are more *willing* because the higher the market price of a particular resource, other things constant, the more goods and services resource owners can buy with the earnings obtained from supplying the resource. Resource prices are signals about the rewards for supplying resources to alternative activities, and higher resource prices will draw resources from lower-valued uses, including leisure. For example, as the wage for carpenters increases, the quantity supplied will increase; some existing carpenters are willing to work more hours and potential carpenters are attracted from alternative occupations.

The second reason a resource supply curve slopes upward is that resource owners are *able* to supply more of the resource at a higher price. For example, some people may have little natural ability as carpenters, but a higher wage justifies the additional training they may need to become carpenters. Likewise, higher paper prices in recent years have increased the market price of timber used to make paper, so logging companies can afford to harvest trees in more remote regions. A higher resource price *enables* resource suppliers to increase their quantity supplied.

Temporary and Permanent Resource Price Differences

Resource owners have a strong interest in selling their resources where they are most valued. *Resources tend to flow to their highest-valued use.* If carpenters, for example, can earn more building homes than making furniture, then carpenters will go into home building. The supply of carpenters will shift out of furniture making and into home building until wages in the two activities are equal. Because resource owners seek the highest pay, *other things constant,* the prices paid for identical resources should, over time, tend toward equality.

For example, suppose an increase in the demand for new housing increases the wage paid to carpenters engaged in home building to $25 per hour, which is $5 more than the wage paid to carpenters who work as furniture makers. This difference is shown in Exhibit 2 by a wage of $25 per hour in panel (a) and a wage of $20 per hour in panel (b). As a result of the difference, some carpenters will move from furniture making to home building. This shift will decrease

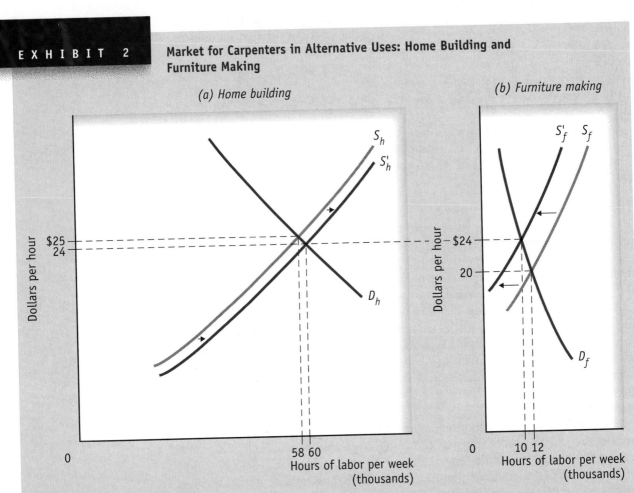

EXHIBIT 2

Market for Carpenters in Alternative Uses: Home Building and Furniture Making

(a) Home building

(b) Furniture making

Suppose the wage offered carpenters is $25 per hour in home building but only $20 per hour in furniture making. As a result of the wage differential, some carpenters will shift from furniture making to home building, and this will continue until the wage offered carpenters is identical in both alternative uses. In panel (b), the reduction in the supply of carpenters to furniture making increases the equilibrium wage from $20 per hour to $24 per hour. In panel (a), the increase in the supply of carpenters to home building decreases the equilibrium wage from $25 per hour to $24 per hour. A total of 2,000 carpenter hours per week are shifted from furniture making to home building.

the wage in home building and increase the wage in furniture making. Carpenters will move into home building until wages equalize. In Exhibit 2, supply shifts until the wage is $24 in both markets. Note that in the adjustment process, 2,000 hours of labor per week shift from furniture making to home building. *As long as the nonmonetary benefits of supplying resources to alternative uses are identical and as long as resources are freely mobile, resources will earn the same in their alternative uses.*

Sometimes, earnings appear to differ between seemingly similar resources. For example, corporate economists on average earn more than academic economists, and land in the city sells for more than land in the country. As you will now see, these differences reflect the workings of demand and supply.

Temporary Differences in Resource Prices. Resource prices sometimes differ temporarily across markets because market adjustment takes time. For example, there are sometimes wage differentials among workers who appear equally qualified. As we have noted, however, a difference between the prices of similar resources prompts resource owners and firms to make adjustments that drive resource prices to equality, as with the carpenters in the previous exhibit. The process may take years, but when resource markets are free to adjust, price differences trigger the reallocation of resources, which equalizes payments for similar resources.

Permanent Differences in Resource Prices. Not all resource price differences cause a reallocation of resources. For example, land along New York's Fifth Avenue sells for as much as $36,000 a *square yard!* For that amount, one could buy several acres of farmland in upstate New York. Yet such a differential does not prompt land owners in upstate New York to supply their land to New York City—obviously that's impossible. The price per acre of farmland varies widely, reflecting differences in the land's productivity and location. Such differences do not trigger actions that result in price equality. Similarly, certain wage differentials stem in part from the different costs of acquiring the education and training required to perform particular tasks. This difference explains why brain surgeons earn more than tree surgeons, why ophthalmologists earn more than optometrists, and why airline pilots earn more than truck drivers.

Other earning differentials reflect differences in the nonmonetary aspects of similar jobs. For example, other things constant, most people require more pay to work in a grimy factory than in a pleasant office. Similarly, corporate economists earn more than academic economists in part because corporate economists typically have less freedom in their daily schedules, attire, and choices of research topics.

Whereas temporary price differentials spark the movement of resources away from lower-paid uses toward higher-paid uses, permanent price differentials cause no such reallocations. Permanent price differentials are explained by *a lack of resource mobility* (rural land versus urban land), *differences in the inherent quality of the resource* (scrubland versus fertile land), *differences in the time and money involved in developing the necessary skills* (file clerk versus certified public accountant), and *differences in nonmonetary aspects of the job* (lifeguard at Malibu Beach versus prison guard at San Quentin).

In 1995, Shaquille O'Neal reportedly earned $22 million, mostly from product endorsements. Because his best alternative to pro basketball would pay far less, most of his earnings consist of economic rent.

Opportunity Cost and Economic Rent

Shaquille O'Neal reportedly earned $22 million in 1995, mostly from product endorsements.[1] But he would likely be willing to play basketball and endorse products for less. The question is, how much less? What is his best alternative? Suppose his best alternative is to devote his energy full time to becoming a rap artist, something he now only dabbles in. Suppose as a full-time rap artist he could earn $2 million per year, including endorsements. Assume too that, if it weren't for the pay difference, he is indifferent between rap and basketball, so the nonmonetary aspects of the two jobs balance out. Thus, he must earn at least $2 million to remain a basketball player. This amount represents his *opportunity cost*—the amount he must be paid to prevent him from supplying his time to rap. The opportunity cost of a resource is what that resource could earn in its best alternative use.

The amount O'Neal earns in excess of his opportunity cost is called *economic rent*. **Economic rent** is that portion of a resource's total earnings that is not necessary to keep the resource in its present use; it is, as the saying goes, "pure gravy." In O'Neal's case, the economic rent is $22 million minus $2 million, or $20 million. Economic rent is a form of producer surplus earned by resource suppliers. The *division* of earnings between opportunity cost and economic rent depends on the resource owner's elasticity of supply. *In general, the less elastic the resource supply, the greater the economic rent as a proportion of total earnings.* To develop a feel for the difference between opportunity cost and economic rent, consider the following three cases.

Case A: All Earnings Are Economic Rent. If the supply of a resource to a particular market is perfectly inelastic, that resource has no alternative uses. Hence, there is no opportunity cost, and all returns are economic rent. For example, scrubland in the high plains of Montana has no use other than for grazing cattle. The supply of this grazing land is depicted by the vertical line in panel (a) of Exhibit 3, which indicates that the 10 million acres have no alternative use. Since the supply is fixed, the amount paid to rent this land for grazing has no effect on the quantity supplied. Since the land has no alternative use, the opportunity cost is zero and all earnings are economic rent, shown by the blue shaded area. Here, *the demand determines the equilibrium price of the resource, but fixed supply determines the equilibrium quantity.*

Case B: All Earnings Are Opportunity Costs. At the other extreme is the case in which a resource can earn as much in its best alternative use as in its present use. This situation is illustrated by the perfectly elastic supply curve in panel (b) of Exhibit 3. Suppose this figure depicts the market for janitors in the local school system. The school system can employ as many janitors as it wants at the market wage of $10 per hour; here, the system demands 100,000 hours of labor per week. If the wage offered to janitors falls below $10 per hour, they will find maintenance jobs elsewhere, perhaps in nearby factories, hospitals, or colleges, where the wage is $10 per hour. In this case, all earnings equal opportunity costs because any reduction in the wage reduces the quantity of labor supplied

Economic rent The portion of a resource's total earnings above its opportunity cost; earnings above the amount necessary to keep the resource in its present use

---

[1]   Randall Lane and Josh McHugh, "A Very Green 1995," *Forbes,* 18 December 1995, p. 214.

Opportunity Cost and Economic Rent

EXHIBIT 3

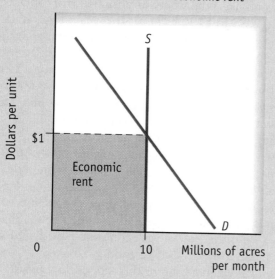

(a) All resource returns are economic rent

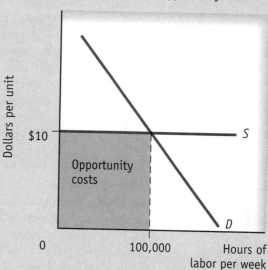

(b) All resource returns are opportunity costs

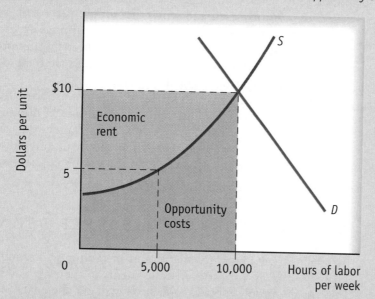

(c) Resource returns are divided between economic rent and opportunity cost

In panel (a), the resource supply curve is vertical, indicating that the resource has no alternative use. The price is de-mand-determined, and all earnings are in the form of economic rent. In panel (b), the supply curve is horizontal, indicat-ing that the resource can earn $10 in its best alternative use. Employment is demand-determined, and all earnings are opportunity costs. Panel (c) shows an upward-sloping supply curve. At the equilibrium wage of $10, resource earnings are partly opportunity costs and partly economic rent. Both supply and demand determine the equilibrium price and quantity.

to this particular use to zero. In this case, *demand determines the equilibrium quantity, but the horizontal supply determines the equilibrium wage.*

Case C: Earnings Include Both Economic Rent and Opportunity Costs. If the supply curve slopes upward, resource owners will earn economic rent in addition to their opportunity cost. For example, if the wage for unskilled work in your college community increases from $5 to $10 per hour, the quantity of labor supplied will increase, as will the economic rent earned by resource suppliers. This situation occurs in panel (c) of Exhibit 3, where the blue area identifies economic rent and the red area identifies opportunity costs. If the wage increases from $5 to $10, the quantity supplied per week will increase by 5,000 hours. For those resource suppliers who had been offering their services at a wage of $5 per hour, the difference between $5 and $10 is economic rent. These workers did not require the higher price to supply their services, but they certainly are not going to turn it down. *In the case of an upward-sloping supply curve and a downward-sloping demand curve, both demand and supply determine the equilibrium price and quantity.*

Note that specialized resources tend to earn a higher proportion of economic rent than do resources with many alternative uses. Thus, Shaquille O'Neal earns a greater *proportion* of his income as economic rent than does the janitor who sweeps up the Orlando Magic locker room.

To review: Given a resource demand curve that slopes downward, when the resource supply curve is vertical (perfectly inelastic), all earnings are economic rent; when that supply curve is horizontal (perfectly elastic), all earnings reflect opportunity cost; and when that supply curve slopes upward (an elasticity greater than zero but less than infinity), earnings are divided between opportunity cost and economic rent. Remember, the opportunity cost of a resource is what that resource could earn in its best alternative use. Economic rent is earnings in excess of opportunity cost.

This completes our introduction to resource supply. In the balance of this chapter, we take a closer look at the demand side of resource markets. The determinants of the demand for a resource are largely the same whether we are talking about land, labor, or capital. The supply of different resources, however, has certain peculiarities depending on the resource, so the supply of specific resources will be taken up in the next three chapters.

A CLOSER LOOK AT RESOURCE DEMAND

In Chapter 2, you learned that the art of economic reasoning involves marginal analysis—that is, focusing on adjustments to the status quo. Although production usually involves many inputs, we will cut the analysis down to size by focusing on a single resource, assuming that the quantities of other resources are constant. As usual, we assume that firms try to maximize profit and households try to maximize utility.

The Firm's Demand for One Resource

You may recall that when we introduced the firm's costs, we considered a moving company, where labor was the only variable resource in the short run. By varying the amount of labor employed, we examined the relationship be-

EXHIBIT 4

The Marginal Revenue Product When a Firm Sells in a Competitive Market

Workers Per Day (1)	Total Product (2)	Marginal Product (3)	Product Price (4)	Total Revenue (5) = (2) × (4)	Marginal Revenue Product (6)
0	0	—	$20	$ 0	—
1	10	10	20	200	$200
2	19	9	20	380	180
3	27	8	20	540	160
4	34	7	20	680	140
5	40	6	20	800	120
6	45	5	20	900	100
7	49	4	20	980	80
8	52	3	20	1040	60
9	54	2	20	1080	40
10	55	1	20	1100	20
11	55	0	20	1100	0
12	53	−2	20	1060	−40

tween the quantity of labor employed and the amount of furniture moved per day. We used the same approach in Exhibit 4, where all but one of the firm's inputs remains constant. The first column in the table lists possible employment levels of the variable resource, in this case measured as workers per day. The second column presents the total output, or total product, and the third column presents the marginal product. The *marginal product* of labor shows how much additional output each additional unit of labor produces.

The first worker has a marginal product of 10 units, the second worker has a marginal product of 9 units, and so on. As the firm hires more workers, the marginal product of labor declines, reflecting the law of diminishing marginal returns. In Exhibit 4, diminishing marginal returns set in immediately—that is, right after the first worker is employed.

Although labor is the variable resource here, we could examine the marginal product of any resource. For example, we could consider how many lawns could be cut per week by varying the quantity of capital employed. We might start off with very little capital—imagine cutting grass with a pair of scissors—then moving up to a push mower, to a power mower, to the Lawn Monster. By holding labor constant and varying the quantity of capital employed, we could compute the marginal product of capital. Likewise, we could compute the marginal product of land by examining crop production for varying amounts of land, holding other inputs, such as the amount of farm labor and capital, constant.

Marginal Revenue Product

The first three columns of Exhibit 4 show what happens to output as the firm hires more workers. The important question is, what happens to the firm's *revenue* as a result of hiring additional workers? The *marginal revenue product* of labor indicates how total revenue changes as more labor is employed, other

Marginal revenue product *The change in total revenue when an additional unit of a resource is hired, other things constant*

things constant. The **marginal revenue product** of any resource is the change in the firm's total revenue resulting from employing an additional unit of the resource, other things constant. You could think of the marginal revenue product as the firm's "marginal benefit" from hiring one more unit of the resource. A resource's marginal revenue product depends on (1) how much additional output the resource produces and (2) the price at which output is sold.

Selling as a Price Taker. The calculation of marginal revenue product is simplest when the firm sells its output in a perfectly competitive market, which is the assumption underlying Exhibit 4. Since an individual firm in perfect competition can sell as much as it wants without affecting the product's price, a perfectly competitive firm is said to be a *price taker*. That firm must accept, or "take," the market price for its product. The marginal revenue product, listed in column (6), is the change in total revenue that results from changing input usage by one unit. For the perfectly competitive firm, the marginal revenue product is simply the marginal product multiplied by the product price of $20. Note that because of diminishing returns, the marginal revenue product falls steadily as the firm employs additional units of the resource.

Selling as a Price Searcher. If the firm has some market power in the product market—that is, some ability to set the price—the demand curve for that firm's output slopes downward. To sell more output, the firm must lower its price. The firm, consequently, must search for the price that maximizes profit. Such a firm is called a *price searcher*. Exhibit 5 reproduces the first two columns of Exhibit 4; the remaining columns reflect the revenue of a firm selling as a price searcher. Together, columns (2) and (3) represent the demand for the product. Total output multiplied by the price at which that output sells yields the firm's total revenue, which appears in column (4).

The marginal revenue product of labor, which is the change in total revenue resulting from a 1-unit change in the quantity of labor employed, appears in column (5). For example, the first worker produced 10 units per day, which sell for $40 each, yielding total revenue of $400. Hiring the second worker adds 9 more units to the total product, but to sell 9 more units, the firm must lower the price of all units from $40 to $35.20. Total revenue increases to $668.80, which means the marginal revenue product of a second worker is $268.80.

Again, the marginal revenue product is the additional revenue that results from employing each additional worker. The profit-maximizing firm should be willing and able to pay as much as the marginal revenue product for an additional unit of the resource. *Since the marginal revenue product of a resource shows how much a firm would be willing and able to pay for each additional unit of the resource, the marginal revenue product curve can be thought of as the firm's demand curve for that resource.*

To review, whether a firm is a price taker or a price searcher, the marginal revenue product of a resource is the change in total revenue resulting from a 1-unit change in that resource, other things held constant. The marginal revenue product curve of a resource is the demand curve for that resource—it shows the most a firm would be willing and able to pay for each successive unit of the resource. For a firm selling as a price taker, the marginal revenue product equals the marginal product times the price. For a firm selling as a price searcher, this

Workers Per Day (1)	Total Product (2)	Product Price (3)	Total Revenue (4) = (2) × (3)	Marginal Revenue Product (5)
0	0	—	—	—
1	10	$40.00	$400.00	$400.00
2	19	35.20	668.80	268.80
3	27	31.40	847.80	179.00
4	34	27.80	945.20	97.40
5	40	25.00	1000.00	54.80
6	45	22.50	1012.50	12.50
7	49	20.50	1004.50	−8.00
8	52	19.00	988.00	−16.50
9	54	18.00	972.00	−16.00
10	55	17.50	962.50	−9.50
11	55	17.50	962.50	0.00

EXHIBIT 5

The Marginal Revenue Product When a Firm Sells as a Price Searcher

simple formula does not apply because that firm can sell more output only if the price of that output falls. *For a price taker in the product market, the marginal revenue product declines only because of diminishing marginal returns. For a price searcher in the product market, the marginal revenue product declines both because of diminishing returns and because additional output can be sold only if the price declines.*

Marginal Resource Cost

Given the firm's marginal revenue product, can we determine how much labor the firm should employ to maximize profit? Not yet, because we know only how much marginal revenue the resource generates. We must also know how much this resource costs the firm. Specifically, what is the **marginal resource cost**—that is, what is the additional cost to the firm of employing one more unit of the resource? The marginal cost of labor, or marginal resource cost, is simplest to calculate when the firm is a price taker in the labor market. A **resource price taker** hires such a tiny fraction of the available resource that its employment decision has no effect on the market price of the resource. Thus, the resource price taker faces a given market price for the resource and decides only on how much to hire at that price.

For example, if the market wage for factory workers is $100 per day, the firm's marginal cost of labor is $100 per day, regardless of how many workers the firm employs. A marginal resource cost of $100 per day appears as the horizontal line drawn at the $100 level in Exhibit 6; this is the resource supply curve. Exhibit 6 also shows the marginal revenue product curve, or resource demand curve, based on the schedule presented in Exhibit 4. The marginal revenue product curve indicates the additional revenue the firm receives as a result of employing each additional unit of labor.

Given a marginal resource cost of $100 per worker per day, how much labor will the profit-maximizing firm purchase? *The firm will hire more labor as long as doing so adds more to revenue than to cost—that is, as long as the marginal revenue*

Marginal resource cost The change in total cost when an additional unit of a resource is hired, other things constant

Resource price taker A firm that faces a constant market price for a resource; the firm can buy any amount of the resource without affecting the resource price

EXHIBIT   6   **Resource Demand of a Competitive Firm Hiring a Resource as a Price Taker**

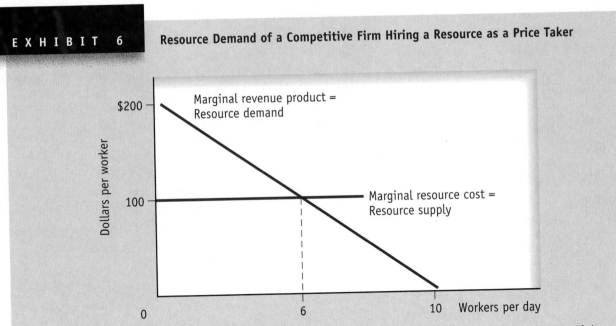

For a competitive firm, the downward-sloping marginal revenue product curve is its demand curve for the resource. If the firm is a price taker in the resource market, it faces a horizontal resource supply curve. It can hire as much of the re-source as it desires at a constant marginal resource cost. The firm will hire up to the point where the marginal revenue product equals the marginal resource cost.

product exceeds the marginal resource cost. The firm will stop hiring labor only when the two are equal. If marginal resource cost is a constant $100 per worker, the firm will hire 6 workers per day because the marginal revenue product of the sixth worker equals $100. The decision rule of equating marginal cost with marginal revenue applies to all the firm's input decisions, just as it did to the firm's output decisions. Stated more formally, the decision rule of resource utilization is that the firm should hire additional inputs up to the level at which

Marginal resource cost = Marginal revenue product

This equality holds for all resources employed. It holds for resource price takers and resource price searchers. It also holds for product price takers and product price searchers. In a competitive labor market, we can say that profit-maximizing employment occurs when the market wage equals the marginal revenue product. Based on data presented thus far, we cannot determine the firm's profit because we don't yet know about the firm's other costs. We do know, however, that in Exhibit 6 a seventh worker would add $100 to cost but would add less than that to revenue, so hiring a seventh worker would reduce the firm's profit (or increase its loss).

Whether the firm sells output as a price taker or as a price searcher, the profit-maximizing level of employment occurs where the marginal revenue product of labor equals its marginal resource cost. Similarly, the profit-maximizing employment of other resources, such as land and capital, occurs where their respective marginal revenue products equal their marginal resource costs. Each resource must "pull its own weight"—it must yield a marginal revenue at least equal to its marginal cost.

In an earlier chapter, we developed a rule for determining the profit-maximizing level of output. Maximum profit (or minimum loss) occurs at the output level where the marginal cost of *output* equals the marginal revenue of *output*. Likewise, maximum profit (or minimum loss) occurs at the resource level where the marginal cost of a *resource* equals the marginal revenue of that *resource*. Though the first rule focuses on output and the second on a resource, the two approaches are equivalent ways of deriving the same principle of profit maximization. For example, in Exhibit 6, the firm maximizes profit by hiring 6 workers when the wage is $100 per day. The details of production were provided in Exhibit 4; specifically, the sixth worker produces an additional 5 units of output, which sell for $20 per unit, for a marginal revenue product of $100. The marginal cost of that output is the change in total cost, $100, divided by the change in output, 5 units; so the marginal cost of output is $100/5, or $20. The marginal revenue of that output is simply its price of $20. Thus, in equilibrium, the marginal cost of output equals its marginal revenue.

Now that you have some idea of how to derive the demand for a resource, let's consider what could shift resource demand.

Shifts in the Demand for Resources

As we have seen, a resource's marginal revenue product consists of two components: the resource's marginal product and the price at which that product is sold. A resource's marginal product will change with a change in the amount of other resources employed or a change in technology. The output's selling price will change with a change in demand for the output. Let's first consider changes that could affect marginal product, then changes that could affect the demand for the final product.

Other Inputs Employed. Although the analysis thus far has focused on a single input, in practice the marginal product of any resource depends on the quantity and quality of other resources used in the production process. Sometimes resources are *substitutes*. For example, coal substitutes for oil in generating electricity. If two resources are substitutes, an increase in the price of one will increase the demand for the other. For example, an increase in the price of oil will increase the demand for coal.

Sometimes resources are *complements,* such as trucks and truck drivers. If the relationship is complementary, a reduction in the price of one increases the demand for the other. If the price of big trucks falls, an increase in the use of big trucks makes drivers more productive, increasing the demand for truck drivers. One reason why U.S. truck drivers earn about $15 an hour and why rickshaw drivers in the Far East earn less than $1 per hour is the *truck*. The rickshaw driver pulls a cart worth maybe $100; the cart can carry relatively little and can move only as fast and as far as the driver's legs will take it. The truck driver is behind the wheel of a $200,000 machine that can haul huge amounts great distances at high speeds. The truck makes the driver more productive.

A valuable resource is one that helps other resources become more productive. In sports, the "most valuable player" is typically a team member who not only contributes directly but makes other players on the team more productive as well. For example, Michael Jordan is such a great scorer that other teams typically "double-team" him—that is, have two players try to prevent him from scoring. This allows Jordan to "assist" other team members who are left open for the shot. *More generally, the greater the quantity and quality of complementary resources used in production, the greater the marginal productivity of the resource in question and the greater the demand for that resource.*

Changes in Technology. *Technological improvements can enhance the productivity of some resources and can make others obsolete.* The development of more fuel-efficient cars increased the productivity of gasoline. Word-processing programs have increased the productivity of authors and typists. Synthetic fibers, such as rayon, have reduced the demand for natural fibers, such as cotton and wool. And fiber optics and satellite communication have reduced the demand for copper wire.

Changes in the Demand for the Final Product. Because the demand for a resource *derives* from the demand for the final output, any change in the demand for output will affect resource demand. For example, an increase in the demand for automobiles will increase their market price and thereby increase the marginal revenue product of auto workers. Let's look at the link between derived demand and employment in the following case study.

CASE STUDY

The Derived Demand for Architects

Location:

To discover more about the state of the architecture industry, visit The American Institute of Architects (AIA) and The American Architectural Foundation (http://www.aia.org/). While the demand for entry-level architects has decreased, the demand for computer-assisted design (CAD) software has increased. To explore a rising software company, visit AutoDesk, Inc., producer of "AutoCAD," the industry-standard design automation software package (http://www.autodesk.com/).

The big drop in real estate prices, particularly commercial real estate prices, that occurred in the late 1980s and early 1990s cut demand for new construction, and in so doing reduced the demand for resources used in construction, such as architects and builders. Consider what happened to the demand for architects.

In New York City, the number of classified ads for architectural positions declined from 5,000 in 1987 to 500 in 1991. Similar drops took place in other major cities. Employment at one national architectural firm shrank from 1,600 to 700 between 1988 and 1992.

Among entry-level architects, job problems were compounded because of changing technology. Drafting jobs long represented the traditional entry-level positions for new architects, but computer-assisted design programs reduced the demand for new architects. Programs such as *Auto-Architect* and *3D Manager* help configure all aspects of a structure and create plans that can be manipulated in three-dimensional space, something impossible with traditional drawings. Programs also help estimate the cost of structures. Design software such as *Design Your Own Home* and *Planix Home Design Kit* even helps amateurs with simple designs. Thus, new software substitutes for entry-level architectural positions.

The declining demand for architects had an interesting impact on the demand for higher education, which itself is a derived demand. Enrollment in undergraduate classes in architecture declined, since entry-level positions disappeared. Enrollments in graduate courses, however, remained relatively stable.

Apparently, many out-of-work architects decided to pursue graduate degrees, since the poor job market reduced their opportunity cost of time. The exception that proves the rule about derived demand is that those architectural firms that specialize in the health-care industry have flourished, because health care has become the fastest-growing sector of the economy.

Sources: D. W. Dunlap, "Recession Is Ravaging Architects' Firms," *New York Times,* 17 May 1992; Cathleen McGuigan, "Stone, Steel, and Cyberspace," *Newsweek,* 27 February 1995; Steven Ross, "Will Amateur CAD Put Residential Architects Out of Business?" *Architectural Record* (April 1994); and Internet site http://www.softdesk.com/index.html.

The Derived Demand for Architects
continued

In summary, the demand for a resource depends on its marginal revenue product. Any change that increases a resource's marginal revenue product will increase resource demand. Let's turn now to factors that influence a resource's price elasticity of demand.

Price Elasticity of Resource Demand

We can examine the price elasticity of demand for a resource, just as we examined the elasticity of demand for final products. The price elasticity of resource demand equals the percentage change in the quantity of the resource demanded divided by the percentage change in its price. A variety of forces influence this price elasticity. Some relate to the derived nature of resource demand; others relate to the productivity of the resource itself.

Demand for the Final Product. Since the demand for a resource derives from the demand for the final product, a resource's price elasticity of demand also derives from the final product's price elasticity. *The more elastic the demand for the final product, other things constant, the more elastic the demand for the resources used to produce it.*

The Resource's Share of Production Cost. *The greater the resource's share of the total production cost, other things constant, the more elastic the demand for that resource.* For example, because lumber is an important component of housing costs, a sharp increase in the price of lumber increases housing prices by a relatively large amount. This increase in the price of housing reduces the quantity of housing demanded and, in turn, reduces the quantity of lumber demanded. On the other hand, the cost of electrical wire makes up only a tiny fraction of the cost of new housing. Therefore, a rise in the price of electrical wire will have little or no impact on the price of housing and, consequently, on the quantity of housing demanded. Since the quantity of housing demanded changes little, neither does the quantity of wire demanded for housing construction. So the demand for electrical wire will be less price elastic than the demand for lumber.

Ease of Substitution. Earlier we mentioned that some resources have close substitutes. *The more easily one resource substitutes for another in production, the more elastic the demand for substitute resources.* For example, to the baker, white eggs and brown eggs are virtually identical, so an increase in the relative price of white eggs will sharply reduce the quantity of white eggs demanded as bakers switch to brown eggs. The demand for white eggs is price elastic, as is the demand for brown eggs. In some cases, resources are substitutes, though not perfect substitutes. For example, an increase in the prevailing wages of security guards could encourage some firms to switch to a more automated security system. At the other extreme, there are no close substitutes for jet fuel, so an increase in its price will not cause airlines to switch to other forms of energy, at least not in the short run. Thus, the demand for jet fuel is relatively inelastic in the short run.

Time. Finally, as with consumer demand, *the longer the time period under consideration, the greater the elasticity of demand for the resource.* For example, if the price of steel increases sharply, auto manufacturers cannot quickly switch to substitutes. Over time, however, they can redesign cars to reduce the amount of steel required. Or consider the nation's experience with oil. Price increases in the 1970s had relatively little effect in the short run on the quantity demanded. In the long run, however, more fuel-efficient engines were developed and coal was substituted for oil in electricity generation.

In summary, other things constant, the price elasticity of demand for a resource will be greater (1) the greater the price elasticity of demand for the final product, (2) the greater the resource cost as a fraction of the total cost of the final product, (3) the more substitutes there are for the resource and the closer these substitutes; and (4) the longer the time period under consideration.

Hiring Resources as a Price Searcher

Determining optimal resource use for a price taker in the resource market is simple, since the firm's marginal resource cost is constant and is equal to the market price of the resource. But what if a firm hires such a large fraction of the available resource that the quantity the firm hires depends on the resource price? If the quantity of the resource supplied to the firm depends on the price the firm pays, the firm is a **resource price searcher.** A resource price searcher typically faces an upward-sloping resource supply curve—that is, the quantity of the resource supplied to the firm increases only if the firm offers a higher resource price. A resource price searcher who is the only buyer of a resource is called a *monopsonist,* such as the only mining company in a mining town. Research suggests monopsony-like behavior for employers of nurses and of college teachers.[2]

Suppose an aircraft manufacturer employs such a large proportion of the total supply of aerospace engineers that the quantity of labor supplied to the firm depends on the wage the firm offers. The first column in panel (a) of Exhibit 7 lists the quantity of engineers hired per day, and the second column shows the daily wage the firm must pay to attract that quantity. Together, the first two columns represent the *supply of labor* faced by a firm that is a price searcher in the resource market. The *supply of labor curve* appears in panel (b) of Exhibit 7. The marginal revenue product for each unit of the resource appears in the final column in panel (a) and as the marginal revenue product curve in panel (b).

Because the labor supply curve slopes upward, the firm must pay a higher wage to employ more labor. To hire another engineer, the firm must increase

Resource price searcher A firm that faces an upward-sloping supply curve for a resource

---

2   See Daniel Sullivan, "Monopsony Power in the Market for Nurses," *Journal of Law and Economics* 32 (October 1989): pp. 135–78; and Michael Ransom, "Seniority and Monopsony in the Academic Labor Market," *American Economic Review* 83 (March 1993): pp. 221–33.

(a)

Workers Per Day (1)	Daily Wage (2)	Total Resource Cost (3)	Marginal Resource Cost (4)	Marginal Revenue Product (5)
0	—	$ 0	—	—
1	$ 80	80	$ 80	$200
2	90	180	100	180
3	100	300	120	160
4	110	440	140	140
5	120	600	160	120
6	130	780	180	100
7	140	980	200	80
8	150	1200	220	60

(b)

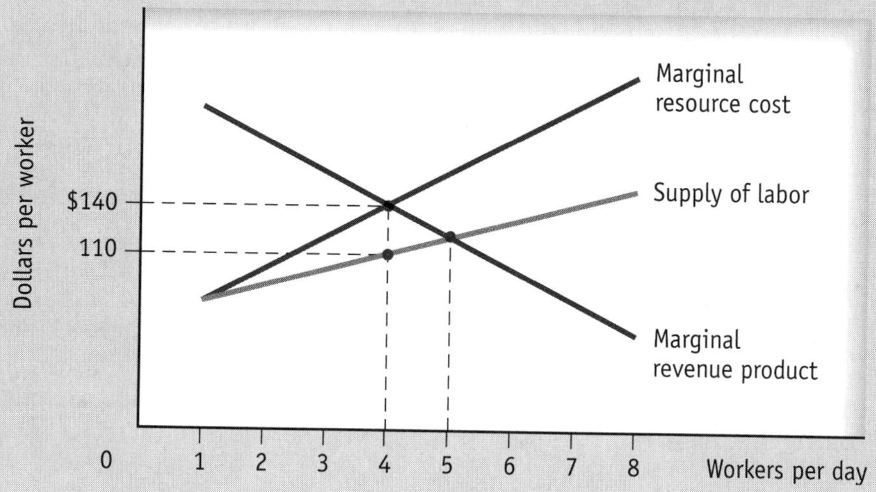

EXHIBIT 7

Resource Demand for a Firm Hiring Workers as a Price Searcher

A resource price searcher faces an upward-sloping supply curve. The marginal resource cost lies above that supply curve. The firm will hire the resource up to the point where the marginal revenue product equals the marginal resource cost (4 workers) and will pay a daily wage based on the resource supply curve ($110).

the wage it pays to all engineers, not just the additional one. For example, a wage of $80 attracts one engineer and a wage of $90 attracts two. So the daily wage must increase by $10 to hire a second engineer. When the firm hires a second engineer, the total resource cost increases from $80 to $180. Thus, the *marginal resource cost* of the second worker is $100, which exceeds the daily *wage* of $90. Likewise, the firm must pay $100 per unit to hire three engineers, for a total labor cost of $300. So the marginal cost of the third one is $120. Compare columns (2) and (4) in panel (a) of Exhibit 7 and you will see that starting with the second engineer, *the marginal resource cost exceeds the wage, and the difference grows as the firm hires more labor.* This growing difference shows in panel (b) as the growing distance between the marginal resource cost curve and the labor supply curve.

The firm maximizes profit by hiring more of a resource as long as each additional unit of that resource adds more to revenue than to cost. Specifically, the firm hires additional workers *until the marginal resource cost equals the marginal revenue product.* In Exhibit 7, the marginal resource cost and the marginal revenue product both equal $140 where 4 engineers are employed. But the wage required to call forth that level of employment is only $110 per day. Thus, *for a resource price searcher, the marginal revenue product exceeds the equilibrium resource price.* For a resource price searcher in the labor market, a worker's marginal revenue exceeds the equilibrium wage.

Summarizing Resource Markets

Let's compare a resource price taker and a resource price searcher. A resource price taker is depicted in panel (a) of Exhibit 8, where the marginal resource cost curve is a horizontal line drawn at the market-determined resource price. A resource price searcher is depicted in panel (b), where the marginal resource cost curve is an upward-sloping line drawn above the resource supply curve. Recall that the resource price searcher's marginal resource cost curve lies above the resource supply curve because the firm, in order to attract more units of the resources, must pay *all* units of the resource the higher supply price.

In each panel, the firm's marginal revenue product curve shows the change in total revenue divided by the change in the quantity of the resource employed. This holds whether the firm is a price taker or a price searcher in the product market. Regardless of the nature of the resource market or the product market, *the profit-maximizing quantity of the resource occurs where the marginal resource cost curve intersects the marginal revenue product curve.* Note that when the firm is a resource price taker, the equilibrium price of the resource equals the marginal resource cost, but when the firm is a resource price searcher, the equilibrium price of the resource is below the marginal resource cost.

Optimal Use: More than One Resource

As long as the marginal revenue product exceeds the marginal resource cost, the firm can increase profit by employing more of the resource. The firm will increase resource use until the marginal revenue product just equals the marginal resource cost, or

$$\text{Marginal revenue product} = \text{Marginal resource cost}$$

Rearranging terms yields:

$$\frac{\text{Marginal revenue product}}{\text{Marginal resource cost}} = 1$$

And this holds for each resource employed. Thus, *to maximize profit, the firm should employ resources so that the last dollar spent on each resource yields one dollar's worth of marginal revenue product.* In other words, profit-maximizing employers will hire any resource up to the point at which the last unit hired adds as much to revenue as it does to cost.

Recall that at the outset of the chapter, you were asked why the buildings at the center of Chicago are taller than those farther out. Land and capital, to a large extent, substitute in the production of building space. Since land is more expensive at the center of the city, builders there substitute additional capital for land, building up instead of out. Hence, buildings are taller when they are closer

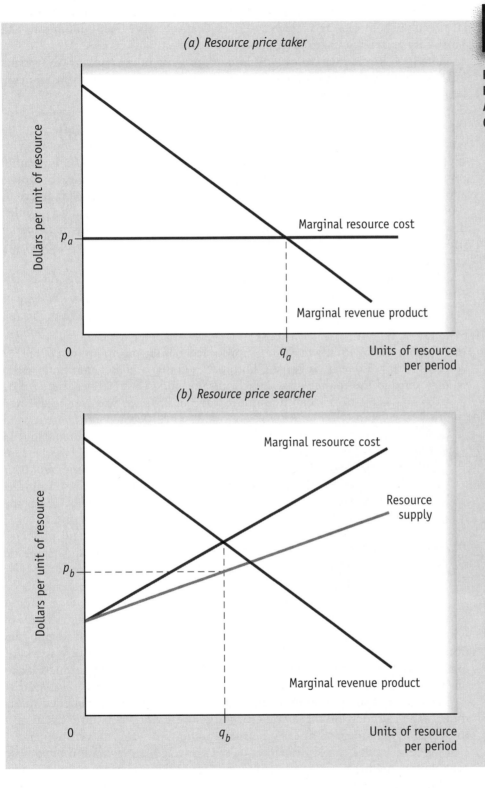

EXHIBIT 8

**Resource Market
Equilibrium under
Alternative Market
Conditions**

(a) Resource price taker

Dollars per unit of resource

Marginal resource cost

p_a

Marginal revenue product

0   q_a Units of resource
per period

(b) Resource price searcher

Dollars per unit of resource

Marginal resource cost

Resource
supply

p_b

Marginal revenue product

0   q_b Units of resource
per period

to the center of the city and are tallest in cities where the land is most expensive. Buildings in Chicago and New York City are taller than buildings in Salt Lake City and Tucson, for example.

The high price of land in metropolitan areas has other implications for the efficient employment of resources. For example, in New York City, as in many large cities, vending carts on street corners specialize in everything from hot dogs to snow cones. Why so many carts? Consider the resources used to supply hot dogs: land, labor, capital, entrepreneurial ability, plus intermediate goods such as hot dogs, buns, and other ingredients. Which of these do you suppose is most expensive in New York City? Retail space along Fifth Avenue rents for as much as $400 a year per square foot. Since a hot dog cart requires about three square yards to operate, it could cost more than $10,000 a year to rent the required commercial space. Aside from the necessary public permits, however, space on the public sidewalk is free to vendors. Profit-maximizing street vendors substitute public sidewalk space, which is free to them, for costly commercial rental space.

Government policy can affect resource allocation in other ways, as is discussed in the following case study.

CASE STUDY

The McMinimum Wage

Location:

Consider two different perspectives about the usefulness of a minimum wage. Browse "Who Wins with a Minimum Wage?", an Economics Policy Institute Briefing Paper written by Lawrence Mishel, Jared Bernstein, and Edith Rasell and maintained by the Electronic Policy Network (http://epn. org/epi/epminw.html), and "President Clinton's Proposal to Increase the Minimum Wage," a testimony by Grant Maloy before the House of Representative's Joint Economic Committee and maintained by the Heritage Foundation (http://www.heritage. org/sbsc/ct2-22-5.html).

In February 1995, President Clinton proposed raising the minimum wage by 90 cents to $5.15 over two years. Clinton argued that a higher minimum wage would "expand the middle class and shrink the underclass." Ever since a federal minimum wage of 25 cents was first established in 1938, economists have debated the benefits and costs of the law. The law initially covered only 43 percent of the work force—primarily workers in large firms involved in interstate commerce. Over the years, the minimum wage has been raised and the coverage has been broadened, so that by 1995 the minimum wage stood at $4.25 per hour and covered 86 percent of the work force (groups still not covered include small-retail employees and domestic workers).

At the time of Clinton's proposed increase, about 4.1 million workers, or 6 percent of the 66.5 million hourly workers, reported earning $4.25 or less. This group consisted mostly of young workers, the majority working part time, primarily in service and sales occupations. A total of 8.5 million workers, or 13 percent of hourly workers, earned less than $5.15, and thus could potentially be affected by an increase to $5.15.

Advocates of the minimum wage argue that an appropriately applied minimum wage can increase the income of the poorest workers at little or no cost to overall employment. Critics argue that a minimum wage above the market-clearing level causes employers either to cut nonwage compensation or to scale back employment.

There have been over 40 published U.S. studies since 1970 looking at the effect of changes in the minimum wage on employment. A few found a small positive effect of the minimum wage on employment, but most found either no effect or a negative effect, particularly among teenage workers. One reason an increase in the minimum wage may not always have the expected negative effect on total employment is that employers often react to a wage increase by substituting part-time jobs for full-time jobs, by substituting more-qualified minimum-wage workers (such as college students) for less-qualified workers (such as high-school dropouts), and by adjusting some nonwage features of the job to reduce costs or increase productivity.

Consider some of the nonwage job features under the employer's control: convenience of work hours, expected work effort, on-the-job training, time allowed for lunch and for breaks, vacation days, paid holidays, sick leave, health-care benefits, tolerance for tardiness, use of the company phone, parking provisions, air conditioning, dress code, and so on. Of most concern to economists is a possible reduction in the provision of on-the-job training to young workers, particularly those with little education.

A higher minimum wage also raises the opportunity cost of staying in school. For example, one study found that an increase in the minimum wage encouraged some 16- to 19-year-olds to quit school to seek work, though many fail to find a job. And those who had already left school were more likely to become unemployed. Thus, there may be significant enrollment effects associated with an increase in the minimum wage.

Although Clinton's proposed legislation went nowhere in 1995, increases in the minimum wage have wide public support. According to one recent poll, the highest support, 81 percent, came from those aged 18 to 29, the group most likely to be affected by a hike in the minimum wage. The typical college student has a part-time job that pays the minimum wage or close to it. An increase in the minimum wage would benefit college students more than high-school dropouts.

Sources: "Minimum Wage, Maximum Fuss," *The Economist,* 8 April 1995; Todd Purdum, "Clinton Asks Rise in Minimum Wage," *New York Times,* 4 February 1995; "Reexamining Methods of Estimating Minimum-Wage Effects," *American Economic Review Papers and Proceedings* 85 (May 1995): pp. 232–49; and "Review Symposium: Myth and Measurement: The New Economics of the Minimum Wage," *Industrial and Labor Relations Review,* 48 (July 1995): pp. 827–49.

The McMinimum Wage
continued

E X H I B I T　9

Functional Distribution of Income: Percentage Share of Each Source of Income

Time Period	Wages and Salaries (1)	Proprietors' Income (2)	Corporate Profits (3)	Interest (4)	Rent (5)
1900–1909	55.0	23.7	6.8	5.5	9.0
1910–1919	53.6	23.8	9.1	5.4	8.1
1920–1929	60.0	17.5	7.8	6.2	7.7
1930–1939	67.5	14.8	4.0	8.7	5.0
1940–1948	64.6	17.2	11.9	3.1	3.3
1949–1958	67.3	13.9	12.5	2.9	3.4
1959–1970	70.9	10.6	11.7	3.7	3.1
1971–1979	74.6	7.4	9.8	6.3	1.9
1980–1989	73.0	7.9	7.9	10.2	1.0
1990–1995	73.0	8.1	8.9	8.2	1.8

Sources: Irving Kravis, "Income Distribution: Functional Shares," *International Encyclopedia of Social Sciences* 7 (New York: Macmillan Co. and Free Press, 1968), p. 134; *Economic Report of the President,* February 1996. Figures after 1970 are not fully consistent with prior figures, but they convey a reasonably accurate picture of income trends.

DISTRIBUTION OF RESOURCE EARNINGS

This chapter showed that firms increase resource employment as long as the resource's marginal revenue product exceeds the marginal resource cost. This employment rule results in an allocation of earnings based on each resource's marginal productivity. So earnings in a market economy are based on the marginal productivity of resources. Resources that are more productive earn more, sometimes much more, than resources that are less productive. Not all are happy with the market outcome, especially those whose resources are not highly valued in the market. In this final section, we examine the distribution of earnings across different kinds of resources in the United States.

Exhibit 9, on page 571, shows the proportion of national income that goes to (1) wages and salaries, (2) proprietors' income, (3) corporate profits, (4) interest, and (5) rent. Proprietors' income consists of incomes of farmers, doctors, lawyers, small-business owners, and other unincorporated business owners. Over time, wages and salaries have claimed by far the largest share of national income, accounting most recently for about three-fourths of the total. But this understates the proportion going to labor, because a portion of proprietors' income consists of labor income as well.

Exhibit 9, on page 571, also shows the decline over time in the share of national income received by proprietors. A generation ago, the income from the corner store was proprietors' income; these stores were named after the owner-operator, such as "Phil's Market" and "Pam's Pantry." Today these corner stores are more likely to be called "7-Eleven" or "Circle K," and the cashier who rings up your Pepsi typically earns a wage paid by the corporate chain.

The column headings "Corporate Profits," "Interest," and "Rent" do not correspond exactly to the terms *profit, interest,* and *economic rent* used by economists, but the definitions in Exhibit 9 are similar enough to the way economists view the world to make the table of interest. *The most important conclusion to draw from Exhibit 9 is that labor's share of total income is relatively large and has grown during this century.* This conclusion still holds even if the definitions of some other income categories do not exactly match our economic definitions. Labor's share has grown primarily because proprietors' income has decreased, as reflected, for example, by the shift from owner-operators to corporate chains.

CONCLUSION

The framework we have developed focuses on the marginal analysis of resource use to determine the equilibrium resource price and quantity. The firm uses each resource up to the point where the marginal revenue product of that resource equals its marginal cost. The objective of profit maximization ensures that to produce any given level of output, firms will employ the least-cost combination of resources and will thereby use the economy's resources most efficiently. Using the least-cost combination of resources implies that the last $1 spent on each resource yields a marginal revenue product of $1. If this were not so, firms could produce the same output at a lower cost by adjusting the resource mix.

Although the focus has been on the marginal productivity of each resource, we should keep in mind that resources combine to produce output, so the marginal productivity of a particular resource will depend in part on what other resources are employed. For example, a baseball player whose teammates get on base more frequently will have more runs batted in during the season and will thereby be considered more productive.

SUMMARY

1. Firms demand resources to maximize profits. Households supply resources to maximize utility. The profit-maximizing goals of firms and the utility-maximizing goals of households harmonize through voluntary exchange in resource markets.

2. Because the value of any resource depends on what it produces, the demand for a resource is a derived demand—derived from the value of the final product. A resource demand curve slopes downward because firms are more willing and able to increase their quantity demanded as the price of a resource declines. A resource supply curve tends to slope upward because resource owners are more willing and able to increase their quantity supplied as their reward for supplying the resource increases.

3. Some differentials in the market prices of similar resources trigger the reallocation of resources to equalize prices for similar resources. Other price differentials do not cause a shift in resources among uses because of a lack of resource mobility, differences in the inherent quality of the resources, differences in the time and money involved in developing the necessary skill, and differences in nonmonetary aspects of the job.

4. Resource earnings can be divided between (1) earnings that reflect the resource's opportunity cost, the amount that must be paid to get a resource owner to supply that resource to a particular use, and (2) economic rent, that portion of a resource's total earnings that exceeds the resource's opportunity cost. If a resource has no alternative uses, earnings consist entirely of economic rent; if a resource has other valued uses, opportunity cost predominates.

5. A firm's demand curve for a resource equals the resource's marginal revenue product curve, which shows the change in total revenue that results from each 1-unit increase in the amount of the resource employed, other things constant. If a firm sells output in a perfectly competitive market, the marginal revenue product curve slopes downward because of diminishing marginal returns. If a firm has some market power in the product market, the marginal revenue product curve slopes downward both because of diminishing marginal returns and because the product price must fall to sell more output.

6. The demand curve for a resource will increase, or shift to the right, if there is an increase either in its marginal productivity or in the price of the output. An increase in the use of a complementary resource or a decrease in the use of a substitute resource will increase a resource's marginal productivity.

7. Marginal resource cost is the change in total cost resulting from employing one more unit of the resource. A firm that hires resources in a competitive resource market is a resource price taker and has no control over resource prices. If the quantity of the resource supplied to the firm depends on the resource price, the firm is a resource price searcher. Both a resource price taker and a resource price searcher maximize profits by employing each resource up to the point where the marginal revenue product equals the marginal resource cost.

8. During this century, wages and salaries have grown as a percentage of total resource income, and they now account for about three-quarters of the total. Proprietors' income and rent have fallen as a percentage of the total.

QUESTIONS AND PROBLEMS

1. **(Elasticity of Resource Demand)** How might the elasticity of demand for a resource depend on the substitutability among resources in the production process?

2. **(Resource Demand and Resource Supply)** Answer each of the following questions about the labor market:
   a. Which economic actors determine the demand for labor?
   b. Which economic actors determine the supply of labor?
   c. What is the goal of the actors on the demand side? On the supply side?
   d. Given the goals of the actors in part c, what decision criteria do they use to meet these goals?
   e. Why is the demand for labor a derived demand?

3. **(Resource Demand)** Suppose that good A has a perfectly inelastic demand. What impact would this have on the price elasticity of demand for resources used to produce A? Explain.

4. **(Market Supply)** Explain why the market supply curve for a resource tends to slope upward.

5. **(Temporary and Permanent Price Differences)** Distinguish between the market reaction to a temporary difference in prices for the same resource and the market reaction to a permanent difference. Explain why the reactions differ.

6. **(Product Price Taker's Marginal Revenue Product)** If a competitive firm hires another full-time worker, total output will increase from 100 units to 110 units *per month*. Suppose the wage is $200 *per week*. What market price will allow the additional worker to be hired?

7. **(Opportunity Cost and Economic Rent)** Define economic rent. In the graph below, assume that the market demand curve for labor is initially D_1.
   a. What are the equilibrium wage rate and quantity hired? What is the amount of economic rent?
   b. Next assume that the price of a substitute resource increases, other things constant. What happens to demand for labor? What are the new equilibrium wage rate and quantity hired? What happens to the amount of economic rent?
   c. Suppose instead that demand for the final product drops, other things constant. Using demand curve D_1 as your starting point, what happens to demand for labor? What are the new equilibrium wage rate and quantity hired? What happens to the amount of economic rent?

8. **(Marginal Revenue Product and Marginal Resource Cost)** Define marginal revenue product and marginal resource cost. How does the marginal revenue product for a price taker in the product market differ from that for a price searcher? How does the marginal resource cost curve for a price taker in the resource market differ from that for a price searcher? Explain.

9. **(Shifts in Resource Demand)** A local pizza establishment hires college students to prepare pizza, wait on tables, take telephone orders, and deliver pizzas. For each situation described below, indicate whether the demand for student employees by the restaurant would increase, decrease, or remain unchanged. Explain each answer.
   a. The demand for pizza increases, other things constant.
   b. The cost of cheese increases, other things constant.
   c. An increase in the minimum wage raises the cost of hiring student employees, other things constant.
   d. The restaurant buys a computer system for taking telephone orders, other things constant.

10. **(Complements in Production)** Many countries are predominantly agrarian. How would the amount of fertilizer available affect the marginal product, and thus the income, of the farmers in such countries?

11. **(Resource Demand)** Use the following data to answer the questions below. Assume a perfectly competitive output market.

Units of Labor	Units of Output
0	0
1	7
2	13
3	18
4	22
5	25

   a. Calculate the marginal revenue product for each unit of labor if output sells for $3 per unit.
   b. If labor costs $15 per hour to a price taker in the labor market, how much labor will get hired?
   c. Construct the demand curve for labor based on the above data and the $3 per unit output price.
   d. Using your answer to part (b), compare total revenue to the total amount paid to labor. Who gets the difference?
   e. What would happen to your answers to parts (b) and (c) if the price of output increased to $5 per unit, other things constant?

12. **(Price Elasticity of Resource Demand)** Indicate whether each of the following would increase or decrease the price elasticity of demand for a resource:

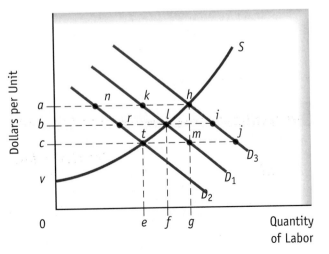

a. The smaller the price elasticity of demand for the final product, other things constant.
b. The less easily another resource substitutes for this resource, other things constant.
c. The longer the time period under consideration, other things constant.
d. The greater the resource's share of the total production cost, other things constant.

13. **(Resource Market Equilibrium)** Consider the graph below.
   a. If the labor market is perfectly competitive, how many workers will be hired and what will the wage rate be?
   b. If demanders in the labor market are resource price searchers, how many workers will be hired and what will the wage rate be?
   c. What is the marginal resource cost of the last worker hired in the perfectly competitive labor market? By the resource price searchers?
   d. For a resource price taker, the marginal resource cost of the last worker hired_____ the equilibrium wage. For a resource price searcher, the marginal resource cost of the last worker hired _____ the equilibrium wage.

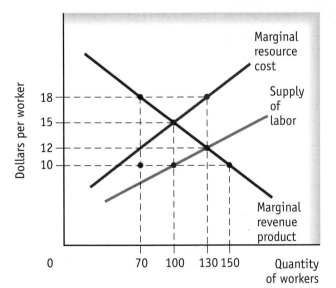

14. **(Optimal Use: More than One Resource)** Explain the rule for obtaining optimal use of each resource when a firm uses multiple resources.

15. **(Distribution of Resource Earnings)** What determines the allocation of earnings in a market economy? In the United States, which resource receives the bulk of national income? What has happened to this resource's share of income during the 20th century?

16. **(Resource Market Equilibrium)** Complete the following table:

Workers per Day	Daily Wage	Total Resource Cost	Marginal Resource Cost	Marginal Revenue Product
1	$ 75	_____	_____	$155
2	80	_____	_____	145
3	85	_____	_____	135
4	90	_____	_____	125
5	95	_____	_____	115
6	100	_____	_____	105

   a. Is the firm illustrated above a price taker or a price searcher in the labor market?
   b. In equilibrium, how many workers will the firm hire per day?
   c. What is the wage rate in equilibrium?
   d. What is the marginal revenue product of the last worker hired? The marginal resource cost?

17. **(Rents Versus Opportunity Cost)** On-the-job work experience typically enhances one's productivity in a particular job. If one's salary increases to reflect this higher productivity, is the increase in opportunity cost or economic rent?

18. **(Resource Demand)** Suppose that a constant-cost competitive industry experiences an increase in demand for its product.
   a. Show what happens to the market for the variable resource in the short run.
   b. What happens to the mix of resources used in the long run?

19. **(The Derived Demand for Architects)** Use a supply-and-demand diagram to illustrate the change in the market for entry-level architects. Explain your diagram.

20. **(The McMinimum Wage)** The case study mentions the "expected negative effect on total employment" of an increased minimum wage. It also mentions the "higher opportunity cost of staying in school." Use a supply-and-demand diagram to illustrate and explain the "expected" effect of the minimum wage.

Using the Internet

21. Visit the Bureau of Labor Statistics (BLS) and look within "Economy at a Glance" (**http://stats.bls.gov/**). Review the latest data on "Average Hourly Earnings." Have these wages tended to increase, decrease, or stay the same? How do they compare to the minimum wage as discussed in the case study "The McMinimum Wage"?

Human Resources: Labor and Entrepreneurial Ability

Because the supply of entry-level lawyers outpaced the demand, salaries for new lawyers remained flat between 1992 and 1995. Perhaps it is no coincidence that the number of law school applications dropped 8 percent in 1995. What determines the wage structure in the economy? You don't need a course in economics to figure out why corporate presidents earn more than file clerks, or why heart surgeons earn more than registered nurses. But why do lawyers earn more than accountants and schoolteachers more than auto mechanics? Will we observe similar patterns in the year 2005? You can be sure of one thing: demand and supply play a central role in the wage structure.

We have already examined what determines the demand for resources. Demand depends on the resource's marginal productivity. In the first half of this chapter, we will focus on the supply of labor, then bring demand and supply together to arrive at the market wage. In the second half of the chapter, we consider another human resource: entrepreneurial ability. As we will see, entrepreneurial ability is in many ways the most important resource for determining the wealth of nations, but it is also the most elusive. Topics discussed in this chapter include:

- Theory of time allocation
- Backward-bending supply curve for labor
- Nonwage factors and labor supply

- Why wages differ
- Entrepreneurial ability and profit
- Theories of profit

LABOR SUPPLY

As a resource supplier, you have a labor supply curve for each of the many possible uses of your labor. To some markets your quantity supplied is zero over the realistic range of wages. The qualifier "over the realistic range" is added because, for a high enough wage (say, $1 million per hour), you might supply labor to *any* activity. In most labor markets, your quantity supplied may be zero either because you are *willing* but *unable* to perform the job (for example: airline pilot, professional golfer, novelist) or because you are *able* but *unwilling* to do so (for example: soldier of fortune, gym teacher, prison guard).

So you have as many supply curves as there are labor markets, just as you have as many demand curves as there are markets for goods and services. Your labor supply to each market depends, among other things, on your ability, your taste for the job in question, and the opportunity cost of your time—how much you could earn in other activities. Your supply to a particular labor market assumes that wages in other markets are constant, just as your demand for a particular product assumes that other prices are constant.

Labor Supply and Utility Maximization

Recall the definition of economics: *the study of how individuals choose to use their scarce resources to produce, exchange, and consume products in an attempt to satisfy their unlimited wants.* That is, individuals attempt to use their limited resources so as to maximize their utility. Two sources of utility are of special interest to us in this chapter: the consumption of goods and services and the enjoyment of leisure. The utility derived from consuming goods and services is obvious and serves as the foundation of consumer demand. Another valuable source of utility is leisure time spent relaxing, sleeping, eating, and in recreational activities. Leisure is a normal good that, like other goods, is subject to the law of diminishing marginal utility. Thus, the more leisure time you have, the less you value each additional unit of leisure. Sometimes you may have so much leisure that you "have time on your hands" and are "just killing time." As that sage of the comic page Garfield the cat once lamented, "Spare time would be more fun if I had less to spare." Or, as Shakespeare wrote in *King John,* "If all the year were playing holidays, to sport would be as tedious as to work." Leisure's diminishing marginal utility explains why some of the so-called "idle rich" grow bored in their idleness.

Three Uses of Time. Some of you are at a point in your career when you have few resources other than time. Time is the raw material of life. You can use your time in three ways. First, you can undertake **market work**—selling your time in the labor market in return for income. When you supply labor, you usually surrender control of your time to the employer in return for a wage. Second, you can undertake what we will call **nonmarket work**—using time to produce your own goods and services. Nonmarket work includes the time you spend doing your laundry, preparing your meals, or typing your term paper. Nonmarket work also includes the time spent acquiring skills and education that enhance your future productivity. Although the time spent studying and attending class provides little immediate payoff, you are betting that the knowledge and perspective you gain will pay off in the future. Third, you can convert time directly into **leisure**—nonwork uses of your time.

Market work Time sold as labor in return for a money wage

Nonmarket work Time spent producing goods and services in the home or acquiring an education

Leisure Time spent on nonwork activities

Work and Utility. Unless you are one of the fortunate few, work is not a pure source of utility, as it often generates some boredom, discomfort, or aggravation. In short, time spent working can be "a real pain," a source of *disutility*—the opposite of utility. You work nonetheless, because your earnings buy goods and services. You expect the utility from these goods and services to more than offset the disutility of work. Thus, the *net utility of work*—the utility of the consumption made possible through work minus the disutility of the work itself—usually makes work an attractive use of your time. In the case of market work, your income buys goods and services. In the case of nonmarket work, either you produce goods and services directly, as in making yourself a tuna sandwich, or you invest your time in education with an expectation of higher future earnings and higher future consumption.

Utility Maximization. Within the limits of a 24-hour day, seven days a week, you balance your time among market work, nonmarket work, and leisure so as to maximize utility. As a rational consumer, *you attempt to maximize utility by allocating your time so that the expected marginal utility of the last unit of time spent in each activity is identical.* Thus, in the course of a week or a month, the marginal utility of the last hour of leisure equals the net marginal utility of the last hour of market work, which equals the net marginal utility of the last hour of nonmarket work. In the case of time devoted to acquiring skills, you must consider the marginal utility expected from the future increase in earnings that will result from your enhanced productivity.

Perhaps at this point you are saying, "Wait a minute. I don't allocate my time with that sort of precision or logic. I just sort of bump along, doing what feels good." Economists do not claim that you are even aware of making such marginal calculations. But as a rational decision maker, you allocate your scarce time to satisfy your wants, or to maximize utility. And utility maximization, or "doing what feels good," implies that you act *as if* you allocated your time to derive the same expected net marginal utility from the last unit of time spent in each alternative use.

You probably have settled into a rough plan (for meals, work, entertainment, study, sleep, and so on) that fits your overall objectives and seems reasonable. This plan is probably in constant flux as you make expected and unexpected adjustments in the use of your time. For example, this morning you may have slept later than you planned because you were up late last night; last weekend you may have failed to crack a book, despite good intentions. Over a week or a month, however, your use of time is roughly in line with an allocation that maximizes utility as you perceive it. Put another way, given the various constraints on your time, money, energy, and other resources, if you could change your use of time to increase your utility, you would do so. Nobody is stopping you! You may emphasize immediate gratification, but that's your choice and you bear the long-term consequences.

This time-allocation process ensures that at the margin, the expected utilities from the last unit of time spent in each activity are equal. Because information is costly and because the future is uncertain, you sometimes make mistakes in allocating time; you do not always get what you expect. Some mistakes are minor, such as going to a movie that proves to be a waste of time. But other mistakes can be costly. For example, you may now be studying for a field that will grow crowded by the time you graduate, or you may be acquiring skills that will become obsolete because of new computer software. New computer programs are changing job prospects in the fields of law, medicine, accounting, architecture, banking, and insurance, to name a few. For example, the computer program *WillMaker* has written more wills than any lawyer alive. In medicine, a program called *Iliad* can, in response to a series of questions, diagnose about 1,000 diseases plus another 1,500 intermediate conditions in a chain of diagnostic deductions. And in accounting, programs like *TurboTax* reduce the demand for CPAs. As the software gets cheaper and better, the demand for some professional skills will diminish, though the demand for computer programmers to write new software will increase.

Implications. The model of time allocation described thus far has several implications for individual choice. First, consider the choice between market and nonmarket work. The higher your market wage, other things constant, the greater the opportunity cost of nonmarket work. Hence, individuals with a high market wage will spend less time in nonmarket activities, other things constant. Surgeons are less likely to mow their own lawns than are butchers. And among those earning the same market wage, people who are handy around the house and are good cooks will tend to do more for themselves and hire fewer household services. Conversely, those who are all thumbs around the house and who have difficulty boiling water will hire more household services and will eat out more frequently. In short, *utility maximization implies that individuals will spend time in nonmarket work if they can produce goods and services more cheaply than the market can.* By the same logic, the higher the expected earnings right out of high school, other things constant, the higher the opportunity cost of attending college. Most young, successful movie stars do not go to college, and the most promising college athletes "turn pro" before completing college.

There is risk involved in allocating time to learn new software programs for your personal computer. Technology changes rapidly and unpredictably; what seems important today may be obsolete tomorrow.

Wages and Individual Labor Supply

To breathe life into the time-allocation problem, consider your choices for the summer. If you can afford to, you can take the summer off, spending it entirely in leisure, perhaps as a fitting reward for a rough academic year. Or you can supply your time to market work. Or you can undertake nonmarket work, such as cleaning the basement or attending summer school. As a rational decision maker, you will select that combination of leisure, market work, and nonmarket work that you expect will maximize your utility. And the optimal combination is likely to involve allocating some time to each activity. For example, even if you work during the summer, you might still consider taking one or two summer courses.

Suppose the only summer job available is some form of unskilled labor, such as working in a fast-food restaurant or for the town parks department. For simplicity, let's assume that you view all available jobs to be equally attractive (or unattractive) in terms of their nonmonetary aspects, such as working conditions, working hours, and so on. (These nonmonetary aspects are discussed in the next section.) Since, in your view, there is no difference among these unskilled jobs, the most important question for you in deciding how much market labor to supply is: What is the market wage for unskilled labor?

Suppose the wage is $5 per hour. At a wage that low, you may decide to work around the house, attend summer school full-time, travel across the country, take a really long nap, or perhaps do some combination of these. In any event, you supply no market labor at such a low wage. The market wage must rise to $6 per hour before you supply any market labor. Suppose that at a wage of $6 per hour, you supply 20 hours per week, perhaps taking fewer summer courses and shorter naps.

As the wage increases, this raises your opportunity cost of time spent in other activities, so you substitute market work for other uses of your time. You decide to work 30 hours per week at a wage of $7 per hour, 40 hours at $8 per hour, 48 hours at $9 per hour, and 55 hours at $10 per hour. At a wage of $11 you go to 60 hours per week; you are starting to earn serious money—$660 per week.

If the wage hits $12 per hour, a wage you consider to be very attractive indeed, you decide to cut back to 58 hours per week, and you earn $696 per week—more than when the wage was $11 per hour. Finally, if the wage is $13 per hour, you cut back your hours supplied to 55 per week and earn $715. To explain why you may eventually reduce the quantity of labor supplied, let's consider the impact of wage increases on your allocation of time.

Substitution and Income Effects. An increase in the wage rate affects your choice between market work and other uses of your time in two ways. First, a higher wage provides you with an incentive to work more, since each hour of work now buys more goods and services. As the wage increases, the opportunity cost of other uses of your time, such as leisure, also increases. Thus, as the wage increases, you substitute market work for other activities; this is the *substitution effect* of a wage increase. But a higher wage means a higher income for the same number of hours, and a higher income means that you demand more of all normal goods. Since leisure is a normal good, a higher income increases your demand for leisure, thereby reducing your allocation of time to market work. The higher wage rate therefore has an *income effect,* which tends to reduce the quantity of market labor supplied.

Consequently, as the wage increases, the substitution effect causes you to supply more time to market work, and the income effect causes you to demand more leisure and, hence, to supply less time to market work. In our example, the substitution effect exceeds the income effect for wage rates up to $11 per hour, resulting in a greater quantity of market labor supplied as the wage increases. When the wage rises above $11 per hour, however, the income effect exceeds the substitution effect, causing a net reduction in the quantity of labor supplied to market work.

Backward-Bending Labor Supply Curve. The labor supply curve that we have described appears in Exhibit 1. As you can see, this supply curve slopes upward until a wage of $11 per hour is reached, and then it begins to bend backward. The **backward-bending supply curve** gets its shape because the income effect of a higher wage eventually exceeds the substitution effect, reducing the quantity of labor supplied. We see evidence of a backward-bending supply curve, particularly among high-wage individuals, who reduce their work and consume more leisure as the wage increases. For example, doctors often play golf on a weekday afternoon. Entertainers typically perform less as they become more successful. Unknown bands play for hours for hardly anything; famous bands play less for more. The income effect of rising real wages helps explain

Backward-bending supply curve of labor Occurs if the income effect of a higher wage dominates the substitution effect of a higher wage

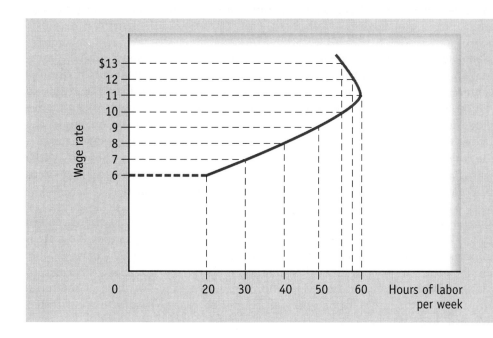

EXHIBIT   1

Individual Labor Supply Curve for Market Work

When the substitution effect of a wage increase outweighs the income effect, the quantity of labor supplied increases with the wage rate. Above some wage (here, $11), the income effect dominates. Above that wage, the supply curve bends backward; further increases in the wage rate reduce the quantity of labor supplied.

the decline in the U.S. work week from an average of 60 hours in 1900 to less than 40 hours today.

Flexibility of Hours Worked. The model we have been describing assumes that workers have some control over the number of hours they work per week. Opportunities for part-time work and overtime allow workers to put together their most preferred quantity of hours (for instance, 30 hours in a restaurant and 15 hours at the college bookstore). Workers also have some control over the timing and length of their vacations. More generally, individuals can control the length of time they stay in school, when and to what extent they enter the work force, and when they choose to retire. Thus, workers actually have more control over the number of hours worked than you might think if you focused on the standard work week of, say, 40 hours per week.

Nonwage Determinants of Labor Supply

The quantity of labor supplied to a particular market depends on a variety of factors other than the wage rate, just as the quantity of a good demanded depends on factors other than the price. As has already been mentioned, the quantity of labor supplied to a particular market depends on wage rates in other labor markets. So what are the nonwage factors that shape a college student's labor supply for the summer?

Other Sources of Income. Although some jobs are rewarding in a variety of nonmonetary ways, the primary reason people work is to earn money to buy goods and services. Thus, the willingness to supply time to the labor market depends on income from other sources, including savings, borrowing, family support, and scholarships. A student who receives a generous scholarship, for example, may feel less need to earn additional income. More generally, wealthy people have less incentive to work. For example, lottery winners often quit their jobs after hitting the jackpot.

Nonmonetary Factors in General. Labor is a special kind of resource. Unlike capital and land, which can be supplied regardless of the whereabouts of the resource owners, time supplied to market work requires the seller of that time to be on the job. Because the individual must be physically present to supply labor, such *nonmonetary factors* as the difficulty of the job and the quality of the work environment have important effects on the labor supply. For example, deckhands on fishing boats in the winter waters of the Bering Sea off Alaska earn $3,000 for five days' work, but the temperature seldom gets above zero and daily shifts are 21 hours long, with only three hours for sleep.

Job Amenities. Consider the different job amenities you might encounter. If you are a college student, a library job that allows you to study much of the time is more attractive than a job that affords no study time. Some jobs have flexible hours; others impose rigid work schedules. Is the workplace air-conditioned or do you have to sweat it out? The more attractive these on-the-job amenities are to you, the more labor you will supply to that particular market, other things constant.

The Value of Job Experience. You are more inclined to take a job that provides valuable experience. Serving as the assistant treasurer for a local business provides more valuable job experience and looks better on a résumé than serving hash at the college cafeteria. Some people are willing to accept relatively low wages now because of the promise of higher wages later. For example, new lawyers are eager to fill clerkships for judges, though the pay is low and the hours long, because these positions provide experience valued by future employers. Thus, *the greater the experience value of a position in terms of enhancing future earning possibilities, the greater the supply of labor to that market, other things constant*. Because of the greater supply of labor to such positions, the pay is lower than for similar jobs that impart less experience.

Taste for Work. Just as the tastes for goods and services differ, tastes for work also differ among labor suppliers. Some people prefer physical labor and would avoid a desk job. Some become surgeons; others can't stand the sight of blood. Some become airline pilots; others are afraid to fly. Many struggling writers and artists could earn more elsewhere, but apparently the satisfaction of the creative process more than offsets the low expected pay. Some people evidently have such a strong preference for certain jobs that they do them for free, such as auxiliary police officers or volunteer fire fighters.

As with the taste for goods and services, economists do not attempt to explain the origin of taste for work. Economists simply argue that your supply of labor will be greater to those jobs that are more in accord with your tastes. Voluntary sorting based on tastes allocates workers among different jobs in a way that tends to minimize the disutility some work generates. This is not to say that everyone will end up in his or her most preferred occupation. The cost of acquiring information about jobs and the cost of changing jobs may prevent some matchups that might otherwise seem desirable. But in the long run, people tend to find jobs that suit them. We are not likely to find tour directors who hate to travel or zoo keepers who are allergic to animals.

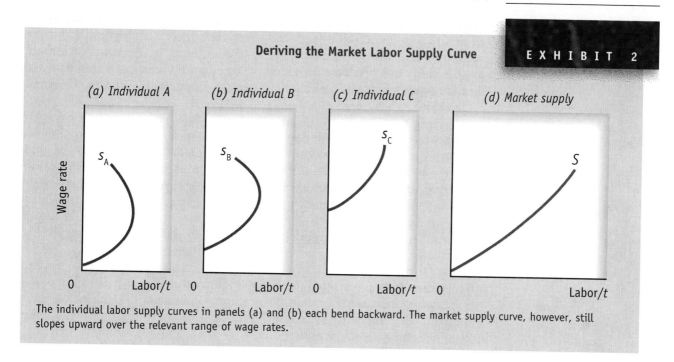

Deriving the Market Labor Supply Curve

EXHIBIT 2

(a) Individual A   (b) Individual B   (c) Individual C   (d) Market supply

The individual labor supply curves in panels (a) and (b) each bend backward. The market supply curve, however, still slopes upward over the relevant range of wage rates.

Market Supply of Labor

In the previous section we considered those factors, both monetary and non-monetary, that influence individual labor supply. *The market supply of labor to a particular market is the horizontal sum of all the individual supply curves.* The horizontal sum is found by adding the quantities at each particular wage level. If an individual supply curve of labor bends backward, does this mean that the market supply curve of labor also bends backward? Not necessarily. Since different individuals have different opportunity costs and different tastes for work, the bend in the supply curve occurs at different wages for different individuals. And for some individuals the labor supply curve may not bend backward, over the realistic range of wages. Exhibit 2 shows how just three individual labor supply curves sum to yield a market supply curve that slopes upward.

Why Wages Differ

Just as both blades of a pair of scissors contribute equally to cutting cloth, both demand and supply determine the market wage. Therefore wage differences across markets can be traced to differences in labor demand, in labor supply, or in both. In the previous chapter we discussed the elements that influence the demand for resources, and we examined labor in particular. In brief, *a profit-maximizing firm hires labor up to the point where labor's marginal revenue product equals its marginal resource cost*—that is, where the last unit employed earns the firm just enough to cover its cost. Since we have already discussed the forces that affect the demand for labor, we focus here primarily on market supply.

Differences in Training, Education, and Experience. Some jobs pay more than others because they require a long and costly training period. Costly training reduces market supply because fewer individuals are willing to incur the time and expense. But the training increases the productivity of labor, thereby increasing the demand for these skills. Reduced supply and increased demand both have a positive effect on the market wage. Certified public accountants earn more than file clerks both because the extensive training of CPAs limits the supply to this field and because this training increases the productivity of CPAs compared to file clerks.

Differences in Ability. Because they are more able and talented, some individuals earn more than others with identical training and education. Two lawyers may have an identical education, but one earns more because of differences in underlying ability. Most executives have extensive training and business experience, but only a few become chief executives of large corporations. In major-league baseball, some players earn up to 50 times more than others. From lawyers to executives to professional athletes, pay differences reflect differing abilities.

Differences in Risk. Research indicates that jobs with a higher probability of injury or death, such as coal mining, pay more, other things constant. Workers also earn more, other things constant, in fields such as construction, where the risks of unemployment are greater.

Geographic Differences. People have a strong incentive to sell their resources in the market where they earn the most, other things constant. For example, place kickers come to the United States from around the world for the attractive salaries available in the National Football League. Likewise, because physicians earn more in the United States than elsewhere, thousands of foreign-trained physicians migrate here each year. The flow of labor is not all one way: some Americans seek their fortune abroad, such as basketball players who head for the high pay in Europe and baseball players who head for Japan. Most workers face migration hurdles if they seek higher pay in another country. Any reduction in these hurdles would reduce wage differentials across countries.

Job Discrimination. Sometimes individuals earn different wages because of racial or sexual discrimination in the job market. Although such discrimination is illegal, history shows that certain groups have systematically earned less than others of apparently equal ability. The reasons underlying the differences in average earnings between males and females are discussed in the following case study.

CASE STUDY

Comparable Worth

Despite laws in this country requiring affirmative action and equal pay for equal work, women on average still earn only 76 percent as much as men. The gap is narrowest for those 20 to 24 years of age and widest for those 45 years of age and older. After adjusting for several factors, such as the tendency of women to interrupt their careers for child rearing, gender differences in pay shrink but do not disappear. Few women rank among the nation's top executives and none are among the 25 top paid executives.

One explanation for this pay gap is that women earn less because they attach greater importance to attractive working conditions, the ability to take time off for child care, and the nearness of the job to home. According to this argument, women value working conditions while men value pay. So the fact that women earn less reflects in part the importance they attach to nonwage characteristics of a job. For example, a study by Eric Solberg and Teresa Laughlin found, for a sample of working men and women between 26 and 34 years of age in 1990, that the average female pay was 87 percent of the average male pay. But when the authors examined total compensation, which includes the value of fringe benefits, they found that the average female pay jumped to 96 percent of the average male pay.

A second explanation for the pay gap is that women crowd into certain occupations, such as secretarial work, nursing, and retail sales, because other job opportunities have been blocked by discrimination and restrictive gender roles. The increased supply of female labor to these crowded professions has lowered the prevailing wage. Some advocates of this crowding explanation have promoted a notion called **comparable worth** as a way of addressing pay differences. The comparable-worth approach calls for evaluating each job based on three criteria: skill required, effort, and responsibility. These evaluations then determine the pay for each job.

Proponents of comparable worth believe that such a system would eliminate situations in which men working in jobs requiring few skills earn more than women working in occupations requiring greater skills. Pay differences were dramatized in a strike of clerical and technical workers at Yale University. Administrative assistants, who were mostly female, performed work that required, in the union's view, at least as much training and experience as the work performed by the university's truck drivers, who were mostly male. Yet the truck drivers earned 38 percent more than the administrative assistants.

Comparable-worth laws have been adopted in more than a dozen states as well as in Australia, Great Britain, and Canada. Some major employers, such as BankAmerica and AT&T, have also begun to introduce comparable worth into their compensation schemes. In Australia, a decade of comparable worth policies closed the ratio between women's and men's hourly wages from 74 percent to 94 percent. In Washington State, the pay gap among state employees closed from 80 percent to 95 percent in the first four years of the program.

These programs have had some unintended consequences. In Australia, the growth rate of female employment slowed somewhat. In Washington State, government pay in some traditionally male fields, such as civil engineering, has fallen so much that government openings are hard to fill. Comparable worth has in some cases also reduced the incentive women have to advance to levels where there are few women. For example, in the past an upwardly mobile clerk-typist working for the state of Washington would seek a job as a fiscal technician, a job category in which the proportion of women is smaller. This job could lead to a still bigger promotion to accountant. But the big pay increase for clerk-typists meant that taking a job as fiscal technician would result in a pay cut. So that path of advancement now seems less attractive. Basing pay

Comparable Worth
continued

Location:

Some employers have begun to develop compensation programs and policies based on principles of comparable worth. For an example, visit "AT&T Employment Opportunities," maintained by AT&T (http://www.att.com/hr/).

Comparable worth The principle that pay should be determined by job characteristics rather than by supply and demand

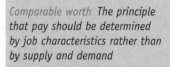

Comparable Worth
continued

on comparable worth may provide for more job equity, but it limits the allocative role of the labor market.

Sources: Lynda Ames, "Fixing Women's Wages: The Effectiveness of Comparable Worth Policies," *Industrial and Labor Relations Review* (July 1995): pp. 709–25; Eric S. Hardy, "America's Highest-Paid Bosses," *Forbes*, 22 May 1995; and Eric Solberg and Teresa Laughlin, "The Gender Pay Gap, Fringe Benefits, and Occupational Crowding," *Industrial and Labor Relations Review* (July 1995): pp. 692–709.

Entrepreneur A profit-seeking decision maker who organizes an enterprise and assumes the risk of its operation

There remains another human resource to discuss, a resource that in some respects is of critical importance: entrepreneurial ability—the wellspring of economic vitality and the source of a rising standard of living.

ENTREPRENEURIAL ABILITY

Though it is difficult to teach, some 400 colleges now offer courses in it. Though it is difficult to measure, business publications look for it in all the rising stars whose success they track. And though it is difficult to analyze, new books on the topic appear almost daily. What is it? *Entrepreneurial ability.* Perhaps no other resource is so poorly understood.

There is no market for entrepreneurial ability in the sense in which we usually think of markets. In fact, one reason firms are formed is because entrepreneurs believe they will be better off creating their own firms than selling their labor in a market. Entrepreneurs are their own bosses—that is, they hire themselves—because there is no formal market for their special kind of ability.

An **entrepreneur** is a profit-seeking decision maker who organizes an enterprise and assumes the risk of its operation. *An entrepreneur pays for the right to direct resources and claims any profit or loss that is left over after all other resources have been paid.* The right to control resources does not necessarily mean that the entrepreneur must manage the firm, but the entrepreneur must have the power to hire, fire, and otherwise control the manager.

The Entrepreneur Can Supply Other Resources

Recall that accounting profit equals a firm's total revenue minus all explicit costs. Economic profit equals total revenue minus all implicit and explicit costs—all opportunity costs. Typically, economic profit goes to the entrepreneur as the reward for entrepreneurial ability. To arrive at economic profit, we must carefully subtract from accounting profit that portion of the entrepreneur's income that is a return for supplying resources other than entrepreneurial ability. For example, suppose the entrepreneur also manages the firm. That entrepreneur's economic profit should exclude any opportunity cost from serving as manager. Managers are, after all, just another form of labor, albeit a rather special kind, so the entrepreneur's opportunity cost as manager should not be confused with profit. *Economic profit excludes the opportunity cost of resources supplied by the entrepreneur other than entrepreneurial ability.* The net result can be an economic loss rather than an economic profit.

Imagine that a new restaurant called The Blue Beagle is opening in your community. Suppose that the entrepreneur, or founder, secures a bank loan, rents a building and restaurant equipment, and hires a manager who, in turn, hires other employees. The entrepreneur promises to pay resource suppliers at

Net Bookmark

The Association of Collegiate Entrepreneurship (ACE) is a student organization, founded through the Management and Human Resources Department at California State Polytechnic University, Pomona. ACE "promotes the spirit of entrepreneurship by guiding and developing creativity and innovation through nontraditional approaches." Toward this goal, ACE provides students with the opportunities and resources needed to start their own businesses. Visit ACE (http://www.csupomona.edu/ace/).

least the market return for putting their resources under the manager's direction. Otherwise, these resources would go elsewhere. The entrepreneur in this example supplies no resources other than entrepreneurial ability.

Since all resources except entrepreneurial ability are either rented or hired, who is The Blue Beagle's owner and what does the owner own? The restaurant's owner is the entrepreneur. *The "firm" owned by the entrepreneur consists of a set of contracts or agreements between the entrepreneur and resource suppliers.* The entrepreneur has acquired the right to direct and control these resources in return for a promise to pay their owners a specified amount. At the end of the year, the entrepreneur can retain as economic profit whatever is left of income after all other resource suppliers have been paid. The entrepreneur is the *residual claimant*—someone who claims the residual left over after all costs, both explicit and implicit, have been subtracted from revenues. If revenues fail to cover outlays, the entrepreneur must make up the shortfall. The entrepreneur is last in line to get paid and is the chief bag-holder should anyone be left holding the bag.

It is not the management of resources that distinguishes the entrepreneur; it is the control over the decision as to who manages resources. Even if the entrepreneur decided to serve as the restaurant's manager, the entrepreneur as manager would likely still delegate to the chef many decisions about resource use—which assistants to hire, what ingredients to purchase, how to combine these ingredients. So don't think entrepreneurs must manage the firm (though they often do); *entrepreneurs must have the power to control the manager and to claim the profit or loss that arises from the manager's decisions.*

As we will see, an entrepreneur is much more than a business owner. An entrepreneur is an idea person, an innovator, and a risk taker who sees new opportunities for profit and goes after them. Entrepreneurs are the pioneers of the economy; they drive the engine of growth.

Why Entrepreneurs Often Invest in the Firm

In our example, the entrepreneur borrowed the funds to start the restaurant. In reality, a bank would be reluctant to finance such a risky undertaking. Although the entrepreneur would promise to repay the bank, the restaurant could go bankrupt. As noted in Chapter 4, under the corporate business structure, an entrepreneur's liability is limited to his or her own investment in the firm. Even if the firm was not incorporated, the entrepreneur, in the face of huge losses, could simply file for personal bankruptcy.

Because of the possibility of bankruptcy and default, lenders typically want entrepreneurs to supply additional resources to the firm. The entrepreneur's supply of funds to the firm reassures wary lenders in at least two ways. First, when the entrepreneur's own assets are tied up in the firm, that individual is likely to exercise greater care and vigilance in shepherding all the firm's resources, including the bank's funds. Second, the entrepreneur's investment in the firm—called *owner's equity*—serves as a buffer, providing lenders and other resource suppliers with some insulation against a default in the event that total cost exceeds total revenue.

Entrepreneurship and Theories of Profit

Profit plays an important role in a market economy because profit incentives direct the allocation of resources. Profit, therefore, deserves special attention.

There is no single theory explaining the source of economic profit in the capitalist system. Rather, there are several theories of profit, each of which focuses on a different role played by the entrepreneur. Here we consider three entrepreneurial roles that represent potential sources of economic profit. These theories are not mutually exclusive—that is, all could apply.

The Entrepreneur as Broker. Perhaps the simplest view of the entrepreneur is that of a broker whose aim is to "buy low and sell high." Entrepreneurs bid against one another for the available resources, and this bidding establishes market prices for those resources. Entrepreneurs contract with resource suppliers and combine the resources to produce goods and services. The difference between the firm's total revenue and total cost is the entrepreneur's economic profit. Thus, *an entrepreneur earns a profit by selling products for more than they cost to produce.* If markets are competitive, economic profit attracts rivals in the long run, forcing profit down to just a normal level. *As brokers, entrepreneurs direct resources to their highest valued use; thus, entrepreneurs promote economic efficiency in the economy.*

The Entrepreneur as Innovator. A variation of the entrepreneur-as-broker view is that an entrepreneur earns a profit from successful innovations. The entrepreneur who makes an existing product for less money than the competition does, or who introduces a successful new product, earns at least short-run economic profits. The possibility of economic profit serves as a powerful motive for innovations. Whether this profit continues in the long run depends on whether other firms can imitate the cost-saving activity or the new product. If there are barriers to entry, such as patents, economic profit can continue into the long run as well.

An enterprising individual who creates a new technology, opens a new market, or introduces a cost-saving efficiency generates economic profit, at least for a while, until imitators swarm in to copy the innovation and drive profit back to the normal level. These path-breaking entrepreneurs are not simply the source of profit. They are the engine of the entire economic system. Innovations are the wellspring of economic growth, and entrepreneurs are the fountainhead of that innovation.

Entrepreneur as Risk Bearer. Some economists think of the profit earned by entrepreneurs as arising from the risk associated with venturing into a world filled with uncertainty. According to this theory of profit, a portion of the return received by entrepreneurs is a payment for their willingness to bear that risk.

Profit and the Supply of Entrepreneurs

The ranks of entrepreneurs are in constant flux, as some emerge from the labor market to form their own enterprises and others return to the labor market after selling successful firms or failing. The supply of entrepreneurial ability is influenced by a variety of forces, such as the pace of technological change, government regulations, tax laws, and the market return on resources other than entrepreneurial ability.

Evidence suggests that a new firm is a risky enterprise. What encourages someone to take on such a risk rather than settle for the predictable salary, vacation time, health benefits, and other amenities that typically come with employment? Why do 25 million people in this country call themselves boss? Many no doubt prefer the individual freedom that comes from self-employment. Some derive satisfaction from the creative process. Some also dream of founding a corporate empire, an empire that can be sold or passed to their heirs. And some may have difficulty finding employment. The bottom line is that people go into business for themselves because this appears more attractive than any other alternative.

One strong economic incentive for founding a firm is that any entrepreneur who develops a profit-making operation can typically sell the firm for a multiple of the firm's expected profit stream. For example, suppose you put together a company that yields an economic profit of $50,000 per year, a stream that is expected to continue indefinitely. The market value of a firm reflects the *capitalized* value of its profit stream. Capitalization converts a future stream of income into a current market value. Though the derivation is discussed in a later chapter, for now we can say that profit of $50,000 per year could have a market value of $1,000,000. The value would be even higher if profit is expected to grow in the future.

Let's close with a case study that follows one successful entrepreneur from the beginning.

Mitch Kapor's background hardly seemed to qualify him for the success that was to come his way. He had held various jobs, ranging from disk jockey to instructor of transcendental meditation. One day he traded his stereo for an Apple computer, and therein lies a tale. He was fascinated by the Apple and soon developed his programming skills to such a level that he reportedly wrote two business applications programs in only two months, programs that sold for more than a million dollars!

With these funds and with additional support, both financial and entrepreneurial, from a *venture capital firm,* he founded the Lotus Development Corporation in 1982. Lotus 1-2-3 quickly became the industry's best-selling business program, with sales of $50 million the first year. In October 1983, the company made its first public offering of stock, making Kapor's stock in the company worth $70 million. In a few short years, Lotus grew out of his basement to become a firm with over 2,200 employees and annual sales of nearly $1 billion.

The other side of this success story is the venture capital firm that invested $2.1 million in Kapor's company in 1982. Venture capitalists shop around, investing in promising new firms. Such investors could be considered entrepreneurs, since they share the responsibility of guaranteeing the payments of the other resources, share in the control of these resources, and are residual claimants of any profit or loss. When Lotus made its public offering in 1983, the stock held by the venture capitalists became worth $70 million, or about 33 times their investment only a year earlier.

In 1985, one of Kapor's software engineers, Raymond Ozzie, came up with

CASE STUDY

IBM's Lotus Position

Location:

Although IBM acquired Lotus Development Corporation in 1995, Lotus continues to have an autonomous presence on the World Wide Web (Lotus founder Mitch Kapor is pictured here). Visit (http://www.lotus.com/). To learn more about venture capitalism, visit "Capital Quest," a web service through ARS Data, Ltd., that showcases new ideas and entrepreneurs directly to potential investors (http://www.usbusiness.com/capquest/home.html).

IBM's Lotus Position
continued

the idea for a program to allow people on different kinds of computers to communicate with one another. Kapor provided Ozzie with the venture capital to start his own company to develop the idea.

In July 1986, Kapor resigned as chairman of Lotus. Evidently, he did not find the job of managing people as attractive as founding a corporate empire. Since Kapor was viewed as the imaginative force behind Lotus, the market price of a share of Lotus stock dropped by 10 percent the day after he resigned. Investors apparently believed that Kapor's special skills could not easily be replaced. But Lotus survived, and in 1994 it paid $84 million to buy the rest of the company Ozzie set up to develop what became known as Lotus Notes—software that allows dozens or even hundreds of people all over the world to share documents, each on his or her own computer.

In 1995 IBM, the world's largest computer company, paid $3.52 billion to buy the Lotus Development Corporation. IBM considered Lotus Notes central to the future of computing. At the time of the IBM offer, Lotus Notes was in use at the White House, the Central Intelligence Agency, Japan's Ministry of International Trade and Industry, and General Motors.

Kapor's initial idea and his subsequent support for Lotus Notes have made a lot of people rich. The same can be said for Steven Jobs at Apple and Bill Gates at Microsoft. Entrepreneurs expand the size of the pie. That's their job.

Sources: "A Software Whiz Logs Off," *Newsweek,* 21 July 1986; "Software Landscape Shifts as IBM Makes Hostile Bid for Lotus," *The Wall Street Journal,* 6 June 1995; and Michael Meyer, "Lou's Big Deal," *Newsweek,* 19 June 1995.

CONCLUSION

The first half of this chapter focused on the supply of labor and on why wages differ both across occupations and among individuals within occupations. The interaction of the demand and supply for labor determines wage rates and the level of employment. The second half of the chapter dealt with another human resource, entrepreneurial ability. If the skills of the entrepreneur could be learned step by step, like the skills of a plumber or an accountant, anyone could complete a course and perhaps strike it rich. Entrepreneurship is a more elusive skill, which is why economic profit is reserved for successful entrepreneurs.

Our emphasis has been on competitive labor markets. To a large extent, we have ignored the influence of institutional forces, such as labor unions and governments. The effect of unions on the labor market is examined in the next chapter.

SUMMARY

1. The demand for labor is the relationship between the wage rate and the quantity of labor producers are willing and able to hire, other things constant. The supply of labor is the relationship between the wage rate and the quantity of labor workers are willing and able to supply, other things constant. The intersection of demand and supply curves determines the equilibrium wage rate.

2. There are three uses of time: market work, nonmarket work, and leisure. People allocate their time so as to maximize utility. The higher the market wage, other things constant, the more goods and services can be purchased with that wage, so a higher wage encourages labor suppliers to substitute market work for other uses of time. But the higher the wage, the higher the income,

and as income increases, people consume more of all normal goods, including leisure. The net effect of a higher wage on an individual's quantity of market labor supplied depends on both the substitution effect and the income effect of a wage increase.

3. The quantity of market labor supplied also depends on factors other than the wage, including (1) other sources of income, (2) job amenities, (3) the future value of job experience, and (4) worker tastes.

4. Market wages differ because of (1) differences in training and education requirements, (2) differences in the skill and ability of workers, (3) differences in the riskiness of the work, both in terms of the workers' safety and the chances of getting laid off, (4) geographic differences, and (5) racial and gender discrimination.

5. Entrepreneurs are profit-seeking decision makers who pay resource suppliers for the right to direct those resources; entrepreneurs also claim any profits or losses. They need not supply any resource other than entrepreneurial ability, though they usually invest in the firm and often manage it as well.

6. There is no single theory explaining the source of profit earned by entrepreneurs. Entrepreneurs have been viewed as brokers who earn a profit by selling output for more than they pay resource suppliers. They have been viewed as innovators who earn a profit by developing new products or by producing existing products for less. And they have been viewed as risk bearers who earn a profit by taking chances.

QUESTIONS AND PROBLEMS

1. **(Uses of Time)** Describe the three possible uses of an individual's time and provide examples of each.

2. **(Labor Supply)** Suppose that the substitution effect of an increase in the wage rate exactly offsets the income effect for all wage levels. What would the market supply of labor look like in this case? Why?

3. **(Labor Supply)** Many U.S. companies have a problem with worker absenteeism. How is this problem related to market labor supply and, in particular, to the level of wages? What other considerations are there?

4. **(Nonwage Determinants of Labor Supply)** (a) Suppose that two jobs are exactly the same except that one is performed in an air-conditioned workplace. How might an economist measure the value workers place on such a job amenity? (b) Suppose that you have a choice between a job that involves the death of one worker in a hundred per year and another job that involves no such risk, other things constant. If the no-risk job pays $20,000 per year, what income would be necessary to induce someone to take the risky job?

5. **(Labor Supply and Utility Maximization)** How does a rational consumer allocate his or her time?

6. **(Equilibrium Wage)** Use a labor supply-demand diagram to predict the impact on the equilibrium wage and quantity of market labor of each of the following:
   a. An increase in the income tax.
   b. A reduction in labor productivity.

c. An increased value of work experience in that market.

7. **(Market Supply of Labor)** The table below indicates the number of hours per week provided to a particular market by three individuals at various wage rates. Calculate the total hours per week (Q_T) provided to the market.

Hourly Wage	Hours per Week			
	Q_1	Q_2	Q_3	Q_T
$ 5	20	0	0	_____
6	25	0	0	_____
7	35	10	0	_____
8	45	25	10	_____
9	42	40	30	_____
10	38	37	45	_____

Which individuals, if any, have backward-bending supply curves in the wage range shown? Does the market supply curve backward in this wage range?

8. **(Why Wages Differ)** What are the various reasons that permanent wage differences may occur among different markets for labor or within the same market?

9. **(Work and Utility)** Explain the concept of the "net utility of work."

10. **(Entrepreneurial Ability and Economic Profit)** Why is an entrepreneur called the "residual claimant"? What costs must be considered in determining the residual amount?

11. **(Theories of Profit)** Explain the three theories of profit discussed in the chapter. How do entrepreneurs promote economic efficiency and growth?

12. **(Profits)** Some people claim that profits are bad or can be excessive. Support or refute this claim in light of the discussion in this chapter.

13. **(The Supply of Entrepreneurs)** How does capitalization act as a catalyst for an entrepreneur to undertake the risk of establishing a new firm?

14. **(Income and Substitution Effects)** Suppose that the cost of living increases dramatically and therefore reduces the purchasing power of your income. If your money wage doesn't increase, you may work *more* hours because of this cost-of-living increase. Is this an income or substitution effect response? Explain.

15. **(Backward–Bending Labor Supply Curve)** Explain why an individual may have a backward-bending labor supply curve.

16. **(Labor Supply)** Is it ever rational to interview for a job for which you are clearly overqualified?

17. **(Comparable Worth)** Suppose legislation were passed mandating equal pay for all jobs that require the same skills and training.
    a. What kinds of problems would this create if such jobs had different nonmonetary attributes?
    b. How might employers respond to the passage of such legislation?

18. **(Comparable Worth)** Suppose that two organizations that are truly identical in terms of job characteristics and skill requirements offer different pay scales. What would you expect to see in terms of relative numbers of job applications for these two organizations? If one of the organizations predominantly hires women and the other predominantly hires men, how could you determine whether job discrimination exists?

19. **(IBM's Lotus Position)** Are the entrepreneurial returns earned by Kapor economic rent or opportunity costs?

20. **(IBM's Lotus Position)** Considering the chapter's discussion of factors affecting the supply of labor, what are possible explanations for Kapor's 1986 decision to resign from Lotus?

Using the Internet

21. Review "U.S. Economy," a summary of economic research conducted by analysts with Bank of America (http://www.bankamerica.com/econ_indicator/econ_indicator.html), and look within "Payroll Employment." What does this report indicate about the current state of the labor market?

Unions and Collective Bargaining

26

Few aspects of the labor market are more in the news than the activities of labor unions. Labor negotiations, strikes, picket lines, confrontations between workers and employers—all of these fit neatly into TV's "action news" format. Each September, for example, we get pictures of striking teachers walking picket lines somewhere in the country. This drama may cause you to miss the real economic significance of unions. Also, you may have developed the mistaken impression that the majority of workers belong to unions and that strikes occur frequently. In fact, fewer than one in six workers belong to unions and well over 95 percent of union agreements are reached without a strike.

In this chapter, we will step back from the charged rhetoric that typically characterizes union-employer relations to review the history of the union movement in the United States, examine more carefully the economic effects of unions, and discuss recent trends in union membership. Topics discussed in this chapter include:

- Craft unions
- Industrial unions
- Collective bargaining

- Bilateral monopoly
- Union objectives
- Union membership trends

A BRIEF HISTORY OF THE U.S. LABOR MOVEMENT

In 1860, before labor unions achieved national prominence, the work day for nonfarm employees averaged about 11 hours, and a 6-day work week was normal. Those employed in steel mills, paper mills, and breweries typically worked 12 hours a day, 7 days a week. Working conditions were often frightful: insurance company records indicate that about one out of 15 workers was seriously injured each year. Mining and metal processing were particularly dangerous. To be compensated for injuries, a worker had to sue the employer and prove the employer's negligence, but most workers did not know how to sue their employers. Child labor was also common. In 1880, a million children between the ages of 10 and 15 were in the work force; this number doubled to 2 million by 1910, when one-fifth of those between 10 and 15 held full-time jobs. Heavy immigration during the period sent millions of new workers streaming into the labor force, competing for jobs and keeping wages relatively low. Thus, *employers had a ready pool of workers, despite the low pay and poor working conditions.*

Early Labor Organizations

A **labor union** is a group of employees who join together to improve their terms of employment. The first labor unions in the United States date back to the early days of national independence, when employees in various crafts, such as carpenters, shoemakers, and printers, formed local groups to seek higher wages and shorter hours. Such **craft unions** confined membership to workers with a particular skill, or craft. In the 1850s, because improved transportation systems extended markets beyond the local level, unions in the same trade began widening their membership to regional and even national levels. The National Typographical Union, formed in 1852, was the first national union and was soon followed by several other national craft unions.

Knights of Labor. The first major national labor organization in the United States was the *Knights of Labor,* formed in 1869. Its objectives were generally more political than economic, but the Knights sought an 8-hour workday and the abolition of child labor. Within 20 years the union had over 750,000 members. But the union lacked focus and tried to include as members both skilled and unskilled laborers, a combination that proved difficult to organize.

American Federation of Labor. The various craft unions that had developed during the 19th century did not find the Knights of Labor suited to their interests. These craft unions formed their own national organization, the *American Federation of Labor (AFL).* The AFL, founded in 1886 under the direction of Samuel Gompers, was not a union but rather an organization of national unions, with each retaining its autonomy. By the beginning of World War I, the AFL, still under the direction of Gompers, was viewed as the voice of labor. The Clayton Act of 1914 exempted trade union negotiations from antitrust laws, meaning that *unions at competing companies could join forces in an attempt to raise wages.* Unions were also tax exempt. Union membership jumped during World War I, but dropped after the war as the government retreated from its support of union efforts. Membership dropped by half between 1920 and 1933.

Labor union A group of employees who join together to improve their terms of employment

Craft union A union whose members have a particular skill or work at a particular craft, such as plumbers or carpenters

Net Bookmark

Under the direction of Samuel Gompers, the American Federation of Labor (AFL) was founded in 1886. In 1955, the AFL merged with the Congress of Industrial Organizations (CIO), creating the AFL-CIO. To learn more about the modern-day activities of the AFL-CIO, visit "Welcome to LaborWEB: The AFL-CIO's Home Page" (http://www.aflcio.org/).

A New Deal for Labor

The Great Depression set the stage for a new era in the labor movement. In 1932, Herbert Hoover signed the *Norris–La Guardia Act,* which sharply limited the courts' ability to stop strikes and banned *yellow-dog contracts,* under which workers had to agree not to join a union as a condition of employment.

Wagner Act. President Franklin D. Roosevelt took office in 1933 and was a strong supporter of unions as one solution to the huge drop in wages and prices that occurred during the Great Depression. The *Wagner Act* of 1935 required employers to bargain in "good faith" with unions that represented the majority of employees. The act also made it illegal for employers to interfere with employees' right to unionize. To investigate unfair labor practices and to oversee union elections, the law established the *National Labor Relations Board.* The Wagner Act has come to be known as the Magna Carta of the U.S. labor movement. Thus, by 1935 workers had the right to unionize, and once the majority of workers selected a union, the employer was required to negotiate in good faith with that union, which was immune from antitrust laws and taxes.

The Congress of Industrial Organizations. Such favorable legislation nourished the growth of a new kind of union, organized along industry lines. The *Congress of Industrial Organizations (CIO)* was established in 1935 to serve as a national organization of unions in mass-production industries, such as autos and steel. Whereas the AFL had organized workers in particular crafts, such as plumbers and carpenters, the CIO was made up of unions whose membership embraced all workers in a particular industry, including unskilled, semiskilled, and skilled workers. Workers in the auto and rubber industries were able to organize through the use of *sit-down strikes,* in which workers occupied the plants but did not work, thereby paralyzing operations. This **industrial union** approach proved successful, and in 1937 the steelworkers' union joined the CIO, bringing more than 200,000 members into the organization. In 1938 the charismatic leader of the United Mine Workers, John L. Lewis, became president of the CIO.

Industrial union A union of both skilled and unskilled workers from a particular industry, such as auto workers or steelworkers

The Labor Movement after World War II

After World War II, economic conditions and public sentiment appeared to turn against unions. Postwar inflation seemed to be aggravated by a series of strikes, and in November 1946 the United Mine Workers defied a court order to return to work after a long and bitter strike. In response, Congress in 1947 passed the *Taft-Hartley Act,* which attempted to limit strikes that would affect the public's safety and welfare. The president, by obtaining a court order, could stop a strike for 80 days, during which time the parties could continue to negotiate.

Despite the Taft-Hartley Act, the union movement flourished right after World War II, with membership growing from less than 4 million in 1930, or about 12 percent of the nonfarm work force, to more than 17 million in 1955, or about 34 percent. The AFL and the CIO merged in 1955, creating the AFL-CIO.

But during the 1950s, organized labor suffered from allegations of corruption and misconduct by union leaders. Congressional investigations led to the passage in 1959 of the *Landrum-Griffin Act* to protect the rights of union members against abuses by union leaders. The act regulated union elections, required union officials to file financial reports, and made theft of union funds a federal offense. *The Landrum-Griffin Act has been called the Bill of Rights for union members because it is aimed at guaranteeing each member's right to fair elections and honest union leadership.*

COLLECTIVE BARGAINING AND OTHER TOOLS OF UNIONISM

Now that you have some idea of the labor movement's history, let's consider the tools used by unions to exert some control over wages and working conditions. We begin with a discussion of collective bargaining.

Collective Bargaining

Collective bargaining is the process by which representatives from the union and management negotiate a mutually agreeable contract specifying wages, employee benefits, and working conditions. The contract can run to many pages of fine print written in language only a lawyer could understand. Once a tentative agreement has been reached, union representatives must present it to the membership for a vote. If the agreement is rejected, the union can vote to continue negotiations or to strike.

Mediation and Arbitration. If negotiations over a contract reach an impasse and the public interest is involved, government officials may ask an independent mediator to step in. A *mediator* is an impartial observer who listens to both sides separately and suggests how each side could adjust its position to resolve differences. If a resolution appears possible, the mediator brings the parties together to iron out a contract. The mediator has no power to impose a settlement on the parties.

In certain critical sectors, such as police and fire protection, where a strike could seriously harm the public interest, an impasse in negotiations is sometimes settled through **binding arbitration,** whereby a neutral third party evaluates both sides of the dispute and issues a decision that the parties are committed to accept. Some disputes skip the mediation and arbitration steps and go directly from impasse to strike.

The Strike

A major source of union power in the bargaining relationship is the threat of a **strike,** which is the union's attempt to withhold labor from the firm. The purpose of a strike is to stop production, thereby forcing the firm to accept the union's position. But strikes can also impose significant costs on union members, who forgo pay and benefits for the duration of the strike and risk losing their jobs. Union funds and other sources, such as unemployment benefits in some states, may provide support during a strike, but the typical striker's income falls substantially.

The most publicized strike in recent years was that by major-league baseball players. That strike, which began in the summer of 1994 and dragged into spring training of 1995, managed to do something that two world wars couldn't—

Collective bargaining The process by which union and management negotiate a labor agreement

Binding arbitration Negotiation in which both parties in a union-management dispute agree to accept an impartial observer's resolution of the dispute

Strike A union's attempt to withhold labor from a firm

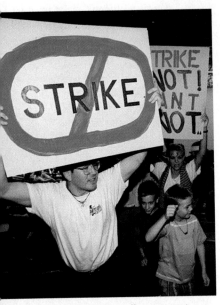

Unions use strikes to exert control over wages and working conditions. By stopping production, unions hope to force firms to make concessions. However, workers on strike forgo pay and risk losing their jobs.

cancel the World Series. The threat of a strike hangs over labor negotiations and can serve as a real spur to reach an accord. *Although neither party usually wants a strike, both sides, rather than concede on key points, typically act as if they could and would endure a strike.*

The strike's success depends on blocking the supply of labor. Unions usually picket the targeted employer to prevent or discourage so-called strikebreakers, or "scabs," from crossing the picket lines to work. But the firm, by hiring temporary workers and nonstriking union workers, can sometimes continue production. Not surprisingly, violence occasionally erupts during confrontations between striking and nonstriking workers. The following case study discusses one company's efforts to continue with business as usual despite a strike.

CASE STUDY

Hard Ball at Caterpillar

Location:

Visit Caterpillar, Inc. (http://www.cat.com/). To learn more about the United Auto Workers (UAW), visit "Welcome to the UAW International Union," maintained by the UAW Public Relations and Publications Department (http://www.uaw.org/).

Labor troubles began for Caterpillar in November 1991, when the company refused to accept the job-security provisions the United Auto Workers (UAW) negotiated with Deere & Co., a rival firm in the heavy equipment industry. In a system called *pattern bargaining,* a union reaching a settlement with one firm in an industry could expect that contract to serve as a model for agreements with other firms in the industry.

Caterpillar's refusal to go along with the Deere settlement prompted the UAW to call a strike against Caterpillar, the nation's largest maker of earth-moving equipment. In an expression of solidarity, Bill Clinton walked the picket line in 1992 while campaigning for president. Five months after the strike began, management threatened to permanently replace any union member who failed to return to work. Faced with the prospect of lost jobs, union members went back to work.

Because union members returned to work without a contract, Caterpillar unilaterally imposed wages and working conditions that were viewed by workers as unfair. Workers tried to pressure the company with a "work-to-rule" slowdown, which meant working according to strict union rules. In a continuing test of wills, various union job actions were countered with disciplinary measures by the company. Claiming "unfair labor practices," some 13,000 UAW members struck all eight Caterpillar plants in June 1994. The reason for the strike was significant because, under labor law, the company could not permanently replace workers striking over unfair labor practices, though the company could replace workers striking for higher wages.

The UAW showed its commitment to strikers by tripling the usual level of monthly strike pay to $1,200. This sweetened strike pay, which would ultimately cost the union over $200 million, was aimed in part at keeping striking workers from crossing picket likes. Strikers believed their skills made them irreplaceable, but, as the strike dragged on, Caterpillar introduced more labor-saving techniques, and skilled workers came from across the country for a chance at these high-paying jobs. By employing a combination of 5,600 temporary workers, plus thousands of salaried workers and UAW members who

Hard Ball at Caterpillar
continued

crossed picket lines, Caterpillar's production rate during the strike exceeded pre-strike levels. In fact, company profits catapulted to record levels during the strike. The company's performance apparently refuted the conventional wisdom that both sides suffer during a long strike.

In December 1995, some 17 months after the walkout began and with no evidence that the company would give in, union officials decided that the 8,700 members still on strike were "available immediately and unconditionally for return to work." This unconditional surrender by the union was a crushing defeat for a union movement badly in need of a victory. Each striking worker had lost on average about $37,000 in wages during the strike. The end of the strike is not likely to mean the end of labor troubles at Caterpillar.

Sources: Robert Rose, "Strike Is Halted at Caterpillar After 17 Months," *The Wall Street Journal,* 4 December 1995; Robert Rose, "Temporary Heaven: A Job at Struck Caterpillar," *The Wall Street Journal,* 29 November 1994; and Ray Long, "Caterpillar Workers Awaiting Recall," *Hartford Courant,* 5 December 1995.

After companies such as Phelps-Dodge Copper, Continental Airlines, Hormel Meatpacking, and Caterpillar successfully broke strikes by hiring replacement workers, other unions became more cautious in calling strikes. Strike activity is way down across the country. During the 1970s, for example, there were an average of 290 strikes a year in the United States involving 1,000 or more workers per strike. During the 1990s, there have been only about 40 such strikes per year on average. The experience at Caterpillar underscores two reasons why unions are more reluctant to strike: (1) the increased willingness of employers to hire strikebreakers, and (2) the increased willingness of workers—both union and nonunion—to cross picket lines.

UNION WAGES AND EMPLOYMENT

Union members, like everyone else, have unlimited wants, but no union can regularly get everything it desires. Because resources are scarce, choices must be made. A menu of union desires includes higher wages, more employee benefits, greater job security, better working conditions, and so on. To keep the analysis manageable, let's focus initially on a single objective: higher wages. We will examine three possible ways of increasing wages: (1) by forming inclusive, or industrial, unions; (2) by forming exclusive, or craft, unions; and (3) by increasing the demand for union labor.

Inclusive, or Industrial, Unions

The first model we will consider describes strong industrial unions, such as the auto and steel unions, which attempt to set an industry-wide wage for each class of labor. In panel (a) of Exhibit 1, the market demand and supply for a particular class of labor are presented as *D* and *S*. In the absence of a union, the equilibrium wage is *W* and the equilibrium employment level is *E*. At the market wage, each individual employer faces a horizontal, or perfectly elastic, supply of labor, as reflected by *s* in panel (b) of Exhibit 1. Thus, each firm, as a labor price taker, can hire as much labor as it wants at the market wage of *W*. The firm hires labor up to the point where the marginal revenue product, which is the

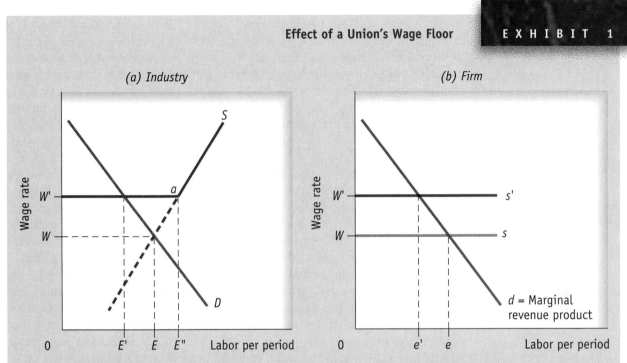

Effect of a Union's Wage Floor   E X H I B I T   1

(a) Industry

(b) Firm

In panel (a), the equilibrium wage rate is W. At that wage, the individual firm of panel (b) hires labor up to the point where the marginal revenue product equals W. Each firm hires quantity e; total employment is E. If a union can negotiate a wage W' above the equilibrium level, the supply curve facing the firm shifts up to s'. The firm hires fewer workers, e', and total employment falls to E'. At wage W' there is an excess supply of labor equal to E" − E'.

firm's demand for labor, equals the marginal resource cost, or the supply of labor to the firm; this amount is represented by quantity e in panel (b). As we saw earlier, in equilibrium each worker hired is paid a wage just equal to the marginal revenue product.

Now suppose that the union is able to negotiate a wage above the market-clearing wage. Specifically, suppose the wage floor negotiated is W', meaning that no labor will be supplied at a lower wage, but any amount desired by the firms, up to the quantity identified at point *a* in panel (a) of Exhibit 1, will be supplied at the wage floor. In effect, the supply of union labor is perfectly elastic at the union wage up to point *a*. If more than E'' workers are demanded, however, the wage floor no longer applies; the upward-sloping portion, *aS*, becomes the relevant part of the labor supply curve. For an industry facing a wage floor of W', the entire labor supply curve is $W'aS$, which has a kink where the wage floor joins the upward-sloping portion of the original supply curve.

Once this wage floor has been established, each individual firm faces a horizontal supply curve for labor at the collectively bargained wage, W'. Since the wage is now higher, the quantity of labor demanded by each employer declines, as reflected by the employment reduction from *e* to *e'* in panel (b) of Exhibit 1. Consequently, the higher wage leads to a reduction in total employment; the quantity demanded by the industry drops from *E* to *E'* in panel (a).

At wage W', the amount of labor workers would like to supply, E'', exceeds the amount demanded, E'. In the absence of a union, this excess quantity of labor supplied would cause unemployed workers to lower their asking wage. But union members agree *collectively* to a wage, so workers cannot individually offer to work for less, nor can employers hire them at a lower wage. Because the number of union members willing and able to work exceeds the number of jobs available, the union must develop some mechanism for rationing the available jobs, such as awarding jobs based on worker seniority or connections within the union. *With the inclusive, or industrial, union that negotiates with the entire industry, wages are higher and total employment lower than they would be in the absence of a union.*

Those who cannot find union employment will look for jobs in the nonunion sector. *The increased supply of labor in the nonunion sector drives down the nonunion wage.* So wages are relatively higher in the union sector: first, because unions bargain for a wage that exceeds the market-clearing wage, and second, because those unable to find employment in the union sector crowd into the nonunion sector. A survey of more than 200 studies concluded that unions increased members' wages by an average of about 15 percent above the wages of similarly skilled nonunion workers.[1] Unions tend to be less successful at raising wages in competitive industries and more successful in heavily regulated, monopolistic industries. For example, unions have little impact on the wages in the garment and textile industries, which tend to be competitive industries, but have greater impact on the wages in airlines, autos, steel, mining, and transportation, which tend to be either regulated or less competitive industries.

Exclusive, or Craft, Unions

One way to increase wages while avoiding the excess quantity of labor supplied which is created by the industrial-union approach is for the union to somehow shift the supply curve of labor to the left, as is shown in panel (a) of Exhibit 2. Successful supply restrictions of this type require that two conditions be met. First, the union must be able to restrict its membership, and second, the union must be able to force all employers in the industry to hire only union members. The union can restrict its membership with high initiation fees, long apprenticeship periods, difficult qualification exams, restrictive licensing requirements, and other devices designed to slow down or discourage new membership. But, as we will see later, unions have difficulty requiring all firms in the industry to hire only union workers.

Whereas wage setting is more typical of the industrial unions, restricting supply (and employment) is more characteristic of the craft unions, such as unions of carpenters, plumbers, and bricklayers. Groups of professionals such as doctors, lawyers, and accountants also impose entry restrictions through education and examination standards. Such restrictions, though usually defended on the grounds that they protect the public, are often no more than self-serving attempts to increase wages by restricting supply.

Increasing Demand for Union Labor

A third way to increase the wage is to increase the demand for union labor by somehow shifting the labor demand curve outward from D to D'' in panel

---

1   See H. Gregg Lewis, *Union Relative Wage Effects: A Survey* (Chicago: University of Chicago, 1986).

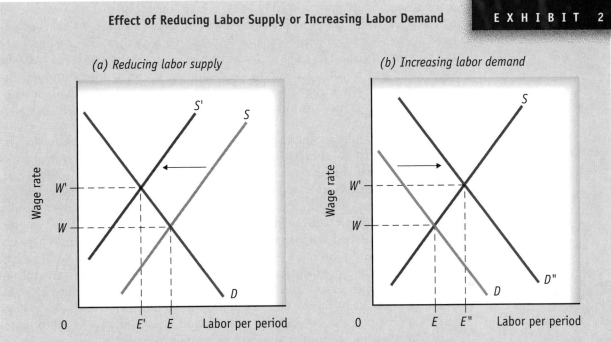

EXHIBIT 2

Effect of Reducing Labor Supply or Increasing Labor Demand

(a) Reducing labor supply

(b) Increasing labor demand

If a union can restrict labor supply to an industry, the supply curve shifts to the left from S to S', as in panel (a). The wage rate rises from W to W', but at the cost of a reduction in employment from E to E'. In panel (b), an increase in labor demand from D to D" raises both the wage and the level of employment.

(b) of Exhibit 2. This approach is an attractive alternative *because it increases both wages and employment,* so there is no need to ration jobs or restrict union membership. Here are some ways unions try to increase the demand for union labor.

Increase Demand for Union-Made Goods. The demand for union labor may be increased through a direct appeal to consumers to buy only union-made products. Because the demand for labor is a derived demand, an increase in the demand for union-made products will increase the demand for union labor.

Restrict Supply of Nonunion-Made Goods. Another way to increase the demand for union labor is to restrict the supply of products that compete with union-made products. Again, this approach relies on the derived nature of labor demand. The United Auto Workers have, for example, supported restrictions on imported cars. Fewer imported cars means a greater demand for cars produced by U.S. workers, who are mostly union members. Now that Japanese and German auto makers also build cars in the United States, the UAW has a trickier problem trying to limit the supply of such cars.

Increase Productivity of Union Labor. Some observers claim that the efficiency with which unions organize and monitor the labor-management relationship increases the demand for union labor. According to this theory, unions increase worker productivity by minimizing conflicts, resolving differences, and at times even straightening out workers who are goofing off. In the absence of a union, a dissatisfied worker may simply look for another job, thereby causing job turnover, which is costly to the firm. With a union, however, workers usually have grievance and arbitration channels through which they can complain, and the negotiated responses they receive may reduce their urge to leave the firm. Quit rates are in fact significantly lower among union workers (though this could be due to the higher pay). If unions increase the productivity of workers in this way, the demand for union labor will increase.

Featherbedding Union efforts to force employers to hire more workers than demanded for the task

Featherbedding. Still another way unions attempt to increase the demand for union labor is by **featherbedding,** which is an attempt to ensure that more union labor is hired than producers would prefer. Featherbedding is often a response to the introduction of labor-saving technology. For example, when the diesel engine replaced the coal-fired engine, locomotives no longer needed someone to shovel coal. For decades after the adoption of the diesel engine, however, the railroad unions required such a crew member. Similarly, painters' unions often prohibit the use of spray guns, limiting members to paintbrushes.

Featherbedding does not create a true increase in demand, in the sense of shifting the demand curve to the right; instead, it forces firms to hire more labor than they really want. The union tries to limit a firm to an all-or-none choice: either hire the number the union requires, or a strike will halt production. Thus, *the union attempts to dictate not only the wage but also the quantity that must be hired at that wage, thereby moving the employers to the right of their labor demand curve.* An example of featherbedding is considered in the following case study.

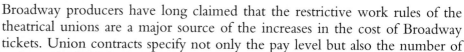

CASE STUDY

Featherbedding on Broadway

Location:

Because of union staffing requirements, stage shows in New York City tend to open off Broadway in theaters with fewer seats. To learn more about on and off Broadway theater, visit "Playbill On-Line," an Internet version of the New York Theater Community's popular news magazine (http://www.playbill.com/).

Broadway producers have long claimed that the restrictive work rules of the theatrical unions are a major source of the increases in the cost of Broadway tickets. Union contracts specify not only the pay level but also the number of workers required for each position. For example, union rules require that each Broadway theater have a permanent "house" carpenter, electrician, and property manager, who help set up scenery and conduct rehearsals. Once the show run begins, these workers appear only on payday. The box office must be staffed by three people. The musicians' union requires that from 9 to 22 musicians be employed at each theater staging a musical, even if the show calls for fewer musicians. Nonplaying musicians required by union rules are called "walkers," a term originating from the days when such musicians signed in each night and then walked away. Today, walkers do not even have to show up at the theater.

To the extent that these union work rules raise ticket prices, the continued employment of union members depends on the elasticity of demand for theater tickets. With the top price per ticket running as high as $100, there is evidence that the demand has been elastic enough to put many theater employees out of work. Less than half of the theaters on Broadway are operating, and many union members are unemployed (only one in seven members of the Actors' Equity union works full time as a stage performer). Featherbedding rules require each theater to hire a specified number of employees, but these rules cannot dictate that theaters stay in business.

Because union staffing requirements are based on the number of seats in the theater, new shows have moved to smaller theaters off Broadway, shifting to the larger Broadway theaters only after their success seems assured. Producers have also reduced staffing requirements by reducing the number of seats that can be sold—in some cases by simply blocking off the balcony (evidently, the marginal cost of those seats exceeded their marginal revenue). Theater owners and unions recently agreed on a special arrangement that would allow theaters that had been empty to stage low-budget plays for bargain ticket prices. For example, under the "special situations" clause negotiated with the musicians' union, producers can request that plays be staged with fewer than the required number of musicians.

Sources: Frank Rich, "Panic on Broadway," *New York Times,* 4 December 1994; Brooke Allen, "Who Killed Broadway?" *City Journal* (Winter 1995); John Tierney, "The Sound of Non-Music," *New York Times Magazine,* 13 March 1994; and Donald McNeil, "New Show Is First Not to Pay Idle Musicians," *New York Times,* 8 February 1995.

Featherbedding on Broadway
continued

We have examined three ways in which unions can try to raise members' wages: (1) by negotiating a wage floor above the equilibrium wage for the industry and somehow rationing the limited jobs among union members, (2) by restricting the supply of labor, and (3) by increasing the demand for union labor. Unions try to increase the demand for union labor in several ways: (1) through a direct public appeal to buy only union-made products, (2) by restricting the supply of products made by nonunion labor, (3) by reducing labor turnover and thereby increasing productivity, and (4) through featherbedding, which forces employers to hire more union workers than they would prefer.

Bilateral Monopoly

Thus far, we have assumed that wages are determined through negotiations between the labor union and the entire industry. Since each firm hires labor as a price taker in the labor market, each firm can hire as much labor as it chooses at the negotiated wage.

More and more, however, negotiations are between a union and an individual employer, such as the UAW's negotiations with Caterpillar. The employer in this case is a price searcher in the labor market, or a **monopsonist.** *A monopsonist faces a labor supply curve that slopes upward.* To establish a frame of reference, we begin with a resource price searcher in the absence of a union, as is depicted in Exhibit 3. The labor supply curve, *S,* determines the wage the firm must pay at each level of employment. Because the quantity of labor supplied to this firm increases only if the wage increases, the firm's marginal resource cost curve for labor is above the labor supply curve. In the absence of a union, the profit-maximizing firm will hire labor up to the point where labor's marginal resource cost equals its marginal revenue product. In Exhibit 3, the profit-maximizing level of employment is *E,* and the profit-maximizing wage as found at point *m* on the supply curve is *W.*

Monopsonist The sole purchaser of a particular resource

EXHIBIT   3   **Bilateral Monopoly**

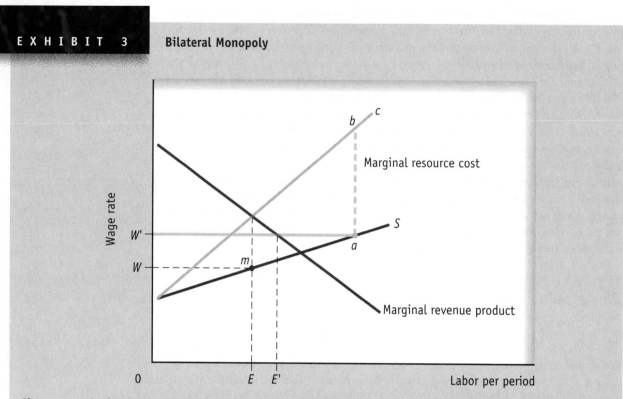

If a monopsonist faces a nonunionized work force, the profit-maximizing employment level occurs where the marginal re-source cost curve intersects the marginal revenue product curve. At that level of employment, E, the equilibrium wage, W, is found at point m, which lies on the labor supply curve, S. If the monopsonist faces a unionized workforce and the union can establish a wage floor, such as W', the labor supply curve consists of the horizontal line W'a plus the upward-sloping segment aS on the labor supply curve. The monopsonist's marginal-resource-cost curve consists of the line segments W'a, ab, and bc. The monopsonist maximizes profits by operating where the marginal resource cost of labor is equal to its mar-ginal revenue product, which yields an employment level E' at the floor wage W'.

Thus, *a profit-maximizing monopsonist pays a wage below labor's marginal revenue product*. In the absence of a union, workers have little power in dealing with the employer. An individual worker can either work or not work at the wage of-fered by the employer. Workers whose opportunity cost is at or below W will work for the firm; those with a higher opportunity cost will not.

In contrast, the union, as a monopoly supplier of labor to the firm, has some power to negotiate the wage. The union's power rests on its willingness and abil-ity to withhold all labor—to strike—if the employer does not comply. So both sides have some economic power: the firm as the only employer of this type of la-bor, and the union as the only supplier of this type of labor. The union will try to push wages up, and the profit-maximizing firm will try to pay no more than it has

Bilateral monopoly A situation in which a single seller, or mo-nopolist, bargains with a single buyer, or monopsonist

to for a given amount of labor. **Bilateral monopoly** describes the situation in which a single seller—in this case, a union as a monopoly supplier of labor—bar-gains with a single buyer—in this case, the firm as a monopsonist. Since both sides have some power, the wage will depend on the relative bargaining skills of each side. Economic theory alone cannot predict what the agreed-upon wage will be.

Of special significance in this bargaining model is the fact that the union, by pushing up wages, can increase both wages *and* employment. Notice in Exhibit

3 that without a union, workers are initially at point m on their supply curve. When the union negotiates a wage floor of W', both the wage and the level of employment increase. The supply curve for union labor is now horizontal at the bargained wage until supply level a is reached. For employment levels greater than a, the supply curve is the upward-sloping line segment aS. Thus, the union's labor supply curve is $W'aS$, with a kink at point a.

Given this kinked supply curve, the monopsonist's marginal resource cost curve for labor consists of two separate segments. For quantities of labor to the left of point a, the marginal resource cost curve is the horizontal segment, $W'a$, which is the wage floor. Within this range of employment, the firm can hire more labor at the wage floor, so the marginal resource cost is constant and equal to that wage. For employment levels greater than a, the labor supply curve slopes upward, so hiring another unit of labor means paying a higher wage to all workers. Thus, for labor quantities to the right of point a, segment bc is the relevant segment of the marginal resource cost curve.

The *marginal resource cost curve* is therefore shown by the line segments $W'a$, ab, and bc, which put together is $W'abc$. The kink in the labor supply curve $W'aS$, creates a gap in the firm's marginal resource cost curve, as reflected by the dashed line segment ab. In Exhibit 3, the intersection of the firm's marginal resource cost curve and the firm's marginal revenue product curve for labor yields a wage of W' and employment of E'. In this example, both the wage and level of employment are higher with a union than without. The union, as a monopoly supplier of labor, is thus able to offset to some extent the monopsony power of the employer.

In summary, when a labor union negotiates with a firm that is the primary employer of that type of labor, a bilateral monopoly exists. The resulting wage will depend on the relative bargaining strength and skills of each side. Both the wage rate and the employment level can be increased over the levels achieved in the absence of a union.

OTHER UNION OBJECTIVES

Thus far, we have assumed that unions attempt to increase wage rates. Although this appears to be a reasonable assumption, union behavior at times suggests other possible objectives, which we will explore in this section. Though we will focus on one objective at a time, keep in mind during this discussion that unions may adopt a variety of goals, depending on the circumstances.

Maximizing the Total Wage Bill

Another possible objective for the union is to maximize the **total wage bill,** which is employment multiplied by the wage rate. Union officials may want to maximize the wage bill as a way of maximizing union dues, which typically are some percentage of pay. Consider the union as a monopoly seller of labor to firms that are resource price takers. To induce firms to hire additional labor, the union must lower the market wage. But as the union lowers the wage, the wage earned by those workers who were already employed in the industry must also fall. As a result, labor's *marginal revenue* will always be less than the wage.

Labor's marginal revenue curve in Exhibit 4 shows how much the total wage bill changes as the wage falls. As long as marginal revenue is positive,

Total wage bill Employment multiplied by the average wage rate

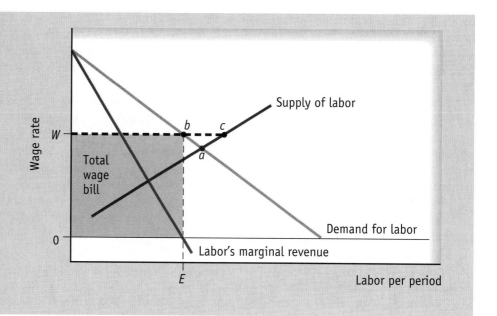

EXHIBIT 4

Maximizing the Total Wage Bill

A union that is interested in maximizing the total wage bill paid to its members should negotiate wage *W*. With employment at *E*, the union's marginal revenue is zero. Further increases in employment will cause the wage bill to decrease. Wage *W* is read off the labor demand curve at point *b*. There is an excess quantity of labor supplied at that wage.

lower wages will increase the total wage bill. Consider the wage rate that maximizes the total wage bill in this example. *The total wage bill is maximized where marginal revenue is equal to zero,* so a wage floor of *W* will maximize the total wage bill. This maximum total wage bill is reflected in Exhibit 4 by the shaded area that results from multiplying the wage of *W* times employment level *E*. But in this example, the wage floor that maximizes the total wage bill results in an excess quantity of labor supplied, identified as *bc,* so jobs must somehow be rationed among union members.

Note, that the wage-bill maximizing solution in Exhibit 4 occurs only as long as the labor supply curve intersects the labor demand curve to the right of the employment level that maximizes the wage bill—that is, to the right of where labor's marginal revenue reaches zero. If the labor supply curve intersected the labor demand curve to the left of where labor's marginal revenue equaled zero, maximizing the wage bill would require a wage below the competitive solution. No union that expects to survive would propose such a low wage.

Maximizing Economic Rent

Some observers have suggested that *union leaders attempt to maximize the difference between the market wage and the opportunity cost of workers' time in its best alternative use*—that is, to maximize the *economic rent* earned by union workers. This approach explicitly takes each member's opportunity cost into account. (Recall that the total earnings of any resource can be divided between opportunity cost and economic rent.) The labor supply curve represents the minimum amount workers must be paid to supply each additional unit of labor to this particular market. The height of the supply curve at each level of employment represents workers' opportunity cost of providing that marginal unit of labor.

For example, the labor supply curve in Exhibit 5 shows that only 10,000 hours of labor are supplied at a wage of $5 per hour because at that wage, most

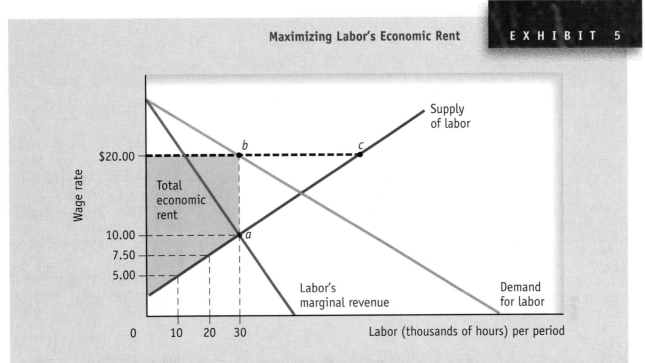

Maximizing Labor's Economic Rent

EXHIBIT 5

At point *a* the union's marginal revenue curve intersects the labor supply curve. The corresponding employment level (here, 30,000 hours) maximizes economic rent to employed workers. However, there is excess supply at the corresponding wage rate (here, $20 per hour).

workers have better things to do. If the wage increases to $7.50 per hour, however, an additional 10,000 hours are supplied per period. All workers who would have supplied their labor at a wage of $5 earn an economic rent of at least $2.50 per hour when the wage is $7.50.

In order to maximize economic rent, the union should expand employment until labor's marginal revenue from supplying additional units equals the opportunity cost of that labor. In Exhibit 5, labor's marginal revenue curve and the labor supply curve intersect at point *a,* where the opportunity cost of time is $10 per hour, and the quantity supplied is 30,000 hours per period. The rent-maximizing wage of $20 per hour is found at point *b* on the labor demand curve. If the union leaders can negotiate a wage floor of $20 per hour, the economic rent earned on the last unit of labor employed is the wage rate of $20 minus the opportunity cost of the last unit hired, $10. So at a wage floor of $20 per hour, each employed worker earns at least $10 per hour in economic rent.

The total economic rent is reflected by the blue shaded area above the supply curve but below the wage floor of $20. This economic rent is "pure gravy" to the workers because it reflects a payment over and above their opportunity cost, the amount required to attract each additional unit of labor to this market.

There are problems with the rent-maximizing solution. Unions are made up of a variety of workers with different backgrounds and different opportunity costs, so it probably would be difficult for a union to pursue such a well-defined objective as rent maximization. And even if rent maximization were achieved, there would likely be an excess quantity supplied of labor (reflected by *bc*) at the wage floor. This excess quantity supplied would create much frustration among unemployed union members.

Summary of Union Objectives

This section explored two possible union goals other than simply maximizing the wage: (1) maximizing the total wage bill and (2) maximizing economic rent. Maximizing the total wage bill is achieved by finding the wage floor that equates labor's marginal revenue from additional employment to zero. Maximizing labor's economic rent requires union leaders to negotiate the wage floor that equates labor's marginal revenue to labor's opportunity cost. Each goal is likely to create excess supply, requiring the union to ration jobs. In reality, unions may adopt a variety of goals, depending on the circumstances.

Some observers believe that union officials pursue wage-employment strategies that ensure the survival and growth of the union, keep most union members happy, and keep the leadership in office. Recent empirical work on union goals suggests that whatever their goals, unions appear to be sensitive to the trade-off between the wage level and the employment level.

RECENT TRENDS IN UNION MEMBERSHIP

In 1955, about one-third of nonfarm wage and salary workers belonged to union. Union membership as a fraction of the work force has declined since then; now only one in seven nonfarm wage and salary workers belongs to a union. The decline in union membership in recent decades is due in part to structural changes in the economy. Unions have long been more important in the industrial sector than in the service sector. But employment in the industrial sector, including manufacturing, mining, and construction, has declined from 37 percent of the nonfarm work force in 1960 to 20 percent today. During the same interval, service employment has increased from 63 percent to 80 percent. These days, union membership rates are highest among government employees, over one-third of whom are unionized, compared to only one-eighth of the private sector. A typical union member these days is a schoolteacher. Union workers are now more likely brain-workers than brawn-workers.

The bar graph in Exhibit 6 indicates recent U.S. union membership rates by age and gender. The rates for men, indicated by the blue shaded bars, are higher than the rates for women, in part because men tend to be employed more in manufacturing and women more in the service sector, where union membership historically has been lower. The highest membership rates are for middle-aged males. Though the exhibit does not show it, blacks have a higher union membership rate than whites (21 percent versus 15 percent), in part because blacks are more often employed by government and by heavy industries such as autos and steel, where union membership rates tend to be higher. In fact, black women have a higher union membership rate (19 percent) than white men (18 percent).

Union membership rates also vary greatly across states. Rates in 1994 were 20 percent or more in the industrial states of the North and 8 percent or less in

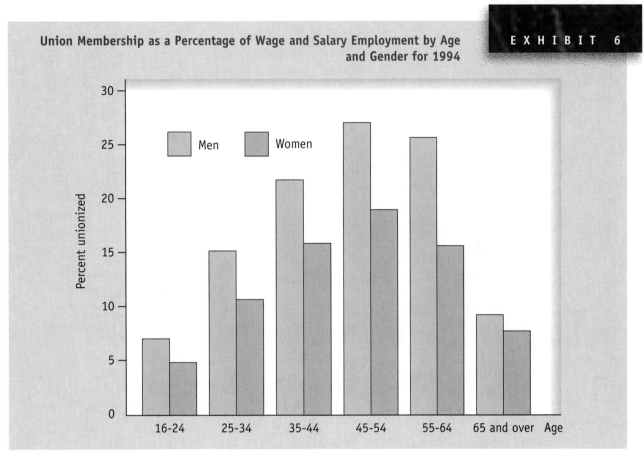

Union Membership as a Percentage of Wage and Salary Employment by Age and Gender for 1994

EXHIBIT 6

Source: Based on data from U.S. Department of Labor, *Employment and Earnings* (January 1995): Table 57.

the South. The highest rate was 29 percent in New York; the lowest was 4 percent in South Carolina.

Compared with those of other industrialized countries, the United States' union participation rate is relatively low. Exhibit 7 shows the trend in union participation rate for eight leading industrial countries. Notice two points: first, only in Sweden did membership rates increase since 1980; and second, U.S. union participation rates are lower than those of all other countries except France. Let's examine recent developments that have contributed to the decline in unionization in the United States.

Public Employee Unions

Union membership among public employees (i.e., employees of local, state, and federal governments) climbed sharply during the 1970s but leveled off during the 1980s. With increased membership in public employee unions has come the ticklish problem of strikes by such groups. Whereas some consumers suffer modest inconveniences if, say, auto workers go on strike, a strike by police personnel or firefighters could jeopardize public safety. Most states have laws restricting strikes by public employees. The issue of public employee strikes was dramatized in 1981, when the Professional Air Traffic Controllers Organization called a strike. As federal employees, they were prohibited by law from strik-

EXHIBIT 7   **Union Membership as a Percentage of the Employed Labor Force: 1980 and 1988**

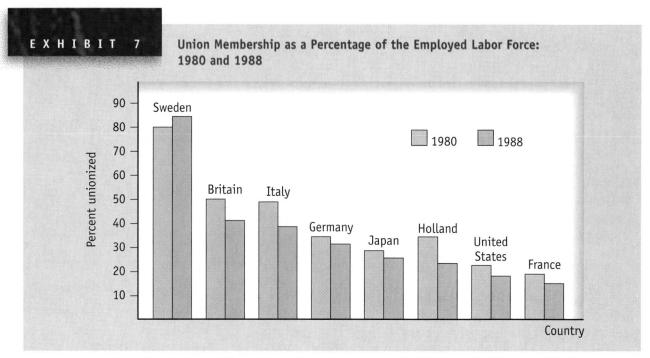

Source: Organization for Economic Cooperation and Development, as reported in *The Economist,* 5 September 1992; figure for the United States is for 1989, not 1988.

ing, and they were fired by President Ronald Reagan. The firings sent a strong signal to other public employee unions.

Competition from Nonunion Suppliers

Since the Middle Ages, craft unions have attempted to increase their wages by restricting output. Weavers from a city would sometimes make forays into the countryside to destroy looms and other weaving devices, eliminating those competitors. Competition from nonunion suppliers is still a major problem facing many unions today. Although unions usually can prevent unionized employers from hiring nonunion workers, they cannot block the entry of new nonunion firms, nor can they always restrict imports. Since 1955, for example, U.S. imports have increased from 5 percent to 12 percent of gross domestic product. The United Auto Workers union has lost over one-third of its membership since 1979. Even more troublesome to the UAW, three Japanese auto makers have established nonunion production facilities in the United States. Unions are now worried about losing jobs to Mexico because of the North American Free Trade Agreement.

Union membership among construction workers fell sharply over the last decade because many union members were unable to find union jobs. In the face of nonunion competition, these unions have been forced to make concessions over wages and work rules. In some parts of the country, unions are permitting construction contractors to hire a larger proportion of apprentices, who are typically paid only half the union scale; unions are also allowing their members to work on the same job sites as nonunion members, which was unheard of a few years ago. Real wages in construction—that is, wages after subtracting the effects of inflation—declined by 9 percent between 1990 and 1995.

Tight times have also caused some union workers to compete among themselves. For example, when General Motors was deciding which plants to close, they let workers in Arlington, Texas, and Ypsilanti, Michigan, know that only one of the two plants would survive. The 3,200 Texas workers went all out, agreeing to a three-shift schedule and to less restrictive work rules. Michigan workers, on the other hand, offered few concessions, so their plant was closed.

Industry Deregulation

For decades, the Teamsters Union negotiated union wages for truckers through a national contract. Government regulations blocked new entry into the industry and prevented existing firms from competing on the basis of price. Thus, trucking regulations, by blocking new entry and banning price competitions, provided an environment conducive to unions. But the deregulation of several major industries, including trucking, airlines, intercity bus lines, and telecommunications, has reduced union power in these industries.

Although the Teamsters Union can prevent unionized firms from hiring nonunion drivers, it cannot prevent nonunion firms from entering the industry. Deregulation of the trucking industry dropped the floor that had propped up the rates charged by all companies, both union and nonunion. The demise of regulation set off rate competition, leading to business failures and eliminating nearly one-third of the jobs controlled by the Teamsters. But, as a result of deregulation, thousands of new nonunion firms entered the industry; the number of firms in the industry has more than doubled since 1980. The union was obliged to give up its automatic cost-of-living adjustment and to agree to lower wages for new employees, creating a *two-tiered wage structure*.

Unions and Technological Change

Some blue-collar workers, such as members of the United Mine Workers, have lost jobs as a result of automation. With employment stagnant in the so-called smokestack industries, leaders of the union movement looked to emerging high-technology areas as a source of new members. Unions made a special effort to organize high-tech workers but were largely unsuccessful. Aside from some defense contractors, the electronics industry remains mostly nonunion. Progressive managers in many high-tech firms encouraged worker participation and often provided employees lavish bonuses and perks. For example, stock options made millionaires of thousands of Microsoft employees. Apple Computer also made many of its employees rich. Workers in such firms were not good prospects for unionization.

A Fight for Survival

With their membership shrinking, unions have adopted new survival tactics. One alternative has been to merge with other unions. Mergers can reduce costs per member by spreading expenses for staff and headquarters, and the larger membership can enhance the union's political clout. Since 1986, over 40 union mergers have occurred in the United States, most involving one union absorbing another. In June 1995, a huge merger was announced among the nation's three largest industrial unions—the United Auto Workers, the United Steel Workers, and the International Association of Machinists and Aerospace Workers. The merger will create a 2-million-worker union by the year 2000. Critics claim this giant merger will simply create a larger, weaker union which, because of its size, will have difficulty keeping in touch with the needs of its members.

Unions are also trying to leverage their political impact by teaming up with other organizations for support. For example, rather than directly attack the free-trade agreement with Mexico, labor unions such as the Steelworkers and the United Auto Workers have encouraged environmental and religious groups to lead the fight. Some U.S. unions have also begun organizing Mexican workers to raise wages and benefits there. Union leaders reason that the more Mexican workers are paid, the less likely they will take jobs from the U.S. workers. And rather than object directly to clothing imports, the Garment Workers Union got help from groups concerned with the destruction of the tropical rain forests. The public responds more readily to environmental appeals than to the special-interest pleadings of union workers.

CONCLUSION

When unions first appeared in our nation's history, working conditions were dreadful. Hours were long, pay was low, and the workplace was often dangerous. The last century brought revolutionary improvements in the conditions of the average worker. The real income of workers has increased more than ninefold since 1860, and the average work week has dropped from 66 hours to about 40 hours. The workplace has also become much safer.

Although union members were always a minority of the work force, never exceeding one-third of the total, just the threat of unionization encouraged some nonunion employers to match benefits available in unionized firms. So the effects of unions spilled over to nonunion firms. Forces in addition to the union movement also helped workers. For example, technological change increased labor productivity, which supported higher wages and better benefits.

The labor movement helped focus attention on the problems of workers and helped develop the political consensus to support employee-oriented legislation. In the last 30 years, the federal government has broadened worker protection against unfair dismissal, plant closings, worker injuries, and unemployment. Social Security, Medicare, and other government transfer programs also buffer workers from the ravages of poor health and old age. *But as government provides a broader menu of worker protection and social insurance, workers feel less compelled to rely on unions for protection.* Unions, to some extent, have become victims of their own success.

At one time, because of government regulations, foreign trade restrictions, the power of the strike threat, and the lack of competition from nonunion firms, unions dominated some key industries. But deregulation, technological change, and growing competition from nonunion firms both here and abroad have seriously challenged union positions in industries such as steel, autos, trucking, airlines, telecommunications, and construction. As global competition intensifies, employers have a harder time passing higher union labor costs along to consumers. Firms have also become more aggressive in replacing striking workers. The threat of losing a job to a replacement worker when well-paying jobs are hard to find has reduced union workers' willingness to strike or to remain on strike. Strikes no longer engender the public support of worker solidarity they once did. Both in the United States and in other industrial economies, labor unions represent a diminishing segment of the labor force.

SUMMARY

1. The formation of labor unions in the United States was in part a response to long hours and poor working conditions in the 19th and early 20th centuries. Unions received a boost from government during the Great Depression, when several laws were passed to improve unions' legal standing.

2. Unions and employers attempt to negotiate a mutually agreeable labor contract through collective bargaining. A major source of union power has been the threat of a strike, which is an attempt to withhold labor from the firm.

3. Inclusive, or industrial, unions attempt to establish a wage floor that exceeds the competitive market wage. But a wage above the market-clearing level creates an excess quantity of labor supplied, so the union must somehow ration jobs among its members. Exclusive, or craft, unions try to raise the wage by restricting the supply of labor. Another way to raise union wages is to increase the demand for union labor.

4. When a labor union negotiates with the only employer of that type of labor, this is a bilateral monopoly situation. The resulting wage will depend on the relative bargaining strengths and skills of each side. Unions may be able to increase both the wage rate and employment level above the levels the monopsonist would choose if labor were not organized.

5. Unions may pursue goals other than maximizing the wage. Unions can try to maximize either the total wage bill or the total economic rent going to labor, but these policies usually create an excess quantity of labor supplied, requiring job rationing. No one goal accounts for all union behavior.

6. Union membership as a percentage of the labor force has been decreasing for decades. Today, only one-seventh of the nonfarm labor force is unionized, compared to one-third in 1955. Unions' problems have included deregulation, a better social safety net, technological change, imports, the willingness of firms to hire replacements for striking workers, and competition from nonunion firms.

QUESTIONS AND PROBLEMS

1. **(U.S. Labor History)** What historical reasons can be given for the development of U.S. labor organizations?

2. **(U.S. Labor History)** Identify which act of the U.S. Congress addressed each of the following issues:
   a. Established the National Labor Relations Board.
   b. Regulated union elections and required union officials to file financial reports.
   c. Limited strikes that would affect public safety and welfare.
   d. Required employers to bargain in good faith with unions representing the majority of employees.
   e. Banned yellow-dog contracts.

3. **(Labor Organizations)** Explain the difference between a craft union and an industrial union. Indicate whether each of the following was formed as a craft union or an industrial union: Knights of Labor, American Federation of Labor, United Mine Workers, and National Typographical Union.

4. **(Strikes)** Why would strikes be most effective in industries where there were very high fixed costs?

5. **(Tools of Unionism)** Distinguish between mediation and binding arbitration. Under what circumstances do firms and unions resort to these tools? What is the role of strikes in the bargaining process?

6. **(Union Tactics)** Will economic rents for union workers increase if unions are successful in raising the demand for the products the workers produce? Will opportunity costs also increase? Why or why not? Illustrate your answer with a demand-and-supply graph.

7. **(Union Objectives)** Show that maximizing the wage bill always leads to greater employment than maximizing economic rent, other things constant.

8. **(Union Tactics)** Why might unions and business lobby together in Washington, D.C. to protect the industry from foreign competition?

9. **(Wage–Bill Maximization)** Use the data below to answer the following questions.

Quantity of Labor	Marginal Revenue Product
0	___
1	$50
2	45
3	40
4	33
5	20
6	5
7	0

a. If the firm's supply of labor is perfectly elastic at $20, how much labor will get hired?
b. What labor price would maximize the total wage bill?
c. Who gains and who loses if a union succeeds in changing the labor price to the level you calculated in part b?

10. **(Wage Differentials)** Using supply-demand diagrams, show what happens to wage differentials between unionized and nonunionized sectors of the labor force when the union negotiates a wage rate for the unionized sector that is above the labor-market equilibrium.

11. **(Union Tactics)** Using a supply-demand diagram for labor, compare the effects on wages and employment in a unionized industry of each of the following:
a. Conducting a "Buy American" plan.
b. Negotiating a wage floor above the market-clearing wage.
c. Restricting labor supply.

12. **(Bilateral Monopoly)** What is the marginal resource cost curve for a monopsonist that faces collective bargaining with a union?

13. **(Bilateral Monopoly)** Define a bilateral monopoly. In the case of a labor market, what impact does a union have on the wage and employment when dealing with a monopsonist? What determines the negotiated wage? What happens to the relationship between the marginal revenue product and the wage for the last unit of labor hired?

14. **(Maximizing Economic Rent)** Answer the following questions on the basis of the graph provided.
a. What are the equilibrium wage and employment levels without a union?
b. What is the level of economic rent at the nonunion equilibrium?
c. If a union negotiates with the employers with the objective of maximizing economic rent, what wage

will the union try to set? What would be the level of employment?
d. What is the level of economic rent at the union wage?
e. What rule does the union follow in order to maximize economic rent?

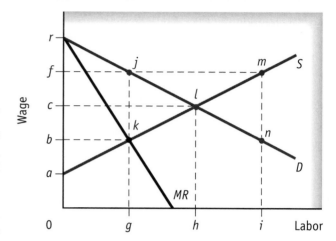

15. **(Recent Membership Trends)** What has happened to membership in U.S. unions in recent decades? What are the main causes of this change?

16. **(Union Tactics)** Define featherbedding. What effect does featherbedding have on labor supply and/or demand curves?

17. **(Union Effects)** Explain how each of the following is likely to affect the impact on employment of a union-backed wage increase in the unionized industry.
a. The ratio of labor used relative to other resources.
b. The elasticity of product demand.
c. Featherbedding.

18. **(Hard Ball at Caterpillar)** What is meant by *pattern bargaining?* What were the consequences of the decision by Caterpillar to "break the pattern"?

19. **(Featherbedding on Broadway)** (a) Has featherbedding had the effect desired by the unions on employment? (b) What would be the impact of convincing people that there is no substitute for seeing a play on Broadway?

20. **(Featherbedding on Broadway)** Broadway show tickets are frequently sold as part of a package that might include transportation, hotel accommodations, and/or other amenities. How would the impact of featherbedding be affected by such package deals?

21. **(Using the Internet)** Visit the Legal Information Institute (LII) at Cornell University and examine the Labor-Management Reporting and Disclosure Act of 1959, or the Landrum-Griffin Act as it is commonly known (**http://www.law.cornell.edu/uscode/** **29/ch11.html**). Why is this Act considered the Bill of Rights for union members? What specific protections does it detail? What economic effect does this Act have on the labor market?

27

Capital, Interest, and Corporate Finance

So far, the discussion of resource markets has focused primarily on human resources. This emphasis is appropriate, since labor income represents more than three-quarters of all resource income. The returns on labor, however, depend in part on the amount and quality of the other resources employed. A farmer driving a huge tractor is more productive than one who scrapes the soil with a stick. In this chapter, we discuss the returns on nonhuman resources, particularly capital. We also take a closer look at how firms are financed and the problems that arise when owners do not control the firm.

One problem that crops up in discussions of resources is that economists sometimes use the same term in slightly different ways. For example, the term *interest* is used to mean both the amount earned for lending money and the return earned by capital as a resource. Another term that may be a source of confusion is *rent*. Earlier we distinguished between opportunity cost, the payment necessary to attract a resource to a particular use, and economic rent, the amount in excess of opportunity cost. Often economists refer to the return on land as rent, because land is typically thought to be in fixed supply and the return on a resource in fixed supply consists entirely of economic rent. Describing the earnings on land as rent is quite appropriate, but land as a resource will not receive special treatment in this book. Topics discussed in this chapter include:

- Consumption, production, and time
- Optimal investment
- Loanable funds

- Present value and discounting
- Corporate finance
- The market for corporate control

THE ROLE OF TIME IN CONSUMPTION AND PRODUCTION

Time plays an important role in both production and consumption. In this section, we first consider the effect of time on the production decision and show why firms are willing to pay for the use of household savings. Next, we consider time in the consumption decision and show why households must be rewarded for saving, or for deferring consumption. Then, bringing together the desires of borrowers and the desires of savers, we examine the equilibrium rate of interest.

Production, Saving, and Time

Suppose Jones is a primitive farmer in a simple economy. Isolated from any neighbors or markets, he literally scratches out a living on a plot of land, using only crude sticks as farm implements. While a crop is growing, none of it is available for present consumption. Since production takes time, Jones must rely on food saved from prior production to support himself during the time required to grow the new crop. The longer the growing season, the more savings required. Thus, even in this simple example, it is clear that *production cannot occur without savings*.

Suppose that with his current resources, consisting of land, labor, seed corn, fertilizer, and some crude sticks, Jones grows about 100 bushels of corn per year. He soon realizes that if he had a plow—a type of investment good, or capital—his productivity would increase. Making a plow in such a crude setting, however, would be time-consuming, keeping him away from the fields for a year. Thus, the plow has an opportunity cost of 100 bushels of corn. Jones will be unable to sustain this temporary drop in production unless he has saved enough food from previous harvests to allow him to forgo the annual crop.

During the time required to produce capital, Jones must rely on his savings from prior production. The question is, should he invest his time making the plow? The answer depends on the costs and benefits of the plow. We already know that the cost is 100 bushels—the forgone output. The benefit depends on how much the plow will increase crop production and how long it will last. Jones figures that the plow will increase production by 20 bushels per year and will last his lifetime. Suppose he decides the benefit of increasing corn production by 20 bushels per year exceeds the one-time cost of 100 bushels sacrificed to make the plow.

In making the plow, he engages in *roundabout production*. Rather than work the farm with his crude sticks, the farmer produces capital, which will increase his future productivity. An increased amount of roundabout production in an economy means that more capital accumulates, so more consumer goods (and capital goods) can be produced in the future. Advanced industrial economies are characterized by much roundabout production and abundant capital accumulation.

You can see why production cannot occur without savings. *Production requires savings because both direct and roundabout production require time—time during which goods and services are not available from current production.* Now let's modernize the example by introducing the ability to borrow. Many farmers visit the bank each spring to borrow enough "seed money" to finance production until their crop is grown and sold. Likewise, other businesses often borrow at least a portion of the start-up funds needed to get going. Thus, in a modern economy, production need not rely exclusively on each producer's prior savings. Banks and other financial institutions accept the deposits of savers to lend to borrowers. Financial markets for trading stocks and bonds also help channel savings to producers.

Consumption, Saving, and Time

Positive rate of time preference A characteristic of consumers, who value present consumption more highly than future consumption

Did you ever burn the roof of your mouth biting into a slice of pizza before it had cooled sufficiently? Have you done this more than once? Why does such self-mutilation persist? It persists because that bite of pizza is worth more to you now than the same bite five minutes from now. In fact, you are even willing to risk burning your mouth rather than wait until the pizza has lost its destructive properties. In a small way, this phenomenon reflects the fact that you and other consumers value *present* consumption more than *future* consumption. You and other consumers have a **positive rate of time preference.**

Because present consumption is valued more than future consumption, you are willing to pay a higher price to consume something now rather than later. And prices often reflect this greater willingness to pay. Consider the movies. You pay more to see a movie at a first-run theater rather than wait until it appears at other theaters. If you are patient, you can wait to rent the video; if you are even more patient, you can wait until it shows up on TV. The same is true for books. If you wait until a new book is available in paperback, you can usually buy it for less than one-third of the hardback price. You also pay more for "instant" pictures (about $1 per picture) than you would for those that must be developed, even though the quality of instant pictures is inferior. Photo developers, dry cleaners, fast-food restaurants, convenience stores, and other suppliers tout the speed of their services, knowing that consumers are willing to pay more for earlier availability, other things constant. Perhaps the T-shirt slogan captures the point: "Life is uncertain. Eat dessert first."

Interest rate The amount of money paid per year to savers as a percentage of the amount saved

Because present consumption is valued more than future consumption, households must be rewarded if they are to postpone consumption; in other words, saving must be rewarded. Saving is income minus consumption. By saving their money in financial institutions such as banks, households refrain from spending a portion of their income on present consumption in return for the promise of a greater ability to consume in the future. Interest is the reward offered households to forgo present consumption. The **interest rate** is the interest per year as a percentage of the amount saved. For example, if the interest rate is 5 percent, the interest is $5 per year for each $100 saved.

The higher the interest rate, other things constant, the more consumers are rewarded for saving. And the more consumers are rewarded for saving, the higher their opportunity cost of present consumption in terms of forgone interest. For example, at an interest rate of 5 percent, a household can place $100 in a savings account and end up with $105 a year from now. So $100 worth of consumption today has an opportunity cost of $105 in consumption a year from now. At an interest rate of 10 percent, $100 worth of consumption today has an opportunity cost of $110 in consumption a year from now.

Consequently, the greater the interest rate offered for saving, other things constant, the greater the amount households are willing to save. Banks are will-

Consumers are willing to pay more for what they can have or do now, like viewing a movie at a first-run theater, than for what they can have or do in the future.

ing to pay interest on consumer savings because the banks can, in turn, lend these savings to those who need credit, such as farmers, home buyers, and entrepreneurs. Banks play the role of *financial intermediaries* in what is known as the market for loanable funds. The **loanable funds market** brings together savers, or suppliers of loanable funds, and borrowers, or demanders of loanable funds, to determine the market rate of interest. The **supply of loanable funds** reflects the positive relationship between the market rate of interest and the quantity of savings, other things constant, as reflected by the usual upward-sloping supply curve. We will see more on that later.

Optimal Investment

In a market economy characterized by specialization and exchange, Farmer Jones no longer needs to produce his own capital, nor does he need to rely on his own savings. He can purchase capital using borrowed funds. Suppose he is interested in buying a tractor. There are many sizes on the market, from the small garden variety to the huge Terminator. Column (1) in panel (a) of Exhibit 1 identifies six tractors, from smallest to largest. The total and marginal products of each tractor are listed in columns (2) and (3). Note that other resources are assumed to be constant (in this case, the farmer's labor, land, seeds, and fertilizer).

Without a tractor, Jones can grow 1,000 bushels of corn per year. The smallest tractor, called the Garden Elf, will allow Jones to double production to 2,000 bushels per year; thus, the Garden Elf yields a marginal product of 1,000 bushels per year. With the next largest size, the Mighty Mouse, total output increases from 2,000 to 2,800 bushels, so its marginal product is 800 bushels. Note that in this example, diminishing marginal returns set in immediately. The marginal product continues to decrease as the tractors get larger, dropping to zero for the largest tractor listed, the Terminator. Though the exhibit does not show it, the marginal product could turn negative for tractors larger than the Terminator. (You might imagine a tractor so large that it would be hard to maneuver on the farmer's relatively small plot.)

Suppose Jones sells corn in a perfectly competitive market, so he is a price taker in the market for corn. He can sell all he wants at the market price of $4 per bushel. This price is multiplied by the marginal product from column (3) to yield each tractor's *marginal revenue product* in column (4). The marginal revenue product in this example is the marginal product times the price, or the change in total revenue resulting from using the next largest tractor size. The marginal revenue product is the amount by which an increment in tractor size increases total revenue each year, assuming the price of corn remains unchanged.

The purchase price of each tractor is listed in column (5). The smallest tractor sells for $10,000, the next largest for $20,000, and so on, with the price increasing by $10,000 for each increase in size. Thus, the marginal cost of buying a larger tractor is $10,000, as listed in column (6). Suppose the tractors are so durable that they last indefinitely, that operating expenses are negligible, and that the price of corn is expected to remain at $4 per bushel in the future. The tractor selected will increase revenue not only in the first year but in every year into the future. Since the tractor costs a sum of money now but yields a stream of revenue this year and in the future, the optimal solution requires Jones to

Loanable funds market **The market in which savers (suppliers of funds) and borrowers (demanders of funds) come together to determine the market rate of interest**

Supply of loanable funds **The relationship between the market rate of interest and the quantity of savings supplied to the economy, other things constant**

EXHIBIT 1   Marginal Rate of Return on Investment

(a)

Tractor Size (1)	Total Product (bushels) (2)	Marginal Product (bushels) (3)	Marginal Revenue Product (4) = (3) × $4	Tractor Cost (5)	Marginal Resource Cost (6)	Marginal Rate of Return (7) = (4)/(6)
No tractor	1,000	—	—	$ 0	—	—
Garden Elf	2,000	1,000	$4,000	10,000	$10,000	40%
Mighty Mouse	2,800	800	3,200	20,000	10,000	32
Crop Meister	3,400	600	2,400	30,000	10,000	24
Field Scout	3,800	400	1,600	40,000	10,000	16
Green Giant	4,000	200	800	50,000	10,000	8
Terminator	4,000	0	0	60,000	10,000	0

(b)

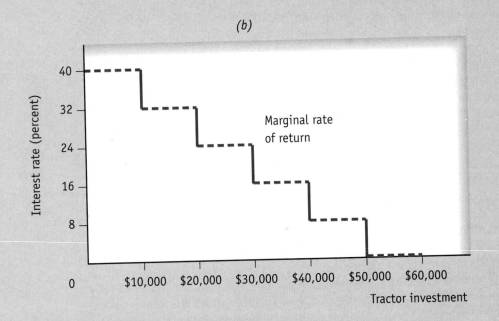

The marginal rate of return shown in column (7) of panel (a) equals the marginal revenue product of each tractor divided by its marginal resource cost. The marginal rate of return curve in panel (b) consists of line segments showing the relationship between the market rate of interest and the amount invested in tractors. This curve is the demand for investment.

take *time* into account. He can't simply equate marginal resource cost with marginal revenue product, because the marginal cost is for a tractor that is expected to last indefinitely whereas the marginal product is an annual amount this year and in the future. As we will see, markets bridge time by use of the interest rate.

Jones must decide how much to invest in a tractor. The first task in determining the optimal investment is to compute the marginal rate of return that could be earned each year by investing in tractors of various sizes. Given the circumstances described thus far, the **marginal rate of return on investment** is equal to capital's marginal productivity (its marginal revenue product) as a percentage of the marginal expenditure on capital (its marginal resource cost). Since the tractor is expected to last indefinitely, Jones wants to know the marginal rate of return he will earn each year from tractors of different sizes.

Marginal rate of return on investment The marginal revenue product of capital expressed as a percentage of its marginal cost

The smallest tractor yields a marginal revenue product of $4,000 per year and has a marginal resource cost of $10,000. Thus, the smallest tractor yields a *marginal rate of return* of $4,000/$10,000, or 40 percent per year, as shown in column (7). The next largest tractor has a marginal revenue product of $3,200 per year and a marginal cost of $10,000, so the marginal rate of return equals $3,200/$10,000, or 32 percent per year. By dividing the marginal revenue product of capital in column (4) by the marginal resource cost of that capital in column (6), we get the marginal rate of return on capital in column (7).

Given the marginal rate of return of tractors, how much should Jones invest in order to maximize profit? Suppose he borrows the money. The amount he must pay to borrow depends on the *market rate of interest,* which is the rate of interest determined by the supply and demand for loanable funds. Ideally, Jones would maximize profit by equating the tractor's marginal rate of return with the market rate of interest. But because tractors are available in only a limited number of sizes, Jones may not be able to match exactly the marginal rates of return with the market rate of interest. Instead, he will find the largest tractor size for which the marginal rate of return equals or exceeds the market rate of interest. For example, if the market rate of interest is 20 percent, Jones will invest $30,000 in the Crop Meister, which yields a marginal return of 24 percent. Investing another $10,000 to buy the Field Scout instead would yield a marginal return of only 16 percent, a rate below the cost of borrowing. If the market rate of interest dropped to 10 percent, the Field Scout would become the most profitable investment. And if the interest rate dropped to 8 percent, Jones would buy the Green Giant for $50,000.

Farmer Jones should increase his investment as long as the marginal rate of return on that investment exceeds the market rate of interest. The data in column (7) are depicted in panel (b) of Exhibit 1 as a steplike curve, where the solid lines reflect the amount that should be invested based on the market rate of interest. The curve steps down to reflect the diminishing marginal productivity as tractor size increases. For example, in the range of market interest rates above 32 percent up to 40 percent, the smallest tractor should be purchased. If the market rate of interest ranges above 24 percent up to 32 percent, the $20,000 tractor should be purchased. Since the marginal rate of return curve shows how much should be invested at each interest rate, this steplike curve represents the farmer's *demand for investment.* This demand is a derived demand, based on each tractor's marginal productivity.

Would the example change if Jones already had the money saved and did not need to borrow? Not as long as he can save at the market rate of interest. For example, suppose Jones has $50,000 in savings that is earning the market rate of interest of 10 percent. He should invest $40,000 of that savings in the Field Scout, which earns a marginal rate of return of 16 percent. Jones should save the remaining $10,000 at the market rate of interest of 10 percent rather than move up to the next largest tractor, which would yield a marginal rate of return of only 8 percent. Thus, as long as he can borrow and save at the same interest rate, Jones ends up with the same tractor whether he borrows funds or draws on his own savings. *Whether Jones borrows the money or has the savings on hand, the market rate of interest represents his opportunity cost of funds.*

Let's review the procedure used to determine the optimal amount of investment. First, compute the marginal revenue product of the investment. Next, divide the marginal revenue product by the marginal resource cost to determine the marginal rate of return on the investment. The firm should increase investment as long as the marginal rate of return on investment exceeds the market rate of interest. The market rate of interest reflects the opportunity cost of investing either borrowed funds or savings. Finally, the marginal rate of return curve is the firm's demand curve for investment—that is, it shows the amount the firm is willing and able to invest at each alternative interest rate.

Investing in Human Capital

The tractor has a substantial impact on the farmer's ability to produce. Similarly, education and training that improve the farmer's knowledge of farming also enhance productivity. Jones could invest in his own education—he could invest in his human capital. For example, by taking agricultural courses at a nearby college, he could increase his knowledge of plant science, fertilizer, soil drainage, agricultural economics, and other subjects that would make him a more productive farmer. He might read through the course descriptions and estimate how valuable each course would be, ranking them from most productive to least productive. The marginal rate of return on each course would equal the marginal revenue product divided by the marginal cost of this investment. (Cost here would include the direct outlays for the course such as tuition and books plus the opportunity cost of time drawn away from production or other valued activities.) How many courses should Jones take? The answer depends on the expected marginal rate of return of each course and the market rate of interest. For the most part, investing in human capital is similar to investing in physical capital. One difference is that a bank may be more inclined to lend for physical capital because that capital, such as a tractor, represents collateral that the bank can claim should the lender default on the loan. With loans to fund human capital, there is no such collateral.

Note that in our simple model, Jones must predict marginal rates of return for tractors and for college courses. To do that, he must predict not only the marginal physical product of these investments but also the price of corn in the future. *Because of technological change and other possible changes in market demand and supply, producers face an uncertain future, so investment decisions are often risky.* In addition, our simple model assumes that Jones can borrow and save at the same interest rate. But financial intermediaries, such as banks, typically charge a higher interest rate to borrowers than they pay to savers. Thus, Jones would likely be charged more interest to borrow than he could earn on savings; consequently, investing with borrowed funds involves a higher opportunity cost. The point is that investment decisions are usually more complicated than those presented here.

The Demand for Loanable Funds

We have now examined why firms are willing to pay interest to borrow money: money gives firms a command over resources that makes roundabout production possible. The simple principles developed for Farmer Jones can be generalized to other firms. The major demanders of loans are firms that borrow to invest in capital goods, such as machines, trucks, and buildings. At any time, each firm has a variety of possible investment opportunities. Each firm ranks its opportunities from highest to lowest, based on the expected marginal rates of return on the investments. Firms will increase their investment until their expected marginal rate of return just equals the market rate of interest. With other inputs held constant, as they were on the farm, the demand curve for investment slopes downward.

For the economy as a whole, if the amount of other resources and the level of technology are fixed, diminishing marginal productivity causes the marginal rate of return curve, which is the demand curve for investment, to slope downward. The **demand for loanable funds** is based on the expected marginal rate of return these borrowed funds yield when invested in capital. Each firm has a downward-sloping demand curve for loanable funds, reflecting a declining marginal rate of return on investment. With some qualifications, the demand for loanable funds by each firm sums horizontally to yield the demand for loanable funds by all firms.

Demand for loanable funds The relationship between the market rate of interest and the quantity of loanable funds demanded, other things constant

But firms are not the only demanders of loanable funds. As we have seen, households value present consumption more than future consumption; they are often willing to pay extra to consume now rather than later. One way to ensure that goods and services are available now is to borrow money for present consumption. Mortgages, car loans, college loans, and credit card purchases are examples of household borrowing. The household's demand curve for loanable funds, like the firm's, slopes downward, reflecting consumers' greater ability and greater willingness to borrow at lower interest rates, other things constant. The government sector and the rest of the world are also demanders of loanable funds. Thus, the market demand curve for loanable funds, presented in Exhibit 2 as *D,* is the total demand by firms, households, governments, and the rest of the world. The supply of loanable funds has already been discussed and is presented as *S* in Exhibit 2.

By bringing the demand and supply for loanable funds together, as in Exhibit 2, we can determine the market rate of interest. The equilibrium interest rate of 8 percent is the only rate that will exactly match the wishes of borrowers and savers. In this case, the equilibrium quantity of loanable funds is $100 billion per period. Any change in the supply or demand for loanable funds will change the equilibrium rate of interest. For example, some major technological breakthrough might increase the productivity of investment, thereby increasing its marginal rate of return and increasing the demand for loanable funds. In such a case, the demand curve for loanable funds would shift out to the right, as shown in the movement from *D* to *D'* in Exhibit 2. Such an increase in the demand for loanable funds would raise the equilibrium rate of interest to 9 percent and increase the quantity of loanable funds to $115 billion per period.

Why Interest Rates Differ

So far, we have been talking about *the* market rate of interest, implying that only one interest rate prevails in the loanable funds market. At any particular time, however, a range of interest rates can be found in the economy. For ex-

EXHIBIT 2

Market for Loanable Funds

Because of the declining marginal rate of return on capital, the quantity of loanable funds demanded is inversely related to the rate of interest. The equilibrium rate of interest, 8 percent, is determined at the intersection of the demand and supply curves for loans. An increase in the demand for loans from *D* to *D'* leads to an increase in the equilibrium rate of interest from 8 percent to 9 percent.

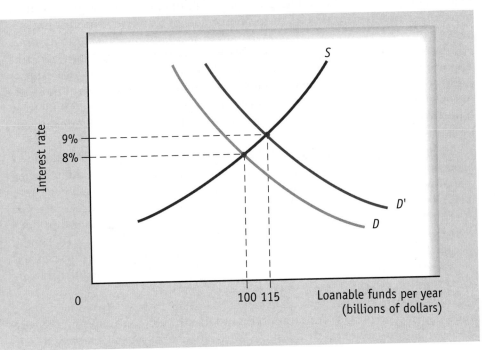

ample, there are interest rates on home mortgages, car loans, and credit cards, as well as the so-called *prime rate,* which is offered to the most trustworthy borrowers. Let's consider some reasons why interest rates differ.

Risk. Some borrowers are more likely than others to repay their loans. Differences in the risk associated with various borrowers are reflected in differences in the interest rate negotiated. As loans become more risky, lenders are less willing to supply loanable funds, so the market interest rate on these loans rises, reflecting the higher risk. For example, a bank would charge more interest on a loan to a new restaurant than to IBM, because IBM is more likely to repay the loan.

Duration of the Loan. The future is uncertain, and the further into the future a loan is to be repaid, the more uncertain that repayment becomes. Thus, as the duration of a loan increases, lenders are less willing to supply loanable funds. Hence loans extended for longer periods usually involve a higher interest rate to compensate the lender for this greater risk. The **term structure of interest rates** refers to the relationship between the duration of a loan and the interest rate charged. This term structure usually indicates that the interest rate increases as the duration of the loan increases.

Term structure of interest rates
The relationship between the duration of a loan and the interest rate charged

Cost of Administration. The costs of executing the loan agreement, monitoring the conditions of the loan, and collecting the payments on the loan are called the *administration costs* of the loan. These costs, as a proportion of the total amount of the loan, decrease as the size of the loan increases. For example, the cost of administering a $100,000 loan will be less than 10 times the cost of administering a $10,000 loan. Consequently, that portion of the interest charge reflecting the cost of administering the loan will be smaller for large loans than for small loans.

Tax Treatment. Differences in the tax treatment of different types of loans will also affect the market rate of interest. For example, the interest earned on funds loaned to state and local governments is not subject to federal income taxes. Since lenders are interested in their after-tax rate of interest, state and local governments can pay lower interest rates than those paid by other borrowers.

PRESENT VALUE AND DISCOUNTING

Because present consumption is valued more than future consumption, present and future consumption cannot be directly compared. A way of standardizing the discussion is to measure all consumption in terms of its present value. **Present value** is the current value of a payment or payments that will be received in the future. For example, how much would you pay now to acquire the right to receive $100 one year from now? Put another way, what is the *present value* to you of receiving $100 one year from now?

Present value The value today of a payment or payments to be received in the future

Present Value of Payment One Year Hence
Suppose that the market interest rate is 10 percent, so you can either lend or borrow money at that rate. One way to determine how much you would pay for the opportunity to receive $100 one year from now is to ask how much you would have to save, at the market rate of interest, to end up with $100 one year from now. Here is the problem we are trying to solve: What amount of money, if saved at a rate of 10 percent, will accumulate to $100 one year from now? We can calculate the answer with a simple formula. We can say

$$\text{Present value} \times 1.10 = \$100$$

or

$$\text{Present value} = \frac{\$100}{1.10} = \$90.91$$

Discounting Determining the present value of a sum of money to be received in the future

Discount rate The interest rate used to convert income to be received in the future into present value

Thus, $90.91 is the present value of receiving $100 one year from now; it is the most you would be willing to pay today to receive $100 one year from now. Rather than pay more than $90.91, you would simply deposit your $90.91 at the market rate of interest and end up with $100 a year from now. The procedure of dividing the future payment by 1 plus the prevailing interest rate in order to express it in today's dollars is called **discounting.** The interest rate that is used to discount future payments is called the **discount rate.**

The present value of $100 to be received one year from now depends on the interest rate used to discount that payment. *The higher the interest rate, or discount rate, the more the future payment is discounted and the lower its present value.* Put another way, the higher the interest rate, the less you need to save now to yield a given amount in the future. For example, if the interest rate is 15 percent, the present value of receiving $100 one year from now is $100/1.15, which equals $86.96. Conversely, the lower the interest rate, or discount rate, the less the future income is discounted and the greater its present value. A lower interest rate means that you must save more now to yield a given amount in the future. As a general rule, the present value of receiving an amount one year from now is

$$\text{Present value} = \frac{\text{Amount received one year from now}}{1 + \text{Interest rate}}$$

For example, when the interest rate is 5 percent, the present value of receiving $100 one year from now is

$$\text{Present value} = \frac{\$100}{1 + 0.05} = \frac{\$100}{1.05} = \$95.24$$

Present Value for Payments in Later Years

Now consider the present value of receiving $100 two years from now. What amount of money, if deposited at the market rate of interest of 5 percent, would yield $100 two years from now? At the end of the first year, the value would be the present value × 1.05, which would then earn the market rate of interest during the second year. At the end of the second year, the deposit would have accumulated to present value × 1.05 × 1.05. Thus, we have the equation

$$\text{Present value} \times 1.05 \times 1.05 = \text{Present value} \times (1.05)^2 = \$100$$

Solving for the present value yields

$$\text{Present value} = \frac{\$100}{(1.05)^2} = \frac{\$100}{1.1025} = \$90.70$$

If the $100 were to be received three years from now, we would discount the payment over three years:

$$\text{Present value} = \frac{\$100}{(1.05)^3} = \$86.38$$

More generally, the present value formula for receiving M dollars in year t at interest rate i may be written as

$$\text{Present value} = \frac{M}{(1 + i)^t}$$

Because $1 + i$ is greater than 1, the more times it is multiplied by itself (as determined by t), the greater the denominator will be and the smaller will be the present value. Thus, *the present value of a given payment will diminish the further in the future that payment is to be received.*

Present Value of an Income Stream

The previous method is used to compute the present value of a single sum to be paid at some point in the future. Most investments, however, yield a stream of payments over time. In cases where the payments are to be made over a period of years, the present value of each payment can be computed individually, and the results summed to yield the present value of the entire payment stream. For example, the present value of receiving $100 next year and $150 the year after is simply the present value of the first year's payment plus the present value of the second year's payment. If the interest rate is 5 percent, the present value equals

$$\text{Present value} = \frac{\$100}{1.05} + \frac{\$150}{(1.05)^2} = \$231.29$$

Present Value of an Annuity

A given sum of money received each year for a specified number of years is called an **annuity**. Such a payment is called a *perpetuity* if it continues indefinitely into the future, as it would in the earlier example of the productivity gain stemming from the purchase of an indestructible tractor. The present value of receiving a certain amount forever seems like a very large sum indeed. But because future payments are valued less the more distant into the future they are to be received, the present value of receiving a particular amount forever is not much more than that of receiving it for, say, 20 years.

To determine the present value of receiving $100 each year forever, we need only ask how much money must be deposited in a savings account to yield $100 in interest per year. When the interest rate is 10 percent, a deposit of $1,000 will earn $100 per year. Thus, the present value of receiving $100 a year indefinitely when the interest rate is 10 percent is $1,000. More generally, the present value equals the amount received each year divided by the interest rate, or discount rate.

The concept of present value is useful in making investment decisions. Farmer Jones, by choosing the Green Giant rather than the next smaller tractor, expected to earn $800 more per year from investing $10,000 more. Thus, his marginal rate of return was 8 percent. At a market rate of interest of 8 percent, the present value of a cash flow of $800 discounted at 8 percent would be $800/0.08, which equals $10,000. Thus, *Jones was willing to invest in capital an amount that at the margin would yield a cash stream with a present value just equal to the marginal amount invested.* To develop a better appreciation for present value and discounting, consider the following case study.

Annuity *A given sum of money received each year for a specified number of years*

CASE STUDY

The Million-Dollar Lottery

Since New Hampshire introduced the first state-run lottery in 1964, 35 states have followed suit, and payoffs of millions of dollars are now common. Some winners of a million-dollar lottery expect to be handed a check for a million dollars. Instead, winners get paid in installments, such as $50,000 per year for 20 years. Though this stream of payments still totals a million dollars, you now know that such a stream has a present value of less than the advertised million. To put this payment schedule in perspective, keep in mind that at a discount rate of 10 percent, the $50,000 received in the 20th year has a present value of only $7,432. If today you deposited $7,432 in an account earning 10 percent interest, you would wind up with $50,000 in 20 years.

If the discount rate is 10 percent, the present value of a $50,000 annuity for the next 20 years is $425,700. Thus, the present value of the actual payment stream is less than half of the promised million, which is why lottery officials

he Million-Dollar Lottery
ontinued

Location:

What is the lottery jackpot in your state or region? To find out, visit "InterLotto: On-Line Lottery Information Service," maintained by I.S. Applications Co. L.L.C. (**http://www.interlotto.com/**). Are you ready to win the lottery? Prosperity Partners, Inc., offers financial advice to lottery winners, including alternative pay-out strategies. Explore "Prosperity Partners, Inc.: Forging New Horizons" (**http://www.note.com/note/pp/**).

pay it out in installments. Incidentally, we might consider the present value of receiving $50,000 per year forever. Using the formula for an annuity discussed earlier, the present value when the interest rate is 10 percent is $50,000/0.10 = $500,000. Since the present value of receiving $50,000 for 20 years is $425,700, continuing the $50,000 annual payment forever after adds only $74,300 to the present value. This shows the dramatic effect of discounting on the present value of payments after year 20.

In some states, lottery winners are allowed to sell their jackpots. Winners typically receive only 40 cents on the dollar for the 20-year annuity. So a million-dollar pot paid out over 20 years could be sold by the winner for only $400,000. At tax rates prevailing in 1996, federal income taxes on $400,000 for a single taxpayer amount to at least $140,000. State and local income taxes could total an additional $50,000. All told, because of time and taxes, the much touted million could shrink to only about $200,000 in after-tax income—a mere one-fifth the amount advertised.

Some observers question the ethics of lottery promotions, which are not subject to state and federal truth-in-advertising standards. Critics point out that lottery officials in some states conceal the huge odds against winning, mail out coupons for free tickets to stimulate gambling, and aim some ads at the poor and the gambling-addicted.

Sources: Lois Gold, "Ticket to Trouble," *New York Times Magazine,* 23 April 1995; Joshua Shenk, "Everyone's a Loser," *Washington Monthly* (July/August 1995); and James Stearns and Shaheen Borna, "The Ethics of Lottery Advertising," *Journal of Business Ethics* (January 1995): pp. 43–51.

This discussion of present value and discounting concludes our treatment of capital and interest. We now have the tools to consider how firms, especially corporations, are financed.

CORPORATE FINANCE

During the Industrial Revolution, labor-saving machinery made large-scale production more profitable, so manufacturing began to require large capital investments. The corporate structure became the easiest way to finance these large investments, and by 1920 corporations accounted for most employment and output in the U.S. economy. In Chapter 4, we examined the pros and cons of the corporate form of business organization, but thus far we have said little about corporate finance.

As was noted in Chapter 4, a corporation is a legal entity, distinct from its shareholders. The corporation may own property, earn a profit, sue or be sued, and incur debt. Stockholders, the owners of the corporation, are liable only to the extent of their investment in the firm. Use of the abbreviation "Inc." or "Corp." in the company name serves as a warning to potential creditors that stockholders will not accept unlimited personal liability for the debts the company incurs. *Corporations acquire funds for investment in three ways: by selling stock, by retaining part of their profit, and by borrowing.*

Stock *A certificate reflecting ownership of a corporation*

Corporate Stock and Retained Earnings

Corporations *issue stock* to raise money for operations and for new plant and equipment. Suppose you have developed a recipe for a hot, spicy chili that your friends have convinced you will be a best-seller. You decide to incorporate and raise $1 million by issuing stock in the company, which you call the Six-Alarm Chili Corporation. To do this, you sell 10,000 shares for $100 per share. A *share* of **stock** represents a claim to a *share* of the company's net assets and earnings, as well as the right to vote on corporate directors and on other important matters. A person who buys 1 percent of the shares issued thereby owns 1 percent of the company, is entitled to 1 percent of any profit, and gets to cast 1 percent of the votes.

Bond *A certificate reflecting a firm's promise to pay the holder a periodic interest payment until the date of maturity and a fixed sum of money on the designated maturity date*

Corporations must pay corporate income taxes on any profits. After-tax profits are either paid as dividends to shareholders or reinvested in the corporation. Reinvested profits, or *retained earnings,* allow the firm to finance expansion. Stockholders expect dividends, but the corporation is not bound by contract to pay dividends. Once shares are issued, their price tends to fluctuate directly with the firm's prospects for profits.

Corporate Bonds

Your corporation can acquire funds by issuing stock and by retaining earnings. A third way to acquire funds is by borrowing. The corporation can go directly to a bank for a loan or can issue bonds. A **bond** is the corporation's promise to pay the holder a fixed sum of money on the designated *maturity date* plus an annual interest payment, or *coupon,* until the date of maturity. For example, a corporation might sell for $1,000 a bond that promises to pay the holder $1,000 at the end of 20 years plus an annual interest payment, or coupon, of, say, $100.

The payment stream for bonds is more predictable than that for stocks. Unless this corporation goes bankrupt, it is obliged to pay bondholders $100 every year for 20 years and to return the $1,000 at the end of that time. In contrast, stockholders are last in line when resource holders get paid, so bondholders get paid before stockholders. Investors consider bonds less risky than stocks.

Securities Exchanges

Once stocks and bonds have been issued and sold, owners of these securities are free to resell them on *security exchanges*. In the United States, there are 10 security exchanges registered with the *Securities and Exchange Commission,* or *SEC,* the federal body that regulates securities markets. The New York Stock Exchange is by far the largest, trading the securities of over 2,000 major companies and handling over 80 percent of U.S. trades. Nearly all the securities traded each day are *secondhand securities* in the sense that they have already been sold by the issuing company. So the bulk of the daily transactions do not provide funds to firms in need of investment capital. Most money goes from a securities seller to a securities buyer. *Institutional investors,* such as banks, insurance companies, and mutual funds, account for over half the trading volume on the New York Stock Exchange. By providing a *secondary market* for securities, exchanges enhance the *liquidity* of these securities—that is, the exchanges make the securities more readily exchangeable for cash.

Net Bookmark

The New York Stock Exchange (NYSE) is the largest organized stock exchange in the world, trading the securities of over 2,000 major companies. Visit NYSENET, the Internet home of the New York Stock Exchange (**http://www.nyse.com/**).

The secondary markets for stocks also determine the current market value of the corporation. The market value of a firm at any given time can be found by multiplying the share price times the number of shares. For example, if your chili company's stock price increases from $100 to $200 per share, the market value of the firm would equal $200 times the 10,000 outstanding shares, or $2 million. The share price reflects the present value of the discounted stream of expected profits. Securities prices give the firm's management some indication of the wisdom of raising new capital through new stock issues or new bond issues. The more profitable the company, other things constant, the higher the value of shares on the stock market and the lower the interest rate that would have to be paid on new bond issues. *Thus, securities markets allocate funds more readily to successful firms than to firms in financial difficulty.* Some firms may be in such poor financial shape that they cannot sell new securities. Securities markets usually promote the survival of the fittest.

So one function of securities markets is to allocate investment funds to those firms that appear in a position to make the most profitable use of those funds. Securities markets also help determine the ownership and control of corporations. We examine this function next.

CORPORATE OWNERSHIP AND CONTROL

We have described the entrepreneur as the individual responsible for guaranteeing payment to owners of the other resources in return for the opportunity to direct the use of these resources in the firm and the right to any profit or loss. We said that the entrepreneur need not actually manage the firm's resources as long as he or she has the power to hire and fire the manager—that is, as long as the entrepreneur controls the manager.

Managerial Behavior in Large Corporations

Up to this point, we have assumed that firms attempt to maximize profits. In a small firm, there is usually little danger that the hired manager will not follow the wishes of the owner; the manager and owner are often the same person. As the modern corporation has evolved, however, its ownership has become widely distributed among many stockholders, leaving no single stockholder with either the incentive or the ability to control the manager.

Portfolio An individual's collection of stocks, bonds, and other financial investments.

Ownership has become widely distributed, in part because individual stockholders prefer to diversify their portfolios across different types of assets rather than purchase shares in just a single company. A **portfolio** is an individual's collection of stocks, bonds, and other financial investments. The exact composition of the portfolio depends on the individual's financial plans and needs. For example, a young family may prefer a portfolio that yields no current income but will grow to finance college costs. An older couple, on the other hand, would prefer a portfolio that provides a reliable stream of retirement income. Even an individual who is wealthy enough to purchase a large fraction of a particular firm usually prefers to buy a small fraction of many firms instead. That way, if a particular firm performs poorly and its share price drops, the portfolio still retains most of its value. Simply put, investors choose a diversified portfolio so as not to put all the eggs in one basket. The upshot is that the ownership of most firms is spread across many stockholders.

Economists since the days of Adam Smith have been concerned with what is known as the **separation of ownership from control** in the large corporation. Various economists have formulated theoretical models suggesting that, when freed from the control of a dominant stockholding influence, managers attempt to pursue their own selfish goals rather than those of the firm's owners. The alternatives vary from model to model, but emphasis has focused on such goals as maximizing the firm's size or increasing the perks and discretionary resources available to the managers, such as attractive surroundings, corporate jets, and other amenities. Managers may try to make the firm larger, even if profits suffer, because they want the power, security, and status associated with a larger firm. As goals other than profit are pursued, so the argument goes, the firm's resources are used less efficiently, resulting in a lower level of profit. Thus, the stockholders—the owners of the firm—suffer because managers are not pursuing the owners' best interests.

Separation of ownership from control **The situation that exists when no single stockholder or unified group of stockholders owns enough shares to control the management of a corporation**

Constraints on Managerial Discretion

Analysts have identified a variety of constraints that can serve as checks on wayward managers. The nature and effectiveness of each constraint will be examined next.

Economics of Natural Selection. Some economists argue that even if managers are freed from the control of a dominant stockholder, the rigors of competition in the product market will force them to maximize profits. This "economics of natural selection," theoretically, ensures that only the most efficient firms will survive; inefficient firms simply will not earn enough profit to attract and retain resources and so will eventually go out of business.

The problem with this argument is that although pressure to pursue profits may arise when firms sell their products in competitive markets, many large corporations are at least partially insulated from intense product competition. Either because government regulations protect their firms from competition or because the firms enjoy some degree of market power, many managers have a certain amount of discretion in how they use their firms' resources. Such managers could divert corporate resources into activities reflecting their own interests, yet still earn enough profit to ensure their firms' survival.

Managerial Incentives. Other economists have examined the manager's incentive structure. If executive pay is linked closely to the firm's profit, the compensation scheme may encourage the manager to pursue profit even in the absence of a dominant stockholder or competition in the product market. Evidence suggests that at least a portion of the typical manager's compensation is tied to the firm's profitability through some type of bonus pay scheme or stock option plan. But even if the manager's income is tied to profit, the manager will not necessarily attempt to maximize profit. The manager in a large corporation who diverts profit to other ends will simply forgo some income. This profit diversion may be "cheap" in view of the small fraction of the firm's shares typically owned by management. For example, if the manager owns 1 percent of the firm's shares and can divert $10,000 of potential profit to buy an antique desk, this diversion will cost the manager only $100 in forgone pretax profit. After corporate taxes and personal income taxes, the cost is less than half that amount.

Thus, the existence of a link between executive pay and firm profit is not necessarily evidence that managers will attempt to maximize profit; it is only evidence that profit diversion will involve some personal cost, but that cost may be quite small.

Stockholder Voting. Each year stockholders have an opportunity to attend the company meeting and elect the board of directors. Couldn't stockholders join forces to oust an inefficient manager? Chances of an effective stockholder revolt are slim. The average stockholder does not have the information, the resources, or the incentive to challenge management. Most shareholders either ignore the election or dutifully pass their votes to the managers.

Dissatisfied stockholders, however, do have one very important alternative. Stockholders can "fire" the manager and the firm simply by selling their shares in the corporation. As dissatisfied stockholders sell their holdings, the share price drops and the firm becomes more attractive as a target for a reform-minded entrepreneur. A so-called *corporate raider* can buy a controlling interest in the firm at a relatively low price, reform or replace the management, and then get rich as the firm's rising profits lead to an appreciation in the value of shares. The effects of this market discipline will be examined next.

The Market for Corporate Control

The market for corporate control has been championed by many economists as an efficient mechanism for allocating corporate assets to those who value them most highly. If the firm's assets are undervalued in the stock market, some entrepreneur has an incentive to "buy low and sell high"—that is, to buy firms that are selling for less than they should be and take measures to increase their value. The effectiveness of this market in checking managerial abuses depends on the existence of someone with (1) the ability to identify firms that are performing below potential, (2) access to the resources necessary to carry off a successful takeover, and (3) the savvy to improve the firm's performance. There are a variety of reasons why this market may not operate perfectly.

One problem with the market for corporate control is that outsiders have difficulty determining whether a firm is being run efficiently. Often when a firm performs poorly, it is unclear whether the management is poor or the assets of the firm are not what they seem. Management is likely to be better informed than a potential corporate raider, but some types of information are more public than others. For example, the value of an oil firm's reserves tends to be widely known in that industry. Thus, when an oil firm's market value falls significantly below the underlying value of the firm's assets, we expect a takeover attempt, as happened frequently in the oil industry during the 1980s.

A corporate raider usually attempts to acquire a majority interest through a public **tender offer** to buy shares. For example, a raider may offer to pay $25 per share for stock that had been trading at $20 per share prior to the takeover attempt. If a majority of shares are "tendered" by shareholders, the raider will purchase them and the takeover will be successful. If too few shareholders agree to sell, however, the deal will fall through and the tender offer will be withdrawn or amended.

A **leveraged buyout** is a corporate takeover that is financed mostly by borrowed funds, or debt. A firm's financial *leverage* is measured by the ratio of its

Tender offer An offer to buy a controlling number (i.e., more than half) of a firm's shares

Leveraged buyout The purchase of controlling interest in a corporation using borrowed funds

debt to its net worth; net worth equals the amount originally invested in the firm plus retained earnings. The higher the ratio of debt to net worth, the more the firm is said to be *leveraged,* or dependent on debt. Corporate acquisitions that are financed primarily by debt result in firms that are highly leveraged, so debt-financed acquisitions are called leveraged buyouts. The debt resulting from a leveraged buyout is often repaid by selling off parts of the acquired company.

Leveraged buyouts allow a corporate raider with little personal wealth to acquire a large corporation by using debt secured with the assets and potential profits of the acquired firm. The gamble, if successful, can yield a huge payoff to the raider. Debt is all the more attractive because interest payments on that debt are tax deductible for the corporation. Not all leveraged buyouts succeed, however, and some of the leveraged buyouts of the 1980s became financial casualties in the 1990s. One such failure is discussed in this closing case study.

CASE STUDY

Campeau Bets the Store

In April 1988, Robert Campeau, a Canadian real estate developer, paid $6.6 billion to acquire Federated Department Stores. A year earlier, he had purchased Allied Stores for $3.7 billion. Both acquisitions were financed by borrowed funds, and thus the deals were leveraged buyouts. As collateral for the loans, Campeau pledged the assets and earnings of the newly acquired companies. To help pay the huge debt, he planned to cut operating costs and sell off parts of the vast retailing empire the two companies composed.

Over 10,000 employees were laid off, and retail chains such as Bonwit Teller and Brooks Brothers were sold. But proceeds from these sales were less than expected, and the remaining stores faced substantial debt payments, which drained the cash needed to pay other bills. By the summer of 1989, suppliers were reluctant to provide goods on credit to Campeau's remaining stores, since suppliers were unsure of payment.

To reduce the debt, Campeau attempted to sell the crown jewel of his acquisitions, Bloomingdale's. But nobody was willing to pay what he thought the chain was worth. Federated and Allied were left in an impossible position since their debt-service requirements far outstripped their expected cash flow. On January 15, 1990, after failing to make scheduled interest payments on $2.3 billion in debt, Federated and Allied filed for bankruptcy protection. The filing affected more than 100,000 employees at 258 stores, about 300,000 suppliers, and bondholders and other creditors. Negotiations with creditors and subsequent debt restructuring permitted Federated Department Stores, the new name of the business, to emerge from bankruptcy in February 1992. In a huge concession, lenders agreed to "forgive" $5 billion in debt; Federated agreed to sever all ties with Campeau.

In 1994, in a bitter takeover battle, Federated acquired R. H. Macy's, which itself was in bankruptcy. Federated closed down some Macy's holdings, such as the I. Magnin chain. In 1995, in an effort to dominate department store retailing in America, Federated acquired other chains including Woodward & Lothrop and Broadway Stores.

Location:

To learn more about Robert Campeau, see "Well-Known People Who Happen to Be Canadians," compiled by Vernon R.J. Schmid (http://calvin.bu.edu/bios/Campeau.html). For further discussion about leveraged buyouts, browse "The Invisible Hand," by Gary Hoover, founder of The Reference Press and "Hoover's Online" (http://www.hoovers.com/inhand.html). Also visit "Leveraged Buyouts," maintained by private investment banker Donald E. Brown (http://www.orci.com/personal/dbrown/lbo.html).

Campeau Bets the Store
continued

At the time they were acquired, Federated and Allied were well managed and highly regarded, but they could not repay the crushing debt that resulted from Campeau's leveraged buyout. Financial analysts argue that Campeau paid too much for the stores, and lenders who financed the costly acquisition were too willing to believe unrealistic profit projections, particularly since Campeau had little experience in retailing. This was not the only leveraged buyout to sour. These defaults cooled the willingness to finance leveraged buyouts in the 1990s.

Sources: "Campeau Bankers Are Posing Some $2.3 Billion Questions," *New York Times,* 14 January 1990; Laura Jereski and Jeff Bailey, "Federated to Acquire Broadway Stores in Stock Swap Valued at $574 Million," *The Wall Street Journal,* 15 August, 1995; and Laura Bird and Jonathan Auerbach, "Federated Group Wins the Auction for Woodward," *The Wall Street Journal,* 22 June 1995.

CONCLUSION

This chapter introduced you to capital, interest, and corporate finance. Capital is a more complicated resource than this chapter has conveyed. For example, the demand curve for investment is a moving target, not the stable relationship drawn in Exhibit 1. An accurate depiction of the investment demand curve calls for knowledge of the marginal product of capital and the price of output in the future. But the marginal product changes with changes in technology and in the employment of other resources. And the future price of the product can vary widely. Consider, for example, the dilemma of someone considering investing in oil wells during the 1980s, when oil prices fluctuated between $10 and $36 per barrel. Although the real world of investment and finance is more complicated than we have let on, this chapter still conveys a reasonable introduction to these topics.

SUMMARY

1. Production cannot occur without savings because both direct production and roundabout production require time—time during which the resources required for production must be paid. Because present consumption is valued more than future consumption, consumers must be rewarded to defer consumption. Interest is the reward paid to savers for forgoing present consumption and is the cost paid by borrowers to increase present consumption.

2. Choosing the profit-maximizing level of capital is complicated because capital purchased today yields a stream of benefit for years into the future. The marginal rate of return of a capital investment equals the marginal revenue product of capital as a percentage of the marginal resource cost of capital. The profit-maximizing firm invests up to the point where its marginal rate of return on capital equals the market rate of interest, which is the opportunity cost of investing savings or borrowed funds.

3. The demand and supply for loanable funds determine the market rate of interest. At any given time, market rates of interest may differ because of differences in risk, maturity, administrative costs, and tax treatment.

4. Corporations secure investment capital from three sources: new stock issues, retained earnings, and borrowing (either directly from a lender or by issuing bonds). Once new stocks and bonds are issued, these securities are bought and sold on securities exchanges. Securities prices tend to vary directly with the firm's expected profitability.

5. The ownership of a large corporation is typically fragmented among many stockholders, with no stockholder owning a dominant share. The fact that a poorly performing firm can be bought at a bargain price, shaped up, and sold for a profit is said to keep management behavior in accord with stockholders' interests.

QUESTIONS AND PROBLEMS

1. **(Capital in Production)** Why would seed also be considered part of Jones' savings? Should seed be considered part of the capital stock? Why or why not?

2. **(Optimal Investment)** Consider Exhibit 1 in this chapter. If the marginal resource cost rose to $24,000 what would be the optimal investment at a market interest rate of 10 percent? If the interest rate then rose to 16.6 percent, what would be the optimal investment?

3. **(Role of Time)** Complete each of the following sentences:
   a. Production cannot occur without _____, because production requires _____ during which current consumption cannot be satisfied with _____ production.
   b. If Bryan values current consumption more than future consumption, he has a _____ _____ _____ _____ _____.
   c. The reward to households for forgoing current consumption is the _____ _____ _____ _____.
   d. Manufacturing capital to increase productivity rather than using resources directly to make final goods is known as _____ _____.
   e. The relationship between the market rate of interest and the quantity of savings, other things constant, is illustrated by the _____ _____ _____ _____.

4. **(Taxes and Investment)** How does the tax deductibility of mortgage interest payments affect the demand for housing and building construction?

5. **(Present Value)** Calculate the present value of each of the following future payments:
   a. A $10,000 lump sum received in 10 years; the market rate of interest is 8 percent.
   b. A $10,000 lump sum received in 10 years; the market rate of interest is 10 percent.
   c. $1,000 received at the end of each year for 3 years; the market rate of interest is 9 percent.
   d. A $25,000 lump sum received in 1 year; the market rate of interest is 12 percent.
   e. A $25,000 lump sum received in 1 year; the market rate of interest is 10 percent.
   f. A perpetuity of $500 per year; the market rate of interest is 6 percent.

6. **(Present Value)** Why is $10,000 a reasonably close approximation of the price of an annuity paying $1,000 each year for 30 years at 10 percent interest?

7. **(Present Value)** Suppose you are hired by your state government to determine the profitability of a lottery offering a grand prize of $10 million paid out in equal installments over 20 years. Show *how* you calculate the cost to the state of paying out such a prize. Assume payments are made at the *beginning* of each year.

8. **(Loanable Funds Market)** Using a supply-demand diagram for loanable funds, show the effect of each of the following on market interest rates:
   a. An increase in the marginal resource cost of capital.
   b. An increase in the productivity of capital.
   c. A decrease in the tax rate on savings.

9. **(Human Capital)** Suppose you are considering enrolling in a graduate school program costing a total of $40,000. You expect that the graduate degree will increase your annual income by $5,000. Calculate the interest rate that would make such an investment in human capital a good one. (Ignore any other costs, including opportunity costs.)

10. **(Corporate Finance)** Describe the three ways in which corporations acquire funds for investment.

11. **(Managerial Behavior)** Why might separation of ownership from control lead to lower profitability for the firm?

12. **(Corporate Finance)** What is the role of securities exchanges in corporate finance?

13. **(Why Interest Rates Differ)** At any given time, there is not a single market rate of interest in the economy, but rather a range of interest rates. Discuss the various factors that contribute to differences in interest rates.

14. **(Constraints on Managerial Discretion)** The separation of ownership from control in a large corporation can cause managers to follow goals other than profit maximization. Discuss reasons why managers may continue to maximize profits. Why might these reasons be insufficient to ensure profit maximization?

15. **(Market for Corporate Control)** How are tender offers and leveraged buyouts used in the market for corporate control?

16. **(Present Value and Risk)** Suppose that the interest rate (discount rate) is not known with certainty, but is expected to fluctuate between 10 percent and 20 percent. Calculate the present value of a $1,000 payment one year in the future at the interest rate at end of the projected range. Do the same for a $1,000 payment two years in the future. Which is more risky?

17. **(Present Value)** Suppose the market rate of interest is 10 percent. Would you be willing to loan out $10,000 if you were guaranteed to receive $1,000 at the end of each of the next twelve years plus a $5,000 payment in 15 years? Why or why not?

18. **(The Role of Time)** Explain why the supply of loanable funds curve slopes upward to the right.

19. **(The Million-Dollar Lottery)** In many states with lotteries, a winner can choose between receiving his or her winnings in a single discounted lump-sum payment or in a series of annual payments for 20 years. What factors should a winner consider in determining how to accept the winnings?

20. **(Campeau Bets the Store)** What would have been the incentive for Robert Campeau to buy Federated Department Stores and Allied Stores in a leveraged buyout? Was his assessment valid?

Using the Internet

21. Visit "Market Reviews," daily market summaries maintained by Knight-Ridder Financial News, the independent newsgathering arm of Knight-Ridder Financial (**http://www.krf.com/KRF/summary. htm**). Examine the "Stock Market Reviews."
    a. How well did U.S. stocks perform? If discussed, which industry or industries have performed well? Which have performed poorly?
    b. Answer the same questions for the Japanese and European stock markets.

Imperfect Information, Transaction Costs, and Market Behavior

28

T he firm has been viewed thus far as a "black box" that hires resources on the basis of their marginal products, combines these resources efficiently to produce the profit-maximizing level of output, and sells this output for the profit-maximizing price. We have assumed that those who run the firm know what resources to employ and in what quantities. We have also assumed that the firm's managers are aware of the latest technology; the price, quality, and availability of all resources; and the demand for its product. Little has been said about the internal structure of the firm, because our objective has been to understand how the price system coordinates the allocation of resources through

markets, not to understand the internal workings of the firm. In the first half of this chapter, we will step inside the factory gates to reconsider some assumptions about the firm and its behavior.

We have also assumed that consumers have all the information they need to make informed choices, including knowledge of the price, availability, and quality of the goods and services they demand. As we will see in the second half of the chapter, participants in most markets do not operate with complete information about the variables that matter most, such as price and quality. To complicate markets further, sometimes sellers know more than buyers about the quality of the product; sometimes it's the other way around. Sometimes the quality of a product becomes obvious only after it has been purchased. In the second half of this chapter, we examine how imperfect information affects the behavior of the market participants and shapes the market outcome. Overall, this chapter should help you develop a deeper understanding of market behavior. Topics discussed in this chapter include:

- Transaction costs and the firm
- Vertical integration
- Economies of scope
- Optimal search
- Winner's curse

- Asymmetric information
- Adverse selection
- Signaling and screening
- Principal-agent problems

THE RATIONALE FOR THE FIRM AND THE SCOPE OF ITS OPERATION

The competitive model assumes that all participants in the market are fully informed about the price and availability of all inputs, outputs, and production processes. Perfect competition assumes that the firm is headed by a decision maker with a computer-like ability to calculate all the marginal productivities of alternative resources. This individual knows everything necessary to solve complex production and pricing problems. But if everyone had easy access to all the information required to make decisions, there would be little need for entrepreneurs.

The irony is that if the black-box characterization of the firm were accurate—that is, if the marginal products of all inputs could easily be measured and if prices for all inputs could be determined without cost—there would be little reason for production to take place in firms. In a world characterized by perfect competition, perfect information, constant returns to scale, and frictionless exchange, the consumer could bypass the firm, purchasing inputs in the appropriate amounts and paying each resource owner accordingly. Someone who wanted a table could buy timber, have it milled, contract with a carpenter, contract with a painter, and end up with a finished product. The consumer could carry out transactions directly with each resource supplier.

The Firm Reduces Transaction Costs

In this section, we explore why production is carried out within firms. The theory we examine argues that the firm is a response to the transaction costs of using the market directly. About 60 years ago, in a classic article entitled "The Nature of the Firm," Nobel Prize winner Ronald Coase asked the fundamental question, "Why do firms exist?"[1] Why do people organize in the hierarchical structure of the firm and coordinate their decisions through a central authority rather than simply relying on market exchange? Coase's answer would not surprise today's students of economics: *Organizing activities through the hierarchy of the firm is often more efficient than market exchange, because production requires the coordination of many transactions among many resource owners.* The costs of transacting business through market relations are, according to Coase, often higher than those of undertaking the same activities within the firm.

Coase's major insight was that economic activity is best understood in terms of the transaction costs involved in any system of exchange between individuals. The exchange relationship between individuals is contractual in nature. When you buy any product, such as a sweat suit, you agree to pay a certain amount—a contract is implicit. With major purchases, such as homes or cars, you actually sign a contract. Many resource owners, such as employees ranging from auto workers to professional athletes, sign contracts specifying the terms of supply. Thus, contractual relationships abound.

The firm itself is most easily understood in terms of a particular kind of contractual relationship, the *authority relationship*. The entrepreneur agrees to pay the resource owner a specified amount in return for the right to direct that resource in the firm. The owner, therefore, sells the right to control the resource

---

1   *Economica* 4 (November 1937): pp. 386–405.

to the entrepreneur, who may do the managing or may hire a manager. In the market, resources are allocated based on prices, but in the firm, resources are guided by the decisions of managers. *Coase argued that firms emerge when the transaction costs involved in using the price system exceed the costs of organizing those same activities through direct managerial controls within a firm.*

Consider again the example of the consumer purchasing a table by contracting directly with all the different resource suppliers, from the grower of timber to the individual who paints the table. Using resource markets directly involves (1) the cost of determining what inputs are needed and how they are combined and (2) the cost of negotiating a separate agreement with each resource owner for each specific contribution to production *over and above* the direct costs of the timber, nails, machinery, paint, and labor required to make the table. Where inputs are easily identified, measured, priced, and hired, production can be carried out through a "do-it-yourself" approach rather than within the firm. For example, getting your house painted is a relatively simple production task: you can buy the paint and brushes and hire painters by the hour. In this case you, the consumer, become your own painting contractor, hiring inputs in the market and combining these inputs to do the job.

Where the costs of determining inputs and negotiating a contract for each specific contribution are high, the consumer minimizes transaction costs by purchasing the finished product from a firm rather than hiring all the inputs directly through markets. For example, although some people serve as their own contractor when it comes to painting a house, few do so when it comes to building a house; most hire general contractors. The more complicated the task, the greater the ability to economize on transaction costs through specialization and centralized control. For example, attempting to buy a car by contracting with the hundreds of resource suppliers required to put one together would be time-consuming and costly. What type of skilled labor should be hired and at what wages? How much steel, aluminum, and other materials should be purchased? How should the resources be combined and in what proportions? The task is impossible for someone who lacks specialized engineering knowledge of auto production. Consequently, it is more efficient for a consumer to buy a car produced by a firm than to contract separately with each resource supplier.

At the margin there will be some activities that could go either way, with some consumers using firms and some hiring resources directly in the markets. The choice will depend on the skill and opportunity cost of time of each consumer. For example, some people may not want to be troubled with hiring all the inputs to get their house painted; instead, they will simply contract with a firm to do the entire job for an agreed-upon price—they will hire a contractor. As we will see later in the chapter, however, hiring a contractor may give rise to other problems of quality control.

The Boundaries of the Firm

So far, the chapter has explained why firms exist: firms minimize both the transaction costs and the production costs of economic activity. Next we ask: What is the efficient scope of the firm? The theory of the firm described in earlier chapters has been largely silent on questions concerning the boundaries of the firm—that is, on the appropriate degree of vertical integration. **Vertical integration** is the expansion of a firm into stages of production earlier or

Vertical integration The expansion of a firm into stages of production earlier or later than those in which it has specialized

later than those in which it has previously specialized. For example, a steel company may decide to mine its own iron ore or to form its steel into various components. A large manufacturer employs an amazing variety of production processes, but on average about half of the cost of production goes to purchasing inputs from other firms. For example, General Motors spends over $50 billion a year on parts and raw materials, an amount that exceeds the total output of many countries.

What determines which activities the firm will undertake and which it will purchase from other firms? Should IBM manufacture its own computer chips or buy them from another firm? The answer depends on a comparison of the costs and benefits of internal production versus market purchases. The point bears repeating: *Internal production and markets are alternative ways of organizing transactions.* The choice will depend on which form of organization is the more efficient way to carry out the transaction in question. Keep in mind that market prices coordinate transactions *between* firms, whereas managers coordinate activities *within* firms. The market coordinates resources by integrating the independent plans of separate decision makers, but a firm coordinates resources through the conscious direction of the manager.

The usual assumption is that transactions will be organized by market exchange unless markets pose problems. Sometimes, for example, it is difficult to use markets because the item in question is not standardized or the exact performance requirements are hard to specify. Consider, for example, one firm contracting with another to supply research and development services. The uncertainty involved in the purchase of such a nonspecific service makes it difficult to write, execute, and enforce contracts covering all possible contingencies that could arise. For example, what if the R&D supplier, in the course of fulfilling the agreement, makes a valuable discovery for an application in an unrelated field? Who has the right to that new application—the firm or the R&D service? And who determines if the field is unrelated? Since incomplete contracts create potentially troublesome situations, conducting research and development *within the firm* often involves a lower transaction cost than purchasing it in the market. Coase's analysis of transaction costs helps explain why production often can be carried out more efficiently inside the firm than through market transactions between the firm and others. His analysis also suggests the appropriate amount of vertical integration in the firm.

At this point, it will be useful to discuss specific criteria the firm considers in deciding whether to purchase a particular input from the market or to produce it internally.

Bounded Rationality of Managers. To direct and coordinate activity in a conscious way in the firm, the manager must understand how all the pieces of the puzzle fit together. As the firm takes on more and more activities, however, the manager starts losing track of things and the quality of managerial decisions suffers. The larger the firm, the longer the lines of communication between the manager and production workers who must implement the decision. One constraint on vertical integration is the manager's **bounded rationality,** which limits the amount of information the manager can comprehend about the firm's operation. When the firm takes on additional functions, it can experience diseconomies similar to those it experiences when it expands output

Bounded rationality The notion that there is a limit to the amount of information an economic agent, such as a manager, can comprehend

beyond the efficient scale of production. Coordination and communication grow more difficult.

Minimum Efficient Scale. As we noted when firm costs were first introduced, the *minimum efficient scale* is the minimum level of output at which economies of scale have been fully exploited. For example, suppose that minimum efficient scale in the production of personal computers is achieved when output reaches 1 million computers per year, as shown by the long-run average cost curve in panel (a) of Exhibit 1. Suppose also that this output rate turns out to be the

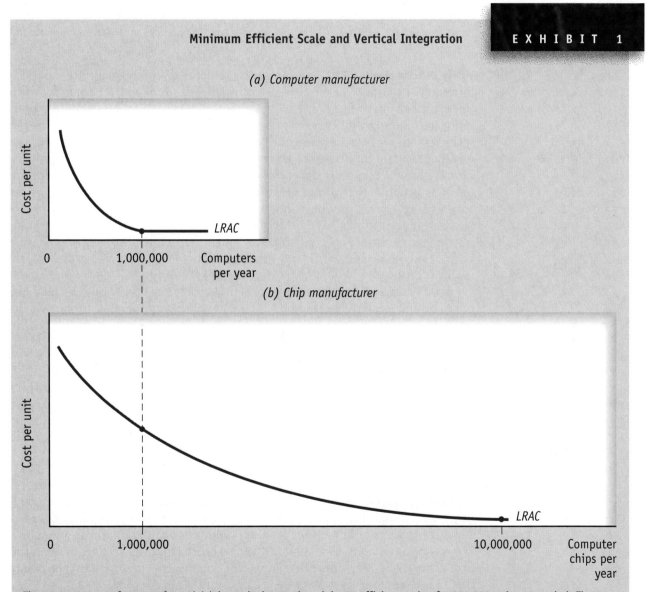

Minimum Efficient Scale and Vertical Integration   **EXHIBIT 1**

(a) Computer manufacturer

(b) Chip manufacturer

The computer manufacturer of panel (a) is producing at the minimum efficient scale of 1,000,000 units per period. That level of production requires 1,000,000 computer chips. If the manufacturer produced its own chips, the cost would be much higher than if it purchased them from a chip manufacturer operating on a much larger scale. As panel (b) shows, at 1,000,000 chips, economies of scale in chip production are far from exhausted.

amount the firm wants to produce to maximize profit. Since the computer chip is an important component in the personal computer, should the PC maker integrate backward into chip production? Suppose that the minimum efficient scale in chip production is not achieved until production reaches a rate of 10 million chips per year. So a PC manufacturer needs only 10 percent of the chips produced at the minimum efficient scale. As you can see in panel (b) of Exhibit 1, if only 1 million chips were produced per year, the cost per chip would be high relative to the cost that could be achieved at minimum efficient scale in chip production. The PC manufacturer therefore minimizes production costs by buying chips from a chip firm of optimal size. More generally, *other things constant, a firm should buy an input if it can buy it for less than it costs to make it.*

Easily Observable Quality. If an input is well defined and its quality is easily determined at the time of purchase, that input is more likely to be purchased in the market than produced internally, other things constant. For example, a flour mill will typically buy wheat in the market rather than grow its own, as the quality of the wheat can be easily assessed upon inspection. In contrast, the quality of certain inputs can be determined only during the production process. Firms whose reputations depend on the operation of a key component are likely to produce that component, especially if the quality of that component varies widely across producers and time and cannot be easily observed by inspection. For example, suppose that the manufacturer of a sensitive measuring instrument requires a crucial gauge, the quality of which can be observed only as the gauge is assembled. If the firm produces the gauge itself, it can closely monitor quality.

Another reason why producers sometimes integrate backward is so they can offer consumers a guarantee about the quality of the components or ingredients in a product. For example, Frank Perdue can talk about the health and quality of the chickens he sells because he raises his own. Kentucky Fried Chicken, however, does not discuss the family background of its chickens because the company makes no claim about raising them. Instead, its ads focus on such things as the secret ingredients used to fry the chicken and the fact that by specializing in chicken preparation, the company does a better job than other fast-food franchises that sell more than chicken.

Number of Suppliers. A firm wants an uninterrupted source of component parts. When there are many interchangeable suppliers of a particular input, a firm is more likely to purchase that input in the market than to produce it internally, other things constant. Not only does the existence of many suppliers ensure a dependable source of components, but competition among the many suppliers keeps the component price down. If the resource market is so unstable that the firm cannot rely on a consistent supply of components, the firm may produce the item to insulate itself from the vagaries of that market.

In summary, the extent to which a firm integrates vertically is limited by the bounded rationality of managers. Other things constant, the firm is more likely to buy a component part rather than produce it if (1) the item can be purchased for less than it would cost the firm to make, (2) the item is well defined and its quality is easily observable, or (3) there are many interchangeable suppliers. These issues are discussed further in the following case study.

Outsourcing occurs when a firm procures services, such as data processing, or products, such as auto parts, from outside suppliers. The firm relies on the division of labor and the law of comparative advantage to focus on what it does best—its "core competency"—while relying on other firms to supply support activities such as payroll services, data processing, and building security. Firms, particularly manufacturing firms, have long purchased some components from other firms, but the outsourcing movement extended these purchases to a broader range of products and activities that typically had been produced by the firm. Japanese firms pioneered outsourcing to reduce production costs and enhance quality. In the United States, outsourcing blossomed in manufacturing during the 1980s and spread to virtually every industry. The boom in outsourcing has created many new firms that specialize in supplying what some firms no longer want to do for themselves.

CASE STUDY

The Trend toward Outsourcing

Location:
Visit "The Outsourcing Institute," a professional association addressing the strategic use of outside resources (**http://www.outsourcing.com/**).

For example, faced with outdated hardware and software, Bethlehem Steel executives realized they could no longer hire and retain enough skilled people to keep up with the changes in such a dynamic field. So Bethlehem outsourced its management information system. Dell Computer, a large mail-order personal computer vendor, turned over all shipping responsibility to an outside firm. Du Pont outsourced responsibility for shipping all imports and exports. In computer operations alone, U.S. outsourcing purchases now exceed $40 billion annually, more than double the 1990 level.

What are the limits to outsourcing? TopsyTail is a Texas company that since 1991 has sold more than $100 million worth of its simple hair-styling gadgets. But the company has virtually no permanent employees. Nearly everything the company does—design, production, marketing, packaging, and distribution—is carried out by subcontractors. The boss claims the company could not have grown so fast in any other way.

One cost of outsourcing can be a loss of control. For example, when Compaq Computer outsourced some laptop-PC production to a Japanese producer, problems mushroomed—in design, production, cost, and quality. Compaq now has a separate management group to oversee outsourced activities. Some companies fear that outsourcing can weaken ties with customers. In 1995, for example, several auto manufacturers had to recall a total of 8 million vehicles because of faulty seat belts from a Japanese supplier. Customers blamed the auto companies, not the subcontractor.

Recently there has been a modest move back to more in-house production. For example, because of better software, some companies are now "insourcing" many of the data processing activities once supplied by other firms. Insourcing reduces the number of times that records must be handled, improving data quality and reducing errors. Chrysler considered outsourcing its data processing, but its own division was the low bidder. Because computer software has made Harley-Davidson more efficient, the company now makes many of the

The Trend toward Outsourcing
continued

components it used to buy from subcontractors. By taking back or keeping key production steps in house, some managers think they can respond more flexibly to custom orders and changing market conditions.

Sources: "The Outing of Outsourcing," *The Economist,* 25 November 1995; Aaron Bernstein, "Outsourced—and Out of Luck," *Business Week,* 17 July 1995; Loise Lee, "Hiring Outside Firms to Run Computers Isn't Always a Bargain," *The Wall Street Journal,* 18 May 1995; and Bart Ziegler, "IBM Offers to Manage and Maintain Personal Computers at Big Companies," *The Wall Street Journal,* 13 March 1995.

Economies of scope Forces that make it cheaper for a firm to produce two or more different products than just one

Net Bookmark

Because all buildings and properties are unique, the real estate market is plagued by imperfect information. To help solve this problem, the National Assocation of Realtors (NAR) offers online solutions. "Multiple Listing Services" (MLSs) available on the World Wide Web provide descriptions for over 600,000 homes. In addition, the NAR has created the "RE-ALTORS Information Network" (RIN), a self-contained online business network for Realtors® to provide buyers and sellers with current, accurate information. To learn more about both, visit the National Association of Realtors (http://www.realtor.com)

Economies of Scope

Thus far, we have considered issues affecting the optimal degree of vertical integration in producing a particular product. Even with outsourcing, the focus is on how best to produce a particular product, such as an automobile or a computer. But sometimes firms branch out into product lines that do not have a vertical relationship. **Economies of scope** exist when it is cheaper to combine two or more product lines in one firm than to produce them separately. Outlays for buildings, research and development, advertising, and product distribution can be minimized when spread over different products. For example, General Electric produces hundreds of products ranging from light bulbs to jet engines. Farmers often grow a variety of crops and raise different kinds of farm animals, animals that recycle damaged crops and food scraps into useful fertilizer. With economies of *scale,* the average cost per unit of output falls as the *scale* of the firm increases; *with economies of scope, average costs per unit fall as the firm produces more types of products.* The cost of some fixed resources, such as specialized knowledge, can be spread across product lines.

Our focus thus far has been on why firms exist, why they often integrate vertically, why they outsource, and why they often produce a whole range of products. These steps toward greater realism move us beyond the simple depiction of the firm employed earlier. In the balance of the chapter, we challenge some simplifying assumptions about how much information is available to market participants.

MARKET BEHAVIOR WITH IMPERFECT INFORMATION

For the most part, our analysis of market behavior has assumed that market participants have full information about products and resources. For consumers, full information reflects knowledge about a product's price, quality, and availability. For firms, full information reflects knowledge about the marginal productivity of various resources, about the appropriate technology for combining them, and about the demand for the firm's product. In reality, *reliable information is costly for both consumers and producers.* What's more, in some markets, one side of a transaction often has better information than does the other side of the transaction. In this section, we examine the impact of less-than-perfect information on market behavior.

Optimal Search with Imperfect Information

Suppose you want to buy a new computer. You need information about the quality and features of each model and the prices of each model at various retail outlets and mail-order firms. To learn more about your choices, you may read advertisements, promotional brochures, and computer publications; you may also talk with experts.

Once you narrow your choice to one or two models, you may price-shop by going from store to store or by letting your fingers do the walking through the *Yellow Pages,* computer catalogs, newspaper ads, and the like. The point is that searching for the lowest price involves a cost. The primary cost of gathering information is usually the opportunity cost of your time. This cost will obviously vary from individual to individual and from item to item. Some people actually enjoy shopping, but this "shop-'til-you-drop" attitude does not necessarily carry over to all items. *For most of us, the process of gathering consumer information can be considered nonmarket work.*

Marginal Cost of Search. In your quest for product information, you gather the easy and obvious information first, such as the types of products on the market and where these products are sold. For example, you may check on the price and availability at the few computer stores at the mall. But as your search widens, the *marginal cost* of acquiring additional information increases, both because you may have to travel greater distances to check prices and services and because the opportunity cost of your time increases as you spend more time acquiring information. Consequently, the marginal cost curve for additional information slopes upward, as is shown in Exhibit 2. Note the assumption in Exhibit 2 is that some amount of information, I_f, is common knowledge and is freely available.

Marginal Benefit of Search. The *marginal benefit* from acquiring additional information is any reduction in price that you are able to uncover because of that additional unit of information. The marginal benefit is relatively large at first, but as you gather more information and grow more acquainted with the mar-

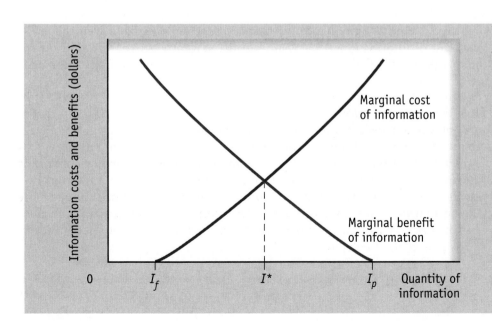

EXHIBIT 2

Optimal Search with Imperfect Information

When information is costly, additional information is acquired as long as its marginal benefit exceeds its marginal cost. Equilibrium, or optimal search, occurs where marginal benefit equals marginal cost.

ket, additional information yields less and less additional benefit. For example, the likelihood of finding a lower price at the second store visited is greater than that of finding a lower price at the 20th store visited. Thus, the marginal benefit curve for additional information slopes downward, as is shown in Exhibit 2.

Optimal Search. Whether we are talking about a consumer attempting to maximize utility or a firm attempting to maximize profit, market participants will continue to gather information as long as the marginal benefit of additional information exceeds its marginal cost. *Optimal search occurs where the marginal benefit just equals the marginal cost,* which in Exhibit 2 occurs where the two curves intersect. Note that at search levels exceeding the equilibrium amount, the marginal benefit of additional information is still positive, but it's below the marginal cost. Note also that full and complete information, what we might call *perfect information,* would occur at level I_p, where the marginal benefit of more information is zero. The high marginal cost of acquiring I_p, however, makes it impractical to become perfectly informed. Thus, firms and consumers, by gathering the optimal amount of information, I^*, have less-than-perfect knowledge about the price, availability, and quality of products and resources.

Implications. The search model we have presented was developed by George Stigler, winner of the Nobel Prize in 1982. Over three decades ago, he showed that the price of a product can differ across sellers because some consumers are unaware of lower prices offered by some sellers.[2] Thus, *search costs result in price dispersion, or different prices, for the same product.* Some sellers call attention to price dispersions by claiming to have the lowest prices around and by promising to match any competitor's price. *Search costs also lead to quality differences across sellers, even for identically priced products.*

There are other implications of Stigler's search model. The more expensive the commodity (a car versus a bag of potato chips), the greater the price dispersion in dollar terms. Thus, the more expensive the item, the greater the incentive to shop around. Also, as the market wage of the consumer rises, the opportunity cost of the consumer's time increases. This shifts the marginal cost of additional information up, resulting in less search and more price dispersion in the market. On the other hand, any change in technology that lowers the marginal cost of information, such as an Internet search program, will shift down the marginal cost of additional information, resulting in more information and less price dispersion.

The Winner's Curse

In 1994, the federal government auctioned off valuable space on the scarce radio spectrum for use in newly invented personal communications services, such as pocket telephones, portable fax machines, and wireless computer networks. The bidding was carried out in the face of much uncertainty about future competition in the industry, the potential size of the market, and forthcoming technological change. Thus, bidders had little experience with the potential value of such leases. If winning bidders turn out like those who won bids in other

---

2   George Stigler, "The Economics of Information," *Journal of Political Economy* (June 1961): pp. 213–25.

auctions for products of uncertain value, such as drilling rights in the Gulf of Mexico, many "winners" will end up losers. How come?

The actual value of space on the radio spectrum was unknown and could only be estimated. For example, suppose the average bid price was, say, $5 million, with some companies bidding more and others bidding less. Suppose also that the winning bid was $10 million. The winning bid was not the average bid, which may have been the most reliable estimate of the lease's true value, but the highest bid, which was the most optimistic estimate. Winners of such bids are said to experience the **winner's curse** because they often lose money after winning the bid. The winner's curse applies to all cases of bidding in which the true value is unknown at the outset. For example, movie companies often bid up the price of screenplays to what many argue are unrealistic ranges. Likewise, publishers get into bidding wars over book manuscripts and even book proposals that are little more than titles. Sports team owners bid for free agents and often overpay. And NBC may have overbid in offering $2.3 billion for the rights to broadcast the Olympics in the years 2002, 2006, and 2008; at the time of the bid, Olympic cities had not even been selected.

If there were perfect information about the market value of a resource, potential buyers would never bid more than the market value. But when competitive bidding is coupled with imperfect information, the winning bidder may lose money on the deal. Once bidders realize that the winning bid will tend to be too high, they may try to scale down their bids. If all bidders scale down by the same amount or by the same proportion, the winning bid should be lower, though the winning bidder should be the same. But such self-restraint is difficult, particularly if a bidder really believes the resource to be more valuable than it actually is.

Will NBC experience the winner's curse? NBC may have overbid in offering $2.3 billion for the right to broadcast the Olympics in 2002, 2006, and 2008.

Winner's curse The plight of the winning bidder for an asset of uncertain value who has overestimated the asset's true value

MARKET BEHAVIOR WITH ASYMMETRIC INFORMATION

Thus far, we have considered the effects of costly information and limited information on market behavior. The issue gets more complicated when one side of the market has more reliable information than does the other side, a situation in which there is **asymmetric information.** In this section, we examine several examples of asymmetric information and its effect on market efficiency.

We can identify two types of information that a market participant may want but lack. First, one side of the market may know about *characteristics* of the product for sale that the other side does not know. For example, the seller of a used car knows more about that car's record of reliability than does the buyer. Likewise, the buyer of a health insurance policy knows more about his or her general state of health than does the insurance company. When one side of the market knows more than the other side about product characteristics that are important in the transaction, the asymmetric information problem involves **hidden characteristics.**

A second type of asymmetric information problem occurs when one side of a transaction can pursue an *action* that affects the other side and that the other side cannot directly observe. For example, the mechanic you hire to check out that strange noise under your car's hood may undertake unneeded repairs,

Asymmetric information A situation in which one side of the market has more reliable information than the other side does

Hidden characteristics A type of asymmetric information problem in which one side of the market knows more than the other side about characteristics that are important to the market exchange

charging you for three hours' work even though the job should have taken only 10 minutes. Whenever one side of an economic relationship can take a relevant action that the other side cannot observe, the situation is described as one of **hidden actions.**

Hidden actions A type of asymmetric information when one side of an economic relationship can take a relevant action that the other side cannot observe

Hidden Characteristics: The "Lemon" Problem

One type of hidden characteristic situation occurs when sellers know more about the quality of the product than do buyers. Consider the market for used cars. The seller of a used car normally has had abundant experience with important *characteristics* of that car: the record of breakdowns, accidents, gas mileage, miles driven, and so on. A prospective buyer can only guess at these, based on the car's appearance and perhaps a test drive. The buyer cannot really know how good a car it is without driving it for several months. So buyers of used cars have less information than sellers.

To simplify the problem, suppose there are only two types of used cars for sale: good ones and bad ones, or "lemons." Again, only the seller knows which type is for sale. Suppose that if buyers were certain about a car's type, they would be willing on average to pay $10,000 for good cars but only $4,000 for lemons. If buyers believed that half the used cars on the market were good ones and half were lemons, buyers would be willing to pay, say, $7,000 for a car of unknown type (since buyers believe this to be the average value of cars on the market). Would $7,000 be the equilibrium price of used cars?

So far, we have ignored the actions of the potential sellers, who know which type of car they have. If potential sellers of good cars can get only $7,000 for a car that they know to be worth $10,000 on average, then many will choose not to sell their cars or will sell them to friends or relatives. But sellers of lemons will find $7,000 an attractive price, since their cars are worth only $4,000 on average. As a result, the proportion of good cars on the market will fall and the proportion of lemons will increase.

As buyers come to realize that the mix has shifted toward lemons, they will reduce the amount they are willing to pay for a car of unknown quality. As the market price of used cars falls, potential sellers of good cars become even more reluctant to sell at such a low price, so the proportion of lemons increases, leading to lower prices still. The process could continue until there were few good cars sold on the open market. More generally, *when sellers have better information about a product's quality than buyers do, lower-quality products tend to dominate the market.*

Hidden Actions: The Principal-Agent Problem

In this age of specialization, there are many tasks we do not do for ourselves because others do them better and because others have a lower opportunity cost of time. Suppose your objective is to get your car repaired, but you have little knowledge of cars. The mechanic you hire may have other objectives, such as maximizing on-the-job leisure or maximizing the garage's revenue. But the mechanic's actions are hidden from you. Even though your car may have only a loose wire, the mechanic could inflate the bill by charging you for services you did not really need or for services that were not performed. This asymmetric information problem occurs because one side of a transaction can pursue *hidden actions* that affect the other side. When buyers have difficulty monitoring and evaluating the quality of goods or services purchased, some suppliers may tend to substitute poor-quality resources or exercise less diligence in providing the service.

The problem that arises from hidden actions is called the **principal-agent problem,** which describes a relationship in which one party, known as the **principal,** makes a contractual agreement with another party, known as the **agent,** in the expectation that the agent will act on behalf of the principal. *The problem arises when the goals of the agent are incompatible with those of the principal and when the agent can pursue hidden actions.* You could confront a principal-agent problem when you deal with a doctor, lawyer, TV repairer, or financial advisor, to name a few. More generally, any employer-employee relationship could potentially be a source of a principal-agent problem. The owners of a corporation are the principals and the managers are the agents. Again, the problem arises because the agent's objectives are not the same as the principal's *and* because the agent's actions are hidden. Note that not all principal-agent relationships pose a problem. For example, when you get your hair cut, there are no hidden actions, and you have the ability to judge the result; thus, you can tip accordingly.

Principal-agent problem A situation in which the agent's objectives differ from those of the principal and the agent can pursue hidden actions

Principal A person who enters into a contractual agreement with an agent in the expectation that the agent will act on behalf of the principal

Agent A person who performs work or provides a service on behalf of another person, the principal

Adverse Selection

When those on the informed side of the market self-select in a way that harms the uninformed side of the market, the problem is one of **adverse selection.** In our earlier example, car sellers, the informed parties, self-select—that is, decide whether to offer their cars for sale—in a way that increases the number of lemons for sale. Because of this adverse selection, car buyers, the uninformed side of the market, end up trading primarily with owners of lemons—exactly the group buyers do not want to deal with.

Adverse selection A situation in which those on the informed side of the market self-select in a way that harms the uninformed side of the market

Adverse selection also creates problems in insurance markets. For example, from an insurance company's point of view, ideal candidates for health insurance are those who lead long, healthy lives, then die peacefully in their sleep. But many people are poor risks for health insurers because of hidden characteristics (bad genes) or hidden actions (smoking and drinking excessively, getting exercise only on trips to the refrigerator, and thinking a seven-course meal consists of some beef jerky and a six-pack of beer). In the insurance market, it is the buyers, not the sellers, who have more information about characteristics and actions that predict their likely need for insurance in the future.

If the insurance company has no way of discriminating among applicants, it must charge the same to those who are poor health risks as to those who are good health risks. This average rate is attractive to poor health risks, but the rate will seem too high to good health risks, some of whom will choose to self-insure. As the number of healthy people who self-insure increases, the insurance pool becomes less healthy on average, so rates must rise, making insurance even less attractive to healthy people. Because of adverse selection, insurance buyers tend to be less healthy than the population as a whole.

Moral Hazard

The insurance problem is compounded by the fact that, once people buy insurance, their behavior may change in a way that increases the probability that a claim will be made. Some people with health insurance may take less care of their health than people without it. This same problem affects other types of insurance such as fire, auto, and theft insurance. For example, after buying theft insurance, people may take less care of their valuables. This incentive problem is referred to as *moral hazard*. **Moral hazard** occurs when an individual's behavior changes in a way that increases the likelihood of an unfavorable outcome.

Moral hazard A situation in which one party to a contract has an incentive after the contract is made to alter behavior in a way that harms the other party to the contract

More generally, *moral hazard results when those on one side of a transaction have an incentive to shirk their responsibilities because the other side is unable to observe them.* The responsibility could be to repair a car or to safeguard valuables. Both the mechanic and the policy buyer may take advantage of the ignorant party. In the car-repair example, the mechanic is the agent; in the insurance example, the policy buyer is the principal. Thus, moral hazard arises on the part of the party that can undertake hidden action; this could be either the agent or the principal, depending on the circumstance.

Coping with Asymmetric Information

There are ways of reducing the consequences of asymmetric information. An incentive structure or an information-revealing system can be developed to reduce the problems associated with the lopsided availability of information. For example, some auto-repair garages provide written estimates before a job is done and return the defective parts to the customer as evidence that the repair was necessary and was completed. Consumers often get multiple estimates for major expenditures and may seek second and third opinions on medical procedures. And several states have passed "lemon laws" that offer compensation to buyers of new or used cars that turn out to be lemons. Used-car dealers also usually offer a warranty to reduce the risk of getting stuck with a lemon.

Health insurance companies deal with adverse selection and moral hazard in a variety of ways. Most require applicants to take a physical exam and to answer questions about their medical histories. A policy often covers all those in a group, such as all company employees, not just those who would otherwise self-select. Such group policies avoid the problem of adverse selection. Insurers reduce moral hazard by making the policyholder pay, say, the first $250 of a claim as a "deductible" and by requiring the policyholder to pay a certain percentage of a claim. Also, the premiums on some automobile and theft policies go up as more claims are filed.

Asymmetric Information in Labor Markets

In our market analysis of the supply and demand for particular kinds of labor, we typically assumed that workers are identical. In equilibrium, each worker in a particular labor market is assumed to be paid the same wage, a wage that for resource price takers is equal to the marginal revenue product of the last unit of labor hired. Here we talk about the problems arising from differences in the ability of workers.

Differences in worker productivity present no particular problem as long as these differences can be readily observed by the employer. If the productivity of each particular worker is easily quantified through a measure such as the quantity of oranges picked, the number of papers typed, or the number of encyclopedias sold, that measure itself can and does serve as the basis for pay. But because production often takes place through the coordinated efforts of several workers, the employer cannot attribute specific outputs to each particular worker. Because information about each worker's marginal productivity is hard to come by, employers usually pay workers by the hour rather than keep track of each worker's contribution to total output.

Often the pay is some combination of an hourly rate and incentive pay linked to a measure of productivity. For example, a sales representative typically receives a base salary plus a commission tied to the amount sold. At times, the task of evaluating performance is left to the consumer rather than to the firm. Workers who provide personal services, such as waiters and waitresses, barbers and beauticians, and bellhops, get paid partly in tips. Since these services are by definition "personal," customers are in the best position to judge the quality of service and to tip accordingly.

Adverse Selection Problems in Labor Markets

An adverse selection problem arises in the labor market when labor suppliers have better information about their own productivities than employers do, because the abilities of workers are not observable prior to employment. Before the individual is hired, that worker's true abilities—motivation, work habits, skills, ability to get along with others, and the like—are *hidden characteristics.*

Suppose an employer wants to hire a program coordinator for a new project, a job that calls for imagination, organizational skills, and the ability to work independently. The employer would like to attract the most qualified person in the market, but the qualities demanded are not directly observable. The employer offers a market wage for such a position. Individual workers have a good idea of their own intelligence and creativity and are able to evaluate this wage in view of their own abilities and opportunities. Talented people will find that the wage is below the true value of their abilities and will be less inclined to apply for the job. Less-talented individuals, however, will find that the offered wage exceeds their marginal productivity, so they will be more likely to seek the job. Because of adverse selection, the employer ends up with a pool of applicants of below-average ability. In a labor market with hidden characteristics, employers might be better off offering a higher wage. The higher the wage, the more attractive the market is to more qualified workers. Paying higher wages to attract and retain more productive workers is called paying **efficiency wages,** an idea also discussed in macroeconomics.

Efficiency wage theory **The idea that offering high wages attracts a more talented labor pool, making it easier for firms to attract and retain more productive workers.**

Signaling and Screening

The side of the market with hidden characteristics and hidden actions has an incentive to say the right thing. For example, a job applicant might say, "Hire me because I am hard-working, reliable, prompt, highly motivated, and just an all-around great employee." Or a producer might say, "At Ford, quality is job one." But such direct claims of quality appear self-serving and therefore are not necessarily believable. Yet both sides of the market have an incentive to develop credible ways of communicating reliable information.

Therefore, adverse selection may give rise to **signaling,** which is the attempt by the informed side of the market to communicate information that the other side would find valuable. Consider signaling in the job market. Because the true requirements for many jobs are qualities that are unobservable on a résumé or in an interview, the job applicant offers evidence of the unobservable

Signaling **Using a proxy measure to communicate information about unobservable characteristics**

features by relying on proxy measures, such as years of education or college grades. A proxy measure is called a *signal,* which is an observable indicator of some hidden characteristic. A signal is sent by the informed side of the market to the uninformed side and may serve as a useful way of sorting out applicants, as long as the signal is a true indicator of the hidden characteristic of interest.

In order to identify the best workers, employers try to *screen* applicants. **Screening** is the attempt by the uninformed side of the market to uncover the relevant but hidden characteristics of the informed party. An initial screen might be to check each résumé for spelling and typographical errors. Although not important in themselves, such errors indicate a lack of attention to detail. The uninformed party must find signals that less-productive individuals will have more difficulty acquiring. A signal that can be sent with equal ease or difficulty by all workers, regardless of their productivity, does not provide a useful way of screening applicants. But if, for example, more productive workers find it easier to succeed in college than do less-productive workers, a good college record is a measure worth using to screen workers. In this case, education may be important, not so much because of its effects on a worker's productivity, but because it enables employers to distinguish among types of workers. To summarize, an employer often cannot directly measure the productivity of job applicants, so the employer must rely on some proxy to screen applicants. Ideally, this proxy is highly correlated with productivity.

The problems of adverse selection, signaling, and screening are discussed in the following case study of McDonald's.

Screening The process used by employers to select the most qualified workers based on readily observable characteristics, such as level of education

CASE STUDY

The Reputation of a Big Mac

Location:

To learn about owning a Mc-Donald's franchise, visit "Franchising Information," maintained by McDonald's Corporation (http://www.mcdonalds.com/a__system/franchise). For more about franchises in general, browse the "Franchise Handbook: On-Line," maintained by Enterprise Magazines, Inc. (http://www.franchise1.com/).

McDonald's has over 15,000 restaurants and is opening more than 500 a year. The secret to their success is that customers can count on product consistency whether they are buying a Big Mac in Anchorage, Moscow, or Singapore.

Since its founding in 1955, McDonald's has grown so fast because it has attracted competent and reliable franchise owners and has provided these owners with appropriate incentives and constraints.

To avoid adverse selection, McDonald's seldom advertises for franchisees (though it does have a web page providing franchising information). Still, each year on average, more than 10 people apply for each new franchise. To be granted an interview, the applicant must show sufficient financial resources and adequate business experience. Those selected after a rigorous screening process must come up with a security deposit and must complete the 12- to 18-month training program involving classroom learning plus 20 hours per week at an established McDonald's. During this time, the individual is paid nothing, not even expenses. Some trainees, after completing thousands of hours without pay, are rejected for a franchise. After completing the program to the satisfaction of the corporation, applicants may wait up to three years to open their own restaurants. Once the restaurant opens, a franchisee is required to work full-time in its daily operation. Franchisees are also encouraged to become involved in community service.

Franchisees make a huge commitment of time and money. About $75,000 toward the $400,000 cost of a new franchise must come from the franchisee's own resources, not from borrowed funds. The franchisee cannot sell the restaurant without prior approval and the company retains the right of first refusal. Any buyer must have company approval and must complete the same training program as all other franchisees.

Since each franchisee gets a large share of the restaurant's operating profit, there is a strong incentive to be efficient. As a further reward, successful operators may apply for and get additional restaurants. If all goes well, the franchise is valid for 20 years and renewable after that, but it can be canceled *at any time* if the restaurant fails the company's standards of quality, pricing, cleanliness, hours of operation, and so on. Thus, the franchisee is bound to the company by highly specific investments, and the loss of a franchise could represent the loss of the individual's life savings. In selecting and monitoring franchises, McDonald's has successfully addressed problems stemming from hidden characteristics and hidden actions.

Source: D. L. Noren, "The Economics of the Golden Arches," *American Economist* (Fall 1990): pp. 60–64; Jeffrey Tannenbaum, "McDonald's Franchise Applicant Seeks Pay for Training," *The Wall Street Journal,* 14 March 1994; Charlene Soloman, "McDonald's Links Franchisees to the Community," *Personnel Journal* (March 1993); and an Internet profile of McDonald's Corporation at http://www.hoovers.com/fortune.html.

CONCLUSION

The firm has evolved through a natural selection process as the form of organization that minimizes both transaction and production costs. According to this theory of natural selection, those forms of organization that are most efficient will be selected by the economic system for survival. Attributes that yield an economic profit will thrive, and those that do not will fall by the wayside. The form of organization selected may not be optimal in the sense that it cannot be improved upon, but it will be the most efficient of those that have been tried. If there is a way to organize production that is more efficient than the firm, some entrepreneur will stumble upon it one day and will be rewarded with greater profit. Thus, the improvement may not be the result of any conscious design. Once a more efficient way of organizing production is uncovered, others will imitate the successful innovation.

Problems created by asymmetric information are not reflected in the simple account of how markets work. In conventional demand-and-supply analysis, trades occur in impersonal markets, and the buyer has no special concern about who is on the selling side. But with asymmetric information, the mix and characteristics of the other side of the market become important. When the problem of adverse selection is severe enough, some markets may cease to function. Market participants try to overcome the limitations of asymmetric information by signaling, screening, and trying to be quite explicit about the terms of the transaction.

SUMMARY

1. According to Ronald Coase, firms exist because production often can be accomplished more efficiently through the hierarchy of the firm than through transactions carried out independently by consumers in markets. Because production requires the extensive coordination of transactions among many resource owners, all this activity can usually be carried out more efficiently under the direction of a manager in a firm than by consumers' specifying detailed performance contracts with many separate suppliers.

2. The extent to which a firm integrates vertically will depend on both the transaction and the production costs of economic activity. Other things constant, the firm is more likely to buy a component part rather than produce it if (1) the item can be purchased for less than it would cost the firm to produce, (2) the item is well defined and its quality is easily observable, and (3) there are a large number of suppliers of the item. Economies of scope exist when it is cheaper to combine two or more kinds of products in one firm than to produce them in separate firms.

3. A buyer acquires additional information as long as the marginal benefit exceeds the marginal cost of searching for that information. In equilibrium, the marginal cost of information equals the marginal benefit. Because information is costly, the same good may sell for different prices across sellers.

4. Asymmetric information occurs when one side of the market is better informed about the quality of a product than the other side. The uninformed party may not know about hidden characteristics or about hidden actions. Because of the problem of adverse selection, those on the uninformed side of the market may find they are dealing with exactly the wrong people.

5. When the productivity of potential employees is not directly observable, employers sometimes try to screen workers based on some signal that appears to be related to productivity, such as education or college grades. This system of screening applicants is effective as long as more productive workers find it easier to send the correct signal than less-productive workers do.

QUESTIONS AND PROBLEMS

1. **(Coase's Theory of the Firm)** Explain Ronald Coase's theory of why firms exist.

2. **(Principal and Agent)** Discuss the meaning of the principal-agent problem. Indicate which is the principal and which is the agent in each of the following relationships.
   a. A firm that produces export goods and the export management company that helps market its goods.
   b. The management of a firm and its stockholders.
   c. A homeowner and the plumber hired to make repairs.
   d. A dentist and his or her patient.
   e. An employee pension management firm and the company using its services.

3. **(Boundaries of the Firm)** Define vertical integration. What are the factors that a firm should consider in determining the amount of vertical integration?

4. **(Internal Production Versus the Market)** Ashland Oil, Inc., is an oil refiner that buys its crude oil in the marketplace. Larger oil companies, such as Texaco, have their own crude oil production facilities. How would you explain this situation?

5. **(Rationale for the Firm)** Complete each of the following sentences:
   a. The notion that a firm has easy access to all the information required to make decisions, such as the marginal products and prices of all inputs, is known as the _____ characterization of the firm.
   b. The particular kind of contractual relationship that occurs within a firm is known as the _____ _____.
   c. Internal production and _____ are alternative ways of organizing transactions.
   d. When it is cheaper to combine the production of two or more different goods in one firm rather than to produce them separately, production of the goods exhibits _____.

6. **(Contracting)** When you deposit money in a bank, you are really lending the money to firms and home purchasers who borrow from the bank. The bank typically makes a profit on this transaction. What is it doing for you? That is, what keeps you from lending your money directly to the borrowers without paying the "middleman"?

7. **(Bounded Rationality)** Distinguish between economies of scale and economies of scope. How does the

technology of information processing influence both economies of scale and economies of scope?

8. **(Optimal Search with Imperfect Information)** The following questions are based on the accompanying graph:
   a. Identify the two curves shown on the graph, explaining the upward or downward slope of each.
   b. Explain why curve A intersects the horizontal axis at point *c*.
   c. What is the significance of quantity *d*?
   d. What does point *e* represent?

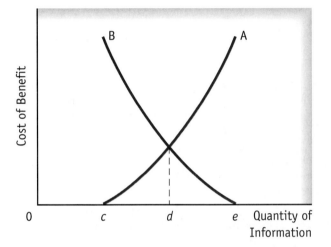

9. **(Optimal Search with Imperfect Information)** Fifty years ago, people often shopped by mail using catalogs from large mail-order houses. In the last few years, catalog shopping has again become a widely used method of buying. What reasons can you suggest for the resurgence of this form of shopping?

10. **(Signaling)** Give an example of signaling for each of the following situations involving information asymmetry.
    a. Choosing a doctor.
    b. Applying to graduate school.

11. **(Economies of Scope)** What are some reasons related to economies of scope that firms produce different product lines? Can you think of any reasons *unrelated* to production costs to produce different products?

12. **(Optimal Search with Imperfect Information)** Indicate whether each of the following would increase or decrease the marginal benefits or marginal costs of searching for additional information. What would be the resulting impact on the optimal quantity of information?

a. The less expensive the commodity that the consumer is buying.
b. A drop in the consumer's income.
c. An improvement in the technology of gathering and transmitting information.

13. **(Winner's Curse)** What are the circumstances in which the winner's curse applies? What is the winner's curse?

14. **(Asymmetric Information)** Define asymmetric information. Distinguish between hidden characteristics and hidden actions. Which type of asymmetric information contributes to the principal-agent problem?

15. **(Adverse Selection and Moral Hazard)** Describe the problems faced by health insurance companies as a result of adverse selection and moral hazard. How might the insurance companies try to reduce these problems?

16. **(Signaling and Screening)** What roles are played by signaling and screening in a labor market with asymmetric information?

17. **(The Trend Toward Outsourcing)** In the movement to downsize government, advocates often recommend turning over some government services to private firms hired by the government. What are the potential benefits and costs of such outsourcing?

18. **(The Reputation of a Big Mac)** Explain how the time and financial requirements involved in obtaining a McDonald's franchise bear on the hidden characteristics problem. Why would each franchise owner have a vested interest in the maintenance of application standards for new franchise owners?

Using the Internet

19. Visit "The Outsourcing Institute's On-line Library," maintained by the Outsourcing Institute, and examine the "Case Studies" (**http://www.outsourcing. com/library/library.html**). Choose a recent case study and answer the following questions.
    a. What functions of the firm have been outsourced? What outsourcing services have been supplied to the firm?
    b. Why were these functions outsourced?
    c. What are the overall benefits/drawbacks of the outsourcing?

29

Economic Regulation and Antitrust Activity

It has been said that business-people praise competition but love monopoly. They praise competition because it harnesses the diverse and often conflicting objectives of various market participants and channels them into the efficient production of goods and services. And competition does this "as if by an invisible hand." They love monopoly because it provides the surest path to economic profit in the long run—and, after all, profit is the name of the game. The fruits of monopoly are so tempting that firms sometimes try to eliminate the competition or to conspire with them. As Adam Smith remarked more than 200 years ago, "People of the same trade seldom meet together, even for merriment or diversion, but the conversation ends in a conspiracy against the public, or in some contrivance to raise prices."

The tendency of firms to seek monopolistic advantage is understandable, but the pursuit of monopoly is often at odds with achieving the most efficient use of the economy's resources. Public policy can play a role by promoting competition in those markets where competition seems desirable and reducing the harmful consequences of monopolistic behavior in those markets where the output can be most efficiently produced by one or a few firms.

This chapter discusses the ways in which government regulates business. As you will see, there is some disagreement about what government is doing and what it should be doing. Topics discussed in this chapter include:

- Market power
- Regulating natural monopolies
- Theories of economic regulation

- Deregulation
- Antitrust activity
- Competitive trends of the economy

BUSINESS BEHAVIOR AND PUBLIC POLICY

You'll recall that a monopolist supplies a product with no close substitutes and so can charge a higher price than would prevail if the market were more competitive. When a few firms account for most of the sales in a market, those firms are sometimes able to coordinate their actions, either explicitly or implicitly, to approximate the behavior of a monopolist. This ability of one or more firms to maintain a price above the competitive level is termed **market power.** The presumption is that a monopoly or firms acting together as a monopoly will restrict output and charge a higher price than competitive firms. With output restrictions, the marginal benefit of the final unit produced exceeds its marginal cost, so social welfare could be increased by expanding output. By failing to expand output to the point where marginal benefit equals marginal cost, monopoly misallocates resources.

Market power The ability of one or more firms to maintain a price above the competitive level

Other distortions have also been associated with monopolies. For example, because monopolies are insulated from competition, many critics argue that they are not as innovative as aggressive competitors would be. Moreover, because of their size and economic importance, monopolies have been said to exert a disproportionate influence on the political system, which they use to protect and even strengthen their monopoly power.

Government Regulation of Business

There are three kinds of government policies designed to alter or control firm behavior: social regulation, economic regulation, and antitrust activity. **Social regulation** consists of government measures designed to improve health and safety, such as control over unsafe working conditions and dangerous products. **Economic regulation** is concerned with controlling the price, the output, the entry of new firms, and the quality of service *in industries in which monopoly appears inevitable or even desirable.* The regulation of natural monopolies, such as electrical utilities, is an example of this type of regulation. Several other industries such as land and air transportation have also been regulated, for reasons that will be discussed later in this chapter. Economic regulation is carried out by various regulatory bodies at the federal, state, and local levels. **Antitrust activity** attempts to prohibit firm behavior aimed at monopolizing or cartelizing markets where competition is desirable. Antitrust activity is pursued in the courts by government attorneys and by individual firms that charge other firms with violations of antitrust laws. Both economic regulation and antitrust activity will be examined in this chapter. Federal spending on economic regulation and antitrust activity has increased on average about 7 percent per year since 1970, after adjusting for inflation.[1] The first type of economic regulation we consider is the regulation of natural monopolies.

Social regulation Government measures aimed at improving health and safety

Economic regulation Government measures aimed at controlling prices, output, market entry and exit, and product quality in situations in which, because of economies of scale, average production costs are lowest when the market is served by only one or a few firms

Antitrust activity Government activity aimed at preventing monopoly and fostering competition

REGULATING NATURAL MONOPOLIES

Because of economies of scale, natural monopolies have a downward-sloping long-run average-cost curve over the entire range of market demand. This

---

1   Computed based on data compiled by Melinda Warren and James Lis, "Regulatory Standstill: Analysis of the 1993 Federal Budget," Center for the Study of American Business, Occasional Paper 105, 1992.

means that the lowest average cost is achieved when one firm serves the entire market. As mentioned earlier, electricity is an example of a good provided by a natural monopoly. The cost per household is lowest when a single company "wires" the community. If two electric companies both strung their own wires through town, the average cost per household would be higher.

Unregulated Profit Maximization

Exhibit 1 shows the demand and cost conditions for a natural monopoly. A natural monopoly usually faces large capital costs, such as those associated with laying the tracks for a railroad, putting a satellite in orbit, building a nuclear power plant, installing a natural gas pipeline, or stringing the wires to transmit electricity, local phone service, or cable TV signals. Because of heavy capital outlays, average cost tends to fall as production increases, so the average cost curve slopes downward over a broad range of output. In this situation, the average cost of production is minimized by having only one producer.

We know that a monopolist, if unregulated, will choose the price-quantity combination that maximizes profit. In Exhibit 1, the monopolist maximizes

EXHIBIT 1   **Regulating the Natural Monopoly**

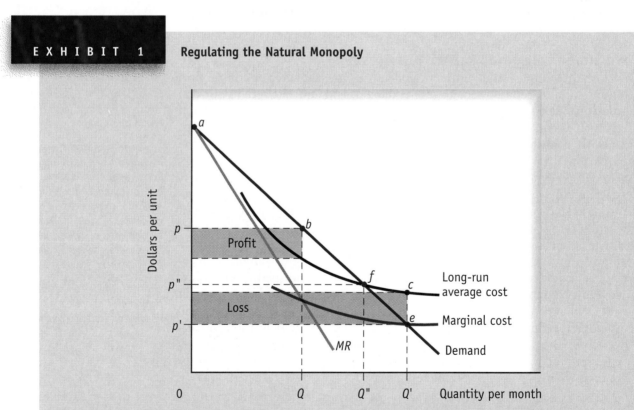

In a natural monopoly, the long-run average-cost curve slopes downward at its point of intersection with the market demand curve. The unregulated firm produces output Q (where marginal cost equals marginal revenue) and charges price p. This situation is inefficient because price exceeds marginal cost. To obtain the efficient level of output, government could regulate the monopolist's price. At price p', the monopoly would produce output Q'—an efficient solution. However, at that price and quantity, the firm would suffer a loss and require a subsidy. As an alternative, the government could set a price of p''. The monopoly would produce output Q''—an inefficient level. Since p'' equals the average cost, the firm would earn a normal profit and no subsidy would be required.

profit by producing where marginal cost equals marginal revenue, which occurs at output level Q. The monopolist will charge price p and earn the economic profit identified by the blue shaded rectangle. The problem is that the monopolist's choice of price and output is inefficient in terms of social welfare: consumers pay a price that is higher than the marginal cost of producing the good. Because the price, which is consumers' marginal valuation of output, exceeds the marginal cost, there is an underallocation of resources to the production of this good. Economic welfare would improve if output were to expand, because at present the marginal valuation of additional output exceeds the marginal cost of that output.

Government has four options for dealing with natural monopolies. First, it can do nothing. If left alone, monopolists will maximize profits, as at price p in Exhibit 1. Second, the government can sell the monopoly rights in this market, such as the rights to run concession stands at the municipal stadium or the regional airport. The winning bidder would still maximize profit at price p in Exhibit 1, but at least the winning monopolist would pay for the privilege. Third, the government can own and operate monopolies, as it does the Tennessee Valley Authority and many urban electricity and transit systems. And fourth, government can *regulate* privately operated monopolies, as it does most electrical utilities and local phone services. Government-owned or -regulated industries have come to be known as *public utilities*. The focus here will be on government regulation rather than government ownership, though the issues discussed are similar whether the government operates as a monopoly or regulates the monopoly. Many facets of natural monopolies have been regulated, but the object of regulation that captures the most attention is the rates, or prices, these utilities can charge.

Setting Price Equal to Marginal Cost

Let's assume that government regulators decide to make the monopolist produce at the level of output that is allocatively efficient—that is, where price, or marginal value, equals marginal cost. That price and output combination is depicted as point e in Exhibit 1, where price equals marginal cost, yielding a price p' and quantity Q'. Consumers will clearly prefer this outcome because the price is lower than when the monopolist is free to maximize profit. The consumer surplus, a measure of consumers' net gain from this market, increases from triangle abp with profit maximization profit to aep' with regulation.

Notice, however, that the monopolist now has a problem. At output level Q', the regulated price, p', is below the firm's average total cost, identified as point c. Rather than earning a profit, the monopolist now suffers a loss, identified by the red shaded rectangle. *Forcing the natural monopolist to produce where marginal cost equals price results in an economic loss.* In the long run, the monopolist would go out of business rather than suffer such losses.

Subsidizing the Natural Monopolist

How can regulators encourage the monopolist to stay in business and yet produce where marginal cost equals price? One way is for the government to compensate the monopolist for the losses—to *subsidize* the firm so that it earns a normal profit. Bus and subway fares are typically set below the average cost of providing the service; the difference is made up through a government subsidy.

For example, in 1996 the Washington, D.C., subway system was to receive over $260 million in subsidies from the federal government; Amtrak also receives substantial federal subsidies. One problem with the subsidy solution is that, to provide the subsidy, the government must raise taxes, borrow more, or forgo spending in some other area.

Setting Price Equal to Average Cost

Although some public utilities are subsidized, most are not. Instead, the regulators attempt to establish a price that will provide the monopolist with a "fair return." Recall that the average total cost curve includes a normal profit. Thus, *setting price equal to average total cost* provides a normal, or "fair," profit for the monopolist. In Exhibit 1, the demand curve and the average cost curve intersect at point *f*, yielding a price of *p″* and a quantity of *Q″*. Such a price will allow the monopolist to stay in business without a subsidy.

Setting price equal to average total cost enhances economic welfare relative to the unregulated situation, but the regulated monopolist would rather earn an economic profit. If given no other choice, however, the monopolist will continue to operate with a normal profit, since that is what could be earned if the resources were redirected to their most profitable alternative use. Still, the marginal value that consumers attach to output level *Q″* exceeds the marginal cost of that output level. Therefore, social welfare could be enhanced by expanding output until consumers' marginal value equals the marginal cost of production at *e*.

The Regulatory Dilemma

Setting price equal to marginal cost yields the *socially optimal* allocation of resources because *the marginal cost of producing the last unit sold equals the consumers' marginal value of that last unit*. Yet with this pricing policy, the monopolist will face recurring losses unless a subsidy is provided. These losses disappear if price is set equal to average cost, thereby ensuring the monopolist a normal profit. But output is still less than would be socially optimal. Thus, the dilemma facing regulators is whether to require a price equal to marginal cost, which is socially optimal but would require a subsidy, or to allow the monopolist to break even by setting price equal to average cost. There is no right answer. Compared to the outcome without regulation, either approach reduces price, increases output, increases consumer surplus, eliminates economic profit, and increases social welfare.

Although Exhibit 1 neatly lays out the options, regulators usually face an unclear picture of things. Demand and costs can only be estimated, and the regulated firm may not always be completely forthcoming with cost information. For example, a utility may overstate its costs so it can charge a higher price.

ALTERNATIVE THEORIES OF ECONOMIC REGULATION

Why does government regulate certain markets? Why not let market forces allocate resources? There are two views of government regulation. The first view has been implicit in the discussion thus far—namely, that economic regulation is in the *public interest*. Economic regulation is designed to promote social welfare by controlling the price and output when the market is most efficiently served by one or just a few firms. A second view of economic regulation is that it is not in the public, or consumer, interest, but rather is in the *special interest* of producers. According to this view, *well-organized producer groups expect to profit from economic regulation and are able to persuade public officials to impose the restrictions existing producers find attractive, such as limiting entry into the industry or preventing competition among existing firms.* Individual producers have more to gain or lose from regulation than do individual consumers; producers typically are also better organized than consumers and therefore better able to bring about regulations that are favorable to them.

Producers Have a Special Interest in Economic Regulation

To understand how producer interests could influence public regulation, consider the last time you had your hair cut. Most states regulate the training and licensing of hair professionals. If any new regulations affecting the profession are proposed, such as entry restrictions or training requirements, who do you suppose has more interest in the outcome of that legislation, you or a person who cuts hair for a living? *Producers have a strong interest in matters that affect their specialized source of income, so they play a disproportionately large role in trying to influence such legislation.* If there are public hearings on haircut regulations, the industry will provide expert witnesses while consumers ignore the proceedings.

As a consumer, you do not specialize in getting haircuts. You purchase haircuts, socks, soft drinks, notebooks, and thousands of other goods and services. You have no *special interest* in legislation affecting hair cutting. Some critics argue that because of this asymmetry in the interests of producers and consumers, business regulations often favor producer interests rather than consumer interests. Well-organized producer groups, as squeaky wheels in the legislative system, receive the most grease in the form of favorable regulations.

Legislation favoring producer groups is usually introduced under the guise of advancing consumer interests. Producer groups may argue that unbridled competition in their industry would lead to results that are undesirable for consumers. For example, the alleged problem of "cutthroat" competition among taxi drivers has led to regulations that fix rates and limit the number of taxis in most large metropolitan areas. Or, regulation may appear under the guise of quality control, as in the case of state control of professional groups such as barbers, doctors, and lawyers, in which case regulations are viewed as necessary to keep unlicensed "quacks" out of these professions.

The special-interest theory may be valid even when the initial intent of the legislation is in the consumer interest. Over time, the regulatory machinery may begin to act more in accord with the special interests of producers, because producers' political power and strong stake in the regulatory outcome lead them, in effect, to "capture" the regulating agency and prevail upon it to serve producers. This *capture theory* of regulation was best explained by George Stigler, a Nobel Prize winner formerly at the University of Chicago, who argued that "as a general rule, regulation is acquired by the industry and is designed and operated for its benefit."[2]

---

2   George Stigler, "The Theory of Economic Regulation," *The Bell Journal of Economics and Management Science* (Spring 1971): 3.

A more complex variant of the capture theory emphasizes the idea that industry members may not all be of one mind regarding the most favorable kind of regulation. For example, large retail stores might support measures that would be opposed by small retail stores; major trucking companies might choose different regulations than would independent truckers. Competing interest groups jockey with one another for the most favorable regulations. Thus, it is not simply a question of consumer interests versus producer interests, but rather of one producer's interest versus another producer's interest.[3]

Perhaps it would be useful at this point to discuss in some detail the direction that economic regulation and, more recently, deregulation have taken in particular industries. We will consider two extensive case studies of regulation and deregulation. The first examines the role of the Interstate Commerce Commission as a regulator of the railroads and trucking.

CASE STUDY ▤

Rail and Truck Regulation and Deregulation

Location:

Despite estimates that total deregulation of the trucking industry would save shippers $35–$40 billion, powerful unions like the International Brotherhood of Teamsters oppose deregulation for the disproportional burdens it would place on unionized truckers. To learn more about the union's perspective, visit the Teamsters Union (http://www.teamster.org/). For more about railroads, visit Conrail (http://www.conrail.com/).

The *Interstate Commerce Commission (ICC),* established in 1887 to regulate the railroads, was the first federal regulatory agency in this country. The major railroads supported formation of the ICC as a way to stabilize rates and reduce "cutthroat" competition by allocating business among the railroads. The ICC was also supposed to ensure that even small towns would receive railroad service. Thus, at the outset, railroad regulations had several objectives. In the 1930s, the railroads began to face vigorous competition from the emerging trucking industry. The railroads wanted to avoid competition with trucks, and in 1935 Congress authorized the ICC to regulate trucking as well. The intent of the regulation was to equalize the prices of the two kinds of transportation, so that the two would not compete directly on the basis of price.

Regulating Entry and Rates. The ICC was able to control the structure of the so-called ground transportation industry by regulating new entry, price competition, and shipping conditions. To control entry, the ICC decreed that no carrier could operate without a license, and it would not issue a new license unless the applicant could show that such entry was "necessary for the public convenience." Existing shippers blocked new entry, so few new licenses were granted. Recall that *the ability to exclude new entrants from a market is a prerequisite for, though not a guarantee of, long-run economic profit.* The ICC had control over shipping rates, but much of this power was relegated to rate-setting committees drawn from the rail and trucking industries, an arrangement that allowed industry members to fix prices legally. Any competitor that wished to charge a lower price had first to receive ICC permission. Because such rulings required hearings and often took up to a year to settle, the system discouraged price competition.

---

3   But just as producer groups may not represent a single interest, consumer groups may not either. For example, major users of electricity prefer rates that decline as usage increases, whereas smaller users prefer uniform rates regardless of usage. Residents of small communities view train service differently than do those from major metropolitan areas.

Regulating Trucking Services. The ICC also regulated the conditions of trucking services, including the kinds of products that could be hauled, the routes that could be taken, and even the number of cities that could be served along the way. The idea was to limit the versatility of trucks by treating them as if they ran on tracks, thereby reducing any advantage trucks had over trains. Truck routes operated on the "gateway" system, similar to railroad junction points. For example, a trucking firm with a license to ship between points A and B and between points B and C could haul from A to C only if it passed through point B first. Other rules allowed trucks to haul from A to B but not from B to A. So a truck could haul a load from St. Louis to Chicago but could not carry a return load. Such restrictions often required trucks to go hundreds of miles out of their way or to travel empty part of the time. Of course, all this added to trucking costs. Despite the higher cost of shipping created by regulation, *the ability of truckers to fix their prices and restrict entry generally ensured their profitability, because transportation services were much in demand and there were no close substitutes except for railroads.* In fact, "shipping rights," or the authority to haul particular goods between cities, became valuable and were bought and sold.

Resulting Inefficiencies. Scholars who examined the issue concluded that regulation kept trucking rates above the competitive level. Intercountry comparisons showed rates 75 percent higher in heavily regulated countries such as the United States and Germany than in unregulated or lightly regulated countries such as Great Britain, Belgium, and the Netherlands. As we have seen, the higher rates resulted in part from the production inefficiency caused by the regulations. Regulation also supported higher wages in the industry, particularly for the members of the truckers' union, the International Brotherhood of Teamsters. Because regulation strictly limited the entry of new firms and prohibited price competition between particular locations, trucking firms could comply with union demands for higher wages without fear of losing business to rivals that charged lower prices. Unionized truck drivers thereby captured some of the producer surplus that resulted from regulation.

Deregulation. During the 1970s, support grew for deregulation in a variety of industries. The Motor Carriers Act of 1980 began the deregulation of trucking. Not only was new entry allowed, but the restrictions on routes, commodities, and the like were reduced. The elimination of "gateways," one-way shipping, and other vestiges of a system aimed at treating trucks like trains reduced duplication and waste. During the first three years after deregulation, an estimated 10,000 small new trucking firms entered the industry. During the same period, trucking rates dropped by an average of 25 percent in inflation-adjusted dollars. Surveys indicated that service improved as well. Service to small communities increased and service complaints decreased.

Winners and Losers. Although consumers benefited from falling prices, deregulation also created some losers. Unionized truckers had been paid 50 percent more than comparable workers in other industries. In the wake of deregulation, Teamsters union members lost jobs, because the number of trucking firms doubled and most new entrants were nonunion. Union workers lost some of their wage premium, and the union share of the trucking work force dropped from

Rail and Truck Regulation and Deregulation
continued

Rail and Truck Regulation and Deregulation
continued

60 percent in 1979 to 28 percent in 1985. Another predictable effect of deregulation was a decline in the value of shipping rights. When entry restrictions were eliminated, their value just about disappeared.

Despite the clear efficiency gains from deregulation, the concentrated allocation of the losses to well-identified groups meant that deregulation measures would be resisted. The losers (owners of shipping rights, unionized truck drivers) were concentrated in well-defined groups and knew they were losers; the winners (purchasers of trucking services, consumers) were widely dispersed and often did not even know that they were winners. As a result, the ICC chairman, supported by the Teamsters union, was slow to push deregulation. In fact, there was so much internal strife within the ICC that the commission met infrequently during the 1980s. In the early 1990s, the Teamsters union was the biggest contributor to Congressional campaigns. Federal law still requires new carriers to apply for a "certificate of public convenience and necessity," and all rates must still be filed with the ICC. These controls create inefficiencies. For example, shipping jeans to Dallas from El Paso costs more than shipping them from Taiwan to Dallas. Studies indicate that complete federal and state deregulation would save shippers another $35 billion to $40 billion per year.

The Railroads and Cross-Subsidization. Deregulation may have promoted thriving competition in trucking, but the railroads faced bigger problems. One such problem was that regulations required them to provide service to remote and rural locations that might not otherwise receive train service based on market demand. The railroads were not allowed to drop unprofitable routes or services, so revenue from profitable routes was used to subsidize operations on unprofitable routes, a policy called **cross–subsidization.** This cross-subsidy from profitable to unprofitable routes contributed to the failure of some railroad companies.

Cross-subsidization A firm's use of revenues from profitable activities to support unprofitable activities

After several railroads in the Northeast went bankrupt, deregulation was introduced in 1980 to promote efficiency and stability in the industry. Railroads were allowed to abandon unprofitable routes, and as a result route mileage fell by 29 percent. The number of major railroads dropped from 37 to 14, employment declined by 52 percent, and labor productivity nearly doubled. For example, Conrail was formed in 1976 from the bankrupt Penn Central Railroad and other ailing Northeast railroads. Conrail went from 100,000 employees in 1976 to only 25,000 in 1992. Because of a greater ability to eliminate unprofitable routes and more aggressive efforts to reduce payroll costs, railroads have become more profitable. And despite the drop in the number of railroad companies, competition among remaining firms has forced down shipping rates in real terms.

Sources: A. F. Friedlaender, E. R. Berndt, and G. McCullough, "Governance Structure, Managerial Characteristics, and Firm Performance in the Deregulated Rail Industry," *Brookings Papers on Economic Activity: Microeconomics,* 1992: pp. 95–186; and Thomas Gale Moore, "Trucking Deregulation," *Fortune Encyclopedia of Economics,* D. R. Henderson, ed. (New York: Warner Books, 1993), pp. 433–37.

The next case study examines regulation and deregulation as they shaped the airline industry.

The interstate airline business was once closely regulated by the *Civil Aeronautics Board (CAB)*, established in 1938. Any potential entrant interested in serving an interstate route had to persuade the CAB that the route needed another airline, a task that proved impossible. During the 40 years prior to deregulation, more than 150 applications for long-distance routes were submitted by potential entrants, *but not a single new interstate airline was allowed*. The CAB also forced strict compliance with regulated prices. A request to lower prices on any route would result in a rate hearing, during which the request was scrutinized by both the CAB and competitors. In effect, the CAB had created a cartel that fixed prices among the 10 existing major airlines.

Although the CAB prohibited price competition in the industry, *nonprice competition flourished*. Airlines competed on the basis of the frequency of flights, the quality of meals, the width of the seats, even the friendliness of the staff. For example, American Airlines put Wurlitzer pianos in its jumbo jet lounges. United Airlines countered with wine tastings and guitarists. Such competition increased operating costs. Costs rose until firms in the industry earned only a normal rate of return. Thus, *air fares set above competitive levels, coupled with entry restrictions, were no guarantee of economic profit as long as airlines were free to compete in other ways, such as in the frequency of flights*. The CAB did not regulate airlines that flew *intrastate* routes. The record shows that fares on intrastate airlines were about 50 percent below fares on identical routes flown by regulated airlines. So regulated airlines were more costly to consumers.

Airline Deregulation. In 1978, despite opposition from the major airlines and relevant labor unions, Congress passed the Airline Deregulation Act, which reduced restrictions on price competition and on new entry. By 1990, airline fares in inflation-adjusted dollars were estimated to be 10 to 18 percent lower because of deregulation. The fall in fares led to a near-doubling of passenger miles flown. The savings to travelers are estimated to be in the range of $5 billion to $10 billion per year. The airlines could afford to lower fares because they became more productive by adding more seats to planes and filling a greater percentage of seats. The hub-and-spoke system developed under deregulation also allowed airlines to route planes more efficiently. Airline routes used to be straight lines from one city to another. Now they radiate like the spokes of a wagon wheel from a "hub" city. From 29 hub airports across the country, airlines send out planes along the spokes to the 400 commercial airports, then quickly bring them back to the hubs.

The insulation from price competition provided by regulation had allowed firms to pay higher wages than they would have in a more competitive industry. The Air Line Pilots Association, the union that represented pilots for all the major airlines prior to deregulation, had been able to negotiate extremely attractive wages for its members, annual wages that reached well into six digits for working less than two weeks a month (many pilots had so much free time, they pursued second careers). Just how attractive a pilot's position was became apparent after deregulation. America West Airlines, a nonunion employer that

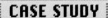

CASE STUDY

Airline Regulation and Deregulation

Location:

The Air Transport Association (ATA), founded in 1936, was the first, and today remains the only, trade organization for U.S. airlines. In that capacity, the ATA has played a role in all major government aviation decisions since its founding, including the creation of the Civil Aeronautics Board (CAB), the creation of the air traffic control system, and airline deregulation. Visit the ATA (**http://www.air-transport.org/**). Also visit the Federal Aviation Administration (FAA) (**http://www.faa.gov/**).

sprouted from deregulation, paid its pilots only $32,000 a year and required them to work 40 hours a week, performing dispatch and marketing tasks when they were not flying. Yet America West received more than 4,000 applications for its 29 pilot vacancies.

Some critics of deregulation were concerned that the government would lose the control it had, under regulation, over the quality and safety of airline service. Despite the demise of the CAB, however, the Federal Aviation Administration (FAA) still regulates the safety and quality of air service. Research indicates that between 1979 and 1990, accident rates declined by anywhere from 10 to 45 percent, depending on the specific measure used. What's more, the lower fares encouraged more people to fly rather than drive, thereby saving lives that would have been lost driving, which is less safe than flying.

Another concern was that smaller communities would no longer be served by a deregulated industry. This has not been a problem; commuter airlines have replaced major airlines in servicing smaller communities. Because of the hub-and-spoke system, the number of scheduled departures from smaller cities and rural communities has actually increased 35 to 40 percent.

Airport Capacity Has Restricted Competition. Competitive trends in the airline industry in recent years raise some troubling questions. Though airline traffic nearly doubled during the 1980s, no new airports were opened during the 1980s (though Denver has since opened a new airport) and the air traffic control system did not expand. Airports and air traffic control are provided by the government. Thus, *the government did not follow up deregulation with an expansion of airport capacity.* Consequently, departure gates and landing rights became the scarce resources in the industry. Those airlines unable to secure such facilities at major airports went out of business. Some argue that the major airlines have not pushed for an expansion of airport facilities because this additional capacity could encourage new entry and greater competition. Deregulation initially promoted a wave of new entry by such upstarts as People Express and New York Air. By the early 1990s, however, most of the new entrants had disappeared or had been absorbed by larger airlines. *New entrants could not acquire the necessary departure gates and landing rights at key airports.* The market share of the five largest airlines climbed from 63 percent before deregulation to 70 percent by the early 1990s, and most key airports came to be dominated by a single airline, such as American Airlines at Dallas/Fort Worth and USAir at Pittsburgh.

Sources: Nancy Rose, "Fear of Flying? Economic Analyses of Airline Safety," *Journal of Economic Perspectives* 6 (Spring 1992): pp. 75–94; "Business Is Picking Up for Airline Industry, Which Looks at Profit," *The Wall Street Journal,* 27 March 1995; and Alfred E. Kahn, "Airline Deregulation," *Fortune Encyclopedia of Economics,* D. R. Henderson, ed. (New York: Warner Books, 1993), pp. 379–84.

The course of regulation and deregulation raises some interesting questions about the true objective of regulation. Recall the competing views of regulation: one holds that regulation is in the public, or consumer, interest; the other holds that regulation is in the special, or producer, interest. In the ground transportation and airline industries, regulation appeared more in accord with producer interests, and producer groups fought deregulation.

This concludes our discussion of economic regulation, which tries to reduce the harmful consequences of monopolistic behavior in those markets where the output can be most efficiently produced by one or a few firms. We now turn to antitrust activity, which tries to promote competition in those markets where competition seems desirable.

ANTITRUST LAWS

Although competition typically ensures the most efficient use of the nation's resources, an individual firm would prefer to operate in a business climate that is more akin to monopoly. If left alone, some competing firms might try to create a monopolistic environment by driving competitors out of business, merging with competitors, or colluding with competitors. In the United States, *antitrust policy* is an attempt to curb these anticompetitive tendencies by (1) promoting the sort of market structure that will lead to greater competition and (2) reducing anticompetitive behavior. Antitrust laws attempt to promote socially desirable market performance.

Origins of Antitrust Policy

A variety of economic events that occurred in the last half of the 19th century created a political climate supportive of antitrust legislation. Perhaps the two most important events were (1) technological breakthroughs that led to more extensive use of capital and a larger optimal plant size in manufacturing industries, and (2) reduced transportation cost as railroads increased from 9,000 miles of road in 1850 to 167,000 miles in 1890. *Economies of scale in production and the cheaper cost of transporting goods extended the geographical reach of markets.* So firms grew larger and reached wider markets.

Declines in the national economy in 1873 and 1883, however, caused panics among these large manufacturers, who were now committed to large-scale production with heavy fixed costs. Their defensive reaction was to lower prices in an attempt to stimulate sales. Price wars erupted, creating economic turmoil. Firms desperately sought ways to stabilize their markets. One solution was for competing firms to form a *trust,* either by merging to form a single enterprise or by simply agreeing on a uniform pricing policy. Early trusts were formed in the sugar, tobacco, and oil industries. Although the activity of these early trusts is still a matter of debate today, they allegedly pursued anticompetitive practices to develop and maintain a dominant market position.

These practices provoked widespread criticism and earned creators of trusts the derisive title of "robber barons." Public sentiment lay on the side of the smaller competitors. Farmers, especially, resented the higher prices of manufactured goods, which resulted from the trusts' activity, particularly since farm prices were declining through the latter part of the 19th century. At the time, farming accounted for 40 percent of the U.S. workforce and thus had political clout. Eighteen states, primarily agricultural, enacted *antitrust* laws in the 1880s, prohibiting the formation of trusts. These laws, however, were largely ineffective because the trusts could simply move across state lines to avoid them.

Sherman Antitrust Act of 1890. In 1888, the major political parties put antitrust planks in their platforms. This consensus culminated in the passage of the *Sherman Antitrust Act* of 1890, the first national legislation against monopoly in the world. The law prohibited the creation of trusts, restraint of trade, and monopolization, though it failed to define what constitutes such activities. Enforcement of the law was hampered by its vague language.

Clayton Act of 1914. Ambiguous language in the Sherman Act let much anticompetitive activity slip by. The *Clayton Act* of 1914 was passed to outlaw certain practices not prohibited by the Sherman Act. For example, the Clayton Act prohibited *price discrimination* when this practice tends to create a monopoly. You'll recall that price discrimination is charging different customers different prices for the same good or charging the same customer different prices for different quantities of a good. The Clayton Act also prohibited *tying contracts* and *exclusive dealing* if they substantially lessened competition. **Tying contracts** require the buyer of one good to purchase another good as well. For example, a seller of a patented machine might require customers to purchase other supplies from the seller as part of the deal. **Exclusive dealing** occurs when a producer will sell a product only if the buyer agrees not to purchase from other manufacturers. For example, a computer-chip maker might sell chips to a computer maker only if the computer maker agrees not to purchase any chips elsewhere. The law also prohibited **interlocking directorates,** whereby the same individual serves on the boards of directors of competing firms. Finally, mergers through the acquisition of the stock of a competing firm were outlawed in cases in which the merger would substantially lessen competition. More on that later.

Tying contract An arrangement in which a seller of one good requires buyers to purchase other goods as well

Exclusive dealing The situation that occurs when a producer prohibits customers from purchasing from other sellers

Interlocking directorate An arrangement whereby one individual serves on the board of directors of competing firms

Federal Trade Commission Act of 1914. The *Federal Trade Commission (FTC)* was established in 1914 to help enforce antitrust laws. The commission consists of five full-time commissioners appointed by the president for 7-year terms and assisted by a staff of mostly lawyers and economists.

The Sherman, Clayton, and FTC acts provided the antitrust framework, a framework that has been clarified and embellished by subsequent amendments. A loophole in the Clayton Act was closed in 1950 with the passage of the *Celler-Kefauver Anti-Merger Act,* which prevents one firm from buying the assets of another firm if the effect is to reduce competition. This law prohibits both horizontal mergers and vertical mergers when these mergers would tend to reduce competition in a particular industry. For example, a merger of Coke and Pepsi would most likely be prohibited.

Antitrust Law Enforcement

Any law's effectiveness depends on the vigor and vigilance of enforcement. The pattern of antitrust enforcement goes something like this. Either the Antitrust Division of the Justice Department or the Federal Trade Commission charges a firm or group of firms with breaking the law. These government agencies are often acting on a complaint by a customer or a competitor. At that point, those charged with the wrongdoing may be able, without admitting guilt, to sign a **consent decree** whereby they agree not to continue doing whatever they had been charged with. If the charges are contested, evidence from both sides is presented in a court trial, and a decision is rendered by a judge. Certain decisions may be appealed all the way to the Supreme Court, and in such cases the high court may render new interpretations of existing law.

Consent decree A legal agreement through which the accused party, without admitting guilt, agrees to refrain in the future from certain illegal activity if the government drops the charges

Per Se Illegality and the Rule of Reason

The courts have interpreted antitrust laws in essentially two ways. One set of practices has been declared illegal **per se**—that is, without regard to economic rationale or consequences. For example, under the Sherman Act, all formal agreements among competing firms to fix prices, restrict output, or otherwise restrain the forces of competition are viewed as illegal *per se*. Under a per se rule, in order for the defendant to be found guilty, the government needs only to show that the offending practice took place; thus, the government needs only to examine the firm's behavior.

Another set of practices falls under the **rule of reason.** Here the courts engage in a broader inquiry into the facts surrounding the particular offense—namely, the reasons why the offending practices were adopted and the effect of these practices on competition. The rule of reason was first set forth in 1911, when the Supreme Court held that the Standard Oil Company had illegally monopolized the petroleum refining industry. Standard Oil allegedly had come to dominate 90 percent of the market by acquiring more than 120 former rivals and by implementing **predatory pricing** tactics to drive remaining rivals out of business, such as by temporarily selling below cost or dropping the price only in certain markets. In finding Standard Oil guilty, the Court focused on both its behavior and the market structure that resulted from Standard Oil's behavior, and the Court found that Standard Oil had behaved *unreasonably*.

But, using the rule of reason, the Court in 1920 found U.S. Steel not guilty of monopolization. In that case, the Court ruled that not every contract or combination in restraint of trade was illegal—only those that "unreasonably" restrained trade violated antitrust laws. The Court said that mere size was not an offense. Although U.S. Steel clearly possessed market power, the company was not in violation of antitrust laws because it had not unreasonably used that power. The Court changed that view 25 years later in reviewing the charges against the Aluminum Company of America (Alcoa). In a 1945 decision, the Supreme Court held that although a firm's conduct might be reasonable and legal, the mere possession of market power—Alcoa controlled 90 percent of the aluminum ingot market—violated the antitrust laws. Here the Court was using market structure rather than the firm's behavior as the test of legality.

Per se illegality A category of illegality in antitrust law, applied to business practices that are deemed illegal regardless of their economic rationale or their consequences

Rule of reason A principle used by a court to examine the reasons for certain business practices and their effects on competition before ruling on their legality

Predatory pricing Pricing tactics employed by a dominant firm to drive competitors out of business, such as temporarily selling below cost and dropping the price only in certain markets

Mergers and Public Policy

Much of what the Justice Department does is approve or disapprove of proposed mergers and acquisitions. In determining the possible detrimental effects a merger might have on competition, one important consideration is the effect of the merger on the level of concentration in that market. The measure of concentration employed until 1982 by the Justice Department was the four-firm **concentration ratio,** which is the sum of the percentage of market share of the top four firms in the market. For example, suppose that 44 firms supply a market. Also suppose that the top four firms account for 23 percent, 18 percent, 13 percent, and 6 percent, respectively, of the total market sales, and the remaining 40 firms account for 1 percent each. The four-firm concentration ratio is the sum of the shares of the top four firms in the market, which in this case is 60 percent. Though definitions are somewhat arbitrary, in markets where the four-firm concentration ratio is above 50 percent, that market may be oligopolistic.

Concentration ratio A measure of the market share of the largest firms in an industry

One problem with the concentration ratio is that it says nothing about the distribution of market share among the four firms. For example, the four-firm concentration ratio is 60 percent if the top four firms each have 15 percent of the market share or if one firm has 57 percent of the market and the next three have 1 percent each. Yet clearly an industry in which one firm captures over half the market is less competitive than an industry in which four firms of identical size compete.

To remedy this lack of precision with the concentration ratio, the Justice Department issued revised merger guidelines in 1982 and 1984 calling for the use of the **Herfindahl index,** which is calculated by squaring the percentage of market share of each firm in the market and then adding those squares. For example, if the industry consists of 100 firms of equal size, the Herfindahl index is 100 $[100 \times (1)^2]$. If the industry is a pure monopoly, the index is 10,000 $[1 \times (100)^2]$. The smaller the index, the more firms there are in the industry and the more equal in size the firms are.

The Herfindahl index provides more information than the four-firm concentration ratio because it gives greater weight to firms with larger market shares and uses all the data, not just information for the top four firms. The Herfindahl index for each of the three examples discussed (where the four-firm concentration ratio is 60 percent) is calculated in Exhibit 2. Although each example has the same four-firm concentration ratio, each yields a different Herfindahl index. Note that the index for Industry III is nearly triple that for the two other industries.

The Justice Department's guidelines also sort all mergers into two bins: horizontal mergers, which involve firms in the same market, and nonhorizontal mergers, which include all others. Of most interest for antitrust purposes are horizontal mergers, such as a merger between competing oil companies. The

Herfindahl index *The sum of the squared percentages of market share of all firms in an industry; a measure of the level of concentration in that industry*

EXHIBIT 2

Computation of the Herfindahl Index Based on Market Share in Three Industries

Firm	Industry I Market Share (percent)	Market Share Squared	Industry II Market Share (percent)	Market Share Squared	Industry III Market Share (percent)	Market Share Squared
A	23	529	15	225	57	3,249
B	18	324	15	225	1	1
C	13	169	15	225	1	1
D	6	36	15	225	1	1
Remaining 40 firms (at 1 percent each)	1 each	40	1 each	40	1 each	40
Four-firm concentration ratio	60		60		60	
Herfindahl index		1,098		940		3,292

Justice Department generally challenges any merger in an industry where two conditions are met: (1) the postmerger Herfindahl index would exceed 1,800 and (2) the merger would increase the index by more than 100 points. Mergers in an industry that would have a postmerger index of less than 1,000 are seldom challenged. Other factors, such as the ease of entry into the market, are considered for intermediate cases.

COMPETITIVE TRENDS IN THE U.S. ECONOMY

For years there has been concern about the sheer size of some firms because of the real or potential power these firms might exercise in both the economic and the political arenas. One way to measure the power of the largest corporations is to calculate the share of the nation's corporate assets controlled by the 100 largest firms. What percentage of the nation's manufacturing assets do the top 100 manufacturing companies own, and how has this share changed over time?

The largest 100 firms now control about half of all manufacturing assets in the United States, up from a 40 percent share after World War II. We should recognize, however, that size alone is not synonymous with market power. A very big firm, such as a large oil company, may face stiff competition from other very big oil companies; on the other hand, the only movie theater in an isolated community may be able to raise its price with less concern about competition.

Market Competition over Time

More important than the size of the largest firms in the nation is the market structure in each industry. Various studies have examined the level of competition and change in industry structure over the years. All have used some variation of the four-firm concentration ratio or the Herfindahl index as a point of departure, sometimes supplementing these measures with data from each industry. Among the most comprehensive of these studies is the research of William Shepherd, of the University of Massachusetts, who relied on many sources to determine the competitiveness of each industry in the U.S. economy.[4]

Shepherd sorted industries into four groups: (1) pure monopoly, in which a single firm controlled the entire market and was able to block entry; (2) dominant firm, in which a single firm had over half the market share and had no close rival; (3) tight oligopoly, in which the top four firms supplied more than 60 percent of the market, with stable market shares and evidence of cooperation; and (4) effective competition, in which firms in the industry exhibited low concentration, low entry barriers, and little or no collusion.

Exhibit 3 presents Shepherd's breakdown of all U.S. industries into the four categories for the years 1939, 1958, and 1988. The table shows a modest trend toward increased competition between 1939 and 1958, with the percentage of those industries rated as "effectively competitive" growing from 52.4 percent

---

4   William G. Shepherd, "Causes of Increased Competition in the U.S. Economy, 1939–1980," *Review of Economics and Statistics* 64 (November 1982); and William G. Shepherd, *The Economics of Industrial Organization,* 3rd ed. (Englewood Cliffs, N.J.: Prentice Hall, 1990), p. 15.

EXHIBIT 3   Competitive Trends in the U.S. Economy

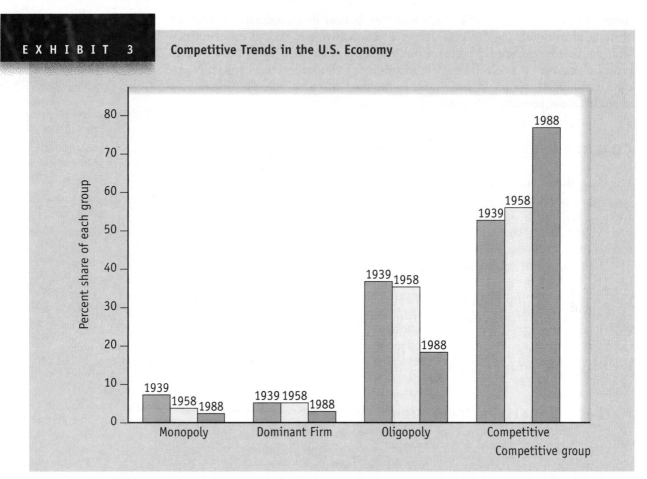

Sources: W. G. Shepherd, "Causes of Increased Competition in the U.S. Economy, 1939–1980," *Review of Economics and Statistics* 64 November 1982); and W. G. Shepherd, *The Economics of Industrial Organization,* 3rd ed. (Englewood Cliffs, N.J.: Prentice Hall, 1990), p. 15.

to 56.3 percent of all industries. Between 1958 and 1988, however, there was a clear increase in competitiveness in the economy, with the percentage of effectively competitive industries jumping from 56.3 percent to 76.7 percent.

According to Shepherd, the growth in competition from 1958 to 1988 can be traced to three primary causes: competition from imports, deregulation, and antitrust activity. Foreign imports between 1958 and 1988 resulted in increased competition in 13 major industries, including autos, tires, and steel. According to Shepherd, the growth in imports accounted for one-sixth of the increase in competition. Imports were attractive to consumers because of their superior quality and lower price. Because they were competing with U.S. producers that often had been tightly knit domestic oligopolies, foreign competitors found these U.S. markets relatively easy to penetrate. Finding themselves at a cost and technological disadvantage, domestic producers initially responded by seeking trade barriers, such as quotas and tariffs, to reduce foreign competition.

Trucking, airlines, and telecommunications were among the industries deregulated between 1958 and 1988. We have already discussed some of the effects of this deregulation in trucking and airlines, particularly in reducing barriers to entry and in eliminating uniform pricing schedules. With regard to telecommunications, in 1982 American Telephone and Telegraph Company was forced to divest itself of 22 companies that provided most of the country's local phone service. As a result, long-distance rates became more competitive, and competition is even creeping into local rates. Deregulation has also occurred in securities trading and banking. According to Shepherd, deregulation accounted for one-fifth of the increase in competition.

Although it is difficult to attribute an increase in competition to specific antitrust activity, Shepherd concludes that about two-fifths of the increase in competition between 1958 and 1988 could be credited to the effects of antitrust activity. He argues that although imports and deregulation were also important, their benefits could be quickly reversed by a shift toward protectionism and a return to regulation. In contrast, the effects of antitrust legislation are more permanent, and a reversal would require a much greater change in both legislation and judicial opinion.

Recent Competitive Trends

Shepherd's data go through 1988. What has been the trend in competition since then? Growing world trade has increased competition in the U.S. economy. But some deregulation has run into snags. Airlines are now more concentrated than they were before deregulation, though plane service is still cheaper and safer than during the regulation era. And the bankruptcy of many savings institutions has been blamed in part on banking deregulation. Thus, the enthusiasm for deregulation has waned in the United States.

Under President Clinton, antitrust policy has been more active than during the Republican administrations of Presidents Reagan and Bush. For example, the Justice Department would not allow Microsoft to acquire Intuit, makers of Quicken personal finance software. The Justice Department also questioned Microsoft's proposed bundling of an on-line service capability in its Windows 95 operating system. The concern was that Microsoft could use its dominance in operating systems, where it controls over 80 percent of the market, to sell other software and services. Industry observers argued that with such consumer convenience, Microsoft could quickly become a market leader in on-line services.

In short, international competition has intensified since 1988, and antitrust activity, though quiet during the 1980s, has stirred in the 1990s.

Problems with Antitrust Legislation

There is growing doubt about the economic value of some of the lengthy antitrust cases pursued in the past. One case against Exxon was in the courts for 17 years before the company was cleared of charges in 1992. Another case began in 1969 when IBM, with nearly 70 percent of domestic sales of electronic data-processing equipment, was accused of monopolizing that market. IBM responded that its large market share was based on its innovative products and on its economies of scale. The trial began in 1975, and the government took nearly three years to present its case. Litigation persisted for years. In the meantime, many other computer manufacturers emerged both in this country and abroad to challenge IBM's dominance. In 1982, the Reagan administration dropped the case, noting that the threat of monopoly had diminished enough that the case was "without merit."

Net Bookmark

The United States Government, through the Antitrust Division of the Justice Department (http://gopher.usdoj.gov/atr/atr.htm) and the Federal Trade Commision (http://www.ftc.gov/) protects and promotes business competition through the enforcement of the antitrust laws. Occasionally, these cases involve high-profile corporations, such as Microsoft, headed by Bill Gates pictured above. To browse the Antitrust Division complaint against Microsoft, visit *U.S.* v. *Microsoft.* (gopher://justice2.usdoj.gov:70/11/atr/cases).

Too Much Emphasis on the Competitive Model. Joseph Schumpeter argued half a century ago that competition should be viewed as a dynamic process, one of "creative destruction." Firms are continually in flux—introducing new products, phasing out old products, trying to compete for the consumer's dollar in a variety of ways. In light of this, antitrust policy should not necessarily be aimed at increasing the number of firms in each industry. In some cases, firms will grow large because they are more efficient than rivals at offering what consumers want. Accordingly, firm size should not be the primary concern. Moreover, the theory of contestable markets, discussed in the monopoly chapter, argues that competition can occur even with only one firm or a few firms in the industry as long as entry and exit barriers are low. And, as noted in the case study in the chapter on perfect competition, economists have shown through market experiments that most of the desirable properties of perfect competition can be achieved with a small number of firms.[5]

Abuse of Antitrust. Parties that can show injury by firms that have violated antitrust laws can sue the offending company and recover three times the amount of the damages sustained. These so-called *treble damage* suits increased after World War II; more than 1,000 cases are initiated each year. Courts have been relatively generous to those claiming to have been wronged. But studies show that such suits can be used to intimidate an aggressive competitor or to convert a contract dispute between, say, a firm and its supplier into treble damage payoffs. The result can have a chilling effect on competition. Many economists now believe that the anticompetitive costs from this abuse of treble damage suits may exceed the procompetitive benefits of these laws.

Growing Importance of International Markets. Finally, a standard approach to measuring the market power of a firm is its share of the market. With the growth of international trade, however, the local or even the national market share becomes less relevant. General Motors may dominate U.S. auto manufacturing, accounting for over half of sales in the United States by domestically owned firms. But when auto sales by Japanese and European producers are included, GM's share of the U.S. auto market falls to about one-third. GM's share of world production has declined steadily since the mid-1950s. Where markets are open to foreign competition, antitrust enforcement that focuses on domestic production makes less economic sense.

Although General Motors may dominate U.S. auto manufacturing, the car company shares only about one-third of the U.S. auto market when Japanese and European car sales are considered as well.

CONCLUSION

If we look at all large corporations, we see evidence that the share of corporate assets controlled by the largest firms has been increasing over time, but if we focus on particular industries, the overall degree of competition in the U.S. economy appears to be increasing. How can this paradox be resolved? Many mergers in the years between World War II and the late 1980s were conglomerate mergers, which joined firms operating in unrelated markets. If two giant firms

---

5   See, for example, Vernon Smith, "Markets as Economizers of Information: Experimental Examinations of the 'Hayek Hypothesis'," *Economic Inquiry* 20 (1982); and Douglas Davis and Charles Holt, *Experimental Economics* (Princeton, N.J.: Princeton University Press, 1993).

from different industries merge, the assets held by the top 100 firms increase, yet because of deregulation, growing global competition, and antitrust legislation, competitiveness in particular industries increases. So it is possible for the share of assets controlled by the largest firms to increase, even though competition in particular markets increases as well.

SUMMARY

1. In this chapter, we examined two forms of government regulation of business: (1) economic regulation, such as the regulation of natural monopolies, and (2) antitrust activity, which promotes competition and prohibits efforts to monopolize or to cartelize an industry.

2. Natural monopolies are regulated by government so that output is greater and prices are lower than they would be if the monopolist were allowed to maximize profits. One problem with regulation is that the price that maximizes social welfare creates an economic loss, whereas the price that allows the firm to earn a normal profit does not maximize social welfare.

3. There are two views of economic regulation. The first is that economic regulation is in the public interest because it controls natural monopolies where production by one or a few firms is most efficient and promotes competition where competition is most efficient. A second view is that regulation is not in the public, or consumer, inter-

est, but is more in the special interest of regulated producers.

4. Both the ground transportation and the airline industry were regulated for much of this century. Regulation had the effect of restricting entry and fixing prices. Both industries underwent deregulation in the early 1980s, which stimulated new entry and reduced prices overall.

5. Antitrust laws are aimed at promoting competition and prohibiting efforts to cartelize or monopolize an industry. The Sherman, Clayton, and FTC acts provided the basic framework for antitrust enforcement, a framework that has been clarified and embellished by subsequent amendments and judicial decisions.

6. Research indicates that competition in U.S. industries has been increasing since World War II. Three reasons for the growth in competition are foreign trade, deregulation, and antitrust activity.

QUESTIONS AND PROBLEMS

1. **(Government Regulation)** What are the three kinds of government policies used to regulate firms' behavior? Indicate which type of regulation is used for each of the following:
   a. The prevention of mergers that the government believes would lessen competition.
   b. The activities of the Food and Drug Administration.
   c. The examination by the Justice Department of possible price fixing.
   d. Regulation of fares charged by a municipal bus company.
   e. The passage in 1996 of a bill to reduce restrictions on entry into the telephone and cable industries.
   f. Occupational Safety and Health regulations affecting working conditions.

2. **(Theories of Regulation)** Why might some industries prefer to be regulated rather than face an unregulated environment?

3. **(Natural Monopoly)** Consider the following graph representing a natural monopoly:

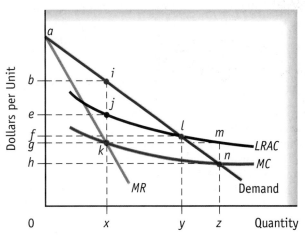

a. Why would this firm be considered a natural monopoly?

b. If the firm is unregulated, what price and output levels would maximize its profit? What would be its profit or loss?

c. If the regulatory commission establishes rates with the goal of maximizing allocative efficiency, what would be the price and output levels? What would be the firm's profit or loss?

d. If the regulatory commission establishes rates with the goal of allowing the firm a "fair return," what would be the price and output levels? What would be the firm's profit or loss?

e. Which of the prices in parts b, c, and d maximizes consumer surplus? What problem, if any, occurs at this price?

4. **(Antitrust Laws)** Indicate which antitrust law forbids each of the following activities:

a. Price discrimination that serves to reduce competition substantially.

b. Vague "restraint of trade" and "monopolization."

c. Mergers through buying the assets of another firm if competition would be reduced substantially.

d. Mergers through buying the stock of another firm if competition would be reduced substantially.

e. Exclusive-dealing contracts that substantially lessen competition.

5. **(Antitrust Activity)** "The existence of only three or four big U.S. auto manufacturers is prima facie evidence that the market structure is anticompetitive and that antitrust laws are being broken." Evaluate this assertion.

6. **(Market Concentration)** Calculate the four-firm concentration ratio and the Herfindahl index for each of the following situations. Which of the industries is the most concentrated according to the four-firm concentration ratio? According to the Herfindahl index?

a. An industry with ten firms with the following market shares: 26 percent, 24 percent, 15 percent, 11 percent, 7 percent, 5 percent, 3 percent, 3 percent, 3 percent, 3 percent.

b. An industry with ten firms with the following market shares: 60 percent, 7 percent, 5 percent for the three largest firms, plus 4 percent each for the other seven firms.

c. An industry with ten firms with the following market shares: 19 percent each for the four largest firms plus 4 percent each for the remaining 6 firms.

d. An industry with 50 firms with the following market shares: 11 percent each for the 5 largest firms plus 1 percent each for the remaining 45 firms.

7. **(Natural Monopoly Regulation)** Explain the regulatory dilemma facing a commission setting the rate structure for a natural monopoly.

8. **(Anticompetitive Behavior)** Identify the type of anticompetitive behavior illustrated by each of the following:

a. A university that requires buyers of season tickets for its basketball games to also buy season tickets for its football games.

b. Collusion by dairies that bid on school contracts to artificially inflate the price of milk sold to the school districts.

c. Placing the same individual on the boards of directors of General Motors and Ford.

d. A large retailer selling merchandise below cost in order to drive competitors out of business.

e. A producer of carbonated soft drinks that sells to a retailer only if the retailer agrees not to buy from the producer's major competitor.

9. **(Discriminating Monopoly)** Using demand and cost curves, show why regulation that forces a perfectly discriminating monopolist to charge everyone the same price could lead to a decrease in economic efficiency. Assume that the firm is permitted to maximize profit as a single-price monopolist.

10. **(Patents and Market Power)** Discuss whether patents, by restricting access to information and product design, have the effect of decreasing competition. What would the optimal patent policy be?

11. **(Antitrust Activity)** A relatively recent development in the theory of economic regulation is the idea of "contestable markets" in which industries with few firms may behave as if they were competitive because of the potential for outside entry. What problems does this create for regulators using, say, four-firm concentration ratio information as a basis for determining whether an antitrust action is warranted?

12. **(Antitrust Law Enforcement)** Discuss the difference between per se illegality and the rule of reason.

13. **(Competitive Trends in the U.S. Economy)** William Shepherd's study of U.S. industries showed a clear increase in competition in the U.S. economy between 1958 and 1988. Discuss the reasons given by Shepherd for this trend.

14. **(Business Behavior and Public Policy)** Define market power. Then, discuss the rationale for government regulation of firms with market power.

15. **(Mergers and Public Policy)** Explain the current guidelines that the Justice Department uses in determining whether to challenge a proposed horizontal merger. Do these guidelines indicate that the Justice Department

is using the per se illegality or rule of reason approach to antitrust enforcement?

16. **(Antitrust Activity)** Define each of the following terms:
    a. Consent decree.
    b. Federal Trade Commission Act.
    c. Treble damages suit.
    d. Trust.

17. **(Rail and Truck Regulation and Deregulation)** What is the Interstate Commerce Commission? What powers did the ICC have before deregulation?

18. **(Rail and Truck Regulation and Deregulation)** Have any consumers or resource providers been hurt by the deregulation of the trucking and rail service industries? Explain.

19. **(Airline Regulation and Deregulation)** What government agency regulated the U.S. airline industry?

Were all airlines regulated? What were the major powers of the regulatory agency before deregulation? Did these powers eliminate competition in the airline industry?

20. **(Airline Regulation and Deregulation)** Since the Airline Deregulation Act of 1978, has concentration in the airline industry increased or decreased? Explain why.

Using the Internet

21. What is the latest news on mergers? Visit "Antitrust Policy: An Online Resource Linking Economic Research, Policy, and Cases," sponsored by, among others, Vanderbilt University. Review "Mergers: In the News" (**http://www.vanderbilt.edu/Owen/ froeb/antitrust/antitrust.html**). Do you notice any trends? Find a story that includes a link to more detailed information. Follow the link and highlight the key points you find.

30

Public Choice

The effects of government are all around us. The clothes you put on this morning were manufactured according to government regulations about everything from the working conditions of textile employees to the label providing washing instructions. Your breakfast cereal was made from grain grown on subsidized farms; the milk and sugar you put on your cereal were also subject to government price supports. The condition of the vehicle in which you rode to campus was regulated by government, as were the driver's speed and sobriety. Your education has been subsidized in a variety of ways by government. Government has a pervasive influence on all aspects of your life and on the economy.

Yes, government is big business. The federal government alone spends over $1,600,000,000,000 per year—over $1.6 *trillion*—including more than $1 million just on paper clips. In addition to federal spending, state and local governments raise and spend nearly $1 trillion on their own. Chapter 4 introduced the roles government plays in the economy, and the role of government has been discussed throughout this book. For the most part, this discussion has assumed that government makes optimal decisions in response to the shortcomings of the private market—that is, when confronted with a failure in the private market, government adopts and implements the appropriate program to address the problem. But this is easier said than done. There are limits to the effectiveness of government activity, just as there are limits to the effectiveness of market activity. Sometimes a government "solution" may be worse than the market failure.

In this chapter, we will trace the government decision-making process and explore problems that arise in this process. Beginning with the problem of majority rule in direct democracy, we proceed to complications that arise when public choices are delegated to elected representatives, who, in turn, delegate the implementation of these choices to government bureaus. Topics discussed in this chapter include:

- The economy as a game
- Median voter model
- Cyclical majority
- Representative democracy
- Rational ignorance

- Special-interest legislation
- Rent seeking
- Underground economy
- Bureaucratic behavior

THE ECONOMY AS A GAME

One useful way of understanding the role of government is to think of the economy as a kind of game, which initially involves two major groups of players: consumers and producers. The players pursue their own self-interests: consumers attempt to maximize utility, and producers attempt to maximize profit. Economic coordination in a market economy hinges on players' ability to secure the rights and obligations of property as well as to enforce contracts. From time to time, disagreements arise about property rights or the interpretations of contracts. For example, a consumer may not want to pay for a roofing job that seems of poor quality. Or an insurance company may not want to pay a fire claim because of the claimant's negligence.

Players can either police themselves, as they do in card games, or have an umpire or referee, as they do in most sports. A market economy often requires some third party (government) to resolve disputes, protect the rights to resources, and enforce contracts. Also, government may provide public goods and services, regulate markets, promote competition, redistribute income, and control activities that involve externalities, which are unpriced by-products of production or consumption.

Fairness of the Game

Participants in a game often value its fairness. Fairness can be viewed from two perspectives. First, are the rules of the game fair to all participants—that is, is the *process* fair? A game may not be fair because the cards are marked, one player can see other players' cards, or a group of players conspires against another player. Fairness can also be viewed in terms of the results of the game. Is the *outcome* of the game fair? Suppose a few skilled or lucky players win all the chips. Some argue that if the rules are fair, then the outcome must by definition be fair, even if there are big winners and losers. Others argue that even fair rules will not result in a fair outcome if the players are not on equal footing at the outset. For example, what if certain players begin the game with fewer chips than the others? Or what if some players lack the skill to play well? Do these differences among players make the game less fair? If fairness means that every player has an equal opportunity to win, differences in the initial endowment of chips or in the ability to play the game need to be taken into account. If players believe it is important that the *result* be fair, the rules can be changed to bring about what is viewed as a fairer outcome.

Kinds of Games

By comparing the total amount of winnings and losses, we can classify games into three categories. If the winnings exceed the losses, the game is a **positive-sum game;** if the winnings are just offset by the losses, it is a **zero-sum game;** and if the losses exceed the winnings, it is a **negative-sum game.** Poker is a zero-sum game because the total amount of the winnings just equals the total amount of the losses. Money is simply redistributed among the players. Most gambling activities, such as horse racing and state lotteries, are negative-sum games because the "house" and the government take a cut of the amount wagered.

Many people mistakenly think of market activity as a zero-sum game. Intuition suggests that the gains from one side of the market must come at the ex-

Positive-sum game A game in which total winnings exceed total losses

Zero-sum game A game in which total winnings just equal total losses

Negative-sum game A game in which total losses exceed total winnings pense of the other side. But a key feature of market activity ensures that most exchanges will yield positive gains. Because market exchange is *voluntary*, participants expect to be at least as well off after engaging in market exchange as before. Product demanders expect consumer surplus, and resource suppliers typically expect producer surplus or profit. Thus, market exchange is usually a positive-sum game.

Rules and Behavior

Rules and rule changes can affect either the way the game is played or the distribution of winnings when the game is over. Laws such as those governing minimum wages, pollution controls, import restrictions, affirmative action, and farm price supports affect the conditions of market production and exchange—that is, the way the game is played. They influence what resources are used, in what quantities, and often at what price. These rules thereby have a direct effect on how the game is played.

Another set of rules redistributes the winnings when the game is over. Taxes and transfers redistribute earnings after production and exchange have taken place. The problem is that the way the winnings are reallocated can also influence the way the game is played. For example, what if all the winnings were divided equally among the players when the game was over? What effect would this have on the intensity and quality of play? It's likely that players would not compete as intensely as they would if the game were "for keeps." Likewise, each individual's incentives to work, to invest, and to take risks will be affected by the redistribution of earnings. Choices about the rules of the game are typically *public choices*—choices that are made collectively by voters, either directly or indirectly. We turn now to a closer examination of the public choice process.

PUBLIC CHOICE IN DIRECT DEMOCRACY

Government decisions about the supply of public goods and services and the collection of revenues are public choices. In a direct democracy, public choices usually require approval by a majority of the voters. As it turns out, we can frequently explain the choice of the electorate by focusing on the preferences of the median voter. The *median voter* is the voter whose preferences lie in the middle of the set of all voters' preferences. For example, if the issue is the size of the government budget, half the voters prefer a larger budget and half prefer a smaller one than is preferred by the median voter.

Median Voter Model

Median voter model Under certain conditions, the preference of the median, or middle, voter will dominate other public choices.

The **median voter model** predicts that under certain conditions, the preference of the median, or middle, voter will dominate other choices. Consider the logic behind the median voter model. Suppose you and two roommates have just moved into an apartment, and the three of you must decide on furnishings. You all agree that the common costs will be divided equally among the three of you and that majority rule will prevail, with one vote per person. The issue at hand is whether to buy a TV and, if so, of what size. The problem is that you each have different preferences. Your studious roommate considers a TV an annoying distraction. Your other roommate, a real TV fan, prefers a 36-inch screen. Although you are by no means a TV addict, you enjoy watching TV as a relief from the rigors of academe; you think a 19-inch screen would be just fine. What to do, what to do?

Exhibit 1 illustrates your preferences and those of your roommates. The horizontal axis specifies the size of the TV screen; we focus on three possibilities: no TV, a 19-inch TV, and a 36-inch TV. The vertical axis indicates, for the different-sized TVs, a ranking of preferences, from most preferred to least preferred. Your studious roommate's preference is shown by the blue line, *SS*; the TV fan's preference is shown by the gold line, *FF*; and your preference is shown by the red line, *YY*. Your studious roommate, shown by *SS*, most prefers the option of no TV, has medium preference for the 19-inch TV, and least prefers the 36-inch TV. The order of preferences of the TV fan, shown by *FF*, are just the opposite. You, shown by *YY*, most prefer the 19-inch screen but would rather have the 36-inch TV than no TV. Spend a moment becoming familiar with the figure. Go ahead.

You all agree to make the decision by voting on two alternatives at a time, then pairing the winning alternative against the remaining alternative until one choice dominates the others. When no TV is paired with the 19-inch set, the 19-inch set wins because this option gets both your vote and the TV fan's vote. When the 36-inch screen is then paired with the 19-inch screen, the 19-inch screen wins a majority again, this time because your studious roommate sides with you rather than voting for the super screen.

Majority voting in effect delegates the public choice to the person whose preference is the median for the group. You, as the median voter in this case, can have your way; if you had wanted a 12-inch screen, you could have received majority support for that size. Similarly, *the median voter in an electorate of-*

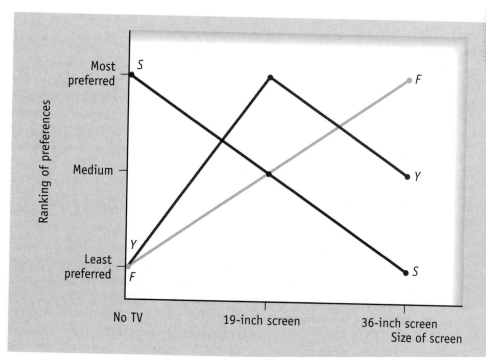

EXHIBIT 1

Preferences for Size of TV Screen

S prefers no TV most and a 36-inch screen least. *F* prefers just the opposite. The median voter, *Y*, prefers a 19-inch screen most and no TV least. In this case, the 19-inch screen will be selected because there are more votes for it than for either of the other two options. The median voter's preference prevails.

ten determines public choices. Political candidates try to get elected by appealing to the median voter. This is one reason why there often seems to be so little difference among candidates, such as Clinton versus Dole.

Note that under majority rule, only the median voter gets his or her way. Other voters are required to go along with what the median voter wants. Thus, other voters usually end up paying for what they consider to be either too much or too little of the good.

Logrolling

Logrolling Vote trading on preferred issues; voter A supports voter B's pet project as long as B supports A's pet project

The outcome preferred by the median voter is less likely to prevail when many issues are subject to public choice. **Logrolling** occurs when voters pledge support for one issue in exchange for support on another issue. Logrolling can result in outcomes that do not reflect the preferences of the median voter. For example, suppose that another choice you and your roommates need to make collectively is that of a stereo system. In this case your studious roommate prefers a powerful, expensive system—one with teeth-rattling speakers. You again prefer a more moderately priced system, and the TV fan prefers no stereo at all, favoring MTV and VH1 to just audio. Thus, you happen to be the median voter in this decision as well.

As the median voter and with no logrolling, you would have your way. If we introduce the possibility of logrolling, however, your choice may no longer dominate. Your two roommates realize that they are not getting their first choices in either decision. Suppose that the studious roommate agrees to vote for the super TV screen in return for the TV fan's vote for the expensive stereo system. By trading votes, or logrolling, each gets a first choice in one of the two decisions. You, as the median voter, no longer cast the deciding vote. This exchange of support usually results in greater outlays for the two items than would have been the case without such logrolling.

Cyclical Majority

Cyclical majority A situation in which no choice dominates all others, and the outcome of a vote depends on the order in which issues are considered

Even without logrolling, a clear majority choice may not emerge. Suppose, for example, that the TV fan, as a purist, prefers having no TV to having any TV smaller than the super size. The TV fan's preference is then shown by the gold line, *FF*, in Exhibit 2; preferences for you and your studious roommate are the same as before. If under these circumstances the 19-inch screen is up for a vote against the giant screen, the 19-inch screen will win a majority, as before. If the option for the 19-inch screen is then paired with the option of no TV, however, the no-TV alternative will gain a majority, winning both the studious roommate's vote and the TV fan's vote. If the no-TV option is then paired with the motion for a 36-inch screen, the large screen will win your vote and the TV fan's vote, thereby gaining a majority.

Note that the 36-inch screen is preferred to no TV, and no TV is preferred to the 19-inch screen, but the 19-inch screen beats the 36-inch screen. There is no dominant choice. No matter which alternative wins in a particular pairing, there is always another option that can beat that winner. Instead of a clear majority, there is a **cyclical majority,** with the outcome depending on the order of voting. What causes this cycle is that the TV fan prefers no TV to any TV smaller than the giant one. Thus the TV fan's preferences are not ordered from most preferred to least preferred based on screen size.

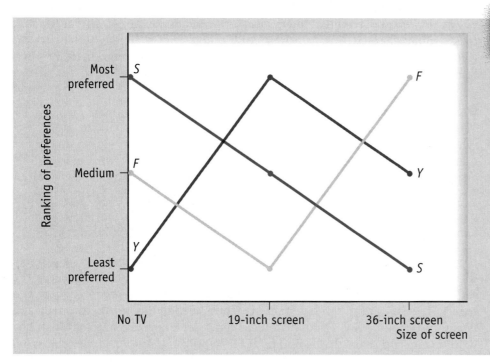

EXHIBIT 2

Preference Pattern That Causes a Cyclical Majority

If voter *F* prefers a 36-inch screen to no TV and no TV to a 19-inch screen, a cyclical majority results. No matter which option is proposed, some other option will be preferred by a majority of voters.

An application to public finance will help clarify the notion of a cyclical majority. Consider the preferences for education in your home town. Suppose that high-income families prefer that the public schools be first-rate. Families of middle income are not able to afford the taxes needed to pay for a top-quality school system and so prefer a moderate school budget. High-income voters believe that if the public schools are not going to be first-rate, then private schools are the appropriate choice for their children. So they send their children to private schools and vote for a low public school budget. This set of preferences will lead to a cyclical majority in public choices regarding the school budget.

You should remember several points from this discussion of majority rule. First, when a single issue is under consideration, majority rule often reflects the views of the median, or middle, voter. Second, under majority rule, all but the median voter will usually be required to purchase either more or less of the public good than they would have preferred. Thus, majority rule means that there are likely to be many dissatisfied voters. Third, because of the possibility of logrolling, the preferences of the median voter may not dominate when several issues are being considered. And fourth, because of the possibility of a cyclical majority, majority rule may result in no dominant choice when issues are voted on two at a time.

REPRESENTATIVE DEMOCRACY

People vote directly on issues at New England town meetings and on the occasional referendum, but direct democracy is not the most common means of public choice. When you consider the thousands of public choices that must be made on behalf of individual voters, it becomes clear that direct democracy through referenda would be unwieldy and impractical. Rather than make decisions by direct referenda, voters elect *representatives,* who, at least in theory, make public choices to reflect their constituents' views. Under certain conditions, the resulting public choices reflect the preferences of the median voter. Some problems of representative democracy will be explored next.

Goals of the Participants

We assume that consumers maximize utility and firms maximize profit, but what about governments? As noted in Chapter 4, there is no common agreement about what governments maximize or, more precisely, what elected officials maximize, if anything. One theory that parallels the rational self-interest assumption employed in private choices is that elected officials attempt to *maximize their political support.* Political support can take the form not only of votes but also of campaign contributions and in-kind support, such as the efforts of campaign workers.

When representative democracy replaces direct democracy, it is possible that elected representatives will cater to special interests rather than serve the interests of the majority. The problem arises because of the asymmetry between special interests and the public interest. Consider only one of the thousands of decisions that are made each year by elected representatives: funding of an obscure federal program that subsidizes U.S. wool production. Under the wool subsidy program, the federal government establishes and guarantees a floor price to be paid to sheep farmers for each pound of wool they produce, a subsidy that costs taxpayers over $75 million per year. During deliberations to renew the program, the only person to testify before Congress was a representative of the National Wool Growers Association, who claimed that the subsidy was vital to the nation's economic welfare. Why didn't a single representative of taxpayer interests testify against the subsidy? Why were sheep farmers able to pull the wool over the taxpayers' eyes?

Rational Ignorance

Households consume so many different public and private goods and services that they have neither the time nor the incentive to understand the effects of public choices on every one of these products. Voters realize that each has only a tiny possibility of influencing the outcome of public choices. Moreover, even if an individual voter is somehow able to affect the outcome, the impact of the chosen policy on that voter is likely to be small. For example, even if a taxpayer could successfully stage a grass-roots campaign to eliminate the wool subsidy, the taxpayer would save, on average, less than $1 per year in federal income taxes. Therefore, unless voters have special interest in the legislation, they adopt a stance of **rational ignorance,** which means that they remain largely oblivious to the costs and benefits of the thousands of proposals considered by elected officials. The costs of acquiring and acting on such information are typically greater than any expected benefits.

In contrast, consumers have a greater incentive to gather and act upon information about decisions they make in private markets because they benefit directly from the knowledge acquired. *In a world where information and the time required to acquire and digest it are scarce, consumers concentrate on private choices rather than public choices because the payoff in making wise private choices is usually more im-*

Rational ignorance A stance adopted by voters when they find that the costs of understanding and voting on a particular issue exceed the expected benefits of doing so mediate, more direct, and more substantial. For example, a consumer in the market for a new car has an incentive to examine the performance records of different models and test drive a few. But the same individual has less incentive to examine the performance records of candidates for public office because that single voter has virtually no chance of deciding the election. What's more, political candidates, who aim to please the median voter, will often take positions that are quite similar anyway.

Distribution of Costs and Benefits

The costs imposed by a particular legislative measure may be either narrowly or widely distributed over the population, depending on the issue. Likewise, the benefits may be conferred on only a small group or on much of the population. The possible combinations of costs and benefits yield four alternative types of distributions: (1) widespread costs and widespread benefits, (2) widespread costs and concentrated benefits, (3) concentrated costs and concentrated benefits, and (4) concentrated costs and widespread benefits.

Traditional public goods, such as national defense and a system of justice, have widespread costs and widespread benefits—nearly everyone pays and nearly everyone benefits from this category of distribution. Provision of traditional public goods is often a positive-sum game because the benefits outweigh the costs. With **special-interest legislation,** benefits are concentrated but costs are widespread. For example, if some special-interest group, such as the wool producers, can get Congress to adopt legislation that fleeces just $1 from each taxpayer and transfers it to wool producers, this yields that special interest over $100 million. Legislation that caters to special interests is often a negative-sum game.

Special-interest legislation Legislation that generates concentrated benefits but imposes widespread costs

Competing-interest legislation involves both concentrated costs and concentrated benefits. Consider, for example, how a tariff affects importers of shoes versus domestic manufacturers of shoes. Competing-interest legislation will be a negative-sum game if the resolution generates economic inefficiencies.

Competing-interest legislation Legislation that imposes concentrated costs on one group and provides concentrated benefits to another group

When legislators try to impose costs in a concentrated way so as to confer benefits widely, the group getting hit with the concentrated costs will object strenuously. Meanwhile, those who will benefit remain rationally ignorant of the proposed legislation, so they will provide little political support for such a measure. For example, whenever Congress considers imposing a tax on a particular industry, that industry floods Washington with lobbyists, phone calls, and mail, usually noting how the tax will lead to economic ruin, not to mention the decline of Western civilization as we know it today. Thus, legislation that imposes costs on a small group but confers benefits widely has less chance of being passed than do measures that confer benefits narrowly but spread costs widely.

In the following case study, we consider the redistributive and efficiency effects of a specific example of special-interest legislation: farm subsidy programs.

CASE STUDY

Farm Subsidies: A Negative-Sum Game

The Agricultural Marketing Agreement Act became law in 1937 to prevent what was viewed as "ruinous competition" among farmers. In the years since, the government has introduced a variety of policies to set floor prices for a wide range of farm products. The federal government spends over $10 billion a year to support higher farm prices on products ranging from wool to peanuts.

Farm Subsidies: A Negative-Sum Game
continued

Location:

Are taxpayers being milked needlessly to subsidize dairy farmers? For one perspective, visit the American Dairy Science Association (ADSA), an international organization for the advancement of the dairy industry (http://orion. animal.uiuc.edu:80/~adsa/). Also visit "Welcome to Cow-Town America!," a site sponsored by the National Cattleman's Beef Association (http://www.cowtown.org/). For another perspective, browse "The Federal Farm Price Support Scandal," a report written by Kristina Hamel and Mark S. Epstein and published by Public Voice for Food and Health Policy, a consumer interest and advocacy group (http://www.hillnet.com/farmbill/issues/hh1.html).

Let's see how price supports work in the dairy industry. Exhibit 3 depicts a simplified view of the market for milk. Suppose that in the absence of government intervention, the market price of milk would be $1.50 per gallon and the equilibrium quantity would be 100 million gallons per week. In long-run equilibrium, dairy farmers would earn a normal rate of return. Consumers as a group would capture the consumer surplus shown by the blue shaded area. Recall that consumer surplus is the difference between the most that consumers would have been willing to pay for each unit of the good and the amount actually paid.

But suppose that dairy farmers persuade Congress that the free-market price was too low, so legislation establishes a price floor for milk of, say, $2.50 per gallon. The higher price floor provides farmers with an incentive to increase the quantity supplied to 150 million gallons per week. In response to the higher price, however, consumers reduce their quantity demanded to 75 million gallons per week. To make the higher price stick, the government must buy the 75 million gallons of "surplus" milk generated by the floor price or somehow get dairy farmers to restrict their output to 75 million gallons per week. For example, the government may pay dairy farmers not to produce or may buy cows from farmers to reduce production (as was done in the 1980s).

Consumers end up paying dearly to subsidize the farmers. First, the price per gallon increases by $1. Second, consumers, as taxpayers, must pay for the surplus milk or otherwise pay farmers not to produce the surplus milk. And third, if the government buys the surplus milk, taxpayers must then pay for storage. So the consumer pays $2.50 per gallon for milk purchased on the market; the consumer as an average taxpayer also pays another $2.50 for each gallon the government buys, plus, say, an extra $0.50 per gallon to convert surplus milk into powder and to store it. Instead of paying just $1.50 for a gallon of milk, which is the price in the absence of government price supports, the typical consumer-taxpayer in our example pays in effect $5.50 per gallon, or an extra outlay of $4.00 per gallon of milk consumed.

How do the farmers make out? Each farmer receives an extra $1 per gallon in additional revenue over the price that would have prevailed in a free market. As farmers increase their output, however, the marginal cost of production increases; at the margin, the higher price the farmer receives is just offset by higher production costs. Still, farmers gain an increase in producer surplus because of the subsidy program, identified in Exhibit 3 by the area above the supply curve that is between the market price of $1.50 and the floor price of $2.50.

The subsidy will increase the value of resources specialized to dairy farming, such as cows and grazing land, and farmers who owned these resources when the subsidy program went into effect will benefit. Farmers who purchase these resources after the subsidy has been introduced will pay more and will end up earning just a normal rate of return on that investment. So with free entry into the dairy industry, most farmers in the long run earn just a normal rate of return, despite the billions of dollars spent on farm subsidies.

If the extra $1 per gallon that farmers receive for milk were pure profit, farm

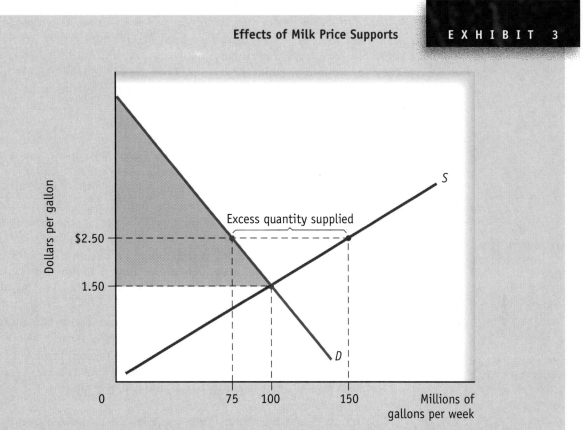

Effects of Milk Price Supports   E X H I B I T   3

In the absence of government intervention, the market price of milk is $1.50 per gallon and 100 million gallons are sold per month. If Congress establishes a floor price of $2.50 per gallon, then the quantity supplied will increase and the quantity demanded will decrease. To maintain the higher price, the government must buy up the excess quantity at $2.50 per gallon.

Consumers are worse off as a result of this policy. In addition to paying an extra $1 per gallon, they must pay for government purchases of surplus milk as well as for storing that milk. In the long run, farmers are no better off, since the policy drives up the prices of resources specialized to dairy farming.

profits would increase by $150 million per week. But consumer–taxpayer costs would increase by $300 million per week ($75 million for the higher price of each of the 75 million gallons consumers purchase, plus $187.5 million in higher taxes for the 75 million surplus gallons purchased by the government, plus $37.5 million to store the 75 million surplus gallons). Thus, consumer–taxpayer costs are double the farmers' maximum possible gain of $150 million. The government subsidy program is therefore a *negative-sum game,* as all the gains and losses sum to less than zero. This does not mean that nobody gains— those who owned specialized resources gained when the subsidy was first introduced. But once the price of farm resources increases, new farmers must pay more to get in a position to reap the subsidies. Ironically, subsidies aimed at preserving the family farm raise the costs of a young person entering the industry. Everyone would be better off if the government made a direct transfer payment to farmers, a payment not tied to milk production or price.

In practice, the milk program combines purchasing surplus milk products

Farm Subsidies: A Negative-Sum Game
continued

Farm Subsidies: A Negative-Sum Game
continued

with paying dairy farmers not to produce and with buying cows from farmers. By the mid-1980s, dairy herds had expanded so much that the government spent more than $1 billion to reduce herd size (herds are now growing again). The dairy industry is supported in other ways. Since 1980, U.S. milk prices have been double or triple the average price on world markets, yet imports are restricted. Regulations also limit farmers in one part of the country from selling their milk in another part of the country. Some state programs support even higher prices. Other laws promote the consumption of dairy products. For example, laws in many states prohibit restaurants from serving margarine unless customers specifically request it instead of butter. Margarine has faced a long history of discrimination dating back a century.

Over the years, government intervention in agricultural markets has grown more complicated. The 1990 Farm Bill was twice the length of its 1985 predecessor. Explaining the intricacies of milk-price supports takes up three volumes of the *Code of Federal Regulation.* (For example, the minimum milk prices in each region around the country are determined by a complicated formula based on the distance from Eau Claire, Wisconsin!) Just to shuffle the paperwork for the program costs the federal government about $1,000 per year for each commercial farm.

Although a direct transfer payment to dairy farmers would be more efficient, such a transparent special-interest proposal could attract the public's attention and be doomed. Special-interest legislation is often promoted under the cover of some greater good. The ostensible goal of farm subsidies, for example, is to save the family farm, but farm households on average earn a higher income than nonfarm households and are wealthier.

The removal of government price supports for butter reduced the average price from $1.45 per pound in 1986 to $0.67 per pound in 1994. Butter sales increased to 1.1 billion pounds in 1994, up 21 percent from 1991. Margarine sales declined. In fact, some butter prices now are lower than margarine prices. So markets, even formerly regulated markets, work when they are allowed to.

Sources: Bruce L. Gardner, "Changing Economic Perspectives on the Farm Problem," *Journal of Economic Literature* 30 (March 1992): pp. 62–101; "Butter's Back," *The Wall Street Journal,* 25 May 1995; Celia Bergoffen, "Margarine Wars," *Audacity,* Summer 1995, pp. 52–61; and Bruce Ingersoll, "Congress Passes New Farm Bill That Dismantles Subsidy Programs After Much Vote Trading," *The Wall Street Journal,* 1 April 1996.

Rent Seeking

An important feature of representative democracy is the incentive and political power it offers participants to employ legislation that increases their wealth, either through direct transfers or through favorable public expenditures and regulations. Special-interest groups, such as farmers, try to persuade elected officials to approve measures that provide the special interest with some market advantage or some outright transfer or subsidy. Such benefits are sometimes called *rents*. The term in this context implies that the government transfer or subsidy constitutes a payment to the resource owner that is over and above the earnings necessary to call forth that resource—*a payment exceeding opportunity cost*. The activity that interest groups undertake to elicit these special favors from government is called *rent seeking*.

The government frequently bestows some special advantage on a producer or group of producers, and abundant resources are expended to secure these rights. For example, *political action committees,* known more popularly as *PACs,* contribute millions to congressional campaigns. More than 4,000 PACs try to shape federal legislation; the top contributors recently included the Teamsters union and the American Trial Lawyers Association. The Teamsters union would like trucking to be reregulated, and lawyers are concerned about legal reforms that would limit lawsuits. The total amount spent by PACs on congressional races in 1994 was a record $724 million.

To the extent that special-interest groups engage in rent-seeking activities, they shift resources from productive endeavors that create income to activities that focus more on transferring income. *Resources that are employed in an attempt to get government to redistribute income or wealth are unproductive because they do nothing to increase output and usually end up reducing it.* And often many firms compete for the same government advantage, thereby wasting still more resources. If the special advantage conferred by government on some special-interest group requires higher income taxes, the net return individuals expect from working and investing will fall, so less work and less investment may occur. If this happens, productive activity will decline.

Competition among groups to obtain rents has been of growing concern among economists. As a firm's profitability becomes more and more dependent on decisions made in Washington, resources are diverted from productive activity to rent seeking, or lobbying. One firm may thrive because it secured some special advantage at a critical time; another firm may fail because its managers were more concerned with productive efficiency than with rent seeking.

As economist Mancur Olson of the University of Maryland notes, special-interest groups typically have little incentive to make the economy more efficient.[1] In fact, special-interest groups will usually support legislation transferring wealth to them even if the measure reduces the economy's overall efficiency. For example, suppose that the American Trial Lawyers Association is able to push through product liability legislation that has the effect of increasing lawyers' incomes by a total of $1 billion per year, or about $1,900 for each lawyer in private practice. Suppose, too, that this measure drives up insurance premiums, raising the total cost of production by, say, $5 billion. Lawyers themselves will have to bear part of this higher cost, but since they account for only about 1 percent of the spending in the economy, they will bear only about 1 percent of the $5 billion in higher costs, or a total of $50 million, which amounts to about $100 per lawyer. Thus, the legislation is a bargain for lawyers because it increases each lawyer's income by an average of about $1,900 but increases each lawyer's costs by only about $100.

There are hundreds of special-interest groups representing farmers, physicians, lawyers, teachers, manufacturers, barbers, and so on. Since there are many competing groups, the situation becomes, in Olson's words, "like a china shop filled with wrestlers battling over the china, and breaking far more than they carry away."[2] Some of the nation's best minds are occupied with devising schemes to avoid taxes and engaging in other practices that transfer income to favored groups at the expense of market efficiency. For example, the

---

1   Mancur Olson, *The Rise and Decline of Nations* (New Haven, Conn.: Yale University Press, 1982).
2   Mancur Olson, "What We Lose When the Rich Go on the Dole," *The Washington Monthly* (January 1984): p. 49.

pursuit of tax loopholes fills up the days of some of the brightest lawyers and accountants.

Think of the economy's output in a particular period as depicted by a pie. The pie is the total value of goods and services produced. In deciding on answers to the "what," "how," and "for whom" questions introduced in Chapter 2, rulemakers have three alternatives: (1) they can introduce changes that will yield a bigger pie (that is, positive-sum changes), (2) they can decide simply to carve up the existing pie differently (zero-sum changes), or (3) they can start fighting over the pie, causing some of it to end up on the floor (negative-sum changes). Much special-interest legislation involves a negative sum.

One way special interests try gain access to the political process is through campaign contributions. The tricky issue of campaign finance reform is discussed in the following case study.

CASE STUDY

Campaign Finance Reform

Location:

To learn more about campaign finance reform, review "In Common: Common Cause News and Issues" (Fall, 1995), the newsletter of Common Cause, a nonpartisan citizens' lobby group actively pursuing campaign reform (http://www.ccsi.com/~comcause/news/f95inc.html). Ross Perot, also known for his reform politics, is pictured here speaking at a rally for Common Cause. Also browse "Campaign Finance Reform: Let the People Do the Talking," written by Tom Edmonds, Republican media consultant and chairman of the American Association of Political Consultants (http://www.newstalk.com/gpp/edmonds.html).

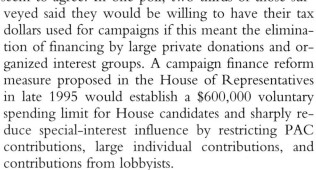

Critics of the current campaign finance system, ranging from Common Cause to Ross Perot, have argued that American politics is awash in special-interest money. Most Americans seem to agree. In one poll, two-thirds of those surveyed said they would be willing to have their tax dollars used for campaigns if this meant the elimination of financing by large private donations and organized interest groups. A campaign finance reform measure proposed in the House of Representatives in late 1995 would establish a $600,000 voluntary spending limit for House candidates and sharply reduce special-interest influence by restricting PAC contributions, large individual contributions, and contributions from lobbyists.

Limits on special-interest contributions may help reduce their influence in the political process, but such limits would heighten the current advantage of incumbency. The overwhelming majority of congressional incumbents are reelected. Observers claim that this results from the unfair advantages that incumbents have in the electoral process, because of taxpayer-funded staff, free mailing privileges (campaign literature masquerading as official communications), and a greater ability to tap special-interest groups for campaign contributions.

Limits on campaign spending would magnify the advantages of incumbency by reducing the funds a challenger has to appeal directly to voters. Some liberal *and* conservative think tanks agree that the supply of political money should be increased, not decreased. As Curtis Gans of the Committee for the Study of the American Electorate argues, "The overwhelming body of scholarly research . . . indicates that low spending limits will undermine political competition by enhancing the existing advantages of incumbency." Money matters more to challengers than to incumbents. One study found a positive relationship between spending by challengers and election success but no relationship between spending by incumbents and their success. So a limit on spending favors incumbents. Challengers must be able to spend enough to get their message out.

Although many decry the amount spent on campaigns, spending is a relative concept. For example, in inflation-adjusted dollars, campaign spending actually declined in 1994. Total direct campaign spending for all congressional races in 1994 averaged about $3 per eligible voter. The cost of the 435 House races and 33 Senate races was roughly double what the makers of the three leading antacids (e.g., Rolaids) budgeted for advertising in 1994. All 1993–1994 PAC contributions for all federal races would barely cover the production costs for the movie *Waterworld*. And more money was spent to syndicate *Seinfeld* than was spent on a presidential election.

The U.S. Supreme Court has struck down mandatory campaign spending limits. According to the Constitution, "Congress shall make no law . . . abridging freedom of speech." The Supreme Court ruled that "dollars are not stuffed in ballot boxes . . . the mediating factor that turns money into votes is speech . . . . Advocacy cannot be proscribed because it's effective."

House Speaker Newt Gingrich argues that because it is so hard to stifle special-interest support, Congress should increase substantially what people can contribute to political parties. Parties could then contribute far more than they now can to help challengers offset the advantage of incumbency by drowning out PAC contributions.

The point is that legislation often has unintended consequences. Efforts to limit campaign spending may or may not reduce the influence of special-interest groups, but a limit would reduce a challenger's ability to reach the voters and thereby increase the advantage of incumbency.

Sources: Joan Claybrook and Ellen Miller, "Who Killed Campaign Finance Reform? (And How to Revive It)," *The American Prospect* (Winter 1995): pp. 16–19 (http://epn.org/prospect/20/20clay.html); David Broder, "Gingrich Is Correct in Proposing More, Not Less, Campaign Spending," *Hartford Courant,* 15 November 1995; Edward Crane, "Testimony before the Committee on House Oversight, U.S. House of Representatives," 16 November 1995; and the *Mother Jones* web site, "The Coin Operated Congress" (http://mojones.com/coinop_congress/coinop_congress.html).

Campaign Finance Reform
continued

THE UNDERGROUND ECONOMY

A government subsidy promotes production, as we saw in the case study on milk price supports. Conversely, a tax discourages production. Perhaps it would be more accurate to say that when government taxes productive activity, less production is *reported*. If you have worked as a waiter or waitress, did you faithfully report all your tips to the Internal Revenue Service? To the extent that you did not, your income became part of the underground economy. The **underground economy** is a term used for all market activity that goes unreported to the government either to avoid taxes or because the activity is illegal. Thus, income arising in the underground economy ranges from unreported tips to the earnings of a drug dealer.

The introduction of a tax on productive activity has two effects. First, resource owners may supply less of the taxed resource because the tax reduces the net return expected from supplying the resource. Second, in an attempt to evade taxes, some market participants will divert their economic activity from the formal, reported economy to an underground, "off-the-books" economy. Thus, when the government taxes market exchange or the income arising from that exchange, less market activity is reported. For example, a plumber and an

Underground economy The portion of the economy that evades taxes and so is not directly measured by government statisticians.

Chefs who work in restaurants make formal, reportable wages. However, if these chefs agree to cook a free meal for their plumber instead of paying for the services, the chefs may be in "hot water" with the IRS.

accountant may barter services to evade taxes, rather than paying each other in money that would have to be reported and taxed as income.

We should take care to distinguish between tax *avoidance* and tax *evasion*. Tax avoidance is a legal attempt to arrange one's economic affairs so as to pay the least tax possible, such as buying municipal bonds because they yield tax-free interest. Tax evasion is illegal; it takes the form of either failing to file a tax return or filing a fraudulent return by understating income or overstating deductions.

Although there are no official figures on the size of the underground economy, federal agencies try to make inferences based on other data. The Commerce Department estimates that its official figures capture only 90 percent of U.S. income. An Internal Revenue Service survey estimated that only 87 percent of tax liabilities are paid. These studies suggest an underground economy amounting to between $600 billion and $800 billion in 1996.

Those who pursue rent-seeking activity and those involved in the underground economy view government from opposite perspectives. Rent seekers want government to become actively involved in transferring wealth to them, but those in the underground economy want to evade any government contact. *Subsidies and other advantages bestowed by government draw some groups closer to government; taxes encourage others to go underground.*

BUREAUCRACY AND REPRESENTATIVE DEMOCRACY

Elected representatives approve legislation, but the task of implementing that legislation is typically left to various government departments and agencies. The organizations charged with implementing legislation are usually referred to as **bureaus,** which are government agencies whose activities are financed by appropriations from legislative bodies.

Ownership and Funding of Bureaus

We can get a better feel for government bureaus by comparing them to corporations. Ownership of a corporation is based on the shares owned by each stockholder. Stockholders are the residual claimants of any profits or losses arising from the firm's operations. Ownership in the firm is *transferable;* the shares can be sold in the stock market. In contrast, taxpayers are in a sense the "owners" of government bureaus in the jurisdiction in which they live. If the bureau earns a "profit," taxes will be reduced; if the bureau operates at a "loss," as most do, this loss must be covered by taxes. Each taxpayer has just one vote, regardless of the taxes paid. Ownership in the bureau is surrendered only if the taxpayer dies or moves out of the relevant jurisdiction; ownership is not transferable—it cannot be bought and sold directly.

Whereas firms receive their revenue when customers voluntarily purchase their products, bureaus are typically financed by a budget appropriation from the legislature. Most of this budget comes from taxpayers. On occasion, bureaus earn revenue through user charges, such as admission fees at state parks or tuition at state colleges, but supplementary funds for these activities often come from budget appropriations. Because of these differences in the forms of ownership and in the sources of revenue, bureaus have different incentives than do profit-making firms, so we are likely to observe different behavior in the two organizations.

Bureaus Government agencies charged with implementing legislation and financed by appropriations from legislative bodies

Ownership and Organizational Behavior

A central assumption of economics is that people behave rationally and respond to economic incentives. The more tightly compensation is linked to individual incentives, the more people will behave in accord with those incentives. If a letter carrier's pay is based on the customers' satisfaction, the carrier will make a greater effort to deliver mail promptly and intact.

The firm has a steady stream of consumer feedback when its product is sold in free markets. If the price is too high or too low to clear the market, the firm will see surpluses or shortages develop. Not only is consumer feedback abundant, but the firm's owners have a profit incentive to act on that information in an attempt to satisfy consumer wants. The promise of profits also creates incentives to produce the output at minimum cost. Thus, the firm's owners stand to gain from any improvement in customer satisfaction or in production efficiency.

Since public goods and services are not sold in free markets, government bureaus receive less consumer feedback. There are no prices and no obvious shortages or surpluses. For example, how would you know whether there was a shortage or a surplus of police protection in your community? (Would gangs of police officers hanging around the doughnut shop indicate a surplus?) Not only do bureaus receive less consumer feedback than do firms, they also have less incentive to act on the information available. Because any "profits" or "losses" arising in the bureau are spread among all taxpayers, and because there is no transferability of ownership, bureaus have less incentive to satisfy customers or to produce their output using the least-cost combination of resources. (Laws prevent bureaucrats from taking home any "profit.")

Some pressure for customer satisfaction and cost minimization may be communicated by voters to their elected representatives and thereby to the bureaus. But this discipline is not very precise, particularly since any gains or losses in efficiency are diffused among all taxpayers. For example, suppose that you are one of a million taxpayers in a jurisdiction and you know about an inefficiency that wastes a million dollars a year. If you undertake measures that succeed in correcting the shortcoming, you save yourself about a dollar per year in taxes.

In a sense, state and local governments compete for households and for firms by trying to offer an attractive bundle of taxes and public services. Yet this mechanism whereby people "vote with their feet" by moving to a more responsive jurisdiction is a rather crude way to approximate voter satisfaction. Moreover, voters dissatisfied with the national government cannot easily vote with their feet.

Because of differences between public and private organizations—in the owners' ability both to transfer ownership and to appropriate profits—we expect bureaus to be less concerned with satisfying consumer demand and minimizing costs than private firms are. A variety of empirical studies have attempted to compare costs for products that are provided by both public bureaus and private firms, such as garbage collection. Of those studies that show a difference, some find public bureaus to be more efficient, but the majority find private firms to be more efficient.

Bureaucratic Objectives

Assuming that bureaus are not simply at the beck and call of the legislature— that is, assuming that bureaucrats have some autonomy—what sort of objectives will they pursue? The traditional view is that bureaucrats are "public servants," who try to serve the public as best they can. No doubt many public employees do just that, but is this a realistic assumption for bureaucrats more generally? Why should we assume self-sacrificing behavior by public-sector employees when we make no such assumption about private-sector employees?

One widely discussed alternative theory of bureaucratic behavior has been proposed by William Niskanen. He argues that bureaus attempt to *maximize their budgets,* for along with a bigger budget comes size, prestige, amenities, and staff, which are valued by bureaucrats.[3] How do bureaucrats maximize the bureau's budget? According to Niskanen, bureaus supply their output to the legislature as monopolists. Rather than charge a price per unit, bureaus offer the legislature the entire amount as a package deal in return for the requested appropriation. According to this theory, the legislature has little ability to dig into the budget and cut particular items (no line-item veto). If the legislature proposes cuts in the bureau's budget, the bureau will threaten to make those cuts as painful to the legislature and its constituents as possible. For example, if city officials attempt to reduce the school budget, school bureaucrats, rather than increasing teaching loads, may threaten to eliminate kindergarten, abolish the high-school football team, or cut textbook purchases. If such threats are effective in forcing the legislature to back off from any cuts, the government budget turns out to be larger than taxpayers would prefer. *Budget maximization results in a budget larger than that desired by the median voter.*

Private Versus Public Production

Simply because public goods and services are financed by the government does not mean that they must be produced by the government. Elected officials may contract directly with private firms to produce public output. Profit-making firms now provide everything from fire protection to prisons to local education. For example, a city council may contract with a firm to handle garbage collection for the city. Elected officials may also use some combination of bureaus and firms to produce desired output. For example, the Pentagon, a giant bureau, hires and trains military personnel, yet contracts with private firms to develop and produce various weapon systems. State governments typically hire private contractors to build roads but maintain roads using state employees. The mix of firms and bureaus varies over time and across jurisdictions, but the trend is toward increased *privatization,* or production by the private sector, of government goods and services. For example, among a sample of a dozen services provided by local governments, the share of services contracted out increased from 24 percent in 1987 to 34 percent in 1992.[4]

When governments produce public goods and services, they are using *the internal organization of the government*—the bureaucracy—to supply the product. When governments contract with private firms to produce public goods and services, they are using *the market* to supply the product. Legislators might prefer dealing with bureaus rather than with firms for two reasons. First, in situations where it is difficult to specify a contract that clearly spells out all the pos-

Net Bookmark

William A. Niskanen—a former defense analyst, business economist, and professor—is chairman of the Cato Institute, a nonpartisan public policy research foundation that advocates limited government, individual liberty, and peace. Niskanen has held this position since stepping down as acting chairman of President Reagan's Council of Economic Advisers in 1985. To learn more about Niskanen's views on bureaucracy, visit the Cato Institute (http://www.cato.org/).

---

3   William A. Niskanen, Jr., *Bureaucracy and Representative Government* (Chicago: Aldine-Atherton, 1971).

4   Robert Barro, "The Imperative to Privatize," *The Wall Street Journal,* 29 June 1995.

sible contingencies, the internal organization of the bureau may be more responsive to the legislature's concerns than the manager of a firm would be. Second, to the extent that bureaus are vehicles for political patronage, legislators may prefer bureaus because bureaus provide opportunities to reward friends and supporters with jobs.

Using market competition to supply services that are not well defined, such as the guidance provided by a social worker, may lead to poor service. A private firm that wins the contract might be tempted to skimp on quality, particularly if the quality of the service can be determined only by direct observation when the service is provided. For example, suppose that government put social work out for bid, selected the lowest bidder, then attempted to monitor the quality of the service through direct observation. The government would find direct monitoring quite costly. These services thus might best be provided by a government bureau. Because the bureau is less concerned with minimizing costs, it has less reason to lower the quality to reduce cost.

CONCLUSION

This chapter examined how individual preferences are reflected in public choices. We began with direct voting based on majority rule, moved on to problems arising from representative democracy, and finally examined bureaus, the organizations that usually implement public choices. We also considered indirect income transfers, which arise because of changes in the rules governing economic activity in the private sector. Price supports, import restrictions, and other indirect transfers are not reflected fully in the government budget but often have profound effects on the economy. Whenever governments become involved in the workings of the economy to favor one group over another, some resources are shifted from productive activity to rent-seeking activity—that is, efforts to persuade the government to confer benefits on certain groups. Individual incentives may also be distorted in a way that reduces the economy's output.

Governments attempt to address market failures in the private economy. But simply turning problems of perceived market failure over to government may not always be the best solution, because government has failings of its own. Participation in markets is based on voluntary exchange. Governments, however, have the legal power to enforce public choices. We should employ at least as high a standard in judging the performance of government, where allocations have the force of law, as we do in judging the private market, where allocations are decided by voluntary exchange between consenting parties.

SUMMARY

1. Under certain conditions, public choice based on majority rule reflects the preferences of the median voter, often requiring other taxpayers to buy either more or less of the public good than they would prefer. Logrolling, or vote trading, produces outcomes that may reflect the preferences, not of the median voter, but some other minority of voters. When a cyclical majority arises, no clear public choice emerges.

2. Producers have an abiding interest in any legislation that affects their livelihood. Consumers, however, purchase thousands of different products and have no special interest in legislation affecting any particular product. Consumers adopt a posture of rational ignorance about producer-oriented legislation, because the costs of keeping up with special-interest issues outweigh the expected benefits.

3. The intense interest that producer groups express in relevant legislation, coupled with rational ignorance of voters on most issues, leaves government officials vulnerable to rent seeking by special interests. Elected officials interested in maximizing their political support may tend to serve producer interests rather than consumer interests—that is, to serve special interests at the expense of the public interest.

4. Much of the redistribution of wealth that occurs through the process of public choice is not from rich to poor but from all taxpayers to some special-interest groups. The harm special-interest groups inflict on the economy often outweighs the benefits they reap, so this type of redistribution is a negative-sum game.

5. Bureaus differ from firms in the amount of consumer feedback they receive, in their incentive to minimize costs, and in the transferability of their ownership. Because of these differences, bureaus may not be as efficient or as sensitive to consumer preferences as firms are.

QUESTIONS AND PROBLEMS

1. **(Median Voter)** In a single-issue vote, such as the television example in the chapter, will the median voter necessarily always get his or her most preferred outcome?

2. **(Kinds of Games)** Indicate the type of game described by each of the following situations. Explain why.
   a. A market for a new product that generates new consumer surplus for the buyers and new producer surplus for the suppliers.
   b. The evolution of a perfectly competitive market into an unregulated, single-price monopoly.
   c. A casual Friday night poker game.

3. **(Representative Democracy)** What would guide a senator in deciding how to vote on an issue that did not directly affect his or her constituency? Is logrolling an important consideration here? Why or why not?

4. **(Majority Rule)** Suppose that the voters on a school property tax issue can be divided into three groups: A, B, and C. The graph below illustrates the preferences of these groups for the size of the school budget. If the budget decision is made by voting on two alternatives at a time, what is the most likely result of the vote?

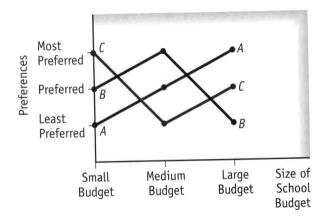

5. **(Distribution of Costs and Benefits)** Why might consumer interest groups in Washington be less effective than producer lobbies?

6. **(Representative Democracy)** Why does 50 percent of the U.S. voting population consistently fail to vote?

7. **(Distribution of Costs and Benefits)** Distinguish among the distribution of costs and benefits for traditional public goods, special-interest legislation, and competing-interest legislation.

8. **(Fairness of the Game)** Discuss the two perspectives by which the fairness of a game can be viewed. Give examples of how the government has tried to affect the fairness of the economy from both perspectives.

9. **(The Underground Economy)** What is the underground economy? What is the impact on the underground economy of instituting a tax on a certain productive activity?

10. **(Distribution of Costs and Benefits)** Suppose that the government decides to guarantee an above-market price for a good by buying up any surplus at that above-market price. Using a conventional supply-demand diagram, illustrate the following gains and losses from a price support:
   a. The loss of consumer surplus
   b. The gain of producer surplus in the short run
   c. The tax cost of running the government program (assuming no storage costs)
   d. What is the total cost to the consumers of the price supports?
   e. Are the costs and benefits of the support program widespread or concentrated?

11. **(Rent Seeking)** Explain how rent-seeking activities can lead to a drop in production. What role might the un-

derground economy play in lessening the drop in productive activities?

12. **(Representative Democracy)** Political parties typically produce "middle of the road" platforms rather than taking extreme positions. Is this consistent with the concepts of the median voter and rational ignorance discussed in the text?

13. **(Bureaucracy)** How do the incentives and feedback for government bureaus differ from those for profit-making firms?

14. **(Majority Rule)** Deciding an issue on the basis of majority vote assumes that everyone has an equal say in the outcome. How does this differ from using markets to allocate resources in private good production? What are the implications of these differences?

15. **(Distribution of Costs and Benefits)** One public choice issue likely to be in the forefront throughout the 1990s is health care—whether to provide universal health, reforms to Medicare and Medicaid, private health insurance reform, and so forth. Who are the interest groups involved in this issue?

16. **(Bureaucracy)** In Chapter 28, the firm was described as combining managerial coordination with market exchange in order to produce its good or service. Does similar behavior occur in the government? Explain.

17. **(The Underground Economy)** Describe the difference between tax avoidance and tax evasion. Which occurs in the underground economy?

18. **(Farm Subsidies)** "To subsidize the price of milk or other agricultural products is not very expensive considering how many consumers there are in the United States. Therefore, there is little harmful effect from such subsidies." Evaluate this point of view.

19. **(Farm Subsidies)** Farm subsidy programs are likely to have a number of secondary or side effects in addition to the direct effect on dairy prices. What impact do you suppose such subsidies are likely to have on the following?
   a. Housing prices
   b. Technological change in the dairy industry
   c. The price of dairy product substitutes

20. **(Campaign Finance Reform)** What are the likely consequences of campaign finance reform to limit contributions?

Using the Internet

21. Review "Alcohol Prohibition Was a Failure," a Cato Institute policy analysis by Mark Thornton (**http://www.cato.org/main/pa-157.html**), and "Ontario's 'Over-Regulation' of Alcohol Beverages Creates Huge Underground Economy," a study by Rich Cartiere addressing Canada's regulation of alcohol (**http://www.smartwired.com/healthy/hd100206.htm**).

   a. For each article, what effects do government alcohol policies have on the underground economy?
   b. Discuss the similarities and differences between Thorton's analysis of the underground economy during the Depression and Cartiere's analysis of present-day Canada.

31

Externalities and the Environment

Toilets in Athens, Greece, flush directly into the Aegean Sea. The river at the port of Bilbao, Spain, is fouled from raw sewage from 110 waste dumps. Breathing the air in Bombay, India, is reportedly equivalent to smoking 10 cigarettes a day. In Mexico City some people buy oxygen in tanks to breathe in their homes. The air in Paris has more lead and carbon monoxide than any other major city in the world. The air in some U.S. cities is also dangerous, and in some areas the ground has been poisoned with toxic waste. The market revolution in Eastern Europe has uncovered deplorable environmental conditions in many of those countries. In Poland, for example, half the lakes and rivers are reportedly too polluted even for industrial use, and what had been East Germany is an environmental disaster area. What does all this have to do with economics? Plenty.

Market prices can efficiently direct the allocation of resources only as long as property rights are well defined and can be easily enforced. But property rights to clean water, air, and soil, to peace and quiet, and to scenic vistas are hard to establish and enforce. This chapter will examine why it is difficult to assign property rights to some key resources, and why a lack of property rights results in inefficient use of these resources. The focus will be on how externalities affect resource allocation and on public policies to promote greater efficiency. As we know from Chapter 4, externalities may be either negative (for example, air pollution) or positive (for example, the general improvement in the civic climate that results from better education). This chapter will concentrate primarily on negative externalities. Topics discussed in this chapter include:

- Private property rights
- Open-access resources
- The common pool problem
- Negative and positive externalities
- Marginal social cost and marginal social benefit
- The market for pollution permits
- The Coase theorem

EXTERNALITIES AND THE COMMON POOL PROBLEM

In a market system, specific individuals usually own the rights to resources and therefore have a strong interest in using those resources efficiently. **Private property rights** allow individuals to control the use of certain resources now and in the future and to charge others for their use. Private property rights are defined and enforced by government, by informal social actions, and by ethical norms. Because specifying and enforcing property rights to certain resources is quite costly, not all resources are owned as private property. For example, how could specific individuals claim and enforce a right to the air, to the fish in the ocean, or to migrating birds? There are usually no individual property rights to such resources because no individual can (1) easily exclude others from using the resource and (2) easily capture the value of the resource by "consuming" it all or selling it all. Thus, we say that some resources are both *nonexcludable* (preventing someone from using the resource is costly if not impossible) and *nonappropriable* (no individual can easily capture the value of the resource).

Private property rights The right of an owner to use or to exchange property

Renewable Resources

Let's begin our discussion of externalities by distinguishing between *exhaustible* resources and *renewable* resources. An **exhaustible resource,** such as oil, coal, or copper ore, does not renew itself, and so is available in a finite amount. Each gallon of oil burned is gone forever. Sooner or later, all oil wells will run dry; oil is exhaustible.

Exhaustible resource A resource available in fixed supply, such as crude oil or copper ore

A resource is **renewable** if periodic use of it can be continued indefinitely. Thus, fish are a renewable resource if the amount taken does not jeopardize the fish stock. Timber is a renewable resource because felled trees can be replaced at rates that provide a steady supply. The atmosphere and rivers are renewable resources to the extent that they can absorb and neutralize pollutants. More generally, biological resources such as fish, game, forests, rivers, grasslands, and agricultural soil are renewable if managed appropriately.

Renewable resource A resource that can regenerate itself and so can be used periodically for an indefinite length of time

Some renewable resources are also **open-access resources,** meaning that it is difficult or costly to exclude individuals from using the resource. An open-access resource is often subject to the **common pool problem,** which results because such a resource will be used until the net marginal value of additional use drops to zero. Consequently, open-access resources tend to be overused or overharvested. Because the atmosphere is an open-access resource, producers tend to use the air as a dump for unwanted gases. Air pollution is a negative externality imposed by polluters on society. As noted in Chapter 4, *negative externalities* are unpriced by-products of production or consumption that impose costs on other consumers or other firms. For example, some spray cans release fluorocarbons into the atmosphere; these gases are said to cause thinning of the ozone layer that protects us from the sun's ultraviolet rays. Carbon dioxide emissions and other gases are said to form a blanket that is trapping the sun's heat and causing global warming. And some scientists claim that the sulfur dioxide emitted from coal-fired power plants located primarily in the Midwest is responsible for the acid rain that is killing lakes and trees in the Northeast (though other scientists aren't so sure).

Open-access resource A type of resource that is difficult or costly to exclude individuals from using

Common pool problem Unrestricted access to a resource results in overuse until the net marginal value of additional use drops to zero

Pollution and other negative externalities arise because there are no practical, enforceable, private property rights to open-access resources, such as the air. Market prices usually fail to reflect the costs that negative externalities impose on society. For example, the cost of a can of hair spray powered by fluorocarbons does not reflect the effect of gas emissions on the ozone layer. The price you pay for gasoline does not reflect the costs imposed by the dirtier air and the traffic congestion your driving creates. And electric rates in the Midwest do not reflect the negative externalities, or *external* costs, that sulfur-dioxide emissions impose on those downwind from power plants. Note that externalities are unintended side effects of an action that in itself is useful and purposeful. The electric utility, for example, did not go into business to pollute. Externalities in the production of electricity are discussed next.

External Costs with Fixed Technology

Suppose the demand curve for electricity in the Midwest is depicted by *D* in Exhibit 1. Recall that demand reflects consumers' marginal benefit for each level of consumption. The lower horizontal curve reflects the *marginal private cost* of production incurred by electricity producers. If producers base their pricing and output decisions on their private marginal costs, the equilibrium quantity of electricity used per month is 50 million kilowatt hours and the equilib-

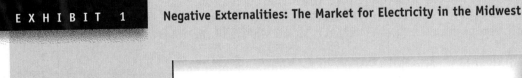

EXHIBIT 1   **Negative Externalities: The Market for Electricity in the Midwest**

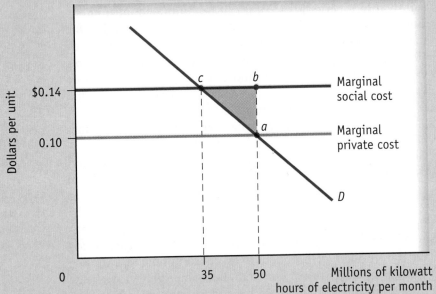

If producers base their output decisions on marginal private cost, 50 million kilowatt hours of electricity are produced per month. The marginal external cost of electricity production reflects the cost of pollution imposed on society. The marginal-social-cost curve includes both the marginal private cost and the marginal external cost. If producers base their output decisions on marginal social cost, only 35 million kilowatt hours are produced, which is the optimal level of output. The total social gain from basing production on marginal social cost is reflected by the blue triangle.

rium price is $0.10 per kilowatt hour. At that price and output level, the marginal private cost of production just equals the marginal benefit enjoyed by consumers of electricity.

But research suggests (though the issue is far from resolved) that the sulfur dioxide emitted by coal-fired power plants during electricity production mixes with moisture in the air to form sulfuric acid, which is carried by the prevailing winds and falls elsewhere as acid rain. Many argue that acid rain has killed lakes and forests and has corroded buildings, bridges, and other structures. Electricity production, therefore, involves not only the private marginal cost of the resources employed but also the external cost of using the atmosphere as a gas dump. Suppose that the marginal external cost imposed on the environment by the generation of electricity is 4 cents per kilowatt hour. If the only way of reducing the emission of sulfur is by reducing the generation of electricity, then the relationship between the production of electricity and the production of pollution is a fixed one. Thus, we say that pollution occurs with **fixed-production technology.**

Fixed-production technology Technology for which the relationship between output and the generation of an externality is a fixed one; the only way to reduce the externality is to reduce the output

The marginal external cost of 4 cents per kilowatt hour is reflected by the vertical distance between the marginal private cost curve and the marginal social cost curve in Exhibit 1. The **marginal social cost** includes both the marginal private cost and the marginal external cost that production imposes on society. Because the marginal external cost is assumed to be constant, the two cost curves are parallel. Notice that at the private-sector equilibrium output level of 50 million kilowatts, the marginal social cost, identified at point *b,* exceeds society's marginal benefit from that unit of electricity, identified at point *a* on the demand curve. The last kilowatt hour of electricity produced costs society 14 cents to produce but has a marginal benefit of only 10 cents. Because the marginal cost to society exceeds the marginal benefit, the firm's choice of output results in a *market failure.* Too much electricity is generated, and too much pollution is produced in the process. What's more, the price of electricity is too low because it fails to reflect the social cost.

Marginal social cost The sum of the marginal private cost and the marginal external cost of production or consumption

The efficient level of output from society's point of view is where the demand, or marginal benefit, curve intersects the marginal social cost curve—a point identified as *c* in Exhibit 1. How could output be restricted to the socially efficient level of 35 million kilowatts per month? If government policymakers knew the demand curve and the marginal cost curves, they could simply require electric utilities to produce no more than the optimal level. Or they could impose on each unit of output a *pollution tax* equal to the marginal external cost of generating electricity. If correctly determined, such a tax would raise the industry supply curve up to the marginal social cost curve, so the marginal private cost of electricity would equal the marginal social cost. The externality would, in effect, be internalized.

With the appropriate tax, the equilibrium combination of price and output moves from point *a* to point *c.* The price rises from 10 cents to 14 cents per kilowatt hour, and output falls to 35 million kilowatts. Setting the tax equal to the marginal external cost results in a level of output that is socially efficient; at point *c,* the marginal social cost of production equals the marginal benefit.

Notice that pollution is not eliminated at point *c,* but the utilities no longer generate electricity whose marginal social cost exceeds its marginal benefit. The total social gain from reducing production to the socially optimal level of output is shown by the blue shaded triangle in Exhibit 1. This triangle also measures the total social cost of ignoring the negative externalities in the production decision; it reflects the total amount by which the social cost exceeds the benefit of the good if 50 million kilowatts are produced. Though Exhibit 1 offers a tidy solution, the external costs of pollution often cannot be easily calculated or taxed. At times, government intervention may result in more or less production than the optimal solution calls for.

External Costs with Variable Technology

The preceding example assumes that the only way to reduce the total amount of pollution is to reduce output. But power companies can usually change the resource mix to reduce emissions, particularly in the long run. Because pollution can be reduced by altering the way electricity is produced rather than simply altering the rate of output, these externalities are said to be produced under **variable technology.** To examine the optimal amount of pollution under variable technology, consider Exhibit 2. The horizontal axis measures the air quality. If all firms made their production decisions based simply on their marginal private cost—that is, if the cost of pollution is external to the firm—then the firm has no incentive to search for ways that reduce pollution, so too much pollution as a by-product of production would occur.

Air quality can be improved by adopting cleaner production technology. For example, coal-burning plants can be fitted with smoke "scrubbers" to reduce toxic emissions. But the production of cleaner air, like the production of other goods, is subject to increasing marginal cost. For example, cutting emissions of the largest particles may involve simply putting a screen over the

Variable technology A technology whose externality can be reduced by altering the production process rather than simply by altering the rate of output

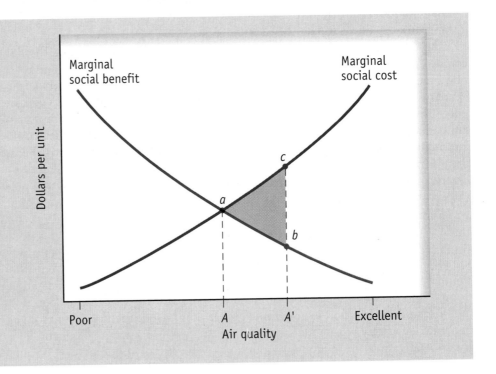

EXHIBIT 2

The Optimal Level of Air Quality

The optimal level of air quality is found at point *a*, where the marginal social cost of cleaner air equals its marginal social benefit. If some higher level of air quality were dictated by the government, the marginal social cost would exceed the marginal social benefit, and social waste would result. The total social waste resulting from a higher-than-optimal air quality is indicated by the red shaded triangle.

smokestack, but eliminating successively finer particles requires more sophisticated and more expensive processes. Thus, the marginal social cost of cleaner air slopes upward, as shown in Exhibit 2.

The **marginal social benefit** curve reflects the additional benefits society derives from improvements in air quality. When air quality is poor, an improvement can save lives and will be valued by society more than when air quality is excellent. Cleaner and cleaner air, like other goods, has a declining marginal benefit to society (though total benefit still increases). The marginal social benefit curve from cleaner air therefore slopes downward, as shown in Exhibit 2. The optimal level of air quality is found at point *a*, where the marginal social cost of cleaner air equals the marginal social benefit of that cleaner air. In this example, the optimal level of air quality is *A*.

Marginal social benefit The sum of the marginal private benefit and the marginal external benefit of production or consumption

What if the government decreed that the level of air quality should exceed *A?* For example, suppose a law were passed setting *A'* as the minimum acceptable level. The marginal social cost, *c,* of achieving that level of air quality exceeds the marginal social benefit, identified as *b.* The total social waste associated with imposing a higher-than-optimal level of air quality is represented by the red shaded triangle, *abc.* This is the total amount by which the social costs of cleaner air (associated with a move from *A* to *A'*) exceed the social benefits.

The idea that all pollution should be eliminated is a popular misconception. If pollution occurs with fixed technology, completely eliminating that pollution would require that output be reduced to zero. Completely eliminating carbon dioxide emissions would require that everyone stop breathing. Even with variable technology, some pollution is consistent with efficiency. *Improving air quality benefits society as a whole as long as the marginal benefit of cleaner air exceeds its marginal cost.*

Consider what would happen to the optimal level of air quality if either the marginal cost or the marginal benefit of cleaner air changes. Suppose, for example, that some technological breakthrough reduces the marginal cost of cleaner air. As shown in panel (a) of Exhibit 3, the marginal social cost of reducing pollution would fall to *MSC',* thereby increasing the optimal level of air quality from *A* to *A'.* The simple logic is that *the lower the marginal cost of reducing pollution, other things constant, the greater the optimal level of air quality.*

An increase in the marginal benefit of air quality would have a similar effect. For example, what if we discovered that air quality affects the incidence of certain types of cancer? The perceived marginal benefit of cleaner air would increase, as reflected in panel (b) of Exhibit 3 by a shift up in the marginal social benefit curve to *MSB'.* As a result, the optimal level of air quality would increase. *The greater the marginal benefit of air quality, other things constant, the greater the optimal level of air quality.*

Resolving the Common Pool Problem

Because property rights do not attach to open-access resources, individual exploiters of fresh air, clean water, wildlife, or other open-access renewable resources tend to ignore the effects of their activities on the resource's renewal ability. As stocks diminish from overuse or overharvesting, the resource grows more scarce. A lack of regulation in the fishing industry allowed years of massive harvesting of the ocean's bounty, which depleted the stock of fish. For example, the Georges Bank off New England, long one of the world's most pro-

EXHIBIT 3

Effect of Changes in Costs and Benefits on the Optimal Level of Air Quality

Either a reduction in the marginal social cost of cleaner air, as shown in panel (a), or an increase in the marginal social benefit of cleaner air, as shown in panel (b), will increase the optimal level of air quality.

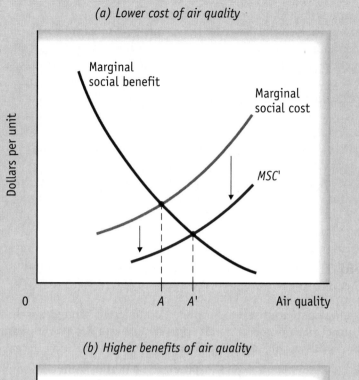

(a) Lower cost of air quality

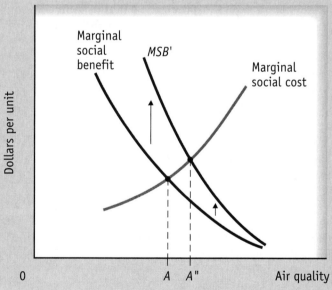

(b) Higher benefits of air quality

ductive fishing grounds, has been so depleted by overfishing that the 1993 catch was down 85 percent from peak years.[1]

The common pool problem of resource exploitation can be reduced if some central authority imposes restrictions on resource use. By restricting output or

---

1   See Deborah Cramer, "Troubled Waters," *The Atlantic* (June 1995): pp. 22–26.

by imposing an appropriate removal, or depletion, tax, a regulatory authority can force competitive firms to use the resource at a rate that is socially optimal. For example, in the face of the tendency to overfish and to catch fish before they are sufficiently mature, the government has imposed a variety of restrictions on the fishing industry. There are limits on the total amount of the catch, on the size of fish that can be caught, on the duration of the fishing season, on the kind of equipment used, and on other aspects of the business.

More generally, *when imposing and enforcing private property rights would be too costly, government regulations may improve allocative efficiency.* For example, stop signs and traffic lights allocate the scarce road space at a road intersection, minimum-size restrictions control lobster fishing, hunting seasons control the stock of game, and official study hours may calm the din in the dormitory.

But not all regulations are equally efficient. For example, fishing authorities sometimes limit the *total* industry catch and allow all firms to fish until that total is reached. Consequently, when the fishing season opens, there is a mad scramble to catch as much as possible before the industry limit is reached. Since time is of the essence, firms make no effort to fish selectively. And the catch reaches processors all at once, creating a problem for all segments of the industry. Also, each firm has an incentive to expand its fishing fleet to catch more in those few weeks. Thus, large fleets of technologically efficient fishing vessels sit in port for most of the year, except during the beginning of the fishing season. Each firm is acting rationally, but the collective effect of the regulation is grossly inefficient in terms of social welfare. Fishing authorities are gradually moving to a quota system that promotes a more efficient allocation of resources.

Fish remain a common-pool resource because the technology has not yet been developed to establish and enforce rights to particular schools of fish. But advances in technology may some day allow the creation of private property rights to ocean fish, migrating birds, and even the air we breathe. At one time, establishing property rights to cattle on the Great Plains seemed impossible, but the invention of barbed wire allowed ranchers to fence the range. In a sense, barbed wire tamed the "Wild West."

The atmosphere has the ability to cleanse itself of some emissions, but a destruction of the tropical rain forest has reduced this ability, as discussed in the following case study.

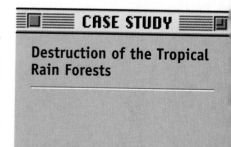

CASE STUDY

Destruction of the Tropical Rain Forests

The tropical rain forests have been called "the lungs of the world" because they naturally recycle carbon dioxide by transforming it into oxygen and wood, thus helping to maintain the world's atmospheric balance. But the world's demand for timber products has caused loggers to cut down much of the tropical forest. Worse yet, farmers burn down these forests to create farmland and pastures. Burning the world's forests has a triple-barreled effect. The loss of trees reduces the atmosphere's ability to cleanse itself, the burning adds yet more harmful gases to the atmosphere, and the forest subsoil usually contains huge quantities of carbon subject to oxidization when the trees are removed. Since the atmosphere is a common pool, the costs of deforestation are imposed on people around the world.

Forest acreage throughout the world has declined by 15 percent over the last decade, and the rate of decline is now accelerating. The amount of Amazon jungle that has been cleared in the last decade is equal to an area the size of

Destruction of the Tropical Rain Forests
continued

Location:

Recently, individuals and organizations, to help deter destructive practices like slash and burn deforestation, have made an effort to promote the beauty and biological diversity of the world's rainforests. For example, visit "The Topical Rainforest in Surinam," a guided multimedia tour around the Surinam rainforest, created and maintained by Marco Bleeker (http://www.euronet.nl/users/mbleeker/suri_eng.html). Also visit the Rainforest Action Network (http://www.wideopen.igc.apc.org/ran/index.html).

France. For example, the north coast of South America contains one of the world's largest unspoiled tropical rain forests, but the governments of Guyana and Suriname have recently opened huge tracks of forest for logging by companies from Korea, Indonesia, and Malaysia. In Central America, the forests have been cleared for cattle ranches. Haiti is now a treeless wasteland, and once-lush El Salvador is a semi-desert. Commercial logging has been so extensive in the African countries of Ghana and the Ivory Coast that the business is already winding down, leaving behind poverty and devastation. According to the World Bank, two-thirds of the countries that export tropical forest products are running out of trees.

The loss of the tropical forests causes other negative externalities as well. As long as the tropical forest has its canopy of trees, it remains a rich, genetically diverse ecosystem. Tropical forests cover only 6 percent of the earth's land surface (down from 12 percent 50 years ago), but they contain *half* of the world's species of plants and animals, thus representing an abundant source of fruits, crops, and medicines. One-fourth of the prescription drugs used in the United States are derived from tropical plants, such as seeds that may help cure some types of cancer. Biologists estimate that 50,000 species are condemned to eventual extinction each year because of deforestation. Yet most tropical plants have not yet been tested for their medicinal properties.

Small-time farmers and wood gatherers and big-time lumber companies are stripping the tropical forests. Once the forests are cut down, the tropical soil is eroded by rains and baked by the sun and soon runs out of nutrients. Once the nutrients are lost, the system is not very resilient. It takes a century for a clear-cut forest to return to its original state. The policy of cutting down everything in sight is of benefit only to loggers, who usually do not own the land and thus have little interest in its future.

The world's rain forests are located in countries that are relatively poor: Brazil, Zaire, Peru, Indonesia, and the Philippines. Environmental quality is a normal good, meaning that as incomes rise the demand for it increases. In very poor countries, however, the priority is not environmental quality but food and shelter. Brazil and other developing countries are destroying their forests to provide jobs. But since the soil quickly loses its nutrients to erosion and the sun, few settlers have become successful farmers.

The tropical rain forests, by serving as the lungs of the world, confer benefits around the globe. But the positive effects that the trees have on the atmosphere tend to be ignored in the decision to clear the land. Worse yet, the taking of timber is often "first come, first served," and government investment programs often subsidize the harvesting of timber. *It is not the greed of peasants and timber companies that leads to inefficient, or wasteful, uses of resource, but the fact that the atmosphere, and, indeed, the rain forests are open-access resources that can be degraded with little immediate personal cost to those who clear the forests.*

What to do? Government programs that encourage selective cutting and replanting would allow the forest to remain an air filter and a renewable source of forest products. International organizations such as the World Bank could award grants or low-interest loans to countries that kept their rain forests unspoiled. Those who benefit from the tropical rain forest should be willing to pay for the benefits.

Sources: Eugene Linden, "Chain Saws Invade Eden," *Time,* 29 August 1994; "Exotic Herb May Speed Colon Cancer Detection," *The Wall Street Journal,* 27 July 1989; Thomas C. Schelling, "Some Economics of Global Warming," *American Economic Review* 82 (March 1992): pp. 1–14; and "Another Green World," *The Economist,* 10 June 1995.

Destruction of the Tropical Rain Forests
continued

The Coase Analysis of Externalities

The traditional analysis of externalities assumes that market failures arise because people ignore the external effects of their actions. Suppose a research laboratory that tests delicate equipment is located next to a manufacturer of heavy machinery. The vibrations caused by the manufacturing process throw off the delicate machinery in the lab next door. Professor Ronald Coase, who won the Nobel Prize in 1991, would point out that the negative externality in this case is not necessarily imposed by the machinery producer on the testing lab— rather, *it arises from the incompatible activities of the two parties.* The externality is the result both of vibrations created by the factory *and* of the location of the testing lab next door. One efficient solution to this externality problem might be to modify the machines in the factory; others might be to make the equipment in the testing lab more shock resistant or to move the lab elsewhere.

According to Coase, the efficient solution to an externality problem depends on which party can avoid the problem at the lower cost. Suppose the factory has determined that it would cost $2 million to reduce vibrations enough to allow the lab to function normally. For its part, the testing lab has concluded that it cannot alter its equipment to reduce the effects of the vibrations (it has fixed technology), so its only recourse would be to move the lab elsewhere at a cost of $1 million. Based on these costs, the efficient resolution to the externality problem is for the testing lab to relocate.

Coase argues that if the government assigns property rights to one party or another, the two parties will agree on the efficient solution to an externality problem as long as transaction costs are low. This efficient solution will be achieved regardless of which party is assigned the property right. Suppose the government grants the testing lab the right to operate free of vibrations from next door, so the testing lab has the right to ask the factory to reduce its vibration. Rather than cut vibrations at a cost of $2 million, the factory can offer to pay the lab to relocate. Any payment by the factory owners that is greater than $1 million but less than $2 million will make both firms better off, since the lab will receive more than its moving cost and the factory will pay less than its cost of reducing vibrations. Thus, the lab will move, which is the efficient outcome.

Alternatively, suppose the factory is granted the right to generate vibrations in its production process. For the factory, this means business as usual. The lab may consider paying the factory to alter its production method, but since the minimum payment the factory will accept is $2 million, the lab would rather move at a cost of $1 million. Thus, whether property rights are granted to the lab or to the factory, the lab will move, which is the efficient outcome. The **Coase theorem** says that as long as bargaining costs are small, the assignment of property rights will generate an efficient solution to an externality problem

Coase theorem The theory that as long as bargaining costs are small, an efficient solution to the problem of externalities will be achieved by assigning property rights

regardless of which party is assigned the property rights. A particular assignment of property rights determines only who incurs the externality costs, not the efficient outcome.

Inefficient outcomes do occur, however, when the transaction costs of arriving at a solution are high. For example, an airport located in a populated area would have difficulty negotiating with all the surrounding residents about noise levels. Or a power plant emitting sulfur dioxide would have trouble negotiating with the millions of people scattered across the downwind states. Or a would-be farmer contemplating clearing a portion of the tropical rain forest cannot negotiate with the millions, and perhaps, billions, of people affected by that decision. When the number of parties involved in the transaction is large, the chance for a voluntary agreement is small.

A Market for Pollution Rights

According to Coase, the assignment of property rights is often sufficient to resolve the market failure typically associated with externalities. Additional government intervention is not necessary. If pollution can be easily monitored and polluters easily identified, the government may be able to achieve an efficient solution to the problem of pollution simply by assigning the right to pollute.

EXHIBIT 4   **Optimal Allocation of Pollution Rights**

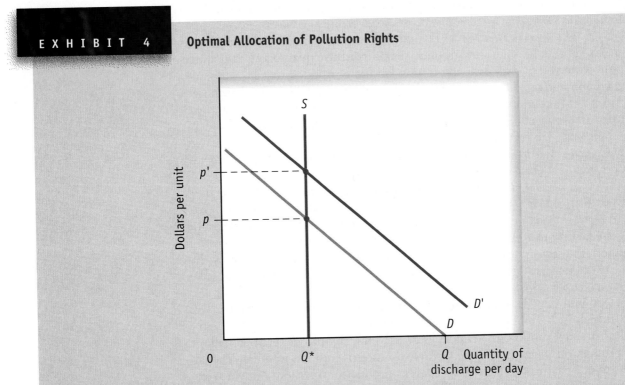

Suppose the demand for a river as an outlet for pollution is D. In the absence of any environmental controls, pollution will occur up to point Q, where the marginal benefit of further pollution equals zero. If regulatory authorities establish $Q*$ as the maximum allowable level of pollution and then sell the rights to pollution, the market for these pollution rights will clear at price p. If the demand for pollution rights increases to D', the market-clearing price will rise to p'.

For example, firms that dump waste into a river evidently value the ability to discharge their waste matter in this way. For them, the river provides an inexpensive outlet for pollutants that otherwise would have to be disposed of at greater cost. The river provides disposal services, and the demand for this pollutant transportation system slopes downward just like the demand for other resources.

The demand for the river as a discharge system is presented as *D* in Exhibit 4. The horizontal axis measures the amount of pollutants dumped into the river per day, and the vertical axis measures firms' marginal benefits of disposing of their pollutants in this way. The demand curve measures the marginal revenue product that comes from dumping in the river. With no restrictions on pollution—that is, if all are free to discharge their wastes into the river—the daily discharge rate can be found where the marginal benefit of discharging wastes goes to zero, which is at output level *Q* in Exhibit 4. Dumping will continue as long as it yields some private marginal benefit. Thus, if dumping remains unregulated, the river must carry away whatever polluters choose to dump there.

The river, like the atmosphere and the soil, can absorb and neutralize a certain amount of pollution per day without deteriorating in quality. Suppose voters in the jurisdiction that encompasses the river make the public choice that the river should be clean enough for swimming and fishing. The maximum level of waste discharge that is consistent with this quality is *Q** in Exhibit 4. Hence, if the river is to be preserved at the specified level of quality, the "supply" of the river as a discharge resource is fixed at *S*.

If polluters can be easily identified and monitored, government regulators can somehow allocate an amount of pollution permits equal to *Q**. If polluters are simply given these permits (that is, if the price of permits is zero), there is excess demand for them, since the quantity supplied is *Q** but the quantity demanded at a price of zero is *Q*. An alternative is to *sell* the specified quantity of pollution permits at the market-clearing price. The intersection of the supply curve, *S*, and the demand curve, *D*, yields a permit price, *p*, which is the marginal value of dumping quantity *Q** into the river each day. Selling the permits ensures that they go to the firms that value them most highly.

The beauty of this system is that those producers that value the discharge rights the most will ultimately end up with them. Producers that attach a lower marginal value to river dumping obviously have cheaper ways of resolving their waste problems, including changing production techniques to reduce their pollution. And if conservation groups wish to maintain a higher river quality than was implied by the government's standard, they can purchase pollution permits but not exercise them.

What if new firms locate along the river and want to discharge wastes? This additional demand for discharge rights is reflected in Exhibit 4 by the higher level of demand, *D'*. This greater demand would bid up the market price of pollution permits to *p'*. Regardless of the comings and goings of would-be polluters, the total quantity of discharge rights is restricted to *Q**, so the river's quality will be maintained. Thus, the value of pollution permits, but not the total amount of pollution, may fluctuate over time.

If the right to pollute could be granted, monitored, and enforced, then what had been a negative externality problem could be solved through market allocation. Historically, the U.S. government has relied on setting discharge standards and fining offenders, and has used pollution rights only in some metropolitan areas. But in 1989, a pollution rights market for fluorocarbon emissions was established and was followed in 1990 by a market for sulfur dioxide. In 1995, the price for the right to emit a ton of sulfur dioxide was $140.[2] So the market for pollution rights is alive and growing.

Unfortunately, legislation dealing with pollution is affected by the same problems of representative democracy that affect other public policy questions. Polluters have a special interest in government proposals relating to pollution, and they will fight measures to limit pollution. But members of the public remain rationally ignorant about pollution legislation. So pollution regulations may be less in accord with the public interest than with the special interests of polluters. This is why pollution permits are often given free to existing firms. For example, under the sulfur dioxide program, the nation's 101 dirtiest power plants receive credits equal to 30 to 50 percent of the pollution they emitted before the program began. Because they receive something of value, polluters are less likely to fight the institution of the program. Once the permits are granted, some recipients find it profitable to sell their permits to other firms that value them more. Thus, a market emerges that leads to an efficient allocation of pollution permits. According to some analysts, the sulfur program will save up to $3 billion annually compared to the old system.[3] More generally, a system of marketable pollution rights can reduce the cost of abatement by as much as 75 percent.

Positive Externalities

Until now, we have considered only negative externalities. Externalities can sometimes be positive, or beneficial. *Positive externalities* are created when the unpriced by-product of consumption or production benefits other consumers or other firms. For example, people who get inoculated against a disease reduce their own likelihood of contracting the disease, but they also reduce the chances of transmitting the disease to others. Inoculations thus provide *external benefits* to others. Education also confers external benefits on society as a whole because those who acquire more education become better citizens, are better able to support themselves and their families, and are less likely to require public assistance or to resort to crime for income. Education confers private benefits but it also confers additional social benefits to others.

The effect of external benefits on the optimal level of consumption is illustrated in Exhibit 5, which presents the supply and demand for education. The demand curve, *D,* represents the private demand for education, which reflects the *marginal private benefit* obtained by those who acquire the education. More education is demanded at a lower price than at a higher price.

The benefits of education, however, spill over to others in society. If we add these positive externalities, or the *marginal external benefit,* to the marginal private benefit of education, we get the marginal social benefit of education. The marginal social benefit includes all the benefit society derives from education, both private and public. The marginal social benefit curve appears above the

2   As found in "Are Regs Bleeding the Economy?" *Business Week,* 17 July 1995.
3   This saving was estimated by Paul R. Portney, "Air Pollution Policy," in P.R. Portney, ed., *Public Policies for Environmental Protection* (Washington, D.C.: Resources for the Future, 1990), pp. 27–96.

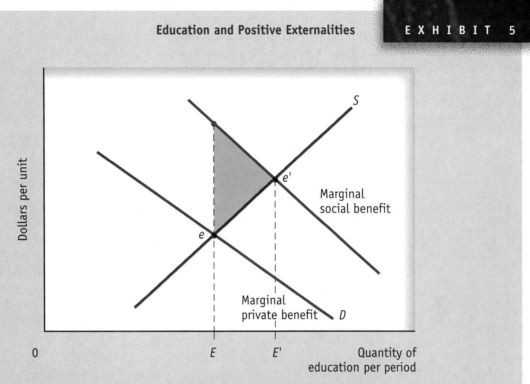

Education and Positive Externalities

EXHIBIT 5

In the absence of government intervention, the quantity of education demanded is *E*, at which the marginal cost equals the marginal private benefit of education. However, education also conveys a positive externality on the rest of society, so the marginal social benefit exceeds the private benefit. At quantity *E*, the marginal social benefit exceeds the marginal cost, so more education is in society's best interest. In such a situation, government will try to encourage an increase in the quantity of education to *E'*, at which point the marginal cost equals the marginal social benefit.

private demand curve in Exhibit 5. At each level of education, the marginal social benefit exceeds the marginal private benefit by the marginal external benefit generated by that particular unit of education.

If education were a strictly private decision, the amount purchased would be determined by the intersection of the private demand curve, *D*, with the supply curve, *S*. The supply curve reflects the marginal cost of producing each unit of the good. This intersection, identified as point *e*, yields education level *E*, where the marginal cost of education equals the marginal private benefit.

But at level *E*, the marginal social benefit of producing an additional unit of education exceeds the marginal cost. Net social welfare will increase if education is expanded beyond *E*. *As long as the marginal social benefit of education exceeds its marginal cost, social welfare is increased by expanding education.* Social welfare is maximized at point *e'* in Exhibit 5, where *E'* units of education are provided—that is, where the marginal social benefit equals the marginal cost, as reflected by the supply curve. The blue shaded triangle identifies the net increase in social welfare that results when the quantity of education increases from *E* to *E'*.

Thus, society is better off if the amount of education provided exceeds the private equilibrium. *When positive externalities are present, decisions based on private marginal benefits result in less than the socially optimal quantity of the good.* Hence, like negative externalities, positive externalities typically point to *market failure,* which is why government often gets into the act. For example, government attempts to encourage education by providing free primary and secondary education, by requiring students to stay in school until they are 16 years old, and by subsidizing public higher education. When there are external benefits, public policy tries to increase the level of output beyond the private optimum.

ENVIRONMENTAL PROTECTION IN THE UNITED STATES

Federal efforts to address the common pool problem of air, water, and soil are coordinated by the *Environmental Protection Agency (EPA).* Four federal laws and subsequent amendments underpin U.S. efforts to protect the environment: the Clean Air Act of 1970, the Clean Water Act of 1972, the Resource Conservation and Recovery Act of 1976 (which governs solid waste disposal), and the *Superfund* law, 1980 legislation focusing on toxic waste dumps. In 1970, the EPA had about 4,000 employees and a budget of $200 million. By the early 1990s, the EPA had about 18,000 employees and a budget of $4.5 billion.

According to EPA estimates, compliance with pollution-control regulations cost U.S. producers and consumers $115 billion in 1990, or 2 percent of GDP.[4] We can divide pollution-abatement spending into three main categories: spending for air pollution abatement, spending for water-pollution abatement, and spending for solid-waste disposal. About 40 percent of the pollution-abatement expenditures in the United States goes toward cleaner air, another 40 percent goes toward cleaner water, and 20 percent goes toward disposing of solid waste. In this section we will consider, in turn, air pollution, water pollution, Superfund activities, and disposing of solid waste.

Air Pollution
In the Clean Air Act of 1970 and in subsequent amendments, Congress set national standards for the amount of pollution that could be emitted into the atmosphere. Congress thereby recognized air as an economic resource, which, like other resources, has alternative uses. The air can be used as a source of life-giving oxygen, as a prism for viewing breathtaking vistas, or as a dump for carrying away unwanted soot and gases. The 1970 act gave Americans the right to breathe air of a certain quality and at the same time gave producers the right to emit certain specified pollutants into the air.

Smog is the most visible form of air pollution. Automobile emissions account for 40 percent of smog. Another 40 percent comes from consumer products, such as paint thinner, fluorocarbon sprays, dry-cleaning solvents, and baker's yeast by-products. Surprisingly, only 15 percent comes from manufacturing. The 1970 Clean Air Act mandated a reduction of 90 percent in auto emissions,

---

4   Other researchers estimate that clean-air and clean-water regulations reduced GDP in 1990 to about 6 percent less than what it would have been in the absence of such regulations. See Michael Hazilla and Raymond Kopp, "Social Cost of Environmental Quality Regulations: A General Equilibrium Analysis," *Journal of Political Economy* 98 (August 1990): pp. 544–51.

leaving it to the auto industry to achieve this target. At the time, auto manufacturers complained that the objective was impossible. Between 1970 and 1990, however, average emissions of lead fell 97 percent, carbon monoxide emissions fell 41 percent, and sulfur oxide emissions fell 25 percent. The 1990 amendment to the Clean Air Act, aimed at reducing acid rain, requires a 10-million-ton reduction in sulfur emissions. Although air pollution is still a problem, U.S. pollution levels are down since the 1970s. And U.S. air quality is relatively good compared to the air in some parts of the world, as is discussed in the following case study.

CASE STUDY

City in the Clouds

Location:

The Global Network of Environment and Technology (GNET), developed and managed by The Global Environment & Technology Foundation and Global Exchange, Incorporated, offers online global information on environmental technologies, business, and news (http://www.gnet.org/). In its own words, GNET is an "interactive community as well as in-depth data source for the environmental marketplace." For information on Mexico and Mexico City, visit "Worldwide Market Information" (http://www.gnet.org/gnet/market/mktinfo/worldindex.htm) and browse "Mexico."

Mexico City has a metropolitan population of 24 million, ranking it the second-largest city in the world. There are 41,000 people per square mile, about four times the density of New York City. The population of Mexico City is expected to grow to 28 million by the end of the decade. More than half the nation's industrial output is produced in or near Mexico City. Millions of vehicles and tens of thousands of small, poorly regulated businesses spew a soup of air pollution. For example, brickmakers fire their kilns with old rubber tires and with sawdust soaked in kerosene oil—fuels that generate black, acrid smoke. A recent study suggests that leaks from tanks of liquefied gas used widely for cooking and heating form the primary component of smog over the city. In all, an estimated 12,000 tons of pollutants are released into the atmosphere each day.

Pollution problems are compounded by the city's geography and altitude. Mexico City is surrounded on three sides by mountains, so the wind that blows in from the north (the open side) traps pollution over the city. Even worse, the city's high altitude reduces the oxygen content of the atmosphere by about one-quarter. The combination of high pollution and low oxygen makes for unhealthy air. In the last decade, the number of days when the city's air quality fell below acceptable levels has doubled. Winter smog sends thousands to the city's hospitals with respiratory problems. Foreign countries advise their diplomats not to have babies while stationed there. Some foreigners who are stationed in Mexico City earn a 10-percent premium as hardship pay.

City officials have taken steps to address the common-pool problem, but their efforts have been halfhearted. The price of gasoline in Mexico City is among the lowest in the world, so price is not much of a check on fuel consumption. Unleaded gas has been introduced but accounts for only 5 percent of the total used. New regulations prohibit 40 percent of the city's 3.5 million cars from traveling the streets during weekdays, yet fuel consumption has actually increased. And although stricter regulations have been imposed on business activity, enforcement has been lax.

Sources: Mark Uhlig, "Under a Cloud," *The Economist*, 4 April 1992; Anthony DePalma, "Cooking Gas, Not Cars, May Cause Mexico Smog," *New York Times*, 18 August 1995; Constance Holden, "Clearing the Air in Mexico City," *Science*, 2 June 1995; and "Petrol Prices," *The Economist*, 17 June 1995.

Water Pollution

Two major sources of water pollution are sewage and chemicals. For decades, U.S. cities had an economic incentive to dump their sewage directly into waterways rather than incur the expense of cleaning it up first. Frequently, the current or tides would carry the waste away to become someone else's problem. Although each community found it rational, based on a narrow view of the situation, to dump into the river or sea, the combined effect of these individual choices was polluted waterways. Water pollution is a negative externality imposed by one community on other communities.

Most federal money over the years has funded sewage treatment plants. Real progress has been made in lessening sewage-related water pollution. Hundreds of once-polluted waterways have been cleaned up enough to permit swimming and fishing. The majority of U.S. cities now have modern sewage control. Notable exceptions include Boston, which still dumps sewage directly into Boston Harbor, and New York City, which teams up with New Jersey to dump raw sewage into the Atlantic Ocean, using a discharge point 106 miles off Cape May, New Jersey. At a huge cost, Boston is in the process of cleaning up its harbor. The typical residential water and sewer bill in Boston is projected to rise from $360 per year in 1990 to $1,620 per year in 2000.[5]

Chemicals are another source of water pollution. Chemical pollution may conjure up an image of a chemical company dumping in the river, but only about 10 percent of water pollution comes from *point* pollution, which means pollution from factories and other fixed industrial sites. About two-thirds of chemical pollutants in water come from what is called *nonpoint* pollution, derived mostly from runoff of pesticides and fertilizer from agriculture. Congress has been reluctant to limit the use of pesticides, though pesticides pollute water and contaminate food. Industrial America seems an easier target than Old MacDonald's farm.

In 1970, Congress shifted control of pesticides from the U.S. Department of Agriculture to the newly formed EPA. But the EPA already had its hands full administering the Clean Water Act, so it turned pesticide regulation over to the states. Most states turned the job over to their departments of agriculture. But these state agencies tend to *promote* the interests of farmers, not *restrict* what farmers can do. The EPA now reports that in most states pesticides have fouled the groundwater. The EPA also argues that pesticide residues on food pose more health problems than do toxic waste dumps or air pollution. Though the facts remain in dispute, according to EPA estimates, some 6,000 cancer deaths a year are caused by just one-third of the *approved* pesticides that have been tested. Over 50,000 pesticides on the market today have never been tested for their long-term health effects.

Hazardous Waste and the Superfund

The U.S. synthetic chemical industry has flourished in the last 40 years, and about 55,000 chemicals are in common use. Some have harmful effects on humans and other living creatures. These chemicals can pose risks at every stage of their production, use, and disposal. New Jersey manufactures more toxic

Net Bookmark

In 1970, the Environmental Protection Agency (EPA) became an independent federal agency, incorporating 15 components from 5 executive departments and independent agencies. The EPA is charged by Congress to protect U.S. land, air, and water systems. To learn more, or to review federal environmental legislation and policies, visit the EPA (http://www.epa.gov/).

---

5   See David Stipp, "Poor Pay a Big Price to Drink Clean Water," *The Wall Street Journal,* 15 January 1992.

chemicals than any other state and, not surprisingly, has the worst toxic waste burden. Prior to 1980, the disposal of toxic waste created get-rich-quick opportunities for anyone who could rent or buy a few acres of land to open a toxic waste dump. One site in New Jersey took in 71 million gallons of hazardous chemicals during a three-year period.[6]

Prior to 1980, once a company paid someone to haul away its hazardous waste, the company was no longer responsible. The Comprehensive Environmental Response, Compensation, and Liability Act of 1980, known more popularly as the *Superfund* law, requires any company that generates, stores, *or* transports hazardous wastes to pay to clean up any wastes that are improperly disposed of. A producer or hauler that is the source of even one barrel of pollution dumped at a site can be held responsible for cleaning up the entire site.

The Superfund law gives the federal government authority over sites contaminated with toxins. But to get an offending company to comply with its edicts, the EPA frequently must sue the company. So the process is slow, and over 80 percent of the Superfund budget, which is financed by a tax on manufacturers, has been spent on court costs and consultants' fees rather than on site cleanups. As of 1995, fewer than 10 percent of the sites designated for cleanup under the Superfund law had actually been cleaned up, though $20 billion had been spent. The law does not require that benefits exceed costs or even that such calculations be attempted.[7] A General Accounting Office study says that the number of cleanup sites could reach 4,000 and the cost could reach $39 billion. An Office of Technology Assessment study says the site count could reach 10,000 and the cost could climb to $100 billion.

A recent EPA study concludes that the health hazards of Superfund sites have been vastly exaggerated. Chemicals in the ground often move very slowly, sometimes taking years to travel a few feet, so any possible health threat may be narrowly confined to the site itself. In contrast, air pollution represents a more widespread threat because the air is so mobile and polluted air is drawn directly into the lungs. Those who are neighbors of toxic waste sites know it and can exert political pressure to get something done. But those who may in the future develop some disease from air- or water-borne pollution do not know it now. Thus, most people see no reason to press public officials for legislation that mandates clean air and clean water. *Because of their greater media appeal and political urgency, toxic waste dumps tend to receive more attention than air or water pollution.*

Solid Waste: "Paper or Plastic?"

Throughout most of history, households tossed their trash outside as fodder for pigs and goats. For example, New York City, like other cities, had no trash collection, so domestic waste was thrown into the street, where it mixed with mud and horse manure; decades of such behavior explains why the oldest Manhattan streets are anywhere from 3 to 15 feet above their original levels. About 200 years ago, people began to bury their trash near their homes or bring it to the

---

6   See Jason Zweig, "Real-Life Horror Story," *Forbes,* 12 December 1988.
7   For a fuller discussion of the costs and benefits of environmental protection, see Maureen L. Cropper and Wallace E. Oates, "Environmental Economics: A Survey," *Journal of Economic Literature* 30 (June 1992): pp. 675–740.

Despite increased attention to the need to recycle, according to the Environmental Protection Agency, only about 13 percent of all garbage generated annually in the United States is recycled.

Recycling The process of converting waste products into reusable material

town dump. Now U.S. households generate about 4.3 pounds of garbage per resident per day—more than double the quantity produced in 1960 and the largest amount per capita in the world. Much of our solid waste is packaging. The question is how to dispose of the 200 million tons of household garbage generated in this country each year.

Advanced economies produce and buy more than less-developed economies, so there is more to throw away. And because of higher incomes in advanced economies, the opportunity cost of time is higher, so there is a tendency to discard items rather than repair or recycle them. A broken toaster, for example, is more likely to be sent to the dump than to the repair shop. It's cheaper to buy a new toaster for $25 than to pay up to $30 per hour to have it repaired, assuming you can find a repair shop. (Look up "Appliance Repair, Small" in the Yellow Pages and see if you can find even one such repair shop in your area.)

About 75 percent of the nation's garbage is bulldozed and covered with soil in landfills. Although a well-managed landfill poses few environmental concerns, at one time communities dumped all kinds of toxic materials in them, materials that could leach into the soil, contaminating wells and aquifers. So landfills developed a bad reputation. The prevailing attitude with landfills is *NIMBY* (Not In My Back Yard). Everybody wants the garbage picked up but nobody wants it put down anywhere nearby.

As the cost of solid-waste disposal increases, state and local governments are instituting economizing measures, such as requiring households to sort their trash, charging households by the pound for trash pickups, and requiring returnable bottles. In 1995, about one third of U.S. households participated in curbside recycling programs. **Recycling** is the process of converting waste products into reusable material. Still, according to the EPA, only about 13 percent of the 200 million tons of garbage generated annually in the United States is recycled. About 14 percent is incinerated and the remaining 73 percent goes into landfills. Of the recycled material, three-quarters consists of corrugated boxes, newspapers, and office paper. Some of the paper product is shipped to Korea and Taiwan, where it becomes packaging material for U.S. imports such as VCRs, CD players, and computer components.

Most of the 14 percent of garbage that is incinerated each year is burned in trash-to-energy plants, which generate electricity using the heat from incineration. Until recently, such plants looked like the wave of the future, but a decline in energy prices, less favorable tax treatment, and environmental concerns over the siting of incinerators have taken the steam out of the trash-to-energy movement.

So about 73 percent of our garbage goes to landfills, and only 27 percent is incinerated or recycled. In contrast, the Japanese recycle 40 percent of their waste and incinerate 33 percent, leaving only 27 percent to be deposited in landfills. Japanese households sort their trash into as many as 21 categories. Because land is more scarce in Japan—we know this because it costs relatively more there—it is not surprising that the Japanese deposit a smaller share of their garbage in landfills.

Some recycling is clearly economical—such as aluminum cans, which are a cheap source of aluminum compared to producing new aluminum. About two out of three aluminum cans now get recycled. Recycling paper and cardboard is also economical and occurred long before the environmental movement. Still, despite promotional efforts, curbside programs account for only one-seventh of U.S. recycling. Such old standbys as paper drives, drop-off bins, and redemption centers still collect more tonnage than curbside programs. Most recycling results from salvaging scrap material from business and industry, a practice that goes back decades.

Governments have tried to stimulate demand for recycled material—for example, by requiring newspapers to use a certain amount of recycled newsprint. A rise in the price of timber used for newsprint has increased the demand for recycled newsprint, raising the price from $30 per ton in 1994 to over $100 per ton in 1995. Other recycled products are not in such demand. In fact, some recycled products have become worthless and must be hauled to the dump.[8] Plastic containers, for example, have limited recycling potential.

Recycling imposes its own cost on the environment. Curbside recycling requires fleets of trucks that pollute the air. Newsprint must first be de-inked, creating a sludge that must be disposed of. But greater environmental awareness has made consumers more receptive to more efficient packaging material. For example, liquid laundry detergent is now available in a more concentrated "ultra" form, which cuts volume in half. And labels for all kinds of products proudly identify the recycled content of the packaging.

CONCLUSION

Over 5.5 billion people inhabit the globe, and the population increases by about 90 million each year. World population is projected to double during the first half of the next century; 90 percent of this growth will occur in less-developed countries, where most people barely eke out a living. Growing population pressure coupled with a lack of incentives to preserve open-access resources results in deforestation, dwindling fish stocks, and polluted air, land, and water.

Ironically, because of tighter pollution controls, developed countries tend to be less polluted than developing countries, where there is more pollution per capita from what little industry there is. Most developing countries have such profound economic problems that environmental quality is not high on their list of priorities. The air in places such as Mexico City and Lagos, Nigeria, is dangerous. Residents of China's cities cover their mouths with masks when the smog is especially thick. Farmers in Central America douse their crops with pesticides long banned in the United States.

Market prices can direct the allocation of resources only as long as property rights are well defined and can be enforced at a reasonable cost. Pollution of air, land, and water arises not so much from the greed of producers and consumers as from the fact that these open-access resources are subject to the common pool problem.

---

8   For example, see the discussion by Jeff Bailey, "Curbside Recycling Comforts the Soul, But Benefits Are Scant," *The Wall Street Journal,* 19 January 1995.

SUMMARY

1. Private choices will result in too little output when positive externalities exist and too much output when negative externalities exist. Public policy should subsidize or otherwise promote the production of goods generating positive externalities and should tax or otherwise discourage the production of goods generating negative externalities.

2. The optimal amount of environmental quality occurs where the marginal social cost of higher quality equals its marginal social benefit. A decrease in the marginal cost or an increase in the marginal benefit of environmental quality increases the optimal level of environmental quality.

3. The world's tropical rain forests have served to recycle noxious gases and convert them into oxygen and wood;

the destruction of these forests reduces the environment's ability to cleanse itself.

4. The Coase theorem argues that as long as bargaining costs are small, assigning property rights to one party leads to an efficient solution to the problem of externalities. An example of the Coase theorem in action is the market for pollution permits.

5. In the last two decades, progress has been made in cleaning up the nation's air and waterways. The air is cleaner because of stricter emissions standards for motor vehicles; the water is cleaner because of billions spent on sewage treatment facilities. Though much of the federal attention and federal budget goes toward cleaning up toxic waste dumps, this pollution source does not pose as great a health threat to the population as a whole as do other forms of pollution such as smog and pesticides.

QUESTIONS AND PROBLEMS

1. **(Types of Resources)** Complete each of the following sentences:
   a. If it is difficult or costly to exclude individuals from using certain resources, they are known as _____ _____ resources.
   b. Resources that are available only in a finite amount are _____ resources.
   c. The possibility that a nonexcludable resource will be used until the net marginal value of additional zero equals zero is known as the _____.
   d. Resources for which periodic use can be continued indefinitely are known as _____ resources.
   e. If no individual can easily capture the value of a resource, it is termed _____.

2. **(Negative Externalities)** Consider the situation illustrated in Exhibit 1, which generates a negative externality. If the government simply sets the price of electricity at the optimal level (that is, where the marginal social cost equals the demand), why is the net gain equal to triangle *abc* even though consumers now pay a higher price for electricity? What would the net gain be if the government set the price above the optimal level?

3. **(External Costs)** Explain the difference between fixed-technology production and variable-technology production. Should the government set a goal of reducing the marginal social cost to zero in polluting industries with

either fixed-technology or variable-technology production?

4. **(Coase Theorem)** Suppose a firm pollutes a stream that has recreational value only when pollution is below a certain level. If transaction costs are low, why does the assignment of property rights to the stream lead to the same (efficient) level of pollution whether the firm or the recreational users own the stream?

5. **(External Costs)** Use the data below to answer the following questions.

Quantity	Marginal Private Benefit (Demand)	Marginal Private Cost (Supply)	Marginal Social Cost
0	—	$ 0	$ 0
1	$10	2	4
2	9	3	5
3	8	4	6
4	7	5	7
5	6	6	8
6	5	7	9
7	4	8	10
8	3	9	11
9	2	10	12
10	1	11	13

   a. What is the external cost per unit of production?

b. At what level will the economy produce if there is no regulation of the externality?

c. At what level should the economy produce to achieve economic efficiency?

d. Calculate the dollar value of the net gain to society from correcting the externality.

6. **(External Costs with Variable Technology)** Consider an industry that pollutes the water and has access to variable technology for reducing the water pollution. Graphically illustrate and explain the impact of each of the following, other things constant, on the optimal level of water quality:

a. New statistical evidence that reduces the estimated cancer danger from water pollution.

b. An increase in the cost of pollution-abatement equipment for the industry with no better technology available.

c. New statistical evidence that increases the estimated danger of typhoid epidemics resulting from water pollution.

7. **(Positive Externalities)** Discuss the following proposition: "Education should be subsidized because external benefits increase when education consumption increases."

8. **(Coase Analysis)** Ronald Coase points out that a market failure does not arise simply from people ignoring the external cost of their actions. What other condition is necessary? What does he consider the efficient solution to a negative externality?

9. **(Reduction of Negative Externalities)** Suppose you wish to reduce a negative externality by imposing a tax on the activity that creates the externality. If the amount of the externality produced per unit of output increases as output increases, show how to determine the correct tax by using a supply-demand diagram. Assume that marginal private cost slopes upward.

10. **(Pollution Rights)** Consider the graph below showing the market for pollution rights.

a. If there are no restrictions on pollution, what will be the amount of discharge?

b. Where is market equilibrium if the government restricts the amount of discharge to Q^* but gives the permits away?

c. Where is market equilibrium if the government sells the permits? Illustrate this on the graph.

d. What happens to market equilibrium if the government reduces the amount of permitted discharge to Q^{**}? Illustrate this on the graph.

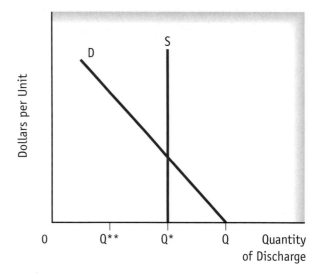

11. **(Resolving the Common Pool Problem)** The Coase theorem advocates solving an externality problem by assigning property rights to one party or another. When would government regulations be more appropriate?

12. **(Pollution Tax)** In Exhibit 1, correction of the negative externality creates a *net* social gain of area *abc*. If the correction is achieved by imposing a tax of 4 cents per kilowatt hour and the tax revenues are rebated back to electricity users, show the gains and losses (if any) that occur as a result of the correction.

13. **(Water Pollution)** What are the two main sources of water pollution in the United States? Explain the difference between point pollution and nonpoint pollution. What type of problem is represented by water pollution?

14. **(Hazardous Waste)** What is the Superfund Law?

15. **(Solid Waste)** What are the economic incentives for households to recycle? To what extent should recycling be encouraged by government policies?

16. **(Tropical Rain Forests)** Can the Coase theorem provide any insight into the problem of the destruction of the world's tropical rain forests?

17. **(Tropical Rain Forests)** Why does a solution involving reduction in the demand for tropical forest lumber require some form of international cooperation? Would this be a sufficient solution to the deforestation problem?

18. **(City in the Clouds)** Which is more visible to the typical citizen of Mexico City, the benefits or costs associated with sources of air pollution?

19. Visit the Chicago Board of Trade Recyclables Exchange (CRE) (http://www.cbot.com/recyclables/).

    a. Discuss briefly how the exchange works. List five types of materials traded on the exchange.

    b. Given the economic factors influencing recycling, what role, if any, does the CRE have in promoting recycling?

Income Distribution and Poverty

The United States produces more output per capita than any other country in the world. The nation also devotes an amount equal to 12 percent of the gross domestic product to public assistance and social insurance programs. Yet poverty remains more prevalent here than in most other industrialized countries. What's more, poverty rates are higher now than they were 25 years ago. Why does the most productive nation on earth experience such poverty, and why have decades of social programs failed to reduce that poverty?

In this chapter, we attempt to answer those questions. To establish a reference point, we first examine the distribution of income in the United States, paying special attention to poverty in recent years. We then discuss and evaluate the "social safety net"—public policies aimed at helping the poor. We also consider the impact of the changing family structure on the incidence of poverty, focusing in particular on the increase in female householders. We will explore the effects of discrimination on the distribution of income and close the chapter by examining recent welfare reforms. Topics discussed in this chapter include:

- Distribution of income
- Lorenz curve
- Official poverty level
- Public policy and poverty

- The feminization of poverty
- Poverty and discrimination
- Recent welfare reforms

THE DISTRIBUTION OF HOUSEHOLD INCOME

In a market economy, household income depends primarily on household earnings, which depend on the productivity of the household's resources. The problem with allocating income according to productivity is that some people have difficulty earning income. Those born with mental or physical disabilities tend to be less productive and may be unable to earn a living. Others may face limited job choices and reduced wages because of advanced age, a poor education, discrimination in the marketplace, or demands of caring for small children.

As a starting point, let's first consider the distribution of income in the economy and see how it has changed over time, focusing on the family as the economic unit. After dividing the total number of families into five groups of equal size, ranked according to income, we can examine what percentage of income is received by each group. Such a division is presented in Exhibit 1 for various years since 1929. Take a moment to look this exhibit over. Notice that in 1929, families in the lowest, or poorest, fifth of the population received only 3.5 percent of the income, whereas families in the highest, or richest, fifth received 54.4 percent of the income. Thus, the richest 20 percent of the families received over half the income. Income here is measured after cash transfer payments have been received but before taxes have been paid.

Notice also that the richest group's share of income dropped from 54.4 percent in 1929 to 43.0 percent in 1947. Why? The Great Depression erased many personal fortunes, and World War II generated jobs and increased wages, pulling more people into the work force. After the war, the distribution of income remained remarkably stable for the next three decades, with about 5 percent going to the bottom fifth and about 41 percent going to the top fifth.

In recent years, the share of income going to the top fifth has increased and the share going to the bottom fifth has declined slightly. Most recently, the top fifth received over 10 times as much income as the bottom fifth. Again, income is measured after cash transfer payments are received but before taxes are paid.

Other evidence tends to support the conclusion that the income going to those at the top has increased. The Census Bureau reported that the percentage of full-time workers who earn less than what would be the poverty level for a family of four increased from 12 percent in 1979 to 18 percent in 1990.[1]

Why has income, when measured before taxes but after cash transfer payments, become more unevenly distributed? Between 1973 and 1993, the wage rate (adjusted for inflation) declined more for poorly educated workers than for well-educated workers. Here are some reasons why. First, new computer-based information technologies increased the demand for skilled labor—for knowledge workers—relative to unskilled workers. The automation accompanying the widespread use of computers and other technological changes has increased demand for skilled workers and simultaneously, because of automation, reduced the demand for less-skilled workers. Second, trends such as deregulation, declining unionization, and greater international trade have reduced the demand for workers with less education. Labor unions, for example, tend to increase the wages for workers who would otherwise end up in the bottom half of the income distribution. The share of the labor force that is unionized has declined

---

1   U.S. Bureau of the Census, *Workers with Low Earnings: 1964 to 1990,* U.S. Department of Commerce, Current Population Reports, Series P-120, No. 178, 1992.

		Percentage Share			
Year	Lowest Fifth	Second-Lowest Fifth	Middle Fifth	Second-Highest Fifth	Highest Fifth
1929	3.5%	9.0%	13.8%	19.3%	54.4%
1947	5.0	11.9	17.0	23.1	43.0
1957	5.1	12.7	18.1	23.8	40.4
1967	5.5	12.4	17.9	23.9	40.4
1977	5.2	11.6	17.5	24.2	41.5
1987	4.6	10.8	16.9	24.1	43.7
1994	4.1	9.9	15.7	23.3	47.0

EXHIBIT 1

The Distribution of Money Income Among Families for Selected Years since 1929

Source: U.S. Bureau of the Census, *Current Population Reports*, Series P-60 (Washington, D.C.: U.S. Government Printing Office, 1995).

from 26 percent in 1973 to 16 percent in 1995. Third, recent U.S. immigrants have tended to be less educated than existing residents, thus increasing the supply of relatively poorly educated workers in the labor force. So economic developments in recent years have benefited the better educated and this helps explain the growing disparity in family income.

Note that it is not necessarily the same families who remain rich or poor over time. Some families drop out of high-income ranks and are replaced by others; likewise, some families work their way out of poverty to be replaced, for example, by young unmarried women who become mothers. So we are not talking about the same families getting richer or poorer over time.

Income in the United States is more concentrated than in other developed countries throughout the world, such as Canada, France, Germany, Great Britain, Japan, Italy, and Australia. But income in the United States is less concentrated than in many developing countries, such as India, Brazil, Turkey, Mexico, and the Philippines. Half or more of all income in developing countries goes to the richest 20 percent of the population.

Lorenz curve A curve showing the percentage of total income received by a given percentage of recipients whose incomes are arranged from smallest to largest

The Lorenz Curve

The Lorenz curve is another way of picturing the distribution of income in an economy. As shown in Exhibit 2, the cumulative percentage of families is measured along the horizontal axis, and the cumulative percentage of income is measured along the vertical axis. The **Lorenz curve** shows the percentage of total income received by any given percentage of recipients when incomes are arrayed from smallest to largest.

Any given distribution of income can be compared to an equal distribution of income among families. If income were evenly distributed, the poorest 20 percent of the population would receive 20 percent of the total income, the poorest 40 percent of the population would receive 40 percent of the income, and so on. The Lorenz curve in this case would be a straight line with a slope equal to 1, as shown in Exhibit 2.

As the distribution becomes more uneven, the Lorenz curve is pulled down and to the right, away from the line of equal distribution. The Lorenz curves in Exhibit 2 were calculated for 1929 and 1994, based on the data in Exhibit 1. As a point of reference, point *a* on the 1929 Lorenz curve indicates that in that year, the bottom 80 percent of families had 45.6 percent of the income and the

E X H I B I T   2

**Lorenz Curves, 1929
and 1994**

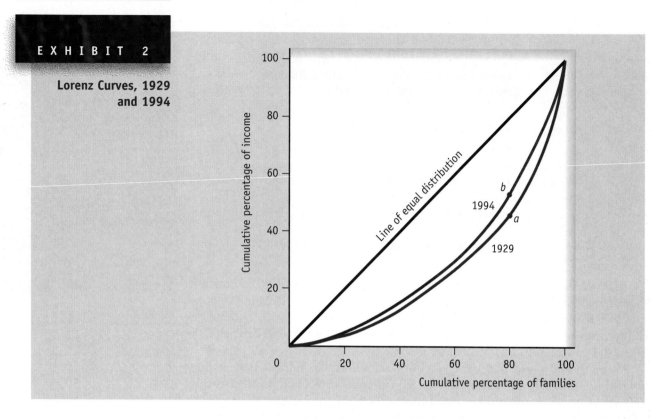

top 20 percent had 54.4 percent of the income. Point *b* on the 1994 Lorenz curve shows that in that year, the bottom 80 percent had 53.0 percent of the income; the income share of the top 20 percent was down to 47.0 percent. The Lorenz curve for 1994 is closer to the center than the one for 1929.

One problem with examining income distributions is that there is no objective standard for evaluating them. The inference thus far is that a more equal distribution of income is more desirable, but is a perfectly even distribution most preferred? If not, then how uneven should the distribution be? For example, among major league baseball players, about 54 percent of the pay goes to 20 percent of the players.[2] So income among major league baseball players is more unevenly distributed than family income in the economy. Does this mean the economy as a whole is "fairer" than professional baseball?

Families receive income from two primary sources: resource earnings and transfer payments from the government. Exhibits 1 and 2 measure money income after cash transfers but before taxes. Thus, the distributions shown in Exhibits 1 and 2 omit the effects of taxes and in-kind transfers, such as food stamps and free medical care for poor families. The tax system as a whole tends to be mildly progressive, meaning that families with higher incomes pay a larger fraction of their incomes in taxes. In-kind transfers benefit the lowest-income groups the most. Consequently, if Exhibits 1 and 2 incorporated the effects of taxes and in-kind transfers, the share of income going to the lower groups would increase, the share going to the higher groups would decrease, and income would be more evenly distributed.

---

2   This statistic was computed by the author based on salaries provided in "Baseball Salaries: Mets Are Leaders of Pack," *USA Today,* 2 April 1992.

Finally, the income distribution figures include only reported sources of income. If people receive payment "under the table" to evade taxes, or if they earn money through illegal activities, their actual income will exceed their reported income. The omission of unreported income will distort the data in the first two exhibits only if unreported income as a percentage of total family income differs across income levels.

Why Do Incomes Differ?

The **median income** of all families is the middle income when incomes are ranked from lowest to highest. In any given year, half the families are above the median income and half are below it. Since most income comes from selling labor, variations in income across families stem primarily from differences in the number of workers in each family. Thus, *one reason family incomes differ is that the number of family members who are working differs.* For example, among families in the bottom 20 percent based on income, only one in five has a full-time, year-round worker. Over two-thirds of families in the bottom 20 percent are headed by an unmarried female.

More generally, the median income for families with two earners is about 68 percent higher than for families with only one earner and nearly *three times* higher than for families with no earners. Incomes also differ for all the reasons labor incomes differ, such as differences in education, ability, job experience, and so on. Exhibit 3 links *education* and *age* to the *median income* of males who were year-round, full-time workers in 1993. Age brackets are measured on the horizontal axis and median money income on the vertical axis. The bottom, middle, and top lines reflect the median money income of those with less than a ninth-grade education, with a high-school diploma, and with a college education or more, respectively.

The relationship between income and education is clear. At every age, those with more education earn more, on average. Age itself also has an important effect on income. As workers mature, they acquire valuable job experience, get promoted, and earn more. Note in Exhibit 3 that the additional earnings from a college education are large at the outset and grow even larger as the workers get older. This suggests that college graduates, who are more likely doing mental work, are rewarded more for their job experience than are others, who are more likely doing physical work.

Differences in earnings based on age and education reflect the normal *life-cycle* pattern of income. In fact, most income differences across households reflect the normal workings of resource markets, whereby workers are rewarded according to their marginal productivity. High-income families often consist of well-educated couples with both spouses employed. Low-income families tend to be headed by single parents who are young, female, poorly educated, and not working. Low incomes are a matter of public concern, especially when children are involved, as we will see in the next section.

On average, high school graduates earn more than those who fail to graduate high school, and college graduates earn more still than high school graduates.

Median income The middle income in a series of incomes ranked from smallest to largest

POVERTY AND THE POOR

Since poverty is such a relative concept, how do we measure it objectively and how do we ensure that our measure can be applied with equal relevance over time? The federal government has developed a method for calculating an offi-

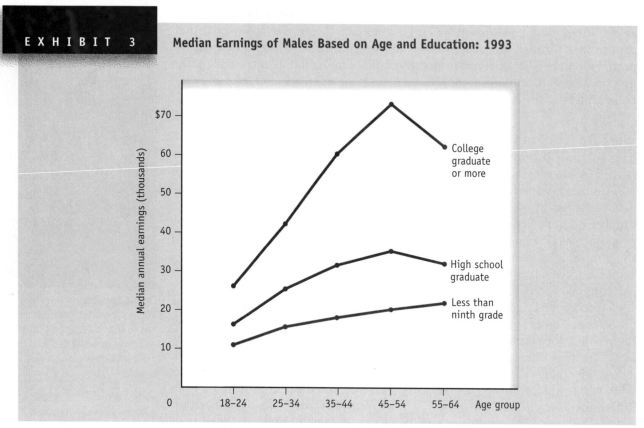

EXHIBIT 3   **Median Earnings of Males Based on Age and Education: 1993**

Source: U.S. Bureau of the Census.

cial poverty level; this level has become the benchmark for poverty analysis in the United States.

Official Poverty Level

To derive the official poverty level, the U.S. Department of Agriculture first estimates the cost of a nutritionally adequate diet. Then, based on the assumption that the poor spend about one-third of their income on food, the official poverty level is calculated by multiplying these food costs by three. Adjustments are made for family size and for inflation over time. The official poverty threshold of money income for a family of four was $15,081 in 1994; a family of four at or below that income threshold was regarded as living in poverty. Poverty thresholds in 1994 ranged from $7,547 for a person living alone to $32,981 for a family with nine or more members. The poverty definition is based on pretax money income, including cash transfers, but it excludes the value of noncash transfers such as food stamps, Medicaid, subsidized housing, or employer-provided health insurance.

Each year since 1959, the Census Bureau has conducted a survey comparing individual families' annual cash incomes to the annual poverty threshold applicable to that family. Results of this survey are presented in Exhibit 4, which indicates both the number of people living below the official poverty level (left-hand scale) and the poverty rate, which is the percentage of the U.S. population below that level (right-hand scale). The biggest decline in the poverty rate occurred prior to 1970; *the poverty rate dropped from 22.4 percent in 1959 to 12.1 percent in 1969.* During that period, the number of poor people dropped from

Number and Percentage of Poor, 1959–1994

EXHIBIT 4

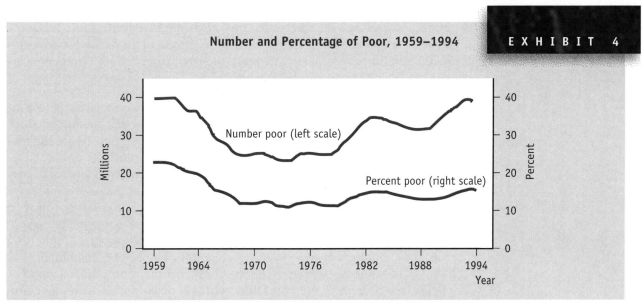

Source: U.S. Bureau of the Census web site (http://www.census.gov/ftp/pub/hhes/www/img/histpov.gif).

about 40 million to 24 million. The poverty rate bottomed out during the 1970s, then rose between 1979 and 1983. After a modest decline between 1983 and 1989, the rate turned up in 1990 and topped out in 1993 at 15.1 percent before falling slightly to 14.5 percent in 1994. The 38.0 million people in poverty in 1994 is down slightly from 39.3 million in 1993.

Poverty is a relative term. If we examined the distribution of income across the countries of the world, we would find huge gaps between rich and poor nations. The official U.S. poverty level of income is many times greater than the average income for three-fourths of the world's population.[3]

An income at the U.S. poverty level today provides a standard of living that would have been considered attractive by most people who lived in the United States at the turn of the century, when only 15 percent of families had flush toilets, only 3 percent had electricity, and only 1 percent had central heating. Finally, the official definition of poverty ignores other assets such as owner-occupied housing or consumer durables such as automobiles. According to one study carried out in the 1980s, three in ten households identified as poor owned their own home and half owned a motor vehicle.

Programs to Help the Poor

What should society's response to poverty be? *Families with a full-time worker are nine times more likely to escape poverty than are families with no worker.* Thus, the government's first line of defense in fighting poverty is to promote a healthy economy and to provide the education and training that enhance job opportunities. Yet even when the unemployment rate is relatively low, some people may remain poor because they lack marketable skills, must care for small children, or face discrimination in the labor market.

Although some government programs to help the poor involve direct mar-

3   See World Bank, *World Development Report 1995* (New York: Oxford University Press, 1995), Table 30.

ket intervention, such as minimum-wage laws, the most visible programs redistribute income after the market has provided an initial distribution. Since the mid-1960s, social welfare expenditures at all levels of government have increased significantly. We can divide social welfare programs into two major categories: social insurance and income assistance.

Social Insurance. The social insurance system is designed to replace the lost income of those who worked but are now retired, temporarily unemployed, or unable to work because of total disability or work-related injury. By far the major social insurance program is *Social Security,* established during the Great Depression of the 1930s to provide retirement income to those with a work history and a record of contributing to the program. *Medicare,* another social insurance program, provides health insurance for short-term medical care to those aged 65 and older, regardless of income. Other social insurance programs include *unemployment insurance* and *worker's compensation,* which supports workers injured on the job; both require that beneficiaries have a prior record of employment.

The social insurance system deducts "insurance premiums" from workers' pay to provide benefits in the event of retirement, disability, or unemployment. These programs protect some families from poverty, particularly the elderly receiving Social Security, but they are aimed more at those with a work history. Still, the social insurance system tends to redistribute income from rich to poor and from young to old. Most Social Security beneficiaries receive far more in benefits than they paid into the program, especially those with a brief work history or a record of low wages.

Income Assistance. Income assistance programs—what we usually call "welfare"—provide money and in-kind assistance to the poor. Unlike social insurance programs, income assistance programs do not require the recipient to have worked or to have contributed to the program. Income assistance programs are means tested. In a **means-tested program,** a household's income and assets must be below a certain level to qualify for benefits. People who qualify for assistance are considered *entitled* to the program; hence, these programs are called *entitlement programs* (though legislation has been recently proposed to eliminate the inherent right, or entitlement, to welfare). The federal government funds two-thirds of welfare spending, and state and local governments fund one-third. Nearly half of all welfare spending pays for medical care.

The two primary *cash transfer* programs are *Aid to Families with Dependent Children (AFDC),* which provides cash to poor families with dependent children, and *Supplemental Security Income (SSI),* which provides cash to the elderly poor and the disabled. Cash transfers vary inversely with family income from other sources. AFDC began during the Great Depression and was originally aimed at providing support for widows with young children. The cost is divided between the state and federal governments, with the federal government paying more than half of the total in poorer states (for example, in Mississippi each dollar of state spending is matched by five dollars of federal spending). In 1994, the AFDC caseload reached 5 million for the first time in history (in all, about 14 million people receive AFDC benefits, of which 9 million are children).

Because AFDC benefit levels are set by each state, they vary widely. For example, benefit levels in California are over five times higher, on average, than those in Alabama. Such differences encourage some poor people to migrate to states where benefit levels are more attractive.

Means-tested program To be eligible for such a program, an individual's income and/or assets must not exceed specified levels

The Supplemental Security Income program provides support for the elderly and disabled poor. SSI is the fastest growing cash transfer program, with outlays increasing from $8 billion in 1980 to $25 billion in 1995. SSI coverage has been broadened to include those addicted to drugs and alcohol, immigrants ineligible for other programs, children with learning disabilities, and, in some cases, the homeless. The federal portion of this program is uniform across states, but states can supplement federal aid. Benefit levels in California average nearly twice those in Alabama. Most states also offer modest *General Assistance* aid to those who are poor but do not qualify for AFDC or SSI.

The federal government also provides an *earned income tax credit* to the working poor. For example, a family with two children and earnings of $11,300 in 1995 would have received a cash transfer of $3,110 as an earned income tax credit. More than 12 million workers received credits.

In addition to cash transfer programs, a variety of *in-kind transfer* programs provide health care, food stamps, and housing assistance to the poor. *Medicaid* pays for medical care for those with incomes below a certain level who are aged, blind, disabled, or in families with dependent children. It is by far the largest welfare program, costing nearly twice as much as all cash transfer programs combined. Medicaid has grown more than any other poverty program, quadrupling in the last decade. It accounts for one-fifth of the typical state's budget. The qualifying level of income is set by each state, and some states are quite strict. Therefore, the proportion of poor covered by Medicaid varies greatly across states. In 1995, about 25 million individuals received Medicaid; outlays averaged about $3,000 per recipient. Spending on the 3.5 million beneficiaries aged 65 and older averaged about $7,000 per year. For many elderly, Medicaid pays for long-term nursing care (Medicaid pays half the nation's nursing home costs). Although half the welfare budget goes for health care, nearly 40 million U.S. residents still have no health insurance.

Food stamps are vouchers that can be redeemed for food. The program is aimed at reducing hunger and providing nutrition to poor families. The cost is paid by the federal government, and benefits are uniform across states. About 1 in 10 Americans received food stamps in 1995, with an average monthly benefit of about $275 per household.

Housing assistance programs include direct assistance for rental payments and subsidized low-income housing. Spending for housing assistance has more than doubled since 1980. About 10 million people received some form of housing assistance.[4] Other in-kind programs include the *school lunch program* for poor children; supplemental food vouchers for pregnant women, infants, and children; *energy assistance* to help pay the energy bills of poor families; and *education and training assistance* for poor families, such as Head Start and the Job Training Partnership Act. In all, there are 77 means-tested federal welfare programs.

Welfare Expenditures and the Rate of Poverty

As noted at the beginning of the chapter, social insurance programs and income assistance programs at all levels of government totaled an amount equal to 12 percent of GDP in 1995. Most of the funding went to social insurance programs rather than to programs aimed more specifically at the poor. Income assistance programs— what we typically think of as welfare programs—claimed about 4 percent of GDP.

---

4   This is an increase of about 50 percent over the number receiving benefits in 1980. About 60 percent of the families in public housing in 1990 had incomes below the poverty level.

The most rapid growth in government outlays aimed specifically at assisting poor people occurred between 1970 and 1981, when expenditures (adjusted for inflation) more than doubled, growing by an average of 9.6 percent per year. But earlier we learned that the greatest drop in poverty occurred prior to 1970. Thus, the improvement in the poverty rate stopped just before government outlays for the poor showed their greatest increase. Why didn't increased spending reduce the poverty rate?

Exclusion of In-Kind Transfers. One reason official poverty statistics seem unaffected by the greater welfare spending between 1970 and 1981 is that the Census Bureau includes only *money transfers* in the definition of income. It ignores the value of in-kind transfer programs, such as Medicaid, food stamps, and housing assistance. When official poverty statistics were first collected in the 1960s, in-kind transfers were minimal, so ignoring these transfers did not seem to matter. But in-kind programs expanded during the 1970s and most recently accounted for about three-fourths of all welfare spending. Ignoring in-kind transfers in the definition of income biases the poverty statistics, making the official figures higher than the actual values. When poverty data include the value of in-kind transfers, the poverty rate drops by about one-fifth.

Despite the growth in in-kind benefit programs, many of the poor still do not receive them (though some families above the poverty line do). Often the poor do not receive benefits because they fail to apply for them, but just as often coverage is limited because of long waiting lists (such as for public housing) or because certain states establish eligibility requirements (such as for Medicaid) that allow only the poorest of the poor to qualify.

Slower Economic Growth. For another explanation of why the war on poverty stalled in the early 1970s, we must look beyond welfare programs to the health of the underlying economy. "A rising tide lifts all boats"—so goes the old saying about the relationship between a thriving economy and rising individual fortunes. A healthy economy can reduce poverty. Between 1959 and 1969, the period during which poverty dropped the most, the economy showed the strongest growth; real family income grew on average by more than one-third. Between 1969 and 1979, however, economic growth slowed. Twice as many people were unemployed in 1979 as in 1969. The effect of the growth in transfer spending during the 1970s may have been to compensate in part for a flat economy, with the result that poverty rates remained relatively unchanged. Poverty rates climbed in the early 1980s because the economy was weakening, then began to fall after 1983 as the economy improved. The poverty rates climbed again in the early 1990s with the recession, then dropped slightly in 1994 as the economy improved.

Perhaps more important than the effect of the economy on poverty has been the change in the family structure. To develop a fuller understanding of the extent and composition of poverty over time, we must look behind the totals and examine the change in the composition of the poor.

WHO ARE THE POOR?

Who are the poor, and how has the composition of this group changed over time? We will slice poverty statistics in several ways to examine the makeup of the group. Keep in mind that we are relying on official poverty estimates,

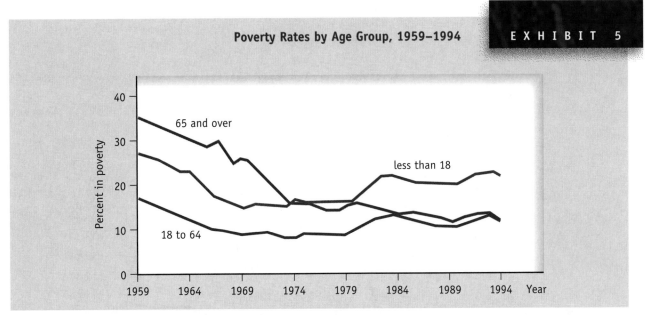

Poverty Rates by Age Group, 1959–1994

EXHIBIT 5

Source: U.S. Bureau of the Census web site (http://www.census.gov/ftp/pub/hhes/www/img/povages.gif).

which ignore the value of in-kind transfers and to that extent overstate the extent of poverty.

Poverty and Age

Earlier we looked at the poverty rate among the entire population. Now we focus on poverty and age. Exhibit 5 presents the poverty rates for three age groups since 1959: those less than 18 years old, those between 18 and 64, and those 65 and older. The poverty rates for each group declined between 1959 and 1968. Since the mid-1970s, the poverty rate among those under 18 years of age has trended upward, except for a decline between 1984 and 1989. In 1994, the poverty rate among people under 18 years of age was 21.8 percent—about twice the rate of those 18 and over.

In 1959, the elderly were the poorest group, with a poverty rate about 35 percent. Since then, elderly poverty has fallen steadily; in 1994, the rate was 11.7 percent, slightly below the rate of 11.9 percent for those 18 to 64 years of age. This reduction in poverty among elderly families can be attributed to a tremendous growth in Social Security and Medicare spending, which grew from $55 billion in 1959 to about $500 billion in 1995 (measured in 1995 dollars). Social Security and Medicare spending is now *triple* what the federal government spends on income assistance, or welfare, programs. *Though not welfare programs in a strict sense, Social Security and Medicare have been extremely successful in reducing poverty among the elderly.*

Poverty and Public Choice

In a democratic country such as ours, public policies depend very much on the political power of the interest groups involved. In recent years, the elderly have become a strong political force. Unlike most interest groups, the elderly are a group we all expect to join one day. The elderly actually are represented by four constituencies: (1) the elderly themselves, (2) those under 65 who are concerned about the current benefits to their parents or other elderly relatives, (3) those under 65 who are concerned about their own benefits in the future, and

EXHIBIT 6

Percentage of Families in Poverty: 1974–1994

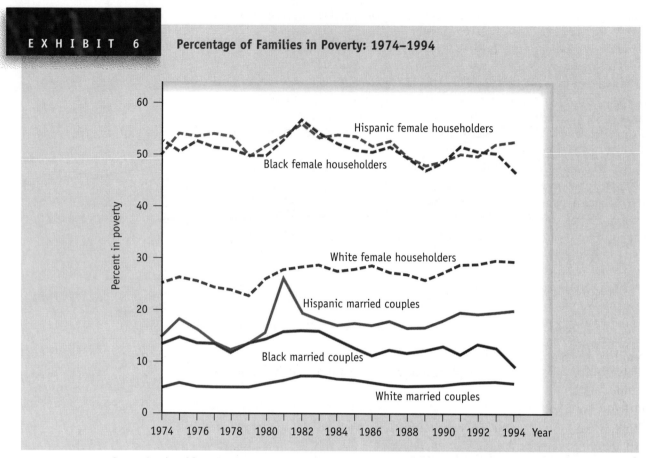

Source: Developed from data found in U.S. Bureau of the Census CD-ROM, Income and Poverty, Table 4, 1995.

(4) those who earn their living by caring for the elderly, such as doctors and nursing home operators.

Moreover, the voter participation rate of those 65 and over tends to be higher than that of other age groups. For example, during the congressional election of 1994, voter participation of those 65 years of age and older was triple that of those between 18 and 24 and four times that of welfare recipients. The political muscle of the elderly has been flexed whenever a question of Social Security benefits has comes up.

Poverty and Gender

One way of classifying the incidence of poverty is by age. Another way is based on the marital status and race of the household head. Exhibit 6 compares, for white, black, and Hispanic families, the poverty rates for married couples with the rates for female householders. Two trends are unmistakable. First, married couples have poverty rates only about one-third of the rate of female householders, and, second, whites have rates only about half those of blacks and Hispanics (individuals of Hispanic origin may be of any race).

During the last two decades, poverty rates for the six groups depicted have fluctuated from year to year, but there has been little long-term trend up or down. *Female householders had a poverty rate in 1994 of 35 percent, which has been the average for this group since 1980.* Not shown in the exhibit are poverty rates among male householders, which are higher than among married couples but still only about half the rates of female householders. The findings show that regardless of race or Hispanic origin, children living in two-parent families are much less likely to be poor than children in one-parent families.

Though the poverty rates among female householders are high, *these rates have increased little since 1969.* What has increased is the *number* of female householders in the economy. The percentage of births to unmarried mothers is five times greater today than in 1960. In 1960, only one in 200 children lived with a single parent who had never married. By 1995, one in ten children lived with a single parent who had never married.

The United States has the highest teenage pregnancy rate in the developed world—twice the level in Great Britain and 15 times the rate in Japan. Since the father in such cases typically assumes little responsibility for child support, children born outside marriage are likely to be poorer than other children. Also, the divorce rate has increased since 1960. Because of the higher divorce rate, even children born to married couples now face a greater likelihood of living in a one-parent household before they grow up. Divorce usually reduces the resources available to the children. *Children of female householders are five times more likely to live in poverty than are other children.*

The increase in the number of unwed mothers and in the divorce rate has doubled the number of female householders since 1969. With a doubling in the number of householders came a doubling in the number of poor people from such families. Thus, even though the poverty *rate* among such families has remained relatively constant since 1969 at about 35 percent, the *number* of poor in families of female householders has increased because the *number* of female householders has increased. Whereas the number of female householders jumped 119 percent between 1969 and 1994, the number of other families grew only 24 percent, and the poverty rate of these other types of families actually *declined* slightly from 6.9 percent to 6.7 percent.

Thus, female householders accounted for nearly all of the increase in poor families since 1969. *The growth in the number of poor families since 1969 resulted overwhelmingly from the growth in the number of female householders.* Since 1969, the U.S. economy has generated over 40 million new jobs. Married couples were in the best position to take advantage of this job growth because they typically had one more potential wage earner than did single female householders.

Young single motherhood is a recipe for instant poverty. Often the young mother drops out of school, which reduces her future earning possibilities when and if she seeks work outside the home. Even a strong economy is little aid to households with nobody in the labor force. Worse yet, young single mothers-to-be are less likely to seek adequate medical care; the result is a higher proportion of premature, underweight babies. This is one reason why the U.S. infant mortality rate ranks above many other industrialized countries.

Each year, about 1.2 million children in the United States are born to single mothers—a number that exceeds the population of 11 states. There is a clear link between unwed parenthood and welfare dependency. Two-thirds of all out-of-wedlock births are to 15- to 24-year olds. Only 57 percent of these mothers have a high-school diploma, and only 28 percent ever worked full time (another 9 percent worked part time). Because of a lack of education and limited job skills, most unwed mothers go on welfare. Once on welfare, unwed mothers tend to stay there. The average never-married mother spends a decade on welfare, twice as long as divorced mothers.

Poverty has therefore become increasingly feminized, mostly because female house-holders have become more common. Because the number of female householders has grown more rapidly among blacks, the feminization of poverty has been more dramatic in black households. Sixty-eight percent of all black births in 1992 were to unmarried women, compared to 39 percent of all births among those of Hispanic origin and 23 percent of births among whites.[5]

Much black poverty occurs in the poorest areas of central cities, where crime, gangs, and drug abuse compound the problem of poverty, creating a group of poor called the *underclass*. The underclass is frequently defined as the poor who live in inner-city neighborhoods where poverty rates are 40 percent or higher. The underclass must cope not only with grinding poverty but also with the daily horror of crime and drug addiction in the neighborhood. Poor job prospects among unskilled young black men in some cases leads to crime and drug addiction—activities that may result in prison terms or even death. Surveys indicate that young black men are more likely now than a decade ago to view crime more rewarding than regular employment.[6] Because so many young black men are unemployed or in prison, marriage prospects of young black females are limited by a shortage of eligible black males.[7]

Some children are born to drug-addicted mothers.[8] The expression "no-parent" households can be used to reflect the sad circumstances of such children. In one inner-city school, half the students lived with neither a mother nor a father. Some schools are trying to adapt to the needs of children from no-parent households by providing more social services such as health care at school. Washington, D.C., even considered operating a boarding school for such children.

The high poverty rate among female householders and the poor job prospects for unskilled black males raise the question whether job discrimination is a contributing factor. In an earlier chapter, we considered discrimination against women and examined the issue of comparable worth. We now consider racial discrimination.

Poverty and Discrimination

Is the lower family income and greater incidence of poverty among blacks the result of discrimination in job markets, or are there other explanations? We should note that discrimination can occur in many ways: in school funding, in housing, in employment, in career advancement. Also, discrimination in one area can affect opportunities in another. For example, housing discrimination may reduce job opportunities because the black family cannot move within commuting distance of the best employers. Moreover, the legacy of discrimination can affect career choices long after discrimination has ceased. Someone whose father and grandfather found job avenues blocked may be less inclined to pursue an education or to accept a job that requires a long training program. Thus, discrimination is a complex topic, and we cannot do it justice in this brief section.

---

5   These figures are from *The American Almanac: Statistical Abstracts of the United States: 1995–1996,* U.S. Bureau of the Census (Austin, Texas: The Reference Press, 1995), Table 88.

6   As reported in *Economic Report of the President* (Washington, D.C.: U.S. Government Printing Office, 1995), p. 180.

7   For an interesting study of the relationship between welfare dependency and the marriage pool of eligible males, see Mwangi S. Kimenyi, "Rational Choice, Culture of Poverty, and the Intergenerational Transmission of Welfare Dependency," *Southern Economic Journal* 57 (April 1991): pp. 947–60.

8   An estimated 10,000 babies were born to substance-abusing mothers in New York City in 1989. See "Crack Mothers, Crack Babies and Hope," *New York Times,* 31 December 1989.

Job market discrimination can take many forms. An employer may fail to hire a black job applicant because the applicant lacks training. But this lack of training may arise from discrimination in the schools, in union apprenticeship programs, or in training programs run by other employers. For example, evidence suggests that black workers receive less on-the-job training than otherwise similar white workers.

Let's first consider the difference between the earnings of nonwhite and white workers. After adjusting for a variety of factors that could affect the wage, such as education and work experience, research shows that whites earn more than blacks, but the wage gap between the two narrowed between 1940 and 1976 to the point where blacks earned only 7 percent less than white workers. However, the gap has since widened again so that by 1990, black workers earned 12 percent less than white workers.[9]

Could explanations besides job discrimination account for the wage gap? Though the data adjust for *years* of schooling, some research suggests that black workers received a lower *quality* of schooling than white workers. For example, black students are less likely to use computers in school. Inner-city schools often have more problems with classroom discipline, which takes time away from instruction. Such quality differences could account for at least a portion of the remaining gap in standardized wages. Although any differences attributable to a poorer-quality education would not necessarily reflect job discrimination, they might well reflect discrimination in the funding of schools.

Affirmative Action

The Equal Employment Opportunity Commission, established by the Civil Rights Act of 1964, monitors cases involving unequal pay for equal work and unequal access to promotion. Executive Order 11246, signed by President Lyndon Johnson, required all companies doing business with the federal government to set numerical hiring, promotion, and training goals to ensure that these firms did not discriminate in hiring on the basis of race, sex, religion, or national origin. For three decades, the order governed employment practices in firms that accounted for one-third of all jobs. Black employment increased sharply in those firms required to file affirmative-action plans.[10] The fraction of the black labor force employed in white-collar jobs increased from 16.5 percent in 1960 to 40.5 percent in 1981—an increase that greatly exceeded the growth of white-collar jobs in the labor force as a whole. Research also suggests that civil-rights legislation played a significant role in narrowing the black-white earnings gap between 1960 and the mid-1970s.[11]

Attention focused on hiring practices and equality of opportunity at the state and local levels as well, as governments introduced so-called "set-aside" programs to guarantee minorities a share of contracts. But in 1989, the U.S. Supreme Court rejected Richmond, Virginia's, set-aside program, which had reserved 30 percent of construction work for minorities. Within a year of the

---

9　See the evidence in M. Boozer, A. Krueger, and S. Wolken, "Race and School Quality Since *Brown v. Board of Education,*" *Brookings Papers on Economic Activity: Microeconomics,* 1992: pp. 269–326.
10　See the evidence provided in James Smith and Finis Welch, "Black Economic Progress After Myrdal," *Journal of Economic Literature* 27 (June 1989): pp. 519–63.
11　See David Card and Alan Krueger, "Trends in Relative Black-White Earnings Revisited," *American Economic Review* 83 (May 1993): pp. 85–91.

Net Bookmark

In June 1995, the U.S. Supreme Court, in *Adarand Constructors, Inc. v. Pena* [115 S. Ct. 2097 (1995)], leveled a blow against affirmative action programs, holding that courts must subject all governmental racial classifications to a standard of strict scrutiny. Thus, governmental affirmative action programs would be illegal unless they respond to specific, provable past discrimination and are narrowly tailored to eliminate that bias. Browse the Court's opinion through Case Western Reserve University, a participant in the Supreme Court's Project Hermes (ftp://ftp.cwru.edu/hermes/ascii/93-1841.ZO.filt).

ruling, many local affirmative action programs, including Richmond's, had been suspended or eliminated.

A 1995 U.S. Supreme Court decision challenged affirmative-action programs more broadly, ruling that Congress must meet a rigorous legal standard in order to justify any contracting or hiring practice based on race, especially programs that reserved job slots for minorities and women. Programs must be shown to be in response to injustices created by past discrimination, said the Court. The ruling could affect the 200,000 federal contractors operating under Executive Order 11246.

In summary, evidence suggests that blacks earn less than whites after adjusting for other factors that could affect the wage, such as education and job experience. Part of this wage gap may reflect differences in the quality of education, differences that could themselves be the result of discrimination. Keep in mind that unemployment rates are twice as high among blacks as among whites and are higher still among black teenagers, the group most in need of job skills and job experience. *But we should also note that black families are not a homogeneous group. In fact, the distribution of income is more uneven among black families than it is among the population as a whole.*

We have already discussed the sad circumstances facing many black households in the inner city. The good news is that there is a growing middle class among black households. The percentage of black families earning more than $35,000, adjusted for inflation, increased from 16 percent in 1982 to 25 percent in 1990. The number of black-owned businesses increased by 46 percent between 1987 and 1992, according to the Census Bureau. Some of the progress among blacks stems from their steady advances in education. In 1970, the percentage of young blacks without a high-school diploma was nearly twice that of whites. By 1990, the percentage of young blacks without diplomas had fallen by half and was nearly identical to that of whites. In 1960, the average black adult had only a junior-high-school education; by 1990, a high-school education was the average. In 1980, only 7 percent of middle-aged blacks had a college degree; by 1990, that figure had jumped to 17 percent. More generally, since 1970, the number of black doctors, nurses, college teachers, and newspaper reporters has more than doubled; the number of black engineers, lawyers, computer programmers, accountants, managers, and administrators has more than tripled; and the number of black elected officials has quadrupled.

UNDESIRABLE CONSEQUENCES OF INCOME ASSISTANCE

On the plus side, antipoverty programs increase the consumption possibilities of poor families, and this is significant, especially since children are the largest poverty group. But programs to assist the poor may have secondary effects that limit their ability to reduce poverty. Here we consider some secondary effects.

Work Disincentives

Society, through government, tries to provide families with an adequate standard of living, but society also wants to ensure that only those in need receive benefits. As we have seen, income assistance consists of a bundle of cash and in-kind transfer programs. Because these programs are designed to help the poor and only the poor, the level of benefits is inversely related to income from other sources. This results in a system in which transfers decline sharply as earned income increases, in effect imposing a high marginal tax rate on that earned income. An increase in earnings may cause a decline in benefits received from AFDC, Medicaid, food stamps, housing assistance, energy assistance, and other programs. If a bite is taken from each transfer program as earned income increases, working may result in little or no increase in total income. In fact, over certain income ranges, the welfare recipient may lose well over $1 in transfer benefits for each $1 increase in earnings. The *marginal tax rate* on earned income could exceed 100 percent!

Since holding even a part-time job involves additional expenses, such as transportation and child-care costs, not to mention the loss of free time, such a system of perverse incentives can frustrate those trying to work their way off welfare. *This high marginal tax rate discourages employment and self-sufficiency.* In many cases, the value of welfare benefits exceeds the disposable income resulting from full-time employment. For example, according to one study, the value of welfare benefits in most states exceeds the full-time earning of a janitor or the starting salary for a secretary.[12]

Just how much the higher marginal tax rates reduce the incentive to work remains unclear. We do know that only about one of every 20 persons receiving AFDC is employed. Twice as many welfare recipients worked in the mid-1970s. These high marginal tax rates also encourage welfare recipients to conceal earned income; some may work "off the books" for cash or may become involved in illegal activities. Research shows that supply of labor is reduced by AFDC and food stamp programs and that higher levels of benefits result in greater participation of these programs.[13] The statistical effect, however, is not great enough to explain the high rates of poverty among female householders.

The longer people are out of the labor force, the more their job skills deteriorate, so when they do seek employment, their marginal product and their pay are lower than when they were last employed. This lowers their expected wage and makes work less attractive. Some economists argue that in this way, welfare benefits can lead to long-term dependency. What seems to be a rational choice in the short run has an unfavorable long-term outcome both for the family and for society.

Does Welfare Cause Dependency?

Does the system of incentives created by high marginal tax rates create dependency among welfare recipients? How could we examine such a question? High turnover among welfare recipients would be evidence of little dependency. If, however, the same families were found to be poor year after year, this would be a matter of concern.

To explore the possibility of welfare dependency in the United States, a University of Michigan study tracked 5,000 families over a number of years, paying particular attention to economic mobility both from year to year and from one generation to the next.[14] The study first examined poverty from year

---

12 See Michael Tanner and Stephen Moore, "Why Welfare Pays," *The Wall Street Journal,* 28 September 1995.

13 See Robert Moffitt, "Incentive Effects of the U.S. Welfare System: A Review," *Journal of Economic Literature* 30 (March 1992): pp. 1–61.

14 Greg J. Duncan, Richard D. Coe, et al., *Years of Poverty, Years of Plenty* (Ann Arbor: University of Michigan Press, 1984).

to year, or dependency within a generation. It found that most recipients received welfare for less than a year, but about 30 percent of all welfare recipients remained on welfare for at least eight years. Thus, there is a core of long-term recipients.

A second and more serious concern is whether the children of the poor end up in poverty as well. Is there a cycle of poverty? Why might we expect such a transmission mechanism? Children in welfare households may learn the ropes about the welfare system and may come to view welfare as a normal way of life rather than as a temporary bridge over a rough patch. Empirical work indicates that daughters from welfare families are more likely to participate in the welfare system themselves and are more likely to have premarital births.[15] The evidence is weaker when it comes to sons from welfare families. What's difficult to say is whether welfare "caused" the link between mother and daughter, since the same factors that contributed to a mother's welfare status could also have contributed to her daughter's welfare status.

WELFARE REFORM

There is much dissatisfaction with the welfare system, both among those who pay for the programs and among direct beneficiaries. A variety of welfare reforms has been suggested in recent years, ranging from dismantling many federal programs to simply shifting responsibility more to the states.

Recent Reforms

Few women on welfare are in the labor force. Some analysts believe that one way to reduce poverty is to provide welfare recipients with job skills and to find jobs for those who are able to work. Some sort of "workfare" component for welfare recipients has been introduced in over 35 states. In such states, as a condition of receiving AFDC, the head of the household must agree to search for work, participate in education and training programs, or take some form of paid or unpaid position. The idea is to acquaint those on welfare with the job market so that they need not depend on welfare. Evidence from various states indicates that programs involving mandatory job searches, short-term unpaid work, and training can be operated at low cost and do increase employment.

Reforms at the state level set the stage for federal reform. Federal welfare reform was debated for nearly two years before a bill was finally passed—the *Family Support Act* of 1988, the first substantial welfare reform since 1935. To increase the incentive to work, welfare recipients were assured one year of day-care assistance and Medicaid after working their way off the AFDC program. The reform was aimed at smoothing the transition from welfare dependency for single mothers on welfare. By providing day care and Medicaid for a year, the measure reduced the marginal tax rate associated with employment.

To encourage spouses to stay together, the act also requires all states to offer benefits for families with dependent children even if an unemployed father is present. (Half the states already provided such coverage in 1988.) An absent parent must provide child support payments that are legally due. But half of the children

---

15 See Moffitt, p. 37.

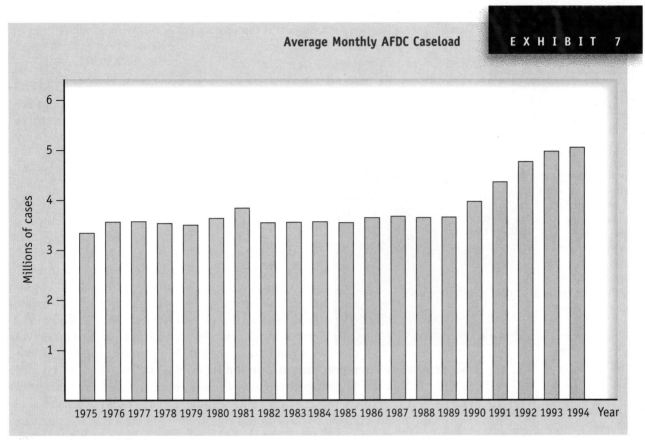

Average Monthly AFDC Caseload

EXHIBIT 7

Source: U.S. Bureau of the Census.

receiving AFDC were born outside marriage, so the whereabouts of the father is often unknown. Also, since AFDC aid is reduced by child support payments, the mother has little economic incentive to identify the father for support.

As shown in Exhibit 7, the AFDC caseload remained relatively constant during the 1980s but began to climb in 1990. The AFDC caseload increased from 3.8 million in 1989 to 5.0 million in 1994. Apparently, the broader required coverage (such as when an unemployed father is present) coupled with a recession in 1990–91 were enough to stimulate the growth in the caseload.

Much of the reform activity lately has been at the state level, where tight budgets have forced some states to cut welfare benefit levels, particularly for able-bodied adults. During the Clinton administration, 50 welfare experiments in 35 states were approved. Most states now limit the length of time that benefits will be provided. Benefit levels have also come to depend more on the behavior of the recipients. In Ohio and Wisconsin, for example, welfare benefits can be withheld if recipients or their children fail to attend school regularly. Some states no longer provide higher benefits to those on welfare who have more children, but those who marry or go to work find their benefit package enhanced. In Wisconsin, adult applicants for AFDC must participate in job orientations and basic skills programs. Many states have also limited the length of AFDC support. Connecticut, for example, now limits benefits to 21 months. So the states have become the test beds of welfare reform. State reforms are in keeping with efforts by the Republican Congress to turn welfare back to the states under a block grant, which is discussed in the following case study.

CASE STUDY

"Ending Welfare as We Know It"

Location:

What types of welfare reforms are necessary? For various opinions on the subject, visit "Welfare Reform: An Analysis of the Issues," edited by Isabel V. Sawhill and maintained by the Urban Institute (**http://www.urban.org/welfare/overview.htm**); "Welfare and Families," part of *Idea Central,* a virtual magazine of the Electronic Policy Network (**http://epn.org/idea/welfare.html**); and "Why Congress Must Reform Welfare," by Robert Rector, Senior Policy Analyst of The Heritage Foundation (**http://www.lead-inst.org/heritage/library/categories/healthwel/bg1063.html**).

During his 1992 presidential campaign, candidate Bill Clinton proposed "ending welfare as we know it." Once elected, he proposed the Work and Responsibility Act of 1994, which, among other things, would have restricted some AFDC recipients to a lifetime maximum of 24 months of cash assistance. Clinton's proposal went nowhere in Congress.

In 1995, the newly seated Republican Congress proposed its own version of welfare reform, the Personal Responsibility Act (PRA), a measure that would repeal the entitlement to welfare benefits (primarily, AFDC, food stamps, and Medicaid) and would fund the federal portion of welfare with a block grant to states. The schedule of block grants to the states would be set in nominal dollars, so states would be on the hook to fund any increase in caseloads should the economy turn sour. Although federal aid under the block grant proposal would grow less than under the existing plan, Republicans argued that the greater discretion provided to the states would allow them to be more flexible and more efficient—hence, states should be able to get by with fewer federal dollars. For example, states could impose a "family cap" to deny additional benefits to poor mothers who have additional children while on welfare.

Other provisions of the PRA included a 60-month limit to federal funds, denial of federal cash to any child born to an unmarried mother under age 18 (until the mother turns 18), and a reduction of federal benefits for children for whom paternity has not been established. In exchange for their welfare benefits, single parents would be expected to work at least 20 hours per week (rising to 35 hours by 2002). The work requirement was to be phased in. All other federal requirements for education and training would be eliminated.

One concern about the PRA was that it would reinforce an existing trend among states to cut benefits as a way to discourage poor people from remaining in the state or migrating to the state. Thus there would be a so-called "race to the bottom," as states jockeyed to become inhospitable to potential welfare recipients. Also, since states would not be required to maintain existing levels of funding, they could cut welfare benefits in response to tough budget times. The PRA would limit welfare benefits to five years, which seems more generous than the Clinton proposal, but Clinton's proposal offered several exceptions. According to Senator Patrick Moynihan, 75 percent of children on welfare remain on welfare more than five years. Thus, he and others argued that the PRA would throw millions of children off welfare.

The PRA passed the House and the Senate in late 1995 but was vetoed by Clinton in January 1996. Republicans in Congress did not appear to have the necessary votes to override the veto, yet Clinton indicated a willingness to compromise on the measure as part of an effort to balance the federal budget in seven years. Republicans were anxious to make good on their Contract with America and Clinton was anxious to make good on his campaign pledge to end welfare as we know it. So, for better or worse, change is on the way. Senator

Moynihan warns that the likely reforms could lead to a national tragedy much worse than the current problem of homelessness, which itself resulted from a flawed social experiment, as we will see in the next case study.

Sources: Martina Shea, *Dynamics of Economic Well-Being,* U.S. Bureau of the Census, Current Population Reports, Household Economic Studies, Series P70–45 (July 1995); "Attack of the Killer Blockheads," *The Economist,* 2 September 1995; "Personal Responsibility and Work Opportunity Act of 1995," *Congressional Record* 141, No. 206, 21 December 1995; and President William J. Clinton, The White House, 9 January 1996 (veto message).

We close this chapter by considering the problem of homelessness.

According to the U.S. Bureau of the Census, during the early morning of March 21, 1990, there were 228,621 homeless people throughout the United States sleeping in shelters, doorways, boxes, or other makeshift quarters. From that number, the Census Bureau estimated there were 400,000 homeless people in the United States. Some critics argue that the census count was much too low. A lawsuit has charged that the census takers did not check rooftops, bushes, trees, cars, and Dumpsters.

Although some homeless are people who became unemployed and could not find a job, most homeless people fall into one of three groups: (1) discharged mental patients, (2) young women who are "run-aways" or young mothers with children who have moved into a shelter, and (3) men who are addicted to drugs or alcohol or who are mentally ill but who have never received any inpatient treatment.

Most studies report that up to one-third of the homeless are deinstitutionalized mental patients. In the mid-1950s, the nation's mental hospitals began releasing patients on a large scale. Newly developed miracle drugs effective in treating mental illness, along with 2,000 community mental-health centers that were projected to be built by 1980, were supposed to follow these patients into society, helping them lead productive lives. Between 1963 and 1993, the number of resident patients in state and county mental hospitals dropped from 500,000 to 77,000. But the community mental-health facilities never materialized—only 400 were built. Some former patients made successful transitions, but many ended up homeless and on the streets. Fewer than one-fourth of those discharged are in any kind of mental health program. When homeless people began showing up in the 1970s, people thought the problem was a lack of affordable housing, not the result of a failed social experiment.

Women and young children make up about one-third of the homeless. Research suggests that homeless families consist mainly of young, single women with children who were receiving AFDC and had received it longer than other welfare families. Homeless families often stay in shelters or in government-funded lodging while waiting for a home.

Since the homeless have no permanent address, they are less likely to register to vote, so they tend to be underrepresented in the political process. Though some homeless receive welfare benefits, especially women with children, those without dependent children may not qualify for much support. There is episodic support, most of it in-kind, from shelters, soup kitchens, and hospital emergency rooms, but coverage varies widely across regions. Many homeless

"Ending Welfare As We Know It"
continued

CASE STUDY

The Homeless

Location:

Numerous public and private groups now handle the growing homeless problem, many of which are on the Internet. One organization, The Emergency Food and Shelter Program (**http://www.efsp.unitedway.org/**), created by Congress in 1983, helps the homeless and hungry by allocating federal funds for the provision of food and shelter. Another group, HomeAid (**http://www.HomeAid.org/**), supported by the National Association of Home Builders, builds and renovates shelters for the homeless. Lastly, the National Coalition for the Homeless (NCH) (**http://nch.ari.net/**), fights homelessness through a national advocacy network of homeless persons, activists, and service providers.

The Homeless
continued

feel safer on the streets even when shelters are available. Some cities fear that the more support they offer the homeless, the more homeless they will attract from other areas. As a way to encourage homeless people to move on, several cities in Southern California prohibit camping in public places.

Homelessness appears to be more prevalent in cities with strong rent-control laws and other housing restrictions. Because the supply of housing is restricted, people who might otherwise move into better housing instead stay put. There is thus little turnover of housing, and less "filtering down" of housing to the low end of the housing market. Affordable housing is therefore more scarce in cities with greater housing restrictions, such as New York and Boston, than in cities with fewer housing restrictions, such as Kansas City and Pittsburgh.

Some remedial programs have met with success. For example, in New York City, a nonprofit agency called Ready, Willing & Able tries to find jobs for homeless men. Even though the program deals with many who have drug problems and prison records, 40 percent of those who enter the program find jobs in the private sector. Another promising solution is the reemergence of single-room-occupancy hotels (SROs). These hotels first appeared in the early part of the 20th century to house railroad workers and other migrant laborers. They all but disappeared because of a changing job market and more restrictive zoning laws. To ease the construction of SROs, cities such as San Diego are easing building codes and zoning laws. The Department of Housing and Urban Development now spends $350 million a year to help nonprofit groups build and operate SROs.

Sources: "Census Bureau Sued Over Homeless Count," *New York Times,* 11 October 1992; David Tucker, *The Excluded Americans: Homelessness and Housing Policy* (Washington, D.C.: Regency Gateway, 1990); Jason DeParle, "Build Single Room Occupancy," *The Washington Monthly,* March 1994; and Eric Pooley, "Can Workfare Work?" *New York Times,* 2 January 1995.

CONCLUSION

Government redistribution programs have been most successful at reducing poverty among the elderly. But poverty rates among children have increased in recent years because of the growth in the number of female householders. We might ask why transfer programs have reduced poverty rates among the elderly but not among female householders. Transfer programs do not encourage people to get old; that process occurs naturally and is independent of the level of transfers. But the level and availability of transfer programs may, at the margin, influence some young unmarried women as they are deciding whether to have a child and may, at the margin, influence a married mother's decision to get divorced.

Most transfers in the economy are not from the government but rather are in-kind transfers within the family, from parents to children. Thus, any change in a family's capacity to earn income has serious consequences for dependent children. Family structure appears to be a primary determinant of family income. The poorest income group, the underclass, consists primarily of minority female householders concentrated in the poorest sections of our central cities. The problem of poverty in the central cities is compounded by the crime and drug addiction that can make daily life there terrifying. Those who suffer most are the children. One-fifth of the children in the United States live in poverty. Children are the innocent victims of the changing family structure.

SUMMARY

1. Money income (before taxes but after cash transfers) in the United States became more evenly distributed across households between 1929 and 1947, remained relatively stable between 1947 and 1977, and has become somewhat less evenly distributed since then.

2. During the 1960s, the economy boomed and the poverty rate fell, reaching a low in 1973. Between 1973 and 1979, the poverty rate fluctuated but showed no substantial decline. Between 1979 and 1983, the poverty rate increased, then declined for the next six years. Poverty rose beginning in 1990, but dropped in 1994. Since 1959, poverty rates have dropped the most among the elderly. Growth in the number of female householders has increased poverty among children.

4. The wage gap between blacks and whites narrowed between 1940 and 1975, but has since increased. Affirmative-action provisions seem to have increased employment opportunities among blacks. Two groups of black households have been growing: (1) a black underclass consisting primarily of female householders living in the poorest part of the inner city and (2) an emerging black middle class employed in professional positions and living in the suburbs.

5. Among the undesirable effects of income assistance is a high marginal tax rate on earned income, which discourages employment and encourages welfare dependency. According to one survey, about 30 percent of families on welfare remain there for eight years or more.

6. Welfare reforms introduced by the states set the stage for federal welfare reforms aimed at promoting the transition from welfare to work. The states have been experimenting with different systems aimed at promoting greater personal responsibility.

QUESTIONS AND PROBLEMS

1. **(Household Income Distribution)** Consider Exhibit 1 in the chapter. What explanations are given for the relatively large shift in income distribution between 1929 and 1947? What has happened to the U.S. income distribution in recent years?

2. **(Lorenz Curve)** Construct a Lorenz curve using the following hypothetical income data for a country with only five households: H1, $10,000; H2, $4,000; H3, $3,000; H4, $2,000; H5, $1,000.

3. **(Official Poverty Level)** How would you explain the drop in Exhibit 4 in the percent of the population below the official poverty level during the 1960s? Why did the percentage rise during the early 1980s? Are these statistics deceptive?

4. **(Poverty and the Poor)** Should the U.S. government attempt to completely eliminate poverty? Why or why not?

5. **(Official Poverty Level)** How does the U.S. Department of Agriculture calculate the official poverty level? What various government assistance programs are considered by the Census Bureau when calculating a household's income? What programs are ignored?

6. **(Poverty and Age)** Poverty among the elderly fell dramatically between 1959 and 1974 and has continued to decline to the present. However, poverty among that portion of the U.S. population that is less than 18 years old has been rising since the mid-1970s. Why have the experiences of these two age groups differed?

7. **(Income Distribution and Poverty)** Complete each of the following sentences:
   a. The _____ shows the percentage of total income received by a given percentage of recipients.
   b. _____ is a government program that provides retirement income to those who have contributed to the program while working.
   c. The poor who live in inner-city neighborhoods where poverty rates are 40 percent or higher are known as the _____.
   d. If family incomes were ranked from highest to lowest, half the families would be above the _____ and half would be below it.
   e. Government programs for which a household's income and assets must be below certain levels in order to qualify for benefits are _____ programs.

8. **(Poverty and Discrimination)** What types of discrimination can drive a wedge between what whites earn and

what nonwhites earn? Consider discrimination in schooling, for example. How could you detect such discrimination?

9. **(Work Disincentives)** How might the implicit tax on earned income (in the form of the loss of benefits from government assistance programs) affect work incentives? How might some people avoid the implicit tax?

10. **(Programs to Help the Poor)** Explain the differences between those who receive benefits in social insurance programs and those who receive them in income assistance programs.

11. **(Poverty and Public Choice)** Why is it difficult to pass legislation to reduce Social Security or Medicare benefits?

12. **(Affirmative Action)** What is meant by affirmative action? Is the movement today toward or away from affirmative action programs?

13. **(Programs to Help the Poor)** Suggest a reason why people who voluntarily give money to charities tend to give less than they give through government.

14. **(Lorenz Curve)** If income were evenly distributed, what would the Lorenz curve look like? Consider the following hypothetical sets of income data for two countries with only five households and total income of $200,000. Construct a Lorenz curve for each distribution. What happens to the shape of the Lorenz curve for more unequal distributions of income?

a. H1:	$ 10,000	b. H1:	$ 12,500
H2:	25,000	H2:	25,000
H3:	25,000	H3:	40,000
H4:	40,000	H4:	55,000
H5:	100,000	H5:	67,500

15. **(Welfare Reform)** What types of welfare reforms have been made at the state level in recent years?

16. **(Why Do Incomes Differ?)** What are the various factors that would tend to increase the income level of a household?

17. **(Income Distribution)** When you look at people's earning patterns over their lifetimes, they tend to be poor when they are young and when they are old and relatively well-off in between. How should this observation affect income assistance programs designed to help the poor?

18. **("Ending Welfare as We Know It")** What are the basic components of welfare reform proposed by the Republican Congress in 1995? Which types of recipients would be most affected by their proposal?

19. **(The Homeless)** What two groups make up the majority of the homeless in the United States? How might welfare reform affect the number of homeless?

20. **(The Homeless)** Does it make sense for policies to assist the homeless to be made at the municipal level or should such policies be made at the state or federal level?

Using the Internet

21. Visit the Housing and Household Economic Statistics Division of the Census Bureau and examine data and analysis for income and poverty (**http://www.census. gov/ftp/pub/hhes/www/incpov.html**).

a. What is the median household income for the most recent year reported? How has this number changed from the previous year?

b. What is the poverty rate for the most recent year reported? How has this number changed from the most recent year?

c. Find the poverty rate for the region including your hometown. How does it compare to the national average?

International Trade

33

This morning you put on your Levi's jeans from Mexico, laced up your Nikes from Indonesia, and pulled on your Benetton sweater from Italy. After a breakfast that included bananas from Honduras and coffee from Brazil, you climbed into your Japanese Toyota fueled by Saudi Arabian oil and headed for a lecture by a visiting professor from London. The world is a giant shopping mall, and Americans are big spenders. Americans buy Japanese cars, French wine, Swiss clocks, European vacations, and thousands of other goods and services from around the globe. But foreigners spend a lot on American products too—grain, personal computers, aircraft, trips to Disney World, and thousands of other goods and services. In this chapter, we examine the gains from international trade and the effects of trade and trade restrictions on the allocation of resources. We base the analysis primarily on the familiar concepts of supply and demand. Topics discussed in this chapter include:

- Gains from trade
- Absolute and comparative advantage
- Tariffs

- Import quotas
- Welfare loss from trade restrictions
- Arguments for trade restrictions

CHAPTER

Net Bookmark

The Foreign Trade Division (FTD), part of the U.S. Bureau of the Census, is the primary source of statistics on foreign trade data. Specifically, the FTD collects and disseminates data regarding U.S. imports and exports. These data are published monthly in the *U.S. International Trade in Goods and Services* report, commonly referred to as the FT900. To view the current FT900, visit "International Trade Reports" (http://www.census.gov/ftp/pub/foreign-trade/www/). In Japan, the Ministry of Finance compiles similar data (http://www.mof.go.jp/).

THE GAINS FROM TRADE

A family from Georgia that sits down for a meal of Kansas prime rib, Idaho potatoes, and California string beans is benefiting from interstate trade. You likely have little difficulty understanding why the residents of one state trade with those of another. Back in Chapter 2, you learned of the gains arising from specialization and exchange. You may recall the discussion of how you and your roommate could maximize output by specializing in typing or ironing. Just as individuals benefit from specialization and exchange, so do states and, indeed, nations. To reap the gains that arise from specialized production, countries engage in international trade. *With trade, each country can concentrate on producing those goods and services that involve the least opportunity cost.*

A Profile of Imports and Exports

Some nations are more involved in international trade than others, just as some states are more involved in interstate trade than others. For example, exports account for about half of the gross domestic product (GDP) in the Netherlands; about one-third of the GDP in Germany, Sweden, and Switzerland; and about a quarter of the GDP in Canada and the United Kingdom. Despite the perception that Japan has a giant export sector, only about 13 percent of Japanese production is exported.

In the United States, exports amounts to about 12 percent of GDP. Though small relative to GDP, exports play a growing role in the U.S. economy. The four main U.S. exports are (1) high-technology manufactured products, such as computers, aircraft, and telecommunication equipment; (2) industrial supplies and materials; (3) agricultural products, especially corn and soybeans; and (4) entertainment products, such as movies and recorded music.

The United States depends on imports for some key inputs. For example, our position as the world's largest producer of aluminum depends upon importing vast amounts of bauxite. Most of our platinum and chromium and all of our manganese, mica, diamonds, and nickel are imported. Two-thirds of U.S. imports are (1) manufactured consumer goods, such as automobiles from Germany and electronic equipment from Taiwan, and (2) capital goods, such as a high-tech printing press.

The big change in U.S. exports over the last two decades has been a growth in the dollar value of machinery exports; nearly half of the capital goods produced in the United States are exported. The primary change in U.S. imports over the last two decades has been the marked increase in spending on foreign oil. Canada is our largest trading partner; Japan is the next largest. Other important trading partners include Mexico, Germany, Great Britain, South Korea, France, Hong Kong, Italy, and Brazil.

Production Possibilities without Trade

The rationale behind some international trade is obvious. The United States grows no coffee beans because our climate is not suited to coffee. It is more revealing, however, to examine the gains from trade where the cost advantage is not so obvious. Suppose that just two goods—food and clothing—are produced and consumed and that there are only two countries in the world—the United States, with a labor force of 100 million workers, and the mythical country of

EXHIBIT 1

Production Possibilities
Schedules for the
United States and
Izodia

(a) United States

Units Produced (per worker per day)		Production Possibilities with 100 Million Workers (millions of units per day)					
		U_1	U_2	U_3	U_4	U_5	U_6
Food	6	600	480	360	240	120	0
Clothing	3	0	60	120	180	240	300

(b) Izodia

Units Produced (per worker per day)		Production Possibilities with 200 Million Workers (millions of units per day)					
		I_1	I_2	I_3	I_4	I_5	I_6
Food	1	200	160	120	80	40	0
Clothing	2	0	80	160	240	320	400

Izodia, with 200 million workers. The conclusions we derive from our simple model will have general relevance to the pattern of international trade.

Exhibit 1 presents each country's production possibilities table, based on the size of the labor force and the productivity of workers in each country. We assume a given technology and that labor is fully and efficiently employed. Since no trade occurs between countries, Exhibit 1 presents each country's *consumption possibilities* table as well, reflecting the country's consumption alternatives.

The production numbers imply that each worker in the United States can produce either 6 units of food or 3 units of clothing per day. If all 100 million U.S. workers produce food, 600 million units can be produced per day, as reflected by combination U_1 in part (a) of Exhibit 1. If all U.S. workers produce clothing, U.S. output is 300 million units per day, as reflected by combination U_6. Combinations in between represent alternatives if some workers produce food and some produce clothing. Because a U.S. worker can produce either 6 units of food or 3 units of clothing, the opportunity cost of 1 more unit of food is $\frac{1}{2}$ unit of clothing.

Suppose Izodian workers are less educated, work with less capital, and farm less fertile land than U.S. workers. So each Izodian can produce only 1 unit of food or 2 units of clothing per day. If all 200 million Izodian workers specialize in food, they can produce 200 million units of food per day, as reflected by combination I_1 in part (b) of Exhibit 1. If all Izodian workers produce clothing, total output is 400 million units of clothing per day, as reflected by combination I_6. Some intermediate production possibilities are also listed in the exhibit. Because an Izodian worker can produce either 1 unit of food or 2 units of clothing, the opportunity cost of 1 more unit of food is 2 units of clothing.

We can convert the data in Exhibit 1 to a production possibilities frontier for each country, as is shown in Exhibit 2. In each diagram, the amount of food produced is measured on the vertical axis and the amount of clothing is mea-

EXHIBIT 2

Production Possibilities Frontiers for the United States and Izodia without Trade

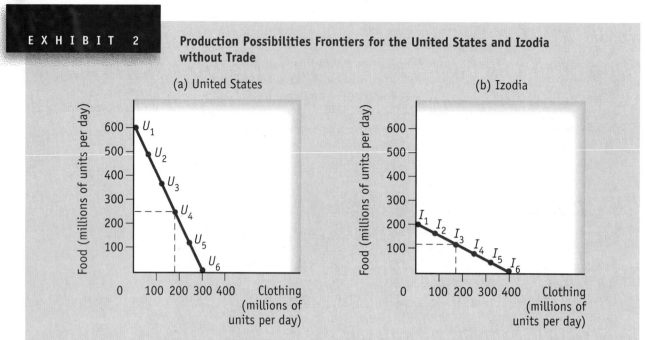

Panel (a) shows the U.S. production possibilities curve; its slope indicates that the opportunity cost of an additional unit of food is $\frac{1}{2}$ unit of clothing. Panel (b) shows production possibilities in Izodia; an additional unit of food costs 2 units of clothing. Food is relatively cheaper to produce in the United States.

sured on the horizontal axis. U.S. combinations are shown in panel (a) by U_1, U_2, and so on; Izodian combinations are designated in panel (b) by I_1, I_2, and so on. Because we assume that resources are perfectly adaptable to the production of each commodity, each production possibilities curve is a straight line.

Exhibit 2 illustrates the possible combinations of food and clothing that residents of each country can produce and consume if all resources are fully and efficiently employed and there is no trade between the two countries. **Autarky** is the situation of national self-sufficiency, in which there is no economic interaction with foreigners. Suppose that U.S. producers maximize profit and U.S. consumers maximize utility with the combination of 240 million units of food and 180 million units of clothing—combination U_4. This combination will be called the *autarky equilibrium*. Suppose also that Izodians have an autarky equilibrium, identified as combination I_3, of 120 million units of food and 160 million units of clothing.

Autarky A situation of national self-sufficiency in which there is no economic interaction with foreigners

Consumption Possibilities Based on Comparative Advantage

In our example, each U.S. worker can produce both more clothing and more food per day than can each Izodian worker. U.S. workers have an *absolute advantage* in the production of both goods because a U.S. worker can produce each good in less time than can an Izodian worker. With an absolute advantage in the production of both commodities, should the U.S. economy remain in autarky—that is, self-sufficient in both food and clothing—or are there gains from trade?

As long as the opportunity costs of the two goods differ between the United States and Izodia, there are gains from specialization and trade. The opportunity cost of producing one more unit of food is fi unit of clothing in the United States, compared to 2 units of clothing in Izodia. *According to the law of comparative advantage, each country should specialize in the good with the lower opportunity cost.* Since the opportunity cost of producing food is lower in the United States than in Izodia, both countries will gain if the United States concentrates on producing food and exports some to Izodia, and Izodia concentrates on producing clothing and exports some to the United States.

Terms of trade How much of one good exchanges for a unit of another good

Before countries can trade, they must somehow determine how much of one good will be exchanged for another—that is, they must establish the **terms of trade.** Suppose that market forces shape terms of trade whereby 1 unit of clothing exchanges for 1 unit of food. Based on those terms of trade, Americans trade 1 unit of food to Izodians for 1 unit of clothing. To produce 1 unit of clothing Americans would have to sacrifice 2 units of food. Likewise, Izodians sacrifice only 1 unit of clothing by trading clothing to Americans for 1 unit of food, which is only half what Izodians sacrifice to produce 1 unit of food.

Exhibit 3 shows that with 1 unit of food trading for 1 unit of clothing, Americans and Izodians can consume anywhere along or below their blue consumption possibilities frontiers. *The consumption possibilities frontier* shows a nation's alternative combinations of goods available as a result of production and

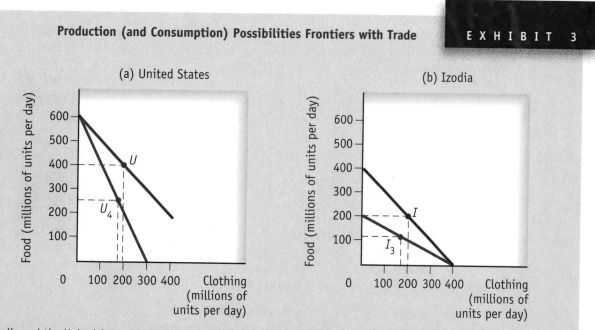

Production (and Consumption) Possibilities Frontiers with Trade   EXHIBIT 3

(a) United States

(b) Izodia

If Izodia and the United States can trade at the rate of 1 unit of clothing for 1 unit of food, both can benefit. Consumption possibilities at those terms of trade are shown by the blue lines. The United States was previously producing and consuming combination U_4. By trading with Izodia, it can produce only food and still consume combination U—a combination that contains more food and more clothing than combination U_4 does. Likewise, Izodia can attain the preferred combination I by trading its clothing for U.S. food. Both countries are better off as a result of international trade.

foreign trade. (Note that the U.S. consumption possibilities curve does not extend to the right of 400 million units of clothing, since that is the most the Izodians can produce.) The amount each country actually consumes will depend on its relative preferences for food and clothing. Suppose Americans select point *U* in panel (a) and Izodians select point *I* in panel (b).

Without trade, the United States produced and consumed 240 million units of food and 180 million units of clothing. With trade, the United States specializes in food by producing 600 million units; Americans eat 400 million units and exchange the remaining 200 million for 200 million units of Izodian clothing. This consumption combination is reflected by point *U* in panel (a). Through exchange, Americans increase their consumption of both food and clothing.

Without trade, Izodians produced and consumed 120 million units of food and 160 million units of clothing. With trade, Izodians specialize in clothing to produce 400 million units; Izodians wear 200 million units of clothing and exchange the remaining 200 million units for 200 million units of food. This consumption combination is reflected by point *I* in panel (b). Izodians, like Americans, are able to increase their consumption of both food and clothing through trade. How is this possible?

Since Izodians are relatively more efficient in the production of clothing and Americans relatively more efficient in the production of food, total world output increases when each country specializes. Specifically, without specialization, total food production was 360 million units and total clothing production was 340 million units. With specialization, food production increases to 600 million units and clothing production increases to 400 million units. The only constraint on trade is that, for each good, *total world production must equal total world consumption*. In our two-country world, this means that the amount of food the United States exports must equal the amount of food Izodia imports. The same goes for Izodia's exports of clothing.

Thus, both countries have more goods and services after trade. *Although the United States has an absolute advantage in both goods, differences in the opportunity cost of production between nations ensure that specialization and exchange can result in mutual gains.* Remember that comparative advantage, not absolute advantage, is the source of gains from trade.

We simplified trade relations in our example to highlight the gains from specialization and exchange. We assumed that each country would completely specialize in producing a particular good, that resources were equally adaptable to the production of either good, that the costs of transporting the goods from one country to another were inconsequential, and that there were no problems in arriving at the terms of trade. The world is not that simple (for example, we don't expect a country to produce just one good), but the law of comparative advantage still points to gains from trade.

Reasons for International Specialization

Countries trade with one another—or, more precisely, people and firms in one country trade with those in another—because each side expects to gain from the exchange. How do we know what each country should produce and what goods should be traded?

Differences in Resource Endowments. Trade is often prompted by differences in resource endowments. Two key resources are labor and capital. Countries differ not only in their amounts of labor and capital but in the qualities of each. A well-educated and well-trained labor force will be more productive than an un-educated and unskilled one. Similarly, capital that reflects the most recent technological developments will be more productive than obsolete capital. Some countries, such as the United States and Japan, have an educated labor force and have accumulated an abundant stock of modern capital. Both resources result in greater productivity per worker, making each nation quite competitive in producing goods that require skilled labor and sophisticated capital.

Some countries are blessed with an abundance of fertile land and favorable growing seasons. The United States, for example, has been called the breadbasket of the world because of its rich farmland. Honduras has the ideal climate for growing bananas. Coffee is grown best in the climate and elevation of Colombia, Brazil, and Jamaica. Thus, the United States exports corn and imports coffee and bananas. Differences in the seasons across countries also serve as a basis for trade. For example, during the winter months, Americans import fruit from Chile and Canadian tourists travel to Florida for sun and fun. During the summer months, Americans export fruit and American tourists travel to Canada for fishing and camping.

Mineral resources are often concentrated in particular countries: oil in Saudi Arabia, bauxite in Jamaica, diamonds in South Africa, coal in the United States. The United States has abundant coal supplies, but not enough oil to satisfy domestic demand. Thus, the United States exports coal and imports oil. More generally, *countries export those products that they can produce more cheaply in return for those that are unavailable domestically or are more costly to produce than to buy from other countries.*

The United States has farming conditions favorable to growing wheat but poor for growing bananas. As a result, the United States exports wheat and imports bananas.

Differences in Tastes. Even if all countries had identical resource endowments and combined those resources with equal efficiency, each country would still gain from trade as long as tastes and preferences differed among countries. Differences in tastes among countries lead to trade. Consumption patterns do appear to differ, often because of custom or religion. For example, the per-capita consumption of beer in Germany is more than double that in Portugal or Sweden. The French drink three times as much wine as do Danes. The Danes consume twice as much pork as do Americans. Americans consume twice as much chicken as do Hungarians. Soft drinks are four times more popular in the United States than in Western Europe. The English like tea; Americans like coffee. Algeria has an ideal climate for growing grapes, but its large Muslim population abstains from alcohol. Thus, Algeria exports wine.

Economies of Scale. If production is subject to *economies of scale*—that is, if the average cost per unit falls as output expands—countries can gain from trade if each nation specializes. Such specialization allows each nation to produce at a higher output level, which reduces average production costs. The primary reason for establishing the single integrated market in Western Europe is to offer European producers a large, open market of over 320 million consumers so that producers can increase production, experience economies of scale, and in the process become more competitive in international markets.

TRADING ON THE WORLD MARKET

So far, we have analyzed the case in which each country fully specializes in the production of a particular good. How does international trade affect prices

World price The price at which a good or service is traded internationally; it is determined by the world supply and demand for a product

and output in domestic markets when two countries both produce a certain good? In this section, we will rely on supply-and-demand analysis to develop an understanding of international markets. The **world price** is the price determined by the world supply and world demand for a product. It is the price at which any supplier can sell output on the world market and at which any demander can purchase output on the world market. Let's consider the market for steel.

What If World Price Is Above Domestic Equilibrium Price?

Panel (a) of Exhibit 4 shows hypothetical curves reflecting the supply and demand for steel in the United States. The U.S. demand curve for steel intersects the U.S. producers' supply curve at a price of $150 per ton. Therefore, a price of $150 per ton is the market-clearing price that would prevail in the United States without international trade. Notice that the world price per ton of steel is measured on the vertical axis in panel (a). What if the world price of steel is $200 per ton—a price *above* the $150-per-ton price that would prevail in the United States in the absence of trade? If U.S. producers cannot export steel, the

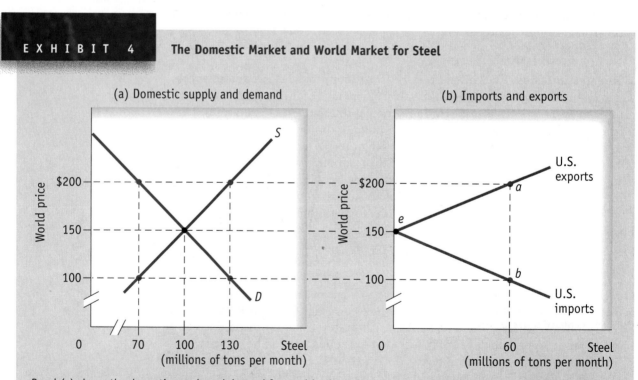

EXHIBIT 4   **The Domestic Market and World Market for Steel**

(a) Domestic supply and demand

(b) Imports and exports

Panel (a) shows the domestic supply and demand for steel in the United States. At a world price of $150 per ton, U.S. consumers demand all the U.S. producers supply. Panel (b) shows that no U.S. steel is exported or imported at that price.

At world prices above $150 per ton, U.S. producers supply more than enough to satisfy domestic quantity demanded. The excess is exported. The U.S. export line in panel (b) shows the volume of exports at prices above $150. If the world price is below $150, domestic quantity demanded exceeds domestic quantity supplied. The difference is made up by imports.

world price is irrelevant, and only the price determined in the United States matters. But if U.S. producers can easily export steel to the rest of the world, they will increase the quantity supplied whenever the world price rises above $150 per ton. You can see from the supply curve in panel (a) that when the world price is $200 per ton, the quantity of U.S. steel produced increases to 130 million tons per month. Because U.S. demanders now face the higher price of $200 per ton, they reduce the quantity they demand to 70 million tons per month.

The amount by which the quantity supplied by U.S. producers exceeds the quantity demanded in the United States equals the amount of steel exported by U.S. producers. Thus, when the world price equals $200 per ton, 60 million tons of steel are exported from the United States. U.S. exports and imports as functions of the world price are illustrated in panel (b) of Exhibit 4. In that panel, the vertical axis again reflects the world price of steel, but the horizontal axis measures U.S. imports or exports of steel based on its world price. At point *e* on the horizontal axis of panel (b), the world price is $150 per ton, which equals the U.S. market-clearing price, so there are no imports or exports. When the world price is $200, the U.S. steel producers export 60 million tons of steel, a combination identified as point *a* in panel (b). By connecting points *e* and *a,* we form an upward-sloping *export line.* At each point on this export line, U.S. exports reflect the difference in panel (a) between the U.S. quantity supplied and the U.S. quantity demanded at that price.

What If World Price Is Below the Domestic Equilibrium Price?

What if the world price is below $150 per ton? If U.S. steel buyers cannot buy from abroad, the world price of steel is irrelevant. If, however, U.S. buyers can purchase foreign output at the world price, the United States will import steel whenever the world price falls below $150 per ton. At a price below $150, U.S. quantity demanded exceeds the quantity supplied by U.S. producers, so *the excess quantity demanded in U.S. markets is satisfied by purchases from foreign producers.* For example, suppose the world price is $100 per ton. In panel (a) of Exhibit 4, you can see that when the price is $100 per ton, the amount U.S. producers are willing to supply drops to 70 million tons, but the U.S. quantity demanded increases to 130 million tons. At that price, 60 million tons of steel are purchased on the world market.

The quantity of steel imported by the United States when the price is $100 per ton is shown by point *b* in panel (b). At prices below $150 per ton, U.S. imports reflect the amount by which U.S. quantity demanded exceeds quantity supplied by U.S. steel producers, shown in panel (a). The *import line* in panel (b) starts at a price of $150 (point *e*) and slopes down to the right.

To summarize: When the world price of steel is $150 per ton, the quantity of steel demanded in the United States equals the quantity supplied by U.S. producers, so steel is neither imported nor exported. When the world price is above $150, the quantity of steel supplied by U.S. producers exceeds the quantity demanded by U.S. buyers, so steel is exported. And when the world price is below $150, the quantity demanded by U.S. buyers exceeds the quantity supplied by U.S. producers, so steel is imported. Therefore, the

EXHIBIT 5   **The Domestic Japanese Market and the World Market for Steel**

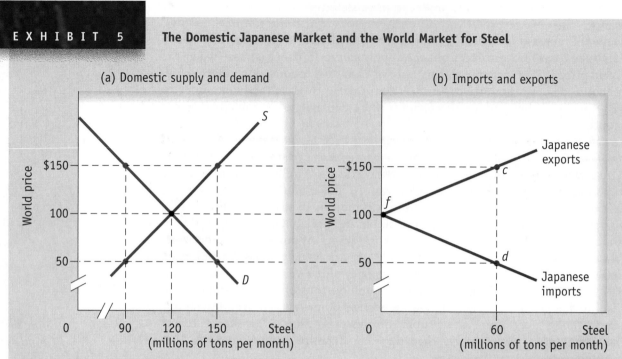

(a) Domestic supply and demand

(b) Imports and exports

At a world price of $100 per ton, Japan neither exports nor imports steel. At prices higher than $100, Japan exports the amount by which domestic production exceeds domestic quantity demanded. At prices below $100, Japan imports steel.

world price determines whether the United States is an importer, an exporter, or neither.

The Rest of the World

To simplify our analysis, let's suppose that there is just one other country in the "rest of the world": Japan, a major producer and user of steel. To keep the accounting manageable, we'll convert all Japanese prices into U.S. dollars. Japan's domestic supply and demand for steel, along with its supply of exports and demand for imports, are presented in Exhibit 5. As you can see from panel (a), when the world price of steel is $100 per ton, the quantity supplied by Japanese producers just equals the quantity demanded in Japan. In panel (b), therefore, there are no imports or exports when the world price is $100 per ton. But at a world price above $100 per ton, Japanese producers supply more steel than is demanded in Japan, so the difference is exported to the world market, as shown in panel (b). The reverse is true for world prices below $100; in that case, the quantity demanded in Japan exceeds the quantity Japanese producers supply, so the difference becomes Japan's imports, as shown in panel (b).

Determining the World Price

The world price of steel is determined by international supply and demand. In our simplified two-country model, *the world price is found where the exports of one country equal the imports of the other country.* To determine the world price of steel,

Determination of the World Price

EXHIBIT 6

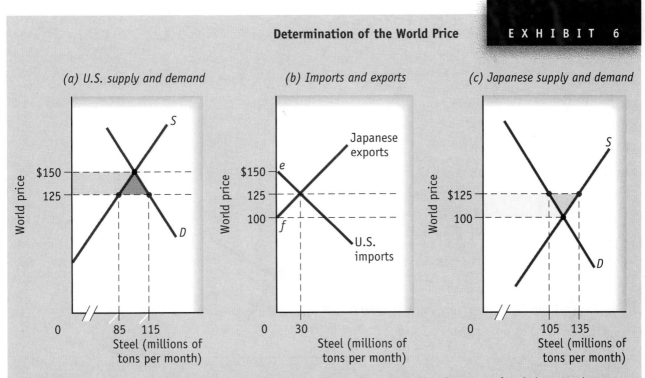

(a) U.S. supply and demand   (b) Imports and exports   (c) Japanese supply and demand

In panel (b), the intersection of the Japanese export and U.S. import lines determines the nature of trade between the two countries. At a world price of $125 per ton, Japan exports 30 million tons of steel to the United States. In the United States, prices are lower and the quantity consumed is greater as a result of trade. The blue shaded areas reflect the gain in consumer surplus. In Japan, prices are higher and the quantity produced is greater. The gold shaded areas indicate the gain in producer surplus. The net gains in the two countries are shown by the darker shaded triangles in panels (a) and (c).

we combine elements of Exhibits 4 and 5. Panel (a) of Exhibit 6 again presents the supply and demand for steel in the United States, and panel (c) presents the same information for Japan.

The U.S. *import* line and the Japanese *export* line are shown in panel (b). The U.S. export line and the Japanese import line are not shown because, given the supply and demand conditions, the United States will not export steel nor will Japan import it. But at a price above $100 per ton, Japanese producers export steel, and at a price below $150 per ton, U.S. buyers import steel. International trade will therefore occur at a world price between $100 and $150 per ton. Specifically, the intersection of the Japanese export line with the U.S. import line yields the world equilibrium price of steel. (Again, we assume that the world market consists of only these two countries.) Given the supply and demand for steel in the two countries, the equilibrium world price will be $125 per ton. At that price, Japan will export 30 million tons of steel per month to the United States.

Consumer and Producer Surplus

Before we consider the net effect of world trade on social welfare, let's develop a framework of describing the benefits that consumers and producers

EXHIBIT   7   **Consumer Surplus and Producer Surplus**

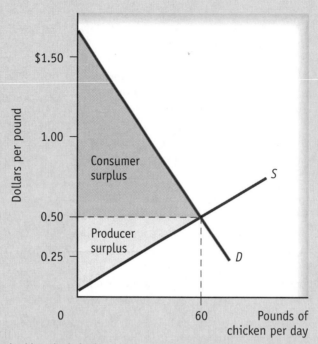

Consumer surplus, shown by the blue shaded triangle, shows the net benefits consumers reap by being able to purchase 60 pounds of chicken at $0.50 per pound. Some consumers would have been willing to pay $1.50 or more per pound for the first few pounds. Consumer surplus measures the difference between the maximum sum of money consumers would pay for 60 pounds of chicken and the actual sum they pay. Producer surplus, shown by the gold shaded triangle, shows the net benefits producers reap by being able to sell 60 pounds of chicken at $0.50 per pound. Some producers would have been willing to supply chicken for $0.25 per pound or less. Producer surplus measures the difference between the actual sum of money producers receive for 60 pounds of chicken and the minimum amount they would accept for this amount of chicken.

derive from exchange. To do this, we consider the hypothetical market for chicken shown in Exhibit 7. The height of the demand curve reflects the amount that consumers are willing and able to pay for each additional pound of chicken. In effect, the height of the demand curve shows the *marginal benefit* consumers expect from each pound of chicken. For example, the demand curve indicates that some consumers are willing to pay $1.50 or more per pound for the first few pounds of chicken. But all consumers get to buy chicken at the market-clearing price, which in Exhibit 7 is only $0.50 per pound. The blue shaded triangle below the demand curve and above the market price reflects the *consumer surplus,* which is the difference between the maximum sum of money consumers would pay for 60 pounds of chicken per day and the actual sum they do pay. Consumers thus get a bonus, or a surplus, from market exchange. We all enjoy a consumer surplus from most products we consume.

There is a similar surplus on the producer side. The height of the supply curve reflects the minimum amount of money that producers are willing and able to accept for each additional pound of chicken. That is, the height of the supply curve shows the *marginal cost* producers incur in supplying each additional pound of chicken. For example, the supply curve indicates that some producers incur a cost of $0.25 or less per pound for supplying the first few pounds of chicken. But all producers get to sell chicken for the market-clearing price—in this case, $0.50 per pound. The gold shaded triangle above the supply curve and below the market price reflects the *producer surplus,* which is the difference between the actual sum of money producers receive for 60 pounds of chicken and the minimum sum they would accept for that quantity.

The point is that market exchange usually yields a surplus, or a bonus, to both producers and consumers. In the balance of the chapter, we focus on how international trade affects consumer surplus and producer surplus.

The Net Effect of Trade on Social Welfare

Now let's return to the market for steel to consider the gains from trade. *The net change in social welfare is determined by summing the net changes in consumer and producer surpluses.* In panel (a) of Exhibit 6, you can see that at a price of $125 per ton, 115 million tons per month are demanded in the United States. At that price, 85 million tons are supplied by U.S. producers and 30 million tons are imported from Japan. In the United States, the price is lower and the quantity consumed is greater than would be the case without trade. U.S. consumers in effect enjoy a bonus, or a consumer surplus, resulting from the lower world price.

The two blue shaded areas in panel (a) reflect the gain in U.S. consumer surplus resulting from a world price below the market-clearing domestic price. But the lower price also means that U.S. producers receive a lower price for their output and thus forgo some producer surplus, as indicated by the light-blue shaded area in panel (a). Hence the light-blue shaded area represents the surplus transferred from domestic steel producers to domestic consumers of steel. But the gain in consumer surplus exceeds the loss in producer surplus, and this net gain is reflected by the dark-blue shaded triangle. Thus, the world price of steel generates a net gain in welfare in the United States equal to the dark-blue shaded triangle.

The gains and losses are reversed in Japan, as is shown in panel (c). At a world price of $125 per ton, Japan produces 105 million tons per month for its domestic market and exports the other 30 million tons to the United States. Japanese producers are better off with international trade because they get to sell more output for a higher price than they could if they were limited to their domestic market. The two gold shaded areas in panel (c) represent the gain in producer surplus for Japanese steelmakers, who can sell steel at a world price of $125 per ton instead of the $100 price prevailing in Japan without international trade. The light-gold shaded area represents the consumer surplus lost as a result of the higher price and reduced domestic consumption. Therefore, that portion of the gain in producer surplus in panel (c) comes at the expense of forgone consumer surplus. But since the gain in producer surplus exceeds the loss in consumer surplus, net social welfare increases in Japan (indicated by the dark-gold shaded triangle). Thus, *trade confers net benefits in both countries.*

TRADE RESTRICTIONS

Despite the benefits of international trade, nearly all countries at one time or another erect barriers to impede or block free trade among nations. Trade restrictions usually benefit domestic producers, but harm domestic consumers. In this section, we will consider the effects of restrictions and the reasons they are imposed.

Tariffs

A *tariff,* a term first introduced in Chapter 4, is a tax on imports. (Tariffs can also be applied to exports, but we will focus on import tariffs.) A tariff can be either *specific,* such as a tariff of $5 per barrel of oil, or *ad valorem,* a percentage of the price of imports at the port of entry. Consider the effects of a specific tariff on a particular good. In Exhibit 8, *D* is the domestic demand for sugar and *S* is the supply provided by domestic producers. Suppose that the world price of sugar is $0.10 per pound, as it was in the early 1990s. With free trade, domestic consumers can buy any amount desired at the world price, so the quantity demanded is 70 million pounds per month, of which 20 million pounds are supplied by domestic producers and 50 million pounds are imported. Domestic producers cannot charge more than the world price, since domestic buyers can purchase as much sugar as they want at $0.10 per pound in the world market.

Now suppose that a specific tariff of $0.05 is imposed on each pound of sugar imported, raising the price of imported sugar from $0.10 to $0.15 per pound. Domestic producers can therefore raise their price to $0.15 per pound as well without losing sales to imports. With the higher price, the quantity supplied by domestic producers increases to 30 million pounds per month, but the quantity demanded by domestic consumers declines to 60 million pounds per month. Because the quantity demanded has declined and the quantity supplied by domestic producers has increased, imports decline from 50 million to 30 million pounds per month.

Since the price is higher after the tariff, consumers are worse off. The loss in consumer surplus is identified in Exhibit 8 by the blue and red shaded areas. Because both the domestic price and the quantity of sugar supplied by domestic producers have increased, the total revenue received by domestic producers increases by the areas *a* plus *b* plus *f.* But only the light-blue shaded area, *a,* represents an increase in producer surplus. The increase in revenue represented by the areas *b* plus *f* just offsets the higher marginal cost of expanding domestic production from 20 million to 30 million pounds. The red shaded triangle, *b,* represents part of the net welfare loss to the domestic economy, because those 10 million pounds could have been purchased from abroad for $0.10 per pound rather than produced domestically at a higher marginal cost.

Government revenue from the tariff is identified by the light-blue shaded area, *c,* which equals the tariff of $0.05 per pound multiplied by the 30 million pounds that are imported. Tariff revenue represents a loss to consumers, but since the tariff is revenue to the government, this loss can potentially be offset by a reduction in taxes or an increase in public services. The red shaded triangle, *d,* represents a loss in consumer surplus reflecting the 10-million-pound drop in quantity demanded that resulted from a higher price. This loss is not

Effect of a Tariff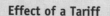

EXHIBIT 8

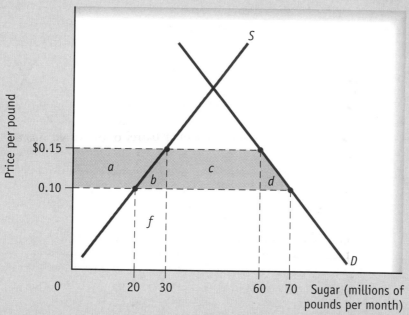

At a world price of $0.10 per pound, domestic consumers demand 70 million pounds per month and domestic producers supply 20 million pounds per month; the difference is imported. With the imposition of a $0.05 per pound tariff, the domestic price rises to $0.15 per pound, domestic producers increase production to 30 million pounds, and domestic consumers cut back to 60 million pounds. Imports fall to 30 million pounds. At the higher domestic price, consumers are worse off; their loss of consumer surplus is the sum of areas *a, b, c,* and *d.* Area *a* represents an increase in producer surplus: a transfer from consumers to producers. Areas *b* and *f* reflect the portion of additional revenues to producers that is just offset by the higher production costs of expanding domestic output by 10 million pounds. Area *c* shows government revenue from the tariff. The net welfare loss to society is the sum of area *d,* which reflects the loss of consumer surplus resulting from the drop in consumption, and area *b,* which reflects the higher marginal cost of producing domestically output that could have been produced more cheaply abroad.

redistributed as a gain to anyone else, so area *d* reflects part of the net welfare loss of the tariff. Therefore, the two red shaded triangles, *b* and *d,* measure the domestic economy's net welfare loss of the tariff; the *two triangles measure a net loss in consumer surplus that is not offset by a net gain to anyone else.*

Of the total loss in consumer surplus (areas *a, b, c,* and *d*) resulting from the tariff, area *a* is redistributed from consumers to domestic producers (and suppliers of resources specific to the industry), area *c* becomes tariff revenue for the government, and the two red shaded triangles, *b* and *d,* reflect a net loss in social welfare because of the tariff.

Import Quotas

An *import quota* is a legal limit on the quantity of a particular commodity that can be imported per year. Quotas often target exports from certain countries.

EXHIBIT 9   **Effect of a Quota**

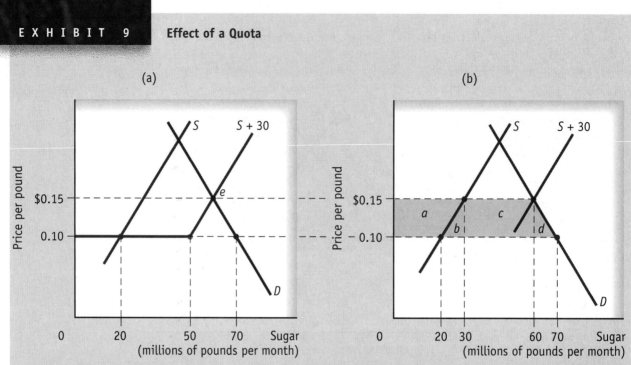

(a)

(b)

In panel (a), *D* is the domestic demand curve and *S* is the domestic supply curve. When the government establishes a sugar quota of 30 million pounds per year, the supply curve from both domestic production and imports becomes horizontal at the world price of $0.10 per pound and remains horizontal until the supply reaches 50 million pounds. For higher prices, the supply curve equals the horizontal sum of the domestic supply curve, *S*, and the quota. The new domestic price, $0.15 per pound, is determined by the intersection of the new supply curve, *S* + 30, with the domestic demand curve, *D*. Panel (b) shows the welfare effect of the quota. As a result of the higher domestic price, consumer surplus is reduced by the amount of shaded area. Area *a* represents a transfer from domestic consumers to domestic producers. Rectangular area *c* shows the gain to those who can import sugar at the world price and sell it at the higher domestic price. Triangular area *b* reflects a net loss; it represents the amount by which the cost of producing an extra 10 million pounds of sugar in the United States exceeds the cost of buying it from abroad. Area *d* also reflects a net loss—a reduction in consumer surplus as consumption falls. Thus, the blue shaded areas illustrate the loss in consumer surplus that is captured by domestic producers and those who are permitted to fulfill the quota, and the red shaded triangles illustrate the minimum net welfare cost.

For example, a quota may limit the number of automobiles that can be imported from Japan or the number of pairs of shoes that can be imported from Brazil. To have an impact on the market, or to be *effective,* a quota must restrict imports to less than would be imported under free trade.

Let's consider the impact of a quota on the domestic market for sugar. In panel (a) of Exhibit 9, the domestic supply of sugar is *S* and the domestic demand is *D*. Suppose that the world price of sugar is $0.10 per pound. With free trade, that price would prevail in the domestic market, and 70 million pounds per month would be demanded. Domestic producers would supply 20 million pounds and importers would supply 50 million pounds. With a quota of 50 million pounds or more per month, the domestic price would be the same as the world price of $0.10 per pound, and domestic sales would be 70 million pounds per month. A more stringent quota, however, would reduce the supply of imports, which, as we will see, would raise the domestic price.

Suppose that a quota of 30 million pounds per month is established. As long as the price in the U.S. market is at or above the world price of $0.10 per pound, foreign producers supply 30 million pounds to the U.S. market. So at prices at or above $0.10 per pound, the total supply of sugar to the domestic market is found by adding 30 million pounds of sugar to the amount supplied by domestic producers. At the world price of $0.10 per pound, domestic producers supply 20 million pounds, and importers supply the quota of 30 million pounds, for a total quantity supplied of 50 million pounds. At prices above $0.10, domestic producers can and do expand their quantity supplied in the U.S. market, but imports are restricted to the quota of 30 million pounds.

Domestic and foreign producers will never sell their output for less than $0.10 per pound in the U.S. market because they can always sell for that price on the world market. Thus, the supply curve that sums both domestic production and imports becomes horizontal at the world price of $0.10 per pound and remains horizontal until the quantity supplied reaches 50 million pounds. For prices above $0.10 per pound, the supply curve equals the horizontal sum of the supply curve of domestic producers, *S,* and the quota of 30 million pounds. The domestic price is found where this new supply curve intersects the domestic demand curve, which in panel (a) of Exhibit 9 occurs at point *e. An effective quota, by limiting imports, raises the domestic price of sugar above the world price and reduces quantity below the free-trade level.* (Note that to compare more readily the effects of tariffs and quotas, this quota was designed to yield the same equilibrium price and quantity as did the tariff we examined earlier.)

Panel (b) of Exhibit 9 focuses on the distributional and efficiency effects of the quota. The decline in consumer surplus after the imposition of the quota is depicted by the blue and red shaded areas. The loss in consumer surplus represented by the blue shaded area *a* is converted into the gain in producer surplus resulting from the higher price. Because the value of area *a* is simply transferred from domestic consumers to domestic producers, area *a* involves no loss in domestic welfare. The blue shaded rectangle *c* shows the gain to those permitted by the quota to sell 30 million pounds per month at the domestic price of $0.15 per pound. To the extent that the gains from the quota go to foreign exporters rather than to domestic importers, area *c* reflects a net loss in domestic welfare.

The red shaded triangle *b* shows the amount by which the marginal cost of producing another 10 million pounds in the United States exceeds the world price of the good. This triangular area represents a welfare loss to the domestic economy, because sugar could have been purchased for $0.10 per pound from abroad, and the domestic resources employed to increase sugar production could have been used more efficiently in the production of other goods. The red shaded triangle *d* also represents a welfare loss, because it reflects a reduction in consumer surplus (resulting from the fact that less sugar is consumed at the higher price) with no offsetting gain to anyone. Thus, the two red shaded triangles in panel (b) of Exhibit 9 measure the minimum welfare cost imposed on the domestic economy by an effective quota. To the extent that the profit from quota rights (area *c*) accrues to foreigners, the welfare loss imposed on the domestic economy is greater than is reflected by the red shaded triangles.

The United States has granted quotas to specific countries. These countries, in turn, award these rights to their exporters through a variety of means. The value of these export rights has been estimated recently to exceed $7 billion, with more than half of this amount due to quotas on textiles and apparel. *By rewarding domestic producers with higher prices and foreign producers with the right to sell goods to the United States, the quota system creates two groups intent on securing and perpetuating these quotas.* Lobbyists for foreign producers work the halls of Congress seeking the right to export to the United States. This strong support from producers, coupled with a lack of opposition from consumers (who remain largely unaware of all this), has resulted in quotas that have lasted for decades. Apparel quotas have been in effect for over 30 years, and sugar quotas for over 50 years.

Some economists have argued that if quotas are to be used, the United States should auction off quota allocations to foreign producers, thereby capturing the difference between the world price and the U.S. price. Auctioning off quotas would not only increase federal revenue, but also would reduce the attractiveness of quotas to foreign exporters to the United States and thereby reduce pressure on Washington to perpetuate quotas.

Consider the similarities and differences between the quota and the tariff we have discussed, both of which raised the domestic price of sugar by the same amount. Since the tariff and the quota have identical effects on the price, they reflect the same change in quantity demanded. In both cases, domestic consumers suffer the same loss in consumer surplus and domestic producers reap the same amount of producer surplus. The primary difference between the two restrictive policies is that the revenue resulting from the tariff goes to the domestic government, whereas the revenue resulting from the quota goes to whoever secures the right to sell foreign goods in the domestic market. If the quota rights accrue to foreigners, then the domestic economy is worse off with a quota than with a tariff.

Other Trade Restrictions

Besides tariffs and quotas, there are a variety of other measures affecting free trade. A country may provide *export subsidies* to encourage firms to export, or *low-interest loans* to foreign buyers to promote exports of large capital goods. Some countries impose *domestic content requirements* specifying that a certain percentage of a final good's value must be produced domestically. Other requirements concerning health, safety, or technical standards often discriminate against foreign goods. For example, European countries prohibit imports of beef from hormone-fed cattle, a measure aimed at U.S. beef producers. Purity laws in Germany bar the importation of many non-German beers. Until uniform standards are adopted by members of the European Community, differing technical standards force manufacturers to make seven different models of the same TV for this market. Even though the U.S. and Mexico have a free trade agreement, Mexican customs agents inspect every package crossing the border. For example, if a shipment contains 20 VCRs, all in identical boxes, customs officials open every box rather than sample them. This inconveniences shippers and slows down free trade. Sometimes exporters will voluntarily agree to limit exports, as when Japanese auto makers agreed to restrain auto exports to the United States. The point is that tariffs and quotas are only two of many devices that restrict foreign trade.

Recent research on the cost of protectionism points to the fact that international trade barriers prevent new goods and new technologies from being introduced into an economy. So rather than simply raising the cost of goods that are currently available, the cost of protection is much higher and helps explain why highly protected developing economies remain extremely poor.

Freer Trade by Multilateral Agreement

Mindful of the welfare loss from trade restrictions, the United States, after World War II, invited its trading partners to negotiate less stringent restrictions. The result was the **General Agreement on Tariffs and Trade (GATT),** which was an international trade treaty adopted in 1947 by 23 countries, including the United States. Each member of GATT agreed to (1) treat all member nations equally with respect to trade, (2) reduce tariff rates through multinational negotiations, and (3) reduce import quotas. The agreement resulted in thousands of tariff reductions.

The greatest improvements in trade liberalization have come through multilateral trade negotiations, or "trade rounds," under the auspices of GATT. Trade rounds offer a package approach to trade negotiations rather than an issue-by-issue approach. Concessions that are necessary but otherwise difficult to defend in domestic political terms can be made more acceptable in the context of a package that also contains politically and economically attractive benefits. Most early GATT trade rounds aimed at reducing tariffs. The Kennedy Round in the mid-1960s included new provisions against **dumping,** which is selling a commodity abroad at a price that is below its cost of production or below the price charged in the home market. The Tokyo Round of the 1970s was a more sweeping attempt to extend and improve the system.

The most recent round of negotiations was launched in Uruguay in September 1986 and ratified by 123 participating countries in April 1994 with 550 pages of legal text spelling out the results of the negotiations. This so-called Uruguay Round created the World Trade Organization to take over from GATT as of January 1, 1995. The new organization is discussed in the following case study.

General Agreement on Tariffs and Trade (GATT) An international tariff-reduction treaty adopted in 1947 that resulted in a series of negotiated "rounds" aimed at freer trade; the Uruguay Round created GATT's successor, the World Trade Organization

Dumping Selling a commodity abroad at a price that is below its cost of production or below the price charged in the domestic market

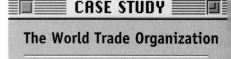

CASE STUDY

The World Trade Organization

The **World Trade Organization (WTO)** is now the legal and institutional foundation of the multilateral trading system. The WTO offers the platform on which trade relations among member countries can evolve through collective debate. Whereas GATT was a multilateral agreement with no institutional foundation, the WTO is a permanent institution with its own secretariat located in Geneva, Switzerland. With an annual budget of $85 million in 1996 and a staff of 450 headed by a director general and four deputies, the secretariat's responsibilities include supporting WTO delegate bodies, providing trade policy analysis, and assisting in the resolution of trade disputes involving the interpretation of WTO rules and precedents. The staff has a special responsibility of providing technical support to the member countries that are least developed.

Whereas GATT involved only merchandise trade, the WTO includes services and trade-related aspects of intellectual property, such as books, movies, and computer programs. For example, the agreement ensures that computer programs will be protected as literary works and specifies which databases

World Trade Organization (WTO) The legal and institutional foundation of the multilateral trading system that succeeded GATT in 1995

The World Trade Organization
continued

Location:

The World Trade Organization (WTO), established in 1995 in Geneva, Switzerland, provides the platform on which trade relations among countries evolve. The essential functions of the WTO are: (1) to administer and implement the trade agreements that make up the WTO; (2) to act as a forum for multilateral trade negotiations; (3) to seek to resolve trade disputes; (4) to oversee national trade policies; and (5) to cooperate with other international institutions involved in global economic policymaking. Visit the World Trade Organization (http://www.unicc.org/wto/).

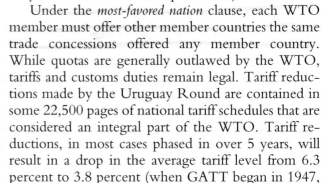

should be protected by copyright. The agreement also requires that a 20-year patent protection be available for all inventions in almost all fields of technology, whether of products or processes (developing-country members that do not currently provide patent protection have up to 10 years to introduce such protection).

Under the *most-favored nation* clause, each WTO member must offer other member countries the same trade concessions offered any member country. While quotas are generally outlawed by the WTO, tariffs and customs duties remain legal. Tariff reductions made by the Uruguay Round are contained in some 22,500 pages of national tariff schedules that are considered an integral part of the WTO. Tariff reductions, in most cases phased in over 5 years, will result in a drop in the average tariff level from 6.3 percent to 3.8 percent (when GATT began in 1947, the average tariff was 40 percent). If the negotiated reforms are implemented by all 123 participating countries, by the year 2005 (the target date for full implementation) world income is projected to rise $510 billion a year because of the Uruguay Round.

Dispute settlements under WTO are expected to be faster, more automatic, and less susceptible to blockage than under the GATT system. The WTO extends and clarifies previous GATT rules regarding two forms of "unfair" competition: dumping and export subsidies. Whereas GATT relied on the voluntary cooperation, the WTO has a permanent Dispute Settlement Body.

Countries that were not parties to the Uruguay Round must negotiate conditions of entry if they want to join the WTO. For example, China is trying to join the WTO and wants to join as a developing country (thereby getting a longer grace period to comply with provisions such as patent laws). But the U.S. government, because of concern about China's violations of human rights as well as widespread pirating of American products there, would like China admitted only as a developed country. That way, China would have less time to comply with WTO standards.

Sources: Kathy Chen, "China Is Faulted by U.S. Group in Piracy Pact," *The Wall Street Journal,* 13 October 1995; Bhushan Bahree, "WTO Panel Rules against U.S. in Dispute over Gasoline Norms," *The Wall Street Journal,* 18 January 1996.

Common Markets

Some countries have considered the success of the U.S. economy, with its free trade within the 50 states, and have developed free-trade pacts. The largest and best known is the European Union, which began in 1958 with a half-dozen countries and has now expanded to more than a dozen. The idea was to create a barrier-free European market like the United States in which goods, services, people, and capital were free to flow to their highest-valued use without restrictions. Another trading bloc has formed among the newly industrialized nations of East Asia. And most recently, the United States, Canada, and Mexico have developed a free-trade pact called the North American Free Trade Agreement, or NAFTA for short. Regional trading bloc agreements such as NAFTA and the European Union require an exception to the World Trade Organization rules because bloc members can make special deals among themselves and can then discriminate against outsiders. Recall that under WTO's most-favored nation clause, any trade concession granted one country must be given to *all other* WTO members.

Through NAFTA, Mexico hopes to increase U.S. investment in Mexico by guaranteeing to those who build manufacturing plants in Mexico duty-free access to U.S. markets, which is where over two-thirds of Mexico's exports go. The United States is interested in NAFTA because Mexico's 95 million people represent an attractive export market for U.S. producers, and Mexico's huge oil reserves could ease U.S. energy problems. The United States would also like to bolster Mexico's move toward a more market-oriented economy, as is reflected, for example, by Mexico's recent privatization of its phone system and banks.

ARGUMENTS FOR TRADE RESTRICTIONS

Trade restrictions often appear to be little more than welfare programs for the protected domestic industries. Given the welfare loss that results from these restrictions, it would be more efficient simply to transfer money from domestic consumers to domestic producers. But such a blatant transfer would probably be politically unpopular. Arguments for trade restrictions avoid mention of transfers to domestic producers and instead cite loftier concerns. As we shall now see, some of these arguments have more validity than others.

National Defense Argument

Certain industries are said to be in need of protection from import competition because they produce products that are vital in time of war. Because of their strategic importance, products such as strategic metals and weapons of war are sometimes insulated from foreign competition by trade restrictions. Thus, national defense considerations outweigh concerns about efficiency and equity.

How valid is this argument? Trade restrictions may shelter the defense industry, but other methods of sheltering it, such as government subsidies to U.S. producers, might be more efficient. Or the government could stockpile basic military hardware so that maintaining an ongoing productive capacity would become less essential, though technological change soon makes many weapons obsolete. Since nearly all industries can make some claim to be vital to national defense, instituting trade restrictions on this basis can get out of hand. For example, one reason U.S. wool producers benefit from protective policies is that wool is said to be critical to the production of military uniforms.

Infant Industry Argument

The infant industry argument was formulated as a rationale for protecting emerging domestic industry from foreign competition. According to this argument, in industries where a firm's average cost per unit falls as production expands, new domestic firms may need protection from foreign competitors until the domestic firms reach sufficient size to be competitive. Trade restrictions are thus viewed as temporary devices for allowing domestic firms to achieve sufficient economies of scale needed to compete with established foreign producers.

One problem is how to identify which industries merit protection. And when do domestic firms become old enough to look after themselves? The very existence of protection may foster production inefficiencies that firms may not be able to outgrow. The immediate cost of such restrictions is the net welfare loss from higher domestic prices. These costs may become permanent if the industry never realizes the expected economies of scale and thus never becomes competitive. As with the national defense argument, policymakers should be careful in adopting trade restrictions based on the infant industry argument. Here again, production subsidies are more efficient than import restrictions.

Antidumping Argument

As we have noted already, *dumping* is selling a commodity abroad at a price that is below its cost of production or below the price charged in the home market. Exporters may be able to sell the good for less overseas because of export subsidies, or firms may simply find it profitable to charge lower prices in foreign markets, where there are more competitors. Critics of dumping recommend applying a tariff to raise the price of dumped goods.

What's wrong with foreign producers selling goods for less in the United States than in their own countries? Why should U.S. consumers be prevented from buying products for as little as possible even if these low prices are the result of a foreign subsidy? If the dumping is *persistent*, the lower price may increase consumer surplus by an amount that will more than offset losses to domestic producers. *Thus, there is no good reason why consumers should not be allowed to buy imports for a persistently lower price.*

An alternative form of dumping, termed *predatory dumping*, is the *temporary* sale of a product at a lower price abroad in order to drive out competing producers. Once the competition has been eliminated, so the story goes, the exporting firm can raise the price. Predatory dumping may also be a way to discourage domestic production of a good. Domestic firms would not find entry into this industry attractive because they would not be able to sell at the low price that results from dumping. By driving out established firms or by discouraging domestic entry, the dumpers try to monopolize the market. The trouble with this argument is that if dumpers try to take advantage of their monopoly position by sharply increasing the price, then other firms may enter the market and sell for less. There are very few documented cases of predatory dumping.

Sometimes dumping may be *sporadic,* as firms occasionally sell at a discount to unload excess inventories; retailers hold periodic "sales" for the same reason. Sporadic dumping can be unsettling for domestic industry, but the economic impact is not a matter of great public concern. Regardless, all dumping is prohibited in the United States by the Trade Agreements Act of 1979, which calls for the imposition of tariffs when a good is sold for less in the United States than in its home market. In addition, WTO rules allow for the imposition of offsetting tariffs when products are sold for "less than fair value" and when there is "material injury" to domestic producers. U.S. producers of lumber and beer have recently accused their Canadian counterparts of dumping.

Jobs and Income Argument

One rationale for trade restrictions that is commonly heard in the United States today is that they protect U.S. jobs and wage levels. Using trade restrictions to protect domestic jobs is a strategy that dates back centuries. One problem with such a policy is that other countries will likely retaliate by restricting their imports to save *their* jobs, so international trade is reduced, jobs are lost in export industries, and potential gains from trade are not realized.

Wages in other countries, especially developing countries, are often a small fraction of wages in the United States. Looking simply at differences in the wage rate, however, narrows the focus too much. Wages represent just one component of the total production cost and may not necessarily be the most important. Employers are interested in the labor cost per unit of output, which depends on both the wage rate and labor productivity.

The high wage rates in the United States exist in part because of the high marginal productivity of U.S. workers. U.S. labor productivity remains the highest in the world. This high productivity can be traced to education and training and to the abundant machines and other physical capital that make workers more productive. Workers in the United States also benefit from a business climate that is relatively stable and that offers appropriate incentives to produce.

But how about the lower wages in many competing countries? These low wages can often be linked to workers' lack of education and training, the meager amount of physical capital that accompanies each worker, and a business climate that is less stable and less attractive. In industries where higher U.S. wages are supported by higher U.S. output per worker, the labor cost per unit of output may be as low, or lower, in the United States as in many countries with low wages and low productivity. For example, although total hourly compensation is more than twice as high at Birmingham Steel, a U.S. corporation, as at South Korean steel plants, Birmingham's labor productivity is four times greater, so the labor cost per ton of steel is lower for Birmingham.[1]

Once multinational firms build plants and provide technological know-how in developing countries, however, U.S. workers lose some of their competitive edge, and their relatively high wages could price some U.S. products out of the world market. This has already happened in the stereo and consumer electronics industries. Over time, as labor productivity in developing countries increases, wage differentials among countries will narrow, much as wage differentials between northern and southern states have narrowed. As technology and capital spread, U.S. workers, particularly unskilled workers, cannot expect to maintain wage levels that are far above those in other countries. The U.S. government may promote research and development to keep U.S. producers on the cutting edge of technological developments, but staying ahead in the technological game is a constant battle.

---

1   Dana Milbank, "U.S. Productivity Gains Cut Costs, Close Gap in Low-Wage Overseas Firms," *The Wall Street Journal,* 23 December 1992.

Domestic producers do not like to compete with foreign producers whose costs are lower, so they often push for trade restrictions. But if restrictions negate any cost advantage a foreign producer might have, the law of comparative advantage becomes inoperative, and domestic consumers are denied access to the lower-priced goods.

Declining Industries Argument

Where an established domestic industry is in jeopardy of being displaced by lower-priced imports, there could be a rationale for *temporary* import restrictions to allow the orderly adjustment of the domestic industry. After all, domestic producers employ many industry-specific resources—both specialized machines and specialized labor. This physical and human capital is worth less in its best alternative use. If the extinction of the domestic industry is forestalled through trade restrictions, specialized machines can be allowed to wear out naturally and specialized workers can retire voluntarily or can gradually pursue more promising careers.

Thus, in the case of declining domestic industries, trade protection is viewed as a temporary measure to help lessen shocks to the economy and to allow for an orderly transition to a new industrial mix. But the protection offered should not be so generous as to encourage continued investment in the industry. Protection should be of specific duration and should be phased out over that period.

The clothing industry is an example of a declining U.S. industry. The 22,000 U.S. jobs saved as a result of trade restrictions pay an average of about $18,000 per year. But a Congressional Budget Office study estimated that because of higher domestic prices, U.S. consumers paid between $39,000 and $74,000 per year for each textile and apparel job saved.

Free trade may displace some U.S. jobs through imports, but it also creates some U.S. jobs through exports. And even where foreign competition appears to have displaced U.S. workers, many foreign companies have built plants in the United States and employ U.S. workers. For example, a dozen foreign television manufacturers and all major Japanese automobile manufacturers have plants in the United States. In fact, a U.S. consumer who buys a Honda Accord is more likely to be getting a car produced in the United States than is a U.S. consumer who buys a Pontiac Le Mans.

Since 1960, the number of jobs in the United States has grown by over 60 million, more than doubling the 1960 total. To recognize this job growth is not to deny the problems facing those workers who are displaced by imports. Some displaced workers, particularly those in blue-collar jobs in steel and other unionized industries, are not apt to find jobs that will pay as well as the jobs they lost. As with infant industries, however, the problems posed by declining industries need not be solved by trade restrictions. To support the affected industry, the government could offer wage subsidies or special tax breaks that decline over time. The government could also fund programs to retrain workers for jobs that are in more demand.

Problems with Protection

Trade restrictions raise a number of problems in addition to the ones already mentioned. First, protecting one stage of production often requires protecting downstream stages of production. Protecting the U.S. textile industry from foreign competition, for example, raises the cost of cloth to U.S. clothing manufacturers, reducing their competitiveness. Thus, if the government protects domestic textile manufacturers, it should also protect the domestic garment industry. Otherwise, foreign manufacturers will fashion lower-priced foreign textiles into garments for export to the United States, where they will sell for less than U.S.-made garments made from higher-priced U.S. textiles.

Second, the cost of protection includes not only the welfare loss arising from the higher domestic price, but also the cost of the resources used by domestic producers and groups to secure the favored protection. The cost of *rent seeking*—lobbying fees, propaganda, legal actions—can amount to as much as or more than the direct welfare loss from restrictions. A third problem with imposing trade restrictions is that other countries often retaliate, thus shrinking the gains from trade. Retaliation can set off still greater trade restrictions, leading to an outright trade war. A final problem with trade restrictions is the complication of policing and enforcing the myriad quotas, tariffs, and other restrictions. Consider the following case study.

CASE STUDY

Enforcing Trade Restrictions

Location:

As the nation's principal border agency, the United States Customs Service, part of the Department of the Treasury, attempts to ensure that all goods entering and exiting the United States do so in accordance with United States laws and regulations. Visit the U.S. Customs Service (http://www.ustreas.gov/treasury/bureaus/customs/customs.html).

The United States is the richest, most attractive market in the world. Trade restrictions often make U.S. markets even more appealing to foreign producers because U.S. prices exceed world prices. With thousands of different tariff classifications and with tariffs ranging from zero to over 100 percent, the U.S. Customs Service has difficulty keeping things straight. We should not be surprised that some U.S. importers try to skirt trade restrictions, either avoiding tariffs or illegally importing goods that are restricted by quotas. A diverse array of goods is imported in violation of quotas, including clothing, sugar, coffee, gems, and steel pipes. It has been estimated that more than 10 percent of all imports are illegal.

Restrictions affect not only the quantity of imports but also the quality. Nearly all schemes to import clothing illegally involve fraudulent documents intended to misrepresent the clothing so that it fits into some quota or qualifies for a lower tariff. Sometimes the garments are altered to evade detection. For example, because imports of men's running shorts are controlled by a quota, manufacturers often add a flimsy inner lining so the shorts could pass for swimming trunks, which face no quotas.

Because the United States allows some countries more generous quotas than others, exporters in a country under tight control sometimes ship their goods through a country with a liberal ceiling. For example, Japan typically makes so little clothing for export that the United States imposes no clothing quota for imports from Japan. As a result, clothing made in Korea is often shipped through Japan to evade U.S. quotas on Korean goods. Similarly, because Nepal is not subject to a clothing quota but India is, India ships clothing to the United States through Nepal.

Enforcing Trade Restrictions
continued

Higher tariffs are often imposed on lower-priced products. Foreign steel companies have been accused of falsely inflating the price of steel to avoid import duties on low-priced steel. Allegedly, part of the higher price paid by importers was secretly rebated by steel producers through a variety of schemes. Producers of other steel products have mislabeled and falsely weighed them to avoid certain restrictions.

Some foreign producers and U.S. importers are said to engage in "port shopping," or testing various ports to see where inspections are most lax. Documents are often forged. U.S. Customs inspectors are responsible for policing all this activity. These inspectors must remain alert because of thousands of tariffs, quotas, and other trade restrictions in effect and the myriad ways to get around them. Add to this the problem of keeping out illegal drugs and counterfeit copies of brand-name products and you can see why Customs inspectors have their hands full.

Sources: Lisa Harrington, "Reinventing the U.S. Customs Service," *Transportation & Distribution,* April 1995; Suzanne McGee, "Customs Service Weighs Duty on Some Gold," *The Wall Street Journal,* 4 November 1994; and James Bovard, "The Customs Service's Fickle Philosophers," *The Wall Street Journal,* 31 July 1991.

CONCLUSION

Comparative advantage, specialization, and trade allow people to use their scarce resources most efficiently to satisfy their unlimited wants. International trade arises from voluntary exchange among buyers and sellers pursuing their self-interest. Despite the clear gains from free trade, restrictions on international trade date back hundreds of years.

Those who benefit from trade restrictions are the domestic producers (and their resource suppliers) who are able to sell their output for a higher price because of the restrictions. Protection insulates an industry from the rigors of global competition, in the process stifling innovation and leaving the industry vulnerable to technological change in other countries. Under a system of quotas, the winners also include those who have secured the right to import the good at the world price and sell it at the domestic price.

Consumers who must pay higher prices for protected goods suffer from trade restrictions, as do the domestic producers who use imported resources. Other losers are U.S. exporters, who face higher trade barriers if foreigners retaliate. Even if other countries do not retaliate, U.S. trade restrictions reduce the gains from comparative advantage and thereby reduce world income. With world income lower, U.S. exporters find that their foreign markets have shrunk. Some of these losers may go out of business; others may never even start producing.

Trade restrictions are often imposed gradually over a period of years. Because the domestic adjustments to restrictions are slow and because the losers are scattered throughout the economy, the losers frequently do not know that they are losers or they fail to connect their troubles with trade policy. On the other hand, those who benefit from trade restrictions are usually a well-defined group who can clearly identify the source of their gains. *One reason trade restrictions exist is that most of those harmed by restrictions do not know they are losers, whereas beneficiaries know what is at stake.* Producers have an interest in trade legislation, but consumers remain largely ignorant. Consumers purchase thousands of different goods and thus have no special interest in the effects of trade policy on any particular good. Congress tends to support the group that makes the most noise, so trade restrictions persist, despite the clear gains from free trade.

SUMMARY

1. Even if a country has an absolute advantage in producing all goods, that country should specialize in producing the goods for which it has a comparative advantage. If each country specializes and trades according to the law of comparative advantage, all countries will have greater consumption possibilities.

2. Tariffs and effective import quotas raise prices in domestic markets. The primary difference between a tariff and a quota is in the distribution of the gains resulting from higher domestic prices.

3. Tariff revenues go to the government and could be used to lower taxes; quotas confer benefits on those with the right to buy the good at the world price and sell it at the higher domestic price. Both restrictions harm domestic consumers more than they help domestic producers, though tariffs at least yield domestic government revenue.

4. Despite the gains from free trade and the net welfare losses arising from tariffs and quotas, trade restrictions have been a part of trade policy for hundreds of years. The General Agreement on Tariffs and Trade (GATT) was an international treaty ratified in 1947 to reduce tariffs. Subsequent rounds of negotiations promoted lower tariffs and discouraged trade restrictions. The Uruguay Round, ratified by 123 countries in 1994, created the World Trade Organization (WTO) to succeed GATT.

5. Some of the reasons given for instituting trade restrictions include promoting national defense, giving infant industries time to grow, preventing foreign producers from dumping goods in domestic markets, protecting domestic jobs, and allowing declining industries time to phase out.

QUESTIONS AND PROBLEMS

1. **(Profile of Imports and Exports)** What are the major exports and imports of the United States? What does this trade do to the U.S. consumption possibilities?

2. **(Gains from Trade)** Complete each of the following sentences:
   a. When a nation has no economic interaction with foreigners and produces everything that it consumes, the nation is in a state of _____.
   b. According to the law of comparative advantage, each nation should specialize in the production of the goods in which it has the lower _____.
   c. The amount of one good that nations will exchange for another good is known as the _____.
   d. Specializing according to comparative advantage and exchange with another nation results in _____ _____ gains from trade.

3. **(Reasons for International Specialization)** What determines the goods in which a country should specialize and export to other nations?

4. **(Absolute and Comparative Advantage)** Suppose that each worker in the United States can produce 8 units of food or 2 units of clothing daily. In Izodia, which has the same number of workers, each worker can produce 7 units of food or 1 unit of clothing daily. Why does the United States have an absolute advantage in both goods? Which country enjoys a comparative advantage in food? Why?

5. **(Gains from Trade)** Why do economists believe that consumers are better off when countries specialize in the goods for which they have a comparative advantage and then trade with each other?

6. **(World Price and Trade)** Diagram the U.S. domestic supply and demand for steel. Assuming that the world equilibrium price is the same as the domestic equilibrium price in both countries, diagram the U.S. import line and the Japanese export line. If there is an increase in Japanese supply, what will happen in the domestic markets for steel and to the world price?

7. **(Tariffs)** Very high tariffs usually cause black markets and smuggling. How is government revenue reduced by such activity? Relate your answer to the graph in Exhibit 8 in this chapter. Does smuggling have any social benefits?

8. **(Effect of Trade on Social Welfare)** Consider a country that is initially in autarky. Indicate the impact on each of the following variables in that country if the country then moves to free trade:
   a. Domestic prices in import-competing industries; in exporting industries.
   b. Consumption in import-competing industries; in exporting industries.
   c. Domestic production in import-competing industries; in exporting industries.
   d. Consumer surplus in import-competing industries; in exporting industries.
   e. Producer surplus in import-competing industries; in exporting industries.
   f. Net social welfare in import-competing industries; in exporting industries.

9. **(Common Markets)** What is a common market? What is NAFTA?

10. **(Efficiency and Production Possibilities)** The data from the production possibilities tables in Exhibit 1 can be used to construct a world production possibilities frontier.
   a. Draw a graph illustrating this joint production possibilities curve. (Hint: Start with all resources producing food and then gradually switch resources into clothing as efficiently as possible.)
   b. Why does this curve have a kink in it?
   c. Explain why it is necessary for one or both countries to specialize in production in order to be on the joint production possibilities curve.
   d. Why does the trading rate between the countries have to fall between 0.5 and 2 units of food per unit of clothing?
   e. How do the relative gains from trade between the two countries depend on what terms of trade are established?

11. **(Arguments for Trade Restrictions)** Explain each of the following arguments for protecting a domestic industry from international competition:
   a. National defense argument.
   b. Declining industries argument.
   c. Infant industry argument.

12. **(Restricting Trade)** Suppose that the world price for steel is below the U.S. domestic price, but the govern-

ment requires that all steel used in the United States be domesticallly produced.
   a. Use a diagram like the one in Exhibit 8 to show the gains and loses from such a policy.
   b. How could you estimate the net welfare loss (deadweight loss) from such a diagram?
   c. What kind of response to such a policy would you expect from industries (like automobile producers) that use U.S. steel?
   d. What government revenues are generated by this policy?

13. **(Restricting Trade)** Industries hurt by cheap imports typically argue that restricting trade will save U.S. jobs. What's wrong with this argument? Are there ever any reasons to support such an argument?

14. **(Consumption Possibilities Frontier)** The consumption possibilities frontiers shown in Exhibit 3 assume terms of trade of 1 unit of clothing for 1 unit of food. What would the consumption possibilities frontiers look like if the terms of trade were 1 unit of clothing for 2 units of food? 3 units of food? $\frac{1}{2}$ unit of food?

15. **(Determining World Price)** Suppose that there is an increase in the U.S. demand for steel. Using Exhibit 6 to illustrate your analysis, show what would happen to the level of world trade and the world price of steel.

16. **(Restricting Trade)** Exhibits 8 and 9 show net loses to the domestic economy of the country imposing tariffs or quotas on imported sugar. What kinds of gains and losses would occur to the economies of countries exporting sugar?

17. **(Restricting Trade)** What kinds of gains and losses are created in importing and exporting countries from export subsidies? From domestic content requirements?

18. **(Import Quotas)** What is meant by an *effective* import quota? Using a supply-and-demand diagram, illustrate and explain the net welfare loss from imposing such a quota. Why might the net welfare loss from an import quota exceed the net welfare loss from an equivalent tariff (one that results in the same price and import level as the quota)?

19. **(World Trade Organization)** What is the World Trade Organization, and how was it established?

20. **(World Trade Organization)** What is the most-favored nation clause? What types of trade restrictions, if any, are allowed under the WTO?

21. **(Enforcing Trade Restrictions)** Increasingly, goods are manufactured using a variety of domestic and imported parts and/or resources. What problem does this create in enforcing trade restrictions?

22. **(Enforcing Trade Restrictions)** What variety of techniques are used to skirt U.S. trade restrictions?

Using the Internet

23. Visit The Office of the U.S. Trade Representative (USTR) (**http://www.ustr.gov/**). The U.S. Trade Representative is a Cabinet member who acts as the principal trade advisor, negotiator, and spokesperson for the president on trade and related investment matters. Find the most recent National Trade Estimate Report on Foreign Trade Barriers (NTE)—listed within "Reports."

   a. For the country of your choice, indicate whether the United States has a trade surplus or deficit, and its amount.

   b. What are the key trade barriers the United States faces with this country?

34

International Finance

A U.S. firm that plans to buy a machine from a British manufacturer will be quoted a price in British pounds. Suppose that machine costs 10,000 pounds. How many dollars will it cost? The cost in dollars will depend on the current exchange rate. When buyers and sellers from two countries trade, two national currencies are almost always involved. Supporting the flows of goods and services are flows of currencies that connect all international transactions. The *exchange rate* between two currencies—the price of one in terms of the other—is the means by which the price of a good in one country is translated into the price to the buyer in another country. The willingness of buyers and sellers to strike deals, therefore, depends on the rate of exchange between currencies. In this chapter we will examine the international transactions that determine the relative value of the dollar. Topics discussed in this chapter include:

- Balance of payments
- Trade deficits and surpluses
- Foreign exchange markets
- Floating exchange rates
- Purchasing power parity

- Fixed exchange rates
- The international monetary system
- Managed float

BALANCE OF PAYMENTS

A country's gross domestic product conveys an idea of the flow of economic activity that occurs within that country during a given period. To account for their dealings abroad, countries also keep track of their international transactions. A country's *balance of payments,* as introduced in Chapter 4, summarizes all economic transactions that occur during a given time period between residents of that country and residents of other countries. *Residents* include individuals, firms, and governments.

International Economic Transactions

Balance of payments statements measure economic transactions that occur between countries, whether they involve goods and services, real or financial assets, or transfer payments. Because the balance of payments reflects the volume of transactions that occur during a particular time period, usually a year, the balance of payments measures a *flow.*

Some transactions included in the balance of payments account do not involve payments of money. For example, if *Time* magazine ships a new printing press to its Australian subsidiary, no money payment occurs, yet an economic transaction involving another country has taken place and must be included in the balance of payments account. Similarly, if you send money to friends or relatives abroad, if CARE sends food to Africa, or if the Pentagon sends military assistance to Bosnia, these transactions must be captured in the balance of payments. So, remember, although we speak of the *balance of payments,* a more descriptive phrase would be the *balance of economic transactions.*

Balance of payments accounts are maintained according to the principles of *double-entry bookkeeping,* in which entries on one side of the ledger are called *debits,* and entries on the other side are called *credits.* As we will see, the balance of payments accounts are made up of several individual accounts; a deficit in one or more accounts must be offset by a surplus in the other accounts. Thus, the total debits must be in balance with, or equal to, the total credits—hence the expression *balance* of payments. The balance of payments involves a comparison during a given time period, such as a year, between the outflow of payments to the rest of the world, which are entered as debits, and the inflow of receipts from the rest of the world, which are entered as credits. The next sections describe the major accounts in the balance of payments.

Although U.S. military aid to Bosnia does not involve direct payments of money, this aid is still an economic transaction.

Merchandise Trade Balance

The *merchandise trade balance,* a term first introduced in Chapter 4, equals the value of merchandise exported minus the value of merchandise imported. The merchandise account reflects trade in tangible products (stuff you can drop on your toe), such as French wine and U.S. computers, and is often referred to simply as the *trade balance.* The value of U.S. merchandise exports is listed as a credit in the U.S. balance of payments account because U.S. residents must *be paid* for the exported goods. The value of U.S. merchandise imports is listed as a debit in the balance of payments account because U.S. residents must *pay* for the imported goods.

If the value of merchandise exports exceeds the value of merchandise imports, there is a *surplus* in the merchandise trade balance, or, more simply, a *trade*

EXHIBIT 1   Merchandise Trade Balance (billions of 1992 dollars)

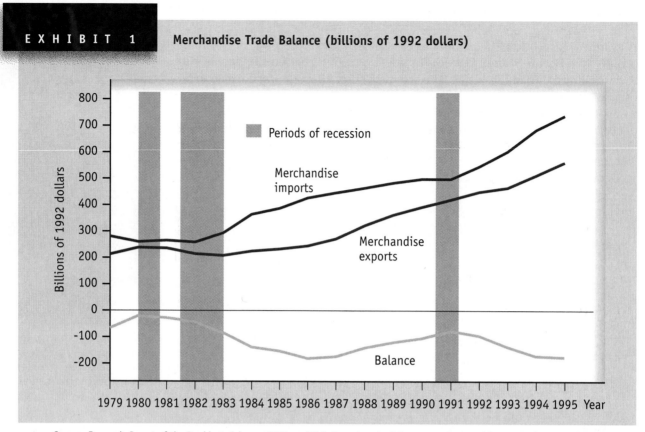

Source: *Economic Report of the President*, February 1996; and U.S. Department of Commerce, *Survey of Current Business*, April 1996.

surplus. If the value of merchandise imports exceeds the value of merchandise exports, there is a *deficit* in the merchandise trade balance, or a *trade deficit*. The merchandise trade balance is reported on a monthly basis; this report influences foreign exchange markets, the stock market, and other financial markets. The trade balance depends on a variety of factors, including the relative strength and competitiveness of the domestic economy compared to other economies and the relative value of the domestic currency compared to other currencies.

The U.S. merchandise trade balance since 1979 is presented in Exhibit 1. Because imports have exceeded exports every year, the balance has been in deficit, as is reflected by the bottom line. Note that during recessions, which are indicated by shading, imports were relatively flat, as was the overall trade deficit. Between 1983 and 1990, the U.S. economy expanded. *When the economy expands, spending on all goods increases, so imports tend to increase.*

Balance on Goods and Services

The merchandise trade balance focuses on the flow of goods, but services are also traded internationally. *Services* are intangibles, such as transportation, insurance, banking, military transactions, and tourist expenditures. Services also include the income earned from foreign investments less the income earned by foreigners from their investment in the U.S. economy. Services are often called "invisibles," because they are not tangible. The value of U.S. service exports, such as when an Irish tourist visits New York City, is listed as a credit in the U.S. balance of payments account because U.S. residents receive payments for these services. The value of U.S. service imports, such as when a computer specialist in Ireland enters claim information for a Connecticut insurer, is listed as a debit in the balance of payments account because U.S. residents must pay for the imported services.

The **balance on goods and services** is the difference between the value of exports of goods and services and the value of imports of goods and services. Currently produced goods and services that are sold or otherwise provided to foreigners form part of U.S. output. The production of these goods and services generates income during the current period. Conversely, imports of goods and services form part of the nation's current expenditures—part of consumption, investment, and government expenditures. Allocating imports to each of the major expenditure components is an accounting nightmare, so we usually just subtract imports from exports to yield *net exports*. Thus, the U.S. gross domestic product in a given year equals total expenditures for consumption, investment, and government purchases, plus net exports.

Balance on goods and services The section of a country's balance of payments account that measures the difference in value between a country's exports of goods and services and its imports of goods and services

Unilateral Transfers

Unilateral transfers consist of government transfers to foreign residents, foreign aid, personal gifts to friends and relatives abroad, personal and institutional charitable donations, and the like. For example, money sent abroad by a U.S. resident to friends or relatives would be included in U.S. unilateral transfers and would be a debit in the balance of payments account. U.S. **net unilateral transfers** equal the unilateral transfers received from abroad by U.S. residents minus the unilateral transfers sent to foreign residents. U.S. net unilateral transfers have been negative each year since World War II, except for 1991, when the U.S. government received sizable transfers from foreign governments to support the Persian Gulf war.

The United States places no restrictions on money sent out of the country.[1] Other countries, particularly developing countries, strictly limit the amount of money that may be sent abroad. More generally, developing countries often restrict the convertibility of their currencies into another country's currency.

Net unilateral transfers The unilateral transfers (gifts and grants) received from abroad by residents of a country minus the unilateral transfers residents send abroad

When we add net unilateral transfers to the exports of goods and services minus the imports of goods and services, we get the **balance on current account,** which is reported quarterly. Thus, *the current account includes all transactions in currently produced goods and services plus net unilateral transfers.* It can be negative, reflecting a current account deficit; positive, reflecting a current account surplus; or zero.

Balance on current account The section of a country's balance of payments account that measures the sum of the country's net unilateral transfers and its balance on goods and services

Capital Account

Whereas the current account records international transactions involving the flow of goods, services, and unilateral transfers, the **capital account** records international transactions involving the flow of financial assets, such as borrowing, lending, and investments. For example, U.S. investors purchase foreign assets in order to earn a higher rate of return and to diversify their portfolios. When

Capital account The record of a country's international transactions involving purchases or sales of financial and real assets

---

1   Federal authorities do, however, require reporting the source of cash exports of $10,000 or more. This measure is aimed at reducing money laundering overseas.

economists talk about capital, they usually mean the physical and human resources employed to produce goods and services. But sometimes *capital* is used as another word for *money*—money used to acquire financial assets, such as stocks, bonds, bank balances, and money used to make direct investments in foreign plants and equipment. U.S. capital outflows result when Americans purchase foreign assets. U.S. capital inflows result from foreign purchases of U.S. assets.

Between 1917 and 1982, the United States was a net capital exporter, and the net return of all this foreign investment over the years improved our balance on current account. In 1983, high real interest rates in the United States (relative to those in the rest of the world) resulted in a net inflow of capital for the first time in 65 years. A net inflow of capital shows up as a surplus in the capital account. Since then, U.S. imports of capital have exceeded exports of capital nearly every year, meaning that Americans owe foreigners more and more. *The United States is now the world's largest net debtor nation.* This is not as bad as it sounds, since foreign investment in the United States adds to America's productive capacity and promotes employment. But the return on foreign investment in the United States flows to foreigners, not to Americans.

The **official reserve transactions account** indicates the net amount of international reserves that shift among central banks to settle international transactions. (Many government publications show this not as a separate account but as part of the capital account.) International reserves consist of gold, dollars, other major currencies, and a special-purpose reserve currency called *Special Drawing Rights,* or *SDRs,* which will be discussed in more detail later.

Official reserve transactions account The section of a country's balance of payments account that reflects the flow of gold, Special Drawing Rights, and currencies among central banks

Statistical Discrepancy

As we have seen, the U.S. balance of payments is a record of all transactions between U.S. residents and foreign residents over a specified period. It is easier to describe this record than to compile it. Despite efforts to capture all international transactions, some go unreported. Yet, as the name *balance of payments* suggests, debits must equal credits—the entire balance of payments account must by definition be in balance. To ensure that the accounts balance, a residual account called the *statistical discrepancy* was created. An excess of credits in all other accounts is offset by an equivalent debit in the statistical discrepancy account, or an excess of debits in all other accounts is offset by an equivalent credit in the discrepancy account. So you might think of the statistical discrepancy as the "fudge factor."

The statistical discrepancy provides analysts with both a measure of the net error in the balance of payments data and a means of satisfying the double-entry bookkeeping requirement that total debits must equal total credits. The positive statistical discrepancy for the United States during most years since 1980 may reflect large, secret money flows into the country. Wealthy people from countries with unstable governments or high taxes may secretly purchase U.S. financial assets to shelter their wealth.

Deficits and Surpluses

Nations, like households, operate under a cash-flow constraint. Expenditures cannot exceed income plus cash on hand and borrowed funds. We have distinguished between *current* transactions, which are the income and expenditures from exports, imports, and unilateral transfers, and *capital* transactions, which reflect international investments and borrowing. Any surplus or deficit in one ac-

Item	Debits	Credits	Balance	
Current Account				**EXHIBIT 2**
1. Merchandise exports		+574.9		
2. Merchandise imports	−749.4			**U.S. Balance of Payments: 1995 (billions of dollars)**
3. Trade balance (1 + 2)			−174.5	
4. Service exports		+390.1		
5. Service imports	−338.5			
6. Goods and services balance (3 + 4 + 5)			−122.9	
7. Net unilateral transfers	−30.0			
8. Current account balance (6 + 7)			−152.9	
Capital Account				
9. Outflow of U.S. capital	−270.3			
10. Inflow of foreign capital		+315.8		
11. Capital account balance (9 + 10)			+45.5	
Official Reserve Transactions Account				
12. Decrease in U.S. official assets abroad	−9.8			
13. Increase in foreign official assets in U.S.		+110.5		
14. Official reserve balance (12 + 13)			+100.7	
15. Statistical discrepancy		+6.7		
TOTAL (8 + 11 + 14 + 15)			**0.0**	

Source: *Survey of Current Business,* U.S. Department of Commerce, April 1996.

count must be balanced by other changes in the balance of payments accounts. The current account has been in deficit since 1982, meaning that the sum of U.S. imports and unilateral transfers to foreigners has exceeded the sum spent by foreigners on our exports and sent as unilateral transfers to us.

Exhibit 2 presents the U.S. balance of payments statement for 1995, the most recent year reported. All transactions requiring payments from foreigners to U.S. residents are entered in the credits column using a plus sign (+), because they result in a flow of funds to U.S. residents. All transactions requiring payments to foreigners from U.S. residents are entered in the debits column using a minus sign (−), because they result in a flow of funds to foreign residents. As you can see, a deficit in the current account was offset by surpluses in the capital account, in the official reserve transactions account, and in the statistical discrepancy.

If a country runs a deficit in its current account, it is because the amount of foreign currency a country gets from exporting goods and services and from receipts of unilateral transfers falls short of the amount of foreign currency, or foreign exchange, needed to pay for its imports and to make unilateral transfers. *Foreign exchange* is the currency of another country that is needed to carry out international transactions. The additional foreign exchange required must be provided by a net capital inflow (international borrowing, foreign purchases of domestic stocks and bonds, and so forth) or through official government transactions in foreign currency. If a country runs a current account surplus, the foreign exchange received from exports and from unilateral transfers exceeds the amount required to pay for imports and to make unilateral transfers. This excess foreign exchange could be held in a bank account, converted to the domestic currency, or used to purchase foreign stocks and bonds.

When all transactions are considered, the balance of payments always balances, though specific accounts may not be in balance. A deficit in a particular account should not necessarily be viewed as a source of concern, nor should a surplus be viewed as a source of satisfaction. The deficit in the U.S. current account in recent years has been offset by a net inflow of capital from abroad. As a result of the net inflow of capital, foreigners are acquiring larger claims on U.S. assets.

FOREIGN EXCHANGE RATES AND MARKETS

Now that you have some idea about the international flow of products and capital, we can take a closer look at the forces that determine the underlying value of the currencies involved in these transactions. We begin by looking at exchange rates and the market for foreign exchange.

Foreign Exchange

Exchange rate The price of one country's currency measured in terms of another country's currency

The **exchange rate** is the price of one country's currency measured in terms of another country's currency. Exchange rates are determined by the interaction of the households, firms, private financial institutions, and central banks that buy and sell foreign exchange. The exchange rate fluctuates to equate the quantity of foreign exchange demanded with the quantity supplied. Typically, foreign exchange is made up of bank deposits denominated in the foreign currency. When foreign travel is involved, foreign exchange may consist of foreign paper money.

The foreign exchange market incorporates all the arrangements used to buy and sell foreign exchange. This market is not so much a physical place as it is a network of telephones, Telex, and computer systems connecting large banks all over the world. Perhaps you have seen pictures of foreign exchange traders in New York, London, or Tokyo amid a tangle of telephones. The foreign exchange market is like an all-night diner—it never closes. Some trading center is always open somewhere in the world.

Currency depreciation An increase in the number of units of a particular currency needed to purchase 1 unit of foreign exchange

Currency appreciation A decrease in the number of units of a particular currency needed to purchase 1 unit of foreign exchange

Consider the market for British pounds in terms of dollars. The price, or exchange rate, is specified in terms of the number of dollars required to purchase one British pound. An increase in the number of dollars needed to purchase a pound indicates a weakening, or a **depreciation,** of the dollar. A decrease in the number of dollars needed to purchase a pound indicates a strengthening, or an **appreciation,** of the dollar. Put another way, a decrease in the number of pounds needed to purchase a dollar is a depreciation of the dollar, and an increase in the number of pounds needed to purchase a dollar is an appreciation of the dollar.

Since the exchange rate is a price, we can explain its determination using the conventional tools of supply and demand: the equilibrium price of foreign exchange is the one that equates quantity demanded with quantity supplied. To simplify the analysis, let's suppose that the United States and Great Britain are the only two countries in the world, so the supply and demand for British pounds in the United States is the supply and demand for foreign exchange from the U.S. perspective.

Demand for Foreign Exchange

U.S. residents need pounds to pay British producers for goods and services, to invest in British assets, to make loans in Great Britain, or simply to send cash gifts to British friends or relatives. Whenever U.S. residents need pounds, they must buy pounds in the foreign exchange market, paying for them with dollars.

Exhibit 3 depicts a market for foreign exchange—in this case, British pounds. The horizontal axis identifies the quantity of foreign exchange, measured here as millions of pounds. The vertical axis identifies the price per unit of foreign exchange, measured here as the number of dollars required to purchase each pound. The demand curve for foreign exchange, identified as *D,* shows the inverse relationship between the dollar price of pounds and the quantity of pounds demanded, other things constant. Some of the factors held constant along the demand curve are the incomes of U.S. consumers, the expected inflation rates in the United States and Britain, the pound prices of British goods, the preferences of U.S. consumers, and interest rates in the United States and Britain. People have many different reasons for demanding foreign exchange, but in the aggregate, the lower the dollar price of foreign exchange, other things constant, the greater the quantity demanded.

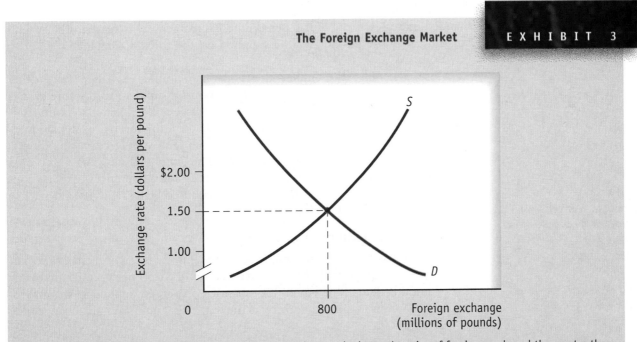

The Foreign Exchange Market   **E X H I B I T   3**

The fewer dollars needed to purchase 1 unit of foreign exchange, the lower the price of foreign goods and the greater the quantity of foreign goods demanded. The greater the demand for foreign goods, the greater the amount of foreign exchange demanded. The demand curve for foreign exchange slopes downward. An increase in the exchange rate makes U.S. products cheaper for foreigners. The increased demand for U.S. goods implies an increase in the quantity of foreign exchange supplied. The supply curve of foreign exchange slopes upward.

A drop in the dollar price of foreign exchange, in this case the pound, means that fewer dollars are needed to purchase each pound, so the dollar prices of British products (including British investment vehicles, such as stocks and bonds), which have price tags listed in pounds, become cheaper. The cheaper it is to buy pounds, the lower the dollar price of British products to U.S. residents, so the greater the quantity of pounds demanded by U.S. residents, other things constant.

Supply of Foreign Exchange

The supply of foreign exchange is generated by the desire of foreign residents to acquire dollars—that is, to exchange pounds for dollars. Foreign residents want dollars to buy U.S. goods and services, to buy U.S. assets, to make loans in dollars, or to make cash gifts in dollars to their U.S. friends and relatives. Also, people from countries suffering from economic and political turmoil may want to buy dollars as a hedge against the inflation and instability of their own currencies. The dollar has long been accepted as an international medium of exchange. It is also the currency of choice in the world market for oil and for illegal drugs.

The British supply pounds in the foreign exchange market to acquire the dollars they need. An increase in the dollar-per-pound exchange rate, other things constant, makes U.S. products cheaper for foreigners, since foreign residents need fewer pounds to get the same number of dollars. For example, suppose a U.S. government security sells for $10,000. When the exchange rate is $1.50 per pound, that bond costs 6,667 pounds; when the exchange rate is $2.00 per pound, it costs only 5,000 pounds. The number of U.S. bonds demanded increases as the dollar-per-pound exchange rate increases, other things constant, so more pounds will be supplied on the foreign exchange market to buy dollars.

More generally, the higher the dollar-per-pound exchange rate, other things constant, the greater the quantity of pounds supplied to the foreign exchange market. The positive relationship between the dollar-per-pound exchange rate and the quantity of pounds supplied on the foreign exchange market is expressed in Exhibit 3 by the upward-sloping supply curve for foreign exchange (again, pounds in our example).[2] The supply curve is drawn holding other things constant, including British incomes and preferences, expectations about the rates of inflation in Britain and the United States, and interest rates in Britain and the United States.

Determining the Exchange Rate

Exhibit 3 brings together the supply and demand for foreign exchange to determine the exchange rate. At an exchange rate of $1.50 per pound, the quantity of pounds demanded equals the quantity of pounds supplied—in our example, 800 million pounds. Once achieved, this equilibrium exchange rate

---

2   As the exchange rate rises, the British have a greater incentive to buy more U.S. goods and services since their prices in terms of pounds have decreased. As more is bought at lower prices, however, the total expenditure of British pounds rises only if the percentage increase in quantities of U.S. products demanded by the British exceeds the percentage decrease in the prices in terms of pounds. If the percentage increase in quantities demanded is less than the percentage decrease in the price in terms of pounds, the supply curve of British pounds will slope downward.

remains constant until a change occurs in one of the factors that affect supply or demand. When the exchange rate is allowed to adjust freely, or to *float*, in response to market forces, the market will clear continually, as the quantities of foreign exchange demanded and supplied are equated.

What if the initial equilibrium is upset by a change in one of the underlying forces that affect supply or demand? For example, suppose an increase in U.S. income causes Americans to increase their demand for all normal goods, including products imported from Britain. An increase in U.S. income will shift the demand curve for foreign exchange to the right, as Americans seek more pounds to buy more cashmere sweaters, Jaguars, trips to London, and British securities.

This increased demand for pounds is shown in Exhibit 4 by a shift to the right in the demand curve for foreign exchange. The supply curve does not change. The shift in the demand curve from D to D' leads to an increase in the exchange rate from $1.50 per pound to $1.55 per pound. Thus, the pound increases in value, or appreciates, while the dollar falls in value, or depreciates. The higher exchange value of the pound prompts some British residents to purchase more American products, which are now cheaper in terms of the pound. In our example, the equilibrium quantity increases from 800 million to 820 million pounds.

Any increase in the demand for foreign exchange or any decrease in its supply, other things constant, causes an increase in the number of dollars required to purchase one unit of foreign exchange, which is a depreciation of the dollar. On the other hand, any decrease in the demand for foreign exchange or any increase in its supply, other things constant, causes a reduction in the number of dollars required to purchase one unit of foreign exchange, which is an appreciation of the dollar.

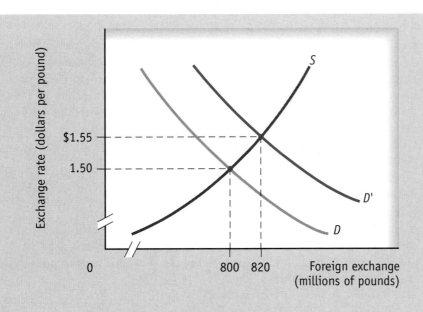

EXHIBIT 4

Effect on the Foreign Exchange Market of an Increase in Demand for Pounds

The intersection of supply curve S and demand curve D determines the exchange rate. At an exchange rate of $1.50 per pound, the quantity of pounds demanded equals the quantity supplied. An increase in the demand for pounds from D to D' leads to an increase in the exchange rate from $1.50 to $1.55 per pound.

Net Bookmark

In 1995, 28 year old trader Nick Leeson, through speculative trading practices, was blamed for bringing down Britain's oldest merchant bank, 233-year-old Barings. Leeson, stationed in Singapore, was trading futures and options on Japanese stocks—trades similar to foreign exchange contracts. Through lack of supervision, Barings failed to realize that Leeson was speculating, and not arbitraging, until Leeson lost approximately $1.4 billion. For differing opinions about the matter, visit "The Barings Affair," maintained by Numa Financial Systems Ltd. (http://www.numa.com/derivs/ref/barings/barx.htm).

Arbitrageur A person who takes advantage of temporary geographic differences in the exchange rate by simultaneously purchasing a currency in one market and selling it in another market

Speculator A person who buys or sells foreign exchange in hopes of profiting from fluctuations in the exchange rate over time

Arbitrageurs and Speculators

Exchange rates between specific currencies are nearly identical at any given time in the different markets around the world. For example, the price of a dollar in terms of the pound is the same in New York, Tokyo, London, Zurich, Istanbul, and other financial centers. This equality is ensured by **arbitrageurs**—dealers who take advantage of any temporary difference in exchange rates across markets by buying low and selling high. Their actions tend to equalize exchange rates across markets. For example, if one pound cost $1.49 in New York and $1.50 in London, an arbitrageur could buy, say, $10,000,000 worth of pounds in New York and at the same time sell these pounds in London for $10,067,114.09, thereby earning $67,114.09 minus the transaction costs of executing the trades. Because exchange rate differences tend to be very small and because of transaction costs, an arbitrageur has to trade huge amounts to make enough profit to survive.

Because an arbitrageur buys and sells simultaneously, no risk is involved. The arbitrageur increases the demand for pounds in New York and increases the supply of pounds in London. Therefore the actions of arbitrageurs tend to increase the dollar price of pounds in New York and decrease it in London. Even a tiny difference in exchange rates across markets will prompt arbitrageurs to act, and this action will quickly eliminate discrepancies in exchange rates across markets. Exchange rates may still change because of market forces, but they tend to change in all markets simultaneously.

The demand and supply of foreign exchange arises from many sources: from importers and exporters, investors in foreign assets, central banks, tourists, arbitrageurs, and speculators. **Speculators** buy and sell foreign exchange in hopes of profiting by trading the currency at a different exchange rate later. By taking risks, speculators aim to profit from market fluctuations—they try to buy low and sell high. In contrast, arbitrageurs take no risks, since they *simultaneously* buy and sell a currency in different markets.

Purchasing Power Parity

As long as trade across borders is unrestricted and as long as exchange rates are allowed to adjust freely, the **purchasing power parity theory** predicts that exchange rates between two national currencies will adjust in the long run to reflect price-level differences in the two countries. *A given basket of internationally traded goods should therefore sell for similar amounts in different countries (except for differences reflecting transportation costs and the like).* Suppose a given basket of internationally traded commodities that costs $1,500 in the United States costs 1,000 pounds in Great Britain. According to the purchasing power parity theory, the equilibrium exchange rate between the United States and Great Britain should be $1.50 per pound. If this were not the case—if the exchange rate were, say, $1.25 per pound—then the basket of goods could be purchased in Great Britain for 1,000 pounds and sold in the United States for $1,500. The $1,500 could then be exchanged for 1,200 pounds, yielding a profit of 200 pounds (minus any transaction costs). Selling dollars and buying pounds drives up the dollar price of pounds.

The purchasing power parity theory is more a predictor of the long-run tendency than of the day-to-day relationship between changes in the price level and the exchange rate. For example, a country's currency generally appreciates when its inflation rate is lower than the rest of the world's and depreciates when its inflation rate is higher. Likewise, a country's currency generally appreciates when its real interest rates are higher than the rest of the world, because capital flows into that country. Foreign investors are attracted by the relatively high interest rates and the currency appreciates, since foreigners are more willing to buy and hold investments denominated in that currency. As a case in point, the dollar appreciated during the first half of the 1980s, when real U.S. interest rates were relatively high, and depreciated in the early 1990s, when real U.S. interest rates were relatively low.

Purchasing power parity theory Exchange rates between two countries will adjust in the long run to reflect price level differences between the countries

Because of trade barriers, central bank intervention in exchange markets, and the fact that many products are not traded or are not comparable across countries, the purchasing power parity theory may not explain exchange rates at a particular point in time. For example, if you went shopping in Tokyo, you would soon see that one dollar's worth of yen buys much less than a dollar will buy in the United States. The following case study considers the theory in light of the price of Big Macs around the globe.

As we have already noted, the theory of purchasing power parity (PPP) says that, in the long run, the exchange rate of two currencies should move towards the rate that would equalize the prices in each country of an identical basket of internationally traded goods. A lighthearted test of the theory has been developed by *The Economist* magazine, which each year compares prices across countries of a "market basket" consisting simply of one McDonald's Big Mac—a product that, though not internationally traded, is made using the same recipe in 79 countries. *The Economist* begins with the price of a Big Mac in the local currency, then converts that price into dollars using the actual exchange rate prevailing at the time. A comparison of the dollar price of Big Macs across countries provides a crude test of the PPP theory, which predicts that these prices should tend toward equality in the long run.

Exhibit 5 lists the dollar price of a Big Mac on April 7, 1995, in each of 32 countries, beginning with the least expensive. By comparing the price of a Big Mac in the United States with prices in other countries, we can derive a crude measure of whether currencies are undervalued or overvalued relative to the dollar. For example, because the price of a Big Mac in Japan, at $4.65, is double the price of $2.32 in the United States, the yen appears to be overvalued by 100 percent compared to the dollar. The same approach suggests the French franc is overvalued by 66 percent, the German mark by 50 percent, and the British pound by 21 percent.

The Economist has been computing the Big Mac price index for a decade, and the index has repeatedly found the dollar to be undervalued against other main currencies, such as the yen and the mark. Some view this persistent misalignment as a rejection of the PPP theory. But that theory relates only to traded goods. The Big Mac is not traded across borders. A large share of the total cost of a Big Mac is rent, which varies substantially across countries. For ex-

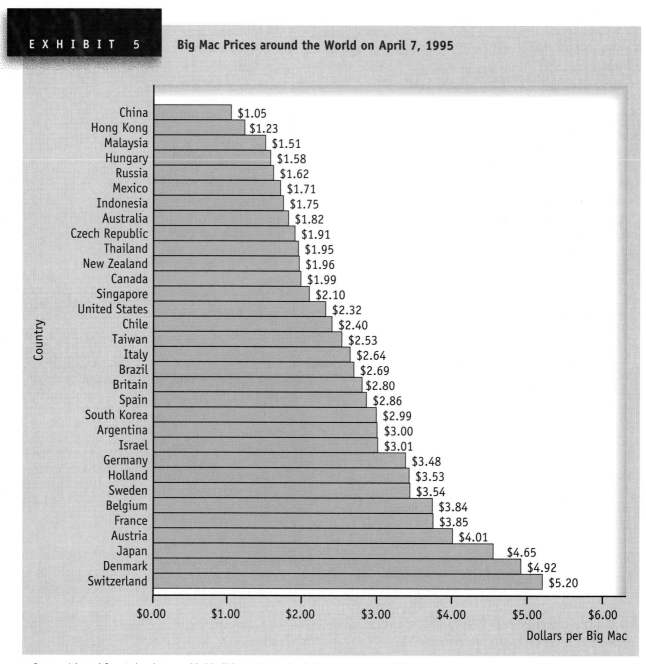

EXHIBIT 5   **Big Mac Prices around the World on April 7, 1995**

Source: Adapted from price data provided in "Big MacCurrencies," *The Economist,* 15 April 1995, p. 74.

The Big Mac Index
continued

ample, rents in Japan are much higher than rents in the United States. Local prices may also be distorted by taxes and trade barriers, such as a tariff on beef. Consequently, although the Big Mac index offers a first cut at the PPP theory, the index may not offer a reliable test of the theory.

Economists who have calculated prices for baskets of traded goods using more refined approaches turn up similar findings. For example, one study found the yen to be overvalued by about 85 percent and the mark by 50 percent. Since, when compared to the main currencies, the dollar remains below the level implied by PPP, some analysts write off the theory of PPP as irrelevant. But if the dollar is undervalued, why does the U.S. current account deficit remain so large? After all, an undervalued dollar should stimulate foreign purchases of U.S. goods and discourage American purchases of foreign goods—thus reducing the U.S. current account deficit.

Another look at Exhibit 5 suggests a possible answer. The dollar may be undervalued compared to the yen, the franc, the mark, and the pound, but many other currencies are undervalued relative to the dollar, such as currencies from Australia, Canada, Mexico, and most of the emerging-market and developing economies. Since over half of U.S. trade is with Canada and with developing countries, the dollar does not appear to be undervalued when currencies from U.S. trading partners are weighted accordingly.

Sources: "Big MacCurrencies," *The Economist,* 15 April 1995; "Burger Devaluation," *The Economist,* 21 October 1995; and Peter Liu and Paul Burkett, "Instability in Short-Run Adjustments to Purchasing Power Parity: Results for Selected Latin American Countries," *Applied Economics,* October 1995, pp. 973–83.

The Big Mac Index
continued

Flexible Exchange Rates

For the most part, we have been discussing a system of **flexible exchange rates,** in which the exchange rate is determined by the forces of supply and demand. Flexible, or *floating,* exchange rates adjust continually to the myriad forces that buffet the foreign exchange market. Consider how the exchange rate is linked to the balance of payments accounts. Debit entries in the current and capital accounts increase the demand for foreign exchange, thereby depreciating the dollar. Credit entries in these accounts increase the supply of foreign exchange, thereby appreciating the dollar.

The wild swings in exchange rates that sometimes occur with flexible exchange rates have caused policymakers to consider alternatives, such as some combination of flexible and fixed exchange rates. Let's look now at how fixed rates work.

Flexible exchange rates Rates determined by the forces of supply and demand without government intervention

Fixed Exchange Rates

When exchange rates are flexible, government officials have little direct role in the foreign exchange market. If government officials try to set, or fix, exchange rates, however, active central bank intervention is necessary to establish and maintain these **fixed exchange rates.** Suppose that monetary officials select what they think is an appropriate rate of exchange between the dollar and the pound. They attempt to *fix,* or to "peg," the exchange rate within a narrow band around the particular value selected. Let's assume that the exchange rate is set at $1.50 per British pound, with a permitted margin of fluctuation of 2 percent on either side of this rate. Therefore, dollars per pound can vary from $1.47 to $1.53. But monetary authorities will not permit the rate to stray outside this narrow band.

To explore the mechanics of fixed exchange rates, let's begin with a situation in which the equilibrium exchange rate is exactly $1.50 per pound, as indicated in Exhibit 6 by point *e,* the intersection of *D* and *S.* Since the fixed rate equals the equilibrium rate, monetary authorities need not intervene in the foreign exchange market.

Fixed exchange rates Rates pegged within a narrow range of values by central banks' ongoing purchases and sales of currencies

EXHIBIT   6   **Central Bank Intervention to Maintain an Exchange Rate Ceiling**

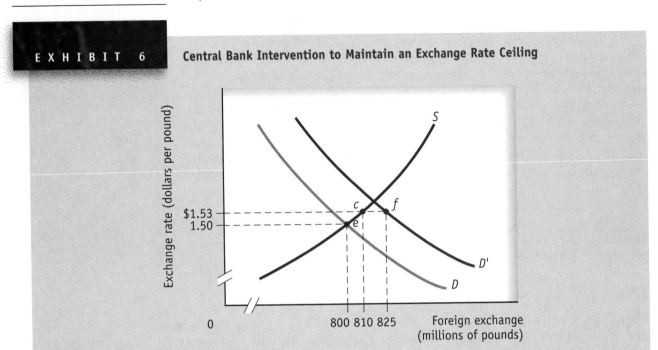

Point *e*, the intersection of demand curve *D* and supply curve *S*, determines an exchange rate within a band of 2 percent on either side of $1.50 per pound. An increase in the demand for foreign exchange from *D* to *D'* would drive the exchange rate above the permitted margin of fluctuation. To maintain the exchange rate within the band, monetary authorities must sell pounds for dollars at an exchange rate of $1.53 per pound. That is, the Federal Reserve must sell 15 million pounds to maintain an exchange rate of $1.53 per pound.

Enforcing a Rate Ceiling

Suppose an increase in British interest rates causes Americans to demand more British securities, thus shifting the demand curve for foreign exchange to the right. If the resulting increase in the equilibrium exchange rate is within the limits set by the government, the increase in demand will prompt no action by monetary authorities. But if the increase in demand is large enough to increase the equilibrium price above $1.53 per pound, monetary authorities will intervene.

The shift to the right from *D* to *D'* in Exhibit 6 would result in an equilibrium exchange rate *above* $1.53. At the ceiling exchange rate of $1.53, 825 million pounds are demanded and 810 million pounds are supplied. Thus, the quantity demanded exceeds the quantity supplied by 15 million pounds. To keep the dollar-per-pound rate from rising above $1.53, monetary authorities must therefore sell 15 million pounds at $1.53 per pound in the foreign exchange market. As long as there is a ready supply of pounds at this ceiling rate, traders will be willing to exchange pounds for dollars at that rate. *By supplying pounds at $1.53, monetary authorities, such as the Federal Reserve in this example, can prevent the exchange rate from rising above the designated rate.* As long as the Federal Reserve is willing to sell pounds at the ceiling price of $1.53, the supply of foreign exchange in effect becomes horizontal where the upward-sloping supply curve reaches $1.53—that is, to the right of point *c*.

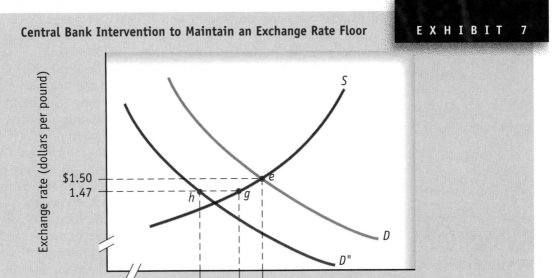

Central Bank Intervention to Maintain an Exchange Rate Floor   E X H I B I T   7

Point e, the intersection of demand curve D and supply curve S, determines an exchange rate within a band of 2 percent on either side of $1.50 per pound. A decrease in the demand for foreign exchange from D to D" would drive the exchange rate below the permitted margin of fluctuation. To maintain the exchange rate within the band, monetary authorities must sell pounds for dollars at an exchange rate of $1.47 per pound. That is, the Federal Reserve must buy 25 million pounds to maintain an exchange rate of $1.47 per pound.

Enforcing a Rate Floor

What if the exchange rate is in danger of falling below the floor rate established by monetary authorities? Suppose that a decline in British interest rates decreases the demand for British securities, thereby reducing the U.S. demand for pounds, reflected in Exhibit 7 by the shift to the left from D to D". At the floor price of $1.47, the quantity of pounds supplied to the market, 785 million pounds, exceeds the quantity demanded in the market, 760 million pounds. Without central bank intervention, this excess supply of pounds at the floor price would force the equilibrium exchange rate lower, to the point where supply and demand intersect. To prevent the value of the pound from slipping below the floor rate, monetary authorities such as the U.S. Federal Reserve or governmental bodies such as the U.S. Treasury must be willing to buy the excess supply of pounds at the floor rate of $1.47. As long as there is a ready demand for pounds at the floor rate, other traders will be unwilling to exchange pounds for dollars at less than that rate. Since the central bank buys, or demands, any excess pounds at the floor rate, then to the right of point h the demand curve becomes horizontal at the floor price.

Through such intervention in the foreign exchange market, monetary authorities can stabilize the exchange rate, keeping it within the specified band. In sum, the situation under fixed exchange rates around a narrow band is as follows: (1) at the exchange rate ceiling, the supply curve is horizontal, since the central bank supplies any excess quantity demanded; (2) within the permitted margin of exchange rate fluctuations, the supply curve slopes upward and the demand curve slopes downward; and (3) at the exchange rate floor, the demand curve is horizontal, since the central bank demands any excess quantity supplied. Government transactions to enforce the fixed exchange rate are recorded as part of the official reserve transactions account of the balance of payments.[3]

If the equilibrium exchange rate is sometimes above and other times below the floor, monetary authorities will be alternatively selling and buying foreign exchange. Their international reserves may therefore fluctuate around a constant average level. The possibility of reserve depletion arises if the equilibrium exchange rate remains continually above the pegged rate on a long-term basis (as we will see in the next case study). When this occurs, the government has several options for eliminating the exchange rate disequilibrium. Suppose there is excess demand for foreign exchange at the ceiling rate, as was the case back in Exhibit 6. First, the pegged exchange rate can be increased, which is a **devaluation** of the domestic currency. (A decrease in the pegged exchange rate is called a **revaluation**.) Second, the government can attempt to reduce the demand for foreign exchange directly by imposing restrictions on imports or on capital outflows. Third, the government can adopt contractionary fiscal or monetary policies that reduce the country's income level, increase interest rates, or reduce inflation relative to that of the country's trading partners, thereby indirectly decreasing the demand for foreign exchange. Finally, the government can allow the disequilibrium to persist and ration the available foreign currency through some form of foreign exchange control.

We have now concluded an introduction to international finance in theory. Let's examine how international finance works in practice, beginning with a case study of Mexico's recent problems with the peso.

Currency devaluation *An increase in the official pegged price of foreign exchange in terms of the domestic currency*

Currency revaluation *A reduction in the official pegged price of foreign exchange in terms of the domestic currency*

CASE STUDY

Mexico's Peso Problems

Location:

In what condition is the current Mexican economy? For an official update on Mexico's economy, as well as background information and economic data, visit the "Official Economic Information of México," coordinated by *Secretaría de Hacienda y Crédito Público* (Ministry of Finance of Mexico) (http://www.shcp.gob.mx/english/).

In early 1994, the Mexican economy was on a roll. Mexico had just signed NAFTA, the free trade agreement with the United States and Canada, and foreign investment poured into what seemed like the world's most promising emerging market. The value of the peso was fixed in terms of the dollar, and the Mexican government supported that rate with its dollar reserves.

One cloud on the horizon was Mexico's growing current account deficit, but even that did not seem alarming—Mexican financial officials explained that the deficit was growing because Mexico was buying the machines needed to build an industrial economy. Mexico could live with a trade deficit as long as foreigners were willing to hold onto pesos or invest them back into Mexico. So Mexico could handle a deficit in its current account as long as the country ran an offsetting capital account surplus.

---

3   Currency transactions by the central bank will affect a country's money supply unless the bank tries to offset, or "sterilize," the transaction by buying or selling other central bank assets. An official reserve transactions surplus increases the money supply; a deficit decreases the money supply.

But the current account deficit continued to grow throughout 1994, totaling $30 billion for the year, which equaled 7.6 percent of Mexico's GDP. To put this in perspective, an equivalent U.S. current account deficit would exceed $500 billion (the U.S. current account deficit in 1994 was $151 billion). As the deficit mounted and as the presidential election neared, other developments began making foreign investors and lenders nervous. First was a fear of devaluation, which would mean foreign investors and lenders could expect less of a return on whatever funds they put into Mexico. For example, American investors could expect to get fewer dollars back. Foreign investors remembered past devaluations that occurred before elections and inaugurations. An uprising in the state of Chiapas and the subsequent assassination of the ruling party's presidential candidate fueled investor uncertainty. Wal-Mart and other U.S. companies put expansion plans in Mexico on hold.

Wealthy Mexicans also tried to hedge their bets by buying foreign assets. According to the finance minister, the equivalent of $30 billion in pesos left Mexico in 1994. This massive capital flight added to the pressure on the peso. Investors lost confidence and the foreign investment and foreign lending dried up. The government tried to finance the trade deficits by drawing down its international reserves. Between February and December of 1994, Mexico's dollar reserves dropped from $30 billion to less than $10 billion.

Finance officials, in trying to support the peso, were fighting a losing battle. On December 20, 1994, Mexico devalued the peso by 13 percent. The thinking was that devaluation would reduce imports, increase exports, and reduce the need for foreign borrowing. The reaction to devaluation was financial panic. The peso became a hot potato. Mexican officials had no choice but to let the peso float; it went into freefall.

In the financial chaos that ensued, Mexico had trouble refinancing short-term foreign borrowing. But a financial bailout of $20 billion from the U.S. government, $18 billion from the International Monetary Fund, and $12 billion from other international lenders helped settle financial markets. All these were loans backed by proceeds from Mexican oil exports.

For its part, Mexico agreed to reduce government spending, curb inflation, accelerate the privatization of key industries, and increase access to Mexican markets by U.S. and other foreign investors. When the dust settled by the summer of 1995, the value of the peso had fallen to half and the devaluation turned the trade deficit into a trade surplus. It turned out that less than a quarter of Mexico's imports in 1994 were capital goods. So most of the deficit had funded consumer goods.

All the financial uncertainty precipitated by the devaluation pushed Mexico into the deepest recession on record. Inflation exceeded 40 percent in 1995. The combination of recession and inflation spelled big trouble for Mexican banks because many loans went into default. The peso problems show Mexico's vulnerability to foreign trade and finance.

Source: "How Mexico's Crisis Ambushed Top Minds in Officialdom, Finance," *The Wall Street Journal*, 6 July 1995; Craig Torres, "The Banking Disaster in Mexico Whipsaws an Ailing Economy," *The Wall Street Journal*, 25 January 1996; and Anthony DePalma, "After the Fall: 2 Faces of Mexico's Economy," *New York Times*, 16 July 1995.

HISTORY AND DEVELOPMENT OF THE INTERNATIONAL MONETARY SYSTEM

Gold standard An arrangement whereby the currencies of most countries are convertible into gold at a fixed rate

From 1879 to 1914, the international financial system operated under a **gold standard,** whereby the major currencies were convertible into gold at a fixed rate. For example, the U.S. dollar could be redeemed at the U.S. Treasury for one-twentieth of an ounce of gold. The British pound could be redeemed at the British Exchequer, or treasury, for one-fourth of an ounce of gold. Since each pound could buy five times as much gold as each dollar, one pound exchanged for $5.

The gold standard provided a predictable exchange rate, one that did not vary as long as currency could be redeemed for gold at the announced rate. But the money supply in each country was determined in part by the flow of gold between countries, so each country's monetary policy was influenced by the supply of gold. A balance of payments deficit resulted in a loss of gold, which theoretically caused a country's money supply to drop. A balance of payments surplus resulted in an increase in gold, which theoretically caused a country's money supply to rise. Also, the supply of money throughout the world depended to some extent on the vagaries of gold discoveries. When gold production was slow so that the money supply did not keep pace with the growth in economic activity, the result was a drop in the price level, or *deflation*. When gold production was up so that the growth of the money supply exceeded the growth in economic activity, the result was a rise in the price level, or *inflation*. For example, gold discoveries in Alaska and South Africa in the late 1890s expanded the U.S. money supply, leading to inflation.

The Bretton Woods Agreement

During World War I, many countries could no longer convert their currencies to gold, and the gold standard eventually collapsed, disrupting international trade during the 1920s and 1930s. Once an Allied victory in World War II appeared certain, the Allies met in Bretton Woods, New Hampshire, in July of 1944 to formulate a new international monetary system. Because the United States was not ravaged by World War II and had a strong economy, the dollar was selected as the key reserve currency in the new international monetary system. All exchange rates were fixed in terms of the dollar, and the United States, which held most of the world's gold reserves, stood ready to convert foreign holdings of dollars into gold at a fixed rate of $35 per ounce. Even though exchange rates were fixed by the Bretton Woods accord, *other* countries could adjust *their* exchange rates relative to the U.S. dollar if there was a fundamental disequilibrium in their balance of payments—that is, if a country faced a large and persistent deficit or surplus.

The Bretton Woods agreement also created the International Monetary Fund (IMF) to set rules for maintaining the international monetary system and to make loans to countries with temporary balance of payments problems. The IMF, which today has more than 150 member countries, also standardized financial reporting for international trade and finance. The IMF now issues paper substitutes for gold called *Special Drawing Rights,* or *SDRs,* which function as international reserves. The value of a unit of SDR is a weighted average of the values of the major national currencies. Whereas the supply of gold depends on discoveries and the cost of production, SDRs can be created by the IMF to satisfy the world's demand for international reserves. Within limits, each central bank can exchange its own currency for SDRs. Note that SDRs are used exclusively to make settlements between central banks.

Demise of the Bretton Woods System

During the latter part of the 1960s, inflation began heating up in the United States, and the higher U.S. prices meant that the dollar did not buy as much as it used to. So those exchanging foreign currencies for dollars at the official exchange rates found these dollars bought less in U.S. goods and services. Because of U.S. inflation, the dollar had become *overvalued* at the official exchange rate, meaning that the gold value of the dollar exceeded the exchange value of the dollar. With the dollar overvalued, foreigners redeemed more dollars for gold. To stop this outflow of gold, something had to give. On August 15, 1971, President Richard Nixon closed the "gold window," refusing to exchange gold for dollars. In December 1971, the 10 richest countries of the world met in Washington and devalued the dollar by 8 percent. The hope at the time was that this devaluation would put the dollar on firmer footing and would save the "dollar standard." With prices rising at different rates around the world, however, an international monetary system based on fixed exchange rates was doomed.

In 1971, U.S. merchandise imports exceeded merchandise exports for the first time since World War II. When the trade deficit tripled in 1972, it became clear that the dollar was still overvalued. In early 1973, the dollar was devalued another 10 percent, but this did not quiet foreign exchange markets. The dollar, for 25 years the anchor of the international monetary system, suddenly looked vulnerable, and speculators began betting the dollar would fall even more. Dollars were exchanged for German marks because the mark appeared to be the most stable currency. Monetary officials at the Bundesbank, Germany's central bank, exchanged marks for dollars to defend the official exchange rate and to prevent an appreciation of the mark. Why didn't Germany want the mark to appreciate? Appreciation of the mark would make their goods more expensive abroad and foreign goods cheaper in Germany, thereby reducing German exports and increasing German imports. But after selling $10 billion worth of marks, the German central bank quit defending the dollar. As soon as the value of the dollar was allowed to float against the mark, the Bretton Woods system, already on shaky ground, collapsed.

The Current System: Managed Float

The Bretton Woods system has been replaced by a **managed float system,** which combines features of a freely floating exchange rate with sporadic intervention by central banks as a way of moderating exchange rate fluctuations among the world's major currencies. Most smaller countries, particularly developing countries, peg their currencies to one of the major currencies (such as the U.S. dollar or the German mark), to Special Drawing Rights, or to a "basket" of major currencies. What's more, in developing countries, private international borrowing and lending are severely restricted; governments may allow residents to purchase foreign exchange only for certain purposes. In some countries, different exchange rates apply to different categories of transactions.

Western European countries in 1979 formed the European Monetary Sys-

Managed float system An exchange rate system that combines features of freely floating rates with intervention by central banks tem, through which they are attempting to align the values of their respective currencies. The members have agreed to fix exchange rates among themselves in an attempt to increase the economic integration among member countries. Members of the European Monetary System have even developed a new monetary unit called the *euro,* which they hope will one day become one of the world's key currencies, perhaps replacing the dollar in international transactions.

Exchange rates between the German mark, the Japanese yen, and the U.S. dollar are relatively unstable, particularly because of international speculation about official efforts to stabilize exchange rates. Major criticisms of flexible exchange rates are that (1) they are inflationary, since they free monetary authorities to pursue expansionary policies, and (2) they have often been volatile, especially since the late 1970s. This volatility creates uncertainty and risk for importers and exporters, increasing the transaction costs of international trade and thus reducing its volume. Furthermore, exchange rate volatility can lead to wrenching changes in the competitiveness of a country's export sector and of those domestic producers who must compete with imports. These changes in competitiveness cause swings in employment, resulting in louder calls for import restrictions.

Policymakers are always on the lookout for an international monetary system that will perform better than the current managed float system, with its fluctuating currency values. *Their ideal is a system that will foster international trade, lower inflation, and promote a more stable world economy.* International finance ministers have acknowledged that the world must find an international standard and establish greater exchange rate stability.

CONCLUSION

At one time, the United States was largely self-sufficient. A technological lead over the rest of the world, an abundance of natural resources, a well-trained work force, a modern and extensive capital stock, and the ability to convert its currency into gold made the United States the envy of the world. The dollar was the world's premier international currency—readily accepted and prized.

The situation has changed. The United States is now very much a part of the world economy, not only as the largest exporter but also as the largest importer in the world. Americans have also borrowed billions from abroad; we are now the world's largest debtor nation. Multinational corporations have spread advanced technology around the world. As a result of the spread of technology and capital, U.S. workers now face stiff competition from abroad.

As a result of chronic balance of payments deficits, enormous numbers of dollars circulate in the world markets. Although the dollar remains the unit of transaction in many international settlements—OPEC, for example, still states oil prices in dollars—the wild gyrations of exchange rates have made those involved in international finance wary of putting all their eggs in one basket. Therefore, traders hedge against a decline in the dollar. The international monetary system is now going through a difficult adjustment period as it gropes for a new source of stability after the collapse of the Bretton Woods agreement.

1. The balance of payments reflects all economic transactions across national borders. The current account measures the flow of (1) merchandise; (2) services, including investment income, military transactions, and tourism; and (3) unilateral transfers, or public and private transfer payments to foreign residents. The capital account reflects international flows involving purchases or sales of investment assets.

2. Currencies support the flow of goods and services across international borders. The interaction of the supply and demand for foreign exchange determines the equilibrium exchange rate.

3. Under a system of floating exchange rates, the value of the dollar relative to foreign exchange varies over time. An increase in the demand for foreign exchange or a reduction in its supply, other things constant, will cause an increase in the value of foreign exchange relative to the dollar, which is a depreciation of the dollar. Conversely, a reduction in the demand for foreign exchange or an increase in its supply will cause a decrease in the value of

foreign exchange relative to the dollar, which is an appreciation of the dollar.

4. Under a system of fixed exchange rates, monetary authorities usually try to stabilize the exchange rate, keeping it between a specified ceiling and floor. At the exchange rate ceiling, the supply of foreign exchange is horizontal, since the central bank supplies any excess quantity demanded. Within the permitted margin of exchange rate fluctuations, the supply curve for foreign exchange slopes upward and the demand curve slopes downward. And at the exchange rate floor, the demand curve for foreign exchange is horizontal, since the central bank demands any excess quantity supplied.

5. For much of this century, the international monetary system was based on fixed exchange rates. A managed float system has been in effect for the major currencies since the demise of the Bretton Woods system in the early 1970s. Although central banks have often tried to stabilize exchange rates, recent swings in exchange rates have troubled policymakers.

1. **(Foreign Exchange)** In general, an American cannot use U.S. currency to buy products in Rome or London. However, businesses in some places, especially border towns such as Windsor, Ontario, and Nuevo Laredo, Mexico, do accept U.S. dollars. Why do businesses in border towns engage in this practice?

2. **(Foreign Exchange Demand)** What is the difference between the foreign exchange demand for the U.S. dollar and the U.S. domestic demand for money? How do the demand curves differ?

3. **(Balance of Payments)** Consider the following hypothetical data for the U.S. balance of payments:

	Billions of Dollars
Merchandise exports	+350.0
Merchandise imports	−425.0
Service exports	+170.0
Service imports	−145.0
Net unilateral transfers	−21.5
Outflow of U.S. capital	−45.0
Inflow of foreign capital	+70.0
Decrease in U.S. official assets abroad	+2.5
Increase in foreign official assets in U.S.	+35.0

Calculate each of the following:
a. Merchandise trade balance.
b. Balance on goods and services.
c. Balance on current account.
d. Capital account balance.
e. Official reserve transactions account balance.
f. Statistical discrepancy.

4. **(Balance of Payments Accounting)** Explain where in the U.S. balance of payments an entry would be made for each of the following:
a. A Hong Kong financier buys some U.S. corporate stock.
b. A U.S. tourist in Paris buys some perfume to take home.
c. A Japanese company sells machinery to a pineapple company in Hawaii.
d. U.S. farmers make a gift of food to starving children in Ethiopia.
e. The U.S. Treasury sells a thirty-year bond to a Saudi Arabian prince.
f. A U.S. tourist flies to France on Air France.
g. A U.S. company sells insurance to a foreign firm.

5. **(Recessions and the Trade Balance)** Explain why recessions in the United States (which are not cur-

rently world recessions) tend to reduce the U.S. trade deficit.

6. **(Fixed Exchange Rates)** The following graph illustrates the foreign exchange market for a foreign currency with a fixed exchange rate against the dollar. The monetary authorities allow the exchange rate to vary only between $2.04 and $1.96 per unit of the other currency. The initial supply curve is S_1; the initial demand curve is D_1.

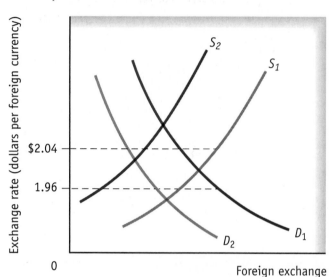

a. Suppose that the supply of foreign currency drops to S_2. What are the possible reasons for the drop in supply? Is the equilibrium exchange rate still within the allowable range? If not, what action must the monetary authority take to keep it within that range?

b. Suppose that the supply of foreign currency is still at S_1 but the demand falls to D_2. What are the possible reasons for the drop in demand? Is the equilibrium exchange rate still within the allowable range? If not, what action must the monetary authority take to keep it within that range?

7. **(Foreign Exchange Rates)** Define the terms *exchange rate* and *depreciation*. What is the difference between a depreciation and a devaluation?

8. **(Foreign Exchange Rates)** Assume that a luxury automobile produced in Japan has a price of 6 million yen. What is the price in U.S. dollars at each of the following exchange rates? What is the price in yen at the different exchange rates of a U.S. product priced at $30?
   a. $1.00 = 100 yen
   b. $1.00 = 120 yen
   c. $1.00 = 90 yen

9. **(Arbitrageurs and Speculators)** Distinguish between arbitrageurs and speculators.

10. **(Bretton Woods Agreement)** What was the role of the U.S. dollar under the Bretton Woods agreement? Why did the agreement fall apart in the 1970s?

11. **(Surplus on Goods and Services Balance)** Suppose the United States ran a balance on goods and services surplus by exporting goods and services while importing nothing.
   a. How would such a surplus be offset elsewhere in the balance of payments accounts?
   b. If the level of U.S. production does not depend on the balance on goods and services, how does running this surplus affect our *current* standard of living?
   c. What is the relationship between total debits and total credits in the goods and services balance? When all international economic transactions are considered, what must be true about the sum of debits and credits? What is the role of the statistical discrepancy account?

12. **(Exchange Rate Determination)** Using a supply-demand diagram for foreign exchange (for example, the pound or yen) against dollars, determine the likely impact of each of the following on the strength of the dollar against foreign exchange, other things constant.
   a. An increase in U.S. interest rates.
   b. An increase in U.S. inflation.
   c. An increase in U.S. productivity.
   d. An increase in U.S. citizens' preferences for imported goods.

13. **(Exchange Rate Determination)** Use the data below to answer the following questions:

Price of pounds (in $)	Q_D (of pounds)	Q_S (of pounds)
$4.00	50	100
3.00	75	75
2.00	100	50

   a. Construct the supply and demand curves for pounds, and determine the equilibrium exchange rate (dollars per pound).
   b. Suppose that the supply of pounds doubles. Draw the new supply curve. What is the new equilibrium exchange rate? Has the dollar appreciated or depreciated? What happens to U.S. imports of British goods?

14. **(Purchasing Power Parity)** According to the theory of purchasing power parity, what will happen to the value of the dollar (against foreign currencies) if the U.S.

price level doubles and price levels in other countries stay constant? Why is the theory more suitable to analyzing events in the long run?

15. **(Managed Float)** What is meant by a managed float? What are the disadvantages of freely floating exchange rates that led countries to the managed float system?

16. **(Exchange Rate Determination)** Floating exchange rates move whenever imbalances in the supply and demand for foreign exchange occurs. Yet the balance of payments is always balanced. Does this mean that exchange rates are always stable?

17. **(Gold Standard)** Explain how a country's monetary policy was subordinate to its balance of payments situation under the gold standard. Assume a balance of payments deficit in your answer.

18. **(Balance of Payments)** According to Exhibit 2, the United States ran a large deficit on its current account, which was largely offset by a surplus in its capital account. Is there any reason to think that a reduction in real U.S. interest rates relative to foreign interest rates would affect these numbers? Explain.

19. **(The Big Mac Index)** The Big Mac Index computed by *The Economist* has consistently found the U.S. dollar to be undervalued against other major currencies, which seems to call for a rejection of the purchasing power parity theory. Explain why the index may not be a true test of the theory.

20. **(Mexico's Peso Problems)** What disadvantages of both fixed and floating exchange rates are illustrated by the 1994–95 Mexican peso crisis?

Using the Internet

21. The International Monetary Fund (**gopher://gopher. imf.org/**) is a permanent organization of 181 member countries working together to stabilize currency exchange. Member nations contribute to a pool of currencies from which all may borrow for a short time to tide them over periods of difficulty in meeting their international obligations (recall Mexico and the peso crisis from the case study). Rather than loan a particular currency, the IMF promises Special Drawing Rights (SDRs), an international reserve asset based on a basket of five main currencies. Look within the "Press Releases" for a recent report on a particular country. Briefly highlight the main points from this report. How much money is the IMF promising to the country? For what reasons? Under what conditions?

35 Developing and Transitional Economies

People around the world face the day under very different circumstances. Many Americans arise from a comfortable bed in a nice home, select the day's clothing from a diverse wardrobe, choose from a variety of foods for breakfast, and drive to school or to work in one of the family's personal automobiles. But most of the 5.8 billion people on earth do not have spacious homes, closets full of clothes, or pantries full of food. They own no automobile, and many have no formal job. Their health is poor, as is their education. Many cannot read or write.

So far this book has focused on the United States, one of the most productive nations on earth. In this chapter, we turn to problems confronting developing and transitional economies. We should acknowledge at the outset that no single theory of economic development has gained general acceptance, so this chapter will focus less on a theory of economic development than on the differences between developed and developing countries.

Although there is no widely accepted theory of economic development, one approach to development that seems to be gaining favor is the introduction of market forces, especially in formerly socialist countries. Around the world, the demise of central planning has been stunning and pervasive. We close the chapter with a discussion of these rich experiments—these works in progress. Topics discussed in this chapter include:

- Third World economies
- Developing countries
- Productivity and development
- Obstacles to development
- Foreign trade and foreign aid
- Transitional economies

WORLDS APART

Countries are classified in a variety of ways based on their level of economic development. The *First World* is the name given to the economically advanced capitalist countries of Western Europe, North America, Australia, New Zealand, and Japan. First World countries were the first to experience long-term economic growth during the 19th century. These countries are more commonly called *industrial market countries* or *developed countries*. The *Second World* is the name given to economically advanced socialist countries, though nearly all these countries have now become more market oriented. The *Third World* consists of more than 100 developing countries in Asia, Africa, Latin America, and Eastern Europe. Third World economies may be capitalist, socialist, or a mix. These countries tend to have a low level of per-capita income, a low standard of living, and a high rate of population growth; they rely on First and Second World countries for technology. Differences in the level of economic development are greater among Third World countries than among industrial countries. Third World countries are also called **developing countries** and *less-developed countries,* or *LDCs*. In this chapter, we will refer to them as *developing countries*.

Developing countries Nations typified by high rates of illiteracy, high unemployment, rapid population growth, and exports of primary products

Developing Countries

The term *developing countries* is an expression adopted by the United Nations to describe countries that usually have a high rate of illiteracy, high unemployment, extensive underemployment, rapid population growth, and exports consisting primarily of agricultural products and raw materials. Typically, more than half the labor force in developing countries is in agriculture. Because farming methods are relatively primitive, farm productivity is low and most people barely subsist.

Differences in economic activity across countries are profound. For example, the United States, with its 265 million people, has a gross domestic product that exceeds the *combined* gross domestic products of 2.65 billion people living in developing countries. The United States, with only 5 percent of the world's population, produces more than does half the world's population put together.

Classifications of Economies

The developing nations vary greatly, ranging from the tragically poor economies of sub-Saharan Africa to the booming economies of the Far East—Taiwan, South Korea, Singapore, and Malaysia (the so-called newly industrialized countries, or NICs). It is helpful, therefore, to draw finer distinctions of development.

The yardstick used most often to compare living standards across nations is gross domestic product per capita. We caution that making intercountry comparisons of GDP is tricky, because countries employ different national income accounting procedures and all measures must be translated into comparable accounting formats and into a common currency. One problem with international comparisons is determining the appropriate exchange rate for putting different countries' GDP statistics on common footing. The exchange-rate problem is compounded when some countries produce a significant amount of

output that is not traded across international boundaries. Furthermore, although official international comparisons based on per-capita GDP usually include an estimate of the value of food produced and consumed by farm households, other nonmarket activity is not always captured by GDP. So international comparisons that employ only GDP per capita tend to underestimate the quantity of goods and services available per person in developing countries, which have more nonmarket production than do industrial nations.

The World Bank, an economic development institution affiliated with the United Nations, attempts to estimate comparable GDP per capita figures for all reporting countries and then uses these figures to classify the economies. The World Bank divides reporting countries with a population of 1 million or more into three major groups based on their per-capita GDP. Most recently, according to the World Bank's tally, there were (1) 45 low-income economies, (2) 63 middle-income economies, and (3) 24 high-income economies. The low- and middle-income countries are usually referred to as *developing* countries, and the high-income countries are usually referred to as *industrial market* countries (though some of the high-income countries have incomes based primarily on oil and are considered to be still developing). Some primarily socialist countries such as Cuba, North Korea, and Libya do not report data on their economic status and consequently are classified by the World Bank as *nonreporting economies*.

Data on total population, GDP per capita, and average growth in real GDP per capita are summarized in Exhibit 1 for all reporting countries with a population of 1 million or more. The GDP per-capita figures have been adjusted by the United Nations to reflect the actual purchasing power of the native currency in its respective economy. The idea is to measure for each country what its per-capita GDP will in fact buy. The per-capita GDP figures reported are for the median country within each classification. For example, the per-capita GDP for the median country among the 45 low-income economies was $1,290 in 1993. Low-income economies make up about 56 percent of the world's population.

The two population giants among the poorest countries are China and India, shown separately in Exhibit 1. Together they account for more than a third of the world's population. China's GDP per capita of $2,330 was nearly double the median of all low-income economies, and its annual growth rate since 1980 of 8.2 percent was more than double the average growth rate for low-income economies. India's GDP per capita was below the median of low-income economies, and its growth rate was below the average for this group.

The per-capita GDP for the median country among the 63 middle-income economies was $4,780 in 1993. The average growth rate between 1980 and 1993 was only 0.2 percent among middle-income economies; this average was pulled down because of the poor performance of former members of the Soviet Union. Middle-income economies make up about 29 percent of the world's population. Developing countries (low- and middle-income economies plus a few high-income countries) account for about 85 percent of the world's population. The per-capita GDP for the median country among the 24 high-income economies was $19,000 in 1993. *The median per-capita GDP among high-income economies was about 15 times greater than the median among the low-income economies—quite a difference.*

| Classification | Population, mid-1993 (millions) | Real GDP per Capita | | EXHIBIT 1 |
		Median 1993 Dollars	Annual Growth Rate, 1980–93 (percent)	Population, GDP per Capita, and Annual Growth Rate (for reporting countries with a population of 1 million or more)
1. Low-income economies	3,092.3	1,290	3.7	
China	1,178.4	2,330	8.2	
India	898.2	1,220	3.0	
2. Middle-income economies	1,596.3	4,780	0.2	
3. High-income economies	812.4	19,000	2.2	

Source: Based on data presented by the World Bank in *World Development Report 1995* (New York: Oxford University Press, 1995), Tables 1 and 30.

Exhibit 2 presents GDP per capita in 1993 for selected countries, arranged from left to right in descending order. Again, figures have been adjusted by the United Nations to reflect the actual purchasing power of the native currency in its respective economy. The United States, the top-ranked country, had a GDP per capita that was about seven times that of Kazakhstan. But GDP per capita in Kazakhstan, in turn, was over seven times that of Mozambique, the poorest country in the world. Residents of Kazakhstan likely feel poor relative to industrialized nations, but they appear well off compared to the poorest developing countries. Per-capita GDP in the United States was 45 times greater than in Mozambique. Thus, there is a tremendous range of productive performance around the world.

Health and Nutrition

Differences in stages of development among countries are reflected in a number of ways besides per-capita income levels. For example, many people in developing countries suffer from poor health as a result of malnutrition and disease. AIDS is devastating some developing countries, particularly those in central and east Africa. Life expectancy in the least-developed African countries averages 48 years, compared with 64 years in other developing economies and 77 years in industrial economies. The average life expectancy at birth in 1993 ranged from 39 years in the African country of Sierra Leone to 80 years in Japan.

Infant Mortality. Health differences among countries are reflected in infant mortality rates. Mortality rates for selected countries are presented as Exhibit 3. By comparing Exhibits 2 and 3, you can see the inverse relationship between per-capita income and infant mortality rates. As might be expected, countries with the longest life expectancies also have the lowest infant mortality rates. Similarly, the countries with the shortest life expectancies have the highest infant mortality rates. Infant mortality rates among the least-developed African countries are more than 20 times those in industrial economies.

Malnutrition. People living in much of Africa, South Asia, and the Indian subcontinent often do not have enough food to maintain good health. Those in

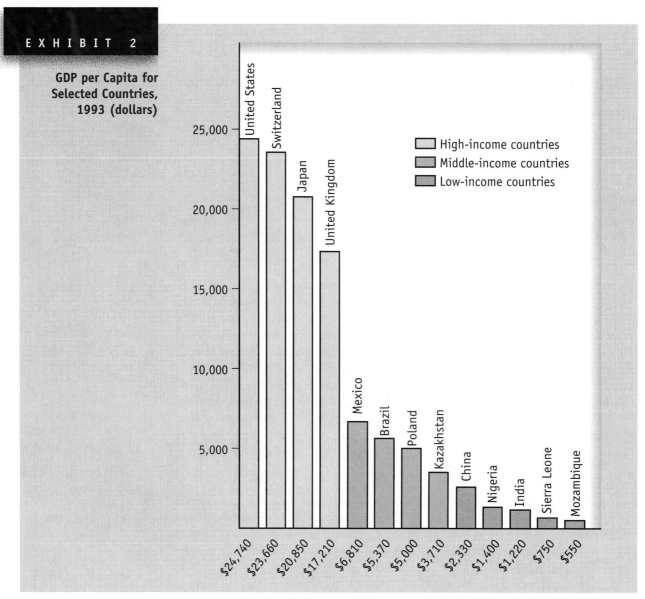

EXHIBIT 2

GDP per Capita for Selected Countries, 1993 (dollars)

High-income countries
Middle-income countries
Low-income countries

United States — $24,740
Switzerland — $23,660
Japan — $20,850
United Kingdom — $17,210
Mexico — $6,810
Brazil — $5,370
Poland — $5,000
Kazakhstan — $3,710
China — $2,330
Nigeria — $1,400
India — $1,220
Sierra Leone — $750
Mozambique — $550

Source: Based on data presented by the World Bank in *World Development Report 1995* (New York: Oxford University Press, 1995), Table 30.

the very poorest countries consume only half the calories of those in high-income countries. Even if an infant survives the first year, malnutrition can turn normal childhood diseases, such as measles, into life-threatening events. Malnutrition is a primary or contributing factor in more than half of all deaths among children under five in low-income countries. Diseases that are well controlled in the industrial countries—malaria, whooping cough, polio, dysentery, typhoid, and cholera—become epidemics in poor countries. Many of these diseases are water borne, and residents of urban areas in less-developed countries are often unable to obtain safe drinking water.

Availability of Physicians. Life expectancy and infant mortality rates are a reflection, in part, of how well the health-care system operates. The number of

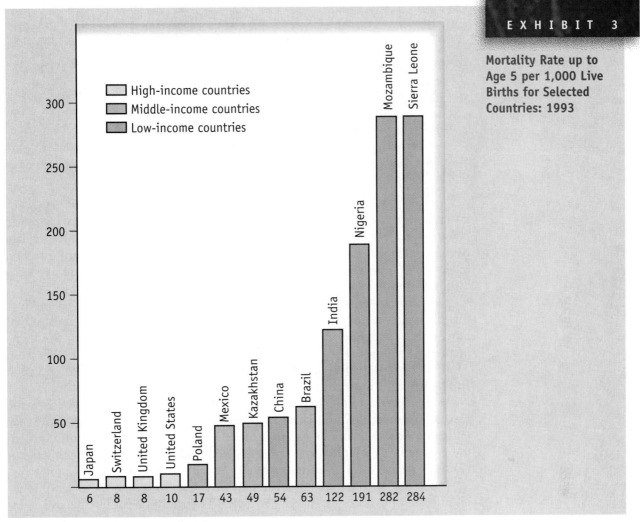

EXHIBIT 3

Mortality Rate up to Age 5 per 1,000 Live Births for Selected Countries: 1993

Source: Based on data presented by the World Bank in *World Development Report 1995* (New York: Oxford University Press, 1995), Table 27.

physicians per capita is one measure of the availability of health care. In high-income economies, the number of physicians per capita is about 12 times greater than in low-income economies. The poorest countries of Africa have the fewest physicians, and industrialized countries have the most. The pattern for nurses is similar to that for physicians.

Not only do developing countries have fewer physicians, but these physicians tend to locate in urban areas, where only about one-fourth of the population lives. Physicians locate near the people who can most afford their services, and higher-income people tend to live in urban areas. For example, only about one-quarter of India's population resides in urban areas, but three-quarters of the physicians practice there.

High Birth Rates

Developing countries are identified not only by their low incomes and high mortality rates but also their high birth rates. This year, about 80 million of the

EXHIBIT 4

Birth Rate per 1,000
Population

Classification	1970	1993
1. Low-income economies	39	28
China	33	19
India	39	29
Sub-Saharan Africa	48	44
2. Middle-income economies	31	23
3. High-income economies	17	13

Source: Based on data presented by the World Bank in *World Development Report 1995* (New York: Oxford University Press, 1995), Table 26.

90 million people added to the world's population will be born in developing countries. In fact, the birth rate is one of the clearest ways of distinguishing between developed and developing countries. Few developing countries have a birth rate of less than 20 per 1,000 population, but no industrial country has a birth rate above that level.

Exhibit 4 presents birth rates per 1,000 population for 1970 and 1993. Note that birth rates for all groups declined between the two periods. Note also that birth rates are highest in the low-income economies and lowest in the high-income economies. The birth rate dropped most in China, where it went from 33 in 1970 to 19 in 1993. The birth rate dropped the least in sub-Saharan Africa, where it went from 48 to 44.

Families tend to be larger in developing countries because children are viewed as a source of farm labor and as economic and social security as the parents age (most developing countries have no pension or social security system for the aged). The higher infant mortality rates in poorer countries also engender higher birth rates, as parents strive to ensure a sufficiently large family.

Much international aid to developing countries has taken the form of medical care and programs to improve hygiene. These advances allow people in developing countries to live longer, but increased longevity has placed a greater strain on the limited resources in those economies. Therefore, improved health does little to avert poverty, at least not in the short run. Despite improvements in medical care, death rates are still higher in developing countries than in developed countries. But these higher death rates are not great enough to offset the higher birth rates. Thus, since 1980, the population in developing countries has grown by an average of 2.0 percent per year, more than triple the 0.6 percent annual growth rate in industrial countries.

Sub-Saharan African countries are the poorest in the world and have the fastest-growing populations. Because of high birth rates in developing countries, children under 15 make up almost half their total population. In industrial countries, children make up only about a quarter of the population. In some developing countries, the growth rate in population has exceeded the growth rate in real GDP, so the standard of living as measured by per-capita GDP has declined. Still, even in the poorest of countries, attitudes are changing about family size. For example, surveys of Kenyan women in the late 1970s showed that they thought the ideal family had more than seven children. A recent Kenyan survey found that between four and five children was the most preferred family size.[1] Evidence from developing countries more generally indicates that when women have better employment opportunities outside the home, fertility rates decline. And as women become better educated, they tend to earn more and have fewer children.

Women in Developing Countries

Throughout the world, poverty is greater among women, particularly women who head households. Because women often must work in the home as well as in the labor market, poverty can impose a special hardship on them. In many cultures, women's responsibilities include gathering firewood and carrying water, tasks that are especially burdensome if firewood is scarce and water is far from home. The percentage of households headed by women varies from country to country, but exceeds 40 percent in some areas of the Caribbean and Africa.

Women in developing countries tend to be less educated than men. In the countries of sub-Saharan Africa and South Asia, for example, only half as many women as men complete high school. Women have fewer employment opportunities and earn lower wages than men do. For example, Sudan's Muslim fundamentalist government bans women from working in public places after 5:00 P.M. In Algeria, Egypt, Jordan, Libya, and Saudi Arabia, the labor participation rate for women in 1995 was 10 percent or less. Women are often on the fringes of the labor market, working long hours in agriculture. They also have less access to other resources, such as land, capital, and technology.

Poverty is especially harsh for women in developing countries. Besides working in the labor market, women often must gather firewood and carry watter for the home.

PRODUCTIVITY: KEY TO DEVELOPMENT

We have examined some of the symptoms of poverty in developing countries, but not why poor countries are poor. At the risk of appearing too simplistic, we might say that poor countries are poor because they do not produce many goods and services. In this section, we will examine why some developing countries experience such low productivity.

Low Labor Productivity

Labor productivity, measured in terms of output per worker, is low in low-income countries. Why? Labor productivity depends on both the quality of the labor and on the amount of capital, land, and other resources that are combined with labor. For example, one certified public accountant with a computer and specialized software can sort out a company's finances more quickly and more accurately than can a hundred high-school-educated file clerks with pencils and paper.

One way a country raises its productivity is by investing more in human and physical capital. This investment must be financed by either domestic savings or foreign funds. Income per capita is often too low in developing countries to permit extensive investments to be financed with internal funds. In poor countries with unstable governments, the wealthy minority frequently invests in more stable foreign economies. Thus, there are few domestic funds available for investment in either human or physical capital; without sufficient capital, workers are less productive.

---

1   As reported in "More Choice, Fewer Babies," *The Economist,* 11 July 1992.

Technology and Education

What exactly is the contribution of education to the process of economic development? Education makes people more receptive to new ideas and methods. Countries with the most advanced educational systems were also the first to develop. In this century, the leader in schooling and economic development has been the United States. In Latin America, Argentina was the most educationally advanced nation 100 years ago, and it is one of the most developed Latin American nations today. The growth of education in Japan during the 19th century contributed to a ready acceptance of technology and thus to Japan's remarkable economic growth in the 20th century.

Knowledge is a resource, and the lack of knowledge can diminish the productivity of other resources. If knowledge is insufficient, other resources may not be used efficiently. For example, a country may be endowed with fertile land, but farmers may lack knowledge of irrigation and fertilization techniques. Or farmers may lack the know-how to rotate crops to avoid soil depletion.

In low-income countries excluding China, over half the adult population was illiterate in 1990 (in China, the illiteracy rate was about one-quarter). Among developed countries, less than 5 percent of the adult population was illiterate. Child labor in developing countries reduces educational opportunities. In Pakistan, for example, the education system can accommodate only one-third of the country's school-age children. More than 10 million Pakistani children work full-time—half of whom are under 10 years old.[2] Worldwide, more than 200 million children under 14 years of age work full-time.

The percentage of the population enrolled in schools at various levels differs sharply across countries. In high-income countries, the total enrollment in post-secondary education was 51 percent relative to the population aged 20 to 24. This compares with only 4 percent for the countries of sub-Saharan Africa. Total post-secondary enrollment as a percentage of those aged 20 to 24 in 1992 is presented in Exhibit 5 for selected countries. Canada and the United States are the leaders by far. Among the poorest countries, enrollment totals 1 percent or less of those aged 20 to 24.

Inefficient Use of Labor

Another feature of developing countries is that they use labor less efficiently than developed nations. Unemployment and underemployment reflect inefficient uses of labor. *Underemployment* occurs when skilled workers are employed in low-skill jobs or when people are working less than they would like—a worker seeking full-time employment may find only a part-time job. *Unemployment* occurs when those who are willing and able to work cannot find jobs.

Unemployment is measured primarily in urban areas, because in rural areas farm work is usually an outlet for labor even if most workers are underemployed there. The unemployment rate in developing nations on average is about 10 to 15 percent of the urban labor force. Unemployment among young workers—those aged 15 to 24—is typically twice that of older workers. In developing nations, about 30 percent of the combined urban and rural work forces is either unemployed or underemployed.

---

2   Pakistani children in the lowest castes become laborers almost as soon as they can walk. See Jonathan Silvers, "Child Labor in Pakistan," *Atlantic Monthly*, February 1996.

Total Post-Secondary Enrollment as Percentage of Population Aged 20–24 in 1992

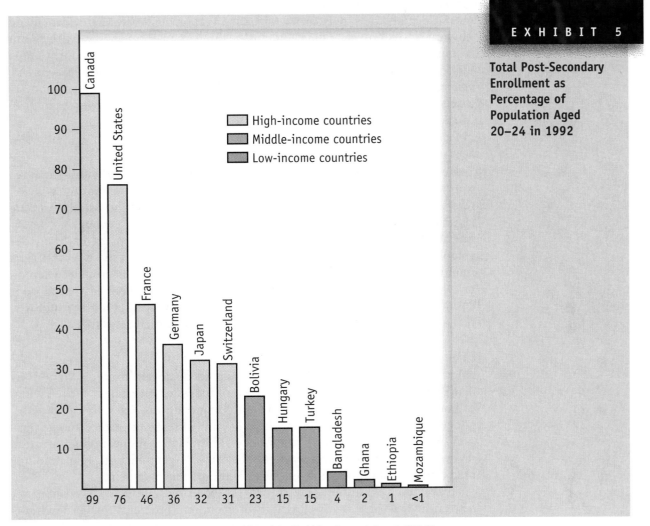

High-income countries
Middle-income countries
Low-income countries

Canada	United States	France	Germany	Japan	Switzerland	Bolivia	Hungary	Turkey	Bangladesh	Ghana	Ethiopia	Mozambique
99	76	46	36	32	31	23	15	15	4	2	1	<1

Source: Based on data presented by the World Bank in *World Development Report 1995* (New York: Oxford University Press, 1995), Table 28.

Agricultural productivity is low in developing countries because of the large number of farmers relative to the amount of land farmed. In some developing countries, the average farm is as small as two acres. Productivity is also low because few other inputs, such as capital and fertilizer, are employed. Even where more land is available, the absence of capital limits the amount of land that can be farmed. *Although about two-thirds of the labor force in developing countries works in agriculture, only about one-third of GDP in these countries stems from agriculture.* In the United States, where farmers account for only 3 percent of the labor force, a farmer with modern equipment can farm hundreds of acres, but in developing countries a farmer with a hand plow or an ox-drawn plow can farm maybe 10 to 20 acres. As you would expect, U.S. farmers, though a tiny fraction of the workforce, grow enough to feed a nation and to make us the largest exporter of farm products in the world.

Low productivity obviously results in low income, but low income can, in turn, affect worker productivity. Low income means less saving and less saving means less investment in human and physical capital. Low income can also mean poor nutrition during the formative years, which can retard mental and physical development. These difficult beginnings may be aggravated by poor diet and insufficient health care in later life, making the worker poorly suited for regular employment. Thus, *low income and low productivity may reinforce each other in a vicious cycle.* Poverty can result in less saving, less capital formation, an inadequate diet, and insufficient attention to health care—all of which, in turn, can reduce a worker's productive ability.

Natural Resources

Some countries are richer than others because they are blessed with natural resources. The difference is most striking when we compare countries with oil reserves and those without. Some developing countries of the Middle East are classified as high-income economies because they are lucky enough to be sitting atop major oil reserves. But oil-rich countries are the exception. Many developing countries, such as Chad and Ethiopia, have little in the way of natural resources. Developing countries without oil reserves were in trouble when oil prices rose. Oil had to be imported, and these imports drained the oil-poor countries of precious foreign exchange. But a few countries, such as South Korea, managed to do very well despite their lack of natural resources.

Financial Institutions

Another requirement for development is an adequate and trusted system of financial institutions. An important source of funds for investment is the savings of households and firms. People in developing countries often have little confidence in their currency because the government tends to finance a large fraction of public outlays by printing money. This practice results in high inflation on average and sometimes very high inflation, or hyperinflation. High and unpredictable inflation discourages saving and hurts development.

Developing countries have special problems because banks are often not held in high regard. At the first sign of economic problems, many depositors withdraw their funds. Since banks cannot rely on a continuous supply of deposits, they cannot make loans for extended periods. Also, governments often impose ceilings on the interest rates that lenders can charge, forcing lenders to ration credit among borrowers. If financial institutions fail to serve as intermediaries between borrowers and lenders, the resulting lack of funds for investment becomes an obstacle to growth.

Capital Infrastructure

Some development economists believe that the most important ingredient in economic development is the administrative competence of the government. Production and exchange often rely on an infrastructure of communication and transportation networks provided by the public sector. Roads, bridges, airports, harbors, and other transportation facilities are vital to commercial activity. Reliable mail service, telephone communication, and a steady supply of water and electricity are also essential for advanced production techniques. Imagine how difficult it would be to run even a personal computer if the supply of electricity were continually interrupted, as is often the case in developing countries. Many developing countries have serious deficiencies in their infrastructures.

And some of the poorest countries in Africa have been ravaged by internal strife. For example, Mozambique, perhaps the poorest country in the world, has been caught up in a bloody civil war since 1975.

Entrepreneurial Ability

An economy can have abundant supplies of land, labor, and capital, but without entrepreneurial ability, the other resources will not be combined efficiently to produce goods and services. Unless a country has a class of entrepreneurs who are able to bring together resources and take the risk of profit or loss, development may never begin. Many developing countries were once under colonial rule, a system of government that offered the local population little opportunity to develop entrepreneurial skills.

Government Monopolies

Government officials often decide that local private-sector entrepreneurs are unable to generate the kind of economic growth the country needs. State enterprises are therefore created to do what government believes the free market cannot do. State-owned enterprises, however, may have objectives other than producing goods efficiently—objectives that could include maximizing employment and providing jobs for friends and relatives of government officials. As we will see later in the chapter, however, many economies are now moving away from government ownership toward private ownership, a process called *privatization.*

INTERNATIONAL TRADE AND DEVELOPMENT

Developing countries need to trade with developed countries in order to acquire the capital and technology that will increase labor productivity on the farm, in the factory, and in the office. To import capital and technology, developing countries must first acquire the funds, or foreign exchange, needed to pay for imports. Exports usually generate more than half of the annual flow of foreign exchange in developing countries. Foreign aid and private investment make up the rest.

Primary products, such as agricultural goods and other raw materials, make up the bulk of exports from developing countries, just as manufactured goods make up the bulk of exports from developed countries. But primary products are worth less than finished products. Consequently, developing countries must export a large amount of raw materials in order to buy back the finished products made from these same materials. Another problem is that the prices of primary products, such as coffee, cocoa, sugar, and rubber, fluctuate more widely than do the prices of finished goods, because crop production fluctuates with the weather.

A third problem of developing countries has been their deteriorating trade position. In recent years, the prices of raw materials have fallen as demand has softened and as substitutes have been developed for products such as rubber. Since the prices of manufactured imported goods have not dropped as much, developing countries have received less money from exports than they have spent on imports, resulting in trade deficits. To reduce these deficits, developing countries have tried to restrict imports. Because imported food often is critical to survival, developing countries are more likely to cut back on imports of capital goods—the very items needed to promote long-term growth and productivity. Thus, many developing countries cannot afford the modern machinery that will help them become more productive. Developing countries often must also confront industrial countries' trade restrictions, such as tariffs and quotas, which often discriminate against primary products. For example, the United States strictly limits sugar imports. *Developing countries' share of world trade has fallen since 1950.*

Import Substitution Versus Export Promotion

Import substitution A development strategy that emphasizes domestic manufacturing of products that are currently imported

Economic development frequently involves a shift from the production of raw materials and agricultural products to manufacturing. If a country is fortunate, this transformation occurs gradually through natural market forces. Sometimes the shift is pushed along by government. Many developing countries, including Argentina and India, have pursued a policy called **import substitution,** whereby the country manufactures products that until then had been imported. To insulate domestic producers from foreign competition, the government imposes tariffs and quotas on imports. This development strategy became popular for several reasons. First, demand already existed for these products, so the "what to produce" question was readily answered. Second, by reducing imports, the approach addressed the balance-of-payments problem so common among developing countries. Third, import substitution nurtured infant industries, providing them the market and the protection to grow. Finally, import substitution was popular with those who supplied capital, labor, and other resources to the favored domestic industries.

Like all protection measures, however, import substitution neglects the gains from specialization and comparative advantage among countries. Often the developing country replaced relatively low-cost foreign goods with high-cost domestic goods. And domestic producers insulated from foreign competition usually failed to become efficient. Even the balance-of-payments picture did not improve, because other countries often retaliated with their own trade restrictions.

Export promotion A development strategy that concentrates on producing for the export market

Critics of the import-substitution approach claim that export promotion is a surer path to economic development. **Export promotion** is a development strategy that concentrates on producing for the export market. This approach begins with relatively simple products, such as textiles. As a developing country builds its technological and educational base, producers can then export more complex products. Economists tend to favor export promotion over import substitution because the emphasis is on comparative advantage and trade expansion rather than trade restriction. Export promotion also forces producers to be more efficient in order to compete on world markets. Recent research shows that global competition has a profound effect on domestic efficiency.[3] What's more, export promotion requires less government intervention into the market than does import substitution.

Export promotion has been the more successful development strategy, as reflected for example by the newly industrialized countries of East Asia. Export-

---

3   See Martin Baily and Hans Gersbach, "Efficiency in Manufacturing and the Need for Global Competition," in *Brookings Papers on Economic Activity: Microeconomics,* M. Baily, P. Reiss, and C. Winston, eds., (Washington, D.C.: Brookings Institution, 1995): pp. 307–47.

promoting economies such as South Korea, China, Malaysia, Singapore, and Hong Kong have in recent decades grown much more quickly than import-substituting countries such as Argentina, India, and Peru. Most Latin American nations, which for decades had favored import substitution, are now pursuing free trade agreements with the United States. Even India is in the process of dismantling trade barriers, though the emphasis has been on importing high-technology capital goods. One slogan of Indian trade officials is "Microchips, yes! Potato chips, no!"

Migration and the Brain Drain

Migration plays an important role in the economies of developing countries. A major source of foreign exchange in some countries is the money sent home by migrants who find jobs in industrial countries. Thus, migration provides a valuable safety valve for poor countries. But there is a downside as well. Often the best and the brightest professionals, such as doctors, nurses, and engineers, migrate to developed countries. Since human capital is such a key resource, this "brain drain" hurts the developing economy.

Trade Liberalization and Special Interests

Though most people would benefit from freer international trade, some would be significantly worse off in the short run. Consequently, governments in some developing countries have difficulty pursuing policies conducive to development. Often the gains from economic development are widespread, but the beneficiaries, such as consumers, do not recognize their potential gains. On the other hand, the losers tend to be concentrated, such as producers in an industry that had been sheltered from foreign competition, and they know quite well the source of their losses. So the government has difficulty removing the impediments to development, because the potential losers fight reforms that might harm their livelihood while the potential winners remain largely unaware of what's at stake. What's more, consumers have difficulty organizing even if they become aware of what's going on. A recent study by the World Bank suggests a strong link in Africa between governments that cater to special-interest groups and low rates of economic growth.

Nonetheless, many developing countries have been opening their borders to freer trade. People around the world have been exposed to information about the opportunities and goods available on world markets. No country can allow its own goods to sell for a multiple of the world price. So consumers want the goods that are available abroad and firms want the technology and capital available from abroad. Both groups want government to ease trade restrictions. Studies by the World Bank and others have underscored the successes of countries that have adopted trade liberalization policies.

FOREIGN AID AND ECONOMIC DEVELOPMENT

We have already seen that because poor countries do not generate enough savings to fund an adequate level of investment, these countries often rely on foreign financing. Private international borrowing and lending are heavily restricted by the governments of developing countries. Governments may allow residents to purchase foreign exchange only for certain purposes. In some developing countries, different exchange rates apply to different categories of transactions. Thus, the local currency is not easily convertible into other currencies. Some developing countries also require foreign investors to find a local partner who must be granted controlling interest. All these restrictions discourage foreign investment. In this section, we will look primarily at foreign aid and its link to economic development.

Foreign Aid

Foreign aid An international transfer made on especially favorable terms for the purpose of promoting economic development

Foreign aid is any international transfer made on *concessional* (especially favorable) terms for the purposes of promoting economic development. Foreign aid includes grants, which need not be repaid, and loans extended on more favorable repayment terms than the recipient could normally secure. Concessional loans have lower interest rates, longer repayment periods, or grace periods during which payments are reduced or waived (similar to student loans). Foreign aid can take the form of money, capital goods, technical assistance, food, and so forth.

Some foreign aid is from a specific country, such as the United States, to a specific country, such as the Philippines. Country-to-country aid is called *bilateral* assistance. Other aid is through international bodies such as the World Bank. Assistance provided by organizations that use funds from a number of countries is called *multilateral*. For example, the World Bank provides loans and grants to support activities that are viewed as prerequisites for development, such as health and education programs or basic development projects like dams, roads, and communications networks.

During the last four decades, the United States has provided the developing world with over $400 billion in aid. Since 1961, most U.S. aid has been coordinated by the U.S. Agency for International Development (AID), which is part of the U.S. Department of State. This agency concentrates primarily on health, education, and agriculture, providing both technical assistance and loans. AID emphasizes long-range plans to meet the basic needs of the poor and to promote self-sufficiency. Foreign aid is a controversial, though relatively small, part of the federal budget. Since 1993, official U.S. aid has been less than 0.2 percent of U.S. GDP, compared to an average of 0.3 percent from 21 other industrialized nations.

Does Foreign Aid Promote Economic Development?

In general, foreign aid provides additional purchasing power and thus the possibility of increased investment, capital imports, and consumption. But it is unclear whether foreign aid *supplements* domestic saving, thus increasing investment, or simply *substitutes for* domestic saving, thereby increasing consumption rather than investment. What is clear is that foreign aid often becomes a source of discretionary funds that benefit not the poor but their leaders. More than 90 percent of the funds distributed by AID go to governments, whose leaders assume responsibility for distributing these funds.

Much bilateral funding is tied to purchases of goods and services from the donor nation, and such programs can sometimes be counterproductive. For example, in the 1950s, the United States began the Food for Peace program, which helped sell U.S. farm products, but some governments sold that food to finance poorly conceived projects. Worse yet, the availability of low-priced food drove down farm prices in the developing country, hurting farmers in the countries that received the aid.

Foreign aid may have raised the standard of living in some developing countries, but it has not necessarily increased their ability to become self-supporting at that higher standard of living. Many countries that receive aid are doing less of what they had done well. Their agricultural sectors have suffered. For example, though we should be careful about drawing conclusions about causality, per-capita food production in Africa has fallen since 1960. Outside aid has often insulated government officials from the troubles of their own economies. No country receiving U.S. aid in the past 20 years has moved up in status from less-developed to developed. Most countries today that have achieved the status of "industrial country" did so without foreign aid.

Because of disappointment with the results of government aid, the trend is towards channeling funds through private nonprofit agencies such as CARE. More than half of the flow of aid now goes through private channels, as is discussed in the following case study.

CASE STUDY

Privatizing Foreign Aid

During the Cold War, foreign aid became another weapon in the clash of East and West. Much of the aid was designed to secure political loyalty. There was often less concern over whether the aid actually helped the poor or simply bought the favor of the ruling elite. Since the Soviet Union no longer exists, and since the United States and other developed countries face severe budget constraints, foreign aid now has a lower priority. Under pressure from the Republican Congress, the federal government is using nongovernment organizations, or NGOs, to "privatize" foreign aid. Between 1993 and 1996, the fraction of U.S. foreign aid channeled through NGOs increased from 17 percent to 40 percent. For example, the Small Enterprise Assistance Fund (SEAF) is a new hybrid—a nonprofit group funded by both government and charities to act as a wheeler-dealer by investing in promising small businesses. There are more than a half-dozen such funds and they are growing.

Location:

With the decline in direct U.S. governmental foreign aid, private groups termed *nongovernmental organizations* (NGOs) have filled in the gaps. InterAction is a coalition of over 150 US-based nonprofit NGOs. Visit InterAction (**http:www. interaction.org/ia/**).

The idea behind these risk-taking private-based aid programs is that the funds will be replenished as investments pay off. The result is a type of *sustainable development,* which means that one investment success can finance another. Money that replenishes itself will not drain scarce public funds.

To be sure, private investors with only profit in mind have long invested in developing countries. The difference is that nonprofits focus on firms that are too small for private investors or for traditional public aid programs. For example, SEAF invested $188,000 to buy one-third of a Polish firm that makes chicken coops. Since the SEAF investment, employment in the firm jumped from 12 to 50. SEAF and similar firms maintain their nonprofit status by reinvesting their earnings.

Sources: Dana Milbank, "Foreign Aid Finds Renewable Resource by Backing Profit-Making Businesses," *The Wall Street Journal,* 19 April 1995; and Robert Greenberger, "Developing Countries Pass Off Tedious Job of Assisting the Poor," *The Wall Street Journal,* 5 June 1995.

The privatization of foreign aid follows a larger trend toward privatization around the world. We discuss that important development in this closing section.

TRANSITIONAL ECONOMIES

As we have noted, there is no widely accepted theory of economic development, but markets around the world are replacing central plans in once-socialist countries. Economic developments in these emerging market economies have tremendous significance for those who study economics. Like geologists, economists must rely primarily on natural experiments to figure out how things work. *The attempt to replace central planning with markets is one of the greatest economic experiments in history.* In the study of geology, this would be comparable to a huge earthquake. In this section, we take a look at these so-called transitional economies.

Types of Economic Systems

First, a brief review of economic systems. In Chapter 2, we considered the three questions that every economic system must answer: what is to be produced, how is it to be produced, and for whom is it to be produced. Laws regarding resource ownership and the role of government in resource allocation determine the "rules of the game"—the incentives and constraints that guide the behavior of individual decision makers. Economic systems can be classified based on the ownership of resources, the way resources are allocated to produce goods and services, and the incentives used to motivate people.

As we discussed in Chapter 2, resources in *capitalist* systems are owned mostly by individuals and are allocated through market coordination. In *socialist* economies, resources other than labor are owned by the state. For example, a country such as Cuba or North Korea carefully limits the private ownership of resources such as land and capital. Each country employs a slightly different system of resource ownership, resource allocation, and individual incentives to answer the three economic questions.

So under capitalism, the rules of the game include private ownership of most resources and the coordination of economic activity by price signals generated by market forces; market coordination answers the three questions. Under socialism, the rules of the game include government ownership of most resources and the allocation of resources through central plans.

Enterprises and Soft Budget Constraints

In the socialist system, enterprises that earn a "profit" see that profit appropriated by the state. Firms that end up with a loss find that loss covered by a state subsidy. Thus, socialist enterprises face what has been called a **soft budget constraint.** This leads to inefficiency, a lack of response to changes in supply or demand, and poor investment decisions. Quality has also been a problem under central planning, because plant managers would rather meet production quotas than satisfy consumer demands. For example, plant managers do not score extra bureaucratic points by producing garments that are in style and in popular sizes. Tales of shoddy products in socialist systems abound.

Most prices in centrally planned economies are determined not by market forces but by central planners. As a result, consumers have little to say about

Soft budget constraint The budget condition faced by socialist enterprises that lose money and then are subsidized

what to produce. Once set, prices tend to be inflexible. For example, in the former Soviet Union, the price of a cabbage slicer was stamped on the metal at the factory. In the spirit of equity, Soviet planners priced most consumer goods below the market-clearing level, so shortages (or "interruptions in supply," as they were called) were common. As of 1990, the price of bread had not changed since 1954, and in 1990 the price amounted to only 7 percent of bread's production cost. Meat prices had not changed since 1962. Rents had not changed in 60 years.

Capitalist economies equate quantity supplied with quantity demanded through the *invisible hand* of market coordination; centrally planned economies use the *visible hand* of bureaucratic coordination assisted by taxes and subsidies. If quantity supplied and quantity demanded are not in balance, something has to give. In a capitalist system, what gives is the price. In a centrally planned economy, what usually gives is the central plan itself. A common problem in the Soviet system was that the amount produced often fell short of planned production. When the quantity supplied fell below the planned amount, central planners reduced the amount supplied to each sector, cutting critical sectors such as heavy industry and the military the least and lower-priority sectors such as consumer products the most. Evidence of shortages of consumer goods included long waiting lines at retail stores; empty store shelves; the "tips," or bribes, shop operators expected for supplying scarce consumer goods; and higher prices for goods on the black market. Shoppers would sometimes wait in line all night and into the next day. Consumers often relied on "connections" through acquaintances to obtain most goods and services. Scarce goods were frequently diverted to the black market.

Another distinction between socialist economies and capitalist economies involves the ownership of resources. The following case study considers the effect of ownership on the efficient use of resources.

Because most property is owned by the state in a socialist economy, nobody in particular owns it. Because there are no individual owners, resources are often wasted. For example, in the former Soviet Union, about one-third of the harvest reportedly deteriorated before it reached retailers. Likewise, to meet Soviet planning goals, oil producers often pumped large pools of oil reserves so quickly that the remaining oil became inaccessible. Soviet workers usually had little regard for equipment that belonged to the state. New trucks or tractors might be dismantled for parts, or working equipment might be sent to a scrap plant. Pilfering of state-owned property, though officially a serious crime, was a high art and a favorite sport.

A narrow focus on meeting the objectives of the central plan also imposed a high cost on the environment. The Aral Sea, which is about the size of Lake Michigan, has been called "a salinated cesspool." Thousands of barrels of nuclear waste were dumped into Soviet rivers and seas. The 1986 Chernobyl reactor meltdown still poses a threat of nuclear contamination; similar reactors continue to

CASE STUDY

Ownership and Resources Use

Location:

Even die-hard socialist countries like Cuba are promoting some free-market activities, including private foreign investment, and are turning to the Internet for help. Visit "Cubaweb," an informational site about Cuban society, culture, and business, supported by various private and public institutions in Cuba (http://www.cubaweb.cu/). In particular, review "Investing in Cuba."

supply energy to Russia, Ukraine, and Lithuania. In a drive for military supremacy, the Soviet government set off 125 nuclear explosions above ground. The resulting bomb craters later filled with water, forming contaminated lakes.

In contrast to the treatment of state property, individual Soviet citizens took extremely good care of their personal property. For example, personal cars were so well maintained that they lasted 20 years or more on average—twice the official projected automobile life. The incentives of private ownership were also evident on the farm. Each farmer on the collective was allowed a small plot of land on which to cultivate crops for personal consumption or for sale at prices determined in unregulated markets. Despite the small size of the plots and the taxes on earnings from these plots, farmers produced a disproportionate share of output on private plots. Privately farmed plots constituted only 3 percent of the Soviet Union's farmland, but they supplied 30 percent of all meat, milk, and vegetables and 60 percent of all potatoes.

Recognizing the incentive power of private property, even the most diehard socialist economies now allow some free-market activity. For example, Cuba welcomes joint ventures funded by private investment in such strategic areas as telecommunication, oil exploration, and mining. Fidel Castro has also authorized condominium sales to foreigners and the sale of farm products in farmers' markets. More than 200 farmers' markets have been established in Cuba since October 1994 to sell everything from live goats to tropical fruit. The point is that the personal incentives provided by private property usually promote a more efficient use of that property than does state ownership.

Sources: Kevin Fedarko, "Open for Business," *Time,* 20 February 1995; Adi Ignatius, "Russia Moves Closer to Ending Collective Farms," *The Wall Street Journal,* 11 March 1994; and Andrei Shleifer and Robert Vishny, "The Politics of Market Socialism," *Journal of Economic Perspective,* Spring 1994, pp. 165–76.

MARKETS AND INSTITUTIONS

A study of economic systems underscores the importance of institutions in the course of development. *Institutions* are the incentives and constraints that structure political, economic, and social interaction. They consist of (1) formal rules of behavior, such as a constitution, laws, and property rights, and (2) informal constraints on behavior, such as sanctions, manners, customs, traditions, and codes of conduct. Throughout history, institutions have been devised by human beings to create order and reduce uncertainty in exchange, among other things. Thus, underlying the surface of economic behavior is a grid of informal, often unconscious, habits, customs, and norms that make the functioning of markets possible. *A reliable system of property rights and enforceable contracts are prerequisites for creating incentives that could support a healthy market economy.*

Together with the standard constraints of economics, such as income, resource availability, and prices, institutions shape the incentive structure of an economy. As the incentive structure evolves, it can direct economic change toward growth, stagnation, or decline. Economic history is largely a story of economies that have failed to produce a set of economic rules of the game that lead to sustained economic growth. After all, three-quarters of the world's economies are still trying to develop.

Customs and conventions can sometimes be obstacles to development. In developed market economies, resource owners tend to supply their resources where they are most valued; but in developing countries, links to the family or clan may be the most important consideration. For example, in some cultures, children are expected to remain in the father's occupation even if they are better suited to some other line of work. Family businesses may resist growth because such growth would involve hiring people from outside the family.

Institutions and Economic Development

Institutions shape the incentive structure of an economy, but, as we have already noted, most countries in the world have failed to produce a set of economic rules of the game that lead to sustained economic growth. Although political and judicial decisions may change formal rules overnight, informal constraints embodied in customs, traditions, and codes of conduct are more immune to deliberate policies. For example, respect for the law cannot be legislated.

Prior to the market reforms in the former Soviet Union, widespread corruption and a lack of faith in formal institutions were woven into the social fabric. Workers bribed officials to get good jobs, and consumers bribed clerks to get desired products. Bribery became a way of life, a way of dealing with the distortions that arise when prices are not allowed to allocate resources efficiently.

In centrally planned economies, the exchange relationship was typically *personal,* based as it was on bureaucratic ties on the production side and inside connections on the consumption side. But in the United States and other market economies, successful institutional evolution permits the *impersonal* exchange necessary to capture the potential economic benefits of specialization and modern technology. Impersonal exchange allows for a far greater division of labor, but it requires a richer and more stable institutional setting.

The "Big Bang" Versus Gradualism

The Hungarian economist Janos Kornai believes that a market order should be grown from the bottom up. First, small-scale capitalism in farming, trade, light manufacturing, and services thrives. These grass-roots markets can serve as a foundation for the privatization of larger industrial sectors. Large industrial enterprises should quickly find the market-clearing price so that input and output decisions are consistent with market preferences. But, according to Kornai, their ownership structure and way of doing business cannot be reformed overnight by legislative mandates. In the meantime, state-owned enterprises should be run more like businesses in which state directors attempt to maximize profit. Money-losing enterprises should be phased out. This "bottom-up" approach proposed by Kornai could be termed *gradualism,* which can be contrasted with a *big-bang* approach, whereby the transition from central planning to a market economy would take place in a matter of months.

One example of gradualism is taking place in China. In 1978, the government began dismantling agricultural communes in favor of a "household-responsibility" system of small-farm agriculture. Land was assigned to individual families, which could keep any excess production after meeting specific state-imposed goals. Initially the system was to be applied only to the poorest 20 percent of the rural areas. Once the positive effects became apparent, however, the system spread on its own. Eventually farmers established their own wholesale and retail marketing systems and were allowed to sell directly to urban areas at market-clearing prices. This gave rise to a market for truckers to buy, transport, and resell farm products. Over the next 7 years, agricultural output increased by an impressive 8 to 10 percent per year. Based in part on China's success, Russia began carving up state-owned farms and giving parts to individual farmers.

In structuring the transition from central planning to a market system, economists are feeling their way. Nobel Prize winner Friedrich von Hayek argued that a fundamental flaw of central planning is that, unlike competitive markets, it provides no way to discover and process localized information about supply and demand. And the more rigid prices become, the less information they convey. Hayek believed that *government's role is to support the dynamic market order by identifying and codifying the conventions of trade and by protecting property rights.* According to Hayek, competition generates market-clearing prices in a discovery process. But the determination of the appropriate rules of the game to support market activity is also a discovery process. Both discovery processes are especially difficult for transitional economies that have no history of market interaction and no established record of codified law or rules of conduct for market participants.

Privatization

Privatization is the process of turning public enterprises into private enterprises. It is the opposite of *nationalization*. For example, Russian privatization began in April 1992 with the sale of municipally owned shops. The government also decreed that state and collective farms must convert into joint-stock companies owned by the workforce and must sell plots of land to anyone who wanted to farm privately.

Privatization The process of turning public enterprises into private enterprises

Although most property in a socialist economy is nominally owned by the state, it often remained unclear who had the authority to sell the property and who was to receive the proceeds. This ambiguity resulted in cases in which the same property was purchased from different officials by different buyers. Yet *there was no clear legal process for resolving title disputes.* Worse still, some enterprises were stripped of their assets by self-serving managers, a process that came to be derisively called "spontaneous" privatization. The necessarily complex process of privatization will be undermined if the general population perceives the process to be unfair.

Privatization requires the development of modern accounting and other information systems, the training of competent managers, and the installation of adequate facilities for telecommunication, computing, travel, and transportation. This transformation cannot be accomplished overnight. Consider just the accounting problem. A market economy depends on financial accounting rules as well as on an independent system for auditing financial reports. The needed information shows up in a company's balance sheet and income statement. Prospective buyers of enterprises need such information, as do banks and other lenders.

By all reports, the accounting systems of socialist firms are almost worthless. For decades, data had been aimed more at central planners, who wanted to know about *physical* flows, than at someone who wanted to know about the efficiency and financial promise of the firm. So there is much information, but little that is relevant. Incidentally, the major advantage of the market economy is that it minimizes the need for the kind of resource-flow data that had been reported under central planning. Prices convey most of the information necessary to coordinate economic activity among firms.

Some may look at the initial instability that resulted from the dismantling of socialist states and argue that the move toward markets has been a failure. But in the former Soviet Union, for example, the state dismantled central controls before institutions such as property rights, customs, codes of conduct, and a legal system were in place. For example, the personal income tax in Russia jumped from a graduated rate topping out at 13 percent to a flat rate of 60 percent and then to a graduated rate topping at 40 percent. As long as taxes seem so arbitrary and capricious, people have less incentive to work, to save, to invest, and more generally to go about the business of building an economy. According to the Russian government, Russian individuals stashed $60 billion in foreign bank accounts between 1991 and 1995.

The road to privatization has nowhere been rockier than in Kazakhstan, the last former Soviet republic to declare independence. Of the 126 large state-owned enterprises targeted for privatization in 1995, only one deal was completed—the nation's largest steel mill was sold for $1 billion to Ispat, a British firm. The new owner expected transition problems but was reportedly stunned by the inefficiency and bureaucratic incompetence of the company's bloated 38,000-person work force.[4] Although the plant had been virtually bankrupt, the plant's directors were living like kings, spending $1 million just on armchairs. According to Ispat's new manager, "Everyone has got his assistant and his assistant and his assistant."[5] On average the new manager had to fire about 100 workers per week for coming to work drunk. Many others were fired for cheating the company by drawing paychecks for two jobs but working only one. The plant's bureaucracy even included more than a dozen KGB agents ensconced in an electronically sophisticated corner office. It took more than two months of negotiations to get them out.

As Kazakhstan's troubled transition shows, the shift from central planning to a market economy is easier said than done. Simply loosening constraints to create private property may not be enough for successful reform. The development of supporing institutions is essential, but *there is no unified economic theory of how to construct the institutions that are central to the success of capitalism.* Most so-called "economists" employed in Soviet-type systems did not understand even the basics of how markets work. They had been trained to regard the alleged "anarchy" of the market as a primary defect of capitalism.

A more fundamental problem is that although Western economic theory focuses on the operation of efficient markets, *even market economists usually do not understand the institutional requirements of efficient markets.* Market economists usually take the necessary institutions for granted. Those involved in the transition must develop a deeper appreciation for the institutions that nurture and support impersonal market activity.

So the jury is still out on the transition to markets. Exhibit 6 presents, for some transitional economies, the GDP per capita in 1992 based on the pur-

---

4   The account of this privatization first appeared in Kyle Pope, "A Steelmaker Built Up by Buying Cheap Mills Finally Meets Its Match," *The Wall Street Journal,* 2 May 1996.
5   As quoted by Kyle Pope.

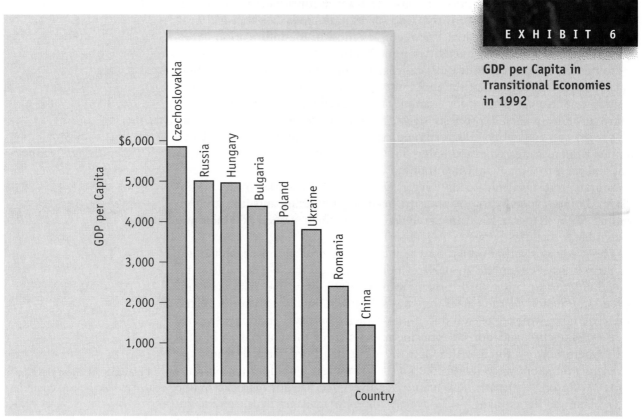

EXHIBIT 6

GDP per Capita in Transitional Economies in 1992

Source: Barry P. Bosworth and Gur Ofer, *Reforming Planned Economies in an Integrating World,* (Washington, D.C.: Brookings Institution, 1995), Table 1-2, p. 33.

chasing power of the domestic currency. For comparison, U.S. GDP per capita in 1992 was $23,500, so even the most successful of transition economies produced only one-quarter as much per capita as the United States. Lessons about the nature of economic processes will likely emerge from the analysis of these transitions. The course of economic reform will provide insights into both the potential and the limits of economics itself.

CONCLUSION

As noted at the outset of the chapter, because no single theory of economic development has become widely accepted, the emphasis has been more descriptive than theoretical. We can readily define the features that distinguish developing and industrial economies, but we are less sure how to foster growth and development. As noted earlier, economic history is largely a story of economies that have failed to produce a set of economic rules of the game that lead to sustained economic growth.

Perhaps the most elusive ingredients for development are the formal and informal institutions that promote economic activity: the laws, customs, conventions, and other institutional elements that encourage people to undertake productive activity. A stable political environment with well-defined property rights is important. Little private sector investment will occur if potential investors believe their capital might be appropriated by government, destroyed by civil unrest, or stolen by thieves. Education is also key to development, both because of its direct effect on productivity and because those who are more educated are more receptive to new ideas. A physical infrastructure of transportation and communication systems and utilities is needed to link economic actors. And trusted financial institutions help link savers and borrowers. Finally, a country needs entrepreneurs with the vision to move the economy forward. The newly emerging industrial countries of South Korea, Taiwan, Singapore, and Malaysia prove that economic development is achievable, though not necessarily easy.

SUMMARY

1. Developing countries are distinguished by low levels of real GDP per capita, poor health and nutrition, high birth rates, low levels of education, and saving rates that are too low to finance sufficient investment.

2. Worker productivity is low in developing countries because the stocks of physical and human capital are low, technological advances are not widely diffused throughout the economy, natural resources and entrepreneurial ability are scarce, financial markets are not well developed, some talented professionals migrate to high-income countries, formal and informal institutions do not provide sufficient incentives for market activity, and governments may serve the interests of the group in power rather than the public interest.

3. The secret to growth and a rising standard of living is increased productivity. To foster productivity, developing nations must stimulate investment, support education and training programs, and provide the infrastructure necessary to support economic development.

4. Increases in productivity do not occur without prior saving, but most people in developing countries have such low incomes that there is little opportunity to save. Also, even if some people had the money to save, financial institutions in developing countries are not well developed, and savings are often sent abroad, where there is a more stable investment climate.

5. Foreign aid has been a mixed blessing for most developing countries. In some cases, that aid has helped countries build the roads, bridges, schools, and other capital infrastructure necessary for development. In other cases, foreign aid has simply increased consumption and insulated government from necessary reforms. Worse still, cheap food from abroad undermined domestic agriculture.

6. Major reforms have been introduced in recent years to decentralize decision making, to provide greater production incentives to workers, and to introduce competitive markets. But in many cases, central controls were dismantled before the institutional framework had developed to support a market economy.

QUESTIONS AND PROBLEMS

1. **(Developing Countries)** How would you explain why agricultural production in developing countries is usually low?

2. **(Classification of Economies)** What arguments are there for using real per capita GDP to compare living standards between countries? What weakness does this measure have?

3. **(International Trade and Development)** How might a country that is predominantly agricultural grow into an industrial economy? Is saving an important feature of growth? What about import substitution, whereby imported products are replaced by domestically produced goods?

4. **(Political Stability and Development)** Why is political stability a key element in a country's ability to grow? Consider the effect of political instability on capital.

5. **(Import Substitution)** Policymakers in many developing countries believe the country must produce steel and

autos in order to experience fast economic growth. Why is this policy usually misguided? Consider the issue of comparative advantage.

6. **(Classification of Economies)** How do differences in each of the following affect the usefulness of per capita real income as a means of comparing living standards across countries?
   a. Income distribution.
   b. The level of nonmarket activity using resources.
   c. The level of negative externalities generated by income production.
   d. The amount of leisure consumption.

7. **(Developing Versus Industrial Market Economies)** Compare developing and industrial market economies on the basis of each of the following general economic characteristics, and relate the differences to the process of development:
   a. Diversity of the industrial base.
   b. Distribution of resource ownership.
   c. Educational level of the labor force.

8. **(Foreign Aid)** Foreign aid, if it is to be successful in enhancing economic development, must lead to a more productive resource base. Describe some of the problems in achieving such an objective through foreign aid.

9. **(Keys to Development)** Among the problems that hinder growth in the developing economies of the world are poor infrastructure, lack of financial institutions and a sound money supply, low savings rate, poor capital base, and lack of foreign exchange. Explain how these problems are interconnected.

10. **(Foreign Aid)** It is widely recognized that aid that promotes productivity in developing economies is superior to merely shipping products like food to these countries. Yet the latter is the approach frequently taken. Why do you think this is the case?

11. **(Developing Countries and the Production Possibilities Frontier)** Growth may be thought of as a shift of the production possibilities frontier outward. Yet in many developing economies, a major problem is simply getting to the frontier in the first place. Explain.

12. **(Developing Countries)** What general characteristics are usually shared by economies described as "developing countries"?

13. **(Classification of Economies)** How are differences in stages of development among countries reflected in ways besides differences in per capital income levels?

14. **(International Trade and Foreign Aid)** Define each of the following terms:
   a. Export promotion.
   b. Brain drain.
   c. Foreign aid.

15. **(Socialism)** Is there any reason why socialist economies couldn't have as much diversity in the production of goods as capitalist economies do? Does your answer depend on how much central planning is undertaken by the government?

16. **(Types of Economic Systems)** One of the questions every economic system must answer is for whom are products produced. How is the answer determined in a market system as compared to a centrally planned system?

17. **(Privatization)** Obviously the conversion to a market-based system of resource allocation, particularly in an economy like that in Russia where consumer goods were priced below production cost, is difficult, and President Yeltsin had a large array of opponents to such change. Who would gain and lose from the conversion?

18. **(Markets and Institutions)** Explain why a system of well-defined and enforceable property rights is crucial when converting to a market-based system of resource allocation.

19. **("Big Bang" Versus Gradualism)** Explain the difference between the "big bang" and gradualism approaches to moving from central planning to market coordination.

20. **(Privatization)** What institutional changes are necessary for a successful transition from central planning to market coordination?

21. **(Privatizing Foreign Aid)** What is the premise for replacing government-funded foreign aid with private-based aid?

22. **(Ownership and Resources Use)** In an economy in which the state owns resources like land and capital, such resources are often wasted. Can you explain such waste in terms of the "common pool problem" discussed in the chapter on externalities and the environment?

23. **(Ownership and Resources Use)** In what ways were the incentives of private ownership evident even in the prereform Soviet Union?

24. Review the most recent "World Bank News," a weekly publication of events, activities, and initiatives involving the World Bank (**http://www.worldbank.org/html/extdr/extcs/news.html**).

a. Review one report specific to a developing country. What is the World Bank doing to help this country? In return for assistance, what has the developing country done, or what does it plan to do?

b. Look within "World Bank Roundup." How much money has the World Bank and its member organizations promised to countries in the last week?

Glossary

A

Absolute advantage The ability to produce something with fewer resources than other producers use

Accounting profit A firm's total revenue minus its explicit cost

Active approach The view that the private sector is relatively unstable and able to absorb economic shocks only with the aid of discretionary government policy

Actual investment The amount of investment actually undertaken during a year; equals planned investment plus unplanned changes in inventories

Adverse selection A situation in which those on the informed side of the market self-select in a way that harms the uninformed side of the market

Adverse supply shocks Unexpected events that reduce aggregate supply, usually only temporarily

Agent A person who performs work or provides a service on behalf of another person, the principal

Aggregate demand The relationship between the price level in the economy and the quantity of aggregate output demanded, other things held constant

Aggregate demand curve A curve representing the relationship between the economy's price level and the amount of aggregate output demanded per period of time, other things held constant

Aggregate expenditure Total spending on final goods and services during a given time period

Aggregate expenditure function A relationship showing, for a given price level, the amount of planned spending for each level of income; the total of $C + I + G + (X - M)$ at each level of income

Aggregate income The sum of all income earned by resource suppliers in an economy during a given time period

Aggregate output The total quantity of final goods and services produced in an economy during a given time period

Aggregate supply curve A curve representing the relationship between the economy's price level and the amount of aggregate output supplied per period of time, other things held constant

Allocative efficiency The condition that exists when firms produce the output that is most preferred by consumers; the marginal cost of each good just equals the marginal benefit that consumers derive from that good

Alternative goods Other goods that use some of the same types of resources used to produce the good in question

Annually balanced budget Budget philosophy prior to the Great Depression; aimed at equating revenues with expenditures, except during times of war

Annuity A given sum of money received each year for a specified number of years

Antitrust activity Government activity aimed at preventing monopoly and fostering competition

Applied research Research that seeks to answer particular questions or to apply scientific discoveries to the development of specific products

Arbitrageur A person who takes advantage of temporary geographic differences in the exchange rate by simultaneously purchasing a currency in one market and selling it in another market

Asset Anything of value that is owned

Association-is-causation fallacy The incorrect idea that if two variables are associated in time, one must necessarily cause the other

Asymmetric information A situation in which one side of the market has more reliable information than the other side does

Autarky A situation of national self-sufficiency in which there is no economic interaction with foreigners

Automatic stabilizers Structural features of government spending and taxation that smooth fluctuations in disposable income over the business cycle

Autonomous A term that means "independent"; autonomous investment is independent of the level of income

Autonomous net tax multiplier The ratio of a change in equilibrium real GDP demanded to the initial change in autonomous net taxes that brought it about; the numerical value of the multiplier is (MPC/(1 − MPC)

Average fixed cost Fixed cost divided by output

Average revenue Total revenue divided by output; in all market structures, average revenue equals the market price

Average total cost Total cost divided by output; the sum of average fixed cost and average variable cost

Average variable cost Variable cost divided by output

B

Backward-bending supply curve of labor Occurs if the income effect of a higher wage dominates the substitution effect of a higher wage

Balance of payments A record of all economic transactions between residents of one country and residents of the rest of the world during a given time period

Balance on current account The section of a country's balance of payments account that measures the sum of the country's net unilateral transfers and its balance on goods and services

Balance on goods and services The section of a country's balance of payments account that measures the difference in value between a country's exports of goods and services and its imports of goods and services

Balance sheet A financial statement that shows assets, liabilities, and net worth at a given point in time

Balanced budget amendment Proposed amendment to the U.S. Constitution requiring a balanced federal budget

Balanced budget multiplier A factor that shows that identical changes in government purchases and net taxes change real GDP demanded by that same amount; the numerical value of the muliplier is 1

Bank holding company A corporation that owns banks

Bank notes Papers promising a specific amount of gold or silver to bearers who presented them to issuing banks for redemption; an early type of money

Barrier to entry Any impediment that prevents new firms from competing on an equal basis with existing firms in an industry

Barter The direct exchange of one good for another without the use of money

Base year The year with which other years are compared when constructing an index; the index equals 100 in the base year, or base period

Basic research The search for knowledge without regard to how that knowledge will be used

Behavioral assumption An assumption that describes the expected behavior of economic actors

Beneficial supply shocks Unexpected events that increase aggregate supply, usually only temporarily

Bilateral monopoly A situation in which a single seller, or monopolist, bargains with a single buyer, or monopsonist

Binding arbitration Negotiation in which both parties in a union-management dispute agree to accept an impartial observer's resolution of the dispute

Bond A certificate reflecting a firm's promise to pay the holder a periodic interest payment until the date of maturity and a fixed sum of money on the designated maturity date

Bounded rationality The notion that there is a limit to the amount of information an economic agent, such as a manager, can comprehend

Bureaus Government agencies charged with implementing legislation and financed by appropriations from legislative bodies

C

Capital All buildings, equipment, and human skill used to produce goods and services

Capital account The record of a country's international transactions involving purchases or sales of financial and real assets

Cartel A group of firms that agree to coordinate their production and pricing decisions, thereby behaving as a monopolist

Change in demand A shift in a given demand curve caused by a change in one of the nonprice determinants of demand for the good

Change in quantity demanded A movement along the demand curve in response to a change in the price, other things constant

Change in quantity supplied A movement along the supply curve in response to a change in the price, other things constant

Change in supply A shift in a given supply curve caused by a change in one of the nonprice determinants of the supply of the good

Checkable deposits Deposits in financial institutions against which checks can be written

Classical economists A group of 18th- and 19th-century economists who believed that recessions and depressions were short-run phenomena that corrected themselves through natural market forces; thus the economy was self-adjusting

Coase theorem The theory that as long as bargaining costs are small, an efficient solution to the problem of externalities will be achieved by assigning property rights

Cold turkey The announcement and execution of tough measures to reduce high inflation

Collective bargaining The process by which union and management negotiate a labor agreement

Command economy An economic system characterized by public ownership of resources and centralized economic planning

Commercial banks Depository institutions that make short-term loans primarily to businesses

Commodity money Anything that serves both as money and as a commodity

Common pool problem Unrestricted access to a resource results in overuse until the net marginal value of additional use drops to zero

Comparable worth The principle that pay should be determined by job characteristics rather than by supply and demand

Comparative advantage The ability to produce something at a lower opportunity cost than other producers face

Competing-interest legislation Legislation that imposes concentrated costs on one group and provides concentrated benefits to another group

Complements Goods that are related in such a way that an increase in the price of one leads to a decrease in the demand for the other

Concentration ratio A measure of the market share of the largest firms in an industry

Conglomerate merger A merger involving the combination of firms producing in different industries

Consent decree A legal agreement through which the accused party, without admitting guilt, agrees to refrain in the future from certain illegal activity if the government drops the charges

Constant-cost industry An industry that can expand or contract without affecting the long-run per-unit cost of production; the long-run industry supply curve is horizontal

Constant elasticity of demand The type of demand that exists when price elasticity is the same everywhere along the curve; the elasticity value is constant

Consumer equilibrium The condition in which an individual consumer's budget is completely spent and the last dollar spent on each good yields the same marginal utility; utility is maximized

Consumer price index (CPI) A measure over time of the cost of a fixed "market basket" of consumer goods and services

Consumer surplus The difference between the maximum amount that a consumer is willing to pay for a given quantity of a good and what the consumer actually pays

Consumption All household purchases of final goods and services

Consumption function The relationship between the level of income in an economy and the amount households spend on consumption, other things constant

Contestable market One in which potential entrants can serve the same market and have access to the same technology as an existing firm

Continuing resolutions Budget agreements that allow agencies, in the absence of an approved budget, to spend at the rate of the previous year's budget

Contractionary gap The amount by which actual output in the short run falls below the economy's potential output

Convergence A theory that economies around the world will grow more alike over time, with poorer countries catching up with richer countries

Coordination failure A state in which workers and employers fail to achieve an outcome that all would prefer because they are unable to jointly choose strategies that would result in a preferred outcome

Corporation A legal entity owned by stockholders whose liability is limited to the value of their stock

Cost-plus pricing A method of determining the price of a good by adding a percentage markup to average variable cost

Cost-push inflation A sustained rise in the price level caused by reductions in aggregate supply

Craft union A union whose members have a particular skill or work at a particular craft, such as plumbers or carpenters

Cross-price elasticity of demand The percent change in the demand of one good (at a given price) as a result of the percent change in the price of another good

Cross-subsidization A firm's use of revenues from profitable activities to support unprofitable activities

Crowding in The potential for government spending to stimulate private investment in an otherwise sluggish economy

Crowding out The displacement of interest-sensitive private investment that occurs when increased government spending drives up interest rates

Currency appreciation A decrease in the number of units of a particular currency needed to purchase 1 unit of foreign exchange

Currency depreciation An increase in the number of units of a particular currency needed to purchase 1 unit of foreign exchange

Currency devaluation An increase in the official pegged price of foreign exchange in terms of the domestic currency

Currency revaluation A reduction in the official pegged price of foreign exchange in terms of the domestic currency

Cyclical majority A situation in which no choice dominates all others, and the outcome of a vote depends on the order in which issues are considered

Cyclical unemployment Unemployment that occurs because of declines in the economy's aggregate production during recessions

Cyclically balanced budget A budget philosophy calling for budget deficits during recessions to be financed by budget surpluses during expansions

D

Deadweight loss A loss of consumer surplus and producer surplus that is not transferred to anyone else; it can result from monopolization of an industry

Decision-making lag The time needed to decide what to do after a macroeconomic problem is identified

Decreasing-cost industry The rare case in which an industry faces lower per-unit production costs as industry output expands in the long run; the long-run industry supply curve slopes downward

Deflation A sustained decrease in the price level

Demand A relation showing the quantities of a good consumers are willing and able to buy at various prices during a given period of time, other things constant

Demand curve A curve showing the quantities of a commodity demanded at various possible prices, other things constant

Demand deposits Accounts at financial institutions that pay no interest and on which depositors can write checks to obtain their deposits at any time

Demand for loanable funds The relationship between the market rate of interest and the quantity of loanable funds demanded, other things constant

Demand-pull inflation A sustained rise in the price level caused by increases in aggregate demand

Demand-side economics Macroeconomic policy that focuses on changing aggregate demand as a way of promoting full employment and price stability

Depository institutions Commercial banks and other financial institutions that accept deposits from the public

Depreciation The value of capital stock used up during a year in producing GDP

Depression A severe reduction in an economy's total production accompanied by high unemployment lasting more than a year

Derived demand The demand for a resource is derived from the demand for the product the resource produces

Developing countries Nations typified by high rates of illiteracy, high unemployment, rapid population growth, and exports of primary products

Discount rate Interest rate charged to member banks by Federal Reserve banks for discount loans; the interest rate used to convert income to be received in the future into present value

Discounting Determining the present value of a sum of money to be received in the future

Discouraged worker A person who has dropped out of the labor force because of lack of success in finding a job

Discretionary fiscal policy The deliberate manipulation of government spending or taxation in order to promote full employment and price stability

Diseconomies of scale Forces that cause a firm's average cost to increase as the scale of operations increases in the long run

Disequilibrium Usually a temporary mismatch between quantity supplied and quantity demanded as the market seeks equilibrium

Disposable income (DI) The income households have available to spend or save after paying taxes and receiving transfer payments

Division of labor The organization of production of a single good into separate tasks in which people specialize

Double coincidence of wants A situation in which two traders are willing to exchange their products directly

Dumping Selling a commodity abroad at a price that is below its cost of production or below the price charged in the domestic market

Duopoly A market with only two producers, who compete with each other; a type of oligopoly market structure

E

Economic fluctuations The rise and fall of economic activity relative to the long-term growth trend of the economy; also called business cycles

Economic profit A firm's total revenue minus its explicit and implicit costs

Economic regulation Government measures aimed at controlling prices, output, market entry and exit, and product quality in situations in which, because of economies of scale, average production costs are lowest when the market is served by only one or a few firms

Economic rent The portion of a resource's total earnings above its opportunity cost; earnings above the amount necessary to keep the resource in its present use

Economic system The set of mechanisms and institutions that resolve the what, how, and for whom questions

Economic theory, economic model A simplification of reality used to make predictions about the real world

Economics The study of how people choose to use their scarce resources in an attempt to satisfy their unlimited wants

Economies of scale Forces that cause reduction in a firm's average cost as the scale of operations increases in the long run

Economies of scope Forces that make it cheaper for a firm to produce two or more different products than just one

Economy The structure of economic life or economic activity in a community, a region, a country, a group of countries, or the world

Effectiveness lag The time necessary for changes in monetary or fiscal policy to have an effect on the economy

Efficiency The condition that exists when there is no way resources can be reallocated to increase the production of one good without decreasing the production of another

Efficiency wage theory The idea that offering high wages attracts a more talented labor pool, making it easier for firms to attract and retain more productive workers

Elastic demand The type of demand that exists when a change in price has a relatively large effect on quantity demanded; the percent change in quantity demanded exceeds the percent change in price

Entitlement programs Guaranteed benefits for those who qualify under government transfer programs such as Social Security and Aid to Families with Dependent Children

Entrepreneur A profit-seeking decision maker who organizes an enterprise and assumes the risk of its operation.

Entrepreneurial ability Managerial and organization skills combined with the willingness to take risks

Equation of exchange The quantity of money, M, multiplied by its velocity, V, equals nominal income, which is the product of the price level, P, and real GDP, Y.

Equilibrium The condition that exists in a market when the plans of the buyers match the plans of the sellers

Excess capacity The difference between a monopolistic competitor's minimum average cost and its profit-maximizing level of output

Excess reserves Bank reserves in excess of required reserves

Exchange rate The price of one country's currency measured in terms of another country's currency

Exclusive dealing The situation that occurs when a producer prohibits customers from purchasing from other sellers

Exhaustible resource A resource available in fixed supply, such as crude oil or copper ore

Expansionary gap The amount by which actual output in the short run exceeds the economy's potential output

Expansion A phase of economic activity during which there is an increase in the economy's total production

Expenditure approach A method of calculating GDP by adding up expenditures on all final goods and services produced during the year

Explicit cost Opportunity cost of a firm's resources that takes the form of cash payments

Export promotion A development strategy that concentrates on producing for the export market

Externality A cost or a benefit that falls on third parties and is therefore ignored by the two parties to the market transaction

F

Fallacy of composition The incorrect belief that what is true for the individual, or part, must necessarily be true for the group, or whole

Featherbedding Union efforts to force employers to hire more workers than demanded for the task

Federal funds market A market for day-to-day lending and borrowing of reserves among financial institutions

Federal funds rate The interest rate prevailing in the federal funds market

Federal Reserve System The central bank and monetary authority of the United States; known as "the Fed"

Fiat money Money not redeemable for any commodity; its status as money is conferred by the government

Final goods and services Goods and services sold to final, or ultimate, users

Financial intermediaries Institutions that serve as go-betweens, accepting funds from savers and lending them to borrowers

Financial markets Banks and other institutions that facilitate the flow of loanable funds from savers to borrowers

Firms Economic units, formed by profit-seeking entrepreneurs, that use hired resources to produce goods and services for sale

Fiscal policy The use of government purchases, transfer payments, taxes, and borrowing to influence aggregate economic activity

Fixed cost Any production cost that is independent of the firm's rate of output

Fixed exchange rates Rates pegged within a narrow range of values by central banks' ongoing purchases and sales of currencies

Fixed-production technology Technology for which the relationship between output and the generation of an externality is a fixed one; the only way to reduce the externality is to reduce the output

Fixed resource Any resource that cannot be varied in the short run

Flexible exchange rates Rates determined by the forces of supply and demand without government intervention

Flow A variable that measures the amount of something over an interval of time, such as the amount of money you spend on food per week

Foreign aid An international transfer made on especially favorable terms for the purpose of promoting economic development

Foreign exchange The currency of another country needed to carry out international transactions

Fractional reserve banking system A banking system in which only a portion of deposits is backed by reserves

Frictional unemployment Unemployment that arises because of the time needed to match qualified job seekers with available job openings

Full employment The level of employment when there is no cyclical unemployment

Functional finance A budget philosophy aiming fiscal policy at achieving potential GDP rather than balancing budgets either annually or over the business cycle

G

Game theory A model that analyzes oligopolistic behavior as a series of strategic moves and countermoves by rival firms

GDP price index A comprehensive price index of all goods and services included in the gross domestic product

General Agreement on Tariffs and Trade (GATT) An international tariff-reduction treaty adopted in 1947 that resulted in a series of negotiated "rounds" aimed at freer trade; the Uruguay Round created GATT's successor, the World Trade Organization

Gold standard An arrangement whereby the currencies of most countries are convertible into gold at a fixed rate

Golden rule of profit maximization To maximize profit or minimize loss, a firm should produce at the level of output where marginal cost equals marginal revenue

Good A tangible item that is used to satisfy wants

Government budget A plan for government expenditures and revenues for a specified period, usually a year

Government budget deficit A flow variable that measures the amount by which total government expenditures exceed total government revenues in a particular period

Government debt A stock variable that measures the net accumulation of prior budget deficits

Government purchase function The relationship between government purchases and the level of income in the economy, other things constant

Government purchases Spending for goods and services by all levels of government

Gresham's Law People tend to trade away inferior money and hoard the best

Gross domestic product, or GDP The market value of all final goods and services produced by resources located in the United States, regardless of who owns those resources

H

Herfindahl index The sum of the squared percentage of market share of all firms in an industry; a measure of the level of concentration in that industry

Hidden actions A type of asymmetric information when one side of an economic relationship can take a relevant action that the other side cannot observe

Hidden characteristics A type of asymmetric information problem in which one side of the market knows more than the other side about characteristics that are important to the market exchange

Horizontal merger A merger in which one firm combines with another firm that produces the same product

Hyperinflation A very high rate of inflation

Hypothesis A statement about relationships among key variables

Hysteresis The argument that a long stretch of high (or low) unemployment can increase (or decrease) the natural rate of unemployment

I

Implementation lag The time needed to introduce a change in monetary or fiscal policy

Implicit cost A firm's opportunity cost of using its own resources or those provided by its owners without a corresponding cash payment

Import substitution A development strategy that emphasizes domestic manufacturing of products that are currently imported

Income approach A method of calculating GDP by adding up all payments to owners of resources used to produce output during the year

Income effect A fall in the price of a good increases consumers' real income, making them more able to purchase all goods, so the quantity demanded increases

Income elasticity of demand The percent change in demand (at a given price) divided by the percent change in income

Income-expenditure model A relationship between aggregate income and aggregate spending that determines, for a given price level, where income equals spending.

Increasing marginal returns Marginal product increases experienced by a firm when another unit of a particular resource is employed, all other resources constant

Increasing-cost industry An industry that faces higher per-unit production costs as industry output expands in the long run; the long-run industry supply curve slopes upward

Industrial policy The policy that government, using taxes, subsidies, and regulations, should nurture the industries and technologies of the future to give domestic industries an advantage over foreign competition

Industrial union A union of both skilled and unskilled workers from a particular industry, such as auto workers or steelworkers

Inelastic demand The type of demand that exists when a change in price has relatively little effect on quantity demanded; the percent change in quantity demanded is less than the percent change in price

Inferior good A good for which demand decreases as consumer income rises

Inflation A sustained increase in the economy's average price level

Injection Any payment of income other than by firms or any spending other than by domestic households; includes investment, government purchases, transfer payments, and exports

Innovation The process of turning an invention into a marketable product

Interest The dollar amount paid to lenders to forgo present consumption and imposed on borrowers; the payment resource owners receive for the use of their capital

Interest rate The amount of money paid per year to savers as a percentage of the amount saved; interest per year as a percentage of the amount loaned

Interlocking directorate An arrangement whereby one individual serves on the board of directors of competing firms

Intermediate goods and services Goods and services purchased for further reprocessing and resale

Inventories Producers' stocks of finished or in-process goods

Investment The purchase of new plants, equipment, buildings and net additions to inventories

Investment function The relationship between planned investment and the level of income, other things constant

K

Kinked demand curve A demand curve that illustrates price stickiness; if one firm cuts its prices, other firms in the industry will cut theirs as well, but if the firm raises its prices, other firms will not change theirs

L

Labor The physical and mental effort of humans used to produce goods and services

Labor force All noninstitutionalized individuals 16 years of age and older who are either working or actively looking for work

Labor force participation rate The ratio of the number in the labor force to the population of working age

Labor union A group of employees who join together to improve their terms of employment

Land Plots of ground and other natural resources used to produce goods and services

Law of comparative advantage The individual or country with the lowest opportunity cost of producing a particular good should specialize in producing that good.

Law of demand The quantity of a good demanded is inversely related to its price, other things constant

Law of diminishing marginal returns When more and more of a variable resource is added to a given amount of a fixed resource, the resulting change in output will eventually diminish and could become negative

Law of diminishing marginal utility The more of a good consumed per period, the smaller the increase in total utility from consuming one more unit, other things constant

Law of increasing opportunity cost As more of a particular good is produced, larger and larger quantities of an alternative good must be sacrificed if the economy's resources are already being used efficiently

Law of supply The quantity of product supplied in a given time period is usually directly related to its price, other things constant

Leakage Any diversion of income from the domestic spending stream; includes saving, taxes, and imports

Legal tender Anything that creditors are required to accept as payment for debts

Leisure Time spent on nonwork activities

Leveraged buyout The purchase of controlling interest in a corporation using borrowed funds

Liability Anything that is owed to another individual or institution

Line-item veto A provision to allow the president to reject particular portions of the budget rather than simply accept or reject the entire budget

Linear demand curve A straight-line demand curve

Liquidity A measure of the ease with which an asset can be converted into money without significant loss in its value

Loanable funds market The market in which savers (suppliers of funds) and borrowers (demanders of funds) come together to determine the market rate of interest

Logrolling Vote trading on preferred issues; voter A supports voter B's pet project as long as B supports A's pet project; a period during which all resources under the firm's control are variable

Long run A period during which all resources under the firm's control are viable; a period during which wage contracts and resource price agreements can be renegotiated

Long-run aggregate supply (LRAS) curve The vertical line drawn at potential output

Long-run average cost curve A curve that indicates the lowest average cost of production at each level of output when the firm's size is allowed to vary

Long-run industry supply curve A curve that shows the relationship between price and quantity supplied once firms fully adjust to any change in market demand

Long-run Phillips curve A vertical line drawn at the economy's natural rate of unemployment that traces equilibrium points that can occur when employers and workers have the time to adjust fully to any unexpected change in aggregate demand

Lorenz curve A curve showing the percentage of total income received by a given percentage of recipients whose incomes are arranged from smallest to largest

M

M1 A measure of the money supply consisting of currency and coins held by the nonbank public, checkable deposits, and travelers checks

M2 A monetary aggregate consisting of M1 plus savings deposits, small time deposits, and money market mutual funds

M3 A monetary aggregate consisting of M2 plus negotiable certificates of deposit

Macroeconomics The study of the economic behavior of entire economies

Managed float system An exchange rate system that combines features of freely floating rates with intervention by central banks

Marginal A term meaning "incremental" or "decremental," used to describe the result of a small change in an economic variable

Marginal cost The change in total cost resulting from a one-unit change in output; the change in total cost divided by the change in output

Marginal product The change in total product that occurs when the usage of a particular resource increases by one unit, all other resources constant

Marginal propensity to consume The fraction of a change in income that is spent on consumption; the change in consumption spending divided by the change in income that caused it

Marginal propensity to save The fraction of a change in income that is saved; the change in saving divided by the change in income that caused it

Marginal rate of return on investment The marginal revenue product of capital expressed as a percentage of its marginal cost

Marginal resource cost The change in total cost when an additional unit of a resource is hired, other things constant

Marginal revenue The change in total revenue resulting from a one-unit change in sales; in perfect competition, marginal revenue equals the market price

Marginal revenue product The change in total revenue when an additional unit of a resource is hired, other things constant

Marginal social benefit The sum of the marginal private benefit and the marginal external benefit of production or consumption

Marginal social cost The sum of the marginal private cost and the marginal external cost of production or consumption

Marginal utility The change in total utility derived from a one-unit change in consumption of a good

Marginal valuation The dollar value of the marginal utility derived from consuming each additional unit of a good

Market A set of arrangements through which buyers and sellers carry out exchange at mutually agreeable terms

Market failure A condition that arises when unrestrained operation of markets yields socially undesirable results

Market power The ability of one or more firms to maintain a price above the competitive level

Market structure Important features of a market, such as the number of firms, uniformity of product among firms, ease of entry, and forms of competition

Market work Time sold as labor in return for a money wage

Means-tested program To be eligible for such a program, an individual's income and/or assets must not exceed specified levels

Median income The middle income in a series of incomes ranked from smallest to largest

Median voter model Under certain conditions, the preference of the median, or middle, voter will dominate other public choices.

Medium of exchange Anything that facilitates trade by being generally accepted by all parties in payment for goods or services

Merchandise trade balance The value of a country's exported goods minus the value of its imported goods during a given time period

Microeconomics The study of the economic behavior in particular markets, such as the market for computers or for unskilled labor

Minimum efficient scale The lowest rate of output at which a firm takes full advantage of economies of scale

Mixed capitalist economy An economic system characterized by private ownership of some resources and public ownership of other resources. Some markets are unregulated and others are regulated.

Monetary aggregates Measures of the economy's money supply

Monetary policy Regulation of the money supply by the Fed in order to influence aggregate economic activity; the Fed's role in supplying money to the economy

Monetary theory The study of the effect of money on the economy

Money market mutual fund A collection of short-term interest-earning assets purchased with funds collected from many shareholders

Money multiplier The multiple by which the money supply increases as a result of an increase in excess reserves in the banking system

Money Anything that is generally acceptable in exchange for goods and services

Monopolistic competition A market structure characterized by a large number of firms selling products that are close substitutes yet different enough that each firm's demand curve slopes downward

Monopoly A sole producer of a product for which there are no good substitutes

Monopsonist The sole purchaser of a particular resource

Moral hazard A situation in which one party to a contract has an incentive after the contract is made to alter behavior in a way that harms the other party to the contract

N

National debt The net accumulation of federal budget deficits

Natural monopoly One firm that can serve the entire market at a lower per-unit cost than can two or more firms

Natural rate hypothesis The natural rate of unemployment is largely independent of the stimulus provided by monetary or fiscal policy

Natural rate of unemployment The unemployment rate that occurs when the economy is producing its potential level of output

Negative-sum game A game in which total losses exceed total winnings

Net domestic product Gross domestic product minus depreciation

Net export function The relationship between net exports and the level of income in the economy, other things constant

Net exports The value of a country's exports minus the value of its imports

Net taxes (NT) Taxes minus transfer payments

Net unilateral transfers The unilateral transfers (gifts and grants) received from abroad by residents of a country minus the unilateral transfers residents send abroad

Net wealth The value of a household's assets minus its liabilities

Net worth Assets minus liabilities

Nominal GDP GDP based on prices prevailing at the time of the transaction; current-dollar GDP

Nominal rate of interest The interest rate expressed in current dollars as a percentage of the amount loaned

Nominal wage The wage measured in terms of current dollars; the dollar amount on a paycheck

Nonmarket work Time spent producing goods and services in the home or acquiring an education

Normal good A good for which demand increases as consumer income rises

Normal profit The accounting profit required to induce a firm's owners to employ their resources in the firm; the accounting profit earned when all resources used by the firm earn their opportunity cost

Normative economic statement A statement that represents an opinion, which cannot be proved or disproved

O

Official reserve transactions account The section of a country's balance of payments account that reflects the flow of gold, Special Drawing Rights, and currencies among central banks; the sum of the current account and the capital account balances

Oligopoly A market structure characterized by a small number of firms whose behavior is interdependent

Open-access resource A type of resource that is difficult or costly to exclude individuals from using

Open-market operations Purchases and sales of government securities by the Federal Reserve in an effort to influence the money supply

Opportunity cost The value of the best alternative foregone when an item or activity is chosen

Other-things-constant assumption The assumption, when focusing on key economic variables, that other variables remain unchanged

P

Partnership A firm with multiple owners who share the firm's profits and each of whom bears unlimited liability for the firm's debts

Passive approach The view that the private sector is relatively stable and able to absorb economic shocks without discretionary government policy

Patent A legal barrier to entry that conveys to its holder the exclusive right to supply a product for a certain period of time

Payoff matrix In game theory, a table listing the payoffs that each player can expect based on the strategy that each player pursues

Per se illegality A category of illegality in antitrust law, applied to business practices that are deemed illegal regardless of their economic rationale or their consequences

Per-worker production function The relationship between the amount of capital per worker in the economy and the output per worker

Perfect competition A market structure in which there are large numbers of fully informed buyers and sellers of a homogeneous product, with no obstacles to entry or exit of firms in the long run

Perfectly discriminating monopolist A monopolist who charges a different price for each unit of the good

Perfectly elastic demand curve A horizontal line reflecting a situation in which any price increase reduces quantity demanded to zero; the elasticity value is minus infinity

Perfectly elastic supply curve A horizontal line reflecting a situation in which any price decrease reduces the quantity supplied to zero; the elasticity value is infinity

Perfectly inelastic demand curve A vertical line reflecting a situation in which price change has no effect on the quantity demanded; the elasticity value is zero

Perfectly inelastic supply curve A vertical line reflecting a situation in which a price change has no effect on the quantity supplied; the elasticity value is zero

Permanent income Income that individuals expect to receive on average over the long term

Phillips curve A curve showing possible combinations of the inflation rate and the unemployment rate

Physical capital Manufactured items used to produce goods and services

Planned investment The amount of investment firms plan to undertake during a year

Political business cycles Economic fluctuations that result when discretionary policy is manipulated for political gain

Portfolio An individual's collection of stocks, bonds, and other financial investments.

Positive economic statement A statement that can be proven or disproven by reference to facts

Positive rate of time preference A characteristic of consumers, who value present consumption more highly than future consumption

Positive-sum game A game in which total winnings exceed total losses

Potential output The economy's maximum sustainable output level, given the supply of resources, technology, and the underlying economic institutions; the output level when there are no surprises about the price level

Predatory pricing Pricing tactics employed by a dominant firm to drive competitors out of business, such as temporarily selling below cost and dropping the price only in certain markets

Present value The value today of a payment or payments to be received in the future

Price ceiling A maximum legal price above which a good or service cannot be sold

Price discrimination Selling the same good for different prices to different consumers as a way to increase profit

Price elasticity formula Percent change in quantity divided by the percent change in price; the average quantity and the average price are used as bases for computing percent changes in quantity and in price

Price elasticity of demand A measure of the responsiveness of quantity demanded to a price change; the percent change in quantity demanded divided by the percent change in price

Price elasticity of supply A measure of the responsiveness of quantity supplied to a price change; the percent change in quantity supplied divided by the percent change in price

Price floor A minimum legal price below which a good or service cannot be sold

Price leader A firm whose price is adopted by the rest of the industry

Price level A composite measure reflecting the prices of all goods and services in the economy relative to prices in a base year

Price searcher A firm that has some control over the price it charges because its demand curve slopes downward

Price taker A firm that faces a given market price and whose actions have no effect on that market price

Principal A person who enters into a contractual agreement with an agent in the expectation that the agent will act on behalf of the principal

Principal-agent problem A situation in which the agent's objectives differ from those of the principal and the agent can pursue hidden actions

Private property rights The right of an owner to use or to exchange property

Privatization The process of turning public enterprises into private enterprises

Producer surplus The amount by which total revenue from production exceeds total variable cost

Product market A market in which goods and services are exchanged

Production possibilities frontier A curve showing all alternative combinations of goods that can be produced when available resources are used efficiently

Productive efficiency The condition that exists when output is produced with the least-cost combination of inputs, given the level of technology

Productivity The ratio of a specific measure of output to a specific measure of input

Profit The return resource owners receive for their entrepreneurial ability; the total revenue from sales minus the total cost of resources employed by the entrepreneur

Public good A good that is available for all to consume, regardless of who pays and who does not

Purchasing power parity theory Exchange rates between two countries will adjust in the long run to reflect price level differences between the countries

Pure capitalism An economic system characterized by private ownership of resources and the use of prices to coordinate economic activity in unregulated markets

Q

Quantity theory of money If the velocity of money is stable or at least predictable, then changes in the money supply have predictable effects on nominal income

Quota A legal limit on the quantity of a particular product that can be imported or exported

R

Rational expectations A school of thought that claims people form expectations based on all available information, including the probable future actions of government policymakers

Rational ignorance A stance adopted by voters when they find that the costs of understanding and voting on a particular issue exceed the expected benefits of doing so

Real business cycle theory Fluctuations in real GDP and employment are caused not by misguided monetary policy but by real shocks to the economy, such as changes in tastes and in technology

Real GDP A measure of GDP that removes the impact of price changes from changes in nominal GDP

Real income Income measured in terms of the goods and services it can buy

Real rate of interest The interest rate expressed in dollars of constant purchasing power as a percentage of the amount loaned; the nominal rate of interest minus the inflation rate

Real wage The wage measured in terms of dollars of constant purchasing power; hence, the wage measured in terms of the quantity of goods and services it will purchase

Recession A period of decline in total output usually lasting at least six months and marked by contractions in many sectors of the economy

Recognition lag The time needed to identify a macroeconomic problem and assess its seriousness

Recycling The process of converting waste products into reusable material

Relevant resources Resources used to produce the good in question

Renewable resource A resource that can regenerate itself and so can be used periodically for an indefinite length of time

Rent seeking Activities undertaken by individuals or firms to influence public policy in a way that will directly or indirectly redistribute income to them

Rent The payment resource owners receive for the use of their land

Required reserve ratio The ratio of reserves to deposits that banks are required, by regulation, to hold

Required reserves The dollar amount of reserves a bank is legally required to hold

Reserves Funds that banks use to satisfy the cash demands of their customers and the reserve requirements of the Fed; reserves consist of deposits at the Fed plus currency physically held by banks

Resource market A market in which resources are exchanged

Resource price searcher A firm that faces an upward-sloping supply curve for a resource

Resource price taker A firm that faces a constant market price for a resource; the firm can buy any amount of the resource without affecting the resource price

Rule of reason A principle used by a court to examine the reasons for certain business practices and their effects on competition before ruling on their legality

S

Saving function The relationship between saving and the level of income in the economy, other things constant

Savings deposits Deposits that earn interest but have no specific maturity date

Scarce When the amount people desire exceeds the amount available at a zero price

Screening The process used by employers to select the most qualified workers based on readily observable characteristics, such as level of education

Seasonal unemployment Unemployment caused by seasonal shifts in labor supply and demand

Secondary effects Unintended consequences of economic actions that develop slowly over time as people react to events

Seigniorage The difference between the face value of money and the cost of supplying it; the "profit" from issuing money

Separation of ownership from control The situation that exists when no single stockholder or unified group of stockholders owns enough shares to control the management of a corporation

Service An intangible activity that is used to satisfy wants

Short run A period during which some resource prices, especially those for labor, are fixed by agreement; a period during which at least one of a firm's resources is fixed

Short-run aggregate supply (SRAS) curve A curve that shows the direct relationship between the price level and the quantity of aggregate output supplied in the short run, other things constant.

Short-run firm supply curve A curve that indicates the quantity a firm supplies at each price in the short run; that portion of a firm's marginal cost curve that intersects and rises above the low point on its average variable cost curve

Short-run industry supply curve A curve that indicates the quantity all firms in an industry supply at each price in the short run; the horizontal sum of each firm's short-run supply curve

Short-run Phillips curve A curve, based on an expected price level, that reflects an inverse relation between the inflation rate and the level of unemployment

Shortage An excess of quantity demanded over quantity supplied at a given price

Signaling Using a proxy measure to communicate information about unobservable characteristics

Simple money multiplier The reciprocal of the required reserve ratio, or $1/r$

Simple spending multiplier The ratio of a change in equilibrium real GDP demanded to the initial change in expenditure that brought it about; the numerical value of the multiplier is $1/(1 - MPC)$

Social regulation Government measures aimed at improving health and safety

Soft budget constraint The budget condition faced by socialist enterprises that lose money and then are subsidized

Sole proprietorship A firm with a single owner who has the right to all profits and who bears unlimited liability for the firm's debts

Special-interest legislation Legislation that generates concentrated benefits but imposes widespread costs

Specialization of labor Focusing an individual's efforts on a particular product or a single task

Speculator A person who buys or sells foreign exchange in hopes of profiting from fluctuations in the exchange rate over time

Stagflation A contraction, or **stag**nation, of a nation's output accompanied by in**flation**

Standard of deferred payment An agreed unit of measure that enables people to contract for future payments and receipts

Stock A certificate reflecting ownership of a corporation; a variable that measures the amount of something at a particular point in time, such as the amount of money you have right now

Store of value Anything that retains its purchasing power over time

Strategy In game theory, the operational plan pursued by a player; for example, one strategy is to avoid the worst outcome

Strike A union's attempt to withhold labor from a firm

Strong version of the natural rate hypothesis The short-run gains in employment resulting from monetary or fiscal surprises diminish as the public comes to expect as much

Structural unemployment Unemployment that arises because (1) the skills demanded by employers do not match the skills of the unemployed, or (2) the unemployed do not live where the jobs are located

Substitutes Goods that are related in such a way that an increase in the price of one leads to an increase in the demand for the other

Substitution effect When the price of a good falls, consumers will substitute it for other goods, which are now relatively more expensive

Sunk Cost A cost that must be incurred no matter what; hence, a cost that is irrelevant when an economic choice is being made

Supply A relation showing the quantities of a good producers are willing and able to sell at various prices during a given time period, other things constant

Supply curve A curve showing the quantities of a good supplied at various prices, other things constant

Supply of loanable funds The relationship between the market rate of interest and the quantity of savings supplied to the economy, other things constant

Supply shocks Unexpected events that affect aggregate supply, usually only temporarily

Supply-side economics Macroeconomic policy that focuses on increasing aggregate supply through tax cuts or other changes to increase incentives to produce

Surplus An excess of quantity supplied over quantity demanded at a given price

T

Tariff A tax on imports or exports

Tastes A consumer's preferences for different goods and services

Tax incidence The distribution of tax burden among taxpayers

Tender offer An offer to buy a controlling number (i.e., more than half) of a firm's shares

Term structure of interest rates The relationship between the duration of a loan and the interest rate charged

Terms of trade How much of one good exchanges for a unit of another good

Thrift institutions, or thrifts Depository institutions that make long-term loans primarily to households

Time deposits Deposits that earn a fixed rate of interest if held for the specified period, which can range anywhere from several months to several years

Time inconsistency problem The problem that arises when policymakers have an incentive to announce one policy to influence expectations but then to pursue a different policy once those expectations have been formed and acted upon

Token money The name given to money whose face value exceeds the cost of producing it

Total cost The sum of fixed cost and variable cost; the opportunity cost of all resources employed by the firm

Total product The total output produced by a firm

Total revenue Price multiplied by the quantity sold at that price

Total utility The total satisfaction a consumer derives from consumption

Total wage bill Employment multiplied by the average wage rate

Transaction costs The costs of time and information required to carry out market exchange

Transactions demand for money The demand for money to support the exchange of goods and services

Transfer payments Cash or in-kind benefits given to individuals as outright grants from the government

Tying contract An arrangement in which a seller of one good requires buyers to purchase other goods as well

U

Underemployment A situation in which workers are overqualified for their jobs or work fewer hours than they would prefer

Underground economy An expression used to describe all market exchange that goes unreported either because it is illegal or because those involved want to evade taxes

Unemployment insurance Temporary income provided to unemployed workers who actively seek employment and who meet other qualifications

Unemployment rate The number of unemployed individuals expressed as a percentage of the labor force

Unit of account A common unit for measuring the value of every good or service

Unit-elastic demand The type of demand that exists when a percent change in price causes an equal (but of opposite sign) percent change in quantity demanded; the elasticity value is minus one

Unit-elastic supply A percent change in price causes an identical percent change in quantity supplied; depicted by a supply curve that is a straight line through the origin; the elasticity value is one

Utility The satisfaction received from consuming a good or service or a collection of goods and services; satisfaction, sense of well-being

V

Value added The difference at each stage of production between the value of a product and cost of intermediate goods bought from other firms

Variable A measure, such as price or quantity, that can take on different possible values.

Variable cost Any production cost that increases as output increases

Variable resource Any resource that can be varied in the short run to increase or decrease the level of output

Variable technology A technology whose externality can be reduced by altering the production process rather than simply by altering the rate of output

Velocity of money The average number of times per year a dollar is used to purchase final goods and services

Vertical integration The expansion of a firm into stages of production earlier or later than those in which it has specialized

Vertical merger A merger in which one firm combines with another from which it purchases inputs or to which it sells output

W

Wages The payment resource owners receive for their labor

Weak version of the natural rate hypothesis Policymakers can trade off between unemployment and inflation in the short run but not in the long run

Winner's curse The plight of the winning bidder for an asset of uncertain value who has overestimated the asset's true value

World price The price at which a good or service is traded internationally; it is determined by the world supply and demand for a product

World Trade Organization (WTO) The legal and institutional foundation of the multilateral trading system that succeeded GATT in 1995

Z

Zero-sum game A game in which total winnings just equal total losses

Index

Note: The letter *d* after an entry indicates marginal *definition; e* indicates *exhibit; i* indicates *Internet address.*

A

Absolute advantage, 29*d,* 29–30
Account(s)
  capital, 777*d,* 777–778, 779*e*
  current, balance on, 777*d*
  negotiable order of withdrawal (NOW), 301
  official reserve transactions, 778*d*
  statistical discrepancy, 778
  unit of, 278*d*
Accounting, national income. *See* National
  income accounting system
Accounting profit, 449*d*
Actual investment, 182*d*
ADSA. *See* American Dairy Science
  Association
Advanced Research Project Agency (ARPA),
  122, 123*i*
Adverse selection, 649*d*
AFDC. *See* Aid to Families with Dependent
  Children
Affirmative action, 735–736
AFL. *See* American Federation of Labor
Agency for International Development (AID),
  812
Agent, 649*d*
Aggregate demand, 98*d,* 98–101, 101*e*
  during Great Depression, 102*e*
  money supply and
    changes in, 324–326, 325*e*
    direct channel to, 330–335
    indirect channel to, 321–330
Aggregate demand curve, 99*d,* 99–100, 100*e*
  and aggregate expenditure function, 216*e,*
    218*e*
  shifts in
    inflation and, 141, 142*e*
    price level changes and, 215–219, 216*e,*
     218*e*
  slope of, money and, 326–328, 327*e*
Aggregate expenditure, 155*d*
  in circular flow, 181–182
  components of, 154–155, 156*e,* 206–207
  consumption part of, 183–191. *See also*
    Consumption
  exports part of, 197–198. *See also* Net
    exports
  government purchases and, 197
  income and, 206–215
  increase in, effect of, 210–211, 211*e*

investment part of, 191–196. *See also*
  Investment
Aggregate expenditure function, 207*d*
  and aggregate demand curve, 216*e,* 218*e*
  algebra for, 227
  construction of, 206–207
  net exports and, 224*e*
  shifts in, effect of, 210–215, 217–219, 218*e,*
    225*e,* 226
Aggregate income, 156*d*
  in circular flow, 179, 812
Aggregate output, 98*d. See also* Gross domestic
  product
  demanded, equilibrium of. *See* Equilibrium,
    of real GDP demanded
Aggregate supply, 98–101, 101*e*
  changes in, factors leading to, 244–248,
    245*e*–246*e*
  and demand, equilibrium of, 100–101, 101*e*
  fiscal policy and, 267
  and labor supply, 231, 245
  long-run, 236–244
  short-run, 231–236
    and money supply, 328–329, 329*e*
Aggregate supply curve, 100*d,* 101*e*
  long-run, 241*d,* 241*e,* 241–242
  shifts in, inflation and, 141, 142*e*
  short-run, 235*d,* 235–236, 236*e. See also*
    Short-run aggregate supply (SRAS)
    curve
Agricultural Economics, 413*i*
Agriculture
  case study: *Farm Subsidies: A Negative-Sum
    Game,* 685–688
  case study: *The Demand for Food and "The
    Farm Problem,"* 412–414
AIA. *See* American Institute of Architects
AID. *See* Agency for International
  Development
Aid
  foreign, 811–814, 812*d*
  government subsidies, 171
Aid to Families with Dependent Children
  (AFDC), 69, 728–729, 738–740, 739*e*
Airbus Industrie, 122
Airline Deregulation Act, 665
Airlines, 118, 394, 535, 665–666
Air Transport Association (ATA), 665*i*
Alcoa (Aluminum Company of America), 517,
  669

Algeria, 72
Allocative efficiency, 495*d,* 495–496
Alternative goods, 53*d*
Aluminum Company of America (Alcoa), 517,
  669
American Airlines, 535*i*
American Architectural Foundation, 564*i*
American Association of Political Consultants,
  690*i*
American Coin-Op Services, 10*i*
American Dairy Science Association (ADSA),
  686*i*
American Federation of Labor (AFL), 594,
  594*i*
American Gem Society, 505*i*
American Institute of Architects (AIA), 564*i*
America's Labor Market Information System
  (ALMIS), 231*i*
AMI. *See* Auction Marketing Institute
Analysis. *See* Economic analysis
Andreessen, Mark, 38
Annually balanced budget, 374*d*
Annuity, 627*d*
Antitrust activity, 657*d*
  and mergers, 668–671
  origins of, 667–668
Antitrust legislation
  and economic competition, 673
  enforcement of, 668
  interpretation of, 669
  problems with, 673–674
Apple Computer, Inc., 6*i,* 6–7, 611
Applied research, 118*d*
Appreciation, 780*d*
Arbitrageur, 784*d*
Architecture industry, 564–565
Argentina's Ministry of Economy and Public
  Works and Services, 332*i*
ARPA. *See* Advanced Research Project
  Agency
ARS Data, Ltd., 589*i*
The Art Bin, 178*i*
Asset, 301*d*
Association-is-causation fallacy, 11*d,* 17
Assumptions
  behavioral, 8*d*
  other-things-constant, 8*d,* 16–17
Asymmetric information, 300*d,* 647*d*
  case study: *The Reputation of a Big Mac,*
    652–653

Asymmetric information (*continued*)
  coping with, 650, 652
  in labor markets, 650–652
  types of, 648–650
ATA. *See* Air Transport Association
Atlantic Monthly, 263*i*
AT&T, 123, 506, 522, 585*i*
Auction(s)
  double continuous, 498
  Dutch, 486
  English open outcry, 486
Auction Marketing Institute (AMI), 486*i*
Auction Web, 486*i*
Australia
  central bank in, 355
  comparable worth policies in, 585
Autarky, 748*d*
AutoDesk, Inc., 564*i*
Automatic stabilizers, 264*d*, 264–265
Automatic teller machines, 290, 301–302
Automobile industry, 71
  case study: *The World of Automobiles,* 84–85
Autonomous, 194*d*
Autonomous investment function, 194, 195*e*
Autonomous net tax multiplier, 258*d*
  algebra for, 273–275
Average fixed cost, 456, 457*e*
  marginal cost and, 456–459, 457*e*–458*e*
Average revenue, 479*d*
Average total cost, 456, 457*e*
  marginal cost and, 456–459, 457*e*–458*e*
Average variable cost, 456, 457*e*
  marginal cost and, 456–459, 457*e*–458*e*

B

Backward-bending supply curve, 580*d,*
  580–581, 581*e*
Balanced budget amendment, 389*d*
Balanced budget multiplier, 259*d,* 259–260,
  274
Balance of payments, 83*d*
  international transactions and, 775–780, 779*e*
Balance on current account, 777*d*
Balance on goods and services, 776–777, 777*d*
Balance sheet, 304*d,* 304*e*
  consolidated, 306*e,* 306–307
Bank(s). *See also* Banking; Depository
    institutions; Financial intermediaries
  balance sheets of, 304*e,* 306*e*
  case study: *Central Bank Independence and
    Price Stability,* 355
  commercial, 284*d*
  Federal Reserve. *See* Federal Reserve System
  formation of, 303–304
  investment by, restrictions on, 289
  liquidity of, versus profitability of, 305–306
  national, 285
  reserves of, 304–305
  role of, 300, 303
  state, 284–285
Bank holding company, 289*d,* 289–290

Banking. *See also* Bank(s)
  branching restrictions on, 289–290
  case study: *Banking on the Net,* 313–314
  deregulation of, 291–292
  dual, development of, 284–285
  Federal Reserve and, 285–289. *See also*
    Federal Reserve System
  fractional reserve system of, 281*d*
  Great Depression and, 286–287
  and money creation, 280–281, 309–317
  and money supply, 300–303
  origins of, 280–281
  problems with, in 1990s, 290–294, 293*e*
  Roosevelt's reforms in, 287–289
Banking Act (1933), 287–289
Banking Act (1935), 287–289
Bank notes, 281*d*
Barriers to entry, 504*d*
  case study: *The Unfriendly Skies,* 535
  and monopoly, 504–505
  and oligopoly, 534–537, 536*e*
  technological change and, 506
  types of, 504–505
Barro, Robert, 387–388
Barter, 30*d,* 277, 283
Base year, 162*d*
  price level and, 99
Basic research, 118*d*
BEA. *See* Budget Enforcement Act
Behavioral assumption, 8*d,* 10
Belgium, national debt of, 384, 385*e*
Big-bang approach, to economic transition, 817
Big Mac Index
  case study: *Big Mac Index,* 785
Bilateral monopoly, 603–605, 604*d,* 604*e*
Binding arbitration, 596*d*
Birth rates, economic development and,
  803–805, 804*e*
Bleeker, Marco, 706*i*
Blockbuster Video, 531*i*
Bond, 629*d*
Bounded rationality, 640*d*
Brain drain, 811
Brazil, 51
  case study: *Hyperinflation in Brazil,* 140–141
  monetary system in, failure of, 283
Brazilian Embassy in London, 140*i*
Bretton Woods agreement, 792–793
Broadway, 602*i*
Brown, Donald E., 633
Brunei, Sultan of, 27–28
Budget. *See also* Federal budget process
  annually balanced, 374*d*
  cyclically balanced, 374*d*
Budget Battle Index, 377*i*
Budget deficit, 103*d*. *See also* Federal budget
  deficit
Budget Enforcement Act (BEA), 375, 388
Budget line, 441*e,* 441–442
  and indifference curves, 442, 442*e*
The Budget of the United States Government, 389*i*
Bundesbank, 355

Bureau of Economic Analysis, 159*i*
Bureau of Engraving and Printing, 308*i*
Bureau of Labor Statistics, 159*i*
Bureau of the Census, 159*i,* 413*i*
Bureaus, 692*d,* 692–695
Bush, George, 12, 148, 255, 269, 348, 349*i,* 375
Business cycles, 93
  political, 269*d*
  real, theory of, 363*d,* 363–364

C

CAASD. *See* Center for Advanced Aviation
    System Development
CAB. *See* Civil Aeronautics Board
Campeau, Robert, 633–634
Capital, 2*d*
  formation (deepening) of, 115
    crowding out and, 386–387
  human, 2, 111, 126
  physical, 2, 111–112, 154*d*
  and productivity, 112–113, 115
  realized gain of, 74*d*
  and technological innovation, 118
Capital account, 777*d,* 777–778, 779*e*
Capitalism
  laissez-faire, 38–39
  mixed, 39–40
  pure, 38*d,* 38–39
  versus socialist economy, 814–816
  venture, 589
Capital Quest, 589*i*
Capture theory of regulation, 661–662
CarMag: Internet CarMagazine Japan, 84*i*
Cartel, 537*d,* 537–539, 538*e*
Carter, Jimmy, 148–149
Case Western Reserve University, 736*i*
Cash transfers, 69
Castro, Fidel, 816
Caterpillar, 597–598
Cato Institute, 694*i*
Causality
  versus association, 11*d,* 17
  slope and, 19
Celler-Kefauver Anti-Merger Act, 668
Center for Advanced Aviation System
    Development (CAASD), 118*i*
Chain-weighted system, 165–166
  index development in, 174*e,* 174–176
Chamberlin, Edward, 527, 533
Change in demand, 48*e,* 50*d*
Change in quantity demanded, 50*d*
Change in quantity supplied, 53*d*
Change in supply, 52*e,* 53*d*
Checkable deposits, 301*d*
China, 801*e,* 804*e,* 806
  gradualism in, 817–818
Choice, 37. *See also* Public choice
  analyses of
    indifference curve, 438–446
    marginal utility, 420–435
  conditions for making, 7

individual, 4
and opportunity cost, 26–28
Chronicle of Higher Education, 26i
CIA World Factbook, 283i
CineMedia, 462i
CIO. *See* Congress of Industrial Organizations
CIO Magazine, 404i
Circular flow, 179–183, 180e
  expenditure half of, 179–181, 180e
  income half of, 179–181, 180e
  simple spending multiplier and, 212–213, 213e
Civil Aeronautics Board (CAB), 665i, 665–666
Classical economists, 178d
Clayton Act (1914), 668
Clean Air Act (1970), 712–713
Clean Water Act (1972), 712
Clinton, Bill, 105–106, 117, 122, 221, 255, 269, 348, 349i, 375–376, 597, 673, 740–741
Coase, Ronald, 638–639, 707–708
Coase theorem, 707d
Coins, 279–280
Cold turkey, 354d
Collective bargaining, 596d
Colligan, Paul, 387
Collusion, 76d
  oligopoly and, 537–540
Columbia University, Bartleby Library, 349i
Command economy, 39d
Commercial banks, 284d
Commodity money, 278d, 278–279
Common Cause, 690i
Common markets, 764–765
Common-pool problem, 699d
  case study: *City in the Clouds,* 713
  case study: *Destruction of the Tropical Rain Forest,* 705–707
  and negative externalities, 700–703
  solutions to, 703–705
    Coase analysis, 707–708
    pollution rights, 707–708
Comparable worth, 584–586, 585d
Comparative advantage, 29d, 29–30
  in international trade, 748–750
Competing-interest legislation, 685d
Competition
  government role in, 76
  monopolistic. *See* Monopolistic competition
  perfect. *See* Perfect competition
  in U.S., 671–674, 672e
Complements, 48d
  and cross-price elasticity of demand, 415
  and resource demand, 563–564
Comprehensive Environmental Response, Compensation, and Liability Act (1980), 715
Computer industry
  case study: *Computer Prices and GDP Estimation,* 165–166
  case study: *Computers and Productivity,* 120–121

case study: *Marginal Analysis in the Computer Industry,* 6–7
Concentration ratio, 669d, 669–670
Concord Coalition, 377i
Conglomerate mergers, 546d
Congress of Industrial Organizations (CIO), 594i, 595
The Connecticut Economy, 215i
Consent decree, 668d
Conservative Generation X, 387i
Constant-cost industry, 492d
Consulate General of Israel, 332i
Consumer equilibrium, 426d
  derivation of, 442e, 442–443
  and income, changes in, 443, 443e
  and price, changes in, 443–445, 444e–445e
Consumer price index (CPI), 99, 142d, 143e, 162d
  development of, 162–163, 163e
  problems with, 163–164
Consumer surplus, 429–431, 430d, 430e
  case study: *The Marginal Value of Free Medical Care,* 432–433
  in competitive market, 496, 496e
  international trade and, 755–757, 756e
  market demand and, 431e, 431–432, 432e
Consumption, 154d, 183–191
  case study: *The Life-Cycle Hypothesis,* 190–191
  case study: *Variability of Consumption and Investment,* 195–196
  expectations and, 190
  income and, 22e, 22–24, 23e, 183e, 183–184, 184e. *See also* Consumption function
  interest rate and, 190
  net wealth and, 188–189
  present, versus future, 618, 625–628
  price level and, 189–190
  and saving, 618–619
  taxes and, 197
  transfer payments and, 197
Consumption function, 184–185, 185d, 185e
  and income, changes in, 189
  shifts in, 188–190, 189e
    versus movement along, 189
  slope of, MPC and, 187, 187e
Consumption possibilities frontier, 748–750, 749d, 749e
Contestable markets, 514d, 514–515
Continuing resolutions, 371d
Contractionary gap, 239e, 240d, 242
  closing of, approaches to, 344e, 344–345
  fiscal policy and, 260–261, 261e
Convergence, theory of, 126d
Cooperative Media Group, 121i
Coordination failure, 242d
Cornell University, Mann Library, 413i
Corporate profits, 173d
Corporation, 74d, 74–75
  control of, market for, 632–634
  financing of, 268–630

management of, constraints on, 631–632
ownership of, 630–631
  separation from control of, 631d
S, 74–75
Cost(s)
  average, 456, 457e
    constant, 463
    long-run. *See* Long-run average cost curve
    marginal cost and, 456–459, 457e–458e
  changes in, output-potential ratio and, 233–235
  explicit, 448d
  fixed, 453d, 455e, 455–456
    average. *See* Cost(s), average
    and loss minimization, 480–481
  implicit, 448d
  in long run, 459–464
  marginal, 454d, 454e, 454–455, 455e, 455–456
    average cost and, 456–459, 457e–458e
    marginal revenue and, 478e, 479, 481–482, 482e
  and oligopoly, 536–537
  opportunity. *See* Opportunity cost
  public, distribution of, 685–688
  resource, marginal, 561d, 561–563, 562e, 566–568, 567e
  in short run, 453–459
  social, marginal, 700e, 700–703, 701d, 702e, 704e
  sunk, 28d. *See also* Cost(s), fixed
  total, 453–454, 454d, 454e–455e, 455–456
    average. *See* Cost(s), average
  transaction, 54d. *See also* Transaction costs
  variable, 453d, 455e, 455–456
    average. *See* Cost(s), average
Cost-of-living adjustments, 144
Cost-plus pricing, 540d, 540–541
Cost-push inflation, 141d, 142e
Cottage industry system, 70
Council of Economic Advisers, 103, 370–371
Counterfeiting, 307
Coupon, 629
CPI. *See* Consumer price index
Craft union(s), 594d, 600
Crane & Company, 307
Cross-price elasticity of demand, 415d
Cross-subsidization, 664d
Crowding in, 380d
Crowding out, 380d
  capital formation and, 386–387
Cuba, 40, 816
Cubaweb, 815i
Currency appreciation, 780d
Currency depreciation, 160d, 780d
Currency devaluation, 790d, 790–791
Currency revaluation, 790d
Current account, balance on, 777d
Cyclically balanced budget, 374d
Cyclical majority, 682d, 682–683, 683e
Cyclical unemployment, 138d

D

Dairy industry, 686–688
Deadweight loss, 516d, 517–518
De Beers Consolidated Mines, 505–506
Decision-making lag, 347d
Decreasing-cost industry, 494d, 494e, 494–495
Defense industry, 122–123
Deferred payment, standard of, 279d
Deficit. See Federal budget deficit; Trade
    deficit
Deflation, 141d
  gold supplies and, 792
Delta Airlines, 394, 394i, 535i
Demand, 44d, 44–47
  aggregate. See Aggregate demand
  changes in, 48e, 50d
    case study: The Market for Professional
        Basketball, 60–61
    factors affecting, 47–50
    impact of, 57e, 57–58, 59e, 59–61, 61e
    and long-run market adjustment,
        488–491, 489e–490e
  cross-price elasticity of, 415d
  derived, 552d, 564–565
  elastic, 396d. See also Cross-price elasticity of
        demand; Income elasticity of demand;
        Price elasticity of demand
  individual, versus market, 47
  inelastic, 396d
  law of, 44d, 44–47
  for loanable funds, 622–623, 623d, 624e
  market, versus individual, 47
  under perfect competition, 475–476, 476e
  versus quantity demanded, 46, 50
  for resources, 551, 552e, 552–553. See also
        Resource demand
  time and, 433–434
  versus wants, 44
Demand curve, 18e, 45–46, 46d, 46e
  aggregate. See Aggregate demand curve
  constant-elasticity, 398–400, 399e
  derivation of, 443–444, 444e
  for investment, 192–193, 193e–194e
  kinked, 542–545, 543d, 543e–544e
  linear, 397d, 397–398
  in monopolistic competition, 528, 529e,
        532, 533e
  in monopoly, 506, 507e
  in perfect competition, 532, 533e
  perfectly elastic, 399d, 399e
  perfectly inelastic, 399d, 399e
  shifts in, 21–22, 22e
Demand deposits, 284d
Demand for loanable funds, 622–623, 623d,
    624e
Demand-management policy, 265
Demand-pull inflation, 141d, 142e
Demand schedule, 45–46, 46e
Demand-side economics, 103d
Demand
  direct, 680–683

representative, 683–691
  and bureaucracy, 692–695
Department of Commerce, 389i
Department of the Treasury, 280i
Dependent variable, 17, 19
Depository institutions, 284d. See also Bank(s);
    Banking
  recent problems with, 290–294
    case study: Easy Money, Empty Buildings,
        292–293
  until 1970s, 290
Deposits
  checkable, 301d
  demand, 284d
  savings, 302d
  time, 302d
  types of, 301–303
Depreciation, 160d, 780d
Depression, 93d. See also Great Depression
Deregulation
  case study: Airline Regulation and Deregulation,
        665–666
  case study: Rail and Truck Regulation and
        Deregulation, 662–664
  and economic competition, 672–673
Derived demand, 552d
  case study: The Derived Demand for Architects,
        564–565
Devaluation, 790d
  case study: Mexico's Peso Problem, 790–791
Developing countries, 799d. See also
    Transitional economies
  education in, 806, 807e
  financial institutions in, 808
  GDP in, 799–801, 801e–802e
  government practices in, 808–809
  health in, 801–803
  international trade and, 809–811
  labor productivity in, 805
  labor use in, 806–808
  population growth in, 800, 801e, 803–805,
        804e
  women in, 805
Development. See Economic development
DI. See Disposable income
Diminishing marginal returns, 451e, 468e,
    469
  law of, 112, 252, 450–453, 452d
Direct democracy, 680–683
Direct relation, between variables, 18
Discounting, 625d, 625–627
  case study: The Million-Dollar Lottery,
        627–628
Discount rate, 286d, 625d
  and money creation, 316–317
Discouraged worker, 132d
Discretionary fiscal policy, 264d, 264–266. See
    also Fiscal policy
  case study: Discretionary Policy and Presidential
        Elections, 269
  versus natural market forces, 344–346
Discrimination, and poverty, 734–736

Diseconomies of scale, 461–462, 462d
  case study: At the Movies, 462–463
  case study: Billions and Billions of Burgers, 464
  and long-run average cost, 463e, 465
  in management of firm, 640–641
Disequilibrium, 61d
  case study: Toys Are Serious Business, 63–64
  of prices, 61–64
  of real GDP, 209
Disinflation, 141d
Disinvestment, 154
Disposable income (DI), 172, 172e, 179d
  in circular flow, 179–182, 180e
  and consumption, 183e, 183–184, 184e,
        185
  and imports, 202e, 202–203
  and investment, 193–194
  and marginal propensity to consume and
        save, 186e–187e
  and saving, 183, 183e
Distribution question, 38
Diversification, risk minimization and, 300
Division of labor, 30–32, 31d
Double coincidence of wants, 277d
Dumping, 763d, 766–767
Duopoly, 541d

E

Earned income tax credit, 729
Earnings, retained, 629
Economic actors
  firms as, 70–75
  foreign countries as, 82–85
  government as, 76–82
  households as, 4, 68–70
  types of, 4
Economic analysis
  as art, 5–7, 9
  case study: A Yen for Vending Machines,
        9–10
  fallacies of, 11–12
  marginal, 5–7
  normative, 10–11
  positive, 10–11
  as science, 7–12
  theory in, 7–8, 91–92
Economic competition
  government role in, 76
  in U.S., 671–674, 672e
Economic development
  factors determining, 805–809, 820–821
  foreign aid and, 811–814
  institutions and, 816–820
  intercountry differences in, 799–805
  international trade and, 809–811
  transitional economies and, 814–816
Economic fluctuations, 93d, 94e
  analysis of, 93–97
  case study: The Global Economy, 96–97, 97e
  indicators for, 98
  in U.S., historical overview of, 94e–95e

Economic growth. *See also* Productivity
  government and, 77
  PPF and, 37
Economic indicators, leading, 98*d*
Economic loss, 477*d*, 477*e*
  minimization of. *See* Loss minimization
Economic model, 7*d*, 108
Economic profit, 449*d*, 477*e*, 477–479, 478*e*.
    See also Profit maximization
  and entrepreneurship, 587–589
  long-run
    monopolistic competition and, 530, 531*e*
    perfect competition and, 487–488, 488*e*
  versus producer surplus, 497
  short run, 479–480
Economic regulation, 657*d*
  alternative theories of, 660–662, 666–667
  case study: *Airline Regulation and Deregulation,*
    665–666
  case study: *Rail and Truck Regulation and*
    Deregulation, 662–664
  of natural monopoly, 657–660, 658*e*
Economic rent, 556*d*
  maximization of, unions and, 606–608, 607*e*
  versus opportunity cost, 556–558, 557*e*
Economic Reports of the President, 106*i*
Economic Research Service (ERS), 413*i*
Economics, 2*d*
  classical, 178
  demand-side, 103*d*
  experimental, case study: *Experimental*
    Economics, 498–499
  Keynesian, 103–104, 178–179
  macroeconomics, 4*d*
  microeconomics, 4*d*
  and politics. *See* Politics, economics and
  supply-side, 105*d*
    case-study: *The Supply-Side Experiment,*
    267–268
Economics of Imperfect Competition (Joan
  Robinson), 527
Economic system(s), 37*d*
  types of, 38–40, 814
Economic theory, 7*d*, 7–8
  testing of, 91–92
  transitional economies and, 814–816
Economies of scale, 461, 462*d*
  and antitrust policy, 667
  case study: *At the Movies,* 462–463
  case study: *Billions and Billions of Burgers,* 464
  and international trade, 752
  and long-run average cost, 463*e*, 465
  and monopoly, 504–505
  and oligopoly, 535–536, 536*e*
Economies of scope, 644*d*
Economy, 413*i*
Economy(ies), 90*d*
  classifications of, 799–801
  command, 39*d*
  convergence of, 125–126
  custom based, 40
  developing. *See* Developing countries

  as game, 679–680
  and human body, comparison of, 90–93
  mixed, 39–40
  national, 90–93
  questions for, 37–38
  of scale. *See* Economies of scale
  of scope, 644*d*
  transitional, 814–816. *See also* Transitional
    economies
  underground, 691*d*, 691–692
EDIMP. *See* Macroeconomic Policy and
  Management Division
Edinburghers, 178*i*
Edison, Thomas, 121
Education
  case study: *The Opportunity Cost of College,*
    26–27
  in developing countries, 806, 807*e*
  government control and, 78
  labor productivity and, 116, 806, 807*e*
  and median income, 725*e*
  as positive externality, 710–712, 711*e*
The Education of David Stockman (William
  Greider), 268*i*
Effectiveness lag, 348*d*
Efficiency, 34*d*
  allocative, 495*d*, 495–496
  firm size and, 641*e*, 641–642
  market exchange and, 496–499
  minimum scale of, 463, 463*e*
  and production function, 468–469
  and production possibilities frontier, 33–34, 37
  productive, 495*d*
  technological, 468
Efficiency wages, 651*d*
Efficiency wage theory, 234*d*
Elastic demand, 396*d*
Elasticity, 393–394
  constant, demand and, 398–400, 399*e*
  cross-price, demand and, 415
  income, demand and, 411–414
  price. *See* Price elasticity of demand; Price
    elasticity of supply
  and tax incidence, 408–411
Electronic Policy Network, 570*i*, 741*i*
Emergency Food and Shelter Program, 742*i*
Emergency Jobs Appropriation Act, 348
Employee compensation, 172
Employment
  full, 138*d*
  government and, 77
  unions and, 600–603, 601*e*
Employment Act (1946), 103, 263, 370–371
Entitlement programs, 372*d*, 728–729
Entrepreneur, 586*d*
  case study: *IBM's Lotus Position,* 589–590
  economic profit and, 587–589
  investment by, 587
  resource control by, 586–587
  transaction costs and, 70
Entrepreneurial ability, 2*d*, 2–3, 586–590
  developing countries and, 809

Envelope curve, 459*d*, 459–461, 460*e*–461*e*
Environment
  and negative externalities, 699–710. *See also*
    Pollution
  protection of, in U.S., 712–717
  socialist economy and, 815–816
Environmental Protection Agency (EPA), 712,
  714*i*, 714–716
Equation of exchange, 330*d*, 330–331
Equilibrium, 55*d*
  case study: *The Market for Professional*
    Basketball, 60–61
  consumer, 426*d*. *See also* Consumer
    equilibrium
  and demand and supply, 55–56, 56*e*
    aggregate, 100–101, 101*e*
    simultaneous changes in, 59*e*, 59–60, 61*e*
  and demand, changes in, 57*e*, 57–58
  of interest rate, 323, 323*e*
  and investment, planned versus actual, 182
  in labor market, 252–252
  long-run, 237, 238*e*–239*e*, 240
  market, 55, 56*e*. *See also* Market equilibrium
  of price and quantity, 55–61
    changes in demand and, 57*e*, 57–58, 59*e*,
      59–61, 61*e*
    changes in supply and, 58*e*, 58–59, 59*e*,
      59–61, 61*e*
  of prices, domestic, 752*e*, 752–754, 754*e*
  of real GDP demanded, 207–210, 208*e*
    algebra for, 227–229
    changes in, 210–215
    income-expenditure approach to,
      207–209, 208*e*
    leakage-injection approach to, 208*e*,
      209–210
    and price level changes, 215–219
  short-run, 237, 238*e*–239*e*, 239–240
  and supply. *See also* Equilibrium, and
    demand and supply
    changes in, 58*e*, 58–59
Ernst & Young, 73
European monetary system, 793–794
European Union, 764–765
Excess capacity, 532*d*
Excess reserves, 305*d*
  and money creation, 309–313
  and money expansion, 314–316
Exchange
  case study: *Experimental Economics,* 498–499
  equation of, 330*d*, 330–331
  foreign. *See* Foreign exchange
  medium of, 278*d*
  personal, versus impersonal, 817
  of securities, 629–630
  specialization and, 28–30
  voluntary, gains from, 496–498
Exchange rate(s), 780*d*
  ceiling on, 788, 788*e*
  current, 338*i*, 785*i*
  determination of, 780–783, 783*e*
  equality of, across countries, 784

Exchange rate(s) (*continued*)
  fixed, 787*d,* 787–790
    and international monetary system, 792–793
  flexible, 787*d,* 793–794
  floor on, 789*e,* 789–790
  gold standard and, 792
  international trade and, 83
  purchasing power parity and, 784–787
Exclusive dealing, 668*d*
Exhaustible resources, 699*d*
Expansion, 93*d*
  path of, long run, 472*e,* 472–473
Expansionary gap, 237*d,* 238*e,* 242
  closing of, approaches to, 345–346, 346*e*
  and fiscal policy, 261–262, 262*e*
  and Phillips curve, 358
Expectations
  consumer, 49
  and consumption, 190
  and investment, 195
  macroeconomics and, 91
  monetary policy and, 350–354, 351*e,* 353*e*
  producer, 53
  rational, 350*d*
    policy rules and, 363
Expenditure
  aggregate. *See* Aggregate expenditure
  algebra for, 227–229
  in circular flow, 179–181, 180*e*
  and income, 207
  for research and development, 118–120
  for welfare, 729–730
Expenditure approach, 153*d,* 154–155
Experimental economics
  case study: *Experimental Economics,* 498–499
Explicit cost, 448*d*
Export promotion, 810*d,* 810–811
Exports. *See also* International trade
  and aggregate expenditure, 197–198
  net, 155*d,* 197–198. *See also* Net exports
  net exports and, 202*e*
  profile of, in U.S., 746, 751
Externality(ies), 77*d*
  and GDP, 160–161
  negative, 699–710
    case study: *Destruction of the Tropical Rain Forest,* 705–707
    Coase analysis of, 707–708
    common pool problem and, 699–700
    and fixed-production technology, 700*e,* 700–702
    and variable technology, 702*e,* 702–703
  positive, 710–712

F

FAA. *See* Federal Aviation Administration
Fairness, 679
Fair, Ray, 269
Fallacy of composition, 11*d*
Family structure, and poverty, 732*e,* 732–734

Family Support Act (1988), 738
FAO. *See* Food and Agriculture Organization
Farm. *See* Agriculture
FDIC. *See* Federal Deposit Insurance Corporation
Featherbedding, 602*d*
  case study: *Featherbedding on Broadway,* 602–603
Federal Advisory Council, 286
Federal Aviation Administration (FAA), 118*i,* 665*i,* 666
Federal budget deficit, 373–381
  case study: *An Intergenerational View of Deficits and Debt,* 387–388
  case study: *The 1996 Federal Budget Deadlock,* 376–377
  factors leading to, 377–378
  and foreign investment, 381, 386
  impact of, 380
  in Keynesian economics, 103
  and labor productivity growth, 117–118
  measures reducing, 375–377, 388–389
  and national debt, 381
  philosophies regarding, 374
  rationale for, 373–374
  since 1980s, 105, 267–268, 374–375, 376*e*
  and trade deficit, 106, 380–381
  U.S., versus other countries, 381, 382*e*
  variables affecting, 378–380, 379*e*
Federal budget process
  congressional role in, 371
  presidential role in, 370–371
  problems with, 371–372
  suggested reforms for, 373
Federal debt. *See* National debt
Federal Deposit Insurance Corporation (FDIC), 288–289, 292*i*
Federal Express Corporation, 518, 518*i*
Federal funds market, 305*d*
Federal funds rate, 306*d*
Federal Open Market Committee (FOMC), 287–288
Federal Reserve Bank of Minneapolis, 243*i,* 308*i,* 337*i*
Federal Reserve Bank of New York, 307*i*
Federal Reserve System, 285*d*
  balance sheet of, 306*e,* 306–307
  Board of Governors of, 287
  case study: *Tracking the Supernote,* 307–309
  goals of, 289, 317
  Great Depression and, 286–287
  open-market operations of, 287*d*
  powers of, 285–286, 307, 317
  reserve requirements of, 288, 304–305
  Roosevelt's reforms in, 287–289
  structure of, 288*e*
Federal Trade Commission (FTC), 668
Feldstein, Martin, 387
Fiat money, 281*d*
Filippello, Ehren, 387
Filo, David, 3
Final goods and services, 153*d*

Finance, functional, 374*d*
Financial intermediaries, 284*d. See also* Bank(s); Banking
  depository institutions as. *See* Depository institutions
  in developing countries, 808
  finance companies as, 300
  in U.S., 284–290
Financial markets, 181*d*
Firm(s), 71*d*
  current market value of, 630
  diseconomies of scale in, 463–464
  as economic actors, 4, 70–75
  economies of scale in, 463–464
  evolution of, 70–71
  perfectly competitive, 475
  rationale for existence of, 638–639
  scope of, 639–644, 641*e*
    case study: *The Trend toward Outsourcing,* 643–644
  specialization by, 70–72
  types of, 73–75
    number and sales of, 75*e*
First Security National Bank, 313*i*
Fiscal policy, 77*d,* 256*d*
  and aggregate supply, 267
  and contractionary gap, 260–261, 261*e*
  discretionary, 264*d,* 264–266
    case study: *Discretionary Policy and Presidential Elections,* 269
    versus natural market forces, 344–346
  and expansionary gap, 261–262, 262*e*
  Great Depression and, 78–79, 263–264
  historical development of, 263–265, 267–269
  lags in, 347–348
  money and, 329–330
  practice of, 263–269
  problems of, 265–266
  theory of, 256–263
  tools of, 264–265
  and unemployment, natural rate of, 265–266
  World War II and, 79–80, 263–264
Fiscal year, 370–371
Fixed cost, 453*d*
  average, 456–459, 457*e*–458*e*
  and loss minimization, 480–481
Fixed exchange rates, 787*d,* 787–790
  and international monetary system, 792–793
Fixed-production technology, 701*d*
  and negative externalities, 700*e,* 700–702
Fixed resources, 450*d*
Fixed-weighted system, GDP and, 165–166
Flexible exchange rates, 787*d,* 793–794
Flow, 91*d,* 321*d*
FOMC. *See* Federal Open Market Committee
Food and Agriculture Organization (FAO), 413*i*
Food stamps, 729
Ford, Gerald, 148
Ford Motor Company, 71*i,* 84–85
Foreign aid, 812*d*
  case study: *Privatizing Foreign Aid,* 813
  and economic development, 811–814

Foreign countries, as economic actors, 82–85
Foreign exchange, 83*d*
    and balance of payments, 779–780
    in developing countries, 809
    market for, 83, 781*e,* 781–782
    rate of, 780–783. *See also* Exchange rate(s)
Foreign investment, 381, 386
45-degree ray, 22–24
    and equilibrium of real GDP demanded,
        207–208, 208*e*
Fractional reserve banking system, 281*d*
Franchise Handbook: On-Line, 652*i*
Frankfurt Money Strategist, 355*i*
Franklin, Benjamin, 433
Frictional unemployment, 137*d*
Friedman, Benjamin, 386
Friedman, Milton, 145, 337, 362, 362*i*
FTC. *See* Federal Trade Commission
Full employment, 138*d*
    government and, 77
Functional finance, 374*d*
Functional relation, variables and, 17
Fusebox, Inc., 219*i*

G

Game(s)
    negative-sum, 679*d,* 685
    positive-sum, 679*d,* 680
    zero-sum, 679*d*
Game theory, 541*d,* 541–542
Gans, Curtis, 690
Gates, Bill, 673
GATT. *See* General Agreement on Tariffs and
    Trade
GDP. *See* Gross domestic product
GDP price index, 99, 164*d,* 164–165
    estimates of, 165–166, 175–176
General Agreement on Tariffs and Trade
    (GATT), 763*d,* 763–764
General Assistance, 729
General Electric, 644
General Motors, 5, 84–85, 540, 611, 640
*General Theory of Employment, Interest, and
    Money* (John Keynes), 103, 178, 190,
    263
Germany
    central bank in, 355, 355*i,* 793
    monetary system in, failure of, 283
Gingrich, Newt, 691
Global Network of Environment and
    Technology (GNET), 713*i*
GNN/Koblas Currency Converter, 785*i*
Golden rule of profit maximization, 479*d*
Gold standard, 792*d*
Gompers, Samuel, 594
Good(s), 3*d*
    alternative, 53*d*
    capital, PPF and, 33–36
    complements, 48*d*
    consumer, PPF and, 32–35
    durable, 70

    inferior, 47*d,* 411
    nondurable, 70
    normal, 47*d,* 411
    private, 76–77
    public, 77*d*
    substitutes, 48*d*
Goods and services, 3–4
    balance on, 776–777, 777*d*
    final, 153*d*
    free, 3–4
    households as demanders of, 70
    intermediate, 154*d*
    market for, 4
    resources and, 2
Government
    in circular flow, 179–181, 180*e*
    in developing countries, 808–809
    as economic actor, 4, 76–82
    objectives of, 78
    policies of. *See also* Economic regulation;
        Policy; Public policy
        productivity and, 116–117, 122–123
    revenue of, sources of, 80–81, 81*e*
    role of, 76–77
        changes in, 78–80
    spending by, 78–80, 79*e*–80*e,* 370*e*
    structure of, 77–78
Government budget, 370*d. See also* Federal
    budget process
    components of, 370*e*
Government budget deficit, 103*d. See also*
    Federal budget deficit
Government debt, 105*d,* 105–106. *See also*
    National debt
Government monopoly, in developing
    countries, 809
Government Printing Office, 106*i*
Government purchase function, 196*d*
Government purchases, 155*d*
    changes in, effects of, 256–257, 257*e,*
        259–260
Government Purchasing Project, 155, 155*i*
Government regulation. *See also* Economic
    regulation
    types of, 657
Government subsidies, 171
Gradualism, in economic transition, 817–818
Graphs, 16*d*
    basics of, 16*e,* 16–17
    drawing of, 17–19, 18*e*
    intercept in, 23
    ray in, 23
    time-series, 16*d*
Great Depression
    aggregate demand during, 102*e*
    banking during, 286–287
    and fiscal policy, 78–79, 263–264
    and Keynesian economics, 178–179
"Green" accounting, 161
Greenspan, Alan, 307, 337–338
Greider, William, 268*i*
Gresham's Law, 279*d*

Gross domestic product (GDP), 78*d,* 153*d. See
    also* Output
    as aggregate output measure, 98–99
    chained-dollar. *See* Gross domestic product,
        real
    and consumption, 195–196, 196*e*
    current-dollar (nominal), 161*d,* 166–167,
        167*e*
    and debt, national, 383*e,* 384
    depreciation and, 160
    expenditure approach to, 154–155, 156*e*
    externalities and, 160–161
    income approach to, 155–157
    intercountry comparisons of, 799–801,
        801*e*–802*e*
    and investment, 195–196, 196*e*
    and leisure, 158–159
    measurement of, 153–154
        case study: *Computer Prices and GDP
            Estimation,* 165–166
        chain-weighted system for, 165
        fixed-weighted system for, 165
        limitations of, 157–161
    nominal (current-dollar), 161*d,* 166–167,
        167*e*
    price index, 99, 164*d,* 164–166, 175–176
    and quality of products, 158–159
    real, 99, 161*d*
        disequilibrium of, 209
        equilibrium of, 207–209, 208*e. See also*
            Equilibrium, of real GDP demanded
        estimates of, 166–167, 167*e*
        index for, 174–175
    in transitional economies, 820, 821*e*
    and variety of product, 158–159
Grossman, Gene, 123
Growth, economic. *See also* Productivity
    government and, 77
    PPF and, 37

H

Handbook of International Economic Statistics,
    283*i*
Health Care Financing Administration
    (HCFA), 433*i*
Health, economic development and, 801–803,
    803*e*
Henry Ford Museum Online, 71*i*
Herfindahl index, 670*d,* 670*e,* 670–671
Heritage Foundation, 570*i,* 741*i*
Hicks, J. R., 518
Hidden actions, 648*d,* 648–649
Hidden characteristics, 647*d,* 648
Holland, auctions in, 486
HomeAid, 742*i*
Hoover, Gary, 633
Hoover, Herbert, 595
Horizontal mergers, 546*d,* 670
Household(s)
    as economic actors, 4, 68–70
    evolution of, 68

Household(s) (*continued*)
    as goods and services demanders, 70
    as resource suppliers, 68–69
Household production
    case study: *The Electronic Cottage,* 73
    opportunity cost and, 72–73
Housing assistance, 729
Housing construction, 492i
Human capital, 2, 111
    and economic convergence, 126
    investment in, 622
Hyperinflation, 141d, 332–333
Hypothesis, 9d
Hysteresis, unemployment rate and, 247d

I

IBM, 6, 461i, 461–462, 589–590
ICC. *See* Interstate Commerce Commission
Identity, 331d
IEM. *See* Iowa Electronic Markets
Ignorance, rational, 684d, 684–685
IMF. *See* International Monetary Fund
Imperfect information, 644–647
Implementation lag, 348d
Implicit cost, 448d
Imports. *See also* International trade
    disposable income and, 202e, 202–203
    and economic competition, 672
    profile of, in U.S., 746, 751
    and quotas, 759–762
Import substitution, 810d, 810–811
Income
    aggregate, 156d, 179, 812
    and aggregate expenditure, 206–215
    algebra for, 227–229
    allocation of, 70
    changes in
        and consumer equilibrium, 443, 443e
        consumption function and, 189
        market demand and, 47–48, 48e
    in circular flow, 179–181, 180e
    and consumption, 22e, 22–24, 23e, 183e,
        183–184, 184e
    disposable, 172, 172e, 179d. *See also*
        Disposable income
    distribution of, 722–726, 723e–724e
        government role in, 77
    education and, 725e
    elasticity of, demand and, 411–414
    functional distribution of, 571e, 572
    and government purchases, 196
    imputed, 158
    and investment, planned, 193–194, 195e
    life-cycle pattern of, 225e, 226
    median, 725d, 725e
    versus money, 276
    national, 171d, 171e, 172–173, 173e
    and net exports, 198, 199e, 202e, 202–203
    nominal, quantity theory of money and,
        331–332
    permanent, discretionary policy and, 266
    personal, 171–172, 172e

present value of, 626–627
and productivity, 807–808
proprietors,' 173d
real, 45d
rental, 173d
sources of, 69e
Income approach, 155–157
    national income accounting and, 153d
Income assistance, 728–729. *See also* Welfare
Income effect, 45d, 444–445, 445e
    and labor supply, 580
    and price elasticity of demand, 401
Income elasticity of demand, 411d, 411–414,
    412e
    case study: *The Demand for Food and "The
        Farm Problem,"* 412–414, 414e
Income-expenditure model, 207d
    and equilibrium of real GDP demanded,
        207–209, 208e
    and price level, changes in, 216e
Increasing-cost industry, 492d, 492–494, 493e
Increasing marginal returns, 451, 451e, 468e, 469
Independent variable, 17, 19
Index
    development of, in chain-weighted system,
        174e, 174–176
    Herfindahl, 670d, 670e, 670–671
    misery, 149
    price. *See* Price index
India, 801e, 804e, 811
Indifference curves, 438e, 438–441, 440e
    and utility analysis, 442e, 442–445
Indifference map, 439d, 440e
Indirect business taxes, 171
Industrial policy, 122d
    case study: *Picking Technological Winners,*
        122–123
Industrial Revolution, 70–71
Industrial union, 595d, 598–600
Industry, 475. *See also specific industries*
    constant-cost, 492d
    cottage, system of, 70
    decreasing-cost, 494d, 494e, 494–495
    increasing-cost, 492d, 492–494, 493e
Industry supply curve
    long-run. *See* Long-run industry supply curve
    short-run, 484d, 485e
Inelastic demand, 396d
Inferior goods, 47d, 411
Inflation, 104d, 140–149, 141d
    anticipated, versus unanticipated, 143–144,
        149
    case study: *Hyperinflation in Brazil,* 140–141
    causes of, 141, 142e
    cost-push, 141d, 142e
    CPI and, 163–164
    demand-pull, 141d, 142e
    effects of, 148–149
    gold supplies and, 792
    and interest rates, 147–148
    international comparisons of, 145, 146e
    money supply and, case study: *The Money
        Supply and Inflation,* 332–333, 333e

and price level, 142–143, 143e
rate of, 141–142, 143e
and relative price changes, 144–145
unanticipated, versus anticipated, 143–144,
    149
and unemployment, 148, 356e, 356–362, 358e
variable, transaction costs of, 144
Information
    asymmetric. *See* Asymmetric information
    and choice making, 7, 27
    imperfect, 644–647
Information Revolution, 73
Injection(s), 182d
    equilibrium of real GDP demanded and,
        208e, 209–210
In-kind transfers, 69, 729
Innovation, 504d
Institutions, 816d
    and economic development, 816–820
    nonprofit, 75
Intel Corporation, 123i
InterAction, 813i
Intercept, in graphs, 23d
Interest, 3d, 147d
Interest rate(s), 147d, 618d
    and consumption, 190
    differences in, reasons for, 623–625
    equilibrium of, 323, 323e
    federal budget deficit and, 378–380, 379e
    inflation and, 147–148
    and investment, 192–195, 193e–194e
        planned, 324–326, 325e, 338
    money demand and, 322e, 322–323
    money supply and, 323e, 323–324, 336–338
    and national debt, 384–385
    nominal, 147d, 147e
    and present value, 625–627
    price level and, 326–328, 327e
    real, 147d
    term structure of, 624d
Interlocking directorates, 668d
Intermediate goods and services, 154d
International Brotherhood of Teamsters, 662i,
    663–664, 689
International Business Machines (IBM), 6,
    461i, 461–462, 589–590
International Journal of Game Theory, 541i
International Monetary Fund (IMF), 792–793
International monetary system, 792–794
International trade, 82–83. *See also* Exports;
    Imports
    and balance of payments, 775–780, 779e
    case study: *The World Trade Organization,*
        763–764
    and economic development, 809–811
    and economies of scale, 752
    gains from, 746–751
    liberalization of, effects of, 811
    multilateral agreement and, 763–764
    restrictions on, 758–763, 770–771. *See also*
        Trade restrictions
    and social welfare, 755e, 757
    world market and, 751–757

International Trade Reports, 746*i*
Internet
　addresses. *See specific organization*
　case study: *Banking on the Net,* 313–314
　Lycos, 32*i*
　Netscape, 38*i*
　specialization and, 32, 55
　World Wide Web Security, 313*i*
　Yahoo, 3*i*
Internet Mall, 32*i*
Interstate Commerce Commission (ICC),
　662–664
Inventories, 154*d*
　disequilibrium of real GDP and, 209
Inverse relation, between variables, 18
Investment, 154*d,* 191–196
　actual, 182*d*
　by banks, restrictions on, 289
　case study: *Variability of Consumption and
　　Investment,* 195–196
　demand curve for, 192–193, 193*e*–194*e*
　disposable income and, 193–194
　entrepreneurship and, 587
　expectations and, 195
　federal budget deficit and, 386–387
　foreign, 381, 386
　gross, 160
　and gross domestic product, 195–196, 196*e*
　in human capital, 622
　interest rate and, 192–195, 193*e*–194*e*
　irreversible, 514–515
　marginal rate of return on, 620*e,* 620–622,
　　621*d*
　and national income accounting system,
　　182–183
　net, 160
　and opportunity cost, 192–193, 193*e*
　optimal, 619–622
　planned, 182*d,* 324–326, 325*e,* 338
　　and income level, 193–194, 195*e*
　　interest rate and, 324–326, 325*e,* 338
　　and profit maximization, 192–193
Investment function, 193–194, 194*d,* 195*e*
Invisibles, 155
Iowa Electronic Markets (IEM), 498*i*
I.S. Applications Co. L.L.C., 628*i*
Isocost lines, 470–471, 471*e*
Isoquants, 469*e,* 469–470
Ispat, 819–820
Israel
　Consulate General of, 332*i*
　inflation in, 332–333
Italy, national debt in, 384, 385*e*

J

Japan
　automobile industry in, 84*i*
　central bank in, 355
　economic fluctuations in, 96–97, 97*e*
　Ministry of Finance of, 746*i*
　recycling in, 716

saving in, 191
　unemployment in, 9–10
Japan Economic Foundation (JEF), 10*i*
Japan External Trade Organization (JETRO),
　191*i*
Jobs, preservation of, and trade restrictions,
　767–768
Johnson, Lyndon, 735
*The Journal of the Experimental Analysis of
　Behavior,* 429*i*

K

Kapor, Mitch, 589–590
Kazakhstan, privatization in, 819–820
Kennedy, John F., 265
Kentucky Fried Chicken, 642
Keynesian economics
　age of, 103–104
　Great Depression and, 178–179
Keynes, John Maynard, 103, 178–179, 190,
　263
Kinked demand curve, 542–545, 543*d,*
　543*e*–544*e*
Kinked labor supply curve, 604*e,* 604–605
Knights of Labor, 594
Kornai, Janos, 817
KPMG's Virtual Office, 73*i*
Kuznets, Simon, 118, 153

L

Labor, 2*d*
　division of, 30–32, 31*d*
　market for, 4, 251–252, 252*e*
　　adverse selection in, 649*d*
　　asymmetric information in, 650–652
　specialization of, 31*d*
　union, increasing demand for, 600–603,
　　601*e*
　use of, in developing countries, 806–808
Labor force, 131*d,* 132*e*
　changes in, 134
　　productivity and, 115–116
Labor force participation rate, 133*d,* 134
Labor movement, 594–596
Labor productivity. *See* Productivity
Labor supply, 251, 252*e*
　and aggregate supply, 231, 245
　backward-bending curve for, 580*d,* 581*e*
　case study: *Comparable Worth,* 584–586
　craft unions and, 600, 601*e*
　income effect and, 580
　market, 583, 583*e*
　nonwage determinants of, 581–582
　substitution effect and, 580
　and utility maximization, 577–579
　wages and, 579–581, 583–584
Labor supply curve, kinked, 604*e,* 604–605
Labor union, 594*d. See also* Union(s)
Lags, problems of, 347–348
Laissez-faire capitalism, 38–39

Laissez-faire philosophy, 178
Landrum-Griffin Act, 596
Latin American Network Information Center,
　332*i*
Laughlin, Teresa, 585
Law of comparative advantage, 29*d*
Law of demand, 44*d,* 44–47
　case study: *Demand in the Animal World,*
　　428–429
　derivation of, 426–428, 428*e*
Law of diminishing marginal rate of
　substitution, 439*d*
Law of diminishing marginal returns, 112, 252,
　450–453, 452*d*
Law of diminishing marginal utility, 421*d,*
　421–422
　and leisure, 577
Law of increasing opportunity cost, 33*e,* 34*d*
Law of supply, 50*d*
Leading economic indicators, 98*d*
Leakage(s), 182*d*
　equilibrium of real GDP demanded and,
　　208*e,* 209–210
Leeson, Nick, 784
Legal tender, 281*d*
Legislation
　antitrust. *See* Antitrust legislation
　competing-interest, 685*d*
　special-interest, 685*d. See also* Special-
　　interest legislation
The Legislative Process, 389*i*
Leisure, 251*d,* 577*d*
　GDP and, 158–159
　law of diminishing marginal utility and,
　　577
"Lemon" problem, 648
Lending. *See* Loanable funds
Leveraged buyout, 632*d*
　case study: *Campeau Bets the Store,* 633–634
Leveraged Buyouts, 633*i*
Lewis, John L., 595
Liability, 301*d*
　limited, 74
　unlimited, 74
Linear demand curve, 397*d,* 397–398
Line-item veto, 388*d,* 388–389
Liquidity, 301*d*
　versus profitability, 305–306
　and securities exchanges, 629
Loanable funds
　demand for, 622–623, 623*d,* 624*e*
　interest rates and, 147, 147*e*
　supply of, 619*d*
Loanable funds market, 619*d*
Logrolling, 682*d*
Long-run, 237*d,* 450*d*
Long-run aggregate supply (LRAS) curve,
　241*d,* 241*e,* 241–242
Long-run average cost curve, 459*d,* 459–461,
　460*e*–461*e*
　and economies and diseconomies of scale,
　　463*e,* 465
　and expansion path, 472–473

Long-run industry supply curve, 491*d*
    for constant-cost industry, 489*e*–490*e*, 492
    for decreasing-cost industry, 494*e*, 494–495
    for increasing-cost industry, 492–494, 493*e*
Long-run Phillips curve, 358*e*, 359–360, 360*d*
Loss, economic, 477*d*, 477*e*
Loss minimization
    in monopolistic competition, 529–530
    in monopoly, 513*e*, 513–514
    in perfect competition, 480–487, 481*e*–482*e*
Lotus Development Corporation, 589*i*, 589–590
LRAS curve. *See* Long-run aggregate supply
    curve
Lucas, Robert E., Jr., 12, 350
Luxuries, and income elasticity, 411
Lycos search engine, 32*i*

M

M1, 301*d*, 302*e*
M2, 302*d*, 302*e*, 302–303
M3, 302*e*, 303*d*
Macroeconomic Policy and Management
    Division (EDIMP), 247*i*
Macroeconomics, 4*d*
Majority rule, 680–683
Managed float system, 793*d*, 793–794
Marginal, 5*d*
Marginal analysis, 5–7
    case study: *Marginal Analysis in the Computer
        Industry,* 6–7
    slope and, 19
Marginal choice, 5–6
Marginal cost, 454*d*, 454*e*, 454–456, 455*e*
    average cost and, 456–459, 457*e*–458*e*
    marginal revenue and, 478*e*, 479
Marginal cost curve, 455*e*, 455–456
Marginal product, 451*d*, 452*e*, 453
Marginal propensity to consume (MPC), 185*d*,
    186*e*, 186–188, 187*e*
    and simple spending multiplier, 214
Marginal propensity to import (MPM), 225*d*,
    225–226
Marginal propensity to save (MPS), 186*d*,
    186*e*, 186–188, 187*e*
    and simple spending multiplier, 214
Marginal rate of return on investment, 620*e*,
    620–622, 621*d*
Marginal rate of substitution (MRS), 439*d*
Marginal rate of technical substitution
    (MRTS), 470
Marginal resource cost, 561*d*, 561–563, 562*e*
    for resource price searcher, 566–568, 567*e*
    for resource price taker, 561–562, 562*e*
Marginal returns, increasing, 451, 451*e*, 468*e*,
    469
Marginal revenue, 479*d*
    versus marginal cost
        loss minimization and, 481–482, 482*e*
        profit maximization and, 478*e*, 479
    in monopoly, 506–510, 507*e*–509*e*

Marginal revenue product, 559*e*, 559–561,
    560*d*, 561*e*
    and marginal resource cost, 561
    resource demand and, 558–561
Marginal social benefit, 702*e*, 703*d*, 704*e*
    education and, 710–712, 711*e*
Marginal social cost, 700*e*, 700–703, 701*d*,
    702*e*, 704*e*
Marginal tax rate, 82
    and work disincentives, 736–737
Marginal utility, 421*d*
    law of demand derivation and, 426–428,
        428*e*
    law of diminishing of, 421*d*, 421–422
Marginal valuation, 429*d*
    case study: *The Marginal Value of Free Medical
        Care,* 432–433
Market(s), 4*d*
    allocative role of, 38–39
    case study: *Auction Markets,* 486–487
    case study: *The Market for Professional
        Basketball,* 60–61
    common, 764–765
    competitive, consumer surplus in, 496,
        496*e*
    contestable, 514*d*, 514–515
    for corporation control, 632–634
    demand and. *See* Market demand
    and economic development, 816–820
    efficiency of, exchange and, 496–499
    federal funds, 305*d*
    financial, 181*d*
    foreign exchange, 83, 781*e*, 781–782
    for goods and services, 4
    labor, 4, 251–252, 252*e*
        adverse selection in, 649*d*
        asymmetric information in, 650–652
        supply for, 583, 583*e*
    loanable funds, 619*d*
    long-run adjustment of, 488–491, 489*e*–490*e*
    money, 290–291, 302
    for pollution rights, 708*e*, 708–710
    resource, 4, 251–254, 550–575
    specialized, 54–55
    supply and. *See* Market supply
    world, trading on, 751–757
Market demand, 54–56
    and consumer surplus, 431*e*, 431–432, 432*e*
    income changes and, 47–48, 48*e*
    versus individual demand, 47
Market equilibrium, 55, 56*e*
    in long run, 487–491, 488*e*–490*e*
    in short run, 484–486, 485*e*
Market failure, 76*d*
    negative externalities and, 701
    positive externalities and, 712
Market forces, versus discretionary fiscal policy,
    344–346
Market power, 657*d*
    size versus structure promoting, 671
Market structure, 475*d*
    perfectly competitive, 475

Market supply, 54–56
    versus individual supply, 51
Market work, 577*d*
Markup, 540–541
McDonald's, 30–31, 464
    case study: *The Big Mac Index,* 785–787
    case study: *The Reputation of a Big Mac,*
        652–653
McGregor Information Services, 505*i*
Means-tested program, 728*d*
Median income, 725*d*
Median voter model, 680*d*, 680–682, 681*e*
Mediator, 596*d*
Medicaid, 69, 432–433, 433*i*, 729
Medicare, 69, 80*e*, 432–433, 433*i*, 728, 731
Medium of exchange, 278*d*
Mercantilism, 153
Merchandise trade balance, 83*d*, 775–776, 776*e*
Mergers, 546
    and antitrust policy, 668–671
    conglomerate, 546*d*
    horizontal, 546*d*, 670
    vertical, 546*d*
Merrill Lynch, 290
Mexico
    case study: *City in the Clouds,* 713
    case study: *Mexico's Peso Problem,* 790–791
    NAFTA and, 765
Mexico Ministry of Finance, 790*i*
Microeconomics, 4*d*
Microsoft Corporation, 6*i*, 212, 313*i*, 611,
    673
Migration, and economic development, 811
Minimum efficient scale, 463, 463*e*
    and firm size, 641*e*, 641–642
Misery index, 149
Mitchell, Wesley C., 93
Mixed capitalist economy, 39*d*
Modigliani, Franco, 386
Mondale, Walter, 375
Monetary aggregates, 301*d*, 302*e*
Monetary policy, 77*d*, 287*d*, 320
    after 1982, 337–338
    anticipated, 352–354, 363
    case study: *Central Bank Independence and
        Price Stability,* 355
    case study: *International Finance,* 338–339
    direct-channel model of, 330–335, 339–340
    and expectations, 350–354, 351*e*, 353*e*
    fixed-growth-rate, 362
    indirect-channel model of, 321–330,
        339–340
    lags in, 347–348
    targets of, 335–339, 336*e*
    until 1982, 337
Monetary system(s)
    case study: *When the Monetary System Breaks
        Down,* 283
    European, 793–794
    failure of, 282–284
    international, 792–794
Monetary theory, 320

Money, 91*d*, 277*d*
  and aggregate demand curve, slope of,
     326–328, 327*e*
  case study: *Tracking the Supernote,* 307–309
  commodity, 278*d*, 278–279
  creation of, banks and, 280–281, 309–317
  evolution of, 277–284
  expansion of, 314–316
  fiat, 281*d*
  and fiscal policy, 329–330
  functions of, 278–279
  versus income, 276
  paper, 281
  quantity theory of, 331*d*, 331–332
  token, 280*d*
  transactions demand for, 321*d*
  value of, 279, 282, 282*e*
  velocity of, 330*d*, 331. *See also* Velocity of
     money
Money demand, 321–322
  and interest rates, 322*e*, 322–323
Money market mutual fund, 290*d*, 290–291,
  302
Money multiplier, 315*d*, 315–316
  simple, 315*d*
Money supply
  and aggregate demand
     direct channel to, 330–335
     indirect channel to, 321–330
  and aggregate supply, 328–329, 329*e*
  banking and, 300–303
  changes in
     aggregate demand and, 324–326, 325*e*
     and aggregate supply, 328–329, 329*e*
  contraction of, 316
  discount rate and, 316–317
  expansion of, 314–316
     limitations on, 316
  and inflation, case study: *The Money Supply
     and Inflation,* 332–333, 333*e*
  and interest rates, 323*e*, 323–324, 336–338
  measures of, 302*e*
Monopolistic competition, 527*d*
  case study: *Fast Forward,* 531–532
  characteristics of, 527
  demand curve in, 528, 529*e*, 532, 533*e*
  in long run, 530
  loss minimization in, 529–530
  versus perfect competition, 532–534, 533*e*
  and product differentiation, 527–528
  profit maximization in, 528–529, 529*e*
  in short run, 528–530
Monopolist, perfectly discriminating, 521*d*,
  521–522
Monopoly, 76*d*
  barriers to entry and, 504–505
  bilateral, 603–605, 604*d*, 604*e*
  case study: *Are Diamonds Forever?,* 505–506
  case study: *The Mail Monopoly,* 518–519
  and contestable markets, 514–515
  demand curve for, 506, 507*e*
  government, in developing countries, 809

  loss minimization in, 513*e*, 513–514
  and market power, 657
  natural, 76*d*, 504
     regulation of, 657–660, 658*e*
  policies against. *See* Antitrust activity;
     Economic regulation
  and price discrimination, 519–522
  profit maximization in, 510–514, 511*e*–512*e*
  resource allocation in, 515–517, 516*e*, 519
  revenue in, 506–510, 507*e*–509*e*
  shutting down in, 513
  welfare cost of, 517–518
Monopsonist, 603*d*
Moral hazard, 649–650, 650*d*
Morgenstern, Oskar, 541
Mori, Taikichiro, 12
Motor Carriers Act, 663
Moynihan, Patrick, 740–741
Mozambique, 802*e*–803*e*, 809
MPC. *See* Marginal propensity to consume
MPM. *See* Marginal propensity to import
MPS. *See* Marginal propensity to save
MRS. *See* Marginal rate of substitution
MRTS. *See* Marginal rate of technical
     substitution
Multiplier(s)
  autonomous net tax, 258*d*, 273–275
  balanced budget, 259*d*, 259–260, 274
  money, 315*d*, 315–316
  simple spending. *See* Simple spending
     multiplier

N

NAFTA. *See* North American Free Trade
     Agreement
NAHB. *See* National Association of Home
     Builders
NAR. *See* National Association of Realtors
National Air Traffic Controllers Association,
  118*i*
National Association of Home Builders
  (NAHB), 492*i*
National Association of Realtors (NAR), 644*i*
National Banking Act (1863), 285
National Basketball Association (NBA), 60*i*,
  60–61
National Bureau of Economic Research
  (NBER), 93, 93*i*, 96
National Cattleman's Beef Association, 686*i*
National Coalition for the Homeless (NCH),
  742*i*
National debt, 381*d*, 381–388
  burden of, 385–388
  case study: *An Intergenerational View of Deficits
     and Debt,* 387–388
  federal budget deficit and, 381
  and GDP, 383*e*, 384
  gross, versus held by public, 381
  interest payments on, 384–385
  international comparisons of, 384, 385*e*
  net, versus total, 384

  seigniorage and, 385
  since World War II, 381–382, 383*e*
  size of, 219*i*
  total, versus net, 384
National Economic Data, 243*i*
National economy, 90–93
National income, 171*d*, 171*e*
  components of, 172–173, 173*e*
National income accounting system,
  152*d*–153*d*
  case study: *Tracking a $7 Trillion Economy,*
     159–160
  development of, 153
  elements of, 171–172
  expenditure approach of, 153–155
  income approach of, 153*d*, 155–157
  investment and, 182–183
  limitations of, 157–161
  price changes and, 161–167
     case study: *Computer Prices and GDP
        Estimation,* 165–167
  summary income statement in, 172–173, 173*e*
Nationalization, 818
Natural monopoly, 76*d*, 504
  regulation of, 657–660, 658*e*
Natural rate hypothesis, 360*d*, 360–361
  strong version of, 360–361
  weak version of, 360
Natural rate of unemployment, 232*d*
  fiscal policy and, 265–266
  Phillips curve and, 360
Natural resources, productivity and, 808
NBA. *See* National Basketball Association
NBER. *See* National Bureau of Economic
     Research
NCH. *See* National Coalition for the
     Homeless
NDP. *See* Net domestic product
Necessities, and income elasticity, 411
Negative externalities. *See* Externality(ies),
     negative
Negative relation, between variables, 18
Negative-sum game, 679*d*, 685
  case study: *Farm Subsidies: A Negative-Sum
     Game,* 685–688
Negotiable order of withdrawal (NOW)
  accounts, 301
Net domestic product (NDP), 160*d*, 171*e*
Net export function, 198*d*, 199*e*
  shifts in, 203, 203*e*
Net exports, 155*d*, 197–198
  and aggregate expenditure function, 224*e*
  income and, 198, 199*e*, 202*e*, 202–203
  nonincome determinants of, 198, 203
  and simple spending multiplier, 225–226
  variable, 224–226
     algebra for, 228, 274
Net interest, 173*d*
Net taxes (NT), 179*d*, 197*d*
  changes in, effect of, 257–260, 258*e*
Net tax multiplier, autonomous, 258*d*
  algebra for, 273–275

Net unilateral transfers, 777*d*
Net wealth, 188*d*
  and consumption, 188–189
Net worth, 303*d*
News From Brazil, 140*i*
New York Stock Exchange (NYSE), 629, 629*i*
New Zealand, central bank in, 355
Nippon Telegraph and Telephone
  Corporation, 10*i*
Niskanen, William, 694
Nisus Publishing, 178*i*
Nixon, Richard, 104, 269, 793
Nobel Laureates in Economic Sciences, 362*i*
Nominal GDP, 161*d*
Nominal rate of interest, 147*d,* 147*e*
Nominal value, 161
Nominal wage, 231*d*
Nonmarket work, 577*d*
Nonprofit institutions, 75
Nordhaus, William, 269
Normal goods, 47*d,* 411
Normal profit, 449*d*
Normative economic statement, 11*d*
Norris-La Guardia Act, 595
North American Free Trade Agreement
  (NAFTA), 764–765
NOW accounts. *See* Negotiable order of
  withdrawal accounts
NPD Toy Services, 63*i*
NT. *See* Net taxes
Numa Financial Systems Ltd., 784*i*
Nutrition, economic development and,
  801–802
NYSE. *See* New York Stock Exchange

O

OECD. *See* Organization for Economic
  Development
Office of Airline Information, 118*i*
Official reserve transactions account, 778*d*
Ohio State University, Fisher College of
  Business, 362*i*
Oligopoly, 534*d*
  barriers to entry and, 534–537, 536*e*
  case study: *The Unfriendly Skies,* 535
  mergers and, 546
  models of, 537–545
  versus perfect competition, 545–546
Olson, Mancur, 689
O'Neal, Shaquille, 556
On Line Banking, 313*i*
ONSALE Interactive Marketplace, 486*i*
OPEC. *See* Organization of Petroleum
  Exporting Countries
Open-access resources, 699*d*
Open-market operations, 287*d,* 309
Opportunity cost, 26*d*
  case study: *The Opportunity Cost of College,*
    26–27
  versus economic rent, 556–558, 557*e*
  and household production, 72–73

investment and, 192–193, 193*e*
  law of increase in, 33*e,* 34*d,* 34–35, 37
  resources and, 448
  subjectivity of, 27–28
Optimal search, 644–646, 645*e,* 646*d*
Organization for Economic Development
  (OECD), 96*i*
Organization of Petroleum Exporting
  Countries (OPEC), 104, 416, 537–539
Other-things-constant assumption, 8*d,* 16–17
Output. *See also* Gross domestic product
  aggregate, 98*d*
  changing composition of, 116
  federal budget deficit and, 378–380, 379*e*
  gaps in, 237*d,* 238*e*–239*e,* 240*d,* 242
    case study: *Output Gaps and Wage*
      Flexibility, 242–244
  per capita, 124–125
  potential, 232*d,* 232–233, 253–254, 254*e*
  profit-maximizing rate of, 476–480
Outsourcing, 643–644
The Outsourcing Institute, 643*i*
Owner's equity, 303*d,* 587
Ozzie, Raymond, 589–590

P

PACs. *See* Political action committees
Pakistan, education in, 806
Panama, monetary system in, failure of, 283
Partnership, 74*d*
Patent(s), 120, 504*d*
Pattern bargaining, 597*d*
Payoff matrix, 541*d,* 542*e*
Payroll taxes, 81
Peninsula Neighborhood Association, 572*i*
Perdue, Frank, 642
Perfect competition, 475*d*
  conditions for, 499
  demand under, 475–476, 476*e,* 532, 533*e*
  and economic profit, long-run, 487–488,
    488*e*
  and efficiency, 495–499
  in long run, 487–495
  loss minimization in, 480–487, 481*e*–482*e*
  versus monopolistic competition, 532–534,
    533*e*
  versus oligopoly, 545–546
  profit maximization in, 476–480, 478*e*
  resource allocation in, 515, 516*e*
  in short run, 476–487
Perfectly discriminating monopolist, 521*d,*
  521–522
Perfectly elastic demand curve, 399*d,* 399*e*
Perfectly elastic supply, 406*d,* 406*e*
Perfectly inelastic demand curve, 399*d,* 399*e*
Perfectly inelastic supply, 406*d,* 406*e*
Perot, Ross, 255, 690*i*
Per se illegality, 669*d*
Perpetuity, 627*d*
Personal income, 171–172, 172*e*
Personal Responsibility Act (PRA), 740–741

Per-worker production function, 112*d,* 112*e,*
  112–113
PhARMA, 404*i*
Pharmaceutical industry, case study:
  Pharmaceutical Prices across Countries,
    403–405, 404*e*
Phillips, A. W., 356
Phillips curve, 356*d,* 356–362
  long-run, 358*e,* 359–360, 360*d*
  short-run, 357–359, 358*e,* 359*d*
Physical capital, 2, 111–112, 154*d*
Planned investment, 182*d,* 324–326, 325*e,* 338
  and income level, 193–194, 195*e*
  interest rate and, 324–326, 325*e,* 338
Planning curve, 459*d,* 459–461, 460*e*–461*e*
Playbill On-Line, 602*i*
Policy. *See also* Economic regulation; Public
  policy
  antitrust. *See* Antitrust activity; Antitrust
    legislation
  fiscal. *See* Fiscal policy
  industrial, 122–123
  monetary. *See* Monetary policy
Political action committees (PACs), 689
Political business cycles, 269*d*
Politics, economics and
  case study: *Campaign Finance Reform,*
    690–691
  case study: *Discretionary Policy and Presidential*
    Elections, 269
  case study: *Presidential Economics,* 349–350
Pollution
  air, 712–713, 715
  hazardous waste, 714–715
  optimal amount of
    under fixed technology, 700*e,* 700–702
    under variable technology, 702*e,*
      702–703, 704*e*
  property rights on, market for, 708*e,*
    708–710
  solid waste, 715–717
  water, 714
Portfolio, 630*d*
Positive economic statement, 11*d*
Positive externalities, 710–712
Positive rate of time preference, 618*d*
Positive relation, between variables, 18
Positive-sum game, 679*d,* 680
Postal services, 518–519
Potential output, 232*d,* 232–233, 253–254,
  254*e*
Poverty
  and age, 731*e,* 731–732
  case study: *The Homeless,* 741–742
  and dependency, 736–738
  and discrimination, 734–736
  and economic growth, 730
  estimates of, 726–727, 727*e*
  and gender, 732*e,* 732–734
  and race, 732, 732*e,* 734–736
  and social welfare programs, 727–729
Poverty level, 726–727

Power Computing Corporation, 6–7
PPF. *See* Production possibilities frontier
PPP. *See* Purchasing power parity
Predatory pricing, 669*d*
Prediction, economic analysis and, 9–10
Preferences. *See* Tastes
Preparing for Change: The Pharmaceutical Industry,
      404*i*
Present value, 625*d*, 625–627
   case study: *The Million-Dollar Lottery,*
      627–628
Price(s)
   case study: *Central Bank Independence and*
      Price Stability, 355
   changes in, 44–45
      and consumer equilibrium, 443–445,
         444*e*–445*e*
      and national income accounting, 161–167
   differences in, resources and, 553–555, 554*e*
   disequilibrium, 61–64
   dispersion of, imperfect information and,
      646
   inflation and, 144–145
   in oligopoly, 537–546
   and quantity, equilibrium of, 55–61. *See also*
      Equilibrium, of price and quantity
   relative, 45, 144–145
   and utility maximization, 424–426, 425*e*,
      427*e*
   world, 752*d*
      determination of, 754–755, 755*e*
      and domestic equilibrium price, 752*e*,
         752–754, 754*e*
Price ceiling, 62*d*, 62*e*, 62–63
Price discrimination, 519*d*, 519–522,
      520*e*–521*e*
   and antitrust policy, 668
Price elasticity formula, 395*d*, 395–396
Price elasticity of demand, 394*d*
   calculation of, 394–396, 395*e*
   case study: *Pharmaceutical Prices across*
      Countries, 403–405, 404*e*
   case study: *The Demand for Food and "The*
      Farm Problem," 412–414, 413*e*
   categories of, 396, 398–400, 399*e*–400*e*
   determinants of, 400–405
   effects of, example of, 408–410, 409*e*
   across goods, 415
   income effect and, 401
   and linear demand curve, 397*e*, 397–398
   long-run, versus short-run, 402–403, 403*e*
   for resources, 565–566
   short-run, versus long-run, 402–403, 403*e*
   substitutes and, 400–401
   and total revenue, 396–398, 397*e*
Price elasticity of supply, 405*d*
   categories of, 405–406, 406*e*
   determinants of, 407*e*, 407–408
   effects of, 410*e*, 410–411
Price floor, 62*d*, 62*e*
Price index
   construction of, 162, 162*e*

consumer, 99, 142*d*, 143*e*, 162*d*, 162–163
   GDP, 99, 164*d*, 164–165
      estimates of, 165–166, 174–176
Price leader, 539*d*, 539–540
Price level, 98*d*, 101*e*
   aggregate output and, 98–99, 235–236
   and base year, 99
   changes in, effects of, 215–221
   and consumption, 189–190
   expected
      changes in, effects of, 252–253, 253*e*
      higher than, 233–234, 237–239
      lower than, 235, 239–240
      and wage determination, 231–232
   federal budget deficit and, 378–380, 379*e*
   inflation and, 142–143, 143*e*
   and interest rate, 326–328, 327*e*
   international comparisons of, 146*e*
   versus relative prices, 145
Price searcher, 510*d*
   and marginal resource cost, 566–568, 567*e*
   and marginal revenue product, 560–561,
      561*e*
Price taker, 475*d*
   and marginal resource cost, 561–562, 562*e*
   and marginal revenue product, 559*e*, 560
Principal, 649*d*
Principal-agent problem, 649*d*
Private property rights, 699*d*, 699–700
   and Coase analysis of externalities, 707–708
   on pollution, 708*e*, 708–710
Privatization, 818*d*, 818–820
Producer surplus, 496*e*, 496–498, 497*d*
   international trade and, 755–757, 756*e*
Product
   marginal, 451*d*, 452*e*, 453
   total, 451*d*, 452*e*, 453
Product differentiation, 527–528
   oligopoly and, 536–537
Production
   disequilibrium of real GDP and, 209
   household, 72–73
   measurement of, 152–160
   roundabout, 617
   and saving, 617–618
   in short run, 450–453
   and time, 617–618
Production function, 451*d*
   and efficiency, 468–469
   per-worker, 112*d*, 112*e*, 112–113
   representations of, 468*e*, 468–471, 469*e*,
      471*e*
Production possibilities frontier (PPF), 33*d*, 33*e*
   as efficiency measure, 33–34, 37
   shape of, 34–35
   shifts in, 35–37, 36*e*
   with trade, 748–750, 749*e*
   without trade, 746–748, 747*e*–748*e*
Productive efficiency, 495*d*
Productivity, 111*d*, 111–113. *See also*
      Economic growth
   capital and, 112–113, 115

   in developing countries, 805
   and division of labor, 31
   education and, 116, 806, 807*e*
   factors affecting, 115–118, 127
   financial institutions and, 808
   government policies and, 116–117, 122–123
   growth in
      and federal budget deficit, 117–118
      long-term, 113–114, 114*e*, 127
      slowdown in, 114–115
   income and, 807–808
   international comparisons of, 124–126, 125*e*
   natural resources and, 808
   and technological change, 116, 118–122
      case study: *Computers and Productivity,*
         120–121
   and use of labor, 806–808
Product market, 4*d*
Profit(s), 3*d*. *See also* Economic profit
   categories of, 448–450, 449*e*
   corporate, 173*d*
   measuring of, 479–480
   normal, 449*d*
Profitability, versus liquidity, 305–306
Profit maximization
   and cost-plus pricing, 541
   firms and, 71
   golden rule of, 479*d*
   input combinations and, 471–472, 472*e*
   investment and, 192–193
   in monopolistic competition, 528–529, 529*e*
   in monopoly, 510–514, 511*e*–512*e*
   in perfect competition, 476–480, 478*e*
   and resource allocation, 568–571
Proprietors, 69*d*
Proprietorship, sole, 73*d*, 73–74
Proprietors' income, 173*d*
Prosperity Partners, Inc., 628*i*
Protectionism. *See* Trade restrictions
Public choice, 680*d*
   in direct democracy, 680–683
   in representative democracy, 683–691
Public good, 77*d*
Public policy. *See also* Economic regulation;
      Government regulation
   active
      versus passive, 344–346, 348–350,
         364–365
      problems with, 346–348
   anticipated versus unanticipated, 350–354,
      363
   credibility of, 354–356
   fiscal. *See* Fiscal policy
   industrial, 122–123
   monetary. *See* Monetary policy
   rules versus discretion in, 363–364
Public Voice for Food and Health Policy, 686*i*
Purchasing power, 45, 282*d*, 282*e*
Purchasing power parity (PPP) theory,
      784–785, 785*d*
   case study: *The Big Mac Index,* 785–787
Pure capitalism, 38*d*, 38–39

Q

Quality of products
    CPI and, 163
    GDP and, 158–159
Quantity demanded. *See also* Demand
    change in, 50*d*
    versus demand, 46, 50
Quantity supplied. *See also* Supply
    change in, 53*d*
    versus supply, 51, 53–54
Quantity theory of money, 331*d*, 331–332
Quesnay, Francois, 153, 178
Quota(s), 83*d*
    effects of, 759–762, 760*e*

R

Rainforest Action Network, 706*i*
Raspyni Brothers Juggling Team, 55*i*
Rate of return, investment and, 192, 193*e*
Rational expectations, 350*d*
    policy rules and, 363
Rational ignorance, 684*d*, 684–685
Rationality, assumptions about, 8–9
Rational self-iterest, 5, 8
Ray, in graphs, 23*d*
Ready, Willing & Able, 742
Reagan, Ronald, 12, 105, 148, 267, 374–375,
    381, 388, 610
Real business cycle theory, 363*d*, 363–364
Real estate market, 644*i*
Real GDP, 99, 161*d*
    disequilibrium of, 209
    equilibrium of, 207–209, 208*e*. *See also*
        Equilibrium, of real GDP demanded
    estimates of, 166–167, 167*e*
    index for, 174–175
Real income, 45*d*
Realized capital gain, 74*d*
Real rate of interest, 147*d*
Real wage, 231*d*
Recession, 93*d*
Recognition lag, 347*d*
Recycling, 716*d*, 716–717
Relevant resources, 53*d*
Renewable resources, 699*d*
Rent, 3*d*
Rental income, 173*d*
Rent seeking, 518*d*, 688*d*, 688–691
    trade restrictions and, 769
Representative democracy, 683–691
Required reserve ratio, 304*d*
Required reserves, 305*d*
Research and development (R&D), 118–122
    expenditures on, 118–120
        relative to GDP, 119*e*
Reserve requirements, 288, 304–305
    money expansion and, 314–315
Reserves, 286*d*
    excess, 305*d*. *See also* Excess reserves

fractional, banking system for, 281*d*
    required, 305*d*
Residual claimant, 587
Resource(s)
    allocation of
        in monopoly, 515–517, 516*e*, 519
        in perfect competition, 515, 516*e*
        and profit maximization, 568–571
    case study: *Ownership and Resources Use,*
        815–816
    categories of, 2–3
    entrepreneur's control of, 586–587
    exhaustible, 699*d*
    fixed, 450*d*
    households as suppliers of, 68–69
    and international specialization and trade,
        751–752
    marginal cost of, 561*d*, 561–563, 562*e*. *See
        also* Marginal resource cost
    market for, 4, 251–254, 550–575
    natural, productivity and, 808
    nonexcludable and nonappropriable, 699
    open-access, 699*d*
    and opportunity cost, 448
    price differentials in, 553–555, 554*e*
    relevant, 53*d*
    renewable, 699*d*
    scarcity of, 2–4
    supply of, 551, 552*e*, 553, 556–558
    variable, 450*d*
Resource demand, 551, 552*e*
    derived nature of, 552–553, 564–565
    and marginal resource cost, 561–563
    and marginal revenue product, 558–561
    price elasticity of, 565–566
    shifts in, 563–565
Resource demand curve, 552*e*, 552–553, 557*e*,
    558
    and marginal revenue product curve, 560,
        562*e*
Resource market, 4*d*, 251–254, 550–575
Resource price searcher, 566*d*, 566–568, 567*e*,
    569*e*
Resource price taker, 561*d*, 568, 569*e*
Resource supply curve, 552*e*, 553, 557*e*, 558
Retained earnings, 629
Returns, diminishing marginal, 451*e*, 468*e*, 469
    law of, 112, 252, 450–453, 452*d*
Revaluation, of currency, 790*d*
Revenue
    average, 479*d*
    marginal, 478*e*, 479*d*
    total, 396*d*
Robinson, Joan, 527, 533
Roosevelt, Franklin D., 287, 595
Rudman, Warren B., 377
Rule of reason, 669*d*
Russia. *See also* Soviet Union
    diamond trade and, 505–506
    monetary system in, failure of, 283
    privatization in, 818–819

S

Saving
    case study: *Not Enough Saving,* 219–221
    case study: *The Life-Cycle Hypothesis,*
        190–191
    in circular flow, 180*e,* 181–182, 212–213
    and consumption, 618–619
    and disposable income, 183, 183*e*
    intercountry comparison of, 220*e*
    and production, 617–618
Saving function, 187*e,* 188*d*
Savings deposits, 302*d*
Scarce, 3*d*
Scarcity
    of goods and services, 3
    PPF and, 37
    of resources, 2–4
    and utility maximization, 424–426, 425*e*
Schmid, Vernon R. J., 633
School lunch program, 729
Schumpeter, Joseph, 519, 674
Scientific method, steps in, 8–9
S corporation, 74–75
Screening, 652*d*
SDRs. *See* Special Drawing Rights
SEAF. *See* Small Enterprise Assistance Fund
Seasonal unemployment, 137*d,* 137–138
SEC. *See* Securities and Exchange Commission
Secondary effects, 12*d*
Securities and Exchange Commission (SEC),
    629
Securities, exchange of, 629–630
Security First Network Bank (SFNB), 313
Seigniorage, 280*d*
    and national debt, 385
Self-interest, rational, 5, 8
Sematech, 123, 123*i*
Separation of ownership from control, 631*d*
Service, 3*d*. *See also* Goods and services
SFNB. *See* Security First Network Bank
Shepherd, William, 671–673
Sherman Antitrust Act (1890), 667–669
Shops.Net, 643*i*
Shortage, 55*d,* 56*e*
Short run, 235*d,* 450*d*
Short-run aggregate supply (SRAS) curve,
    235*d,* 235–236, 236*e*
    money supply and, changes in, 328–329,
        329*e*
    and short-run Phillips curve, 358*e*
Short-run cost curves, 455–459, 465
    and long-run planning curve, 460*e*–461*e*
Short-run firm supply curve, 483*d,* 484*e*
Short-run industry supply curve, 484*d,* 485*e*
Short-run Phillips curve, 357–359, 359*d*
    historical evidence for, 361*e,* 361–362

and short-run aggregate supply curve, 358e
Shutting down
    in monopoly, 513
    in short run, 483, 484e
Signaling, 651d, 651–652
Simple money multiplier, 315d
Simple spending multiplier, 211d
    and autonomous net tax multiplier, 258–259
    case study: *Hard Times in Connecticut,* 214–215
    and circular flow, 212–213, 213e
    formula for, 213–214
    and marginal propensity to consume, 214
    and marginal propensity to save, 214
    net exports and, 225–226
Single-room-occupancy hotels (SROs), 742
Slope, 19
    of aggregate demand curve, 326–328, 327e
    of consumption function, 187, 187e
    of curved lines, 19–21, 21e–22e
    of saving function, 187e, 188
    of straight lines, 19, 20e
    units of measure and, 19, 21e
Small Enterprise Assistance Fund (SEAF), 813
Smith, Adam, 39, 102, 178, 656
Smith, Vernon, 498
Social benefits
    distribution of, 685–688
    marginal, 702e, 703d, 704e, 710–712, 711e
Social insurance, 727–728
Socialism, and economic development, 814–816
Social regulation, 657d
Social Security, 69, 80e, 728, 731
Social Security Act (1935), 138
Social welfare. *See also* Welfare loss
    international trade and, 755e, 757
    monopoly and, 517–518
Solberg, Eric, 585
Sole proprietorship, 73d, 73–74
Soviet Union. *See also* Russia
    case study: *Ownership and Resources Use,* 815–816
    institutional setting in, 817
    market planning in, 815
Special Drawing Rights (SDRs), 778, 792–793
Special-interest legislation, 685d
    case study: *Campaign Finance Reform,* 690–691
    case study: *Farm Subsidies: A Negative-Sum Game,* 685–688
Specialization, 28–32
    case study: *Evidence of Specialization,* 31–32
    degree of, extent of market and, 54
    firms and, 70–72
    international trade and, 748–752
    and Internet, 32, 55
    of labor, 31d
    and money evolution, 277
Speculator, 784d
Spending multiplier. *See* Simple spending multiplier

SRAS curve. *See* Short-run aggregate supply curve
SROs. *See* Single-room-occupancy hotels
SSI. *See* Supplemental Security Income
Stagflation, 104d
    and Phillips curve, 358
Standard of deferred payment, 279d
Standard Oil Company, 669
Statistical discrepancy account, 778
Steel industry, 136
Stigler, George, 646, 661
Stock, 91d, 321d, 629d
Stockman, David, 268
Store of value, 278d
Strategy, 541d, 542e
Strike(s), 596d
    case study: *Hard Ball at Caterpillar,* 597–598
    recent trends in, 598
Structural unemployment, 137d
Substitutes, 48d
    and cross-price elasticity of demand, 415
    and price elasticity of demand, 400–401
    and resource demand, 563
Substitution effect, 45d, 444–445, 445e
    and labor supply, 580
Sunk cost, 28d
Sun Microsystems, Inc., 212, 212i
Superfund law, 715
Supplemental Security Income (SSI), 728–729
Supply, 50d, 50–51
    aggregate. *See* Aggregate supply
    changes in, 52e, 53d
        and changes in demand, 59e, 59–60, 61e
        equilibrium and, 58e, 58–59, 59e, 59–61, 61e
        factors affecting, 51–54
    and demand, equilibrium of, 55–56, 56e, 59e, 59–60, 61e
    increase in, technological change and, 52–53
    individual, versus market, 51
    of labor. *See* Labor supply
    law of, 50d
    market, versus individual, 51
    of money. *See* Money supply
    perfectly elastic, 406d, 406e
    perfectly inelastic, 406d, 406e
    price elasticity of, 405d. *See also* Price elasticity of supply
    versus quantity supplied, 51, 53–54
    of resources, 551, 552e, 553, 556–558
    unit elastic, 406d, 406e
Supply curve, 50d, 51e
    aggregate, 100d, 101e. *See also* Aggregate supply curve
    long-run, 241d, 241e, 241–242
    short-run, 235d, 235–236, 236e. *See also* Short-run aggregate supply curve
    backward-bending, 580d, 580–581, 581e
    firm, short-run, 483d, 484e

industry
    long-run, 491d. *See also* Long-run industry supply curve
    short-run, 484d, 485e
    labor, kinked, 604e, 604–605
    resource, 552e, 553, 557e, 558
Supply of loanable funds, 619d
Supply schedule, 50, 51e
Supply shocks, 244d
    adverse, 246e, 247d
    beneficial, 245d, 246e
Supply-side economics, 105d
    case-study: *The Supply-Side Experiment,* 267–268
Supreme Court, Project Hermes, 736i
Surinam, 706i
Surplus, 55d, 56e
    consumer, 429–431, 430d, 430e. *See also* Consumer surplus
    producer, 496e, 496–498, 497d
    trade, 775–776, 778–780
Switzerland, central bank in, 355

T

Tableau Économique (Francois Quesnay), 153
Taco Bell, 121
Taft-Hartley Act, 595
Takeovers, 546
Tariff, 83d
    effects of, international trade and, 758–759, 759e
Tastes, 49d, 421d
    changes in, 49–50
    and indifference curves, 438–441
    and international specialization and trade, 752
    and work choice, 582
Taxation, principles of, 81–82
Taxes
    as automatic stabilizers, 264
    avoidance of, versus evasion of, 691–692
    and consumption, 197
    earned income credit, 729
    evasion of, versus avoidance of, 691–692
    household production and, 72
    indirect business, 171
    net, 179d, 197d
        autonomous multiplier for, 258d, 273–275
        changes in, effect of, 257–260, 258e
    payroll, 81
    progressive, 82
    proportional (flat-rate), 82
        net-tax multiplier and, 274
    regressive, 82
Tax incidence, 82d
    elasticity and, 408–411
Teamsters. *See* International Brotherhood of Teamsters
Technical substitution, marginal rate of, 470

Technological change
  and antitrust policy, 667
  and barriers to entry, 506
  capital and, 118
  government involvement in, 122
    case study: *Picking Technological Winners,*
      122–123
  and household production, 72–73
  and labor productivity, 116, 118–122
    case study: *Computers and Productivity,*
      120–121
  and per-worker production function,
      112–113, 113e
  and resource demand, 564
  and shifts in PPF, 36e, 37
  and supply, increase in, 52–53
  and unemployment, 123–124
  and unions, 611
Technological efficiency, 468
Technology
  fixed-production, 700e, 700–702, 701d
  variable, 702d, 702e, 702–703
Technology for Netscape Communications, 38i
Telecommunication industry, 672
Tender offer, 632d
Terms of trade, 749d
Term structure of interest rates, 624d
The Invisible Hand (Gary Hoover), 633i
Theory, in economic analysis, 7–8, 91–92
Theory of convergence, 126d
Theory of Games and Economic Behavior (John
  von Neumann and Oskar Morgenstern),
  541
Theory of Monopolistic Competition (Edward
  Chamberlin), 527
The Tropical Rainforest in Surinam (Marco
  Bleeker), 706i
Thierman Virtual Law Firm, 73i
Third Millennium, 387i
Third World, 799. *See also* Developing
  countries
Thrift institutions (Thrifts), 284d, 291–292
Time
  allocation of, and utility maximization,
      577–579
  and choice making, 7, 27
  constraints of, 27–28
  and consumption, 618
  and demand, 433–434
  and price elasticity of demand, 401–403,
      402e, 566
  and price elasticity of supply, 407e, 407–408
  and production, 617–618
  as resource, 2
Time deposits, 302d
Time inconsistency problem, 352d
Time preference, positive rate of, 618d
Time-series graphs, 16d
Token money, 280d
Topsy Tail, 643i
Total cost, 453–456, 454d, 454e–455e
  average, 456–459, 457e–458e

Total cost curve, 455e, 455–456
Total product, 451d, 452e, 453
Total revenue, 396d
  in monopoly, 507–510, 508e–509e
Total utility, 421d, 423e–424e
Total wage bill, 605d
  maximization of, 605–606
Toy industry, 63–64
Toyota Motor Corporation, 84i
Trade. *See also* International trade
  merchandise balance in, 83d, 775–776, 776e
  terms of, 749d
Trade Agreements Act (1979), 766
Trade balance, merchandise, 83d, 775–776, 776e
Trade deficit, 83, 776, 778–780
  and federal budget deficit, 106, 380–381
Trade restrictions, 83–85
  arguments for, 765–768
    case study: *Enforcing Trade Restrictions,*
      769–770
    case study: *The World of Automobiles,* 84–85
  and multilateral agreement, 763–764
  problems with, 768–771
  types of, 758–763
  welfare loss from, 758–763, 765–771
Trade surplus, 775–776, 778–780
Transaction costs, 54d
  and evolution of firm, 70–71
  household production and, 72
  of inflation, 144
  reduction of, firms and, 638–639
Transactions demand for money, 321d
Transfer payments, 69d
  consumption and, 197
  in-kind, 69, 729
Transitional economies, 814–816. *See also*
  Developing countries
  GDP in, 820, 821e
  institutions in, 817
  privatization and, 818–820
  theories about, 817–818
Treble damage suits, 674
Trucking industry, 672
Trusts, 667. *See also* Antitrust activity
Tsongas, Paul E., 377
Tying contracts, 668d

U

UN. *See* United Nations
Underclass, 734
Underemployment, 806
Underground economy, 158d, 691d, 691–692
Unemployment, 131–140
  case study: *Why Is Unemployment so High in
    Europe?,* 247–248
  cyclical, 138d
  in developing countries, 806
  duration of, 135
  frictional, 137d
  geographic differences in, 135
    case study: *Poor King Coal,* 136

  and inflation, 356e, 356–362, 358e
  versus inflation, 148
  international comparisons of, 139
  in Japan, 9–10
  measurement of, 131–133, 132e
  natural rate of, 232d
    fiscal policy and, 265–266
    Phillips curve and, 360
  seasonal, 137d, 137–138
  statistics for, problems with, 139–140
  structural, 137d
  technological change and, 123–124
  types of, 136–138
Unemployment insurance, 138d, 138–139, 728
  as automatic stabilizer, 264d
Unemployment rate, 131d
  calculation of, 132
  changes in, 17e, 133–134, 134e
  civilian, 133
  hysteresis and, 247d
  population groups and, 134, 135e
Unilateral transfers, net, 777d
Unilever, 536
Union(s)
  and bilateral monopoly, 603–605, 604e
  craft, 594d, 600
  and employment level, 600–603, 601e
  history of, in U.S., 594–596
  industrial, 595d, 598–600
  membership in, recent trends in, 608–613,
      609e–610e
  and nonunion competition, 610
  objectives of, 605–608
  practices of, 596–598
  and technological change, 611
  and wage rates, 598–600, 599e
United Airlines, 535i
United Auto Workers (UAW), 597i, 597–598,
  601, 610–611
United Kingdom
  auctions in, 486
  economic fluctuations in, 96–97, 97e
United Nations (UN), 800i
United Parcel Service (UPS), 518, 518i
United States Customs Service, 769i, 769–770
United States Department of Agriculture, 413i
United States Department of Education, 26i
United States Department of Labor, 231i
United States economy
  in age of Keynes, 103–104
    case study: *A Half Century of Price Levels and
      Real GDP,* 106–107, 107e
  competitive trends in, 671–674, 672e
  exports in, 746, 751
  financial intermediaries in, 284–290
  fluctuations in, 96–97, 97e
  Great Depression and, 101–103, 102e
  historical overview of, 94e–95e, 101–107
  imports in, 746, 751
  in 1970s, 104, 105e
  since 1980s, 104–106
United States Geological Survey, 269i

United States House of Representatives, 389*i*

United States Mint, 280

United States Postal Service, 518*i*, 518–519

United Technologies Corporation (UTC), 214–215, 215*i*

Unit elastic demand, 396*d*, 404

Unit elastic supply, 406*d*, 406*e*

Unit of account, 278*d*

Universal Studios Florida, 422*i*

University of Iowa, College of Business Administration, 498*i*

University of Michigan, 338*i*

UPS, 518–519

Urban Institute, 741*i*

USA Today, 196*i*, 377*i*

U.S. Steel, 540, 546, 669

UTC. *See* United Technologies Corporation

Utility, 68*d*
  marginal, 421*d*, 423*e*–424*e*
    law of demand derivation and, 426–428, 428*e*
    law of diminishing of, 421*d*, 421–422
    total, 421*d*, 423*e*–424*e*
    units of, 422–423

Utility analysis, 421–422
  and indifference curves, 438–446
  marginal, 420–435

Utility maximization
  conditions of, 426
  by households, 68
  indifference curves and, 442*e*, 442–443
  labor supply and, 577–579
  price and, 424–426, 425*e*, 427*e*

V

Value
  of firms, current market, 630
  of money, 279, 282, 282*e*
  nominal, 161
  present, 625*d*, 625–627
    case study: *The Million-Dollar Lottery,* 627–628
  store of, 278*d*

Value added, 156*d*, 156–157
  computation of, 157*e*

Variable(s), 8*d*
  dependent, 17, 19
  independent, 17, 19

Variable cost, 453*d*, 455*e*, 455–456
  average, 456–459, 457*e*–458*e*

Variable resources, 450*d*

Variable technology, 702*d*
  and negative externalities, 702*e*, 702–703

Variety of products, GDP and, 158–159

Vegetarian Resource Group (VRG), 464*i*

Velocity of money, 330*d*, 331
  determinants of, 333–334
  stability of, 334–335, 335*e*

Vending machines, 8
  case study: *A Yen for Vending Machines,* 9–10

Venture capitalism, 589

Vertical integration, 639*d*, 640–644

Vertical mergers, 546*d*

Virtual Africa, 505*i*

Virtual office, 73

Volcker, Paul, 337–338, 364

von Hayek, Friedrich, 818

von Neumann, John, 541

Vote maximization, 78

VRG. *See* Vegetarian Resource Group

W

Wage(s), 3*d*
  adjustment of, 242
  case study: *Output Gaps and Wage Flexibility,* 242–244
  case study: *The McMinimum Wage,* 570–571
  determinants of, 583–586
  determination of, and expected price level, 231–232
  efficiency, 651*d*
  efficiency theory of, 234*d*
  and labor supply, 579–581, 583–584
  nominal, 231*d*
  real, 231*d*
  unions' impact on, 598–605, 599*e*

Wage bill, total, 605*d*, 605–606

Wagner Act, 595

WAICENT. *See* World Agricultural Information Center

Wal-Mart Stores, Inc., 572*i*

Wants
  and demand, 44
  double coincidence of, 277*d*
  resources and, 2

Wealth, net, 188*d*
  and consumption, 188–189

The Wealth of Nations (Adam Smith), 102, 178

Welfare, 80*e*, 727–729
  case study: *"Ending Welfare as We Know It,"* 740–741
  expenditures for, 729–730
  reforms in, 738–742
  undesirable consequences of, 736–738

Welfare and Families, 741*i*

Welfare loss, 516*d*, 517–518. *See also* Social welfare
  from trade restrictions, 758–763, 765–771

Welfare Reform: An Analysis of the Issues, 741*i*

Well-Known People Who Happen to Be Canadians (Vernon R. J. Schmid), 633*i*

Wendy's, 464

West Virginia Web, 136*i*

Winner's curse, 646–647, 647*d*

Women
  in developing countries, 805
  and poverty, 732–734

Work. *See also* Labor supply
  disincentives for, welfare and, 736–737
  market, 577*d*
  nonmarket, 577*d*
  utility and, 578

Worker, discouraged, 132*d*

Worker's compensation, 728

World Agricultural Information Center (WAICENT), 413*i*

World Bank, 247*i*, 800, 800*i*, 812

World Bank Group, 800*i*

World Factbook, 283*i*

World price, 752*d*
  determination of, 754–755, 755*e*
  and domestic equilibrium price, 752*e*, 752–754, 754*e*

The World's Economic Outlook (John Maynard Keynes), 263*i*

World Trade Organization (WTO), 763*d*, 763–764, 764*i*

World War II
  and fiscal policy, 79–80, 263–264
  and income distribution, 722
  labor movement after, 595–596
  national debt since, 381–382, 383*e*

Worldwide Market Information, 713*i*

World Wide Web. *See* Internet

World Wide Web Security, 313*i*

Worth, comparable, 584–586, 585*d*

WTO. *See* World Trade Organization

Y

Yahoo, 3*i*

Yang, Jerry, 3

Z

Zero-sum game, 679*d*

Photo Credits

Page   1 © Stewart Cohen/Tony Stone Images

3 Courtesy of Yahoo

6 © David Young-Wolff/Tony Stone Images

10 © Dean Siracusa 1993/FPG International

12 APP/BETTMANN

25 © Richard Clintsman/Tony Stone Images

26 © Loren Santow/Tony Stone Images

32 © Don Smetzer/Tony Stone Images

38 © AP/Wide World Photos

43 © Ron Chapple 1993/FPG International

47 © Bill Losh 1995/FPG International

55 © Scott Dietrich/Tony Stone Images

60 © Jonathan Daniel/Allsport

63 © Alan Levenson/Tony Stone Images

67 © Alan Levenson/Tony Stone Images

71 Courtesy Ford Motor Company

73 © Jon Riley/Tony Stone Images

76 © Andy Sacks/Tony Stone Images

84 © David Doody 1992/FPG International

89 © Ken Biggs/Tony Stone Images

93 © UPI/Bettmann

96 © Richard During/Tony Stone Images

102 © FPG International

106 © Wide World Photos

110 © Baron Wolman

118 © David Ximeno Tijada/Tony Stone Images

121 © Tony Freeman/Photo Edit

123 Courtesy Intel Corporation (top)

123 © Gerard Fritz/FPG International (bottom)

130 © Dennis O'Clair/Tony Stone Images

131 © Andy Sacks/Tony Stone Images

133 © Ron Chapple/FPG International

136 © Larry Ulrich/Tony Stone Images

140 © Ary Diesendruck/Tony Stone Images

152 © Andy Sacks/Tony Stone Images

154 © Robert E. Daemmrick/Tony Stone Images

155 © Nikolay Zurek 1988/FPG International

159 © Bette S. Garber

165 © FPG International

177 © Wendt Worldwide

178 © The Bettmann Archive

181 © FPG International

191 © TravelPix/FPG International

196 © Myrleen Ferguson/PhotoEdit

205 © Chronis Jons/Tony Stone Images

212 © Doug Menuez/SABA

215 NASA

217 © Jeff Zaruba/Tony Stone Images

219 © 1992 T. Corner/Unicorn Stock Photos

230 © Charles Thatcher/Tony Stone Images

231 © Wide World Photos

234 © UPI/Bettmann

243 © Mark Richards/PhotoEdit

247 © WEKA Publishing, Inc.

255 © Maxwell MacKenzie/Tony Stone Images

256 © Ross Harrison Koty/Tony Stone Images

263 © UPI/Bettmann

268 © UPI/Corbis-Bettmann

269 © Reuters/Bettmann

276 © Donald Johnston/Tony Stone Images

278 © David Schultz/Tony Stone Images

280 © Superstock

283 © Wide World Photos

292 © Superstock

299 © Kaluzny/Thatcher/Tony Stone Images

301 © Poulides/Thatcher/Tony Stone Images

307 © Superstock

308 © Jed Share/Liaison International

313 © Michael Newman/PhotoEdit

320 © Scott Goldsmith/Tony Stone Images

332 © Claudia Conteris/Prisma/Impact Visuals

337 © Wide World Photos

338 © WEKA Publishing, Inc.

343 © Will & Deni McIntyre/Tony Stone Images

347 © Wide World Photos

349 © Wide World Photos

355 © Wide World Photos

362 © Wide World Photos

369 © Dennis O'Clair/Tony Stone Images

372 © William H. Allen, Jr.

377 © Wide World Photos

387 © Frank Herholdt/Tony Stone Images

389   © Wide World Photos
393   © Joseph Probereskin/Tony Stone Images
394   © Terry Qing/FPG International
401   Joe Higgins
404   © Rich Iwasaki/Tony Stone Images
413   © Michael Goldman 1994/FPG International
420   © Rick Rusing/Tony Stone Images
422   © Superstock
429   © 1988 Bob Gomel
433   © Tom McCarthy/Unicorn Stock Photos
434   © Elena Rooraid/PhotoEdit
447   © Jeff Corwin/Tony Stone Images
448   © Michael Newman/PhotoEdit
461   © Superstock
462   © Jim Shippee/Unicorn Stock Photos
464   © Mary Kate Denny/PhotoEdit
474   © Andy Sacks/Tony Stone Images
480   Courtesy Toyota
486   © Reuters/Corbis-Bettmann
498   © AP/Wide World Photos
503   © Patrick Clark/Photonica
504   © PhotoDisc
505   © Jason Lauré
517   © Reuters/Corbis-Bettmann
518   Courtesy United States Postal Service
526   Keith Wood/Tony Stone Images
535   © Cameramann International, Ltd.
550   © Andy Sacks/Tony Stone Images
556   © Allsport USA
564   Courtesy Hewlett Packard
570   Courtesy Kelley Services
576   © Jake Rajs/Photonica
579   © Jim Leavitt/Impact Visuals
585   © PhotoDisc
586   © Marc Asnin/SABA
589   © Martin Simon/SABA
593   © Bruce Forster/Tony Stone Images
594   © UPI/Corbis-Bettmann
596   © AP/Wide World Photos
597   © Jim West/Impact Visuals
602   © Leland Bobbe/Tony Stone Images
616   © Andy Sacks/Tony Stone Images
618   Don Smetzer/Tony Stone Images

628   © AP/Wide World Photos
629   Courtesy of New York Stock Exchange
633   Reuters/Corbis-Bettmann
637   © WEKA Publishing, Inc.
643   © Steve Foxall
647   © Robert Tringali/Sports Chrome
656   © Charles Thatcher/Tony Stone Images
662   © PhotoDisc
665   © PhotoDisc
673   © AP/Wide World Photos
674   © Jeff Greenberg
678   © Janet Gill/Tony Stone Images
686   © David Addison/Visuals Unlimited
690   © Najlah Feanny/SABA Press Photos
692   © Alan Levenson/Tony Stone Images
694   © AP/Wide World Photos
698   © Bruce Forster/Tony Stone Images
706   © Jacques Jangoux/Tony Stone Images
713   © AP/Wide World Photos
714   © PhotoDisc
716   © Jeff Greenberg
721   © Index Stock
725   © PhotoDisc
736   Photography by Alan Brown/Photonics
       Graphics
740   © Kevin Horan/Tony Stone Images
741   © Emily Strong/Visuals Unlimited
745   © Trevor Wood/Tony Stone Images
746   © PhotoDisc
751   © Ron Spomer/Visuals Unlimited
764   © Claude Berger
769   © Jeff Greenberg
774   © Mike Blank/Tony Stone Images
775   © Reuters/Corbis-Bettmann
784   © Action Press/SABA Press Photos
785   © Michael Newman/PhotoEdit
790   © Keith Dannemiller/SABA Press Photos
798   Courtesy KFC Corporation
800   Courtesy World Bank Organization
805   © Alan Oddie/PhotoEdit
813   © Amy Etra/PhotoEdit
815   © Najlah Feanny/SABA Press Photos